5, 6, 7 Years

Aardema, Verna. *Borreguita and the Coyote.* Illustrated by Petra Mathers. Knopf, 1991.

Ahlberg, Janet, and Allan Ahlberg. *The Jolly Postman.* Little, Brown, 1986.

Anno, Mitsumasa. *Anno's Counting Book.* Crowell, 1977.

Coffelt, Nancy. *The Dog Who Cried Wolf.* Gulliver, 1995.

Cooney, Barbara. *Miss Rumphius.* Viking, 1982.

de Paola, Tomie. *Strega Nona.* Prentice Hall, 1975.

Gershator, Phillis. *Rata-Pata-Scata-Fata.* Illustrated by Holly Meade. Little, Brown, 1994.

Gray, Libba Moore. *Small Green Snake.* Illustrated by Holly Meade. Orchard, 1994.

Henkes, Kevin. *Owen.* Greenwillow, 1993.

Hong, Lily Toy. *Two of Everything.* Whitman, 1993.

Huck, Charlotte. *Princess Furball.* Illustrated by Anita Lobel. Greenwillow, 1989.

Hutchins, Pat. *The Doorbell Rang.* Greenwillow, 1986.

Hyman, Trina Schart. *Little Red Riding Hood.* Holiday House, 1983.

King-Smith, Dick. *All Pigs Are Beautiful.* Illustrated by Anita Jeram. Candlewick, 1994.

Lobel, Arnold. *Frog and Toad Are Friends.* Harper & Row, 1970.

Pomerantz, Charlotte. *Here Comes Henny,* Illustrated by Nancy Winslow Parker. Greenwillow, 1994.

Prelutsky, Jack. Ed. *The Random House Book of Poetry for Children.* Illustrated by Arnold Lobel. Random House, 1983.

Sendak, Maurice. *Where the Wild Things Are.* Harper & Row, 1963.

Silverman, Erica. *Don't Fidget a Feather.* Illustrated by S. D. Schindler. Macmillan, 1994.

Steig, William. *Doctor De Soto.* Farrar, Straus & Giroux, 1982.

Steptoe, John. *Mufaro's Beautiful Daughter: An African Tale.* Lothrop, Lee & Shepard, 1987.

Stevens, Janet. *Tops and Bottoms.* Harcourt Brace, 1995.

Wilder, Laura Ingalls. *The Little House in the Big Woods.* Illustrated by Garth Williams. Harper & Row, 1953.

Williams, Vera. *A Chair for My Mother.* Greenwillow, 1982.

Yolen, Jane. *Owl Moon.* Illustrated by John Schoenherr. Philomel, 1987.

7, 8, 9 Years

Aardema, Verna. *Misoso: Once Upon a Time Tales from Africa.* Illustrated by Reynolds Ruffins. Applesoup, 1994.

Ahlberg, Alan. *The Giant Baby.* Illustrated by Fritz Wegner. Viking, 1995.

Best, Carrie. *Taxi! Taxi!* Illustrated by Dale Gottlieb. Little, Brown, 1994.

Buehner, Caralyn. *Fanny's Dream.* Illustrated by Mark Buehner. Dial, 1996.

Burnett, Francis Hodgson. *The Secret Garden.* Illustrated by Tasha Tudor. Harper & Row, 1987.

Cameron, Ann. *The Most Beautiful Place in the World.* Illustrated by Thomas B. Allen. Knopf, 1988.

Cleary, Beverly. *Ramona Quimby, Age 8.* Illustrated by Alan Tiegreen. Morrow, 1981.

Cole, Joanna. *The Magic School Bus Inside the Human Body.* Illustrated by Bruce Degen. Scholastic, 1989.

de Regniers, Beatrice Schenk, ed. *Sing a Song of Popcorn.* Scholastic, 1988.

Doherty, Berlie. *Willa and Old Miss Annie.* Illustrated by Kim Lewis. Candlewick, 1994.

Fleischman, Sid. *The Whipping Boy.* Illustrated by Peter Sis. Greenwillow, 1986.

Fritz, Jean. *Where Do You think You're Going, Christopher Columbus?* Illustrated by Margot Tomes. Putnam, 1980.

Greenfield, Eloise. *Honey I Love and Other Poems.* Illustrated by Leo and Diane Dillon. Crowell, 1978.

Grimm, Jacob, and Wilhelm Grimm. *Snow White and the Seven Dwarfs.* Illustrated by Nancy Ekhom Burkert. Farrar, Straus & Giroux, 1972.

Lester, Julius. *The Tales of Uncle Remus: The Adventures of Brer Rabbit.* Illustrated by Jerry Pinkney. Dial, 1987.

Lewis, C. S. *The Lion, the Witch, and the Wardrobe.* Illustrated by Pauline Baynes. Macmillan, 1961.

Lisle, Janet Taylor. *A Message from the Match Girl.* Orchard, 1995.

MacLachlan, Patricia. *Sarah, Plain and Tall.* Harper & Row, 1985.

McKay, Hilary. *Dog Friday.* McElderry, 1995.

Osborne, Mary. *American Tall Tales.* Illustrated by Michael McCurdy. Knopf, 1990.

Rathman, Peggy. *Officer Buckle and Gloria.* Putnam, 1995.

San Souci, Robert D. *Kate Shelley, Bound for Legend.* Illustrated by Max Ginsburg. Dial, 1995.

Stanley, Diane, and Peter Vennema. *Cleopatra.* Illustrated by Diane Stanley. Morrow, 1994.

Williams, Karen Lynn. *Galimoto.* Illustrated by Catherine Stock. Lothrop, Lee & Shepard, 1990.

Wolff, Patricia Rae. *The Toll-Bridge Troll.* Illustrated by Kimberly Bucken Root. Browndeer, 1995.

The child on the cover represents every child who has ever opened a book and discovered the power of reading. The open window/border surrounding the child allows a free flow of fresh air, new ideas, and information. The child's curiosity/creativity is the trailing vine reaching out as it grows and moves into new spaces where it blooms.

—Denise Fleming

Children's Literature
in the Elementary School SIXTH EDITION

Charlotte S. Huck
Professor Emeritus
The Ohio State University

Susan Hepler
Children's Literature Specialist
Alexandria, Virginia

Janet Hickman
The Ohio State University

Barbara Z. Kiefer
Teachers College Columbia University

Brown & Benchmark
PUBLISHERS

Madison, WI Dubuque Guilford, CT Chicago Toronto London
Mexico City Caracas Buenos Aires Madrid Bogotá Sydney

Book Team

Executive Publisher *Edgar J. Laube*
Managing Editor *Sue Pulvermacher-Alt*
Developmental Editor *Suzanne M. Guinn*
Production Editor *Karen A. Pluemer*
Proofreading Coordinator *Carrie Barker*
Designer *Jamie O'Neal*
Art Editor *Miriam Hoffman*
Permissions Coordinator *Patricia Barth*
Production Manager *Beth Kundert*
Production/Costing Manager *Sherry Padden*
Production/Imaging and Media Development Manager *Linda Meehan Avenarius*
Marketing Manager *Amy Halloran*
Copywriter *Jennifer Smith*
Proofreader *Ann Morgan*

Basal Text *10/12 Goudy*
Display Type *Bell Gothic Black*
Typesetting System *Macintosh™ QuarkXPress™*
Paper Stock *45# Bulkton*

Brown & Benchmark
PUBLISHERS

Executive Vice President and General Manager *Bob McLaughlin*
Vice President, Business Manager *Russ Domeyer*
Vice President of Production and New Media Development *Victoria Putman*
National Sales Manager *Phil Rudder*
National Telesales Director *John Finn*

A Times Mirror Company

Cover illustration by Denise Fleming

Copyedited by Wendy Nelson; proofread by Wendy M. Christofel

Composition by TMHEG Imaging Group; compositor/pager Deb E. Motsch

Library of Congress Catalog Card Number: 95–83874

ISBN 0–697–27960–X

Printed in the United States of America by Times Mirror Higher Education Group, Inc.,
2460 Kerper Boulevard, Dubuque, IA 52001

10 9 8 7 6 5 4 3 2 1

To all those students and teachers whom we have taught and from whom we have learned . . .

brief contents

part one

*Learning About Books
and Children* 3

chapter one
Knowing Children's Literature 4

chapter two
*Understanding Children's Responses
to Literature* 38

chapter three
*The Changing World of Children's
Books* 81

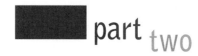

part two

*Exploring Children's
Literature* 135

chapter four
Books to Begin On 136

chapter five
Picture Storybooks 196

chapter six
Traditional Literature 265

chapter seven
Modern Fantasy 339

chapter eight
Poetry 389

chapter nine
Contemporary Realistic Fiction 453

chapter ten
Historical Fiction 513

chapter eleven
Biography 551

chapter twelve
Informational Books 577

part three

*Developing a Literature
Program   619*

chapter thirteen
*Planning the Literature
Program   620*

chapter fourteen
*Extending and Evaluating Children's
Understandings of Literature   667*

appendix a
Children's Book Awards   722

appendix b
Book Selection Aids   732

appendix c
Publishers' Addresses 741

contents

preface xiii
acknowledgments xv

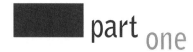

part one

Learning About Books and Children 3

chapter one
Knowing Children's Literature 4
Children's Literature Defined 5
  What Is Children's Literature? 6
  Writing for Children 7
Valuing Literature for Children 8
  Personal Values 8
  Educational Values 11
Evaluating Children's Fiction 18
  Plot 18
  Setting 19
  Theme 20
  Characterization 21
  Style 23
  Point of View 24
  Additional Considerations 26
  Comparison with Other Books 27
Classics in Children's Literature 28
The Book Awards 28
  The Newbery and Caldecott Medals 30
  International Book Awards 30
  Lifetime Contribution Awards 31

chapter two
Understanding Children's Responses to Literature 38
Reading Interests and Preferences 40
  Age and Gender Differences 40
  Other Determinants of Interest 41
  Explaining Children's Choices 42
Growth Patterns That Influence Response 43
  Physical Development 44
  Cognitive Development 45
  Language Development 48
  Moral Development 49
  Personality Development 50
  Guides for Ages and Stages 51
Response in the Classroom 51
  Theories of Response 51
  Types of Response 60
  Interpreting Children's Responses 61
  Collecting Children's Responses 64

chapter three
The Changing World of Children's Books 81
Early Beginnings: The Middle Ages 84
  The Oral Tradition 84
  The Earliest Manuscripts 84
  Caxton Begins English Printing 85
  Hornbooks, ABCs, and Primers 85
  Lasting Contributions of the Period 86
Children's Books: The Seventeenth and Eighteenth Centuries 86
  The "Goodly Godly" Books of the Puritans 86
  Chapbooks: Forerunners of Comics 87
  Nursery Rhymes or Mother Goose 88
  Fairy Tales and Adventure 88
  Newbery Publishes for Children 89
  Didactic Tales 90
  Poetry and Pictures 91
Children's Literature: The Nineteenth Century 92
  Books of Instruction and Information 92
  Folktale Collections 92
  Family Stories 93
  Tales of Adventure 95
  Animal Stories 96
  The Rise of Fantasy and Humor 96

Poetry 98
Magazines 99
Illustrators of the Nineteenth Century 100
Children's Literature: The Twentieth Century 102
Recognition of Children's Literature 102
The Rise of the Picture Storybook 103
The Growth of Informational Books 105
The Proliferation of Series Books 107
Folktales of the World 108
Fantasy 109
Poetry 110
Realistic Fiction 111
An International Literature for Children 113
Recent Trends in Children's Books 114
Children's Books: Big Business 114
New Books for New Markets 118
Shifts in Publishing Emphases 119
Changes in Writing and Illustration 120
Increased Use in Schools 122
Increased Censorship 123
The Need for Multicultural Books 123
The Development of a Multiliterate Society 124

part two

Exploring Children's Literature 135

chapter four
Books to Begin On 136

Developing Initial Literacy 137
Babies' First Books 139
Toy Books 140
Finger Rhymes and Nursery Songs 141
Mother Goose 146
The Appeal of Mother Goose 146
Different Editions of Mother Goose 147
Alphabet Books 154
Counting Books 156
Concept Books 163
Wordless Books 168
Books About the Common Experiences of the Young Child 170
Books for the Beginning Reader 174
Predictable Books 174
Big Books 180
Controlled-Vocabulary Books 182

chapter five
Picture Storybooks 196

The Picture Storybook Defined 198
The Art and Artists of Picture Storybooks and Illustrated Books 199
Creating Meaning in Picture Storybooks 199
The Artist's Choice of Media 202
Elements of Design 210
The Matter of Style 212
The Format of the Book 218
The Language of Picture Storybooks 222
The Content of Picture Storybooks 222
Themes and Subjects in Picture Storybooks 225
Family Stories 225
Familiar Everyday Experiences 227
Picture Storybooks About Older People 228
The Child's World of Nature 229
Animals as People 230
Modern Folktale Style 236
Humor 237
Fantasy 239
Appreciating Cultural Diversity 241
Social and Environmental Concerns 248
War and Its Aftermath 249

chapter six
Traditional Literature 265

A Perspective on Traditional Literature 266
The Origin of Folk Literature 266
The Value of Folk Literature for Children 268
Folktales 268
Types of Folktales 269
Characteristics of Folktales 273
Folktales of the World 280
Fables 310
Characteristics of Fables 310
Editions 310
Myths 313
Types of Myths 313
Greek Mythology 314
Norse Mythology 317
Epic and Legendary Heroes 318
The Iliad and the Odyssey 318
The Ramayana 318
Heroes of the Middle Ages 319
The Bible as Literature 321
Collections of Bible Stories 321
Single Bible Stories 322

chapter seven
Modern Fantasy   339
Fantasy for Today's Child   341
Modern Fairy Tales   343
    The Beginnings of the Modern Fairy Tale   343
    Fairy Tales Today   345
Modern Fantasy   346
    Evaluating Modern Fantasy   346
    Animal Fantasy   347
    The World of Toys and Dolls   353
    Eccentric Characters and Preposterous Situations   355
    Extraordinary Worlds   357
    Magical Powers   360
    Suspense and the Supernatural   361
    Time-Shift Fantasy   363
    Imaginary Realms   367
    High Fantasy   369
Science Fiction   373
    Through the Door   374
    Visitors to Earth   375
    Outer Space and Cyberspace   375
    Views of the Future   376

chapter eight
Poetry   389
The Meaning of Poetry   390
    Poetry for Children   391
The Elements of Poetry   392
Forms of Poetry for Children   399
Selecting Poetry for Children   403
    Children's Poetry Preferences   403
    Poets and Their Books   404
    Anthologies of Poems for Children   413
Sharing Poetry with Children   418
    Creating a Climate for Enjoyment   424
    Finding Time for Poetry   426
    Reading Poetry to Children   432
    Involving Children in Poetry   433

chapter nine
Contemporary Realistic Fiction   453
Realism in Contemporary Children's Literature   454
    The Value of Contemporary Fiction   454
    Issues Relating to Realistic Fiction   456
Becoming One's Own Person   459
    Living in a Family   459
    Living with Others   466
    Growing Toward Maturity   468
Coping with Problems of the Human Condition   475
    Physical Disabilities   475
    Developmental and Learning Disabilities   476
    Mental Illness   477
    Aging and Death   478

Living in a Diverse World   482
    Appreciating Racial and Ethnic Diversity   483
    Understanding Various World Cultures   488
Popular Types of Realistic Fiction   491
    Humorous Stories   492
    Animal Stories   496
    Sports Stories   498
    School Stories   499
    Mysteries   501

chapter ten
Historical Fiction   513
Historical Fiction for Today's Child   514
    The Value of Historical Fiction   515
    Types of Historical Fiction   516
    Criteria for Historical Fiction   517
Stories of Prehistoric Times   520
Stories of the Old World   521
    Ancient Times   521
    Tales of Early Britain   521
    Medieval Times and Tales   521
    The Emergence of the Modern World   523
Stories of the New World   524
    Colonial America   524
    The Revolutionary Era   528
    Native Americans   529
    The American Frontier   531
    The Civil War Era   533
Into the Twentieth Century   536
    Immigrants   536
    African Americans   537
    The World at War   538

chapter eleven
Biography   551
Biography for Today's Child   552
Criteria for Juvenile Biography   554
    Choice of Subject   554
    Accuracy and Authenticity   554
    Style   556
    Characterization   556
    Theme   557
Types of Presentation and Coverage   559
    Picture-Book Biographies   559
    Simplified Biographies   562
    Partial Biographies   563
    Complete Biographies   564
    Collective Biographies   567
Autobiographies and Memoirs   569

chapter twelve
Informational Books   **577**
Trends in Informational Books   578
  Increased Quantity and Quality   578
  A New Focus on the Very Young   579
  The Growing Importance of Illustration   580
  Unconventional Formats and Approaches   580
  Specialized Topics   581
  Recognition and Awards   581
Criteria for Evaluating Informational Books   581
  Accuracy and Authenticity   581
  Content and Perspective   585
  Style   588
  Organization   589
  Illustrations and Format   590
Types of Informational Books   593
  Concept Books   593
  Informational Picture Storybooks   594
  Photographic Essays   596
  Identification Books   598
  Life-Cycle Books   598
  Experiment and Activity Books   598
  Documents and Journals   599
  Survey Books   600
  Specialized Books   601
  Craft and How-to Books   602
Using Literature Across the Curriculum   602
  Informational Books in the Classroom   602
  Choosing Informational Books for the Classroom   604
  Integrating Fact and Fiction   605

part three
Developing a Literature Program   619

chapter thirteen
Planning the Literature Program   **620**

Purposes of the Literature Program   622
  Discovering Delight in Books   622
  Linking Literature to Life   623
  Developing Literary Awareness   623
  Developing Appreciation   625
Different Plans for Literature Programs   625
  Literature with a Basal Reading Program   625
  Literature Programs Using Real Books   626
  *Making the Transition to a Literature-Based
    Approach*   627

The Components of a Literature Program   629
  An Enthusiastic Teacher   629
  The Classroom Book Collection   630
  Creating a Classroom Reading Center   630
  Display Techniques   631
Sharing Literature with Children   632
  Reading to Children   632
  Storytelling   634
Providing Time to Read Books   637
Talking About Books with Children   638
  Guided Discussion   639
  Working in Small Groups   641
Literature and the Writing Program   642
  Helping Children Write About Books   643
  Helping Children Become Authors   645
Guiding the In-Depth Study of Books   645
  Making and Using Guides   645
  Webbing Curriculum Possibilities   646
The School and the Community   648
  The Whole-School Program   648
  Involving Administrators   652
  Planning Author/Illustrator Visits   652
  The School Library Media Center   653
  The Library Media Specialist   654
  Selecting Materials   655
  Selection versus Censorship   656
  Dealing with Censorship   657
  Working with Parents and the Community   658
  Working with the Public Library   659

chapter fourteen
Extending and Evaluating Children's Understandings of Literature   **667**

Active Learning in the Classroom   669
Exploring Literature Through Art and Media   669
  Pictures and Collage   670
  Murals   671
  Media Exploration   671
  Displays, Dioramas, and Museums   674
  Story-Retelling Aids   676
  Graphic Organizers   677
  Videos and Computers   678
Making Things   680
  Sewing   680
  Crafts and Construction   681
  Cooking   682
  Games   683
Singing and Movement in the Classroom   684
  Picture-Book Editions of Single Songs   684
  Matching Music and Literature   685
  Composing Music   685
  Movement and Literature   685

Connecting Literature and Life   686
    Artifacts and Collections   686
    Maps and Time Lines   686
    Jackdaws   687
Extending Literature Through Drama   688
    Pantomime   688
    Dramatizing Stories   689
    Improvisation   690
    Readers' Theater   690
    Puppetry   691
Writing from Children's Books   692
    Developing Sensitivity to Language   692
    Single Books as Springboards   694
    Experimenting with Literary Patterns   695
    Extending Forms of Writing   699
    Expository Writing   700
    Making Books   704
Assessment and Evaluation   704
    Determining Children's Literacy Background   705
    Record Keeping   706
    Student and Parent Conferences   707
    Evaluating Children's Literary Understandings   708
    Evaluating Children's Growth as Readers   709
    Evaluating the Literature Program   709
    Developing Lifetime Readers   709

appendix a
Children's Book Awards   722

appendix b
Book Selection Aids   732

appendix c
Publishers' Addresses   741

name index   744
subject index   778

preface

The sixth edition of *Children's Literature in the Elementary School* is written for all adults with an interest in providing good literature for children. It also provides a rationale and suggestions to teachers for planning and evaluating a literature-based curriculum. The text is designed for classes in children's literature at the preservice and graduate levels in education or English departments and in library schools in colleges and universities. It can also be used for in-service courses and as a useful resource for the school professional library.

Purposes

Our primary purpose in writing this textbook is the same as in the previous five editions—to share our knowledge and enthusiasm for the literature of childhood with students, teachers, and librarians in the hope that they, in turn, will communicate their excitement about books to the children they teach. As a nation, we have become so concerned with teaching the skills of reading that we have often neglected to help children discover the joys of reading. We, the authors of this text, believe that children become readers only by reading many books of their own choosing and by hearing high-quality literature read aloud with obvious delight and enthusiasm. It is our hope that the students, teachers, and librarians who read this book will be able to create in children a love of good books and a joy in reading them.

The growth of the field of children's literature has been phenomenal since the first edition of this text was published in 1961. With more than ninety thousand children's books in print, prospective and in-service teachers and librarians need a guide for selecting the best ones, based on a knowledge of book selection criteria and an understanding of children's responses to literature. Chapter 1 and the genre chapters provide guidelines for evaluating books; Chapter 2 presents current research on children's responses to books.

Educators have finally realized the importance of story and real books in developing readers who not only *know how* to read but *do* read. Increasingly, teachers are using children's literature across the curriculum. Superb informational books and biographies can enhance every subject taught in the curriculum by providing readers with the most up-to-date information and facts. Chapters on developing early literacy, evaluating informational books and biography, and planning and evaluating the literature program all speak to the development of readers.

Organization

The three-part organization of *Children's Literature in the Elementary School* emphasizes the triple focus of this text: the reader, the book, and teaching. Part One emphasizes the values and criteria for choosing and using literature with children at various stages in their development. It also includes a historical overview of the ways in which children's literature has changed over the years. Part Two provides an in-depth look at the various genres of children's literature and establishes evaluative criteria for each genre. Part Three focuses on teaching children, structuring learning in classrooms, using literature across the curriculum, and evaluating literature-based reading programs.

New to This Edition

For this edition we have considered the changes that have occurred in approaches to teaching and in the publishing and marketing of children's books over the last thirty years. We realize that as the research base supporting the centrality of good literature has grown, as more teachers have been putting this research into practice in literature-based classrooms, and as more and more books have been published for children, we have been reluctant to leave out any of the good news about good practice and good books. For the sixth edition, however, we have realized that there is a limit to the amount of information and the number of pages we can ask readers to absorb. Therefore we have carefully considered what has always been the central purpose of this text—the sharing of our knowledge and enthusiasm for the literature of childhood—and we have attempted to refine the sixth edition to that end.

Readers will find the substance of the text and the basic format unchanged from previous editions. For the sixth edition we have added Chapter 11, "Biography," to highlight the many excellent biographies and autobiographies available for children. Several curriculum webs that were previously clustered in the third section have been updated and placed in relevant chapters to strengthen the connections we hope to make between books, children, and classroom practice. Two new webs have been added, "Brian Pinkney—A World of Possibilities" in Chapter 5 and "In Praise of Poetry" in Chapter 8. We have added new Resources for Teaching boxes, including "Picture Storybooks About the Everyday World of the Child" and "Picture Storybooks About the Child's Imaginary World" in Chapter 5 and " 'To be Continued'—Popular Series Books for Children" in Chapter 9.

We have also continued to give attention to literature that reflects a variety of cultures. Rather than devote a single chapter to multicultural and cross-cultural literature, however, we maintain that such literature should be integrated into all areas of the curriculum. In this textbook, we have discussed multicultural literature as a part of each genre or subject area. Students are introduced to picture storybooks, poetry, novels, informational books, and biographies about people of all races and all cultural backgrounds. We believe that this approach assures that the literature and accomplishments of all groups will be a part of every subject taught instead of separated out from the heart of the curriculum.

Although the title of this book is *Children's Literature in the Elementary School*, throughout the book we have attempted to include titles that reflect the interests and developmental needs of children from birth through middle school. Each chapter has been rewritten to include the latest research and the latest books. Over eight hundred new titles have been added to this edition, and new color pictures have been used throughout the text.

Finally, a new author joins us for this edition. Barbara Kiefer, an associate professor at Teachers College, Columbia University, did her doctoral work under the guidance of Charlotte Huck and studied with Susan Hepler and Janet Hickman. Along with the other three authors, she has taught in the elementary schools as well as at the university level, and she brings to this edition her understanding of children and teachers in various areas of the country and her passionate love for books.

As children's literature becomes more central to the curriculum, teachers and librarians need a book that will serve for many years as a reference as well as provide thorough coverage of the issues and genres in children's literature. We have hoped to produce, from endpaper to endpaper, a practical textbook that will serve as a resource both for students who are just beginning their teaching and for teachers and librarians already in the field. We believe teachers and librarians are professional people who want a book of substance, documented with pertinent research and based on real practice in the classroom. This is the kind of book we have tried to write.

Special Features

- *Teaching Features* focus on ways teachers have actually used literature as the heart of curriculum.
- *Guidelines* provide criteria for evaluating books within each genre, as well as suggestions and criteria for evaluating children's responses to literature and literature-based programs.
- *Resources for Teaching* present a wide variety of useful information regarding children, book titles, and curriculum concerns in a compact, easily accessible format.
- *Related Readings* at the end of each chapter present annotated selections of books, articles, and research relevant to the chapter discussion.
- *Learning Experiences* at the end of each chapter serve as built-in study guides for sharing and comparing books with elementary-age children or university students.
- There are three *Appendixes:* "Children's Book Awards," "Book Selection Aids," and "Publishers' Addresses" (including book club addresses).
- *Endpapers* serve as an introductory core to the field of children's literature by providing an updated list of 150 books to read aloud to six overlapping age groups.

Instructor's Manual

The instructor's manual is a valuable resource for teaching and evaluating students' understanding of literature.

Each chapter corresponds to a text chapter to provide valuable teaching tips for all topic areas. Activities and strategies focus on both lectures and participatory activities and are geared to undergraduate and graduate students. Recommendations for poetry and brief readings to stimulate chapter discussion also accompany each chapter. Assessment suggestions are also included in each chapter.

acknowledgments

No one writes a book of this magnitude without the help of friends. We are deeply indebted to many people: the teachers, librarians, and children in the schools where we have always been welcomed; our students at The Ohio State University, Teachers College, and elsewhere, both undergraduates and graduate students, who have shared with us their insights into children's responses and interpretations of literature; and those teachers who have sent pictures of, and allowed us to take pictures in, their classrooms. We thank them all and hope they continue to share their classroom experiences and enthusiasm for children's literature.

Specifically, we wish to express our appreciation to the following teachers and schools who shared their teaching ideas, children's work, and classroom photos with us: Mary Sullivan Gallivan at PS 124 and Ilana Dubin-Spiegel at PS 116 in New York City; Faye Freeman of William B. Ward Elementary School in New Rochelle, New York; Jean M. Norman of Anna Maria College, Paxton, Massachusetts; Marlene Harbert and other faculty members at Barrington Road School, Upper Arlington, Ohio; Diane Driessen, librarian, and Jean Sperling, Peggy Harrison, Sheryl Reed, and other faculty members at Wickliffe Alternative School, Upper Arlington, Ohio; Kristen Kerstetter and the staff at Highland Park School, Grove City, Ohio; Marilyn Parker at Columbus School for Girls; Arleen Stuck, Richard Roth, and Melissa Wilson at Columbus Public Schools; Lisa Dapoz and Joan Fusco at Emerson Elementary School, Westerville, Ohio; Linda Woolard at Miller Elementary School, Newark, Ohio; Rebecca Thomas, Shaker Heights Public Schools, Ohio; Barbara Friedberg and other faculty members at the Martin Luther King, Jr., Laboratory School, Evanston Public Schools, Illinois; Joan Manzione, librarian, and Susan Steinberg, Marci El-Baba, and other staff members at George Mason Elementary School, Alexandria City Public Schools, Virginia; Shirley Bealor at Fairfax County Public Schools, Virginia; Nancy Anderson and Joan Schleicher at Mission School, Redlands Public Schools, California; Sharon Schmidt and other faculty members at Idyllwind Elementary School, Idyllwind, California: Janine Batzle at Esther L. Watson School, Anaheim, California; Joan Nassam and other faculty members at Mt. Eden Normal School in Auckland, New Zealand; Colleen Fleming at Mangere Bridge School, Auckland, New Zealand; and Roy Wilson, formerly at Dhahran Hills Elementary School, Dhahran, Saudi Arabia. We are also grateful to Valerie and Hans Bang-Jensen and their daughter Bree, and Dawn Person-Hampton, Harold Hampton, and their son Bryson, for their contributions. We are grateful to The Ohio State University photography department, to photographers Linda Rozenfeld, of Images Marmor Rozenfeld, and Larry Rose, of Redlands, California, for their careful work in creating many of the photographs used in this edition. We also wish to thank Connie Compton and Regina Weilbacher for special photographs. We are also grateful to Stacey Watt Kumor, Maria Lutz, and A. Ann Redpath, for their help with the research for and preparation of the manuscript.

We express gratitude to the following reviewers of this edition whose comments and suggestions were most helpful:

Jane White
Drury College

Linda Burns
Southeast Missouri State
University

Lenore D. Parker
Lesley College

Alice M. Denham
Texas Tech University

Gary D. Schmidt
Calvin College

Paul Dale Hauser
Kirkwood College

Anita Price Davis
Converse College

Carol J. Fuhler
Northern Arizona
University

James E. Twining
Community College of
Rhode Island

June G. Hornsby
William Carey College

Jance A. DeLong
Liberty University

Rebecca S. Compton
East Central University

We give special thanks to our friends at Brown & Benchmark, including Sue Pulvermacher-Alt, Suzanne Guinn, Karen Pluemer, Wendy Nelson, Jamie O'Neal, Patricia Barth, and Miriam Hoffman.

Finally, we want to thank our families for their patience, tolerance, and sheer endurance. There is no adequate way to thank friends and family except to wonder at the glory of having had their company and support in creating this text.

Charlotte S. Huck   Susan Hepler   Janet Hickman   Barbara Z. Kiefer

Children's Literature
in the Elementary School SIXTH EDITION

part one

Learning About Books and Children

chapter one

Knowing Children's Literature

Children's Literature Defined 5

What Is Children's Literature? 6
Writing for Children 7
Valuing Literature for Children 8

Personal Values 8

Enjoyment 8
Narrative as a Way of Thinking 9
Imagination 9
Vicarious Experience 10
Insight into Human Behavior 11
Universality of Experience 11

Educational Values 11

Literature in the Home 12
Literature in the School 13
Evaluating Children's Fiction 18

Plot 18
Setting 19

Theme 20
Characterization 21
Style 23
Point of View 24
Additional Considerations 26
Comparison with Other Books 27
Classics in Children's Literature 28
The Book Awards 28
Guidelines: Evaluating Children's Fiction 29
The Newbery and Caldecott Medals 30
International Book Awards 30
Lifetime Contribution Awards 31
Learning Experiences 32
Related Readings 32
Children's Literature 33

W as there ever a baby who didn't giggle with delight when her toes were touched to the accompaniment of "This little pig went to market"? Children's introduction to literature comes in the crib as babies listen to Mother Goose rhymes and nursery songs. It continues with the toddler's discovery of Eric Carle's *The Very Hungry Caterpillar* or Keiko Narahashi's *Is That Josie?* Later, children beg to hear Margaret Wise Brown's *Goodnight Moon* or Beatrix Potter's *The Tale of Peter Rabbit* just one more time.

If he is fortunate in his teachers, the primary-age child will hear stories two and three times a day. He will see his own reaction to a new baby in the family mirrored in *Julius, the Baby of the World* by Kevin Henkes or *Harry and Arney* by Judith Caseley. He will identify with the feelings of Max, who, when scolded, takes off in his imagination in *Where the Wild Things Are* by Maurice Sendak. And somewhere in those early years he will discover that he can read, and the magical world of literature will open before him.

The growing child experiences loneliness and fear as she imagines what it would be like to survive alone on an island for eighteen years as Karana did in *Island of the Blue Dolphins* by Scott O'Dell. She encounters personal toughness and resiliency as she lives the life of Gilly in Katherine Paterson's *The Great Gilly Hopkins*, the story of a foster child of today. She can taste the bitterness of racial prejudice in Mildred Taylor's *Roll of Thunder, Hear My Cry*, and she can share in the courage and determination of young people who helped others escape the Holocaust in *Number the Stars* by Lois Lowry.

A vast treasure of thoughts, deeds, and dreams lies waiting to be discovered in books. Literature begins with Mother Goose. It includes Sendak as well as Shakespeare, Milne as much as Milton, and Carroll before Camus. Children's literature is a part of the mainstream of all literature, whose source is life itself.

Children's Literature Defined

In the introduction to his book *The Call of Stories*, noted child psychiatrist Robert Coles tells how, during his childhood, his mother and father would read aloud to each other every evening. They were convinced that the great novels of Dickens, Tolstoy, and others held "reservoirs of wisdom." "Your mother and I feel rescued by these books," his father told him. "We read them gratefully."[1]

What is it about literature that can inspire such passionate attention? What *is* literature? And with more than 90,000 titles for boys and girls now in print, how can we choose the books that will bring the full rewards and pleasures of literature to children?

There are many ways of defining literature. Our ideas about what should be included have changed over time; definitions vary a bit from culture to culture, from critic to critic, and from reader to reader. In this book we think of literature as the imaginative shaping of life and thought into the forms and structures of language. Where appropriate, we consider pictures as well as words, asking how both sets of symbols work to produce an aesthetic experience. How do they help the reader perceive pattern, relationships, and feelings that produce an inner experience of art? This aesthetic experience might be a vivid reconstruction of past experience, an extension of experience, or the creation of a new experience.

[1]Robert Coles, *The Call of Stories: Teaching and the Moral Imagination* (Boston: Houghton Mifflin, 1989), p. xii.

We all have, in our experience, memories of certain books that changed us in some way—by disturbing us, or by gloriously affirming some emotion we knew but could never shape in words, or by revealing to us something about human nature. Virginia Woolf calls such times "moments of being," and James Joyce titles them "epiphanies."[2]

The province of literature is the human condition. Literature illuminates life by shaping our insights. W. H. Auden differentiated between first-rate literature and second-rate literature, writing that the reader responds to second-rate literature by saying, "That's just the way I always felt." But first-rate literature makes one say: "Until now, I never knew how I felt. Thanks to this experience, I shall never feel the same way again."[3]

The experience of literature always involves both the book and the reader. Try as we might to set objective criteria, judgments about the quality of literature must always be tempered by an awareness of its audience. Some critics consider Lewis Carroll's *Alice in Wonderland* the greatest book ever written for children. However, if the child has no background in fantasy, cannot comprehend the complexity of the plot, nor tolerate the logic of its illogic, *Alice in Wonderland* will not be the greatest book for that child.

What Is Children's Literature?

It might be said that a child's book is a book a child is reading, and an adult book is a book occupying the attention of an adult. Before the nineteenth century only a few books were written specifically for children. Children read books written for adults, taking from them what they could understand. Today, children continue to read some books intended for adults, such as the works of Stephen King and *All Creatures Great and Small* by James Herriot. And yet some books first written for children—such as Margery Williams's *The Velveteen Rabbit*, A. A. Milne's *Winnie the Pooh*, and J. R. R. Tolkien's *The Hobbit*—have been claimed as their own by college students.

Books *about* children might not necessarily be *for* them. Richard Hughes's adult classic *A High Wind in Jamaica* shows the "innocent" depravity of children in contrast to the group of pirates who had captured them. Yet in Harper Lee's novel *To Kill a Mockingbird*, also written for adults, 8-year-old Scout Finch reveals a more finely developed conscience than the small southern

town in which she is raised. The presence of a child protagonist, then, does not assure that the book is for children. Obviously, the line between children's literature and adult literature is blurred.

Children today appear to be more sophisticated and knowledgeable about certain life experiences than children of any previous generation. They spend a great deal of time within view of an operating television. According to *Nielsen Media Research*, actual time watching television for children ages 2 to 11 averages almost 23 hours per week.[4] The evening news shows them actual views of war while they eat their dinners. They have witnessed air strikes, assassinations, and starvation. While most modern children are separated from first-hand knowledge of birth, death, and senility, the mass media bring vicarious and daily experiences of crime, poverty, war, death, and depravity into the living rooms of virtually all American homes. This generation is exposed to more violence in the name of entertainment than any other generation in the past.

Such exposure has forced adults to reconsider what seems appropriate for children's literature. It seems unbelievable that only a generation ago Madeleine L'Engle's *Meet the Austins* was rejected by several publishers because it began with a death; or that some reviewers were shocked by a mild "damn" in *Harriet the Spy* by Louise Fitzhugh. Such publishing taboos have long since moderated. Children's books are generally less frank than adult books, but contemporary children's literature does reflect the problems of today, the ones children read about in the newspapers, see on television and in the movies, and experience at home.

However, the content of children's literature is limited by children's experience and understanding. Certain emotional and psychological responses seem outside the realms of childhood. For example, nostalgia is an adult emotion that is foreign to most boys and girls. Children seldom look back on their childhood, but always forward. Stories that portray children as "sweet" or that romanticize childhood, like the Holly Hobbie books that go with cards and gift products, have more appeal for adults than for children. Likewise, a sentimental book like *Love You Forever* by Robert Munsch, despite its popularity with teachers, is really not for children. Its themes of the passing of childhood and the assumption of responsibility for an aging parent both reflect adult experiences. The late Dr. Seuss (Theodor S. Geisel) also took an adult perspective in books such as *Oh, the Places You'll Go*. His enduring place in children's literature rests on earlier titles such as *And to Think That I Saw It on Mulberry Street* and *The Cat in the*

---

[2]Frances Clarke Sayers, *Summoned by Books* (New York: Viking, 1965), p. 16.

[3]W. H. Auden, as quoted by Robert B. Heilman in "Literature and Growing Up," *English Journal* 45 (September 1956): 307.

[4]Nielsen Media Research, November 1994.

Now you get settled in bed,
I'll tell you a story.

Literature such as Kim Stafford's *We Got Here Together* reflects the universal need for story.
Illustration from *We Got Here Together* by Kim R. Stafford, illustration copyright © 1994 by Debra Frasier, reproduced by permission of Harcourt Brace & Company.

Hat, books that are filled with childlike imagination and joyful exuberance.

Cynicism and despair are not childlike emotions and should not figure prominently in a child's book. Even though children are quick to pick up a veneer of sophistication, of disillusionment with adults and authority, they still expect good things to happen in life. And although many children do live in desperate circumstances, few react with real despair. They may have endured pain, sorrow, or horror; they may be in what we would consider hopeless situations; but they are not without hope. The truth of the Russian folktale by Becky Reyher, *My Mother Is the Most Beautiful Woman in the World*, shines clear. Children see beauty where there is ugliness; they are hopeful when adults have given up. This is not to suggest that all stories for children must have happy endings; many today do not. It is only to say that when you close the door on hope, you have left the realm of childhood. The only limitations, then, that seem binding on literature for children are those that appropriately reflect the emotions and experiences of children today. Children's books are books that have the child's eye at the center.

Writing for Children

Editor William Zinsser says:

> No kind of writing lodges itself so deeply in our memory, echoing there for the rest of our lives, as the books that we met in our childhood. . . . To enter and hold the mind of a child or a young person is one of the hardest of all writers' tasks.[5]

[5]William Zinsser, ed., *Worlds of Childhood: The Art and Craft of Writing for Children* (Boston: Houghton Mifflin, 1990), p. 3.

The skilled author does not write differently or less carefully for children just because she thinks they will not be aware of style or language. E. B. White asserts:

🐝 Anyone who writes *down* to children is simply wasting his time. You have to write up, not down. . . . Some writers for children deliberately avoid using words they think a child doesn't know. This emasculates the prose and . . . bores the reader. . . . Children love words that give them a hard time, provided they are in a context that absorbs their attention.[6]

Authors of children's literature and those who write for adults should receive equal approbation. C. S. Lewis[7] maintained that he wrote a children's story because a children's story was the best art form for what he had to say. Lewis wrote for both adults and children, as have Rumer Godden, Madeleine L'Engle, Paula Fox, E. B. White, Isaac Bashevis Singer, Penelope Lively, and many other well-known authors.

The uniqueness of children's literature, then, lies in the audience that it addresses. Authors of children's books are circumscribed only by the experiences of childhood, but these are vast and complex. Children think and feel; they wonder and they dream. Much is known, but little is explained.

Children are curious about life and adult activities. They live in the midst of tensions, of balances of love and hate within the family and the neighborhood. The author who can bring these experiences imagination and insight, give them literary shape and structure, and communicate them to children is writing children's literature.

Valuing Literature for Children

Because children naturally take such delight in books, we sometimes need to remind ourselves that books can do more for children than entertain them. Values inherent in sharing literature with children include personal qualities that might be difficult to measure as well as qualities that result in important educational understandings.

---

[6]E. B. White, "On Writing for Children," quoted in *Children and Literature: Views and Reviews*, ed. Virginia Haviland (Glenview, Ill.: Scott, Foresman, 1973), p. 140.

[7]C. S. Lewis, "On Three Ways of Writing for Children," *Horn Book Magazine* 39 (October 1963): 460.

Personal Values

Literature should be valued in our homes and schools for the enrichment it gives to the personal lives of children, as well as for its proven educational contributions. We will consider these affective values of literature before we discuss the more obvious educational ones.

Enjoyment

First and foremost, literature provides delight and enjoyment. Much of what is taught in school is not particularly enjoyable. Our Puritan backgrounds have made literature somewhat suspect. If children enjoy it, we reason, it can't be very good for them. Yet literature can educate at the same time as it entertains.

Children need to discover delight in books before they are asked to master the skills of reading. Then learning to read makes as much sense as learning to ride a bike; they know that eventually it will be fun. Four- and 5-year-olds who have laughed out loud at Judi Barrett's funny book *Animals Should Definitely Not Wear Clothing* can hardly wait to read it themselves. After hearing the ugly troll's cry of "Who's that tripping over my bridge?" children are eager to take parts in playing out *The Three Billy Goats Gruff* by P. C. Asbjørnsen and Jorgen Moe. They respond to the distinctive rhythm of the poem "Deer Mouse" by Marilyn Singer as the tiny creature goes scurrying for food, or to the sound of David McCord's "The Pickety Fence." Six- and 7-year-olds giggle at the silly antics in Arnold Lobel's Frog and Toad books, and they laugh uproariously when Ramona, in Beverly Cleary's *Ramona Quimby, Age 8*, mistakenly cracks a raw egg on her head thinking it is hard-boiled. Later they empathize with her when she overhears her teacher calling her a nuisance and a show-off.

Bingo Brown, a funny and genuine preadolescent first brought to life by Betsy Byars in *The Burning Questions of Bingo Brown*, is popular with middle graders. This age group also identifies with Anastasia in Lois Lowry's *Anastasia Krupnik*, a fourth grader who is horrified that her parents are having another baby. A warm, loving family relationship helps her to change her mind in this very funny yet touching novel. Sad books also bring a kind of enjoyment, as the children who have read *Bridge to Terabithia* by Katherine Paterson or *Stone Fox* by John Gardiner will tell you. Most children love being frightened by a story. Watch 6- and 7-year-olds respond to a scary sharing of Joanna Galdone's *The Tailypo* or Eve Bunting's *Night of the Gargoyles* and you will have no doubt of their shivery delight. Many older

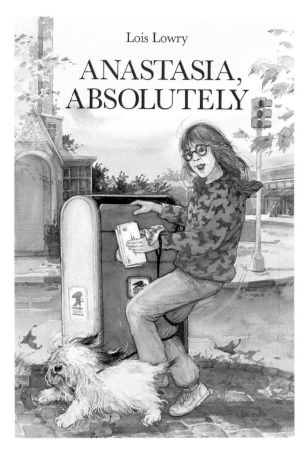

Middle-grade readers find delight in reading about characters like Anastasia in Lois Lowry's *Anastasia Absolutely*.

Cover from *Anastasia, Absolutely* by Lois Lowry. Jacket art © 1995 by Diane de Groat. Reprinted by permission of Houghton Mifflin Company. All rights reserved.

children revel in tales of suspense such as Betty Ren Wright's *The Ghost Comes Calling* or Donna Jo Napoli's haunting *The Magic Circle*.

The list of books that children enjoy can go on and on. There are so many fine ones—and so many that children won't find unless teachers, librarians, and parents share them with children. A love of reading and a taste for literature are the finest gifts we can give to our children, for we will have started them on the path of a lifetime of pleasure with books.

Narrative as a Way of Thinking

Storytelling is as old as human history and as new as today's gossip. Ask any of your friends about their weekends or last vacations, and they will organize their remarks in narratives about when their car stalled in the middle of a freeway or their child broke his leg or the marvelous places they stayed at the ocean. Barbara Hardy of the University of London suggests that all our constructs of reality are in fact stories that we tell ourselves about how the world works. She maintains that the narrative is the most common and effective way of ordering our world today:

> We dream in narrative, day-dream in narrative, remember, anticipate, hope, despair, believe, doubt, plan, revise, criticize, construct, gossip, learn, hate, love by narrative. In order really to live, we make up stories about ourselves and others, about the personal as well as the social past and future.[8]

If thinking in narrative form is characteristic of adult thought, it is even more typical of children's thinking. Watch young children and observe all the stories that they are playing out in their lives. When they are naughty and sent to their rooms, they tell themselves a story about how they will run away—and then won't their parents be sorry? Does this plot sound familiar? Of course, for it is the basis for Maurice Sendak's modern classic *Where the Wild Things Are*. Part of this book's tremendous popularity no doubt rests on the fact that it taps the wellsprings of the stories children have been telling themselves for years. Because it is literature, however, this story brings order and structure to the imagined events. Max returns to his room after his fantastic dream, "where he finds his supper waiting for him—and it was still hot."[9] Ask 5- or 6-year-olds who brought Max his supper and they will reply, "His mother." Then ask them what this ending means, and they will answer, "That she's not mad at him anymore." Critics will call the hot meal a symbol of love and reconciliation, but children are simply satisfied that all is well. The book narrative has provided a reassuring ending for the inner story that they have told themselves.

Imagination

Literature develops children's imagination and helps them to consider nature, people, experiences, or ideas in new ways. Children love to discover secrets hidden in certain illustrations: the little secondary story of the mouse in the informational book *Charlie Needs a Cloak* by Tomie de Paola; subplots and other small details in the borders of Jan Brett's *Town Mouse, Country Mouse*; or the shipwreck seen through the window of Sendak's *Outside Over There*.

[8]Barbara Hardy, "Narrative as a Primary Act of the Mind," in *The Cool Web: The Pattern of Children's Reading,* ed. Margaret Meek, Aidan Warlow, and Griselda Barton (New York: Atheneum, 1978) p. 13.

[9]Maurice Sendak, *Where the Wild Things Are* (New York: Harper & Row, 1963), unpaged.

Candace Whitman imagines night as a gentle bear in *The Night Is Like an Animal.*
Illustration from *The Night Is Like an Animal* by Candace Whitman. Copyright © 1995 by Candace Whitman. Reprinted by permission of Farrar, Straus & Giroux, Inc.

Good writing can pique the child's curiosity just as much as intriguing art can. Literature helps children entertain ideas they never considered before—"to dwell in possibility," as one of Emily Dickinson's poems suggests. Literature frequently provides answers to the child's "What if?" questions. *The Indian in the Cupboard* by Lynne Banks answers the question, What if I could bring my plastic toys to life? Then it asks another of Omri, the protagonist: What responsibility do I have for a live two-inch Indian? Madeleine L'Engle explores the idea of changing the past in *A Swiftly Tilting Planet.* What if we could enter history? Could we change certain major decisions? Charles Wallace has to find that out, and so does the reader. Literature explores possibility.

One of the values of fairy tales and myths is that they stretch the child's imagination. How many children would imagine creating a coach out of a pumpkin, horses from mice, and coachmen from lizards? Yet they readily accept it all in the well-loved tale of Cinderella. Bettelheim maintains: "Fairy tales have unequaled value, because they offer new dimensions to the child's imagination which would be impossible for him to discover as truly on his own."[10]

Today television has made everything so explicit that children are not developing their power to visualize. Teachers need to help them see with their inner eye to develop a country of the mind. Mollie Hunter, whose books such as *A Stranger Came Ashore* and *Mermaid Summer,* has this power to create the visual image in the mind of the reader and to stretch the imagination, says that the whole reward of reading is

to have one's imagination carried soaring on the wings of another's imagination, to be made more aware of the possibilities of one's mind . . .; to be thrilled, amazed, amused, awed, enchanted in worlds unknown until discovered through the medium of language, and to find in those worlds one's own petty horizons growing ever wider, ever higher.[11]

Vicarious Experience

The experiences children have with literature give them new perspectives on the world. Good writing can transport readers to other places and other times and expand their life space. Readers feel connected to the lives of others as they enter an imagined situation with their emotions tuned to those of the story. One 10-year-old boy, sharing his love of Jean George's survival story *My Side of the Mountain,* said, "You know, I've always secretly felt I could do it myself." This boy had vicariously shared Sam Gribley's adventure of "living off the land" in his tree home in the Catskill Mountains. Sam's experiment in self-sufficiency had strengthened the conviction of a 10-year-old that he, too, could take care of himself. James Britton points out that "we never cease to long for more lives than the one we have . . . [and a reader can] participate in an infinite number.[12]

How better can we feel and experience history than through a well-told story of the lives of its people and times? Readers of Lois Lowry's *Number the Stars* hold their breath as Nazi soldiers ask questions about 10-year-old Annemarie's dark-haired "sister." The girl is really Annemarie's Jewish friend Ellen, whose Star of David necklace is at that moment hidden in Annemarie's hand. Fear and courage become very real to the reader in this story of the Danish Resistance in World War II. A social studies textbook might simply list dates and facts related to this episode in history; a quality piece of imaginative writing has the power to make the reader

[10]Bruno Bettelheim, *The Uses of Enchantment: The Meaning and Importance of Fairy Tales* (New York: Knopf, 1976), p. 7.

[11]Mollie Hunter, *The Pied Piper Syndrome* (New York: HarperCollins, 1992), p. 92.

[12]James Britton, *The Dartmouth Seminar Papers: Response to Literature,* ed. James R. Squire (Champaign, Ill.: National Council of Teachers of English, 1968) p. 10.

feel, to transport her to Ellen's hiding place and allow her to feel the terror of Nazi persecution.

Literature provides vicarious experiences of adventure, excitement, and sometimes struggle. In fantasy, Will Stanton, seventh son of a seventh son, must do battle against the forces of evil, the power of the dark, and the unbelievably intense cold before he can complete his quest. The strength of this fantasy, *The Dark Is Rising* by Susan Cooper, is the degree to which the author involves the reader in Will's struggle.

Insight into Human Behavior

Literature reflects life, yet no book can contain all of living. By its very organizing properties literature has the power to shape and give coherence to human experience. It might focus on one aspect of life, one period of time in an individual's life, and so enable a reader to see and understand relationships that she had never considered. In *Dicey's Song* by Cynthia Voigt, a 13-year-old girl learns to release her brothers and sisters to the care of her independent, feisty grandmother. Only as she grows into loving and respecting this eccentric mother of her own mentally ill mother does Dicey begin to understand her grandmother's advice to reach out and let go. Gradually Dicey realizes how hard it is for Gram, whose own three children are lost to her, to reach out to this new family, to let herself love again. As Dicey sands down the rough places on the old derelict boat she has found, she symbolically smooths out her own rough life and readies herself for her independent voyage into maturity.

So much of what we teach in school is concerned with facts. Literature is concerned with feelings, the quality of life. It can educate the heart as well as the mind. Chukovsky, the Russian poet, says:

> The goal of every storyteller consists of fostering in the child, at whatever cost, compassion and humanness, this miraculous ability of man to be disturbed by another being's misfortune, to feel joy about another being's happiness, to experience another's fate as your own.[13]

Literature can show children how others have lived and "become," no matter what the time or place. As children gain increased awareness of the lives of others, as they vicariously try out other roles, they may develop a better understanding of themselves and those around them. Through wide reading as well as living, they acquire their perceptions of literature and life.

[13]Kornei Chukovsky, *From Two to Five*, trans. Miriam Morton (Berkeley: University of California Press, 1963), p. 138.

Universality of Experience

Literature continues to ask universal questions about the meaning of life and our relationships with nature and other people. Every story provides a point of comparison for our own lives. Are we as courageous as Irene in William Steig's *Brave Irene?* As troubled as Vinnie in Katherine Paterson's *Flip-Flop Girl?* Are we willing to go as far as Donald is to get revenge in Dennis Haseley's *Getting Him*, and are we willing to face the consequences that arise?

We also learn to understand the common bonds of humanity by comparing one story with another. Pride of accomplishment is strong for Ahmed when he learns to write his name in *The Day of Ahmed's Secret* by Florence Parry Heide and Judith Gilliland, and no less so for Kondi, who makes his own toy car from discarded wire in *Galimoto* by Karen Williams.

The story of Max leaving home to go to the island in Sendak's *Where the Wild things Are*, follows the ancient pattern of Homer's *Iliad* and *Odyssey*. This pattern is repeated again and again in myth and legend and seen in such widely divergent stories as *Homecoming* by Cynthia Voigt, *A Wrinkle in Time* by Madeleine L'Engle, and *Park's Quest* by Katherine Paterson. These are all stories of a journey through trials and hardship and the eventual return home. The pattern reflects everyone's journey through life.

War stories frequently portray acts of compassion in the midst of inhumanity. *The Upstairs Room* by Johanna Reiss and *Rose Blanche* by Christophe Gallaz and Roberto Innocenti both tell of the uncommon bravery of common people to do what they can to right a wrong. Children's literature is replete with stories of true friendships, as seen in Katherine Paterson's *Bridge to Terabithia*, E. B. White's *Charlotte's Web*, and picture books such as *Ernest and Celestine* by Gabrielle Vincent and *Willy and Hugh* by Anthony Browne. Other stories reflect the terrible renunciation of friendship, as found in *Friedrich* by Hans Richter or *The Friendship* by Mildred Taylor. Literature illumines all of life; it casts its light on all that is good, but it can also spotlight what is dark and debasing in the human experience. Literature enables us to live many lives, good and bad, and to begin to see the universality of human experience.

Educational Values

The intrinsic values of literature should be sufficient to give it a major place in the curriculum. Unfortunately, our society assigns a low priority to such aesthetic experiences. Only when literature is shown to be basic to the development of measurable skills does it receive attention in the elementary schools. Fortunately, research has proven the essential value of literature in helping children learn to read and write. There is now a wide body of evidence that supports the importance of literary experiences both before and after children come to school.

Literature in the Home

Characteristic of the development of all children is the phenomenal growth of language during the preschool years. Kornei Chukovsky, the Russian poet, refers to the tremendous "speech-giftedness of the pre-school child" and maintains that "beginning with the age of two, every child becomes for a short period of time a linguistic genius."[14]

Literature clearly plays an important role in all aspects of oral language development. We now know, for example, that when young children are read to, their own phonological production—the number and range of sounds that they produce—increases significantly.[15] Reading aloud has significant effects on the complexity of children's sentence structures[16] and also has an important influence on the development of their vocabulary.[17]

Reading a variety of books with children helps build important concepts about story structure[18] and expository text.[19] Moreover, the conversations that take place as children and adults read together also cement understandings about interactional patterns.[20]

In a study of 3-year-old Anna and her mother, Henrietta Dombey has described the characteristics that are typical of read-aloud sessions among preschoolers and parents or caregivers. As Anna and her mother discuss a story, we see how the mother uses stress and intonation as she reads and speaks to familiarize Anna with new syntactic forms. She also encourages Anna to take an active language role, to ask questions, and to test her own predictions.[21]

Reading aloud in the home has also been shown to be powerfully connected to later success in learning to read and in attitude toward reading. For example, in studies conducted in the United States[22] and in Britain, researchers found a strong correlation between reading in the home and children who learned to read before they entered school. Margaret Clark's study of young fluent readers in Scotland confirmed the value of being read aloud to at an early age.[23] Not all of the children in her study came from wealthy homes, but they all came from homes that valued books. The families made good use of the local library, and one father was a superb storyteller, telling his family fairy tales every night. Thorndike's study[24] of reading in fifteen different countries also found that books in the home and reading aloud were potent factors in children's learning to read.

An important longitudinal study by Gordon Wells showed that hearing many stories in the preschool years can have lasting benefit. The amount of experience that 5-year-old children in this study had had with books was directly related to their reading comprehension at age 7 and, even later, at age 11. Wells concluded, "Of all the activities that had been considered as possibly helpful preparation for the acquisition of literacy only one was significantly associated with later test scores. . . . That activity was listening to stories."[25]

A long-term effect of reading to children was also determined by Judith Sostarich, who compared sixth-grade "active readers" with nonactive readers in the same class.[26] In every instance the active readers had been read to from the time they were 3 years old, and some of their families were still sharing books aloud.

[14]Ibid., pp. 7, 9.

[15]O. C. Irwin, "Infant Speech: Effect of Systematic Reading of Stories," *Journal of Speech and Hearing Research* 3 (June 1960): 187–190.

[16]Courtney B. Cazden, "Environmental Assistance to the Child's Acquisition of Grammar" (Ph.D. dissertation, Harvard University, 1965).

[17]A. Ninio and J. Bruner, "The Achievement and Antecedents of Labelling," *Journal of Child Language* 5 (1973):1–15.

[18]Arthur N. Applebee, *The Child's Concept of Story: Ages Two to Seventeen* (Chicago: University of Chicago Press, 1978).

[19]Christine C. Pappas and Elga Brown, "Learning to Read by Reading: Learning How to Extend the Functional Potential of Language," *Research in the Teaching of English* 21 (1987):160–174.

[20]Catherine E. Snow and Beverly Goldfield, "Turn the Page Please: Situation Specific Language Learning," *Journal of Child Language* 10 (1983):551–570.

[21]Henrietta Dombey, "Learning The Language of Books," in *Opening Moves: Work in Progress in the Study of Children's Language Development* (Bedford Way Papers no. 17), ed. Margaret Meek (Portsmouth, N.H.: Heinemann, 1985), pp. 26–43.

[22]Dolores Durkin, *Children Who Read Early* (New York: Columbia Teachers College Press, 1966).

[23]Margaret Clark, *Young Fluent Readers* (London: Heinemann Educational Books, 1976), p. 102.

[24]Robert Ladd Thorndike, *Reading Comprehension, Education in 15 Countries: An Empirical Study*, vol. 3, International Studies in Education (New York: Holstead Wiley, 1973).

[25]Gordon Wells, *The Meaning Makers* (Portsmouth, N.H.: Heinemann, 1986), p. 151.

[26]Judith Sostarich, "A Study of the Reading Behavior of Sixth Graders: Comparisons of Active and Other Readers" (Ph.D. dissertation, Ohio State University, 1974).

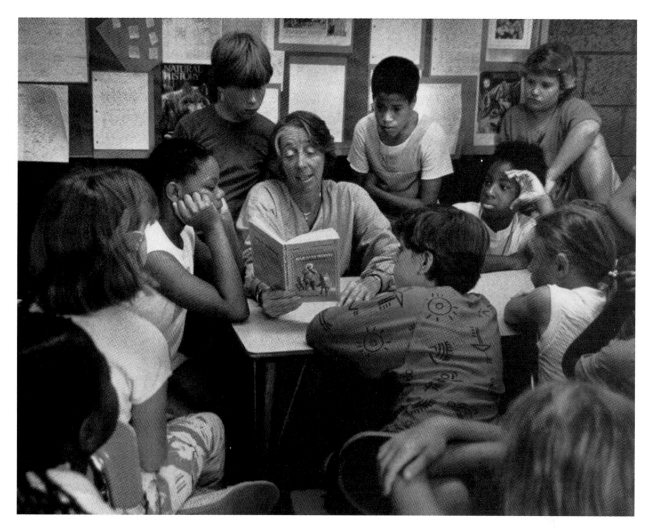

Reading aloud to older children gives the teacher a chance to introduce and discuss more complex stories than the ones they choose themselves.

Martin Luther King, Jr., Laboratory School, Evanston, Illinois, Public Schools. Barbara Friedberg, teacher. Photo by James Ballard.

Literature in the School

It is clear that experiences with literature at an early age can benefit children in many ways. Once children enter school, they also benefit when literature is placed at the center of the curriculum.

Reading Aloud and Learning to Read

The powerful influence of books on children's language and literacy continues once they enter school. Studies with school-age children show that reading aloud can result in significant increases in their reading achievement. Dorothy Cohen sought to determine if reading aloud to 7-year-olds who had not previously been exposed to literature would make a difference in their

ability to read.[27] Books were read aloud to children in ten experimental classrooms in New York City on a daily basis for a period of one year. Following the 20-minute story time, the children were asked to do something with the book to make it memorable. For example, they might act out the story, draw a picture of their favorite characters, or compare the story with a similar story—something to make them think about the story and revisit the book several times. At the end of the year, Cohen found that the children in the

[27]Dorothy Cohen, "The Effect of Literature on Vocabulary and Reading Achievement," *Elementary English* 45 (February 1968): 209–213, 217.

experimental group were significantly ahead of the control group on their individual reading vocabulary and reading comprehension. Evidently, reading *to* children and giving them a chance to work with real books had helped them learn to read.

In the past ten years many teachers have written articles for professional journals about their successes with using children's trade books in their reading programs. These reports confirm the research that links literature with success in learning to read. They also stress that increased enjoyment and interest in reading are important outcomes of regularly reading aloud to children.

Developing a Sense of Book Language

Hearing books read aloud is a powerful motivation for the child to begin to learn to read. Children learn that reading provides enjoyment, and they want to learn to read themselves. They also see someone important in their lives valuing books. Too frequently we tell children that reading is important, but we show by our actions that we really value other activities more.

Exposure to books also provides a rich input of literary language. Frank Smith maintains:

> Children need to become acquainted with the language of books; it is not the language they hear spoken around them in their daily life, and it is unrealistic to expect them to learn this unfamiliar style at the same time they learn to read.[28]

Listening to stories introduces children to patterns of language and extends vocabulary and meaning. Young children love to repeat such refrains as "Not by the hair on my chinny chin chin" from Paul Galdone's *The Three Little Pigs* or the well-loved rhyme from Wanda Gág's *Millions of Cats*:

> Cats here, cats there,
> Cats and kittens everywhere,
> Hundreds of cats,
> Thousands of cats,
> Millions and billions and trillions of cats.[29]

They delight in new words, such as *humiliated* in Lynd Ward's *The Biggest Bear* or the line from Beatrix Potter's

The Tale of Peter Rabbit in which the friendly sparrows "implored him to exert himself" when Peter was caught in the gooseberry net. A first-grade teacher read to her class Charlotte Zolotow's *Say It!* in which a mother and her little girl go for a walk on a beautiful autumn day—a "splendiferous day," the mother calls it. Later on, a child asked her to reread the "splendiferous book." Children love the sounds of words and enjoy repeating them over and over.

Knowing the structure of a story and being able to anticipate what a particular character will do helps young children predict the action and determine the meaning of the story they are reading. For example, children quickly learn the rule of three that prevails in most folktales. They know that if the first Billy Goat Gruff goes trip-trapping over the bridge, the second Billy Goat Gruff will go trip-trapping after him, and so will the third. In reading or listening to the story of the Gingerbread Boy, the child who has had a rich exposure to literature can anticipate the ending on the basis of what he knows about the character of foxes in stories. As one little boy said, "Foxes are clever. He won't be able to get away from him!"

This understanding of literary patterns extends to expository text as well as to narrative. In her studies of kindergartners' pretend reading of information books and storybooks, Christine Pappas found that young children are equally successful in taking on textual properties of both narrative and expository texts.[30] Furthermore, she found that the kindergartners often preferred informational books to storybooks. She suggests that

> to become literate the young child has to come to terms with certain important characteristics of written language that are different from spoken language—its sustained organization, its disembedded quality. And children need to understand that different conventions, rhythms, and structures are expressed in different written genres to meet various social purposes in our culture. (p. 126)

The more experience children have with literature—with fiction, folktales, poetry, biography, and informational books—the greater their ability will be to grasp the meaning of the text and understand the way the author tells it. This helps them become successful readers.

[28]Frank Smith, *Reading Without Nonsense* (New York: Teachers College Press, 1979), p. 136.

[29]Wanda Gág, *Millions of Cats* (New York: Coward McCann, 1928), unpaged.

[30]Christine C. Pappas, "Is Narrative 'Primary'? Some Insights from Kindergartners' Pretend Readings of Stories and Information Books," *Journal of Reading Behavior* 25 (1993): 97–129.

Developing Fluency and Understanding

The reading of many books is essential to the development of expert readers. This was the kind of reading, even rereading, of favorite stories that Margaret Clark found to be characteristic of her avid readers.[31] Such reading is characteristic of middle-grade students who get "hooked" on a particular author or series of books. Frequently, a sign of a good reader is the rereading of favorite books.

In a year-long study of children's reading behavior in a literature-based program in a fifth- and sixth-grade class, Susan Hepler found that these children read an average of 45 books a piece for the year, with the range being 25 to 122 books.[32] Compare this record with the usual two basal texts read in a year by children in the typical basal reading programs. Only wide reading will develop fluency.

Such assumptions are supported by studies that link diverse reading experiences to reading proficiency and comprehension.[33] Many researchers have concluded that the extent to which children read is a significant contributor to their developed reading ability. The National Assessment of Educational Progress (NAEP) found a clear relationship between wide reading experiences and reading ability and suggested that reading outside of school for enjoyment and reading self-selected books in school, including information books as well as stories, were important to growth in reading.[34]

With all the many demands on their time outside of school, we cannot always be sure that children will read at home. It is even more important, then, for teachers at every grade level—from preschool on up—to enable children to spend time with books every day. If they do not have the opportunity to read widely at school, children probably will not become fluent readers.

Literature and Writing

Teachers have always believed that there is a relationship between reading and writing—that the good writers are avid readers, and that good readers often are the best writers. Now we have research that validates those observations and explores how reading and writing develop together.

Walter Loban conducted one of the most extensive studies of the relationship between reading achievement as measured by reading scores and the ratings of writing quality. He discovered a high correlation, particularly in the upper elementary grades, and concluded: "Those who read well also write well; those who read poorly also write poorly."[35]

Glenda Bissex studied the evolution of her own child's writing and published the results in a book titled after the sign 5-year-old Paul posted over his workbench: ""DO NAT DSTRB GNYS AT WRK"[36] This "genius" learned to write and read at the same time. Reading appeared to have a broad influence on the forms of writing Paul did. He first demonstrated his awareness of print by making signs, labels, and advertisements. He then went on to write shopping lists, little stories, notes, newspapers, and a science fiction book. Books at all times served as models for Paul's increasing sense of form.

If reading provides models for children's writing, then the kinds of reading children are exposed to become even more important. Exposure to much good literature appears to make a difference in children's writing abilities, just as it does in their linguistic abilities. Fox and Allen maintain: "The language children use in writing is unlikely to be more sophisticated in either vocabulary or syntax than the language they read or have had someone else read to them."[37]

The content of children's stories also reflects the literature they have heard. Whether consciously or unconsciously, children pick up words, phrases, parts of plots, even the intonation pattern of dialogue from books they know. A second grader wrote the following when a researcher asked him to "write a story." No other directions were given. Notice the number of stories that he "borrows" from in telling his own. The titles of his probable sources are given at right.

---

[31]Margaret Clark, *Young Fluent Readers*, p. 103.

[32]Susan Hepler, "Patterns of Response to Literature: A One-Year Study of a Fifth- and Sixth-Grade Classroom" (Ph.D. dissertation, Ohio State University, 1982).

[33]Jim Cipielewski, and Keith E. Stanovich, "Predicting Growth in Reading Ability from Children's Exposure to Print," *Journal of Experimental Child Psychology* 54 (1992):74–89.

[34]Jay Campbell and Kent P. Ashworth, eds., *Interviewing Children About Their Literary Experience: Report in Brief* (Washington, D.C.: U.S. Department of Education, 1995).

[35]Walter Loban, *The Language of Elementary School Children*, Research Report No. 1 (Urbana, Ill.: National Council of Teachers of English, 1963) p. 75.

[36]Glenda Bissex, *GNYS AT WRK: A Child Learns to Write and Read* (Cambridge, Mass.: Harvard University Press, 1980), p. 197.

[37]Sharon Fox and Virginia Allen, *The Language Arts: An Integrated Approach* (New York: Holt, Rinehart & Winston, 1983), p. 206.

The Lonesome Egg

Once there lived a Lonesome Egg

    And nobody liked him because he was ugly. And there was an Ugly duck too but they didn't know each other.

    One day while the Lonesome Egg was walking, he met the Ugly duck. And the Egg said to the Duck,

    "Will you be my friend?"

    "Well, O.K."

    "Oh, thank you."

    "Now let's go to your house, Duck"

    "No, let's go to your house"

    "No, we'll go to your house first and my house too."

    "O.K."

    And while they were walking they met a Panda Bear and they picked it up and took it to Duck's house. And then the baby Panda Bear said: "I'm tired of walking." So they rested.

    And soon came a tiger. And the tiger ate them up except for Duck. And right as he saw that he ran as fast as he could until he saw a woodcutter and he told the woodcutter to come very quickly. And when they got there the tiger was asleep. So the woodcutter cut open the tiger and out came Egg and Baby Panda Bear. And they ate the tiger and lived happily ever after.[38]

The Golden Egg Book (Brown)

The Ugly Duckling (Andersen)

Do You Want to Be My Friend? (Carle)

Dialogue from the Frog and Toad series (Lobel)

The Fat Cat (Kent)

The Gingerbread Boy (Galdone)

Little Red Riding Hood (Grimm brothers)

    Not only the content of this writing, but also certain conventions of the text reflect previous exposure to literature. The conventional beginning, "Once there lived," and the traditional ending, "lived happily ever after," are obvious examples. Phrases such as "and soon came a tiger" and "out came Egg and Baby Panda Bear"

have a literary ring to them. Discussion of whose house they will go to echoes the many conversations in the Frog and Toad series by Arnold Lobel. There can be little doubt about the influence of other stories on the shape and content of this 7-year-old's writing. The role of literature, then, is significant to the development of writing. For as Frank Smith wrote,

> the development of composition in writing cannot reside in writing alone, but requires reading and being read to. Only from the written language of others can children observe and understand convention and idea together.[39]

Literature and Critical Thinking

Recent calls for reform in education have stressed the need for children to become better critical thinkers and problem solvers. Many schools have set goals for developing these abilities, which has resulted in the publication of special practice materials and packaged programs as well as tests to measure specific skills. One of the benefits of using literature in the elementary school is that it encourages critical and creative thinking in a more natural way than worksheet exercises in logic do.

    Comparing, summarizing, and finding the main idea are generally recognized as components of critical thinking. These are also built-in features of good book discussions and other literature activities. As children compare many variants of the Cinderella story, for instance, they will identify similarities and differences and weigh the comparative merits of each. Talking about the moral of a fable, or the theme of a story, such as what lesson the animals learned in the tale "The Little Red Hen," is a way of exploring a story's main idea. Children might also consider which of two biographies of Christopher Columbus presents the more balanced view of the famous explorer, or which of several books about the Civil War presents the most complete picture of the issues behind the conflict. Because of its variety in content and the availability of many books on one topic, literature provides great opportunity for thinking critically and making judgments.

Literature Across the Curriculum

The widely read person is usually the well-informed person. The content of literature educates while it entertains. Fiction includes a great deal of information about the real world, present and past.

    A 10-year-old reading *Julie of the Wolves* by Jean George learns much that is authentic and true about

---

[38]"Study of Cohesion Elements on Three Modes of Discourse," NIE Research project, Martha L. King and Victor Rentel, co-researchers, Ohio State University, 1983.

[39]Frank Smith, *Writing and the Writer* (New York: Holt, Rinehart & Winston, 1982).

wolf behavior. Written by a naturalist who has studied animal behavior, this story includes information about wolf communication, the hierarchy of the pack, and the division of labor within the pack. More important than the factual information, however, is the story's theme of the significance of choice and growing up.

My Brother Sam Is Dead by the Colliers gives authentic information about one part of the American Revolution while it contrasts different points of view held by the various characters toward the war itself. This story helps the reader imagine what it was like to live in a family torn apart by divided loyalties. And it raises the larger political question concerning the role of neutrality in a revolution.

Information books can also add both facts and human perspective to the curriculum. In *Across America on an Emigrant Train*, Jim Murphy weaves excerpts from the diary of Robert Louis Stevenson together with material about the building of the transcontinental railroads. However, this is really the story of the courage of the diverse groups of people who went looking for a better life in the American West in the late 1800s.

Picture books, too, offer important understandings across subject areas and grade levels. In Anne Shelby's *Homeplace*, a grandmother tells her young granddaughter about the ancestors who built their home. Wendy Anderson Halperin's beautiful illustrations add a wealth of details about aspects of family life from the early

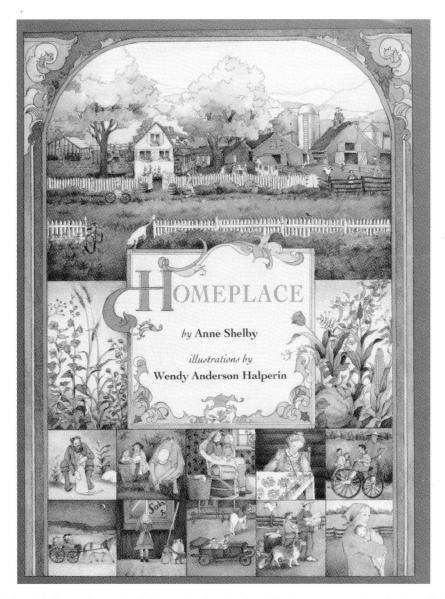

Wendy Anderson Halperin's illustrations help children visualize details of life in other generations in Anne Shelby's *Homeplace*.
From *Homeplace* by Anne Shelby, illustrated by Wendy Anderson Halperin. Jacket illustration copyright © 1995 by Wendy Anderson Halperin. Reprinted by permission of the Publisher, Orchard Books, New York.

1800s to the present. Anita Lobel's lovely alphabet book *Alison's Zinnia* or Lois Ehlert's *Growing Vegetable Soup* can help young children learn the names of flowers and vegetables. Dick King-Smith's *All Pigs Are Beautiful* compares similarities and differences between people and pigs in an information book that is as visually appealing as it is engaging to read. The story of *The Doorbell Rang* by Pat Hutchins incorporates a math problem about sharing Grandma's cookies that children will want to solve.

All areas of the curriculum can be enriched through literature. Children might start with a story and research the facts; or they might start with the facts and find the true meanings in the stories surrounding those facts. Literature has the power to educate both the heart and the mind.

Introducing Our Literary Heritage

In general, the educational values of literature described here center on learning *through* literature. We must never forget, however, that as children have experiences with books, they are also learning *about* literature. As they enjoy nursery rhymes, traditional literature, and well-loved classics, they build a background for understanding genre, story structure, and many literary allusions.

Through in-depth discussions of such books as *Missing May* by Cynthia Rylant, *Julie of the Wolves* by Jean George, and *Tuck Everlasting* by Natalie Babbitt, children become aware of what constitutes fine writing. While children usually will focus on plot or story, teachers can help them see Summer's growing acceptance of May's death, or ask them why they think Jean George began her book when Julie was lost on the vast tundra rather than starting with the beginning of her story. Children can be led to discover the recurring references to the wheel, the toad, and the music box in *Tuck Everlasting* as a way of shedding light on their understanding of this lovely fantasy. Children's appreciation for literature and knowledge of their literary heritage should be developed gradually in the elementary school as a way to add to the enjoyment of literature rather than as an end in itself.

Evaluating Children's Fiction

What makes a good children's book? Who will read it? Why? Whose purposes will it serve? All these are important considerations to be taken up in later sections of this chapter and throughout the book. The primary concern of evaluation, however, is a book's literary and aesthetic qualities. Children show what they think of books through their responses, but they are not born critics in the conventional sense. Teachers and librarians need to value children's own interpretations and judgments. At the same time, they need to help children discover what practiced readers look for in a well-written book.

The traditional criteria by which we evaluate a work of fiction look at such elements as plot, setting, theme, characterization, style, point of view, and format. Special criteria need to be applied to different types of literature, such as picture storybooks, biographies, and informational books. For example, in picture books it is important that the verbal text and illustrations interact harmoniously. Modern fantasy has to establish believability in a way that realistic fiction does not. Historical fiction requires added criteria for authenticity of setting. Perhaps the most important task for critics of any age is to identify the kind of book they are reading in order to apply the appropriate criteria for evaluation. In general, though, the following elements are crucial to good works of fiction.

Plot

Of prime importance in any work of fiction for children is the plot. Children ask first, "What happens? Is it a good story?" The plot is the plan of action; it tells what the characters do and what happens to them. It is the thread that holds the fabric of the story together and makes the reader want to continue reading.

A well-constructed plot is organic and interrelated. It grows logically and naturally from the action and the decisions of the characters in given situations. The plot should be credible and ring true rather than depend on coincidence and contrivance. It should be original and fresh rather than trite, tired, and predictable.

In books that have substance, obstacles are not quickly overcome, and choices are not always clear-cut. In C. B. Christiansen's *I See the Moon*, 12-year-old Bitte struggles to reconcile her desire to play the role of aunt with her older sister's decision to put her baby up for adoption. It is not an easy decision for her sister, and Bitte's eventual acceptance of this difficult choice represents a new, more mature perspective that is won at the cost of much anguish.

Plot is the chief element of appeal in stories of mystery and suspense. In series mysteries, the action is frequently predictable; Nancy Drew never fails, and the Hardy Boys move smoothly from one major feat to the next. The action is usually beyond the capabilities of the characters and becomes contrived and sensational. In contrast, Avi's *The True Confessions of Charlotte Doyle* is a tautly constructed story of suspense. In this nineteenth-century shipboard murder mystery, events become increasingly surprising although the author makes them seem inevitable. The action begins sedately but then moves at breakneck speed to the climax. As in

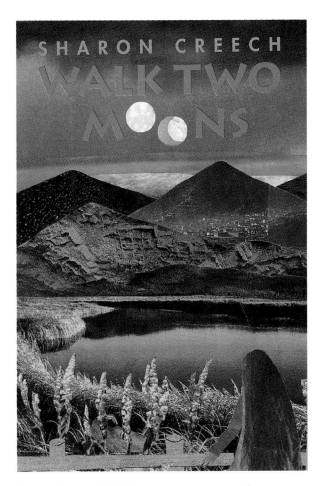

Sharon Creech's *Walk Two Moons* involves children in several levels of plot structure.
Copyright © 1994 by Sharon Creech. Used by permission of HarperCollins Publishers, New York, NY.

other well-plotted books, the climax develops naturally from the interaction of characters and events. Children prefer a swift conclusion following the climax. The purpose of this brief denouement is to knot together the loose ends of the story.

Most plots in children's literature are presented in a linear fashion. Frequently children find it confusing to follow several plot lines or to deal with flashbacks in time and place. However, several excellent books for middle graders do make use of these devices. Multiple stories are interwoven in the Newbery Medal book *Walk Two Moons* by Sharon Creech. On a cross-country trip with her grandparents, Salamanca Tree Hiddle regales them with the somewhat wacky adventures of her friend Phoebe. As the narrative moves back and forth between the car journey and Phoebe's adventures, however, Sal's own story is revealed. These different plots represent the layers of self-understanding that Salamanca must uncover in order to accept the major changes that have occurred in her life.

In *Cousins*, Virginia Hamilton dramatically portrays the grief and guilt young Cammy feels when her cousin, spoiled Patty Ann, is drowned on a day-camp excursion. Although the book is a short one, it has multiple plot lines. The reader's attention is also drawn to Cammy's concern over the time her brother spends with troublesome cousin Richie and to her own attempts to brighten the life of Gram Tut, who is in the Care Home. The author uses remembered and imagined events, making part of the "action" take place in Cammy's head. This gives the story a wonderfully rich texture but makes it more challenging. The effectiveness of structure in stories like these depends on the clarity of the author's presentation and the child's ability to comprehend complexity.

Plot is but one element of good writing. If a book does not have a substantial plot, it will not hold children's interest long. But well-loved books are memorable for more than plot alone.

Setting

The structure of a story includes both the construction of the plot and its setting. The setting may be in the past, the present, or the future. The story may take place in a specific locale, or the setting may be deliberately vague to convey the universal feeling of all suburbs, all large cities, or all rural communities.

The setting for Cynthia Rylant's *Missing May* is contemporary rural West Virginia. Summer, an orphan who was bounced from home to home until May and Ob took her into their lives, learns to accept the death of her beloved May and to trust in the strong connections of people who care for one another. The story's power lies in a setting that is more than a mere geographical place. The real setting here is a community of living people who care deeply for one another, and it is this place and the strength of the story's theme that suggest the universality of this story and its setting.

Both the time and the place of the story should affect the action, the characters, and the theme. Place, time, and people are inextricably bound together in Pam Conrad's *Prairie Songs*. Although Louisa's family see the huge Nebraska prairie with its endless skies as home, their new neighbor Mrs. Berryman is driven mad by its isolation and hardships. The setting that the author constructs includes geography, weather, the news of the day, and the details of everyday life. Pam Conrad drew on the work of original journals and a pioneer photographer in supplying these elements for *Prairie Songs*. Readers can compare their mental images of sod houses and prairie grass with the actual photographs in Conrad's nonfiction book *Prairie Visions: The Life and Times of Solomon Butcher*.

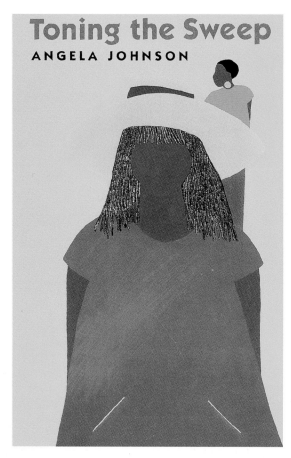

Angela Johnson creates a vivid southwestern setting in *Toning the Sweep*.
From *Toning the Sweep* by Angela Johnson. Jacket painting copyright © 1993 by Synthia Saint James. Reprinted by permission of the Publisher, Orchard Books, New York.

Stories of the present often seem to occur in homogenized settings that have little impact on character and action. There are notable exceptions, of course. When Brian's plane crashes at the edge of a wilderness lake in Gary Paulsen's *Hatchet*, the rigors of that setting dictate the terms of the tense survival story that follows. Jamal and Tito in *Scorpions* by Walter Dean Myers lead lives circumscribed by their urban ghetto environment. The desert of the Southwest, or "the dry," is both a memorable background and the focus of Emily's videotaping project in *Toning the Sweep* by Angela Johnson. As she seeks to record her Grandmama Ola's story and to understand her own place in it as an outsider from Cleveland, Emily comes to know the desert and the people who have made it a community for her grandmother. Books that provide a unique sense of place are more memorable than those that do not.

The imaginary settings of fantasy must be carefully detailed in order to create a believable story. In *Charlotte's Web*, E. B. White has made us see and smell Wilbur's barnyard home so clearly that it takes little stretch of the imagination to listen in on the animals' conversations. In *A Wizard of Earthsea*, a more serious fantasy by Ursula Le Guin, the tale of wizards, dragons, and shadows is played out in an archipelago of imagined islands. Ruth Robbins has provided a map of Earthsea, for its geography is as exact as the laws and limits of magic used by the wizards of the isles. The setting of a story, then, is important in creating mood, authenticity, and credibility. The accident of place and time in a person's life might be as significant as the accident of birth, for places can have tremendous significance in our life stories.

Theme

A third point in the evaluation of any story is its overarching theme, or themes, the larger meanings that lie beneath the story's surface. Most well-written books can be read for several layers of meaning—plot, theme, or metaphor. On one level the story of *Charlotte's Web* by E. B. White is simply an absurd but amusing tale of how a spider saves the life of a pig; on another level, it reveals the meaning of loneliness and the obligations of friendship. A third layer of significance can be seen in the acceptance of death as a natural part of the cycle of life. Finally, E. B. White himself wrote that it was "an *appreciative* story. . . . It celebrates life, the seasons, the goodness of the barn, the beauty of the world, the glory of everything."[40]

The theme of a book reveals something of the author's purpose in writing the story. Katherine Paterson eloquently states how authors and readers are partners in calling up true meaning:

> We are trying to communicate that which lies in our deepest heart, which has no words, which can only be hinted at through the means of a story. And somehow, miraculously, a story that comes from deep in my heart calls from a reader that which is deepest in his or her heart, and together from our secret hidden selves we create a story that neither of us could have told alone.[41]

Theme provides a dimension to the story that goes beyond the action of the plot. The theme of a book might be the acceptance of self or others, growing up,

[40]Dorothy L. Guth, ed., *Letters of E. B. White* (New York: Harper & Row, 1976), p. 613.

[41]Katherine Paterson, "Hearts in Hiding," in *Worlds of Childhood: The Art and Craft of Writing for Children*, ed. William Zinsser (Boston: Houghton Mifflin, 1990), p. 153.

the overcoming of fear or prejudice. This theme should be worth imparting to young people and be based on justice and integrity. Sound moral and ethical principles should prevail. However, one danger in writing books for children is that the theme will override the plot. Authors might be so intent on conveying a message that they neglect story or characterization. Didacticism is still alive and well in the twentieth century. It might hide behind the facade of ecology, drug abuse, or alienation, but it destroys fine writing.

Some well-written stories do make their themes fairly explicit, however. In Natalie Babbitt's *Tuck Everlasting*, three motifs provide meaningful threads that keep reappearing: a toad, a music box, and the concept of a wheel. The wheel represents the theme of this gentle fantasy, the cycle of life and death that the Tuck family can never experience because they have drunk by accident from a spring that has frozen them in time, to live forever. As Angus Tuck tries to persuade young Winnie Foster not to drink from this water, he uses the example of a wheel to carry his message about life:

> It's a wheel, Winnie. Everything is a wheel, turning and turning, never stopping. The frog is part of it, and the bugs, and the fish and the wood thrush, too. And people. But never the same ones. Always coming in new, always growing and changing, and always moving on. That's the way it's supposed to be. That's the way it *is*.[42]

Children in the middle grades can comprehend symbolic meaning and recurring motifs that are woven so beautifully into the fabric of the theme. Literary symbols are the fusion of some concrete object with an abstract concept or meaning. Eight- and 9-year-olds, for example, link the significance of Jean Fritz's title *The Cabin Faced West* with the brothers' admonition that no one was to mention their former home on the eastern side of the mountain. Children as young as 7 and 8 realize the symbolic meaning of the cloak Sarah Noble's mother had given her to wear when she went into the wilderness with her father in *The Courage of Sarah Noble* by Alice Dalgliesh.

Characterization

True characterization is another hallmark of fine writing. The people portrayed in children's books should be as convincingly real and lifelike as our next-door neighbors. Many of the animal characters in modern fantasy also

Arnold Lobel created two memorable animal characters in the *Frog and Toad* series.
Copyright © 1970 by Arnold Lobel. Used by permission of HarperCollins Publishers, New York, NY.

have human personalities. The credibility of characters depends on the author's ability to show their true natures, their strengths, and their weaknesses.

Just as it takes time to know a new friend in all his various dimensions, so, too, does an author try to present many facets of a character bit by bit. In revealing character, an author might tell about the person through narration, record the character's conversation with others, describe the thoughts of the character, show the thoughts of others about the character, or show the character in action. A character who is revealed in only one way is apt to lack depth. If a single dimension of character is presented, or one trait overemphasized, the result is likely to be stereotyped and wooden. One-dimensional characters are the norm in folk and fairy tales, where witches are prototypes of evil and youngest children are deserving and good. However, modern fiction requires multidimensional characters whose actions and feelings grow out of the

---

[42]Natalie Babbitt, *Tuck Everlasting* (New York: Farrar, Straus & Giroux, 1975), p. 62.

circumstances of the story. Books are usually more satisfying when readers feel they are discovering the character through the story rather than relying on authors' labels, like *jealous, troublesome,* or *shy.* Children do not need to be told that Gus overcomes his fear of the dark in *The Stone-Faced Boy* by Paula Fox; he shows his bravery by rescuing a dog for his sister in the middle of the night.

In addition to depth in characterization, there should be consistency in character portrayal. Everything characters do, think, and say should seem natural and inevitable. We can expect them to act and speak in accordance with their age, culture, and educational background. For the fictionalized voice of young Harriet in *Letters from a Slave Girl: The Story of Harriet Jacobs,* author Mary E. Lyons used spelling and grammar patterns that were based on authentic letters of Harriet and her brother. In a note Lyons explains:

> The younger Harriet would have spoken and written in the southern black dialect of her native state—a dialect somewhat diluted by spending eight childhood years with white mistresses. To recreate this voice I flavored letters with folk expressions inspired by the rich oral language of former North Carolina slaves.[43]

Patricia McKissack uses similar speech patterns in *Mirandy and Brother Wind,* a tale with origins in the rural South. Grandmama Beasley, the oldest character, uses the most pronounced version of this dialect: "Can't nobody put shackles on Brother Wind, chile. He be special. He be free."[44]

Another aspect of sound characterization is growth and development. Do the characters change in the course of the story, or are they untouched by the events in which they have a part? In picture books and short tales, we might expect characters to be fully described but not to change much. In longer fiction, however, characters have time to learn and grow. Many characters are best remembered for the turnarounds they have made or the way they have matured. Readers do not quickly forget the struggle of headstrong, self-centered Jo of Louisa May Alcott's *Little Women* in taming her rebellious ways. Marguerite de Angeli has created a vivid character study of Robin in her outstanding book *The Door in the Wall.* Robin, crippled son of a great lord,

---

[43]Mary E. Lyons. *Letters from a Slave Girl: The Story of Harriet Jacobs* (New York: Scribner's, 1992), p. 137.

[44]Patricia C. McKissack, *Mirandy and Brother Wind* (New York: Knopf, 1988), unpaged.

Beverly Cleary's Ramona has come alive for millions of children in books like *Ramona and Her Father.*
Illustration from *Ramona and her Father* by Beverly Cleary, illustrated by Alan Tiegreen. Copyright © 1975, 1977 by Beverly Cleary. By permission of Morrow Junior Books, a division of William Morrow & Company, Inc.

must learn to accept his infirmity and find a useful place in life. The gradual development of his character is made clear as he solves these problems. Another character who grows before the reader's eyes in a gradual and convincing manner is the title character of Katherine Paterson's *Lyddie.* A nineteenth-century New England girl who becomes a mill worker in an effort to save the family farm, Lyddie is courageous and determined throughout the story. The change comes in her ability to see the options of her life realistically and in her growing sense of the possibilities of her future as she sets off to attend the first women's college in the nation.

Not all characters change, though. A character might be well developed, multidimensional, and interesting and yet seem to remain frozen in that particular time of her or his life. Such characters are common in humorous stories. In Robert McCloskey's *Homer Price* and Astrid Lindgren's *Pippi Longstocking,* the title characters remain consistent to their natures in all their adventures. Some stories, then, might be notable for character delineation rather than character development.

Long after we have forgotten their stories, we can recall some of the personalities of children's literature. We recognize them as they turn the corner of our memories, and we are glad for their friendship. The line is long; it includes animals and people. It is hard to tell where it begins, and we are happy that is has no end. In our mind's eye we see the three loyal friends Mole, Toad, and Rat returning from their adventures on the open road; Mary Poppins flies by holding tightly to her large black umbrella with one hand and carrying her carpet-bag in the other; she passes right over those comic friends Frog and Toad, who are out looking for the cor-ner that spring is just around; meanwhile Georgie hops down the road announcing "New folks coming" and nearly interrupts Pooh and Piglet in their search for a Woozle. In the barnyard Wilbur has just discovered a wonderful new friend, Charlotte A. Cavatica, much to the amusement of the wise geese and the sly rat, Tem-pleton. If we look closely, we can see tiny Arrietty and Pod, out for a Borrower's holiday; Stuart Little paddles his souvenir canoe along the drainage ditch; and our fa-vorite Hobbit, Bilbo Baggins, outwits the terrifying Gol-lum. Gathered in the schoolyard are the Great Gilly Hopkins and her tag-along friend, Agnes Stokes; Meg Murry is consulting with the principal, Mr. Jenkins, about her little brother, Charles Wallace. Ramona comes by wearing the crown of burrs she had made so she can star in a TV commercial; Harriet, with flash-light and notebook, is just beginning her spy route, and Jeffrey "Maniac" Magee comes loping along with his sneaker soles slapping.

The line is long in this procession of real personages in children's literature. It reaches back in our memories to include Beth, Jo, Amy, and Meg; it stands outside the Secret Garden and listens to the laughing voices of Mary, Colin, and Dickon; and, with Laura, it delights in the warm coziness of the fire and the sound of Pa's fid-dling in Laura Ingalls Wilder's *Little House in the Big Woods*. We know all these characters well because their authors blew the breath of life into each one of them. They have come alive in the pages of books, and they will live forever in our memories.

Style

An author's style of writing is simply selection and arrangement of words in presenting the story. Good writing style is appropriate to the plot, theme, and char-acters, both creating and reflecting the mood of the story. Although some authors develop a style so distinc-tive that it is easily recognizable, their work might show variation from book to book. Gary Paulsen's *Hatchet* is a survival story told as a continuous record of the

thoughts and actions of Brian, the survivor. The brief sentences arranged as individual paragraphs are choppy, breathless, tense:

> I was flying to visit my father and the plane crashed and sank in a lake.
>
> There, keep it that way. Short thoughts.
> I do not know where I am.
> Which doesn't mean much. More to the point, *they* do not know where I am.[45]

Paulsen's *The Winter Room* is a more lyrical story that takes as its backdrop the changing seasons of a northern Minnesota farm. Carefully placed sentence fragments punctuate this narrative also, but here they are con-trasted to long chains of sensory details. The following is only a part of a sentence:

> . . . [when] Rex moves into the barn to sleep and Father drains all the water out of all the radiators in the tractors and the old town truck and sometimes you suck a quick breath in the early morning that is so cold it makes your front teeth ache; when the chickens are walking around all fluffed up like white balls and the pigs burrow into the straw to sleep in the corner of their pen, and Mother goes to Hem-ings for the quilting bee they do each year that lasts a full day—when all that happens, fall is over.
> But it still isn't winter.[46]

Most children do not enjoy a story that is too de-scriptive, but they can appreciate figurative language, especially when the comparisons are within their back-ground of understanding. Natalie Babbitt's vivid pro-logue to *Tuck Everlasting* invites children to visualize the intense images by describing the month of August as curiously silent "with blank white dawns and glaring noons and sunsets smeared with too much color."[47]

Patricia MacLachlan's style effectively mirrors the setting of the story and the background of its characters in *Sarah, Plain and Tall*. The writing reflects the prairie setting and the straightforward manner of Sarah, a mail-order bride from Maine. The tension of the story lies in its themes of longing and belonging—Sarah's under-stated longing for the sea and the children's longing for

---

[45]Gary Paulsen, *Hatchet* (New York: Bradbury, 1987), p. 47.

[46]Gary Paulsen, *The Winter Room* (New York: Orchard, 1989), p. 62.

[47]Natalie Babbitt, *Tuck Everlasting*, p. 3.

a mother. The beauty of the sea is contrasted with that of the prairie; the light after a prairie storm reminds Sarah of a sea squall. At the end of the story, when Sarah has decided to stay, the child-narrator, Anna, reflects on the future:

> Autumn will come, then winter, cold with a wind that blows like the wind off the sea in Maine. . . . There will be Sarah's sea, blue and gray and green, hanging on the wall. And songs old and new. And Seal with yellow eyes. And there will be Sarah, plain and tall.[48]

The repeated phrases in this passage have a rhythm like music, a cadence that is very satisfying, especially when the book is read aloud.

There is no one style or set of language patterns that is more appropriate than others for a children's book. Yet children's tastes do place some demands on the writer. Because young readers tend to prefer action over description or introspection, those elements must be handled with special skill. Children crave dialogue, like readers of all ages. They feel as Alice in Wonderland did when she looked into her sister's book and said, "What's the use of a book without pictures or conversation?" Masters at writing dialogue that sounds natural and amusing include Rosemary Wells in her picture books such as *Max's Dragon Shirt*, Cynthia Rylant in *Henry and Mudge Take the Big Test*, and Judith Caseley in *Harry and Arney*. Writing the dialogue for a book of contemporary realistic fiction is particularly difficult because slang and popular expressions are quickly dated. Betsy Byars is one writer who skillfully captures the sound of today's idiom in her stories. Ron Koertge makes talk sound real in books like *Tiger, Tiger, Burning Bright*, and Walter Dean Myers captures the sound of urban street language in books like *The Mouse Rap*.

The best test of an author's style is probably oral reading. Does the story read smoothly? Does the conversation flow naturally? Does the author provide variety in sentence patterns, vocabulary, and use of stylistic devices?

Although it is difficult for children to analyze a particular author's style, they do react to it. Children are quick to detect the patronizing air of an author who talks down to them in little asides, for example. They dislike a story that is too sentimental; and they see through the disguise of the too-moralistic tales of the past. Adults are more responsive than children to the

clever, the slyly written, and the sarcastic. Frequently children are better able to identify what they dislike about an author's style than to identify what they like. Obviously, the matter of style is important when adults evaluate books for children.

Point of View

The term *point of view* is often used to indicate the author's choice of narrator(s) and the way the narrator reveals the story. Whose story is it? Who tells it? In folk and fairy tales, for instance, the storyteller tells the tale, and the storyteller knows the thoughts and actions of all the characters. The storyteller's voice is also used in modern fiction, for books in which the author reports the comings and goings, the conversations, and the feelings of all the characters, villains as well as heroes. We say that such stories have an omniscient, or all-knowing, narrator. C. S. Lewis presents his Narnia series in this way. In *The Lion, the Witch, and the Wardrobe*, we are sometimes with Lucy, sometimes with Edmund, sometimes with all four of the adventuring children, and occasionally in places where they can never go. With the use of the third person, the omniscient point of view allows the author complete freedom to crawl inside the skins of each of the characters, thinking their thoughts, speaking their words, and observing the action of the story. It also allows the author to speak directly to the reader, if she or he chooses, just as a storyteller would in a face-to-face situation. C. S. Lewis comments to his readers in parentheses, a practice that some children and adults find detracts from their enjoyment of the story.

Many children's books take a point of view that also uses the third person but gives the author less freedom. This limited-omniscient, or concealed, narrator view does, however, provide closer identification with a single character. The author chooses to stand behind one character, so to speak, and tell the story from over his or her shoulder. The story is then limited to what that character can see, hear, believe, feel, and understand. Katherine Paterson has told the story of *The Great Gilly Hopkins* from this perspective. Gilly is "on stage" throughout, and we see the world as Gilly sees it. We know what others think about her through their reactions to her and her interpretations of their thoughts. For example, Gilly is having her first dinner at the home of Trotter, her latest foster mother:

> The meal proceeded without incident. Gilly was hungry but thought it better not to seem to enjoy her supper too much. William Ernest ate silently and steadily with only an occasional glance at Gilly. She could tell that the child was scared silly of her.

[48]Patricia MacLachlan, *Sarah, Plain and Tall* (New York: Harper & Row, 1985), p. 58.

It was about the only thing in the last two hours that had given her any real satisfaction. Power over the boy was sure to be power over Trotter in the long run.[49]

William Mayne, a British writer, helps the reader see the world from the limited point of view of a magical being in *Hob and the Goblins* and thus makes the fantasy more believable. Hob, a brownie-like creature, suddenly finds himself in the modern-day London and does not understand that the world has changed from horse-and-buggy days. When a "noisy red house" appears, he climbs "up the big steps," thinking he has found a new home.

🌿 Hob went straight for the staircase, all among the feet of people, and up to see the bedrooms. There were narrow beds, with people sitting on them, looking out of windows. "What a lot live here," said Hob. "Hob will stay downstairs until I know them better."[50]

While it might take children a few pages to catch on to Hob's unusual way of looking at the world of humans, Mayne's consistent point of view adds to the delight of the story.

The more direct narrative voice of the first person, once considered unusual in children's books, is quite common today. In contemporary realism it is almost the norm. Judy Blume helped to popularize this kind of storytelling with books like *Are You There God? It's Me, Margaret* and *Blubber*. Blume's stories are not known for strong characterization, but they do reveal the author's ability to recreate the everyday language of children.

The advantage of using first-person narrative is that it can make for easy reading. It attempts to invite its audience by taking a stance that says, "Look—we speak the same language." In many cases this sort of writing does not stretch the reader's vocabulary or imagination. The short, choppy sentences simply reflect a 10-year-old's idiom's and grammatical errors. Moreover, children's perspectives on the world are limited by their lack of experience, just as their vocabulary is. This is an added challenge for an author writing in the first person; for although it might be easy to present the narrator's thoughts and feelings in an appealing way, it will be more difficult to show that the narrator's view might be narrow, misguided, or simply immature when seen from a broader perspective.

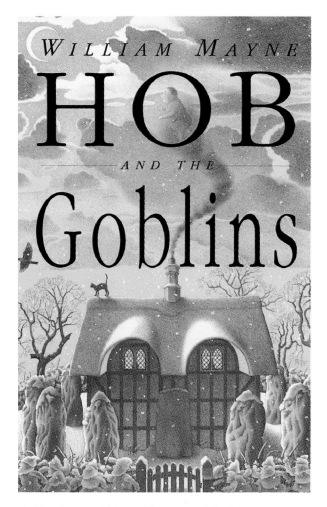

Hob's unique worldview adds a sense of the fantastic to William Mayne's *Hob and the Goblins*.
From *Hob and the Goblin,* by William Mayne. Copyright © 1994 by Dorling Kindersley, Inc., New York, NY. Reprinted by permission of the publisher.

Stories told by older characters, or those who are especially intelligent or sensitive, usually do a better job of dealing with complex issues. In books such as *Missing May* by Cynthia Rylant or *Catherine, Called Birdie* by Karen Cushman, the authors have created believable characters and lent power to the story through the use of first-person narration.

Catherine, Called Birdy, a story set in the Middle Ages, begins with a journal entry:

🌿 I am commanded to write an account of my days: I am bit by fleas and plagued by family. That is all there is to say.[51]

---

[49]Katherine Paterson, *The Great Gilly Hopkins* (New York: Harper & Row, 1978), p. 14.

[50]William Mayne, *Hob and the Goblins* (New York: Dorling Kindersley, 1994), p. 9.

[51]Karen Cushman, *Catherine, Called Birdy* (New York: Clarion, 1994), p. 1.

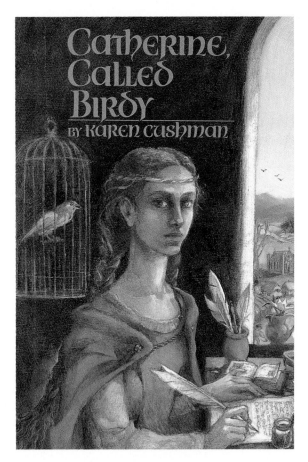

Karen Cushman's *Catherine, Called Birdy* speaks to today's middle grader from the Middle Ages.
Cover from *Catherine, Called Birdy*. Copyright © 1994 by Karen Cushman. Jacket illustration copyright © 1994 by Trina Schart Hyman. Reprinted by permission of Clarion Books/Houghton Mifflin Company. All rights reserved.

This strong first-person voice evokes a rich sense of the thirteenth century but also resonates with the sensibilities of a 13-year-old of today. Though Catherine tells her story with a great deal of earthy humor, the narrative also reveals a gradual coming of age and an understanding of her complex role as an adult woman.

At times authors counter the limitations of a single point of view by alternating the presentation of several views within the same story or changing points of view. *Morning Girl*, by Michael Dorris, alternates the stories of a young girl and her brother, who describe their life in an island culture at an unnamed time. Their voices represent typical sibling relationships at the same time that they add depth to the strong family bonds that shape this community. At the end of the story, however, Morning Girl sees an unusual "canoe" approaching her island.

All the fat people in the canoe began pointing at me and talking at once. In their excitement they almost turned themselves over, and I allowed my body to

sink beneath the waves for a moment in order to hide my smile. One must always treat guests with respect I reminded She Who Listens, even when they are as brainless as gulls.[52]

The book ends with a third and chilling voice, that of Christopher Columbus, in a journal entry dated 11 October, 1492. In it he suggests that the people of the island he has "discovered" will make good servants because they "say very quickly everything that is said to them." By adding this third viewpoint at the close of *Morning Girl*, Dorris forces us to reconsider the tales told in our history books and to understand the perspective of peoples who have had no voice for centuries.

Style, structure, and revelation of character necessarily are influenced by the author's choice of point of view (or points of view). In evaluating books, we need to ask not just who is telling the story, but how this influences the story. What perspective does the narrator bring to events, and what vision of the world does that offer to children?

Additional Considerations

The books we think of as truly excellent have significant content, and, if illustrated, fine illustrations. Their total design, from the front cover to the final endpaper, creates a unified look that seems in character with the content and invites the reader to proceed. Today we have so many picture storybooks and so many beautifully illustrated books of nonfiction, poetry, and other genres that any attempt to evaluate children's literature should consider both the role of illustration and the format of the book. We will discuss these criteria in greater depth in chapters 5 and 12. In general, however, we should consider what function the art in a book is intended to have. Are the pictures meant to be decorations? Were they designed to complement or clarify the text? Are they so much a part of the story that you cannot imagine the book without them?

Most novels for older readers have no illustrations, although some include decorative designs to mark chapter breaks or an occasional drawing. Shorter chapter books for younger readers generally do have pictures. These pictures enrich the story but are not essential to the telling as they would be in a picture storybook. In picture storybooks, the words and the illustrations share the job of storytelling, of communicating the mood and message. In a wordless picture book the illustrations must do the job by themselves.

[52]Michael Dorris, *Morning Girl* (New York: Hyperion, 1992), p. 70.

In considering illustration, then, we need to look at its purpose in a particular book. In every case we would look for art that is aesthetically pleasing and carefully crafted. Are the pictures consistent with the story or intended as a deliberate counterpoint to it? Do they present a unique, aesthetically satisfying vision of the world of the story? Naturally, we need to give more attention to illustrations in books where the pictures play a more important role.

The format of a book includes its size, shape, page design, illustrations, typography, paper quality, and binding. Frequently, some small aspect of the format, such as the book jacket, will be an important factor in a child's decision to read a story.

All types of books—novels, picture books, poetry, biography, informational books—should be well designed and well made. Many factors other than illustration are important. The type should be large enough for easy reading by children at the age level for which the book is intended. At the same time, if the type is too large, children might see the book as "babyish." Space between the lines (leading) should be sufficient to make the text clear. The paper should be of high quality, heavy enough to prevent any penetration of ink. Off-white with a dull finish prevents glare, although other surfaces are used for special purposes. The binding should be durable and practical, able to withstand hard use. Publishers produce many books in alternate bindings, one for the trade (bookstore sales) and an extra-sturdy version for library use. However, a book should never be selected on the basis of format alone. No book is better than its content.

A book that features careful attention to format throughout is Diana Appelbaum's *Giants in the Land* with scratchboard illustrations by Michael McCurdy. The tall, slender shape of the book evokes the giant pine trees of the title that once covered all of New England and that were cut down to make the masts for British warships in the eighteenth century. The book's cloth cover, embossed with a single gold pine tree, the deep red endpages, the black-and-white illustrations, and the careful page design all lend a sense of quiet majesty to this environmental history and invite children to linger over Appelbaum's poetic text.

Comparison with Other Books

A book should be considered not in isolation but as a part of the larger body of literature. Individual books need to be compared with others on the same subject or theme. Is this just another horse story, or does it make a distinctive contribution? Every teacher and librarian should know some books well enough to develop a personal list of books of excellence that can serve as models

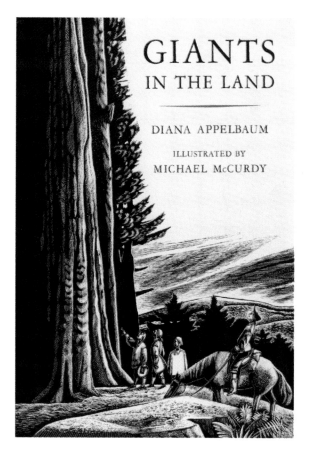

Giants in the Land is a fine example of excellence in total book design.

Cover from *Giants in the Land* by Diana Appelbaum, illustrated by Michael McCurdy. Jacket art © 1993 by Michael McCurdy. Reprinted by permission of Houghton Mifflin Company. All rights reserved.

for comparison. How does this adventure story compare with Armstrong Sperry's *Call It Courage*, or this fantasy with *A Wrinkle in Time* by Madeleine L'Engle, or this historical fiction with Elizabeth George Speare's *The Sign of the Beaver*? These reference points of outstanding books help to sharpen evaluations.

An author's new book should be compared with her or his previous works. Contributions by the same author might be inconsistent in quality. What is the best book Jean George has written? Is *On the Far Side of the Mountain* as good as *My Side of the Mountain*? How does *Water Sky* compare with *Julie of the Wolves*? Too frequently, books are evaluated on the basis of the author's reputation rather than for their inherent worth.

Many informational and biographical series are written by different authors. The quality of the book varies with the ability of the writer, despite similarities in approach and format. Rather than condemning or approving an entire series, evaluate a book on its own merits.

A book needs to be compared with outstanding prototypes, with other books written by the same author, and with other books in the same series. It may also be helpful to become familiar with some of the review journals in the field of children's literature and to compare reviews of a given book. What have reputable reviewers said about this book? Where have they placed it in relation to others of its type? Have they singled it out for special notice by starring it or providing a special focus? A comparison of reviews of one book usually reveals more similarities than differences, although reviewers have personal preferences just as other readers do. Appendixes A and B provide sources that will be helpful in evaluating and selecting children's books.

In summary, the basic considerations for the evaluation of fiction for children are a well-constructed and well-paced plot, a significant theme, an authentic setting, a credible point of view, convincing characterization, appropriate style, and an attractive format. Not all books achieve excellence in each of these areas. Some books are remembered for their fine characterizations, others for their exciting plots, and others for the evocation of the setting. The Guidelines "Evaluating Children's Fiction" on page 29 may help the reader look at a book more carefully. However, not all questions will be appropriate for each book.

Classics in Children's Literature

Knowledge of children's classics—those books that have stood the test of time—can provide further guidance for evaluating children's books. What makes a book endure from one generation to another? Alice Jordan states: "Until a book has weathered at least one generation and is accepted in the next, it can hardly be given the rank of a classic."[53]

Many books and poems have achieved an honored position in children's literature through a combination of adult adoration, parent perpetuation, and teacher assignments. Most adults remember with nostalgia the books they read as children. They tend to think that what they read was best and ignore the possibility that any better books might be produced. It is easy to forget that every "classic" was once a new book, that some of today's new books will be tomorrow's classics. Teachers and librarians should begin with modern children and their interests, not adults' interests when *they* were children.

Certain books became classics when there were very few books from which children could choose. In fact, many classics were not children's books at all, but were written for adults. In their desire to read, children claimed these adult books, struggled through the difficult parts, and disregarded what they did not understand. They had no other choice. Today's children are not so persevering, because they see no reason to be. The introductory sentence of *Robinson Crusoe* runs the length of the entire first page and contains difficult vocabulary and syntax. Defoe wrote the story in 1719 for adult readers, but children quickly discovered this story of shipwreck and adventure and plunged into it. However, they can find the same tingling excitement and more readable prose in modern survival stories like Avi's *The True Confessions of Charlotte Doyle* or Cynthia DeFelice's *Lostman's River*.

The classics should not be exempted from reevaluation by virtue of their past veneration. They should be able to compete favorably with contemporary books. Unimpressed by vintage or lineage, children seldom read a book because they think they should. They read more for enjoyment than for edification. Some books have been kept alive from one generation to the next by the common consent of critics and children; these are the true classics of children's literature. No teacher or parent has to cajole a child into enjoying the adventure and suspense in Robert Louis Stevenson's *Treasure Island*, the mystery and excitement of *The Secret Garden* by Frances Hodgson Burnett, or the memorable characters in Alcott's *Little Women* or A. A. Milne's *Winnie the Pooh*. These books can hold their own amid today's ever-increasing number of new and beautiful books.

The Book Awards

Teachers and librarians will find it helpful to be familiar with books that have won awards.[54] These awards, which have been established for various purposes, provide criteria for what experts consider to be the best in children's literature. Such awards have helped to counteract the judgment of the marketplace by focusing attention on beautiful and worthwhile books. In an age of mass production, they have stimulated artists, authors, and publishers to produce books of distinction and have helped children's literature achieve a worthy status.

---

[53]Alice M. Jordan, *Children's Classics* (Boston: Horn Book, 1974), p. 4.

[54]See Appendix A for various children's book awards, criteria, and winners. For a complete listing of awards for children's books, consult *Children's Books: Awards and Prizes* published by the Children's Book Council. Information also appears in *Children's Books in Print* (New York: R. R. Bowker).

Guidelines:
Evaluating Children's Fiction

- Before reading:

What kind of book is this?

What does the reader anticipate from the

    title?

    dust jacket illustration?

    size of print?

    illustrations?

    chapter headings?

    opening page?

For what age range is this book intended?

- Plot:

Does the book tell a good story?

Will children enjoy it?

Is there action? Does the story move?

Is the plot original and fresh?

Is it plausible and credible?

    Is there preparation for the events?

    Is there a logical series of happenings?

Is there a basis of cause and effect in the happenings?

Is there an identifiable climax?

How do events build to a climax?

Is the plot well constructed?

- Setting:

Where does the story take place?

How does the author indicate the time?

How does the setting affect the action, characters, or theme?

Does the story transcend the setting and have universal implications?

- Theme:

Does the story have a theme?

Is the theme worth imparting to children?

Does the theme emerge naturally from the story, or is it stated too obviously?

Does the theme overpower the story?

Does it avoid moralizing?

How does the author use motifs or symbols to intensify meaning?

- Characterization:

How does the author reveal characters?

    Through narration?

    In conversation?

    By thoughts of others?

    By thoughts of the character?

    Through action?

Are the characters convincing and credible?

Do we see their strengths and their weaknesses?

Does the author avoid stereotyping?

Is the behavior of the characters consistent with their ages and background?

Is there any character development or growth?

Has the author shown the causes of character behavior or development?

- Style:

Is the style of writing appropriate to the subject?

Is the style straightforward or figurative?

Is the dialogue natural and suited to the characters?

How did the author create a mood? Is the overall impression one of mystery? gloom? evil? joy? security?

- Point of view:

Is the point of view from which the story is told appropriate to the purpose of the book?

Does the point of view change?

Does the point of view limit the reader's horizon, or enlarge it?

Why did the author choose this particular point of view?

- Additional considerations:

Do the illustrations enhance or extend the story?

Are the illustrations consistent with the story?

Are the pictures aesthetically satisfying?

How well designed is the book?

Is the format of the book related to the text?

What is the quality of the paper?

How sturdy is the binding?

How does the book compare with other books on the same subject?

How does the book compare with other books written by the same author?

How have other reviewers evaluated this book?

What age range would most appreciate this story?

The award books are not always popular with children. However, most of the awards are based not on popularity but on recognized excellence. They were never intended to rubber-stamp the tastes of children; they were intended to raise them. Children's reactions to books are significant, and many awards, particularly state awards, are voted on by children. However, popularity of a book, whether for children or for adults, is not necessarily a mark of distinctive writing or artistic achievement. How many best-sellers win a Pulitzer Prize for literature? Because there are now so many awards in so many categories of children's literature, only the best-known ones will be discussed here.

The Newbery and Caldecott Medals

Two of the most coveted awards in children's literature are the Newbery and Caldecott Medals. Winners are chosen every year by two committees of the Association for Library Service to Children, a division of the American Library Association. A candidate for either of the awards must be a citizen or resident of the United States.

The John Newbery Medal, established in 1922, is the oldest award for children's books. It is named for John Newbery, a British publisher and bookseller of the eighteenth century. Appropriately called the "father of children's literature," he was the first to publish books expressly for children. The Newbery Medal is awarded to the author of the most distinguished contribution to American literature for children published in the preceding year. Although the award is occasionally given to a book with outstanding illustrations, such as Nancy Willard's *A Visit to William Blake's Inn*, with pictures by Alice and Martin Provensen, the Newbery Medal honors the quality of the writing. Many age ranges are represented, but most of the Newbery Medal books are for able, mature readers. Frequently children need to hear these books read aloud and discuss them with an adult before they develop a taste for their excellence.

The Randolph J. Caldecott Medal is named in honor of a great English illustrator of the nineteenth century, Randolph Caldecott. Caldecott was well known for his sprightly picture books depicting the country life of England. The Caldecott Medal, established in 1938, is awarded to the most distinguished American picture book for children chosen from those first published in the United States during the previous year. The text should be worthy of the illustrations, but the award is made primarily for the artwork.

Students of children's literature would do well to acquaint themselves with some of these medal-winning books and their authors and illustrators. The Honor Books for each award are also worth knowing. Since the selection for the awards must be limited to books published during one year, the quality of the award books varies, for certain years produce a richer harvest than others. In the majority of cases, the passage of time has shown the choices to have been wise ones, but there have been a few surprises. In 1953, for instance, the highly praised *Charlotte's Web* was a Newbery Honor Book, edged out in the medal competition by Ann Nolan Clark's *Secret of the Andes*, a beautifully written but far less popular story. Books by Laura Ingalls Wilder were in the Honor Book category five different years, but never received the medal. Final restitution was made, perhaps, by the establishment of the Laura Ingalls Wilder Award, which serves a different purpose.

The list of Caldecott Medal winners shows great variety as to type of artwork, media used, age appeal, and subject matter. The range of artwork includes the lovely winterscapes by John Schoenherr for Jane Yolen's *Owl Moon*; the comic, almost cartoon, style of William Steig's *Sylvester and the Magic Pebble*; Ed Emberley's stylized patterns in *Drummer Hoff* by Barbara Emberley; the surrealism of Chris Van Allsburg's *Jumanji* or David Wiesner's *Tuesday*; and the expressionistic collages of David Diaz in *Smoky Night* by Eve Bunting. Various media are represented among the medal winners, including woodcut, watercolor, opaque paint, collage, and various combinations of pen and ink and paint. Marcia Brown has won the Caldecott Medal three times; Chris Van Allsburg, Robert McCloskey, Nonny Hogrogian, Leo and Diane Dillon, and Barbara Cooney have been honored twice. Joseph Krumgold, Elizabeth Speare, and Katherine Paterson have each received two Newbery Medals; Robert Lawson continues to be the only person who has won both the Newbery and the Caldecott Medals.

International Book Awards

The Hans Christian Andersen Medal was established in 1956 as the first international children's book award. It is given by the International Board on Books for Young People every two years to a living author and (since 1966) an illustrator, in recognition of his or her entire body of work. Meindert DeJong, Maurice Sendak, Scott O'Dell, Paula Fox, and Virginia Hamilton are the only Americans to have received this medal so far.

The Mildred L. Batchelder Award was established to honor the U.S. publication of the year's most outstanding translated book for children. Like the Newbery and Caldecott Medals, this award is given by the Association

In this Caldecott Medal-winning book, *Ox-Cart Man* by Donald Hall, the father loads up his ox-cart with the many things his family has been making and growing all year to take to market. Barbara Cooney's paintings accurately reflect the New England landscapes and early American primitive art.

From *Ox-Cart Man* by Donald Hall, illustrated by Barbara Cooney. Copyright © 1979 by Barbara Cooney Porter, illustrations. Used by permission of Viking Penguin, a division of Penguin books, USA Inc.

for Library Service to Children of the American Library Association. Appropriately, it is always presented on International Children's Book Day, 2 April, which was Hans Christian Andersen's birthday.

Lifetime Contribution Awards

The Laura Ingalls Wilder Award honors an author or illustrator for a substantial and lasting contribution to children's literature. It was established in 1954 by the Association for Library Service to Children and was presented first to Laura Ingalls Wilder herself, for her *Little House* books. First presented every five years, and now every three, the award makes no requirement concerning the number of books that must be produced, but

a body of work is implied and the books must be published in the United States. The recipients of the award, including Beverly Cleary, Theodor S. Geisel (Dr. Seuss), Maurice Sendak, Jean Fritz, Virginia Hamilton, and Marcia Brown, all are creators who have made an indelible mark on American children's literature.

Some of the other awards presented for a body of work are the Catholic Library Association's Regina Medal and the University of Mississippi's Children's Collection Medallion. The Kerlan Award, which honors "singular attainments" in children's literature, also recognizes the donation of original manuscripts, as resource material, to the Kerlan Collection at the University of Minnesota.

There was no major award for children's poetry until 1977, when the National Council of Teachers of English established the Award for Excellence in Poetry for Children, to be given to a living American poet. This award recognizes the writer's entire body of work. Octogenarian David McCord was the first recipient; others have included Aileen Fisher, Karla Kuskin, Myra Cohn Livingston, Eve Merriam, John Ciardi, Lilian Moore, Arnold Adoff, Valerie Worth, and Barbara Esbensen.

Several other awards, like the Scott O'Dell Award for Historical Fiction and the Edgar Allen Poe Award of the Mystery Writers of America, honor particular kinds of writing. These prizes are given for individual books rather than for a body of work, however.

No one but the most interested follower of children's literature would want to remember all the awards that are given for children's books. And certainly no one should assume that the award winners are the only children's books worth reading. Like the coveted Oscars of the motion picture industry and the Emmys of television, the awards in children's literature focus attention not only on the winners of the year but also on the entire field of endeavor. They recognize and honor excellence and also point the way to improved writing, illustrating, and producing of worthwhile and attractive books for children.

Learning Experiences

1. Write your reading autobiography. What memories do you have of your early reading? Did either of your parents read to you? Do you recall any of the books they read? Did any teachers or librarians read aloud to you? What books did you own as a child? What were some of your favorites? Do you recall any that you did not like? Do you know why?

2. Can you think of any one book that you read and reread as a child? What particular qualities of the story appealed to you? Reread it and evaluate it according to the criteria established in this chapter. Would you still recommend it for children?

3. Interview two or three classmates, colleagues, or family members about the influence of literature in their lives. In what way(s) have books been important to them? What titles are most memorable? Why?

4. Read one of the series books: for instance, one from the Baby-Sitters Club, Sweet Valley High, Boxcar Children, or Nancy Drew series. Look closely at the literary craftsmanship of the book. How many contrived incidents can you find? Do the characters have real strengths *and* weaknesses? If you read this book aloud, how would it sound?

5. Form a mock Newbery award committee and review the medal winners and Honor Books for one year. Do you agree with the opinions of the actual judges? Be prepared to state your reasons.

6. Read a recently published children's book and write a brief reaction to it. Then find two or more published reviews. List the criteria that seem important to the reviewers. How are their criteria like or different from yours?

Related Readings

Butler, Dorothy. *Cushla and Her Books*. Boston: Horn Book, 1980.

A moving account of the power of books in the life of a little girl with multiple handicaps. Charts at the end of the report show all of Cushla's interactions with books for one typical day; another chart lists the books shared with her for the first four years of her life.

Cameron, Eleanor. *The Seed and the Vision: On the Writing and Appreciation of Children's Books*. New York: Dutton, 1993.

This collection of essays by a noted children's author and scholar looks at writing for children, aiming a critical lens at many classic works.

Coles, Robert. *The Call of Stories: Teaching and the Moral Imagination*. Boston: Houghton Mifflin, 1989.

A noted child psychiatrist describes the influence of literature in his own life and its impact on the young adults he has taught at Harvard University and elsewhere.

Egoff, Sheila, G. T. Stubbs, and L. F. Ashley. *Only Connect: Readings on Children's Literature*. 2nd ed. Toronto: Oxford University Press, 1980.

An excellent collection of essays on children's literature, encompassing literary criticism, standards, changing tastes, children's responses to books, and writing and illustrating books. Many of the contributors are well known, including Rumer Godden, Nat Hentoff, C. S. Lewis, and John Rowe Townsend.

Hearne, Betsy. *Choosing Books for Children: A Commonsense Guide*. New York: Delacorte, 1990.

This guide for parents features top-quality selections and graceful style.

Hunt, Peter. *Criticism, Theory, and Children's Literature*. Cambridge, Mass.: Basil Blackwell, 1991.

A fresh examination of important questions and issues, such as what children's literature is, the nature of reading, and the role of style and narrative in children's books. Much attention goes to the underlying assumptions of critics and other adults regarding children and their reading, with emphasis on the relationship between ideology and literature. These complex ideas are presented in generally readable terms and will spark discussion and debate.

Kingman, Lee, ed. *Newbery and Caldecott Medal Books 1976–1985*. Boston: Horn Book, 1985.

The acceptance speeches of the medal winners are included, along with biographical sketches, photographs, and illustrations or quotes from their work. In addition there are critical essays by Barbara Bader, Ethel Heins, and Zena Sutherland. Speeches of recent medal winners are published each year in the July/August issue of the *Horn Book Magazine*.

Landsberg, Michele. *Reading for the Love of It: Best Books for Young Readers*. New York: Prentice Hall, 1987.

Lively writing and strong convictions make this guide to choosing children's books exceptionally readable for parents as well as professionals. Landsberg does not hesitate to give low marks to popular authors like Judy Blume or to make clear her distinction between good books and bad books. Ten chapters organized around elements of reader interest are followed by an annotated "treasury" of four hundred titles.

Lukens, Rebecca J. *A Critical Handbook of Children's Literature*. 5th ed. New York: HarperCollins, 1994.

A careful examination of literary elements in children's books. Lukens concentrates on E. B. White's *Charlotte's Web* to show how elements like characterization, style, and point of view are developed in good children's books.

Trelease, Jim. *The New Read-Aloud Handbook*. 4th rev. ed. New York: Penguin Books, 1995.

Written for a popular audience by a father who discovered what fun it was to share books with his family, this book is a delight to read and a good gift for parents. The selection is highly personal.

Vandergrift, Kay E. *Child and Story: The Literary Connection*. New York: Neal-Schuman, 1986.

Literary form, critical theory, and elements of story are some of the topics explored in this discussion of the aesthetics of children's literature. One of the book's strengths is that the author sustains her critical perspective without losing sight of contemporary children.

Zinsser, William, ed. *Worlds of Childhood: The Art and Craft of Writing for Children*. Boston: Houghton Mifflin, 1990.

Essays by six gifted writers for children—Jean Fritz, Jill Krementz, Maurice Sendak, Jack Prelutsky, Rosemary Wells, and Katherine Paterson—reveal individual personality and a common concern for the needs of their audience. A special bibliography lists books that were childhood favorites of each author or ones that have influenced their adult lives and work.

Children's Literature

Books listed at the end of each chapter are recommended, subject to qualifications noted in the text. See Appendix C for publishers' complete addresses. In the case of new editions, the original publication date appears in parentheses.

Alcott, Louisa May. *Little Women*. Dell Yearling, 1987 [1868].

Andersen, Hans Christian. *The Ugly Duckling*. Retold and illustrated by Troy Howell. Putnam, 1990.

Appelbaum, Diana. *Giants in the Land*. Illustrated by Michael McCurdy. Houghton Mifflin, 1993.

Asbjørnsen, P. C., and Jorgen E. Moe. *The Three Billy Goats Gruff*. Illustrated by Marcia Brown. Harcourt Brace, 1957.

Avi. *The True Confessions of Charlotte Doyle*. Orchard, 1990.

Babbitt, Natalie. *Tuck Everlasting*. Farrar, Straus & Giroux, 1985.

Banks, Lynne Reid. *The Indian in the Cupboard*. Doubleday, 1981.

Barrett, Judi. *Animals Should Definitely Not Wear Clothing*. Illustrated by Ron Barrett. Atheneum, 1970.

Blume, Judy. *Are You There, God? It's Me, Margaret*. Bradbury, 1970.

———. *Blubber*. Bradbury, 1974.

Brett, Jan. *Town Mouse, Country Mouse*. Putnam, 1994.

Brown, Margaret Wise. *Goodnight Moon*. Illustrated by Clement Hurd. Harper & Row, 1947.

———. *The Golden Egg Book*. Illustrated by Leonard Weisgard. Golden Press, 1976.

Browne, Anthony. *Willy and Hugh*. Knopf, 1991.

Bunting, Eve. *Night of the Gargoyles*. Illustrated by David Wiesner. Clarion, 1994.

———. *Smoky Night*. Illustrated by David Diaz. Harcourt Brace, 1994.

Burnett, Frances Hodgson. *The Secret Garden*. Illustrated by Shirley Hughes. Viking, 1989 [1910].

Byars, Betsy. *The Burning Questions of Bingo Brown*. Viking, 1988.

Carle, Eric. *Do You Want to Be My Friend?* Crowell, 1971.

———. *The Very Hungry Caterpillar*. Philomel, 1969.

Carroll, Lewis. *Alice's Adventures in Wonderland* and *Through the Looking Glass*. Illustrated by John Tenniel. Macmillan, 1963 [First published separately, 1866 and 1872].

Caseley, Judith. *Harry and Arney*. Greenwillow, 1994.

Christiansen, C. B. *I See the Moon*. Atheneum, 1994.

Clark, Ann Nolan. *Secret of the Andes*. Illustrated by Jean Charlot. Viking, 1952.

Cleary, Beverly. *Ramona and Her Father*. Illustrated by Alan Tiegreen. Morrow, 1977.

———. *Ramona Quimby, Age 8*. Illustrated by Alan Tiegreen. Morrow, 1981.

Collier, James Lincoln, and Christopher Collier. *My Brother Sam Is Dead*. Four Winds, 1974.

Conrad, Pam. *Prairie Songs*. Illustrated by Darryl Zudeck. Harper & Row, 1985.

———. *Prairie Visions: The Life and Times of Solomon Butcher*. HarperCollins, 1991.

Cooper, Susan. *The Dark Is Rising*. Illustrated by Alan Cober. Macmillan, 1973.

Creech, Sharon. *Walk Two Moons*. HarperCollins, 1994.

Cushman, Karen. *Catherine, Called Birdy*. Clarion, 1994.

Dalgliesh, Alice. *The Courage of Sarah Noble*. Illustrated by Leonard Weisgard. Scribner's, 1954.

de Angeli, Marguerite. *The Door in the Wall*. Doubleday, 1949.

DeFelice, Cynthia. *Lostman's River*. Macmillan, 1994.

Defoe, Daniel. *Robinson Crusoe*. Houghton Mifflin, 1972 [1719].

de Paola, Tomie. *Charlie Needs a Cloak*. Prentice Hall, 1974.

Dorris, Michael. *Morning Girl*. Hyperion, 1992.

Ehlert, Lois. *Growing Vegetable Soup*. Harcourt Brace, 1990.

Emberley, Barbara. *Drummer Hoff*. Illustrated by Ed Emberley. Simon & Schuster, 1974.

Fitzhugh, Louise. *Harriet the Spy*. Harper & Row, 1964.

Fox, Paula. *The Stone-Faced Boy*. Illustrated by Donald A. Mackay. Bradbury, 1968.

Fritz, Jean. *The Cabin Faced West*. Illustrated by Feodor Rojankovsky. Putnam, 1958.

Gág, Wanda. *Millions of Cats*. Putnam, 1977 [1928].

Galdone, Joanna. *The Tailypo*. Clarion, 1984.

Galdone, Paul. *The Gingerbread Boy*. Clarion, 1983.

———. *The Three Little Pigs*. Clarion, 1979.

Gallaz, Christophe, and Roberto Innocenti. *Rose Blanche*. Creative Education, 1985.

Gardiner, John. *Stone Fox*. Illustrated by Marcia Sewall. Crowell, 1980.

George, Jean. *Julie of the Wolves*. Illustrated by John Schoenherr. Harper & Row, 1972.

———. *My Side of the Mountain*. Dutton, 1988 [1959].

———. *On the Far Side of the Mountain*. Dutton, 1990.

———. *Water Sky*. Harper & Row, 1987.

Grimm, Jacob, and Wilhelm Grimm. *Little Red Riding Hood*. Illustrated by Trina Schart Hyman. Holiday, 1983.

Hall, Donald. *Ox-Cart Man*. Illustrated by Barbara Cooney. Viking, 1979.

Hamilton, Virginia. *Cousins*. Philomel, 1990.

Haseley, Dennis. *Getting Him*. Farrar, Straus & Giroux, 1994.

Heide, Florence Parry, and Judith Heide Gilliland. *The Day of Ahmed's Secret*. Illustrated by Ted Lewin. Lothrop, Lee & Shepard, 1990.

Henkes, Kevin. *Julius, the Baby of the World*. Greenwillow, 1990.

Herriot, James. *All Creatures Great and Small*. St. Martin's Press, 1972.

Hughes, Richard. *A High Wind in Jamaica*. Harper & Row, 1989 [1929].

Hunter, Mollie. *Mermaid Summer*. Harper & Row, 1988.

———. *A Stranger Came Ashore*. Harper & Row, 1974.

Hutchins, Pat. *The Doorbell Rang*. Greenwillow, 1986.

Johnson, Angela. *Toning the Sweep*. Orchard, 1993.

Kent, Jack. *The Fat Cat: A Danish Folktale*. Parents Magazine Press, 1971.

King-Smith, Dick. *All Pigs Are Beautiful*. Illustrated by Anita Jeram. Candlewick, 1993.

Koertge, Ron. *Tiger, Tiger, Burning Bright*. Orchard, 1994.

L'Engle, Madeleine. *Meet the Austins*. Vanguard, 1960.

———. *A Swiftly Tilting Planet*. Farrar, Straus & Giroux, 1978.

———. *A Wrinkle in Time*. Farrar, Straus & Giroux, 1962.

Le Guin, Ursula. *A Wizard of Earthsea*. Illustrated by Ruth Robbins. Parnassus, 1968.

Lewis, C. S. *The Lion, the Witch, and the Wardrobe*. Illustrated by Pauline Baynes. Macmillan, 1986 [1961].

Lindgren, Astrid. *Pippi Longstocking*. Translated by Florence Lamborn. Illustrated by Louis Glanzman. Viking Penguin, 1950.

Lobel, Anita. *Alison's Zinnia*. Greenwillow, 1990.

Lobel, Arnold. *Days with Frog and Toad*. Harper & Row, 1976.

———. *Frog and Toad All Year*. Harper & Row, 1976.

———. *Frog and Toad Are Friends*. Harper & Row, 1972.

———. *Frog and Toad Together*. Harper & Row, 1972.

Lowry, Lois. *Anastasia Absolutely*. Houghton Mifflin, 1995.

———. *Anastasia Krupnik*. Houghton Mifflin, 1979.

———. *Number the Stars*. Houghton Mifflin, 1989.

Lyons, Mary E. *Letters from a Slave Girl: The Story of Harriet Jacobs*. Scribner's, 1992.

MacLachlan, Patricia. *Sarah, Plain and Tall*. Harper & Row, 1985.

Mayne, William. *Hob and the Goblins*. Illustrated by Norman Messenger. Dorling Kindersley, 1994

McCloskey, Robert. *Homer Price*. Viking, 1943.

McCord, David. "The Pickety Fence." In *Every Time I Climb a Tree*. Illustrated by Marc Simont. Little, Brown, 1985.

McKissack, Patricia. *Mirandy and Brother Wind*. Illustrated by Jerry Pinkney. Knopf, 1988.

Milne, A. A. *Winnie the Pooh*. Illustrated by Ernest H. Shepard. Dutton, 1988 [1926].

Munsch, Robert. *Love You Forever*. Illustrated by Sheila McGraw. Firefly Books, 1986.

Murphy, Jim. *Across America on an Emigrant Train*. Clarion, 1993.

Myers, Walter Dean. *The Mouse Rap*. HarperCollins, 1990.

———. *Scorpions*. Harper & Row, 1988.

Napoli, Donna Jo. *The Magic Circle*. Dutton, 1993.

Narahashi, Keiko. *Is That Josie?* McElderry, 1994.

O'Dell, Scott. *Island of the Blue Dolphins*. Illustrated by Ted Lewin. Houghton Mifflin, 1990 [1960].

Paterson, Katherine. *Bridge to Terabithia*. Illustrated by Donna Diamond. Crowell, 1977.

———. *Flip-Flop Girl*. Lodestar, 1994.

———. *The Great Gilly Hopkins*. Crowell, 1978.

———. *Lyddie*. Lodestar, 1991.

———. *Park's Quest*. Lodestar, 1988.

Paulsen, Gary. *Hatchet*. Bradbury, 1987.

———. *The Winter Room*. Orchard, 1989.

Potter, Beatrix. *The Tale of Peter Rabbit*. Warne, 1902.

Reiss, Johanna. *The Upstairs Room*. Crowell, 1972.

Reyher, Becky. *My Mother Is the Most Beautiful Woman in the World*. Illustrated by Ruth Gannett. Lothrop, Lee & Shepard, 1945.

Richter, Hans Peter. *Friedrich*. Penguin, 1987.

Rylant, Cynthia. *Henry and Mudge Take the Big Test*. Illustrated by Suçcie Stevenson. Bradbury, 1991.

———. *Missing May*. Orchard, 1992.

Sendak, Maurice. *Outside Over There*. Harper & Row, 1981.

———. *Where the Wild Things Are*. Harper & Row, 1988 [1963].

Seuss, Dr. [Theodor S. Geisel]. *And to Think That I Saw It on Mulberry Street*. Random House, 1989 [1937].

———. *The Cat in the Hat*. Random House, 1966 [1957].

———. *Oh, the Places You'll Go*. Random House, 1990.

Sewell, Anna. *Black Beauty*. Grosset & Dunlap, 1945 [1877].

Shelby, Anne. *Homeplace*. Illustrated by Wendy Anderson Halperin. Orchard, 1995.

Singer, Marilyn. "Deer Mouse." In *Turtle in July*. Illustrated by Gary Blythe. Dial, 1977.

Speare, Elizabeth George. *The Sign of the Beaver*. Houghton Mifflin, 1983.

Sperry, Armstrong. *Call It Courage*. Macmillan, 1940.

Stafford, Kim R. *We Got Here Together*. Illustrated by Debra Fraser. Harcourt Brace, 1994.

Steig, William. *Brave Irene*. Farrar, Straus & Giroux, 1986.

———. *Sylvester and the Magic Pebble*. Simon & Schuster, 1969.

Steptoe, John. *Stevie*. Harper & Row, 1969.

Stevenson, Robert Louis. *Treasure Island*. Illustrated by N. C. Wyeth. Scribner's, 1981 [1883].

Taylor, Mildred. *The Friendship*. Illustrated by Max Ginsburg. Dial, 1987.

———. *Roll of Thunder, Hear My Cry*. Illustrated by Jerry Pinkney. Dial, 1976.

Tolkien, J. R. R. *The Hobbit*. Houghton Mifflin, 1938.

Van Allsburg, Chris. *Jumanji*. Houghton Mifflin, 1981.

Vincent, Gabrielle. *Ernest and Celestine*. Morrow, 1986.

Voigt, Cynthia. *Dicey's Song*. Atheneum, 1982.

———. *Homecoming*. Atheneum, 1981.

Ward, Lynd. *The Biggest Bear*. Houghton Mifflin, 1952.

Wells, Rosemary. *Max's Dragon Shirt*. Dial, 1991.

White, E. B. *Charlotte's Web*. Illustrated by Garth Williams. Harper & Row, 1952.

Whitman, Candace. *The Night Is Like an Animal*. Farrar, Straus & Giroux, 1995.

Wiesner, David. *Tuesday*. Clarion, 1991.

Wilder, Laura Ingalls. *Little House in the Big Woods*. Illustrated by Garth Williams. Harper & Row, 1953 [1932].

Willard, Nancy. *A Visit to William Blake's Inn*. Illustrated by Alice and Martin Provensen. Harcourt Brace, 1981.

Williams, Karen. *Galimoto*. Illustrated by Catherine Stock. Lothrop, Lee & Shepard, 1990.

Williams, Margery. *The Velveteen Rabbit*. Illustrated by William Nicholson. Doubleday, 1969 [1922].

Wright, Betty Ren. *The Ghost Comes Calling*. Scholastic, 1994.

Yolen, Jane. *Owl Moon*. Illustrated by John Schoenherr. Philomel, 1987.

Zolotow, Charlotte. *Say It!* Illustrated by James Stevenson. Greenwillow, 1980.

chapter two

Understanding Children's Responses to Literature

Reading Interests and Preferences 40

Age and Gender Differences 40
Other Determinants of Interest 41
Explaining Children's Choices 42

Growth Patterns That Influence Response 43

Teaching Feature: Asking Children to Tell About Themselves as Readers 44

Physical Development 44
Cognitive Development 45
Language Development 48
Moral Development 49
Personality Development 50
Guides for Ages and Stages 51

Response in the Classroom 51

Theories of Response 51

Resources for Teaching: Books for Ages and Stages 52

Types of Response 60

Interpreting Children's Responses 61

Recognizing Patterns of Change 61
Younger Children (Preschool to Primary) 61
Children in Transition (Primary to Middle Grades) 62
Older Children (Middle Grades to Middle School) 63

Collecting Children's Responses 64

Observing Children 64
Eliciting Responses 64
Studying Concepts About Literature 65
Learning from Literary Miscues 68
Keeping Track 68

Learning Experiences 69
Related Readings 70
Children's Literature 71

ive-year-old Michael hurried to the block corner from the story circle, where his teacher had just told "Little Red Riding Hood." He whispered parts of the story under his breath as he worked to build a low enclosure around himself. When an aide walked by, Michael stood and made a growling noise. "I'm the big bad wolf!" he announced.

One rainy noon hour Sean and Dan, both 7, found a quiet corner of the bookcase and read to each other from Shel Silverstein's book of verse *Where the Sidewalk Ends*. "Listen to this one!" (Giggles.) "I can read this one!" (More giggles.) Two other children discovered the fun and joined them. All four were soon arguing heatedly about which poem was "the best one."

A small group of 9- and 10-year-olds searched the well-stocked library corner of their own classroom for something to read at sustained silent-reading time. Jason picked a book, glanced at the cover, and quickly reshelved it. "Who would want to read a book like *that*?" he muttered. Emily whispered to Julie that she had found another Lois Lowry book about Anastasia Krupnik. "I get it next," the friend said, and went on looking for a book about horses.

At regular silent-reading time, 10-year-old Evie curled up in her class's reading-and-rocking chair to finish Katherine Paterson's book *The Great Gilly Hopkins*. "The way it ended wasn't fair," Evie later protested to her teacher. "Gilly should have gone back to Trotter. This way just isn't right!"

A teacher asked her sixth graders to explain why they thought Jean George had written *Cry of the Crow*. Katie wrote: "I think what the author was trying to tell you is that once something has lived in the wild, it should stay there even if it's just like your brother or sister. . . . When you catch a bird and try to make it do something, it is like being in prison for the bird."

These glimpses of children responding to literature show some of the many different ways in which they may express their preferences, thoughts, and feelings. Although each of these responses is personal and unique, each also reflects the child's age and experience. Young children like Michael are often so totally involved in a story that they relive it through dramatic play. Those like Dan and Sean, who are developing independent reading skills, seem particularly eager to demonstrate that ability and to share newly discovered favorites. Middle graders choosing books, like Jason, Emily, and Julie, show definite preferences. Both Evie's expectation of a happy ending and her concern with injustice in a character's life are typical of middle childhood. Katie's success in generalizing a theme about all wild things from the story of one crow and her fluency in discussing the author's purpose are representative of older children's growing ability to deal with abstract ideas about a story.

To have a successful literature program, teachers and librarians must know books well, but that is only half the task. It is also necessary to understand children and the changing patterns of their responses to literature.

Reading Interests and Preferences

The phrase *response to literature* is used in a variety of ways. Theoretically, *response* refers to any outward sign of that inner activity, something said or done that reveals a reader's thoughts and feelings about literature. A 6-year-old's drawing of a favorite character and a book review in the *New York Times* are both responses in this sense. Teachers or librarians who predict that a book will bring "a good response" use the term in a different way, focusing on the likelihood that children will find a book appealing and will be eager to read and talk about it.

Most of the early research on children and literature focused on this third area of response to discover what reading material children like or dislike. Children's interests and preferences are still a major concern for teachers, librarians, parents, publishers, and booksellers. Everyone who selects children's books can make better choices by knowing which books are likely to have immediate appeal for many children and which ones might require introduction or encouragement along the way.

Studies of reading interests over the years have consistently identified certain topics and elements of content that have wide appeal.[1] Researchers have found that *animals* and *humor*, for instance, are generally popular across age levels. Among other elements that are frequently mentioned for reader appeal are *action*, *suspense*, and *surprise*. Sales figures, too, can reflect children's reading interests. A recent survey by *Publisher's Weekly* magazine showed that tie-ins to popular movies or television shows and series books, particularly those with supernatural or horror themes, were among the bestselling children's books.[2]

Even though we can identify commonly chosen topics and story features that have wide general appeal, it is still impossible to concoct a formula for books that would have unfailing popularity with *all* children. Teachers and librarians need to be sensitive to children's individual tastes, which often are unique and very particular. Nevertheless, the variations in interests among different *groups* of children seem to be linked to age, gender, and certain other influences.

Age and Gender Differences

The most obvious change in children's interest patterns occurs with age as children take on more complex material and new areas of concern. Good book choices for first and sixth graders seldom overlap, even when the general topic is the same. Robert McCloskey's picture book *Make Way for Ducklings* is a favorite animal story among 4- and 5-year-olds; 12-year-olds prefer their animal characters to be part of something more dramatic, as in Wilson Rawls's story about two coon dogs, *Where the Red Fern Grows*. Seven-year-olds laugh at Peggy Parish's *Amelia Bedelia* and her literal interpretation of instructions like "Draw the drapes" and "Dress the chicken." Eleven-year-olds like "funny" books, too, but prefer a different brand of humor, such as the wisecracking dialogue in *Tiger, Tiger, Burning Bright* by Ron Koertge or the comic situations in Barbara Park's *Skinnybones*.

Some of the broader shifts in preference that mark the elementary school years include a move away from a preference for fairy tales toward more interest in realistic subject matter. According to many studies, adventure becomes more important through the middle grades. Research continues to confirm older children's liking for adventure, mystery, and contemporary realistic stories. All of these studies also show that upper-grade students begin to show marked content preferences according to their sex.[3]

The influence of gender differences on reading interests is not entirely clear. In general, studies have found the following:

- Interests of children vary according to age and grade level.
- Girls read more than boys, but boys have a wider interest range and read a greater variety.
- Girls show an earlier interest in adult fiction of a romantic type than boys do.

[1]Angela M. Broening, "Factors Influencing Pupils' Reading of Library Books," *Elementary English Review* 11 (1934): 155–158; Fannie Wyche Dunn, *Interest Factors in Reading Materials* (New York: Teachers College, Columbia University, 1921); Jeanie Goodhope, "Into the Eighties: BAYA's Fourth Reading Interest Survey," *School Library Journal* 29 (December 1982): 33; S. A. Graham, "Assessing Reading Preferences: A New Approach," *New England Reading Association Journal* 21 (winter 1986): 8–11; George W. Norvell, *What Boys and Girls Like to Read* (Morristown, N.J.: Silver Burdett, 1958); Alan Purves and Richard Beach, *Literature and the Reader: Research in Response to Literature, Reading Interests, and the Teaching of Literature* (Urbana, Ill.: National Council of Teachers of English, 1972), pp. 69–71.

[2]*Publishers Weekly* (March 20, 1995), pp. 517–521.

[3]B. A. Bundy, *The Development of a Survey to Ascertain the Reading Preferences of Fourth, Fifth, and Sixth Graders*, Dissertation Abstracts 44 (1983), University Microfilms No. DA 8312392; J. W. Coomer and K. M. Tessmer, "1986 Books for Young Adults Poll," *English Journal* 75 (November 1986): 58–66.

Choosing favorites and interpreting them are both a part of response to literature. Notice how the details of the modern playroom setting in this child's illustration for *The Velveteen Rabbit* provide a glimpse of her unique personal perspective on the book.
Martin Luther King, Jr., Laboratory School, Evanston, Illinois, Public Schools.

- Boys tend to prefer nonfiction from an early age.
- Boys seldom show preference for a "girl's" book, but girls will read a "boy's" book more often.[4]

What we do not know about gender differences in children's choices is whether they reflect a "natural" interest or conformity to cultural expectations. We might suspect that boys' demand for informational books is in part a learned preference. In school and home settings where traditional sexual stereotypes are downplayed, boys and girls share enthusiasm for many common favorites. It is important to give children many options for book choice so that boys and girls can have a chance to explore each other's perspectives. It is just as unfortunate for girls to miss the excellent nonfiction being published today as it is for boys to turn away from fine fiction that offers insight into human relationships.[5]

Other Determinants of Interest

Many factors other than age and gender have been investigated in relation to children's reading interests. At one time the influence of mental age as measured by standardized tests received considerable attention. Now, however, we believe that children of varying academic abilities still are more alike than different in the character of their reading interests. It is more likely that the quantity of books involved and the rate at which interests develop may vary widely.

Illustrations, color, format, length, and type of print can also influence children's choices. It would be unwise, however, to oversimplify the effect of these factors on children's book choices, especially since so much of the research has been done outside the context of normal reading and choosing situations. When children choose and use books in their own classrooms, their reactions to books are more complex than controlled experiments or surveys could reveal.[6]

[4]Glenda Childress, "Gender Gap in the Library: Different Choices for Boys and Girls," *Top of the News* 42 (fall 1985): 69–73; Helen Huus, "Interpreting Research in Children's Literature," in *Children, Books and Reading* (Newark, Del.: International Association, 1964), p. 125.

[5]Elizabeth Segel, "Choices 'For Girls'/'For Boys': Keeping Options Open," *School Library Journal* 28 (March 1982): 106.

[6]Barbara Z. Kiefer, "Envisioning Experience: The Potential for Picture Books," *Publishing Research Quarterly* 7, no. 3 (1991): 63–75.

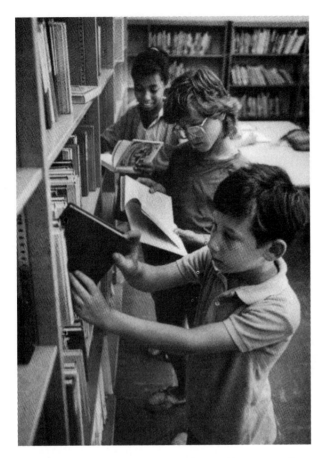

Although reading preferences are influenced by age, gender, and many other factors, children often make specific choices based on the book itself—its length, format, cover, or the appeal of a sample paragraph.
Martin Luther King, Jr., Laboratory School, Evanston, Illinois, Public Schools. Photo by James Ballard.

Social and environmental influences also affect children's book choices and reading interests. Many teachers and librarians feel that cultural and ethnic factors are related to reading interests. One of the arguments for providing culturally authentic picture books and novels about Asian, Hispanic, African American, and Native American children is that readers from a particular culture will find material drawn from their own culture more interesting. One study of American Indian and Anglo children in grades 2 and 3 found that Native American children preferred to read about Indian characters over Anglo characters, although they preferred stories that had characters from both races over those that had only members of one race.[7] The relationship

between interests and culture does not seem to be simple, however, and unfortunately there is not yet much research to clarify this point.

While interests do not seem to vary greatly according to geographical location, the impact of the immediate environment—particularly the availability and accessibility of reading materials in the home, classroom, and public and school libraries—can be very strong. Children in classrooms where books are regularly discussed, enjoyed, and given high value tend to show livelier interest in a wider range of literature than do children from situations where books are given less attention. It is hard to tell how much of this effect is due to contact with the books and how much is social. Teachers' favorite books are often mentioned by children as their own favorites, perhaps because these are the stories closest at hand, or perhaps because of positive associations with the teacher.

Children frequently influence each other in their choice of books. In the culture of the classroom, a title or an author or a topic may rise to celebrity status for a time. Shel Silverstein's *A Light in the Attic* might be "the book" to read in one group of third graders, or children might make their own sign-up sheets to read the classroom's only copy of Judy Blume's *Fudge-a-Mania*. Younger children might spend time on a study of bears and long afterward point out "bear stories" to each other. Media presentations like the prime-time TV dramatization of Patricia MacLachlan's *Sarah, Plain and Tall*, the "Reading Rainbow" series, or "Storytime" from the Public Broadcasting System create demand for specific books.

Peer recommendations are especially important to middle graders in choosing what to read. Some fifth and sixth graders are very candid:

> "Everyone else in the class read it, so I figured I ought to, too." . . . "I usually read what Tammy reads." ". . . most of my friends just like the same type of book I like. So, if they find a book, I'll believe them and I'll try it."[8]

Explaining Children's Choices

How can children influence each other's book choices so readily? Part of the answer may be simply that agemates are likely to enjoy the same kinds of stories because they share many developmental characteristics. As children grow and learn, their levels of understanding change, and so do their favorites in literature. A few

[7]Deborah Lowther and Howard J. Sullivan, "Reading Preferences of American Indian and Anglo Children for Ethnicity, Gender and Story Setting," paper presented at the meeting of the Association for Educational Communications and Technology, 13–17 January 1993, New Orleans.

[8]Susan I. Hepler and Janet Hickman, " 'The Book Was Okay. I Love You'—Social Aspects of Response to Literature," *Theory into Practice* 21 (autumn 1982): 279.

thought-provoking studies have suggested that children prefer those stories that best represent their own way of looking at the world.

André Favat has argued that children reach the peak of their liking for fairy tales between 6 and 8 years old because the reasoning and belief systems in the tales are compatible with the child's thinking pattern.[9] Favat analyzed well-known fairy tales and then compared characteristics of the stories to characteristics of young children's thinking as described by noted psychologist Jean Piaget. Favat found several similarities. For example, young children seem to believe that unrelated objects or actions can have magical influence on each other, just as, in the fairy tales, the kiss of the prince magically wakens Sleeping Beauty. Young children also tend to think that inanimate objects have human characteristics and that questions of right and wrong can be settled by swift punishment. Both of these situations are common in fairy tales. Although most 6- to 8-year-olds are growing beyond this way of thinking, Favat maintained that children find comfort in stepping back, through the story, into old familiar patterns of belief.

Norma Schlager's study of literature choices in middle childhood reaches a similar conclusion: books with main characters who reflect the emotional and psychological aspects of the reader are the ones that gain a wide readership.[10] Schlager compiled behavioral characteristics of 7- to 12-year-olds based on the developmental theories of Piaget and Erikson. Then she analyzed Newbery Medal books that showed the highest and lowest circulations in a large library system. She found that the most popular books portray the world of childhood much as children see it, according to the child development experts, while the least popular books show a different view.

The analysis of Scott O'Dell's *Island of the Blue Dolphins*, the most widely circulated book in Schlager's study, shows that Karana, the story's main character, displays many of the mental attributes common in 7- to 12-year-olds. Karana lives virtually alone on her island off the California coast for eighteen years and must learn to survive without adult help. Children in the middle grades are also concerned with testing their own self-sufficiency, although the circumstances are usually much less dramatic. Karana's success is due to her ability to plan ahead, think logically, and work to make the things she needs. Schlager points out that children in the 7- to 12-year-old age range are also developing the power of

syllogistic reasoning, which allows preplanning and problem solving, and that they too are task-oriented, with newfound abilities in craftsmanship. Schlager suggests that middle-grade readers showed little interest in the least-circulated book (*Dobry* by Monica Shannon) because it does not include the characteristic behavior and thinking of their age level.

There are many things to consider in explaining children's book choices. One of the most important is prior experiences with literature. Some children have heard many stories read aloud at home or have been introduced by their teachers to many different authors and genres. These children are likely to have tastes and preferences that seem advanced compared to children their age who have had less exposure to books. Children's personal experiences influence their interests in ways that teachers and librarians might never be able to discover. And sometimes apparent interests are only the product of which books are available and which are not.

We must be careful not to oversimplify the reasons for children's book choices. Even so, it is important not to underestimate a developmental perspective that takes into account both experience and growth. This is a powerful tool for predicting reading interests and for understanding other ways in which children respond.

Growth Patterns That Influence Response

The child-development point of view begins with recognizing and accepting the uniqueness of childhood. Children are not miniature adults but individuals with their own needs, interests, and capabilities—all of which change over time and at varying rates.

In the early decades of child study, emphasis was placed on discovery of so-called normal behavior patterns for each age. Growth studies revealed similarities in patterns of physical, mental, and emotional growth. More recently, longitudinal studies have shown wide variations in individual rates of growth. One child's growth might be uneven, and a spurt in one aspect of development might precede a spurt in another. Age trends continue to be useful in understanding the child, but recent research has also been concerned with the interaction of biological, cultural, and life-experience forces. We know, for example, that development is not simply the result of the maturation of neural cells but evolves as new experience reshapes existing structures. Experience affects the age at which development appears.

Studies in children's cognitive and language growth, as well as in other areas of human development, have direct application for the choice of appropriate books

---

[9]André Favat, *Child and Tale: The Origins of Interest* (Urbana, Ill.: National Council of Teachers of English, 1977).

[10]Norma Marian Schlager, "Developmental Factors Influencing Children's Responses to Literature" (Ph.D. dissertation, Claremont Graduate School, 1974.)

Fourth-grade teacher Roberto Sbordone asks his students to write a "Reader's Portrait" each year to help them reflect on themselves as readers. As Bree, one of his students, reveals her journey to becoming a book lover, she shows how personal each child's responses to books can be.

A Reader's Portrait by Bree Bang-Jensen

I guess I've always loved stories because long before I knew how to read I would listen to a story tape over and over and over again for hours.

My parents used to read to me from a very early age. When I was three my parents read Laura Ingalls books to me.

Years passed, and I had no desire to learn to read. I hated those books called "Easy Readers," because to me they had no point.

In first grade it made no sense to me that I had to learn this bizarre system called reading. Then, in the Thanksgiving vacation of second grade, suddenly it all clicked in place. I was reading the first Boxcar Children Book. I was IN the book! From then on, I spent all my time reading.

For a while, my mother had to make me go outside for half an hour everyday.

My favorite book author is Jean Little, and my favorite book is *Mine for Keeps*. My ninth birthday party was a "Book Party" where we had a book obstacle course, played charades from books, made bookmarks and used books with "treasure" in the title for a treasure hunt. There were even books in the goody bags.

You know what I like about reading? You can take a vacation almost anywhere for a dollar or two—you buy a book and read it. In reading you can be anyone, anywhere, in any situation!

Bree Bang-Jensen, Age 9
Springhurst School, Dobbs Ferry, N.Y.
Teacher, Roberto Cecere Sbordone

and the understanding of children's responses. Although this text can highlight only a few recent findings, it can serve to alert the student of children's literature to the importance of such information.

As we begin, it seems worthwhile to offer a word of caution about graded school organization, which falsely appears to provide homogeneous classroom groups. Not only might there be a two- to three-year chronological age range within one class, but children of the same age will reflect wide and varied levels of individual development. Many of our schools have developed multi-age units or family groupings that further increase diversity of interest and ability. To provide appropriate literature experiences for these children, the teacher needs to know each of them as individuals—their level of development, their rate of development, and their varying interests. To meet their needs, the school must provide an extensive collection of books and media covering a wide range of topics at various interest and reading levels.

Physical Development

Children's experiences with literature can begin at a very early age. Studies of infant perception show that even tiny babies hear and see better than was thought possible a few decades ago. For instance, newborns show more response to patterned, rhythmic sounds than to continuous tones. They also show preferences for the sound frequencies of the human voice.[11] This supports the intuition of parents who chant nursery rhymes or sing lullabies that the sound of songs and rhymes provides satisfaction even for the youngest.

Infants gain visual perception very rapidly within their range of focus. According to Leslie Cohen's summary of research, babies in their first months of life see lines, angles, and adjacent areas of high contrast and prefer black and white to muted colors up to about 2 months of age.[12] They progress to seeing simple dimensions such as forms or colors, and before 6 months are perceiving more complex patterns (faces or colored shapes) as whole units. Books designed for babies and toddlers, like Tana Hoban's *Red, Blue, Yellow Shoe*, often acknowledge this developmental pattern by featuring simple, clearly defined pictures with firm outlines, uncluttered backgrounds, and bright colors.

As visual perception develops, children begin to show fascination with details and often enjoy searching for specific objects in illustrations. One 18-month-old

[11]Aidan Macfarlane, *The Psychology of Childbirth* (Cambridge, Mass.: Harvard University Press, 1977).

[12]Leslie B. Cohen, "Our Developing Knowledge of Infant Perception and Cognition," *American Psychologist* 34 (1979): 894–899.

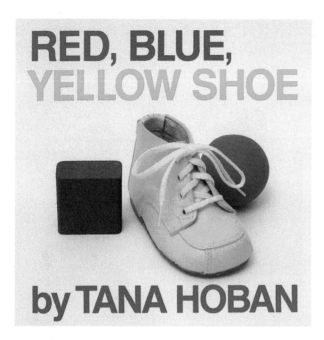

Sturdy books like Tana Hoban's *Red, Blue, Yellow Shoe* are just right for little ones' hands (and teeth).
Cover photograph by Tana Hoban from her *Red, Blue, Yellow Shoe.* Copyright © 1986 by Tana Hoban. By permission of Greenwillow Books, a division of William Morrow & Company, Inc.

boy spotted a clock in Margaret Wise Brown's *Goodnight Moon* and subsequently pointed out clocks in other books when he discovered them. Older preschoolers make a game of finding "hidden" things in pictures, like the Mother Goose and fairy tale characters tucked into each illustration of Janet and Allan Ahlberg's *Each Peach Pear Plum.*

Children's attention spans generally increase with age as well as interest. In their first school experiences some young children have trouble sitting quietly for even a 20-minute story. It is better to have several short story times for these children than to demand their attention for longer periods and so lose their interest. Some kindergarten and primary teachers provide many opportunities for children to listen to stories in small groups of two or three by using the listening center or asking parent aides or student teachers to read to as few as one or two children.

Physical development influences children's interests as well as their attention span. Growth in size, muscularity, and coordination is often reflected in children's choice of a book in which characters share their own newly acquired traits or abilities. *Whistle for Willie* by Ezra Jack Keats, for example, seems most rewarding for young children who have just learned to whistle. The demand for sports books increases as boys and girls gain the skills necessary for successful participation.

American children are growing up faster, both physically and psychologically, than they ever have before. By sixth grade almost all girls have reached puberty, although very few boys have.[13] The age of onset of puberty figures prominently in early adolescents' self-concept and influences book choices. Girls are still reading Judy Blume's *Are You There God? It's Me, Margaret* (1970) because it reflects their own concerns about menstruation. Margaret has frequent chats with God, which include such pleas as: "Are you there God? It's me, Margaret. I just told my mother I want a bra. Please help me grow God. You know where."[14]

Both physical maturity and social forces have led to the development of sexual interests at a younger age. Sophisticated 7-year-olds are teased about their "boyfriends" or "girlfriends." One report indicates that every day 7,742 U.S. teenagers become sexually active.[15] It is somehow as if childhood were something to be transcended rather than enjoyed. One result of this shortened childhood is a decrease in the length of time in which boys and girls are interested in reading children's literature. Many of them turn to reading teenage novels or adult fiction before they have read such fine books as *A Question of Trust* by Marion Dane Bauer or *Jericho* by Janet Hickman, both well-written, complex stories about young adolescents.

Cognitive Development

The work of the great Swiss psychologist Jean Piaget has had a great influence on educators' understanding of children's intellectual development.[16] Piaget proposed that intelligence develops as a result of the interaction of environment and the maturation of the child. In his view, children are active participants in their own learning.

Piaget's observations led him to conclude that there are distinct stages in the development of logical thinking. According to his theory, all children go through these stages in the same progression, but not necessarily at the same age. He identified these stages as the

[13]Frederick C. Howe, "The Child in the Elementary School: Developmental Trends," *Child Study Journal* 23 (1993): 327–346.

[14]Judy Blume, *Are You There God? It's Me, Margaret* (Englewood Cliffs, N.J.: Bradbury Press, 1970), p. 37.

[15]Children's Defense Fund, *Children, 1990: A Report Card, Briefing Book, and Primer,* (Washington, D.C.: Children's Defense Fund, 1990).

[16]Barbel Inhelder and Jean Piaget, *The Growth of Logical Thinking* (New York: Basic Books, 1962); John Flavell, *The Developmental Psychology of Jean Piaget* (Princeton, N.J.: Van Nostrand, 1963); Hans G. Furth, *Piaget for Teachers* (Englewood Cliffs, N.J.: Prentice Hall, 1970).

sensory-motor period, from infancy to about 2 years of age; *the preoperational period,* from approximately 2 to 7 years; the *concrete operational period,* from about 7 to 11; and a two-phase development of *formal operations,* which begins around age 11 and continues throughout adult life. It will be useful for us to look at some of the characteristics of children's thinking described by Piaget and consider how these are related to the books children like and to their responses to literature.

During the sensory-motor period, infants and toddlers learn through coordinating sensory perceptions and motor activity. By the end of their first year, most children enjoy the action or game rhymes of Mother Goose. They delight in the rhythm of "Pat-a-Cake, Pat-a-Cake" and anticipate the pinching and patting that accompanies the rhyme. Tactile books such as *Pat the Bunny* by Dorothy Kunhardt or *Goodnight, Teddy Bear* by Lynne Bertrand appeal to their sensory perceptions by encouraging them to touch special materials pasted on the page. Such an introduction to books incorporates what the young child responds to best—sensory-motor play and participation with a loving adult.

Preschool and kindergarten children fall into Piaget's stage of preoperational thinking, during which children learn to represent the world symbolically through language, play, and drawing. Thinking is based on direct experience and perception of the present moment. Many of the particular features ascribed to this stage of thought seem to be reflected in young children's response to literature. For instance, preoperational children are not yet able to "conserve." That is, they are unable to hold an idea or image constant in their mind as it changes in shape or form. (If they pour the same amount of water into a tall, slim container and into a short, stout container, they are still likely to report there is more water in the tall container.) This model might explain why young children so enjoy cumulative stories like "The Gingerbread Boy" or *Shoes from Grandpa* by Mem Fox. The built-in repetition in these stories carries the sequence of the action along from page to page. Children who have learned to conserve can remember the events without aid and often say that the repetitious language is boring.

Egocentrism is another characteristic of the thinking of children during the preoperational period. Egocentrism, in this sense, does not imply selfishness or putting one's own desires ahead of others'. It simply means that the young child is not capable of assuming another person's point of view. Piaget maintained that preschoolers cannot figure out, in the literal sense, what objects will be seen from vantage points different from their own. However, work by Margaret Donaldson and others suggests that children as young as 3 or 4 *can* demonstrate

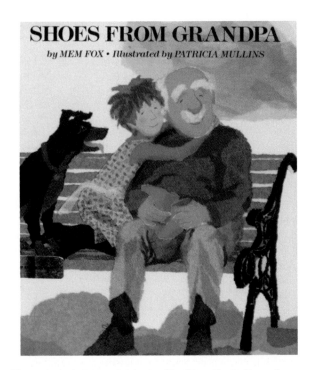

The repeated phrases in stories like Mem Fox's *Shoes from Grandpa* help young children gain control of story patterns.
From *Shoes From Grandpa* by Mem Fox, illustrated by Patricia Mullins. Illustration copyright © 1990 by Patricia Mullins. Reprinted by permission of the Publisher, Orchard Books, New York.

this ability when the situation is concrete and has meaning for them.[17]

Most children of elementary-school age would be described as concrete operational thinkers in Piaget's model. Classifying and arranging objects in series are important abilities within children's command during this period, making them more systematic and orderly thinkers. Their thought also becomes flexible and reversible, allowing them to unravel and rearrange a sequence of events. It is no surprise, then, that elementary-age children begin to like mysteries and to understand stories with more complex plot features such as flashbacks or a story within a story. Shifting from an egocentric pattern of thought, children in the concrete operational stage also seem to identify more spontaneously with different points of view. A book like *The True Story of the Three Little Pigs* by Jon Scieszka suits this developmental level well because readers understand what the author has done with the structure of a familiar tale and can also begin to see the events through the eyes of a new narrator, in this case the wolf.

[17]Margaret Donaldson, *Children's Minds* (New York: Norton, 1979), chap. 2.

One interesting aspect of concrete operational children's thinking is described by psychologist David Elkind as "cognitive conceit."[18] As children begin to have some success in reasoning and problem solving, they tend to get the idea that they must be as able as adults, or even smarter. They enjoy besting an older child, parent, or teacher. Although children's visions of superiority may seldom come true in real experience, books for middle graders often feature young protagonists on their own who manage just as well as, or better than, their elders. In E. L. Konigsburg's *From the Mixed-Up Files of Mrs. Basil E. Frankweiler,* for instance, young Claudia is clever enough to outwit adults by living undetected in New York's Metropolitan Museum of Art and shrewd enough to make an important discovery about one of the statues there.

The last stage of cognitive development described by Piaget is that of formal operations, which begins with a transitional period that corresponds roughly to the middle school years. Students begin to develop abstract theoretical thought; they are no longer dependent on concrete evidence but can reason from hypotheses to logical conclusions. This allows them to think of possibilities for their lives that are contrary to their prior experience and enables them to see the future in new ways. Complex novels and science fiction in particular begin to have appeal for students at this level. Also, students gain understanding of the use of symbols for symbols, such as letters for numbers in algebra or symbolic meanings in literature. While they have understood the use of obvious symbols like the broom in *Hurry Home, Candy* by Meindert DeJong, they can now deal with the layers of meaning found in some poetry and complex stories like Tim Wynne-Jones's *Some of the Kinder Planets* or Lois Lowry's *The Giver.*

This would appear to be the time, then, when literary criticism would be most appropriately introduced. Although teachers at every grade level would have been steadily building some knowledge and appreciation of literature, detailed analysis of a work would probably not be undertaken before this period of intellectual development. Even then, teachers would want such a discussion to arise from the child's personal response to the book.

It is important to remember that not all young people entering middle schools or junior high schools have reached the level of formal operations.[19] At the same

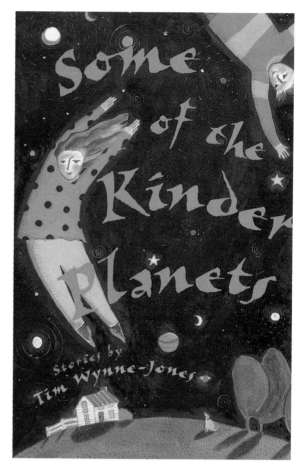

The subtle humor and quirky situations in *Some of the Kinder Planets* demand a more mature reader.
From *Some of the Kinder Planets* by Tim Wynne-Jones. Jacket illustration copyright © 1995 by Christian Potter Drury. Reprinted by permission of the Publisher, Orchard Books, New York.

time, some young children demonstrate considerable analytical competence as they talk about books that are familiar and meaningful to them.

Educators today express many concerns about the interpretation of Piaget's theory. The whole idea of stages, for instance, suggests a progression of development that might be far more orderly than what occurs in real life. Some feel that the theory fails to describe the intricacy and complexity of children's thinking and might lead teachers to focus on what children are supposedly not able to do, thus falsely lowering expectations. We need to keep these cautions in mind if we look to Piagetian theory for guidance in selecting books for children and planning literature experiences.

Other views of cognitive development can help us broaden our base for understanding children and their response to literature. Russian psychologist Lev Semenovich Vygotsky, for instance, stresses the ties between

[18]David Elkind, *Children and Adolescents* (New York: Oxford University Press, 1970).

[19]David Elkind, "Investigating Intelligence in Early Adolescence," in *Toward Adolescence: The Middle School Years,* ed. Mauritz Johnson and Kenneth J. Rehage. Seventy-Ninth Yearbook of the National Society for the Study of Education (Chicago: University of Chicago Press, 1980), pp. 282–294.

development of thought and language, the social aspect of learning, and the importance of adult-child interaction.[20] One crucial idea is that children grow in their thinking abilities within a "zone of proximal development," an area in which they are asked to stretch their ability, but not too far. For example, if students can identify the similarities in two versions of a familiar folktale like "Little Red Riding Hood," they might also be able to see how these stories are related to Ed Young's *Lon Po Po: A Red Riding Hood Tale from China*. However, they might not yet be ready to connect these tales to the modern spoof *Ruby*, by Michael Emberley, which draws its humor from sly references to Red Riding Hood.

American psychologist Howard Gardner has proposed that there is no single "intelligence," but a cluster of at least seven intellectual abilities, or "multiple intelligences": linguistic, musical, spatial, logical-mathematical, bodily, knowledge of self, and understanding of others.[21] The stages of development he sees for each of these are different. Appreciation of literature falls into the category of linguistic intelligence. Increasing sensitivity to balance, composition, style, and sound of language characterize growth within this domain. The idea of multiple intelligences would help to explain why some children breeze through math but blank out during discussions of literature, and vice versa.

However we look at cognitive development, we need to remember that it is only one part of a much larger picture of growth patterns that influence interests and responses.

Language Development

The pattern of early language learning moves from infant babbling and cooing to the use of single words, frequently ones that name familiar people or things, like *Mama* or *kitty*. Next, somewhere around 2 years, children begin to use two-word utterances. They develop the ability to change inflection, intonation, or word order to expand their range of meaning ("Daddy go?" "*Bad* kitty!"). Theorists disagree on just how children are able to acquire a functional command of such a complex system as language so early in life. There is strong evidence, however, that the child is more than just an imitator. Children seem to construct on their own the system for making themselves understood; M. A. K. Halliday calls this "learning how to mean."[22] To do so they must *use* language—talk as well as listen.

Verbal participation with an adult is an important element in young children's experience with literature. ABC or picture identification books like Margaret Miller's *Guess Who?* provide special opportunities if they are "talked through" rather than simply read as a string of nouns. Toddlers learn more than vocabulary from such encounters. Very early experiences with books encourage many aspects of language development. (See Chapters 1 and 4 for more on this point.)

Language development proceeds at a phenomenal pace during the preschool years. By the end of that time children will have learned to express their thoughts in longer sentences that combine ideas or embed one idea within another. In short, they will have gained access to the basic structure of grammar—all this by about age 4, and regardless of native language.[23]

Children improvise and explore words as they learn, chanting and playing with language as they gain confidence.[24] Rhythmic rhymes and nonsense verses are natural choices for preschoolers because they fit this pattern so well. However, children's fun in playing with language as various forms are mastered is not limited to the very young. Middle-grade children, with their wider range of language competence, are fascinated by the variety of jokes, riddles, tongue twisters, and folklore miscellany offered by Alvin Schwartz in collections like *Tomfoolery: Trickery and Foolery with Words*. They are also intrigued by ingenious uses of language in a story context, as in Norton Juster's *The Phantom Tollbooth*, Ellen Raskin's *The Westing Game*, or *The BFG* by Roald Dahl.

We know that children's language growth continues through the elementary grades and beyond, although the rate is never again as dramatic as during the preschool years. The average length and complexity of their statements, both oral and written, increase as children progress through school.[25] We also know, however, that children's capacity to produce language consistently lags behind their ability to understand it. This suggests that we owe students of all ages the opportunity

[20]L. S. Vygotsky, *Thought and Language* (Cambridge, Mass.: MIT Press, 1962; idem *Mind in Society: The Development of Higher Psychological Processes* (Cambridge, Mass.: Harvard University Press, 1978).

[21]Howard Gardner, *Frames of Minds* (New York: Basic Books, 1983).

[22]M. A. K. Halliday, *Learning How to Mean: Explorations in the Functions of Language* (New York: Elsevier, 1974).

[23]Dan I. Sobin, "Children and Language: They Learn the Same Way All Around the World," in *Contemporary Readings in Child Psychology*, ed. E. Mavis Hetherington and Ross D. Parke, 2nd ed. (New York: McGraw-Hill, 1981), pp. 122–126.

[24]Ruth Weir, *Language in the Crib* (The Hague: Mouton, 1970).

[25]Walter Loban, *Language Development: Kindergarten Through Grade Twelve* (Urbana, Ill.: National Council of Teachers of Enligsh, 1976).

to read and hear good writing that is beyond the level of their own conversation. Seven-year-olds, for instance, cannot speak with the eloquence and humor that characterize William Steig's picture books, such as *Zeke Pippin* or *Doctor De Soto*. Still, they can understand the language in its story context, and hearing it will add to their knowledge of how language sounds and works. Books by Virginia Hamilton or Natalie Babbitt might serve the same function for older students. Unlike novels that do little more than mirror contemporary speech, the work of these and other fine writers can give children a chance to consider the power of language used with precision and imagination.

Moral Development

Piaget's extensive studies of children included special attention to their developing ideas about fairness and justice. According to Piaget, the difference between younger and older children's concepts is so pronounced that there are really "two moralities" in childhood.[26] Lawrence Kohlberg's studies of moral development build on Piaget's work, providing a hierarchy of six stages reaching into adulthood.[27]

According to both Piaget's and Kohlberg's descriptions of the general direction of elementary children's development, as children grow in intellect and experience, they move away from ideas of morality based on authority and adult constraint and toward morality based on the influence of group cooperation and independent thinking. Carol Gilligan adds a dimension based on gender to the later stages of this development.[28] She suggests that as girls mature, their sense of their identity is influenced by interconnections with others to a greater degree than for boys. Consequently, their moral judgment develops along lines of an enhanced sense of responsibility and caring for others. Girls might seem less decisive than boys in discussing moral dilemmas because they are trying to take into account a whole network of people who may be affected by a choice. This concern for others is present in boys' thinking as well, but seldom takes precedence over their ideas about what is "fair."

Some of the contrasts between the moral judgment of younger and older children are as follows:

- Young children judge the goodness or badness of an act according to its likelihood of bringing punishment or reward from adults; in other words, they are constrained by the rules that adults have made. Older elementary-age children usually understand that there are group standards for judging what is good or bad and by then are very conscious of situations where they can make their own rules.

- In a young child's eyes, behavior is totally right or totally wrong, with no allowance for an alternate point of view. More mature children are willing to consider that circumstances and situations make for legitimate differences of opinion.

- Young children tend to judge an act by its consequences, regardless of the actor's intent. By third or fourth grade, most children have switched to considering motivation rather than consequences alone in deciding what degree of guilt is appropriate.

- Young children believe that bad behavior and punishment go together; the more serious the deed, the more severe the punishment they would prescribe. Its form would not necessarily be related to the offense, but it would automatically erase the offender's guilt. Older children are not so quick to suggest all-purpose pain. They are more interested in finding a "fair" punishment, one that somehow fits the crime and will help bring the wrongdoer back within the rules of the group.

These developmental differences are apparent in the responses of two groups of children to Taro Yashima's *Crow Boy*. When asked what the teacher in the story should do about shy Chibi, who hid under the schoolhouse on the first day, many first graders said "Spank him!" Nine- and 10-year-olds, however, suggested explaining to him that there was nothing to be afraid of or introducing him to classmates so he wouldn't be shy.

Many stories for children present different levels of moral complexity that have the potential for stimulating rich discussions among children. Erica Silverman's picturebook *Don't Fidget a Feather* provides younger children with a chance to consider the impulse to help another over the need to compete to be the best. *On My Honor* by Marion Dane Bauer provides older elementary readers with a chance to discuss the complexities of a tragic personal experience. Avi's *Nothing but the Truth* also poses many questions on values for middle-school readers to debate.

Working through dilemmas, the experts suggest, allows us to move from one level of moral judgment

[26]Jean Piaget, *The Moral Judgment of the Child*, trans. M. Gabain (New York: Free Press, 1965).

[27]Lawrence Kohlberg, "Development of Moral Character and Moral Ideology," in *Review of Child Development Research*, ed. M. L. Hoffman and L. W. Hoffman. (New York: Russell Sage Foundation, 1964).

[28]Carol Gilligan, *In a Different Voice: Psychological Theory and Women's Development* (Cambridge, Mass.: Harvard University Press, 1982.)

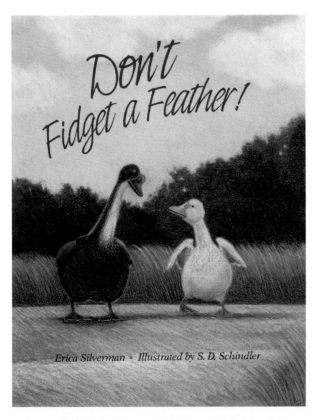

The characters in Erica Silverman's *Don't Fidget a Feather* face a moral dilemma that will be familiar to many children.
Reprinted with permission of Simon & Schuster Books for Young Readers from *Don't Fidget a Feather* by Erica Silverman, illustrated by S. D. Schindler. Illustrations copyright © 1994 S. D. Schindler.

toward another. Literature provides a means by which children can rehearse and negotiate situations of conflict without risk, trying out alternative stances to problems as they step into the lives and thoughts of different characters.

Personality Development

Every aspect of a child's growth is intertwined with every other. All learning is a meshing of cognitive dimensions, affective or emotional responses, social relationships, and value orientation. This is the matrix in which personality develops. The process of "becoming" is a highly complex one indeed. For children to become "fully functioning" persons, their basic needs must be met. They need to feel they are loved and understood; they must feel they are members of a group significant to them; they must feel they are achieving and growing toward independence. Psychologist Abraham Maslow's research suggests that a person develops through a "hierarchy of needs" from

basic animal-survival necessities to the "higher" needs that are more uniquely human and spiritual.[29] Self-actualization might take a lifetime, or it might never be achieved. But the concept that the individual is continually "becoming" is a more positive view than the notion that little change can take place in personality. Literature can provide opportunities for people of all ages to satisfy higher-level needs, but it is important to remember that books alone cannot meet children's basic needs.

Psychologist Erik Erikson sees human emotional and social development as a passage through a series of stages.[30] Each stage centers around the individual's meeting a particular goal or concern associated with that stage. Erikson theorized that accomplishments at later stages depend on how well the individual was able to meet the goals of preceding stages. According to this theory, a sense of *trust* must be gained during the first year; a sense of *autonomy* should be realized by age 3; between 3 and 6 years the sense of *initiative* is developed; and a sense of duty and *accomplishment* or *industry* occupies the period of childhood from 6 to 12 years. In adolescence a sense of *identity* is built; while a sense of *intimacy*, a parental sense of *productivity*, and a sense of *integrity* are among the tasks of adulthood.

The elementary school audience for children's books can be grouped according to the categories *initiative*, *accomplishment*, and *identity*. Preschool and early primary children can be described as preoccupied with first ventures outside the circle of familiar authority. Most elementary children are caught up in the period of industry, or "task orientation," proud of their ability to use skills and tools, to plan projects, and to work toward finished products. Middle school students are more concerned with defining values and personal roles.

Writers of children's books sometimes suggest a natural audience for their work by bringing one of these orientations into the foreground. In Beatrix Potter's *The Tale of Peter Rabbit*, Peter's adventures demonstrate a developing sense of initiative like that of the preschoolers listening to the story. *Jackson Jones and the Puddle of Thorns*, by Mary Quattlebaum, focuses on the industriousness of its middle-childhood protagonist; Maude Casey's *Over the Water* speaks directly to the adolescent's struggle for identity.

In considering any theory of development, we need to remember that children's prior experiences with books and their individual backgrounds can have an

[29]Abraham H. Maslow, *Motivation and Personality*, rev. ed. (New York: Harper & Row, 1970).

[30]Erik H. Erikson, *Childhood and Society*, rev. ed. (New York: W. W. Norton, 1964).

Jackson assumes responsibility for organizing a community garden in Mary Quattlebaum's *Jackson Jones and the Puddle of Thorns.*

From *Jackson Jones and the Puddle of Thorns (Jacket)* by Mary Quattlebaum. Copyright © 1994 by Mary Quattlebaum. Illustration copyright © 1994 by Melodye Rosales. Used by permission of Bantam Doubleday Dell Books for Young Readers.

impact in their responses to literature. For instance, a child who has read stories of King Arthur and Lloyd Alexander's Prydain series will have a different understanding of what constitutes a hero in literature than someone who has not read beyond the Hardy Boys. Every child brings to literature a different lifetime of experiences and a set of constructs that is not quite the same as any other's. Whenever we consider the broad outlines of similarity that mark developmental levels, we have to remember that each reader is also one of a kind.

Guides for Ages and Stages

Adults who are responsible for children's reading need to be aware of child development and learning theory and of children's interests. They must keep in mind

characteristics and needs of children at different ages and stages of development. At the same time, it is important to remember that each child has a unique pattern of growth. Resources for Teaching, "Books for Ages and Stages," (see pages 52–59) summarizes some characteristic growth patterns, suggests implications for selection and use of books, and provides examples of suitable books for a particular state of development. Remember that the age levels indicated are only approximate. Also, books suggested as appropriate for one category may fit several other categories as well.

Response in the Classroom

Understanding children's responses to literature would be much easier if it were possible to peer inside children's heads. Then we might see firsthand what concept of story guides progress through a book or just what children are thinking as a story unfolds. Instead, teachers must be satisfied with secondary evidence. Children's perceptions and understandings are revealed in many different ways—as they choose and talk about books, and as they write, paint, play, or take part in other classroom activities.

Classroom responses can be obvious and direct (primary children have been known to kiss a favorite book) or hidden within a situation that appears to have little to do with literature (such as block corner play). Many responses are verbal, many come without words. Some are spontaneous, bubbling up out of children too delighted to be still, or shyly offered in confidence. Other responses would not be expressed at all without the direct invitation of teachers who plan extension activities or discussions (see Chapters 13 and 14) to generate thoughtful reaction to literature. To understand any of these observed responses, it is helpful to be acquainted with a few basic theoretical perspectives.

Theories of Response

What really goes on between a reader and a story or poem is a complex question with many answers. Theories about reader response draw from many disciplines, including psychology, linguistics, aesthetics, and, of course, literature and education.

Some theories focus on what is read; others focus on the reader. For instance, some researchers have examined in careful detail the structure of stories, noting the precise arrangement of words and sequence of ideas.

Resources for Teaching
Books for Ages and Stages: Before School—Infancy, Ages 1 and 2

Characteristics	Implications	Examples
Rapid development of senses. Responds to sound of human voice, especially rhythmic patterns. Vision stimulated by areas of color and sharp contrast; increasingly able to see detail.	Enjoys rhymes, songs, and lullabies. Likes simple, bright illustrations. Looks for familiar objects.	*Tomie de Paola's Mother Goose* (dePaola) *Hush, Little Baby: A Folk Lullaby* (Aliki) *What Is It?* (T. Hoban) *Night Becomes Day* (McGuire) *Time for Bed* (M. Fox)
Uses all senses to explore the world immediately at hand; learns through activity and participation.	Gets maximum use from sturdy books with washable pages. Needs to participate by touching, pointing, peeking, moving.	*Rain Feet* (Johnson) *Where's Spot?* (Hill) *Pat the Bunny* (Kunhardt) *Tickle, Tickle* (Oxenbury) *Where Is the Green Parrot?* (Zacharias)
Very limited attention span; averts eyes or turns away when bored.	Needs books that can be shared a few pages at a time or in a brief sitting; many short story times are better than one long one.	*Babies* (Isadora) *Max's Ride* (Wells) *Dear Zoo* (Campbell) *1, 2, 3* (T. Hoban)
Building foundations of language; plays with sounds, learns basic vocabulary along with concepts, begins to learn implicit "rules" that govern speech and conversation.	Needs to hear many rhymes and simple stories. Needs encouragement to use language in labeling pictures and in sharing dialogue with adults as they read aloud.	*Splash, Splash* (Sheppard) *Catch Me and Kiss Me and Say It Again* (Watson) *Sam Who Never Forgets* (Rice) *Baby Says* (Steptoe)
Building basic trust in human relationships.	Needs love and affection from caregivers, in stories as well as in life. Thrives on dependable routines and rituals such as bedtime stories.	*Goodnight Moon* (Brown) *The Blanket* (Burningham) *Tom & Pippo's Day* (Oxenbury) *Asleep, Asleep* (Ginsburg)
Limited mobility and experience; interests centered in self and the familiar.	Needs books that reflect self and people and activities in the immediate environment.	*The Baby's Catalogue* (Ahlberg and Ahlberg) *The Cupboard* (Burningham) *How Many?* (MacKinnon) *Things to Play With* (Rockwell)
Learning autonomy in basic self-help skills.	Enjoys stories of typical toddler accomplishments such as feeding self or getting dressed.	*Can You Guess?* (Miller) *Alfie's Feet* (Hughes) *I Can* (Oxenbury) *Going to the Potty* (F. Rogers)

Preschool and Kindergarten—Ages 3, 4, and 5

Characteristics	Implications	Examples
Rapid development of language.	Interest in words, enjoyment of rhymes, nonsense, and repetition and cumulative tales. Enjoys retelling simple folktale and "reading" stories from books without words.	*Random House Book of Mother Goose* (Lobel) *Oh, What a Noisy Farm* (Zeifert) *Mr. Grumpy's Outing* (Burningham) *Millions of Cats* (Gág) *The Three Bears* (Rockwell) *Sunshine* (Ormerod)
Very active, short attention span.	Requires books that can be completed in one sitting. Enjoys participation such as naming, pointing, singing, and identifying hidden pictures. Should have a chance to hear stories several times each day.	*The Very Hungry Caterpillar* (Carle) *Each Peach Pear Plum* (Ahlberg and Ahlberg) *The Wheels on the Bus* (Zelinsky) *Have You Seen My Duckling?* (Tafuri) *Small Green Snake* (Gray)

Resources for Teaching
Preschool and Kindergarten—Ages 3, 4, and 5 (continued)

Characteristic	Implications	Examples
Child is center of own world. Interest, behavior, and thinking are egocentric.	Likes characters that are easy to identify with. Normally sees only one point of view.	*Noisy Nora* (Wells) *Fix-It* (McPhail) *Hi!* (Scott) *A Baby Sister for Frances* (R. Hoban)
Curious about own world.	Enjoys stories about everyday experiences, pets, playthings, home, people in the immediate environment.	*The Snowy Day* (Keats) *Jesse's Daycare* (Valens) *Building a House* (Barton) *Trucks* (Rockwell) *Feast for Ten* (Falwell)
Beginning interest in how things work and the wider world.	Books feed curiosity and introduce new topics.	*My Visit to the Dinosaurs* (Aliki) *I Want to Be an Astronaut* (Barton) *Is This a House for a Hermit Crab?* (McDonald) *Little Elephant* (Ford)
Building concepts through many firsthand experiences.	Books extend and reinforce child's developing concepts.	*Eating the Alphabet* (Ehlert) *Freight Train* (Crews) *Spirals, Curves, Fanshapes, and Lines* (T. Hoban) *Trucks* (Gibbons)
Has little sense of time. Time is "before now," "now," and "not yet."	Books can help children begin to understand the sequence of time.	*Homeplace* (Shelby) *A Year of Beasts* (Wolff) *The Little House* (Burton) *When You Were a Baby* (Jonas) *Clocks and More Clocks* (Hutchins)
Learns through imaginative play; make-believe world of talking animals and magic seems very real.	Enjoys stories that involve imaginative play. Likes personification of toys and animals.	*Hi, Pizza Man!* (Walter) *May I Bring a Friend?* (DeRegniers) *We're Going on a Bear Hunt* (Rosen) *Corduroy* (Freeman)
Seeks warmth and security in relationships with family and others.	Likes to hear stories that provide reassurance. Bedtime stories and other read-aloud rituals provide positive literature experiences.	*The Runaway Bunny* (Brown) *Guess How Much I Love You* (McBranty) *Little Bear* (Minarik) *Ten, Nine, Eight* (Bang) *Julius, the Baby of the World* (Henkes)
Beginning to assert independence. Takes delight in own accomplishments.	Books can reflect emotions. Enjoys stories where small characters show initiative.	*Will I Have a Friend?* (M. Cohen) *I Hate to Go to Bed* (Judi Barrett) *Alfie Gets in First* (Hughes) *Titch* (Hutchins) *Julius* (Johnson)
Makes absolute judgments about right and wrong.	Expects bad behavior to be punished and good behavior to be rewarded. Requires poetic justice and happy endings.	*The Three Billy Goats Gruff* (Asbjørnsen and Moe) *The Little Red Hen* (Barton) *The Tale of Peter Rabbit* (Potter) *Maxi, the Hero* (Barracca and Barracca) *Farmer Duck* (Waddell)

Resources for Teaching
Primary—Ages 6 and 7

Characteristics	Implications	Examples
Continued development and expansion of language.	Frequent story times during the day provide opportunity to hear the rich and varied language of literature. Wordless books and simple tales encourage storytelling.	*Sylvester and the Magic Pebble* (Steig) *Rachel Fister's Blister* (MacDonald) *Strega Nona* (de Paola) *The Royal Nap* (Black) *Chicka Chicka Boom Boom* (Martin and Archambault) *The Little Old Lady Who Was Not Afraid of Anything* (L. Williams) *The Snowman* (Briggs)
Attention span increasing.	Prefers short stories; may enjoy a continued story provided each chapter is a complete episode.	*Frog and Toad Together* (Lobel) *Willa and Old Miss Annie* (Doherty) *The Courage of Sarah Noble* (Dalgliesh) *The Stories of Julian Tells* (Cameron) *Ramona the Brave* (Cleary)
Striving to accomplish skills expected by adults.	Proud of accomplishments in reading and writing. Needs reassurance that everyone progresses at own rate. First reading experiences should be enjoyable, using familiar or predictable stories.	*When Will I Read?* (M. Cohen) *Leo the Late Bloomer* (Kraus) *The Day of Ahmed's Secret* (Heide and Gilliland) *The Bee Tree* (Polacco) *Brown Bear, Brown Bear, What Do You See?* (Martin) *The Napping House* (Wood) *Cookie's Week* (Ward)
Learning still based on immediate perception and direct experiences.	Uses information books to verify as well as extend experience. Much value in watching guinea pigs or tadpoles *before* using a book.	*My Puppy Is Born* (Cole) *I Love Guinea Pigs* (King-Smith) *Bugs* (Parker and Wright) *Summer* (Hirschi)
Continued interest in own world; more curious about a wider range of things. Still sees world from an egocentric point of view.	Needs wide variety of books. TV has expanded interests beyond home and neighborhood.	*Rata-Pata-Scata-Fata* (Gershator) *Fish Is Fish* (Lionni) *How My Parents Learned to Eat* (Friedman) *What Happened to the Dinosaurs?* (Branley) *Up Goes the Skyscraper!* (Gibbons)
Vague concepts of time.	Needs to learn basics of telling time and the calendar. Simple biographies and historical fiction may give a feeling for the past, but accurate understanding of chronology is beyond this age group.	*Nine O'Clock Lullaby* (Singer) *The Grouchy Ladybug* (Carle) *Ox-Cart Man* (D. Hall) *The House on Maple Street* (Pryor) *The Days Before Now* (Brown) *When I Was Young in the Mountains* (Rylant) *Little House in the Big Woods* (Wilder)
More able to separate fantasy from reality; more aware of own imagination.	Enjoys fantasy. Likes to dramatize simple stories or use feltboard, puppets.	*Where the Wild Things Are* (Sendak) *Tops and Bottoms* (Stevens) *Sam, Bangs, and Moonshine* (Ness) *I Know an Old Lady* (Karas)

Resources for Teaching
Primary—Ages 6 and 7 (continued)

Characteristics	Implications	Examples
Beginning to develop empathy and understanding for others.	Adults can ask such questions as "What would you have done?" "How do you think Stevie felt about Robert?"	*Stevie* (Steptoe) *Fly Away Home* (Bunting) *When I Am Old with You* (Johnson) *Crow Boy* (Yashima)
Has a growing sense of justice. Demands application of rules, regardless of circumstances.	Expects poetic justice in books.	*Flossie and the Fox* (McKissack) *Python's Party* (Wildsmith) *Once a Mouse* (Brown) *Too Many Tamales* (Soto)
Humor is developing.	Needs to hear many books read aloud for pure fun. Enjoys books and poems that have surprise endings, plays on words, incongruous situations, and slapstick comedy. Likes to be in on the joke.	*Amelia Bedelia* (Parish) *The Bone Stranger* (Remkiewicz) *The Stupids Have a Ball* (Allard) *Alexander and the Terrible, Horrible, No Good, Very Bad Day* (Viorst) *Proud Rooster and the Fox* (Threadgill)
Shows curiosity about gender differences and reproduction.	Teachers need to accept and be ready to answer children's questions about sex.	*How I Was Born* (Wabbes) *The Story of Birth* (Abel-Prot) *How You Were Born* (J. Cole)
Physical contour of the body is changing; permanent teeth appear; learning to whistle and developing other fine motor skills.	Books can help the child accept physical changes in self and differences in others.	*You'll Soon Grow into Them, Titch* (Hutchins) *One Morning in Maine* (McCloskey) *Whistle for Willie* (Keats) *Hue Boy* (Phillips)
Continues to seek independence from adults and to develop initiative.	Needs opportunities to select own books and activities. Enjoys stories of responsibility and successful ventures.	*Galimoto* (K. Williams) *Ira Sleeps Over* (Waber) *Max Found Two Sticks* (Pinkney) *By Myself* (Hopkins) *Raymond's Best Summer* (J. Rogers) *Amazing Grace* (Hoffman)
Continues to need warmth and security in family relationships.	Books may emphasize universal human characteristics in a variety of lifestyles.	*Willie's Not the Hugging Kind* (Barrett) *A Chair for My Mother* (V. Williams) *The Relatives Came* (Rylant) *Osa's Pride* (Grifalconi) *Chickens! Chickens!* (Porte)

Middle Elementary—Ages 8 and 9

Characteristics	Implications	Examples
Attaining independence in reading skill. May read with complete absorption; or may still be having difficulty learning to read. Wide variation in ability and interest.	Discovers reading as an enjoyable activity. Prefers an uninterrupted block of time for independent reading. During this period, many children become avid readers.	*Kids of Polk Street School* series (Giff) *Rats on the Range* (Marshall) *Sunken Treasure* (Gibbons) *Ramona Quimby, Age 8* (Cleary) *Harry and Arnie* (Caseley) *Charlotte's Web* (White)
Reading level may still be below appreciation level.	Essential to read aloud to children each day in order to extend interests, develop appreciation, and provide balance.	*Sing a Song of Popcorn* (DeRegniers) *Dawn* (Bang) *Sarah, Plain and Tall* (MacLachlan) *Hob and the Goblins* (Mayne)

Resources for Teaching
Middle Elementary—Ages 8 and 9 (continued)

Characteristics	Implications	Examples
Peer group acceptance becomes increasingly important.	Children need opportunities to recommend and discuss books. Sharing favorites builds sense that reading is fun, has group approval. Popular books may provide status, be much in demand.	*How to Be Cool in the Third Grade* (Duffey) *Fudge-a-Mania* (Blume) *A Light in the Attic* (Silverstein) *Bunnicula* (Howe and Howe) *Ozzie on His Own* (Hurwitz)
Developing standards of right and wrong. Begins to see viewpoints of others.	Books provide opportunities to relate to several points of view.	*Guests* (Dorris) *The Indian in the Cupboard* (Banks) *Molly's Pilgrim* (B. Cohen) *Danny, the Champion of the World* (Dahl)
Less egocentric, developing empathy for others. Questioning death.	Accepts some books with a less than happy ending. Discussion helps children explore their feelings for others.	*Flip-Flop Girl* (Paterson) *Blackberries in the Dark* (Jukes) *Stone Fox* (Gardiner) *The War with Grandpa* (R. Smith)
Time concepts and spatial relationships developing. This age level is characterized by thought that is flexible and reversible.	Interested in biographies, life in the past, in other lands, and the future. Prefers fast-moving, exciting stories.	*Night Crossing* (Ackerman) *Cleopatra* (Stanley and Vennema) *What's the Big Idea, Ben Franklin?* (Fritz) *The Secret Soldier* (McGovern) *Trouble for Lucy* (Stevens) *The Green Book* (Walsh)
Enjoys tall tales, slapstick humor in everyday situations. Appreciates imaginary adventure.	Teachers need to recognize the importance of literature for laughter, releasing tension, and providing enjoyment.	*The Blood and Thunder Adventures on Hurricane Peak* (Mahy) *The Not-So-Jolly Roger* (Scieszka) *Skinnybones* (Park) *American Tall Tales* (Osborne)
Cognitive growth and language development increase capacity for problem solving and word play.	Likes the challenge of solving puzzles and mysteries. High interest in twists of plot, secret codes, riddles, and other language play.	*Zoom* (Banyai) *Anno's Math Games III* (Anno) *The Banshee Train* (Bodkin) *The Dollhouse Murders* (Wright) *A Basket Full of White Eggs* (Swann)
Improved coordination makes proficiency in sports and games possible and encourages interest in crafts and hobbies.	Interest in sports books; wants specific knowledge about sports. Enjoys how-to-do-it books.	*The Young Rider* (Green) *Be the Best You Can Be* (Puckett) *The Paper Airplane Book* (Simon) *Playing with Plasticine* (Reid) *The Little House Cookbook* (B. Walker)
Sees categories and classifications with new clarity; interest in collecting is high.	Likes to collect and trade paperback books. Begins to look for books of one author, series books.	*Meet Addy* (the American Girl Collection) (Porter) *Ramona Forever* and others (Cleary) *Zero's Slider* and others (M. Christopher) *101 Questions and Answers About Dangerous Animals* (Simon)
Seeks specific information to answer questions; may go to books beyond own reading ability to search out answers.	Enjoys books that collect facts, informational identification books. Requires guidance in locating information within a book and in using the library.	*The Magic Schoolbus in the Time of the Dinosaurs* (Cole) *The Way Things Work* (Macaulay) *Dinosaurs Walked Here* (Lauber) *Insect Zoo* (Meyers) *George Washington's Breakfast* (Fritz)

Resources for Teaching
Later Elementary—Ages 10 and 11

Characteristics	Implications	Examples
Rate of physical development varies widely. Rapid growth precedes beginning of puberty. Girls are about two years ahead of boys in development; both increasingly curious about all aspects of sex.	Guide understanding of growth process and help children meet personal problems. Continued differentiation in reading preferences of boys and girls.	*Asking About Sex and Growing Up* (J. Cole) *Are You There God? It's Me, Margaret* (Blume) *I See the Moon* (Christiansen) *My Buddy, the King* (Brittain)
Understanding of sex role is developing; boys and girls form ideas about their own and each other's identity.	Books may provide identification with gender roles and impetus for discussion of stereotypes.	*Alice in Between* (Naylor) *The Burning Questions of Bingo Brown* (Byars) *Roses Sing on New Snow* (Yee) *Flour Babies* (Fine) *Maphead* (Howarth)
Increased emphasis on peer group and sense of belonging.	Book choices often influenced by peer group; many requests for books about "kids like us."	*Libby on Wednesday* (Snyder) *Risk 'N Roses* (Slepian) *The Battle for the Castle* (Winthrop) *The Mouse Rap* (Myers)
Deliberate exclusion of others; some expressions of prejudice.	Books can emphasize unique contributions of all. Discussion can be used to clarify values.	*Mayfield Crossing* (Nelson) *Roll of Thunder, Hear My Cry* (Taylor) *Alan and Naomi* (Levoy) *The Man from the Other Side* (Orlev)
Family patterns changing; may challenge parents' authority. Highly critical of siblings.	Books may provide some insight into these changing relationships.	*Baby* (MacLachlan) *Western Wind* (Fox) *Dear Mr. Henshaw* (Cleary) *Dicey's Song* (Voigt) *Cousins* (Hamilton)
Begins to have models other than parents drawn from TV, movies, sports figures, books. Beginning interest in future vocation.	Biographies may provide models. Career books broaden interests and provide useful information.	*Franklin Delano Roosevelt* (Freedman) *Little by Little* (Little) *Jim Abbott: Major League Pitcher* (Macht) *My Mom's a Vet* (Horenstein)
Sustained, intense interest in specific activities.	Seeks book about hobbies and other interests.	*Stamp Collecting* (Granger) *Crazy About German Shepherds* (Ashabranner) *Drawing from Nature* (Arnosky) *Amazing Bikes* (Lord)
A peak time for voluntary reading.	Avid readers welcome challenges, repeated contact with authors, genres.	Prydain series (Alexander) Narnia series (Lewis) *The Bellmaker* (Jacques) *Julie* (George) *Prairie Songs* (Conrad) *Darnell Rock Reporting* (Myers)
Seeks to test own skills and abilities; looks ahead to a time of complete independence.	Enjoys stories of survival and "going it alone."	*Hatchet* (Paulsen) *Monkey Island* (P. Fox) *The Fear Place* (Naylor) *The Exiles* (McKay) *The Sign of the Beaver* (Speare)

Resources for Teaching
Later Elementary—Ages 10 and 11 (continued)

Characteristics	Implications	Examples
Increased cognitive skill can be used to serve the imagination.	Tackles complex and puzzling plots in mysteries, science fiction, fantasy. Can appreciate more subtlety in humor.	*The Westing Game (Raskin)* *The Haunting* (Mahy) *The Dark Is Rising* (Cooper) *The Daydreamer* (McEwan) *The Watchers* (Cresswell)
Increased understanding of the chronology of past events; developing sense of own place in time. Begins to see many dimensions of a problem.	Literature provides opportunities to examine issues from different viewpoints. Guidance needed for recognizing biased presentations.	*The Shadow Children* (Schnur) *My Daniel* (Conrad) *Homesick* (Fritz) *Shades of Gray* (Reeder) *Morning Girl* (Dorris) *Now Is Your Time!* (Myers)
Highly developed sense of justice and concern for others.	Willing to discuss many aspects of right and wrong; likes "sad stories," shows empathy for victims of suffering and injustice.	*Cat Running* (Snyder) *Shiloh* (Naylor) *On My Honor* (Bauer) *Missing May* (Rylant) *Pink and Say* (Polacco) *Journey to Jo' Burg* (Naidoo) *Number the Stars* (Lowry)
Searching for values; interested in problems of the world. Can deal with abstract relationships; becoming more analytical.	Valuable discussions may grow out of teacher's reading aloud prose and poetry to this age group. Questions may help students gain insight into both the content and the literary structure of a book.	*Sadako* (Coerr) *Tuck Everlasting* (Babbitt) *Getting Him* (Haseley) *The Great Gilly Hopkins* (Paterson) *A Tree Place and Other Poems* (Levy)

Middle School—Ages 12, 13, and 14

Characteristics	Implications	Examples
Wide variation in physical development; both boys and girls reach puberty by age 14. Developing sex drive; intense interest in sexuality and world of older teens.	Books provide insight into feelings, concerns. Guidance needed to balance students' desire for frank content with lack of life experience.	*It's Perfectly Normal* (Harris) *The Goats* (B. Cole) *A Couple of Kooks* (Rylant) *Peter* (K. Walker) *Alice the Brave* (Naylor)
Self-concept continues to grow. Developing a sense of identity is important.	Books help students explore roles, rehearse journey to identity. Many stories based on myth of the hero.	*The Crying for a Vision* (Wangerin) *Bearstone* (Hobbs) *Dogsong* (Paulsen) *A Wizard of Earthsea* (LeGuin) *Dragonsong* (McCaffrey) *The Hero and the Crown* (McKinley)
Peer group becomes increasingly influential; relationships with family are changing.	Concerns about friends and families reflected in books. School should provide chance to share books and responses with peer group.	*Scorpions* (Myers) *Over the Water* (Casey) *The Eagle Kite* (P. Fox) *Baseball in April* (Soto) *Maniac Magee* (Spinelli) *Walk Two Moons* (Creech) *Grandpa's Mountain* (Reeder)

Resources for Teaching
Middle School—Ages 12, 13, and 14 (concluded)

Characteristics	Implications	Examples
New aspects of egocentrism lead to imagining self as center of others' attention and feeling one's own problems are unique.	Students begin to enjoy introspection; may identify with characters who are intense or self-absorbed.	*3 NB's of Julian Drew* (Deem) *Adam and Eve and Pinch Me* (J. Johnston) *Jacob Have I Loved* (Paterson) *A Ring of Endless Light* (L'Engle)
Cognitive abilities are increasingly abstract and flexible, but not consistently so. New capacity to reason from imaginary premises, manipulate symbolic language, and make hypothetical judgments.	Students read more complex stories, mysteries, and high fantasy that call for complex logic; enjoy science fiction and high adventure. Metaphor, symbols, and imagery are understood at a different level.	*Saturnalia* (Fleischman) *The True Confessions of Charlotte Doyle* (Avi) *The Ear, the Eye and the Arm* (Farmer) *A Swiftly Tilting Planet* (L'Engle) *The Place My Words Are Looking For* (Janeczko)
Able to apply ideas of relativity to questions of values; girls might see moral issues differently than boys do.	Students need discussion time to negotiate meanings in stories that pose moral dilemmas.	*I Hadn't Meant to Tell You This* (Woodson) *Shabanu* (Staples) *Taste of Salt* (Temple) *The Giver* (Lowry) *Rice Without Rain* (Ho) *Make Lemonade* (Wolff)
Sensitive to great complexity in human feelings and relationships.	Students seek richer and more complex stories.	*The Glory Field* (Myers) *Jericho* (Hickman) *The Leaving* (Wilson) *The Master Puppeteer* (Paterson) *Toning the Sweep* (Johnson) *I Am Wings* (Fletcher)
Cumulative effects of development and life experience produce wide variation among individuals in abilities and interests.	Reading ability and interests in one class may range from early elementary to adult.	*The Stinky Cheese Man* (Scieszka) *Unsolved! Famous Real-Life Mysteries* (Sullivan) *Nightjohn* (Paulsen) *The Hobbit* (Tolkien) *The Beekeeper's Apprentice* (King)

These patterns are called "story grammars," and studies indicate that they can affect the way readers understand and recall a story.[31] Other theorists are more concerned with individual readers and how their personalities can influence their ideas about what they read.[32] Still other researchers emphasize the cultural or social aspects of response. According to Richard Beach, "While all these theoretical perspectives rest on different assumptions about meaning, they ultimately intersect and overlap. The local—the focus on reader's textual knowledge and experience—is embedded within the global, larger social and cultural contexts." All categories of reader response research focus on the reader's textual knowledge and experience but they are embedded within larger social and cultural contexts.[33]

One important point on which scholars agree is that the process of reading and responding is active rather

[31]Nancy L. Stein and Christine G. Glenn, "An Analysis of Story Comprehension in Elementary School Children," in *New Dimensions in Discourse Processing,* ed. Roy O. Freedle (Norwood, N.J.: Ablex, 1977); Bertram Bruce, "What Makes a Good Story?" *Language Arts* 55 (April 1978): 460–466.

[32]Norman H. Holland, *Five Readers Reading* (New Haven, Conn.: Yale University Press, 1975).

[33]Richard Beach. *A Teacher's Introduction to Reader-Response Theories* (Urbana, Ill.: National Council of Teachers of English, 1993), p. 9.

than passive. The words and ideas in the book are not transferred automatically from the page to the reader. Rather, as Louise Rosenblatt has argued,

> The literary work exists in the live circuit set up between reader and text: the reader infuses intellectual and emotional meanings into the pattern of verbal symbols, and those symbols channel his thoughts and feelings.[34]

Response is dynamic and open to continuous change as readers anticipate, infer, remember, reflect, interpret, and connect. The "meaning" and significance of a story like Patricia MacLachlan's *Journey* will vary from reader to reader, depending on age and personal experience as well as experience with literature. However, each reader's response will also change, given time for reflection, discussion, or repeated readings.

Reader response theory also points out that readers approach works of literature in special ways. James Britton proposes that in all our uses of language we can be either *participants* or *spectators*.[35] In the participant role we read in order to accomplish something in the real world, as in following a recipe. In the spectator role we focus on what the language says as an end in itself, attending to its forms and patterns, as we do in enjoying poetry.

Rosenblatt suggests that reading usually involves two roles, or stances, and that we shift our emphasis from one to the other according to the material and our purposes for reading it.[36] In the *efferent* stance we are most concerned with what information can be learned from the reading. In the *aesthetic* stance our concern is for the experience of the reading itself, the feelings and images that come and go with the flow of the words. Most readers, of course, find themselves switching back and forth from one of these stances to the other as they read. One thing that teachers can do to help children share the world the author has created is to help them find an appropriate stance as they begin to read.

Types of Response

Teachers who are familiar with reader response theories and who study children's responses to literature will discover that they provide a basis for deepening children's

satisfaction with books and for supporting children's growth in interpretation.

The most common expressions of response to literature are statements, oral or written. In their most polished form such responses are known as literary criticism, and for many years research in literature involved measuring young people's statements against a standard of mature critical ability.

Recently researchers have been more interested in the process of response and have looked at verbal responses in a number of ways. Many researchers begin with a system developed by Alan Purves from the responses of three hundred teenagers in four countries.[37] All of the categories in this system have descriptive labels. They help teachers see what *kinds* of statements about literature are made by students without indicating whether the statements are "right" or "wrong."

Although early studies of response involved high school students or young adults, there have been a number of studies that provide information about the responses of elementary or preschool children. Arthur Applebee's study of children's statements about stories, the base for his work on the concept of story, shows how characteristics of responses change as students gain in age and experience.[38] Other researchers have looked carefully at what elementary children have to say about literature, often collecting data from intensive interviews, response journals, or long periods of observation.[39]

Susan Lehr talked with children about the interpretation of story themes ("The Three Little Pigs," for instance) in kindergarten, second, and fourth grades.[40] Although she noted some differences across age levels in the statements children made, she found that previous high exposure to literature enabled them to make more sophisticated statements than might have been expected. She also noted that the content and structure of interview questions and the presence of the actual book during the discussion could make an important difference in the substance of their responses.

---

[34]Louise M. Rosenblatt, *Literature as Exploration*, 3rd ed. (New York: Noble & Noble, 1976), p. 25.

[35]James Britton et al., *The Development of Writing Abilities (11–18)*, Schools Council Research Studies (London: Macmillan Education Limited, 1975).

[36]Louise M. Rosenblatt, *The Reader, the Text, the Poem: The Transactional Theory of the Literary Work* (Carbondale: Southern Illinois University Press, 1978).

[37]Alan C. Purves with Victoria Rippere, *Elements of Writing About a Literary Work: A Study of Response to Literature* (Urbana, Ill.: National Council of Teachers of English, 1968).

[38]Arthur Applebee, *The Child's Concept of Story: Ages Two to Seventeen* (Chicago: University of Chicago Press, 1978).

[39]Lee Galda, "Assuming the Spectator Stance: An Examination of the Responses of Three Young Readers," *Research in the Teaching of English* 16 (February 1982): 1–20; Marjorie R. Hancock, "Exploring the Meaning Making Process Through the Content of Literature Response Journals," *Research in the Teaching of English* 27 (December, 1993): 335–368; Rudine Sims, "Strong Black Girls: A Ten Year Old Responds to Fiction About Afro-Americans," *Journal of Research and Development in Education* 16 (spring 1983): 21–28.

[40]Susan Lehr, *The Child's Developing Sense of Theme: Responses to Literature* (New York: Teachers College Press, 1991).

"William Ernest lay a bolster pillow behind Mrs Trotter's back like

Children's pictures or other classroom work can furnish important evidence about their understanding of literature.
Martin Luther King, Jr., Laboratory School, Evanston, Illinois, Public Schools. Ellen Esrick, teacher.

Where children are concerned, it is important to remember that direct comment is only one of many ways of revealing what goes on between the book and its audience. Language used in other ways—to tell or write stories based on other stories, for instance—often provides good clues about a child's feelings and understandings about the original. Parents and teachers of young children also recognize nonverbal behaviors as signs of response. For instance, young listeners almost always show their involvement, or lack of it, in body postures and facial expressions. Children's artwork, informal drama, and other book extension activities (see Chapter 14) also provide windows on response.

Interpreting Children's Responses

Previous research in response to literature provides teachers and librarians with a framework for interpreting their students' reactions to books. This classroom-based research can give us a deeper understanding of children's responses.

Recognizing Patterns of Change

Teachers and researchers alike have observed that when children at different grade levels read and respond in ways that are comfortable for them, their responses will be alike in some ways and different in others. What might teachers expect to see in a fourth-grade classroom? What are typical first-grade responses? No one can answer these questions with exactness, for every child is a unique reader and every classroom represents a different composite of experiences with literature and with the world. Even so, it is helpful to know what researchers and teachers have discovered about the responses of their students at various grade levels. This section outlines some of these findings to provide information on the patterns of change in responses that usually take place as children have experiences with literature in the elementary school.[41] Although these findings are presented in an age-level sequence, keep in mind that any of these characteristics can be seen at other ages, depending on the child, the situation, and the challenge presented by the material. Like the Resources for Teaching chart, (pp. 52–59), this guide is more useful for making predictions about a class than for making predictions about an individual child.

Younger Children (Preschool to Primary)

Younger children are *motor-oriented*. As listeners, they respond with their whole selves, chiming in on refrains or talking back to the story. They lean closer to the book, point at pictures, clap their hands. They use body movements to try out some of the story's action, "hammering"

[41]This section is based on observations with reference to the work of Arthur Applebee, *The Child's Concept of Story*, pp. 123–125; Janet Hickman, "A New Perspective on Response to Literature," *Research in the Teaching of English* 15 (1981): 343–354; and others.

Teachers need to listen carefully to children's responses to literature in order to discover their thinking strategies.
Mission School, Redlands Public Schools, Redlands, California. Joan Schleicher, teacher. Photo by Larry Rose.

along with *John Henry* by Ezra Jack Keats or making wild faces to match the illustrations in Ruth Park's *When the Wind Changed*. Actions to demonstrate meaning ("Like this") may be given as answers to a teacher's questions. These easily observable responses go undercover as children mature; older children reveal feelings through subtle changes of expression and posture.

At this age, children spontaneously act out stories or bits of stories using actions, roles, and conventions of literature in their *dramatic play*. Witches, kings, "wild things," and other well-defined character types appear naturally, showing how well children have assimilated elements of favorite tales. Examples of story language ("We lived happily ever after") are sometimes incorporated. Spontaneous dramatic play disappears from the classroom early in the primary years (although it persists out of school with some children) and is replaced by more structured drama of various kinds. Older children are usually much more conscious of their own references to literature.

These children respond to stories piecemeal. Their responses deal with *parts rather than wholes*. A detail of

text or illustration might prompt more comment than the story itself, as children make quick associations with their own experience: "I saw a bird like that once" or "My sister has bunk beds just like those." This part-by-part organization can also be seen in very young children's art, where the pictures show individual story items without any indication of relationship ("This is the baby bear's chair, and this is Goldilocks, and this is the house the bears lived in, and here is the bed . . ."). This is the same sort of itemization or cataloging of characters, objects, and events that children sometimes use when asked to tell something about a story. Young children are more likely to respond to the story as a whole if they have heard it many times or if an adult provides that focus by asking good questions.

Children at this age use *embedded language* in answering direct questions about stories. Because young children see the world in literal, concrete terms, their answers are likely to be couched in terms of the characters, events, and objects found in the story. One first grader made a good attempt to generalize the lesson of "The Little Red Hen," but couldn't manage without some reference to the tale: "When someone already baked the cake and you haven't helped, they're probably just gonna say 'No'!" A teacher or other adult who shares the child's context—who knows the story, has heard or read it with the child, and knows what other comments have been made—will understand the intent of such a statement more readily than a casual observer will.

Children in Transition (Primary to Middle Grades)

Children in transition from the primary to the middle grades develop from being listeners to becoming readers. They go through a period of focus on the *accomplishment of independent reading*. They make many comments about quantity—number of pages read, the length of a book, or the number of books read. Conventions of print and of bookmaking may draw attention. One third grader refused to read any of the poems from Shel Silverstein's *Where the Sidewalk Ends* without locating them in the index first; a classmate was fascinated with the book's variety of word and line arrangements for poetry. Another child studied the front matter of a picture book and pronounced it "a dedicated book." So-called independent reading may be more sociable than it sounds, since many children like to have a listener or reading partner and begin to rely on peers as sounding boards for their response.

At this age, children become more adept at *summarizing* in place of straight retelling when asked to talk about stories. This is a skill that facilitates discussion and becomes more useful as it is developed. Summarizing is one of the techniques that undergirds critical commentary, but adults use it more deliberately and precisely than children do.

These children classify or *categorize* stories in some of the same ways that adults do. Middle graders who are asked to sort out a random pile of books use categories like "mysteries," "humorous books," "make-believe," and "fantasy." If you ask kindergartners to do the same, they are more likely to classify the books by their physical properties ("fat books," "books with pretty covers," "red books") than by content.

Children at this age *attribute personal reactions to the story* itself. A book that bores an 8-year-old will be thought of as a "boring book," as if "boring" were as much a property of the story as its number of pages or its first-person point of view. Children judge a story on the basis of their response to it, regardless of its qualities as literature or its appeal to anyone else. This is a very persistent element in response; it affects the judgment of students of children's literature and of professional book reviewers as well as children in elementary school. Personal response can never be totally eliminated from critical evaluation; but with experience, readers can develop more objectivity in separating a book's literary characteristics from its personal appeal.

These children also *use borrowed characters, events, themes, and patterns from literature in their writing,* just as younger children do in dramatic play. In the earliest stages, much of this is unconscious and spontaneous. One example is a 7-year-old who was convinced that her story about a fish with paint-splashed insides was "made up out of my own head," even when reminded that the class had just heard Robert McCloskey's *Burt Dow, Deep Water Man.* A 9-year-old spontaneously combined a favorite character with a field-trip experience in his story "Paddington Bear Goes to Franklin Park Conservatory," but he was aware of his idea sources. Other children produce their own examples of patterns, forms, or genres. The direction of growth is toward more conscious realization of the uses of literature in writing (see Chapter 14).

Older Children (Middle Grades to Middle School)

Older children express *stronger preferences,* especially for personal reading. Younger children seem to enjoy almost everything that is reasonably appropriate, but older ones do not hesitate to reject books they do not like. Some children show particular devotion to certain authors or genres or series at this time. Some children also become more intense and protective about some of their reactions, and they should not be pressed to share those feelings that demand privacy.

At this age, children are more skillful with language and more able to deal with abstractions. They can *disembed ideas* from a story and put them in more generalized terms, as in stating a universal moral for a particular fable.

These children also begin to *see* (but not consistently) *that their feelings about a book are related to identifiable aspects of the writing.* Responses like "I love this book because it's great" develop into "I love this book because the characters say such funny things" or "*Strider* [Cleary] is my favorite because Leigh is a lot like me."

Older children go beyond categorizing stories *toward a more analytical perception* of why characters behave as they do, how the story is put together, or what the author is trying to say. They begin to test fiction against real life and understand it better through the comparison. They use some critical terminology, although their understanding of terms may be incomplete. In talk and writing, children who are encouraged to express ideas freely begin to stand back from their own involvement and take an evaluative look at literature. One sixth grader had this to say about *A Taste of Blackberries* by Doris Buchanan Smith:

> I thought the author could have put more into it. I really didn't know much about the kid who died. I mean, it really happened fast in the book. It started out pretty soon and told about how sad he was and what they used to do. All the fun things they used to do together. I wished at the beginning they would have had all the things that he talked about and then have him thinking about what a good friend he is and then all of a sudden he dies—a little closer to the end. Because when he died, you didn't much care 'cause you didn't really know him. But I guess the author wanted to talk about how it would be, or how people feel, or maybe what happened to her— how it felt when one of her friends died like that.[42]

In general, children's responses move toward this sort of conscious comment. Young children sometimes make stunningly perceptive observations about stories, but they are not usually able to step back and see the importance of what they have said. Older children begin to know what they know, and can then take command of it. This allows them to layer mature appreciation on top of the beginner's natural delight.

However, older children's increasing capacity for abstraction, generalization, and analysis should *not* be interpreted as a need for programs of formal literary

---

[42]Recorded in the classroom of Lois Monaghan, teacher, Barrington School, Upper Arlington, Ohio.

analysis or highly structured study procedures. Opportunities to read, hear, and talk about well-chosen books under the guidance of an interested and informed teacher will allow elementary school children to develop their responses to their full potential.

Children, no matter what their age, will respond to a story on their own terms of understanding. It does little good (and can be destructive to the enjoyment of literature) if younger children are pushed to try to formulate the abstractions achieved by more mature children. However, James Britton maintains that teachers may refine and develop the responses that children are already making by gradually exposing them to stories with increasingly complex patterns of events.[43]

Collecting Children's Responses

Finding out how children understand literature and which books they like is such basic information for elementary teachers and librarians that it should not be left to chance. Luckily there are good techniques for discovering responses that are simple and fit naturally into the ongoing business of classrooms and library media centers.

Observing Children

Regardless of how much we know about the general characteristics and interest patterns of children at various age levels, it is only after studying individual children that we can begin to think: "David loved Madeleine L'Engle's *A Wrinkle in Time*. I must tell him about the sequel, *A Wind in the Door*. Beth enjoys ballet so much—I wonder if she has seen Mark Helprin's *Swan Lake* with the Chris Van Allsburg illustrations. Peter is somewhat slow in reading, but he enjoyed hearing the informational book on snakes we read during our science unit. Maybe he would feel successful with an easy book like *Snakey Riddles* by Katy Hall and Lisa Eisenberg."

A better understanding of the child and the accumulated effect of past experiences can be gained through observation in many situations. As teachers or librarians observe children choosing books, studying or reading alone, responding to books, reacting to others in work and play situations, and meeting problems, they will note what the child does not do or say, as well as active behavioral responses. Through these observations teachers also seek to understand a child's perception of self, for this self-concept influences behavior and choices as well as achievement.

Obviously teachers will not have time for daily, detailed observation of each child. One efficient primary teacher in a classroom busy with activities takes a moment as she moves from one group to another to stand back and focus on what just one child is doing. A teacher might single out certain children to watch when they seem to be having difficulties or when they are having special success. Some teachers find that a self-designed checklist is a useful tool. This gives some structure to the observation (Chooses fiction _____; chooses nonfiction _____; reads alone _____; reads with a friend . . . , etc.) and makes it possible to share the task with classroom aides or parent volunteers. Chapters 13 and 14 provide more information about observing children's responses to literature.

Eliciting Responses

Children do not always express their ideas about literature spontaneously, and even when they do, the teacher might not be there to see or hear them. However, there are many ways to deliberately evoke children's responses.

Talking over a story that has just been read aloud or one that a child has just read independently is a natural and satisfying thing to do. Such discussions are a primary teaching tool in helping children build a framework for literature (see Chapter 13). Discussions with a slightly different tone are just as useful in helping teachers get a more complete picture of where the children are to start. When the focus is on finding out what children are thinking, it is important to begin with general questions that invite talk and do not suggest their own answers: What do you like about the story? What do you notice about it? How does it make you feel? What does this story make you think of? Many comments might not seem relevant from an adult perspective, but the careful listener will find out what is in the foreground of the children's perception of the story. This is a time when it is especially important to be accepting, to offer encouraging comments, nods, and other signals of affirmation. Children who fear giving a "wrong" answer will say what they think the teacher wants to hear or perhaps not say much at all. It takes time for readers of any age to frame their thoughts about a book; a little reflection time between reading and discussion may make for a more productive session.

More-directive questioning can also be used to explore a particular area of children's understanding. Again, however, the emphasis should be on discovering children's own ideas and not on reaching predetermined answers. To find out more about her children's perception of fantasy, one teacher asked, about Maurice Sendak's *Outside over There*, "Just where *is* 'outside over there'?" and encouraged them to explain their answers. Another teacher, wanting clues to the sense of moral

[43]James Britton, in *Response to Literature*, ed. James R. Squire, (Champaign, Ill.: National Council of Teachers of English, 1968), p. 4.

judgment her second graders brought to stories, asked them why they thought Jack's mother in Steven Kellogg's *Jack and the Beanstalk*, which she had just read aloud, did not punish Jack for stealing from the giant.

Book extension activities such as the ones described in Chapter 14 are also important contexts for eliciting information about children's responses. For instance, making a gameboard that traces the adventures of the three animal companions in Sheila Burnford's *The Incredible Journey* requires deciding which events are important enough to represent and remembering their sequence—or referring back to the book to check. Watching the work in progress allows the teacher to see false starts and self-corrections as well as to note how the child uses the book for information. It is a bonus if two or three students are working together, for then the teacher can listen as they negotiate next steps. Sometimes the most revealing comments a child makes about literature are offered to another child in just such a setting.

Teachers can direct many extension activities to bring out certain aspects of response. One strategy is to ask children to translate meaning from a story through artwork using other characters, incidents, or settings to represent their understanding of the author's message.

The pictures on page 66 show two children's responses to the story *The Biggest House in the World* by Leo Lionni. After reading this book, the children were asked to choose any animal and grant it the same wish as the little snail had—namely, that it could change itself in any way. Julia, age 8, chose a bird, and she made his tail large, more elaborate, and more colorful. Rick, age 10, also drew a bird. He used the vocabulary of the story, saying: "The bird twitched his tongue in order to make his beak bigger so he could eat more." Finally, his beak becomes so heavy that he can't see over it or lift it up. The boy's comment was: "He'll have to get a derrick to lift it up now." This 10-year-old got the notion of the bird's becoming the cause of its own self-destruction, as in the story of the snail, whereas the 8-year-old girl saw only the change of size and the elaboration of color. Both had translated the story into their own creative drawings, but one child appeared to have a fuller understanding of the meaning of the story.

A middle school teacher whose students had heard *Tuck Everlasting* by Natalie Babbitt asked them to chart out, with words and pictures, the cycle of their own lives, including what they knew of their past and what they predicted for the future. Many of the children could not transfer the ideas about life and death from the book to their own speculations. They did not get beyond young adulthood in their plans, skipping directly from getting a job and getting married to death at an advanced age. Of those who revealed a deeper connection with the book, some portrayed the possibility that their lives might be troubled or brief; some represented life as

a circle with themselves in the older generation giving way to the new. The teacher then used these charts to begin a discussion relating the book to the students' own lives.

Writing activities can easily be tailored to bring out personal responses. A letter of advice to a friend about what to read helps the teacher judge what kinds of books are important to the writer. Asking a middle grader to write an updated folktale or a story based on the information about medieval times in Sheila Sancha's *The Luttrell Village* will show something about the child's knowledge of genre as well as a more general concept of story. Children should *never* have to be subjected to formal testing to determine their response. The number of ways for inviting natural responses in the classroom is limited only by the teacher's ingenuity.

Studying Concepts About Literature

The way children's concepts of written language grow and change is central to their response to literature, and these understandings apply to expository text as well as to narrative. The work of several researchers can provide a framework for teachers to study children's developing sense of book language and their responses to different genres in a more systematic way.

The most comprehensive research on children's sense of story has been done by Arthur Applebee.[44] Because young children do not easily examine or explain their own ideas, Applebee drew inferences about their understanding of story structure from the patterns he found in stories told by 2- to 5-year-olds. These patterns reflect an increasing ability to chain events together and to develop a thematic center at the same time. Their stories showed that children seem to move toward an awareness of the "grammar" or structure of story. For example, 50 percent of the 5-year-olds intuitively understood that stories had formal beginnings and endings and were told in the past tense.

According to Applebee, children also develop expectations for character roles and begin to distinguish between the real world and the story world. When 6- and 9-year-olds were asked what they thought certain characters were "usually like" in a story, the 9-year-olds were much more confident than the younger group about the stock roles that lions play (brave) and the fact that fairies should be good. Half the 6-year-olds expected witches to be wicked, but with 9-year-olds it was unanimous.[45] It is sometimes much later, however, before students begin to notice and expect multiple dimensions in characterization.

[44]Applebee, *The Child's Concept of Story.*
[45]Ibid., p. 42.

When asked to replicate Leo Lionni's story of *The Biggest House in the World* using a new main character, these two children demonstrated different levels in their understanding of the theme. The 8-year-old (top picture) showed a bird growing more elaborate; the 10-year-old (bottom picture) portrayed a change leading to the bird's self-destruction.
Tremont Elementary School, Upper Arlington, Ohio, Public Schools. Jill Boyd, teacher.

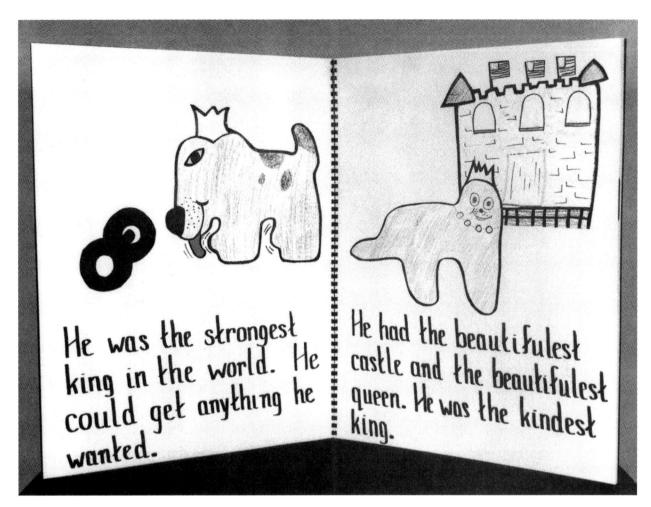

Children's expectations about stories are influenced by the stories they know. "Spot the King" was composed by first graders who combined their knowledge of fairy tales with a favorite character from the books of Eric Hill.
Dana Avenue Elementary School, Columbus, Ohio, Public Schools. Elizabeth Strong, research participant.

Asking children to retell books that have been read to them is another way to reveal understandings about literary structures and elements. On three subsequent occasions Christine Pappas asked kindergartners to "pretend to read" an information book or a story that she had read to them.[46] Their retellings showed that children were as successful at reconstructing the information books as they were at retelling the stories. They took on the languages of literature with equal facility and even seemed to prefer rereading the information books.

Another way to study growth in concept of literature is by keeping track of a broad range of data from one or a few children. This might include contacts with literature, responses, and developing skills in reading and writing. One such study, *Books Before Five*, is Dorothy White's diary account of her daughter Carol's experiences with books.[47] It shows the beginnings of Carol's curiosity about authorship and the origin of stories, her concern about whether things represented in stories are "real" or "true," and other aspects of her changing ideas about literature.

Like other areas of response, continued growth in concept of story and other literary forms depends on the interaction of new capabilities and experiences. Children must be steadily nurtured with books that help them discover new possibilities and increasing complexity in literature.

[46]Christine C. Pappas, "Is Narrative 'Primary'? Some Insights from Kindergartners' Pretend Readings of Stories and Information Books," *Journal of Reading Behavior* 25 (1993): 126–127.

[47]Dorothy White, *Books Before Five* (Portsmouth, N.H.: Heinemann, 1954, 1984).

Learning from Literary Miscues

In one sense, it is impossible for any child to make a "wrong" response to literature. Each reader's own feelings and personal interpretations are valid, because each reader is different. After all, everyone has a different correct answer for the question "What do *you* think?" But some responses that readers make, although they may reflect true feelings, contradict the evidence of the text.

In the teaching of reading, deviations from the text in oral reading are sometimes called *miscues*. According to Goodman and others who have developed this idea, it is not very useful to see miscues as mistakes.[48] It is more profitable to see them as clues that reveal what thinking process or cueing systems the child uses during reading. An example of this is the child who reads "Daddy" for "Father," cueing on the meaning but not paying attention to the form of the word. The whole notion of miscues focuses the teacher's attention on the kind of thinking children are doing, not just on the errors they make.

This positive point of view is just as important in considering children's efforts at making meaning from whole stories or episodes as it is at the level of words and phrases. We cannot say that a 6-year-old is wrong, for instance, in calling "The Three Little Pigs" a sad story, but the label does not really seem to fit a tale of diligence, cleverness, and success. If we take the attitude that this is a literary miscue and not simply a lack of understanding, we will go on to try to find out what kind of thinking led to that response. The child in this example explained to his teacher that he thought it would be terrible to fall into a pot of boiling water, and it was sad for the wolf. This helped the teacher to see that he was basing his judgment on a part of the story rather than the whole; other observations showed that this was often the strategy behind his responses.

Many other examples of response can be profitably interpreted as literary miscues. A group of third graders who were reading and discussing Laura Ingalls Wilder's *By the Shores of Silver Lake* misread the passage that describes the death of Jack, the Ingalls family's beloved dog. Ingalls describes the dog's body laying "stiff and cold" and explains that Pa "buried it on a low slope above a wheat field." Pa comforts Laura by telling her that Jack "has gone to the Happy Hunting Grounds."[49]

Misunderstanding the meaning of these phrases, the children told their teacher that Jack was stiff and cold when he woke up because of the weather, and that later he was out chasing rabbits in the Happy Hunting Grounds. These students seem to have reacted to part of the clues in the text while blocking out others. Their concept of story included such a firm expectation that things in stories will work out all right (a phenomenon that James Squire called "happiness binding")[50] that they didn't see the dog's death as a possible meaning for the text at all. Children who make responses like this one are not so much slow to pick up meaning as they are quick to operate out of trust in what they already know. Their teacher's questioning acknowledged their competence but refocused their attention on other details that changed their perception of "stiff" and "cold."

This group of students also struggled with another passage in the same book that deals with Pa Ingalls' receiving government land from "Uncle Sam." Laura's Aunt Docia is a prominent character in the same chapter, and some children identified Uncle Sam as Aunt Docia's husband. The logic was sound, but based on insufficient world knowledge. This type of literary miscue is common in the reading of historical fiction or other books with unfamiliar background context.

Recognizing the origin of children's interpretations is important, because it suggests how teachers can intervene to help students clarify their thinking or adjust their expectations for certain types of stories. Sometimes, however, the evidence will suggest that more conventional interpretation is not within reach for a particular child or group at a particular time. Sensitive teachers accept this and do not press for signs of superficial understanding but go on to selections that may be more suitable.

Keeping Track

Observing and inviting children's responses have more value if the teacher can somehow keep track of what has been discovered. Because of the time demands that exist in all classrooms, it is wise to use the simplest methods. Many teachers take advantage of existing reading records (see Chapter 14) to jot down brief notes about children's responses. A teacher's journal or log, even one with brief entries, provides a good overview account of classroom responses. It can also be narrowed in focus to record children's changing attitudes and understandings during a theme of study or to collect information about interests and preferences.

Personal portfolios of children's writing and work samples are even easier to maintain than notes, although they require space. A real advantage of this sort

---

[48]Yetta M. Goodman and Carolyn L. Burke, *Reading Miscue Inventory* (Chicago: Richard C. Owen, 1972).

[49]Laura Ingalls Wilder, *By the Shores of Silver Lake* (New York: Harper & Row, 1953), pp. 12–13.

[50]James R. Squire, *The Responses of Adolescents While Reading Four Short Stories* (Urbana, Ill.: National Council of Teachers of English, 1964).

of file is that it provides a history of growth in response that can be accessible to the child as well as the teacher. Children who have this concrete evidence of how far they have come are helped in their progress toward self-awareness and are assured that their work is valued.

A camera can be used to record evidence of art work and other artifacts that children create. Photographs can also capture the setting of response or the larger context of an activity and serve as a reminder of what prompted this particular work or how it was tied to other concerns in the classroom.

Audiotape recordings of read-aloud sessions and the talk that follows gives the teacher a chance to sort out patterns of comments that are not easy to catch while in the midst of leading the discussion. Two or more children might record their private small-group discussion about a book with the idea that the teacher will hear it later. Or the teacher might tape book conferences with one or two children to save for comparison with later responses.

Videotape equipment can be used to record drama experiences or other large-scale activities. Even though video can capture nonverbal responses beautifully, the apparatus is too intrusive (and expensive) to make this an everyday possibility for most classrooms. However, some teachers have had great success with getting children to watch tapes of their own activities or discussions and then to reflect on their own responses. This is a technique that helps students develop the ability to step back from a story and from their own experience of it.

Teachers and children can also use a classroom computer to help keep track of reading experiences and record responses. For instance, the class could keep a cumulative file of readers' comments about particular books on a disc for other students' reference. If children enter specific information about their free-reading choices into a database program, it will be possible to sort out the class's favorite authors and genres or differences in boys' and girls' reading patterns as well as other summaries. If children have access to the Internet, they can join literature discussion groups or post questions for e-mail conversations. A child might post a question such as "I'm reading *Julie of the Wolves* by Jean George and I want to know what other people think." These conversations can be saved on the computer and downloaded to a child's portfolio.

As elementary teachers become aware of the way they can tune in to children's responses to literature, they will see the value of examining the nature of children's thinking about it. We all believe that literature is important for children, but we do not truly know what difference it makes in a child's life, if any. An in-depth study of children's responses to books is just as important as, if not more important than, the studies of children's interests in books. We should explore the developmental nature of response and conduct longitudinal studies of a child's responses over the years. As teachers and librarians, we need to be still and listen to what the children are telling us about their involvement with books and what it means to them.

Learning Experiences

1. If there is a young child in your household, keep a log for four to five weeks of her or his interaction with literature. What do the child's choices, reactions, comments, and questions reveal about cognitive skills or moral judgment? Do you see any changes that reflect experiences with books?

2. Observe young children as a parent or teacher reads to them. Note as many behaviors (verbal, nonverbal, or artistic/creative) as you can. What clues do you get about the value of reading aloud and about means of effective presentation?

3. Ask three children of various ages (e.g., 5, 7, 9) to retell the story "Goldilocks and the Three Bears" from the point of view of Baby Bear. Who is able to begin the story as Baby Bear? Who can maintain the role change? What problems do 5-year-olds have with language that 9-year-olds seem to solve easily?

4. Set up a play corner in a primary classroom, including props from stories such as a magic wand, a witch's hat, a cardboard crown. What happens over time? What seem to be the sources for children's imaginative play?

5. Choose one of the book extension activities described in Chapter 14 and try it with two or more children. Pay careful attention to their working procedures and analyze the products. What variations or individual differences do you see among the children? What similarities?

Continued

Learning Experiences

6. In a middle-grade class-room, assemble twenty to thirty books that are mostly familiar to the children. Ask a small group to categorize and label these for a tabletop display. Tape their comments as they work. What do you notice about their categories? About the process? If possible, repeat the activity with younger children and books that they have heard read aloud. What differences do you notice? Arrange to see the Weston Woods film *What's a Good Book?* Discuss the categories suggested by the children in contrast to those mentioned by the adult experts interviewed in the film. (For more information about the Weston Woods film, please call 1–800–243–5020.)

7. If you can meet with a class of children, ask them to submit the names of their ten favorite books. How do their choices seem to reflect their particular ages and stages of development?

8. Visit the children's room of a public or school library to watch children in the process of choosing books. Keep a list, if you can, of the books examined and rejected, as well as those finally chosen. What factors seem to influence the children's choices?

9. With a small group of fellow students or teachers, read and discuss an award-winning children's book. Working together, plan two sets of questions that could be used with children, one to discover children's initial response to the story, the other to direct their thinking toward the characters' motivations and decisions, the author's effective use of language, or other noteworthy features of the writing.

10. Arrange to talk with one or more readers in the 11-to-13 age range about a book that you and the child or children have read individually—for example, Jerry Spinelli's *Maniac Magee*. Plan questions and comments that will encourage the students to share their own interpretations of characters and events. How are their ideas about the book similar to or different from your own? How could you use this information in planning for teaching?

Related Readings

Applebee, Arthur. *The Child's Concept of Story: Ages Two to Seventeen.* Chicago: University of Chicago Press, 1978.

A report of systematic research on children's developing perceptions of stories. Applebee provides fresh insight on the child's sense of story and response to literature. Among the contributions of this important work are a description of organization and complexity in the structure of stories children tell and a model of developmental stages in the formulation of children's responses.

Carlsen, G. Robert, and Anne Sherrill. *Voices of Readers: How We Come to Love Books.* Urbana, Ill.: National Council of Teachers of English, 1988.

Drawing on "reading autobiographies" collected over a thirty-year period, the authors have synthesized and categorized more than a thousand reports of young people's reading experiences. Many excerpts preserve the individual "voices of readers" in a book that provides evidence of the paradoxical uniqueness and similarity of human responses.

Elkind, David. *The Hurried Child: Growing Up Too Fast Too Soon.* Reading, Mass.: Addison-Wesley, 1981.

In a book addressed mainly to parents, a noted psychologist argues that contemporary children are under too much pressure. They are rushed toward adulthood both at home and at school without regard for normal patterns of development or individual differences. Chapters 5 and 6 present a very readable overview of intellectual, emotional, and social development, with particular reference to Piaget. Chapter 4, which deals with the influence of books and media in "hurrying" children, provides good discussion material for adults considering selection policies.

Holland, Kathleen E., Rachael A. Hungerford, and Shirley B. Ernst. eds. *Journeying: Children Responding to Literature*. Portsmouth, N.H.: Heinemann, 1993.

This collection provides a comprehensive view of recent research in children's response to literature. Chapters in four sections deal with responses of children in grades K through 8 in a variety of settings. Authors describe children's responses to different literary genres, and show how variables such as age, culture, and mode shape children's understanding.

Langerman, Deborah. "Books and Boys: Gender Preferences and Book Selection." *School Library Journal* 36 (March 1990):132–136.

This brief but thought-provoking look at recent evidence on what boys and girls like to read considers several explanatory theories and raises many issues relevant to the classroom as well as the library.

Lehr, Susan. *The Child's Developing Sense of Theme: Responses to Literature*. New York: Teachers College Press, 1991.

The author provides a background of discussion and research as well as a report of her own work in discovering the interpretations of story meaning held by preschool and elementary children. Her findings suggest that adults need to be very good listeners when talking to children about literature. Many examples of children's talk and an engaging, conversational tone make this scholarly work particularly readable.

Martinez, Miriam, and Nancy Roser. "Children's Responses to Literature." In *Handbook of Research on Teaching the English Language Arts*, In ed. James Flood et al. New York: Macmillan, 1991.

This comprehensive review of research since the 1960s is organized around three major categories of factors that affect children's response—characteristics of the reader, context factors, and the nature of the text. Included among the many other sections of this reference volume are the essays "Response to Literature" by Robert Probst and "Reading Preferences" by Dianne Monson and Sam Sebesta, and articles on child development in the preschool, elementary, and middle school years.

Purves, Alan C., Theresa Rogers, and Anna O. Soter. *How Porcupines Make Love II: Teaching a Response-Centered Literature Curriculum*. New York: Longman, 1990.

This lively book for teachers is designed to explain the implications of reader response theory for literature instruction. Although this book deals with the adolescent years, teachers of older elementary students find many of the ideas and principles discussed here to be useful.

Rosenblatt, Louise M. *The Reader, the Text, the Poem: The Transactional Theory of the Literary Work*. Carbondale: Southern Illinois University Press, 1978.

A scholarly discussion of the reader's role in evoking a literary work from an author's text. The distinction between aesthetic and efferent reading stances is clearly explained. Although elementary children are seldom mentioned, the book gives a valuable basis for understanding the responses of readers at any age.

Tucker, Nicholas. *The Child and the Book: A Psychological and Literary Exploration*. Cambridge: Cambridge University Press, 1981.

A British psychologist with wide knowledge of literature outlines the "changing imaginative and intellectual outlook" of children from infancy to age 14. Although his major concern is explaining why certain types of stories are popular at various ages, he also considers why some children show more general interest in reading than others do.

Children's Literature

Abel-Prot, Viviane. *The Story of Birth*. Illustrated by Rozier Gaudriault. Translated by Vicki Bogard. Young Discovery, 1991.

Ackerman, Karen. *Night Crossing*. Illustrated by Elizabeth Sayles. Knopf, 1994.

Ahlberg, Janet, and Allan Ahlberg. *The Baby's Catalogue*. Little, Brown, 1983.

——. *Each Peach Pear Plum*. Viking, 1978.

Alexander, Lloyd. *The Book of Three* (Book 1 in *The Chronicles of Prydain*). Holt, 1964.

Aliki. *Hush, Little Baby: A Folk Lullaby*. Simon & Schuster, 1992.

——. *My Visit to the Dinosaurs*. 2nd ed. Harper & Row, 1987.

Allard, Harry. *The Stupids Have a Ball*. Illustrated by James Marshall. Houghton Mifflin, 1978.

Anno, Mitsumasa. *Anno's Math Games III*. Philomel, 1991.

Arnosky, Jim. *Drawing from Nature*. Lothrop, Lee & Shepard, 1983.

Asbjørnsen, P. C., and Jorgen E. Moe. *The Three Billy Goats Gruff*. Illustrated by Marcia Brown. Harcourt Brace, 1957.

Ashabranner, Brent. *Crazy About German Shepherds*. Photos by Jennifer Ashabranner. Cobblehill, 1991.

Avi. *Nothing but the Truth*. Orchard, 1991.

————. *The True Confessions of Charlotte Doyle*. Orchard, 1990.

Babbitt, Natalie. *Tuck Everlasting*. Farrar, Straus & Giroux, 1975.

Bang, Molly. *Dawn*. Morrow, 1983.

————. *Ten, Nine, Eight*. Greenwillow, 1983.

Banks, Lynne Reid. *The Indian in the Cupboard*. Doubleday, 1981.

Banyai, Ivan. *Zoom*. Viking, 1995.

Barracca, Debra, and Sal Barracca. *Maxi, the Hero*. Illustrated by Mark Buehner. Dial, 1991.

Barrett, Joyce D. *Willie's Not the Hugging Kind*. Illustrated by Pat Cummings. Harper & Row, 1989.

Barrett, Judi. *I Hate to Go to Bed*. Illustrated by Ray Cruz. Four Winds, 1977.

Barton, Byron. *Building a House*. Greenwillow, 1981.

————. *I Want to Be an Astronaut*. Crowell, 1988.

————. *The Little Red Hen*. HarperCollins, 1993.

Bauer, Marion Dane. *On My Honor*. Clarion, 1986.

————. *A Question of Trust*. Scholastic, 1994.

Bertrand, Lynne. *Goodnight, Teddy Bear*. Illustrated by Janet Street. Chapters, 1992.

Black, Charles C. *The Royal Nap*. Illustrated by James Stevenson. Viking, 1995.

Blume, Judy. *Are You There, God? It's Me, Margaret*. Bradbury, 1970.

————. *Fudge-a-Mania*. Dutton, 1990.

Bodkin, Odds. *The Banshee Train*. Illustrated by Ted Rose. Clarion, 1995.

Branley, Franklyn. *What Happened to the Dinosaurs?* Illustrated by Marc Simont. Crowell, 1989.

Briggs, Raymond. *The Snowman*. Random House, 1978.

Brittain, Bill. *My Buddy, the King*. Harper & Row, 1984.

Brown, Marcia. *Once a Mouse*. Scribner's, 1961.

Brown, Margaret Wise. *The Days Before Now*. Adapted by Joan W. Blos. Illustrated by Thomas B. Allen. Simon & Schuster, 1994.

————. *Goodnight Moon*. Illustrated by Clement Hurd. Harper & Row, 1947.

————. *The Runaway Bunny*. Illustrated by Clement Hurd. Harper & Row, 1942.

Bunting, Eve. *Fly Away Home*. Illustrated by Ron Himler. Clarion, 1991.

Burningham, John. *The Blanket*. Crowell, 1976.

————. *Mr. Gumpy's Outing*. Holt, 1971.

————. *The Cupboard*. Crowell, 1975.

Burnford, Sheila. *The Incredible Journey*. Illustrated by Carl Burger. Bantam, 1990.

Burton, Virginia Lee. *The Little House*. Houghton Mifflin, 1942.

Byars, Betsy. *The Burning Questions of Bingo Brown*. Viking, 1988.

Cameron, Ann. *The Stories Julian Tells*. Illustrated by Ann Strugnell. Knopf, 1987.

Campbell, Rod. *Dear Zoo*. Four Winds, 1983.

Carle, Eric. *The Grouchy Ladybug*. Crowell, 1977.

————. *The Very Hungry Caterpillar*. Philomel, 1969.

Caseley, Judith. *Harry and Arnie*. Greenwillow, 1994.

Casey, Maude. *Over the Water*. Holt, 1994.

Christiansen, C. B. *I See the Moon*. Atheneum, 1994.

Christopher Matt. *Zero's Slider*. Illustrated by Molly Delaney. Little, Brown, 1994.

Cleary, Beverly. *Dear Mr. Henshaw*. Illustrated by Paul O. Zelinsky. Morrow, 1983.

———. *Ramona the Brave*. Illustrated by Alan Tiegreen. Morrow, 1975.

———. *Ramona Forever*. Illustrated by Alan Tiegreen. Morrow, 1984.

———. *Ramona Quimby, Age 8*. Illustrated by Alan Tiegreen. Morrow, 1981.

———. *Strider*. Illustrated by Paul O. Zelinsky. Morrow, 1991.

Coerr, Eleanor. *Sadako*. Illustrated by Ed Young. Putnam, 1993.

Cohen, Barbara. *Molly's Pilgrim*. Illustrated by Michael Deraney. Lothrop, Lee & Shephard, 1983.

Cohen, Miriam. *When Will I Read?* Illustrated by Lillian Hoban. Greenwillow, 1977.

———. *Will I Have a Friend?* Illustrated by Lillian Hoban. Macmillan, 1971.

Cole, Brock. *The Goats*. Farrar, Straus & Giroux, 1987.

Cole, Joanna. *Asking About Sex and Growing Up: A Question and Answer Book for Boys and Girls*. Illustrated by Alan Tiegreen. Morrow, 1988.

———. *How You Were Born*. Morrow, 1984.

———. *The Magic Schoolbus in the Time of the Dinosaurs*. Illustrated by Bruce Degen. Scholastic, 1994.

———. *My Puppy Is Born*. Photos by Margaret Miller. Morrow, 1990.

Conrad, Pam. *My Daniel*. Harper & Row, 1989.

———. *Prairie Songs*. Illustrated by Darryl Zudeck. Harper & Row, 1985.

Cooper, Susan. *The Dark Is Rising*. Illustrated by Alan Cober. Atheneum, 1973.

Creech, Sharon. *Walk Two Moons*. HarperCollins, 1994.

Cresswell, Helen. *The Watchers: A Mystery at Alton Towers*. Macmillan, 1994.

Crews, Donald. *Freight Train*. Greenwillow, 1978.

Dahl, Roald. *The BFG*. Illustrated by Quentin Blake. Farrar, Straus & Giroux, 1982.

———. *Danny, the Champion of the World*. Illustrated by Jill Bennett. Knopf, 1975.

Dalgliesh, Alice. *The Courage of Sarah Noble*. Illustrated by Leonard Weisgard. Scribner's, 1954.

Deem, James M. *3 NB's of Julian Drew*. Houghton Mifflin, 1994.

DeJong, Meindert. *Hurry Home, Candy*. Illustrated by Maurice Sendak. Harper & Row, 1953.

de Paola, Tomie. *Strega Nona*. Prentice Hall, 1975.

———. *Tomie de Paola's Mother Goose*. Holiday House, 1984.

DeRegniers, Beatrice Schenk. *May I Bring a Friend?* Illustrated by Beni Montesor. Atheneum, 1964.

———. *Sing a Song of Popcorn: Every Child's Book of Poems*. Illustrated by Caldecott-Medal–winning artists. Scholastic, 1988.

Doherty, Berlie. *Willa and Old Miss Annie*. Illustrated by Kim Lewis. Candlewick, 1994.

Dorris, Michael. *Guests*. Hyperion, 1994.

———. *Morning Girl*. Hyperion, 1992.

Duffey, Betsy. *How to Be Cool in the Third Grade*. Illustrated by Janet Wilson. Viking, 1993.

Ehlert, Lois. *Eating the Alphabet*. Harper & Row, 1989.

Emberley, Michael. *Ruby*. Little, Brown, 1990.

Falwell, Cathryn. *Feast for Ten*. Clarion, 1993.

Farmer, Nancy. *The Ear, the Eye and the Arm*. Orchard/Jackson, 1994.

Fine, Anne. *Flour Babies*. Little, Brown, 1994.

Fleischman, Paul. *Saturnalia*. HarperCollins, 1990.

Fletcher, Ralph. *I Am Wings: Poems About Love*. Photographs by Joe Baker. Bradbury, 1994.

Ford, Miela. *Little Elephant*. Photos by Tana Hoban. Greenwillow, 1994.

Fox, Mem. *Shoes from Grandpa*. Illustrated by Patricia Mullins. Orchard, 1990.

————. *Time for Bed*. Illustrated by Jane Dyer. Gulliver, 1993.

Fox, Paula. *The Eagle Kite*. Orchard/Jackson, 1995.

————. *Monkey Island*. Orchard, 1991.

————. *Western Wind*. Orchard, 1993.

Freedman, Russell. *Franklin Delano Roosevelt*. Clarion, 1990.

Freeman, Don. *Corduroy*. Viking, 1968.

Friedman, Ina. *How My Parents Learned to Eat*. Illustrated by Allen Say. Houghton Mifflin, 1984.

Fritz, Jean. *George Washington's Breakfast*. Illustrated by Paul Galdone. Putnam, 1984.

————. *Homesick: My Own Story*. Illustrated by Margot Tomes. Putnam, 1982.

————. *What's the Big Idea, Ben Franklin?* Illustrated by Margot Tomes. Coward, 1976.

Gág, Wanda. *Millions of Cats*. Coward, 1956 [1928].

Gardiner, John. *Stone Fox*. Illustrated by Marcia Sewall. Harper & Row, 1980.

George, Jean. *Cry of the Crow*. HarperCollins, 1980.

————. *Julie*. Illustrated by Wendell Minor. HarperCollins, 1994.

————. *Julie of the Wolves*. Illustrated by John Schoenerr. Harper & Row, 1972.

Gershator, Phillis. *Rata-Pata-Scata-Fata: A Caribbean Story*. Illustrated by Holly Meade. Little, Brown, 1994.

Gibbons, Gail. *Sunken Treasure*. HarperCollins, 1990.

————. *Trucks*. Crowell, 1981.

————. *Up Goes the Skyscraper!* Macmillan, 1990.

Giff, Patricia Reilly. *Kids of Polk Street School* (series). Dell, 1988.

Ginsburg, Mirra. *Asleep, Asleep*. Illustrated by Nancy Tafuri. Greenwillow, 1992.

Granger, Neill. *Stamp Collecting*. Millbrook, 1994.

Gray, Libba Moore. *Small Green Snake*. Illustrated by Holly Meade. Orchard, 1994.

Green, Lucinda. *The Young Rider*. Dorling Kindersley, 1993.

Grifalconi, Ann. *Osa's Pride*. Little, Brown, 1990.

Hall, Donald. *Ox-Cart Man*. Illustrated by Barbara Cooney. Viking, 1979.

Hall, Katy, and Lisa Eisenberg. *Snakey Riddles*. Dial, 1990.

Hamilton, Virginia. *Cousins*. Philomel, 1990.

Harris, Robie H. *It's Perfectly Normal: A Book About Changing Bodies, Growing Up, Sex, and Sexual Health*. Illustrated by Michael Emberley. Candlewick, 1994.

Haseley, Dennis. *Getting Him*. Farrar, Straus & Giroux, 1994.

Heide, Florence Parry, and Judith Heide Gilliland. *The Day of Ahmed's Secret*. Illustrated by Ted Lewin. Lothrop, Lee & Shepard, 1990.

Helprin, Mark. *Swan Lake*. Illustrated by Chris Van Allsburg. Houghton Mifflin, 1989.

Henkes, Kevin. *Julius, the Baby of the World*. Greenwillow, 1990.

Hickman, Janet. *Jericho*. Greenwillow, 1994.

Hill, Eric. *Where's Spot?* Putnam, 1980.

Hirschi, Ron. *Summer*. Photos by Thomas D. Mangelson. Cobblehill, 1991.

Ho, Minfong. *Rice Without Rain*. Lothrop, Lee & Shepard, 1990.

Hoban, Russell. *A Baby Sister for Frances*. Illustrated by Lillian Hoban. Harper & Row, 1964.

Hoban, Tana. *1, 2, 3*. Greenwillow, 1985.

———. *Red, Blue, Yellow Shoe*. Greenwillow, 1986.

———. *Spirals, Curves, Fanshapes, and Lines*. Greenwillow, 1992.

———. *What Is It?* Greenwillow, 1985.

Hobbs, Will. *Bearstone*. Atheneum, 1989.

Hoffman, Mary. *Amazing Grace*. Illustrated by Caroline Binch. Dial, 1991.

Hopkins, Lee Bennett. *By Myself*. Illustrated by Glo Coalson. Crowell, 1980.

Horenstein, Henry. *My Mom's a Vet*. Candlewick, 1994.

Howarth, Lesley. *Maphead*. Candlewick, 1994.

Howe, James, and Deborah Howe. *Bunnicula*. Illustrated by Alan Daniel. Atheneum, 1979.

Hughes, Shirley. *Alfie Gets in First*. Lothrop, Lee & Shepard, 1981.

———. *Alfie's Feet*. Lothrop, Lee & Shepard, 1983.

Hurwitz, Johanna. *Ozzie on His Own*. Illustrated by Eileen Keating. Morrow, 1995.

Hutchins, Pat. *Clocks and More Clocks*. Macmillan, 1994 [1970].

———. *Rosie's Walk*. Macmillan, 1968.

———. *Titch*. Macmillan, 1971.

———. *You'll Soon Grow into Them, Titch*. Greenwillow, 1983.

Isadora, Rachel. *Babies*. Greenwillow, 1990.

Jacques, Brian. *The Bellmaker*. Philomel, 1995.

Janeczko, Paul. *The Place My Words Are Looking For: What Poets Say About and Through Their Work*. Bradbury, 1990.

Johnson, Angela. *Julius*. Illustrated by Dave Pilkey. Orchard, 1993.

———. *Rain Feet*. Illustrated by Rhonda Mitchell. Orchard, 1994.

———. *Toning the Sweep*. Orchard/Jackson, 1993.

———. *When I Am Old with You*. Illustrated by David Soman. Orchard, 1990.

Johnston, Julie. *Adam and Eve and Pinch Me*. Little, Brown, 1994.

Jonas, Ann. *When You Were a Baby*. Greenwillow, 1982.

Jukes, Mavis. *Blackberries in the Dark*. Illustrated by Thomas B. Allen. Knopf, 1985.

Juster, Norton. *The Phantom Tollbooth*. Random House, 1961.

Karas, Brian. *I Know an Old Lady*. Scholastic, 1995.

Keats, Ezra Jack. *John Henry: An American Legend*. Pantheon, 1965.

———. *The Snowy Day*. Viking, 1962.

———. *Whistle for Willie*. Viking, 1964.

Kellogg, Steven. *Jack and the Beanstalk*. Morrow, 1991.

King, Laurie. *The Beekeeper's Apprentice, or on the Segregation of the Queen*. St. Martin's Press, 1994.

King-Smith, Dick. *I Love Guinea Pigs*. Illustrated by Anita Jeram. Candlewick, 1995.

Koertge, Ron. *Tiger, Tiger, Burning Bright*. Orchard, 1994.

Konigsburg, E. L. *From the Mixed-Up Files of Mrs. Basil E. Frankweiler*. Atheneum, 1967.

Kraus, Robert. *Leo the Late Bloomer*. Illustrated by Jose Aruego. Windmill, 1971.

Kunhardt, Dorothy. *Pat the Bunny*. Golden Press, 1962 [1940].

Lauber, Patricia. *Dinosaurs Walked Here and Other Stories Fossils Tell*. Bradbury, 1987.

Le Guin, Ursula. *A Wizard of Earthsea*. Illustrated by Ruth Robbins. Parnassus, 1968.

L'Engle, Madeleine. *A Ring of Endless Light*. Farrar, Straus & Giroux, 1980.

———. *A Swiftly Tilting Planet*. Farrar, Straus & Giroux, 1978.

———. *A Wind in the Door*. Farrar, Straus & Giroux, 1973.

———. *A Wrinkle in Time*. Farrar, Straus & Giroux, 1962.

Levoy, Myron. *Alan and Naomi*. Harper & Row, 1978.

Levy, Constance. *A Tree Place and Other Poems*. Illustrated by Robert Sabuda. McElderry, 1994.

Lewis, C. S. *The Lion, the Witch, and the Wardrobe*. (Book 1 of *The Chronicles of Narnia*). Illustrated by Pauline Baynes. Macmillan, 1961.

Lionni, Leo. *The Biggest House in the World*. Pantheon, 1968.

———. *Fish Is Fish*. Pantheon, 1970.

Little, Jean. *Little by Little: A Writer's Education*. Viking, 1987.

Lobel, Arnold. *Frog and Toad Together*. Harper & Row, 1972.

———. *The Random House Book of Mother Goose*. Random House, 1986.

Lord, Trevor. *Amazing Bikes*. Knopf, 1992.

Lowry, Lois. *The Giver*. Houghton Mifflin, 1993.

———. *Number the Stars*. Houghton Mifflin, 1989.

Macaulay, David. *The Way Things Work*. Houghton Mifflin, 1988.

MacDonald, Amy. *Rachel Fister's Blister*. Illustrated by Marjorie Priceman. Houghton Mifflin, 1990.

Macht, Norman. *Jim Abbott: Major League Pitcher*. Chelsea, 1994.

MacKinnon, Debbie. *How Many?* Photographs by Anthea Sieveking. Dial, 1993.

MacLachlan, Patricia. *Baby*. Delacorte, 1993.

———. *Journey*. Delacorte, 1991.

———. *Sarah, Plain and Tall*. Harper & Row, 1985.

Mahy, Margaret. *The Blood and Thunder Adventures on Hurricane Peak*. McElderry, 1989.

———. *The Haunting*. Atheneum, 1982.

Marshall, James. *Rats on the Range*. Dial, 1993.

Martin, Bill, Jr. *Brown Bear, Brown Bear, What Do You See?* Illustrated by Eric Carle. Holt, 1983.

Martin, Bill, Jr., and John Archambault. *Chicka Chicka Boom Boom*. Illustrated by Lois Ehlert. Simon & Schuster, 1989.

Mayne, William. *Hob and the Goblins*. Illustrated by Norman Messenger. Dorling Kindersley, 1994.

McBranty, Sam. *Guess How Much I Love You*. Illustrated by Anita Jeram. Candlewick, 1995.

McCaffrey, Anne. *Dragonsong*. Illustrated by Laura Lydecker. Atheneum, 1976.

McCloskey, Robert. *Burt Dow, Deep Water Man*. Viking, 1963.

———. *Make Way for Ducklings*. Viking, 1941.

———. *One Morning in Maine*. Viking, 1952.

McDonald, Megan. *Is This a House for a Hermit Crab?* Illustrated by S. D. Schindler. Orchard, 1990.

McEwan, Ian. *The Daydreamer*. Illustrated by Anthony Browne. HarperCollins, 1994.

McGovern, Ann. *The Secret Soldier: The Story of Deborah Sampson*. Illustrated by Ann Grifalconi. Four Winds, 1975.

McGuire, Richard. *Night Becomes Day*. Viking, 1994.

McKay, Hilary. *The Exiles*. McElderry, 1992.

McKinley, Robin. *The Hero and the Crown*. Greenwillow, 1984.

McKissack, Patricia C. *Flossie and the Fox*. Illustrated by Rachel Isadora. Dial, 1986.

McPhail, David. *Fix-It*. Dutton, 1984.

Meyers, Susan. *Insect Zoo*. Photos by Richard Hewett. Lodestar, 1991.

Miller, Margaret. *Can You Guess?* Greenwillow, 1993.

———. *Guess Who?* Greenwillow, 1994.

Minarik, Else Holmelund. *Little Bear*. Illustrated by Maurice Sendak. Harper & Row, 1957.

Myers, Walter Dean. *Darnell Rock Reporting*. HarperCollins, 1994.

———. *The Glory Field*. Scholastic, 1994.

———. *The Mouse Rap*. HarperCollins, 1990.

———. *Now Is Your Time! The African-American Struggle for Freedom*. HarperCollins, 1991.

———. *Scorpions*. Harper & Row, 1988.

Naidoo, Beverley. *Journey to Jo'Burg: A South African Story*. Illustrated by Eric Velasquez. Lippincott, 1986.

Naylor, Phyllis Reynolds. *Alice the Brave*. Atheneum, 1995.

———. *Alice in Between*. Atheneum, 1994.

———. *The Fear Place*. Atheneum, 1994.

———. *Shiloh*. Atheneum, 1991.

Nelson, Vaunda Micheaux. *Mayfield Crossing*. Illustrated by Leonard Jenkins. Putnam, 1993.

Ness, Evaline. *Sam, Bangs, and Moonshine*. Holt, 1966.

O'Dell, Scott. *Island of the Blue Dolphins*. Houghton Mifflin, 1990 [1960].

Orlev, Uri. *The Man from the Other Side*. Houghton Mifflin, 1991.

Ormerod, Jan. *Sunshine*. Lothrop, Lee & Shepard, 1981.

Osborne, Mary Pope. *American Tall Tales*. Illustrated by Michael McCrudy. Knopf, 1991.

Oxenbury, Helen. *I Can*. Candlewick, 1995.

———. *Tickle, Tickle*. Macmillan, 1988.

———. *Tom & Pippo's Day*. Macmillan, 1989.

Parish, Peggy. *Amelia Bedelia*. Illustrated by Fritz Siebel. Harper & Row, 1963.

Park, Barbara. *Skinnybones*. Knopf, 1982.

Park, Ruth. *When the Wind Changed*. Illustrated by Deborah Niland. Coward, 1981.

Parker, Nancy Winslow, and Joan R. Wright. *Bugs*. Illustrated by Nancy Winslow Parker. Morrow, 1988.

Paterson, Katherine. *Flip-Flop Girl*. Lodestar, 1994.

———. *The Great Gilly Hopkins*. Crowell, 1978.

———. *Jacob Have I Loved*. Crowell, 1980.

———. *The Master Puppeteer*. Illustrated by Haru Wells. Crowell, 1976.

Paulsen, Gary. *Dogsong*. Bradbury, 1985.

———. *Hatchet*. Bradbury, 1987.

———. *Nightjohn*. Delacorte, 1993.

Phillips, Rita Mitchell. *Hue Boy*. Illustrated by Caroline Binch. Dial, 1993.

Pinkney, Brian. *Max Found Two Sticks*. Simon & Schuster, 1994.

Polacco, Patricia. *The Bee Tree*. Philomel, 1993.

———. *Pink and Say*. Philomel, 1994.

Porte, Barbara Ann. *Chickens! Chickens!* Illustrated by Greg Henry. Orchard, 1995.

Porter, Connie. *Meet Addy* (the American Girl collection). Illustrated by Nancy Niles. Pleasant, 1990.

Potter, Beatrix. *The Tale of Peter Rabbit*. Warne, 1902.

Pryor, Bonnie. *The House on Maple Street*. Illustrated by Beth Peck. Morrow, 1987.

Puckett, Kirby. *Be the Best You Can Be*. Illustrated by Tim Houle. Waldman, 1993.

Quattlebaum, Mary. *Jackson Jones and the Puddle of Thorns*. Delacorte, 1994.

Raskin, Ellen. *The Westing Game*. Dutton, 1978.

Rawls, Wilson. *Where the Red Fern Grows*. Doubleday, 1961.

Reeder, Carolyn. *Grandpa's Mountain*. Macmillan, 1991.

———. *Shades of Gray*. Macmillan, 1989.

Reid, Barbara. *Playing with Plasticine*. Morrow, 1989.

Remkiewicz, Frank. *The Bone Stranger*. Lothrop, Lee & Shepard, 1994.

Rice, Eve. *Sam Who Never Forgets*. Greenwillow, 1977.

Rockwell, Anne. *Things to Play With*. Dutton, 1988.

———. *The Three Bears and Fifteen Other Stories*. Crowell, 1975.

———. *Trucks*. Dutton, 1984.

Rogers, Fred. *Going to the Potty*. Illustrated by Jim Judkis. Putnam, 1986.

Rogers, Jean. *Raymond's Best Summer*. Illustrated by Marilyn Hafner. Greenwillow, 1990.

Rosen, Michael. *We're Going on a Bear Hunt*. Illustrated by Helen Oxenbury. McElderry, 1989.

Rylant, Cynthia. *A Couple of Kooks and Other Stories About Love*. Orchard, 1990.

———. *Missing May*. Orchard, 1992.

———. *The Relatives Came*. Illustrated by Stephen Gammell. Bradbury, 1985.

———. *When I Was Young in the Mountains*. Illustrated by Diane Goode. Dutton, 1982.

Sancha, Sheila. *The Luttrell Village: Country Life in the Middle Ages*. Crowell, 1982.

Schnur, Steven. *The Shadow Children*. Morrow, 1994.

Schwartz, Alvin. *Tomfoolery: Trickery and Foolery with Words*. Illustrated by Glen Rounds. Harper & Row, 1973.

Scieszka, Jon. *The Not-So-Jolly Roger*. Illustrated by Lane Smith. Viking, 1991.

———. *The Stinky Cheese Man and Other Fairly Stupid Tales*. Illustrated by Lane Smith. Viking, 1992.

———. *The True Story of the Three Little Pigs*. Illustrated by Lane Smith. Viking, 1989.

Scott, Ann Herbert. *Hi!* Illustrated by Glo Coalson. Philomel, 1994.

Sendak, Maurice. *Outside over There*. Harper & Row, 1981.

———. *Where the Wild Things Are*. Harper & Row, 1963.

Shannon, Monica. *Dobry*. Illustrated by Atanas Katchamakoff. Viking, 1934.

Shelby, Anne. *Homeplace*. Illustrated by Wendy Anderson Halperin. Orchard, 1995.

Sheppard, Jeff. *Splash, Splash*. Illustrated by Dennis Panek. Macmillan, 1994.

Silverman, Erica. *Don't Fidget a Feather*. Illustrated by S. D. Schindler. Macmillan, 1994.

Silverstein, Shel. *A Light in the Attic*. Harper & Row, 1981.

———. *Where the Sidewalk Ends*. Harper & Row, 1963.

Simon, Seymour. *101 Questions and Answers About Dangerous Animals*. Illustrated by Ellen Friedman. Macmillan, 1985.

———. *The Paper Airplane Book*. Illustrated by Byron Barton. Viking, 1971.

Singer, Marilyn. *Nine O'Clock Lullaby*. Illustrated by Frané Lessac. HarperCollins, 1991.

Slepian, Jan. *Risk 'N Roses*. Philomel, 1990.

Smith, Doris Buchanan. *A Taste of Blackberries*. Illustrated by Charles Robinson. Crowell, 1973.

Smith, Robert. *The War with Grandpa*. Illustrated by Richard Lauter. Delacorte, 1984.

Snyder, Zilpha Keatley. *Cat Running*. Delacorte, 1994.

———. *Libby on Wednesday*. Doubleday, 1990.

Soto, Gary. *Baseball in April and Other Stories*. Harcourt Brace, 1990.

———. *Too Many Tamales*. Illustrated by Ed Martinez. Putnam, 1993.

Speare, Elizabeth George. *The Sign of the Beaver*. Houghton Mifflin, 1983.

Spinelli, Jerry. *Maniac Magee*. Little, Brown, 1990.

Stanley, Diane, and Peter Vennema. *Cleopatra*. Illustrated by Diane Stanley. Morrow, 1994.

Staples, Suzanne. *Shabanu: Daughter of the Wind*. Knopf, 1989.

Steig, William. *Amos & Boris*. Farrar, Straus & Giroux, 1971.

———. *Doctor De Soto*. Farrar, Straus & Giroux, 1982.

———. *Sylvester and the Magic Pebble*. Windmill, 1969.

———. *Zeke Pippin*. HarperCollins, 1994.

Steptoe, John. *Baby Says*. Lothrop, Lee & Shepard, 1988.

———. *Stevie*. Harper & Row, 1969.

Stevens, Carla. *Trouble for Lucy*. Illustrated by Ronald Himler. Clarion, 1979.

Stevens, Janet. *Tops and Bottoms*. Harcourt Brace, 1995.

Sullivan, George. *Unsolved! Famous Real Life Mysteries*. Scholastic, 1992.

Swann, Brian. *A Basket Full of White Eggs: Riddle-Poems*. Illustrated by Ponder Goembel. Orchard, 1988.

Tafuri, Nancy. *Have You Seen My Duckling?* Greenwillow, 1984.

Taylor, Mildred. *Roll of Thunder, Hear My Cry*. Dial, 1976.

Temple, Frances. *Taste of Salt: A Story of Modern Haiti*. Orchard/Jackson, 1992.

Threadgill, Colin. *Proud Rooster and the Fox*. Tambourine, 1992.

Tolkien, J. R. R. *The Hobbit*. Illustrated by Michael Hague. Houghton Mifflin, 1989 [1938].

Valens, Amy. *Jesse's Daycare*. Houghton Mifflin, 1990.

Viorst, Judith. *Alexander and the Terrible, Horrible, No Good, Very Bad Day*. Illustrated by Ray Cruz. Atheneum, 1972.

Voigt, Cynthia. *Dicey's Song*. Atheneum, 1982.

Wabbes, Marie. *How I Was Born*. Tambourine, 1991.

Waber, Bernard. *Ira Sleeps Over*. Houghton Mifflin, 1973.

Waddell, Martin. *Farmer Duck*. Illustrated by Helen Oxenbury. Candlewick, 1992.

Walker, Barbara. *The Little House Cookbook: Frontier Foods from Laura Ingalls Wilder's Classic Stories*. Illustrated by Garth Williams. Harper & Row, 1979.

Walker, Kate. *Peter*. Houghton Mifflin, 1993.

Walsh, Jill Paton. *The Green Book*. Illustrated by Lloyd Bloom. Farrar, Straus & Giroux, 1982.

Walter, Virginia. *"Hi, Pizza Man!"* Illustrated by Ponder Goembel. Orchard, 1995.

Wangerin, Walter. *The Crying for a Vision*. Simon & Schuster, 1994.

Ward, Cindy. *Cookie's Week*. Illustrated by Tomie de Paola. Putnam, 1988.

Watson, Clyde. *Catch Me and Kiss Me and Say It Again*. Illustrated by Wendy Watson. Philomel, 1978.

Wells, Rosemary. *Max's Ride*. Dial, 1979.

————. *Noisy Nora*. Dial, 1973.

White, E. B. *Charlotte's Web*. Illustrated by Garth Williams. Harper & Row, 1953.

Wilder, Laura Ingalls. *By the Shores of Silver Lake*. Illustrated by Garth Williams. Harper & Row, 1953 [1939].

————. *Little House in the Big Woods*. Illustrated by Garth Williams. Harper & Row, 1953 [1932].

Wildsmith, Brian. *Python's Party*. Watts, 1975.

Williams, Karen. *Galimoto*. Illustrated by Catherine Stock. Lothrop, Lee & Shepard, 1990.

Williams, Linda. *The Little Old Lady Who Was Not Afraid of Anything*. Illustrated by Megan Lloyd. Crowell, 1986.

Williams, Vera B. *A Chair for My Mother*. Greenwillow, 1982.

Wilson, Budge. *The Leaving*. Philomel, 1992.

Winthrop, Elizabeth. *The Battle for the Castle*. Holiday, 1993.

Wolff, Ashley. *A Year of Beasts*. Dutton, 1986.

Wolff, Virginia Euwer. *Make Lemonade*. Holt, 1993.

Wood, Audrey. *The Napping House*. Illustrated by Don Wood. Harcourt Brace, 1984.

Woodson, Jacqueline. *I Hadn't Meant to Tell You This*. Delacorte, 1994.

Wright, Betty Ren. *The Dollhouse Murders*. Holiday, 1983.

Wynne-Jones, Tim. *Some of the Kinder Planets*. Orchard, 1995.

Yashima, Taro. *Crow Boy*. Viking, 1955.

Yee, Paul. *Roses Sing on New Snow*. Illustrated by Harvey Chan. Macmillan, 1992.

Young, Ed. *Lon Po Po: A Red Riding Hood Story from China*. Philomel, 1989.

Zacharias, Thomas. *Where Is the Green Parrot?* Doubleday, 1990.

Zeifert, Harriet. *Oh, What a Noisy Farm!* Illustrated by Emily Bolam. Tambourine, 1995.

Zelinsky, Paul O. *The Wheels on the Bus*. Dutton, 1990.

© James L. Shaffer

chapter three

The Changing World of Children's Books

Early Beginnings: The Middle Ages 84

The Oral Tradition 84
The Earliest Manuscripts 84
Caxton Begins English Printing 85
Hornbooks, ABCs, and Primers 85
Lasting Contributions of the Period 86

Children's Books: The Seventeenth and Eighteenth Centuries 86

The "Goodly Godly" Books of the Puritans 86
Chapbooks: Forerunners of Comics 87
Nursery Rhymes or Mother Goose 88
Fairy Tales and Adventure 88
Newbery Publishes for Children 89
Didactic Tales 90
Poetry and Pictures 91

Children's Literature: The Nineteenth Century 92

Books of Instruction and Information 92
Folktale Collections 92
Family Stories 93
Tales of Adventure 95
Animal Stories 96
The Rise of Fantasy and Humor 96
Poetry 98
Magazines 99
Illustrators of the Nineteenth Century 100

Children's Literature: The Twentieth Century 102

Recognition of Children's Literature 102
The Rise of the Picture Storybook 103
The Growth of Informational Books 105
The Proliferation of Series Books 107
Folktales of the World 108
Fantasy 109
Poetry 110
Realistic Fiction 111

Teaching Feature: Studying Books of the Past 112

An International Literature for Children 113

Recent Trends in Children's Books 114

Children's Books: Big Business 114

Resources for Teaching: Landmarks in the Development of Books for Children 115

New Books for New Markets 118
Shifts in Publishing Emphases 119
Changes in Writing and Illustration 120
Increased Use in Schools 122
Increased Censorship 123
The Need for Multicultural Books 123
The Development of a Multiliterate Society 124

Learning Experiences 124
Related Readings 125
Children's Literature 126

"Cruel Boys" from *Sunnybank Stories: My Teacher's Gem*. Boston, Mass.: Lee & Shepard, 1863.

"GOOD-BYE!"
"GOOD-BYE!"

"Cruel Boys"

"O, what a shame!" a kind child may be ready to say on looking at this picture. You see these boys, little as they are, have hard and cruel hearts. They have been robbing a happy little bird family of one of the young ones; and now they will so hurt it that it will die, or they will let it starve to death. And they have robbed another pair of birds of their nest and eggs. How unhappy must all these birds now be! and how wicked it is to give such needless pain to any of God's creatures! No kind child can think of hurting a dear, innocent little bird. But those who delight in such sport will very likely grow up to be capable of injuring their fellowmen in the various ways of which we so often hear and read. Let us be kind to every thing that lives.

And this isn't the whole story about these wicked boys. Don't you see they are in a *quarrel*, how they shall divide what they have so cruelly stolen from the birds? Ah, that is the way in doing wrong—one wrong step leads on to another; and robbing birds' nests does not usually go alone—a quarrel, or some other wickedness, usually follows it. Beware, then, of the *beginnings* of cruelty and wickedness.[1]

[1]Asa Bullard, *Sunnybank Stories: My Teacher's Gem* (Boston: Lee & Shepard, 1863), pp. 22–24.

Excerpt from *Let's Be Enemies*

James used to be my friend.
But today he is my enemy.
James always wants to be the boss.
James carries the flag.
James takes all the crayons.
He grabs the best digging spoon
and he throws sand. . . .
I'm going right over to James' house and tell him. . . .
"Hullo, James."
"Hullo, John."
"I came to tell you that I'm not your friend any more."
"Well then, I'm not *your* friend either."
"We're enemies."
"All right!"
"GOOD-BYE!"
"GOOD-BYE!"
"Hey, James!"
"What?"
"Let's roller skate."
"O.K. Have a pretzel, John."
"Thank you, James."[2]

[2]Janice May Udry, *Let's Be Enemies*, illustrations Maurice Sendak (New York: Harper & Row, 1961). Text copyright © 1961 by Janice May Udry. Used by permission of HarperCollins Publishers, New York, NY.

Compare the language, the content, and the illustrations in these two stories—the ways in which society has changed its cultural values and its attitude toward children are strikingly apparent. "Cruel Boys" is taken from *Sunnybank Stories: My Teacher's Gem*, a collection of moralistic stories printed in 1863. Its purpose was to instruct the young by first describing a horrible example of misbehavior (in this instance, stealing) and then warning of its dire consequences. It is told in the third person from the point of view of an adult admonishing all children. The moral of the story is explicitly stated.

The story "Cruel Boys" contains only one print, black and white, the one pictured here. This same illustration was used in many different books at that time. The "pirating" of pictures and stories from other books was a common practice.

Let's Be Enemies (1961), on the other hand, captures the experience, the feelings, and the language of the young child. The story is told in the first person from the point of view of the child protagonist, which makes it easier for the reader to identify with John's growing anger. But 5-year-olds' quarrels are as fleeting as the brief showers that Sendak includes in his childlike illustrations. The sun soon comes out; and true to the nature of young children, John and James are fast friends by the end of the story.

The contrast between these stories mirrors the changes in literature for children. In *Let's Be Enemies*, children are allowed their childhood; they can be their 5-year-old selves. Their private feelings, thoughts, and language are considered worthy of attention. As much care has gone into conveying the meaning of the story through the pictures as through the text. It has taken a very long time for children's books to move from the didactic and moralistic to books that delight and entertain.

The literature intended for children always reflects society's changing attitude toward childhood and the family. Philippe Ariès contends that the idea of childhood itself was a seventeenth-century invention that has been transformed and reconstituted in every subsequent historical period.[3] Books for children provide a fascinating record of society and the values it has wished to inculcate in its youth.

Children's literature has a relatively brief history. Nevertheless, it has evolved from a rich and interesting background. Literature reflects not only the values of society but also the books that have preceded it—the literature of one generation builds on the literature of the past generation. An understanding of family stories of today is enriched by an acquaintance with the family stories of the past. How, for example, do the Beverly Cleary stories of the Quimby family (such as *Ramona and Her Father*, 1977) or Cynthia Voigt's descriptions of the Tillermans in *Homecoming* (1981) compare with *The Moffats* (1941) by Eleanor Estes or Edith Nesbit's Bastable children in *The Story of the Treasure-Seekers* (1899) or even that earliest of well-loved family stories, *Little Women* (1868), by Louisa May Alcott?

One danger in evaluating stories of the past is the tendency to use contemporary criteria rather than to recognize the prevailing values of the period in which a book was published. Some modern-day critics see *Little Women* as being antifeminist, but at the time of its publication in 1868 its main character was considered much too independent and

---

[3]Philippe Ariès, *Centuries of Childhood: A Social History of Family Life*, trans. from the French by Robert Baldick (New York: Knopf, 1962).

tomboyish. Obvious as this might seem, books for children are products of their times. They need to be evaluated in relationship to the other books of the day and against the social and political values of the period. Only then is it possible to identify the books that were real breakthroughs in the changing literature of childhood.

Early Beginnings: The Middle Ages

Today's literature for children has grown out of oral traditions that exist in every society. Stories and poems that were passed on by bards and retold by the common people were eventually recorded in manuscripts for a wide audience of adults and children.

The Oral Tradition

Before there were books, there were stories. In the medieval days—from the fifth to the fifteenth century—stories were told around the fires in cottages or sung in the great halls of castles. Young and old alike listened, with no distinction made between stories for children and stories for adults, just as there was little difference in the work they did, the food they ate, or the clothes they wore. All gathered to listen, to be entertained after a hard day's labor. A comparison can be made between this time of the oral tradition and today, when an entire family gathers to view a television show. True, there are children's programs, but many surveys show that children watch what adults watch. All are exposed to the same stories.

In the Middle Ages, there were differences between the kinds of stories told in the cottages and the kinds told in the castles, and in the ways they were told. In the castles and great manor houses, wandering minstrels or bards told the heroic tales of Beowulf or King Arthur or the ballad of Fair Isabella, whose stepmother had her cooked and served in a pie. Often these tales were sung, accompanied by harp or lyre. By contrast, the tales told around the peat fires in the cottages or at the medieval fairs were about simple folk—farmers, woodcutters, and millers—or beast tales about wolves, foxes, and hens. Frequently, the stories portrayed the poor peasant outwitting the lord of the manor or winning the hand of the princess by a daring deed. These tales were told over and over for generations until they were finally collected by scholars and thus passed into recorded literature.

It is important to remember that the oral tradition did not cease with the invention of the printing press. Most common folk could not read or afford to buy books. And the first books were not intended for entertainment; they were for religious or instructional purposes—frequently both. It was the told tale that continued to delight far into the nineteenth century. Today the storyteller is still a welcome visitor in the classroom, library, or home. The increased number of storytelling festivals today signals a revival of interest in this art.

The Earliest Manuscripts

Before the invention of movable type, the first books available for children were lesson books handwritten in Latin by monks. Mostly religious or instructional, these were intended only for the wealthy or for use by teachers in monastery schools. Such handwritten books were extremely valuable; houses and lands were often exchanged for a single volume.[4]

Most early lesson books followed one of two forms, which continued in popularity up to the early twentieth century: (1) a dialogue between the pupil and teacher, usually in the form of questions and answers, or (2) rhymed couplets, which made for easy memorization. Aldhelm, abbot of Malmesbury during the seventh century, is credited with introducing the question-and-answer approach. Also during this century, the Venerable Bede translated and wrote some forty-five books for his students at the monastery at Jarrow in England.

Another type of book, the *Elucidarium*, or book of general information for young students, was developed by Anselm, archbishop of Canterbury during the twelfth century. This type of book, a forerunner of the encyclopedia, treated such topics as manners, children's duties, the properties of animals and plants, and religious precepts.

---

[4]Louise Frances Story Field [Mrs. E. M. Field], *The Child and His Book*, 2nd ed. (London: Wells Gardner, 1892; reprint: Detroit: Singing Tree Press, 1968), p. 13.

Early lesson books are important to the history of children's literature only in that they represent some concession to developing specific books for the *instruction* of children. Another six centuries would pass before John Newbery would add the word *amusement* to the word *instruction*.

The Gesta Romanorum (Deeds of the Romans), compiled in Latin about 1290, served as a sourcebook of stories for the clergy for instruction and for enlivening sermons. This compilation of stories included many myths, fables, and tales from as far away as the Orient. Both Chaucer and Shakespeare drew incidents and stories from the *Gesta*. For example, it contained anecdotes of the three caskets and the pound of flesh found in *The Merchant of Venice* and a synopsis of the medieval romance in *Guy of Warwick*. These tales were often dressed up with suitable morals and then told to children.

Only one well-known work remains from these early manuscripts, Chaucer's *Canterbury Tales*. Although written for adults in 1387, the tales are full of legendary stories and folktales that were known to children as well as adults of the period.

Caxton Begins English Printing

Some historians maintain that Western printing first began in Holland sometime between 1380 and 1420.[5] However, in the 1450s, Gutenberg in Germany devised a practical method for using movable metal type, far superior in quality to the early Dutch type. William Caxton, an English businessman, went to Cologne, Germany, to learn the printing trade. Returning to England, he set up a printing press in Westminster about 1476. Among the first books he published were *A Book of Curteseye* (1477), *The Historye of Reynart the Foxe* (1481), and *Aesop's Fables* (1484). Malory's *Le Morte d'Arthur* first appeared in printed form in 1485. Caxton is credited with publishing some 106 books, including traditional romance literature, ballads, texts, and religious books. His books were of high quality and expensive, which made them available only to wealthy adults, not children. The impact of the printing press can be seen, however, in the number of books owned by some individuals. Before its invention in the 1450s, even scholars and physicians possessed only a few books. A century later, to give one example, Columbus of Seville (the son of Christopher Columbus) owned a library of more than 15,000 titles.

canne in to the forst / And whanne the wylom knefes sawe hym come / they were so fердful that they alle веganne to flee / For they wenдr / that it had be the lyon / And the mapfter of the affe ferchдr and foughдr his affe in euery place al аbout And as he had foughдr longe/he thoughдt that he wolдr go in to the forst for to fee yf his affe were there/And as soone as

Woodcut and type for Caxton's version of *Aesop's Fables* in 1484.

Hornbooks, ABCs, and Primers

The first children's books to be influenced by the invention of printing were then the only children's books: lesson books or textbooks. Young children learned to read from "hornbooks." A hornbook was really not a book at all but a little wooden paddle to which was pasted a sheet of parchment printed with the alphabet, the vowels, and the Lord's Prayer. A thin sheet of transparent protective horn bound with strips of brass covered the text. Most hornbooks were tiny, measuring 2¾ by 5 inches. Sometimes a hole in the handle made it possible for the child to carry the book on a cord around his or her neck or waist. What made these little "books" unique was that now the child could handle them and see the print close up, rather than merely look at a manuscript held by the teacher. Hornbooks were also made of leather, silver, copper, ivory, and sometimes gingerbread! First appearing in the 1440s, they served for over two hundred years as tools of instruction for young children. Brought to this country, they were used by the Puritans and in the colonial dame schools.

Children advanced from the hornbooks to ABC books and primers. These had more text than the hornbooks but were still of a religious nature. The first primers developed from the books of hours, which were intended as private devotionals for laypeople, with prayers for eight specified times of the day. In 1514 an alphabet was added to a book of hours for use by children. When Henry VIII came to the throne, he authorized printing a set of English primers for children that presented his religious

[5]Elva S. Smith, *Elva S. Smith's History of Children's Literature*, rev. Margaret Hodges and Susan Steinfirst (Chicago: American Library Association, 1980), p. 38.

During the fifteenth and sixteenth centuries, hornbooks were often the child's first introduction to literature.
This facsimile of a colonial hornbook was ordered from The Horn Book, Inc., 11 Beacon Street, Boston, MA 02108.

beliefs. These little books, appropriately called King Henry's Primers, appeared about 1548.

Johann Amos Comenius, a Moravian bishop, planned a book for schools that has often been called the first picture book. Titled *Orbis Pictus* (The World Illustrated), the book was translated into English in 1658 and published with many woodcuts illustrating everyday objects.

Lasting Contributions of the Period

Children were not much better off after the invention of printing than before. They still derived their enjoyment from the told story. True, some concession had been made to their youth in devising special books of instruction for them. But only crudely written and printed chapbooks provided a kind of underground literature of enjoyment for both adults and children. The two lasting books of this period are Chaucer's *Canterbury Tales* and Thomas Malory's collection of Arthurian legends, later published in 1485 by Caxton under the title *Le Morte d'Arthur*. Neither of these books was written for children, but children probably knew the stories from hearing them told by bards and minstrels.

What strikes a twentieth-century reader as remarkable about this period is how few books there were and how long they stayed in print. Many of the books published by Caxton in the 1440s were still in print in the late 1600s, more than two hundred years later. This seems almost unbelievable when compared with today's publishing world, where some books go out of print in less than a year.

Children's Books: The Seventeenth and Eighteenth Centuries

In the seventeenth and eighteenth centuries, many books for children were meant to be educational rather than entertaining. Over time, however, authors, illustrators, and publishers began to present children with books that were meant to delight as well as to inform.

The "Goodly Godly" Books of the Puritans

Books of the seventeenth century were dominated by the stern spiritual beliefs of Puritanism. As William Sloane has put it, "Nothing in our own diffuse civilization holds quite the pivotal position, the centrality, which religion held in seventeenth-century England and America. To man's relationship with God all the other circumstances of his life were peripheral."[6]

Children were considered to be miniature adults by the Puritans, and they were thus equally subject to sin and eternal damnation. Concern for the salvation of their souls became the central goal of their parents and teachers. Given the high mortality rate of infants and young children (more than half did not live to reach the age of 10), instruction in the fear of God began early.

Children were expected to memorize John Cotton's catechism, *Spiritual Milk for Boston Babes in Either England, Drawn from the Breasts of Both Testaments for*

[6]William Sloane, *Children's Books in England and America in the 17th Century* (New York: King's Press/Columbia University Press, 1955), p. 12.

Their Souls' Nourishment. Originally published in England in 1646, it was revised for American children in 1656, the first book written and printed for children in the American colonies. Later books followed its question-and-answer approach. For example, there was the question "How did God make you?" The child had to memorize the accompanying answer: "I was conceived in sin and born in iniquity." Even alphabet rhymes for the youngest emphasized the sinful nature of humans. *The New England Primer*, first advertised in 1683, includes "In Adam's fall/We sinned all." This primer also provided a catechism, the Ten Commandments, verses about death, and a woodcut of the burning at the stake of the Martyr John Foxe, watched by his wife and nine children. This primer was in print for more than a century and sold about three million copies.

In England in 1671, James Janeway published his book of gloomy joy titled *A Token for Children, Being an Exact Account of the Conversions, Holy and Exemplary Lives and Joyful Deaths of Several Young Children.* In his preface to Part 1, he reminds his readers that they are "by Nature, Children of Wrath." Cotton Mather added the life histories of several New England children and published an American edition of Janeway's book in Boston in 1700 under the title *A Token for Children of New England, or Some Examples of Children in Whom the Fear of God Was Remarkably Budding Before They Died.* Virginia Haviland describes the American edition: "An account of youthful piety, in tune with the doctrine of original sin, this is the first of the few narratives that were available to 18th century children in America and undoubtedly the most widely read children's book in the Puritan age."[7]

Religious leaders also could give approval to the moral and spiritual instruction in John Bunyan's *Pilgrim's Progress*, first printed in 1678. No doubt children skipped the long theological dialogues as they found adventure by traveling with the clearly defined characters. Another book by John Bunyan, evidently written *for* children, was first published in 1686 under the title *A Book for Boys and Girls or Country Rhymes for Children*, then changed to *Divine Emblems or Temporal Things Spiritualized.* F. J. Harvey Darton states that this particular emblem book was popular with both children and "ignorant folk" throughout the eighteenth century and remained in common use until at least the middle of the nineteenth century.[8]

This woodcut from a seventeenth-century chapbook has two episodes, "Tom Thumb running a tilt" and "how Tom Thumb did take his sickness, and of his death and burial." c. 1650–1660.
The Walter Havighurst Special Collections, Miami University Libraries, Oxford, Ohio.

Chapbooks: Forerunners of Comics

Luckily, there was some relief from the doom and gloom of the religion-oriented books of the Puritans. Chapbooks—small, inexpensive, folded-paper booklets sold by peddlers, or chapmen—first appeared in the late 1500s, but they achieved real popularity in the seventeenth and eighteenth centuries. Sold for a few pennies, these crudely printed little books brought excitement and pleasure into the lives of both children and adults with tales about Dick Whittington, Sir Guy of Warwick, Robin Hood, and other heroes. A ballad of a "most strange wedding of the froggee and the mouse" was licensed as early as 1580. "The Death and Burial of Cock Robin" was another early chapbook that children must have enjoyed. One of the most popular was about

---

[7]Virginia Haviland and Margaret N. Coughlan, *Yankee Doodle's Literary Sampler of Prose, Poetry and Pictures* (New York: Crowell, 1974), p. 11.

[8]F. J. Harvey Darton, *Children's Books in England*, 3rd ed., revised by Brian Alderson (Cambridge: Cambridge University Press, 1932, 1982), p. 64.

Tom Hickathrift, a giant-sized man who accomplished Paul Bunyan–like feats like pulling up trees and felling four highwaymen with a single blow. By contrast, a 1630 story of the tiny Tom Thumb shows him disappearing into a bowl of pudding when he was young and later bravely riding into battle astride a mighty warhorse. The earliest known edition of "Jack the Giant Killer" seems to have been in a chapbook of 1711. Other chapbooks gave accounts of crimes and executions, descriptions of the art of making love, and riddles.

While these books were decried by the Puritans, they were read and reread by the common people of England and America. Their popularity with children is said to have influenced John Newbery's decision to publish a book solely for children. The chapbooks' greatly abbreviated texts and crude woodcut illustrations suggest that they were forerunners of today's comic strips, still read by both adults and children.

Nursery Rhymes or Mother Goose

No one knows for sure the exact origin of nursery rhymes. Apparently, the rhymes we know as Mother Goose, including counting-out rhymes, finger plays, and alphabet verses, originated in the spoken language of both common folk and royalty. Some have been traced as far back as the pre-Christian era. A few writers theorize that "Jack and Jill" refers to the waxing and waning of the moon. It is believed that many of the verses were written as political satires or told of tragedy. "Mary, Mary, Quite Contrary," for example, has been said to date back to the turbulent reign of Mary Queen of Scots. "Ring Around the Rosie" may have referred to the pink ringlike rash that marked the early signs of bubonic plague. People carried "posies" of herbs for protection, and "We all fall down," of course, refers to the final demise of the victims. Katherine Thomas cites the account of a deed in the possession of a Horner family signed by Henry VIII that was a "plum" pulled out of the pie—the King's collection of deeds.[9] However, other scholars have found little evidence of these relationships.[10]

Shakespeare evidently knew these nursery rhymes, for they are referred to in *King Lear* and other of his plays. Yet the oldest *surviving* nursery rhyme book was

published by Mary Cooper in 1744 in two or perhaps three little volumes under the title *Tommy Thumb's Pretty Song Book;* a single copy of volume 2 is a treasured possession of the British Museum. John Newbery is supposed to have published *Mother Goose's Melody or Sonnets for the Cradle* about 1765, although the book was not advertised until 1780, which is the more likely date of its publication. No copy of this edition exists. However, Isaiah Thomas of Worcester, Massachusetts, produced a second edition of *Mother Goose's Melody* in 1794. Many of his books were pirated from Newbery, and it is assumed that his first edition of about 1786 was a copy of the lost Newbery book.

The legend that Dame Goose is buried in Boston is kept alive for tourists and children who visit the Boston burying grounds, but it has created confusion regarding the origin of the verses. Even the publication of *Songs for the Nursery, or Mother Goose's Melodies* by the son-in-law of Dame Goose is itself a legend. According to the story, Thomas Fleet tired of the good woman's frequent renditions of the ditties as she cared for his children, so he decided to collect and publish them in 1719. No actual evidence of this edition has been found.

Other verses and rhymes were later added to Mother Goose after their publication as small separate books. *The Comic Adventures of Old Mother Hubbard and her Dog* by Sarah Martin first appeared in 1805. During the same year *Songs from the Nursery Collected by the Most Renowned Poets* was published. For the first time, "Little Miss Muffett" and "One, Two Buckle My Shoe" were included in a Mother Goose book. *The History of Sixteen Wonderful Old Women*, issued by J. Harris and Son in 1820, contains the earliest examples of what we now call the limerick.

Uncertain of her origin as they are, historians do recognize that the venerable Mother Goose became a welcome part of the nursery on both sides of the Atlantic during the eighteenth century. Since then she has never left her post.

Fairy Tales and Adventure

Another source of enjoyment for children came in the form of fairy tales; the first was printed in France in 1697 by Charles Perrault. Titled *Histoires ou contes du temps passé; avec des moralités* (Stories or Tales of Times Past, with Morals), the collection included "The Sleeping Beauty," "Cinderella or the Glass Slipper," "Red Riding Hood," "Puss-in-Boots," and "Blue Beard." These tales were in fashion at the French court of the Sun King, Louis XIV, where they were told to adults. The frontispiece of Perrault's book, however, showed an old woman spinning and telling stories to children.

---

[9]Katherine Elwes Thomas, *The Real Personages of Mother Goose* (New York: Lothrop, 1930).

[10]Iona and Peter Opie, *The Oxford Nursery Rhyme Book* (London: Oxford University Press, 1952). William S. Baring-Gould and Ceil Baring-Gould, *The Annotated Mother Goose* (New York: Charles N. Potter, 1962).

The caption read *Contes de ma Mère l'Oye* (Tales of Mother Goose), which was the first reference to Mother Goose in children's literature. Translated into English in 1729, these fairy tales have remained France's gift to the children of the world.

Following the success of Perrault, other French authors, including Mme. d'Aulnoy, created original fairy tales. Only one remains well known today and that is "Beauty and the Beast," rewritten from a longer version by Mme. de Beaumont.

The Arabian Nights is a collection of old tales from India, Persia, and North Africa. Galland published these tales in French in 1558, but not until about 1706 were they available in English. Intended for adults, such stories as "Aladdin," "Ali Baba," and "Sinbad the Sailor" were appropriated by children. Ridley also published a series of tales modeled after *The Arabian Nights* under the title *The Tales of the Genii* (1766).

Defoe did not write his account of the eighteenth-century hero Robinson Crusoe for them, but children made his story part of their literature. *The Life and Strange and Surprising Adventures of Robinson Crusoe* (1719) was later printed in an abridged and pocket-size volume that became a "classic" of children's literature. This book was so popular that it spawned many imitations—so many, in fact, that a word, *Robinsonades*, was coined for them.

Children, no doubt, did not understand the scathing satire about high society in Swift's *Gulliver's Travels*, but they did find enjoyment in the hero's adventures with the huge and tiny folk and the talking horses. Thus young and old alike enjoyed this tale of adventure, first published in 1726.

Newbery Publishes for Children

The concept of a literature for children usually dates from 1744, the year the English publisher John Newbery printed *A Little Pretty Pocket-Book*. The title page is shown here. Newbery included Locke's advice that children should enjoy reading. The book itself attempted to teach the alphabet "by Way of Diversion," including games, fables, and little rhymes about the letters of the alphabet. What was significant about the book was that Newbery deliberately and openly set out to provide amusement for children, something no other publisher had had the courage or insight to do.

No documentary evidence is available to determine whether John Newbery or Oliver Goldsmith wrote *The History of Little Goody Two Shoes*, published by Newbery in 1765. London records do show that Newbery gave Goldsmith lodging above his shop, called "The Bible and the Sun." It is probable that Goldsmith was

Title page of *A Little Pretty Pocket-Book* published by John Newbery in 1744.

the author of some of the two hundred books published by Newbery. In *Little Goody Two Shoes*, Margery Meanwell and her brother are turned out of their home after the death of her parents, for "Her father had succumbed to a fever, in a place where Dr. James' Powder was not to be had." (Newbery also sold Dr. James' Powder and other medicines in his store.) At first the children are taken in by a kind parson, who properly clothes Tommy and sends him off to sea and provides Margery with two shoes instead of the poor one left to her after their eviction. This kind man hopes to take her into his family, but the evil Graspall threatens to reduce his tithe if he does. Eventually Margery becomes a tutor who moralizes as she teaches her young pupils to read. She marries a wealthy squire and continues to carry on her good works. *Little Goody Two Shoes* was read for well over a century. A modern eight-page version of it was sold to be read in air-raid shelters in England in the 1940s.

Newbery was obviously impressed with the advice given by the famous English philosopher John Locke in

The title character of *Little Goody Two Shoes* points to her two shoes in a facsimile reprint of John Newbery's best-known publication.

his *Thoughts Concerning Education* (1693). Locke maintained that as soon as children know their alphabet they should be led to read for pleasure. He advocated the use of pictures in books and deplored the lack of easy, pleasant books for children to read, except for *Aesop's Fables* and *Reynard the Fox*, both dating back to Caxton's times.

Newbery's books were all illustrated with pictures based on the text, rather than just any woodcuts available as was the custom of other printers of the day. Many of his books were bound with Dutch gilt paper covers, which made for a gay appearance. Even though moral lessons were clearly there for young readers, his stories did emphasize love and play rather than the

wrath and punishment of God. Except for *Little Goody Two Shoes*, none of his work has lasted, but we honor the man who was the first to recognize that children deserve a literature of their own.

Didactic Tales

During the last half of the eighteenth century, women writers entered the field of juvenile literature determined to influence the moral development of children. In 1749, Mrs. Sarah Fielding published *The Governess*, which included character-building stories about Mrs. Teachum's School for Girls. *Easy Lessons for Children*, published in 1760 by Mrs. Barbauld, contained moral stories supposedly written for children as young as 2 to 3 years. Mrs. Sarah Trimmer published a magazine titled *Guardian of Education*, which contained articles on moral subjects and book reviews. Mrs. Trimmer did not approve of fairy tales or Mother Goose. "All Mother Goose tales . . . were only fit to fill the heads of children with confused notions of wonderful and supernatural events brought about by the agency of imaginary beings."[11] She saw no inconsistency, however, in writing a story in which a family of robins could talk about day-to-day problems in their lives. First titled *Fabulous Histories* (1786), it was published for many years afterward under the title *The Robins*. The conversation between the parent robins and their offspring (called Flapsy, Pecksy, Dicky, and Robin) is stilted and lofty, indeed. Robin, the eldest, is portrayed as a conceited young bird who will take no advice. His parents discuss his behavior in this way:

"You have been absent a long time, my love," said her mate, "but I perceive that you were indulging your tenderness towards that disobedient nestling, who has rendered himself unworthy of it; however, I do not condemn you for giving him assistance, for had not you undertaken the task, I would myself have flown to him instead of returning home; how is he, likely to live and reward your kindness?"

"Yes," said she, "he will, I flatter myself, soon perfectly recover, for his hurt is not very considerable, and I have the pleasure to tell you he is extremely sensible of his late folly, and I dare say will endeavor to repair his fault with future good behaviour."[12]

[11]Darton, *Children's Books in England*, p. 97.

[12]Mrs. Trimmer, *The Robins, or Domestic Life Among the Birds*, rev. ed. (New York: C. S. Francis, 1851), p. 93.

Poor Mrs. Trimmer justified the use of this anthropomorphized bird family by calling the stories "fables" and stating that she was following the advice of John Locke, who had advocated the use of *Aesop's Fables* with children. No wonder Beatrix Potter recalled hating this book and refusing to learn to read from it.[13] Some memory of it must have lingered with her, however, for there is a strong resemblance in the sound of names of the young robins to her famous rabbit family, Flopsy, Mopsy, Cottontail, and Peter.

Other didactic writers of this period maintained that they followed Rousseau's theory of education by accompanying children in their natural search for knowledge. These stories frequently contained lengthy "conversations" that tried to conceal moral lessons under the guise of an exciting adventure. The priggish children found in these books served as models of behavior for nearly a hundred years.

Poetry and Pictures

In this period, poetry for children also emphasized religion and instruction. However, John Newbery printed *Pretty Poems for Children Three Feet High* and added this inscription: "To all those who are good this book is dedicated by their best friend."

Although Isaac Watts spent most of his time writing hymns, he did write some poetry for children. In the preface to *Divine and Moral Songs Attempted in Easy Language for Use of Children* (1715), Watts wrote that his songs were to be memorized, which was how children were to be given "a relish for virtue and religion." Though written by a Puritan, these hymns were kind and loving, and the collection made up a real child's book. Altogether Watts wrote about seven hundred hymns, some of which are still sung today, notably "Joy to the World," "O God Our Help in Ages Past," and the lovely "Cradle Hymn," which begins "Hush, my dear, lie still and slumber."

The engraver and artist William Blake wrote poetry that children enjoyed, but the poems constituting *Songs of Innocence* (1789) were not specifically written for children. Blake's poetry was filled with imagination and joy and made the reader aware of beauty without preaching. Children still respond to his happy poem that begins "Piping down the valleys wild,/Piping songs of pleasant glee." His desire to open the "doors of

SELECT FABLES.

THE FOX AND THE CROW.

A white-line woodcut of "The Fox and the Crow" from *Select Fables,* designed and engraved by Thomas and John Bewick, c. 1784.
The Walter Havighurst Special Collections, Miami University Libraries, Oxford, Ohio.

perception" is reflected in his well-known poem "To see a World in a Grain of Sand."

One British artist, Thomas Bewick, emerged during this period as an illustrator of books for boys and girls. He perfected the white-line method of engraving on the end grain of a block of wood to achieve a delicacy of line not found in usual carved woodblock designs. Bewick's *The New Lottery Book of Birds and Beasts* (1771) was one of the first instances of a master illustrator's putting his name on a book for children. Among his other works were *A Pretty Book of Pictures for Little Masters and Misses; or Tommy Trip's History of Beasts and Birds* (1779), which was a variation of one of Newbery's titles of the early 1760s, and several books of fables, including his own *Fables of Aesop and Others* (1818).

As the century neared its end, most of the stories for children were about how to live the "good life." Information about the natural world was peddled in didactic lectures sugarcoated with conversational style. Little prigs were models for young people to follow. However, there was now a literature for children. Authors and publishers were aware of a new market for books. Parents and teachers were beginning to recognize the importance of literature for children.

[13]Janet Crowell Morse, ed., *Beatrix Potter's Americans: Selected Letters* (Boston: Horn Book, 1982).

Children's Literature: The Nineteenth Century

In the nineteenth century, children could choose to read about a wide variety of topics. Books and magazines sought to present children with works of literature that celebrated their unique enthusiasms and explored their special worlds.

Books of Instruction and Information

During the period immediately following the American Revolution, there was a rush to publish textbooks that reflected the changing social purposes and interests of the new nation. A picture of George Washington was substituted for the woodcut of George III in *The New England Primer.* The alphabet no longer intoned "In Adam's fall/We sinned all" but started with a less pious rhyme: "A was an Angler and fished with a hook./B was a Blockhead and ne'er learned his book."

Noah Webster's *Blue Backed Speller, Simplified and Standardized,* first published in 1783, was widely used. Revised many times, the third part of the series contained stories and became America's first secular reader. It sold more than 80 million copies during the nineteenth century.

Reading for patriotism, good citizenship, and industry was the purpose of the well-loved *Eclectic Readers* by William H. McGuffey. They were used so widely from 1834 to 1900, one could almost say these readers constituted the elementary curriculum in literature. A glance at the *Fifth Reader* reflects the type of material included: speeches by Daniel Webster; essays by Washington Irving; selections from Shakespeare (although the play is often not identified); narrative, sentimental, and patriotic poetry, and many didactic essays with titles like "Advantages of a Well-educated Mind," "Impeachment of Warren Hastings as reported in the *Edinburgh Review*," and "Eulogy on Candlelight."

In the early nineteenth century Samuel Goodrich was responsible for eliminating the British background in books for American children. Influenced by both the English and the American Sunday school movement, which produced moral tales for the uneducated masses of children who could attend school only on Sunday, Goodrich wrote more than a hundred books for children. He created the venerable Peter Parley, an elderly gentleman who told stories to children based on his travels and personal experiences. History, geography, and science were included in his *Tales of Peter Parley About America* (1827). Nearly a million copies of *Peter*

Parley's Method of Telling About Geography to Children (1829) were published. This series became so popular that Goodrich employed a writing staff to help him, which included Nathaniel Hawthorne and his sister, Elizabeth. Peter Parley books sold over 7 million copies, and they were frequently pirated and issued abroad.

The Little Rollo series by Jacob Abbott became as popular as the Peter Parley books. Abbott wrote about Little Rollo learning to talk, Rollo learning to read, and Rollo's travels to Europe. In the first books of the series, published in 1834, Rollo was a natural little boy, but as he became older and traveled about the world he became another little prig.

Only a few writers and publishers seemed to realize that children want to learn about their world. Children had to plod through pages of tiresome conversations with moralistic overtones to gain the information they sought. It was not until much later that informational books on almost every subject were placed on bookshelves for boys and girls.

Folktale Collections

Early in the nineteenth century two German brothers went about asking servants and peasants to recall stories they had heard. In 1812 Jacob and Wilhelm Grimm published the first volume of *Kinder und Hausmärchen* (Household Stories). These serious scholars tried to preserve the form as well as the content of the old tales that were translated and published in England by Edgar Taylor from 1823 to 1826. "The Elves and the Shoemaker," "Rumpelstiltskin," and "Snow White," in addition to many others, became part of the literature of childhood.

In America, Washington Irving included "Rip Van Winkle" and "The Legend of Sleepy Hollow" in his 1819 *Sketch Book.* These tales, written mainly for adults, were also enjoyed by older children.

The origin of the story "The Three Bears" has been questioned by various authorities. It was first credited to the poet Robert Southey, who published it in *The Doctor* (1837). Later, Edgar Osborne, the famous English collector of children's books, found the story handwritten in verse by Eleanor Mure in 1831. Both these early versions portray a wicked old woman who comes to visit the bears, which are described as wee, middle-sized, and huge. Through various retellings, the story has been changed to the more familiar fair-haired Goldilocks visiting a *family* of bears.

In 1846 Mary Howitt translated Hans Christian Andersen's fairy tales under the title *Wonderful Stories for Children.* Now both English and American children could enjoy "The Princess and the Pea," "Thumbelina," and "The Emperor's New Clothes." In these stories, inanimate objects and animals like the heroic Tin Soldier and the Ugly Duckling come to life. The values and foibles of human life are presented in the stories with action and rich language.

Not until the last half of the nineteenth century were folktales and fairy tales completely accepted for children. John Ruskin was influenced by the Grimm tales as he wrote his *King of the Golden River* (1851). Charles Dickens's *The Magic Fishbone* appeared first as a serial in 1868. *The Wonder Book for Boys and Girls* was published by Nathaniel Hawthorne in 1852, followed by *Tanglewood Tales* in 1853. Now children had the Greek myths written especially for them. Sir George Dasent translated *Popular Tales from the North* in 1859, making it possible for children to enjoy more tales from Scandinavia. *The Nürnberg Stove* was another favorite, first published by Louise de la Ramee in a collection of children's stories in 1882. Joel Chandler Harris collected stories from the South for *Uncle Remus, His Songs and Sayings*.

Andrew Lang's famous series of collections of folktales began with *The Blue Fairy Book*. The Red, Green, and Yellow fairy books followed the 1889 publication of the first volume of folklore. Joseph Jacobs was also interested in retelling folktales especially for children. *English Fairy Tales* was published in two volumes between 1890 and 1894; *Celtic Fairy Tales*, also in two volumes, appeared in 1892 and 1894; *Indian Fairy Tales* was written in 1892. All these tales were important contributions to the realm of folklore. As the merits of folklore were recognized everywhere, there was increasing interest in such volumes as Howard Pyle's collections of original stories titled *Pepper and Salt* (1886) and *The Wonder Clock* (1888).

Family Stories

In the first half of the nineteenth century the didactic school of writing continued to flourish. Women writers, wielding influential pens, still condemned fairy stories and relentlessly dispensed information in lengthy dialogues between parent and child. Mrs. Martha Sherwood, a prolific writer, produced over 350 moralizing books and religious tracts. While living in India, she wrote *Little Henry and His Bearer* (1814). This story illustrates her missionary theme by telling how little Henry converted his Indian servant to Christianity. However, Sherwood is remembered best for a series of stories including *The Fairchild Family;* the first part of which was published in 1818, the third and last in 1847. Considered one of the first "family" stories, it contained some frighteningly realistic passages. In one scene, in order to teach his quarreling children a lesson, Mr. Fairchild takes them to see something "very dreadful,

. . . a gibbet on which the decomposed body of a man still hangs in irons. The face of the corpse was so shocking the children could not look at it." Later revisions of this story omitted the grim scene. However, even without this passage *The Fairchild Family* was a dramatic, vital story, and it was known on both sides of the Atlantic.

In contrast to the religious severity of *The Fairchild Family*, Charlotte Yonge described the milder Victorian experiences of the eleven motherless children of the May family in *The Daisy Chain* (1856). Women were always portrayed in the Victorian novel as inferior to men. This attitude is reflected in *The Daisy Chain* when Ethel May is advised not to try to keep up with her brother Norman in his university studies because "a woman cannot hope to equal a man in scholarship." In *The Clever Woman of the Family* (1865) Yonge devotes nearly the whole book to making the heroine "realize how much better and deeper were her husband's ideas than her own."[14] Yonge had an ear for dialogue and frequently recorded her friends' conversations. She was a superb storyteller and wrote over 120 books.

American children wept pools of tears over the pious, sentimental *Elsie Dinsmore*. Writing under her maiden name, Martha Farquharson, Martha Finley initiated the Elsie Dinsmore series in 1867. The best-known scene is the one in which Elsie's father demands that she play the piano and sing for a group of his friends. Because it is the Sabbath, Elsie refuses. Her father will not have his authority questioned and makes her sit on the piano stool for hours until she finally faints and cuts her head in the fall. Filled with remorse, her father gently carries her upstairs, only to have her insist that she be allowed to pray before going to bed. Elsie at all times is righteous and good. Her favorite book is the Bible, which she knows by heart and quotes regularly. The series contains eighteen books, published from 1867 to 1905, that follow Elsie from girlhood through motherhood and widowhood and into grandmotherhood. Unbelievable as the stories seem to us today, the Elsie Dinsmore books were tremendously popular.

The next year saw the publication of *Little Women* (1868) by Louisa May Alcott. This story must have blown like a fresh breeze through the stifling atmosphere of pious religiosity created by books like *Elsie Dinsmore*. As described by the irrepressible Jo (who was Louisa May Alcott herself), the March family were real people who faced genteel poverty with humor and fortitude. Louisa May Alcott didn't preach moral platitudes, but described the joys, the trials, and the fun of growing up in a loving family. Jo, one of the first tomboys in

[14]Cornelia Meigs, et al., *A Critical History of Children's Literature*, rev. ed. (New York: Macmillan, 1969), p. 158.

The first edition of *Little Women* (published as a single book in 1868) was illustrated by May Alcott, the author's sister.
The Walter Havighurst Special Collections, Miami University Libraries, Oxford, Ohio.

Jessie Wilcox Smith pictured slightly older girls for the eight full-color illustrations she painted in oils for the popular 1915 edition of *Little Women*.

children's literature, hates the false Victorian standards of the day. When her older sister Meg tells her that she should remember she is a young lady, this follows:

> "I'm not! and if turning up my hair makes me one, I'll wear it in two tails till I'm twenty," cried Jo, pulling off her net and shaking down a chestnut mane. "I hate to think I've got to grow up and be Miss March, and wear long gowns and look prim as a China-aster. It's bad enough to be a girl, anyway, when I like boys' games and work and manners!"[15]

Little Women was not an immediate success with the critics of the time. One of the first reviewers wrote: "They [*Little Women* was originally two books] are not religious books, should not be read on Sunday, and are not appropriate for the Sunday School. This is the character of the book before us. It is lively, entertaining, and not harmful."[16]

Children loved it and have read it every day, including Sundays, since its publication. The first edition of volume 1 of *Little Women* (which ended before Beth's death) was sold out within two months of printing. The publisher asked for a second volume, which was ready the next year. Later the two books were combined into one. *Little Men* and *Jo's Boys* were sequels to this American family classic. Still loved today, *Little Women* has been translated into many languages, including Russian, Arabic, Bengali, and Urdu.

Another vivacious heroine appeared in the celebrated Katy stories written by Susan Coolidge (pseudonym of Sarah Chauncey Woolsey). This series included such titles as *What Katy Did* (1872), *What Katy Did at School* (1873), and *What Katy Did Next* (1886). Susan

[15]Louisa May Alcott, *Little Women* (Boston: Little, Brown, 1922, [1868]), p. 3.

[16]Lavinia Russ, " 'Not to Be Read on Sunday,' Centenary of *Little Women*, 1868–1968," *Horn Book Magazine*, (October 1968), pp. 521–526.

Coolidge also wrote many other stories. Harriet Lathrop, under the pseudonym Margaret Sidney, presented a lively family story about a widowed mother and her five children in a series starting in 1881 with *Five Little Peppers* and concluding in 1916 with *Our Davie Pepper*.

Other authors wrote dramatic family stories with foreign settings. In *Hans Brinker, or the Silver Skates*, Mary Mapes Dodge gave accurate glimpses of Dutch life in 1865. The skating race is actually less important than the daring brain surgery performed on Father Brinker, who had been mentally incompetent for several years after an accident. The bravery and courage of Hans and his sister in facing poverty, scorn, and their father's illness provided further examples for child behavior.

Johanna Spyri's well-loved *Heidi* was translated from the German by Louise Brooks and published in this country in 1884. Not only did readers share the joys and sorrows of Heidi's life with her grandfather, they "breathed" the clear mountain air and "lived" in Switzerland.

Frances Hodgson Burnett described family conflict within the English aristocracy in *Little Lord Fauntleroy* (1886). Although born in England, Mrs. Burnett was an American citizen. Burnett's second book, *Sara Crewe* (1888), told of the pitiful plight of a wealthy pupil who is orphaned and reduced to servitude in a boarding school. Its Cinderella ending delights children and adults, and it was made into a very successful play. Mrs. Burnett then expanded the play into a longer novel under the title *The Little Princess* (1905). A new edition of *Sara Crewe* was published as recently as 1981, illustrated with appropriate Dickensian pictures by Margot Tomes. Mrs. Burnett's best-written and most popular book is *The Secret Garden* (1910), which presents an exciting plot in a mysterious setting. This story depicts the gradual change wrought in two lonely and selfish children by a hidden garden and the wholesome influence of the boy Dickon. It is still read and loved by children today.

Tales of Adventure

The rise of family stories and series books for girls prompted more attention to tales of adventures and the development of so-called boys' series. The best known of the Robinsonades, *The Swiss Family Robinson*, was written by Johann David Wyss, a Swiss pastor, and translated into English in 1814. Inaccurate in its description of flora and fauna (almost everything grew on that tropical island), it still delighted children's imaginations. Sir Walter Scott's novels *Rob Roy* (1818) and *Ivanhoe* (1820), while intended for adults, were frequently appropriated by young people. James Fenimore Cooper's Leatherstocking novels of exciting tales of Indians and pioneers in North America were avidly read by young and old alike. The bloody incidents and

tragedy of *The Last of the Mohicans* (1826) brought a sense of tingling adventure to all readers. Richard Henry Dana's *Two Years Before the Mast* (1840) describes the author's own adventures as a young seaman sailing around Cape Horn to California. Also written for adults, it provided adventure for children.

British writers such as Captain Frederick Marryat and George A. Henty wrote books based on military histories and adventures that were read with enthusiasm by American children. At the same time the American names Horatio Alger, Jr., Oliver Optic, and Harry Castlemon were well known to English readers. The emphasis in American series was more on individual achievement, usually against unbelievable odds. The stories by Horatio Alger epitomized this rags-to-riches theme. In fact, because his first successful novel, *Ragged Dick* (1868), was based on this formula, he saw no reason to change it in the more than a hundred books that followed.

Harry Castlemon (pseudonym of Charles Austin Fosdick) based his book *Frank on a Gunboat* (1864) on his own experiences in the Civil War. He wrote fifty-eight more volumes in his Gunboat, Rocky Mountain, Sportsman Club, Boy Trapper, Rod and Gun, and Pony Express series. His stories were exciting, as incident followed incident. He is quoted as saying: "Boys don't like fine writing. What they want is adventure, and the more of it you can get into 250 pages of manuscript, the better fellow you are."[17]

Though most of these series books did provide plenty of adventure, the characters and plots tended to be superficial and predictable. However, there was one superb adventure story written during the last half of the nineteenth century that included not only a bloody, exciting, and tightly drawn plot but also well-depicted characters. Serialized in an English magazine called *Young Folks* in 1881 and 1882, Robert Louis Stevenson's *Treasure Island* was published in book form in 1883. For the first time adults were drawn to a children's book for adventure, a reverse of the pattern of children reading adults' books. *Treasure Island* was an immediate success.

Gradually books written for boys changed in their portrayal of childhood, and little prigs became real live boys. Thomas Bailey Aldrich's *The Story of a Bad Boy* (1870) was based on his own life in Portsmouth, New Hampshire. The tale of this Tom's pranks and good times paved the way for another story of a real boy's adventures in Hannibal, Missouri. *The Adventures of Tom Sawyer* was published in 1876 by Mark Twain (pseudonym of Samuel Clemens). This book was soon followed by an American classic, *The Adventures of Huckleberry Finn* (1884). Mark Twain combined realism, humor,

---

[17]Jacob Blanck, compiler, *Harry Castlemon: Boys' Own Author* (New York: R. R. Bowker, 1941), pp. 5–6.

and adventure in these realistic portrayals of growing up in a small town near the end of the nineteenth century. Although *Huckleberry Finn* has won literary acclaim, children prefer *The Adventures of Tom Sawyer*. This seems only natural, since Tom's adventures involve children their age.

The beginnings of science-fiction adventure stories came to us from France in the translations of Jules Verne's *Journey to the Center of the Earth* (1864), *Twenty Thousand Leagues Under the Sea* (1869), and *Around the World in Eighty Days* (1872). Modern readers may be surprised to note the early dates of these books.

Animal Stories

In *A Dog of Flanders and Other Stories* (1872), Louise de la Ramee presented a collection of stories that included the sad tale of a Belgian work dog and his friend, a boy artist. It has been considered the first modern dog story. *Black Beauty* appeared in 1877 as a protest against cruel treatment of horses. Children skipped the lectures calling for more humane treatment of animals and read the compelling first-person story of the life of Black Beauty. Some children today continue to enjoy Anna Sewell's rather overdrawn and sentimental tale. Rudyard Kipling's *The Jungle Books* (1894–1895) were exciting animal stories. Many children today know the story of Mowgli, a child raised by a wolf family, a bear, and a panther, although they might be more familiar with the animated movie than with the original book.

The Rise of Fantasy and Humor

Even though many of the early books for children included the word *amusing* in their titles, their main purpose was to instruct or moralize. Undoubtedly, children enjoyed the broad humor in some of the folktales and the nonsense in Mother Goose, but few books used humor or nonsense before the middle of the nineteenth century.

The first stirrings of modern fantasy can be seen in a tale written by an English clergyman and scientist in 1863. *The Water Babies* by Charles Kingsley is a strange mixture of the fanciful overladen with heavy doses of morality. It is the story of a chimney sweep who has become a water baby with gills. Hidden within this little tale was Kingsley's social concern for the plight of the chimney sweeps, plus his attempt to reconcile the new science (Darwin's *The Origin of Species* had been published in 1859) with his religious belief that salvation can be obtained through love and compassion as easily as through punishment.

On a summer day in 1862 an Oxford professor of mathematics, Charles Dodgson, told a story to three little

Although many artists (including Lewis Carroll himself) have illustrated *Alice's Adventures in Wonderland*, it is Tenniel who created the best-known images of Alice and her many adventures in nonsense.

girls on a picnic. According to Meigs, this "was the real beginning of modern literature for children."[18] For the tale that was told was about Alice, who followed a white rabbit down a rabbit hole and found herself a part of a remarkable adventure. At the children's request, Dodgson wrote down that story (as *Alice's Adventures Underground*) and presented it to his young friends as a Christmas gift in 1864. At the insistence of others, he decided to have it published. By 1865 the artist John Tenniel had completed the drawings, and *Alice's Adventures in Wonderland*, published under the pseudonym Lewis Carroll, was ready for the host of readers to come. What made this story absolutely unique for its time was that it contained not a trace of a lesson or a moral. It was really made purely for enjoyment, and it has delighted both children and adults ever since. Allusions to this book and its companion title, *Through the Looking-Glass* (1871), have become a part of our everyday speech: "curiouser and curiouser"; "much of a muchness"; "begin at the beginning, then go on until you've come to the end: then stop"; "I've believed as many as six impossible things before breakfast"; "O frabjous day"; and many more.

Other well-known fantasies were published near the end of the century. George MacDonald was a friend of Lewis Carroll's; in fact he was one of the persons who had urged the publication of Alice. However, his own

18Meigs, *A Critical History*, p. 194.

Ernest Nister's bicycling bears are on their way to *The Animals' Picnic* in one of today's numerous reissues of Victorian pop-up books.

From *The Animals' Picnic*, by Ernest Nester. Copyright © 1988 by The Putnam & Grosset Group, New York, NY. Reprinted by permission.

"invented fairy-tale" *At the Back of the North Wind* (1871) has much more of the sad spiritual quality found in many of Hans Christian Andersen's fairy tales than the mad inconsistencies of the world of Lewis Carroll. MacDonald's other works include *The Princess and the Goblin* (1872) and *The Princess and the Curdie* (1883). "The Light Princess" and "The Golden Key" are well-known stories from his other books.

The Adventures of Pinocchio by Carlo Collodi first appeared in a children's newspaper in Rome in 1881. Translated into many languages, it was issued in English in 1891 under the title *The Story of a Puppet*, but the title was soon changed back to the original *Pinocchio*. Children still enjoy this story of the mischievous puppet whose nose grew longer with each lie he told the Blue Fairy. Collodi's real name was Carlos Lorenzini.

The prototype for Mary Poppins, Amelia Bedelia, Miss Pickerell, and all the other eccentric women characters in children's literature can be found in the nonsensical antics of Mrs. Peterkin and her family.

Published in 1880 by Lucretia Hale, *The Peterkin Papers* provided children with real humor. One of the most amusing stories, "The Lady Who Put Salt in Her Coffee," appeared in a juvenile magazine as early as 1868. Mrs. Peterkin mistakenly substitutes salt for sugar in her coffee. The whole family troops to the chemist and the herb lady to find out what to do. Finally "the lady from Philadelphia" provides the answer—make another cup of coffee! The antics of the Peterkin family were just as exaggerated and as much fun in 1880 as McCloskey's *Homer Price* was in the 1940s.

Also in the category of books for fun may be included the many books with movable parts. Harlequinades, or turn-ups, first appeared in 1766. They consisted of pages of pictures that could be raised or lowered to create other scenes. Later (from the 1840s through the 1890s) pictures were made like Venetian blinds to create another scene. Circular wheels could be turned to provide more action, and whole pop-up scenes created miniature stages.

Poetry

Poetry for children began to flourish in the nineteenth century. In the first part of the century, poetry, like prose, still reflected the influence of religion and moral didacticism. The Taylor sisters, Ann and Jane, emphasized polite behavior, morals, and death in the poetry for their first book, *Original Poems for Infant Minds* (1804). While Jane Taylor wrote the often parodied "Twinkle Twinkle Little Star" for this collection and Ann provided the lovely "Welcome, welcome little stranger, to this busy world of care," the book also included morbid poems such as this example:

> You are not so healthy and gay
> So young, so active and bright,
> That death cannot snatch you away,
> Or some dread accident smite.
>
> Here lie both the young and the old,
> Confined in the coffin so small
> The earth covers over them cold,
> The grave-worms devour them all.

William Roscoe's *The Butterfly's Ball and the Grasshopper's Feast* (1807) provided pure nonsense, rhyme, and rhythm that delighted children. There were no moral lessons here, just an invitation: "Come take up your hats and away let us haste/To the Butterfly's Ball and the Grasshopper's Feast." The arrival of each guest was illustrated by copper engravings (a "snail person," a "bumble bee child") by William Mulready. Roscoe, a historian and botanist, wrote the book for the pleasure of his own child. It was so fresh and different that it generated many imitations.

Clement Moore, a professor who also wrote to please his own children, gave the world the Christmas classic *A Visit from St. Nicholas.* One of the first American contributions to a joyous literature for children, it was published with this title in 1823, but it is now known by the title *The Night Before Christmas.* Tasha Tudor, Michael Hague, and Tomie de Paola have all created beautifully illustrated editions of this well-loved poem for today's children. *Mary Had a Little Lamb,* first written by Sarah Josepha Hale in 1830, was included in McGuffey's reader in 1837 and has since been recited by generations of American schoolchildren.

Dr. Heinrich Hoffman's *Struwwelpeter* (Shock-Headed Peter) was translated from the German in about 1848. His subjects included "Shock-Headed Peter," who wouldn't comb his hair or cut his nails; Harriet, who played with fire; and Augustus, who would not eat his

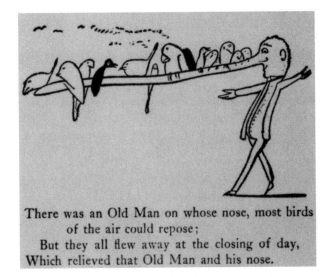

There was an Old Man on whose nose, most birds of the air could repose; But they all flew away at the closing of day, Which relieved that Old Man and his nose.

Edward Lear's laughable limericks and humorous illustrations in *A Book of Nonsense* are over a hundred years old, but they are still enjoyed today.

nasty soup and he became as "thin as a thread/and the fifth day was dead." These cautionary tales in verse were meant to frighten children into good behavior. Instead, children loved the pictures and gruesome verse. Surely these poems are the forerunners of some of the modern verse by Shel Silverstein and Jack Prelutsky.

The century's greatest contribution to lasting children's poetry was the nonsense verse of Edward Lear, a poet who, like Lewis Carroll, wrote only to entertain. Lear was by profession a landscape painter and illustrator. He wrote his first book, *A Book of Nonsense,* in 1846 for his child friends; *More Nonsense* (1877) appeared twenty-six years later. Generations have delighted in the elderly "Quangle Wangle" and "The Owl and the Pussycat." Lear did not invent the limerick, but he certainly became master of the form. His black-line illustrations are as clever as his poetry.

Most of Lewis Carroll's nonsense verse is included in *Alice's Adventures in Wonderland* and *Through the Looking-Glass.* Many of Carroll's poems were parodies of the popular poems of his time. "The Lobster Quadrille" mimics Mary Howitt's "The Spider and the Fly," "Father William" copies Southey's "The Old Man's Comforts," and "How Doth the Little Crocodile" parodies Watts's "How Doth the Busy Bee." Interest in the original poems has all but disappeared, but the parodies continue to delight. The sound and play of words must have fascinated Carroll, for his poems and books abound with puns, double meanings, coined words, and wonderful nonsense.

Some of Christina Rossetti's poetry is reminiscent of Mother Goose, such as the well-loved "Mix a pancake/Stir a pancake/Pop it in the pan;/Fry the pancake/Toss the pancake/Catch it if you can." Others such as "Who has seen the wind?" gave children vivid descriptions of the world around them. Many poems from her book *Sing Song* (1872) are found in anthologies today.

William Allingham's name is always associated with the poem "The Fairies," which begins "Up the airy mountain,/Down the rushy glen,/We daren't go a hunting,/For fear of little men." It appeared in his book *In Fairyland* (1870), which was beautifully illustrated in colored pictures by Richard Doyle. Allingham's *Ballad Book*, published in 1865, contained "Fourscore of the best of the old ballads," as stated in his preface. John Greenleaf Whittier included some of his own poems in his anthology *Child Life, a Collection of Poems* (1871) as well as some by Blake, Shakespeare, Tennyson, Keats, Shelley, Browning, and Wordsworth. He thought children were capable of understanding poetry of literary merit.

The century ended with a unique volume of poetry that celebrated the everyday life and thought of the child. *A Child's Garden of Verses* (1885) by Robert Louis Stevenson was first published under the title *Penny Whistles*. Stevenson was a poet who could discover joy in child's play and enter the child's imaginings in such well-loved poems as "My Shadow," "Bed in Summer," "The Swing," "Windy Nights," and "My Bed Is a Boat."

Two notable American poets were writing for children at the close of the nineteenth century. Eugene Field's *Poems of Childhood* (1896) included "The Sugar Plum Tree" and "The Duel." James Whitcomb Riley employed dialect as he described local incidents and Indiana farm life. This Hoosier dialect has made most of his poems seem obsolete, except for "Little Orphant Annie" and "The Raggedy Man," which continue to give children pleasure.

Magazines

Magazines formed a significant part of the literature for children in the last half of the nineteenth century. The first magazines, which grew out of the Sunday school movement, were pious in their outlook. The first true children's magazine for English children appeared in 1853 under the title *Charm*. Stating that there would always be room for stories of the little people or fairies on its pages, it was ahead of its time and lasted only two years. Charlotte Yonge's own stories appeared in her magazine *The Monthly Packet*. In 1866, Mrs. Gatty

started *Aunt Judy's Magazine,* which began the policy of reviewing children's books, reporting enthusiastically on *Alice's Adventures in Wonderland* and Hans Christian Andersen's stories.

The first magazine planned for children in America was published in 1826. *The Juvenile Miscellany* was edited by Lydia Maria Child, a former teacher who wanted to provide enjoyable material for children to read. The magazine was very successful until Child, an ardent abolitionist, spoke out against slavery. Sales dropped immediately, and the magazine stopped publication in 1834. *The Youth's Companion* survived the longest of all the children's magazines in America, beginning in 1827 and merging with *The American Boy* in 1929, which in turn ceased publication in 1941. It published such well-known writers as Kipling, Oliver Wendell Holmes, Jack London, Mark Twain, and Theodore Roosevelt, among others. *The Youth's Companion* had a definite editorial policy. It proposed to "exile death from its pages"; tobacco and alcohol were not to be mentioned, and love figured in some of the stories only after 1890. Part of the popularity of this magazine can be attributed to the inviting prizes that were offered each week.

In 1873 Mary Mapes Dodge, author of *Hans Brinker, or the Silver Skates,* became editor of the most famous magazine for children, *St. Nicholas Magazine.* The publisher announced that in this magazine "there must be entertainment, no less than information; the spirit of laughter would be evoked; there would be 'no sermonizing, no wearisome spinning out of facts, no rattling of dry bones of history,' while all priggishness was condemned."[19] A promising young writer, Frank Stockton, became Dodge's assistant, and together they published a magazine that would become known throughout the English-speaking world. They attracted well-known artists and writers such as Arthur Rackham, Reginald Birch, Howard Pyle, Frances Hodgson Burnett, Rudyard Kipling, Robert Louis Stevenson, and Louisa May Alcott. Many of the novels that were first serialized in *St. Nicholas Magazine* were published as books and became classics of their day. These included Louisa May Alcott's *An Old-Fashioned Girl* (1870) and *Jo's Boys* (1873) and Frances Hodgson Burnett's *Little Lord Fauntleroy* (1886) and *Sara Crewe* (1888). This magazine guided children's reading for over three-quarters of a century and set standards of excellence for the whole publishing field.

---

[19]Alice M. Jordan, *From Rollo to Tom Sawyer* (Boston: Horn Book, 1948), p. 134.

Illustrators of the Nineteenth Century

During the nineteenth century, the illustrators of children's books began to achieve as much recognition as the authors. In the early part of the century, crude woodcuts were still being used, illustrators were not identified, and pictures were frequently interchanged among books. Gradually, however, several outstanding artists emerged as illustrators of children's books. The engraver George Cruikshank illustrated the English edition of *Grimm's Fairy Tales* in 1823. His tiny detailed pictures portrayed much action and humor, real characters, and spritely elves and fairies. His interpretations were so appropriate and seemed so much a part of these tales that they were republished in Germany with the original text. In 1853–1854 he published four volumes of his *Fairy Library*, which contain some of his best artwork. Cruikshank was a friend of Dickens and his most famous illustrator, although they had a falling out over Cruikshank's rewriting of the fairy tales to include temperance messages. Fortunately, he is remembered for his enchanting illustrations, not his rewritten texts.

The three best-known illustrators of the nineteenth century are Walter Crane, Randolph Caldecott, and Kate Greenaway. All three were fortunate indeed to have as their engraver Edmund Evans, the best color printer in England. Walter Crane, the son of a portrait painter, knew that Evans wanted to print some quality illustrated books for children, something that interested Crane also. Crane created beautifully designed pictures for four nursery-rhyme books, *Sing a Song of Sixpence, The House That Jack Built, Dame Trot and Her Comical Cat,* and *The History of Cock Robin and Jenny Wren.* Evans and Crane convinced Warne to publish these high-quality "toy books" during the years 1865–1866. They were very successful, and Crane went on to design some thirty-five other picture books, including two well-known nursery-rhyme collections with music and illustrations, *The Baby's Opera* (1877) and *The Baby's Bouquet* (1878). Crane had a strong sense of design and paid particular attention to the total format of the book, including the placement of the text, the quality of the paper, and even the design at the beginning and end of the chapters. He characteristically used flat colors with a firm black outline, and his pages usually were decorated with elaborate borders. He made a point of studying the Victorian child's attitude toward art, saying: "Like the Ancient Egyptians, children appear to see most things in profile and like definite statements in design. They prefer

Walter Crane's decorative borders and fine sense of design are seen in this frontispiece for *The Baby's Own Aesop.*

well-defined forms and frank colour. They don't want to bother about three dimensions."[20]

The picture books by Randolph Caldecott established new standards of illustration for children's books. His drawings were filled with action, the joy of living, and good fun. His love of animals and the English countryside is reflected in his illustrations, which seem to convey much meaning through a few lines. Although Caldecott, like Crane, illustrated many books, he is best remembered for his series of picture books. These included *The House That Jack Built* (1878), *The Diverting History of John Gilpin* (1878), *Sing a Song of Sixpence* (1880), and *Hey Diddle Diddle Picture Book* (1883). On the Caldecott Medal for distinguished illustrations there is a reproduction of one of his pictures showing John Gilpin's ride, a reminder of this famous illustrator of the nineteenth century.

Kate Greenaway's name brings visions of English gardens, delicate prim figures, and the special style of costume worn by her rather fragile children. Her art defined the fanciful world of Victorian sentimentality. After the publication of her first book, *Under the Window* (1878), it became the fashion to dress children in Greenaway costumes with large floppy hats. Greeting

[20]As quoted by Bryan Holme in his preface to *An Alphabet of Old Friends and the Absurd ABC* by Walter Crane (New York: Metropolitan Museum of Art, 1981), unpaged.

Randolph Caldecott was one of the first illustrators for children to show action in his pictures. The design for the Caldecott Medal is taken from this scene in *The Diverting History of John Gilpin.*

cards, wallpaper, and even china were made with designs copied after Greenaway. Her best-known works include *Marigold Garden* (1885), *A Apple Pie* (1886), and *The Pied Piper of Hamelin* (1888). The Kate Greenaway Medal, similar to our Caldecott Medal, is given each year to the most distinguished British picture book.

From France came the remarkable work of Maurice Boutet de Monvel, best remembered for the superb pictures for *Jeanne d'Arc*, (Joan of Arc) which he wrote and illustrated in 1896. The power of these paintings—the massed groupings of men and horses and the mob scenes in which every person is an individual yet the focus is always on the Maid of Orleans—made this a distinctive book for young and old alike. It was translated into English in 1897 and reissued in 1980 by Viking Press in cooperation with the Pierpont Morgan Library.

In America, Howard Pyle was writing and illustrating his versions of *The Merry Adventures of Robin Hood of Great Renown* (1883), *Pepper and Salt* (1886), and *The Wonder Clock* (1888). He created *real* people in his illustrations for these collections of folktales and legends. His characters from the Middle Ages were strong; the life of the times was portrayed with interesting, clear

detail. In 1903, Pyle published the first of four volumes of *The Story of King Arthur and His Knights,* which was reissued by Scribner's in 1984. He also illustrated and wrote for *Scribner's Monthly Magazine* and *St. Nicholas Magazine.* Another of his important contributions was establishing classes for illustrators of children's books. Some of his students included N. C. Wyeth, Maxfield Parrish, and Jessie Wilcox Smith, all of whom became well-known illustrators in the twentieth century.

By the close of the nineteenth century, children's literature was alive and flourishing. Pious, moralistic, didactic books were no longer being written. Gone were the make-believe accounts of impossible children. In their place were real live persons living in fun-loving families. Pure nonsense and the fanciful were welcomed in both poetry and fantasy. The old folktales and the fairies were accepted once again. Children's books were more beautiful, with illustrations by recognized artists. A few magazines had given consideration to the place of literary criticism. Much would need to be done to bring books to all children in the next century, but a literature for children, designed to bring them joy and happiness, was now firmly in place.

Without alerting Joan, the French had attacked the English bastion of Saint-Loup. The attack failed; the French were retreating in disorder. Joan rushed up, rallied them, and led them once more to the very foot of the bastion. The English, under their commander Talbot, fought back desperately for three hours, but despite their resistance the French overcame them and captured the bastion.

The extraordinary illustrations by Maurice Boutet de Monvel for the picture book *Jeanne d'Arc* (Joan of Arc) created in 1896 had a pervasive influence on the children's books that followed.

Children's Literature: The Twentieth Century

The nineteenth century saw the firm establishment of a literature for children; the twentieth has been characterized by the recognition of literary and artistic quality in children's books, the growth of children's book departments in publishing houses, and the expansion of both public and school library service to all children. Technological improvements made it possible to create beautifully illustrated, well-bound books for children and just as easy to mass-produce shoddy, cheap editions. The picture book as we know it today was created early in this century, as were fine informational books for all ages.

Recognition of Children's Literature

Disturbed by the influence of the cheaply produced fifty-cent books for juveniles, Franklin K. Mathiews, chief librarian for the Boy Scouts, sought to raise the level of reading for children. His suggestion to establish Children's Book Week was promoted in 1919 by Frederick Melcher as a project of the American Booksellers Association. Schools, libraries, newspapers, and bookstores supported the event, which became a significant stimulant to the development of children's literature. In 1945 the Children's Book Council was established to promote Children's Book Week and to distribute information on children's books throughout the year.

Melcher also promoted another event that has encouraged the development of children's literature. He proposed the presentation of an annual award for the most distinguished book for children. Initiated in 1922, the Newbery Medal was the first award in the world to be given for "distinguished contribution to literature for children." The Caldecott Medal for the most distinguished illustration of the year was first given in 1938. Both these awards have had great influence in raising the standards of writing and illustrating in children's books. They also gave prestige to the idea of creating books for children.

The addition of children's departments to publishing firms indicated the growing importance of literature for the young. In 1919 Macmillan made Louise Seaman its children's editor, and other companies were quick to follow this innovation. May Massee became editor of children's books at Doubleday in 1922. The first critical reviews of children's books appeared in *The Bookman* in 1918. Anne Carroll Moore continued this influential work in her *New York Herald Tribune* column, "The Three Owls." *The Horn Book Magazine*, a publication devoted solely to children's literature, was first published in 1924 under the editorship of Bertha Mahony.

Public libraries instituted children's rooms, and many elementary schools had libraries. By 1915 the American Library Association had established a School Library division. The enactment of the Elementary and Secondary Education Act of 1965 made the concept of school library media centers for *every* elementary school a viable possibility.

The Junior Literary Guild was established in 1929 and was the first to send children selected books each month. In the late 1950s, paperback book clubs made it possible for more children to own books and increased their enthusiasm for reading. Currently, many book clubs offer selections of children's literature.

The Rise of the Picture Storybook

One of the best-loved stories for children is Beatrix Potter's tale of Peter Rabbit, who appeared in Mr. MacGregor's garden at the turn of the century. After writing a short version of the tale in a letter to the ill son of a former governess, Potter expanded the story and submitted it to Warne Publishers. When they rejected it, she had it published privately in 1901. Warne finally accepted and published *The Tale of Peter Rabbit* with the author's own watercolor illustrations in 1902. Potter later introduced stories of many other animals, such as Jemima Puddleduck, Benjamin Bunny, and Mrs. Tittlemouse, but the Cottontail family is the best known and loved.

A trusting fowl listens to a "foxy-whiskered gentleman" in this scene from *Jemima Puddle-Duck*. Beatrix Potter created real personalities in both the text and the pictures of her many books.

At the same time as Potter was writing and illustrating, Leslie Brooke was creating wonderfully humorous pictures for his nursery-rhyme picture books. No one could draw such expressive faces on pigs as Brooke did in "This Little Pig Went to Market," which first appeared in *The Golden Goose Book* (1905). Brooke added whimsical details to his illustrations, like a picture of "Home Sweet Home" hanging inside the pigs' house showing a mother pig and her little ones. Leslie Brooke's animals in the popular *Johnny Crow's Garden* (1903) were costumed and personified. They included the lion with a "green and yellow tie on" and the bear in his striped pants and tailcoat.

The other well-known English illustrator of this period was Arthur Rackham. He is recognized for the imaginative detail of his pictures, which frequently portrayed grotesque people and humanlike trees, evoking an eerie atmosphere. His illustrations for *Mother Goose* (1913) show imaginative elves and gnomes hiding under mushrooms and in the roots of trees. He illustrated many other books, including Hans Christian Andersen's *Fairy Tales*, *Cinderella*, *Peter Pan in Kensington Gardens*, *Aesop's Fables*, and many more.

Arthur Rackham became known for his imaginative worlds of gnomes and anthropomorphized trees. His illustrations appeared in magazines as well as books.

For many years these English books, along with those of Caldecott, Crane, and Greenaway, supplied the American picture book market. So there was much rejoicing when, in 1923, C. B. Falls's *ABC Book* with its boldly colored woodcuts was published in this country. Only a few persons knew that it was a rather poor copy of William Nicholson's *Alphabet* (1898) and his *Square Book of Animals*, both published in England.[21]

William Nicholson is credited with creating the first true picture book, *Clever Bill*, published in England in 1926 and in New York in 1927. Farrar, Straus reissued this book in 1972, including the following statement by Maurice Sendak on the jacket flap: "*Clever Bill*, I have long felt, is among the few perfect picture books ever created for children." At most, the text of this book is only two long run-on sentences. The illustrations carry the story of a little girl who goes to visit her aunt and leaves her favorite toy soldier at home. The toy runs after her and is "just in time to meet her train at Dover." Wanda Gág's delightful tale *Millions of Cats*, published in 1928, has been called the first American picture storybook. This is an outstanding example of how text and pictures work together. In the unfolding drama a very old man goes in search of the most beautiful cat in the world. The long horizontal format enabled Gág to spread the journey over both pages. Like a folktale with its repetition and refrain of "hundreds of cats, thousands of cats, millions and billions and trillions of

[21]See discussion and illustrations in Barbara Bader's *American Picturebooks from Noah's Ark to the Beast Within* (New York: Macmillan, 1976), p. 24.

Wanda Gág's delightful tale *Millions of Cats*, published in 1928, has been called the first American picture storybook.
From *Millions of Cats* by Wanda Gág. Copyright © 1977 The Putnam & Grosset Group, New York, NY. Reprinted by permission.

cats," the story is still popular with children today. It opened the door to what was to become a treasure house of beauty and enjoyment for children, the modern picture storybook.

Progressive education and the growth of the nursery school movement made an impact on the development of books for the preschool child. Lucy Sprague Mitchell of the Bank Street School published her *Here and Now Story Book* in 1921. She pointed out the young child's preoccupation with self and interest in daily experiences. Her collection of stories provided simple little tales of the small child's everyday activities. None of them have lasted, but Mitchell did conduct classes on writing for children, which Margaret Wise Brown attended. When William Scott and his partner decided to start a new firm to publish books just for the very young child, Mrs. Mitchell recommended Margaret Wise Brown. Their first success and breakthrough book for young children was Brown's *The Noisy Book* (1939). In this story a little dog has bandaged eyes and must guess at the noises he hears, as must the child listening to the story. These books (there are seven in the series) invited participation by the child reader-listener.

Writing under her own name and three pseudonyms, Margaret Wise Brown created nearly a hundred books. Her most frequent illustrator was Leonard Weisgard, who won the Caldecott Medal for their book *The Little Island* (1946). Many of her books are still popular today, including *Goodnight Moon* (1947), the most favorite bedtime story of all, and *The Runaway Bunny* (1942) and *The Little Fur Family* (1946). After Brown's untimely death at 42, William Scott wrote: "All her books have an elusive quality that was Margaret Wise Brown. . . . [They have] simplicity, directness, humor, unexpectedness, respect for the reader and a sense of the importance of living."[22]

Other author-illustrators of this period include Marjorie Flack, who, like Margaret Wise Brown, knew how to tell a good story for preschoolers. Her *Angus and the Ducks* (1930) and *Ask Mr. Bear* (1952) are still shared with youngsters. Kurt Wiese illustrated her popular *The Story About Ping* (1933), the little runaway duck on the Yangtze River. Lois Lenski began creating her picture storybooks *The Little Family* (1932) and *The Little Auto* (1934) at about this time. These pictured 5-year-olds as little adults doing what young children wished they could do, such as drive a car, sail a boat, or be a fireman.

Machines became popular characters in such books as Watty Piper's *The Little Engine That Could* (1929), Hardie Gramatky's *Little Toot* (1930), and Virginia Lee Burton's *Mike Mulligan and His Steam Shovel* (1939). In *The Little House* (1942), Burton personified a house, which was first built in the country, then engulfed by the city, and finally rescued and returned to the country again. This story, which won the Caldecott Medal, has been called a child's first sociology book.

Dr. Seuss wrote and illustrated the first of many hilarious rhymed stories for children, *And to Think That I Saw It on Mulberry Street*, in 1937. That delightful daredevil Madeline appeared on the Paris streets in 1939. Though *Madeline* was not Ludwig Bemelmans's first book, it is certainly his best known. Robert McCloskey's ducklings made their difficult journey across Boston streets in 1941. *Make Way for Ducklings* richly deserved the Caldecott Medal it received. In the same year H. A. Rey introduced the antics of everyone's favorite monkey in *Curious George*.

During the late 1930s and early 1940s the United States benefited from the influx of many fine European artists seeking political refuge in this country. These artists found a legitimate outlet for their creative talents in the field of children's literature. Picture storybooks were greatly enriched through their unique contributions. A glance at a roster of some of the names of well-known illustrators indicates the international flavor of their backgrounds: d'Aulaire, Duvoisin, Eichenberg, Mordvinoff, Petersham, Rojankovsky, Simont, Shulevitz, Slobodkin, and many more. Certainly the variety of their national backgrounds has added a flavor to our picture books that is unprecedented in both time and place. American children have become the beneficiaries of an inheritance from the whole artistic world.

The Growth of Informational Books

Increased understanding of human development brought the recognition that the child was naturally curious and actively sought information. No longer did a discussion of nature have to be disguised as "an exciting walk with Uncle Fred," who lectured on the flowers and trees. Children enjoy facts, and they eagerly accept information given to them in a straightforward manner.

E. Boyd Smith created some of the earliest information picture books in *The Farm Book* (1910), *Chicken World* (1910), *The Seashore Book* (1912), and *The Railroad Book* (1913). The illustrations for these stories were large, colored double-page spreads filled with fascinating

---

[22]Louise Seaman Bechtel, "Margaret Wise Brown, 'Laureate of the Nursery,'" *Horn Book Magazine*, June 1958, p. 184.

E. Boyd Smith was one of the first Americans to produce artistic and accurate informational picture books. *The Railroad Book* was first published in 1913.

detail. His *Chicken World* tells the life story of a chick, ending with a roast bird on a platter. *The Railroad Book* helps its readers visualize all the details of a train trip, whether they have had that experience or not.

From Sweden came a translation of *Pelle's New Suit* (1929) by Elsa Beskow. Large colored pictures illustrate the process of making clothes, beginning with the shearing of Pelle's lamb, carding the wool, spinning it, dyeing it, weaving the cloth, and making the suit, and ending with a bright Sunday morning when Pelle wears his new suit. It is interesting for children to compare this book, which can still be found in libraries today, with Tomie de Paola's *"Charlie Needs a Cloak"* (1974). Maud and Miska Petersham used rich vivid colors on every page of their informational books, which frequently described processes. Their books *The Story Book of Things We Use* (1933), *The Story Book of Wheels, Trains, Aircraft* (1935), *The Story Book of Foods from the Field* (1936), and *The Story Book of Things We Wear* (1939) spawned

some fifteen smaller books and were the predecessors of Holling C. Holling's beautifully illustrated story of the travels of a little carved canoe, *Paddle to the Sea* (1941), which gave rich geographical information on the Great Lakes region, and *Tree in the Trail* (1942), which provided much information of historical interest about the Southwest.

W. Maxwell Reed, a former professor at Harvard, started to answer his nephew's questions in a series of letters that resulted in two books, *The Earth for Sam* (1932) and the popular *Stars for Sam* (1931). These books exemplify the beginnings of accurate informational books written by recognized authorities in the field.

As a result of the preschool movement with its emphasis on the "here and now," very young children also had their informational books. Mary Steichen Martin produced *The First Picture Book: Everyday Things for Babies* (1930) and *The Second Picture Book* (1931); while her photographer father, Edward Steichen, provided the pictures of such common objects as a cup of milk with a slice of bread and butter, a faucet with a bar of soap, a glass holding a toothbrush, and a brush and comb set. No text accompanied these pictures, which were clear enough to provoke recognition and discussion for the child. Their books paved the way for other photographic information books, such as Lewis W. Hine's *Men at Work* (1932), which pictured train engineers, workers on a skyscraper, and cowboys. Harriet Huntington's book *Let's Go Outdoors* (1939) portrayed close-up pictures of bugs and flowers just as a child might discover them on a nature walk. Her style of contrasting a primary object in sharp focus against a blurred background is similar to the contemporary work of Tana Hoban. Henry Kane's fine close-ups of a mouse and frog in his *Tale of the Whitefoot Mouse* (1940) and *The Tale of a Bullfrog* (1941) started the trend to create photographic stories of individual animals.

New books for social studies included *America: Adventures in Eyewitness History* (1962) and *Africa: Adventures in Eyewitness History* (1963), both by Rhoda Hoff. These books, based on original sources, recognized children's ability to read complex materials and draw their own conclusions about history. Alex Bealer's *Only the Names Remain: The Cherokees and the Trail of Tears* (1972) was representative of a new emphasis on readable, carefully documented history. It also attempted to balance recorded history by presenting a Native American point of view.

Biographies appeared to satisfy children's interest in national heroes. Ingri and Edgar Parin d'Aulaire, who had lived in Norway and in many other parts of Europe, were fascinated with the heroes of the New World. They presented somewhat idealized images in their large picture-book biographies *George Washington* (1930), *Abraham Lincoln* (1939), *Leif the Lucky* (1941), *Pocahontas* (1949), and many more. These stories were new to them, so they were perhaps freer to interpret the lives afresh, seeing them as a child discovers them for the first time. James Daugherty portrayed many American pioneers with strong vibrant pictures and ringing epic prose. His *Daniel Boone* (1939) was awarded the Newbery Medal.

The Childhood of Famous Americans series initiated the trend of publishing biographies for boys and girls in series form. By the 1960s, biographies gave less emphasis to the early years of great men and women. More biographies for young children became available, including such lively and authentic books as Jean Fritz's *And Then What Happened, Paul Revere?* (1973) and *Poor Richard in France* (1973) by F. N. Monjo. Biographies of civil rights leaders honored Martin Luther King, Jr., and

Rosa Parks. There was more concern to publish biographies about women, and Crowell began their Women in America series.

Early in the twentieth century, historical fiction also served to give children details about the past. Laura Richards quoted from diaries and letters as she wrote *Abigail Adams and Her Times* (1909). A historical overview was provided in Hendrik Van Loon's *The Story of Mankind* (1921), the first Newbery Medal winner. Starting with *Little House in the Big Woods* (1932), Laura Ingalls Wilder gave children detailed descriptions of life on the midwestern frontier in her remarkable series of Little House books. Elizabeth Coatsworth began her Away Goes Sally series in 1934. Carol Ryrie Brink wrote of a vivacious tomboy in *Caddie Woodlawn* the following year. Forty years later, most historical fiction was more concerned with social conscience than with personal issues. The Newbery Medal winner for 1974, *The Slave Dancer* by Paula Fox, realistically faced up to the wrongs of the past. Celebration of the Bicentennial spurred publication of many attractive and authentic books on eighteenth-century America.

There is no accurate accounting of the number of nonfiction children's titles that are published, in contrast to fiction titles, but a survey of the new titles would suggest that most of the children's books published today could be classified as informational.

The Proliferation of Series Books

The dime novel was initiated in the nineteenth century, and the series books of George Henry, Oliver Optic, and Horatio Alger introduced the repetitive incident plot and stereotyped characters. In the twentieth century, "fiction factories" were developed by Edward Stratemeyer, who manufactured the plots for literally hundreds of books, including *The Rover Boys* (1899–1926), *The Bobbsey Twins* (1904–   ), the Tom Swift series (1910–1941), and *The Hardy Boys* (1927–   ), to name just a few. Using a variety of pseudonyms, Stratemeyer would give hack writers a three-page outline of characters and plot to complete. When he died in 1930, a millionaire, he had himself written or conceived for others to write more than 1,300 fifty-cent juveniles. His daughter, Harriet Stratemeyer Adams, continued his work, writing nearly 200 children's books, including the well-known Nancy Drew series (1930–   ), until her death at 89 in 1982. In all her books, Mrs. Adams portrayed an innocent, affluent, and secure world. The original Nancy Drew could be kidnapped, knocked unconscious, and locked in a room with no way to escape, but she always solved the crime and survived to spend another day chasing villains in her blue roadster. Although modern versions of the series books deal with nuclear war, space flights, and submarines, the plots and characters are much the same. The hero or heroine is always a child or adolescent acting with adult wisdom and triumphing over all obstacles—unaided, undaunted, undefeated. Despite bitter criticism from literary critics, these books have been translated into many languages and continue to be sold in our country and throughout the world. They have found their modern-day counterparts in Ann Martin's Baby-Sitters Club series, R. L. Stine's Goosebump series, and other popular series.

Books that met with literary approval were also sold in series. The Lucy Fitch Perkins Twins series, beginning in 1911 with *The Dutch Twins*, provided authentic information on children of other lands in the form of an interesting realistic story. The series included books at various levels of difficulty; the story of *The Scotch Twins* (1919) was more complex, for example, than that of *The Dutch Twins*. The author also wrote stories of twins living in various historical periods, such as *The Puritan Twins* (1921) and *The Pioneer Twins* (1927).

Folktales of the World

The publication of Grimm's *Household Tales* in the early part of the nineteenth century represented only the beginning of interest in recording the told tale. Not until the twentieth century would children have access to the folktales of almost the entire world. A famous storyteller, Gudrun Thorne-Thomsen, recorded stories from Norway in *East o' the Sun and West o' the Moon* in 1912. Kate Douglas Wiggin edited tales from the *Arabian Nights* in 1909, and Ellen Babbitt brought forth *Jataka Tales*, a collection of tales from India, in 1912. Constance Smedley provided children with stories from Africa and Asia in her *Tales from Timbuktu* (1923). The next year, Charles Finger published stories that he had collected from Indians in South America in his Newbery Medal book *Tales from Silver Lands* (1924).

Pura Belpré grew up in Puerto Rico in a family of storytellers and later told these stories to American children in library story hours. Finally they were published in a collection called *The Tiger and the Rabbit* (1946). Philip Sherlock, vice principal of the University College of the West Indies in Jamaica, told stories of his homeland at a meeting of the American Library Association. A children's book editor heard him and persuaded him to write them down; they were published as *Anansi: The Spider Man* in 1954. Harold Courlander, a folklorist and musicologist, gathered many fine collections of stories in West Africa, Ethiopia, Indonesia, Asia, and the islands of the Pacific. His first collection of tales for children was *Uncle Bouqui of Haiti* (1942).

Courlander worked like the Grimm brothers, collecting his stories from the native storytellers of the country. The tales in *The Terrapin's Pot of Sense* (1957) were collected from African American storytellers in Alabama, New Jersey, and Michigan. Courlander related these stories to their origins in Africa in his interesting notes at the back of the book.

Lim Sian-Tek, a Chinese writer, spent ten years gathering many different Chinese myths, legends, and folktales from her country. These were introduced to American children in *Folk Tales from China* (1944). Frances Carpenter made "Grandmother" collections, such as her *Tales of a Chinese Grandmother* (1949). *The Dancing Kettle and Other Japanese Folk Tales* (1949) contains the favorite stories from Yoshiko Uchida's childhood. She also adapted old Japanese tales for American children in her popular *Magic Listening Cap* (1955) and *The Sea of Gold* ([1965] 1985). Alice Geer Kelsey introduced American children to the humorous tales of the Hodja of Turkey and the Mullah of Persia in *Once the Hodja* (1943) and *Once the Mullah* (1954).

Many other collections continue to be published each year, presenting American children with the folklore of the world. They also serve as source material for the many individual folktale picture storybooks that became so popular in the second half of the century.

Marcia Brown developed this trend of illustrating single folktales in a picture-book format with her publication of the French tale of trickery *Stone Soup* (1947). Her *Cinderella* (1954) and *Once a Mouse* (1961) won

Marcia Brown's portrayal of three soldiers clever enough to make soup from a stone helped start a trend toward illustrating single folktales as picture books.

Caldecott Medals; her other fairy tales, *Puss in Boots* and *Dick Whittington and His Cat,* were Caldecott Honor Books. Other illustrators who have brought children richly illustrated picture-book fairy tales include Felix Hoffman, Adrienne Adams, Paul Galdone, Errol LeCain, Nonny Hogrogian, Margot Zemach, and Steven Kellogg.

Greater emphasis was placed on individual African folktales, Jewish folktales, and legends of Native Americans during the decades of the 1960s and 1970s. Gail Haley won the Caldecott Medal in 1971 for *A Story, a Story,* an African tale of Anansi; *Anansi the Spider* by Gerald McDermott won an Honor Medal in 1973. Leo and Diane Dillon were Caldecott Medal winners for *Why Mosquitoes Buzz in People's Ears* (1975), an African tale retold by Verna Aardema. Two Jewish tales, *The Golem* (1976) by Beverly Brodsky McDermott and *It Could Always Be Worse* (1977) by Margot Zemach, were Honor Books. Folktales from around the world are not only an established part of children's literature but a frequently honored genre.

Fantasy

Fantasy for children in the first half of the twentieth century seemed to come mainly from the pens of English writers. Kipling stimulated the child's imagination with his *Just So Stories* (1902), humorous accounts of the origins of animal characteristics—how the elephant got a trunk or the camel a hump. Much of the delight of these stories is in Kipling's use of rich language like "great grey-green, greasy Limpopo River all set about with fever-trees."

Another English storyteller, Kenneth Grahame, brought to life for his son the adventures of a water rat, a mole, a toad, and a badger. *The Wind in the Willows* was published in 1908 with pictures by Ernest Shepard. This story of four loyal friends became a children's classic and has been reissued in a variety of editions. Individual chapters have also been published as picture books. Obviously *The Wind in the Willows* continues to delight new generations of children.

The boy who refused to grow up and lose the beauties of Never Never Land, Peter Pan, first appeared in a London play by J. M. Barrie in 1904. Later the play was made into a book titled *Peter Pan in Kensington Gardens* (1906), with elaborate illustrations by Arthur Rackham. Darton maintains that *Peter Pan,* though in the form of a play, "has influenced the spirit of children's books, and the grown-up view of them, more powerfully than any other work except the *Alices* and Andersen's *Fairy Tales.*"[23]

The Wizard of Oz by L. Frank Baum has been called the first American fantasy. Published in 1900, this highly inventive story of the Cowardly Lion, the Tin Woodsman, the Scarecrow, and Dorothy in the Land of Oz has been enjoyed by countless children. Several publishers felt *The Wizard of Oz* was too radical a departure from the literature of the day and refused to publish it. Baum and the illustrator W. W. Denslow finally agreed to pay all the expenses if one small Chicago firm would print it. Within two months of publication, the book had been reprinted twice. The first book of the series is the best and might well have sufficed, but Baum created thirteen more titles; and after his death at least twenty-six others were added to the series by Ruth Plumly Thompson, John R. Neill, and others. The 1939 film version of *The Wizard of Oz,* starring Judy Garland, has helped to keep interest in this book alive.

Talking animals have always appealed to children. Hugh Lofting created the eccentric Dr. Dolittle, who could talk to animals as well as understand their languages. In *The Story of Dr. Dolittle* (1920), Lofting describes the way Dolittle learns the animals' languages with the help of the parrot Polynesia and begins his animal therapy. There were ten books in this series; the second one, *The Voyages of Doctor Dolittle* (1922), won the Newbery Medal. Later readings would reveal racial stereotypes in these books, but readers in the 1920s were not alert to such flaws in writing.

Remembering her love of toys, Margery Williams wrote *The Velveteen Rabbit* (1922) while living in England. This story, with its moving description of what it means to be real, has delighted children and adults. It was first illustrated by William Nicholson. More recent editions display the work of Michael Hague (1983), David Jorgensen (1985), and Ilse Plume (1987).

One of the most delightful stories of well-loved toys is A. A. Milne's *Winne the Pooh,* which he wrote for his son in 1926. Eeyore, Piglet, and Pooh may be stuffed animals, but they have real, believable personalities. Their many adventures in the "100 Aker Wood" with Christopher Robin have provided hours of amusement for both children and the parents and teachers fortunate enough to have shared these stories with boys and girls. Ernest Shepard created unsurpassed illustrations of these lovable toys.

Many American children found the books by Walter Brooks about Freddy the Pig highly entertaining. Starting with *To and Again* (1927), Brooks created some twenty-five novels about high jinks on Mr. Bean's farm. Some of these books were reissued in 1986. Robert Lawson's *Rabbit Hill* (1944) and *The Tough Winter* (1954) captured the feelings and thoughts of the little wild animals that lived in the Connecticut meadows, farms, and woods near his house.

---

[23]Darton, *Children's Books in England,* p. 309.

All these stories paved the way for the most loved animal fantasy to be written by an American, E. B. White's *Charlotte's Web* (1952). This book, with its multiple themes of friendship, loyalty, and the celebration of life, is now delighting new generations of children.

Other significant fantasy appearing in the twentieth century certainly must include J. R. R. Tolkien's *The Hobbit* (1937), first discovered by college students and only recently shared with children, and *The Little Prince* by Antoine de Saint-Exupéry, which also appealed primarily to adults. Translated in 1943 from the French, this tale of a pilot's encounter with a Little Prince, who lived alone on a tiny planet no larger than a house, is really a story of the importance of uniqueness and love.

Fantasy in the third quarter of the century emphasized serious themes. C. S. Lewis's *The Lion, the Witch, and the Wardrobe* (1950) was the first of seven books about the imaginary kingdom of Narnia. These popular fantasy adventure tales reflect the author's background as a theologian and carry strong messages about right and wrong. The term *high fantasy* came into use during the 1960s to describe books that took as their themes the battle between good and evil and other cosmic issues. The most memorable works of high fantasy in the United States were written by Madeleine L'Engle, Lloyd Alexander, Susan Cooper, and Ursula Le Guin (see Chapter 7 for further discussion of their work).

Poetry

The turn of the century saw the publication of the first work by a rare children's poet, Walter de la Mare's *Songs of Childhood* (1902). This was a poet who understood the importance and meaning of early childhood experiences. His poems can be mysterious, humorous, or delightfully realistic. De la Mare was also a master of lyric imagery; his often anthologized "Silver" paints a picture of the beauty of a moonlit night. In 1913 his *Peacock Pie* brought readers new melodies, nursery rhymes, and poems of enchantment.

Eleanor Farjeon, also English, was writing merry imaginative verse for children at the same time Walter de la Mare was creating his poetry. Her first published work was *Nursery Rhymes of London Town* (1916). *Joan's Door* was published ten years later and *Over the Garden Wall* in 1933. Many of these poems later appeared in a collection titled *Eleanor Farjeon's Poems for Children* ([1931, 1951] 1984). We remember her for such poems as "Mrs. Peck Pigeon," "Tippetty Witchet," and "The Night Will Never Stay."

Still another Englishman brought joy and fun into the nursery with *When We Were Very Young* (1924) and *Now We Are Six* (1927). A. A. Milne could tell a rollicking story, as in "Bold Sir Brian" or "The King's Breakfast" or "Sneezles," or he could capture a child's imaginative play, as in "Lines or Squares" and "Binker."

In the United States, Rachel Field, Dorothy Aldis, and Aileen Fisher were interpreting the delight of the child's everyday world. Frances Frost and Elizabeth Coatsworth were writing lyrical poems about nature. The transition in children's poetry from the didactic to the descriptive, from moralizing to poems of fun and nonsense, had at last been achieved. No longer were poems *about* children; they were *for* children.

The 1930s and 1940s saw many collections of poetry selected especially for children from the works of well-known contemporary poets. These included Edna St. Vincent Millay's *Poems Selected for Young People* (1917), Vachel Lindsay's *Johnny Appleseed and Other Poems* (1928), Carl Sandburg's *Early Moon* (1930), Sara Teasdale's *Stars Tonight* (1930), Emily Dickinson's *Poems for Youth* (1934), Robert Frost's *Come In and Other Poems* (1943) and later his *You Come Too* (1959), and Countee Cullen's *The Lost Zoo* (1940).

Hildegarde Hoyt Swift gave a poetic interpretation of African American experience in her book *North Star Shining* (1947), illustrated with powerful pictures by Lynd Ward. The Pulitzer Prize–winning African American poet Gwendolyn Brooks presented the poignant poems of *Bronzeville Boys and Girls* in 1956. Each of these poems carries a child's name as the title and is written as the voice of that child. Selected works by noted African American poet Langston Hughes were published for young readers in *The Dream Keeper* (1962).

Two fine poets for children, Harry Behn and David McCord, emerged during the early 1950s. Harry Behn's first book, *The Little Hill* (1949), consisted of thirty-three poems written for his three children. His other books of poetry ranged from pure nonsense to childhood memories to lyrical poems about nature. David McCord's poetry is more playful and humorous. McCord's verse includes poems about nature and everyday experiences and an interest in language and the various forms of poetry. His first book of poetry was *Far and Few: Rhymes of Never Was and Always Is* (1952).

In the 1960s, the publication of several collections of poems written by children reflected new interest in poetry. In 1966, Richard Lewis published his first volume of children's writing from around the world, *Miracles*. That same year the poignant poetry and drawings of the children imprisoned at the Theresienstadt concentration camp between 1942 and 1944 were published under the title *. . . I Never Saw Another Butterfly*. The strident voices of the protest of the 1960s were heard in *Young Voices* (1971), an anthology of poems written by fourth-, fifth-, and sixth-grade children. Nancy Larrick published a collection of poems written by American youth titled *I Heard a Scream in the Street* (1970).

Specialized collections of poetry celebrating the uniqueness of African Americans, Native Americans, Eskimos, and others were published in the 1960s and 1970s. These included Arnold Adoff's collection *I Am the Darker Brother: An Anthology of Modern Poems by Negro Americans*; Hettie Jones's *The Trees Stand Shining* (1971), a collection of Papago Indian poems; and Knud Rasmussen's recordings of virile Eskimo poetry in his *Beyond the High Hills: A Book of Eskimo Poems* in 1961. Two books about the uniqueness of girls marked a new awareness of feminist perspectives. *Girls Can Too* (1972) was edited by Lee Bennett Hopkins; *Amelia Mixed the Mustard and Other Poems* (1975) was selected and edited by Evaline Ness.

With such increased interest in poetry for children, it seems particularly fitting that the National Council of Teachers of English established the Excellence in Poetry for Children Award in 1977.

Realistic Fiction

One characteristic of books in the past was that they stayed in print for a long time and were read by generations of children. In the beginning of the twentieth century, children continued to derive pleasure from *Little Women* (1868) and the other Alcott books, Dodge's *Hans Brinker, or the Silver Skates* (1865), Spyri's *Heidi* (1884), and all the Frances Hodgson Burnett books, including *Little Lord Fauntleroy* (1886), *The Little Princess* (1905), and *The Secret Garden* (1910). Many of these titles continue to bring pleasure to children today.

Perhaps the success of the orphaned Little Princess accounted for the number of stories about orphans. L. M. Montgomery wrote the very popular story *Anne of Green Gables* (1908) about a young orphan girl living on Prince Edward Island in Canada. Seven sequels covered Anne's growing up, her adulthood, and her children. Montgomery also wrote *Emily of New Moon* (1923), the story of an orphan who had to draw straws to see which of the family relations would take her. Books were never written in the first person at this time, but Emily's letters to her dead father and her journal allowed the reader to enter into her thoughts and feelings in a way that anticipated the many first-person stories of contemporary children's books. Jean Webster's *Daddy-Long-Legs* (1912) is also a story of an orphan and her benefactor. *Pollyanna* (1913) by Eleanor H. Porter was another popular story of an orphan who must learn to live with two disagreeable spinster aunts. Her unfailingly optimistic way of coping made her name last longer than her story. The child in Dorothy Canfield's *Understood Betsy* (1917) was not an orphan, she was a sickly city child sent to live with relatives on a Vermont farm in order to regain her health. Lucinda of Ruth Sawyer's *Roller Skates* (1936) was not an orphan either but was left with her teacher and sister while her father and mother went abroad for a year in the late 1890s. Lucinda was an unforgettable character who loved life and people. Sawyer won the Newbery Medal for this book in 1937.

Kate Douglas Wiggin's *Rebecca of Sunnybrook Farm* (1903) epitomizes the happy family stories that were characteristic of the first half of the century. Carolyn Haywood began her many Betsy and Eddie stories, for younger children, in 1939 with *B is for Betsy*; these stories tell of simple everyday doings of children at school and home. In *Thimble Summer* (1938) Elizabeth Enright told an entertaining family story set on a Wisconsin farm. Enright's *The Saturdays* (1941) was the first of several stories capturing the joyous life of the four children of the Melendy family. In three books, *The Moffats* (1941), *The Middle Moffats* (1942), and *Rufus M* (1943), Eleanor Estes detailed the delights of growing up in West Haven, Connecticut. The four children, Jane, Rufus, Sylvie, and Joey, are clearly realized as individuals and grow up in ways consistent with their characters. Sydney Taylor's *All-of-a-Kind Family* (1951) and its sequels presented the adventures of five Jewish girls growing up on New York's Lower East Side.

Two humorous stories appeared at this time: Robert McCloskey's classic tale *Homer Price* (1943) about Homer's amusing adventures in Centerburg, and Beverly Cleary's *Henry Huggins* (1950). Both centered around all-American boys growing up in small towns, and they have remained popular with children for half a century.

Not all realistic fiction told happy or humorous tales of growing up in mainstream America. Realistic fiction often reflected war, depression, and contemporary social problems. As authors began to write more about the various ethnic and regional groups in our nation, children's books also reflected this interest. Lois Lenski pioneered in presenting authentic, detailed descriptions of life in specific regions of the United States. By living in the communities, observing the customs of the people, and listening to their stories, she was able to produce a significant record of American life from the 1940s into the 1960s. Her first book, *Bayou Suzette* (1943), was set in the Louisiana bayou country; *Strawberry Girl* (1945), which won the Newbery Medal, told of life among the Florida Crackers. *Judy's Journey* (1947), her most forceful book, concerned the plight of migratory workers. Doris Gates also dramatized the problems of migratory workers in her classic story *Blue Willow* (1940), named after the family's one prized possession, a blue willow plate. Eleanor Estes was one of the first to write about poverty and children's interrelationships in their closed society. Her book *The Hundred Dresses* (1944) enabled teachers to undertake and guide frank discussions of the problem of being "different."

Teaching Feature   Studying Books of the Past

Children in the fourth grade at the Martin Luther King, Jr., Laboratory School in Evanston, Illinois, were studying the past through the history of their families. Their teacher, Barbara Friedberg, shared with them books like *Miss Rumphius* by Barbara Cooney, *When I Was Young in the Mountains* by Cynthia Rylant, *Three Names* and *Sarah, Plain and Tall*, both by Patricia MacLachlan, and *The Night Journey* by Kathryn Lasky.

Together the teacher and children developed questions they could ask their parents or grandparents in an interview or letter. Here are some of the questions they included on their lists:

What were their favorite foods as children?

What did they do on their birthdays or special days?

What did they remember about their schools?

What were their favorite books to read?

What historic days do they remember?

The students made graphs and charts to depict what they found out. Some children, remembering the story of the samovar that the family saved in *The Night Journey*, asked their parents what was the oldest thing they had in their homes that had belonged to the family.

Frequently, the oldest things were books. Several children brought in the favorite children's books of both their parents and grandparents. They were excited to find out that their grandparents had read and enjoyed *The Secret Garden* by Frances Hodgson Burnett and *Little Women* by Louisa May Alcott. The children made a display of the old editions compared with their new editions. They also exhibited some of the textbooks that were used for reading instruction, including an old McGuffey Reader belonging to a great-grandparent, several Elson Readers that a grandmother had in her basement, and their parents' Dick and Jane readers.

Dating and labeling these books for display helped the students see how books had changed over the years. They became aware of how many more books they had than their grandparents had had, for example. But probably the greatest value of this focus unit lay in the discussions that took place between family members recounting the traditions and excitement of the "olden days."

Barbara Friedberg
Martin Luther King, Jr., Laboratory School
Evanston, Illinois

Until the 1950s and 1960s very few books portrayed African Americans or other racial minorities. Books that did portray blacks showed stereotypes—the bandanna-wearing fat mammy and the kinky-haired, thick-lipped "funny" boy. Such stereotypes were epitomized in the Nicodemus series written by Inez Hogan in the late 1930s with such titles as *Nicodemus and the Gang* (1939). The jacket of this book quotes part of a *New York Herald Tribune* review that said: "A story that will get itself remembered when some longer and louder ones are forgotten." Fortunately, Nicodemus and his gang, with their stereotyped names and exaggerated black dialect, have been forgotten. African American poet Arna Bontemps drew on authentic language patterns of the rural South in *You Can't Pet a Possum* (1934) and *Sad-Faced Boy* (1937). Unfortunately, his work has also been largely forgotten.[24]

The segregation of blacks was clearly shown in *Araminta* (1935) by Eva Knox Evans and the photographic essay *Tobe* (1939) by Stella Sharpe. It was nearly ten years later that blacks and whites were shown participating in activities together. The theme of *Two Is a Team* (1945) by the Beims is revealed in both the title and the action as a black boy and a white boy play together. Prejudice was openly discussed for the first time in Jesse Jackson's *Call Me Charley* (1945) and Marguerite de Angeli's *Bright April* (1946).

Mary Jane (1959) by Dorothy Sterling, *The Empty Schoolhouse* (1965) by Natalie Carlson, and *Patricia Crosses Town* (1965) by Betty Baum discussed the new social problems caused by school integration. By the mid 1960s, a few books showed African American characters in the illustrations, but they did not mention race in the text. Examples include *The Snowy Day* (1962) by Ezra Jack Keats, *Mississippi Possum* (1965) by Miska Miles, and Louisa Shotwell's *Roosevelt Grady* (1963). In the 1970s such books were criticized for "whitewashing" African Americans and attempting to make everyone the same. Books such as *Zeely* (1967) by Virginia Hamilton and *Stevie* (1969) by John Steptoe,

[24]See Violet J. Harris, "From Little Black Sambo to Popo and Fifina: Arna Bontemps and the Creation of African-American Children's Literature," *The Lion and the Unicorn*, 14 (June 1990): 108–127.

John Steptoe's *Stevie* was one of the first picture books to present an African American family through an insider's eyes. It was published before this gifted author/illustrator was 20 years old.

Copyright © 1969 by John L. Steptoe. Used by permission of HarperCollins Publishers, New York, NY.

both written by African American authors, captured something of the special pride of the African American experience in children's literature.

M. C. *Higgins the Great* by Virginia Hamilton, an African American author, won the Newbery Medal for distinguished writing in 1975. Two years later, *Roll of Thunder, Hear My Cry* by Mildred D. Taylor, another fine African American author, won the Medal. Books by and about African Americans had at long last received recognition. However, even today the number of African American authors is small when compared to the African American population of this country.

The "new freedoms" of the 1960s were reflected in both adult and children's books. The so-called new realism in children's literature can probably be dated from the publication of *Harriet the Spy* (1964) by Louise Fitzhugh. Harriet is an 11-year-old antiheroine who keeps a notebook in which she records with brutal honesty her impressions of her family and friends and characters in her New York neighborhood. Unlike Lucinda, who made friends with the people she met in *Roller*

Skates, Harriet spies on them. Harriet's parents are psychologically absent, being too engrossed in their own affairs to be overly concerned about their daughter's activities. Children readily identified with Harriet, for she had the courage to think *and* say the things they didn't dare to say, including swearing. Following the breakthrough made by *Harriet the Spy,* many long-standing taboos in children's literature came tumbling down.

Vera and Bill Cleaver wrote about death and suicide in *Where the Lilies Bloom* (1969) and *Grover* (1970); alcoholism and homosexuality are described in *I'll Get There, It Better Be Worth the Trip* (1969) by John Donovan; and *George* (1970) by E. L. Konigsburg includes divorced parents, a psychologically disturbed child, and LSD. In Judy Blume's popular novel *Are You There God? It's Me, Margaret* (1970), Margaret's vague interest in religion is overshadowed by the more immediate concern of when she will start menstruating. Blume's *Deenie* (1973) is primarily the story of a beautiful girl who discovers she must wear a back brace for four years. This story contains several references to masturbation. Even picture books reflected the impact of this new freedom. Mickey falls out of bed and out of his clothes in Maurice Sendak's *In the Night Kitchen* (1970). In *My Special Best Words* (1974) by John Steptoe, bodily functions are discussed naturally, as a slightly older sister tries to toilet train her younger brother.

The literature published for the child's expanding world reflected the changes and challenges of life in the mid twentieth century. Just as adult literature mirrored the disillusionment of depression, wars, and materialism by becoming more sordid, sensationalist, and psychological, children's literature became more frank and honest, portraying situations like war, drugs, divorce, abortion, sex, and homosexuality. No longer were children protected by stories of happy families. Rather, it was felt that children would develop coping behaviors as they read about others who had survived similar problems.

All these problems are legitimate concerns of childhood. They have always existed, but only in the last twenty-five years have they been openly and honestly written about in books for children. Further discussion of realism in children's literature will be found in Chapter 9.

An International Literature for Children

An exciting development in children's literature was the rise of international interest in children's books during the years after World War II. This was indicated by an increased flow of children's books between countries.

In 1950 *Pippi Longstocking,* by the Swedish author Astrid Lindgren, arrived in our country and was an immediate success. This was the beginning of many such exchanges.

The Mildred L. Batchelder Award for the most outstanding translated children's book, originally published abroad and then published in the United States, was established in 1966 by the Association for Library Service to Children of the American Library Association. It honored their retiring executive secretary, who had worked tirelessly for the exchange of books. This award has served as an impetus in promoting the translation of fine children's books from abroad. Such excellent books as *Friedrich* (1970) by Hans Richter of Germany and *Hiroshima No Pika* (The Flash of Hiroshima) (1980) by Toshi Maruki of Japan have been the recipients of this award.

Another indicator of the growing internationalism of children's literature during the 1950s was the number of congresses, book fairs, and exhibitions of children's books that were held around the world. The first general assembly of the International Board on Books for Young People (IBBY) was held in 1953. Jella Lepman, founder of the IBBY, maintained that the organization should serve as a world conscience for international children's books and call attention to the best in the field by awarding international prizes. Consequently, the IBBY awarded its first Hans Christian Andersen Medal to Eleanor Farjeon in 1956. In 1966 the IBBY decided to extend the award to include a medal for the most outstanding artist as well as author of children's books. Alois Carigiet was the first artist to receive this award. Then, in 1967, Jella Lepman created the annual International Children's Book Day, which was appropriately established on 2 April, Hans Christian Andersen's birthday.

In 1967 the Biennale of Illustrations in Bratislava, Czechoslovakia, (BIB) held its first exhibition. It is now scheduled to meet in the odd-numbered years, alternating with the IBBY congress. Other international displays include the annual Frankfurt Book Fair in September of each year and the Bologna Children's Book Fair in April.

The 1950s and 1960s, then, saw the formation of international organizations for the exchange and appreciation of children's books throughout the world. These developments paved the way for UNESCO to designate 1972 as International Book Year. Almost 250 years from the time Newbery first conceived of it, literature especially for children's enjoyment had achieved worldwide recognition. Literature for children has indeed come of age. The Resources for Teaching box "Landmarks in the Development of Books for Children" lists significant books and other events in the development of children's literature.

Recent Trends in Children's Books

As the twentieth century nears its end, several trends seem to be affecting the future direction of children's books. Changes in the way books are marketed, produced, and used by children are likely to affect the types of literature that children will enjoy in the twenty-first century.

Children's Books: Big Business

The publication and distribution of children's books is now big business. Enormous growth in children's book publishing occurred in the late 1980s; children's book sales skyrocketed to a billion dollars in 1990. The number of juveniles published in 1993 was over twenty times the number published in 1880.

The following statistics show the increased rate of growth in the publication of juveniles for over a century:[25]

1880	270
1890	408
1900	527
1910	1,010
1920	477
1930	933
1940	984
1950	1,059
1960	1,725
1970	2,640
1980	2,895
1990	5,000
1993	5,469

Recent years have also seen a dramatic increase in both high-quality and inferior paperbacks for children. Individual publishing houses are selecting some of the best of their previously published titles for reissue in paperback form. Increasingly, publishers are bringing out new titles in hardcover and paperback simultaneously. Some have instituted new divisions devoted exclusively to paperbacks. In addition, many paperback houses have started commissioning their own original books to be published directly in paperback. Some of these originals qualify as imaginative writing, but many of them are written to formula. Reminiscent of the many series churned out by the Stratemeyer Syndicate beginning in 1885, these books promise to be almost as popular.

[25]*The Bowker Annual of Library and Book Trade Information* (New York: Bowker, 1983, 1989, 1995).

Resources for Teaching
Landmarks in the Development of Books for Children

Before 1700

Oral stories told by minstrels—Beowulf, King Arthur, ballads, etc.

c. 700   Question-and-answer form of instruction—Aldhelm
c. 1200   *Elucidarium*, Anselm
c. 1290   *Gesta Romanorum* (Deeds of the Romans)
1387   *Canterbury Tales*, Geoffrey Chaucer
c. 1440   Hornbooks developed
1447   *A Book of Curteseye*, published by Caxton
1481   *Historye of Reynart the Foxe*, published by Caxton
1484   *The Fables of Aesop*, published by Caxton
1485   *Le Morte d'Arthur* (The Death of King Arthur), Malory
1548   *King Henry's Primer*
c. 1580s   Beginnings of chapbooks

Seventeenth Century

1646   *Spiritual Milk for Boston Babes . . .*, John Cotton
1659   *Orbis Pictus* (The World Illustrated), Johann Amos Comenius
1678   *The Pilgrim's Progress*, John Bunyan
c. 1686   *The New England Primer*
1697   *Histoires ou Contes du Temps Passé* (Stories of Times Past), Charles Perrault

Eighteenth Century

c. 1706   *The Arabian Nights*, translated into English
1715   *Divine and Moral Songs*, Isaac Watts
1719   *Robinson Crusoe*, Daniel Defoe
1726   *Gulliver's Travels*, Jonathan Swift
1729   *Perrault's Fairy Tales*, translated into English
1744   *A Little Pretty Pocket-Book*, John Newbery
1765   *The History of Little Goody Two Shoes*, published by John Newbery
1771   *The New Lottery Book of Birds and Beasts*, Thomas Bewick
c. 1780   *Mother Goose's Melody* (may have been Newbery)
c. 1786   *Mother Goose's Melodies*, Isaiah Thomas, American publisher
1789   *Songs of Innocence*, William Blake

Nineteenth Century

1804   *Original Poems for Infant Minds*, Ann and Jane Taylor
1807   *The Butterfly's Ball*, William Roscoe
1823   *A Visit from St. Nicholas*, Clement C. Moore
1823   *Grimm's Popular Stories*, translated by Edgar Taylor, illustrated by George Cruikshank
1846   *Book of Nonsense*, Edward Lear
1846   *Fairy Tales of Hans Christian Andersen*, translated by Mary Howitt
1848   *Struwwelpeter* (Shock-Headed Peter), Heinrich Hoffman (English translation)
1861   *Seven Little Sisters Who Live on the Big Round Ball That Floats in the Air*, Jane Andrews
1865   *The House That Jack Built, Sing a Song of Sixpence*, illustrated by Walter Crane
1865   *Alice's Adventures in Wonderland*, Lewis Carroll, illustrated by John Tenniel
1865   *Hans Brinker, or the Silver Skates*, Mary Mapes Dodge
1868   *Little Women*, Louisa May Alcott
1869   *Twenty Thousand Leagues Under the Sea*, Jules Verne
1871   *At the Back of the North Wind*, George MacDonald
1872   *Sing Song*, Christina Rossetti
1873   *St. Nicholas Magazine* begun, Mary Mapes Dodge, editor
1876   *The Adventures of Tom Sawyer*, Mark Twain

Resources for Teaching
Landmarks in the Development of Books for Children (continued)

1878   *Under the Window*, Kate Greenaway
1878   *The Diverting History of John Gilpin*, illustrated by Randolph Caldecott
1880   *The Peterkin Papers*, Lucretia Hale
1881   *Uncle Remus Stories*, Joel Chandler Harris
1883   *The Merry Adventures of Robin Hood*, adapted and illustrated by Howard Pyle
1883   *Treasure Island*, Robert Louis Stevenson
1884   *Heidi*, Johanna Spyri, translated by Louise Brooks
1884   *The Adventures of Huckleberry Finn*, Mark Twain
1885   *A Child's Garden of Verses*, Robert Louis Stevenson
1889   *The Blue Fairy Book*, Andrew Lang
1892   *The Adventures of Pinocchio*, Carlo Collodi
1894   *The Jungle Book*, Rudyard Kipling
1897   *Jeanne d'Arc* (Joan of Arc), Maurice Boutet de Monvel (English translation)
1898   *Wild Animals I Have Known*, Ernest Thompson Seton

First Half of the Twentieth Century

1900   *The Wizard of Oz*, L. Frank Baum
1902   *The Tale of Peter Rabbit*, Beatrix Potter
1902   *Songs of Childhood*, Walter de la Mare
1902   *Just So Stories*, Rudyard Kipling
1903   *Johnny Crow's Garden*, L. Leslie Brooke
1903   *The Call of the Wild*, Jack London
1903   *Rebecca of Sunnybrook Farm*, Kate Douglas Wiggin
1906   *Peter Pan in Kensington Gardens*, J. M. Barrie, illustrated by Arthur Rackham
1908   *The Wind in the Willows*, Kenneth Grahame, illustrated by Ernest H. Shepard
1910   *The Secret Garden*, Frances Hodgson Burnett
1910   *The Farm Book* and *Chicken World*, E. Boyd Smith
1921   *Here and Now Story Book*, Lucy Sprague Mitchell
1922   *Rootabaga Stories*, Carl Sandburg
1922   Newbery Medal established for most distinguished book for children
1924   *When We Were Very Young*, A. A. Milne, illustrated by Ernest H. Shepard
1926   *Winnie the Pooh*, A. A. Milne, illustrated by Ernest H. Shepard
1926   *Clever Bill*, William Nicholson
1928   *Millions of Cats*, Wanda Gág
1932   *What Whiskers Did*, Ruth Carroll
1932   *Little House in the Big Woods*, Laura Ingalls Wilder
1934   *The Little Auto*, Lois Lenski
1934   *Mary Poppins*, Pamela Travers
1935   *Caddie Woodlawn*, Carol Ryrie Brink
1936   *The Story of Ferdinand*, Munro Leaf, illustrated by Robert Lawson
1936   *Roller Skates*, Ruth Sawyer
1937   *And to Think That I Saw It on Mulberry Street*, Dr. Seuss
1937   *The Hobbit*, J. R. R. Tolkien
1938   Caldecott Medal established for most distinguished picture book for children
1939   *Madeline*, Ludwig Bemelmans
1939   *The Noisy Book*, Margaret Wise Brown, illustrated by Leonard Weisgard
1939   *Mike Mulligan and His Steam Shovel*, Virginia Lee Burton
1940   *Blue Willow*, Doris Gates
1941   *The Moffats*, Eleanor Estes
1941   *Make Way for Ducklings*, Robert McCloskey
1941   *Paddle to the Sea*, Holling C. Holling
1941   *In My Mother's House*, Ann Nolan Clark
1941   *Curious George*, H. A. Rey
1942   *The Little House*, Virginia Lee Burton

Resources for Teaching
Landmarks in the Development of Books for Children (concluded)

1943	*Johnny Tremain*, Esther Forbes
1943	*Homer Price*, Robert McCloskey
1944	*The Hundred Dresses*, Eleanor Estes, illustrated by Louis Slobodkin
1945	*Call Me Charley*, Jesse Jackson
1946	*Bright April*, Marguerite de Angeli
1947	*Stone Soup*, Marcia Brown
1947	*White Snow, Bright Snow*, Alvin Tresselt, illustrated by Roger Duvoisin
1947	*Judy's Journey*, Lois Lenski
1947	*The Twenty-One Balloons*, William Pène DuBois

Second Half of the Twentieth Century

1952	*A Hole Is to Dig*, Ruth Krauss, illustrated by Maurice Sendak
1952	*Charlotte's Web*, E. B. White, illustrated by Garth Williams
1952	*Anne Frank: The Diary of a Young Girl*, Anne Frank
1956	*Bronzeville Boys and Girls*, Gwendolyn Brooks
1957	*The Cat in the Hat*, Dr. Seuss
1959	*Tom's Midnight Garden*, Philippa Pearce
1962	*A Wrinkle in Time*, Madeleine L'Engle
1962	*The Snowy Day*, Ezra Jack Keats
1963	*Where the Wild Things Are*, Maurice Sendak
1964	*Harriet the Spy*, Louise Fitzhugh
1965	*Dorp Dead*, Julia Cunningham
1966	Mildred L. Batchhelder Award established for most outstanding translated book
1969	Coretta Scott King Award established for best African American children's literature
1969	*Stevie*, John Steptoe
1969	*Where the Lilies Bloom*, Vera and Bill Cleaver
1970	*Are You There God? It's Me, Margaret*, Judy Blume
1970	*In the Night Kitchen*, Maurice Sendak
1971	*Journey to Topaz*, Yoshiko Uchida, illustrated by Donald Carrick
1974	*Where the Sidewalk Ends*, Shel Silverstein
1974	*My Brother Sam Is Dead*, James and Christopher Collier
1974	*The Blanket*, John Burningham
1974	*M. C. Higgins the Great*, Virginia Hamilton
1975	*Why Mosquitoes Buzz in People's Ears*, retold by Verna Aardema, illustrated by Leo and Diane Dillon
1977	Excellence in Poetry for Children Award established by the National Council of Teachers of English
1980	*Hiroshima No Pika* (The Flash of Hiroshima), Toshi Maruki
1981	*A Visit to William Blake's Inn*, Nancy Willard, illustrated by Alice and Martin Provensen
1982	*Yeh-Shen: A Cinderella Story from China*, Ai-Ling Louie, illustrated by Ed Young
1985	*The Polar Express*, Chris Van Allsburg
1985	*Sarah, Plain and Tall*, Patricia MacLachlan
1986	*The Magic School Bus at the Waterworks*, Joanna Cole, illustrated by Bruce Degan
1987	*Lincoln: A Photobiography*, Russell Freedman
1987	*Mufaro's Beautiful Daughters: An African Tale*, John Steptoe
1988	*Stringbean's Trip to the Shining Sea*, Vera B. Williams, illustrated by Vera B. and Jennifer Williams
1990	*Baseball in April and Other Stories*, Gary Soto
1990	Orbis Pictus Award for outstanding children's nonfiction established by the National Council of Teachers of English
1990	*Black and White*, David Macaulay
1991	*Maniac Magee*, Jerry Spinelli
1991	*The Wall*, Eve Bunting, illustrated by Ronald Himler
1994	*Guests*, Michael Dorris
1994	*I Hadn't Meant to Tell You This*, Jacqueline Woodson
1994	*Earthshine*, Theresa Nelson
1994	*Christmas in the Big House, Christmas in the Quarters*, Patricia and Frederick McKissack

In 1994 one title of Ann Martin's Baby-Sitters Club, *The Baby-Sitters Remember*, sold 228,000 copies. A new phenomenon is the interest in ghost and horror stories, particularly R. L. Stine's Goosebump series. Of the top fifteen best-selling paperbacks in 1994, thirteen were Goosebump titles. At that point the series, which was begun in 1993, had sold 13,880,000 copies.[26]

Another factor hidden in the statistics is the large number of titles that go out of print each year. Although it appears that many more books are being published, title turnover is far greater today. The life of a modern book is seldom more than 5 years, in contrast to the 10- to 20-year life span of books in the mid twentieth century, or, in the case of the very early books, a 200-year life span. However, certain books do stay in print and continue to sell and sell. Judy Blume's publishers report that all her books have sold over 25 million copies. Shel Silverstein's poetry books have also sold over 25 million copies. The *Bowker Annual* listed nearly fifty hardcover children's books that had sold over 750,000 copies by 1985.[27] Heading the list was Beatrix Potter's *Tale of Peter Rabbit*, with 8 million copies; E. B. White's *Charlotte's Web* had sold over 1.5 million copies, and *Where the Wild Things Are* by Maurice Sendak had sold 1 million. Books by Dr. Seuss, Marguerite Henry, and Laura Ingalls Wilder are among the other titles in that rarefied company.

The health of children's literature can also be seen in the increasing number of children's bookstores and children's book fairs. Ten years ago the number of independent children's bookstores in the United States was less than a dozen or so; today the number is close to four hundred, not including the children's departments of larger bookstores and chains. Unfortunately, many large chain stores buy the cheaper books produced for mass marketing. This also applies to the jobbers whose entire business is supplying book fairs. Generally, book fairs sponsored by independent stores are more responsive to the schools' needs and provide better-quality books.

Another trend in publishing is the increased number of mergers between publishing houses and large conglomerates. Few independently owned publishing companies are left today. A publishing company owned by a large conglomerate must show a profit; it is measured against the success of other companies in the corporation, most of which have nothing to do with publishing. Many of these changes began in the late 1970s, when the cutback in federal assistance to education was felt in schools throughout the United States. To counteract the loss of school sales, publishers put more emphasis on the trade book market than ever before. In spite of the additional mergers and company changes needed to meet the economic pressures of recent years, children's book publishing was close to a $2 billion business in 1994.[28]

New Books for New Markets

As publishers have sought continued profits, they have searched for new markets. In the 1980s, as a result of the many research studies showing the value of reading aloud to young children and the interest of baby boomers in their new offspring, publishers discovered the infant market. Many companies are producing their own line of books for babies and toddlers. Helen Oxenbury's series of board books titled *Friends, Working, Playing, Dressing,* and *Family,* all published in 1981, were the first to portray the infant with her or his concerns and accomplishments. Oxenbury's husband, John Burningham, had done the same thing for toddlers in his little books *The Blanket* and *The Cupboard,* first published in England in 1974. The creation of these new books for the very young, plus the publication of such popular titles as Jim Trelease's *The Read-Aloud Handbook* (1995), contributed to a new awareness among conscientious parents of the value of reading aloud to youngsters.

Wordless books (many of them do contain some print in the introduction or afterword) first made their appearance in 1932 with *What Whiskers Did* by Ruth Carroll. This story of the adventures of a little Scottie dog was reprinted in 1965, when there was a greater emphasis on the importance of "reading pictures" in preparation for learning to read. The wordless books caught on, and the 1960s and 1970s saw a flood of them. Some of them, such as Mercer Mayer's series that included *A Boy, a Dog and a Frog* (1967), were amusing cartoon sequences; others, such as *The Snowman* (1978) by Raymond Briggs, reached a fine artistic level. Wordless books are no longer only for beginning readers—watch adults and older children pore over *Anno's Journey* (1978) by Mitsumasa Anno, David Wiesner's Caldecott Medal winner, *Tuesday* (1991), or *Window* (1991) by Jeannie Baker.

Some of today's "new" books are old books revisited. Toy books, including pop-up books and books with revolving pictures, are once again delighting children. Modern pop-ups tell a continuous story like Margaret Wise Brown's *Goodnight Moon Room* (1984) or they allow an artist to explore paper engineering through

---

[26] Diane Roback, "Lion King Roars, Goosebumps Soar," *Publishers Weekly,* 20 March 1995, pp. 517–523.

[27] *Bowker Annual* (1985).

[28] M. P. Dunleavey, "The Squeeze is On," *Publishers Weekly,* 9 January 1995, pp. 44–46.

Engineering techniques allow artists such as Robert Sabuda to experiment with three dimensional forms in *The Christmas Alphabet*.
From *The Christmas Alphabet* by Robert Sabuda. Copyright © 1994 by Robert Sabuda. Reprinted by permission of the Publisher, Orchard Books, New York.

such forms as alphabet books like Robert Sabuda's exquisite *The Christmas Alphabet* (1994). Unless very well designed and sturdy, these manipulative books are more appropriate for the entertainment of one child than for library use.

In general, reissues and new editions of old favorites appeal to adult book buyers because they are familiar. Today's editions of classic stories often have the added attraction of appearing with fresh illustrations. Recently even a few critically acclaimed picture books such as Alvin Tresselt's *Wake Up, City!* ([1957] 1989) have been reillustrated. Although Louis Slobodkin won the Caldecott Medal for his pictures in James Thurber's *Many Moons* (1943), the 1990 version of this book is newly illustrated by Marc Simont, another Caldecott Medal winner.

Walt Disney was the first to establish movie-related books, rewriting old classics to suit himself and giving them titles like *Walt Disney's Cinderella*. In 1994, books connected to the Disney movie *The Lion King* sold just under 10 million copies.[29] It is particularly unfortunate when this practice results in the distortion of a book noted for its literary merit. Robert O'Brien's *Mrs. Frisby and the Rats of NIMH* (1971), a Newbery Medal winner, appeared on the screen and then reappeared in book form as *The Secret of NIMH*. The focus of the story is changed, and even "Mrs. Brisby's" attempt to save her son Timothy's life relies on magic rather than on her own bravery, as in O'Brien's original book. A real concern is that children who read these spin-off books are under the impression that they have read the story as it was originally conceived—which is not true.

Another trend is the publication of the print book as a secondary form, a book based on a popular television show, film, or even video game. Frequently the result of this market-oriented approach to publishing is the packaging of cheaply produced books with other items such as plush toys, T-shirts, or greeting cards. Quality writing is seldom part of such a package. More and more often, however, even well-written books seem to have toys or games packaged with them. Major publishers such as Little, Brown and E. P. Dutton have established marketing partnerships with toy companies that make Legos and Playskool toys.

Shifts in Publishing Emphases

One of the most notable trends in children's books today is the dominance of picture storybooks and picture-book formats. Many publishers' catalogs show that a majority of their new titles are picture storybooks or profusely illustrated books. Also, editors report that it is typical to print many more copies of a new picture book than of a novel because picture storybooks are in far greater demand.

This emphasis on the visual is also evident in the tremendous increase in informational books published. It seems likely that the eye appeal of books like David Macaulay's *The Way Things Work* (1988) or the Eyewitness series from Dorling Kindersley Publishers has a lot to do with their success. Along with the increase in the number of high-quality nonfiction books has come increased recognition of their place as literature. Russell Freedman's *Lincoln: A Photobiography* (1987) was a Newbery Medal winner, and many other nonfiction titles are earning critical acclaim.

[29] Roback, "Lion King Roars, Goosebumps Soar," p. 517.

The publication of poetry books also enjoyed a growth spurt in recent years. Like informational books, most of these new titles, both collections and single poems in book form, feature attractive illustrations that claim as much attention as the words. The production of new editions of folk and fairy tales has expanded to include many more multicultural and global folktales. At the same time, myths, tall tales, and other lesser-known forms of traditional literature seem to be gaining ground. Two tall tales—Anne Isaacs's *Swamp Angel*, illustrated by Paul O. Zelinsky, and Julius Lester's *Iron John*, illustrated by Jerry Pinkney—were among the Caldecott Honor Books for 1994.

In books for middle-grade readers, recent years have seen greater emphasis on contemporary realistic fiction. The immensely popular series books, such as the Baby-Sitters Club, Sweet Valley Twins, and even the Kids of Polk Street School and the Pee Wee Scouts series for younger readers, are marketed directly to their audiences through paperback book clubs and bookstores. Hardcover titles cater to this "more of the same" impulse in middle-grade readers by providing many sequels, such as Betsy Byars's four books about Bingo Brown and James Howe's several Sebastian Barth mysteries. In general the content of realistic fiction has moved away from the narrowly focused "problem novel" of the 1960s and 1970s. The lighter fiction for elementary school readers today seems more innocent, and the serious fiction more realistically balanced, with characters less prone to despair than in the books of a decade or two ago.[30] Many sober themes remain, of course. Published in the mid 1990s, Theresa Nelson's *Earthshine* (1994) and Barbara Ann Porte's *Something Terrible Happened* (1994) dealt with parents with AIDS, and Jaqueline Woodson's *I Hadn't Meant to Tell You This* (1994) focused on sexual abuse.

Book Links editor Barbara Elleman suggests that as a result of the increased interest in multicultural literature, there has been a rise in historical fiction offerings in the 1990s.[31] Titles like Patricia and Frederick McKissack's *Christmas in the Big House, Christmas in the Quarters* (1994), Walter Dean Myers's *The Glory Field* (1994), and Laurence Yep's *Dragon's Gate* (1993) are examples of books by minority writers who are examining the stories of their own families and their ancestors, no matter how painful. In addition, authors are looking at other time periods as a way of examining concerns like gender issues. Avi's *The True Confessions of Charlotte Doyle*

(1990) and Karen Cushman's *The Midwife's Apprentice* (1995) and *Catherine Called Birdy* (1994) focus attention on women's roles in other centuries without sacrificing strength of character.

The return of many classic titles reflected the shift of the 1980s toward conservative values as well as a concern that children should not miss out on their literary heritage. It is a joy to have such books as *Treasure Island* and *Robinson Crusoe* back in print with their handsome N. C. Wyeth illustrations and to see new editions of *The Velveteen Rabbit* and others. At the same time, most of these books are available in libraries, and costly new editions might mean that new authors and artists are not being published. How many different editions of *The Secret Garden* do we need?

Changes in Writing and Illustration

Although conservative trends have influenced the content of recent books, writers and illustrators today have great freedom to experiment with style and format. For years it was assumed that all books for children should be told in the third person, past tense; children were not supposed to like introspective first-person accounts. The recognition and popularity of such books as *Meet the Austins* (1960) by Madeleine L'Engle and Judy Blume's *Are You There God? It's Me, Margaret* (1970) certainly put an end to this myth. Even historical fiction and biography have assumed this point of view in such books as *My Brother Sam Is Dead* (1974) by the Colliers and the biography *I'm Deborah Sampson* (1977) by Patricia Clapp. Some authors have also begun to make greater use of the present tense. Patricia MacLachlan's *The Facts and Fictions of Minna Pratt* (1988) and Crescent Dragonwagon's *Winter Holding Spring* (1990) both demonstrate how this device gives a sense of immediacy and intimate participation in the character's experience.

Another trend in writing can be seen in the books told from various points of view. Mary Stolz wrote two books about the same events but told from the different protagonists' points of view: *A Dog on Barkham Street* ([1960] 1985) and *The Bully of Barkham Street* ([1963] 1985). *The True Story of the 3 Little Pigs as Told by A. Wolf* (1989) by Jon Scieszka is a picture storybook that offers an unusual and very funny point of view. The use of shifting points of view, which can heighten the suspense of a story, serves the same purposes as flashbacks, cut-ins, and other devices on TV and in films. Avi's *Nothing but the Truth* (1991), a novel for older readers, uses this technique throughout.

Other experimentation in writing includes the telling of stories through letters and journals. Such an approach is not necessarily new. In *Little Women* (1868) Alcott

[30]See Liz Rosenberg, "It's All Right to Be Innocent Again," *New York Times Book Review*, 21 May 1989, p. 46.

[31]Barbara Elleman, "Toward the 21st Century—Where Are Children's Books Going?" *New Advocate* 8 (summer 1995): 151–165.

9

Nine mortars and some pestles were lined up in rows at the end of the market.

"Some of those would be good for Granny's kitchen," thought Emeka. "Then, when I visit her with my cousins, we could help her to pound up yams for supper.

"But with no money, I can't give her anything." He walked slowly up to his grandmother's house.

Pestles and mortars

Pestles and mortars are used for grinding up food. The wood-carver makes them from a tree trunk, hollowing out a piece very carefully to make the mortar. The pestle is shaped to make it easy to handle and to grind up different kinds of food.

In Ifeoma Onyefulu's *Emeka's Gift: An African Counting Story,* photographs convey detailed information and provide children with a pleasing visual experience.
From *Emeka's Gift: An African Counting Story* by Ifeoma Onyefulu. Copyright © 1995 by Ifeoma Onyefulu. Copyright © 1995 by Frances Lincoln Limited. Used by permission of Cobblehill Books, an affiliate of Dutton Children's Books, a division of Penguin USA Inc.

included a copy of the "Pickwick Portfolio," a newspaper the four sisters created, a round-robin story they all composed, many letters, and a copy of Amy's "will." The Newbery Medal winner *A Gathering of Days* (1979) by Joan Blos consists of imaginary entries from a New England girl's diary for the years 1830–1832. Karen Cushman's *Catherine Called Birdy*, the journal of a 14-year-old in the year 1290, received a Newbery honor medal in 1994. Beverly Cleary won the Newbery Medal in 1984 for her story *Dear Mr. Henshaw*, which consists mostly of a boy's letters to his favorite author and later of entries in his own journal. *Stringbean's Trip to the Shining Sea* (1988) by Vera Williams tells its story through the words and pictures on a sequence of postcards.

As authors tell stories in intriguing new ways, they may create books that are hard to classify according to traditional definitions of genre. For instance, several recent books have combined fantasy with historical fiction. *The Root Cellar* (1983) by Janet Lunn provides a mixture of modern-day living and the Civil War era. *The Devil's Arithmetic* (1988) by Jane Yolen takes a contemporary Jewish girl bored with her family's emphasis on their heritage and thrusts her back in time into a Polish village during World War II. However, Hannah does not lose the knowledge of her own time and is able to anticipate her own fate as she relives the heroic story of her namesake. These books use an element of fantasy to unite the past with the present and to capture contemporary children's interest in an earlier time.

Current books cross conventional genre lines in other ways as well. For instance, the boundaries between fact and fiction are crossed and recrossed by Joanna Cole and illustrator Bruce Degen in *The Magic*

School Bus Inside the Human Body (1989). In this informational adventure, Ms. Frizzle takes her young students on a fantasy field trip through the circulatory system of one of their classmates and brings them home again to an everyday world of group projects and science reports. Blends of story and information for younger children are offered in Lois Ehlert's *Feathers for Lunch* (1990) and other concept books. Books like this use a playful approach to draw readers into a content topic.

Illustrators have also departed from old notions about what is appropriate for a children's book. Earlier in this century, for instance, experts advised against photography in children's books. Photos were not clear enough or appealing enough for a young audience. Now, thanks to improved quality of reproduction and rising standards of artistry, informational books like Ifeoma Onyefulu's beautifully designed *Emeka's Gift* (1995) offer photos that are clear and aesthetically satisfying. Technological advances have also lifted restrictions and encouraged experimentation with new tools for picture making. Daniel Pinkwater illustrated his story *The Muffin Fiend* (1986) on his Macintosh computer. Alan Lee's illustrations for *The Mirrorstone* (1986) by Michael Palin and Marcus Pfister's *The Rainbow Fish* (1992) make use of holography. Paul Morin is able to use various materials in his textured paintings for books like Julie Lawson's *The Dragon's Pearl* (1993) because cameras, scanners, and other equipment, which can now efficiently reproduce illustrations created in any medium, have replaced the laborious hand preparation of color separations for the printer.

Although new uses of media may be the most noticeable change in illustrations, artists have also established a more important role for the visual element in telling

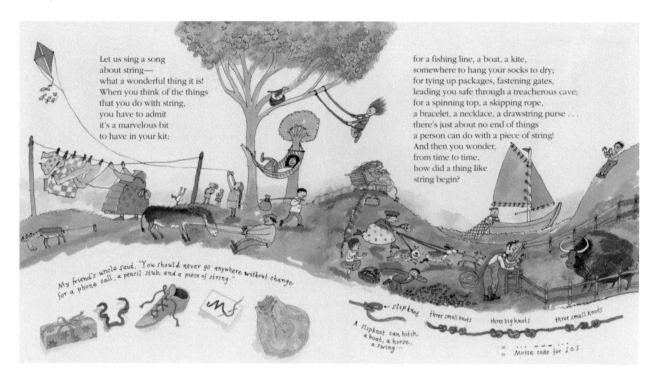

Margaret Chamberlain's lively drawings and pleasing composition bring the everyday topic of string to life in Judy Hindley's *A Piece of String Is a Wonderful Thing.*

A Piece of String Is a Wonderful Thing. Text copyright © 1993 by Judy Hindley. Illustration copyright © 1993 by Margaret Chamberlin. Reprinted by permission.

stories. In picture storybooks, some artists are creating more and more complex interactions between pictures and print, as David Macaulay does with the four intertwined, separately illustrated threads of story in his Caldecott Medal winner, *Black and White* (1990). Other generously illustrated books of the past decade or so stretch our ideas about what constitutes a picture storybook. In *City of Light, City of Dark: A Comic Book Novel* (1990), Avi, author of other innovative works such as *Nothing But the Truth*, teams with illustrator Brian Floca to stretch our ideas of what constitutes a novel. Margaret Chamberlain's beautiful illustrations for Judy Hindley's *A Piece of String Is a Wonderful Thing* are as well designed and artistically pleasing as any good picture storybook. Although these books can be classified as realistic fiction and nonfiction, they are also picture books in their own ways.

Increased Use in Schools

A noteworthy trend of the past several years is the growing use of children's trade books in classrooms—for reading instruction, integrated language arts programs, and a variety of uses across the curriculum. The whole language movement and new understandings about children's literacy learning have brought the use of real literature to the classrooms of many schools.

Unlike the 1960s, this is not a trend nurtured by government funds (which are largely unavailable now); it is nurtured by the grassroots interest of teachers and the encouragement of professional associations.

The actual extent of the use of children's books in instructional programs across the country is difficult to estimate, however, because many teachers use trade books on an individual basis rather than as part of a recognized program. Another complicating factor is that teachers and supervisors often use the same terminology to describe widely different practices.

The disturbing side of this trend is that some instructional programs use literature without regard for its imaginative and aesthetic characteristics. Some stories selected for "literature-based" basal texts are revised and adapted in ways that destroy their original merits.[32] In other instances, students read "real" books, but still use the same skill and drill activities that teachers were trying to avoid by switching from the basal textbooks. Uses of literature that ruin children's enjoyment of good books are a real disservice to children and to literature.

Children's books are now also part of many community literacy programs. During the 1980s, problems of

[32]Kenneth S. Goodman, et al., *Report Card on the Basal Readers* (Katonah, N.Y.: Richard C. Owen, 1988).

illiteracy in the United States were widely acknowledged. Government agencies with an eye to tight budgets worked to involve corporations and private foundations in assisting community and school efforts, particularly among the poor. First Lady Barbara Bush made the encouragement of family literacy a key project. Libraries, neighborhood groups, and businesses continue to sponsor a wide variety of reading-incentive programs like "Book It," which rewards children's reading accomplishments with free pizza from a nationwide chain.

Increased Censorship

An account of trends from the 1960s to the present would be incomplete without mention of the increase in censorship of books in schools and libraries. The number of book challenges has increased every decade since the 1950s. According to the American Library Association, about half of the censorship attempts in the United States succeed. It should be emphasized that censorship refers to an attempt to have a book removed from a library, not simply a complaint or challenge.

Most book challenges are directed at young adult books. However, as the new freedoms of the 1960s were reflected in children's books, censorship and book bannings became more common. Books can be objected to for almost any reason. Edward B. Jenkinson lists 116 targets of the censors, including profanity, conflicts with parents, drug use and abuse, homosexuality, violence, depressing stories of the ghetto, realistic dialogue, secular humanism, values clarification—and the list goes on.[33] Dictionaries, textbooks, trade books, and nursery rhymes have all come under attack.

Of all the children's authors who have come under attack, Judy Blume is cited most frequently. Her books have been challenged in Hanover, Pennsylvania, Peoria, Illinois, and Casper, Wyoming, to name just a few places. In some instances the books have been removed from the library; in other cases children have had to obtain parental consent to read them.[34] A survey in Ohio showed that even Newbery Medal–winning books like Jean George's *Julie of the Wolves* and Madeleine L'Engle's *A Wrinkle in Time* have been objects of censorship.[35] Jack Prelutsky's poetry books *Nightmares: Poems to Trouble Your Sleep* (1976) and *The Headless Horseman Rides Tonight* (1980) have also weathered attempts at censorship.

There is no doubt that censorship has been on the rise in American elementary schools during the last thirty years. The censors represent both conservatives and liberals. Many of them are administrators, teachers, and librarians themselves![36] For a further discussion of censorship and what you can do about it, see "Dealing with Censorship" in Chapter 13.

The Need for Multicultural Books

During the 1960s and early 1970s, federal support for children's libraries encouraged publishers to produce books about many ethnic groups. When these funds were drastically cut and bookstore sales began to play a bigger part in a book's success, publishers found that so-called ethnic books, which were selling poorly in the stores, were not profitable, and their publication figures dropped. In the wake of the civil rights movement, the influential Council on Interracial Books for Children had encouraged minority authors to write about their own cultures, yet by the late 1970s almost no new authors of color were being published. There are shockingly few books available that provide culturally authentic characters from African American, Hispanic, Asian, and Native American groups. Consider as an example the eligibility list for the Coretta Scott King Award. Every new publication by an African American author or illustrator is automatically considered. In 1985 only 18 books were eligible, and in 1990 the award committee could pick from only 38 titles out of the well over 4,000 books published in 1989.[37]

Some changes for the better began with the new decade. Predictions about the changing demographics of the school population and renewed demand by schools and libraries for multicultural books have led to more-active recruitment of authors from a variety of ethnic backgrounds and to better recognition of high-quality titles.[38] There is still a lack of cultural diversity among editors and other publishing professionals who make decisions about what books will be published and how they will be marketed. However, small presses such as Carolrhoda or Children's Book Press, with a commitment to multicultural publishing, have begun to make some impact, particularly in the realm of picture storybooks.

[33]Edward B. Jenkinson, *Censors in the Classroom: The Mind Benders* (New York: Avon, 1982).

[34]Judith F. Krug, ed., *Newsletter on Intellectual Freedom* 14 (March 1985): 1, 58.

[35]Amy McClure, "Censorship in Ohio: It *Is* Happening Here," *Ohio Reading Teacher* 16 (April 1982): 1–6.

[36]Lee Burress, "Appendix B," in *Battle of the Books* (Metuchen, N.J.: Scarecrow Press, 1989).

[37]Kathleen Horning and Clare Seguin, "The Search for Multiculturalism in Children's Books," *Rethinking Schools* (January/February 1991): 16.

[38]See titles such as Rudine Sims Bishop, ed., *Kaleidoscope: A Multicultural Booklist* (Urbana, Ill.: National Council of Teachers of English, 1994) and other books listed in Appendix B.

The recognition of need in the United States for literature that reflects cultural diversity extends to books from and about other countries. Global education is a curriculum concept that has made itself felt in the world of children's books. One result is a renewed interest in international literature, particularly in books like Beverley Naidoo's South African story *Journey to Jo'burg* (1986), Nina Ring Aamundsen's *Two Short and One Long* (1991), or Frances Temple's *Taste of Salt* (1993), which explore the human side of political conflicts and questions of justice.

The Development of a Multiliterate Society

Dire predictions have been made about the death of the book as we know it today; our society has been called a postliterate society. Modern technology has certainly affected literature and the arts, with developments like interactive fiction, where the "reader" responds to and actually creates plot variations for the story that appears on her computer screen. Computers can be programmed to generate poetry, pictures, and music. Some of these works meet high standards of artistry and receive appropriate critical recognition. With the rise of CD-ROMs, more publishers are putting popular books on disks. At this point, however, many of these programs represent glorified games rather than literary or artistic encounters.

Charles Suhor, deputy executive director of the National Council of Teachers of English, projects four possible scenarios for the role of print in the future, ranging from a technological takeover to books' remaining the core of educational material. His most recent conclusion is that "Ultimately, the new technologies will not be revolutionary, transforming, or pervasive in the schools. They will have a place, but that place will resemble at best a modified media center in which books, machinery, teachers, and students find more varied ways of relating to each other."[39]

It seems likely, then, that today's youth will become multiliterate, using the new technologies for the rapid retrieval of information of all kinds, for writing and editing their thoughts, for communicating about books with children in distant places, and for creating original programs of their own. But they will still need reading for a wide range of skills, and they will need books for pleasure. Just as many youth today are multilingual, so the youth of the future will become multiliterate, reading a wide variety of formats.

As we move toward the close of the century, the future of the book is uncertain. Computers, videotapes, cassettes, films, cable TV—all have the potential to give us instant information in many forms. Will the book be as important in the twenty-first century as it is today? Those of us who love literature and have witnessed its positive influence on children's lives can only hope that it will be—that it will continue to live and flourish.

[39]Charles Suhor, draft of unpublished paper, "The Role of Print as a Medium in Our Society," 41 pp., 1984.

Learning Experiences

1. Interview five adults of different ages and ask about their favorite childhood books and reading interests. How similar are their responses? How much overlapping of titles is there?

2. Conduct a survey of your literature class to find out how many students have read *Little Women, Alice's Adventures in Wonderland, The Wind in the Willows, Charlotte's Web,* or one of Judy Blume's books. Make a chart of your findings.

3. Prepare a display of early children's books; note the printing and binding, the illustrations, the subject matter. Display a varied selection of recent books as well. What contrasts do you see, and what similarities?

4. Identify adult purposes in several recent books for children. Can you find any examples of didactic stories written in the last ten years? Be sure to look at several books dealing with current social problems and environmental concerns.

5. Read and compare two books of realistic fiction with African Americans as major characters—one published within the last five years, the other published before 1960. How does each book specifically reflect the time in which it was written?

Continued

Learning Experiences

6. If possible, read two books aloud to a group of children. Choose one old book and one new, but on a similar theme, such as the books about quarreling in the introduction to this chapter. Elicit the children's responses. What do they see as differences? Which book do they prefer?

7. Read one of the new original paperbacks produced for a series. Compare it with a Nancy Drew book or a Sue Barton book. What similarities and differences do you see? Another person could compare it with a modern realistic story for children like those by Cynthia Voigt or Katherine Paterson. Again, how do they compare?

8. Plan a panel discussion on the role of the book in the future. What would you lose if you didn't have books?

9. Read a book that has been the object of censorship. Act out a meeting between a teacher or librarian and a concerned citizen. What are the steps that should be taken when someone objects to a book?

Related Readings

Ariès, Philippe. *Centuries of Childhood: A Social History of Family Life*. Translated from the French by Robert Baldick. New York: Knopf, 1962.

A definitive study of the development of the concept of childhood. Ariès maintained that childhood was not discovered until the seventeenth century. While some have disputed this claim, Ariès's book has formed the basis of most historical studies of childhood.

Bader, Barbara. *American Picturebooks from Noah's Ark to the Beast Within*. New York: Macmillan, 1976.

A comprehensive historical study of American picture books, including the influence of foreign artists, the impact of motion pictures and comic books, and the social scene. Over seven hundred illustrations, some in color, enable the author to discuss and show various styles of art. The emphasis is on books produced from the 1920s to the 1970s.

Bingham, Jane, and Grayce Scholt. *Fifteen Centuries of Children's Literature*. Westport, Conn.: Greenwood Press, 1980.

An indispensable reference book for the historical scholar of children's literature, providing an annotated chronology of both British and American books from A.D. 523 through 1945. The chronology is divided into six time segments. Historical background, the development of books, and general attitudes toward children are presented for each time period. Information is included on series books as well as those that became classics.

Carpenter, Humphrey, and Mari Prichard. *The Oxford Companion to Children's Literature*. Oxford: Oxford University Press, 1984.

An excellent reference source on many aspects of children's literature, including authors, illustrators, titles, and characters. The historical span stretches from early chapbooks through books published in the 1980s. Nearly two thousand entries are included in this one-volume reference source to children's literature.

Darton, F. J. Harvey. *Children's Books in England: Five Centuries of Social Life*. 3rd ed. Revised by Brian Alderson. Cambridge: Cambridge University Press, 1982 [1932].

This updated version of a well-recognized text on the history of children's literature in England makes fascinating reading. Darton had great respect for children's books, seeing their relationship to the history of children, the socioeconomic situation of the times, the cultural-religious beliefs of the period, and the history of publishing. Alderson added detailed notes to each chapter, but he did not revise the text. Therefore the reader does need to remember that the text's "now" and "today" refer to Darton's time, 1932.

Jackson, Mary V. *Engines of Instruction, Mischief, and Magic: Children's Literature in England from Its Beginnings to 1839*. Lincoln: University of Nebraska Press, 1990.

This readable scholarly work focuses on the economic, sociopolitical, and religious forces that helped to shape early children's books. Jackson's attention to issues of class distinction and debates about education provides a useful way to look at recent trends as well as titles of the eighteenth and nineteenth centuries.

Johnson, Diedre. *Stratemeyer Pseudonyms and Series Books*. Westport, Conn.: Greenwood Press, 1982.

This book provides an annotated checklist of the Stratemeyer syndicated publications, plus historical information on the growth of the company. The bibliography is arranged alphabetically by authors and pseudonyms, thus it is possible to see how many Laura Lee Hope books were published and note the various authors and publishers.

Lurie, Alison. *Don't Tell the Grown-Ups: Subversive Children's Literature*. Boston: Little, Brown, 1990.

In a collection of essays from the 1980s, this well-known scholar and novelist demonstrates that the enduring works of children's literature have been books that did not conform to the ideal values of their own time. She points to characters who are disobedient and who mock adult hypocrisy from folklore and fairy tales to the middle of the twentieth century.

Lystad, Mary. *From Dr. Mather to Dr. Seuss: 200 Years of American Books for Children*. Cambridge, Mass.: Schenkman, 1980.

Basing her conclusions on a content analysis of a thousand books chosen from a random sample of the juveniles in the Rare Book Collection of the Library of Congress, Lystad determined the social values and social behavior reflected in American children's books over the last two hundred years. She traces the changes in children's literature from the religious admonitions of Dr. Mather to the nonsense of Dr. Seuss.

Marcus, Leonard S. *Margaret Wise Brown: Awakened by the Moon*. Boston: Beacon Press, 1992.

Marcus's exhaustive, well-written, and engaging biography has detailed not only a writer's life but also a much broader portrait, one of the progressive education movement and of the major figures who created, influenced, and guided children's books during a most fertile period.

Meigs, Cornelia, et al. *A Critical History of Children's Literature*. Rev. ed. New York: Macmillan, 1969.

First published in 1953, this comprehensive history of children's literature was written and revised by four recognized authorities in the field: Cornelia Meigs, Anne Thaxter Eton, Elizabeth Nesbitt, and Ruth Hill Viguers. The organization by four chronological periods emphasizes the social trends influencing children's literature in England and America from earliest times to 1967.

Silvey, Anita, ed. *Children's Books and Their Creators*. Houghton Mifflin, 1995.

This beautiful book focuses on twentieth-century American children's books. It includes overviews of the types of books written for various ages; essays on issues, history, and genres; biographical information on important authors and illustrators; and essays by creators of children's books.

Smith, Elva S. *Elva S. Smith's History of Children's Literature*. Revised by Margaret Hodges and Susan Steinfirst. Chicago: American Library Association, 1980.

This very useful reference book on American and English children's books has been revised and enlarged by Hodges and Steinfirst. An introduction and outline for each period, ranging from Anglo-Saxon times to the close of the nineteenth century. Annotated references are provided for general works and individual writers of each period.

Townsend, John Rowe. *John Newbery and His Books*. Metuchen, N.J.: Scarecrow Press, 1994.

This collection of essays includes background and commentary on John Newbery by Townsend, edited chapters of Charles Welsh's 1885 biography of Newbery, and selections by Newbery contemporaries Samuel Johnson and George Coleman that give glimpses of this important figure in children's literature.

Townsend, John Rowe. *Written for Children: An Outline of English Children's Literature*. 4th ed. Revised. New York: HarperCollins, 1990.

Townsend supplies a readable overview of the development of children's books in England and America, with a brief nod at Canada and Australia. His critical comments add interest to the text and help to put the books in perspective. The survey ranges from before 1840 into the 1980s.

Children's Literature

The references for this chapter are limited to books still in print as the decade of the 1990s began. The dates in square brackets refer to the original publication of the text portion of the book.

Aamundsen, Nina Ring. *Two Short and One Long*. Houghton Mifflin, 1990.

Aardema, Verna. *Why Mosquitoes Buzz in People's Ears.* Illustrated by Leo and Diane Dillon. Dial, 1975.

Adoff, Arnold. *I Am the Darker Brother: An Anthology of Modern Poems by Negro Americans.* Macmillan, 1968.

Alcott, Louisa May. *Jo's Boys.* Penguin, 1984 [1873].

———. *Little Men.* Scholastic, 1987.

———. *Little Women.* Illustrated by Jessie Wilcox Smith. Little, 1968 [1868].

———. *An Old-Fashioned Girl.* Dell Yearling, 1987 [1870].

Alger, Horatio, Jr. *Struggling Upward.* Galloway, 1971 [n.d.].

Anno, Mitsumasa. *Anno's Journey.* Putnam, 1981 [1978].

Avi. *City of Light, City of Dark: A Comic Book Novel.* Illustrated by Brian Floca. Orchard, 1993.

———. *Nothing but the Truth.* Orchard, 1991.

———. *The True Confessions of Charlotte Doyle.* Orchard, 1990.

Baker, Jeannie. *Window.* Greenwillow, 1991.

Barrie, J. M. *Peter Pan in Kensington Gardens.* Illustrated by Arthur Rackham. Buccaneer Books, 1980 [1906].

Baum, L. Frank. *The Wizard of Oz.* Illustrated by Michael Hague. Holt, 1982 [1900].

Bealer, Alex. *Only the Names Remain: The Cherokees and the Trail of Tears.* Illustrated by William S. Bock. Little, Brown, 1972.

Bemelmans, Ludwig. *Madeline.* Viking Penguin, 1958 [1939].

Beskow, Elsa. *Pelle's New Suit.* Harper & Row, 1929.

Blos, Joan. *A Gathering of Days.* Macmillan, 1979.

Blume, Judy. *Are You There God? It's Me, Margaret.* Bradbury Press, 1970.

———. *Deenie.* Bradbury Press, 1973.

Briggs, Raymond. *The Snowman.* Random House, 1978.

Brink, Carol Ryrie. *Caddie Woodlawn.* Macmillan, 1970 [1935].

Brooke, Leslie. *Johnny Crow's Garden.* Warne, 1986 [1903].

Brooks, Gwendolyn. *Bronzeville Boys and Girls.* Illustrated by Ronni Solbert. Harper & Row, 1956.

Brooks, Walter. *Freddy and the Perilous Adventure.* Illustrated by Leslie Morrill and Kurt Wiese. Knopf, 1986.

Brown, Marcia. *Cinderella.* Macmillan, 1954.

———. *Dick Whittington and His Cat.* Macmillan, 1988 [1950].

———. *Once a Mouse.* Macmillan, 1961.

———. *Stone Soup.* Macmillan, 1947.

Brown, Margaret Wise. *Goodnight Moon Room.* Illustrated by Clement Hurd. Harper & Row, 1984.

———. *Goodnight Moon.* Illustrated by Clement Hurd. Harper & Row, 1947.

———. *The Little Fur Family.* Illustrated by Garth Williams. Harper & Row, 1985 [1946].

———. *The Noisy Book.* Illustrated by Leonard Weisgard, Harper & Row, 1939.

———. *The Runaway Bunny.* Illustrated by Clement Hurd. Harper & Row, 1942.

Bullard, Asa. *Sunnybank Stories: My Teacher's Gem.* Lee & Shepard, 1863.

Bunting, Eve. *The Wall.* Illustrated by Ron Himler. Clarion, 1991.

Burnett, Frances Hodgson. *Little Lord Fauntleroy.* Godine, 1993 [1886].

———. *The Little Princess.* Illustrated by Jamichael Henterly. Grossett, 1995 [1905].

———. *Sara Crewe.* Scholastic, 1986 [1888].

———. *The Secret Garden.* Illustrated by Tasha Tudor. Harper & Row, 1987.

Burningham, John. *The Blanket*. Harper & Row, 1976.

——— . *The Cupboard*. Harper & Row, 1976.

Burton, Virginia Lee. *The Little House*. Houghton Mifflin, 1978 [1942].

——— . *Mike Mulligan and His Steam Shovel*. Houghton Mifflin, 1939.

Byars, Betsy. *Bingo Brown and the Language of Love*. Viking, 1989.

Caldecott, Randolph. *Sing a Song of Sixpence*. Barron, 1988 [1880].

Canfield, Dorothy. *Understood Betsy*. Buccaneer, 1981 [1917].

Carlson, Natalie. *The Empty Schoolhouse*. Illustrated by John Kaufman. Harper & Row, 1965.

Carroll, Lewis [Charles Dodgson]. *Alice's Adventures in Wonderland*. Illustrated by Anthony Browne. Knopf, 1988 [1865].

——— . *Through the Looking-Glass*. Illustrated by John Tenniel. St. Martin's Press, 1977 [1871].

Cleary, Beverly. *Dear Mr. Henshaw*. Illustrated by Paul O. Zelinsky. Morrow, 1983.

——— . *Henry Huggins*. Illustrated by Louis Darling. Morrow, 1950.

——— . *Ramona and Her Father*. Illustrated by Alan Tiergreen. Morrow, 1977.

Cleaver, Vera, and Bill Cleaver. *Grover*. Illustrated by Frederic Marvin. Harper & Row, 1970.

——— . *Where the Lilies Bloom*. Lippincott, 1970.

Cole, Joanna. *The Magic School Bus at the Waterworks*. Illustrated by Bruce Degen. Scholastic, 1986.

——— . *The Magic School Bus Inside the Human Body*. Illustrated by Bruce Degen. Scholastic, 1989.

Collier, James L., and Christopher Collier. *My Brother Sam Is Dead*. Macmillan, 1974.

Collodi, Carlo. *The Adventures of Pinocchio*. Illustrated by Roberto Innocenti. Knopf, 1988 [1891].

Cooney, Barbara. *Miss Rumphius*. Viking, 1982.

Cooper, James Fenimore. *The Last of the Mohicans*. Illustrated by N. C. Wyeth. Scribner's, 1986 [1826].

Cunningham, Julia. *Dorp Dead*. Illustrated by James Spanfeller. Knopf, 1987 [1965].

Cushman, Karen. *Catherine Called Birdy*. Clarion, 1995.

——— . *The Midwife's Apprentice*. Clarion, 1995.

Dana, Richard Henry. *Two Years Before the Mast*. Airmont, 1985 [1840].

D'Aulaire, Ingri, and Edgar Parin d'Aulaire. *Abraham Lincoln*. Doubleday, 1957 [1939].

de la Mare, Walter. *Peacock Pie*. Illustrated by Edward Ardizzone. Faber & Faber, 1988 [1913].

——— . *Songs of Childhood*. Dover, n.d. [1902].

de Paloa, Tomie. *"Charlie Needs a Cloak."* Simon & Schuster, 1974.

de Saint-Exupéry, Antoine. *The Little Prince*. Harcourt Brace, 1943.

Dickinson, Emily. *Poems for Youth*. Illustrated by Doris Hauman and George Hauman. Little, 1934.

Disney, Walt (production staff). *Walt Disney's Cinderella*. Random House, 1974.

Dixon, Franklin W. *The Hardy Boys: Demon's Den*. 1984.

Dodge, Mary M. *Hans Brinker, or the Silver Skates*. Scholastic, 1988 [1865].

Donovan, John. *I'll Get There, It Better Be Worth the Trip*. Harper & Row, 1969.

Dorris, Michael. *Guests*. Hyperion, 1994.

Dragonwagon, Crescent. *Winter Holding Spring*. Illustrated by Ronald Himler. Macmillan, 1990.

DuBois, William Pène. *The Twenty-One Balloons*. Viking, 1947.

Ehlert, Lois. *Feathers for Lunch*. Harcourt Brace, 1990.

Enright, Elizabeth. *The Saturdays*. Holt, 1988.

——— . *Thimble Summer*. Holt, 1938.

Estes, Eleanor. *The Hundred Dresses*. Illustrated by Louis Slobodkin. Harcourt Brace, 1974 [1944].

——— . *The Middle Moffats*. Dell, 1989 [1942].

——— . *The Moffats*. Illustrated by Louis Slobodkin. Harcourt Brace, 1941.

——— . *Rufus M*. Illustrated by Louis Slobodkin. Harcourt Brace, 1943.

Farjeon, Eleanor. *Eleanor Farjeon's Poems for Children*. Harper & Row, 1984 [1931, 1951].

Field, Eugene. *Poems of Childhood*. Armont, 1969 [1896].

Finger, Charles. *Tales from Silver Lands*. Illustrated by Paul Honore. Doubleday, 1965 [1924].

Fitzhugh, Louise. *Harriet the Spy*. Harper & Row, 1964.

Flack, Marjorie. *Angus and the Ducks*. Macmillan, 1989 [1930].

——— . *Ask Mr. Bear*. Macmillan, 1986 [1932].

——— . *The Story About Ping*. Illustrated by Kurt Wiese. Viking Penguin, 1933.

Forbes, Esther. *Johnny Tremain*. Illustrated by Lynd Ward. Houghton, 1943.

Fox, Paula. *The Slave Dancer*. Illustrated by Eros Keith. Bradbury, 1973.

Frank, Anne. *Anne Frank: The Diary of a Young Girl*. Rev. ed. Doubleday, 1967 [1952].

Freedman, Russell. *Lincoln: A Photobiography*. Clarion, 1987.

Fritz, Jean. *And Then What Happened, Paul Revere?* Illustrated by Margot Tomes. Putnam, 1973.

Frost, Robert. *You Come Too*. Illustrated by Thomas W. Nason. Holt, 1959.

Gág, Wanda. *Millions of Cats*. Putnam, 1928.

Gates, Doris. *Blue Willow*. Viking Penguin, 1940.

George, Jean. *Julie of the Wolves*. Illustrated by John Schoenherr. Harper & Row, 1972.

Grahame, Kenneth. *The Wind in the Willows*. Illustrated by Ernest H. Shepard. Scribner's, 1983 [1908].

——— . *The Wind in the Willows*. Illustrated by Alex Tsao. Signet, 1989 [1908].

Gramatky, Hardie. *Little Toot*. Putnam, 1978 [1930].

Grimm, Jacob, and Wilhelm Grimm. *Grimm's Fairy Tales*. Illustrated by George Cruikshank. Dover, n.d. [1823].

Hale, Lucretia P. *The Peterkin Papers*. Sharon, 1981 [1880].

Hale, Sarah Josepha. *Mary Had a Little Lamb*. Illustrated by Tomie de Paola. Holiday House, 1984 [1830].

Haley, Gail. *A Story, a Story*. Atheneum, 1970.

Hamilton, Virginia. *M. C. Higgins the Great*. Macmillan, 1974.

——— . *Zeely*. Illustrated by Simeon Shimin. Macmillan, 1967.

Harris, Joel Chandler. *Uncle Remus*. Illustrated by A. B. Frost. Schocken, 1987 [1881].

Hawthorne, Nathaniel. *Tanglewood Tales*. Sharon, 1981 [1853].

——— . *The Wonder Book for Boys and Girls*. White Rose, 1987 [1852].

Haywood, Carolyn. *B Is for Betsy*. Harcourt Brace, 1987 [1939].

Hindley, Judy. *A Piece of String Is a Wonderful Thing*. Illustrated by Margaret Chamberlain. Candlewick, 1993.

Holling, Holling C. *Paddle to the Sea*. Houghton Mifflin, 1980 [1941].

——— . *Tree in the Trail*. Houghton Mifflin, 1990 [1942].

Hope, Laura L. *The Bobbsey Twins*. Simon & Schuster, 1990.

Hughes, Langston. *The Dream Keeper*. Illustrated by Helen Sewell. Knopf, 1962.

Irving, Washington. *Sketch Book*. New American Library, 1961 [1819].

Isaacs, Anne. *Swamp Angel*. Illustrated by Paul O. Zelinsky. Dutton, 1994.

Jackson, Jesse. *Call Me Charley*. Illustrated by Doris Speigel. Harper & Row, 1945.

Jacobs, Joseph, ed. *Celtic Fairy Tales*. Illustrated by John D. Batten. Dover, n.d. [1890–1894].

———, ed. *English Fairy Tales*. Illustrated by John D. Batten. Dover, n.d. [1890–1894].

———, ed. *Indian Fairy Tales*. Illustrated by John D. Batten. Roth, 1976 [1892].

Jones, Hettie. *The Trees Stand Shining: Poetry of the North American Indians*. Illustrated by Robert A. Parker. Dial, 1993 [1971].

Keats, Ezra Jack. *The Snowy Day*. Viking Penguin, 1962.

Kellogg, Steven. *Johnny Appleseed*. Morrow, 1988.

Kingsley, Charles. *The Water Babies*. Penguin, 1986 [1863].

Kipling, Rudyard. *Just So Stories*. Woodcuts by David Frampton. HarperCollins, 1991 [1902].

——— . *The Jungle Books*. Illustrated by Fritz Eichenberg. Grossert, 1950 [1894–1895].

Konigsburg, E. L. *George*. Dell, 1985 [1970].

Krauss, Ruth. *A Hole Is to Dig*. Illustrated by Maurice Sendak. Harper & Row, 1952.

Lang, Andrew, ed. *The Blue Fairy Book*. Airmont, 1969 [1889].

Lasky, Kathryn. *The Night Journey*. Illustrated by Trina Schart Hyman. Viking, 1986.

Lawson, Julie. *The Dragon's Pearl*. Illustrated by Paul Morin. Clarion, 1993.

Lawson, Robert. *Rabbit Hill*. Viking Penguin, 1944.

——— . *The Tough Winter*. Viking Penguin, 1979 [1954].

Leaf, Munro. *The Story of Ferdinand*. Illustrated by Robert Lawson. Viking, 1936.

L'Engle, Madeleine. *Meet the Austins*. Dell, 1981 [1960].

——— . *A Wrinkle in Time*. Farrar, Straus & Giroux, 1962.

Lenski, Lois. *Judy's Journey*. Harper & Row, 1947.

——— . *The Little Auto*. McKay, 1980 [1934].

——— . *Strawberry Girl*. Harper & Row, 1988 [1945].

Lester, Julius. *Iron John*. Illustrated by Jerry Pinkney. Dial, 1994.

Lewis, C. S. *The Lion, the Witch, and the Wardrobe*. Illustrated by Pauline Baynes. Macmillan, 1988 [1950].

Lindgren, Astrid. *Pippi Longstocking*. Illustrated by Louis S. Glanzman. Translated by Florence Lambron. Viking Penguin, 1950.

Lindsay, Vachel. *Johnny Appleseed and Other Poems*. Buccaneer, 1981 [1928].

Lofting, Hugh. *The Story of Dr. Dolittle*. Delacorte, 1988 [1920].

——— . *The Voyages of Dr. Dolittle*. Delacorte, 1988 [1922].

London, Jack. *The Call of the Wild*. Macmillan, 1963 [1903].

Louie, Ai-Ling. *Yeh-Shen: A Cinderella Story from China*. Illustrated by Ed Young. Philomel, 1982.

Lunn, Janet. *The Root Cellar*. Macmillan, 1983.

Macaulay, David. *Black and White*. Houghton Mifflin, 1990.

——— . *The Way Things Work*. Houghton Mifflin, 1988.

MacDonald, George. *At the Back of the North Wind*. Illustrated by Lauren Mills. Godine, 1988 [1871].

——— . *The Princess and Curdie*. Dell Yearling, 1987 [1883].

——— . *The Princess and the Goblin*. Dell Yearling, 1986 [1872].

MacLachan, Patricia. *The Facts and Fictions of Minna Pratt*. Harper & Row, 1988.

——— . *Sarah, Plain and Tall*. Harper & Row, 1985.

——— . *Three Names*. Illustrated by Alexander Pertzoff. HarperCollins, 1991.

Martin, Ann. *The Baby-Sitters Remember*. Scholastic, 1994.

Maruki, Toshi. *Hiroshima No Pika* (The Flash of Hiroshima). Lothrop, Lee & Shepard, 1980.

Mayer, Mercer. *A Boy, a Dog and a Frog*. Dial, 1967.

McCloskey, Robert. *Homer Price*. Viking Penguin, 1943.

———. *Make Way for Ducklings*. Viking Penguin, 1941.

McDermott, Beverly Brodsky. *The Golem*. Lippincott, 1976.

McDermott, Gerald. *Anansi the Spider*. Holt, 1972.

McKissack, Patricia C., and Frederick L. McKissack. *Christmas in the Big House, Christmas in the Quarters*. Illustrated by John Thompson. Scholastic, 1994.

Millay, Edna St. Vincent. *Edna St. Vincent Millay's Poems Selected for Young People*. Illustrated by Ronald Keller. Harper & Row, 1979 [1917].

Milne, A. A. *Now We Are Six*. Illustrated by Ernest H. Shepard. Dutton, 1988 [1927].

———. *When We Were Very Young*. Illustrated by Ernest H. Shepard. Dutton, 1988 [1924].

———. *Winnie the Pooh*. Illustrated by Ernest H. Shepard. Dutton, 1988 [1926].

Monjo, F. N. *Poor Richard in France*. Dell, 1990 [1973].

Montgomery, L. M. *Anne of Green Gables*. Bantam, 1976 [1908].

———. *Emily of New Moon*. Bantam, 1991 [1923].

Moore, Clement. *The Night Before Christmas*. Illustrated by Tasha Tudor. Macmillan, 1975 [1823].

———. *The Night Before Christmas*. Illustrated by Michael Hague. Holt, 1981 [1823].

———. *The Night Before Christmas*. Illustrated by Tomie de Paola. Holiday House, 1980 [1823].

Myers, Walter Dean. *The Glory Field*. Scholastic, 1994.

Naidoo, Beverley. *Journey to Jo'burg*. Illustrated by Eric Velasquez. Harper & Row, 1986.

Nelson, Theresa. *Earthshine*. Orchard, 1994.

Nister, Ernest. *The Animals' Picnic*. Putnam, 1988 [reissue].

O'Brien, Robert. *Mrs. Frisby and the Rats of NIMH*. Illustrated by Zena Bernstein. Macmillan, 1971.

———. *The Secret of NIMH*. Scholastic, 1982.

Onyefulu, Ifeoma. *Emeka's Gift: An African Counting Story*. Cobblehill, 1995.

Oxenbury, Helen. *Dressing*. Simon & Schuster, 1981.

———. *Family*. Simon & Schuster, 1981.

———. *Friends*. Simon & Schuster, 1981.

———. *Playing*. Simon & Schuster, 1981.

———. *Working*. Simon & Schuster, 1981.

Palin, Michael. *The Mirrorstone*. Illustrated by Alan Lee. Knopf, 1986.

Pearce, Philippa. *Tom's Midnight Garden*. Harper & Row, 1984 [1959].

Pfister, Marcus. *The Rainbow Fish*. North-South, 1992.

Pinkwater, Daniel. *The Muffin Fiend*. Lothrop, Lee & Shepard, 1986.

Piper, Watty. *The Little Engine That Could*. Putnam, 1990 [1929].

Porte, Barbara Ann. *Something Terrible Happened*. Orchard, 1994.

Porter, Eleanor H. *Pollyanna*. Yearling Classics, 1987 [1913].

Potter, Beatrix. *Jemima Puddle-Duck*. Warne, 1994 [1908].

———. *The Tale of Peter Rabbit*. Warne, 1972 [1902].

Prelutsky, Jack. *The Headless Horseman Rides Tonight*. Illustrated by Arnold Lobel. Greenwillow, 1980.

———. *Nightmares: Poems to Trouble Your Sleep*. Illustrated by Arnold Lobel. Greenwillow, 1976.

Pyle, Howard. *The Merry Adventures of Robin Hood of Great Renown*. Dover, 1968 [1883].

———. *The Story of King Arthur and His Knights*. Scribner's, 1984 [1903].

———. *The Wonder Clock*. Dover, n.d. [1888].

Rey, H. A. *Curious George*. Houghton, 1973 [1941].

Richter, Hans. *Friedrich*. Penguin, 1987 [1970].

Rossetti, Christina. *Sing Song*. Illustrated by Arthur Hughes. Dover, 1969 [1872].

Ruskin, John. *King of the Golden River*. Illustrated by Richard Doyle. Dover, 1974 [1851].

Rylant, Cynthia. *When I Was Young in the Mountains*. Illustrated by Diane Goode. Dutton, 1982.

Sabuda, Robert. *The Christmas Alphabet*. Orchard, 1994.

Sandburg, Carl. *Early Moon*. Illustrated by James Daughterty. Harcourt Brace, 1978 [1930].

———. *Rootabaga Stories*. Illustrated by Michael Hague. Harcourt Brace, 1989 [1922].

Sawyer, Ruth. *Roller Skates*. Illustrated by Valenti Angelo. Penguin, 1986 [1936].

Scieszka, Jon. *The True Story of the 3 Little Pigs as Told by A. Wolf*. Illustrated by Lane Smith. Viking, 1989.

Scott, Walter. *Ivanhoe*. Airmont, 1964 [1820].

Sendak, Maurice. *In The Night Kitchen*. Harper & Row, 1970.

———. *Where the Wild Things Are*. Harper & Row, 1988 [1963].

Seton, Ernest Thompson. *Wild Animals I Have Known*. Creative Arts, 1987 [1898].

Seuss, Dr. [Theodor S. Geisel]. *And to Think That I Saw It on Mulberry Street*. Random House, 1989 [1937].

———. *The Cat in the Hat*. Random House, 1957.

Sewell, Anna. *Black Beauty*. Grosset, 1945 [1877].

Sherlock, Philip. *Anansi: The Spider Man*. Illustrated by Marcia Brown. Harper & Row, 1954.

Sidney, Margaret. *Five Little Peppers and How They Grew*. Puffin, 1990 [1881].

Silverstein, Shel. *Where the Sidewalk Ends*. Harper & Row, 1974.

Smith, E. Boyd. *The Farm Book*. Houghton Mifflin, 1990 [1910].

———. *The Railroad Book*. Houghton Mifflin, 1983 [1913].

———. *The Seashore Book*. Houghton Mifflin, 1985 [1912].

Soto, Gary. *Baseball in April and Other Stories*. Harcourt Brace, 1990.

Spier, Peter. *Noah's Ark*. Doubleday, 1977.

Spinelli, Jerry. *Maniac Magee*. Little, Brown, 1991.

Spyri, Johanna. *Heidi*. Illustrated by Troy Howell. Messner, 1982 [1884].

Steptoe, John. *Mufaro's Beautiful Daughters: An African Tale*. Lothrop, Lee & Shepard, 1987.

———. *Stevie*. Harper & Row, 1969.

Stevenson, Robert Louis. *A Child's Garden of Verses*. Illustrated by Michael Foreman. Delacorte, 1985 [1885].

———. *Treasure Island*. Illustrated by N. C. Wyeth. Scribner's, 1981 [1883].

Stolz, Mary. *The Bully of Barkham Street*. Illustrated by Leonard Shortall. Harper & Row, 1985 [1963].

———. *A Dog on Barkham Street*. Illustrated by Leonard Shortall. Harper & Row, 1985 [1960].

Taylor, Mildred. *Roll of Thunder, Hear My Cry*. Illustrated by Jerry Pinkney. Dell, 1976.

Taylor, Sydney. *All-of-a-Kind Family*. Illustrated by John Helen. Dell, 1980 [1951].

Temple, Frances. *Taste of Salt*. Orchard, 1993.

Thurber, James. *Many Moons*. Illustrated by L. Slobodkin. Harcourt Brace, 1943.

———. *Many Moons*. Illustrated by Marc Simont. Harcourt Brace, 1990 [1943].

Tolkien, J. R. R. *The Hobbit.* Illustrated by Michael Hague. Houghton Mifflin, 1989 [1937].

Travers, P. L. *Mary Poppins.* Harcourt, 1934.

Trelease, Jim. *The Read-Aloud Handbook.* Penguin, 1995.

Tresselt, Alvin. *Wake Up, City!* Illustrated by Carolyn Ewing. Lothrop, Lee & Shepard, 1989 [1947].

——— . *White Snow, Bright Snow.* Illustrated by Roger Duvoisin. Lothrop, Lee & Shepard, 1989 [1947].

Twain, Mark [Samuel Clemens]. *The Adventures of Huckleberry Finn.* Scholastic, 1982 [1884].

——— . *The Adventures of Tom Sawyer.* Illustrated by Barry Moser. Morrow, 1989 [1876].

Uchida, Yoshiko. *The Dancing Kettle and Other Japanese Folk Tales.* Creative Arts, 1986 [1949].

——— . *Journey to Topaz.* Illustrated by Donald Carrick. Scribner's, 1971.

——— . *The Magic Listening Cap.* Creative Arts, 1987 [1955].

Udry, Janice May. *Let's Be Enemies.* Illustrated by Maurice Sendak. Harper & Row, 1961.

Van Allsburg, Chris. *The Polar Express.* Houghton Mifflin, 1985.

Van Loon, Hendrik. *The Story of Mankind.* Updated in a new version for the 1980s. Liveright, 1985 [1921].

Verne, Jules. *Around the World in Eighty Days.* Illustrated by Barry Moser. Morrow, 1988 [1872].

——— . *Journey to the Center of the Earth.* Penguin, 1986 [1864].

——— . *Twenty Thousand Leagues Under the Sea.* Airmont, 1964 [1869].

Voigt, Cynthia. *Homecoming.* Atheneum, 1981.

Webster, Jean. *Daddy-Long-Legs.* Dell Yearling, 1987 [1912].

White, E. B. *Charlotte's Web.* Illustrated by Garth Williams. Harper & Row, 1952.

Wiesner, David. *Tuesday.* Clarion, 1991.

Wiggin, Kate Douglas. *Rebecca of Sunnybrook Farm.* Penguin, 1986 [1903].

Wilder, Laura Ingalls. *Little House in the Big Woods.* Illustrated by Garth Williams. Harper & Row, 1953 [1932].

Willard, Nancy. *A Visit to William Blake's Inn.* Illustrated by Alice and Martin Provensen. Harcourt Brace, 1981.

Williams, Margery. *The Velveteen Rabbit.* Illustrated by William Nicholson. Doubleday, 1969 [1922].

——— . *The Velveteen Rabbit.* Illustrated by Michael Hague. Holt, 1983 [1922].

——— . *The Velveteen Rabbit.* Illustrated by David Jorgensen. Knopf, 1985 [1922].

——— . *The Velveteen Rabbit.* Illustrated by Ilse Plume. Harcourt Brace, 1987 [1922].

Williams, Vera B. *Stringbean's Trip to the Shining Sea.* Illustrated by Jennifer Williams and Vera B. Williams. Greenwillow, 1988.

Woodson, Jacqueline. *I Hadn't Meant to Tell You This.* Delacorte, 1994.

Wyss, Johann. *The Swiss Family Robinson.* Sharon, 1981 [1814].

Yep, Laurence. *Dragon's Gate.* HarperCollins, 1993.

Yolen, Jane. *The Devil's Arithmetic.* Viking, 1988.

Zemach, Margot. *It Could Always Be Worse.* Farrar, Straus & Giroux, 1990 [1977].

part two

❋ *Exploring Children's Literature*

chapter four

Books to Begin On

Developing Initial Literacy 137
Babies' First Books 139
Toy Books 140
Finger Rhymes and Nursery Songs 141
Guidelines: Evaluating Books for the Very
    Young Child 142
Mother Goose 146

The Appeal of Mother Goose 146
Different Editions of Mother Goose 147

Collections 147
Guidelines: Evaluating Mother Goose
    Books 149

Single-Verse Editions 149
Nursery-Rhyme Collections from Other Lands 150
Resources for Teaching: Mother Goose
    Books 152
Alphabet Books 154
Counting Books 156
Resources for Teaching: ABC Books 157

Resources for Teaching: Counting
    Books 160
Concept Books 163
Guidelines: Evaluating ABC and Counting
    Books 164
Wordless Books 168
Books About the Common Experiences of
    the Young Child 170
Books for the Beginning Reader 174

Predictable Books 174
Resources for Teaching: Predictable
    Books 180

Big Books 180

Controlled-Vocabulary Books 182

Teaching Feature: Creating Big Books with
    Emergent Readers 183
Learning Experiences 184
Related Readings 185
Children's Literature 186

One of our colleagues is a proud new grandfather. Every time we meet him, he regales us with tales of his granddaughter's progress in "reading"—Laura is 18 months old. However, he is determined that Laura will grow into reading as naturally as she is learning to speak. So he floods her house with books; he mixes books with her blocks so she will think of them as toys; he built her a special bookshelf for her books; he bought a miniature supermarket basket that he filled with books so she can have books available in every room in the house; he takes her to the library frequently. Of course, whenever he visits he is greeted with the welcome words, "Grandpapa, read!" And he always does. Laura's mother and father read to her also, so it is not unusual for Laura to hear six to ten stories a day.

Laura has favorite books, which she can readily find, and she asks to hear them over and over again. She relates books to her own life. For example, when she lost her teddy bear and finally found it, she went to her bookshelf and pulled out the story *The Blanket* by John Burningham and laughed. In that story a little boy loses his blanket and the whole family searches for it. Laura had obviously connected it with her family's search for her bear. Each night when she hears *Goodnight Moon* by Margaret Wise Brown, she softly whispers, "Night night, chair, night night, Bear." Laura's grandfather is achieving his purpose. Laura is learning to love books and learning to read naturally in the process.

Developing Initial Literacy

What a lot Laura already knows about books and reading at 18 months! First, she knows books are enjoyable, and she even has particular favorites. She also knows that adults hold the key to reading and can give meaning to the text. She herself knows how to hold a book and that it has to be right-side-up to read the print. She is beginning to relate books to her own life. If at 18 months she knows this much about how to read a book, think what she will know when she enters school.

At a year and a half, Laura already has entered the world of literature. She is learning to love books, as she has many opportunities to snuggle up close to her mother, father, and grandfather for story time. She is also increasing her vocabulary as she points to pictures and names them or hears new words used in the context of the story. The language development of children this age is phenomenal; preoccupation with words and the sounds of language is characteristic of the very young child. Books help to fulfill this insatiable desire to hear and learn new words. Hearing literature of good quality helps children to develop to their full language potential.

Children cannot be introduced to books too soon. The human baby is attuned to various sound patterns almost from the moment of birth. She will be startled by a cross word or a loud noise, soothed by a gentle loving voice or a softly sung lullaby. Gradually the baby begins to develop comprehension skills as she attaches meaning to the sounds around her. Talk is essential at this time. In *A Language for Life*, an educational report from England, parents are advised to "bathe the child with language."[1] One parent read a best-selling novel to her infant son just so he could hear the sound of her voice. Primarily, however, the very young child listens for the "quack quack" of a duck in a picture book or the "roar" of a lion. Singing simple nursery rhymes or playing such finger rhymes as "This little pig went to market" will make the baby giggle with delight. Increasingly, publishers are producing books for babies' enjoyment, for, in Dorothy Butler's words, "Babies need books."[2]

[1] *A Language for Life: The Bullock Report* (London: H.M.S.O., 1975).
[2] Dorothy Butler, *Babies Need Books* (New York: Atheneum, 1980).

Research suggests that one of the most important gifts a family can give to children is an early love of books.
Photo by Larry Rose.

The young child who has the opportunity to hear and enjoy many stories is also beginning to learn to read. No one taught Laura how to hold a book or where to begin to read the text. Through constant exposure to stories, Laura is learning about book handling and developing some beginning concepts about the print.[3] She is spontaneously learning some of the attitudes, concepts, and skills that Don Holdaway describes as a "literacy set," including a positive attitude toward books, an understanding about the sense-making aspect of stories, the stability of print to tell the same story each time, and the form and structure of written language itself. All of this learning occurs at the prereading stage—what Holdaway refers to as the "emergent level of reading"—and seems to be essential for later success in reading.[4]

We have previously discussed, in Chapter 1, the research that shows the importance of books in the young child's life. It is clear that hearing many stories in the preschool years can have lasting benefit for children. Boys and girls who enter school having had many experiences with books are well prepared to acquire

literacy,[5] and these children are more likely to remain active readers well into late elementary and middle school.[6]

During the times in which they share books with their young children, parents appear to use consistent language patterns when labeling objects in a picture book. Even before the baby can talk, the child and mother (or father) take turns engaging in a dialogue and collaboratively make meaning out of the text. As they read Margaret Wise Brown's *Goodnight Moon* over the course of many bedtimes, the mother points to a picture and says, "Can you find the red balloon? Where's the mouse?" and the baby delightedly points to these tiny objects. As the child acquires a simple vocabulary, the parent might ask, "What's this?" or respond to the same query from the child with the name of the object. This book-reading context is unique because the attention of both participants is focused on pictures and words that stay the same for each rereading. Thus the child can predict the story and build up vocabulary over numerous readings.

While the way parents share these books follows a distinctive pattern, the quality of the read-aloud time varies tremendously according to the parents' patience and ingenuity in holding the youngster's interest.[7] In the best read-aloud situations, parents take time with the book, giving children opportunities to look at the pictures and to talk about the story. They wait long enough to see if the children can name objects in identification books, and they elaborate on the child's response to pictures or story by repeating or extending the child's language.[8] The length of time spent with the book and this type of quality read-aloud experience is as important for the young child as the selection of the book.

Early exposure to books and plenty of time for talk and enjoyment of the story appear, then, to be key factors in the child's acquisition of literacy. One father whose child has been exposed to books from infancy said, "You know, I haven't the slightest doubt that David will learn to read, any more than I was concerned that he would talk."

[3]See Marie Clay, *The Early Detection of Reading Difficulties*, 3rd ed. (Portsmouth, N.H.: Heinemann Educational Books, 1985), for a description of her Concepts About Print test.

[4]Don Holdaway, *The Foundations of Literacy* (Sydney: Ashton Scholastic, 1979).

[5]Gordon Wells, *The Meaning Makers: Children Learning Language and Using Language to Learn* (Portsmouth, N.H.: Heinemann Educational Books, 1986), p. 151 (emphasis added).

[6]Judith Sostarich, "A Study of the Reading Behavior of Sixth Graders: Comparisons of Active and Other Readers" (unpublished Ph.D. dissertation, Ohio State University, 1974).

[7]Linda Lamme and Pat Olmsted, "Family Reading Habits and Children's Progress in Reading," paper presented at the Annual Meeting of the International Reading Association, Miami Beach, 2–6 May 1977. ERIC Document ED 138 963.

[8]Barry J. Guinagh and R. Emile Jester, "How Parents Read to Children," *Theory into Practice* 11, no. 3 (1972): 171–177.

Babies' First Books

First books for young children are frequently identification books, "naming books," or books with simple narrative lines that allow a child to point to one picture after another, demanding to know "wha dat?" It is probably this give-and-take of language between the adult and the child that makes sharing books at this age so important. Recognizing the need for the young child to identify and name objects, publishers have produced many of these simple, sturdy "first books." The growth of good books for babies and toddlers was a publishing phenomenon of the 1980s. As part of the interest in books for babies, publishers reissued well-known nursery classics or enlisted well-known illustrators or writers in creating series of baby books. These books can be pouffy, made of foam-filled cloth pages that are washable, or they might be constructed with heavy laminated cardboard or plastic pages that will withstand teeth or sticky fingers. Illustrations for these books need to be simple, uncluttered, and easily identifiable.

Tana Hoban's photographic concept books such as *What Is It?* and *Red, Blue, Yellow Shoe* present clear, colored photographs of familiar objects like a sock, a shoe, a bib, a cup, and a spoon. Only one object is pictured on a page, shown against a plain white background, in these sturdy first books. Hoban's *Black on White* and *White on Black* picture everyday objects in high contrast and are aimed at very young infants.

Helen Oxenbury has a series of "Baby Board Books" titled *Playing, Dressing, Working, Friends,* and *Family.* These books feature a delightfully droll round-headed infant doing what toddlers do, such as banging on pots, messily eating food, or sitting on the potty. A single noun such as *bowl, potty,* or *dog* represents the action on the page in much the same way that the young child uses a single word to carry the force of a sentence. The simplicity of the illustrations is just right for the audience—plain white backgrounds, clearly outlined figures, single-focus composition, attractive but not distracting color. In *Tickle Tickle, Clap Hands,* and *Say Goodnight,* the author-artist portrays wonderful babies of several races playing together. Oxenbury continues the exploration of the toddler's world in her Baby Board series with *I Can, I Hear, I See,* and *I Touch.*

Jan Ormerod's "Baby Books" are unique in that they portray the special relationships between babies and fathers. The series includes *Dad's Back, Messy Baby, Reading,* and *Sleeping.* In *Reading,* for example, a bearded father attempts to read his book while a toddler crawls in and out of his legs, peeps over this book, and finally ends up resting in his arms, reading too.

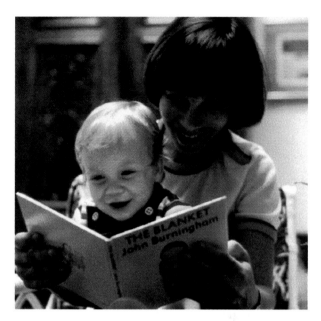

It's never too early to begin reading to children.

The representation of more African American children in board books can be seen in John Steptoe's story *Baby Says,* which shows a toddler learning to endure the antics of his baby brother. Angela Johnson's four Joshua books—*Joshua by the Sea, Joshua's Night Whispers, Rain Feet,* and *Mama Bird, Baby Birds*—also feature an African American boy. With their poetic text and satisfying emotional vignettes, these are sure to keep parents and toddlers interested through repeated readings. *Babies* by Rachel Isadora shows solitary children of different races eating, laughing, reading, playing, sleeping; Isadora's *Friends* depicts multicultural pairs and groups of youngsters sharing typical activities such as drawing, building, or waving good-bye. Parents, preschool teachers, and librarians enjoy sharing these books that portray joyful activities in the child's day.

Rosemary Wells's little board books about Max, a lovable rabbity creature, are labeled "Very First Books." However, the humor is for slightly older toddlers. In *Max's First Word,* Max's sister tries to get him to talk. She names everything she shows him, and Max always responds with "Bang." Giving him an apple, Ruby suggests he say "Yum, yum," but Max surprises her with "Delicious." Other stories continue big sister Ruby's struggle to get Max to eat an egg for breakfast, take a bath, and go to bed. Max manages to outsmart her at every move.

Garden and *Seashore* are two Fingerwiggle Books by Julie Lacome that invite toddlers to interact with the brightly colored collage pictures by inserting fingers or hands to help fish glide and bees flee. *Hey Diddle Diddle*

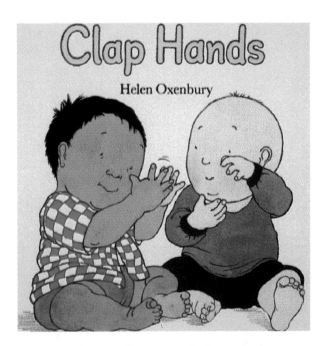

Delightful babies of different racial backgrounds play together happily in *Clap Hands* by Helen Oxenbury.
Reprinted with permission of Little Simon, an imprint of Simon & Schuster from *Clap Hands* by Helen Oxenbury. Copyright © 1987 Helen Oxenbury.

by James Marshall has interactive sound devices to add to the delight of Marshall's amusing pictures.

Other series books for toddlers carry more text than board books and often have heavier stock to withstand repeated readings. *The Blanket*, describing a whole family's frantic search for a lost blanket, is one of a series by the British artist-author John Burningham. These squarish-shaped books portray the activities and interests of a 2- or 3-year-old. For example, in *The Baby*, a child details what the baby does at his house, such as eating, sleeping, and going for a walk. It concludes with the candid statement "Sometimes I like the baby, and sometimes I don't." In these simple stories the young child is always at the center of the action, reflecting the ego-centered way of thinking that is characteristic of this age group. The plot line is not sequential; episodes could be interchanged at will. This is characteristic of the kind of stories the young children tell themselves.

There are many fine picture books that appeal to babies and toddlers and that introduce them to the rhythms and forms of literature from an early age. These are often the books that, like Margaret Wise Brown's *Goodnight Moon*, become bedtime classics although they don't have to be about going to sleep. Favorites with toddlers include Robert Kraus's *Whose Mouse Are You?* Vera Williams's *"More More More," Said the Baby*, and Trish Cooke's *So Much*, illustrated by Helen Oxenbury.

These are books that often invite babies' participation in the form of finding hidden objects in the pictures, repeating simple refrains like "more, more, more" or "so much," or getting tummy tickles and hugs and kisses.

Toy Books

Young children can respond to a book by pointing or labeling, but some books have a kind of "built-in participation" as part of their design. These books have flaps to lift up and peek under, soft flannel to touch, or holes to poke fingers through. Such books can serve as the transition between toys and real books. *Pat the Bunny* by Dorothy Kunhardt has been a best-seller for very young children for more than fifty years. In this little book the child is invited to use senses other than sight and sound. A "pattable" bunny made of flannel is on one page, and Daddy's unshaven face, represented by rough sandpaper, is on another. Young children literally wear out this tactile book. Kunhardt's daughter Edith has created a sequel to this classic called *Pat the Puppy*.

An increasing number of sophisticated cutout books and "lift the flap" stories are appearing on the market. In *Where Can It Be?* Ann Jonas uses cleverly designed half pages to open closets, cupboards, and refrigerator doors to further a little girl's search for her beloved lost blanket. Lucy Cousins's *Maisy* is the appealing mouse heroine in several books in which Maisy goes swimming, to school, and to other familiar places. In *Maisy Goes to Bed*, Maisy goes to a potty that "flushes," puts on her pajamas, and ends up in bed reading a bedtime book. Eric Hill's "lift the flap" stories about the dog Spot never fail to intrigue young children. In *Where's Spot?* Spot's mother, Sally, searches for her puppy behind a door, inside a clock, under the stairs, in the piano, and under the rug. As the child opens doors and lifts up flaps to join in the search, highly unlikely creatures such as monkeys, snakes, and lions answer no to the question "Is he in here?" Since *no* is one of 2-year-olds' favorite words, they love to chime in on the refrain. These books are sturdily made, the pictures are bright and clear, and the stories are imaginative. Other titles in the series include *Spot Bakes a Cake* and *Spot Goes to School*. These books are also available in Spanish editions.

Eric Carle's story *The Very Hungry Caterpillar* is a favorite with children ages 3 through 6. This imaginative tale describes the life cycle of a ravenous caterpillar who leaves behind a trail of holes in all the food that he eats. Children love to stick their fingers through the holes and count them. In Carle's multisensory story *The Very Busy Spider*, children are invited to feel the pictures as well as see them. Brilliant collages depict familiar animals whose questions are never answered by the spider,

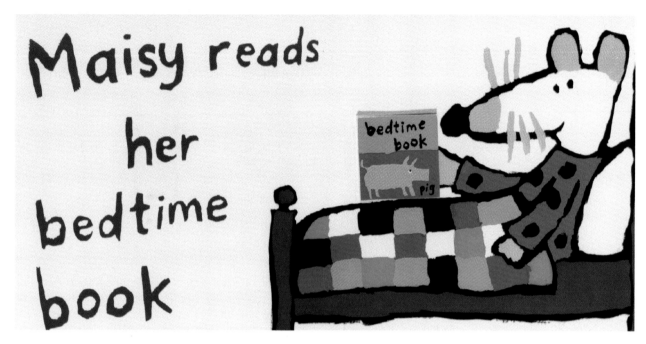

Lucy Cousins recreates familiar bedtime scenes in *Maisy Goes to Bed*.
From *Maisy Goes To Bed* by Lucy Cousins. Copyright © 1990 by Lucy Cousins. By permission of Little, Brown and Company.

who is too busy spinning her tactile web. Carle's *The Very Quiet Cricket* and *The Very Lonely Firefly* have technological support that brings each tale to its conclusion. The sound of the cricket coming from a computer chip imbedded in the pages of the cricket book and tiny blinking lights in the fireflies' bodies surprise and delight children in these multisensory books.

Books that describe different kinds of sounds invite their own special kind of noisy participation. *Noisy* by Shirley Hughes pictures the noises a baby and a toddler can make, as well as the noises they hear. Realistic pictures show a frustrated mother holding a bawling baby while the telephone rings and the stew boils over. Peter Spier's book of animal sounds is titled *Gobble Growl Grunt*, while in *Crash! Bang! Boom!* the reader may compare the quiet crunch of new boots in the snow with the police siren's commanding cry of "you, yo-u, y-o-u." *Pigs Say Oink* by Martha Alexander includes sounds of many animals, trains, and children at a nursery school, and the quietest sound of all, when everyone is asleep. *Early Morning in the Barn* by Nancy Tafuri begins with a large double-page spread picturing a rooster waking the barnyard with his "cock-a-doodle-doo," which awakens his brother and sister. All three run out of the henhouse into the barnyard, where they are greeted by an array of animals each making their familiar noise. Finally the story comes full circle as the chicks meet their mother hen. Lovely sunny pictures add to the fun of this noisy book.

If a book does not provide for participation, the adult reader can stimulate it by the kinds of questions he or she asks. For example, when sharing the old favorite *Caps for Sale* by Esphyr Slobodkina, the parent might say to the child, "Find the monkey—not the one in the red hat, not the one in the blue hat, but the one in the green hat!" Such participation will help children develop visual discrimination, but, more importantly, it will add to the fun of the story time. The Guidelines box "Evaluating Books for the Very Young" lists criteria for the best books for infants and toddlers.

Finger Rhymes and Nursery Songs

Finger rhymes are one traditional way to provide for young children's participation as they play "Five Little Pigs" or sing "Where Is Thumbkin?" and the ever popular "Eensy, Weensy Spider." Finger plays date back to the time of Friedrich Froebel, the so-called father of the kindergarten movement, who collected the finger plays and games that the peasant mothers in the German countryside were using with their children.

Sarah Hayes selected over twenty favorite finger rhymes to include in her book *Clap Your Hands*. Toni Gaffe provided the lively step-by-step illustrations to demonstrate the action of such rhymes as "Little Turtle," "Incey Wincey Spider," and "Ten Fat Sausages."

Guidelines:
Evaluating Books for the Very Young Child

The best books for babies and toddlers should:

Relate to familiar life experiences

Provide clear uncluttered illustrations with little or no distracting background

Be well constructed with sturdy, durable pages

Use clear, natural language

Have predictable stories

Provide some humor, especially so the child will feel superior

Offer opportunities for participation and interaction

Hold the child's attention

Tom Glazer's *Eye Winker Tom Tinker Chin Chopper* provides the music and verbal directions for some fifty finger plays. His collection includes some for the youngest, such as "Eye Winker," "Pat-a-Cake," and "Here Is the Church," and some longer cumulative songs for older children, such as "I Know an Old Lady Who Swallowed a Fly" and "There's a Hole in the Bottom of the Sea." Piano arrangements and guitar chords accompany each of these rhymes.

Babies and young toddlers often first respond to the sounds of music and singing. Aliki's spirited song *Go Tell Aunt Rhody* is a bit of authentic Americana that will be familiar to many parents. Starting with brilliant endpapers of quilt blocks, this illustrated songbook tells the familiar tale of the death of the old gray goose. The gander and the goslings mourn the death of the old gray goose, but Aunt Rhody is pleased indeed with her new feather bed. Jakki Wood and Melissa Sweet have both illustrated *Fiddle-I-Fee*, another American folksong with a cumulative pattern that children enjoy. Sweet's version shows a little boy trying to feed the animals on his farm. As each animal is fed, it joins an ever longer parade through the countryside. When the boy's bucket is empty, his parents appear on a tractor and drive everyone back to the farm house for a final feast. Wood's version has less narrative and focuses on close-ups of a blonde-haired child and the animals. It also ends with an owl rather than a cow.

Nadine Westcott creates a hilarious tale to accompany the old nursery song in *Skip to My Lou*. When his parents leave a young boy in charge of the farm, the animals take over and chaos ensues. But fifteen minutes before his parents return, the boy ends the romp and the animals all help clean up the mess.

Children love to make up additional verses to the rollicking old folksong adapted by John Langstaff in *Oh,*

A-Hunting We Will Go. Nancy Winslow Parker's childlike illustrations are carefully arranged so as not to give away the last lines of each verse. Once children have determined the pattern of the song, they can guess what will be seen in the next picture. They easily predict the goat will end up "in a boat," but they laugh at the bear who gets put "in underwear."

Counting rhymes have also been made into individual songbooks. *Roll Over!* by Merle Peek shows a little boy in bed with nine animals. Each time they roll over, one animal falls out of bed. As the number of animals in the bed dwindles, children can look to see where they have found resting places in the room. Finally, when only the boy is asleep in his bed, a lion in a picture in his room appears to be winking and all the other animals are seen on a wall frieze that rings the ceiling. The music accompanies this tale of a young child's imaginary game. Mordicai Gerstein's *Roll Over!* is a small-sized book featuring a fold-out flap on each page. As a little boy calls out "Roll over!" the reader lifts the flap to discover which of his animal friends has fallen out of the huge bed. After the little boy is asleep alone in his bed, all the animals come creeping back.

Eileen Christelow illustrates another patterned rhyme in her amusing *Five Little Monkeys Jumping on the Bed*. Young children love to chant this story along with you. The surprise ending when Mama monkey jumps on her bed sends them into fits of laughter.

Ezra Jack Keats illustrated an old counting rhyme in *Over in the Meadow* with collage pictures in jewel-like colors. The fine recording by Marvin Hayes increases children's enjoyment of the lilt and rhythm of this favorite nursery song. Other versions have been illustrated by Paul Galdone and Louise Voce. Feodor Rojankovsky also illustrated a version retold by John Langstaff.

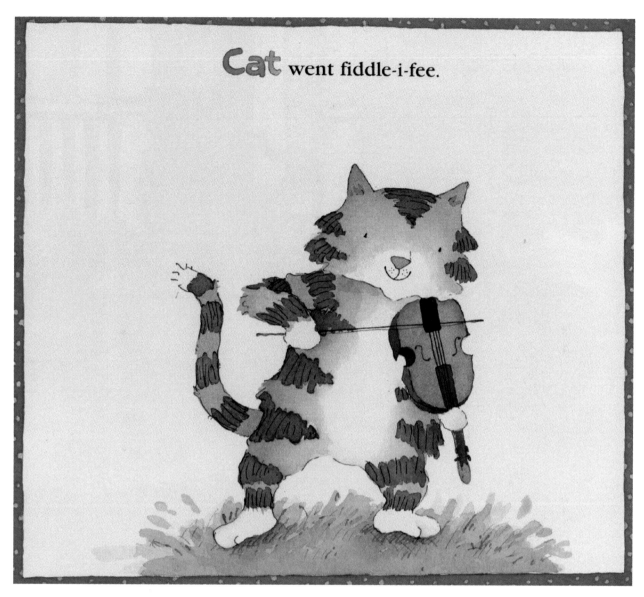

Cat went fiddle-i-fee.

A musical cat begins a long chain of events in Melissa Sweet's version of an American folk rhyme, *Fiddle-I-Fee*.
From *Fiddle-I-Fee: A Farmyard Song For the Very Young* by Melissa Sweet. Copyright © 1992 by Melissa Sweet. By permission of Little, Brown and Company.

In *We're Going on a Bear Hunt*, Michael Rosen recounts a popular action rhyme as an exciting adventure tale. Pictures by Helen Oxenbury portray a father and his four children (including the baby) crossing a field of waving grass ("Swishy, swashy"), wading in the mud ("Squelch, squerch"), and braving a snowstorm ("Hoooo, woooo") until they reach a gloomy cave and see a bear! Oxenbury alternates black-and-white pictures with sweeping landscapes in full color. Children will relish the sound effects, the humor, and the drama of this tale.

Christopher Manson used an 1898 book of nursery rhymes and songs as the source for his version of *The Tree in the Wood*, "the finest tree that you ever did see, and the green grass grew all around." In this cumulative song, each new addition to the verse is highlighted and framed on the right-hand page and the words are framed to the left. Manson's hand-painted woodcuts add a lovely antique feel to this familiar song.

In *The Fox Went Out on a Chilly Night*, Peter Spier's setting for the nursery rhyme song portrays the colorful autumn countryside outside of a New England village.

Helen Oxenbury portrays a father and his four children splashing through the deep cold river in Michael Rosen's retelling of *We're Going on a Bear Hunt*. The onomatopoetic text, lovely large watercolors, and surprise ending make this a favorite to read aloud.
Reprinted with permission of Margaret K. McElderry Books, an imprint of Simon & Schuster from *We're Going on a Bear Hunt* by Michael Rosen, illustrated by Helen Oxenbury. Illustrations copyright © 1989 Helen Oxenbury.

Shimmering moonlit pictures won this book a Caldecott Honor Award. The complete text of the song is provided at the end of the book. Youngsters can sing along with a second sharing of the story or join in while viewing the excellent filmstrip from Weston Woods.

Children have their choice of many editions of *Old MacDonald Had a Farm*. Lorinda Cauley portrays a patient rotund farmer who does his best to get his chores done despite the interfering animals. By way of contrast, Glen Rounds uses bold primitive drawings to depict his bowlegged farmer and angular animals, including a

skunk! Cleverly designed die-cut pages add an animal each time you turn a page in Nancy Hellen's version of this cumulative song. Carol Jones creates a peephole on each page of her engaging version. The first peephole view shows just a part of a chicken. Turn the page and you see the whole chicken in the hen house. While these books differ in their numbers and kinds of animals, they all, except for Jones's version, provide music along with the words.

In *I Know an Old Lady Who Swallowed a Fly*, Nadine Westcott illustrates the traditional version of the

Two children practice reading the speech balloons in their nursery-rhyme mural.
Mission School, Redlands Public Schools, Redlands, California. Nancy Anderson, teacher. Photo by Larry Rose.

popular song. After using seven cans of bug spray to kill the fly she swallowed, the old lady reels from one Epicurean delight to another. Devouring the horse, she dies of course! Colin and Jacqui Hawkins have the old lady sneeze after swallowing the horse and up come all the animals. By lifting up the old lady's apron, the reader can see all the animals in her stomach. This would make an excellent model for an enlarged old lady that children could then put their drawn animals into. A sealed sandwich bag stapled behind her apron would make a good imitation stomach. Open the bag and you could remove the animals. Also, the speech balloons in the Hawkinses' tale encourage children's own original writing. Brian Karas has a slightly more macabre version of this tale in which a young child reporter makes notes, draws sketches, and takes photographs as a slightly sinister old woman chases around the countryside after bigger and bigger meals.

One of primary children's favorite songs is "The Wheels on the Bus." In *The Wheels on the Bus*, Maryann Kovalski provides a London setting for her picture story of Jenny and Joanna and their grandma, who sing this song as they wait for their bus. They become so involved with their actions and singing, they miss their bus and have to take a taxi. Paul Zelinsky's interpretation of this song features paper engineering—wheels spin, the windshield wipers go "swish, swish, swish," and flaps and pullouts provide other items to manipulate. Well constructed, this movable version captivates children.

Nancy Larrick compiled *Songs from Mother Goose*, illustrated by Robin Spowart. Designed as a lap book, the book gives each verse its own illustration and traditional melody. Parents and teachers will find this collection very useful. Tom Glazer also collected forty-four popular rhymes with their melodies in his *Mother Goose Songbook*. Large humorous illustrations by David McPhail enhance each verse.

All children need to hear songs, from the time they are babies right through school. Many emergent readers' first books are shared nursery rhymes and songs or chants. Children "read" the familiar words as they sing the songs. Just as families have favorite songs that they sing in the bath or in the car, classes should have favorite songs to start the day or to sing while they are waiting to go to lunch or outside to play. A class without favorite songs is as sad as a class without favorite books.

Mother Goose

For many children, Mother Goose is their first introduction to the world of literature. Even a 1-year-old child will respond with delight to the language games of "Pat-a-Cake! Pat-a-Cake!" or "This Little Pig Went to Market." Many of the Mother Goose rhymes and jingles continue to be favorites of children 4 and 5 years old. What is the attraction of Mother Goose that makes her so appealing to these young children? What accounts for her survival through these many years? Much of the language in these rhymes is obscure; for example, modern-day children have no idea what curds and whey are, yet they delight in Little Miss Muffet. Nothing in current literature has replaced the venerable Mother Goose for the nursery school age.

The Appeal of Mother Goose

Much of the appeal of Mother Goose lies in the musical quality of the varied language patterns, the rhythm and rhyme of the verses, the alliteration of such lines as "Wee Willie Winkie runs through the town" or "Deedle, deedle, dumpling, my son John."

Researchers have now linked children's experience with nursery rhymes and speech play to the development of sensitivity to the sounds within words, an ability they call "phonemic awareness." This ability to manipulate the sounds of words as they sing and chant nursery rhymes is a necessary foundation for understanding relationships between letters and sounds and contributes to children's emergent literacy development.[9]

More importantly, however, children love the sounds of the words, for they are experimenting with language in this period of their lives. The child learns new words every day; he likes to try them out, to chant them while playing. Mother Goose rhymes help the young child satisfy this preoccupation with language patterns and stimulate further language development.

Mother Goose rhymes also offer young children many opportunities for active participation and response. The young child loves to get bounced on Daddy's knee to the rhythm of "Ride a Cock Horse" or clap hands to the sound of "Pat-a-cake, pat-a-cake, baker's man." Some of the rhymes—such as "Pease Porridge Hot," "London Bridge," or "Ring a Ring o' Roses"—are games or involve direct action from the child. Other verses include counting rhymes—as in "1, 2, buckle my shoe, 3, 4, shut the door." Slightly older children enjoy answering the riddles in some of the Mother Goose verses or attempting to say their favorite tongue twisters. Every child likes to fool someone with the well-known riddle: "As I was going to St. Ives, I met a man with seven wives." And they never fail to delight in successful recitation of the entire verse of "Peter Piper picked a peck of pickled peppers."

Another attraction of many of the Mother Goose rhymes is their narrative quality; they tell a good story with quick action. In just six lines "Little Miss Muffet" proves to be an exciting tale with action, a climax, and a satisfying conclusion. This is also true of "Simple Simon," "Sing a Song of Sixpence," "The Old Woman in the Shoe," and "Three Blind Mice." Preschool and kindergarten children enjoy pantomiming or dramatizing these well-known verse stories.

Many of the characters in Mother Goose have interesting, likable personalities: Old King Cole *is* a merry old soul; Old Mother Hubbard not only tries to find her poor dog a bone but she runs all over town at his special bidding; and although Tommy Lynn puts the pussy in the well, Johnny Stout pulls her out! Unpleasant but intriguing character traits are suggested by "Crosspatch," "Tom, the Piper's Son," and "Lazy Elsie Marley."

The content of the verses reflects the interests of young children. Many favorites are rhymes about animals—"The Three Little Kittens," "The Cat and the Fiddle," and the story of the mouse that ran up the clock in "Hickory Dickory Dock." Some of the verses are about simple everyday experiences and include such incidents as Lucy Locket losing her pocket, the Three Little Kittens losing their mittens, and Little Bo Peep losing her sheep. Children's pranks are enacted in "Ding, Dong, Bell!" and "Georgie Porgie." Peter, Peter, Pumpkin-Eater has a housing problem, as does the Old Woman in the Shoe. There are many verses about seasons and the weather, a concern of both young and old. The pleading request of one child in "Rain, Rain, Go Away" reflects the universal feelings of all children.

A major appeal of Mother Goose is the varied humor. There is the jolly good fun of a ridiculous situation:

One misty, moisty morning
When cloudy was the weather,
I chanced to meet an old man
Clothed all in leather;
He began to compliment
And I began to grin—
"How do you do" and "How do you do"
And "How do you do" again!

---

[9]Morag Maclean, Peter Bryant, and Lynette Bradley, "Rhymes, Nursery Rhymes, and Reading in Early Childhood," *Merrill-Palmer Quarterly, Journal of Developmental Psychology* 33 (July 1987): 255–281.

Two 6-year-olds interpreted this verse in action by pretending to pass each other; as one moved to the left, the other moved in the same direction. Their movements were perfect for this amusing and familiar situation.

The young child's rather primitive sense of humor, which delights in other persons' misfortune, is satisfied by the verses in "Jack and Jill" and "Dr. Foster":

> Doctor Foster went to Gloucester
> In a shower of rain;
> He stepped in a puddle up to his middle
> And never went there again.

The pure nonsense in Mother Goose tickles children's funny bones. Chukovsky, a Russian poet, reminds us that there is sense in nonsense; a child has to know reality to appreciate the juxtaposition of the strawberries and the herrings in this verse:[10]

> The man in the wilderness asked me
> How many strawberries grow in the sea.
> I answered him as I thought good,
> As many as red herrings grow in the wood.

Different Editions of Mother Goose

Today's children are fortunate in being able to choose among many beautifully illustrated Mother Goose editions. There is no *one* best Mother Goose book, for this is a matter for individual preference. Some Mother Goose books seem to stay in print indefinitely. Each generation may have its favorite edition, yet older versions remain popular. The children in every family deserve at least one of the better editions, however. Preschool and primary teachers will also want to have one that can be shared with small groups of children who might not have been fortunate enough ever to have seen a really beautiful Mother Goose.

Collections

One of the most glorious nursery-rhyme collections is *Tomie de Paola's Mother Goose*. Each of the more than two hundred verses is illustrated with brilliant jewel tones against a clear white background. Characters of many races are included quite naturally. Pictures are large enough to be shared with a large group of children. Several include a full-page spread; many show a

[10]Kornei Chukovsky, *From Two to Five*, trans. Miriam Morton (Berkeley: University of California Press, 1963), p. 95.

sequence of action. Careful placement of the rhymes provides interesting artistic contrasts, such as the jagged lines of the crooked man's house next to the rounded haystack of Little Boy Blue. The total format of this comprehensive Mother Goose is pleasing to the eye.

Wendy Watson's Mother Goose incorporates more than two hundred traditional verses along with some well-known rhymes. Set in rural America, each verse is illustrated with small pictures of animal characters or round-figured rustic folk. A unique feature of this book is that the illustrations span the seasons of a year, beginning with a frosty morning and ending with a chilly midnight New Year's Eve.

The Random House Book of Mother Goose should have been named for its editor/illustrator, Arnold Lobel, for it was one of the last books published before his death in 1987. Lobel illustrated over three hundred rhymes in this lively collection. Filled with fresh images and spontaneity, Lobel's Mother Goose book is a lasting contribution to children from this talented and well-loved illustrator. *Whiskers and Rhymes*, also by Lobel, is a lively collection of rhymes about cats. Although it features only several dozen rhymes, *James Marshall's Mother Goose* provides young children with a fresh and funny look at the venerable Old Goose. Most of the rhymes included in this collection are humorous, with hilarious illustrations to match. Children clever enough to spy the knife slipping through the pumpkin shell will realize that Peter is not going to be able to keep his wife forever, despite the last line of the rhyme. Sharing Marshall's funny parody on "Hey Diddle Diddle" might inspire older children to create their own original Mother Goose rhymes.

A recent collection by Zena Sutherland consists of some seventy-five verses under the title *The Orchard Book of Nursery Rhymes*. Brilliant detailed illustrations by Faith Jaques depict an eighteenth-century setting of rural England, the source of many of these verses. A few, such as "How much wood would a woodchuck chuck," reveal their American origin. Adding to the authenticity of this edition are the carefully researched notes on the sources and variants of these verses by both author and illustrator.

Scholars of nursery rhymes are all indebted to Iona and Peter Opie for their definitive work *The Oxford Dictionary of Nursery Rhymes*, in which they assembled almost everything known about these verses. In order to support the gift of their large children's literature collection to the Bodleian Library of Oxford, the Opies selected many previously unpublished rhymes for their book *Tail Feathers from Mother Goose: The Opie Rhyme Book*. Beginning with a cover by Maurice Sendak, each verse is illustrated by a different well-known artist.

Jan Ormerod has illustrated a short collection of Mother Goose rhymes for the very young in *To Baby with Love*.
Illustration by Jan Ormerod from her *To Baby With Love*. Copyright © 1994 by Jan Ormerod. By permission of Lothrop, Lee & Shepard Books, a division of William Morrow & Company, Inc.

Some of these little-known rhymes delight slightly older children. Sendak illustrated a new version of the Opies' first collection, *I Saw Esau*, which includes 170 rhymes, tongue twisters, jeers, and jump-rope rhymes. The many small pictures are just as sly and naughty as the children's rhymes. Only 7½ by 5 inches, this "Schoolchild's Pocket Book" is a superb example of fine bookmaking.

The Rooster Crows by Maud and Miska Petersham is sometimes called an American Mother Goose, for it includes many well-known American rhymes and jingles, such as "A bear went over the mountain" and "How much wood would a woodchuck chuck." Another bit of Americana is found in the highly original *Father Fox's Pennyrhymes*, written by Clyde Watson and illustrated by her sister, Wendy Watson. These nonsense rhymes and jingles have the lilt and rhythm of traditional verses of folklore. The little watercolor-and-ink illustrations detail the antics of Father Fox and his friends and relatives in old-fashioned pictures.

Guidelines:
Evaluating Mother Goose Books

With so many editions of Mother Goose, what factors should be considered when evaluating them? The following points might be useful in studying various editions:

• Coverage
How many verses are included? Are they well-known rhymes, or are there some fresh and unusual ones?

• Illustrations
What medium has been used? What colors? Are the illustrations realistic, stylized, or varied? Are the illustrations consistent with the text? Do they elaborate the text? What is the mood of the illustrations (humorous, sedate, high-spirited)? Has the illustrator created a fresh approach, avoiding cliché-ridden images?

• Text
Does the text read smoothly, or have verses been altered? Is the text all on the same page, or fragmented by turning the page?

• Setting
What background is presented—rural or urban? Does the book take place in any particular country? Is the setting modern or in the past? What does the setting add to the collection?

• Characters
Do the characters come from a variety of ethnic backgrounds? Do the characters have distinct personalities? Are adults and children featured? Only children? How are animals presented—as humans or realistically?

• Arrangement
Is there a thematic arrangement of the verses? Is there a feeling of unity to the whole book, rather than just separate verses? Are pictures and verses well spaced or crowded? Is it clear which picture illustrates which verse?

• Format
What is the quality of the paper and the binding? Is the title page well designed? Is there an index or table of contents? Is there harmony among endpapers, cover, and jacket?

No matter what edition is selected, children should be exposed to the rhythm and rhyme of Mother Goose. It is part of their literary heritage and might be their first introduction to the realm of literature.

With such a proliferation of nursery-rhyme books, parents, teachers, and librarians will want to examine a variety of collections before sharing them with their children. Even though you might have a favorite collection, try new ones with fresh images and unfamiliar rhymes after you have read the more traditional ones. Mother Goose should never be enjoyed only once, but read over and over again. See Guidelines, "Evaluating Mother Goose Books," for some considerations to take into account when selecting Mother Goose editions.

Single-Verse Editions

A recent publishing trend has been the production of picture books portraying only one Mother Goose rhyme or a limited number of rhymes around a single theme.

Maurice Sendak was one of the first to extend the text of two single verses with illustrations in his *Hector Protector and As I Went Over the Water*. The rhyme about Hector Protector is only five lines in length, but

twenty-four action-filled pictures expand the story behind this five-line verse. Sendak has also combined two unrelated rhymes in *We Are All in the Dumps with Jack and Guy*. With its images of rats, box cities, and homeless people, this book is for older children, but Sendak's illustrations create strong visual links to the darker social and political origins of some of the earliest rhymes.

In his foreword to Sarah Hale's *Mary Had a Little Lamb*, Tomie de Paola reminds us that this well-loved verse was first written by Sarah Josepha Hale in 1830 and then appeared in a McGuffey Reader. Since that time, however, it has been included in many Mother Goose collections. In illustrating a single edition of this verse, de Paola is faithful to the time and historical setting of the original poem. Bruce McMillan uses full-color photos of an African American child who poses for a rural Mary in his artfully crafted version of Hale's verse. Sally Mavor has used all kinds of fabrics and

Mary had a little lamb,   its fleece was white as snow.

Sally Mavor's fabric and stitchery illustrations add a sense of authenticity to Sarah Hale's *Mary Had a Little Lamb*.
From *Mary Had a Little Lamb* by Sarah Hale, illustrated by Sally Mavor. Illustration copyright © 1995 by Sally Mavor. Reprinted by permission of the Publisher, Orchard Books, New York.

stitchery to construct the pictures for her version of Mary's tale. The old-fashioned costumes and setting and the subtle links to woolly fibers and American folk art add surprising depth to the familiar rhyme. Equally faithful, in very different ways, to the historical context of this verse, all three books would be good choices for sharing with children.

Two recent books make a kind of game based on children's knowledge of Mother Goose. The easiest one, Eric Hill's *Nursery Rhyme Peek-a-Book*, asks rhyming questions such as "Hickory, dickory, dock, what ran up the clock?" Lifting the flap covering the face of the clock, the child discovers not only a little mouse, but the text of the whole rhyme printed on the inside of the flap. Ten well-known rhymes, such as "Old Mother Hubbard," "Sing a Song of Sixpence," "Humpty Dumpty," and "Little Miss Muffet," are included. If children don't know these verses, they will after hearing this book. Sturdily made with lively, clear pictures, it provides for much participation and learning.

Each Peach Pear Plum by the Ahlbergs pulls together characters from Mother Goose and traditional folktales in a kind of "I Spy" game. Starting with Little Tom Thumb, each successive picture hides a new character somewhere in its design. Thus the picture of Baby Bunting carries the text "Baby Bunting fast asleep, I spy

Bo-Peep," while the next picture of Bo-Peep challenges the viewer to find Jack and Jill. Children delight in playing this game, and they particularly love the ending, which pictures all of the characters together, eating plum pie, of course.

In *The Missing Tarts*, B. G. Hennessy creates a believable story about what happened to some tarts. All the Mother Goose characters search diligently, only to discover that the Knave of Hearts had given them to the children of the Old Woman in the Shoe. Like *Each Peach Pear Plum*, this story synthesizes children's knowledge of Mother Goose.

Nursery-Rhyme Collections from Other Lands

Nursery rhymes are difficult to translate because they are based on sound and nonsense, but several collections capture the elements of rhythm and sound that are so appealing to young children.

Barbara Cooney creates authentic settings for her pictures of Latin American rhymes collected from Spanish-speaking communities in the Americas. Each rhyme in *Tortillitas Para Mama* by Margot Griego and others is written in both Spanish and English. The English verses do not rhyme, but the Spanish ones do.

La loba

La loba, la loba,
le compró al lobito,
un calzón de seda
y un gorro muy bonito.

La loba, la loba
se fue de paseo,
con su gorro lindo
y su hijito feo.

ARGENTINA

The universal appeal of rhymes for children can be seen in such books as Lulu Delacre's *Arroz Con Leche*.
From *Arroz Con Leche: Popular Songs and Rhymes From Latin America* by LuLu Delacre. Copyright © 1989 by LuLu Delacre. Reprinted by permission of Scholastic Inc.

Arroz Con Leche: Popular Songs and Rhymes from Latin America, collected by Lulu Delacre, is another source of rhymes of Spanish origin.

Robert Wyndham's *Chinese Mother Goose Rhymes* has been reissued. Each page shows a rhyme in English and then in Chinese characters. Strikingly illustrated by Ed Young, this collection includes rhymes about dragons as well as counting-out rhymes.

In *Dragon Kites and Dragonflies*, Demi presents some twenty-two nursery rhymes illustrated with brilliant full-page watercolors. In this collection only the rhymed English versions are given. Students involved in a study of China could well begin with these rhymes about dragon boats, the Great Wall, and a Chinese wedding procession.

No Hickory No Dickory No Dock by John Agard and Grace Nichols is a collection of folk rhymes from the Caribbean that is full of energy in both its rhymes and its illustrations. This collection includes playful variations on "London Bridge," rhymes out of the Creole tradition, and many that have been recalled and rewritten by the authors from their childhood. Cynthia Jabar's bright scratchboard illustrations add a sense of island sizzle to the collection.

Sharing rhymes from other countries lets children of many cultures tap into their parents' memories to find rhymes in a variety of languages. The creation of nursery rhymes for the young child is a universal activity.

Young children enjoy all kinds of poetry besides nursery rhymes. See Chapter 8 for more about poetry. For a comparison of the unique features of various Mother Goose editions, see the Resources for Teaching box "Mother Goose Books."

Resources for Teaching
Mother Goose Books

Author, Illustrator	Title	Unique Features
Traditional Collections		
Leslie Brooke	*Ring o' Roses*	Published in 1923, this was the first collection to include humorous animals.
Kate Greenaway	*Mother Goose, or the Old Nursery Rhymes*	This has been a treasured classic since 1901. Tiny format and precise old-fashioned pictures of proper children.
Arthur Rackham	*Mother Goose, or the Old Nursery Rhymes*	Small eerie pictures of pointed-eared elves and personified trees.
Feodor Rojankovsky	*The Tall Book of Mother Goose*	The illustrations depict natural-looking children showing real emotions. Humpty Dumpty is portrayed as Hitler, appropriate to the time of this book's publication in 1942.
Blanche Fisher Wright	*The Real Mother Goose*	With pale flat traditional pictures, this book has been divided into four narrow-sized board books with checkered covers.
Contemporary Collections		
Raymond Briggs	*The Mother Goose Treasury*	Contains over 400 rhymes and twice as many illustrations. A lively vibrant presentation by a British illustrator.
Marguerite de Angeli	*The Book of Nursery and Mother Goose Rhymes*	Some 250 soft watercolor illustrations portray the English countryside and show the author's love for and knowledge of children.
Tomie de Paola	*Tomie de Paola's Mother Goose*	See text.
Eric Hill	*The Nursery Rhyme Peek-a-Book*	See text.
Arnold Lobel	*The Random House Book of Mother Goose*	See text.
James Marshall	*James Marshall's Mother Goose*	See text.
Iona and Peter Opie, Maurice Sendak	*I Saw Esau*	See text.
Iona and Peter Opie	*Tail Feathers from Mother Goose*	See text.
Jan Ormerod	*To Baby with Love*	Four rhymes for baby. A short collection but perfect for bedtime reading. The Ormerods' brightly colored illustrations will attract babies *and* parents.
Helen Oxenbury	*The Helen Oxenbury Nursery Rhyme Book*	Over fifty verses are illustrated with humorous, droll pictures of common folk.
Maud and Miska Petersham	*The Rooster Crows*	See text.
Alice and Martin Provensen	*The Mother Goose Book*	By grouping rhymes around various subjects, the artists have made one large picture serve several verses. Victorian dress reflects the period and origin of Mother Goose.
Liz Rosenberg, Janet Street	*Mama Goose*	These rhymes were chosen for their positive and playful content. Rhymes with violence or sexist views are not included.
Richard Scarry	*Richard Scarry's Best Mother Goose Ever*	Large brilliant-colored illustrations of animal characters make this a Mother Goose book that captures the attention of the youngest child.

Resources for Teaching
Mother Goose Books (concluded)

Author, Illustrator	Title	Unique Features
Zena Sutherland, Faith Jaques	*The Orchard Book of Nursery Rhymes*	See text.
Tasha Tudor	*Mother Goose*	Small, soft pastel pictures are quaint and charmingly reminiscent of the work of Kate Greenaway.
Wendy Watson	*Wendy Watson's Mother Goose*	See text.
Brian Wildsmith	*Brian Wildsmith's Mother Goose*	Pictures are glowing watercolors with the typical Wildsmith trademarks seen in the harlequin designs on clothing and the frequency with which he portrays people's backs.

Single Verse Editions

Author, Illustrator	Title	Unique Features
Lorinda Bryan Cauley	*The Three Little Kittens*	Appealing kittens that delight very young children.
Sarah Josepha Hale, Tomie de Paola	*Mary Had a Little Lamb*	See text.
Sarah Josepha Hale, Bruce McMillan	*Mary Had a Little Lamb*	See text.
Sarah Josepha Hale, Sally Mavor	*Mary Had a Little Lamb*	See text.
Susan Ramsay Hoguet	*Solomon Grundy*	The life span of a nineteenth-century New England baker provides authentic period detail.
Susan Jeffers	*Three Jovial Huntsmen*	Three bumbling hunters search and search for their quarry and never see the many hidden animals watching them.
Julie Lacome	*Walking Through the Jungle*	A traditional rhyme in an exotic setting with a toddler exploring jungle habitat and beasts.
Tracey Campbell Pearson	*Sing a Song of Sixpence*	Children could compare this humorous version with Lubin's interpretation.
Rodney Peppe	*The House That Jack Built*	Splendid bold collage pictures illustrate this favorite cumulative rhyme.
Janet Stevens	*The House That Jack Built*	Bright red, yellow, and black pictures portray the characters as country bumpkins.
Maurice Sendak	*Hector Protector and As I Went Over the Water*	See text.
Maurice Sendak	*We Are All in the Dumps with Jack and Guy*	See text.
Peter Spier	*London Bridge Is Falling Down*	Notes on the back page provide the history of London Bridge and the music.
Ashley Wolff	*The Bells of London*	Full-color linoleum block prints tell a story of friendship and freedom and at the same time illustrate verses for the traditional "Bells of London."

Alphabet Books

In colonial days, children were first taught their ABCs from cautionary rhymes like "In Adam's Fall/we sinned all," which combined early literacy and religion. Later, pictures of animals beginning with certain letters were added to hornbooks and early primers for younger children. Alphabet books today can be equally deceptive. Many of them have moved beyond teaching children their alphabet to serving as a format to present detailed information about a particular subject for older boys and girls, to showcase an art book, or to create complicated puzzles. Most of the alphabet books and criteria for their evaluation discussed in this chapter are directed at ABC books for the young child, however. Ages are given when an older audience is implied.

Besides teaching the names and shapes of the letters, ABC books can also be used for identification or naming, as they provide the young child with large, bright pictures of animals or single objects to look at and talk about. One of the liveliest and jazziest alphabet books is Bill Martin, Jr., and John Archambault's *Chicka Chicka Boom Boom*, illustrated with vibrant colors by Lois Ehlert. An alphabet chant, this book helps children memorize the letters and identify them. It does not provide an object or animal that goes with a beginning sound as most alphabet books do, but it does provide for much fun and merriment as children chant these active letters.

Certain factors need to be considered in selecting alphabet books. Objects should be clearly presented on the page, and these should be easily identifiable and meaningful for the intended age level. Only one or two objects should be shown for the very young child, and it is best to avoid portraying anything that might have several correct names. For example, if a rabbit is presented for *R*, the very young child might refer to it as a "bunny." Since text is necessarily limited, the pictures usually "carry" the story. For this reason they should be both clear and consistent with the text, reflecting and creating the mood of the book.

Alphabet books vary, in both their texts and their pictorial presentation, from very simple to intricate levels of abstraction. Authors and illustrators use a variety of organizing structures to create ABC texts. Four types of ABC books are discussed here (some books incorporate several types): (1) word-picture formats, (2) simple narratives, (3) riddles or puzzles, and (4) topical themes. Today there are so many alphabet books that only outstanding examples of each type are described here.

Striking pictures of realistic animals climb, poke through, or push large black block letters in *Animal Alphabet* by Bert Kitchen. A giraffe chins himself on the huge G, while a small snail climbs up the *S*. Each page contains only the letter and the picture of the animal.

Names of animals are given on a page at the end of this handsome book.

Suse MacDonald creates an original and imaginative book in *Alphabatics*. Each letter grows or tilts to become part of a beautifully clear graphic picture on the next page. For example, a C moves sideways, stretches, and becomes the smile on the clown's face. The Y moves off one page to become the head and horns of the yak on the other side. Children enjoy seeing the letters evolve and then finding them in the opposite picture.

At first glance Kate Duke's *The Guinea Pig ABC* looks like a one-word, one-picture identification book. A closer look reveals that the child must interpret the action and meaning of each small vignette on a page. Thus M stands for "mean" and shows one guinea pig about to pull a chair out from under another. The vignettes are clear and cleverly done, but interpreting a story is a more difficult task than simply identifying an object or animal.

Arnold and Anita Lobel combined their many talents to create a handsome and unique alphabet book. Starting with the picture of a small Victorian boy determinedly lacing up his high shoes, sailor hat ready to go and purse fat with change, we follow him on his journey to the page displaying the title, *On Market Street*. Then he proceeds on his way through the shops from A to Z. He returns home in the evening exhausted, with an empty purse but a gorgeous array of gifts, each purchased from a different shop. Rather than portray all the stores, Anita Lobel creates tradespeople and shopkeepers out of their own wares, making intriguing characters from books, clocks, eggs, quilts, toys, or zippers.

In brilliant watercolor collages, Lois Ehlert introduces children to a wide variety of fruits and vegetables in her book *Eating the Alphabet*. Sometimes as many as four vegetables appear on a single page, but they are clearly depicted. Children might not know all the items pictured, but it would extend their knowledge and be an excellent book to use prior to a trip to the grocery store.

In Anne Shelby's *Potluck*, Alpha and Betty decide to have a party, so they call all of their friends. Action-filled pictures by Irene Trivas show children of various racial and ethnic backgrounds bringing a variety of delectable foods. The foods are not stereotyped as to the child's background—for example, Ben, an African American child, brings bagels—but Hispanic triplets do turn up with tacos. Finally, they all sit down to a glorious feast, eating everything from A to Z. Children can also eat their way through the alphabet in Bonnie Christiansen's *An Edible Alphabet* and Crescent Dragonwagon's *Alligator Arrived with Apples*. Christiansen creates lovely wood engravings to illustrate twenty-six edible plants, including eggplant, tomatoes, and zucchini. Each picture is full of narrative detail that shows the plant in context; for "Eggplant," a chicken picks through the garden beside the purple plants while children in the background play in a windy field. Dragonwagon's alliterative tale can serve as a model for children's own alphabet books.

Anita Lobel's *Alison's Zinnia* is a brilliant alphabet book glowing with flower paintings. Listen to the carefully planned sentences in this book:

> Alison acquired an Amaryllis for Beryl
> Beryl bought a Begonia for Crystal

and so it goes until

> Yolanda yanked a Yucca for Zena
> Zena zeroed in on a Zinnia for Alison.

Some alphabet books incorporate riddles or hidden puzzles in their formats. *Anno's Alphabet*, by one of Japan's leading illustrators and designers, Mitsumasa Anno, is filled with quirky illusions and puzzles. Each large letter looks three-dimensional, as if it has been carefully carved from wood. Suddenly, however, its perspective will appear to change and surprise you. The M is only half there as it disappears into its mirror image. Each letter is matched with a clear yet amusing picture, and hidden in all of the borders are even more surprises. A glossary at the end provides clues to the hidden pictures in this visually exciting ABC book.

The Z Was Zapped by Chris Van Allsburg is a highly sophisticated alphabet drama presented in twenty-six acts. The large black-and-white picture of a letter on a stage appears before the sentence describing how it meets its sinister demise. For example, a pair of gloved hands picks up the *K*; turn the page to find "The K was quietly Kidnapped." Older children delight in guessing what happened to each letter and may want to create their own alphabet drama.

Topical themes are frequently used to tie the alphabet together. For example, *V for Vanishing: An Alphabet of Endangered Animals* by Patricia Mullins and Ann Jonas's *Aardvarks Disembark!* provide information on endangered or extinct animals. In *A Caribou Alphabet*, Mary Beth Owens portrays the world of the caribou, from "A for Antlers" to "Z for Below Zero Weather." A compendium at the end gives even more information about this endangered species. Older students studying the Middle Ages will want to look at *Illuminations* by Peter Hunt. From *alchemist* to *zither*, Hunt depicts many aspects of the life, architecture, and legends of these times in a format that reflects the illuminated manuscripts. This is an excellent example of a theme alphabet book.

Children can explore the world around them or beyond their borders through alphabet books like Nikki

Grimes's *C Is for City*, illustrated by Pat Cummings. Through rhyming text and detailed paintings, the two show the lively multicultural world of a big city. In this urban setting, for example, *H* is for handball, hopscotch, hot dogs, and Hasidim. In Anita Lobel's *Away from Home*, children travel to the far corners of the earth, beginning with Adam, who "arrived in Amsterdam," and ending with Zachary, who "zigzagged in Zaandam." Background paintings show scenes from each of the locations. Older children might enjoy creating their own alphabet book based on a chosen subject, using these two books as models. Another interesting alphabet book for older students is *ABC Americana* by Cynthia Rubin with illustrations of folk art from the National Gallery of Art. Such theme books suggest ways for older students to organize material they might be presenting for a particular study. Children could make their own ABC books of "Life at the Seashore," "Pioneer Life," or their favorite books. For a description of the unique features of many ABC books, see the Resources for Teaching box "ABC Books."

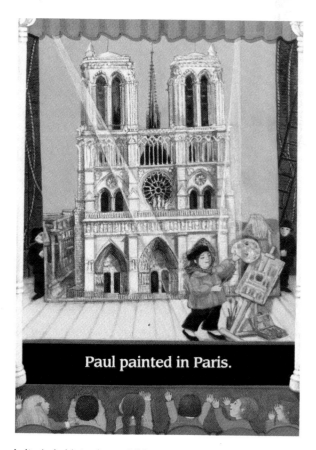

Paul painted in Paris.

Anita Lobel introduces children to ABC wonders of the world in *Away from Home*.

Illustration by Anita Lobel from her *Away From Home*. Copyright © 1994 by Anita Lobel. By permission of Greenwillow Books, a division of William Morrow & Company, Inc.

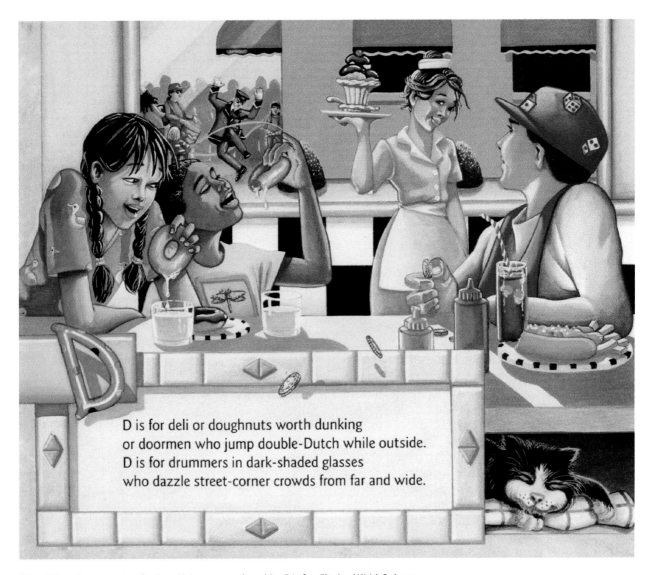

D is for deli or doughnuts worth dunking
or doormen who jump double-Dutch while outside.
D is for drummers in dark-shaded glasses
who dazzle street-corner crowds from far and wide.

The alliterative aspects of urban living are explored in *C Is for City* by Nikki Grimes.
Illustration from *C is for City* by Nikki Grimes, illustrated by Pat Cummings. Illustration copyright © 1995 by Pat Cummings. By permission of Lothrop, Lee & Shepard Books, a division of William Morrow & Company, Inc.

Counting Books

Ideally, girls and boys should learn to count by playing with real objects like blocks, boxes, bottle caps, or model cars. They can manipulate and group these as they wish, actually seeing what happens when you add one more block to nine or divide six blocks into two groups. Since time immemorial, however, we have been providing children with counting books, substituting pictures for real objects. Young children can make this transition from the concrete to its visual representation if they first experience the real objects and the visual illustrations are clearly presented.

In evaluating counting books, then, we look to see if the objects to be counted stand out clearly on the page.

Groupings of objects should not look cluttered or confusing. Illustrations and page design are most important in evaluating counting books. Accuracy is essential.

Counting books, too, vary from the very simple to the more complex. For the purposes of this text they are discussed under three categories: (1) one-to-one correspondence, (2) other simple mathematical concepts, and (3) number stories and puzzles. Examples of each category are given; Resources for Teaching, "Counting Books," lists other titles by structure.

Tana Hoban's *1, 2, 3* is a sturdy, well-designed first counting book that presents simple one-to-one correspondence. Colored photographs picture well-known objects like two shoes, five small fingers, six eggs, seven animal crackers, and ten toes. Numbers and names of the numerals are given in this first board book for very

Resources for Teaching
ABC Books

Author, Illustrator	Title	Age Level	Unique Features
Word/Picture Identification			
Bonnie Christiansen	An Edible Alphabet	2–5	See text.
Tana Hoban	A, B, See!	2–4	Black-and-white photograms illustrate familiar objects. The page for L depicts a piece of lace, a lollipop, a lock, and two leaves.
John Burningham	John Burningham's ABC	2–4	One clear picture for each letter. Unusual choices: T is for tractor; V shows a volcano.
Bert Kitchen	Animal Alphabet	2–5	See text.
Suse MacDonald	Alphabatics	3–6	See text.
Helen Oxenbury	Helen Oxenbury's ABC of Things	3–6	Provides a small vignette for each letter. H is represented by a very funny picture of a hare and a hippopotamus lying in bed in a hospital.
Simple Narrative			
Crescent Dragonwagon, Jose Aruego and Ariane Dewey	Alligator Arrived with Apples	6–10	See text.
Kate Duke	The Guinea Pig ABC	4–6	See text.
Wanda Gág	The ABC Bunny	2–4	A little rabbit provides the story line for each letter. Beautifully designed woodcuts in black and white illustrate this classic ABC. Each letter is brilliant red, reminiscent of a child's block.
Anita Lobel, Arnold Lobel	On Market Street	5–7	See text.
Tim Mahurin	Jeremy Kooloo	5–7	A cat's quest for milk. Sentences created from words in ABC order.
Anne Shelby, Irene Trivas	Potluck	6–10	See text.
Clyde Watson, Wendy Watson	Applebet	5–7	A farmer and her daughter take a cart full of apples to the country fair. The accompanying verse asks the child to find the apple hidden in each picture. Illustrations and verse celebrate a bit of rural Americana that will delight young children.
Riddles or Puzzles			
Mitsumasa Anno	Anno's Alphabet	5–10	See text.
Jan Garten	The Alphabet Tale	5–7	Each letter is introduced on the preceding page by showing just the tail of an animal; turn the page and you see the whole animal. Children can predict the next animal by the rhyming verse, the picture of the tail, and the beginning letter.
Lucy Mickelwait	I Spy: An Alphabet in Art	5–10	Children are invited to play "I Spy" and find objects in famous paintings.
Anne Rockwell	Albert B. Cub and Zebra	5–8	This wordless alphabet book is both a puzzle and a story. Albert B. Cub's beloved zebra is abducted. Albert's search for his friend takes him around the world and through the alphabet.
Chris Van Allsburg	The Z Was Zapped	7–12	See text.

Resources for Teaching
ABC Books (continued)

Author, Illustrator	Title	Age Level	Unique Features
Topical Themes			
Jim Aylesworth, Stephen Gammell	*Old Black Fly*	6–10	Marvelously funny illustrations portray this tiresome fly as he buzzes around the alphabet.
Mary Azarian	*A Farmer's Alphabet*	5–12	A handsome book that celebrates rural life in Vermont. Striking black-and-white woodcuts portray a barn, quilt, and a wood stove, for example.
Betsy Bowen	*Antler, Bear, Canoe*	6–10	Hand-colored woodcuts show the four seasons in the North woods. Compare to Azarian's Vermont woodcuts.
Jo Bannatyne-Cugnet, Yvette Moore	*A Prairie Alphabet*	6–12	Highly detailed paintings provide a tour of the seasons and people of the northern prairie.
Lois Ehlert	*Eating the Alphabet*	4–7	See text.
Nikki Grimes, Pat Cummings	*C Is for City*	6–10	See text.
Muriel Feelings, Tom Feelings	*Jambo Means Hello*	6–12	Muriel Feelings gives children a simple lesson in Swahili while introducing some important aspects of the geography and culture of East Africa. Tom Feelings has produced soft, luminous gray, black, and white illustrations of the people and their villages.
Lee Bennett Hopkins, Barry Root	*April, Bubbles, Chocolate*	6–10	Favorite poems to highlight the alphabet. Selections include "Foghorns" by Lilian Moore and Richard Brautigan's "Xerox Candy Bar."
Ted Harrison	*A Northern Alphabet*	7–12	This striking book about northern Canada and Alaska describes people, places, animals, and objects for each letter. Place names beginning with the appropriate letter form a frame around each picture. The flowing lines of the pictures recall Inuit art.
Peter Hunt	*Illuminations*	8–12	See text.
Rachel Isadora	*City Seen from A to Z*	6–9	Captures the action of the city through body postures and storytelling vignettes. This is a city bustling with people—all ages, all races, all enjoying their city.
Stephen Johnson	*Alphabet City*	6–10	Photo-realistic paintings capture the lines, shapes, and textures of the city.
Ann Jonas	*Aardvarks Disembark!*	7–12	See text.
Frané Lessac	*Caribbean Alphabet*	6–10	From airport arrivals to a trip to the zoo, this is a visual tour of the Caribbean. A glossary at the end provides information on unfamiliar words.
Anita Lobel	*Alison's Zinnia*	7–12	See text.
Anita Lobel	*Away from Home*	7–12	See text.

Resources for Teaching
ABC Books (concluded)

Author, Illustrator	Title	Age Level	Unique Features
Patricia Mullins	*V is for Vanishing*	6–12	See text.
Margaret Musgrove, Leo and Diane Dillon	*Ashanti to Zulu: African Traditions*	7–12	This is the only alphabet book to have won the Caldecott Medal. Musgrove describes many of the customs of 26 African tribes; the Dillons create stunning illustrations picturing the people, their homes, and an artifact and animal for each tribe. Pictures are framed and tied together at the corners with a design based on the Kano Knot, which symbolizes endless searching.
Ifeoma Onyefulu	*A Is for Africa*	6–12	Striking photographs and pleasing page design introduce African cultures and customs.
Mary Beth Owens	*A Caribou Alphabet*	7–12	See text.
Alice Provensen, Martin Provensen	*A Peaceable Kingdom: The Shaker ABCEDARIUS*	6–12	The Provensens illustrated this old 1882 alphabet verse of the Shakers in a way that depicts the rhyme of the animals but also provides much information about the way the Shakers lived. Richard Barsan concludes the book with a note on Shaker history and education.
Cynthia Rubin	*ABC Americana*	7–12	See text.
Marilyn Sanders, Eve Sanders	*What's Your Name? From Ariel to Zoe*	6–10	Twenty-six children from a variety of cultures talk about their names. Each class will want to create their own name alphabet book.
Luci Tapahonso, Eleanor Schick	*Navajo ABC*	6–12	Beginning with A for Arroyo, lovely realistic illustrations give information about the Navajo, or Diné, culture. A glossary provides further information about symbols, values, and language.
Tasha Tudor	*A Is for Annabelle*	5–7	Delicate watercolors portray an old-fashioned doll with her different belongings representing different letters.

young children. Such a beginning counting book might serve more for identification of the object than for actual counting. Certainly it requires a lower level of associative thinking for the very young child.

Keith Baker's *Big Fat Hen* will attract children with its richly textured paintings and its familiar counting rhyme "1, 2, buckle my shoe." Bright white eggs are pictured on one double-page spread with numerals to match. Then on the next two pages the eggs have hatched into little chicks who act out buckling the shoe, shutting the door, and so on. The bright yellow chicks and white eggs stand out on the pages, making them easy to count. They also make a nice contrast to the beautifully patterned multicolored chickens.

Tana Hoban's *26 Letters and 99 Cents* is really two books in one. Clear magnetic letters are photographed with equally clear pictures of toys or objects beginning with that letter. Turn the book around and you have number concepts with photos of magnetic numbers and all the possible sets of coins to make up that number. Although the number section is far more difficult than the alphabet section, primary children who are learning to count lunch money would find it very useful.

Patricia MacCarthy creates beautiful batik paintings of patterned fish for her number book *Ocean Parade*. Every page swirls before your eyes as you look at three flat fish, twenty sea horses, and one hundred silverfish.

Resources for Teaching
Counting Books

Author, Illustrator	Title	Age Level	Unique Features
One-to-One Correspondence			
Jim Aylesworth, Ruth Young	*One Crow, a Counting Rhyme*	5–7	The farm provides much to count, both in the summer and then again in the winter.
Keith Baker	*Big Fat Hen*	4–6	See text.
Molly Bang	*Ten, Nine, Eight*	4–6	Starting with her ten toes, a father begins a countdown until his daughter is in bed. One of the few number books to portray a black father and daughter.
Eric Carle	*1, 2, 3, to the Zoo*	4–6	A circus train serves as the vehicle for this counting book as each passing car contains an increasing number of animals, such as two hippos and nine snakes.
Kathleen Sullivan Carroll, Suzette Barbier	*One Red Rooster*	4–6	Bright clear paintings picture farm animals, beginning with one red rooster who "went cock-a-doodle-do." The rhyming text also stresses colors and animal sounds.
Cathryn Falwell	*Feast for Ten*	4–7	Beginning with one grocery cart, these bold textured collages show an African American family shopping for, preparing, and eating a feast for ten.
Muriel Feelings, Tom Feelings	*Moja Means One*	7–12	This is more an informational book on East Africa and the Swahili language than a counting book. For example, the number 6 is represented by six persons in different kinds of dress, but only five kinds of clothing are identified.
S. T. Garne, Lisa Etre	*One White Sail*	6–8	Rhyming text and vivid watercolors reflect the climate and culture of the Caribbean.
Arthur Geisert	*Pigs from 1 to 10*	5–9	Detailed etchings hide pigs to count and adventures to follow.
Tana Hoban	*1, 2, 3*	1–3	See text.
Bert Kitchen	*Animal Numbers*	5–9	A stunning counting book that begins with one baby kangaroo in its mother's pouch and ends with a hundred baby tadpoles and frogs' eggs.
Patricia MacCarthy	*Ocean Parade*	5–8	See text.
Helen Oxenbury	*Numbers of Things*	4–6	Delightfully amusing illustrations add to the fun of this number book. Fifty is represented by the appropriate number of ladybugs; the final page pictures an astronaut on the moon and asks "How many stars?"
John J. Reiss	*Numbers*	3–5	Clear drawings of such common objects as shoes, kites, baseball players, etc., make this well within the young child's experience. The book ends with a picture representing a thousand raindrops.
Ann Herbert Scott	*One Good Horse: A Cowpuncher's Counting Book*	5–9	From one good horse to a hundred cattle, this book provides a unique territory for a counting book. The last double-page spread shows everything that has been counted on this western landscape.

Resources for Teaching
Counting Books (continued)

Author, Illustrator	Title	Age Level	Unique Features
Peter Sis	*Waving: A Counting Book*	5–7	Mary's mother waved to a taxi. Two bicyclists waved back to her while three boys waved to the bicyclists. A city background provides even more to count.

Other Mathematical Concepts

Author, Illustrator	Title	Age Level	Unique Features
Mitsumasa Anno	*Anno's Counting Book*	4–7	See text.
Mitsumasa Anno	*Anno's Counting House*	5–8	Ten little people living in a furnished house move to an empty house next door, taking their belongings with them. Concepts of addition and subtraction can be developed. Die-cut windows pique the child's curiosity to see inside.
Donald Crews	*Ten Black Dots*	4–8	A graphic counting book that shows what you can do with ten black dots. One can make a sun, two become fox's eyes, or eight the wheels of a train. Would make an interesting design assignment.
Olivier Dunrea	*Deep Down Underground*	5–8	See text.
Lois Ehlert	*Fish Eyes: A Book You Can Count On*	6–8	See text.
Paul Giganti, Jr., Donald Crews	*How Many Snails?*	4–8	A counting book that asks increasingly difficult questions: not only how many snails, but how many snails with stripes? how many striped snails with their head stuck out?
Tana Hoban	*26 Letters and 99 Cents*	6–8	See text.
Ann Jonas	*Splash!*	6–10	See text.
Eve Merriam, Bernie Karlin	*12 Ways to Get to 11*	5–7	In an imaginative introduction to sets, eleven different combinations of things add up to twelve.
Bruce McMillan	*Eating Fractions*	6–10	Bright photographs show something good to eat. On the left-hand page is a picture of the food divided into parts. Under this picture is the name of the part (whole, thirds, fourths, etc.) and a schematic drawing of each fractional part with its proper numeral. On the right-hand page two children are having a wonderful time eating up the parts.
Lloyd Moss, Marjorie Priceman	*Zin! Zin! Zin! A Violin*	6–10	Musical instruments come together to count to ten through musical groups, from solo to nonet to a chamber group that performs a stellar concert.
Pam Munoz Ryan, Benrei Huang	*One Hundred Is a Family*	5–8	The rhyming text first counts to ten, illustrated with pictures of families from many cultures. Then counting by tens shows families as larger communities working together for a better world.
Peter Sis	*Going Up! A Color Counting Book*	5–8	Ordinal numbers are presented as various costumed persons get on an elevator going up to a surprise party on the tenth floor.

Resources for Teaching
Counting Books (concluded)

Author, Illustrator	Title	Age Level	Unique Features
Number Stories and Puzzles			
Eric Carle	*The Very Hungry Caterpillar*	5–7	See text.
Shari Halpern	*Moving from One to Ten*	5–8	It's moving day and there are plenty of things to count on the way to a new house.
Sarah Hayes	*Nine Ducks Nine*	5–7	Nine ducks go for a walk, followed by a fox. One by one the ducks take off for the rickety bridge where Mr. Fox receives his comeuppance. A wonderful story that helps children count down.
Pat Hutchins	*1 Hunter*	5–7	See text.
Pat Hutchins	*The Doorbell Rang*	5–7	See text.
Ifeoma Onyefulu	*Emeka's Gift*	6–10	Beautiful photographs celebrate family and community in a Nigerian village.
Charlotte Pomerantz, Jose Aruego and Ariane Dewey	*One Duck, Another Duck*	5–7	A grandmother owl teaches her grandson to count to ten. Easy and entertaining story.
Maurice Sendak	*One Was Johnny*	5–7	Part of the small "Nutshell Library," this is the story of a small boy visited by many obnoxious animals. He threatens to eat them all if they are not gone by the time he counts down from ten.

A watery theme can also be found in Lois Ehlert's *Fish Eyes: A Book You Can Count On*, illustrated with brilliant colored graphics. A little black fish takes the reader on a journey through the ocean to discover "one green fish, two jumping fish, three smiling fish." Always the black fish adds himself to the group: "Three smiling fish plus me makes 4." Children delight in the spots and stripes of these gleaming fish with die-cut eyes.

Captivating language characterizes Olivier Dunrea's counting book *Deep Down Underground*. Moudiewort (pronounced "moo-dee-wort") is a Scottish word for "mole." In this cumulative story, ten little creatures "deep down underground" hear the digging mole and "wriggle and wrangle," "burrow and scrape," "scrooch and scrunch" to get out of his way. Children will love to chant the verses while learning to count from one to ten and back again.

Many mathematical concepts are developed in one of the most inventive and perfect counting books of recent years, *Anno's Counting Book* by Mitsumasa

Anno. Delicate watercolors portray a landscape changing with the various times of day, seasons, and year. The clock in the church steeple tells the time of day while adults, children, and animals go about their daily activities. As the buildings in the village increase, so do the groups and sets of children, adults, trees, trains, boats, and so on. This is one of the few counting books to begin with zero—a cold winter landscape showing only the river and the sky, no village. It ends with a picture of the twelfth month, a snowy Christmas scene and twelve reindeer in the sky. *Anno's Counting Book* requires real exploration to find the sets of children, adults, buildings, and animals, generating a higher level of thought and discussion about numerical concepts than a simple one-to-one counting book.

Pat Hutchins provides both a number story and a puzzle in her creative book *1 Hunter*. This is an account of a hunter's humorous walk through a jungle filled with hidden animals. The hunter determinedly stalks past two trees; turn the page and "the trees" are the legs of

In *Anno's Counting Book,* Mitsumasa Anno's delicate watercolors portray a landscape changing with the various times of day, seasons, and year. The clock in the church steeple tells the time of day while sets of adults, children, and animals go about their daily activities. How many sets of nine can you discover on this page?
Copyright © 1995 by Mitsumasa Anno. Used by permission of HarperCollins Publishers, New York, NY.

two elephants. The hunter is oblivious to all he is missing, until the very last page when the animals come out of hiding and the one hunter runs away.

Hutchins's well-loved story *The Doorbell Rang* could also be used for its math concepts. Victoria and Sam's mother makes them a dozen cookies just like Grandmother's to share (six each). The doorbell rings and two friends are welcomed in to share the cookies (three each). The doorbell rings twice more until there are a dozen children and a dozen cookies. The doorbell rings again. Should they answer it? They do, and it is their grandmother with an enormous tray of cookies!

Ann Jonas's *Splash!* will challenge primary children learning about adding and subtracting. The book begins on a lazy summer day at a backyard pond where two catfish and four goldfish swim lazily. On the bank three frogs, one turtle, and one dog are napping while one robin rests on a bird house. When one cat comes home, she startles the turtle, who jumps in the water. "How many are in my pond?" becomes the refrain that carries through the rest of the book as animals, amphibians, fish, birds, and insects get in and out of the pond.

Certainly there is no dearth of counting books and books that can be used for the development of math concepts. Because the criteria for evaluating counting books are similar to those for alphabet books, we have combined the criteria for both in the Guidelines box "Evaluating ABC and Counting Books."

Concept Books

A concept book describes various dimensions of an object, a class of objects, or an abstract idea. Concepts need to grow from firsthand experience as children gradually perceive common characteristics and relationships such as color, size, weight, or location. Some concepts, like shape or color, can be more easily presented in a book than abstract concepts like growth, time, or distance. Certain concepts, like the concept of love or death, develop gradually over years and might be best understood in the themes of storybooks or informational books for older children.

The books discussed in this chapter are written for young children with the specific purpose of developing concepts. A concept book is really a young child's first informational book. It should stimulate much talk and help children develop their vocabularies while at the same time helping to sharpen their perceptions and enlarge their growing understanding of the world. Well-defined concepts are necessary for children's linguistic and cognitive development.

Notice how young children struggle to define their understanding of the concept "dog." At first "doggies" includes all dogs and maybe even a few cats and squirrels. Later, after they have abstracted the essential qualities of "dogginess," young children can tell the difference. Still later, they can make finer differentiations

Children can count, add, and subtract in Ann Jonas's *Splash!*.

Illustration by Ann Jonas from her *Splash!*. Copyright © 1995 by Ann Jonas. By permission of Greenwillow Books, a division of William Morrow & Company, Inc.

Guidelines:
Evaluating ABC and Counting Books

ABC Books

The objects or animals should be presented clearly.

For very young children, only one or two objects should be pictured on a page.

Common objects or animals that are easily identifiable are best for the young child.

ABC books should avoid the use of objects that might be known by several names.

The author/illustrator's purpose for the book should be clear.

The illustrations should be consistent with the text and reflect the mood of the book.

The organizing principle of the presentations should be clear.

The intended age level should be considered in both pictures and text.

Counting Books

Objects to be counted should stand out clearly.

Accuracy is essential.

Common objects that children know, such as fingers, toes, and eggs, are usually best for the young child.

Groupings or sets should be clearly differentiated.

Number concepts should not be lost in the story.

The level of thinking required should be challenging for appropriate ages.

Vividly colored photographs portray a full spectrum of color in Tana Hoban's *Colors Everywhere*.
Illustration by Tana Hoban from her *Colors Everywhere*. Copyright © 1995 by Tana Hoban. By permission of Greenwillow Books, a division of William Morrow & Company, Inc.

—among a St. Bernard, a cocker spaniel, and a German shepherd, for example. Concept books help children identify these essential elements of an object or a class of objects.

ABC books and counting books are really concept books. So, too, are the books that help children identify and discriminate colors. John Reiss illustrates his book *Colors* for very young children with clear, bright graphics showing several pages of familiar objects for each color; for example, the various shades of green are shown by green leaves, grass, a green snake, a frog, a turtle, pickles, cucumbers, gooseberries, and peas. It is appropriate that a first book on colors should be as aesthetically pleasing to the eye as this one is.

In *Colors Everywhere* Tana Hoban places photographs of a basket of buttons, a peacock in a field of daffodils, a carnival, and a pile of autumn leaves next to separate bands of color that a child could name and match in each picture. This task requires more-advanced perceptual skills, but even the very young child will be attracted to these brightly colored photographs.

Color Dance by Ann Jonas shows what happens when you mix colors, using four young dancers with colored scarves. The red dancer and yellow dancer unfurl their scarves to create orange. This is a joyous book of colors.

Tana Hoban has written four books on shapes. The first, *Shapes and Things*, uses black-and-white photograms of real objects like scissors and a hammer to help children identify unique shapes. Each page shows sets of generic objects; for instance, shapes of tools are arranged on one page, and objects used in sewing are on the opposite page. *Circles, Triangles and Squares* uses photographs of familiar objects to present these particular concepts. Full-color photographs illustrate Hoban's two other books, *Shapes, Shapes, Shapes* and *Spirals, Curves, Fanshapes, and Lines*.

Color Zoo and *Color Farm*, both by Lois Ehlert, use sophisticated die-cut graphics to create the heads of stylized animals out of various shapes. A square, a triangle, and a circle produce a picture of a tiger's head. When you turn the page, each shape is then clearly shown and identified. Primary and even older children might use shapes to make their own animals after looking at these brilliant pictures. In *Sea Shapes*, Suse MacDonald shows how abstract geometric shapes can be found in natural forms. In three small vignettes a circle becomes a whale's eye or a crescent turns into a leaping dolphin. A large picture facing each transformation shows the creature in its watery world.

In another fine photo concept book, *Is It Larger? Is It Smaller?* Tana Hoban looks at relative size. Showing such familiar objects as three vases of flowers, or a large snowwoman and a baby snowman, she presents the concept of size in a way children can easily understand. In *Exactly the Opposite,* Hoban uses a variety of situations to show open and shut, front and back, empty and full, and far and near. Large colored photos capture children running up the stairs and the same children coming down the stairs. Children push a wagon, children pull a wagon. As always Hoban is inclusive of various races and avoids any gender stereotyping. Using her book *All About Where,* primary children could work in groups to see how many of the location words alongside the pictures apply to each color shot. Since there is no one right answer, they would have much fun generating a variety of sentences. Again this would be too abstract for most preschoolers.

Ann Morris has brought an international focus to the concepts of family, food, transportation, and the like in *Loving, Bread, Bread, Bread,* and *Houses and Homes.* In each of her books she provides photographs of children from a multitude of cultures. Simple text accompanies the pictures, and a simple glossary at the end matches photo to country with a brief fact.

Margaret Miller explores professions and trades in two well-conceived concept books, *Whose Hat?* and *Who Uses This?* A clear colored picture shows just a chef's hat. Turn the page and there is a picture of a chef in his kitchen. The opposite page pictures white and African American girls stirring a big pot, each wearing chef's hats. Nine professions are introduced by their hats. In *Who Uses This?* bakers, football players, and a conductor are identified by the tools of their trades. Miller has developed a similar question-and-answer format in *Can You Guess?* ("What do you comb in the morning?"), *Guess Who?* ("Who flies an airplane?"), and *Where Does It Go?* ("Where does a sock go?"). Photographs of four silly answers follow each question before the page is turned to reveal the correct response.

Many of Donald Crews's books, such as *Freight Train, Truck, School Bus,* and *Harbor,* could be classified as concept books or easy informational books. Certainly all of them explore the various dimensions of their subjects. In the first one, Crews pictures an empty track, then each of the different cars: the red caboose, orange tank car, yellow hopper car, green cattle car, blue gondola, purple box car, and finally the black steam engine. The train goes faster and faster through the tunnels and over bridges until it becomes a rainbow of speeding colors and then fades out of sight. Both colors and specific names for the cars provide real information for young children. In *Truck,* using bold graphics, Crews swings a big red truck across the country from east to west through cities, small towns, night and day, rain and shine. No text appears in this concept book except for

A toddler shares his interest in *Machines at Work* by Byron Barton with his Raggedy Andy.
Photo by Susan Fertig.

all the environmental print one naturally encounters on a trip, such as names of other trucks, traffic signs, highway exit signs, tunnels, and truck stops. In *School Bus* children again have an opportunity to see common signs and symbols: the green "Walk" sign, the red "Don't walk" sign, the school bus stop, and others. The yellow buses are large and small, but all pick up students and bring them home when school is over.

Other equally well-designed concept books by Crews include *Flying* and *Sail Away.* While these books seem geared for young children, some of them contain hidden messages that intrigue older children and adults.[11] For example, *Harbor* is dedicated "to the women in my life and Malcolm." Each boat is named after a woman: his wife, his daughter, his editor, and so on. Malcolm is his nephew.

Many of Lois Ehlert's books convey concepts for primary children as well as tell little stories. *Feathers for Lunch,* written with a rhyming text, tells about a little cat who would like to catch all the different birds that he sees, but luckily his bell frightens them away. The birds are pictured with life-size brilliant collages, and plants and trees are labeled. In *Red Leaf, Yellow Leaf* Ehlert uses collage again to tell the story of her favorite maple tree. Using natural objects, fibers, and painted paper forms, she describes all the parts of the tree and the creatures it affects—at its beginning as a seed on the

[11]See Susan Hepler, "Books in the Classroom," *Horn Book Magazine,* September/October 1988, pp. 667–669.

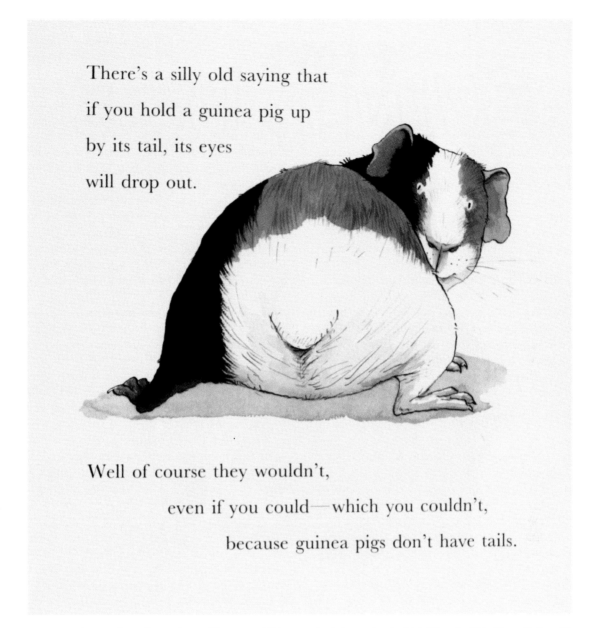

There's a silly old saying that
if you hold a guinea pig up
by its tail, its eyes
will drop out.

Well of course they wouldn't,
even if you could—which you couldn't,
because guinea pigs don't have tails.

Anita Jeram's appealing illustrations will attract children to the information in Dick King-Smith's *I Love Guinea Pigs*.
I Love Guinea Pigs, copyright © 1994 by Foxbusters Ltd. Illustrations copyright © 1994 by Anita Jeram. Reprinted by permission.

forest floor, then as a tree sprout in the nursery, and finally in her garden. In both books a brief appendix gives
information about the concept dealt with in the story.

Aliki's two informational concept books, *My Feet*
and *My Hands* from the Let's-Read-and-Find-Out Science Books series, seem just right for preschoolers. In
simple words and with clear, attractive pictures, Aliki
explores all of the things hands do and feet do. As always, Aliki pictures children of different races and cuts
across gender stereotypes. For example, the title page of
My Hands shows a young boy doing cross-stitching.

Dick King-Smith's *I Love Guinea Pigs* and *All Pigs
Are Beautiful* are a particularly delightful pair from the
Read and Wonder series, books that convey simple concepts in the context of stories or poems. King-Smith's
chatty format and his enthusiasm for his subjects provide just enough information for young children. For example, he explains immediately that guinea pigs aren't
pigs but rodents. In smaller hand-printed captions he
provides information about a major characteristic of rodents and mentions that guinea pigs and pigs have in
common the fact that males and females are called

"boars" and "sows." Anita Jeram's watercolor pictures add to the appeal of both books.

Concept books are really children's first informational books. They help children see relationships between objects, develop awareness of similarities and differences, and grasp the various dimensions of an abstract idea. Often these books begin with the familiar and move to the unfamiliar or more complex. Many of them appear to be moving from totally obvious concepts for younger children to more abstract and less obvious concepts for older children. Concepts for the younger child should be presented in a clear, unconfusing manner, with one or more examples given. Where appropriate, the functions of objects should be made clear. Concepts should be within the developmental scope of the child. Concept books can be used to enrich or reinforce an experience, not substitute for it. Young children enjoy hearing these beginning nonfictional books along with fictional stories, for young children are curious and seek information. They want to know the *names* of things, *how* they work, and *why* this is so. Evaluative criteria for informational books are presented in Chapter 12.

Wordless Books

Wordless books are picture books in which the story line is told entirely through pictures. They are increasingly popular with today's TV-oriented child. Many of them are laid out in the same sequential story as comic books and have wide appeal to different age levels.

Textless books are surprisingly helpful in developing some of the skills necessary for reading. Handling the book, turning the pages, beginning at the left-hand side and moving to the right are all skills that give the young child a sense of directionality and the experience of acting like a reader. These books are particularly useful in stimulating language development through encouraging children to take an active part in storytelling. As the child relates the story, she will become aware of beginnings, endings, the sequence of the story, the climax, the actions of the characters—all necessary for learning how a story works, for developing a sense of story. "Reading" or telling what is happening in the pictures in a wordless book also requires specific comprehension skills. Teachers may want to record children's stories in language experience booklets. Older children might want to write their own creative stories to accompany the illustrations. To help the child tell the story, pictures must show action and sequence clearly so children will not be confused in their tellings. Also, children should be given an opportunity to examine the

book and look through it completely before they try to tell the story orally. Otherwise, they will describe the action on each page but not understand the sequential relationship of the events.

In *Do You Want to Be My Friend?* Eric Carle gives the child latitude to create his own story about a little mouse who in seeking a friend follows the lead of one tail after another, only to be very surprised at what is at the other end! The brilliant collage pictures will delight children and provide the opportunity to tell their own versions of this story.

Nancy Tafuri provides an exciting wordless adventure story in *Junglewalk*. A boy puts down his book, "Jungles of the World," and turns off his light just as his cat slips out the window. The tail of the cat becomes a tiger, and the boy is off on his dream adventure seeing monkeys, elephants, zebras, and many other creatures in this brilliant jungle. The tiger brings him home, and the boy wakes from his dream just as his cat bounds in the window. In another wordless book, Tafuri uses exquisite large watercolors to show the explorations of a baby sea lion following a baby crab. Behind the baby sea lion is his mother carefully following him. When the crabs jump in the ocean, mother and child return to the herd. Tafuri's *Follow Me!* is a simple love story without words.

Alexandra Day tells a series of humorous stories about an almost human Rottweiler dog named Carl. In each wordless story, when Carl is left to mind the baby, he gives the child a marvelous time and manages to keep the grown-ups ignorant of their escapades. This is the plot of *Good Dog, Carl*. In *Carl Goes Shopping*, Carl takes care of the baby in the lobby of an elegant department store. In *Carl's Birthday*, Carl and the baby sample preparations for a surprise party without giving away the fact that they're in on the surprise. It is hard to tell who is the most lovable, dependable Carl or the delightful baby.

A highly original wordless book is *Changes, Changes* by Pat Hutchins. Here, two wooden dolls arrange and rearrange wooden building blocks to tell a fast-paced circular story. When their block house catches fire, the resourceful couple dismantle it and build a fire engine, whose hose quickly douses the fire, thereby creating a flood! Undaunted, the wooden dolls then build a boat, which becomes a truck, which is changed to a train, until eventually they reconstruct their original block house. In *Rosie's Walk*, Hutchins has written and illustrated an even funnier story with the use of only one sentence. In this book Rosie—a very determined, flat-footed hen—goes for a walk, unmindful of the fact that she is being stalked by a hungry fox. At every turn of Rosie's walk, the hen unwittingly foils the fox in his plans to catch her. The brightly colored comic illustrations help youngsters tell Rosie's story. Primary children enjoy retelling this story from the point of view of the fox.

The first waking thought of a plump little lady is that this is the morning to have pancakes for breakfast. In *Pancakes for Breakfast*, Tomie de Paola pictures her persistent efforts to make the pancakes despite the fact that she has to gather the eggs from the hen house, milk the cow, and churn the butter. Finally thinking she has all the ingredients, she discovers she must go and buy some maple syrup. She returns with a self-satisfied expression on her face, only to discover that her dog and cat have tipped over the milk and flour and eaten the eggs. All is not lost, however, for from her neighbor's house comes the delicious aroma of pancakes. The recipe for the pancakes is given and asks to be tried out.

Two outstanding wordless books, *Sunshine* and *Moonlight* by Jan Ormerod, celebrate a small girl's joy in the simple pleasures of morning and nighttime rituals. In a series of watercolor vignettes, often several to a page, a lovable little girl "helps" her mother and father get up in the morning. The little girl wakens first, reads her book, and then gets dressed in a wonderful sequence of twelve narrow pictures across two pages. She looks at her clock and goes in to alert her parents that they have overslept. They both dash back and forth in various stages of getting dressed. Finally, her father kisses her good-bye, and the little girl goes off with her schoolbag and her mother. The sunshine of this story streams through the windows and the radiant love of this family. *Moonlight* concludes the day with dinner, bath, bedtime story, and stalling ploys familiar to all children and parents. Once again the illustrator captures the shining glow of moonlight with beautifully soft watercolors.

It is interesting to see when children recognize that *Deep in the Forest* by Brinton Turkle is really a variant of "Goldilocks and the Three Bears," with the unique twist that a baby bear wreaks havoc in a pioneer cabin. Usually when the children see baby bear eating porridge from three different-size bowls, they recall having "heard" something like this before.

Mercer Mayer was one of the first illustrators to create wordless books. His series that includes *A Boy, a Dog, and a Frog* is very popular with children aged 5 and up. Simple line drawings in green and black portray the friendship between a boy, his dog, his frog, and a turtle. The stories are amusing and full of slapstick fun, particularly *Frog Goes to Dinner*, in which frog hides in the boy's pocket and goes to the restaurant with the family. Jealousy is the theme of *One Frog Too Many* when the boy is given a new baby frog. These stories are humorous and easily told from their pictures.

Emily McCully tells delightful stories of a large mouse family and their seasonal fun in *Picnic, First Snow,* and *School.* In *Picnic* a little mouse falls out of the truck when they go down a bumpy road. Her absence is not discovered until all eight of her brothers and sisters are ready to eat. Then the whole family piles into the truck to go find her. In *School,* the little mouse runs off to join her eight brothers and sisters. When the teacher discovers her, she calls her mother, only to have the little mouse cry. But after she holds the pointer, passes out milk and cookies, and listens to the teacher share *Picnic,* the little mouse is comforted and ready to go home with her mother. These books provide real narratives, with identifiable characters, exciting plots, and lush watercolors.

Peter Spier's Rain captures the delight of a sister and brother thoroughly enjoying playing in a rain-puddled day. It begins with just a few drops on the title page. The children's mother calls them into the house to get their macintoshes, rubber boots, and umbrella and then sensibly sends them outside to play. And play they do! The children see the shimmering beauty of drops of rain caught in a spider's web, check on where other animals and birds hide in the rain, and feed the ducks, geese and swans, who are in their element as much as the children are. Finally a strong wind comes up and the children run for home, where they enjoy all the cozy indoor treats of a rainy day: cocoa and cookies, a hot bath, reading, and bed.

The story of Noah's ark has been translated from the Dutch by Peter Spier in *Noah's Ark* and appears in verse form on the first page. What follows, however, is the virtually wordless story of all that transpires both inside and outside the ark for forty days and forty nights. Various-size pictures portray Noah's many activities on the ark and capture his every mood, from deep concern to jubilant rejoicing over the dove's return with the olive branch. Mrs. Noah's washline of clothes contrasts sharply with the dirty, messy interior of the ark at the end of its long voyage. Humorous touches run throughout this book, including the number of rabbits that leave the ark and the slow final departure of the snails and tortoise. Each viewing of the book reveals more of Spier's wit and artistic talent. This book richly deserved the Caldecott Medal it received.

Another beautiful wordless book is Raymond Briggs's *The Snowman.* Using soft colored pencils in a comic strip format, Briggs tells the story of a small boy and his snowman who comes to life one night. The boy invites the snowman inside to see the house but warns him away from the fireplace, the stove, and the hot water tap. The snowman has a childlike fascination for such simple things as an electric light switch, a skateboard, the father's false teeth in a glass, and the family car. The boy and the snowman share a meal and a fantastic predawn flight before returning to bed and the front lawn. In the morning the sun awakens the boy, and his first thought is for his snowman. He looks out the window—alas, his friend has melted. Children who have seen this lovely picture book want to look at it over and over again. It is the kind of story that invites revisiting and discussing all the details Briggs has included.

David Wiesner's fascinating book *Tuesday* is the second almost wordless book to receive the Caldecott Medal. On "Tuesday evening, around eight," all the frogs take off from their lily pads. Brilliant watercolors portray their joyous flight as they zoom through a house, chase birds and a dog, and return home at dawn. The next Tuesday evening, the pigs fly! Children could easily tell their own stories to accompany these action-filled pictures.

Free Fall by David Wiesner is based on a dream in which a boy's quilt becomes cultivated fields, then a chess board of five knights and queens who escort him into a castle with a magician and hidden dragon. Episodes flow into each other from the previous illustrations. The final picture shows the boy waking in bed surrounded by many of the objects in his dream. The age of the boy and his adventures would suggest that this wordless book is for older children.

Two other wordless picture books that also feature imaginary journeys play with unusual points of view. *Zoom* by Istvan Banyai begins in a barn with a close-up of a rooster's comb. The artist's eye pulls back like a movie camera to show the rooster and then moves back again to picture children looking through the barn window at the rooster. Banyai never lets viewers take the scenes for granted and includes many visual surprises as he takes the viewer farther and farther away from the barn until we are in outer space looking at Earth as a tiny dot of light. Steve Jenkins's *Looking Down* begins where *Zoom* ends, out in space looking at Earth. Now, however, we move in closer and closer through tissue paper clouds to the Maryland and South Carolina coasts, to cities and countrysides, to neighborhoods, to a small boy's house, and to the small boy who is looking at a ladybug through a magnifying glass. The last page pictures a close-up of that ladybug. These inventive books are lovely complements to one another and can help make the idea of point of view concrete for younger children while they will intrigue and instruct an older audience.

There appear to be fewer wordless books published today than five years ago. Increasingly, those being produced seem geared to an older audience than preschool or even kindergarten children.

Istvan Banyai's quaint illustrations belie the visual surprises in store in the wordless picture book *Zoom*.
From *Zoom* by Istvan Banyai. Copyright © 1995 by Istvan Banyai. Used by permission of Viking Penguin, a division of Penguin USA Inc.

Books About the Common Experiences of the Young Child

Increasingly, publishers are producing books that mirror the everyday common experiences and feelings of the preschooler. In these books for 2- through 5-year-olds the illustrations are simple and clear. The young child's activities and concerns are at the center of the action, but frequently the humor is directed at the parent reader.

Anne and Harlow Rockwell collaborated on producing the My World series, including the titles *Sick in Bed*, *I Play in My Room*, *Happy Birthday to Me*, and *Can I Help?* The text in these squarish books presents a straightforward first-person account of a child's response to these experiences. The Rockwells effectively cut across stereotyping; in *Sick in Bed* the doctor is a woman, and when the child returns to nursery school, her teacher is a man. A little girl helps her father polish the car in *Can I Help?* but it is her mother who helps her fly a kite.

"Open the door, Alfie," said Mom.

But Alfie didn't know how to open the door from the inside. The catch was too high up. Mom looked into the mail slot.

"Try to reach the catch and turn it," she said. Alfie tried but he couldn't quite reach it.

"Can you put the key through the mail slot?" asked Mom. But Alfie couldn't reach the mail slot either.

Shirley Hughes ingeniously uses the gutter of the book to represent the door separating Alfie from his mom. Increasing frustration is shown on both sides of the door, until Alfie solves the problem himself.
Illustration by Shirley Hughes from her *Alfie Gets in First*. Copyright © 1981 by Shirley Hughes. By permission of Lothrop, Lee & Shepard Books, a division of William Morrow & Company, Inc.

Children frequently experience childcare outside their homes before they are old enough to attend school and can find this experience reflected in their picture books. In *Jesse's Daycare* by Amy Valens, Jesse is busy sharing toys and playing with Sara while his mom is busy working at her computer in a downtown office. The author describes Jesse's and Mom's parallel feelings and activities in a quiet, reassuring way. Michelle Magorian gently explores a young boy's courage to stand on his own in her book *Who's Going to Take Care of Me?* When Eric and his big sister went to daycare together, Karin taught him words to the songs and let him sit by her during story time. Now Karin is going to school and Eric feels small and wonders who will care for him, until he discovers a new child in his daycare who needs his special care.

Shirley Hughes's Alfie is a delightful preschooler whose everyday adventures are captured in several books. In *Alfie Gets in First*, Alfie is so excited to be the first one home from a shopping trip that he races in the door as soon as his mother opens it and locks himself in. Hughes ingeniously uses the center gutter of the book as the door dividing the outside of the house from the inside. In this way the reader can see all the people who come to try to help open the door and at the same time see what Alfie is doing. Just at the moment when the window cleaner is about to climb up his ladder and go through a bathroom window, Alfie gets a chair, reaches

the lock himself, and grandly opens the door. Other books about this enterprising toddler include *Alfie's Feet*, *Alfie Gives a Hand*, and *An Evening at Alfie's*. The *Big Alfie and Annie Rose Storybook* provides five delightful stories and three poems about Alfie and his younger sister, Annie Rose.

Marisabina Russo also has a talent for tapping into the way a young child feels. In *Time to Wake Up!* a mother and her little boy carry on a dialogue as the mother tries to get the sleepy boy up and ready for school. It is obvious from the pictures that the child is not really sleepy but loves the attention and the ritual involved in this little game. *Waiting for Hannah* is a loving story in which a mother recounts to her daughter all the things she did during the long hot summer while she was expecting her arrival. In *Why Do Grown-Ups Have All the Fun?* Hannah lies in bed imagining the wonderful things her parents must be doing, like playing with her building blocks or Play-Doh. She then slips downstairs, only to discover her mother writing a letter and her father doing a crossword puzzle. So Hannah curls up on the couch with her parents and eventually falls asleep. Russo's bright childlike illustrations match the young child's naive perceptions of what her parents do for fun.

Eve Rice captures the feelings of a child whose birthday is almost a disaster. In *Benny Bakes a Cake*, Benny has a wonderful time helping his mother make his birthday cake. But when they go for a walk, Ralph, their dog, eats the cake. Benny is disconsolate until his father comes home with presents, birthday hats, *and* a beautiful birthday cake. A young child can easily follow the action of this story by looking at the large flat primary-color pictures against the clear white background.

Learning to get along in the family is another developmental task of the young child. In *They Really Like Me!* Anna Hines tells the story of Joshua, who is left home alone with his two older sisters. They won't let him watch television or share their popcorn, and when they play tricks on him Joshua isn't sure they like him. However, when Joshua out-tricks them and they can't find him, he learns that they really do like him.

In *Sam*, an African American child, the youngest of his family, feels rejected by the members of his family—all are so engrossed in their own activities that they tell him to go somewhere else to play. Finally, completely frustrated, Sam begins to cry. Then everyone in the family comes together and realizes the cumulative effect they have had on Sam. Consoled at last, Sam helps his mother make raspberry tarts. Symeon Shimin's illustrations portray the nuances of feelings in this fine book by Ann Herbert Scott.

The youngest child frequently feels left out, the tag end of the family. Pat Hutchins captures these feelings in her well-loved books *Titch*, *You'll Soon Grow into Them, Titch*, and *Tidy Titch*. In the first book Titch is too small to ride a two-wheel bicycle or fly a kite or use a hammer. But he is not too small to plant a seed, and Titch's plant grows and grows. The ending of the story is a classic example of poetic justice for the youngest and smallest of a family. The classic story *The Carrot Seed* by Ruth Krauss has a theme similar to that in *Titch*. Here, the smallest in the family triumphs over all the doubts raised by his family. Little children need to feel big, if only through their stories.

A family of birds gives much encouragement to a baby seagull longing to fly. His mother tells him he will fly, his father says "By and by," and his sister tells him, "Flap your wings and try." Written by Charlotte Pomerantz and beautifully illustrated by Nancy Tafuri, *Flap Your Wings and Try* has a dedication reading: "For All of Us Who Are Still Trying."

Young children also need much love and reassurance that they will always be needed and belong to their family. This is the theme of the favorite story *The Runaway Bunny* by Margaret Wise Brown. A little bunny announces that he is going to run away, and his mother tells him that she will run after him. The little bunny thinks of all the things he will become—a fish in a stream, a crocus, a sailboat. His mother in turn says she will become a fisherman, a gardener, the wind, and

come after him. The little rabbit decides just to stay and be her little bunny, after all. This story might seem suffocating for older children, but it is just what the preschool child wants to hear.

Bedtime stories provide the comfort and reassurance that children need to face the dark alone. There are several recent bedtime books that have the potential to become modern-day classics, although probably no book for the very young child will ever replace Margaret Wise Brown's *Goodnight Moon*. First published in 1947, it was reissued in 1975 in paperback and made into a pop-up book, *The Goodnight Moon Room*, in 1984.

The lyrical text of Mem Fox's *Time for Bed* with Jane Dyer's lovely watercolor illustrations will no doubt have a similar soothing effect on toddlers. Beginning with a tiny mouse, animal and insect families get ready for sleep. Finally, a human mother wishes her baby sweet dreams against the background of a starry pillow and a starry sky: "The stars on high are shining bright—Sweet dreams, my darling, sleep well . . . good night!" Molly Bang has written and illustrated both a counting book and a loving bedtime story in *Ten, Nine, Eight*. Starting with his daughter's ten toes, a daddy counts backward until she is ready for bed. This is a warm reassuring story of an African American father and his daughter.

Young children love the lilt and rhyme of *Jesse Bear, What Will You Wear?* by Nancy Carlstrom. Jesse Bear wears not only his red shirt but also such unusual things as "the sun on his legs that run" or the three kisses and bear hug that his dad gives him at night. Exuberant paintings of Jesse Bear's day make this a very special book to share with preschoolers and kindergarten children. The two sequels are not as good as the first story.

Jonathon London's *Like Butter on Pancakes* is another book that follows a child from morning to night. Beginning with first light that "melts like butter on pancakes, spread warm and yellow across your pillow," the bright golden yellows and soothing gray purples of G. Brian Karas's illustrations depict the activities of a little farm boy from his sleepy waking, through his action-packed day, to his tired goodnight. As the sun sleeps "beyond the rim of evening" and the spoons are "nestled in the kitchen drawers," the child is tucked into his bed by his loving parents.

Goodnight, Gorilla by Peggy Rathmann is an almost wordless book that is sure to delight toddlers. A sleepy zookeeper is locking up for the night when a gorilla baby takes his keys. As the keeper says good night to the animals, one by one, the gorilla opens their cages and the animals all follow the keeper home and bed down in his room. His sleepy wife suddenly realizes what has

A baby gorilla and a tiny mouse lead a parade of animals home with the zookeeper in *Goodnight, Gorilla.*
From *Goodnight, Gorilla*, by Peggy Rathmann. Copyright © 1994 by The Putnam & Grosset Group, New York, NY. Reprinted by permission.

happened and takes all the animals back to their cages—except for the little gorilla and a tiny mouse, who manage to follow her back to bed and slide in under the covers.

Martin Waddell's *Owl Babies* might be the perfect book to reassure a toddler who fears the nighttime separation from mother. In this charming predictable book, three little owl siblings find themselves alone on their leafy branch. "Where's Mommy?" asks Sarah, "Oh my goodness!" exclaims Percy, and "I want my mommy," wails Bill, the smallest. Patrick Benson's expressive illustrations lend just the right amount of suspense to the story, in which the night seems to get darker and darker. Sarah and Percy try to reassure each other that Mom will be back, while Bill continues to cry for Mother until she swoops "soft and silent" through the trees and home to her children. Bill's plaintive wail will resonate with every child who is frightened of the dark, and the message that mother is never far away is a reassuring finale that will linger in sleepy memories.

In *Close Your Eyes* by Jean Marzollo, Susan Jeffers's pictures show two stories going on simultaneously. Rhyming text suggests things that a little girl can do in her dreams, such as play with "wooly lambs on a lazy day." Jeffers's large, beautifully composed pictures will intrigue both children and their parents. In *The Biggest Boy* by Kevin Henkes, the toddler is so big he can eat with a fork and put on his own boots and buckle them. When he tells his mother and father that he will soon be the biggest boy in the world, they suggest that he can

then wear their roof as a hat, hang the rainbow around his neck, and wear the moon as a moustache. As he lies in bed that night, he holds a hand up to the moon, which he sees out his window, and frames it between his two fingers. He decides he really *is* the biggest boy. Nancy Tafuri's lovely close-ups of Billy are the perfect accompaniment to Henkes's poetic text.

With glowing colors and verse, Gloria Kamen describes all that goes on from dawn until dusk in the lives of birds, animals, and a sleepy baby in her book *"Paddle," Said the Swan*. She also provides some of the sounds of animals that always intrigue toddlers. As the sun sets, the fireflies say "Glow," and mother and baby prepare for bed. Repetition and soothing language characterize the story of *Where Does the Brown Bear Go?* by Nicki Weiss. When the sun sinks behind the seas, all the animals are on their way home. Shown against a darkened sky, a cat, a monkey, a camel, and a stray dog make their way home. In the last picture, all the animals are seen as plush toys surrounding a sleeping boy.

Stories that have no relationship to bedtime of course make fine reading at this time, too. So young children should see many of the appropriate picture storybooks described in Chapter 5 and hear the well-loved traditional tales of "The Three Bears," "The Three Billy Goats Gruff," and "The Gingerbread Man" discussed in Chapter 6. For although young children need books that mirror their own feelings and experiences, they also need books to take them beyond those experiences and to help their imaginations soar.

Books for the Beginning Reader

Learning to read begins at home with children hearing stories on their parents' laps and seeing loved persons in their lives valuing books. The child lucky enough to have had such a wide exposure to books will usually learn to read easily and fluently. The importance of reading aloud to young children, if they are to be successful in learning to read, has been consistently proven by researchers in this country and abroad.[12]

The books for the very young child that have been discussed in this chapter can be read again when children of 5 or 6 start to become readers. Increasingly, theories of reading emphasize the importance of reading for meaning and enjoyment from the very start of learning to read. Many preprimers and primers that are part of reading textbook series have stilted, unnatural language and pointless plots that thwart the child's spontaneous attempts to read; on the other hand, stories that children love and have heard over and over again have natural language and satisfying plots that encourage reading. Many of these books utilize repetitious language and story patterns that help children learn to read naturally as they join in on the refrains or predict the action of the story.

Jerome Bruner was the first to use the term *scaffold* to characterize adult assistance to children's language development.[13] Some books can also be an instructional scaffold or a temporary help in the child's first attempts to read. Such books include familiar texts like Mother Goose rhymes or songs that children know by heart and can easily "read"; or they might be books with repetitive language or story patterns that help children remember or predict the story easily.[14]

Primary children need to hear many stories read several times a day by an enthusiastic teacher.
Highland Park Elementary School, South-Western City Schools, Grove City, Ohio. Kristen Kerstetter, teacher.

Margaret Meek points out that as children explore a variety of texts, they learn how books work.[15] She also emphasizes the importance of repeated readings, maintaining that each time a book is revisited, new understandings are gained.[16]

Predictable Books

Books that can help an emergent reader can be identified by such characteristics as repetitive language patterns or story patterns or the use of familiar sequences like numbers, the days of the week, or hierarchical patterns. Frequently texts combine several of these characteristics in a single story.

Many stories include repetitive words, phrases, or questions that invite children to share in the reading. Children quickly learn the language pattern of Eric Hill's *Where's Spot?* and chime in as the word *no* is revealed under each lifted flap. They will want to join in and repeat the word *suddenly!* in Colin McNaughton's delightful book entitled *Suddenly!* They will also be tickled by the suspenseful plot as an ingenuous pig is set upon by a nasty wolf on his way home from school.

[12]See Margaret Clark, *Young Fluent Readers* (London: Heinemann Educational Books, 1976); Dorothy Cohen, "The Effect of Literature on Vocabulary and Reading Achievement," *Elementary English* 45 (February 1968): 209–213; Dolores Durkin, *Children Who Read Early* (New York: Columbia Teachers College Press, 1966); Robert Ladd Thorndike, *Reading Comprehension, Education in 15 Countries: An Empirical Study*, vol. 3, International Studies in Education (New York: Holstead Wiley, 1973); Gordon Wells, *The Meaning Makers* (Portsmouth, N.H.: Heinemann, 1986).

[13]Identified by C. B. Cazden, "Adult Assistance to Language Development: Scaffolds, Models, and Direct Instruction," in *Developing Literacy: Young Children's Use of Language* ed. R. P. Parker and F. A. Davis, (Newark, Del.: International Reading Association, 1983), pp. 3–18.

[14]Connie A. Bridge, et al., "Using Predictable Materials vs. Preprimers to Teach Beginning Sight Words," *Reading Teacher* 36 (May 1983): 884–891.

[15]Margaret Meek, *How Texts Teach What Readers Learn* (London: Thimble Press, 1988).

[16]See also Miriam Martinez and Nancy Roser, "Read It Again: The Value of Repeated Readings During Storytime," *Reading Teacher* 38 (1985): 782–786.

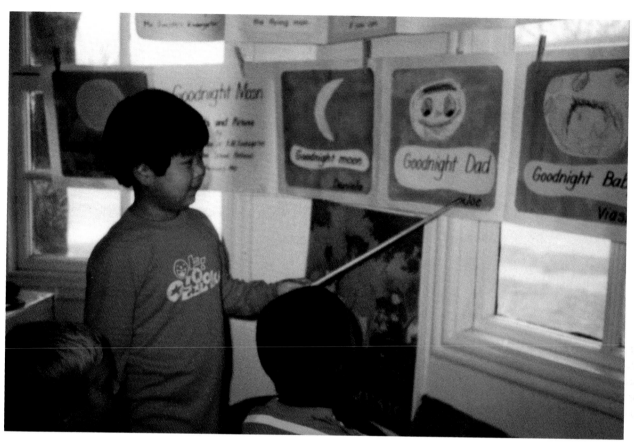

Kindergarten children enjoy reading their alternative version of *Goodnight Moon* by Margaret Wise Brown.
Mission School, Redlands Public School, Redlands, California. Nancy Anderson, teacher and photographer.

Prestin the pig escapes from each increasingly bizarre assault, seemingly unaware that the wolf is after him. The illustrations here, like those in Pat Hutchins's *Rosie's Walk*, give the real story away, including the last funny surprise.

Children will quickly pick up the language patterns in Martin Waddell's *Farmer Duck*. "How goes the work?" asks an exceedingly lazy farmer. "Quack!" squawks an increasingly exhausted duck who must perform all the work around the farm while the farmer lies in bed eating chocolates. Helen Oxenbury's wonderfully expressive illustrations bring these characters to life in a story with an ending that is highly satisfying for any child (or adult) who has ever felt overburdened by chores.

A well-liked patterned question-and-answer book is *Brown Bear, Brown Bear, What Do You See?* by Bill Martin, Jr. The question in the title is put to a large brown bear, who replies that he sees a redbird looking at him. The question is then directed at the redbird: "Redbird, redbird, what do you see?" He sees a yellow duck, who

in turn sees a blue horse, and so on. Identification of animal and color on the picture allows the child to chime in on the answer for each page. The large, bold collage pictures by Eric Carle are a perfect match for the text and support the child's reading of the story. Author and illustrator have followed the same pattern of text in *Polar Bear, Polar Bear, What Do You Hear?*

Another excellent story similar to *Brown Bear, Brown Bear* is Sue Williams's *I Went Walking*. A vivacious redheaded boy goes walking and sees a variety of animals. The phrase *I went walking* is always followed by the question "What did you see?" Looking closely at Julie Vivas's charming illustrations, the reader can discover the next animal or bird partially hidden. Turn the page and you see the whole animal. Each animal joins the little boy, making the large pictures cumulative. A subplot reveals the little boy discarding his jacket, his sweater, and his shoes and socks as he continues on his walk. This story leads children into reading as easily as the animals follow the boy on his adventuresome walk.

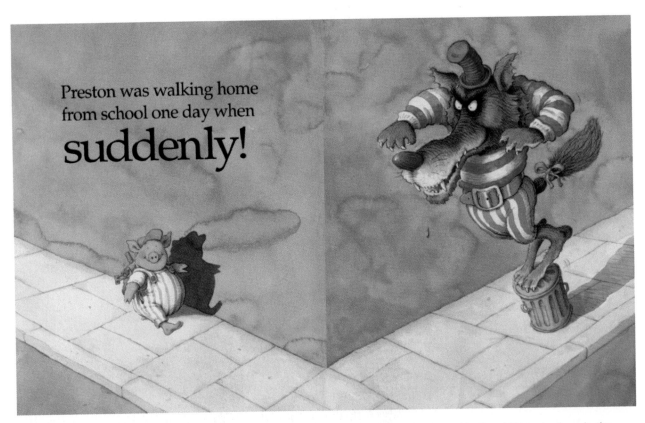

Preston was walking home from school one day when **suddenly!**

In Colin McNaughton's funny book *Suddenly!* the repeated word draws attention to print and invites children to share in the reading.

Illustration from *Suddenly!*, copyright © 1994 by Colin McNaughton, reproduced by permission of Harcourt Brace & Company. First published in Great Britain in 1994 by Andersen Press Limited.

In Mirra Ginsburg's *The Chick and the Duckling*, the title characters play a delightful game of follow-the-leader. Each thing the duckling does is copied by the chick, who echoes, "Me too." However, when the duck decides to take a *second* swim, the chick has learned his lesson and says, "Not me." Both the refrain and the repetitive action in the story make this a very predictable book. Other patterned language books might repeat certain words many times, as in *Snow on Snow on Snow* by Cheryl Chapman. In this simple narrative a little boy wakes up "under blankets under blankets under blankets" on a wintry day and goes sledding with his friends and his dog Clancy, who gets lost. The children look "behind trees behind trees behind trees" and "tears on tears on tears" result when they can't find him. Clancy finally appears from under a snowdrift to a triple happy-ever-after ending.

Rather than simply repeat words and phrases, some books play with the sounds of language in a more complex way. Many of Bill Martin, Jr.'s, books have refrains or patterns in which beginnings, endings, or internal parts of words are manipulated. In *The Happy Hippopotami*, "hippopotamuses climb aboard their picnic buses" for a trip to the beach. There are hippopotamamas

wearing pajamas and hippopotapoppas who give their hippopotadaughters and their hippopotasons dimes and nickels to buy poppasicles, and they all give a "Hippo-ray! Hip-hippocheer!" for a jolly good time. Charlotte Pomerantz's *The Piggy in a Puddle* and *Here Comes Henny* also have irresistible refrains that will have children chanting along with enthusiasm. Piggy is in the middle of a "muddy little puddle" and dawdles and diddles there while daddy, mommy, and brother try to convince her to come out. In a rollicking ending they all dive in and join her in the "squishy-squashy, mooshy-squooshy, ooffy-poofy" mud. Henny is a mother chicken who plans a picnic for her chickies and packs it in her backpack,

 which she carries
pickabacky

back and forth
and forth and backy.[17]

---

[17]Charlotte Pomerantz, *Here Comes Henny*, illus. Nancy Winslow Parker (New York: Greenwillow, 1994), p. 5.

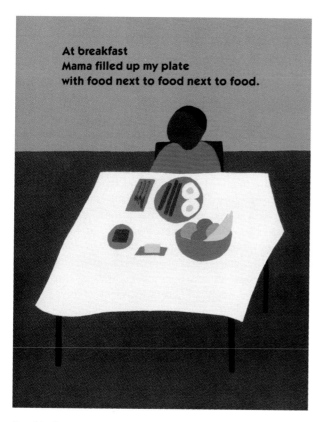

**At breakfast
Mama filled up my plate
with food next to food next to food.**

Synthia Saint James's bold collages reinforce the repetition of phrases in *Snow on Snow on Snow.*
From *Snow on Snow on Snow* by Cheryl Chapman, illustrated by Synthia Saint James. Copyright © 1994 by Synthia Saint James on illustrations. Used by permission of Dial Books for Young Readers, a division of Penguin Books USA Inc.

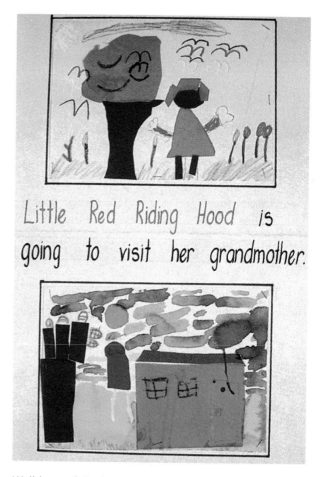

Little Red Riding Hood is going to visit her grandmother.

Well-known folktales such as "Little Red Riding Hood" make easy reading for beginners. Here 6-year-olds have retold the story and illustrated it with tissue paper collage, paints, and crayons.
Mt. Eden Normal School, Auckland, New Zealand. Ava McGregor, teacher.

These are picky chickies, however, and they will only eat snacky snickies, not the snicky snackies that Henny has packed. In the end the chicks collect their own pack of snackies and have a happy picnic-nicky. In addition to being irresistible fun for children, this type of sound play helps make them more aware of the internal sounds of words and the fact that language is made up of individual sounds. This understanding—phonemic awareness—seems to be crucial to emergent reading strategies. Hallie Kay Yopp and other researchers suggest that a certain level of phonemic awareness is necessary for children to benefit from more-formal reading instruction.[18]

Building on children's knowledge of numbers and the days of the week provides a kind of scaffold for reading. Clear pictures by Tomie de Paola illustrate the predictable book *Cookie's Week* by Cindy Ward. If a child knows the days of the week, she can easily read the

description of everything a mischievous little black-and-white cat does each day. Much to children's delight, it begins with "On Monday . . . Cookie fell in the toilet." The next page sets the pattern of the book: "And there was water everywhere." Knowledge of the days of the week and numbers help children read *The Very Hungry Caterpillar* by Eric Carle. They particularly enjoy reciting the part where the caterpillar eats through *one* apple on *Monday,* *two* pears on *Tuesday,* *three* plums on *Wednesday,* until he has a huge feast on *Sunday.* In *Today Is Monday* Carle illustrates the familiar nursery song with different animals. A snake eats spaghetti, a porcupine munches string beans, and so on. The last picture shows children from many cultures, including a child in a wheelchair, sitting around a table for a feast. In Maurice Sendak's rhyming *Chicken Soup with Rice,* each verse begins with the month and ends with doing something to the soup, such as blowing on it or sipping it. Some groups have made up their own verses for the months,

[18]Hallie Kay Yopp, "Developing Phonemic Awareness in Young Children," *Reading Teacher* 45 (May 1992): 696–703.

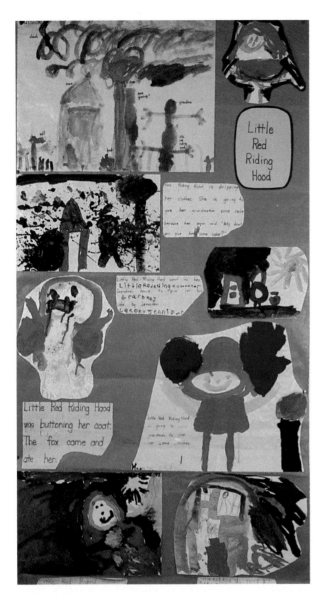

A kindergarten/first-grade teacher honors all stories and interpretations of "Little Red Riding Hood" by cutting around the most important part of children's pictures and displaying them on this very tall mural.
Highland Park Elementary School, South-Western City Schools, Grove City, Ohio. Kristen Kerstetter, teacher.

using Sendak's pattern and repeated phrases. Hierarchies based on size, such as those in the tales about the three bears and the three Billy Goats Gruff, help children to read these stories. With one reading, children easily discern the pattern of being the littlest in Pat Hutchins's story *Titch*. They know that if his brother has a *great big bike* and his sister a *big bike*, then Titch will have a *tricycle*.

Repetitive story patterns also help the child predict the action in the plot. The easy folktales with their patterns of three, such as *The Three Billy Goats Gruff* by Glen Rounds, *The Three Little Pigs* and *The Three Bears*

by Paul Galdone, and *The Little Red Hen* by Byron Barton, support the child's reading. For once children recognize the story structure, they know that if the great big bear says, "Someone has been tasting my porridge," then the middle-size bear and the baby bear will both say the same thing. In Deborah Guarino's *Is Your Mama a Llama?* a baby llama asks the repetitive question "Is your mama a llama?" of each animal he meets. They in turn provide factual and rhyming clues that make it easy to guess the identities of their mothers. Children love these riddle rhymes by Guarino and the endearing pictures of baby animals by Steven Kellogg. Cumulative tales have repeated patterns and phrases that become longer and longer with each incident. In Mem Fox's *Shoes from Grandpa* a simple gift for Jessie turns into a whole wardrobe as different members of her family decide to buy her an article of clothing "to go with the shoes from grandpa." There are lots of rhyming pairs here, such as "mittens soft as kittens" and a "skirt that won't show the dirt," that will invite children to make up their own special wardrobes. Patricia Mullins's lively collages include bits of fabric that reflect the theme and add to the humor of the story.

The familiar patterns of the nursery rhyme "This Is the House that Jack Built" can be found in many illustrated retellings and several modern-day variants. Children love Don and Audrey Wood's *The Napping House*, in which an old lady, a boy, a dog, a cat, and a mouse are sleeping until a flea "bites the mouse who scares the cat," and so on, until everyone wakes to a glorious day. Rose Robart creates a rollicking cumulative tale in *The Cake That Mack Ate*. Even though every verse ends in the title phrase, it is only in the last few pictures that children discover the identity of Mack, a huge dog.

Some modern stories contain predictable plots, also. Certainly one of the easiest is Brian Wildsmith's *The Cat on the Mat*. In this simple yet beautifully illustrated book, one animal after another comes and sits on the mat until the cat thinks there are too many. With one hiss he frightens them all away and once again he is left with complete ownership of the mat. *Rosie's Walk* by Hutchins is better for telling than reading, since the entire text is only one sentence long. However, children can learn how to predict what is going to happen to the fox by careful observation of where the unsuspecting hen takes her walk. Another tale of a narrow escape, *Across the Stream* by Mirra Ginsburg, is the story of a hen and chicks who cross a stream and foil the hungry fox. These and other stories like Colin McNaughton's *Suddenly!* help children begin to develop an understanding of how the character of a fox or a wolf will act in an animal tale. This developing sense of story also begins to help them predict action.

Familiar Mother Goose rhymes such as "Little Miss Muffet" or "Old Mother Hubbard" or the popular song

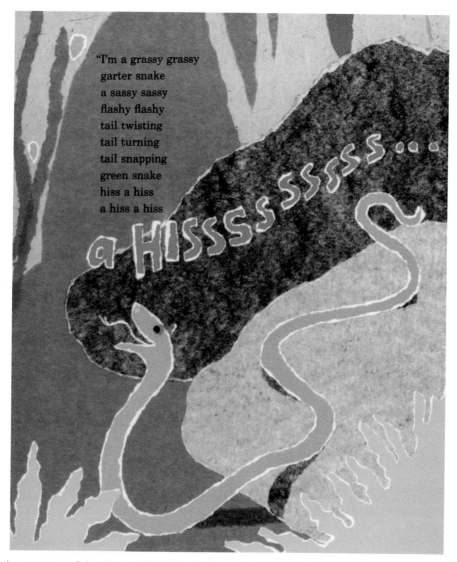

"I'm a grassy grassy
garter snake
a sassy sassy
flashy flashy
tail twisting
tail turning
tail snapping
green snake
hiss a hiss
a hiss a hiss

a HISSSS SSSSS...

The printed words become part of the visual art in Holly Meade's lively illustrations for Libba Moore Gray's *Small Green Snake*.
From *Small Green Snake* by Libba Moore Gray, illustrated by Holly Meade. Jacket illustration copyright © 1994 by Holly Meade. Reprinted by permission of the Publisher, Orchard Books, New York.

reprised in *Mary Wore Her Red Dress* by Merle Peek all enable the child to assume the role of reader. Children can hold the books or point to a large chart and "read the words" because they know the verse or song. As they match sentences and phrase cards or point to individual words in the text, they begin to read the story. In the meantime, they are learning that those symbols stand for the words they already know. This enables them to behave like readers.

Denise Fleming's books, such as *In the Tall Tall Grass*, have predictable refrains that also convey simple concepts about animal behavior and habitats. In *In the Small Small Pond*, "wiggle, jiggle, tadpoles wriggle," and in *Barnyard Banter* "pigs in the wallow, muck muck muck." These visually appealing books also offer children interesting vocabulary within the context of the predictable text.

Some concept books, like *Truck* by Donald Crews or *My Kitchen* by Harlow Rockwell, give children an opportunity to read environmental print. Tana Hoban's books *I Read Signs* and *I Read Symbols* provide excellent photographs of the signs in their environmental context. Other books use print as an important part of the visual art and thus draw children's attention to letters and words. In Pat Hutchins's predictable *Little Pink Pig*, Mother Pig searches for her baby pig at bedtime. As she asks each animal for help, their animal responses are printed in a more decorative, larger, colored type. In Libba Moore Gray's *Small Green Snake*, Holly Meade uses torn-paper collage for some of the words as well as the images and thus highlights important action and dialogue. With its wordplay and the large and colorful torn-paper words, the book will have children begging to join in the reading. In addition to being wonderful literature, books like these strengthen children's concepts about print and they can also help teachers see how aware of print children are becoming.

As more and more primary teachers begin to use real books for teaching children to read, textbook publishers are beginning to produce made-to-order predictable books written to a formula. These "little books" frequently lack the imaginative quality of true literature. They might use repetitive phrases or questions, but they have deadly dull plots and the unnatural language of primers. Look rather for imaginative trade books with natural language, a creative plot, and real child appeal. Look, too, for fine artwork such as that found in the books by Eric Carle, Denise Fleming, Pat Hutchins, Marisabina Russo, and many more outstanding author/illustrators.

The titles we have discussed here are all trade books that meet the criteria we have suggested. They help the emergent reader learn to read naturally and with real delight. For a list of predictable books by their characteristics, see Resources for Teaching, "Predictable Books."

Big Books

As primary teachers begin to use real books to teach emergent readers, some of them put favorite stories and poems on large charts so that everyone in the class can see them. During shared reading time, the children read them together as one of them points to the words. Frequently, children illustrate these homemade charts with their own drawings and then the teacher puts them together as a big book. Teachers might chat about the words and ask a child to point to a particular word that they are certain the child knows, or to find all the words that begin the same as their name. At other times, children might create their own original version of a favorite story. One group transposed the popular tale *Five Minutes' Peace* by Jill Murphy, which tells of a harassed mother elephant who could not get away from her family, to a schoolroom setting and a teacher's need for five minutes' peace.

Children love these alternative stories that they have a part in producing either by illustrating or by writing. They take ownership of them and read them to each

---

Resources for Teaching
Predictable Books

Language Patterns: Repetitive Words, Phrases, Questions

Jill Bennett, *Teeny Tiny*

Ruth Brown, *A Dark Dark Tale*

Marilee Robin Burton, *Tail Toes Eyes Ears Nose*

Rod Campbell, *Dear Zoo*

Eric Carle, *Do You Want to Be My Friend?*

————, *Have You Seen My Cat?*

————, *The Very Busy Spider*

————, *The Very Quiet Cricket*

————, *The Very Lonely Firefly*

Mirra Ginsburg, *The Chick and the Duckling*

————, *Good Morning, Chick*

Eric Hill, *Where's Spot?*

Robert Kraus, *Where Are You Going, Little Mouse?*

————, *Whose Mouse Are You?*

Bill Martin, Jr., *Brown Bear, Brown Bear, What Do You See?*

Charlotte Pomerantz, *Here Comes Henny*

————, *The Piggy in a Puddle*

Nancy Shaw, *Sheep in a Jeep*

Nancy Tafuri, *Have You Seen My Duckling?*

Martin Waddell, *Farmer Duck*

Sue Williams, *I Went Walking*

Familiar Sequences: Numbers, Days of Week, Months, Hierarchies

Eric Carle, *The Very Hungry Caterpillar*

————, *Today Is Monday*

Eileen Christelow, *Five Little Monkeys Jumping on the Bed*

Paul Galdone, *The Three Bears*

————, *The Three Billy Goats Gruff*

Nancy Hellen, *The Bus Stop*

Resources for Teaching
Predictable Books (concluded)

Pat Hutchins, *Titch*

Maurice Sendak, *Chicken Soup with Rice*

Uri Shulevitz, *One Monday Morning*

Cindy Ward, *Cookie's Week*

Ashley Wolff, *A Year of Beasts*

————, *A Year of Birds*

Repetitive Story Patterns

Byron Barton, *Buzz Buzz Buzz*

Glen Rounds, *The Three Billy Goats Gruff*

Margaret Wise Brown, *Four Fur Feet*

Paul Galdone, *The Three Bears*

————, *The Little Red Hen*

————, *The Three Little Pigs*

Deborah Guarino, *Is Your Mama a Llama?*

Pat Hutchins, *Little Pink Pig*

Ruth Krauss, *The Carrot Seed*

Dee Lillegard, *Sitting in My Box*

Jeff Sheppard, *Splash Splash*

Nancy Van Laan, *This Is the Hat: A Story in Rhyme*

Cumulative Tales

Maggie Duff, *Rum, Pum, Pum*

Barbara Emberley, *Drummer Hoff*

Paul Galdone, *The Gingerbread Boy*

Sarah Hayes, *This Is the Bear*

Jack Kent, *The Fat Cat*

Rose Robart, *The Cake That Mack Ate*

Nancy Van Laan, *The Tiny Tiny Boy and the Big Big Cow*

Elfrida Vipoint, *The Elephant and the Bad Baby*

Linda Williams, *The Little Old Lady Who Was Not Afraid of Anything*

Audrey Wood, *The Napping House*

Predictable Plots

Margaret Wise Brown, *Goodnight Moon*

John Burningham, *Mr. Gumpy's Outing*

Pat Hutchins, *Good-Night, Owl!*

————, *Happy Birthday, Sam*

————, *Rosie's Walk*

————, *You'll Soon Grow Into Them, Titch*

Eve Rice, *Benny Bakes a Cake*

————, *Sam Who Never Forgets*

Brian Wildsmith, *The Cat on the Mat*

Familiar Songs and Rhymes

Aliki, *Go Tell Aunt Rhody*

Colin Hawkins, and Jacqui Hawkins, *Old Mother Hubbard*

————, *I Know an Old Lady Who Swallowed a Fly*

Eric Hill, *Nursery Rhyme Peek-a-Book*

Carol Jones, *Old MacDonald Had a Farm*

————, *This Old Man*

Merle Peek, *Mary Wore Her Red Dress and Henry Wore His Green Sneakers*

————, *Roll Over! A Counting Song*

Raffi, *Down By the Bay: Songs to Read*

————, *Five Little Ducks*

Nadine Bernard Westcott, *Peanut Butter and Jelly: A Play Rhyme*

————, *Skip to My Lou*

Artistic Use of Print

Donald Crews, *School Bus*

————, *Truck*

Libba Moore Gray, *Small Green Snake*

Anna Grossnickle Hines, *Rumble Thumble Boom*

Tana Hoban, *I Read Symbols*

————, *I Read Signs*

Pat Hutchins, *Little Pink Pig*

Gail Jorgensen, *Crocodile Beat*

Karla Kuskin, *Roar and More*

Patricia Lillie, *When the Rooster Crowed*

Harlow Rockwell, *My Kitchen*

First graders show much interest in reading the Big Book they have created.
Idyllwild Elementary School, Idyllwild, California. Sharon Schmidt, teacher.
Photo by Larry Rose.

other over and over again. In two trips we made to New Zealand to visit schools, these homemade big books were the only ones we saw.

Since that time, publishers have recognized a need for commercial big books and predictable books and created their own. Commercial big books are necessarily expensive and do not provide the same sense of ownership that comes with the class-made books. This cost needs to be balanced against the number of trade books that can be purchased with the money. Some of the commercial big books use the same illustrations as the trade books; others have new illustrations. Almost all of the traditional tales, such as "The Three Bears," are available in big books. Teachers need to ask if this is the version they want to share with their class, or if they would prefer a different one. Also, they must evaluate the text for ease of reading. Is this a version that helps students read the text? Does the placement of the text show the repetitious phrases, for example? Do the illustrations help the children read the story? Big books need to be evaluated before their purchase. The best of the commercial ones are those that replicate good predictable trade books exactly; examples are *The Chick and the Duckling* by Mirra Ginsburg and *Rosie's Walk* by Pat Hutchins.

Controlled-Vocabulary Books

Most basal reading series control the number of words, the sounds of the words, and the length of the stories for beginning readers. Until the advent of books for babies

and preschoolers, most picture storybooks were written to be read *to* children and thus were at a reading level of at least third grade. They were geared to the young child's interest and appreciation level, not reading ability level. That left very little for the beginning reader to read, except for preprimers and primers. This is no longer true, with the number of easy predictable books available today.

A new genre of book was created when Dr. Seuss wrote *The Cat in the Hat* in 1957. This book was written with a controlled vocabulary (derived from the Dolch vocabulary list of 220 words) for the young child to read independently. Since then many publishers have developed "easy reading" books. In format, such books tend to look more like basal readers than picture storybooks, although they do have illustrations on every page. Some of these books, such as *Little Bear* by Else Minarik and illustrated by Sendak, and the superb Frog and Toad series by Arnold Lobel, are easy-reading books that do not use controlled vocabulary. They can take their rightful place in children's literature. In fact, *Frog and Toad Are Friends* was a Caldecott Honor Book and *Frog and Toad Together* was a Newbery Honor Book two years later, suggesting that quality writing can be achieved with a limited vocabulary.

Cynthia Rylant's Henry and Mudge series features Henry and his lovable 180-pound dog, Mudge. In *Henry and Mudge*, short episodes about these two inseparable friends are divided into chapters, just right for the newly independent readers who love them. The language is simple, but it has an almost poetic quality, particularly when the author contrasts Henry's life before and after acquiring Mudge. Before he had Mudge, he had to walk to school alone and he worried about "tornadoes, ghosts, biting dogs and bullies." But after he got Mudge, he'd think about "vanilla ice cream, rain, rocks and good dreams." Other well-loved Mudge stories include *Henry and Mudge and the Happy Cat, Henry and Mudge Take the Big Test,* and *Henry and Mudge and the Best Day of All.*

Today there are literally hundreds of these easy-reading books. Some are stories, some appeal to special interests such as sports, mysteries, science, or history. Not all achieve the literary excellence of the Little Bear series, Frog and Toad series, or Henry and Mudge series. Some appear contrived and restricted by the controlled vocabulary. Research has shown that the meaning of the story is far more important for ease of reading than limiting vocabulary. We should not accept a book just because it has a beginning-to-read label. Each book must be evaluated for literary qualities, child appeal, and difficulty of reading.

Teaching Feature | Creating Big Books with Emergent Readers

At the end of the year, Nancy Anderson's group of kindergartners/first graders at Mission School in Redlands, California, did a unit on insects. They read informational books on insects and Eric Carle's stories about insects, including *The Very Hungry Caterpillar*, *The Very Busy Spider*, and *The Very Quiet Cricket*.

Using the structure of *Brown Bear, Brown Bear, What Do You See?* by Bill Martin, Jr., they wrote and illustrated their own big book with insects as their main characters. They read this together in shared reading time.

Later they decided to write their own story about a ladybug and illustrate it the way Eric Carle illustrated his stories. Using their fingerpaint pictures, they cut out butterflies, ladybugs, and bumblebees to illustrate their story:

Lady Bug Saves the Day

Once there was a red shiny spotted ladybug. She lived in the forest. She kept busy eating aphids off the flowers and bushes.

Along came a black and orange butterfly who was being chased by a fierce mean bumblebee. The ladybug heard a terrible buzzing sound. The butterfly cried, "Help Help!" The ladybug waved and whispered, "Come over here, hide with me. Come in my house, it's safe."

The butterfly followed the ladybug to her house. She said, "Thank you for saving my life."

Both big books reflect what the children learned about insects. The first one shows how a book helped to provide structure to their story; the second one gives them an opportunity to illustrate like Eric Carle, their favorite illustrator.

Nancy Anderson, teacher
Mission School
Redlands, California

Using the structure of *Brown Bear, Brown Bear, What Do You See?* first graders created their own story about insects.
Mission School, Redlands, California. Nancy Anderson, teacher. Photo by Larry Rose.

The cover and one page from the story created by kindergarten and first graders about "Lady Bug Saves the Day." Notice their use of fingerpaint paper in their collage pictures, which they tried to do in the same way Eric Carle makes his.
Mission School, Redlands Public Schools, Redlands, California. Nancy Anderson, teacher. Photo by Larry Rose.

It is important to remember that no matter what we read, we are helping the child learn to read. Children need to hear many books. Frequently they want to reread a book. Sometimes children have a fascination with a long book in which they search for familiar words and teach themselves to read, so we need not limit the emergent reader's book exposure to just predictable books. One child, with whom one of the authors read in England, had taught himself to read with the Frances stories by Russell Hoban. He had learned to read *Bread and Jam for Frances* and was working on *A Baby Sister for Frances*. These are difficult books, but Gerald wanted to read them, and that is the key to helping children learn to read.

Today, with the number of fine trade books available, it is quite possible to find books that children want to read and that they find pleasure in learning to read.

Beginning readers are supported by such "easy-reading" books as Cynthia Rylant's Henry and Mudge series.
Reprinted with permission of Simon & Schuster Books for Young Readers from *Henry and Mudge: The First Book* by Cynthia Rylant, illustrated by Suçie Stevenson. Illustrations copyright © 1987 by Suçie Stevenson.

Learning Experiences

1. Share several stories with a child under 1 year of age. What appears to capture her or his attention? How many different ways can you provide for the child's active participation in the story?

2. Learn several finger plays to try with young children. Can they do them? What is difficult for them? Teach these finger plays to your classmates.

3. Working in pairs and using the evaluative criteria established in this chapter, compare three different editions of Mother Goose, ABC, or counting books.

4. Select a wordless picture book to use with children of various ages. Record the retelling of the story by each child, noting differences in language development, sense of story, descriptive phrases, and complexity of plot. Be sure to let the child look through the book once before beginning to tell the story.

5. Assume you are going to compile a small Mother Goose book of twenty to twenty-five rhymes.

Which ones would you choose? How would you arrange them in your book?

6. Find a concept book about one particular subject. *Before* you read it, list all the possible dimensions of that concept. Then compare your list with what the author/artist chose to include.

7. Read three or four bedtime stories to one child or several children. Which ones do they ask to hear repeatedly? Can you find any patterns among their favorites?

8. Select what you consider to be a predictable book. Share it with 5- and 6-year-olds, then reread it, waiting for them to join in at various places. What did you learn about your selection?

9. Interview a nursery school teacher. How often does he or she read aloud to the group? How do the teachers select the books? Do they have any favorites? What are they? What recommendations for change could you make?

10. Compare several preprimers and primers with the books for the beginning reader described in this text. What do you notice as being different or significant for an emerging reader?

Related Readings

Butler, Dorothy. *Babies Need Books*. New York: Atheneum, 1980.

A firm believer in the importance of books for the young child, this New Zealander writes from her experience as a mother, grandmother, and children's bookseller. She not only recommends books for ages 1 through 5, but she gives practical suggestions about when and how to read to wiggly children.

Cochran-Smith, Marilyn. *The Making of a Reader*. Norwood, N.J.: Ablex, 1984.

This book focuses on how adults and children observed over an eighteen-month period in a preschool collaborated on building meaning in books. It emphasizes what the children know about books and ways they seem to be coming to know it. The observational charts will prove useful to other researchers.

Fisher, Bobbi. *Joyful Learning*. Portsmouth, N.H.: Heinemann Educational Books, 1991.

———. *Thinking and Learning Together*. Portsmouth, N.H.: Heinemann Educational Books, 1995.

Written by an experienced primary-grade teacher, these two books describe a rich literature-based environment for children's literacy development. Practical suggestions are offered about organizing the day, developing emergent reading and writing activities, carrying out evaluation and portfolio assessment, and communicating with parents.

Goelmann, Hillel, Antoinette Oberg, and Frank Smith, eds. *Awakening to Literacy*. Portsmouth, N.H.: Heinemann Educational Books, 1984.

Based on a literacy symposium held at the University of Victoria, the fourteen papers in this book provide a thorough review of the research on literacy before schooling. Articles by Yetta Goodman, Frank Smith, and Jerome Bruner are particularly significant. William H. Teale's paper on the importance of reading aloud to young children supports the point of view presented in this chapter.

Hill, Mary W. *Home: Where Reading and Writing Begin*. Portsmouth, N.H.: Heinemann Educational Books, 1989.

Written for parents, this book is filled with children's literature titles and helpful suggestions of ways to create literate environments in the home.

Hart-Hewins, Linda, and Jan Wells. *Real Books for Reading: Learning to Read with Children's Literature*. Portsmouth, N.H.: Heinemann Educational Books, 1990.

The subtitle of this book evolved from the extensive experience of two former teachers in Canada using children's literature as the core of their classroom reading program. Practical suggestions for reading aloud, buddy reading, conferencing with children, and writing opportunities are all given. An extensive bibliography of books for children is also included.

McConaghy, June. *Children Learning Through Literature*. Portsmouth, N.H.: Heinemann Educational Books, 1990.

A Canadian describes her experience of teaching first graders to read by using literature. She emphasizes discussing children's responses to books rather than quizzing them with questions. She describes literature's influence on children's writing and gives examples of children's stories. She also provides samples from her own journal entries to show her growth as a teacher and researcher.

Short, Kathy Gnagey, and Kathryn Mitchell Pierce, eds. *Talking About Books: Creating Literate Communities*. Portsmouth, N.H.: Heinemann Educational Books, 1990.

Teachers and educators focus on the kinds of learning communities that support readers as they read and interact with others, particularly as they discuss literature. Emphasis is placed on collaborative learning from kindergarten through high school. Practical suggestions are provided about ways to organize the classroom to encourage talk about literature.

Strickland, Dorothy S., and Lesley Mandel Morrow, eds. *Emerging Literacy: Helping Young Children Learn to Read and Write*. Newark, Del.: International Reading Association, 1989.

This book contains the International Reading Association's influential statement "Literacy Development and Prefirst Grade: A Joint Statement of Concerns About Present Practices in Prefirst Grade Reading Instruction and Recommendations for Improvement." Strickland's excellent chapter enlarges on this statement to provide a model for change in the curriculum.

Taylor, Denny, and Catherine Dorsey-Gaine. *Growing Up Literate: Learning from Inner-City Families*. Portsmouth, N.H.: Heinemann Educational Books, 1988.

These authors describe how children can grow up poor and black in an urban environment and still grow up literate. It presents a devastating picture of the economic poverty and in many instances (see the chapter "Shanna's Day at School") the educational poverty of these children's lives. Yet despite it all, these children become literate. One needs to ask how.

Taylor, Denny, and Dorothy S. Strickland. *Family Storybook Reading*. Portsmouth, N.H.: Heinemann Educational Books, 1986.

These authors provide real-life experiences and photographs of the various ways parents share books in the home. Astute observers, the authors focus on the natural ways parents lead children to develop literacy.

Teale, William H., and Elizabeth Sulzby, eds. *Emergent Literacy: Writing and Reading*. Norwood, N.J.: Ablex, 1986.

A fine collection of articles about literacy by such well-known researchers as Emilia Ferreioro, Shirley Brice Heath, Catherine Snow, and Anat Ninio. Teale's last article sums up the research on children's home background and emergent literacy development.

Wells, Gordon. *The Meaning Makers: Children Learning Language and Using Language to Learn*. Portsmouth, N.H.: Heinemann Educational Books, 1986.

Wells reports on the importance of story and reading aloud to preschoolers for their later educational attainment. Based on fifteen years of longitudinal research, this is a significant book.

White, Dorothy. *Books Before Five*. Portsmouth, N.H.: Heinemann Educational Books, 1984 [1954].

A reissue of the first longitudinal study of a young child's response to books. Written by a young mother who was a former librarian, this book records how she and her daughter Carol explored books from the time Carol was 2 until she went to school. Long out of print, this new edition has a foreword by Marie Clay.

Children's Literature

Agard, John, and Grace Nichols. *No Hickory No Dickory No Dock*. Illustrated by Cynthia Jabar. Candlewick, 1995.

Ahlberg, Janet, and Allan Ahlberg. *Each Peach Pear Plum*. Viking, 1979.

Alexander, Martha. *Pigs Say Oink*. Random House, 1978.

Aliki [Aliki Brandenberg]. *Go Tell Aunt Rhody*. Macmillan, 1986 [1974].

———. *My Feet*. Crowell, 1990.

———. *My Hands*. Crowell, 1990.

Anno, Mitsumasa. *Anno's Alphabet*. Crowell, 1975.

———. *Anno's Counting Book*. Crowell, 1977.

———. *Anno's Counting House*. Crowell, 1982.

Aylesworth, Jim. *Old Black Fly*. Illustrated by Stephen Gammell. Holt, 1992.

———. *One Crow, a Counting Rhyme*. Illustrated by Ruth Young. Lippincott, 1988.

Azarian, Mary. *A Farmer's Alphabet*. Godine, 1981.

Baker, Keith. *Big Fat Hen*. Harcourt Brace, 1994.

Bang, Molly. *Ten, Nine, Eight*. Greenwillow, 1983.

Bannatyne-Cugnet, Jo. *A Prairie Alphabet*. Illustrated by Yevette Moore. Tundra Books, 1992.

Banyai, Istvan. *Zoom*. Viking, 1995.

Barton, Byron. *Buzz Buzz Buzz*. Macmillan, 1973.

———. *The Little Red Hen*. HarperCollins, 1994.

———. *Machines at Work*. Crowell, 1987.

Bennett, Jill. *Teeny Tiny*. Illustrated by Tomie de Paola. Putnam, 1986.

Bowen, Betsy. *Antler, Bear, Canoe: A Northwoods Alphabet Year*. Little, Brown, 1991.

Briggs, Raymond. *The Mother Goose Treasury*. Coward-McCann, 1966.

———. *The Snowman*. Random House, 1978.

Brooke, Leslie. *Ring o'Roses*. Clarion, 1992 [Warne, 1923].

Brown, Margaret Wise. *Four Fur Feet*. Watermark, 1989. [William R. Scott. (Hopscotch Books), 1961].

———. *Goodnight Moon*. Illustrated by Clement Hurd. Harper & Row, 1947.

———. *The Goodnight Moon Room*. Illustrated by Clement Hurd. Harper & Row, 1984.

———. *The Runaway Bunny*. Illustrated by Clement Hurd. Harper & Row, 1972 [1942].

Brown, Ruth. *A Dark Dark Tale*. Dial, 1981.

Burningham, John. *The Baby*. Candlewick, 1994 [Crowell, 1975].

———. *The Blanket*. Candlewick, 1994 [Crowell, 1976].

———. *Mr. Gumpy's Outing*. Holt, 1971.

———. *John Burningham's ABC*. Crown, 1993 [1986].

———. *The Rabbit*. Crowell, 1975.

Burton, Marilee Robin. *Tail Toes Eyes Ears Nose*. Harper & Row, 1989.

Campbell, Rod. *Dear Zoo*. Four Winds, 1983.

Carle, Eric. *1, 2, 3, to the Zoo*. Philomel, 1968.

———. *Do You Want to Be My Friend?* Harper & Row, 1971.

———. *The Grouchy Ladybug*. Harper & Row, 1977.

———. *Have You Seen My Cat?* Picture Book Studio, 1987.

———. *Today Is Monday*. Philomel, 1993.

———. *The Very Busy Spider*. Philomel, 1984.

———. *The Very Hungry Caterpillar*. Philomel, 1969.

———. *The Very Lonely Firefly*. Philomel, 1995.

———. *The Very Quiet Cricket*. Philomel, 1990.

Carlstrom, Nancy White. *Jesse Bear, What Will You Wear?* Illustrated by Bruce Degen. Macmillan, 1986.

Carroll, Kathleen Sullivan. *One Red Rooster*. Illustrated by Suzette Barbier. Houghton Mifflin, 1992.

Cauley, Lorinda Bryan. *Old MacDonald Had a Farm*. Putnam, 1989.

———. *The Three Little Kittens*. Putnam, 1982.

Chapman, Cheryl. *Snow on Snow on Snow*. Illustrated by Synthia St. James. Dial, 1994.

Christelow, Eileen. *Five Little Monkeys Jumping on the Bed*. Clarion, 1989.

Christiansen, Bonnie. *An Edible Alphabet*. Dial, 1994.

Cooke, Trish. *So Much*. Illustrated by Helen Oxenbury. Candlewick, 1994.

Cousins, Lucy. *Maisy Goes to Bed*. Little, Brown, 1990.

Crews, Donald. *Flying*. Greenwillow, 1986.

———. *Freight Train*. Greenwillow, 1978.

———. *Harbor*. Greenwillow, 1982.

———. *Sail Away*. Greenwillow, 1995.

———. *School Bus*. Greenwillow, 1984.

———. *Ten Black Dots*. Greenwillow, 1986 [1968].

———. *Truck*. Greenwillow, 1980.

Day, Alexandra. *Carl Goes Shopping*. Farrar, Straus & Giroux, 1989.

———. *Carl's Birthday*. Farrar, Straus & Giroux, 1995.

———. *Good Dog, Carl*. Green Tiger Press, 1985.

de Angeli, Marguerite. *The Book of Nursery and Mother Goose Rhymes*. Doubleday, 1954.

Delacre, Lulu, ed. *Arroz Con Leche: Popular Songs and Rhymes from Latin America*. Scholastic, 1989.

Demi. *Dragon Kites and Dragonflies: A Collection of Chinese Nursery Rhymes*. Harcourt Brace, 1986.

de Paola, Tomie. *The Comic Adventures of Old Mother Hubbard and Her Dog*. Harcourt Brace, 1981.

———. *Pancakes for Breakfast*. Harcourt Brace, 1978.

———. *Tomie de Paola's Mother Goose*. Putnam, 1985.

Dragonwagon, Crescent. *Alligator Arrived with Apples.* Illustrated by Jose Aruego and Ariane Dewey. Macmillan, 1987.

Duff, Maggie. *Rum, Pum, Pum.* Macmillan, 1978.

Duke, Kate. *The Guinea Pig ABC.* Dutton, 1983.

Dunrea, Olivier. *Deep Down Underground.* Macmillan, 1989.

Ehlert, Lois. *Color Farm.* Lippincott, 1990.

———. *Color Zoo.* Lippincott, 1990.

———. *Eating the Alphabet.* Harcourt Brace, 1989.

———. *Feathers for Lunch.* Harcourt Brace, 1990.

———. *Fish Eyes: A Book You Can Count On.* Harcourt Brace, 1990.

———. *Red Leaf, Yellow Leaf.* Harcourt Brace, 1991.

Emberley, Barbara. *Drummer Hoff.* Illustrated by Ed Emberley. Prentice Hall, 1967.

Falwell, Cathryn. *Feast for Ten.* Clarion, 1993.

Feelings, Muriel. *Jambo Means Hello: Swahili Alphabet Book.* Illustrated by Tom Feelings. Dial, 1974.

———. *Moja Means One: Swahili Counting Book.* Illustrated by Tom Feelings. Dial, 1971.

Fleming, Denise. *Barnyard Banter.* Holt, 1993.

———. *In the Small Small Pond.* Holt, 1993.

———. *In the Tall Tall Grass.* Holt, 1991.

Fox, Mem. *Shoes from Grandpa.* Illustrated by Patricia Mullins. Orchard, 1990.

———. *Time for Bed.* Illustrated by Jane Dyer. Harcourt Brace, 1993.

Gág, Wanda. *The ABC Bunny.* Coward-McCann, 1933.

Galdone, Paul. *The Gingerbread Boy.* Clarion, 1975.

———. *The House That Jack Built.* McGraw-Hill, 1961.

———. *The Little Red Hen.* Clarion, 1973.

———. *Old Mother Hubbard and Her Dog.* McGraw-Hill, 1960.

———. *Over in the Meadow.* Prentice Hall, 1986.

———. *The Three Bears.* Clarion, 1972.

———. *The Three Billy Goats Gruff.* Clarion, 1981.

———. *Three Little Kittens.* Clarion, 1986.

———. *The Three Little Pigs.* Clarion, 1970.

Garne, S. T. *One White Sail: A Caribbean Counting Book.* Illustrated by Lisa Etre. Simon & Schuster, 1994.

Garten, Jan. *The Alphabet Tale.* Illustrated by Muriel Batherman. Random House, 1964.

Geisert, Arthur. *Pigs from 1 to 10.* Houghton Mifflin, 1992.

Gerstein, Mordicai. *Roll Over!* Crown, 1984.

Giganti, Paul, Jr. *Each Orange Had 8 Slices.* Illustrated by Donald Crews. Greenwillow, 1992.

———. *How Many Snails?* Illustrated by Donald Crews. Greenwillow, 1988.

Ginsburg, Mirra. *Across the Stream.* Illustrated by Nancy Tafuri. Greenwillow, 1982.

———. *The Chick and the Duckling.* Illustrated by Jose Aruego and Ariane Dewey. Macmillan, 1972.

———. *Good Morning, Chick.* Illustrated by Byron Barton. Greenwillow, 1980.

Glazer, Tom. *Eye Winker Tom Tinker Chin Chopper.* Doubleday, 1973.

———. *The Mother Goose Songbook.* Illustrated by David McPhail. Doubleday, 1990.

Gray, Libba Moore. *Small Green Snake.* Illustrated by Holly Meade. Orchard, 1994.

Greenaway, Kate. *Mother Goose, or the Old Nursery Rhymes.* Warne, n.d.

Griego, Margot C., et al. *Tortillitas Para Mama and Other Nursery Rhymes/Spanish and English.* Illustrated by Barbara Cooney. Holt, 1981.

Grimes, Nikki. *C Is for City.* Illustrated by Pat Cummings. Lothrop, Lee & Shepard, 1995.

Guarino, Deborah. *Is Your Mama a Llama?* Illustrated by Steven Kellogg. Scholastic, 1989.

Hale, Sarah Josepha. *Mary Had a Little Lamb.* Illustrated by Tomie de Paola. Holiday House, 1984.

———. *Mary Had a Little Lamb.* Illustrated by Sally Mavor. Orchard, 1995.

———. *Mary Had a Little Lamb.* Photo-illustrated by Bruce McMillan. Scholastic, 1990.

Halpern, Shari. *Moving from One to Ten.* Macmillan, 1993.

Harrison, Ted. *A Northern Alphabet.* Tundra, 1982.

Hawkins, Colin, and Jacqui Hawkins. *I Know an Old Lady Who Swallowed a Fly.* Putnam, 1987.

Hayes, Sarah. *Clap Your Hands.* Illustrated by Toni Gaffe. Lothrop, Lee & Shepard, 1988.

———. *Nine Ducks Nine.* Lothrop, Lee & Shepard, 1990.

———. *This Is the Bear.* Illustrated by Helen Craig. Lippincott, 1986.

Hellen, Nancy. *The Bus Stop.* Orchard, 1988.

———. *Old MacDonald Had a Farm.* Orchard, 1990.

Henkes, Kevin. *The Biggest Boy.* Illustrated by Nancy Tafuri. Greenwillow, 1995.

Hennessy, B. G. *The Missing Tarts.* Illustrated by Tracey Campbell Pearson. Viking Kestrel, 1989.

Hill, Eric. *Nursery Rhyme Peek-a-Book.* Price, Stern, 1982.

———. *Spot Bakes a Cake.* Putnam, 1994.

———. *Spot Goes to School.* Putnam, 1994.

———. *Where's Spot?* Putnam, 1980.

Hines, Anna Grossnickle. *Rumble Thumble Boom.* Greenwillow, 1992.

———. *They Really Like Me!* Greenwillow, 1989.

Hoban, Russell. *A Baby Sister for Frances.* Illustrated by Lillian Hoban. Harper & Row, 1964.

———. *Bread and Jam for Frances.* Illustrated by Lillian Hoban. Harper & Row, 1964.

Hoban, Tana. *1, 2, 3.* Greenwillow, 1985.

———. *26 Letters and 99 Cents.* Greenwillow, 1987.

———. *A, B, See!* Greenwillow, 1982.

———. *All About Where.* Greenwillow, 1991.

———. *Black on White.* Greenwillow, 1993.

———. *Circles, Triangles and Squares.* Macmillan, 1974.

———. *Colors Everywhere.* Greenwillow, 1995.

———. *Exactly the Opposite.* Greenwillow, 1983.

———. *I Read Signs.* Greenwillow, 1983.

———. *I Read Symbols.* Greenwillow, 1983.

———. *Is It Larger? Is It Smaller?* Greenwillow, 1985.

———. *Red, Blue, Yellow Shoe.* Greenwillow, 1986.

———. *Shapes, Shapes, Shapes.* Greenwillow, 1986.

———. *Shapes and Things.* Macmillan, 1970.

———. *Spirals, Curves, Fanshapes, and Lines.* Greenwillow, 1992.

———. *What Is It?* Greenwillow, 1985.

———. *White on Black.* Greenwillow, 1993.

Hoguet, Susan Ramsay. *Solomon Grundy*. Dutton, 1986.

Hopkins, Lee Bennett. *April, Bubbles, Chocolate: An ABC of Poetry*. Illustrated by Barry Root. Simon & Schuster, 1994.

Hughes, Shirley. Nursery collection. *Bathwater's Hot. Noisy. When We Went to the Park*. All Lothrop, Lee & Shepard, 1985.

———. *The Big Alfie and Annie Rose Storybook*. Lothrop, Lee & Shepard, 1989.

———. *Alfie Gets in First*. Lothrop, Lee & Shepard, 1982.

———. *Alfie Gives a Hand*. Lothrop, Lee & Shepard, 1983.

———. *Alfie's Feet*. Lothrop, Lee & Shepard, 1983.

———. *An Evening at Alfie's*. Lothrop, Lee & Shepard, 1992.

Hunt, Peter. *Illuminations*. Bradbury, 1989.

Hutchins, Pat. *1 Hunter*. Greenwillow, 1982.

———. *Changes, Changes*. Macmillan, 1971.

———. *The Doorbell Rang*. Greenwillow, 1986.

———. *Good-Night, Owl!* Macmillan (Penguin), 1972.

———. *Happy Birthday, Sam*. Penguin, 1981.

———. *Little Pink Pig*. Greenwillow, 1994.

———. *Rosie's Walk*. Macmillan, 1968.

———. *Tidy Titch*. Greenwillow, 1991.

———. *Titch*. Macmillan, 1971.

———. *You'll Soon Grow into Them, Titch*. Greenwillow, 1983.

Isadora, Rachel. *Babies*. Greenwillow, 1990.

———. *City Seen from A to Z*. Greenwillow, 1983.

———. *Friends*. Greenwillow, 1990.

Jeffers, Susan. *Three Jovial Huntsmen*. Macmillan, 1989.

Jenkins, Steve. *Looking Down*. Houghton Mifflin, 1995.

Johnson, Angela. *Joshua by the Sea*. Illustrated by Rhonda Mitchell. Orchard, 1994.

———. *Joshua's Night Whisper*. Illustrated by Rhonda Mitchell. Orchard, 1994.

———. *Mama Bird, Baby Birds*. Illustrated by Rhonda Mitchell. Orchard, 1994.

———. *Rain Feet*. Illustrated by Rhonda Mitchell. Orchard, 1994.

Johnson, Stephen T. *Alphabet City*. Viking, 1995.

Jonas, Ann. *Aardvarks Disembark!* Greenwillow, 1989.

———. *Color Dance*. Greenwillow, 1989.

———. *Splash!* Greenwillow, 1995.

———. *Where Can It Be?* Greenwillow, 1986.

Jones, Carol. *Old MacDonald Had a Farm*. Houghton Mifflin, 1989.

———. *This Old Man*. Houghton Mifflin, 1990.

Jorgensen, Gail. *Crocodile Beat*. Illustrated by Patricia Mullins. Simon & Schuster, 1989.

Kamen, Gloria. *"Paddle," Said the Swan*. Atheneum, 1989.

Karas, G. Brian. *I Know an Old Lady*. Scholastic, 1994.

Keats, Ezra Jack. *Over in the Meadow*. Four Winds, 1971.

Kent, Jack. *The Fat Cat*. Parents Magazine Press, 1971.

King-Smith, Dick. *All Pigs Are Beautiful.* Illustrated by Anita Jeram. Candlewick, 1993.

———. *I Love Guinea Pigs.* Illustrated by Anita Jeram. Candlewick, 1995.

Kitchen, Bert. *Animal Alphabet.* Dial, 1984.

———. *Animal Numbers.* Dial, 1987.

Kovalski, Maryann. *The Wheels on the Bus.* Little, Brown, 1987.

Kraus, Robert. *Where Are You Going, Little Mouse?* Illustrated by Jose Aruego and Ariane Dewey. Greenwillow, 1986.

———. *Whose Mouse Are You?* Illustrated by Jose Aruego and Ariane Dewey. Macmillan, 1970.

Krauss, Ruth. *The Carrot Seed.* Illustrated by Crockett Johnson. Harper & Row, 1945.

Kunhardt, Dorothy. *Pat the Bunny.* Golden, 1962 [1940].

Kunhardt, Edith. *Pat the Puppy.* Golden, 1993.

Kuskin, Karla. *Roar and More.* HarperCollins, 1990.

Lacome, Julie. *Garden.* Candlewick, 1993.

———. *Seashore.* Candlewick, 1993.

Langstaff, John. *Oh, A-Hunting We Will Go.* Illustrated by Nancy Winslow Parker. Atheneum, 1974.

———. *Over in the Meadow.* Illustrated by Feodor Rojankovsky. Harcourt Brace, 1967.

Larrick, Nancy. *Songs from Mother Goose.* Illustrated by Robin Spowart. Harper & Row, 1989.

Lessac, Frané. *Caribbean Alphabet.* Tambourine, 1989.

Lillegard, Dee. *Sitting in My Box.* Illustrated by Jon Agee. Dutton, 1989.

Lillie, Patricia. *When the Rooster Crowed.* Illustrated by Nancy Winslow Parker. Greenwillow, 1991.

Lobel, Anita. *Alison's Zinnia.* Greenwillow, 1990.

———. *Away from Home.* Greenwillow, 1994.

Lobel, Arnold. *Days with Frog and Toad.* Harper & Row, 1979.

———. *Frog and Toad All Year.* Harper & Row, 1976.

———. *Frog and Toad Are Friends.* Harper & Row, 1970.

———. *Frog and Toad Together.* Harper & Row, 1972.

———. *On Market Street.* Illustrated by Anita Lobel. Greenwillow, 1981.

———. *Whiskers and Rhymes.* Greenwillow, 1985.

———, ed. and illus. *The Random House Book of Mother Goose.* Random House, 1986.

London, Jonathon. *Like Butter on Pancakes.* Illustrated by G. Brian Karas. Viking, 1995.

MacCarthy, Patricia. *Ocean Parade: A Counting Book.* Dial, 1990.

MacDonald, Suse. *Alphabatics.* Bradbury, 1986.

———. *Sea Shapes.* Gulliver, 1994.

Magorian, Michelle. *Who's Going to Take Care of Me?* Illustrated by James Graham Hale. HarperCollins, 1990.

Mahurin, Tim. *Jeremy Kooloo.* Dutton, 1995.

Manson, Christopher. *The Tree in the Wood: An Old Nursery Song.* North-South, 1993.

Marshall, James. *Hey Diddle Diddle.* Farrar, Straus & Giroux, 1994.

———. *James Marshall's Mother Goose.* Farrar, Straus & Giroux, 1979.

Martin, Bill, Jr. *Brown Bear, Brown Bear, What Do You See?* Illustrated by Eric Carle. Holt, 1983.

———. *The Happy Hippopotami.* Illustrated by Betsy Everitt. Harcourt Brace, 1991.

———. *Polar Bear, Polar Bear, What Do You Hear?* Illustrated by Eric Carle. Holt, 1991.

Martin, Bill, Jr., and John Archambault. *Chicka Chicka Boom Boom*. Illustrated by Lois Ehlert. Simon & Schuster, 1989.

Marzollo, Jean. *Close Your Eyes*. Illustrated by Susan Jeffers. Dial, 1978.

Mayer, Mercer. *A Boy, a Dog, and a Frog*. Dial, 1967.

———. *Frog Goes to Dinner*. Dial, 1974.

———. *One Frog Too Many*. Dial, 1975.

McCully, Emily Arnold. *First Snow*. Harper & Row, 1985.

———. *Picnic*. Harper & Row, 1984.

———. *School*. Harper & Row, 1987.

McMillan, Bruce. *Eating Fractions*. Scholastic, 1991.

McNaughton, Colin. *Suddenly!* Harcourt Brace, 1994.

Merriam, Eve. *12 Ways to Get to 11*. Illustrated by Bernie Karlin. Simon & Schuster, 1993.

Mickelwait, Lucy. *I Spy: An Alphabet in Art*. Greenwillow, 1992.

Milhous, Katherine, and Alice Dalgliesh. *The Turnip*. Illustrated by Pierr Morgan. Putnam, 1990.

Miller, Margaret. *Can You Guess?* Greenwillow, 1993.

———. *Guess Who?* Greenwillow, 1994.

———. *Where Does It Go?* Greenwillow, 1992.

———. *Whose Hat?* Greenwillow, 1988.

———. *Who Uses This?* Greenwillow, 1990.

Minarik, Else Holmelund. *Father Bear Comes Home*. Illustrated by Maurice Sendak. Harper & Row, 1959.

———. *A Kiss for Little Bear*. Illustrated by Maurice Sendak. Harper & Row, 1968.

———. *Little Bear*. Illustrated by Maurice Sendak. Harper & Row, 1957.

———. *Little Bear's Friend*. Illustrated by Maurice Sendak. Harper & Row, 1960.

———. *Little Bear's Visit*. Illustrated by Maurice Sendak. Harper & Row, 1961.

Morris, Ann. *Bread, Bread, Bread*. Photographs by Ken Heyman. Lothrop, Lee & Shepard, 1989.

———. *Houses and Homes*. Photographs by Ken Heyman. Lothrop, Lee & Shepard, 1992.

———. *Loving*. Photographs by Ken Heyman. Lothrop, Lee & Shepard, 1990.

———. *On the Go*. Photographs by Ken Heyman. Mulberry, 1994.

Moss, Lloyd. *Zin! Zin! Zin! A Violin*. Illustrated by Marjorie Priceman. Simon & Schuster, 1995.

Mullins, Patricia. *V for Vanishing: An Alphabet of Endangered Animals*. HarperCollins, 1993.

Murphy, Jill. *Five Minutes' Peace*. Putnam, 1986.

Musgrove, Margaret. *Ashanti to Zulu: African Traditions*. Illustrated by Leo and Diane Dillon. Dial, 1976.

Onyefulu, Ifeoma. *A Is for Africa*. Cobblehill, 1993.

———. *Emeka's Gift: An African Counting Story*. Cobblestone, 1995.

Opie, Iona, and Peter Opie. *I Saw Esau*. Illustrated by Maurice Sendak. Candlewick Press, 1992.

———. *The Oxford Dictionary of Nursery Rhymes*. Oxford, 1951.

———. *Tail Feathers from Mother Goose: The Opie Rhyme Book*. Little, Brown, 1988.

Ormerod, Jan. Jan Ormerod Baby Books. *Dad's Back. Messy Baby. Reading. Sleeping*. All Lothrop, Lee & Shepard, 1985.

———. *Moonlight*. Lothrop, Lee & Shepard, 1982.

———. *Sunshine*. Lothrop, Lee & Shepard, 1981.

———. *To Baby with Love*. Lothrop, Lee & Shepard, 1994.

Owens, Mary Beth. *A Caribou Alphabet*. Illustrated by Mark McCollough. Tilbury House, 1988.

Oxenbury, Helen. Baby Board Books. *Dressing. Family. Friends. Playing. Working*. All Simon & Schuster, 1995 [1981].

———. Baby Board Books. *I Can. I Hear. I See. I Touch*. All Candlewick, 1995 [Random House, 1986].

———. *Clap Hands*. Macmillan, 1987.

———. *Helen Oxenbury's ABC of Things*. Watts, 1972.

———. *The Helen Oxenbury Nursery Rhyme Book*. Morrow, 1986.

———. *Numbers of Things*. Watts, 1968.

———. *Say Goodnight*. Macmillan, 1987.

———. *Tickle Tickle*. Macmillan, 1988.

Pearson, Tracey Campbell. *Sing a Song of Sixpence*. Dial, 1988.

Peek, Merle. *Mary Wore Her Red Dress and Henry Wore His Green Sneakers*. Clarion, 1985.

———. *Roll Over! A Counting Song*. Clarion, 1981.

Peppe, Rodney. *The House That Jack Built*. Delacorte, 1985.

Petersham, Maud, and Miska Petersham. *The Rooster Crows*. Macmillan, 1945.

Pomerantz, Charlotte. *Flap Your Wings and Try*. Illustrated by Nancy Tafuri. Greenwillow, 1989.

———. *Here Comes Henny*. Illustrated by Nancy Winslow Parker. Greenwillow, 1994.

———. *One Duck, Another Duck*. Illustrated by Jose Aruego and Ariane Dewey. Greenwillow, 1984.

———. *The Piggy in a Puddle*. Illustrated by James Marshall. Macmillan, 1974.

Provensen, Alice, and Martin Provensen. *The Mother Goose Book*. Random House, 1976.

———. *A Peaceable Kingdom: The Shaker ABCEDARIUS*. Viking, 1978.

Rackham, Arthur. *Mother Goose, or the Old Nursery Rhymes*. Appleton, 1913.

Raffi. *Down By the Bay: Songs to Read*. Illustrated by Nadine Bernard Westcott. Crown, 1987.

———. *Five Little Ducks*. Illustrated by Jose Aruego and Ariane Dewey. Crown, 1989.

Rathmann, Peggy. *Goodnight, Gorilla*. Putnam, 1994.

Reiss, John J. *Colors*. Bradbury, 1969.

———. *Numbers*. Bradbury, 1971.

Rice, Eve. *Benny Bakes a Cake*. Greenwillow, 1981.

———. *Sam Who Never Forgets*. Greenwillow, 1977.

Robart, Rose. *The Cake That Mack Ate*. Illustrated by Maryann Kovalski. Joy Street/Little, Brown, 1986.

Rockwell, Anne. *Albert B. Cub and Zebra: An Alphabet Storybook*. Crowell, 1977.

Rockwell, Harlow. *My Kitchen*. Greenwillow, 1980.

Rockwell, Anne, and Harlow Rockwell. *Happy Birthday to Me*. Simon & Schuster, 1981.

———. *Can I Help?* Simon & Schuster, 1982.

———. *How My Garden Grows*. Simon & Schuster, 1982.

———. *I Play in My Room*. Simon & Schuster, 1981.

———. *Sick in Bed*. Simon & Schuster, 1982.

Rojankovsky, Feodor. *The Tall Book of Mother Goose*. Harper & Row, 1942.

Rosen, Michael. *We're Going on a Bear Hunt*. Illustrated by Helen Oxenbury. Macmillan, 1989.

Rosenberg, Liz. *Mama Goose: A New Mother Goose*. Illustrated by Janet Street. Philomel, 1994.

Rounds, Glen. *Old MacDonald Had a Farm*. Holiday House, 1981.

———. *The Three Billy Goats Gruff*. Holiday House, 1993.

Rubin, Cynthia, ed. *ABC Americana from the National Gallery of Art*. Harcourt Brace, 1989.

Russo, Marisabina. *Time to Wake Up!* Greenwillow, 1994.

———. *Waiting for Hannah*. Greenwillow, 1989.

———. *Why Do Grown-Ups Have All the Fun?* Greenwillow, 1987.

Ryan, Pam Munoz. *One Hundred Is a Family*. Illustrated by Benrei Huang. Hyperion, 1994.

Rylant, Cynthia. Henry and Mudge books. *Henry and Mudge*, 1987. *Henry and Mudge in Puddle Trouble*, 1987. *Henry and Mudge in the Green Time*, 1987. *Henry and Mudge Under the Yellow Moon*, 1987. *Henry and Mudge in the Sparkle Days*, 1988. *Henry and Mudge and the Forever Sea*, 1989. *Henry and Mudge Get the Cold Shivers*, 1989. *Henry and Mudge and the Happy Cat*, 1990. *Henry and Mudge Take the Big Test*, 1991. *Henry and Mudge and the Long Weekend*, 1992. *Henry and Mudge and the Wild Wind*, 1993. *Henry and Mudge and the Careful Cousin*, 1994. *Henry and Mudge and the Best Day of All*, 1995. All illustrated by Suçie Stevenson and published by Bradbury Press.

Sanders, Marilyn. *What's Your Name? From Ariel to Zoe*. Photographs by Eve Sanders. Holiday House, 1995.

Scarry, Richard. *Richard Scarry's Best Mother Goose Ever*. Golden Press, 1970.

Scott, Ann Herbert. *One Good Horse: A Cowpuncher's Counting Book*. Illustrated by Lynn Sweat. Greenwillow, 1990.

———. *Sam*. Illustrated by Symeon Shimin. McGraw-Hill, 1992 [1967].

Sendak, Maurice. *Chicken Soup with Rice*. Harper & Row, 1962.

———. *Hector Protector and As I Went over the Water*. HarperCollins, 1990 [1965].

———. *One Was Johnny* (Nutshell Library, vol. 3). Harper & Row, 1962.

———. *We Are All in the Dumps with Jack and Guy: Two Nursery Rhymes with Pictures*. HarperCollins, 1993.

Seuss, Dr. [Theodor S. Geisel]. *The Cat in the Hat*. Beginner Books, 1957.

Shaw, Nancy. *Sheep in a Jeep*. Illustrated by Margot Shaw. Houghton Mifflin, 1986.

Shelby, Anne. *Potluck*. Illustrated by Irene Trivas. Orchard, 1991.

Sheppard, Jeff. *Splash, Splash*. Illustrated by Dennis Panek. Macmillan, 1994.

Shulevitz, Uri. *One Monday Morning*. Scribner's, 1967.

Sis, Peter. *Going Up! A Color Counting Book*. Greenwillow, 1989.

———. *Waving: A Counting Book*. Greenwillow, 1988.

Slobodkina, Esphyr. *Caps for Sale*. Addison, 1947.

Spier, Peter. *Crash! Bang! Boom!* Doubleday, 1972.

———. *The Fox Went Out on a Chilly Night*. Doubleday, 1961.

———. *Gobble Growl Grunt*. Doubleday, 1971.

———. *London Bridge Is Falling Down*. Doubleday, 1967.

———. *Noah's Ark*. Doubleday, 1977.

———. *Peter Spier's Rain*. Doubleday, 1982.

Steptoe, John. *Baby Says*. Lothrop, Lee & Shepard, 1988.

Stevens, Janet. *The House That Jack Built*. Greenwillow, 1983.

Sweet, Melissa. *Fiddle-I-Fee*. Little, Brown, 1992.

Sutherland, Zena. *The Orchard Book of Nursery Rhymes*. Illustrated by Faith Jaques. Orchard, 1990.

Tafuri, Nancy. *Early Morning in the Barn*. Greenwillow, 1983.

———. *Follow Me!* Greenwillow, 1990.

———. *Have You Seen My Duckling?* Greenwillow, 1984.

———. *Junglewalk*. Greenwillow, 1988.

Tapahonso, Luci, and Eleanor Schick. *Navajo ABC: A Diné Alphabet Book*. Illustrated by Eleanor Schick. Little, Brown, 1995.

Tudor, Tasha. *A Is for Annabelle*. Walck, 1954.

———. *Mother Goose*. Walck, 1944.

Turkle, Brinton. *Deep in the Forest*. Dutton, 1976.

Valens, Amy. *Jesse's Daycare*. Illustrated by Richard Brown. Houghton Mifflin, 1990.

Van Allsburg, Chris. *The Z Was Zapped: A Play in Twenty-Six Acts*. Houghton Mifflin, 1987.

Van Laan, Nancy. *A Mouse in My House*. Illustrated by Marjorie Priceman. Knopf, 1990.

———. *This Is the Hat: A Story in Rhyme*. Illustrated by Holly Meade. Little, Brown, 1992.

———. *The Tiny Tiny Boy and the Big Big Cow*. Illustrated by Marjorie Priceman. Knopf, 1993.

Vipoint, Elfrida. *The Elephant and the Bad Baby*. Illustrated by Raymond Briggs. Coward-McCann, 1969.

Voce, Louise. *Over in the Meadow: A Traditional Counting Rhyme*. Candlewick, 1994.

Waddell, Martin. *Farmer Duck*. Illustrated by Helen Oxenbury. Candlewick, 1993.

———. *Owl Babies*. Illustrated by Patrick Benson. Candlewick, 1992.

Ward, Cindy. *Cookie's Week*. Illustrated by Tomie de Paola. Putnam, 1988.

Watson, Clyde. *Applebet*. Illustrated by Wendy Watson. Farrar, Straus & Giroux, 1982.

———. *Father Fox's Pennyrhymes*. Illustrated by Wendy Watson. Crowell, 1971.

Watson, Wendy. *Wendy Watson's Mother Goose*. Edited by Dorothy Briley. Lothrop, Lee & Shepard, 1989.

Weiss, Nicki. *Where Does the Brown Bear Go?* Greenwillow, 1989.

Wells, Rosemary. Very First Books. *Max's Bath*, 1985. *Max's Bedtime*, 1985. *Max's Birthday*, 1985. *Max's Breakfast*, 1985. *Max's First Word*, 1979. *Max's Ride*, 1979. *Max's Toys*, 1979. All Dial.

Westcott, Nadine Bernard. *Peanut Butter and Jelly: A Play Rhyme*. Dutton: 1987.

———. *I Know an Old Lady Who Swallowed a Fly*. Little, Brown, 1980.

———. *Skip to My Lou*. Joy Street/Little, Brown, 1989.

Wiesner, David. *Free Fall*. Lothrop, Lee & Shepard, 1988.

———. *Tuesday*. Clarion, 1991.

Wildsmith, Brian. *Brian Wildsmith's Mother Goose*. Watts, 1963.

———. *The Cat on the Mat*. Oxford University Press, 1983.

Williams, Linda. *The Little Old Lady Who Was Not Afraid of Anything*. Illustrated by Megan Lloyd. Harper & Row, 1986.

Williams, Sue. *I Went Walking*. Illustrated by Julie Vivas. Harcourt Brace, 1990.

Williams, Vera B. *"More More More," Said the Baby*. Greenwillow, 1990.

Wolff, Ashley. *The Bells of London*. Dodd, Mead, 1985.

———. *A Year of Birds*. Putnam, 1984.

———. *A Year of Beasts*. Dutton, 1986.

Wood, Audrey. *The Napping House*. Illustrated by Don Wood. Harcourt Brace, 1984.

Wood, Jakki. *Fiddle-I-Fee*. Bradbury, 1994.

Wright, Blanche Fisher. *The Real Mother Goose*. Rand McNally, 1965 [1916].

Wyndham, Robert. *Chinese Mother Goose Rhymes*. Illustrated by Ed Young. Philomel, 1989 [1968].

Zelinsky, Paul O. *The Wheels on the Bus*. Dutton, 1990.

chapter
five

Picture Storybooks

Courtesy of Linda Rozenfeld/Images Marmor Rozenfeld

The Picture Storybook Defined   198
The Art and Artists of Picture
     Storybooks and Illustrated Books   199
Creating Meaning in Picture Storybooks   199
The Artist's Choice of Media   202
Woodcuts and Similar Techniques   203
Collage and Construction   204
Paints and Pen and Ink   207
Crayon, Chalk, Charcoal, and Pencil   209
Elements of Design   210
Line and Shape   210
Use of Color   210
Space   211
Point of View or Perspective   211
The Matter of Style   212
Realism, or Representational Art   212
Impressionism   213
Expressionism   214
Surrealism   214
Naive or Folk Art   215
Cartoon Style   216
Cultural Connections   217
Personal Styles   217
The Format of the Book   218
Web: Brian Pinkney—A Web of
     Possibilities   219
Teaching Feature: Learning About the Art
     of Picture Storybooks   221

The Language of Picture
     Storybooks   222
The Content of Picture Storybooks   222
Guidelines: Evaluating Picture
     Storybooks   223
Themes and Subjects in Picture
     Storybooks   225
Family Stories   225
Familiar Everyday Experiences   227
Picture Storybooks About Older People   228
The Child's World of Nature   229
Animals as People   230
Resources for Teaching: Picture Storybooks
     About the Everyday World of the
     Child   231
Modern Folktale Style   236
Humor   237
Fantasy   239
Appreciating Cultural Diversity   241
Resources for Teaching: Picture Storybooks
     About the Child's Imaginary World   242
Social and Environmental Concerns   248
War and Its Aftermath   249
Learning Experiences   251
Related Readings   251
Children's Literature   252

Some primary children in the Midwest were studying trees and autumn as a special unit.[1] Their teacher read them *Say It!* by Charlotte Zolotow, illustrated by James Stevenson. The children reviewed what the mother and the little girl had seen on their walk on that windy day. They talked about the words in the story they liked, particularly the word *splendiferous*. Then *Say It!* was placed on the display table with the other books about autumn.

The next week the teacher shared the book again. The children then took clipboards, pencils, and paper and went outside. Each chose a favorite tree to sit under and record what they saw, heard, smelled, thought, felt, or wished. They worked like this for about fifteen minutes. Then they made a giant pile of leaves and jumped and played in them.

That afternoon the teacher read *Say It!* again to the children. They selected their favorite words and phrases to be listed on the board. These included *swirled, wondrous, dazzling, zigzagging, streaks of color,* and *scrunching.*

The following day they gave detailed attention to each of the illustrations, talking about the medium and the way James Stevenson had made the pictures. The children were given watercolors and an opportunity to paint what they had seen outside or a favorite part of the story. They were also asked to write about their paintings. Here are some of their comments:

🍂 This is a pond of floating colors. The mother said it is a wonderful pond.

James Stevenson's impressionistic watercolors create the illusion of a windy autumn day—"a splendiferous day" in *Say It!* by Charlotte Zolotow.

Illustration from *Say It!* by Charlotte Zolotow, illustrated by James Stevenson. Illustration copyright © 1980 by James Stevenson. By permission of Greenwillow Books, a division of William Morrow & Company, Inc.

🍂 It was a golden splendiferous day in this town and the mommie and the girl walked down the road and saw lots of leaves.

🍂 The little girl and her mother went on a walk. And on the walk they found a little floating cloud of seeds.

[1]This account is based on a much longer article by Joetta M. Beaver, "*Say It!* Over and Over," *Language Arts* 59 (February 1982): 143–148.

Say It! became one of their favorite books. It was read frequently, and many of the children chose to share it with their "book buddies" in third grade.

What a wonderful way this teacher related a book to life experiences, and life experiences back to a book! Repeated readings heightened the children's appreciation for the language and art of the story. Their experiences with watercolors helped them see what they could do with that medium, and talking and writing about their own pictures enhanced their vocabularies.

In the process of looking at one book in depth, children learned much about the way text and illustrations work together to create a story. A picture storybook had provided for the development of these students' visual, mental, and verbal imaginations.

The Picture Storybook Defined

Although we discuss books in which pictures play a vital role in Chapters 4, 6, and 12, this chapter is primarily concerned with picture storybooks. The picture storybook conveys its messages through two media, the art of illustrating and the art of writing. In a well-designed book in which the total format reflects the meaning of the story, both the illustrations and the text must bear the burden of narration. Barbara Bader maintains:

> As an art form it [the picture storybook] hinges on the interdependence of picture and words, on the simultaneous display of two facing pages, and on the drama of the turning of the page.[2]

In discussing the narrative art of children's picture storybooks, Perry Nodelman states:

> We perceive new experiences in terms of the experiences preceding them. . . . Each picture in a picture book establishes a context for the picture that follows—it becomes a schema that determines how we will perceive the next picture.[3]

Some persons differentiate between the picture book and the picture storybook; others maintain that any book with a picture-book format can be included under the umbrella term *picture book*. Yet a picture storybook places special demands on the artist.

A picture book might be an alphabet book, a counting book, a first book, or a concept book (the books discussed in Chapter 4). In these the pictures must be accurate and synchronized with the text; however, it is not essential that they provide the continuity required by a story line. The illustrations for a concept book or an alphabet book can depict a different object or an animal on each page, providing for much variety in the pictures. Examples would be Bert Kitchen's *Animal Alphabet*, which shows large individual pictures for each letter, or Tana Hoban's *Shadows and Reflections*, which explores various dimensions of a concept with stunning photographs. In a picture storybook, pictures must help to tell the story, showing the action and expressions of the characters, the changing settings, and the development of the plot.

Paul O. Zelinsky's illustrations for *Swamp Angel* by Anne Isaacs are a fine example of the integral partnership between pictures and text. This original story is based on a particularly American folktale form, the tall tale. In a tall tale, heroes and heroines are larger than life and perform impossible feats, all in a spirit of comic horseplay that children love. For his illustrations, Zelinsky has looked to another American folk art that has been identified with America's past, the landscapes and portraits done during the colonial period by mostly untrained painters called limners. Inspired by their style, Zelinsky chose to work in oils on wood veneers that subtly recall the tall forests of the Appalachian mountains of Tennessee where the story takes place. On these warm and glowing woods, he paints the story of Angelica Longrider, who is "born scarcely taller than her mother" but grows up to save the people of Tennessee from Thundering Tarnation, a bear so big that his pelt covered the entire state of Montana and his bear soul became the big dipper. The portrait of Angelica opposite the title page introduces the wide-eyed heroine, and the look of unassuming innocence on her face sets the tone of the story; what is to come is good fun and not to be taken seriously. Throughout the book Zelinsky adds a wealth of visual detail to Isaacs's story. On the first double-page spread, for example, he shows Angelica stopping a flash flood with her apron, harnessing a rain cloud to put out a cabin fire, and knitting herself striped pantaloons with two tree trunks. His choice of color scheme creates a sense of lively action throughout the book. To heighten the excitement, aqua blue skies and soft grey-green mountains are set against the warm reds and oranges of his figures and the oak, ash, and cherry veneers of the background. In addition, the page design also has great energy. Zelinsky varies the frame for each picture from oval to semicircle to rectangle. On some double-page spreads he shows multiple scenes; on

[2]Barbara Bader, *American Picturebooks from Noah's Ark to the Beast Within* (New York: Macmillan, 1976), Introduction.

[3]Perry Nodelman, *Words About Pictures* (Athens: University of Georgia Press, 1988), p. 176.

Paul Zelinsky's richly layered paintings extend and enhance the written text of Anne Isaacs's *Swamp Angel.*
From *Swamp Angel* by Anne Isaacs, illustrated by Paul O. Zelinsky. Copyright © 1994 by Paul O. Zelinsky. Used by permission of Dutton Signet, a division of Penguin USA Inc.

The Art and Artists of Picture Storybooks and Illustrated Books

A picture storybook, then, must be a seamless whole conveying meaning in both the art and the text. An illustration for such a book does not merely reflect the action on that page but shares in moving the story forward and in engaging the reader with the narrative on both an intellectual and an emotional level. Throughout the narration the pictures should convey and enhance the meaning behind the story. Artists do this in a variety of subtle and interesting ways.

Creating Meaning in Picture Storybooks

An outstanding example of illustrations that help to move the plot can be found in the classic *Blueberries for Sal* by Robert McCloskey. This is a story that children can tell by themselves just by looking at the clear blue-and-white pictures. The illustrations help the reader anticipate both the action and the climax as Sal and her mother are seen going berry picking up one side of Blueberry Hill, and Little Bear and his mother are seen coming up the other side. McCloskey uses a false climax, a good storytelling technique. Sal hears a noise and starts to peer behind an ominously dark rock; the reader expects her to meet the bears, but instead she sees a mother crow and her children. On the next page she calmly meets Mother Bear and tramps along behind her. A parallel plot gives Little Bear a similar experience, but Sal's mother is not so calm about meeting him! The human expressions of surprise, fear, and consternation on the faces of both mothers express emotion as well as action.

Artwork might show mounting tension by increasing the size of the pictures. One of the best-known examples of this is in Maurice Sendak's fine story *Where the Wild Things Are*. The pictures in this book become larger and larger as Max's dream becomes more and more fantastic. Following the climactic wild rumpus, which is portrayed on three full-sized spreads with no text whatsoever, Max returns home. The pictures decrease in size, although never down to their original size—just as, symbolically, Max will never be quite the same again after his dream experience.

Picture-book artists also provide clues to the future action of a story. A close look at the first and second pages of *Where the Wild Things Are* shows the mischievous Max dressed in his wild-thing suit and stringing up

others he highlights the action in single frames. He also moves the story along by varying the point of view from a close-up to a distant shot and from looking straight at the scene to looking down from a bird's-eye view. Zelinsky's artistic choices add to the delight of the story so that the reader closes the book with an experience that is more than the sum of its parts. This book represents the type of real marriage between pictures and text that we hope to find in good picture storybooks.

An illustrated book is different from either a picture book or a picture storybook. In an illustrated book only particular incidents in the story might be illustrated to create interest. Chris Van Allsburg, noted for his fine picture storybooks, provided a dozen full-color plates for the illustrated edition of *Swan Lake* by Mark Helprin. This retelling of the classic ballet is a beautiful example of fine bookmaking with its cloth cover, gold imprinted title, endpapers with floating feathers, and two-color borders. It is indeed a handsome illustrated edition, but it is not a picture storybook.

a homemade tent. A plush toy looking vaguely like a wild thing hangs nearby. Later the tent and wild things appear in Max's dream trip to the far-off land of the wild things. His drawing of a wild thing on page 2 shows his preoccupation with creating these creatures that later inhabit his dreams.

Some picture-book illustrations use visual metaphors in the same way that poets add to the image-making qualities of their poems. In *Once a Mouse* Marcia Brown reinforces the drama of the little mouse who is about to be snatched up in the beak of a crow by making the shape of a hill in the background look like an open beak. Again, as she creates shadows of the animals, the reader can see that the shadow of the tiger is that of a dog, his former self before the hermit transformed him.

Sendak's book *Outside Over There* is filled with visual metaphor and symbols. A comparison of the half title page and the last picture in the book reveals that the entire action of Ida's dream story happened in one moment of time, the time when her baby sister took one small step. The storm at sea and the shipwreck that the viewer can see outside the window accompany and intensify with Ida's fury over the goblin's stealing her baby sister. Edmund Spenser used the same metaphor of a safe sea journey to accompany his telling of the story of Saint George and the dragon. Trina Schart Hyman faithfully reproduced it in the borders of her superb illustrations for that story as retold by Margaret Hodges in *Saint George and the Dragon*.

Uri Shulevitz chronicles the demise of a tiny small-town post office in his picture storybook *Toddlecreek Post Office*. To the villagers of Toddlecreek, the post office was a special place for friends to gather and tell stories and was the hub of activity until the day a postal inspector came and closed it forever. Expressive watercolors help tell this tale of the end of an era. The pictures, which are wreathed in warm golden light for most of the story, suddenly become dark and dim with the arrival of the postal inspector. This creative use of color signals the sad climax of this story. Shulevitz also used increasing light and color in *Dawn* to portray his quietly beautiful story of a man and his grandson rowing out on a lake to see the dawn break. Don Wood used a similar technique in illustrations for *The Napping House* by Audrey Wood. When everyone in the house is sleeping, the overall color is a restful blue-gray. As the house's inhabitants wake up, the illustrations move to all the bright colors of the rainbow that appears on the final page.

Pictures not only should reflect the action and climax of the plot, they should help to create the basic mood of the story. In a perfection of words and watercolors, Robert McCloskey captures the changing moods of the Maine coast in his *Time of Wonder*. Using soft grays and yellow, he conveys the warmth and mystery of the early-morning fog in the woods. His ocean storm scene, on the other hand, is slashed with streaks of dark blues and emerald greens, highlighted by churning whites. The text is no longer quiet and poetic, but races along with "the sharp choppy waves and slamming rain." The storm subsides; the summer ends; and it is time to leave the island. The beauty of this book will not reach all children, but it will speak forever to young and old alike who have ever intensely loved a particular place on this earth.

Besides creating the basic mood of a story, illustrations also help create convincing character delineation and development. The characterization in the pictures must correspond to that in the story. There is no mistaking the devilish quality of the incorrigible Madeline as she balances herself on the ledge of the Pont des Arts in Paris or says "pooh-pooh to the tiger in the zoo." Madeline is always her roguish self in *Madeline* and the four other books that Ludwig Bemelmans wrote about her.

Expression and gesture can also reveal character and move the action forward. In *Just Plain Fancy*, Patricia Polacco tells the story of Naomi, an Amish girl, and her little sister, who hatch a peacock from a fancy egg they

Uri Shulevitz shows Toddlecreek Post Office suffused with a warm golden glow until the arrival of the postal inspector, who decides to close this small community center.
Illustration from *Toddlecreek Post Office* by Uri Shulevitz. Copyright © 1990 by Uri Shulevitz. Reprinted by permission of Farrar, Straus & Giroux, Inc.

find. Frightened that their bird is too fancy for Amish ways, they decide to hide it. The expression of awe and amazement on their faces when they first see Fancy raise his peacock feathers provides the emotional climax of this delightful story. Peggy Rathmann's comical drawings carry the weight of the narrative in *Officer Buckle and Gloria,* the Newbery Medal-winning story of two friends who learn the value of partnership. The expressions on the faces of these characters convey a range of emotions and help the reader to empathize with the predicament of Officer Buckle.

One of the few picture storybooks to portray character development is the Japanese story *Crow Boy* by Taro Yashima. In the very first picture of this wonderfully sensitive story, Chibi is shown hidden away in the dark space underneath the schoolhouse, afraid of the schoolmaster, afraid of the children. Once Chibi is inside the school, he and his desk are pictured as being far removed from all the other children. The artist's use of space helps to emphasize Chibi's isolation and intensifies the representation of his feelings of loneliness. In subsequent pictures Chibi is always alone, while the other children come to school in twos and threes. With the arrival of the friendly schoolmaster and his discovery of Chibi's ability to imitate crows, we see Chibi grow in stature and courage.

In illustrating Paul Hein's version of the Grimm brothers' *Snow White,* Trina Schart Hyman shows the

gradual deterioration of the stepmother until, in the last picture, she has the stare of a mad woman as she stands in front of a mirror framed with skulls and jeering faces. Nancy Burkert, on the other hand, in her interpretation of *Snow White* by the Grimm brothers,

Patricia Polacco captures the expression of amazement and concern on the faces of the two young Amish girls when they see their peacock spread his tail feathers for the first time.
From *Just Plain Fancy* by Patricia Polacco. Copyright © 1990 by Patricia Polacco. Used by permission of Bantam Books, a division of Bantam Doubleday Dell Publishing Group, Inc.

That night, Officer Buckle watched himself on the 10 o'clock news.

Peggy Rathmann portrays a wealth of emotions with a few tiny lines in *Officer Buckle and Gloria.*
From *Officer Buckle and Gloria* by Peggy Rathmann. Copyright © 1995 by The Putnam & Grosset Group, New York, NY. Reprinted by permission.

Sometime in the early morning hours, the train comes to rest. All is quiet. Suddenly, the door of the compartment slides open. The conductor leans in, announces that something is blocking the tracks, and disappears. A few minutes later, an old woman enters the compartment and sits down opposite the boy. She says nothing.

Every morning at seven o'clock they leave for their offices in the city.

The worst thing about Holstein cows is that if they ever get out of the field, they're almost impossible to find.

A double-page spread of David Macaulay's award-winning book *Black and White* shows four different stories done in four different media; or are there connections in this intriguing book?
Illustration from *Black and White*. Copyright © 1990 by David Macaulay. Reprinted by permission of Houghton Mifflin Company. All rights reserved.

never shows the evil queen's face, only her back. But on the queen's workbench is every conceivable symbol of evil and death, including deadly nightshade, the thirteenth tarot card, a skull, spiders, bats, mushrooms, and an open book of formulas for poisonous concoctions. These symbols of evil are as eloquent as the mad queen's face. Each illustrator manages to bring a very personal interpretation to this old tale.

Another requirement of an excellent picture book is that the art be accurate and consistent with the text. If the story states, as in Ludwig Bemelmans's *Madeline*, "In an old house in Paris that was covered with vines lived twelve little girls in two straight lines," children are going to look for the vines, they are going to count the little girls, and they are going to check to see that the lines are straight. Bemelmans was painstakingly careful to include just eleven little girls in his picture after Madeline goes to the hospital. Six-year-olds are quick to point out his one failure in a small picture that shows twelve girls breaking their bread, even though Madeline was still hospitalized. Accuracy is a requirement of both picture storybooks and informational picture books.

The Artist's Choice of Media

Children accept and enjoy a variety of media in the illustrations of their picture books. Many artists today are using the picture book as a vehicle for experimentation with new and interesting formats and media. (See also "Exploring Literature Through Art and Media" in Chapter 13.) For example, David Macaulay's award-winning *Black and White* is really four stories, elements of which enter each story. Each story uses different media, including transparent watercolors, torn paper, opaque paint, and pen and sepia ink. This highly inventive book is like a game or puzzle. *Black and White* appeals to older children capable of interpreting four stories at the same time.

Illustrators are also experimenting with interesting materials that would have been difficult to reproduce prior to modern printing technology. Molly Bang has used a variety of materials to construct the pictures for *One Fall Day*. In this picture storybook, a mother's recounting of her young child's busy day is given depth by Bang's meticulously constructed characters and settings.

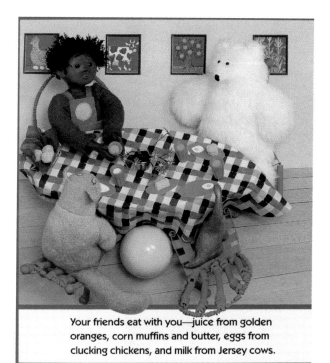

Your friends eat with you—juice from golden oranges, corn muffins and butter, eggs from clucking chickens, and milk from Jersey cows.

Molly Bang experiments with constructions that recreate the intensely imaginative world of the child in *One Fall Day*.
Illustration by Molly Bang from her *One Fall Day*. Copyright © 1994 by Molly Garrett Bang. By permission of Greenwillow Books, a division of William Morrow & Company, Inc.

A doll plays the part of the main character. A plush toy cat, a furry polar bear, a clay dinosaur, a tiny white paper crane, a yellow ball, and a handmade car are her companions as she plays inside and outside the house. The illustrations reflect the intensely imaginative world of the young child, yet the reader *believes* in this created world, just as this child believes that her toys are alive. In addition to her highly inventive use of materials, Bang has added visual references to her other books that will please those children who love to find little details in books. In this kind of creative experimentation that is taking place in picture storybooks today, what medium the artist uses is not nearly as important as the appropriateness of the choice for a particular book and how effectively the artist uses it. Nevertheless, teachers and children are fascinated with the hows of illustrating and always ask what medium is used. This is becoming increasingly difficult to answer, as artists these days use a combination of media and printing techniques to achieve a particular effect. Some publishing houses provide information on the art techniques of some of their outstanding books. This might be found in a foreword, on the copyright page, or on a jacket flap. It is a service that teachers and librarians hope more companies will provide.

The following section gives a brief overview of some of the media choices open to the artist.

Woodcuts and Similar Techniques

In the beginning of the history of printing, the woodcut or wood engraving was the only means of reproducing art. It is still used effectively today. In the making of a woodcut, the nonprinting areas are cut away, leaving a raised surface that, when inked and pressed on paper, duplicates the original design. If color is to be used, the artist must prepare as many woodcuts as colors, or the printed picture can be painted by hand. Woodcut illustrations produce a bold simplicity and have a power not found in any other medium.

David Frampton uses this traditional medium in a fresh way to illustrate Jim Aylesworth's retelling of the traditional rhyme "Diddle Diddle Dumpling" in *My Son John*. The text for each of these fourteen new verses is cut into a wood block and is accompanied by pictures of fourteen lively children, each with a rhyming verse for her or his name. In *Once a Mouse*, a fable of India, Marcia Brown takes full advantage of her medium, allowing the texture or grain of the wood to show through. This adds depth and interesting patterns to these dramatic illustrations.

Wood engravings are cut on the end grain of very hard wood (usually boxwood) rather than with the grain on the plank side of a soft wood. This process of wood engraving gives a delicate, finer line to the illustrations than a woodcut has. Barry Moser has used this technique to illustrate Patricia MacLachlan's *What You Know First*, an evocative memoir that examines the importance of one's roots.

Etching is another type of engraving technique. A design is drawn with a tool on a waxed metal plate, then the plate is dipped in acid, which eats thin lines into the metal. The wax is removed, and prints are then made from the inked plate. Arthur Geisert makes use of this medium for several of his books. His puzzle alphabet book *Pigs from A to Z* is illustrated with detailed etchings of seven little pigs constructing a tree house. Each picture shows five hidden forms of the letter and the seven pigs, and part of the fun of the book is to find them. The fine lines of these intricate etchings make superb hiding places for the letters. Geisert uses the same technique in his comic picture books for younger children simply titled *Oink* and *Oink Oink*.

Linoleum block prints also give a finer line than woodcuts. Mary Wormell uses this technique to create a lively charm to her stories of a sweet, rather egocentric hen in *Hilda Hen's Search* and *Hilda Hen's Happy Birthday*. Ashley Wolff's glowing linoleum block prints illustrate *A Year of Birds* and *A Year of Beasts*. The crisp

Michael McCurdy's scratchboard illustrations evoke a lovely sense of the past in *Lucy's Summer* by Donald Hall.
Illustration from *Lucy's Summer* by Donald Hall, illustrations copyright © 1995 by Michael McCurdy, reproduced by permission of Harcourt Brace & Company.

black lines of the linoleum cuts seem to make the animals, birds, and people stand out in relief against brilliant skies and seasonal landscapes.

Scratchboard illustrations can be confused with wood engravings, because their appearance is similar. However, the process of making them is very different. In the making of scratchboard illustrations, a very black ink is usually painted on the smooth white surface of a drawing board or scratchboard. When the ink is thoroughly dry, the picture is made by scratching through the black-inked surface with a sharp instrument. Color can be added with a transparent overlay, painted on the white scratchboard prior to applying the black ink or applied after the drawing is complete. Scratchboard techniques produce crisply textured illustrations. Michael McCurdy, who has been a wood engraver for many years, uses a similar painstaking technique for the scratchboard drawings in two books by Donald Hall, *Lucy's Christmas* and *Lucy's Summer*. These stories have personal connections to Hall's mother's childhood in New Hampshire, and the fine linear work that McCurdy achieves on scratchboard resembles old wood engravings and evokes a lovely sense of the past as well as the hardy nature of family connections. Brian Pinkney creates stunning effects with scratchboard in books like *Max Found Two Sticks* and Robert D. San Souci's *Sukie and the Mermaid*. By adding color in inventive ways, he

creates interesting textures that give his illustrations drama and excitement. Barbara Cooney has achieved an equally dramatic effect with this technique combined with brilliant color overlays for her award-winning book *Chanticleer and the Fox*.

Collage and Construction

The use of collage for illustrating children's books has become very popular. The effect of this medium is simple and childlike, not unlike pictures children might make themselves. The word *collage*, derived from the French verb *collar*, meaning "to paste," refers to the kind of picture that is made by cutting out a variety of different kinds of materials—newspaper clippings, patterned wallpaper, fabric, and the like—and assembling them into a unified, harmonious illustration. Ezra Jack Keats proved himself a master of this technique with his award-winning *The Snowy Day*. Using patterned and textured papers and pen and ink, Keats captured young Peter's delight in a snowy day.

Leo Lionni is known for his highly original use of collage in his many books. Circles of torn paper convey a satisfying story of families in *Little Blue and Little Yellow*. Lionni also uses his familiar collage techniques and brilliant colors to tell a fable of art, love, and the role of the imagination in seeing beauty in all things in

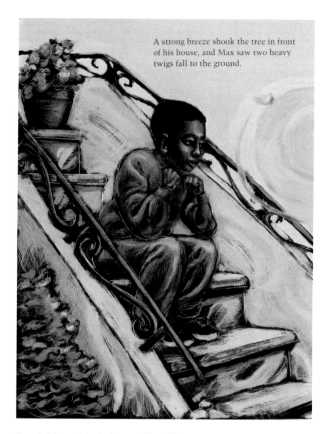

A strong breeze shook the tree in front of his house, and Max saw two heavy twigs fall to the ground.

Scratchboard techniques allow illustrator Brian Pinkney to explore a range of textures and colors in books like *Max Found Two Sticks*.
Reprinted with permission of Simon & Schuster Books for Young Readers from *Max Found Two Sticks* by Brian Pickney. Copyright © 1994 Brian Pickney.

Patricia Mullins creates sumptuous collage illustrations in *V for Vanishing: An Alphabet of Endangered Animals* and other books.
Copyright © 1994 by Patricia Mullins. Used by permission of HarperCollins Publishers, New York, NY.

Matthew's Dream. In *An Extraordinary Egg* three frogs find what they believe to be a chicken egg. When the egg hatches into an alligator, they continue to believe it is a chicken, despite evidence to the contrary. In this book Lionni uses collage with oil pastels, a mixture that adds texture to the pictures but allows the white of the paper to show through, giving a much lighter tone to this funny story.

Eric Carle first paints many sheets of paper with various colors to achieve texture. Then he cuts them out and pastes them together to create interesting characters, as in *The Very Hungry Caterpillar*. Australian artist Patricia Mullins uses brilliant tissue-paper collages to create the animals in Gail Jorgensen's foot-stomping *Crocodile Beat* and Mem Fox's whimsical tale *Hattie and the Fox*.

Marcia Brown made sophisticated use of collage in her stunning interpretation of *Shadow* by the French poet Blaise Cendrars. Rich backgrounds of textured painted shapes have been cut out to form purple and orange mountains; the people and their shadows are done in black and tissue-paper silhouettes. Some woodcuts printed in white represent the eerie spirits in this tale of

Africa where shadows are both respected and feared. Ann Grifalconi, who is perhaps best known for her vibrant pastel illustrations, has made innovative use of collage in another tale set in Africa, *The Lion's Whiskers* by Nancy Raines Day. For this folktale about a stepmother who risks her life to win her stepson's love, Grifalconi combines cutout photographs, handmade papers, and natural materials to visually represent the complicated family relationships dealt with in the story. Other artists who make skillful use of collage include Elizabeth Cleaver, Lois Ehlert, Bettina Paterson, and Susan Roth.

Modern reproduction techniques have freed illustrators to go beyond collage, which is relatively flat, and work in three dimensions. Jeannie Baker makes what she calls "collage constructions" or "assemblage" to illustrate her fine books. Made from a multitude of materials, including modeling clay, papers, textured materials, preserved grass, leaves, feathers, hair, and paints, her pictures stand out in relief. In *Where the Forest Meets the Sea*, a story of a visit to a tropical rain forest in North Queensland, Australia, a young boy imagines who else might have played there before him, including the dinosaurs and later the aboriginal children. Baker also uses this technique effectively for her environmental statements in *The Story of Rosy Dock* and *Window*, a wordless book.

Children will be intrigued by Barbara Reid's plasticine, or modeling clay, art for her books. In *Effie*, by Beverly Allinson, an ant with a loud voice frightens the other insects away, but she is instrumental in preventing

Victoria Raymond uses modeling compounds to create pictures that seem to jump off the page in Ellen Jackson's *Brown Cow, Green Grass, Yellow Mellow Sun.*
From *Brown Cow, Green Grass, Yellow Mellow Sun* by Ellen Jackson. Reprinted by permission of Hyperion Books for Children.

David Wisniewski's intricate cut-paper illustrations add excitement to books like *The Wave of the Sea-Wolf.*
Illustration from *The Wave of the Sea-Wolf.* Copyright © 1994 by David Wisniewski. Reprinted by permission of Clarion Books/Houghton Mifflin Company. All rights reserved.

an elephant from stepping on all of them. Reid's *Two by Two* introduces more animals, those who sailed with Noah on the Ark. The detail Reid can achieve with this modeling clay material is quite amazing. Victoria Raymond used a similar modeling compound for Ellen Jackson's *Brown Cow, Green Grass, Yellow Mellow Sun.* The objects in this simple story about making butter for a pancake breakfast seem to jump off the page of the book, and by the end children will all be drooling for their own stack of pancakes.

Other artists are working in innovative ways with paper. Molly Bang, who used found-object constructions to illustrate Sylvia Cassedy's collection of haiku *Red Dragonfly on My Shoulder* and her own original story *One Fall Day*, used folded-paper sculpture, cutout figures, and furniture for her modern folktale *The Paper Crane.* This medium seems the perfect choice to illustrate the story of the folded-paper bird who comes to life and restores the restaurant bypassed by a freeway. True to so many Chinese fairy tales, the owner of the restaurant receives his good reward as payment for his kindness to a gentle stranger.

Another master with the art of cut-paper sculpture is David Wisniewski. *The Wave of the Sea-Wolf* is one of his many stories illustrated with intricately cut paper. Placed in layers that provide a feeling of depth to the pictures and add excitement and tension, the meticulously cut shapes tell an original story of a young Tlingit princess who saves her people from natural and human threats. *Sundiata: Lion King of Mali*, the true story of an African king's rise to power, is given dramatic life through Wisniewski's detailed art.

Other artists have used the traditional Asian technique of paper cutting to create their illustrations. Ed Young's illustrations for Jane Yolen's *The Emperor and the Kite* imply a subtle relationship to the paper kite that is at the center of the story. The lacy linear design that results also gives a feeling of airy lightness that suits the book's ending. Aki Sogabe illustrated *Cinnamon, Mint, and Mothballs* by Ruth Tiller and *The Loyal Cat* by Lensey Namioka using single sheets of black paper that she cut freehand and then placed over hand-painted rice papers. The result is a jewel-like quality well suited to both these stories.

Denise Fleming works with cotton rag fibers colored with pigments to create handmade papers for the illustrations in such books as *Where Once There Was a Wood* and *Barnyard Banter*. Debra Frasier has experimented with paste paper cutouts in William Stafford's *The Animal That Drank Up Sound* and with collages made from tie-dyed papers for Kim Stafford's *We Got Here Together*. In all these books the abstracted shapes and the textures that result from these artistic processes match the poetic texts of the printed words.

Paints and Pen and Ink

The vast majority of illustrations for children's books are done in paint, pen and ink, or combinations of these media. The creation of materials like plastic paints, or acrylics, and new techniques frequently make it very difficult to determine the medium used.

Generally, paint can be divided into two kinds: paint that is translucent and has a somewhat transparent quality, such as watercolor, and paint that is opaque and impenetrable to light, such as tempera, gouache, and oils.

The transparency of watercolor can be seen in books like Uri Shulevitz's *Rain Rain Rivers* and Norma Simon's *Wet World*, illustrated by Alexi Natchev. For both books, watercolor is the perfect choice of medium, for it allows the artists to convey the feeling of clouds bleeding into rainy skies and light reflected in watery puddles. Allen Say makes fine use of transparent watercolor in his many books. In *Grandfather's Journey*, the effect of the medium conveys a sense of quiet dignity to his grandfather's memory. David Small's soft watercolor washes seem just right for the gently humorous stories of such quirky characters as Elizabeth Brown in *The Librarian* by Sarah Stewart and Imogene in Small's *Imogene's Antlers*.

We might think of old-fashioned, delicate pictures when we think of watercolor, but watercolors are not necessarily like that. Edward Ardizzone, England's master of watercolor and pen-and-ink sketches, has produced full-color watercolor seascapes that have tremendous vitality and movement for his *Little Tim and the Brave Sea Captain*. The storm scenes in McCloskey's *Time of Wonder* have this same power, contrasted with the soft, diffused light of the fog scene.

Ted Rand's dark, ominous watercolors for *The Ghost-Eye Tree*, by Bill Martin, Jr., and John Archambault, create just the right spooky mood for this tale of two children's journey down a lonely road on a dark windy night. We can almost hear the huge black tree creak and groan as it bends in the wind. Bathed in eerie moonlight, the children's faces reflect their fear of the ghost-eye tree. Ted Lewin's vivid watercolor washes in

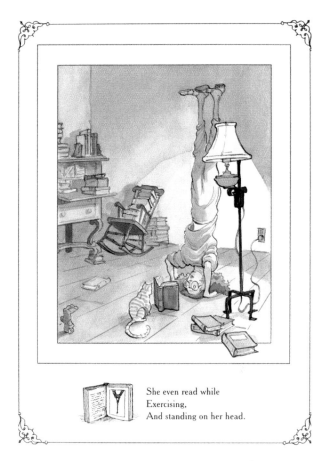

She even read while
Exercising,
And standing on her head.

The softened hues in David Small's watercolors for Sarah Stewart's *The Librarian* lend his pictures a sense of lighthearted charm.
Illustration by David Small from *The Library* by Sarah Stewart. Copyright © 1995 by David Small. Reprinted by permisison of Farrar, Straus & Giroux.

Florence Parry Heide and Judith Heide Gilliland's *Sami and the Time of the Troubles* add an emotional punch to this story about a young boy trying to grow up normally in war-torn Lebanon.

Watercolors can be warm and cozy, too, as we see in Vera Williams's *A Chair for My Mother*. In this story of a family's struggle to recover from a household fire, we celebrate the day they have saved enough money to buy a big fat comfortable chair for the little girl's mother. Watercolors create the symbolic borders of these pictures and the velvet texture of the chairs in the furniture store.

Opaque paints can give an intense brilliant look, like Leonard Weisgard achieved in Golden MacDonald's *The Little Island*, or they can produce the rather somber colors of Leo Politi's *Song of the Swallows*. Maurice Sendak contrasted dark green and blue tempera with shades of purple to create Max's weird fantasy world in

In books like *Coming Home: From the Life of Langston Hughes,* Floyd Cooper builds up many layers of transparent oil washes to give figures and landscapes a warm glow.

From *Coming Home: From the Life of Langston Hughes,* by Floyd Cooper. Copyright © 1994 by The Putnam & Grosset Group, New York, NY. Reprinted by permission.

Where the Wild Things Are. Texture and shading are achieved with pen-and-ink crosshatch strokes. The characters in Sendak's *In the Night Kitchen* are painted in bold flat colors that resemble a comic book world; details are reserved for the intricate labels and pictures on the cartons, bottles, and jars that make up the city of the night kitchen.

Gouache (pronounced "gwash") paint is watercolor with the addition of chalk and has an effect similar to tempera. Marisabina Russo uses gouache to produce vivid paintings for books like *I Don't Want to Go Back to School* and *Time to Wake Up!* Russo's subject matter is the everyday world of the younger child, and the choice of medium allows a style that is childlike and suits the subject matter perfectly. The use of gouache is also characteristic of the many books illustrated by Alice and Martin Provensen, including their well-known *A Visit to William Blake's Inn* by Nancy Willard (see Chapter 8) and the Caldecott Medal winner *The Glorious Flight: Across the Channel with Louis Blériot*.

Acrylics (plastic paints) produce vibrant, almost glowing colors. When mixed with water, acrylics resemble transparent watercolors. More often acrylics are used straight from the tube. Like oils, they can be built up on the painting surface to give a dense texture; however,

they dry faster than oils. Barbara Cooney used acrylic paints to create the pictures for her well-loved *Miss Rumphius*. After her many travels throughout the world, Miss Rumphius settles down in her little gray house in Maine beside a shimmering ocean. Crisp clear colors beautifully capture the Maine landscape, with its purple and blue blooming lupines.

Increasingly, we are seeing picture books illustrated with full-color oil paints. Trina Schart Hyman, who for many years worked in acrylics, used oils to illustrate Eric Kimmel's version of the Grimm brothers' *Iron John*. Here the use of oils allowed her to create a feeling of depth in both her landscapes and her figures. Floyd Cooper uses oil paint on canvas board and works back into the paint with a soft malleable eraser before the paint dries. This technique gives his paintings layers of subtle color tones that seem to glow with a rich sheen and that add depth and drama to his scenes. This medium is particularly suited to the warm human stories Cooper illustrates, such as *Coming Home: From the Life of Langston Hughes* and Sandra Belton's *From Miss Ida's Front Porch*.

Thomas Locker, a well-known landscape artist, illustrates his picture books with majestic full-color oil paintings. Locker's rendering of light in such books as *Where the River Begins, The Mare on the Hill, Family*

Farm, and *Sky Tree* reminds us of the early landscape painters of the Hudson River School. Two other stories illustrated by Locker, *The Young Artist* and William H. Hooks's *The Boy Who Held Back the Sea*, reflect the influence of the early Dutch masters.

Crayon, Chalk, Charcoal, and Pencil

Crayon and soft-pencil illustrations are frequently employed for children's books. The subtle texture of crayon is easily discernible. In *Fish Is Fish*, Leo Lionni creates an underwater world with crayons, but he portrays the fish's conception of the frog's world with the brilliant colors of acrylics. The difference in color and media helps to separate the imagined world from the real one.

Pastels and charcoal are most appropriate media for Thomas Allen's rich illustrations for books that have strong connections to people and places. Told from a young girl's point of view, *In Coal Country* and *Up the Tracks to Grandma's* by Judith Hendershot are evocative accounts of growing up in a small Ohio coal-mining town of the 1930s. *Climbing Kansas Mountains* by George Shannon tells of a long-ago summer on a Kansas farm where the only mountains to climb were the grain elevators. The colored pastels are built up from the surface of the page, and the rich textures mingle with the tinted charcoal papers like the love that surrounds these families. Ed Young also uses pastel effectively in books like *Little Plum* and Rafe Martin's *Foolish Rabbit's Big Mistake*. Here he makes full use of brilliant color applied thickly to add intensity and life to the stories. In stories that convey a quieter mood, Young chooses softer tones and applies the colors more delicately. He often keeps his edges rough and lets the texture of the paper show through. This gives his illustrations something of a dreamlike quality and is very effective for stories like *While I Sleep* by Mary Calhoun.

Stephen Gammell's soft-pencil drawings create a mystical mood for the legend *Where the Buffaloes Begin* by Olaf Baker. The large full-page and double-page pictures capture the wide sweep of the prairie and the immensity of the buffalo. Yet the impressionistic, indefinite shapes suggest the legendary nature of a story in which the buffalo arise from a misty lake and stampede an enemy tribe, thereby saving Little Wolf's people. Wendy Anderson Halperin's pencil drawings overlayed with soft watercolor washes in Tres Seymour's *Hunting the White Cow* and Anne Shelby's *Homeplace* convey the lovely pastoral settings that frame these two folksy stories.

Using a conté pencil, a rather hard drawing pencil, Chris Van Allsburg creates a surrealistic world for the playing of the game in *Jumanji*. Sand-papering the conté

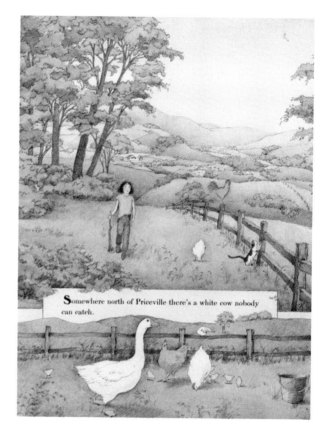

Wendy Anderson Halperin uses colored pencils to capture the soft light of a sleepy countryside in Tres Seymour's *Hunting the White Cow*.
From *Hunting the White Cow* by Tres Seymour, illustrated by Wendy Anderson Halperin. Illustrations copyright © 1993 by Wendy Anderson Halperin. Reprinted by permission fo the Publisher, Orchard Books, New York.

pencil and applying the dust with cotton balls, he gives the pictures a spooky, dreamlike feeling. Van Allsburg is adept in the use of a variety of drawing materials; he used carbon pencil for his first book, *The Garden of Abdul Gasazi*, full-color pastels for *The Wreck of the Zephyr*, and oil pastels for *The Polar Express*.

Increasingly artists are using combinations of many media. John Burningham creates the visual jokes in his book *Come Away from the Water, Shirley* by using crayons to depict Shirley's father and mother as they sit in their beach chairs giving frequent admonitions to Shirley. On the opposite page he employs rich paints, collage, and crayon to develop the wonderful pirate adventure story that Shirley creates in her imagination. The use of different media and color tones helps to create the humor of this juxtaposition of parents' and child's thinking. In *Time to Get Out of the Bath, Shirley*, Burningham uses the same technique for Shirley's exciting adventures down the bath drain.

Elements of Design

Crucial to the visual meaning in a picture storybook are the choices artists make about certain elements of design, particularly the use of line, shape, color, and space, as they decide what to illustrate in the story and how best to do it.

Line and Shape

Line is so inherently a part of every illustration that we forget that this element, too, can convey meaning. A horizontal line suggests repose and peace, a vertical line gives stability, and a diagonal line suggests action and movement. Uri Shulevitz has used diagonal rain lines superbly in the pictures and even endpapers of his book *Rain Rain Rivers*. Even the size of a line can convey meaning. In *Stevie*, John Steptoe uses a heavy black outline for his figures to emphasize Robert's resentment of Stevie, the little boy his mother takes care of during the day. The tiny, sketchy lines in Marcia Brown's version of Perrault's *Cinderella* suggest the somewhat fussy elegance of the story's setting at the sixteenth-century French court.

A line that encloses space creates shape, and this element is equally evocative of meaning. Richard McGuire chooses line and shape to create the flowing movement in two picture books, *Night Becomes Day* and *What Goes Around Comes Around*. In both these books the reliance on line and shape rather than on realistic depiction of objects creates pictorial designs that subtly evoke themes of change.

Shapes with sharp edges and corners can evoke tension and movement, as they do in Janina Domanska's version of the Grimm brothers' *Bremen Town Musicians*. On the other hand, when shapes have nongeometric curving forms found in nature, they can breathe a sense of life into illustrations. Peter Parnall's many horizontal lines convey movement and create rounded womblike shapes for Byrd Baylor's *Your Own Best Secret Place* and *The Way to Start a Day*. These reaffirm Baylor's reverence for the natural world and suggest peace and a tapping of inner strength.

Use of Color

Many classic picture storybooks did not use color in the illustrations—the sepia pictures of Robert McCloskey's *Make Way for Ducklings*, the black-and-white humorous illustrations by Robert Lawson for *The Story of Ferdinand* by Munro Leaf, and the well-loved black-and-white illustrations for *Millions of Cats* by Wanda Gág.

Illustrators today are successfully using black-and-white graphics to create exciting picture books. The unique story *Round Trip* by Ann Jonas describes a trip to the city past farms, silos, and steel highway wires, to

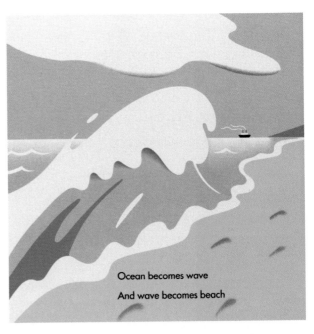

The clean-edged shapes in Richard McGuire's *Night Becomes Day* echo the simple text and create a feeling of movement throughout the book.
From *Night Becomes Day* by Richard McGuire. Copyright © 1994 by Richard McGuire. Used by permission of Viking Penguin, a division of Penguin USA Inc.

ride on the subway; turn the book around and the reader returns in the dark. The farm and silos become factories, the highway poles support the freeway, and the subway becomes a parking garage. Black and white are the appropriate colors for this triumph of design. David Weisner uses black and white to spooky effect for Eve Bunting's *Night of the Gargoyles*, a story of stone sculptures that come alive to roam the city after the sun goes down. Chris Van Allsburg's black-and-white illustrations help to create an eerie otherworldly cast in *The Garden of Abdul Gasazi*, *Jumanji*, and *The Mysteries of Harris Burdick*.

The choice of colors depends on the theme of the book. Certainly, the choice of blue for both pictures and text in *Blueberries for Sal* by McCloskey was appropriate. Tawny yellow and black were the natural choices for Don Freeman's wonderfully funny *Dandelion*, the story of Dandelion the lion who suddenly decided to live up to the double meaning of his name. Quiet or nostalgic stories, such as Cynthia Rylant's *When I Was Young in the Mountains*, demand soft tones that suggest the haze of memory. Diane Goode's gentle pictures for this story celebrate the love of an extended family and the beauty of a remote Appalachian mountain region. By way of contrast, Rodney A. Greenblat uses brilliant electric colors for his zany story *Uncle Wizzmo's New Used Car*. Weird cars that look like turtles, rabbits, and a bowl of fruit are on the showroom floor. Uncle Wizzmo finally chooses a brilliant blue one, and off he zooms with his delighted niece and nephew. Choice of color, then, can set the mood of the story.

Certain artists have made effective use of color to show a change in mood for the story. In *Dawn* by Uri Shulevitz, a grandfather takes his grandson camping by a lake. Early in the morning while it is still dark, they rise and row out to the center of the lake, where they can see the beauty of the sunrise. Gradually, almost in slow-motion cinematic fashion, the pictures move from deep blues to subdued gray-greens and finally to the blazing full color of the sunrise. Different perspectives show the boy and the old man moving farther and farther out on the lake, until they almost appear to be swallowed up by the brilliance of the sun on the final page. Interest is created by changing the shapes of the pictures. One child, when asked why the artist chose to shape some of the pictures the way he did, noted that many were ovals, "like egg shapes because eggs are beginnings and this story is about a day's beginning."

Allen Say uses color most effectively in his picture-book biography of the very first Chinese matador. Titled *El Chino*, it is the account of a Chinese American who longs to be a great athlete. He is an ace basketball player in high school but too short to compete in college. Following his graduation as an engineer, he goes on a vacation in Spain and falls in love with bullfighting. For the first half of the book, the pictures are in brownish-gray tones reminiscent of old photographs. However, after Billy Wong finds his true vocation, the pictures change to full color, symbolizing his joy at finding his life's work. To signify danger, Marcia Brown has added red to her pictures for *Once a Mouse*. Starting with cool forest green, mustard yellow, and a trace of red, the red builds up in increasing amounts until the climax is reached and the tiger is changed back to a mouse. Only cool green and yellow are seen in the last picture as the hermit is once again "thinking about big—and little."

It is this rich use of many layers of color to create meaning that helps to distinguish the really fine picture storybooks. The splashy use of color for color's sake, so frequently seen in the grocery store or mass-produced books, does little to develop children's artistic eye. It is the appropriate use of color that is significant.

Space

The creative use of space can produce a feeling of isolation, as we have seen in Taro Yashima's *Crow Boy*, or the blurred line between reality and legend, as in the illustrations by Stephen Gammell for *Where the Buffaloes Begin* by Olaf Baker. Shirley Hughes uses the gutter between pages to represent the door into the house in *Alfie Gets in First*. In John Burningham's *Granpa*, when the little girl becomes angry at her grandfather, the

artist places the two characters on either edge of a large double-page spread with their backs to each other. Plain white in the middle emphasizes the distance between them. Lisbeth Zwerger uses pen and ink and soft watercolor wash to reduce her backgrounds to almost nothing, making the realistic wistful figures in the Grimm brothers' fairy tales stand out. In *The Seven Ravens*, she pictures the little girl who goes in search of her brothers as sitting on a little chair looking as if she were alone on the edge of the world.

Molly Bang makes use of negative space in her surrealistic wordless book *The Grey Lady and the Strawberry Snatcher*. The gray lady appears to fade into the background of trees as she runs away from the strawberry snatcher. Part of the fun of David Macaulay's experimental book *Black and White* is his use of negative space to hide an escaping convict in a herd of Holstein cows.

The decision to use borders also involves the artist's use of space. The borders in Vera Williams's *A Chair for My Mother* or Trina Hyman's interpretation of *Little Red Riding Hood* provide a kind of coziness to these stories and help to create a unified whole to each double-page spread.

In inexpensive mass-marketed books, which frequently must conform to one size for all, artists cannot afford the creative use of space. In a well-designed picture storybook, however, the illustrators can use space to enhance the meaning of the story.

Point of View or Perspective

Just as an author decides what would be the best point of view from which to tell a story, so too does an artist think about perspective. One way to obtain action in what might otherwise be a static series of pictures is to change the focus, just as a movie camera changes perspective or shows close-ups and then moves back to pan the whole scene. In *The Napping House* by Audrey Wood, for example, the scene is almost always in the bedroom, where the granny, the dog, the cat, the mouse, and the flea are seen in various postures as they sleep during the quiet rain. Don Wood shows us a fish-eye view of the scene, with the bed growing increasingly concave until its final collapse. As the story progresses, Wood moves the point of view slowly upward until he is directly above the sleeping figures for the climax, when the flea bites the cat and wakes them all up and the bed falls down.

Part of the perfection of the poetic Caldecott Medal book *Owl Moon* by Jane Yolen is the way John Schoenherr uses shifting perspectives to provide the action. It is the quiet story of a child and her father who go out late one snowy night to look for owls. Starting with an owl's view of the farm bathed in moonlight, the artist shifts his focus, showing the pair trudging through the snow from the side, from the front, and finally looking up in

John Schoenherr uses shifting perspectives to provide action in Jane Yolen's quiet story *Owl Moon*.

From *Owl Moon* by Jane Yolen, illustrated by John Schoenherr. Copyright © 1987 by The Putnam & Grosset Group, New York, NY. Reprinted by permission.

awe at the huge owl landing on the tree. This picture of the owl is the only close-up in the story, a fact that underlines the climax of the story and intensifies the excitement of finally seeing the owl.

The perspective in Chris Van Allsburg's surrealistic pictures for *Jumanji* changes from a worm's-eye point of view to a bird's-eye view, adding to the constant shifts between reality and fantasy in that story. Seen from the floor level of an ordinary living room, two charging rhinoceroses look much more frightening than in the zoo! Again in *The Polar Express*, Van Allsburg shows dramatic shifts in perspective from the aerial views from Santa's sleigh to the floor-level view of the children opening their presents.

Not all artists work with changing perspectives, but when they do, it is interesting to ask why and look to see how this adds to the meaning of the story.

The Matter of Style

Style is an elusive quality of an artist's work based on the arrangement of line, color, and mass into a visual image. An illustrator's style will be influenced by her or his own skill as an artist and the vision of the story that is being interpreted. The primary decision for the artist to make is how to create visual images that will harmonize with and enhance the meaning of the text. The illustrator also needs to consider how the art might extend or add a new dimension to the message of the story.

Style can also refer to the particular artistic properties associated with eras, like Renaissance art or Impressionism, or with cultures, such as the culture of the

people of Tibet or of Northern Plains Indian tribes. Pictorial styles can be distinguished by certain constant elements or "umbrella conventions," which are widely accepted ways of depicting.[4] Illustrators often borrow these conventions to enhance or extend their visual message. Teachers might want to know these terms and conventions, just as they develop an understanding of literary terms for more careful evaluation of books for children. However, it is more important to teach children to look and really see how an illustrator creates meaning than it is to be glib with terms they might not understand. Also, these terms were developed to describe the art of a single picture, not the cumulative effect of many images seen by turning the pages of a picture book.

Realism, or Representational Art

No designation of an art style can be precise, because of the infinite variation within styles; however, realism is perhaps the easiest to recognize, because it presents a picture of the world as we see it in real life. Of course, the pictures still incorporate the artist's interpretation of the story, the choice of scenes to visualize, point of view, expressions, and so forth. Barry Moser's realistic watercolor illustrations for Cynthia Rylant's *Appalachia: The Voices of Sleeping Birds* have the feeling of arrested motion, almost like Depression-era photographs. The beauty of the countryside contrasts sharply with the harshness of the life, as seen in the exhausted-looking face of the coal miner. Realism also emphasizes the message of family ties and warm affection in Mike Wimmer's glowing paintings for Patricia MacLachlan's *All the Places to Love*. In this story a young boy recalls the places his family introduced him to when he was born and plans in turn to show these special spots to his new baby sister.

Canadian illustrator Ron Lightburn creates detailed drawings that have a wonderful three-dimensional quality. *Eagle Dreams*, written by Sheryl McFarlane, tells of a young farm boy who fights to save a wounded bald eagle and return it to the wild. Lightburn's rectangular pictures actually look like photographs and add believability to this story's important theme. These two also collaborated on *Waiting for Whales*, a lovely story about a grandfather who teaches his young granddaughter the mysteries of the natural world.

Donald Carrick illustrated his wife's real-life stories about children sleeping out in the woods for the first time and climbing mountains, and their beloved dog being run over. His brown and green natural watercolors realistically portray these experiences in *Sleep Out*,

[4]Barbara Z. Kiefer, *The Potential of Picturebooks: From Visual Literacy to Aesthetic Understanding* (Columbus, Ohio: Merrill/Prentice Hall, 1995), pp. 118–120.

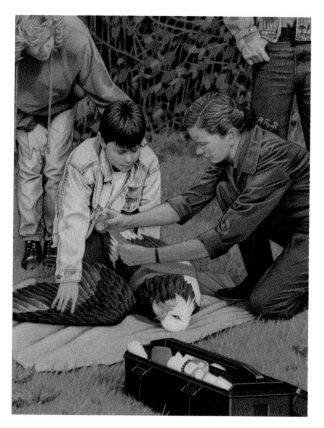

Ron Lightburn's realistic drawings provide an intense immediacy to Sheryl McFarlane's *Eagle Dreams*.
From *Eagle Dreams* by Sheryl McFarlane, illustrated by Ron Lightburn. Copyright © 1995 by The Putnam & Grosset Group, New York, NY. Reprinted by permission.

Raúl Colón's impressionistic paintings in Libba Moore Gray's *My Mama Had a Dancing Heart* recall the figures of Edgar Degas.
From *My Mama Had a Dancing Heart* by Libba Moore Gray, illlustrated by Raúl Colón. Jacket illustration copyright © 1995 by Raúl Colón. Reprinted by permission of the Publisher, Orchard Books, New York.

The Climb, The Accident, and other titles. Carol and Donald Carrick's love of nature is reflected in these representational illustrations. Such illustrations have an immediacy about them and help readers to enter more fully into an experience they could actually have. Although Donald Carrick's work is generally representational, his illustrations for their last book, *In the Moonlight, Waiting,* seem almost impressionistic. This is because the art was photographed from his preliminary sketches for the book that he never had time to finish. The hazy first impressions add charm to the story of a little girl waking in the middle of the night and joining her parents to witness the birth of a lamb. It seems appropriate that at the time of Carrick's death, these illustrations reinforce the theme of birth and new life.

Impressionism

Impressionism is associated with the French artists who worked in and around Paris in the latter part of the nineteenth century, including such well-known painters as Monet, Sisley, and Pissarro. They were concerned with observing nature as it really was and so attempted to capture their first visual impressions before intellect or emotion could define the image further.

A wonderful example of an homage to Impressionism can be found in the Monet-like paintings by Maurice Sendak for *Mr. Rabbit and the Lovely Present,* written by Charlotte Zolotow. In luscious shades of blues and greens, Sendak has created a dreamlike world where a very sophisticated rabbit and a little girl wander about the countryside looking for presents of red, yellow, green, and blue (her mother's favorite colors) for the little girl's mother. The dappled endpapers for this book are examples of impressionistic techniques in themselves.

Lloyd Bloom's oil paintings for the prose poem *Yonder* by Tony Johnston seem most appropriate for this nostalgic story of one family's history. To commemorate the births of his children, one nineteenth-century farmer always plants a plum tree. The plum trees grow and blossom pink with the arrival of more children and even grandchildren. Finally the grandfather who planted the first tree dies and the family remembers him by planting another tree. Bloom's impressionistic paintings capture the family's activities throughout the seasons. For example, one lovely picture shows the mother making a patchwork quilt; the one on the facing page shows the farmer plowing his patchwork fields. Always the plum trees "yonder way over yonder" define the passing seasons. Impressionistic paintings have a way of distancing viewers, placing them outside the action while at the same time their luminous beauty draws them in.

Expressionism

Aspects of expressionistic art include shocking colors, figures slightly out of proportion, and rough, rapid brushwork. The emphasis is on the artist's own inner emotions and on self-expression rather than the reproduction of what he or she sees.

In illustrations for children's books, expressionism may take the form of brilliant blue horses or blue cats, as seen in some of Eric Carle's pictures for very young children. The abstracted shapes and bright but unusual colors of the four animals in Janina Domanska's interpretation of the Grimms' *Bremen Town Musicians* are another fine example of expressionistic paintings. Here the striking colors and unusual abstracted shapes used for both animals and robbers help to create the excitement and

The intense colors and thick textures in Susan Guevara's paintings for Gary Soto's *Chato's Kitchen* convey the culture of East Los Angeles.

From Chato's Kitchen, by Gary Soto, illustrated by Susan Guevara. Copyright © 1995 by The Putnam & Grosset Group, New York, NY. Reprinted by permission.

action of this robust folktale. In *Chato's Kitchen* Gary Soto tells the tale of a low-riding cat from East L.A. who has designs on a family of mice who move in. The mice find an ally in Chorizo, the dog, and Chato and his friend Novio Boy decide to have a fiesta instead of fight. Susan Guevara's paintings add heat to this lively tale and visually convey a wonderful rhythm of the barrio.

David Diaz's illustrations for *Smoky Night* are aptly suited to Eve Bunting's story of a community torn apart by riots. This is a difficult subject to present to children, and Bunting's text is quietly understated. She provides a glimpse of these upheavals through the eyes of a young narrator who is puzzled, then frightened, by events but also concerned about his missing cat. Diaz's paintings, framed in collages of papers, broken glass, shoe leather, and other found objects, provide emotional punch to the story without overwhelming children with concepts that might be beyond them. The faces of the people are done in vivid greens, purples, and blues that heighten the tensions yet avoid racial stereotypes. The thick paint and black lines that frame the figures add movement and texture that also increase the emotional power of the illustrations.

Surrealism

Surrealism is characterized more by subject matter than by technique, for the surrealist combines realistic yet incongruous images in unnatural juxtapositions. To make the viewer believe in this unreal scene, the artwork will be meticulously realistic in detail. Anthony Browne creates a surreal world in his picture storybooks *The Big Baby, Changes,* and *The Piggybook.* In *The Tunnel,* Jack and his sister Rose do not get along. She wants to read fairy tales while he insists on exploring a tunnel. Finally, when he doesn't come back, Rose must go through the frightening tunnel and find him. Once on the other side, she enters a dark forest of trees whose roots and branches form weird, threatening shapes. Finally, in a clearing, she spies the figure of her brother Jack, turned to stone. Fearing she is too late, she throws her arms around him and he is slowly transformed back to his original self. The transformation is also apparent in their friendship. This modern fairy tale becomes very real and frightening in this surrealistic setting.

In explaining his choice of surrealism, Browne is quoted as saying:

🐾 It's a part of not losing that visual openness that kids have . . . surrealism corresponds to a childlike view of the world, in that everything can be made new by putting unrelated objects together.[5]

---

[5]In Douglas Martin's *The Telling Line* (New York: Delacorte Press, 1990), p. 283.

Chris Van Allsburg's surrealistic world in *Jumanji* is certainly well known, since this story won a Caldecott Medal. The fourteen pictures that make up *The Mysteries of Harris Burdick* are beautiful examples of surrealism. Houses on Maple Street lift off, schooners magically appear, and a nun sits in a chair suspended thirty feet above the cathedral floor! Even though the pictures have no connecting narrative, they stimulate children to tell their stories. Van Allsburg is a master of juxtaposition of the real with the unreal.

Naive or Folk Art

One form of naive art is the style often found in self-taught artists like Grandma Moses, Henri Rousseau, and the itinerant painters, or limners, of colonial America.

It can be characterized by a lack of such conventions as perspective and so-called real appearances.

We have seen how Paul Zelinsky used these conventions in Anne Isaacs's *Swamp Angel*. Barbara Cooney also adapted her style to imitate that of the early American limners for *Ox-Cart Man* by Donald Hall. Tomie de Paola uses gouache paints reminiscent of the paintings on wood done by the early itinerant painters for *The Quilt Story* by Tony Johnston and the lively tale of *Tattie's River Journey* by Shirley Murphy. His illustrations for *Mary Had a Little Lamb* by Sarah Josepha Hale and his brightly colored illustrations for *Tomie de Paola's Mother Goose* all echo the early folk art style.

Kathy Jakobsen's folk art paintings for Reeve Lindbergh's narrative poem *Johnny Appleseed* seem most appropriate for celebrating the life of one of America's

Kathy Jakobsen uses a folk art style to express her very personal view of New York City.
From *My New York* by Kathy Jacobsen. Copyright © 1994 by Kathy Jacobsen. By permission of Little, Brown and Company.

legendary heroes. Brightly colored pictures show Johnny's journeys through the seasons; the poetry page is bordered with scenes of apple trees and blossoms tied together with the star quilt pattern in which an apple forms the center. Jakobsen's *My New York* is a feast of visual details that represent a personal view of her years in New York City. Although set in modern times, the story is told in the form of a letter to a friend from a child who has moved from the Midwest to the city. Jakobsen's childlike paintings are appropriate to the theme and invite children everywhere to represent their own home places in art and writing.

Frané Lessac's brilliantly colored paintings represent naive art and capture her love for her native islands in the West Indies in such books as *My Little Island*, *Caribbean Carnival*, and *Caribbean Alphabet*. *Caribbean Canvas* portrays the people, places, sights, and sounds of the islands while illustrating West Indian proverbs and poetry. Lessac also illustrated *The Chalk Doll* by Charlotte Pomerantz, in which a mother tells her daughter stories of her happy childhood growing up in Jamaica. These detailed paintings are childlike and beautiful in their simplicity of style.

Cartoon Style

Many children's books are illustrated in a style that depends on a lively line to create movement and humor. Certainly the gross exaggerations of the zany animals of Dr. Seuss are representative of this style, which is often referred to as cartoon art. From the weird birds in *Scrambled Eggs Super!* to the mess created in *The Cat in the Hat*, Seuss utilized cartoon art to tell his far-fetched stories. Sendak used this style very effectively in some of his early art for *A Hole Is to Dig* and *A Very Special House*, both by Ruth Krauss. The little boy who swings on doors and jumps on beds in *A Very Special House* is the only one painted in color, so the reader knows that all the other goings-on in this very special house are "root in the noodle" of his "head head head."

Steven Kellogg's wonderful drawings are fine examples of the expression and humor that can be achieved with this style of art. *The Rattlebang Picnic* by Margaret Mahy is surely the silliest of summer getaways, and the McTavish family manages to escape from an erupting volcano none too soon. Kellogg's illustrations for Tom Paxton's *Engelbert the Elephant* are as hilarious as the story of this elephant who is invited to the queen's ball. Bursting with action and slapdash humor, Kellogg's illustrations always fill in many details that are never mentioned in the text.

William Steig creates his sophisticated dressed animals in line-and-wash drawings for *Zeke Pippin*, *The*

William Steig's fine style lends a sense of lighthearted farce to *Zeke Pippin,* the story of a musician who puts his audiences to sleep with his music.
Copyright © 1995 by William Steig. Used by permission of HarperCollins Publishers, New York, NY.

Amazing Bone, *Gorky Rises*, and *Doctor DeSoto*. Although Steig uses background in many of his pictures, the flat-looking characters and clever lines remind us of cartoon art. Certainly in *Shrek!* the greenheaded ugliest creature in the swamp comes straight from cartoon art.

James Stevenson, a fellow cartoonist at the *New Yorker*, has also created many books utilizing the cartoon style of art. His tall-tale stories about Grandpa use cartoon balloons for speech and watercolor illustrations. All children enjoy Grandpa's story in *That Terrible Halloween Night* when as a child he went into a haunted house and was so frightened he came out an old man. Cartoon art requires skilled drawing and vivid imagination. It creates and extends much of the humor in children's books.

Several artists have made use of the visual layout and linear qualities of the art found in comic books. The flat painted figures and speech balloons that are typical of this cultural icon can be seen in the pictures for *In the Night Kitchen* by Maurice Sendak and works by British artist Raymond Briggs. Briggs's *Father Christmas* and *Fungus the Bogeyman* are masterpieces of visual irony that have great appeal for older children. *The Bear* is a gentler story about a little girl who is convinced that a huge polar bear has come to live with her. As in his wordless book *The Snowman*, in *The Bear* Briggs gives a unique visual interpretation to a common childhood fantasy.

Cultural Connections

Many artists illustrating folktales or legends make use of the conventions found in art forms of their respective countries or cultures. In *Children of the Yukon* and *A Northern Alphabet*, Ted Harrison uses bright flat colors for his stylized paintings of children's play and activities throughout the year in the lonely settlements of the Yukon. The simple lines of his illustrations suggest the art of the Inuit tribes. Paul Goble's use of Plains Indian designs in his folktales, such as *Star Boy* and *Iktomi and the Buzzard*, recall the hide paintings of these Native Americans. Just as they made use of African motifs and art in Margaret Musgrove's *Ashanti to Zulu*, Leo and Diane Dillon have created vibrant, powerful illustrations for Leontyne Price's retelling of the opera *Aïda*, using borders and motifs from the one-dimensional Egyptian style of art. Deborah Nourse Lattimore always uses the style of art of the culture from which her tales come. For example, her Mayan tale *Why There Is No Arguing in Heaven* is illustrated with many bluish-gray figures that suggest the stone carvings of the ancient Mayas. In *The Sailor Who Captured the Sea*, she recreates the extraordinary art and design of the ancient Irish Book of Kells while telling its story.

Personal Styles

Few picture-book artists use only one style of art; they adapt their work to meet the requirements of a particular story. At the same time, many of them do develop a recognizable personal style that can be identified by their preference for a particular pictorial style of art, use of medium, even choice of content. Thus we have come to associate the use of collage with Leo Lionni, Ezra Jack Keats, and Eric Carle, even though they differ in how they use it. The delicate, old-fashioned style of Tasha Tudor's watercolors is as easily recognizable as the flowing, massive look of Warwick Hutton's watercolors. Tomie de Paola's use of the symbols of folk art, such as hearts, doves, and rabbits, is another recognizable mark of his work. The amusing animals in the stories by Pat Hutchins are frequently stylized with patterned fur and feathers. Her birds and animals in *What Game Shall We Play?* and that self-assured hen in *Rosie's Walk* are obviously vintage Hutchins. Frequently hers are the first illustrations children can identify by the artist's name. And yet Hutchins employs a very different style in *The Very Worst Monster* and *Where's the Baby?* Roy Gerrard always paints little chunky people, as in his riotous spoof on westerns in *Rosie and the Rustlers*, his hero's tale *Mik's Mammoth*, and his journey in Ancient Egypt in *Croco'nile*. Wordplay and visual fun are also characteristic of Gerrard's books.

Several artists are experimenting with both style and media and seem to gather strength with each new book. Paul O. Zelinsky is a talented artist who is able to choose styles that are beautifully suited to the mood and meaning of each of his books. His *The Maid, the Mouse and the Odd Shaped House* is a lighthearted tale, based on an old nursery rhyme, about an old woman and her pet mouse who make themselves at home in a very odd house. Zelinsky's softened tints and stylized figures evoke the decorative arts of the nineteenth century. He also relies primarily on the elements of line and shape to reveal clues to the real nature of the odd house as the story progresses. On the other hand, he uses oil paints and borrows conventions from Renaissance art to retell *Hansel and Gretel* and *Rumpelstiltskin*, two stories by the Grimm brothers. This style beautifully evokes the setting and the origin of these old tales. His illustrations for *Swamp Angel* by Anne Isaacs are more playful, and here his style makes a direct connection to Early American art and folklore.

Maurice Sendak's pictures for *Mr. Rabbit and the Lovely Present* by Charlotte Zolotow, *Where the Wild Things Are*, *In the Night Kitchen*, *Outside Over There*, and *We Are All in the Dumps with Jack and Guy* vary, despite the fact that each has a moonlight setting. The impressionistic Monet-like pictures for Zolotow's *Mr. Rabbit and the Lovely Present* are easily identifiable. The trees and endpapers of *Where the Wild Things Are* have been compared to Henri Rousseau's French primitive paintings. However, Max with his roguish smile and the big ludicrous beasts with their "terrible eyes and terrible teeth" are very much Sendak. While the illustrations for *In the Night Kitchen* reflect the influence that Disney and the comics had on Sendak in his youth, they are very definitely Sendak's own creation. Max has now become Mickey, who sheds the last of his inhibitions in a dream in which he falls out of his clothes and into the night kitchen. Comic book characters have been refined into a work of art that captures the feelings and dream wishes of childhood. The lush watercolors in *Outside Over There* represent another direction in Sendak's work. Here he is reaching the child at a deeper psychological level through symbolic art. His artistic metaphors call forth the same inner feelings that Ida is struggling with as she imagines in a momentary daydream what it would be like to be rid of the responsibility of her baby sister. Even though the art is very different in *Where the Wild Things Are, In the Night Kitchen*, and *Outside Over There*, Sendak refers to these books as a trilogy, all united by the fact that they represent childhood dreams. Each new book of Sendak's seems to represent a deeper involvement with his "child within."

His illustrations for *We Are All in the Dumps with Jack and Guy* and *The Miami Giant* by Arthur Yorinks are superbly drawn and represent the full scope of Sendak's imagination. *We Are All in the Dumps* shows Sendak's unique ability to grasp children's innermost fears and give them visual form. The two unrelated nursery rhymes that are tied together through his illustrations are the basis for commenting on modern society with all its terrible ills. We see homeless people wrapped in newspapers that proclaim stories of greed and calamity. Giant rats play a game of bridge in front of Trump Tower, and Jack and Guy journey past the Auschwitz ovens to rescue a homeless child. There are also suggestions of hope and redemption, however, in the form of visual references to Renaissance religious art and in the final scene where the homeless baby sleeps cradled in Jack's arms. Sendak has never been one to lie to children, and this book is truthful about a world they know but that most adults refuse to acknowledge.

The Miami Giant is Sendak at his funniest, an influence of Yorinks's comic story. These two obviously had a wonderful time with this silly story of Giuseppe Giaweeni, an unheralded Christopher Columbus who set out to sail to China and discovered a tribe of dancing giants in Miami Beach instead. In this book Sendak's colors are more vivid, in keeping with the mood of the story. His strong linear designs and his talent with caricature are in full bloom here.

Style, then, is an elusive quality. It includes signature features like the big hands and feet that Sendak always draws and the small chunky figures in Roy Gerrard's amusing illustrations. Style can be the use of characteristic media, like Eric Carle's collages or Pat Hutchins's patterned animals and birds or Anthony Browne's surrealism. Style is an elusive quality of the artist, which changes and varies over the years and with the particular demands of the work. Today there is more freedom to experiment in illustrating children's picture storybooks. Many of our artists are taking advantage of this new freedom and producing fresh and original art.

Exposure to a variety of art styles through fine picture storybooks can help children develop visual maturity and appreciation. Certainly there is no *one* style that is appropriate for children or preferred by children. The major consideration in evaluating style is how well it conveys and enhances *meaning*. Exploring the work of an illustrator through an intense classroom study can give children time to articulate their responses to an artist's work and to identify some of the many components that can be part of an illustrator's style. The web "Brian Pinkney: A Web of Possibilities" shows how teachers might plan to study the work of Brian Pinkney.

The Format of the Book

A picture storybook is not made up of single illustrated pictures but conveys its message through a *series* of images. The impact of the total format of the book is what creates the art object known as the picture storybook.

Book size and shape are often decisions made jointly by the illustrator and the art director of the publishing house. They might search for a size that will enhance the theme of the story. *The Bear* by Raymond Briggs is almost fifteen inches tall—big enough, it seems, to contain the huge bear within. *The Biggest Boy* by Kevin Henkes is also a large book, and Nancy Tafuri's close-up pictures make the little boy character seem even bigger, in keeping with his lively imagination. *Noisy Nora* by Rosemary Wells is a very small book and certainly in keeping with the way middle sister Nora, a small mouse, felt about being left out. The size of Ellen Raskin's amusing story *Nothing Ever Happens on My Block* reflects the narrow viewpoint of dull Chester, who misses the many exciting events that *are* occurring all around him.

The shape of some books suggests their content. The horizontal shape of Donald Hall's *Ox-Cart Man*, illustrated by Barbara Cooney, is very appropriate for portraying the long trek to the Portsmouth market to sell the family's produce in the early fall and the long walk home through leafless trees in late autumn after the father has sold everything, including the ox and his cart. *Giants in the Land* by Diana Applebaum, illustrated by Michael McCurdy, and *A Tree Is Nice* by Janice Udry, illustrated by Marc Simont, are tall and vertical in shape, much like the trees described in the books. The shape of *Fish Eyes* by Lois Ehlert is long and narrow like that of a fish or small aquarium.

Both the cloth cover and dust jacket of a book should receive careful attention. The primary purpose of the jacket is to call attention to the book. The jacket for the award-winning *Puss in Boots* illustrated by Fred Marcellino certainly calls attention to itself, for it features the huge head of a hat-bedecked puss in a ruffled collar that could only be the famous *Puss in Boots* by Charles Perrault. But the cover carries no title. Turn the book over and there is the title on the back. A dark brown cloth cover and golden brown endpapers harmonize well with the picture on the jacket. The cover for Maurice Sendak's *We Are All in the Dumps with Jack and Guy* is heavier than normal and is meant to evoke the cardboard boxes of the homeless depicted in the story. Sometimes the cloth cover has a design imprinted in it. Good cloth designs are usually small and symbolic of the content. For example, for *A Chair for My Mother*, Vera Williams uses an imprint of a chair, heart-shaped to show the family's intense desire

Art Techniques

Celebrate Brian Pinkney's work. Set up an illustrator corner with books he has illustrated as well as work done by the children.

How does Pinkney's work convey the theme of each book? affect its mood?

Display art media used in his illustrations.

Create your own scratchboard pictures. Use oil pastel, paint, or other media to color the picture.

Compare Pinkney's scratchboard illustrations to those by other illustrators such as Barbara Cooney or Marcia Sewall.

Compare the techniques of scratchboard with block prints, wood engravings, and etchings. How are they similar/different? Can you tell the difference between these art techniques?

All in the Family

Explore the life of the illustrator through members of his family:
Father: Jerry Pinkney (illustrator)
Mother: Gloria Jean Pinkney (writer)
Wife: Andrea Davis Pinkney (writer and editor).

Make a comparison chart of various books created by each family member, comparing story content, art techniques, and connection to authors.

Collect data in the library involving the work of the illustrator.

Write a letter to editors who publish the works of the Pinkney family to obtain background information.

Research how and why authors and illustrators work together on projects.

Sing and Swing to the Beat

Alvin Ailey (A. Pinkney)
Make a time line of the life of Alvin Ailey.
Visit a ballet class.
Listen to the music of jazz and blues bands. Create your own dance style.

Max Found Two Sticks (Pinkney)
Make a list of the sounds that are similar to the sounds Max's sticks made.
Collect different natural objects to represent different instruments.

The Story Drum

Cut from the Same Cloth (San Souci)
Make a graph of the most popular characters/tall tales among the boys and girls in the class.
Label the locations of each legendary character on a map.
Read *Herstories* (Hamilton). Try to find more female characters in other folklore, or create a heroine in your own tall tale.

The Elephant's Wrestling Match (Sierra)
Write your own talking-drum story with animal characters from Africa.
Make a story drum. Try using various containers with string or bands wrapped from end to end

Sukey and the Mermaid (San Souci)
Following Pinkney's scratchboard technique, create a picture of the mermaid's world.
Explore and compare other tales of mermaids. Find their origins.

Magic, Mystery, & Discovery

The Faithful Friend (San Souci)
The Ballad of Belle Dorcas (Hooks)
The Dark Thirty (McKissack)
The Boy and the Ghost (San Souci)
Compare southern tales with tales from other regions or cultures.
Have a ghost story celebration at a pretend "dark-thirty" time, a half hour of supernatural stories.
List the spells and the effects of each.
Find other folktales that contain three characters similar to the three witches, spells, or transformations.

Where Does the Trail Lead? (Albert)
Take a nature walk by the seashore.
Go on a scavenger hunt looking for specific objects along the trails.
Follow a guide book of trails along seashores and sand dunes.

Celebrate!

Seven Candles for Kwanzaa (A. Pinkney)
Discuss the seven principles of Kwanzaa, and discover the origins of Kwanzaa.
Weave your own straw "mkeka" (placemat).
Make some Kwanzaa gifts: a fabric doll or a bead necklace.

Day of Delight (Schur)
Examine Jewish traditions. How are they like and different from other religious traditions?
Discover kosher recipes.

Happy Birthday, Martin Luther King (Marzollo)
Plan a birthday celebration in honor of Martin Luther King, Jr.

Brian Pinkney
A Web of Possibilities

Poetry

The Dream Keeper (Hughes)
I Never Told (cover art) (Livingston)
A Time to Talk (Livingston)
Find favorite poems to read aloud.
Create scratchboard pictures for individual poems.
Research the lives of the poets Langston Hughes and Myra Cohn Livingston. What are the similarities and differences between the two? in their work?

A Wave in Her Pocket (Joseph)
Ask a family member or relative to come into class to tell stories passed down from generation to generation.

Discovering People in the Past

Alvin Ailey (A. Pinkney) (see "Sing and Swing to the Beat")
Dear Benjamin Banneker (A. Pinkney)
Happy Birthday, Martin Luther King (Marzollo)
Harriet Tubman (Carter)
Make a time line of African Americans' contributions to American life and history.

Web prepared by Jean M. Norman

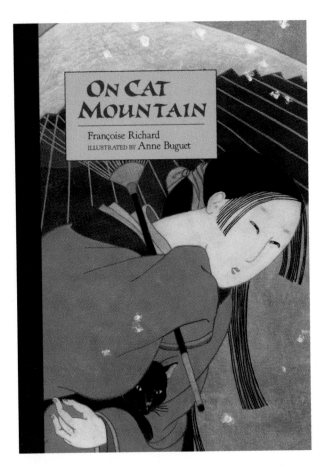

On Cat Mountain by Françoise Richard is an artifact of excellent design that recalls handmade Japanese books.
From *On Cat Mountain*, by Françoise Richard, illustrated by Anne Buguet. Copyright © 1994 by The Putnam & Grosset Group, New York, NY. Reprinted by permssion.

for a beautiful, comfortable chair for their mother. On the other hand, there is no dust jacket at all on Françoise Richard's *On Cat Mountain*, a folktale set in ancient Japan and illustrated by Anne Buguet. Instead, the cover is carefully designed to resemble a handmade book; a two-inch-wide cloth strip covers the binding, and the cover picture looks like a Japanese wood-block print. This attention to detail is a subtle yet effective beginning for a story whose illustrations also pay homage to Japanese art forms.

The endpapers of a picture book can also add to its attractiveness. These are the first and last pages of the book; one half of each is glued to the inside of the cover, while the other is not pasted down. Endpapers are usually of stronger paper than printed pages. In picture books, endpapers are often of a color that harmonizes with the cover or other pictures in the book, and frequently they are illustrated. Decorated endpapers can reflect the setting, the theme, or the content of the book and serve as a special invitation into the book.

Judith Caseley has visually surveyed the contents of Mama's purse on the endpapers of *Mama Coming and Going*. Car keys, a bottle of aspirin, a Band-Aid, and a piece of old pizza are among the many objects pictured on the endpapers and featured in this warm and funny story of a highly disorganized mother. Leo and Diane Dillon created stylized lotus blossoms and seedpods on marbleized paper for *Aïda*, retold by Leontyne Price. Tomie de Paola made an Italian setting for *Strega Nona* by showing the arched piazza and tile roofs of Strega Nona's Calabrian town. The endpapers of *Crow Boy* by Taro Yashima show a flower and a butterfly alone against a dark background. They seem to symbolize the metamorphosis of Crow Boy's life from dark despair to brilliant hope.

Even the title page of a picture storybook can be beautiful and symbolic. Marcia Brown has created a striking title page for Cendrars's *Shadow*. She portrays a young boy in silhouette anxiously looking back at his long shadow, which falls across a double-page spread, while the spirits of his ancestors, shown as white masks, look on. This primitive fear of and respect for shadows permeates the book. William Steig emphasizes the friendship of a mouse and a whale at the same time as he contrasts their size with his title page for *Amos & Boris*. The title page of *Just Plain Fancy* by Patricia Polacco provides the clue to the origin of the fancy peacock egg that Naomi and Ruth found in the tall grass by the drive. All aspects of a book can reinforce or extend the meaning of the story.

The layout of pictures and text on each double-page spread and on succeeding pages can have an important impact on the meaning and movement of a story. Full-size pictures might be interspersed with smaller ones, or a page might show a sequence of pictures. Beatriz Vidal's placement of pictures and use of shapes complement the rhythm of Verna Aardema's *Bringing the Rain to Kapiti Plain*. This African tale from the Nandi tribe is cumulative, reminiscent of the nursery rhyme "The House That Jack Built." First, Vidal shows a verdant plain mostly on the right-hand page; then she switches to the left, while the third page rests the eye with a double-page spread showing a heavy cloud mass spreading over the entire plain. Then once again she places her masses on the right and then left page—readers anticipate this shift just as they anticipate the cumulative rhyme. This is not done throughout the book, however; it would be too monotonous. This is a beautiful example of how one image on a page blends into the next to create the total impact of the book.

The spacing of the text on the page, the choice of margins, and the white space within a book contribute to the making of a quality picture storybook. In Virginia Lee Burton's *The Little House*, the arrangement of the text on the page suggests the curve of the road in the

Teaching Feature

Learning About the Art of Picture Storybooks

During Book Week in the fall, teachers in the Highland Park School in Grove City, Ohio, presented several minicourses on the making of books. One minicourse gave an overview of all the kinds of books a child might want to write. The teacher showed the children various kinds of ABC books and counting books. They looked at concept books for the young child, collections of poetry, and many informational books, from Aliki's simple books *My Feet* and *My Hands* to more complicated books such as Patricia Lauber's *The News About Dinosaurs*. Special books that are takeoffs on fairy tales, such as *The Jolly Postman* by the Ahlbergs or *The Principal's New Clothes* by Stephanie Calmenson, were discussed. Children then started to write their own stories in their classrooms.

Another minicourse emphasized the use of art media, introducing children to the collages of Eric Carle, Ezra Jack Keats, and Jeannie Baker. The teachers had cloth and newspapers available as they discussed the material Keats used in *The Snowy Day* or *Whistle for Willie*. They had fingerpaint paper to make large animals like those in Eric Carle's stories, and natural materials like the grasses, sponges, and mosses that Jeannie Baker uses.

Another teacher had collected books with interesting endpapers, like *The Great White Man-Eating Shark* by Margaret Mahy, *At Grammy's House* by Eve Rice, and *Henny Penny* by Stephen Butler. Then children made stamps from inner tubes, vegetables, or plastic foam meat trays to create their own endpapers. This same teacher had a collection of books with interesting title pages. In all instances, the teacher talked about the ways the artwork strengthened the theme of the book.

Another minicourse emphasized different ways to bind books with cloth or wallpaper covers.

At the end of the week, the children had all created their own books. More importantly, they had learned about the ways text and art work together to create a unified impression. They had developed a greater appreciation for picture storybooks and the amount of work involved in creating a fine book, and they looked at books differently after this experience.

Faculty of Highland Park School
Kristen Kerstetter, project coordinator
Grove City, Ohio

---

opposite picture. In the very funny story of the dog poet in *Max Makes a Million* by Maira Kalman, Max dreams of going to Paris. These longings are printed on the paper in the shape of the Eiffel Tower.

It is important also that the text can easily be read and is not printed on dark paper. In Paul Goble's *The Girl Who Loved Wild Horses*, the text was changed to white when it was placed on the dark pages that represented night.

Appropriate type design is also a matter for consideration. *Type* is the name given to all printed letters, and *typeface* refers to the more than six thousand different styles available today. Typefaces vary in legibility and the feeling they create. Some seem bold; others delicate and graceful, some crisp and businesslike. Nicolas Sidjakov describes the difficulty he and his editor had in finding a suitable typeface for Ruth Robbins's *Baboushka and the Three Kings*. When they did find one they liked, it was obsolete and not easily available. They finally located enough fonts to handset *Baboushka* a page at a time.[6] Aliki maintains that the illustrator must think of

the text on the page as a part of the art itself. She hand-lettered the text for her book *Feelings* so that the appearance of the words would convey a more personal expression.[7]

Other factors in a picture book must be considered from a utilitarian standpoint. The paper should be dull enough so that it does not easily reflect light, opaque enough to prevent print from showing through, and strong enough to withstand heavy usage. Side sewing in the binding of many picture books makes them more durable, but it might distort double-page spreads unless the artwork is prepared with the gutter separation in mind. Tall narrow books with side sewing will not lie flat when the book is open. Many librarians complain that today's bindings are of poor quality and will not last for the life of the book. These, then, are some of the practical considerations that can affect a book's beauty and durability.

In sum, no single element creates an outstanding picture book. What does create one is all elements' working together to create a cohesive whole that pleases the eye and delights the imagination.

[6]Nicolas Sidjakov, "Caldecott Award Acceptance," in *Newbery and Caldecott Medal Books: 1956–1965*, ed. Lee Kingman (Boston: Horn Book, 1965), pp. 223–225.

[7]Aliki Brandenberg, in a speech given at the Children's Literature Conference at Ohio State University, Columbus, 1989.

The Language of Picture Storybooks

The words of picture storybooks are as important as the illustrations; they can help children develop an early sensitivity to the imaginative use of language and add to their overall experience with a picture storybook. Since most of these books are read to children rather than by them, there is no reason to oversimplify or write down to today's knowledgeable and sophisticated child. Beatrix Potter knew that, given the context of *The Tale of Peter Rabbit* and the picture of Peter caught in the gooseberry net, most children would comprehend the words "his sobs were overheard by some friendly sparrows, who flew to him in great excitement, and implored him to exert himself" (p. 45).

Steig's *Amos & Boris* is a comical story of the unlikely friendship between a mouse and a whale. Amos, the mouse, delighted by all things nautical, builds himself a jaunty little boat, which he names *Rodent*. Admiring the starry skies one night, he rolls overboard and is saved by a huge whale, who is amazed to find that the mouse is also a mammal. He gives him a ride to safety, and, true to the lion and rat fable on which the story is based, Amos is able to reciprocate at a later time. Steig's luxuriant use of language and superb pictures make this an unusual picture storybook. The description of their trip home details their growing friendship:

> Swimming along, sometimes at great speed, sometimes slowly and leisurely, sometimes resting and exchanging ideas, sometimes stopping to sleep, it took them a week to reach Amos's home shore. During that time, they developed a deep admiration for one another. Boris admired the delicacy, the quivering daintiness, the light touch, the small voice, the gemlike radiance of the mouse. Amos admired the bulk, the grandeur, the power, the purpose, the rich voice, and the abounding friendliness of the whale. (unpaged)

While these words may seem difficult words to understand, children do make sense of the story, using the context of both the pictures and the text. They sweep back and forth from one to the other, obtaining the general feeling for this unusual friendship even if they do not know the exact meaning of every single word. This is the way children increase their vocabularies—by hearing or reading words they do not know but in a context that provides a general sense of the meaning.

In contrast to Steig's exuberant use of words in *Amos & Boris*, the well-known New England poet Donald Hall portrays the journey of *Ox-Cart Man* in cadenced language that is as slow and deliberate as the pace of the ox on the ten-day journey to Portsmouth. When the father packs the family's products, which had taken them a whole year to make, the author describes them in a kind of litany of words:

> He packed a bag of wool he sheared from the sheep in April.
>
> He packed a shawl his wife wove on a loom from yarn spun at the spinning wheel from sheep sheared in April.
>
> He packed five pairs of mittens his daughter knit from yarn spun at the spinning wheel from sheep sheared in April. (unpaged)

All children can appreciate figurative language, provided the comparisons are within the realm of their experience. The vivid word pictures in Alvin Tresselt's *White Snow, Bright Snow* are thoroughly enjoyed by 5- and 6-year-olds and reflect a child's point of view:

> In the morning a clear blue sky was overhead and blue shadows hid in all the corners. Automobiles looked like big fat raisins buried in snow drifts.
>
> Houses crouched together, their windows peeking out from under great white eyebrows. Even the church steeple wore a pointed cap on its top. (p. 20)

The dialogue of a story can be rich and believable or it can be stilted, as in a Dick and Jane basal reader. Arnold Lobel was a master at creating understated humorous dialogue in his Frog and Toad series. Similarly, part of the charm of the Frances stories by Russell Hoban is the natural-sounding dialogue of everybody's favorite badger, Francis. The expressive pictures are as humorous as the dialogue in both of these well-written series.

In evaluating picture storybooks, it is good to remember that the story should be told quickly because the action must be contained within a 32- to 64-page book. Even with this limitation, the criteria developed in Chapter 1 for all fiction apply equally well to picture storybooks. Both text and illustrations should be evaluated. The artistry of the words should be equal to the beauty of the illustrations. See the Guidelines box "Evaluating Picture Storybooks" for some questions that can help you evaluate picture storybooks.

The Content of Picture Storybooks

Several recent changes can be noted in the content of picture storybooks. One is the increasing publication of books that are based on sharing memories of times past with children. Frequently these are told by grandparents, much as they might once have been told around

Guidelines:
Evaluating Picture Storybooks

The following questions are meant to help the reader determine the strengths of the book. Not every question is appropriate for every book.

Content

How appropriate is the content of the book for its intended age level?

Is this a book that will appeal to children, or is it really written for adults?

When and where does it take place? How has the artist portrayed this?

Are the characters well delineated and developed?

Are race, gender, and other stereotypes avoided?

What is the quality of the language of the text?

How is the theme developed through text and illustrations?

Illustrations

In what ways do the illustrations help to create the meaning of the text?

How are pictures made an integral part of the text?

Do the illustrations extend the text in any way? Do they provide clues to the action of the story?

Are the pictures accurate and consistent with the text?

Where the setting calls for it, are the illustrations authentic in detail?

Medium and Style of Illustrations

What medium has the illustrator chosen to use? Is it appropriate for the mood of the story?

How has the illustrator used line, shape, and color to extend the story?

How would you describe the style of the illustrations? Is the style appropriate for the story?

How has the illustrator varied the style and technique? What techniques seem to create rhythm and movement?

How has the illustrator created balance in composition?

Format

Does the size of the book seem appropriate to the content?

Does the jacket design express the theme of the book?

Do the cover design and endpapers convey the spirit of the book?

In what way does the title page anticipate the story to come?

Is the type design well chosen for the theme and purpose of the book?

What is the quality of the paper?

How durable is the binding?

Overall Evaluation

How is this work similar to or different from other works by this author and/or illustrator?

How is this story similar to or different from other books with the same subject or theme?

What comments have reviewers made about this book? Do you agree or disagree with them?

What has the artist said about her or his work?

Will this book make a contribution to the growing body of children's literature? How lasting do you think it will be?

---

the dinner table. Perhaps these books compensate for the lack of frequent contact with extended families in our fast-paced lives. These books seldom have a real plot but are based on what life was like when grandfather, or grandmother, or parents were children.

Another development in the content of picture storybooks is a tremendous increase in books that are geared to children in the middle grades and older. This seems appropriate for today's visually minded child. As the age range for picture storybooks increases, it becomes imperative to evaluate the appropriateness of the content for the age level of its intended audience. You do not want to share *Hiroshima No Pika* (The Flash of

Hiroshima) by Toshi Maruki with young children any more than you would read *Goodnight Moon* by Margaret Wise Brown to older children.

Other considerations regarding the content of picture storybooks need to be examined. For example, does the book avoid race, gender, and age stereotyping? Gender stereotyping begins early. Examples can be found in pictures as well as in text. In the imaginative story *Can I Keep Him?* by Steven Kellogg, Albert asks his mother if he can keep one pet after another, ranging from real to imaginary to human. His distraught mother is always pictured attending to such household chores as scrubbing, ironing, and cleaning the toilet bowl. She explains in very literal terms why Albert cannot keep his pets; for example, a snake's scales could clog the vacuum. While the contrast between Albert's highly original ideas and his mother's mundane preoccupation with household duties is funny, it is also a stereotyped image of the traditional housewife.

An increasing number of books have been published that counteract gender stereotyping. In *William's Doll*, by Charlotte Zolotow, a little boy who desperately wants a doll is misunderstood by family and teased by friends. Only his grandmother understands how he feels, and so she brings him a baby doll "to hug . . . so that when he's a father . . . he'll know how to care for his baby."

More and more books portray characters who are willing to step outside of traditional roles to have fulfilling lives. In *Max* by Rachel Isadora, a young baseball player decides to take ballet lessons. He finds that it is a super way to warm up for baseball. Arnold Adoff, the well-known poet, cuts across several stereotypes in his story *Hard to Be Six*. He presents an affectionate view of sibling rivalry in a loving interracial family where the 6-year-old brother always kisses his sister goodnight and his father does the cooking.

We have picture books that portray the experiences of more diverse cultures than ever before, although the total number of multicultural books is still small compared to the proportion of ethnic and racial groups in the population.[8] Native Americans, who have been maligned in print, on television, and in commercial games as bloodthirsty warriors, are still underrepresented in books. *In My Mother's House* by Ann Nolan Clark, a poetic story of life among Pueblo Indians, has been reissued with handsome black-and-white and colored illustrations by Velino Herrera. *This House Is Made of Mud*, by Ken Buchanan, celebrates the joy of living in a Navajo hogan. The desert is its yard, the mountains its fence, and all the animals and birds are welcome visitors. Lovely clear watercolors by Libba Tracy add to the beauty of this simple story. A few stories attempt to tell stories of family relationships in Native American communities, with mixed results. *Annie and the Old One*, by Miska Miles, is a story of a Navajo girl and her grandmother. However, this book has been criticized by Native Americans for not being authentic in its representation of the Navajo way of life. Bill Martin, Jr., and John Archambault's *Knots on a Counting Rope* tells about a warm relationship between a blind child and

his grandfather. Text and illustrations suggest that this is a story about a Native American family, but Native Americans have objected to the portrayal of tribal life in this book.[9] The popularity of books like these continues to suggest the need for Native American authors, or at least that teachers have resources on Native Americans to consult for authenticity.

The last few years have seen an increase in books about Latino cultures, in bilingual books and translated books. A picture book can often bridge linguistic barriers and introduce all children to cultures and languages other than their own. Brilliant collage paintings by Elisa Kleven illustrate the imaginary trips Rosalba and her grandmother take in *Abuela* and *Isla*. Rosalba narrates their marvelous journeys in English spiced with Spanish phrases that children who do not speak Spanish can easily understand in the context of these jewel-like settings. The author, Arthur Dorros, provides a glossary and pronunciation guide at the end.

Con Mi Hermano: With My Brother by Eileen Roe relates the joyous times that a little boy spends with his older brother—playing ball, helping him deliver newspapers, and sharing picture books together. *Family Pictures: Cuadros de Familia* by Carmen Lomas Garza is like a family album of all the special events the author remembers from her childhood days of growing up in Kingsville, Texas. We need more such books written in both English and Spanish that celebrate our cultural diversity.

While there are more books about elderly people than ever before, we can find stereotypes among these, too. One young-appearing grandfather went to a bookstore recently and said he wanted "a book about a grandfather in which the main character doesn't die." Many grandparents today in their sixties and seventies are vigorous and healthy; we might well ask if they are being portrayed this way.

Picture storybooks frequently give children their first impressions of various ethnic and racial groups. Only when our books portray characters of both sexes, all ages, and all ethnic and racial groups in a wide range of occupations and from a great variety of socioeconomic backgrounds and settings will we have moved away from stereotyping to a more honest portrayal of the world for children.

---

[8]See *New Advocate* 8 (Winter 1995) and *Horn Book Magazine*, May/June 1995, for several articles on multicultural literature.

[9]Native Americans maintain that Native American children would not interrupt their grandfather as the boy does in this story, because elders are always respected. Clothing and hairstyles are not authentic to any one nation, and the naming ceremony is incorrect. See "Book Reviews" in Beverly Slapin and Doris Seale, eds., *Books Without Bias: Through Indian Eyes* (Berkeley, Calif.: Oyate, 1988), pp. 273–278.

In Arthur Dorros's *Isla*, vibrant paintings by Elisa Kleven sparkle like an island in the sea.
From Isla by Arthur Dorros, illustrated by Elisa Kleven. Copyright © 1995 by Elisa Kleven, illustrations. Used by permission of Dutton Children's Books, a division of Penguin USA Inc.

Themes and Subjects in Picture Storybooks

It is important that we, as teachers and librarians, know all the criteria by which to judge a quality picture book. Children are most interested in one criterion—does it tell a good story? They will respond most deeply to books that touch their interests and their imagination with words and pictures. In this section we discuss picture storybooks by theme for the benefit of those selecting particular books or preparing units of study.

Family Stories

Family stories today include single-parent families, divorced and remarried (blended) families, adoptive and foster families, and the extended family. Children always beg to hear stories about when their parents were small. The little African American girl in *Tell Me a Story, Mama* by Angela Johnson knows exactly what family stories she wants to hear, and she knows them so well that she can tell them herself with her mother adding just the right comment. This is the story of a tender parent-child relationship.

Taxi Taxi by Carrie Best is a story of the loving relationship between a little girl and her father. Every Sunday Tina, a child of divorced parents, waits for Papi to come in his yellow taxi. Their day together in the country is filled with simple pleasures, and it ends with all Tina's neighbors piled into the taxi for a ride home. Dale Gottlieb's vivid paintings convey the excitement of this special day and the warm feelings that radiate from family and community.

Sibling rivalry is a common theme in picture storybooks. Peter in *Peter's Chair* by Ezra Jack Keats decides to run away before all of his possessions are painted pink for his new baby sister. However, when he discovers that he no longer fits in his chair, he decides that maybe it would be fun to paint it pink himself. The collage pictures add greatly to this universally loved story. Sibling rivalry is also portrayed in *She Come Bringing Me That Little Baby Girl* by Eloise Greenfield. Kevin dislikes all the attention given to his new sister. Then his uncle tells him how he used to take care of his baby sister, and Kevin is surprised to learn that his mother was once a baby girl. Kevin gets over his resentment and goes to get his friends to show them his new sister. Illustrations by John Steptoe capture Kevin's changing emotions in this warm, loving story.

Dale Gottlieb's warm colors and simple shapes convey the special relationship of father and daughter in Carrie Best's *Taxi Taxi*.
From *Taxi! Taxi!* by Carrie Best. Text copyright © 1994 by Carrie Best; illustrations copyright © 1994 by Dale Gottlieb. By permission of Little, Brown and Company.

Sibling conflict is portrayed more frequently in picture storybooks than love and compassion are. In Shirley Hughes's *Dogger*, a big sister, Bella, lovingly gives up the huge teddy bear she won at the fair in order to obtain her little brother's lost, much-loved plush-toy dog. Hughes always portrays real, believable characters in messy, confusing households in both her pictures and her text. In this story Bella shows her love for Dave in her actions, whereas many family mood stories only talk about love.

Relatives are an important part of a child's world, and many picture storybooks explore the closeness between children and the members of their extended families. The warm, jubilant picture storybook by Cynthia Rylant, *The Relatives Came*, celebrates the joys of family reunions. Illustrated by Stephen Gammell, the book describes the summer some six or seven relatives arrive, having driven up from Virginia in an old station wagon. The relatives stay for weeks and weeks, helping tend the garden and mend any broken things. Stephen Gammell used brightly colored pencil drawings for this award-winning book.

There are increasingly more stories about grandparents. Several themes can be discerned in these. One is the sharing of family stories, frequently including the cultural feeling for the country from which the grandparents emigrated. Another theme is helping the child overcome a fear or learn something new, or just enjoyment of the relationship. The third type is learning to say good-bye and adjusting to the death of a grandparent.

In *Grandaddy's Place* by Helen Griffith, Janetta meets her granddaddy for the first time. She is apprehensive about staying at his house, which is way out in the country. Her grandfather understands her fears and helps her make friends with all the animals on his place. A special closeness develops between the two of them. In *Georgia Music*, by Griffith, Janetta's grandaddy's health is failing and he has been brought to live with her family in the city. This time it is Janetta who helps him learn to accept his new situation. James Stevenson's full-color watercolors create the settings for these two loving stories.

In *Storm in the Night* by Mary Stolz, a storm has cut off the electricity, so a grandfather and grandson sit together in the dark and enjoy the sounds and smells of the rain. The grandfather recounts the story of a stormy night from his childhood and how he overcame his fear of the dark. Pat Cummings's pictures show a loving relationship in an African American family. Patricia Polacco tells a memorable story of how a little girl is terrified of thunder until her Russian "babushka" (grandmother) teaches her to make a special *Thunder Cake*. As child and grandmother scurry around to get the ingredients for the Thunder Cake, the little girl doesn't have time to be frightened of the storm.

Food is often a way for families to share love and mark special occasions. In Jama Kim Rattigan's *Dumpling Soup*, little Marisa is old enough to help her relatives prepare dumplings for the New Year festival in Hawaii, but she worries that no one will eat her funny-looking "mandoo." When it is midnight and time for dumpling soup, however, her relatives proclaim hers the best they've ever tasted. Lillian Hsu-Flanders's charming watercolor paintings picture a family as colorful and multicultural as their individual recipes for a happy new year.

Tomie de Paola has written two grandmother stories. In *Watch Out for the Chicken Feet in Your Soup*, Joey warns his friend Eugene, as they go to visit his Italian grandmother, about the chicken feet in her soup. Eugene gets to help the well-meaning grandmother make bread dolls (a recipe is provided in the text) and thoroughly enjoys his visit. The second story, *Nana Upstairs & Nana Downstairs*, is more serious, describing a boy's

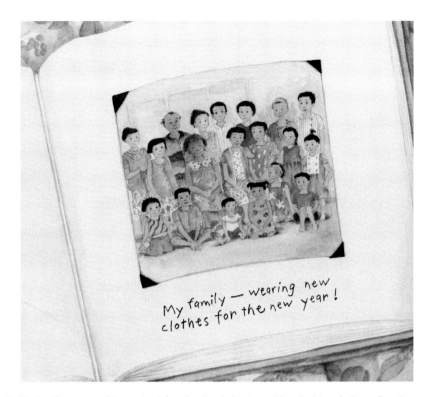

My family — wearing new clothes for the new year!

Lillian Hsu-Flanders's illustrations record important family rituals in Jama Kim Rattigan's *Dumpling Soup*.
From *Dumping Soup* by Jama Kim Rattigan. Text copyright © 1993 by Jama Kim Rattigan; illustrations copyright © 1993 by Lillian Hsu-Flanders. By permission of Little, Brown and Company.

visits with his bedridden great-grandmother. *Now One Foot, Now the Other* is de Paola's story of the little boy helping his grandfather recover from a stroke and learn to walk again. *Tom* describes his relationship with his irrepressible maternal grandfather, who must have given him his sense of humor as well as his name.

Every family makes its own history, creates its own mythology by retelling family stories many times over. Three stories of African American families carry on this theme. In Valerie Flournoy's *The Patchwork Quilt*, Tanya loves to hear her grandmother tell the stories of the material she is using to make a quilt. She helps her cut the squares and listens to her story of the quilt of memories. Flournoy's story and the realistic pictures by Jerry Pinkney capture a young girl's love for her treasured grandmother. In Elizabeth Fitzgerald Howard's *Aunt Flossie's Hats (and Crab Cakes Later)*, Sarah and Susan hear the history of their Great-Great-Aunt Flossie's many hats, including the time a dog retrieved her "favorite best Sunday hat" from the water. Sumptuous oil paintings by James Ransome convey the joy of the children's visit to their very special aunt. Howard's own 98-year-old aunt who never threw anything away was the inspiration for this delightful family story. In *Uncle Jed's Barbershop*, by Margaree King Mitchell, Sarah Jean remembers her uncle who sacrificed dreams of

having his own barbershop to help his family and neighbors. Uncle Jed, a remarkable man, struggled through the Great Depression and the years of segregation in the South until finally, at the age of seventy-nine, he opened his barbershop. James Ransome's richly textured paintings add to the warmth of this lovely story.

In *The Keeping Quilt* by Patricia Polacco, Great Gramma Anna, a Russian Jew who was an immigrant to this country, made a quilt to help the family always remember their homeland. Through four generations the quilt is a Sabbath tablecloth, a wedding canopy, and a blanket that welcomes babies warmly into the world. To this day, Patricia Polacco still treasures this family quilt. The warm sepias of the drawings set against the full color in the quilt itself visually recreate the textures of memory and the fabric of tradition.

Familiar Everyday Experiences

Everything is new to the young child the first time it happens—going to school, making friends, losing teeth, taking a trip, moving away, the death of a pet. Children soon become accustomed to familiar experiences; nevertheless, books can help keep alive the wonder and anticipation of many such experiences. They can also alleviate some of their concerns and worries about the new and unknown.

Ezra Jack Keats has used collage and bright acrylic paints for his well-loved stories of Peter and his friends. Beginning with *The Snowy Day, Peter's Chair, Whistle for Willie,* and *A Letter to Amy,* the stories deal with simple events that are central to a young child's life. As Peter grows up, he is joined by his friend Archie in *Goggles, Hi Cat!* and *Pet Show!* All these stories take place in the inner city and have exciting story lines and convincing characterization. In *Goggles,* Peter, Archie, and Willie, Peter's dachshund, fool some big boys who want to take away the motorcycle goggles that the two friends have found. In *Hi Cat!* Peter is adopted by a crazy cat. In *Pet Show!* the crazy cat disappears just when Archie needs him for his entry. Being highly creative, Archie substitutes an empty bottle that contains his pet, a germ! He receives an award for the quietest pet.

Birthdays are extra-special events for children, and Vera Williams's brightly colored paintings add extra warmth to her stories about Rosa and her family. In *Something Special for Me,* Williams makes very real the decision that Rosa, the little girl in *A Chair for My Mother,* must make. Soon it will be her birthday, and this time she can have the money in the large money jar that contains her mother's waitressing tips to buy anything she wants. After much soul-searching, Rosa decides to spend the money on a used accordion. In *Music, Music for Everyone,* Rosa's grandmother becomes ill and the money jar is empty from paying her bills, so Rosa uses her birthday accordion to earn money.

Children facing the death of a pet may find comfort in books by Carol and Donald Carrick such as *The Accident.* This story describes Christopher's dismay when his dog, Bodger, is run over by a truck and killed. In *The Foundling,* Christopher's dad takes him to the local animal shelter hoping that a dog there will attract his attention. However, Christopher feels that adoption would be unfaithful to Bodger's memory and can't respond to any of the dogs. Later, an abandoned pup that he thinks belongs next door starts waiting for him after school. When Christopher finds that the pup doesn't belong to anyone, he decides to keep it. These stories are part of a series of books about Christopher and his family. Donald Carrick's expressive watercolors authentically portray the people and settings of New England villages and the seacoast.

Picture Storybooks About Older People

For many years we believed that children identified only with stories about children their own age. More recently we have given them literature that includes persons of all ages.

Mem Fox's *Wilfrid Gordon McDonald Partridge* is the story of a small redheaded boy who makes friends with the old folks who live next door in a home for people who are elderly. He likes them all, but his particular friend is 96-year-old Miss Nancy. When he hears his parents say she has lost her memory, he decides to help her find it. Julie Vivas's exuberant pictures provide unique characterizations that are painted almost larger than life and seen from unusual perspectives.

Fox and Vivas teamed up again for the loving and wonderfully funny *Our Granny.* The book is as much a positive look at older women as it is a celebration of one grandmother. Vivas's quirky illustrations and varied points of view show grannies who come in all shapes and sizes and do all manner of interesting things. They exercise, they drive trucks, they march in demonstrations, and they tuck their grandbabies in at night. Fox's descriptions of grannies who wear "jeans and sneakers, pantsuits, silky dresses, big bras, and baggy underwear" will delight children as much as Vivas's zany pictures.

Vivas also illustrated Margaret Wild's book *The Very Best of Friends,* which describes the loving friendship between James and Jessie, and James and his cat, William. Jessie doesn't like cats. When elderly James dies suddenly, Jessie locks the cat outside and herself inside. William becomes a mean, lean cat and bites her one morning. That shocks Jessie into taming and feeding the cat and restoring her own life. Vivas's illustrations are full of expression and show this life cycle superbly.

Barbara Cooney illustrated two popular stories about older people, *Emma* and *Miss Rumphius. Emma,* written by Wendy Kesselman, is about a woman the author knew who didn't start painting until she was in her late eighties. In this story Barbara Cooney depicts her as a kind of Grandma Moses character who creates many primitive paintings based on her memories of her town. Cooney's *Miss Rumphius* is a fine model of an independent older person. As a youngster she told her grandfather that she, too, wished to travel to faraway places as he had and live by the sea. He told her there was a third thing she must do—make the world more beautiful. And so, years later she planted lupine all over her little seacoast village. Repetition of the story line is reflected as a very elderly Miss Rumphius passes along her grandfather's advice to her grandniece. The continuity of life is nicely portrayed by the many objects that we first saw in the grandfather's house, or on her travels, and that now comfortably reside in Miss Rumphius's home by the sea.

Another remarkable person who dreams of going to faraway places is Arizona in Gloria Houston's *My Great-Aunt Arizona.* Born in a log cabin in the Blue Ridge Mountains, Arizona never goes to those faraway places. Instead she stays at home and becomes one of

Julie Vivas's illustrations show grandmothers with unique personalities and "can-do" attitudes in Mem Fox's *Our Granny*.
Illustration by Julie Vivas from *Our Granny* by Margaret Wild. Illustration copyright © 1994 by Julie Vivas. Reprinted by permission of Houghton Mifflin Company/Ticknor & Fields Books for Young Readers. All rights reserved.

those special teachers whom fortunate students hold in their hearts. Great-Aunt Arizona dies on her ninety-third birthday, but she goes to those faraway places with all of the students she taught. "She goes with us in our minds."

Blow Me a Kiss, Miss Lilly is a touching story by Nancy White Carlstrom of Sara's friendship with the very old lady who lives across the street from her. Miss Lilly tells Sara that you can be different when you are very old and even eat ice cream for breakfast. One day Miss Lilly doesn't feel well, and Sara's father takes her to the hospital, where she dies. Sara takes in her cat, visits her garden, and always blows her a kiss the way she did when she was alive. Small, precise illustrations by Amy Schwartz make this story particularly appealing.

The Child's World of Nature

Sometimes young children seem more attuned to the world about them than adults do. Watch children on the first day of snow, for example, and see the excitement in their eyes and their eagerness to go outside. Adults might complain about having to shovel the snow or getting the car stuck, but for children a snowstorm is pure joy. It is this very contrast between adults' and children's reactions to snow that formed the basis for Alvin Tresselt's well-loved book *White Snow, Bright Snow*, illustrated with Roger Duvoisin's sparkling pictures. Repeating the same pattern in *Hide and Seek Fog*, Tresselt describes the children's joyous response to a fog that came and stayed for three days in a little seaside village on Cape Cod, while their parents grumbled about spending their vacations in the middle of a cloud. Duvoisin's hazy pearl-gray illustrations effectively convey the mystery of a fog-shrouded day.

Anyone who has ever seen a child go out of his way to walk through a puddle knows that children are fascinated with bodies of water. In *Pond Year* Katherine Lasky details the changes that occur in the ecology of a backyard pond and describes the rich playground it provides for two friends. Mike Bostock's transparent watercolors are the perfect medium to show the two girls collecting tadpoles in May, catching salamanders in August, looking for muskrats in October, and skating on the ice in January.

The various sounds the rain makes are explored in the poetic picture book *Rain Talk* by Mary Serfozo. A young child hears the "first fat raindrops" fall on the summer dust of a country road. She smells the wet dust. Eventually she and her dog make their way home after enjoying their rainy day walk. Bright yellow and green illustrations by Keiko Narahashi portray the child's delight in this summer rain. In the well-known story *Umbrella* by Taro Yashima, a little Japanese American girl is impatient for rain because she wants to wear her new red rubber boots and carry her new umbrella to nursery school. At last the rain comes, and Momo walks straight like a lady, listening to the rhythmic patter of raindrops on her new umbrella.

Mike Bostock's lovely watercolors bring the wonders of a backyard pond to life in Katherine Lasky's *Pond Year.*
Pond Year text copyright © by Kathryn Lasky. Illustrations copyright © 1995 by Mike Rostock. Reproduced by permission of the publisher Candlewick Press, Cambridge, MA.

Byrd Baylor's long narrative free verse reflects her love and appreciation for the western setting where she makes her home. The sweeping fluid lines of Peter Parnall's pen and ink and paints beautifully illustrate such titles as *Everybody Needs a Rock, Your Own Best Secret Place,* and *The Other Way to Listen.* In *The Way to Start a Day,* Baylor celebrates the way people all over the world have paid their respects to the wonder of each new sunrise. In her words: "You have to make a good day . . . you have to make a good world for the sun to live its one-day life in."

Rachel Carson tells us in the sensitive essay that she wrote about her grandnephew Roger just a few years before her death: "If a child is to keep alive his inborn sense of wonder . . . he needs the companionship of at least one adult who can share it, rediscovering with him the joy, excitement and mystery of the world we live in."[10] Books are not a substitute for real experiences, but through the sharing of beautiful picture storybooks, teachers can enhance a real experience and keep the wonder of it alive with their own enthusiasm and appreciation for nature. See Resources for Teaching, "Picture Storybooks About the Everyday World of the Child," for a list of many picture storybooks about children's everyday experiences.

[10]Rachel Carson, *The Sense of Wonder,* photographs by Charles Pratt and others (New York: Harper & Row, 1956, 1965), p. 45.

Animals as People

Ever since the day Peter Rabbit disobeyed his mother and squeezed through Mr. MacGregor's garden fence, children have enjoyed stories in which animals act like people, frequently like small children. In fact, many of these stories would be listed as family stories if you read just the text, since only in the pictures are the characters revealed as animals. Usually the animals are dressed and live in cozy furnished homes, hollow trees, or burrows and face the same problems as their child readers, whose lives are mirrored in these stories.

Small Green Snake by Libba Moore Gray is really Peter Rabbit in reptilian guise. Holly Meade's expressive collages add to the fun of this story of a little garter snake who is "grassy," "sassy," and "flashy" and likes to wander far from home. Despite his mother's warning, he is tempted over the garden wall and is captured in a glass jelly jar. A striped yellow cat provides the exciting climax and the means of escape for this wily snake, who is only slightly chastened by his adventures. Gray's vivid writing makes this a particularly wonderful book to read aloud.

Rosemary Wells creates many lovable animal characters that mirror the behavior of young children. In *Noisy Nora,* as the middle sister in a mouse family, Nora has to find some unusual way to gain the attention of her parents—and this she does with a flourish. With simple verse and beguiling illustrations, Rosemary Wells has created a very lovable animal character who will gain the attention of every child lucky enough to hear this amusing story. *Shy Charles* is the intersting tale of a shy mouse who doesn't want to take ballet lessons or play football. He just wants to stay home and play by himself. However, in an emergency Charles comes through as a real hero, but still a shy one. Wells is also the creator of *Stanley and Rhoda,* about an older brother/sister combination, in which Stanley shows he knows all the ploys of handling his toddler sister. Facial expressions and very funny dialogue make these books popular with 5-, 6-, and 7-year-olds.

Kevin Henkes is the creator of a remarkable mouse child named Lilly, who was the very best until the arrival of her baby brother in *Julius, the Baby of the World.* Lilly thinks he is disgusting and hopes he will go away; she hates Julius and the way her parents fawn over him. When no one is looking, Lilly pinches his tail, teaches him his numbers backward, and tells him, "If he was a number, he would be zero." Lilly spends a great deal of time in what her parents call "the uncooperative chair." But then Cousin Garland comes to visit and says Julius is disgusting. Suddenly Lilly has a complete change of heart.

Resources for Teaching
Picture Storybooks About the Everyday World of the Child

Author, Illustrator	Title	Description
Family Stories		
Carrie Best, Dale Gottlieb	*Taxi Taxi*	See text.
Jeannette Caines, Ron Himler	*Daddy*	Himler's illustrations capture the joy and delight that an African American little girl and her father feel for the one day a week they have together.
Judith Caseley	*Mama Coming and Going*	Mama is distracted by a new baby and doesn't know if she's coming or going. A warm and funny story about imperfections and affections.
Angela Johnson, David Soman	*Tell Me a Story, Mama*	See text.
Mavis Jukes, Lloyd Bloom	*Like Jake and Me*	Bloom's bold illustrations capture the strong personalities in a sensitive story about stepfather and son.
Patricia MacLachlan, Ruth Lercher Bornstein	*Mama One and Mama Two*	A foster child is reassured that she will be loved and cared for until her real mother recovers from her mental depression and the two of them can be together again.
John Steptoe	*Daddy Is a Monster . . . Sometimes*	Prismatic pictures capture the feelings and tension in a household where the single parent is a father.
Ann Turner, James-Graham Hale	*Through Moon and Stars and Night Skies*	Lovely, tender, but not sentimental watercolor pictures illustrate this story of a brave little boy coming to a strange land to his adoptive parents.
Sibling Rivalry		
Martha Alexander	*When the New Baby Comes, I'm Moving Out*	The anticipation of a new baby in the family is clearly expressed through words and humorous pictures.
Martha Alexander	*Nobody Asked Me If I Wanted a Baby Sister*	Indignant at all the attention the new baby receives, Oliver tries to give her away. Pictures show childlike, but real, feelings.
Eloise Greenfield, John Steptoe	*She Come Bringing Me That Little Baby Girl*	See text.
Elizabeth Starr Hill, Sandra Speidel	*Evan's Corner*	Evan takes a corner of his family's two-room apartment for his special place and then decides to help his brother fix up his own place.
Shirley Hughes	*Dogger*	See text.
Ezra Jack Keats	*Peter's Chair*	See text.
Jeanne Titherington	*A Place for Ben*	Ben invites his baby brother to come and play in his special place.
Mildred Pitts Walter, Pat Cummings	*My Mama Needs Me*	Bright illustrations show an African American older child's desire to be of help, as well as his resentment, when a baby sister arrives.
Relatives		
Eve Bunting, Donald Carrick	*The Wednesday Surprise*	For Dad's birthday surprise Anna teaches her grandmother to read by sharing books every Wednesday night when she comes to babysit.
John Burningham	*Granpa*	A moving story of the many experiences a little girl and her grandfather share and the changing relationship as the grandfather ages and finally dies.
Jeannette Caines, Pat Cummings	*Just Us Women*	Realistic illustrations detail the fun that African American women plan to have on their special trip to North Carolina in Aunt Martha's new car.

Resources for Teaching
Picture Storybooks About the Everyday World of the Child (continued)

Author, Illustrator	Title	Description
Judith Caseley	*Dear Annie*	Annie's grandfather celebrates his love for her through his many letters and postcards.
Tomie de Paola	*Watch Out for the Chicken Feet in Your Soup* *Nana Upstairs & Nana Downstairs* *Now One Foot, Now the Other Tom*	See text.
Helen Griffith, James Stevenson	*Grandaddy's Place* *Georgia Music*	See text.
Mary Hoffman, Caroline Binch	*Amazing Grace* *Boundless Grace*	Remarkably expressive watercolors help convey the story of an African American child whose mother and grandmother tell her she can be anything she wants to be, including Peter Pan in the school play. The sequel follows Grace to a visit with her father and his new family in Africa.
Patricia MacLachlan, Deborah Ray	*Through Grandpa's Eyes*	A tender story in which the grandson realizes that his blind grandfather has many ways of seeing.
Pat Mora, Cecily Lang	*Pablo's Tree*	Pablo's grandfather planted a tree when Pablo was born, and each year he decorates it as Pablo's special birthday surprise.
Susan Pearson, Ronald Himler	*Happy Birthday, Grampie*	Lovely realistic watercolors capture a moment of love when a little girl makes a very special birthday card that her blind grandfather can feel.
Patricia Polacco	*Thunder Cake*	See text.
Jama Kim Rattigan, Lillian Hsu-Flanders	*Dumpling Soup*	See text.
Eve Rice, Nancy Winslow Parker	*At Grammy's House*	Simple childlike illustrations seem just right for this cheerful book about two children who visit their French grandmother every week for Sunday dinner.
Cynthia Rylant, Stephen Gammell	*The Relatives Came*	See text.
Mary Stolz, Pat Cummings	*Storm in the Night*	See text.

Family History

Barbara Cooney	*Island Boy*	Stunning pictures portray seascapes and the family members who make up four generations of a New England family who settled on Tibbett's Island.
Barbara Cooney	*Hattie and the Wild Waves*	Cooney describes the affluent life of her mother growing up in Brooklyn and then Long Island while searching for her life's work.
Elizabeth Fitzgerald Howard, James Ransome	*Aunt Flossie's Hats (and Crab Cakes Later)*	See text.
Valerie Flournoy, Jerry Pinkney	*The Patchwork Quilt*	See text.

Resources for Teaching
Picture Storybooks About the Everyday World of the Child (continued)

Author, Illustrator	Title	Description
Ina Friedman, Allen Say	*How My Parents Learned to Eat*	Delicate watercolors illustrate a young girl's story about her parents' meeting. Her father, an American sailor, learned to eat with chopsticks in order to invite his future wife, a Japanese girl, out to dinner.
Riki Levinson, Diane Goode	*Watch the Stars Come Out*	Impressionistic watercolors detail the journey two young children made alone on a ship from Europe to their strange new home in America.
Margaree King Mitchell, James Ransome	*Uncle Jed's Barbershop*	See text.
Patricia Polacco	*The Keeping Quilt*	See text.

Familiar Experiences

Carol Carrick, Donald Carrick	*The Accident* *The Foundling*	See text.
Miriam Cohen, Lillian Hoban	*Will I Have a Friend?* *The New Teacher* *When Will I Read?* *Best Friends* and others	Illustrations of a multicultural first-grade classroom are as warm and reassuring as Jim's teachers and friendly classmates as they face the everyday worries of young children.
Paul B. Johnson and Celeste Lewis	*Lost*	A child never gives up hope that her lost dog will be found.
Ezra Jack Keats	*The Snowy Day* *Peter's Chair* *Whistle for Willie* and others	See text.
Robert McCloskey	*One Morning in Maine*	Sal announces her loose tooth to anyone who will listen. Story and illustrations show how important such changes are to young children.
John Steptoe	*Stevie*	Robert resents Stevie, who stays at their house every day while his mother goes to work, but he realizes that he misses him after he goes back to his family.
Judith Viorst, Ray Cruz	*Alexander and the Texrrible, Horrible, No Good, Very Bad Day* and others	Cruz's illustrations add to the wonderfully funny stories about the frustrations of being a kid.
Judith Viorst, Erik Blegvad	*The Tenth Good Thing About Barney*	The little black-and-white ink sketches by Erik Blegvad underscore the sincerity of this story of a boy's first experience with death.
Bernard Waber	*Ira Sleeps Over*	Illustrations reflect Ira's dilemma as he tries to decide if he will take his teddy bear to his first sleep over.
Vera Williams	*Something Special for Me* *A Chair for My Mother* *Music, Music for Everyone*	See text.

Books About Older People

Nancy White Carlstrom, Amy Schwartz	*Blow Me a Kiss, Miss Lilly*	Small, precise illustrations add to the appeal of this story of a friendship between a young child and a very old lady. After Lilly's death, young Sara remembers her in a special way.

Resources for Teaching
Picture Storybooks About the Everyday World of the Child (concluded)

Author, Illustrator	Title	Description
Mem Fox, Terry Denton	*Night Noises*	Strange noises can't wake Lily Laceby, who has drifted off to sleep. Finally the commotion wakes her, and she discovers that her family has come to wish her a happy birthday.
Mem Fox, Julie Vivas	*Wilfrid Gordon McDonald Partridge* *Our Granny*	See text.
Gloria Houston, Susan Condie Lamb	*My Great-Aunt Arizona*	See text.
Wendy Kesselman, Barbara Cooney	*Emma*	See text.
Barbara Cooney	*Miss Rumphius*	See text.
Jenny Wagner, Ron Brooks	*John Brown, Rose, and the Midnight Cat*	An amusing story about a dog who is jealous of his mistress's attention to a stray cat. Lovely landscapes place the story in Australia.
Margaret Wild, Julie Vivas	*The Very Best of Friends*	See text.

The Child's World of Nature

Author, Illustrator	Title	Description
Byrd Baylor, Peter Parnall	*Everybody Needs a Rock* *Your Own Best Secret Place* *The Other Way to Listen* *The Way to Start a Day*	See text.
Sheila Cole, Virginia Wright-Frierson	*When the Tide Is Low*	The illustrations provide watery seascapes and accurate pictures of sea animals and shells for this quiet story of a mother and daughter's delightful day.
Katherine Lasky, Mike Bostock	*Pond Year*	See text.
Joanne Ryder, Catherine Stock	*When the Woods Hum*	The hatching of seventeen-year cicadas is shared first between father and daughter and then between that daughter and her son seventeen years later.
Allen Say	*The Lost Lake*	Glowing watercolors portray the wilderness trip that a Japanese American father and his son take to a lost lake.
Mary Serfozo, Keiko Narahashi	*Rain Talk*	See text.
Uri Shulevitz	*Rain Rain Rivers*	Watercolors in greens and blues are the appropriate medium and colors for a book that expresses the mood of a rainy day in the city and the country.
Peter Spier	*Peter Spier's Rain*	All the dimensions of a rainstorm are included here—children's and animals' reactions, indoor and outdoor fun in the rain.
Alvin Tresselt, Roger Duvoisin	*White Snow, Bright Snow* *Hide and Seek Fog*	See text.
David Wiesner	*Hurricane*	Detailed watercolors capture all of the excitement of two boys waiting out a hurricane in their snug home.
Taro Yashima	*Umbrella*	See text.

Lilly is a real character wearing her queen's crown and red cowboy boots. She was first introduced in *Chester's Way*, a story of the friendship between Chester and Wilson and, finally, Lilly. The title character in Henkes's *Chrysanthemum* is another lively mouse who thinks her name is "absolutely perfect" until she goes to school and is teased about her long flower name. Mrs. Twinkle, the music teacher, saves the day and restores Chrysanthemum's love for her name. In Henkes's *Owen*, the title character must deal with an interfering neighbor, Mrs. Tweezers, who convinces Owen's parents that he is too old for his security blanket. Owen's mother finally comes up with a solution that allows Owen to keep his dignity *and* his security. These are real stories with genuinely humorous plots that appeal to adults as well as children. Henkes's illustrations provide additional details and are as clever as the text in these wonderful mouse stories.

The series of stories about a young pig by David McPhail delights young children. In *Pig Pig Grows Up*, a very overprotected pig refuses to grow up and act his age. His indulgent mother pushes him in a stroller and falls exhausted to the ground. When the stroller rolls downhill, Pig Pig acts swiftly and averts a crash into a baby buggy. Suddenly Pig Pig has grown up. In *Pig Pig Goes to Camp*, only the pictures reveal what camp is really like for Pig Pig. McPhail has also written a series of imaginative small books about a bear titled *The Bear's Toothache, Henry Bear's Park,* and *Stanley, Henry Bear's Friend*. These books have far more text than the Pig Pig series and appeal more to primary children. McPhail's illustrations are tremendously engaging and make Stanley and Henry Bear well worth knowing.

First graders faced with the (for some of them) formidable task of learning to read can sympathize with *Leo the Late Bloomer* by Robert Kraus. Leo, a baby tiger, can't do anything right; he can't read, write, or draw; he is a sloppy eater and never talks. His mother assures his father that Leo is a late bloomer. And she is right. Eventually, and in his own good time, Leo blooms! Stunning pictures by José Aruego add much to the humor of this story.

Children might also recognize a familiar situation in Erica Silverman's *Don't Fidget a Feather*. Gander and Duck are so full of self-adulation that they hold contests to see who is the best swimmer and who can fly the highest. When neither of these competitions has a clear winner, Duck suggests a freeze-in-place contest. Through many distractions they don't "fidget a feather," even when a fox takes the two back to his stew pot. When the fox prepares to cook Gander, however, Duck decides that winning the contest is not as important as saving Gander's life. S. D. Schindler's pastel drawings manage to maintain a state of high tension and add a note of realism to this story with its underlying note of conflict.

Petra Mathers creates appealing animal characters whose experiences will resonate with slightly older children. In *Sophie and Lou*, Sophie is a contemplative mouse who is also dreadfully shy. When a dance school is built across the street, she watches the goings-on from behind her curtain. She is so intrigued, however, that she gets up her courage and asks the librarian for a book on learning to dance and secretly follows the book as she continues to watch the dance class. Soon Sophie's confidence has grown, and she finds the perfect partner

S. D. Schindler shows that Gander and Duck won't let even hurricane-force winds interfere with their contest of wills in *Don't Fidget a Feather* by Erica Silverman.

in Lou, the gentleman mouse who has had his eye on her all along. *Victor and Christobel* are alligator characters who meet through more magical circumstances. Victor is a guard in an art museum and falls in love with the beautiful alligator lying on her sick bed in a painting. Christobel has been trapped in the painting by her evil magician cousin Anatole. As in other Mathers stories, true love wins all and Victor gets Christobel out of her frame-up. Visual references to real paintings and other pop culture icons add to the fun.

Modern Folktale Style

Perhaps Rudyard Kipling started the trend of writing modern folktales. The humor of his pourquoi tales, *Just So Stories*, is based on his wonderful use of words and his tongue-in-cheek asides to the reader. A favorite with children is *The Elephant Child*, the story of how a young elephant got his trunk. Originally his nose was no bigger than a bulgy boot. His "satiable curiosity" causes him all kinds of trouble and spankings. To find out what the crocodile has for dinner, he departs for the "banks of the great grey-green, greasy Limpopo River, all set about with fever-trees." Here he meets the crocodile, who whispers in his ear that today he will start his meal with the elephant's child! Then the crocodile grabs his nose and pulls and pulls. When the poor elephant is free, he has a trunk for a nose.

Some of these stories—such as *The Elephant's Child*, *How the Camel Got His Hump*, and *How the Leopard Got His Spots*—have been attractively illustrated in single picture-book editions by Jan Mogensen, Lorinda Cauley, Caroline Ebborn, and Quentin Blake. The language in these tales deserves to be heard read aloud by an enthusiastic teacher or librarian.

Tricky Tortoise, Lazy Lion, Hungry Hyena, and other stories written by Mwenye Hadithi have the sound and plot of the told tale. Tricky Tortoise, tired of being stepped on by the elephant, tells him his head (which the elephant can't see, of course) is "tiny and stupid." And then, by enlisting his look-alike brother, he proves he can jump over the elephant's head. Lazy Lion decides he needs a house for the rainy season, so he demands that the other animals and insects build him one. None of the houses they build suit him, so he still stands out on the plains in the sun and the rain. Hungry Hyena is so greedy that he tricks Fish Eagle out of a meal. He ends up chastened and minus his tail when the eagle tricks him in turn. And that is why, to this day, hyenas slink low to the ground and have no tails. Adrienne Kennaway's stunning watercolors portray stylized African plains and jungles.

Leo Lionni frequently writes modern folktales. His *Alexander and the Wind-Up Mouse* includes a purple pebble, a magic lizard, and a transformation. Alexander envies a wind-up mouse, Willie, and wants to become one himself. However, fortunes change and in order to save his friend, Alexander asks the magic lizard to make Willie a real mouse, just like Alexander. In *Frederick* Lionni creates his own version of the fable of the ant and the grasshopper, only this tale celebrates the contribution of Frederick, a mouse poet. The other mice bring in the harvest for the long winter, but Frederick does not work. He is gathering a harvest of sights and feelings. When the wind is cold and there is no food, Frederick shares his contribution of words and colors with his friends. He makes up poetry about the sun and the flowers and warms their souls. Lionni's statement about the role of the artist in society is direct and to the point.

Certain contemporary stories provide modern twists on well-loved tales and require a previous knowledge of the folktales. Steven Kellogg's retelling and illustrations for *Chicken Little* are very funny indeed. The story starts out with Chicken Little's famous warning that "The sky is falling" after she has been hit on the head by an acorn. Foxy Loxy hears the animals cry for the police and quickly changes his "poultry" truck sign to read "poulice." Thinking his Thanksgiving dinner is safely locked in the truck, he shows the foolish fowls the harmless acorn and tosses it up in the air. It gets caught in Sergeant Hippo Hefty's helicopter, which crashes to the earth, landing on the truck and freeing all the birds while Sergeant Hefty "flattens the fleeing fox." Foxy Loxy is sent to prison and Chicken Little plants the acorn. It grows into a fine tall tree by the side of her house, where her grandchildren come to hear her retell her famous story. Action-packed illustrations accompany this hilarious retelling of the Chicken Little story.

Other books take known characters or the bones of a traditional tale and flesh them out in new and intriguing ways. In Eugene Trivias's *The Three Little Wolves and the Big Bad Pig*, three wolf cubs go out into the world and build a house of bricks, only to have a mean pig attack it with a sledge hammer. Their next house, of concrete, is no match for the pig's pneumatic drill, and their metal bunker succumbs to his dynamite. Finally, they try a house of flowers. When the bad pig huffs to blow it down, he is transformed by the floral scents, and the four live happily ever after. This modern-day story about the power of aroma therapy is made all the more appealing through Helen Oxenbury's expressive characterizations.

Author Jon Scieszka and illustrator Lane Smith have great fun playing with traditional tales in *The True Story of the Three Little Pigs* and *The Stinky Cheese Man and Other Fairly Stupid Tales*. Their hilarious version of "The Three Pigs" is told from the wolf's point of view. His explanation is that he just wanted to borrow a cup of sugar to bake a cake for his old granny, when he accidentally sneezed and blew the pigs' houses down. It seemed like a shame to leave a perfectly good warm dinner lying there in the straw. So he eats one pig, and the second one too. He blames the whole bad rap on the reporters and the fact that when the third pig insulted his granny, he went berserk. Older students love this retelling, which easily invites them to write from a different point of view. In *The Stinky Cheese Man* the two turn ten familiar tales, such as "The Ugly Duckling," "Chicken Little," and "Jack and the Bean Stalk," inside out and upside down. They do the same thing and more with the format of the picture storybook, inserting the endpapers in the middle of the book, moving the table of contents to page 9, altering typeface, and changing size. Scieszka continues the silliness in *The Frog Prince Continued*, illustrated by Steve Johnson. Here he carries on from the traditional ending, "They lived happily ever after," to show that every marriage has its rocky places. The pictures by Steve Johnson are a fascinating mix of old and new that will appeal to students ages 8 and up.

As we have seen in Chapter 4, the nursery rhyme "The House That Jack Built" has provided many authors and illustrators with a model for inventive new versions. Will Hillenbrand's delightfully ghoulish illustrations for Judy Sierra's *The House That Drac Built* are scary enough to please the horror story crowd without sending them to bed with nightmares. As one might expect, the house that Drac built has a mummy, a manticore, and other monsters who precipitate a chain of events that is put to rights by a group of Halloween trick-or-treaters. In *The Book That Jack Wrote*, Jon Scieszka takes traditional nursery rhyme characters and creates a series of cause-and-effect events that will have readers wondering if they are coming or going. Daniel Adel manipulates the visual images in equally intriguing ways. Rather than looking like illustrations in a picture book, these framed paintings seem to hang on the page like pictures on a wall. But are these illusions or the real thing? Such questions will surely intrigue older readers.

One of children's favorite modern retellings involves a roundup of fairy tale characters on the postman's route in *The Jolly Postman* by Janet and Allan Ahlberg. In this rhymed tale, a postman delivers letters that readers can remove from real envelopes (which form the actual page), such as a letter of apology from Goldilocks to the Three Bears, a postcard from Jack to the Giant, and a business letter to the Wolf from the Three Pigs' lawyer representing the firm of Meany, Miny, Mo, and Company. This cleverly designed book synthesizes children's knowledge of folktales besides providing them a model for writing all kinds of letters and making them laugh in the process. (See "Fooling with Folktales, Fables, and Myths" in Chapter 14.)

In *The Book That Jack Wrote*, Jon Scieszka alters a familiar folk rhyme and illustrator Daniel Adel plays with visual reality.
From *The Book That Jack Wrote* by Jon Scieszka, illustrated by Dan Adel. Copyright © 1994 by Jon Scieszka. illustrations copyright © 1994 by Dan Adel. Used by permission of Viking Penguin, a division of Penguin Books USA Inc.

Humor

Young children's sense of fun is simple and obvious. Illustrations in picture storybooks often provide the humor that they might miss through words alone. Steven Kellogg is a master at drawing utter confusion and slapstick. A bored young girl gives her mother a deadpan account of the class trip to the farm in the hilarious story of *The Day Jimmy's Boa Ate the Wash* by Trinka Noble. The contrast between the girl's reporting of the events and the exuberant illustrations is extreme. The same approach is used in *Jimmy's Boa Bounces Back*, written and illustrated by the same team. The low-key narration is nicely balanced by the action-packed pictures. Kellogg has also produced many books of his own, which are equally funny. The tales of his own Great Dane in *Pinkerton, Behave!*, *A Rose for Pinkerton*, and *Prehistoric Pinkerton* provide the frame for his madcap pictures.

Martha is another indomitable dog who takes matters into her own paws in Susan Meddaugh's *Martha Speaks*. When Martha swallows a bowl of alphabet soup, the letters go straight to her brain and convert Woof to English. At first her family is delighted, but soon Martha won't shut up and becomes an embarrassment. Her talents are finally appreciated when she saves the family treasures from a burglar. Martha in turn learns to appreciate the finer points of conversational etiquette. Martha's adventures are continued in *Martha Calling*, when Martha again takes charge, this time of the family vacation.

Hally is the pet dog of the Tosis family; she has breath problems instead of language problems. Like Martha, she also encounters burglars in Dav Pilkey's extremely silly *Dog Breath*. It doesn't take a genius to figure out that she conquers the crooks not with words but with odors. When the family finds the thieves passed out cold as a result of Hally's big doggy kiss, they decide that living without Hally just wouldn't make any "scents." Both Meddaugh and Pilkey sustain much of the slapstick humor in their books through their droll illustrations as well as their wordplay. Two of Pilkey's other animal takeoffs, *Dogzilla* and *Cat Kong*, are illustrated with painted photo-collages and pay homage to their horror movie predecessors. Older children, especially those familiar with old movies, will find Pilkey's wit infectious.

Children also enjoy books about funny weird characters who appear in a series of stories. Seven- and 8-year-olds find the deadpan humor of Harry Allard's *The Stupids Die* very funny. When the lights go out, the Stupids decide that they have died. When the lights come back on, they think they are in heaven, until Grandpa sets them right: "This isn't Heaven—This is Cleveland." Children love to look for the visual jokes in the Stupids' house; for example, the framed picture of beach balls is labeled "The Pyramids" and one of a dog is titled "Fish." *The Stupids Have a Ball* and *The Stupids Step Out* are other titles in this series. James Marshall's lumpy figures seem just right for the Stupid family. Marshall has created his own funny friends in his many stories, such as *George and Martha*, about two large hippopotamuses. Each book contains about five episodes, which gives the feeling of a chapter book for 6- and 7-year-olds. The two hippo friends continue their antics in *George and Martha Tons of Fun*, *George and Martha Round and Round*, and *George and Martha Back in Town*.

Marc Brown's Arthur stories are equally popular and include a variety of animal characters. Arthur bears the brunt of a good deal of teasing in *Arthur's Nose* and *Arthur's Eyes* (when he must wear glasses). Never very brave, Arthur is seen as very courageous when he goes into a large spooky house on Halloween to find his baby sister in *Arthur's Halloween*. A surprise ending to *Arthur's Valentine* delights children, who have to guess the identity of his secret admirer. In *Arthur's Chicken Pox*, Arthur is afraid his spots will keep him from going on the annual family outing to the circus. All these Arthur books satisfy 6- and 7-year-olds' sense of humor and demand for poetic justice.

Another favorite character of children this age is Harry Allard and James Marshall's Miss Nelson, the lovely sweet teacher who cannot make the class behave. In *Miss Nelson Is Missing*, she is replaced by Miss Viola Swamp, who wears a dark black dress and is a witch, the

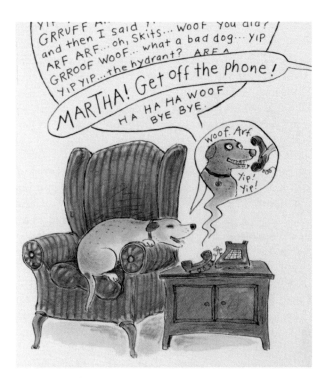

After Martha the dog swallows alphabet soup, her ability to communicate takes an unusual turn in Susan Meddaugh's *Martha Calling.*

children decide. After one week with Miss Swamp's rules and homework, the children are delighted to welcome Miss Nelson back. At home Miss Nelson takes off her coat and hangs it right next to an ugly black dress. Viola Swamp returns to coach the worst team in the state in *Miss Nelson Has a Field Day*. Readers will be delighted with the coach's ugly black sweatshirt, which reads "Coach and Don't You Forget It." Children will have to solve the puzzle of how Miss Nelson and her alter ego can be in the same place at the same time.

Young children are masters at exaggeration, so they appreciate the humor of the tall tale. James Stevenson's *Could Be Worse!* is titled after Grandpa's laconic comment on anything that ever happened to anyone. One day Grandpa hears Mary Ann asking Louie why Grandpa always says the same thing, and Louie says it is probably because nothing very interesting ever happened to him. The next morning Grandpa tells the children a tall tale that is unsurpassed, and their comment is most predictable: "Could be worse." Stevenson continues Grandpa's epic adventures, recounting the dreadful things that his baby brother did in *Worse Than Willy!* and Grandpa's Halloween experiences in *That Terrible Halloween Night*. It is hard ever to get the best of

Grandpa! Stevenson's watercolor and cartoon-style illustrations are as funny as his tales. For example, he always pictures young Grandpa and his baby brother, Wainey, with moustaches. Children can't seem to hear enough of Grandpa's tall tales.

Fantasy

The line is blurred between humorous picture stories for children and fanciful ones. Talking beasts and modern spin-offs on folktales are certainly fanciful stories, yet they can be very humorous. However, children appear to see a difference between the make-believe story and the funny one.

John Burningham contrasts daydreams with reality in his books *Come Away from the Water, Shirley* and *Time to Get Out of the Bath, Shirley*. The first book has already been described in this chapter. In the second one, Shirley is taking a bath while her mother busies herself in the bathroom, admonishing Shirley most of the time for being so messy. Meanwhile, Shirley, in her imagination, shown in richly colored dream pictures, has ridden her duck down the drain and out onto a wide river. The contrast between Shirley's vivid imagination and her mother's preoccupation with mundane matters is very funny indeed. The endpapers of this book also deserve mention, as they combine pipes and sewers with all of Shirley's adventures. Burningham uses this same technique in his wonderful story *John Patrick Norman McHennessy—The Boy Who Was Always Late*, about a boy whose teacher never believes his improbable excuses. The pictures of John's adventures are in full color, while the school punishments are in black and white. This book is a natural to compare with the well-known *And to Think That I Saw It on Mulberry Street* by Dr. Seuss.

Imaginary trips are a common theme in picture storybooks. In Arthur Dorros's *Abuela* and *Isla*, discussed previously, Rosalba and her grandmother visit favorite places in the city and Abuela's island home by flying over them. In Faith Ringgold's *Tar Beach*, Cassie Louise Lightfoot has a dream to be free, to go anywhere she wants. One night up on Tar Beach, the rooftop of her family's Harlem apartment building, her dream comes true. Cassie can fly over the city. This magical story was originally written by Ringgold for a story quilt of the same name.

In *How to Make Apple Pie and See the World* by Marjorie Priceman, an ordinary recipe for apple pie is made extraordinary when the grocery store is closed and the young heroine must seek the ingredients at their origin. She travels to Italy for semolina wheat, to Sri Lanka for cinnamon, to Jamaica for sugar, and so on.

Not content with their own backyard, two Holsteins dance on the moon in Barry Root's illustrations for Toby Speed's *Two Cool Cows*.
From *Two Cool Cows* by Toby Speed, illustrated by Barry Root. Copyright © 1995 by The Putnam & Grosset Group, New York, NY. Reprinted by permission.

The childlike paintings echo the narrator's voice and make a nice model for researching and writing other imaginary cooking trips.

Toby Speed has imagined an out-of-this-world adventure in *Two Cool Cows*. Millie and Maude, two Holsteins, break the contented-cow stereotype in their sunglasses and black boots. They are ready for high jinks as they travel to the other side of the moon, where vacationing bovines picnic on buttercups and columbine and dance the bunny hop. Called back to Earth by the four Huckabuck kids, whose boots they have borrowed, the cows are just in time for one last fling. Children will find the wordplay in Speed's text as amusing as Barry Root's lively paintings.

In the story *George Shrinks* by William Joyce, George dreams he is small and wakes to find it is true. He discovers a note from his parents listing his chores. The words of the note become the text of the story; the illustrations show how George deals with each task. He uses a sponge to surf across the dishes as he cleans them. He has a wonderful time flying in a model airplane until it is knocked down by the cat. Suddenly George is his own size again, with his parents at his side, but as in so many other fantasies, he has the damaged plane to remind him of the adventure and to make readers wonder if maybe it really did happen.

Another popular book by Joyce is *Dinosaur Bob and His Adventures with the Family Lazardo*. Bob is discovered while the family is on a safari in Africa. They bring him home by boat and train. Bob can scare off burglars, dance, and play baseball. The latter talent saves the day for the Pimlico Pirates and Bob. In Joyce's *A Day with Wilbur Robinson*, one weird thing after another happens. Wilbur greets his friend at the door while an octopus takes his bag, Aunt Billie is playing with her life-size train set, cousin Pete is walking the cats (which are tigers), and Uncle Gaston is sitting in the family cannon—and that's just the beginning. There is no plot, just strange incongruities that will intrigue some children.

Another form of young children's fantasy involves anthropomorphism, or the personification of inanimate objects, such as toys and machines. Most children know and love Watty Piper's story *The Little Engine That Could* and Hardie Gramatky's story *Little Toot*. Most of the books written by Virginia Lee Burton contain personification: *Katie and the Big Snow*, *The Little House*, and *Mike Mulligan and His Steam Shovel*. The modern problem of obsolescence is solved easily in the story of Mike and his beloved steam shovel, Mary Ann. After proving that Mary Ann could dig a basement for the new town hall in a day, Mike is forced to convert her into a furnace, since he has neglected to plan a way for Mary Ann to get out of the excavation. Katie is a snowplow who saves the day by plowing out a whole village. The encroachment of the city on the country is portrayed in Burton's classic story *The Little House*, about a house that stands on the hill and watches day and night as the seasons pass. Gradually a road is built and cars come, and soon the city grows up around the little house. Elevated cars speed by her; subway trains speed under her; and people rush to and fro in front of her. One day the great-great-granddaughter of the original owner sees the little house, buys her, and has her moved back to the country where she can once again see the stars.

Several picture books personify toys and dolls. In *The Tub People* and *The Tub Grandfather*, Pam Conrad tells the story of seven wooden toys, including a father, mother, grandmother, boy, dog, doctor, and policeman. Perhaps more than any other picture books, these show the helplessness of dolls. In *The Tub People* the little tub boy is sucked down the drain and the other tub people

Brian Selznick gives a party-planning doll an uncommon personality in Pam Conrad's *Doll Face Has a Party*.
Illustrations copyright © 1994 by Brian Selznick. Used by permission of HarperCollins Publishers, New York, NY.

no longer smile or wink at each other. When the plumber finally finds him, the tub people are all removed to a shelf in a bedroom. They line up the same way they always had on the edge of the tub, but each morning the little tub boy person is found between his parents, their sides just barely touching. *The Tub Grandfather*, missing for years, is found sleeping under the radiator. The family members attempt to revive him, with happy results. Richard Egielski's detailed watercolors show the tub people as rounded wooden dolls—or are they? In Conrad's *Doll Face Has a Party*, Doll Face clearly is a doll. As she makes preparations for a tea party, her expression never changes, her porcelain fingers never move, and her legs hang in impossible positions when she sits on a chair. However, Brian Selznick's illustrations animate this character and bring the story to life through the use of bizarre close-ups and unusual points of view.

There are many editions of Margery Williams's sentimental classic *The Velveteen Rabbit: Or How Toys Become Real*. The most attractive ones are those illustrated by Michael Hague, Ilse Plume, and David Jorgensen. Any child who has loved a stuffed animal of her own will understand the conversation between the old skin horse and the velveteen rabbit on the subject of becoming real.

Today there might be more stories about monsters than there are about toys and dolls. Pat Hutchins's monster books present a family that is monstrously delightful. Sibling rivalry is the theme of Hutchins's *The Very Worst Monster*. When Billy monster was born, Billy's sister Hazel is afraid she won't be the worst child in the family anymore. Every time Billy does something awful, Hazel does something even worse. No one notices—until Hazel gives her baby brother away, thereby achieving her goal. In *Where's the Baby?* mother monster, grandmother monster, and Hazel (sister monster) all search for the baby. All they can find are clues to where he had been by the monstrous messes he left behind. At last they find him safe in bed—but not for long. Hutchins's green-colored monsters live in very cozy, well-furnished houses.

Chris Van Allsburg is certainly the best-known creator of fantasy in children's picture storybooks. *Jumanji* has been discussed previously. *The Garden of Abdul Gasazi* was Van Allsburg's first book. Children are intrigued with the stark black-and-white pictures portraying the strange garden and huge house of the magician. The puzzling ending of the story gives them much to discuss. *Two Bad Ants* provides a useful perspective on another point of view. The ending for *The Wreck of the Zephyr* is another of Van Allsburg's puzzles. Superb full-color pictures illustrate this fantasy of the one time a boat could fly. The identity of the title character (who might be a relative of Jack Frost) is never fully revealed in the mysterious tale *The Stranger*. *The Polar Express* by Van Allsburg is a haunting Christmas story for all children and for those who remain children at heart. This picture storybook richly deserved the Caldecott Medal it received. In *Just a Dream*, Van Allsburg predicts the kind of future we are going to have if we keep polluting the earth. *The Wretched Stone* is another message book that suggests the evils of watching television. In *The Sweetest Fig* a little dog receives poetic justice after years of mistreatment by a despicable dentist, while in *The Widow's Broom* the title character needs a little help from the Widow Shaw to overcome its tormentors. In *Bad Day at Riverbend*, Van Allsburg is at his artistic best. In this story a mysterious light appears over the town of Riverbend, and a slimy substance begins to attack people, beasts, and countryside. The brave sheriff rides out after the villain in the best Hollywood tradition, but unlike Wyatt Earp, he doesn't save the day. In this book Van Allsburg creates an intellectual puzzle and challenges our visual thinking. He has become so well known for his highly three-dimensional style and his dramatic use of contrasting values that it is a shock to see his flat linear drawings in this book that resemble coloring book art. That is all part of the fun, of course, and once

Chris Van Allsburg combines visual styles to manipulate reality in *Bad Day at Riverbend*.

again Van Allsburg presents us with a stimulating visual and verbal puzzle. See Resources for Teaching, "Picture Storybooks About the Child's Imaginary World," for a list of many picture storybooks exploring children's imaginary experiences.

Appreciating Cultural Diversity

American children of the twenty-first century will need to develop a worldview that appreciates the richness of other cultures at the same time as they preserve and celebrate their uniqueness. In this text we integrate multiracial and ethnic stories throughout chapters just as we would hope they will be used in schools. A global view requires books about other cultures and countries that children may not be able to visit. Fortunately, we have an increasing number of titles of both nonfiction and fiction that will introduce children to others who share this earth.

Resources for Teaching
Picture Storybooks About the Child's Imaginary World

Author, Illustrator	Title	Description
Animals as People		
Jean de Brunhoff	*The Story of Babar*	Well-loved stories about an elephant king and his friends and family. Continued in sequels by de Brunhoff's son, Laurent.
Roger Duvoisin	*Petunia*	A silly goose thinks she has acquired wisdom when she finds a book but does not know that it is important to learn to read what is in the book.
Mem Fox, Pamela Lofts	*Koala Lou*	A little koala bear feels neglected when new brothers and sisters arrive, and she tries to win her mother's attention. Her mother assures her that she always has, and always *will*, love her.
Don Freeman	*Dandelion*	The story of a lion who becomes such a "dandy" in order to go to a party that his hostess does not recognize him and shuts the door in his face.
Kevin Henkes	*Julius, the Baby of the World* *Chester's Way* *Chrysanthemum* *Owen*	See text.
Russell Hoban, Garth Williams	*Bedtime for Frances* and other Frances stories	Frances is an engaging, uproariously funny badger who mirrors the behavior of young children.
Pat Hutchins	*Good-Night, Owl!*	A beautifully designed book about a poor owl who is kept awake by noisy animals during the day and then gets his revenge at night.
Robert Kraus, José Aruego	*Leo the Late Bloomer*	See text.
Robert Kraus, José Aruego and Ariane Dewey	*Owliver* *Milton the Early Riser*	More charming animal stories.
Petra Mathers	*Sophie and Lou*	See text.
David McKee	*Elmer*	Lovely story about a patchwork-colored elephant who wanted to be gray like all the other elephants.
David McPhail	*Pig Pig Grows Up* *Pig Pig Goes to Camp* *The Bear's Toothache* *Henry Bear's Park* *Stanley, Henry Bear's Friend*	See text.
Else Minarik, Maurice Sendak	Little Bear series	The illustrations are in perfect harmony with the tone of these gentle stories about a little Victorian bear and his family.
H. A. Rey	*Curious George*	A comical monkey has one escapade after another, but the man in the yellow hat always manages to save him from real danger.
Dr. Seuss	*Horton Hatches the Egg* *Thidwick, the Big-Hearted Moose*	These two are among the many wonderfully original stories by a favorite author of young children.
Gabrielle Vincent	*Ernest and Celestine* and other stories	The humorous stories of mouse-child Celestine and her adventures with a warm, understanding, avuncular bear named Ernest. Delicate expressive watercolors beautifully convey these characters.
Bernard Waber	*The House on East 88th Street* *Lyle, Lyle Crocodile*	Lyle, a performing crocodile, lives happily with the Pimm family in several comic stories.

Resources for Teaching
Picture Storybooks About the Child's Imaginary World (continued)

Author, Illustrator	Title	Description
Rosemary Wells	*Noisy Nora* *Shy Charles* *Stanley and Rhoda*	See text.

Modern Folktale Style

Author, Illustrator	Title	Description
Janet and Allan Ahlberg	*The Jolly Postman*	See text.
Raymond Briggs	*Jim and the Beanstalk*	A sequel to "Jack and the Beanstalk."
Stephanie Calmenson, Denise Brunkus	*The Principal's New Clothes*	Hysterically funny modern-day version of "The Emperor's New Clothes."
Mem Fox, Julie Vivas	*Possum Magic*	Grandma Poss and Hush set off on what becomes a culinary visit of the cities of Australia to find the proper magic food to turn Hush from invisible to visible.
Mwenye Hadithi, Adrienne Kennaway	*Tricky Tortoise* *Lazy Lion* *Hungry Hyena*	See text.
Steven Kellogg	*Chicken Little*	See text.
Ken Kesey, Barry Moser	*Little Tricker the Squirrel Meets Big Double the Bear*	A wonderful tall tale of how a little squirrel bamboozles a grizzly bear.
Rudyard Kipling, various illustrators	*How the Camel Got His Hump* *The Elephant's Child* *How the Leopard Got His Spots*	See text.
Leo Lionni	*Alexander and the Wind-Up Mouse* *Frederick*	See text.
Arnold Lobel	*Fables*	These modern fables include a pirouetting camel in a tutu and an elephant reading the *Daily Trumpet*.
Mary Rayner	*Mr. and Mrs. Pig's Evening Out* *Garth Pig and the Ice Cream Lady* *Mrs. Pig's Bulk Buy*	A family of pigs outsmarts the wicked wolf at every funny turn.
Jon Scieszka	*The True Story of the Three Little Pigs* *The Frog Prince Continued* *The Stinky Cheese Man*	See text.
Judy Sierra, Will Hillenbrand	*The House That Drac Built*	See text.
William Steig	*Sylvester and the Magic Pebble* *The Amazing Bone* *Doctor DeSoto* *Brave Irene* *Shrek!* *Zeke Pippin*	Steig continues to enchant children with his superbly written stories and appealing illustrations.
Eugene Trivias, Helen Oxenbury	*The Three Little Wolves and the Big Bad Pig*	See text.
Nancy Van Laan, George Booth	*Possum Come A-Knockin'*	Booth's wry cartoons illustrate this silly story about a little old possum just trying to have fun.

Resources for Teaching
Picture Storybooks About the Child's Imaginary World (continued)

Author, Illustrator	Title	Description
Brian Wildsmith	*The Owl and the Woodpecker*	A troublesome woodpecker keeps the owl awake all day with his loud drumming, but saves him when Owl's tree blows down in a storm.
Brian Wildsmith	*Python's Party*	A beautiful example of double trickery in this story about a wily python.

Humorous Picture Storybooks

Author, Illustrator	Title	Description
Harry Allard and James Marshall, James Marshall	*Miss Nelson Is Missing* *Miss Nelson Has a Field Day*	See text.
Harry Allard, James Marshall	*The Stupids Die* *The Stupids Have a Ball* *The Stupids Step Out*	See text.
Judi Barrett, Ron Barrett	*Animals Should Definitely Not Wear Clothing* *Animals Should Definitely Not Act Like People*	Children love the visual ridiculousness of animals garbed in highly inappropriate clothing.
Marc Brown	*Arthur's Chicken Pox* and other Arthur stories	See text.
Beatrice Schenk de Regniers, Beni Montresor	*May I Bring a Friend?*	Slapstick and nonsense are the order of the day.
Steven Kellogg	*Pinkerton, Behave!* and other stories	See text.
Margaret Mahy, Jonathan Allen	*The Great White Man-Eating Shark*	Norvin, a boy who looks rather like a shark, takes to swimming with a dorsal fin strapped to his back. He has the beach to himself until a female shark falls in love with him.
James Marshall	George and Martha stories	See text.
Susan Meddaugh	*Martha Speaks* *Martha Calling*	See text.
Trinka Noble, Steven Kellogg	*The Day Jimmy's Boa Ate the Wash* *Jimmy's Boa Bounces Back*	See text.
Tom Paxton, Steven Kellogg	*Engelbert the Elephant*	The illustrations are as uproarious as the antics of the guests when Engelbert crashes the queen's party.
Dav Pilkey	*Dog Breath*	See text.
James Stevenson	*Could Be Worse!* *That Terrible Halloween Night* *What's Under My Bed?* *Worse Than Willy!* *That Dreadful Day* *Grandpa's Too-Good Garden*	Children appreciate the humor of Grandpa's exaggerated tall tales. Stevenson's watercolor and cartoon-style illustrations are as funny as his stories.

Fantasy in Picture Storybooks

Author, Illustrator	Title	Description
John Burningham	*Come Away from the Water, Shirley* *Time to Get Out of the Bath, Shirley* *John Patrick Norman McHennessy—The Boy Who Was Always Late*	See text.

Resources for Teaching
Picture Storybooks About the Child's Imaginary World (concluded)

Author, Illustrator	Title	Description
Virginia Lee Burton	*Katie and the Big Snow* *The Little House* *Mike Mulligan and His Steam Shovel*	See text.
Pam Conrad, Richard Egielski	*The Tub People* *The Tub Grandfather*	See text.
Pam Conrad, Brian Selznick	*Doll Face Has a Party*	See text.
Robert Crowe	*Clyde Monster*	Clyde is afraid to go to bed because people might be hiding in his cave.
Don Freeman	*Corduroy*	A completely satisfying story of a plush-toy bear who waits patiently in the department store for someone to buy him.
Pat Hutchins	*The Very Worst Monster* *Where's the Baby?*	See text.
William Joyce	*George Shrinks* *Dinosaur Bob and His Adventures with the Family Lazardo* *A Day with Wilbur Robinson*	See text. See text. See text.
Maira Kalman	*Max Makes a Million* *Ooh La La, Max in Love* *Max in Hollywood*	The wacky adventures of Max, a dog, a poet, and a dreamer.
Leah Komaiko	*My Perfect Neighborhood*	A young girl describes her walk down the wackiest street in the world.
Rafe Martin, Stephen Gammell	*Will's Mammoth*	Wonderful action-filled pictures capture this joyous imaginary adventure of Will and his very own mammoth.
Mercer Mayer	*There's a Nightmare in My Closet*	A small boy who is afraid of the dark ends up comforting a monster who has a nightmare.
Marjorie Priceman	*How to Make Apple Pie and See the World*	See text.
Faith Ringgold	*Tar Beach*	See text.
Toby Speed, Barry Root	*Two Cool Cows*	See text.
Chris Van Allsburg	*Jumanji* *The Garden of Abdul Gasazi* *Bad Day at Riverbend* *Two Bad Ants* *The Wreck of the Zephyr* *The Stranger* *The Polar Express* *Just a Dream* *The Wretched Stone*	See text.
Margery Williams, Michael Hague, Ilse Plume, David Jorgensen	*The Velveteen Rabbit*	See text.

Holly Keller captures the essence of Vietnamese culture in her illustrations for *Grandfather's Dream*.
Illustration by Holly Keller from her *Grandfather's Dream*. Copyright © 1994 by Holly Keller. By permission of Greenwillow Books, a division of William Morrow & Company, Inc.

Galimoto is titled after a popular toy car that boys in Malawi, Africa, make out of scraps of wire. In this story by Karen Williams, Kondi, a resourceful 7-year-old boy, is determined to make one. He persists in finding enough wire and finally constructs what looks like a pickup truck from scraps and bits he has scavenged from various places. Vibrant watercolors by Catherine Stock portray this ingenious young boy and reflect her weeks spent sketching in Malawi. Stock has also told and illustrated the story of another African child in *Where Are You Going, Manyoni?* Manyoni wakes early. After breakfast, when the sun is just rising, she sets out on a journey. She travels past the baobab tree, across a ridge, under the wild fig trees, past the malala palms, through the fever-tree pan, over the place where impala feed beside the red sandstone, above the dam, and on and on until finally, when the sun is high over the veld, she arrives at the end of her journey. She has come to school. The lovely watercolor illustrations give us an education while Manyoni travels to hers. We learn about the flora and fauna of Zimbabwe and come to appreciate the very real effort children like Manyoni must make to get an education.

In Florence Parry Heide and Judith Heide Gilliland's *The Day of Ahmed's Secret*, Ahmed, a young *butagaz* boy in Cairo, Egypt, makes his daily rounds through sun-bleached streets and daily market stalls to deliver cooking oil. Ahmed hugs a special secret to his heart. Home, at last, he can finally show his newly acquired skill to his family: Ahmed has learned how to write his name. In *Sami and the Time of the Troubles* Heide and Gilliland tell of a young boy who must struggle to maintain a normal life during the war in Lebanon. In both books, Ted Lewin's realistic watercolors capture the sounds and sights of these two countries and visually convey the emotional power of the two stories.

In Holly Keller's *Grandfather's Dream*, the war in Vietnam is over and Nam's family is rebuilding their lives. As the rice fields are replanted, Grandfather hopes that the beautiful Saurus cranes will return to nest in the wetlands. Some of the villagers think the land should be used for planting and not set aside for wildlife. Keller's lovely watercolors evoke the patterns of Vietnamese art and convey the beauty of the rural setting. Although the book has a happy ending, in reality the Vietnamese are still waiting for the cranes to return.

Keller is honest about the dilemmas that face a community that has been torn apart by war.

Ann Grifalconi illustrated her *Osa's Pride* with brilliant pastels on variously colored papers. Osa is proud, just a little too proud to make friends with the rest of the children in her Cameroon village. Her grandmother tells her a story about another proud girl, using her storytelling cloth. As her grandmother unrolls the scenes, Osa learns as much about herself as about the girl in the story. In *Darkness and the Butterfly,* the Wise Woman helps Osa learn to overcome her fear of the dark. Grifalconi is also the author-illustrator of the well-known story *The Village of Round and Square Houses.* Her illustrations glow with the beauty of the African world and the affection of a nurturing family.

Grifalconi has also illustrated Lynn Joseph's *Jasmine's Parlour Day,* a warm family story set in Trinidad. Jasmine looks forward to helping her mother sell fish and sugar cakes at their own wooden "parlour" at a roadside market on Maracas Bay, but she also loves the hustle and bustle of the noises and neighbors they find there. Joseph's text captures the sounds of the island just as Grifalconi's bright paintings evoke the sunny setting.

In Lulu Delacre's *Vejigante Masquerader,* Ramón prepares for the important Puerto Rican carnival that is celebrated during all of February. He has saved for, and sewn, his own costume so that he can dress up and join the festivities. More important, he hopes to be asked to be part of the group of older boys whom he idolizes. Delacre's dual-language story and her watercolor paintings convey a warm understanding of family and community spirit and the persistence of one determined little boy.

A mother shares stories of her growing up in Jamaica with her little daughter, Rose, in *The Chalk Doll* by Charlotte Pomerantz. She describes the wonderful fun she had playing with the things she made herself, such as her rag doll. Rose in her rich American environment feels deprived because, while she has had many chalk dolls, she has never had a rag doll. And so together they make one. Frané Lessac's brightly colored paintings show the contrast between Rose's childhood and her mother's.

Riki Levinson has told a more serious story of the families who lived on the boats in Hong Kong harbor in *Our Home Is the Sea.* The boy journeys from his school through the bustling city down to his family's houseboat. He can't wait for the day when he too will be a fisherman. Dennis Luzak's handsome oil paintings portray the huge gray city of Hong Kong and the boat the boy calls home. Eve Bunting has written a moving story of the flight of a Cuban family to America in their very small boat. These people are pilgrims in their search for freedom, so Bunting titled her story *How Many Days to America? A Thanksgiving Story.*

Chicken Man by Michelle Edwards describes the rotation of work that is characteristic of some of the kibbutzim in Israel. The chicken man, Rody, is so happy doing his work that everyone wants his job. But then Rody is cheerful about ironing and gardening. Finally, when the chickens stop laying, Rody is assigned to work permanently in the chicken house and he couldn't be happier. A map of Kibbutz Hanan gives children a picture of the size of this community and the way the kibbutzniks live. The joy the chicken man takes in all his jobs is worthy of discussion.

In the *Very Last First Time,* Jan Andrews gives us a picture of life in the Inuit village of Ungava Bay in northern Canada. This is a special day for Eva Padlyat, for she is going to go alone below the sea ice and gather mussels. Eva is so intrigued with all she sees that she nearly doesn't make it back up before the tide comes in again. When at last she is safe with her mother, she says, "That was my very last *first* time for walking alone on the bottom of the sea." Ian Wallace's full-color illustrations picture an Inuit family, with their modern-day kitchen but still gathering food in the traditional manner.

Rachel Isadora tells of a joyful reunion in *At the Crossroads.* A young boy tells how he, his brother and sister, and his friends wait all day and all night for their fathers to come home after ten months of working in the mines in South Africa. Underneath their anticipation and joy is the terrible injustice of apartheid that kept families separated for such a long time. Glowing double-page watercolors contrast the swirling colors of the children's clothing and the red of the sun with the somber grayness of the corrugated iron shacks the children live in. This simple story of joy reveals the cruelty of prejudice in a way that could be discussed with children of all ages.

Naomi Shihab Nye makes connections between two countries half a world apart in *Sitti's Secret.* Back home in America, after a trip to Palestine, Mona recalls her experiences and thinks about Sitti, her grandmother who lives on the West Bank. Although the two speak different languages and have very different ways of life, they are joined by universal bonds of family feeling and the wish for peace. Like the secrets Sitti hears her lemon tree whisper each morning, Nancy Carpenter's illustrations have secrets, too. Maps, pieces of fabric, and photographs of cityscapes, desert mountains, and the planets form the background for the textured paintings of Mona and Sitti's world and reinforce the connections these two share.

Nigel Gray contrasts the story of two children, one black, one white, who wake, sleep, play, eat, and share in family life on opposite sides of the globe. The fascinating contrast between an African boy in his village and a Western child in his suburb is made clear by Philippe Dupasquier's detailed illustrations for *A Country Far Away.*

Nancy Carpenter's collages and pencil drawings speak of the special intimacy that unites a grandmother and granddaughter in Naomi Shihab Nye's *Sitti's Secret*.
Reprinted with permission of Simon & Schuster Books for Young Readers from *Sitti's Secret* by Naomi Shihab Nye, illustrated by Nancy Carpenter. Illustrations copyright © 1994 Nancy Carpenter.

This story could lead to much discussion of the contrast between wealthy Western countries and those of the third world. Children need to develop a world vision at an early age.

Social and Environmental Concerns

As more and more picture storybooks are written for older children, more are dealing with major social and environmental concerns.

Eve Bunting's moving story *Fly Away Home* tells of a homeless boy and his father who live in a large airport, moving from terminal to terminal and trying never to be noticed. A trapped bird who finally manages to fly free becomes the boy's metaphor for hope. Ronald Himler's watercolors are as understated and honest as this story. In *Uncle Willie and the Soup Kitchen* by DyAnne DiSalvo-Ryan, a young boy goes with his uncle who volunteers at a soup kitchen. They stop and pick up chickens at the butcher shop. Then the boy meets the other volunteers and helps set tables for "the guests" as Uncle Willie calls them. Uncle Willie is a wonderful model as he stands at the door and greets the guests and shares his zest for living. The warm, sensitive story and pictures were inspired by the author's own experience as a soup kitchen volunteer.

In *The Auction* by Jan Andrews, Todd's grandfather has to sell his farm. Both of them recall happier days when Todd's grandmother was living and the farm was thriving. Remembering the different kind of scarecrows she used to make, they cheer themselves up by making straw people for the combine and rocking chair. Yet both are dreading the inevitable auction the next day.

Several books portray the wrenching changes that often occur in the name of progress. In Jane Yolen's *Letting Swift River Go*, the change is bittersweet. Barbara Cooney's lovely transparent watercolors portray the landscapes that will remain in memory long after a little girl's community is drowned beneath the reservoir created by a new dam. She realizes in the end that although she has lost a physical place, she has not lost the stories of that place. In *Shaker Lane*, Alice and Martin Provensen describe the people and the shacks they lived in alongside Shaker Lane. Yet these people also formed a community of their own until the new reservoir was built and flooded it forever. What was left of Shaker Lane became Reservoir Road with beautiful suburban homes and swimming pools.

Ann Turner's *Heron Street* provides a tale of so-called progress from wilderness to the arrival of settlers, the Revolutionary War, and the coming of houses, gaslights, cars, trolleys, and airplanes. One night a heron circles the house and flies higher and higher, "its legs like a long, thin good-bye." Lisa Desimini's jewel-like paintings perfectly complement this progression of change. Jeannie Baker's collage pictures for *Where the Forest Meets the Sea* combine both the past and the future. As the young boy explores the forest, shadows of dinosaurs can be seen in the trees; and on the last page, shadows of a future Star Hotel, skyscrapers, homes, and swimming pools are superimposed on the picture of the beach and bay. *Window*, also by Jeannie Baker, is a wordless book that depicts the view from a boy's window changing from wilderness, to country, to small town, to city. The boy, now 25 and with a baby of his own, looks through a window in his new house in the country and sees an ominous sign advertising "House blocks for sale," suggesting that the whole destructive cycle will continue. Other books previously discussed, such as Van Allsburg's *Just a Dream* and Allen Say's *The Lost Lake*, also have an environmental theme.

A story with a happier outcome is Lynne Cherry's *A River Ran Wild*. This stunning book details the history of the Nashua River in New Hampshire. Beginning long ago when the river ran so clear that its pebbled bottom was visible, Cherry shows how the ecology of the river gradually changed as the land was colonized and then industrialized. Eventually the river became so badly polluted that nothing lived in it. However, a community campaign led by one determined woman reversed this terrible decline and the river became a thriving ecosystem once again. The book is a model for action in other

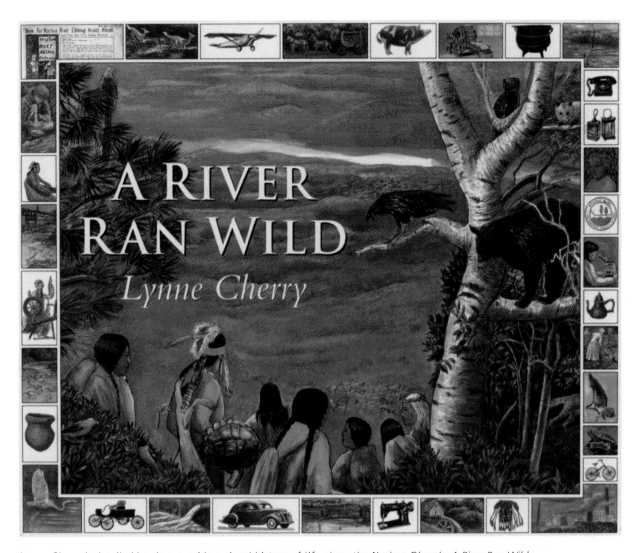

Lynne Cherry's detailed borders provide a visual history of life along the Nashua River in *A River Ran Wild.*
Illustration from *A River Ran Wild,* copyright © 1992 by Lynne Cherry, reproduced by permission of Harcourt Brace & Company.

communities, and Cherry's illustrations, and her detailed borders showing wildlife and other artifacts from various eras, will invite children to create similar social and ecological histories.

War and Its Aftermath

Art can portray the devastation of war in ways that mere words cannot. Picture storybooks that tell of effects of war in times past and present may help a new generation to bring about a peaceful future. Patricia Polacco's *Pink and Say* is a tremendously moving book based on events that happened to her great-grandfather during the American Civil War. Sheldon Russell Curtis was a young white Union soldier badly wounded in Georgia and left to die when he was found by young

Pinkus Aylee, an African American soldier. Pink risks his life to take Sheldon, or Say, to his mother, Moe Moe, who nurses him at great danger to herself. As he recuperates, the two share family stories and memories of the war. Say tells the two of shaking President Lincoln's hand before the Battle of Bull Run. Before they can get to safety, however, southern marauders kill Moe Moe, and on their way to rejoin their units, Pink and Say are captured by Confederate soldiers. In their last moments together, Pink reaches out to touch Say's hand, the hand that touched Mr. Lincoln. An afterword tells that Say survived (barely) the terrible Andersonville prison and that Pink was hanged. Polacco meant the book to serve as a written memory since Pinkus had no descendants to preserve it for him.

My Hiroshima by Junko Morimoto describes Junko's life before the war and immediately after the atomic

A close-up of two hands is a particularly moving climax to Patricia Polacco's *Pink and Say*.

From *Pink and Say*, by Patricia Polacco. Copyright © 1994 by The Putnam & Grosset Group, New York, NY. Reprinted by permission.

bomb was dropped. She was the youngest in a family of four children. Miraculously they all escaped being killed. Pictures and photographs of the events, in which 70,000 persons died instantly and another 70,000 died by the end of the first year, are devastating. This story is not as moving, however, as that told by Toshi Maruki in *Hiroshima No Pika* (The Flash of Hiroshima). Seven-year-old Mii and her family are calmly eating their breakfast of sweet potatoes on 6 August 1945, at 8:15 A.M., when the flash occurs. Mii's mother carries her wounded husband to the river. There they all sleep for four days. Mii's father recovers, only to die later from radiation sickness. Mii herself never grows in mind or body beyond her seven years. The expressionistic pictures of the fires, the thunder and lightning, and the wounded and dying all recreate the horror of an atomic attack. Yet the book was written in the hope that such horrors would never happen again. This, of course, is the reason teachers should share this book. For somehow when pain is particularized for a specific family it becomes more real and immediate than when it is depersonalized into mass numbers who were killed that day.

For many years children have been moved by Eleanor Coerr's chapter book *Sadako and the Thousand Paper Cranes*. In the picture book *Sadako*, Coerr rewrote the story of a young girl who died of leukemia as a result

of the atomic bomb. Ed Young created the moving illustrations that are a fine example of how visual art can work with and empower fine writing. Young's soft pastels mediate this tragic story for children but do not lessen its emotional impact. Figures are hazily drawn, particularly when the most frightening scenes are rendered. Instead of using realistic depictions, Young lets color convey the feelings that underlie the story. As Sadako gets sicker and sicker, the colors darken, until the pages on which she dies are predominantly the blue-black color of night. On the following page, however, Young changes the colors to the soft blues and peaches of a sunrise. The paper cranes that Sadako tried so hard to make have become real cranes flying toward heaven. Young's moving artwork and Sadako's statue in Hiroshima suggest that Sadako left behind a powerful legacy of peace.

The kindness of one child who cared for and provided food for children in a concentration camp is told in the moving story *Rose Blanche* by Christophe Gallaz and Roberto Innocenti. Illustrated with paintings of almost photographic clarity, this picture book is certainly for older children. The courage of Rose Blanche and all persons who in their small ways try to maintain humanity in the midst of inhumanity is something that needs to be discussed with older children.

In *The Wall*, a little boy visits Washington, D.C., with his father and they find the name of his grandfather on the Vietnam Memorial. Eve Bunting tells this poignant story, and Ronald Himler creates stark watercolor pictures for it. The pain the boy's father feels is contrasted with the young child's comments. His father tells him he is proud that his grandfather's name is on this wall. The boy replies:

 "I am, too."
  I am.
  But I'd rather have my grandpa here, taking me to the river, telling me to button up my jacket because it's cold.
  I'd rather have him here. (p. 32)

Picture storybooks are for all ages and they can be about all subjects. They can enlarge children's lives, stretch their imaginations, increase their sensitivity, and enhance their living. The phenomenal growth of beautiful picture storybooks for children of all ages is an outstanding accomplishment of the past fifty years of publishing. Children do not always recognize the beauty of these books, but early impressions do influence the development of children's permanent tastes as they grow up.

Learning Experiences

1. Look closely at three or more picture storybooks to discover how the illustrations extend the story's meaning beyond the words. Note the effect of the artist's choice of medium, style, and color; look for content details present in the pictures but not in the text.

2. Study the work of one Caldecott Medal–winning illustrator. What medium does this artist use? What terms would you use to describe the style? How do earlier books compare to the artist's most recent ones? Read the artist's acceptance speech for the Caldecott. How has the illustrator's style been influenced by her or his concepts of childhood?

3. Form a mock Caldecott award committee and review the Honor Books and Medal-winning book for one specific year. Would you have made the same decision as the ALA committee? Why or why not?

4. Find three or four books that are examples of the use of one medium, such as scratchboard or collage. Experiment with the materials used in this medium to make a picture of your own.

5. Find examples of picture storybooks that you think might increase children's sensitivity to well-used language. Look for vivid descriptions, repetition of unusual words or phrases, and figures of speech within the child's experience.

6. Select a group of stories based on a single subject or theme, such as stories about grandparents, "Be yourself" themes, or environmental concerns. Discuss which ones you would use to introduce a unit, which ones you would read aloud as a teacher, and which ones would be appropriate for children's reading.

7. Collect stories written by one author, such as Mem Fox, Eve Bunting, or Cynthia Rylant, but illustrated by different artists. How do the artists' visions affect the moods of the stories?

8. If possible, read several stories to a group of children over a period of weeks. Select different kinds of stories: humorous, folktale-style, or nostalgic stories recalling the past. What are children's responses to these books? What do they single out to comment on? Record their comments and share these with your children's literature class. What conclusions can you draw?

Related Readings

Brown, Marcia. *Lotus Seeds: Children's Pictures and Books.* New York: Scribner's, 1986.

A noted illustrator writes eloquently on picture books, the hero within, publishing, and her own work. Her three Caldecott acceptance speeches are included among these thought-provoking essays.

Cianciolo, Patricia. *Picture Books for Children.* 3rd ed. Chicago: American Library Association, 1990.

A thorough discussion of the art of picture books with an annotated listing of all kinds of picture books for children. Particular attention is given to the media and style of illustrating for each entry as well as the ethnic and racial backgrounds of the characters in the stories.

Kiefer, Barbara. *The Potential of Picturebooks: From Visual Literacy to Aesthetic Understanding.* Columbus, Ohio: Merrill/Prentice Hall, 1995.

This book discusses classroom research on children's responses to picture books, provides a history of picture books, looks at some of the modern-day artists who create them, and suggests a theory for evaluating the art of the picture book. The last section provides practical suggestions for classroom activities.

Lacy, Lyn Ellen. *Art and Design in Children's Picture Books: An Analysis of Caldecott Award Winning Illustrations.* Chicago: American Library Association, 1986.

An intelligent review of the art of over four dozen illustrators who have won the Caldecott Medal. The author also provides real guidance in how to understand pictures and the ways they create meaning.

Kingman, Lee, ed. *Newbery and Caldecott Medal Books: 1956–1965*. Boston: Horn Book, 1965.

———. *Newbery and Caldecott Medal Books: 1966–1975*. Boston: Horn Book, 1975.

———. *Newbery and Caldecott Medal Books: 1976–1985*. Boston: Horn Book, 1985.

These volumes contain the acceptance speeches and biographies of the Newbery and Caldecott Medal winners, reprinted from the August issue of *Horn Book Magazine*. In the most recent volume, Barbara Bader gives a very critical review of the committee's choices. She far prefers some of the Honor Books over the Medal winners and tells you why.

Martin, Douglas. *The Telling Line*. New York: Delacorte Press, 1989.

Thoughtful essays on fifteen contemporary British illustrators. Based on interviews the author had with all of them, he quotes them regularly. Illustrated in color and black and white, this text makes a fine contribution to the story of twentieth-century illustration.

Nodelman, Perry. *Words About Pictures: The Narrative Art of Children's Picture Books*. Athens: University of Georgia Press, 1988.

Nodelman explores the various means by which pictures tell stories. These elements include design, style, code, tension, action, irony, and rhythm. Nodelman draws on a number of aesthetic and literary theories in his discussions. Unfortunately this significant book contains few pictures.

Schwarcz, Joseph H., and Chava Schwarcz. *The Picture Book Comes of Age*. Chicago: American Library Association, 1991.

A remarkable book that reveals knowledge of the creative process, children, artistic and literary expertise, and books from several different countries. A professor at the University of Haifa, Joseph Schwarcz taught children's literature for many years before his death in 1988.

Children's Literature

Aardema, Verna. *Bringing the Rain to Kapiti Plain*. Illustrated by Beatriz Vidal. Dial, 1981.

Adoff, Arnold. *Hard to Be Six*. Illustrated by Cheryl Hanna. Lothrop, Lee & Shepard, 1991.

Ahlberg, Janet, and Allan Ahlberg. *The Jolly Postman*. Little, Brown, 1986.

Albert, Burton. *Where Does the Trail Lead?* Illustrated by Brian Pinkney. Simon & Schuster, 1993.

Alexander, Martha. *When the New Baby Comes, I'm Moving Out*. Dial, 1979.

———. *Nobody Asked Me if I Wanted a Baby Sister*. Dial, 1971.

Aliki [Aliki Brandenberg]. *Feelings*. Greenwillow, 1984.

———. *My Feet*. Crowell, 1990.

———. *My Hands*. Crowell, 1990.

Allard, Harry. *The Stupids Die*. Illustrated by James Marshall. Houghton Mifflin, 1981.

———. *The Stupids Have a Ball*. Illustrated by James Marshall. Houghton Mifflin, 1977.

———. *The Stupids Step Out*. Illustrated by James Marshall. Houghton Mifflin, 1978.

Allard, Harry, and James Marshall. *Miss Nelson Has a Field Day*. Illustrated by James Marshall. Houghton Mifflin, 1985.

———. *Miss Nelson Is Missing*. Illustrated by James Marshall. Houghton Mifflin, 1977.

Allinson, Beverly. *Effie*. Illustrated by Barbara Reid. Scholastic, 1991.

Andrews, Jan. *The Auction*. Illustrated by Karen Reczuch. Macmillan, 1991.

———. *Very Last First Time*. Illustrated by Ian Wallace. McElderry, 1985.

Applebaum, Diana. *Giants in the Land*. Illustrated by Michael McCurdy. Houghton Mifflin, 1993.

Ardizzone, Edward. *Little Tim and the Brave Sea Captain*. Penguin, 1983.

Aylesworth, Jim. *My Son John*. Illustrated by David Frampton. Henry Holt, 1994.

Baker, Jeannie. *The Story of Rosy Dock*. Greenwillow, 1995.

———. *Window*. Greenwillow, 1991.

———. *Where the Forest Meets the Sea*. Greenwillow, 1987.

Baker, Olaf. *Where the Buffaloes Begin*. Illustrated by Stephen Gammell. Warne, 1981.

Bang, Molly. *The Grey Lady and the Strawberry Snatcher*. Four Winds, 1980.

———. *One Fall Day*. Greenwillow, 1994.

———. *The Paper Crane*. Greenwillow, 1985.

Barrett, Judi. *Animals Should Definitely Not Act Like People*. Illustrated by Ron Barrett. Atheneum, 1980.

———. *Animals Should Definitely Not Wear Clothing*. Illustrated by Ron Barrett. Atheneum, 1970.

Baylor, Byrd. *Everybody Needs a Rock*. Illustrated by Peter Parnall. Scribner's, 1974.

———. *The Other Way to Listen*. Illustrated by Peter Parnall. Scribner's, 1978.

———. *The Way to Start a Day*. Illustrated by Peter Parnall. Scribner's, 1978.

———. *Your Own Best Secret Place*. Illustrated by Peter Parnall. Scribner's, 1979.

Belton, Sandra. *From Miss Ida's Front Porch*. Illustrated by Floyd Cooper. Four Winds, 1993.

Bemelmans, Ludwig. *Madeline*. Viking, 1962 [1939].

Best, Carrie. *Taxi Taxi*. Illustrated by Dale Gottlieb. Little, Brown, 1994.

Briggs, Raymond. *The Bear*. Random House, 1994.

———. *Father Christmas*. Random House, 1973.

———. *Fungus the Bogeyman*. Random House, 1979.

———. *Jim and the Beanstalk*. Coward-McCann, 1970.

———. *The Snowman*. Random House, 1978.

Brown, Marc. *Arthur's April Fool*. Little, Brown, 1983.

———. *Arthur's Chicken Pox*. Little, Brown, 1994.

———. *Arthur's Eyes*. Little, Brown, 1979.

———. *Arthur's Halloween*. Little, Brown, 1983.

———. *Arthur's Nose*. Little, Brown, 1976.

———. *Arthur's Valentine*. Little, Brown, 1980.

Brown, Marcia. *Once a Mouse*. Scribner's, 1961.

Brown, Margaret Wise. *Goodnight Moon*. Illustrated by Clement Hurd. Harper & Row, 1975 [1947].

Browne, Anthony. *The Big Baby: A Little Joke*. Knopf, 1994.

———. *Changes*. Knopf, 1986.

———. *The Piggybook*. Knopf, 1986.

———. *The Tunnel*. Knopf, 1990.

Buchanan, Ken. *This House Is Made of Mud*. Illustrated by Libba Tracy. Northland, 1991.

Bunting, Eve. *Fly Away Home*. Illustrated by Ronald Himler. Clarion, 1991.

———. *How Many Days to America? A Thanksgiving Story*. Illustrated by Beth Peck. Houghton Mifflin, 1988.

———. *Night of the Gargoyles*. Illustrated by David Weisner. Clarion, 1994.

———. *Smoky Night*. Illustrated by David Diaz. Harcourt Brace, 1994.

———. *The Wall*. Illustrated by Ronald Himler. Clarion, 1990.

———. *The Wednesday Surprise*. Illustrated by Donald Carrick. Clarion, 1989.

Burgie, Irving. *Caribbean Carnival: Songs of the West Indies*. Illustrated by Frané Lessac. HarperCollins, 1992.

Burningham, John. *Come Away from the Water, Shirley*. Harper & Row, 1977.

———. *Granpa*. Crown, 1985.

————. *John Patrick Norman McHennessy—The Boy Who Was Always Late*. Crown, 1987.

————. *Time to Get Out of the Bath, Shirley*. Harper & Row, 1978.

————. *Would You Rather. . . .* Harper & Row, 1978.

Burton, Virginia Lee. *Katie and the Big Snow*. Houghton Mifflin, 1943.

————. *The Little House*. Houghton Mifflin, 1942.

————. *Mike Mulligan and His Steam Shovel*. Houghton Mifflin, 1939.

Butler, Stephen. *Henny Penny*. Tambourine, 1991.

Caines, Jeanette. *Daddy*. Illustrated by Ronald Himler. Harper & Row, 1977.

————. *Just Us Women*. Illustrated by Pat Cummings. Harper & Row, 1982.

Calhoun, Mary. *While I Sleep*. Illustrated by Ed Young. Morrow, 1992.

Calmenson, Stephanie. *The Principal's New Clothes*. Illustrated by Denise Brunkus. Scholastic, 1989.

Carle, Eric. *The Very Hungry Caterpillar*. World, 1968.

Carlstrom, Nancy White. *Blow Me a Kiss, Miss Lilly*. Illustrated by Amy Schwartz. HarperCollins, 1990.

Carrick, Carol. *The Accident*. Illustrated by Donald Carrick. Clarion, 1976.

————. *The Climb*. Illustrated by Donald Carrick. Clarion, 1984.

————. *The Foundling*. Illustrated by Donald Carrick. Clarion, 1977.

————. *In the Moonlight, Waiting*. Illustrated by Donald Carrick. Clarion, 1990.

————. *Sleep Out*. Illustrated by Donald Carrick. Clarion, 1973.

Carter, Polly. *Harriet Tubman*. Illustrated by Brian Pinkney. Silver Press, 1992.

Caseley, Judith. *Dear Annie*. Greenwillow, 1991.

————. *Mama Coming and Going*. Greenwillow, 1994.

————. *Mr. Green Peas*. Greenwillow, 1995.

Cassedy, Sylvia, and Suetake Kunihiro, trans. *Red Dragonfly on My Shoulder*. Illustrated by Molly Bang. HarperCollins, 1992.

Cendrars, Blaise. *Shadow*. Illustrated by Marcia Brown. Scribner's, 1982.

Cherry, Lynne. *A River Ran Wild*. Gulliver/Harcourt, 1992.

Clark, Ann Nolan. *In My Mother's House*. Illustrated by Velino Herrera. Viking, 1991 [1941].

Coerr, Elanor. *Sadako*. Illustrated by Ed Young. Putnam, 1993.

————. *Sadako and the Thousand Paper Cranes*. Illustrated by Ron Himler. Putnam, 1977.

Cohen, Miriam. *Best Friends*. Illustrated by Lillian Hoban. Macmillan, 1971.

————. *It's George!* Illustrated by Lillian Hoban. Greenwillow, 1988.

————. *The New Teacher*. Illustrated by Lillian Hoban. Macmillan, 1972.

————. *When Will I Read?* Illustrated by Lillian Hoban. Greenwillow, 1977.

————. *Will I Have a Friend?* Illustrated by Lillian Hoban. Macmillan, 1967.

Cole, Sheila. *When the Tide Is Low*. Illustrated by Virginia Wright-Frierson. Lothrop, Lee & Shepard, 1985.

Conrad, Pam. *Doll Face Has a Party*. Illustrated by Brian Selznick. HarperCollins, 1994.

————. *The Tub Grandfather*. Illustrated by Richard Egielski. HarperCollins, 1993.

————. *The Tub People*. Illustrated by Richard Egielski. Harper & Row, 1989.

Cooney, Barbara. *Chanticleer and the Fox*. Crowell, 1958.

————. *Hattie and the Wild Waves*. Viking, 1990.

————. *Island Boy*. Viking, 1988.

————. *Miss Rumphius*. Viking, 1982.

Cooper, Floyd. *Coming Home: From the Life of Langston Hughes*. Philomel, 1994.

Crowe, Robert. *Clyde Monster*. Illustrated by Kay Chorao. Dutton, 1976.

Day, Nancy Raines. *The Lion's Whiskers*. Illustrated by Ann Grifalconi. Scholastic, 1995.

de Brunhoff, Jean. *The Story of Babar*. Random House, 1960.

de Paola, Tomie. *Nana Upstairs & Nana Downstairs*. Penguin, 1978.

————. *Now One Foot, Now the Other*. Putnam, 1981.

————. *Strega Nona*. Prentice Hall, 1975.

————. *Tom*. Putnam, 1993.

————. *Tomie de Paola's Mother Goose*. Putnam, 1985.

————. *Watch Out for the Chicken Feet in Your Soup*. Prentice Hall, 1974.

de Regniers, Beatrice Schenk. *May I Bring a Friend?* Illustrated by Beni Montresor. Atheneum, 1964.

Delacre, Lulu. *Vejigante Masquerader*. Scholastic, 1993.

DiSalvo-Ryan, DyAnne. *Uncle Willie and the Soup Kitchen*. Morrow, 1991.

Dorros, Arthur. *Abuela*. Illustrated by Elisa Kleven. Dutton, 1991.

————. *Isla*. Illustrated by Elisa Kleven. Dutton, 1995.

Duvoisin, Roger. *Petunia*. Knopf, 1950.

Edwards, Michelle. *Chicken Man*. Lothrop, Lee & Shepard, 1991.

Ehlert, Lois. *Fish Eyes*. Harcourt Brace, 1990.

Fleming, Denise. *Barnyard Banter*. Holt, 1994.

————. *Where Once There Was a Wood*. Holt, 1996.

Flournoy, Valerie. *The Patchwork Quilt*. Illustrated by Jerry Pinkney. Dial, 1985.

Fox, Mem. *Hattie and the Fox*. Illustrated by Patricia Mullins. Bradbury, 1988.

————. *Koala Lou*. Illustrated by Pamela Lofts. Harcourt Brace, 1989.

————. *Night Noises*. Illustrated by Terry Denton. Harcourt Brace, 1989.

————. *Our Granny*. Illustrated by Julie Vivas. Ticknor & Fields, 1994.

————. *Possum Magic*. Illustrated by Julie Vivas. Harcourt Brace, 1990.

————. *Wilfrid Gordon McDonald Partridge*. Illustrated by Julie Vivas. Kane Miller, 1985.

Freeman, Don. *Corduroy*. Viking, 1968.

————. *Dandelion*. Viking, 1964.

————. *A Pocket for Corduroy*. Viking, 1978.

Friedman, Ina. *How My Parents Learned to Eat*. Illustrated by Allen Say. Houghton Mifflin, 1984.

Gág, Wanda. *Millions of Cats*. Coward-McCann, 1928.

Gallaz, Christophe, and Roberto Innocenti. *Rose Blanche*. Illustrated by Roberto Innocenti. Creative Education, 1985.

Garza, Carmen Lomas. *Family Pictures: Cuadros de Familia*. Children's Book Press, 1990.

Geisert, Arthur. *Oink*. Houghton Mifflin, 1991.

————. *Oink Oink*. Houghton Mifflin, 1993.

————. *Pigs from A to Z*. Houghton Mifflin, 1986.

Gerrard, Roy. *Croco'nile*. Farrar, Straus & Giroux, 1994.

————. *Mik's Mammoth*. Farrar, Straus & Giroux, 1990.

————. *Rosie and the Rustlers*. Farrar, Straus & Giroux, 1989.

Goble, Paul. *The Girl Who Loved Wild Horses*. Bradbury, 1978.

————. *Iktomi and the Buzzard: A Plains Indian Story*. Orchard, 1994.

————. *Star Boy*. Bradbury, 1983.

Gramatky, Hardie. *Little Toot*. Putnam, 1939.

Gray, Libba Moore. *My Mama Had a Dancing Heart*. Illustrated by Raúl Colón. Orchard, 1995.

————. *Small Green Snake*. Illustrated by Holly Meade. Orchard, 1994.

Gray, Nigel. *A Country Far Away*. Illustrated by Philippe Dupasquier. Orchard, 1989.

Greenblat, Rodney A. *Uncle Wizzmo's New Used Car*. HarperCollins, 1990.

Greenfield, Eloise. *She Come Bringing Me That Little Baby Girl*. Illustrated by John Steptoe. Lippincott, 1974.

Grifalconi, Ann. *Darkness and the Butterfly*. Little, Brown, 1987.

————. *Osa's Pride*. Little, Brown, 1990.

————. *The Village of Round and Square Houses*. Little, Brown, 1986.

Griffith, Helen. *Georgia Music*. Illustrated by James Stevenson. Greenwillow, 1986.

————. *Grandaddy's Place*. Illustrated by James Stevenson. Greenwillow, 1987.

Grimm brothers. *The Bremen Town Musicians*. Translated by Elizabeth Shub. Illustrated by Janina Domanska. Greenwillow, 1980.

————. *Hansel and Gretel*. Retold by Rika Lesser. Illustrated by Paul Zelinsky. Dodd Mead, 1984.

————. *Rumpelstiltskin*. Retold and illustrated by Paul O. Zelinsky. Dutton, 1986.

————. *The Seven Ravens*. Translated by Elizabeth D. Crawford. Illustrated by Lisbeth Zwerger. Morrow, 1981.

————. *Snow White*. Translated by Randall Jarrell. Illustrated by Nancy Ekholm Burkert. Farrar, Straus & Giroux, 1972.

————. *Snow White*. Translated by Paul Heins. Illustrated by Trina Schart Hyman. Little, Brown, 1974.

Hadithi, Mwenye. *Hungry Hyena*. Illustrated by Adrienne Kennaway. Little, Brown, 1994.

————. *Lazy Lion*. Illustrated by Adrienne Kennaway. Little, Brown, 1990.

————. *Tricky Tortoise*. Illustrated by Adrienne Kennaway. Little, Brown, 1988.

Hale, Sarah Josepha. *Mary Had a Little Lamb*. Illustrated by Tomie de Paola. Holiday House, 1984.

Hall, Donald. *Lucy's Christmas*. Illustrated by Michael McCurdy. Browndeer/Harcourt Brace, 1994.

————. *Lucy's Summer*. Illustrated by Michael McCurdy. Browndeer/Harcourt Brace, 1995.

————. *Ox-Cart Man*. Illustrated by Barbara Cooney. Viking, 1979.

Hamilton, Virginia. *Her Stories: African American Folktales, Fairy Tales and True Tales*. Illustrated by Leo and Diane Dillon. Scholastic, 1995.

Harrison, Ted. *Children of the Yukon*. Tundra, 1977.

————. *A Northern Alphabet*. Tundra, 1989.

Heide, Florence Parry, and Judith Heide Gilliland. *The Day of Ahmed's Secret*. Illustrated by Ted Lewin. Lothrop, Lee & Shepard, 1990.

————. *Sami and the Time of the Troubles*. Illustrated by Ted Lewin. Clarion, 1992.

Helprin, Mark. *Swan Lake*. Illustrated by Chris Van Allsburg. Houghton Mifflin, 1989.

Hendershot, Judith. *In Coal Country*. Illustrated by Thomas B. Allen. Knopf, 1987.

————. *Up the Tracks to Grandma's*. Illustrated by Thomas B. Allen. Knopf, 1993.

Henkes, Kevin. *Chester's Way*. Greenwillow, 1988.

————. *Chrysanthemum*. Greenwillow, 1991.

————. *Julius, the Baby of the World*. Greenwillow, 1990.

———. *Owen*. Greenwillow, 1993.

———. *The Biggest Boy*. Illustrated by Nancy Tafuri. Greenwillow, 1995.

Hill, Elizabeth Starr. *Evan's Corner*. Illustrated by Sandra Speidel. Viking, 1991 [1967].

Hoban, Russell. *A Baby Sister for Frances*. Illustrated by Lillian Hoban. Harper & Row, 1964.

———. *A Bargain for Frances*. Illustrated by Lillian Hoban. Harper & Row, 1970.

———. *Bedtime for Frances*. Illustrated by Garth Williams. Harper & Row, 1960.

———. *Best Friends for Frances*. Illustrated by Lillian Hoban. Harper & Row, 1969.

———. *A Birthday for Frances*. Illustrated by Lillian Hoban. Harper & Row, 1968.

Hoban, Tana. *Shadows and Reflections*. Greenwillow, 1990.

Hodges, Margaret. *Saint George and the Dragon*. Illustrated by Trina Schart Hyman. Little, Brown, 1984.

Hoffman, Mary. *Amazing Grace*. Illustrated by Caroline Binch. Dial, 1991.

———. *Boundless Grace*. Illustrated by Caroline Binch. Dial, 1995.

Hooks, William H. *The Ballad of Belle Dorcas*. Illustrated by Brian Pinkney. Knopf, 1990.

———. *The Boy Who Held Back the Sea*. Illustrated by Thomas Locker. Dial, 1986.

Houston, Gloria. *My Great-Aunt Arizona*. Illustrated by Susan Condie Lamb. HarperCollins, 1992.

Howard, Elizabeth Fitzgerald. *Aunt Flossie's Hats (and Crab Cakes Later)*. Illustrated by James Ransome. Houghton Mifflin, 1991.

Hughes, Langston. *The Dream Keeper*. Illustrated by Brian Pinkney. Knopf, 1994.

Hughes, Shirley. *Alfie Gets in First*. Lothrop, Lee & Shepard, 1981.

———. *Dogger*. Lothrop, Lee & Shepard, 1988.

Hutchins, Pat. *Good-Night, Owl!* Macmillan, 1972.

———. *Rosie's Walk*. Macmillan, 1968.

———. *The Very Worst Monster*. Greenwillow, 1985.

———. *What Game Shall We Play?* Greenwillow, 1990.

———. *Where's the Baby?* Greenwillow, 1988.

Hyman, Trina Schart. *Little Red Riding Hood*. Holiday House, 1983.

Isaacs, Anne. *Swamp Angel*. Illustrated by Paul O. Zelinsky. Dutton, 1994.

Isadora, Rachel. *At the Crossroads*. Greenwillow, 1991.

———. *Max*. Macmillan, 1976.

Jackson, Ellen. *Brown Cow, Green Grass, Yellow Mellow Sun*. Illustrated by Victoria Raymond. Hyperion, 1995.

Jakobsen, Kathy. *My New York*. Little, Brown, 1993.

Johnson, Angela. *Tell Me Story, Mama*. Illustrated by David Soman. Orchard, 1989.

Johnson, Paul Brett and Celeste Lewis. *Lost*. Illustrated by Paul Brett Johnson. Orchard, 1996.

Johnston, Tony. *The Quilt Story*. Illustrated by Tomie de Paola. Putnam, 1985.

———. *Yonder*. Illustrated by Lloyd Bloom. Dial, 1988.

Jonas, Ann. *Round Trip*. Greenwillow, 1983.

Jorgensen, Gail. *Crocodile Beat*. Illustrated by Patricia Mullins. Bradbury, 1989.

Joseph, Lynn. *Jasmine's Parlour Day*. Illustrated by Ann Grifalconi. Lothrop, Lee & Shepard, 1994.

———. *A Wave in Her Pocket: Stories from Trinidad*. Illustrated by Brian Pinkney. Clarion, 1991.

Joyce, William. *A Day with Wilbur Robinson*. HarperCollins, 1990.

———. *Dinosaur Bob and His Adventures with the Family Lazardo*. Harper & Row, 1988.

———. *George Shrinks*. Harper & Row, 1985; miniature edition, 1991.

Jukes, Mavis. *Like Jake and Me*. Illustrated by Lloyd Bloom. Knopf, 1984.

Kalman, Maira. *Max in Hollywood*. Viking. 1995.

———. *Max Makes a Million*. Viking, 1990.

———. *Ooh La La, Max in Love*. Viking, 1991.

Keats, Ezra Jack. *Goggles*. Macmillan, 1969.

———. *Hi Cat!* Macmillan, 1970.

———. *A Letter to Amy*. Harper & Row, 1968.

———. *Peter's Chair*. Harper & Row, 1967.

———. *Pet Show!* Macmillan, 1972.

———. *The Snowy Day*. Viking, 1962.

———. *Whistle for Willie*. Viking, 1964.

Keller, Holly. *Grandfather's Dream*. Greenwillow, 1994.

Kellogg, Steven. *Can I Keep Him?* Dial, 1971.

———. *Chicken Little*. Morrow, 1985.

———. *Pinkerton, Behave!* Dial, 1979.

———. *Prehistoric Pinkerton*. Dial, 1987.

———. *A Rose for Pinkerton*. Dial, 1981.

Kesey, Ken. *Little Tricker the Squirrel Meets Big Double the Bear*. Illustrated by Barry Moser. Viking, 1990.

Kesselman, Wendy. *Emma*. Illustrated by Barbara Cooney. Doubleday, 1980.

Kipling, Rudyard. *The Elephant's Child*. Illustrated by Jan Mogensen. Crocodile Books/Interlink, 1989.

———. *The Elephant's Child*. Illustrated by Lorinda B. Cauley. Harcourt Brace, 1983.

———. *How the Camel Got His Hump*. Illustrated by Krystyna Turska. Warne, 1988.

———. *How the Camel Got His Hump*. Illustrated by Quentin Blake. Bedrick, 1985.

———. *How the Leopard Got His Spots*. Illustrated by Caroline Ebborn. Bedrick, 1986.

———. *Just So Stories*. Illustrated by David Frampton. HarperCollins, 1991 [1983].

Kitchen, Bert. *Animal Alphabet*. Dial, 1984.

Komaiko, Leah. *My Perfect Neighborhood*. Illustrated by Barbara Westman. Crowell, 1971.

Kraus, Robert. *Leo the Late Bloomer*. Illustrated by José Aruego. Crowell, 1971.

———. *Milton the Early Riser*. Illustrated by José Aruego and Ariane Dewey. Windmill, 1972.

———. *Owliver*. Illustrated by José Aruego and Ariane Dewey. Windmill, 1974.

Krauss, Ruth. *A Hole Is to Dig*. Illustrated by Maurice Sendak. Harper & Row, 1952.

———. *A Very Special House*. Illustrated by Maurice Sendak. Harper & Row, 1953.

Lasky, Katherine. *Pond Year*. Illustrated by Mike Bostock. Candlewick, 1995.

Lattimore, Deborah Nourse. *The Sailor Who Captured the Sea*. HarperCollins, 1991.

———. *Why There Is No Arguing in Heaven*. Harper & Row, 1989.

Lauber, Patricia. *The News About Dinosaurs*. Bradbury, 1989.

Leaf, Munro. *The Story of Ferdinand*. Illustrated by Robert Lawson. Viking, 1936.

Lessac, Frané. *Caribbean Alphabet*. Tambourine, 1994.

———. *Caribbean Canvas*. Lippincott, 1989.

———. *My Little Island*. Tambourine, 1985.

Levinson, Riki. *Our Home Is the Sea*. Illustrated by Dennis Luzak. Dutton, 1988.

———. *Watch the Stars Come Out*. Illustrated by Diane Goode. Dutton, 1985.

Lindbergh, Reeve. *Johnny Appleseed*. Illustrated by Kathy Jakobsen. Little, Brown, 1990.

Lionni, Leo. *Alexander and the Wind-up Mouse*. Pantheon, 1969.

———. *An Extraordinary Egg*. Knopf, 1994.

———. *Fish Is Fish*. Pantheon, 1970.

———. *Frederick*. Pantheon, 1967.

———. *Little Blue and Little Yellow*. Astor-Honor, 1959.

———. *Matthew's Dream*. Knopf, 1991.

Livingston, Myra Cohn. *A Time to Talk: Poems of Friendship*. Illustrated by Brian Pinkney. McElderry, 1992.

———. *I Never Told and Other Poems*. Cover art by Brian Pinkney. McElderry, 1992.

Lobel, Arnold. *Days with Frog and Toad*. Harper & Row, 1979.

———. *Fables*. Harper & Row, 1980.

———. *Frog and Toad All Year*. Harper & Row, 1976.

———. *Frog and Toad Are Friends*. Harper & Row, 1970.

———. *Frog and Toad Together*. Harper & Row, 1972.

Locker, Thomas. *Family Farm*. Dial, 1988.

———. *The Mare on the Hill*. Dial, 1985.

———. *Sky Tree*. With Candace Christiansen. HarperCollins, 1995.

———. *Where the River Begins*. Dial, 1984.

———. *The Young Artist*. Dial, 1989.

Macaulay, David. *Black and White*. Houghton Mifflin, 1990.

MacDonald, Golden [Margaret Wise Brown]. *The Little Island*. Illustrated by Leonard Weisgard. Doubleday, 1946.

MacLachlan, Patricia. *All the Places to Love*. Illustrated by Mike Wimmer. HarperCollins, 1994.

———. *Mama One, Mama Two*. Illustrated by Ruth Lercher Bornstein. Harper & Row, 1982.

———. *Through Grandpa's Eyes*. Illustrated by Deborah Ray. Harper & Row, 1979.

———. *What You Know First*. Illustrated by Barry Moser. HarperCollins, 1995.

Mahy, Margaret. *The Great White Man-Eating Shark*. Illustrated by Jonathan Allen. Dial, 1990.

———. *The Rattlebang Picnic*. Illustrated by Steven Kellogg. Dial, 1994.

Marshall, James. *George and Martha*. Houghton Mifflin, 1972.

———. *George and Martha Back in Town*. Houghton Mifflin, 1984.

———. *George and Martha Round and Round*. Houghton Mifflin, 1984.

———. *George and Martha Tons of Fun*. Houghton Mifflin, 1972.

Martin, Bill, Jr., and John Archambault. *The Ghost-Eye Tree*. Illustrated by Ted Rand. Henry Holt, 1985.

———. *Knots on a Counting Rope*. Illustrated by Ted Rand. Henry Holt, 1987.

Martin, Rafe. *Foolish Rabbitt's Big Mistake*. Illustrated by Ed Young. Putnam, 1985.

———. *Will's Mammoth*. Illustrated by Stephen Gammell. Putnam, 1989.

Maruki, Toshi. *Hiroshima No Pika* (The Flash of Hiroshima). Lothrop, Lee & Shepard, 1980.

Marzollo, Jean. *Happy Birthday, Martin Luther King*. Illustrated by Brian Pinkney. Scholastic, 1993.

Mathers, Petra. *Sophie and Lou*. HarperCollins, 1991.

———. *Victor and Christobel*. Knopf, 1993.

Mayer, Mercer. *There's a Nightmare in My Closet*. Dial, 1968.

McCloskey, Robert. *Blueberries for Sal*. Viking, 1963.

————. *Make Way for Ducklings*. Viking, 1941.

————. *One Morning in Maine*. Viking, 1952.

————. *Time of Wonder*. Viking, 1957.

McFarlane, Sheryl. *Eagle Dreams*. Illustrated by Ron Lightburn. Philomel, 1995.

————. *Waiting for Whales*. Illustrated by Ron Lightburn. Philomel, 1993.

McGuire, Richard. *Night Becomes Day*. Viking, 1994.

————. *What Goes Around Comes Around*. Viking, 1995.

McKee, David. *Elmer*. Lothrop, Lee & Shepard, 1989 [1968].

McKissack, Patricia C. *The Dark Thirty: Southern Tales of the Supernatural*. Illustrated by Brian Pinkney. Knopf, 1992.

McPhail, David. *The Bear's Toothache*. Little, Brown, 1972.

————. *Henry Bear's Park*. Little, Brown, 1976.

————. *Pig Pig Goes to Camp*. Dutton, 1983.

————. *Pig Pig Grows Up*. Dutton, 1980.

————. *Stanley, Henry Bear's Friend*. Little, Brown, 1979.

Meddaugh, Susan. *Martha Calling*. Houghton Mifflin, 1994.

————. *Martha Speaks*. Houghton Mifflin, 1992.

Miles, Miska. *Annie and the Old One*. Illustrated by Peter Parnall. Little, Brown, 1971.

Minarik, Else. *Father Bear Comes Home*. Illustrated by Maurice Sendak. Harper & Row, 1959.

————. *A Kiss for Little Bear*. Illustrated by Maurice Sendak. Harper & Row, 1968.

————. *Little Bear*. Illustrated by Maurice Sendak. Harper & Row, 1957.

————. *Little Bear's Friend*. Illustrated by Maurice Sendak. Harper & Row, 1960.

————. *Little Bear's Visit*. Illustrated by Maurice Sendak. Harper & Row, 1961.

Mitchell, Margaree King. *Uncle Jed's Barbershop*. Illustrated by James Ransome. Simon & Schuster, 1993.

Mora, Pat. *Pablo's Tree*. Illustrated by Cecily Lang. Macmillan, 1994.

Morimoto, Junko. *My Hiroshima*. Viking, 1987.

Murphy, Shirley Rousseau. *Tattie's River Journey*. Illustrated by Tomie de Paola. Dial, 1983.

Musgrove, Margaret. *Ashanti to Zulu: African Traditions*. Illustrated by Leo and Diane Dillon. Dial, 1976.

Namioka, Lensey. *The Loyal Cat*. Illustrated by Aki Sogabe. Browndeer/Harcourt Brace, 1995.

Noble, Trinka H. *The Day Jimmy's Boa Ate the Wash*. Illustrated by Steven Kellogg. Dial, 1980.

————. *Jimmy's Boa Bounces Back*. Illustrated by Steven Kellogg. Dial, 1984.

Nye, Naomi Shihab. *Sitti's Secret*. Illustrated by Nancy Carpenter. Four Winds, 1994.

Paxton, Tom. *Engelbert the Elephant*. Illustrated by Steven Kellogg. Morrow, 1990.

Pearson, Susan. *Happy Birthday, Grampie*. Illustrated by Ronald Himler. Dial, 1987.

Perrault, Charles. *Cinderella*. Illustrated by Marcia Brown. Scribner's, 1954.

————. *Puss in Boots*. Illustrated by Fred Marcellino. Farrar, Straus & Giroux, 1990.

Pilkey, Dav. *Cat Kong*. Harcourt Brace, 1993.

————. *Dog Breath: The Horrible Trouble with Hally Tosis*. Blue Sky, 1994.

————. *Dogzilla*. Harcourt Brace, 1993.

Pinkney, Andrea Davis. *Alvin Ailey*. Illustrated by Brian Pinkney. Hyperion, 1993.

———. *Dear Benjamin Banneker*. Illustrated by Brian Pinkney. Harcourt Brace, 1994.

———. *Seven Candles for Kwanzaa*. Illustrated by Brian Pinkney. Dial, 1993.

Pinkney, Brian. *Max Found Two Sticks*. Simon & Schuster, 1994.

Piper, Watty. *The Little Engine That Could*. Illustrated by George Hauman and Doris Hauman. Platt & Munk, 1954 [1930].

Polacco, Patricia. *The Keeping Quilt*. Simon & Schuster, 1988.

———. *Just Plain Fancy*. Bantam/Doubleday, 1990.

———. *Pink and Say*. Philomel, 1994.

———. *Thunder Cake*. Philomel, 1990.

Politi, Leo. *Song of the Swallows*. Scribner's, 1949.

Pomerantz, Charlotte. *The Chalk Doll*. Illustrated by Frané Lessac. Lippincott, 1989.

Potter, Beatrix. *The Tale of Peter Rabbit*. Warne, 1902.

Price, Leontyne. *Aïda*. Illustrated by Leo and Diane Dillon. Harcourt Brace, 1990.

Priceman, Marjorie. *How to Make Apple Pie and See the World*. Knopf, 1994.

Provensen, Alice, and Martin Provensen. *The Glorious Flight: Across the Channel with Louis Blériot*. Viking, 1983.

———. *Shaker Lane*. Viking, 1987.

Raskin, Ellen. *Nothing Ever Happens on My Block*. Macmillan, 1989 [1966].

Rathmann, Peggy. *Officer Buckle and Gloria*. Putnam, 1995.

Rattigan, Jama Kim. *Dumpling Soup*. Illustrated by Lillian Hsu-Flanders. Little, Brown, 1993.

Rayner, Mary. *Garth Pig and the Ice Cream Lady*. Atheneum, 1977.

———. *Mr. and Mrs. Pig's Evening Out*. Atheneum, 1976.

———. *Mrs. Pig's Bulk Buy*. Atheneum, 1981.

Reid, Barbara. *Two by Two*. Scholastic, 1992.

Rey, H. A. *Curious George*. Houghton Mifflin, 1941.

Rice, Eve. *At Grammy's House*. Illustrated by Nancy Winslow Parker. Greenwillow, 1990.

Richard, Françoise. *On Cat Mountain*. Adapted by Arthur A. Levine. Illustrated by Anne Buguet. Putnam, 1994.

Ringgold, Faith. *Tar Beach*. Crown, 1991.

Robbins, Ruth. *Baboushka and the Three Kings*. Illustrated by Nicholas Sidjakov. Parnassus, 1960.

Roe, Eileen. *Con Mi Hermano: With My Brother*. Illustrated by Robert Casilla. Bradbury, 1991.

Russo, Marisabina. *I Don't Want to Go Back To School*. Greenwillow, 1994.

———. *Time to Wake Up!* Greenwillow, 1994.

Ryder, Joanne. *When the Woods Hum*. Illustrated by Catherine Stock. Morrow, 1991.

Rylant, Cynthia. *Appalachia: The Voices of Sleeping Birds*. Illustrated by Barry Moser. Harcourt Brace, 1991.

———. *The Relatives Came*. Illustrated by Stephen Gammell. Bradbury, 1985.

———. *When I Was Young in the Mountains*. Illustrated by Diane Goode. Dutton, 1982.

San Souci, Robert D. *The Boy and the Ghost*. Illustrated by Brian Pinkney. Simon & Schuster, 1989.

———. *Cut from the Same Cloth: American Women of Myth, Legend, and Tall Tale*. Illustrated by Brian Pinkney. Putnam/Philomel, 1993.

———. *The Faithful Friend*. Illustrated by Brian Pinkney. Simon & Schuster, 1995.

———. *Sukey and the Mermaid*. Illustrated by Brian Pinkney. Four Winds, 1992.

Say, Allen. *El Chino*. Houghton Mifflin, 1990.

———. *Grandfather's Journey*. Houghton Mifflin, 1993.

———. *The Lost Lake*. Houghton Mifflin, 1989.

Schur, Maxine R. *Day of Delight*. Illustrated by Brian Pinkney. Dial, 1994.

Scieszka, Jon. *The Book That Jack Wrote*. Illustrated by Daniel Adel. Viking, 1994.

———. *The Frog Prince Continued*. Illustrated by Steve Johnson. Viking, 1991.

———. *The Stinky Cheese Man and Other Fairly Stupid Tales*. Illustrated by Lane Smith. Viking, 1992.

———. *The True Story of the Three Little Pigs*. Illustrated by Lane Smith. Viking, 1989.

Sendak, Maurice. *In the Night Kitchen*. Harper & Row, 1970.

———. *Outside Over There*. Harper & Row, 1981.

———. *We Are All in the Dumps with Jack and Guy*. HarperCollins, 1993.

———. *Where the Wild Things Are*. Harper & Row, 1963.

Serfozo, Mary. *Rain Talk*. Illustrated by Keiko Narahashi. McElderry Books/Macmillan, 1990.

Seuss, Dr. [Theodor S. Geisel]. *And to Think That I Saw It on Mulberry Street*. Vanguard, 1937.

———. *The Cat in the Hat*. Random House, 1957.

———. *Horton Hatches the Egg*. Random House, 1993 [1940].

———. *Scrambled Eggs Super!* Random House, 1953.

———. *Thidwick, the Big-Hearted Moose*. Random House, 1948.

Seymour, Tres. *Hunting the White Cow*. Illustrated by Wendy Anderson Halperin. Orchard, 1993.

Shannon, George. *Climbing Kansas Mountains*. Illustrated by Thomas B. Allen. Bradbury, 1993.

Shelby, Anne. *Homeplace*. Illustrated by Wendy Anderson Halperin. Orchard, 1995.

Shulevitz, Uri. *Dawn*. Farrar, Straus & Giroux, 1974.

———. *Rain Rain Rivers*. Farrar, Straus & Giroux, 1969.

———. *Toddlecreek Post Office*. Farrar, Straus & Giroux, 1990.

Sierra, Judy. *The Elephant's Wrestling Match*. Illustrated by Brian Pinkney. Lodestar/Dutton, 1992.

———. *The House That Drac Built*. Illustrated by Will Hillenbrand. Gulliver, 1995.

Silverman, Erica. *Don't Fidget a Feather*. Illustrated by S. D. Schindler. Macmillan, 1994.

Simon, Norma. *Wet World*. Illustrated by Alexi Natchev. Candlewick, 1995.

Small, David. *Imogene's Antlers*. Crown, 1986.

Soto, Gary. *Chato's Kitchen*. Illustrated by Susan Guevara. Putnam, 1995.

Speed, Toby. *Two Cool Cows*. Illustrated by Barry Root. Putnam, 1995.

Spier, Peter. *Peter Spier's Rain*. Doubleday, 1982.

Stafford, Kim. *We Got Here Together*. Illustrated by Debra Frasier. Harcourt Brace, 1992.

Stafford, William. *The Animal That Drank Up Sound*. Illustrated by Debra Frasier. Harcourt Brace, 1992.

Steig, William. *The Amazing Bone*. Farrar, Straus & Giroux, 1976.

———. *Amos & Boris*. Farrar, Straus & Giroux, 1971.

———. *Brave Irene*. Farrar, Straus & Giroux, 1986.

———. *Doctor DeSoto*. Farrar, Straus & Giroux, 1982.

———. *Gorky Rises*. Farrar, Straus & Giroux, 1980.

———. *Shrek!* Farrar, Straus & Giroux, 1990.

———. *Sylvester and the Magic Pebble*. Windmill, 1979.

———. *Zeke Pippin*. HarperCollins, 1994.

Steptoe, John. *Daddy Is a Monster . . . Sometimes*. Lippincott, 1980.

————. *Stevie*. Harper & Row, 1969.

Stevenson, James. *Could Be Worse!* Greenwillow, 1977.

————. *The Dreadful Day*. Greenwillow, 1985.

————. *Grandpa's Too-Good Garden*. Greenwillow, 1988.

————. *That Terrible Halloween Night*. Greenwillow, 1983.

————. *We Hate Rain*. Greenwillow, 1989.

————. *What's Under My Bed?* Greenwillow, 1983.

————. *Worse Than Willy!* Greenwillow, 1984.

Stewart, Sarah. *The Librarian*. Illustrated by David Small. Farrar, Straus & Giroux, 1995.

Stock, Catherine. *Where Are You Going, Manyoni?* Morrow, 1993.

Stolz, Mary. *Storm in the Night*. Illustrated by Pat Cummings. Harper & Row, 1988.

Tiller, Ruth. *Cinnamon, Mint, and Mothballs: A Visit to Grandmother's House*. Illustrated by Aki Sogabe. Browndeer/Harcourt Brace, 1993.

Titherington, Jeanne. *A Place for Ben*. Greenwillow, 1987.

Tresselt, Alvin. *Hide and Seek Fog*. Illustrated by Roger Duvoisin. Lothrop, Lee & Shepard, 1988 [1965].

————. *White Snow, Bright Snow*. Illustrated by Roger Duvoisin. Lothrop, Lee & Shepard, 1988 [1947].

Trivias, Eugene. *The Three Little Wolves and the Big Bad Pig*. Illustrated by Helen Oxenbury. McElderry, 1993.

Turner, Ann. *Heron Street*. Illustrated by Lisa Desimini. Harper & Row, 1989.

————. *Through Moon and Stars and Night Skies*. Illustrated by James-Graham Hale. HarperCollins, 1990.

Udry, Janice May. *A Tree Is Nice*. Illustrated by Marc Simont. Harper & Row, 1956.

Van Allsburg, Chris. *Bad Day at Riverbend*. Houghton Mifflin, 1995.

————. *The Garden of Abdul Gasazi*. Houghton Mifflin, 1979.

————. *Jumanji*. Houghton Mifflin, 1981.

————. *Just a Dream*. Houghton Mifflin, 1990.

————. *The Mysteries of Harris Burdick*. Houghton Mifflin, 1984.

————. *The Polar Express*. Houghton Mifflin, 1985.

————. *The Stranger*. Houghton Mifflin, 1986.

————. *The Sweetest Fig*. Houghton Mifflin, 1993.

————. *Two Bad Ants*. Houghton Mifflin, 1988.

————. *The Widow's Broom*. Houghton Mifflin, 1992.

————. *The Wreck of the Zephyr*. Houghton Mifflin, 1983.

————. *The Wretched Stone*. Houghton Mifflin, 1991.

Van Laan, Nancy. *Possum Come A-Knockin'*. Illustrated by George Booth. Knopf, 1990.

Vincent, Gabrielle. *Ernest and Celestine*. Greenwillow, 1982.

————. *Ernest and Celestine's Picnic*. Greenwillow, 1982.

————. *Feel Better, Ernest!* Greenwillow, 1988.

————. *Merry Christmas, Ernest and Celestine*. Greenwillow, 1984.

————. *Smile, Ernest and Celestine*. Greenwillow, 1982.

Viorst, Judith. *Alexander and the Terrible, Horrible, No Good, Very Bad Day*. Illustrated by Ray Cruz. Atheneum, 1972.

————. *Alexander Who Used to Be Rich Last Sunday*. Illustrated by Ray Cruz. Atheneum, 1978.

————. *The Tenth Good Thing About Barney*. Illustrated by Erik Blegvad. Atheneum, 1971.

Waber, Bernard. *The House on East 88th Street*. Houghton Mifflin, 1962.

————. *Ira Sleeps Over*. Houghton Mifflin, 1972.

————. *Lyle, Lyle Crocodile*. Houghton Mifflin, 1965.

Wagner, Jenny. *John Brown, Rose, and the Midnight Cat*. Illustrated by Ron Brooks. Bradbury, 1978.

Walter, Mildred Pitts. *My Mama Needs Me*. Illustrated by Pat Cummings. Lothrop, Lee & Shepard, 1983.

Wells, Rosemary. *Noisy Nora*. Dial, 1973.

————. *Shy Charles*. Dial, 1988.

————. *Stanley and Rhoda*. Dial, 1978.

Wiesner, David. *Hurricane*. Clarion, 1990.

Wild, Margaret. *The Very Best of Friends*. Illustrated by Julie Vivas. Harcourt Brace, 1990.

Wildsmith, Brian. *The Owl and the Woodpecker*. Watts, 1972.

————. *Python's Party*. Oxford University Press, 1974.

Willard, Nancy. *A Visit to William Blake's Inn*. Illustrated by Alice and Martin Provensen. Harcourt Brace, 1981.

Williams, Karen Lynn. *Galimoto*. Illustrated by Catherine Stock. Lothrop, Lee & Shepard, 1990.

Williams, Margery. *The Velveteen Rabbit: Or How Toys Become Real*. Illustrated by David Jorgensen. Knopf, 1985.

————. *The Velveteen Rabbit: Or How Toys Become Real*. Illustrated by Ilse Plume. Harcourt Brace, 1987.

————. *The Velveteen Rabbit: Or How Toys Become Real*. Illustrated by Michael Hague. Henry Holt, 1983.

————. *The Velveteen Rabbit: Or How Toys Become Real*. Illustrated by William Nicholson. Doubleday, 1958 [1922].

Williams, Vera B. *A Chair for My Mother*. Greenwillow, 1982.

————. *Music, Music for Everyone*. Greenwillow, 1984.

————. *Something Special for Me*. Greenwillow, 1983.

Wisniewski, David. *Sundiata: Lion King of Mali*. Clarion, 1992.

————. *The Wave of the Sea-Wolf*. Clarion, 1994.

Wolff, Ashley. *A Year of Beasts*. Dutton, 1989.

————. *A Year of Birds*. Dutton, 1984.

Wood, Audrey. *The Napping House*. Illustrated by Don Wood. Harcourt Brace, 1984.

Wormell, Mary. *Hilda Hen's Happy Birthday*. Harcourt Brace, 1995.

————. *Hilda Hen's Search*. Harcourt Brace, 1994.

Yashima, Taro [Jun Iwamatsu]. *Crow Boy*. Viking, 1955.

————. *Umbrella*. Viking Penguin, 1958.

Yolen, Jane. *The Emperor and the Kite*. Illustrated by Ed Young. Philomel, 1988 [1967].

————. *Letting Swift River Go*. Illustrated by Barbara Cooney. Little, Brown, 1992.

————. *Owl Moon*. Illustrated by John Schoenherr. Philomel, 1987.

Yorinks, Arthur. *The Miami Giant*. Illustrated by Maurice Sendak. HarperCollins, 1995.

Young, Ed. *Little Plum*. Philomel, 1994.

Zelinsky, Paul O. *The Maid, the Mouse and the Odd Shaped House*. Dodd Mead, 1981.

Zolotow, Charlotte. *Mr. Rabbit and the Lovely Present*. Illustrated by Maurice Sendak. Harper & Row, 1962.

————. *Say It!* Illustrated by James Stevenson. Greenwillow, 1980.

————. *William's Doll*. Illustrated by William Pène duBois. Harper & Row, 1972.

chapter six

Traditional Literature

A Perspective on Traditional Literature 266

The Origin of Folk Literature 266

The Value of Folk Literature for Children 268

Folktales 268

Types of Folktales 269

Cumulative Tales 269

Pourquoi Tales 269

Teaching Feature: Creating Pourquoi Stories with Fifth Graders 270

Beast Tales 270

Wonder Tales 271

Realistic Tales 271

Resources for Teaching: A Cross-Cultural Study of Folktale Types 272

Characteristics of Folktales 273

Plot Structures 273

Characterization 274

Style 274

Themes 275

Motifs 276

Variants 278

Resources for Teaching: A Cross-Cultural Study of Folktale Motifs 279

Folktales of the World 280

British Folktales 280

Resources for Teaching: A Cross-Cultural Study of Folktale Variants 281

German Folktales 283

Scandinavian Folktales 285

French Folktales 286

Russian Folktales 287

Jewish Folktales 289

Folktales from the Middle East and India 290

Folktales from Asia 292

Folktales from Africa 295

Folktales of North America 297

Resources for Teaching: Some Native American Folktales by Region 299

Resources for Teaching: A Study of Folktales by Culture 302

Folktales from Central and South America 307

Resources for Teaching: Some American Tall-Tale Heroes 308

Fables 310

Characteristics of Fables 310

Editions 310

Web: Folktales 311

Myths 313

Types of Myths 313

Creation Myths 313

Nature Myths 314

Hero Myths 314

Greek Mythology 314

Resources for Teaching: Some Gods and Goddesses of Greek and Roman Mythology 315

Norse Mythology 317

Epic and Legendary Heroes 318

The *Iliad* and the *Odyssey* 318

The *Ramayana* 318

Heroes of the Middle Ages 319

The Bible as Literature 321

Collections of Bible Stories 321

Single Bible Stories 322

Learning Experiences 324

Related Readings 324

Children's Literature 325

Ever since human beings realized they were unique among animals in that they could think and talk, they have tried to explain themselves and their world. Who were the first humans? How did they come to be? What made the sun and the moon and the stars? Why are the animals made the way they are? What caused night and day, the seasons, the cycle of life itself? Why are some people greedy and some unselfish, some ugly and some handsome, some dull and some clever? As people pondered these questions and many more, they created stories that helped explain the world to their primitive minds. The storytellers told these tales again and again around the fires of the early tribes, by the hearths of humble cottages, before the great fire in the king's hall; they told them as they sat in the grass huts of the jungle, the hogans of the southern plains, and the igloos of the northern tundra. Their children told them, and their children's children, until the stories were as smooth and polished as the roundest stones in a stream. And so people created their myths and their folktales, their legends and epics—the literature of the fireside, the poetry of the people, and the memory of humankind.

A Perspective on Traditional Literature

Traditional literature can provide a window on cultural beliefs and on the spiritual and psychological qualities that are part of our human nature. These stories also form the basis for many works of more-modern literature, drama, and other art forms. It is important to help children become familiar with the rich heritage of stories that have come down to us from cultures around the world.

The Origin of Folk Literature

We have no one word that encompasses all of the stories born of the oral tradition. The stories most often are labeled "folklore," "folk literature," or "mythology." Generally we say that myths are about gods and the creation of things; legends are about heroes and their mighty deeds before the time of recorded history; and folktales, fairytales, and fables are simple stories about talking beasts, woodcutters, and princesses who reveal human behavior and beliefs while playing out their roles in a world of wonder and magic.

Children sometimes identify these stories as "make-believe," as contrasted with "true" or "stories that could really happen." Unfortunately, the word *myth* sometimes has been defined as "imagined event" or "pagan falsehood" and contrasted with "historical fact" or "religious truth." In literary study, however, a myth is not "untrue"; rather, it is a story with a generalized meaning, or a universal idea, that expresses a significant truth about humans and their lives. A single myth is a narrative that tells of origins,[1] explains natural or social phenomena, or suggests the destiny of humans through the interaction of people and supernatural beings. A *mythology* is a group of myths of a particular culture. Myth making is continuous and still in process today.[2] Usually myth is a product of a society rather than of a single author.

The origin of the myths has fascinated and puzzled folklorists, anthropologists, and psychologists. How, they wonder, can we account for the similarities among these stories that grew out of ancient cultures widely separated from each other? The Greek myth in Margaret Hodges's *The Arrow and the Lamp: The Story of Psyche* is very much like the Norwegian tale told in George Dasent's *East o' the Sun and West o' the Moon.* The Chinese "Cinderella" story recounted in Ai-Ling Louie's *Yeh-Shen* is similar to Perrault's French *Cinderella* except that a fish acts on the poor girl's behalf. And the

[1] X. J. Kennedy, *Literature: An Introduction to Fiction, Poetry and Drama* (Boston: Little, Brown, 1983), p. 610.

[2] Joseph Campbell, with Bill Moyers, *The Power of Myth* (New York: Doubleday, 1988).

Readers will recognize many aspects of the "Cinderella" story in the Ojibwa tale *Sootface* by Robert D. San Souci.
From *Sootface* by Robert D. San Souci. Copyright text © 1994 by Robert D. San Souci, illustration by Daniel San Souci. Used by permission of Bantam Books, a division of Bantam Doubleday Dell Publishing Group, Inc.

Cinderella story is found throughout the world, with nearly five hundred variants in Europe alone.

In trying to explain this phenomenon, one group of early mythologists proposed the notion of *monogenesis*, or inheritance from a single culture. The Grimm brothers, who were among the first nineteenth-century scholars of folklore, theorized that all folktales originated from one prehistoric group called Aryans, later identified as Indo-Europeans by modern linguists. As this group migrated to other countries, the scholars reasoned, they took their folklore with them; such reasoning led scholars to the theory of *diffusion*.

Another approach to folklore involves the theory of *polygenesis*, or multiple origins. It is argued that each story could have been an independent invention growing out of universal human desires and needs. Early anthropologists viewed myth as the religion of the people derived from rituals that were recounted in drama and narratives. They identified recurrent themes in myths of different cultures. Clyde Kluckhohn's study of the myths of fifty cultures revealed recurring themes like the flood, the slaying of monsters, incest, sibling rivalry, and castration.[3] Kluckhohn also found several patterns repeated in the myth of the hero. Sir James Frazer's twelve-volume analysis of ritual, taboos, and myths, *The Golden Bough*,[4] was of major importance. This anthropological study ascribed sexual symbolic meaning to primitive myths and greatly influenced modern literature.

Sigmund Freud's analysis of myth as dream, or disguised wish fulfillment, was the beginning of psychological literary criticism.[5] Freud held the view that all myths expressed the Oedipus theme with its incest motive, guilt, and punishment. Another psychological viewpoint was that of Carl Jung, a contemporary of Freud, who thought that a "collective unconscious" is "inherited in the structure of the brain."[6] These unconscious, recurring images created the primitive mythic heroes and still exist as individual fantasies for the civilized person as a kind of "race memory," according to Jung. The folklorist, however, might disagree with such psychological interpretations. Richard Dorson argues that "folk literature cannot all be prettily channeled into the universal monomyth" and that "the folklorist looks with jaundiced eye at the excessive straining of mythologists to extort symbols from folk tales."[7]

Folktales are also of special interest to scholars of narrative theory. Because of the way the tales are honed by many generations of telling, only the most important elements of the story survive. Close study of the patterns of action and character relationships show how language shapes a form we recognize as a story. Vladimir Propp, for instance, analyzed Russian tales and identified a set sequence of thirty-one "functions" that might occur in a tale, such as these: The hero leaves home (departure); one member of a family lacks or desires something (lack); or a villain attempts to deceive his victim (trickery).[8] Other researchers have used simplified folktale structures to develop models of children's story comprehension. Although looking at tales in such a technical way is definitely an adult perspective, children who have heard and enjoyed many traditional stories begin to discover for themselves that folktales seem to follow certain structural rules. One 10-year-old girl who wrote instructions for "making a fairy story" summed up by saying, "Fairy tales have to have a sort of pattern or they would just be regular stories."

However scholars choose to look at them, folktales and myths are literature derived from human imagination to explain the human condition. Literature today continues to express our concern about human strengths

[3]Clyde Kluckhohn, "Recurrent Themes in Myth and Mythmaking," in *The Making of Myth*, ed. Richard M. Ohrmann (New York: Putnam, 1962), pp. 52–65.

[4]Sir James Frazer, *The Golden Bough*, 3rd ed. (London: Macmillan, 1911–1915).

[5]Stanley E. Hyman, *The Armed Vision*, rev. ed. (New York: Vintage, 1955).

[6]Carl C. Jung, "On the Relation of Analytic Psychology to Poetic Art," in *Modern Continental Literary Criticism*, ed. O. B. Hardison, Jr. (New York: Appleton, 1962), pp. 267–288.

[7]Richard Dorson, "Theories of Myth and the Folklorist," in *The Making of Myth*, p. 45.

[8]Vladimir Propp, *The Morphology of the Folktale* (Austin: University of Texas Press, 1968).

and weaknesses and the individual's relationships to the world and to other people. Traditional literature forms the foundation of understandings of life as expressed in modern literature.

The Value of Folk Literature for Children

When Jacob and Wilhelm Grimm published the first volume of their *Household Stories* in 1812, they did not intend it for children. These early philologists were studying the language and grammar of such traditional tales. In recent years, as we have seen, anthropologists study folklore in order to understand the inherent values and beliefs of a culture. Psychologists look at folktales and myths and discover something of human motivation and feelings. Folklorists collect and categorize various stories, types, and motifs from around the world. These are all adult scholars of folk literature, which itself was first created by adults and usually told to an adult community. How, then, did folk literature become associated with children's literature, and what value does this kind of literature have for children?

Originally folklore was the literature of the people; stories were told to young and old alike. Families or tribes or the king's court would gather to hear a famous storyteller in much the same way that an entire family today will watch their favorite television program together. With the age of scientific enlightenment, these stories were relegated to the nursery, often kept alive by resourceful nursemaids or grandmothers, much to the delight of children.

Children today still enjoy these tales because they are good stories. Born of the oral tradition, these stories are usually short and have fast-moving plots. They frequently are humorous and almost always end happily. Poetic justice prevails; the good and the just are eventually rewarded; the evil are punished. This appeals to children's sense of justice and their moral judgment. Wishes come true, but usually not without the fulfillment of a task or trial. The littlest child, the youngest child, or the smallest animal succeeds; the oldest or the largest is frequently defeated. Youngsters, who are the little people of their world, thrive on such turns of events.

Beyond the function of pure entertainment, folktales can kindle the child's imagination. Behind every great author, poet, architect, mathematician, or diplomat are that person's dreams of what she or he hopes to achieve. These dreams or ideals have been created by the power of imagination. If we always give children stories of "what is," stories that only mirror the living of today, then we have not helped them to imagine what "might have been" or "what might be."

Bruno Bettelheim, in his remarkable book *The Uses of Enchantment*, maintains that fairy tales help children cope with their dreams and inner turmoil. "Each fairy tale," he says, "is a magic mirror which reflects some aspects of our inner world and of the steps required by our evolution from immaturity to maturity."[9]

Kornei Chukovsky, the Russian poet, tells of a time when it was proposed that all folktales and fairy tales be eliminated from the education of the Russian child in favor of simple realistic stories. Then one of the major Russian educators began keeping a diary of her child's development. She found that her child, as if to compensate for the loss of the fairy tales he had been denied, began to make up his own. He had never heard a folktale, but his world became peopled with talking tigers, birds, and bugs. Chukovsky concludes: "Fantasy is the most valuable attribute of the human mind and should be diligently nurtured from earliest childhood."[10]

Our speech and vocabulary reflect many contributions from traditional literature. Think of the figures of speech that come from Aesop's fables: "sour grapes," "dog in the manger," "boy who cried wolf." Our language is replete with words and phrases from the myths—*narcissistic, cereal, labyrinth, siren*, and many more.

Traditional literature is a rightful part of a child's literary heritage and lays the groundwork for understanding all literature. Poetry and modern stories allude to traditional literature, particularly the Greek myths, Aesop's fables, and Bible stories. Northrop Frye maintains that "all themes and characters and stories that you encounter in literature belong to one big interlocking family."[11] As you meet recurring patterns or symbols in mythlike floods, savior heroes, cruel stepmothers, the seasonal cycle of the year, the cycle of a human life, you begin to build a framework for literature. Poetry, prose, and drama become more emotionally significant as you respond to these recurring archetypes.

Folktales

Folktales have been defined as "all forms of narrative, written or oral, which have come to be handed down through the years."[12] This definition would include epics, ballads, legends, and folk songs, as well as myths

---

[9]Bruno Bettelheim, *The Uses of Enchantment* (New York: Knopf, 1976), p. 309.

[10]Kornei Chukovsky, *From Two to Five*, trans. and ed. Miriam Morton (Berkeley: University of California Press, 1963), p. 119.

[11]Northrop Frye, *The Educated Imagination* (Bloomington: Indiana University Press, 1964), p. 48.

[12]Ibid.

and fables. In using folk literature in the elementary school, we have tended to confine the rather simple folktales—such as the popular "Three Billy Goats Gruff," "Little Red Riding Hood," and "Rumpelstilt-skin"—to the primary grades; we recommend the so-called fairy tales—such as "Snow White" and "Cinderella"—for slightly older children, since these tales are longer and contain romantic elements. Such a division appears arbitrary; it is based more on use than on any real difference in the stories. To complicate matters even further, modern fanciful stories created by known authors are often also referred to as fairy tales. Hans Christian Andersen's stories are becoming part of the heritage that might be described as folktales, but *many originated in written rather than oral form.* Thus they are distinguished from the stories told by the common folk that were finally collected and recorded. Stories that are written in a folktale style but originated in an author's imagination are often referred to as "literary folktales" (see "Modern Folktale Style" in Chapter 5).

Questions often arise about which of the available print versions of a tale is the "correct" or authentic text. From a folklorist's point of view, a tale is recreated every time it is told and therefore *every* telling is correct in its own way. A great deal of variation is also acceptable in print versions, where literary style carries the same uniqueness as the teller's voice. Authors and illustrators may also add original twists, customize their stories for a chosen audience, or adapt a familiar tale to an unfamiliar setting, as oral storytellers do. There might be a problem, however, when a print version suggests by its title, or lack of an author's note, that it represents a tale derived directly from a previously printed source. Readers of a story identified as recorded and published by the Grimm brothers, for instance, have a right to find that this tale has been subsequently published without major additions, omissions, or distortions.

This chapter discusses folktales in children's literature that come from the oral tradition. It also includes a description of epics, myths, and stories from the Bible, which are all a part of traditional literature. Modern fanciful stories written by known authors are discussed in Chapter 7.

Types of Folktales

The many folktales that have found their way into the hands and hearts of children come from many cultures. There will be features of these stories that are unique to each culture, but children will also find particular aspects of plot or characterization that occur across cultures. Recognizable literary patterns can be found in cumulative tales, beast tales, pourquoi tales, wonder tales, and realistic tales.

Cumulative Tales

Very young children are fascinated by such cumulative stories as Anne Rockwell's "The Old Woman and Her Pig" with its "Rat! rat! gnaw rope; rope won't hang butcher; butcher won't kill ox; ox won't drink water; water won't quench fire; fire won't burn stick; stick won't beat dog; dog won't bite pig; piggy won't get over the stile; and I shan't get home tonight." The story itself is not as important as the increasing repetition of the details building up to a quick climax. The story of the gingerbread boy who ran away from the old woman defiantly crying "Catch me if you can," as in Paul Galdone's *The Gingerbread Boy,* has been told in many different versions, including Arnica Esterl's English version *The Fine Round Cake* and Ruth Sawyer's Appalachian version *Journey Cake, Ho!*

In another familiar cumulative tale, one day an acorn falls on Henny Penny (see Stephen Butler's *Henny Penny* and the version in Helen Oxenbury's *Nursery Story Book*). Thinking the sky is falling down, she persuades Cocky-Locky, Ducky-Daddles, Goosey-Poosey, and Turkey-Lurkey to go along with her to tell the king. Children delight in the sound of the rhyming double names, which are repeated over and over. Young children, especially, enjoy extending and personalizing these cumulative tales through dramatic play. Certainly the best known of all cumulative tales is the one told in William Stobbs's *The House That Jack Built.* You will find repetitive stories in practically all folklore.

Pourquoi Tales

Some folktales are "why," or *pourquoi,* stories that explain certain animal traits or characteristics or human customs. In "How the Animals Got Their Tails" in *Beat the Story-Drum, Pum-Pum,* Ashley Bryan tells an African tale of a time when all animals were vegetarians. Then Raluvhimba created a mistake, the flies who were flesh eaters and bloodsuckers. "I can't take back what I've done. After all, that's life," the god said. But he did give the rest of the animals tails with which to swish away the flies.

Many Native American stories are "why" stories that explain animal features, the origin of certain natural features, or how humans and their customs came to be. Paul Goble's retelling of a Sioux myth in *The Great Race of the Birds and the Animals* explains the origins of the Milky Way and the reason why the magpie's tail feathers are iridescent. In *The Story of Light,* Susan Roth uses dramatic black-and-white woodcuts with yellow to highlight a Cherokee myth that explains how each animal was marked in its failure to capture light for the earth until the tiny spider

Teaching Feature   Creating Pourquoi Stories with Fifth Graders

A fifth-grade teacher assembled many African *pourquoi* stories and led her class in reading and discussing the patterns. Children noted that most explained animal characteristics or habits and natural phenomena. Children also discussed the illustrations and were particularly impressed with the clear colors and white-outlined shapes that Leo and Diane Dillon used for the Caldecott Medal–winning pictures in Verna Aardema's *Why Mosquitoes Buzz in People's Ears*. When the teacher asked children to produce their own "how" or "why" stories and illustrate them, here is what one child created:

Why Flies Eat Rotten Food

A long time ago, in a jungle, Fly was very hot. So he flew to the river and rolled around in the mud. After that Fly was very hungry so he flew home. On the way he looked down and saw a big juicy steak lying on the ground.

Now fly was *very* hungry so he flew down and started eating it. But he was so dirty that when he landed he got mud on the steak and as he walked around eating it he got even more mud on it.

By the time Fly was done eating, the whole steak was covered with mud. Just then King Lion (the owner of the steak who had been taking a nap) walked into the clearing. "What have you done to my steak you stupid fly?" roared his majesty.

"Oh," said Fly, "I was just—." Then he looked at the steak. "Oh your majesty! I am very sorry. So very sorry," apologized Fly.

Then the King said, "As a punishment you can never eat fresh food again. You must always eat things like this steak."

Fly was so ashamed that he flew off with his head down but because he does not dare oppose King Lion he has eaten dirty and rotten food ever since.

Allison Fraser, fifth grade
Susan Steinberg, teacher
George Mason Elementary School
Alexandria, Virginia

succeeded. It also explains how dark Earth received the first sunlight.[13]

Beast Tales

Probably the favorite folktales of young children are beast tales in which animals act and talk like human beings. The best known of these frequently appear in newly illustrated versions. In his version of *The Three Little Pigs*, Paul Galdone portrays the wolf as a ferocious doggy creature. Lorinda Bryan Cauley's illustrations for Joseph Jacobs's version present the wolf as a country gentleman among bumpkins. James Marshall's red-capped wolf looks like a thug in his red-striped polo shirt. And in his *The Three Pigs*, Tony Ross shows a modern-day wolf in a gray flannel topcoat pursuing the pigs, who have moved to the country to escape an over-crowded city high-rise apartment! Other beast tales found in several versions include *The Three Billy Goats Gruff* (versions by Asbjørnsen and Moe, and Glen Rounds), *The Little Red Hen* (Paul Galdone, Margot Zemach), and *Puss in Boots* (Galdone, Fiona Moody). In *The Three Bears and Fifteen Other Stories*, Anne Rockwell has included many of these favorite beast stories in a delightful collection for the very young child. Clear, glowing watercolors are used throughout to help the child follow the action of the stories.

Many African stories are "wise beast/foolish beast" tales of how one animal, such as a spider or rabbit, outwits a lion, hyena, leopard, or other foe. In Verna Aardema's *Rabbit Makes a Monkey of Lion*, Rabbit and Turtle steal Lion's honey and continually trick him into letting them go. So Lion hides in Rabbit's house in hopes of eating him for supper. But Rabbit notices the beast's footprints and calls out, "How-de-do, Little House." When the house doesn't reply, Rabbit pretends to be puzzled. "Little House, you always tell me *how-de-do*. Is something wrong today?" Of course, the confused Lion answers for the house, reveals his presence, and is tricked once again. Many beast tales that traveled to the United States with enslaved Africans were collected by Joel Chandler Harris in the late 1800s. These have been retold in two series, one by Julius Lester that begins with *The Tales of Uncle Remus: The Adventures of Brer Rabbit*, and the other by Van Dyke Parks, beginning with *Jump: The Adventures of Brer Rabbit*.

Talking animals appear in folktales of all cultures. Fish are often in English, Scandinavian, German, and South Seas stories. Tales of bears, wolves, and the firebird are found in Russian folklore. Spiders, rabbits, tortoises, crocodiles, monkeys, and lions are very much a part of African tales; rabbits, badgers, monkeys, and even bees are represented in Japanese stories. A study of just the animals in folklore would be fascinating.

[13]For modern pourquoi tales, see the section on Rudyard Kipling's *Just-So Stories* in Chapter 5.

Demi's *The Firebird* is a wonder tale—a story that involves romance, magic, and difficult tasks.
From *The Firebird* by Demi. Copyright © 1994 by Demi. Reprinted by permission of Henry Holt and Co., Inc.

Wonder Tales

Children call wonder tales about magic and the super-natural "fairy tales." Very few tales have fairies or even a fairy godmother in them, but the name persists. These are the stories that include giants, such as Steven Kellogg's *Jack and the Beanstalk*, or fairies, as in Susan Cooper's *Tam Lin*. Wicked witches, Baba Yaga in Russian folklore, demons such as the *oni* of Japanese tales, or monsters and dragons abound in these stories. Traditionally we have thought of the fairy tale as involving romance and adventure. "Cinderella," "Snow White and the Seven Dwarfs," and "Beauty and the Beast" all have elements of both. The long quest tales—such as the Russian tale told in Demi's *The Firebird* or the Norwegian tale told in George Dasent's *East o' the Sun and West o' the Moon*—are complex wonder tales in which the hero, or heroine, triumphs against all odds to win the beautiful princess, or handsome prince, and makes a fortune. Children know that these tales will end with " . . . and they lived happily ever after." In fact, part of the appeal of the fairy tale is the secure knowledge that no matter what happens, love, kindness, and truth will prevail—and hate, wickedness, and evil will be punished. Wonder tales have always represented the glorious fulfillment of human desires.

Realistic Tales

Surprisingly, there are a few realistic tales included in folklore. The story in Marcia Brown's *Dick Whittington and His Cat* could have happened; in fact, there is evidence that a Richard Whittington did indeed live and was mayor of London. Like the American story in Reeve Lindbergh's *Johnny Appleseed*, the tale began with a real person but has become so embroidered through various tellings that it takes its place in the folklore of its culture.

"Zlateh the Goat," the title story in a collection of Jewish tales by Isaac Bashevis Singer, is a survival story. The son of a poor peasant family is sent off to the butcher to sell Zlateh, the family goat. On the way, he and the goat are caught in a fierce snowstorm. They take refuge in a haystack, where they stay for three days. Zlateh eats the hay while the boy survives on Zlateh's milk and warmth. When the storm is over, they return home to a grateful family. No one ever again mentions selling Zlateh.

Two Japanese stories are very different in feeling but are realistic nonetheless. In *The Boy of the Three-Year Nap*, Diane Snyder tells how a poor mother tricks her lazy son into a marriage and employment. In the story Margaret Hodges retells in *The Wave*, a poor man sacrifices his own rice fields in order to warn other villagers of an approaching tidal wave. Blair Lent worked in a technique rarely seen in children's books, using card-board cutouts to print the illustrations for the story.

Resources for Teaching, "A Cross-Cultural Study of Folktale Types," is the first of three boxes in this chapter that groups folktales from various countries in specific ways to help teachers more easily plan curricula. This box groups together titles that tell similar tales. The other two boxes group tales by motif and by variants.

Resources for Teaching
A Cross-Cultural Study of Folktale Types

Type of Folktale	Tale, Author	Culture
Cumulative tales	"The Old Woman and Her Pig" (Rockwell)	England
	Henny Penny (Butler)	England
	One Fine Day (Hogrogian)	Armenia
	Knock, Knock, Teremok! (Arnold)	Russia
	The Rooster Who Went to His Uncle's Wedding (Ada)	Cuba
	The Fine Round Cake (Esterl)	England
Pourquoi tales	*The Great Ball Game* (Bruchac)	Native American
	"Jack and the Devil," in *The People Could Fly* (Hamilton)	African American
	The Cat's Purr (Bryan)	West Indian
	Why the Sun and the Moon Live in the Sky (Dayrell)	Africa
	How Summer Came to Canada (Toye)	Native American
	"Tia Miseria's Pear Tree," in *The Magic Orange Tree* (Wolkstein)	Puerto Rico
	"How Animals Got Their Tails," *Beat the Story-Drum* (Bryan)	Africa
	Feathers Like a Rainbow (Flora)	South America
	A Song of Stars (Birdseye)	China/Japan
	Why Ducks Sleep on One Leg (Garland)	Vietnam
Beast tales	*The Three Billy Goats Gruff* (Absjørnsen and Moe)	Norway
	The Bremen-Town Musicians (Grimm brothers)	Germany
	Rabbit Makes a Monkey of Lion (Aardema)	Africa (Tanzania)
	Three Little Pigs and the Big Bad Wolf (Rounds)	England
	Foolish Rabbit's Big Mistake (Martin)	India
	"Brer Terrapin," in *Jump!* (Parks and Jones)	African American
	Beat the Story-Drum, Pum-Pum (Bryan)	Africa
	Rockaby Crocodile (Aruego and Dewey)	Philippines
Wonder tales	*Lily and the Wooden Bowl* (Schroeder)	Japan
	Ali Baba and the Forty Thieves (McVitty)	Middle East
	Jack and the Beanstalk (Kellogg)	England
	Beauty and the Beast (de Beaumont)	France
	Snow White (Grimm brothers)	Germany
	Momotaro, the Peach Boy (Shute)	Japan
	Tam Lin (Cooper)	Scotland
	Vasilissa the Beautiful (Winthrop)	Russia
Realistic tales	*Fire on the Mountain* (Kurtz)	Ethiopia
	Dick Whittington and His Cat (Brown)	England
	Something from Nothing (Gilman)	Jewish
	The Boy of the Three-Year Nap (Snyder)	Japan
	"The Case of the Uncooked Eggs," in *The Magic Orange Tree* (Wolkstein)	Haiti
	Brothers (Freedman)	Jewish
	My Mother Is the Most Beautiful Woman in the World (Reyher)	Russia
	"Zlateh the Goat" (Singer)	Jewish
	The Empty Pot (Demi)	China

Characteristics of Folktales

Since folktales have been told and retold from generation to generation within a particular culture, we may ask how they reflect the country of their origin and its oral tradition. An authentic tale from Africa will include references to the flora and fauna of Africa and to the tribespeople's food, huts, customs, foibles, and beliefs. And it will sound like it is being *told*. Although folktales have many elements in common, it should not be possible to confuse a folktale from Japan with a folktale from the fjords of Norway. What then are the characteristics common to all folktales?

Plot Structures

Of the folktales best known in children's literature, even the longer stories are usually simple and direct. A series of episodes maintains a quick flow of action. If it is a "wise beast/foolish beast" story, the characters are quickly delineated, the action shows the inevitable conflict and resolution, and the ending is usually brief. If the tale is a romance, the hero or heroine sets forth on a journey, often helps the poor on the way, frequently receives magical power, overcomes obstacles, and returns to safety. The plot that involves a weak or innocent child going forth to meet the monsters of the world is another form of the "journey-novel." In the Grimm brothers' *Hansel and Gretel* the children go out into a dark world and meet the witch, but goodness and purity triumph. Almost all folktale plots are success stories of one kind or another.

Repetition is a basic element in many folktale plots. Frequently three is the magic number. There are three little pigs whose three houses face the puffing of the wolf. The wolf gives three challenges to the pig in the brick house—to get turnips and apples and to go to the fair. In the longer tales each of the three tasks becomes increasingly more difficult, and the intensity of the wonders becomes progressively more marvelous. This repetition satisfies listeners or readers with its orderliness.

The repetition of responses, chants, or poems is frequently a part of the structure of a tale. "Mirror, mirror on the wall, who is fairest of them all?" And "Fee, fi, fo, fum" are repetitive verses familiar to all. Some versions of *Hansel and Gretel* end with a storyteller's coda, such as Elizabeth Crawford's: "My tale is done, and there a mouse does run. Whoever catches it can make a big fur cap of it." These serve both the storyteller and the listener as memory aids and familiar markers of the unfolding plot.

Time and place are established quickly in the folktale. Suzanne Crowder Han's *The Rabbit's Judgment*, a Korean tale, begins: "Long, long ago, when plants and animals talked, a tiger fell into a deep pit while roaming through the forest in search of food." Time is always past, and frequently described by such conventions as "Once upon a time" or "In olden times when wishing still helped." Time also passes quickly in the folktale. In Trina Schart Hyman's version of *Sleeping Beauty*, the woods and brambles encircled Sleeping Beauty's palace in a quarter of an hour, and "when a hundred years were gone and passed," the prince appeared at the moment the enchantment ended. The setting of the folktale is not specific, but in some faraway land, in a cottage in the woods, in a beautiful palace.

The introduction to the folktale usually presents the conflict, characters, and setting in a few sentences. In "Anansi and Nothing Go Hunting for Wives" (in Courlander and Herzog's *The Cow-Tail Switch*) the problem is established in the first two sentences:

> It came to Anansi one time, as he sat in his little hut, that he needed a wife. For most men this would have been a simple affair, but Anansi's bad name had spread throughout the country and he knew that he wouldn't be likely to have much luck finding a wife in near-by villages. (p. 95)

With little description, the storyteller goes to the heart of his story, capturing the interest of his audience.

The conclusion of the story follows the climax very quickly and includes few details. In the Grimm brothers' *The Seven Ravens*, after the small sister finds her brothers who have been bewitched as ravens, she leaves her tiny ring in the cup belonging to one of the ravens. He sees it and makes a wish:

> . . . "Would God that our own little sister were here, for then we should be free. . . !"
>
> When the maiden, who was standing behind the door listening, heard the wish, she came out, and then all the ravens regained human forms again. And they embraced and kissed one another and went joyfully home. (unpaged)

Even this is a long ending compared with "And so they were married and lived happily ever after."

The structure of the folktale, with its quick introduction, economy of incident, and logical and brief conclusion, maintains interest through suspense and repetition. Because the storyteller has to keep the attention of the audience, each episode must contribute to the theme of the story. Written versions, then, should follow the oral tradition, adding little description and avoiding lengthy asides or admonitions.

Characterization

Characters in folktales are shown in flat dimensions, symbolic of the completely good or entirely evil. Character development is seldom depicted. The beautiful girl is usually virtuous, humble, patient, and loving. Stepmothers are ugly, cross, and mean. The hero, usually fair-haired or curly-haired, is strong, virile, brave, kind, and sympathetic. The poor are often kind, generous, and long-suffering; the rich are imperious, hardhearted, and often conniving, if not actually dishonest. Physical characteristics may be described briefly, but readers form their own pictures as they read. In describing the daughter of the Dragon King, the Chinese grandmother says: "Now this young woman was poorly dressed, but her face was as fair as a plum blossom in spring, and her body was as slender as a willow branch."[14]

Qualities of character or special strengths or weaknesses of the characters are revealed quickly, because this factor will be the cause of conflict or lead to resolution of the plot. The lazy daughter and virtuous stepdaughter are contrasted in Samuel Marshak's Russian tale *The Month-Brothers*: "The daughter used to loll about the whole day long on a featherbed devouring sweetmeats, while the stepdaughter never got a chance to rest from morn to night." The trickster character of Brer Rabbit in Van Dyke Parks's *Jump Again!* is established in a few swift phrases: "Brer Rabbit could cut more capers than a hive has bumbly-bees. Under his hat, Brer Rabbit had a mighty quick thinking apparatus" (p. 2).

Seeing folktale characters as symbols of good, evil, power, trickery, wisdom, and other traits, children begin to understand the basis of literature that distills the essences of human experience.

Style

Folktales offer children many opportunities to hear rich qualitative language and a wide variety of language patterns. Story introductions may range from the familiar "Once upon a time" to the Persian "There was a time and there wasn't a time"; and then there is the African tale that starts: "We do not mean, we do not really mean that what we are going to say is true."

The introductions and language of the folktale should maintain the "flavor" of the country but still be understood by its present audience. Folktales should not be "written down" to children, but they might need to be simplified. Wanda Gág describes her method of simplification in adapting folktales for children:

🐜 By simplification I mean:

(a) freeing hybrid stories of confusing passages
(b) using repetition for clarity where a mature style does not include it
(c) employing actual dialogue to sustain or revive interest in places where the narrative is too condensed for children.

However, I do not mean writing in words of one or two syllables. True, the careless use of large words is confusing to children; but long, even unfamiliar words are relished and easily absorbed by them, provided they have enough color and sound value.[15]

Some folktales include proverbs of the country. For example, in Diane Wolkstein's *The Magic Orange Tree* a king says to his followers after hearing a story of a man whose second wife murdered his son: "Choose whom you want to marry, but if you choose a tree that has fruit, you must care for the fruit as much as for the tree" (p. 97). In Elizabeth Winthrop's Russian story *Vasilissa the Beautiful,* a small doll counsels the sorrowful Vasilissa to shut her eyes and sleep, for "The morning is wiser than the evening."

Although there is a minimum of description in the folktale, figurative language and imagery are employed by effective narrators. In *Mazel and Shlimazel,* Isaac Singer uses delightful prose to introduce the Jewish tale about the wager between the spirits of good luck and bad luck:

🐜 In a faraway land, on a sunny spring day, the sky was as blue as the sea, and the sea was as blue as the sky, and the earth was green and in love with them both. (p. 1)

In Verna Aardema's East African story *Bimwili & the Zimwi,* a little girl, Bimwili, was playing by the ocean, and "something that looked like a daytime moon came rolling in with a wave, and it tumbled at Bimwili's feet." The daytime moon, a simile for a seashell, begins all of Bimwili's many nights of troubles.

Frequently storytellers imitate the sounds of the story. In Katherine Paterson's poetic translation from Sumiko Yagawa's traditional Japanese tale *The Crane*

---

[14]Frances Carpenter, *Tales of a Chinese Grandmother,* illustrations Malthe Hasselriis (New York: Doubleday, 1949), p. 75.

[15]Wanda Gág, *Tales from Grimm* (New York: Coward-McCann, 1936), p. ix.

Wife, Yohei goes out into the winter snow on an errand. "Suddenly, *basabasa*, he heard a rustling sound. It was a crane dragging its wing, as it swooped down and landed on the path." In Verna Aardema's retelling of a West African tale in *Why Mosquitoes Buzz in People's Ears*, a python slithers into a rabbit's hole *wasawusu, wasawusu, wasawusu*, and the terrified rabbit scurries away *krik, krik, krik*. These onomatopoeic words help listeners hear the story and are wonderful additions for those who tell and read stories to children.

When the tales are written as though the storyteller is speaking directly to the reader, the oral tradition is more clearly communicated. Joyce Arkhurst uses this style effectively in *The Adventures of Spider:*

🕷 I have already told you, and you have already seen for yourselves, that Spider was very full of mischief. He was often naughty and always greedy. But sometimes, in his little heart, he wanted very much to be good. . . . He tried hard, but his appetite almost always got in the way. In fact, that is why Spider has a bald head to this day. Would you like to hear how it got that way? (p. 21)

Surely children in the primary grades would be cheated linguistically if the only version they heard was Gerald McDermott's *Anansi the Spider:*

🕷 One time Anansi went a long way from home. Far from home. He got lost. He fell into trouble. Back home was See Trouble. "Father is in danger!" he cried. He knew it quickly and he told those other sons. (unpaged)

This kind of simplification of text deprives children not only of the meaning but also of the language of the folktale, a key feature of literature based on an oral tradition. Without the pictures, it would be difficult to comprehend McDermott's story.

Dialect enhances a story, but it is difficult for children to read. The teacher will need to practice reading or telling a story with dialect, but it is worth the effort if it is done well. Richard Chase recorded stories from the Appalachian mountain folk in *The Jack Tales*. He notes: "The dialect has been changed enough to avoid confusion to the reading eye; the idiom has been kept throughout." In this dialogue from "The Heifer Hide" the mountaineer vocabulary and dialect are clear:

🕷 "Well, now," she says, "hit's just a little I was a-savin' for my kinfolks comin' tomorrow."

"Me and Jack's your kinfolks. Bring it on out here for us."

So Jack and him eat a lot of them good rations. Jack was awful hungry, and he knowed she hadn't brought out her best stuff yet, so he rammed his heifer hide again, says, "You blabber-mouthed thing! I done told you to hush. You keep on tellin' lies now and I'll put you out the door." (p. xi)

Julius Lester, in his retellings of the Uncle Remus stories collected by Joel Chandler Harris, tried to do what Harris had done: namely, to write tales "so that the reader (listener) would feel as if he or she were being called into a relationship of warmth and intimacy with another human body."[16] His contemporary storyteller communicates through asides, imagery, and allusions. For instance, in "Brer Rabbit Gets Even," in *The Tales of Uncle Remus*, Brer Rabbit decides to visit with Miz Meadows and the girls:

🕷 . . . "Don't come asking me who Miz Meadows and her girls were. I don't know, but then again, ain't no reason I got to know. Miz Meadows and the girls were in the tale when it was handed to me, and they gon' be in it when I hand it to you. And that's the way the rain falls on that one. . . ." (p. 16)

The major criteria for style in the written folktale, then, are that it maintain the atmosphere of the country and culture from which it originated and that it sound like a tale *told* by a storyteller.

Themes

The basic purpose of the folktale is to tell an entertaining story, yet these stories do present important themes. Some tales might be merely humorous accounts of foolish people who are so ridiculous that the listeners see their own foolish ways exaggerated in them. Many of the stories once provided an outlet for feelings against the kings and nobles who oppressed the poor. Values of the culture are expressed in folklore. Humility, kindness, patience, sympathy, hard work, and courage are invariably rewarded. These rewards reflect the goals of people—long life, a good spouse, beautiful homes and fine clothing, plenty of food, freedom from fear of the ogre or giant. The power of love, mercy, and kindness is one of the major themes of folktales. The thematic wisdom of Mme. de Beaumont's *Beauty and the Beast* and Alan Schroeder's *Lily and the Wooden Bowl* is that we should not trust too much to appearances. The valuing of the

[16]Julius Lester, "The Storyteller's Voice: Reflections on the Rewriting of Uncle Remus," *New Advocate* 1, no. 3 (summer 1988): 144.

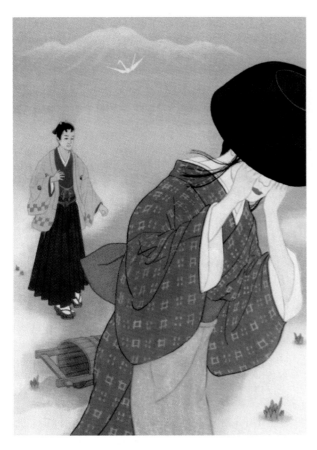

Inner beauty being valued over outward appearances is a
common theme in such folktales as *Lily and the Wooden Bowl*
by Alan Schroeder.
From *Lily and the Wooden Bowl* by Alan Schroeder. Illustrations by Yoriko
Ito. Copyright © 1994 by Alan Schroeder. Used by permission of Bantam
Doubelday Dell Books for Young Readers.

inner qualities of kindness and a loving heart above outward appearance is dramatically presented.

Many folktales feature the small and powerless
achieving good ends by perseverance and patience. In
the traditional Japanese tale recounted by Linda Shute
in *Momotaro, the Peach Boy*, a peasant must battle
wicked demons, but courage and quick wits help him
persevere. In Gail Haley's African tale *A Story, a Story*,
Anansi the spider man wins stories for his people by
outsmarting a leopard, the hornets, and a fairy, and presenting them all to the Sky God. Both Marina, the
good child in Eric Kimmel's *Baba Yaga*, and Sasha, the
kind girl in Joanna Cole's *Bony-Legs*, have good luck
when they are kind to objects and animals. Thus they
are able to outwit the formidable old Russian witch,
Baba Yaga.

Feminists have expressed concern that folktale
themes most often favor courageous, independent boy
adventurers and leave girl characters languishing at
home. Though it is true that it is easier to find tales that

feature plucky boys, there are folktales that portray resourceful, courageous, clever, and independent girls. In
Jane Yolen's *Tam Lin*, an outspoken heroine perseveres
in saving a young man bewitched by the fairies even
though they change him into many fearsome animals.
In the Grimm brothers' *Princess Furball*, the heroine
doesn't need a fairy godmother; she wins a prince because of her own cleverness. In Harve Zemach's *Duffy
and the Devil*, the heroine makes a pact with the devil,
but she finally outwits him—and manages to get out of
spinning and knitting for the rest of her days. Tales that
feature spirited and courageous heroines have been
gathered in several collections. Robert D. San Souci's
*Cut from the Same Cloth: American Women of Myth, Leg-
end and Tall Tale*, Virginia Hamilton's *Her Stories:
African American Folktales*, Ethel Johnston Phelps's *The
Maid of the North*, and Rosemary Minard's *Womenfolk
and Fairy Tales* are examples of collections from the
world over that preserve and honor stories of strong,
clever, and often brave women.

Parents, teachers, and some psychologists have expressed concern about themes of cruelty and horror in
folktales. "Little Red Riding Hood," for example, has
been rewritten so that the wolf eats neither the grandmother nor the heroine. Goals are not accomplished easily in folktales; they frequently require sacrifice. But usually harsh acts occur very quickly with no sense of pain
and no details. In the Grimm brothers' *Seven Ravens*, no
blood drips from the sister's hand when she cuts off a finger; not an "ouch" escapes her lips. Children accept
these stories as they are—symbolic interpretations of life
in an imaginary land of another time.

Motifs

Folklorists analyze folktales according to motifs or patterns, numbering each tale and labeling its episodes.[17]
Motif has been defined as the smallest part of a tale that
can exist independently. Motifs can be seen in the recurring parade of characters in folktales—the younger
brother, the wicked stepmother, the abused child, the
clever trickster—or in supernatural beings like the fairy
godmother, the evil witch, and the terrifying giant. The
use of magical objects (a slipper, a doll, a ring, a tablecloth) is another pattern found in many folktales. Stories of enchantment, long sleeps, or marvelous transformations are typical motifs. Some motifs have been
repeated so frequently that they have been identified as
a type of folk story. Thus we have beast tales about talking animals and wonder tales about supernatural beings.

Even the story plots have recurring patterns—three
tasks to be performed, three wishes that are granted,

[17]Stith Thompson, *Motif Index of Folk-Literature* (Bloomington:
Indiana University Press, 1955–1958), 6 vols.

three trials to be endured. A simple tale will have several motifs; a complex one will have many. Recognizing some of the most common motifs in folklore will help a teacher to suggest points of comparison and contrast in a cross-cultural approach to folk literature.

Magical Powers

Magical powers are frequently given to persons or animals in folktales. A common motif in folklore is the presence of "helpful companions" who all have magical talents. In Arthur Ransome's *The Fool of the World and the Flying Ship*, the fool sails away with eight companions who can eat huge quantities, hear long distances, and drink whole lakes. Later these talents help them overcome trials the czar imposes on the fool. In the tale of "The Month-Brothers," recounted by Samuel Marshak and by Beatrice de Regniers, the brothers have magical powers to control the coming of the seasons, and each brother oversees his month. In William Hooks's *Moss Gown*, the gris-gris woman can make a girl fly as well as create a gown for her out of moss, in which she is able to attend the Carolina plantation owner's ball. Of course, Rumpelstiltskin (see, for instance, Alison Sage's version) can spin straw into gold. The possessors of magical powers always aid heroes and heroines in obtaining their goals.

Transformations

The transformation of an animal into a person, or the reverse, is a part of many folktales. Mme. de Beaumont's *Beauty and the Beast* and the Grimm brothers' *The Princess and the Frog* are perhaps the best known of tales in which a bewitched animal is transformed by love. A crane turns into a woman and back into a crane when her spouse is disloyal in the Japanese tale recounted in Sumiko Yagawa's *The Crane Wife*. "Selkies" are seals that have shed their skins and assumed human form in Jane Yolen's *Greyling*, Susan Cooper's *Selkie Girl*, and Mordicai Gerstein's *The Seal Mother*. Children who feel caught between two cultures or between the world of childhood and the world of adolescence might see themselves reflected in such stories. In fact, in *The Star Fisher*, a work of historical fiction, Lawrence Yep uses a tale similar to *The Crane Wife* to represent the conflict felt by a young Chinese girl whose family moves to West Virginia from China.

Magical Objects

Magical objects are essential aspects of many tales that also reflect other themes or motifs. Both a ring and a lamp play essential parts in the story recounted in Andrew Lang's *Aladdin*. In Elizabeth Winthrop's *Vasilissa the Beautiful*, the heroine is able to outwit Baba Yaga's demands with the help of a magical little doll given to her by her mother. In Tomie de Paola's *Strega Nona*, the title character owns a magical cooking pot that can be started by saying "Bubble, bubble, pasta pot" to make all the pasta anyone needs. But Big Anthony, a true noodlehead, starts the pot without observing Strega Nona's method of getting it to stop: blowing three kisses. The title character of Arlene Mosel's *The Funny Little Woman* has a magical rice paddle that she uses to good advantage both underground and above. Other magical objects that figure in folktales are purses, harps, hens that lay golden eggs, tables, sticks, and tinderboxes. A magical object often heightens a good character's courage and cleverness, while in other stories the misuse of a magical object can cause disaster for a bad character.

Wishes

Many stories are told of wishes that are granted and then used foolishly or in anger or greed. In *The Three Wishes* Margot Zemach recounts the tale of the woodsman who was so hungry that he wished for a sausage; his wife was so angry at this wish that she wished the food would stick to his nose; then, of course, they have to use the third wish to get it off. In Gerald McDermott's *The Stonecutter*, a character wishes to have more power but ends up in a position of powerlessness. In the Grimm brothers' *The Fisherman and His Wife*, as in these other stories, greed destroys any gains a character might make.

Trickery

Both animals and people trick their friends and neighbors in folk literature. The wolf tricks Little Red Riding Hood into believing he is her grandmother; Hansel and Gretel trick the mean old witch into crawling into the oven.

Almost every culture has an animal trickster in its folklore. In European folktales it is usually a wolf or a fox; in Japan it is a badger or a hare; Indonesia has Kantjil, a tiny mouse deer; Africa has three well-known tricksters—Anansi the spider, Zomo the rabbit, and Ijapa the tortoise. Coyote and Raven play this role in Native American tales.

Two realistic tales feature humans tricking others. In the familiar tale in Marcia Brown's *Stone Soup*, three poor soldiers dupe greedy peasants into contributing all of the ingredients for a pot of soup, save one—a stone, with which they generously start off the pot. In Diane Snyder's *The Boy of the Three-Year Nap*, the lazy boy tricks a rich merchant, but then is tricked into a lifetime occupation by his wise old mother.

Magical powers, transformations, the use of magical objects, wishes, and trickery are just a few of the motifs

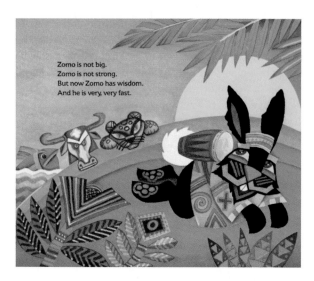

Zomo is not big.
Zomo is not strong.
But now Zomo has wisdom.
And he is very, very fast.

Tricksters like Zomo, in Gerald McDermott's *Zomo the Rabbit,* a West African story, are found in almost every culture.

Illustration from *Zomo the Rabbit: A Trickster Tale From West Africa,* copyright © 1992 by Gerald McDermott, reproduced by permission of Harcourt Brace & Company.

that run through the folklore of all countries, as we have seen. Others might include the power of naming, as in Paul Galdone's *Rumpelstiltskin;* the ability to make yourself invisible, as the man did in Marianna Mayer's *The Twelve Dancing Princesses;* becoming stuck to a person or object, as in the African American tale "The Wonderful Tar-Baby Story" in Van Dyke Parks's *Jump Again;* or an enchanted or lengthy sleep, as in "Urashimo Taro and the Princess of the Sea," in Yoshiko Uchida's *The Dancing Kettle;* or in the Grimms' *Snow White.* One way to understand the common elements of all folklore is to make your own lists of motifs or have the children in your classroom do so.

The Resources for Teaching box "A Cross-Cultural Study of Folktale Motifs" mentions both well-known and lesser-known tales as a beginning for those wishing to pursue a study of motifs. There are many other titles that could be listed for these five motifs, and, of course, there are many more motifs around which to group folklore.

Variants

The number of variants of a single folktale can fascinate beginning students of folklore. Each variant has basically the same story or plot as another, but it might have different characters and a different setting or it might use different motifs. For example, in Robert D. San Souci's retelling of an African American story in *The Talking Eggs,* a poor girl is kind to an old woman and in return is given some plain eggs that become

riches when tossed behind her. Later her greedy stepsister is critical and unhelpful to the old woman. She chooses to take fancy eggs instead of plain ones, but when these are tossed, out come stinging insects. In the Philippine tale retold by Jose Aruego and Ariane Dewey in *Rockaby Crocodile,* a kind boar and a greedy one end up in similar situations when one rocks a cranky baby crocodile while the other ignores it. The theme of rewards for a generous and willing person and punishment for a greedy and disobedient one seems to be universal.

A comparison of the variants of the Cinderella story illustrates differences in theme and motif. Scholars have found versions of this story in ancient Egypt, in ninth-century China, and in tenth-century Iceland. Cinderella receives her magical gifts in many different ways. In the French and most familiar version (see Charles Perrault's), a fairy godmother gives them to her; in the Grimms' version, a dove appears on the tree that grew from the tears she had shed on her mother's grave; in the English version in Joseph Jacobs's *Tattercoats,* she receives her beautiful gowns from a herdboy; in the Chinese version in Ai-Ling Louie's *Yeh-Shen,* magical fish bones bestow gifts on her. She attends three balls in some stories, and her treatment of the stepsisters varies from blinding them to inviting them to live at the palace. The Vietnamese version, "The Brocaded Slipper," recounted by Lynette Dyer Vuong, is made longer by the narrative of the stepsister's finally meeting her own death after "killing" her Cinderella sister, Tam, three times. In Rafe Martin's *The Rough-Face Girl,* an Algonquin story, the daughter of a poor man is made to sit by the fire by her cruel elder sisters. After a time her face and hands become horribly scarred and she is rejected by the villagers. For this reason she is often called "Little Burnt Face" in other versions of this tale.

Variants of the Rumpelstiltskin story (see the retelling by Paul Zelinsky) include the hero's need to know the antagonist's name in order to have his services or to be safe from his magical powers. A character in these stories is able to discover the name and trick an imp, dwarf, or devil. Variations on this theme can be found in Harve Zemach's Cornish *Duffy and the Devil,* Evaline Ness's English *Tom Tit Tot,* and the Scottish "Whippety Stourie" (see Barbara Wilson's *Scottish Folk-Tales and Legends*), all of which are discussed later in this chapter in the section entitled "British Folktales."

Trickery also appears in "helpful companion" stories in which friends have magical powers that assist the hero in completing his quest. The tale of "Jack and the Beanstalk" comes in many versions—for instance, Lorinda Cauley gives a British version. But Appalachian variants change not only the language of the telling but also the typical objects that Jack covets, such as a coverlet with small bells on it and a rifle. Humorous literary

Resources for Teaching
A Cross-Cultural Study of Folktale Motifs

Sample Motifs	Tale, Author	Culture
Magical powers	*The Fool of the World and the Flying Ship* (Ransome)	Russia
	Rumpelstiltskin (Galdone)	Germany
	The Month-Brothers (Marshak)	Russia
	Raven's Light (Shetterly)	Native American
	The Seven Chinese Brothers (Mahy)	China
	Moss Gown (Hooks)	United States
	Yeh-Shen (Louie)	China
	Uncegila's Seventh Spot (Rubalcaba)	Native American
Transformations	*The Girl, the Fish, and the Crown* (Heyer)	Spain
	Beauty and the Beast (de Beaumont)	France
	The Crane Wife (Yagawa)	Japan
	The Story of Jumping Mouse (Steptoe)	Native American
	The Little Snowgirl (Croll)	Russia
	The Hedgehog Boy (Langton)	Latvia
	Cinderella (Perrault)	France
	Tam Lin (Yolen)	Scotland
	Snow White and Rose Red (Grimm brothers)	Germany
	The Princess and the Frog (Grimm brothers)	Germany
	The Selkie Girl (Cooper)	Scotland
	The Orphan Boy (Mollel)	Africa (Kenya)
Magical objects	*The Fish Skin* (Oliviero)	Native American
	The Talking Eggs (San Souci)	African American
	Vasilissa the Beautiful (Winthrop)	Russia
	Aladdin (Lang)	Middle East
	Two of Everything (Hong)	China
	The Twelve Dancing Princesses (Mayer)	France
	The Magic Purse (Uchida)	Japan
	The Three Princes (Kimmel)	Middle East
Wishes	*The Stonecutter* (McDermott)	Japan
	The Fisherman and His Wife (Grimm brothers)	Germany
	The Seven Ravens (Grimm brothers)	Germany
	Momotaro, the Peach Boy (Shute)	Japan
	The Three Wishes (M. Zemach)	Germany
	The Fool and the Fish (Afanasyev)	Russia
	Gluskabe and the Four Wishes (Bruchac)	Native American
Trickery	*The Man Who Tricked a Ghost* (Yep)	China
	The Tale of Rabbit and Coyote (Johnston)	Mexico
	"Shrewd Todie and Lyzer, and Mizer," in *When Shlemiel Went to Warsaw* (Singer)	Jewish
	Rabbit Makes a Monkey of Lion (Aardema)	Africa (Tanzania)
	Stone Soup (Brown)	France
	The Boy of the Three-Year Nap (Snyder)	Japan
	"Firefly and the Apes," in *More Stories to Solve* (Shannon)	Philippines
	Clever Tom and the Leprechaun (Shute)	Ireland
	The Merry Pranks of Till Eulenspiegel (Zwerger)	Germany
	Lon Po Po (Young)	China
	Three Sacks of Truth (Kimmel)	France
	Sungura and the Leopard (Knutson)	Africa (Tanzania)
	"Ticky-Picky Boom-Boom," in *Anansi the Spider Man* (Sherlock)	Jamaica

variants on this tale can be found in Raymond Briggs's *Jim and the Beanstalk* and Gayle Haley's *Jack and the Bean Tree*.

The variants on a folktale make excellent comparison material, and elementary children enjoy discovering the similarities and differences. Classroom-made charts, with the tale titles going down the left margin and topics listed across the top, allow children to compare aspects like these:

- Opening and ending conventions
- Origin of the tale
- Clues to the country or region of origin
- Talents of the characters
- Tasks to be done
- Verses, refrains, chants, and their outcomes
- Illustrations
- Special or unique vocabulary

Each group of variants will have other categories to compare as well. For example, categories might be "Instructions for Stopping a Pot from Cooking," "How Rumpelstiltskin's Name Is Discovered," or "Greedy Person's Reward." Children should be encouraged to develop their own category titles whenever possible.

Knowledge of the variants of a tale, common motifs, and common types of folktales enable a teacher to help children see similar elements in folktales across cultures. Knowledge of the folklore of a particular country or cultural group aids in identifying the uniqueness and individuality of that group. Both approaches to a study of folklore seem essential. The Resources for Teaching box "A Cross-Cultural Study of Folktale Variants" can help the teacher organize tales by variants for classroom presentation.

Folktales of the World

Every culture has produced folklore. A study of the folktales of West Africa, Russia, Japan, or North America can provide insights into the beliefs of these peoples, their values, their jokes, their lifestyles, their histories. At the same time, a cross-cultural study of folk literature can help children discover the universal qualities of humankind.

British Folktales

The first folktales that most children in the United States hear are the English ones. This is because Joseph Jacobs, the folklorist who collected many of the English tales, deliberately adapted them for young children, writing them, he said, "as a good old nurse will speak when she tells Fairy Tales." His collection includes cumulative tales such as "The Old Woman and Her Pig," "Henny Penny," and the much-loved talking-beast stories "The Little Red Hen," "The Three Bears," and "The Three Little Pigs." Both Helen Oxenbury, in her *Nursery Story Book*, and Anne Rockwell, in *The Old Woman and Her Pig* and *The Three Bears*, have retold and illustrated these in excellent collections. James Marshall's flippant tellings of several of these tales seldom stray in content from the "bones" of the originals yet are wonderfully humorous in their visual portrayals. His Goldilocks cries "Patooie" as she tastes the too-hot porridge, and his cartoonish illustrations show Baby Bear's room as a mess of football pennants, books, and toys. Marshall has also given *The Three Little Pigs* verbal and visual topspin.

In the original British tale recounted in Gavin Bishop's *Chicken Licken* and in Stephen Butler's *Henny Penny*, the fox eats the accumulation of animals rushing to tell the king that the sky is falling. However, Steven Kellogg gives Foxy Loxy his comeuppance in *Chicken Little* by having a police helicopter pilot, a hippopotamus, fall onto the fox's poultry truck. The hapless fox is sentenced to jail and a diet of green bean gruel, and the foolish fowl are freed. While purists may object, these humorous treatments of well-known beast tales keep the stories alive for slightly older elementary school audiences who are familiar with the original story from having heard it in preschool, on television, or at library story hours. (For more about folktale spin-offs, see "Fooling with Folktales, Fables, and Myths" in Chapter 14.)

An element of realism runs through some English folktales. The story of Dick Whittington and his cat has its basis in history. There was once a real Richard Whittington who was three times mayor of London, in 1396, 1406, and 1419. And what an exceptional mayor he must have been—enacting prison reforms, providing the first public lavatory and drinking fountain, and building a library and a wing on the hospital for unmarried mothers. It is no wonder that the common people made him the popular hero of one of their most cherished tales. The story "Dick and His Cat" was found in some of the very earliest chapbooks of the day. Marcia Brown's picture storybook *Dick Whittington and His Cat* portrays this realistic tale with handsome linoleum block prints appropriately printed in gold and black.

Joseph Jacobs's British version of Cinderella, *Tattercoats*, is a more poignant romance than the better-known French story, for in this tale the prince falls in love with Tattercoats even when she is dirty and wearing an old, torn petticoat. To prove his love, he invites her to come as she is to the king's ball. Only after the prince greets her and presents her to the king is she revealed as the true princess that she really is. Margot Tomes's illustrations depict this story of a former

Resources for Teaching
A Cross-Cultural Study of Folktale Variants

Theme	Culture

Cinderella

Cinderella (Perrault)	France
Tattercoats (Jacobs)	England
Yeh-Shen (Louie)	China
Soot Face (San Souci)	Native American
The Egyptian Cinderella (Climo)	Egypt
The Korean Cinderella (Climo)	Korea
Moss Gown (Hooks)	United States
Vasilissa the Beautiful (Winthrop)	Russia
Princess Furball (Grimm brothers)	Germany
The Girl Who Wanted to Hunt (Bernhard)	Siberia

Jack and the Beanstalk

Jack and the Beanstalk (Cauley)	England
The History of Mother Twaddle and the Marvelous Achievements of Her Son Jack (Galdone)	England
Jim and the Beanstalk (Briggs)	Modern Literary
The Giant's Toe (B. Cole)	Modern Literary
"Jack and the Bean Tree," in *The Jack Tales* (Chase)	Appalachian American
Jack and the Bean Tree (Haley)	Appalachian American

Magical Gifts

The Table, the Donkey, and the Stick (Grimm brothers)	Germany
"The Lad Who Went to the North Wind," in *East o' the Sun and West o' the Moon* (Asbjørnsen and Moe)	Norway
"Jack and the North West Wind," in *The Jack Tales* (Chase)	Appalachian American

Magical Pots

The Magic Porridge Pot (Galdone)	Germany
Strega Nona (de Paola)	Italy
The Funny Little Woman (Mosel)	Japan

Generous Person/Greedy Person

On Cat Mountain (Richard)	Japan
Mufaro's Beautiful Daughters (Steptoe)	Africa (Zimbabwe)
Baba Yaga (Kimmel)	Russia
The Talking Eggs (San Souci)	African American
Rockaby Crocodile (Aruego and Dewey)	Philippines
Toads and Diamonds (Bender)	France
The Tongue-Cut Sparrow (Ishii)	Japan
Mother Holly (Grimm brothers)	Germany
The Month-Brothers (Marshak)	Russia

Helpful Companions

The Loyal Cat (Namioka)	Japan
The Seven Chinese Brothers (Mahy)	China
The Fool of the World and the Flying Ship (Ransome)	Russia
Anansi the Spider (McDermott)	West Africa
The Boy and the Giants (Moody)	Scotland
Rum Pum Pum (Duff)	India
Iron John (Kimmel)	Germany

Resources for Teaching
A Cross-Cultural Study of Folktale Variants (concluded)

Theme	Culture
Rumpelstiltskin	
Rumpelstiltskin (Grimm brothers)	Germany
Duffy and the Devil (H. Zemach)	England
"Whippety Stourie," in *Scottish Folk-Tales and Legends* (Wolkstein)	Scotland
Tom Tit Tot (Ness)	England
Tucker Pfeffercorn (Moser)	Modern Literary
Stone Soup	
Stone Soup (Brown)	France
The Soup Stone (Van Rynbach)	Modern Literary
Stone Soup (T. Ross)	Modern Literary
Nail Soup (H. Zemach)	Sweden
Stone Soup (Stewig)	France
Burgoo Stew (Patron)	Appalachian

princess reduced to and rescued from poor circumstances in warm earthy tones of charcoals and browns with tints of rose and rust.

A Cornish variation on the German Rumpelstiltskin is presented in Harve Zemach's *Duffy and the Devil*. Illustrator Margot Zemach depicts the devil as a "squinny-eyed creature"; he dances and sings:

> Tomorrow! Tomorrow! Tomorrow's the day!
> I'll take her! I'll take her! I'll take her away!
> Let her weep, let her cry, let her beg, let her pray—
> She'll never guess my name is Tarraway! (unpaged)

However, Duffy's outwitting of the devil makes all of her husband's handspun clothes disappear! Both the language and the pen-and-wash illustrations retain the Cornish flavor of this folklore comedy. In the Scottish "Whippety Stourie" (see Barbara Wilson's *Scottish Folk-Tales and Legends*), six wee ladies help a young wife outmaneuver her husband.

Three versions of the story told in the Scottish ballad "Tamlane" show how storytellers and illustrators give new meanings to a story. In Jane Yolen's *Tam Lin*, Jennet MacKenzie has a mind of her own: "No man would want her, even for all her beauty and her father's name. For she always spoke what she thought. And *what* she thought was never quite proper for a fine young lady." On her sixteenth birthday, she wishes to claim her inheritance, the ancient family home of Carterhaugh

stolen by the fairies many years ago and left in ruins. In the garden she plucks a rose, the only thing of beauty left, and suddenly a young man appears. Claimed by the fairies over a hundred years ago, he is Tam Lin, and if she cannot save him by Hallow's Eve, he will die. The way she must save him is to pull him from his horse when the fairy procession passes, and hold him no matter what shape he assumes. Vivid and bold illustrations by Charles Mikolaycak depict Tam Lin's transformation from a serpent still partially clad in tartan to a lion. Jennet perseveres, outwits the fairies, and wins herself a husband and a home.

In Susan Cooper's retelling, Margaret meets Tam Lin in the forest in June and must save him by Midsummer's Eve. Warwick Hutton's ethereal watercolors give this version a more dreamlike appearance, and his depiction of Tam Lin's transformation is dramatically rendered over three pages. In a third variation, Susan Jeffers's *Wild Robin*, a young girl saves her impetuous brother from the fairies. Children might compare the moods created by different illustrators, the character of the girl, the relationship of the two characters, the supernatural aids or advice given, and the outcomes. Yolen's version includes an informative note about the history of this ballad.

In *The Selkie Girl*, Cooper and Hutton present another legend of Scottish or Irish origin, concerning a man who takes as his wife a selkie, who is a gray seal in the water but a woman on land. He hides her sealskin and for many years the woman lives as his wife and mother to their five children. But when the youngest child finds his mother's sealskin, she confesses that she also has a family of five children in the sea, bids farewell to her landbound family, and disappears into the sea. Mordicai Gerstein's *The Seal Mother* softens the ending by having the son accompany his mother under water. Each Midsummer's Eve thereafter, the human and the selkie branches of the family meet to cavort on the rocks. Jane Yolen's *Greyling* is yet a third variation. Children familiar with Tam Lin or selkie stories can recognize the shape-changing or transformation motif, which is found in ancient mythology as well as modern fantasy (see Chapter 7). Cooper and Hutton have produced a third tale of transformation in their Welsh story *The Silver Cow*. In this story the Scottish fairies, the Fey, turn cows into waterlilies when a farmer's greed gets the better of his judgment.

British folklore includes giants and wee folk but has developed relatively few of the complicated wonder tales that abound in French and Russian folklore. It is often more robust and humorous than some other European tale traditions. Its greatest contribution has been made to the youngest children in providing such nursery classics as "The Three Little Pigs," "Henny Penny," and "The Little Red Hen."

German Folktales

Next in popularity to the English folktales are those of German origin. Jacob and Wilhelm Grimm spent over twelve years collecting the tales they published in 1812 as the first volume of *Kinder und Hausmärchen* (Household Stories). They did not adapt their stories for children, as Joseph Jacobs did for British folktales, but were very careful to preserve (without benefit of a tape recorder) the form and content of the tales as they were told. In 1823 to 1826, these were then translated into English by Edgar Taylor.

New and beautiful collections and single tales of the Grimms' stories continue to be published. Maurice Sendak visited Kassel, Germany, before illustrating his two volumes of *The Juniper Tree and Other Tales from Grimm*. In the museum there he was fortunate to find a version illustrated by the Grimms' younger brother, Ludwig. The size of this little-known version with only six engravings served as the inspiration for Sendak's small volumes. Mindful of the fact that these tales were told to country folk, Sendak used adults as his subjects. His view of Rapunzel is from within her room looking out, rather than the cliché of Rapunzel hanging her hair out of the castle window. Sendak has pictured a pregnant Rapunzel, for the story states that she had her twin babies with her when she was at last united with her prince. This is an authentic and distinguished edition of Grimm that reflects the origin of the stories yet makes us look at them with new wonder and delight.

German folklore is enlivened by elves, dwarfs, and devils, rather than the fairies of other cultures. The Grimm brothers' *The Elves and the Shoemaker* tells of a kindly but poor shoemaker who is aided in his work by elves until he and his wife return the favor by making the elves clothes. Then, off the elves scamper, never to be seen again. Elegant marbleized endpapers with a hairy tail curling around the margins introduce Nonny Hogrogian's *The Devil with the Three Golden Hairs*. Similar to the Russian story in Sally Scott's *The Three Wonderful Beggars*, it tells of a boy who wins the hand of the king's daughter by obtaining three hairs from the devil. In addition, he discovers the answers to three questions that enable him to return with four gold-laden donkeys and a way of outwitting the greedy king.

Alison Sage's *Rumpelstiltskin* presents another well-known tale that features a clever but demanding tiny man. He agrees to help the miller's daughter spin straw into gold to save her life, as her father has bragged too loudly to the king about her talents. Gennady Spirin's illustrations feature sharply delineated characters and settings in the manner of Brueghel's sixteenth-century paintings. Paul O. Zelinsky's elegant paintings for his Grimm brothers' edition set the tale in a medieval castle, and the gold of the spun straw shines richly from the pages. Paul Galdone's version presents a weepier daughter, a less elegant castle, and a more dwarflike little man. In comparing these three versions, children would discover these subtle differences in aspects of the illustrations, as well as the demise of the little man, the verse in which he reveals his name, and the name guesses the miller's daughter offers.

Many children know a version of "Snow White" only from the cartoon story created by Walt Disney Studios. However, Nancy Ekholm Burkert's illustrations and Randall Jarrell's retelling in *Snow-White and the Seven Dwarfs* more faithfully recreate the original Grimm story. Burkert used her own 14-year-old daughter as the model for Snow White. Her drawings of dwarfs are based on weeks of medical library research studying characteristic proportions of dwarfs. And so Burkert's dwarfs are not grotesque elves, but real people who are loving and proud. The medieval cottage of the dwarfs is an authentic depiction; every architectural detail, the rich fabrics on floor and wall, the very plates and mugs on the table were copied from museum pieces. In keeping with artistic styles of the late middle ages, Burkert used images symbolically: the white dog, the basket of cherries, and the lilies on the table signify virginity; the meadow rue embroidered on the girl's apron was supposed to protect the wearer against witches; a Tarot card, the red mushrooms, spiders, and other articles in the witch's workroom signify evil. In Disney's version, a "Sleeping Beauty" kiss awakes the sleeping girl. But Randall Jarrell was true to the Grimm story, in which the apple lodged in Snow White's throat is shaken free when the prince carries her off to Italy. Such a beautiful edition of this story restores its dignity, beauty, and symbolic meaning. Another edition of *Snow White* has been faithfully translated by Paul Heins and illustrated with robust, more romantic pictures by Trina Schart Hyman. In this version, the artist skillfully portrays the ravaging effects of the queen's jealous madness through the changing appearance of her face.

The villain in the few beast tales in German folklore is usually a wolf. Perhaps the best-known wolf appears in the Grimm story "Little Red Cap." In the familiar story, the heroine ignores her mother's warnings, and as a result she and her grandmother are eaten. Both escape through the intervention of a passing hunter who thinks that the wolf's loud snores couldn't be coming from a healthy grandmother. After her adventure, the little girl vows always to obey her mother's advice. Lisbeth Zwerger, in *Little Red Cap*, and Trina Schart Hyman, in *Little Red Riding Hood*, have portrayed this story with striking but differing illustrations. Hyman presents a younger, more innocent child distracted by the wolf. Small vignettes depicting household details, wildflowers, and insects are enclosed in changing border frames, giving the whole book a delightfully old-fashioned look. Beautiful, spare watercolors by Zwerger portray a contrastingly older Red Cap and only essential props are set against a soft and muted backdrop. James Marshall has illustrated his version of this tale in his characteristically humorous way.

Some of the Grimm tales can be grim, dark, and forbidding. Small children can be frightened by *Hansel and Gretel*, the somber tale of a brother and sister abandoned in the woods by their parents and nearly eaten by a horrible witch. However, justice does prevail in this wonder tale: the witch dies in the same way as she had intended to kill the children; the stepmother also dies, and the children, laden with wealth, are reunited with their joyful father. Several very different illustrated versions present this tale to children. Paul Zelinsky's oil paintings somberly recreate the forest settings and interior of the poor woodcutter's house, and we can almost smell the witch's tasty house. Lisbeth Zwerger's illustrations portray characters against a brown wash that gives the action a dreamlike, long-ago appearance. Anthony Browne, in his startling contemporary illustrations, makes a visual connection between the stepmother and the witch by placing a mole on each woman's cheek. Browne's illustrations are full of reflected images, symbols of cages and flight, and the triangular shape that resembles a witch's hat. While adults might feel that Browne's interpretation brings the story too close to children today, this violation of the folktale convention of distancing in "a long time ago" might be treated by older children simply as one more interesting variation.

Other Grimm stories featuring witches have been illustrated and retold. In *Rapunzel*, a witch, though never unkind to Rapunzel, nevertheless keeps her locked in a tower until a prince climbs her braids. When the witch discovers the prince, she throws him from the tower and he is blinded by the sharp thorns below. A year later, he and Rapunzel are reunited and her tears restore his sight. Trina Schart Hyman's dark and mysterious illustrations for this story have a Slavic appearance and owe a debt to Russian illustrator Ivan Biliban's use of small rectangular vignettes and borders. In Alix Berenzy's version, the illustrations and page design recall the miniatures and decorations in illuminated manuscripts.

In Randall Jarrell's translation of a well-known morality tale *The Fisherman and His Wife*, a foolish woman wishes her way from living in a smelly pigsty to being the pope. When her husband spares the life of an enchanted flounder, the wife insists that the fish owes him a wish. The husband dutifully asks for the wish, but the woman goes too far when she asks to control the sun and the moon. The two end up, predictably, in the pigsty where they started. In Margot Zemach's watercolor illustrations, the dwellings of the peasant couple go through several transformations before their clothes catch up to their circumstances. In a Grimm version, with more orderly depictions by Margot Tomes, reds and pinks replace browns and blues as the woman's desires escalate. In contrast, Zemach crowds her scenes with jumbles of people while angry swirls of black watercolor wash depict the increasing agitation of the fish over the woman's unreasonable demands.

Another Grimm tale with a moral is *The Frog Prince*, which stresses the importance of keeping a promise, even if it is made by a princess to a frog. So the king makes his daughter honor her promise to welcome a frog that has retrieved her golden ball from a deep, dark pond. After the princess lets the frog sit by her side, eat from her plate, and sleep in her bed for three nights, the frog becomes a prince and the two are married. While some versions end with the princess dashing the frog against a wall, or beheading it, Jan Ormerod chose a gentler ending for her version. A similar Grimm tale, *The Princess and the Frog* with illustrations by Rachel Isadora, pictures a redheaded princess in turn-of-the-century attire.

Wicked enchantments and magical transformations are typical of German folktales. In the Grimms' *The Seven Ravens*, seven boys are changed into ravens by their father's curse when they break a jug of water that was to be used to christen their new baby sister. When the sister is old enough to realize what has happened, she sets off for the glass mountain to find them. Coming at last to a locked door, she must cut off her finger in order to pass through. There she is able to release her brothers.

Charlotte Huck's "Cinderella" variation on the Grimm story of "many Furs" is titled *Princess Furball*. A cruel king betroths his motherless daughter to an ogre in exchange for fifty wagonloads of silver. But the princess hopes to foil his plan by first demanding that her father give her three dresses, one as golden as the sun, another as silvery as the moon, and the last as glittering as the stars, as well as a coat made of a thousand pieces of fur, one from every animal in the kingdom. When the king actually fulfills these demands, the princess runs away with her dresses and three tiny treasures that had belonged to her mother. Disguised in her fur coat, she is discovered and taken to another king's castle, where she becomes a scullery maid known as Furball. When the king gives a ball, she appears in one of her dresses and the following day leaves a token in the king's soup. At the third ball, the king slips a ring on Furball's finger and is later able to identify the scullery maid as his own true love, saying, "You are as clever as you are lovely." Practical, independent, and resourceful, Furball has capably managed to create a happy future. Anita Lobel uses opening portraits to personify Furball's dead mother, while a portrait of the ogre looks like the father-king. A series of imprisoning enclosures such as long hallways, deep forests, and windowless kitchens symbolically give way to more open scenes in lighter and brighter colors, with more windows, and finally to the fresh air of an outdoor wedding. In contrast to many other Cinderella characters, Princess Furball is a strong, responsible female who actively brings about her own happy end.

Although there is little mercy for the wicked in these German tales, there is much joy for the righteous. The plots are exciting, fast-moving, and a little frightening. Evil stepmothers, wicked witches, and an occasional mean dwarf hold princes and princesses in magical enchantments that can be broken only by kindness and love. Such were the dreams and wishes of the common folk of Germany when the Grimm brothers recorded their tales.

Scandinavian Folktales

Most of the Scandinavian folktales are from the single Norwegian collection titled *East o' the Sun and West o' the Moon*. These stories were gathered in the early 1840s by Peter Christian Asbjørnsen and Jorgen Moe. The collection ranks in popularity with the Grimms' fairy tales for much the same reason; they capture the vigorous language of the storyteller. Ten years after their publication in Norway, they were ably translated by an Englishman, George Dasent, and made available to the English-speaking world.

Perhaps the best known of all of these stories is *The Three Billy Goats Gruff* (see the versions by Asbjørnsen and Moe and by Glen Rounds). These billy goats "trip-trapped" across the troll's bridge to eat the green grass on the other side in a tale that is a perfect example of folktale structure: the use of three billy goats, the increasing size of each one, and the anticipated downfall of the mean old troll. Fast action and an economy of words lead directly to the storyteller's conventional ending: "Snip, snap, snout/This tale's told out." Marcia Brown's matchless illustrations for the version by Asbjørnsen and Moe is faithful to the Norwegian origin of this tale in both the setting of her lively illustrations and in the text. Paul Galdone's picture-book version, showing large close-up illustrations of the goats and the troll, will appeal particularly to the younger child.

Another story that delights young children is Nancy Polette's *The Little Old Woman and the Hungry Cat*. When his owner leaves him alone, the cat eats the sixteen cupcakes she left cooling and proceeds down the road eating everyone and everything in his path. When he meets his owner, he gobbles her up as well. But her sewing scissors save the day when she is able to cut her way out, and she and the rest of the cat's victims escape. Now free, all have a party except for the hungry cat who has to stitch himself up.

George Dasent's *East o' the Sun and West o' the Moon* is a complex tale in which a poor man gives his youngest daughter to a white bear, who promises to make the family rich. The white bear comes to her every night and throws off his beast shape, but he leaves before dawn so she never sees him. When her mother tells her to light a candle and look into his face, she sees a handsome prince, but three drops of hot tallow awaken him. He then tells her of his wicked enchantment in which for one year he must be a bear by day. Now that she has seen him, he must return to the castle that lies east of the sun and west of the moon and marry the princess with a long nose. So the girl seeks the castle, finally arriving there on the back of the North Wind. Before the prince will marry, he sets one condition: he will only marry the one who can wash out the tallow spots on his shirt. Neither his long-nose troll bride-to-be nor an old troll hag can do it, but the girl who has posed as a beggar can wash it white as the snow. The wicked trolls burst, and the prince and princess marry and leave the castle that lies east of the sun and west of the moon. Gillian Barlow's framed paintings in the style of folk art glow with warm colors. Children who know the Greek myth of Cupid and Psyche (see Margaret Hodges's *The Arrow and the Lamp*) will recognize similarities in the girl's nighttime curiosity and the trouble it begets. Kathleen and Michael Hague's retelling in their *East of the Sun and West of the Moon* follows the original structure of the story faithfully.

In many of the Norwegian tales the hero is aided in the accomplishment of such seemingly impossible tasks by animals or people that he has been kind to. The hero of Eric Kimmel's *Boots and His Brothers* sets out with his two brothers, Peter and Paul, to seek his fortune. They meet an old woman along the way who tells them that their fortune can be gained from an old king who needs an oak tree chopped down and a well dug. The two older boys push the old woman out of the way and hurry off. But because Boots stops and takes time to talk to her, she gives him three magical objects and some good advice. These help him to chop down the enchanted oak tree, dig a well in iron rocks, and fill it with cool clear water from a hundred leagues away. The king is so delighted with Boots, he gives him his weight in gold and half his kingdom. For the greedy brothers, the king has a job as dogkeepers.

Scandinavian tales often seem to reflect the harsh elements of the northern climate. Animal helpmates assist heroes in overcoming giants or wicked trolls. Frequently heroes are human beings who are held by an evil spell. The Scandinavian tales, characterized by many trolls, magical objects, and enchantments, often are also humorous, exciting, and fast-moving. The youngest son performs impossible tasks with ease and a kind of practical resourcefulness.

French Folktales

French folktales were the earliest to be recorded, and they are also the most sophisticated and adult. This is probably because these tales were the rage among the court society of Louis XIV. In 1697, Charles Perrault, a distinguished member of the French Academy, published a little volume of fairy tales. The title page bore no name, and there has been some debate as to whether they were the product of Charles Perrault or his son, Pierre. While the stories were probably very close to the ones told to Pierre by his governess, they have the consciously elegant style of the "literary tale" rather than the "told tale" of the Grimms.

The fairy godmother in Cinderella is Perrault's invention, as are the pumpkin coach, the six horses of dappled mouse gray, and the glass slipper. In this French version Cinderella is kind and forgiving of her two stepsisters, inviting them to live at the palace with her. Marcia Brown was faithful to both the French setting and the original text in her Caldecott Medal–winning illustrations for Perrault's *Cinderella*. Ethereal illustrations in delicate blues and pinks portray the splendid palace scenes. Cinderella's stepsisters are haughty and homely, but hardly cruel. Another beautiful picture-book *Cinderella* has been created by Errol Le Cain. The rich, lavish illustrations are interesting to compare with Brown's delicate ones. Younger children will enjoy James Marshall's colorful and humorous illustrations in a version retold by Barbara Karlin.

The sister story to "Cinderella" is the well-known "Sleeping Beauty," and Perrault's version closely parallels the one collected by the Grimms. It is interesting to compare the wishes that the fairies gave to the newborn baby. In the German tale they endow Briar Rose with virtue, beauty, riches, and "everything in the world she could wish for"; in the French version they bestow her with beauty, an angelic disposition, and the abilities to dance, sing, and play music. In both versions the jealous uninvited fairy predicts that the child will prick her finger on a spindle and die. This wish is softened by the last fairy, who changes it to the long sleep of a hundred years to be broken by the kiss of a prince.

Several beautiful picture-book editions of "Sleeping Beauty" have been published. Margaret Early, an Australian, illustrated Perrault's *The Sleeping Beauty* with beautiful paintings filled with details of French costume design and architecture. The elaborate borders that frame the text and illustrations recall the interlacing of a French Book of Hours. English artist Errol Le Cain went to the Brothers Grimm for his retelling of the German *Thorn Rose or the Sleeping Beauty*. His opulent pictures give the impression of Northern Renaissance paintings and royal tapestries. Trina Schart Hyman has painted robust romantic scenes for her interpretation of the Grimm's *Sleeping Beauty*. Her many close-up pictures of the characters place the reader in the midst of the scenes rather than providing the distancing and mystical mood of the others.

On the cover of the version of Perrault's *Puss in Boots* illustrated by Fred Marcellino, a very French Puss looks out past the reader as if plotting his next moves. While he is the only inheritance of the youngest son of a poor miller, he proves his worth by fooling the king into believing the miller's son is the imaginary Marquis of Carabas. He then tricks an ogre out of his gold and proclaims the ogre's castle as his master's. The king is delighted to give his daughter in marriage to the "Marquis," and Puss retires to a life of luxury. Marcellino's illustrations and large type crowd the page as if the story would burst the confines of the book. Children familiar with this version and with Alain Vaës's elegant illustrations could compare it with Lorinda Cauley's colored-pencil renditions of the sleek cat or with Paul Galdone's swashbuckler.

The French telling of "The Twelve Dancing Princesses" is more ornate than the German version. Errol Le Cain illustrated the Grimm version of *The Twelve Dancing Princesses* for this story of the poor soldier who discovers the underground kingdom where the twelve girls dance their shoes to pieces nightly. However, the depictions of tapestry borders, powdered wigs, and the elegant dress of the masked ball give Le Cain's version a very French look. Marianna Mayer's cumbersome retelling of the story introduces new elements as well, but Kinuko Y. Craft's luminous paintings are well suited to the spirit of the original tale.

The best-known French wonder tale, other than those by Perrault, is "Beauty and the Beast," adapted from a long story written in 1757 by Madame de Beaumont. This story of love based on essence rather than appearance has been variously illustrated. Mordicai Gerstein's illustrations feature pastel-tinted line drawings that reveal their source as an animated film. In Gerstein's version, a courageous Beauty rides to the Beast's castle by herself, while in Warwick Hutton's version, a more timid Beauty is accompanied by her father. Jan Brett's economical text and rich illustrations are framed in jeweled borders, and the elegant tapestries in the background reveal the boar-beast's true identity.

Marcia Brown's *Stone Soup* has long been staple primary-grade fare. As the French villagers clad in wooden shoes and smocks hurry their contributions to the huge soup kettle, the three soldiers maintain a subtly earnest but amused look. In John Stewig's version, Grethel is a solo hungry traveler. When villagers turn down their mouths "like unlucky horseshoes" at her request for food, the girl goes to work with her magic stone and soon has created an evening, and a soup, to remember. Margot Tomes's soft flat tones give the story a homespun look.

Eric Kimmel's *Three Sacks of Truth* also revolves around trickery and contains many other traditional folktale motifs as well. In Kimmel's retelling, a greedy king declares that he will marry his daughter to the suitor who brings him the perfect peach. When Petit Jean, the youngest of three brothers, does just that, the king finds additional tasks for him to perform. With the aid of a magical fife, given to him by an old woman he helped, Jean outwits the king and then performs one last difficult task. When the king asks him to show him three sacks of truth, Jean reveals that he knows a highly embarrassing truth—the king has kissed his donkey's muzzle. To save face, the king insists that Jean and the princess marry immediately. In *Three Perfect Peaches*, by Cynthia De Felice and Mary DeMarsh, the tale is retold from the same source, but in this version Jean receives a magical whistle instead of a fife and must fill a glass bucket to overflowing with truth. In addition, the king's secret is a bit more ribald—he has kissed the other end of his donkey. Both versions are sure to delight children.

The folktales of France are usually not the tales of the poor but those of the rich. Most have all the trappings of the traditional fairy tale, including fairy godmothers, stepsisters, and handsome princes. Tales of romance and sophisticated intrigue, they must surely have been the "soap operas" of their day.

Petit Jean's kindness to an old woman is rewarded in Eric Kimmel's *Three Sacks of Truth: A Story From France.*

Russian Folktales

Folktales from Russia feature universal patterns of tasks and trials, tricks, and transformations. Russian folktales are often longer and more complicated than those of other countries and frequently involve several sets of tasks. In Demi's *The Firebird*, Dimitri, an archer, comes upon the feather of the firebird in the forest. His Horse of Power warns him to let it lie or he will know the meaning of fear, but Dimitri thinks only of Tsar Ivan's reward. The tsar is not content with the firebird's feather, however, and sets increasingly impossible tasks for Dimitri. He must capture the firebird, bring back the fairy Princess Vasilisa for his bride, and find her wedding gown at the bottom of the sea. Dimitri's magic horse helps him complete each of these tasks. Finally Vasilisa insists she will not marry until Dimitri jumps into a pot of boiling water. Dimitri is sure that this will be the end of him and bemoans the fact that he ever picked up the firebird's feather. The horse, knowing that Vasilisa has sprinkled the boiling water with fairy dust, tells Dimitri to jump into the pot. When Dimitri emerges from the pot transformed into the handsomest prince in all the world, the vain old tsar jumps in after him. The magic dust is used up, however, and the tsar disappears forever, leaving Dimitri and Vasilisa to marry and the horse to live in a golden stable. Demi's intricately patterned illustrations, accented with gold and other jewel-like colors, capture the feel of Russian embroideries and architecture. Margaret Hodges's retelling of the story, *The Little Humpbacked Horse*, is even more complex and begins with a tale of how a more modest hero, Ivan the Fool, obtained the magic horse—in this version a little pony with two humps on his back. Chris Conover's illustrations recall the stylized forms of Russian icons and integrate the flowing lines of Eastern calligraphy.

Sally Scott's precise and richly textured paintings for *The Three Wonderful Beggars* tell the story of Vassili, a seventh son of a villager whose destiny is foretold by three old beggars. Mark the Rich does everything he can to thwart the prophecy, but Vassili is able to trick Mark, and win his daughter and riches as well, by outwitting the Serpent King. As for Vassili, "he never turned a beggar from his door." As in many Russian folktales, the greedy rich and the heartless nobility are soon brought down by honest and hardworking commoners.

Russian folklore is replete with stories of poor but lucky men. In Harve Zemach's *Salt*, Ivan the fool takes the ship his father has given him and, much to his father's surprise, returns as the richest of the three brothers who started out. With the help of an irresistible magic sack, an old soldier outwits some devils in Michael McCurdy's *The Devils Who Learned to Be Good*, and another soldier saves a helpless tsar in Uri Shulevitz's *Soldier and Tsar in the Forest*. In Arthur Ransome's *The Fool of the World and the Flying Ship*, a youngest son goes forth, accompanied by eight companions, each of whom has a magical power that helps in outwitting the treacherous tsar. The fool wins the princess and riches for them both in this Caldecott Medal book. A poor archer in Diane Wolkstein's *Oom Razoom, or Go I Know Not Where, Bring Back I Know Not What* keeps his beautiful wife from the clutches of the king while gaining riches and a magical servant.

The witch Baba Yaga is a complex character who figures in many Russian tales, including Eric Kimmel's *Go I Know Not Where, Bring Back I Know Not What* and Diane Wolkstein's *Oom Razoom*.[18] Elizabeth Winthrop's *Vasilissa the Beautiful* is often called "the Russian Cinderella." In this tale, Vasilissa is sent by her stepmother to Baba Yaga to get a light for the cottage with the hope that the witch will eat her up. But Vasilissa carries with her a doll that her mother gave her before she died. When Baba Yaga gives Vasilissa impossible tasks to perform, the unfortunate girl is saved by the doll's magic and its advice to go to sleep for "the morning is wiser than the evening." The renowned Russian illustrator Alexander Koshkin richly paints the story in a seventeenth-century setting. The arrival of Baga Yaga in her mortar and pestle is boldly lit by the glowing eyes of the picketed skulls surrounding her chicken-footed house. K. Y. Craft's paintings for Marianna Mayer's *Baba Yaga and Vasilisa the Brave* are reminiscent of the miniatures found on Russian lacquer boxes.

In *Vassilisa the Wise*, a retelling by Josepha Sherman, Vassilisa is now presented as the loving wife of the merchant Staver. When Staver's bragging about his wife's beauty and wisdom causes him to be imprisoned by the legendary prince Vladimir, Vassilisa disguises herself as a Tartar prince. She outwits Vladimir and wins the release of her now contrite husband by performing three tasks. Daniel San Souci's use of rich browns, blues, and rose hues, bordered illustrations, and illuminated capitals reinforces the medieval setting of this tale.

Other stories about Baba Yaga present the fearsome witch in less frightening terms. Joanna Cole's *Bony-Legs* tells how Sasha meets Baba Yaga under a different name but escapes being eaten by the witch because she is kind to a cat, a dog, and a squeaky gate. In *Baba Yaga*, Eric Kimmel adds a "generous person/greedy person" motif in this story of Marina, a child with a horn growing out of her forehead, who is sent by her stepmother to Baba Yaga to get a needle. Her kindness to a frog earns her good advice in tricking the witch and good luck in having her horn removed. But when the stepsister Marusia rudely ignores the frog on her way to visit Baba Yaga so as to become "just like my stepsister," she is sent away with a horn on her forehead. Humorous illustrations in both stories remove some of the power of Baba Yaga's evil while providing an invitation to younger children to meet a well-known witch.

The same characters reappear in different guises in many Russian tales, and one story often braids into another. In J. Patrick Lewis's *The Frog Princess*, Prince Ivan marries a frog who sheds her skin and turns into the beautiful Princess Vasilisa at night. Ivan burns her frog skin, thinking this will keep her in the guise of a woman, only to find that he has interfered with the working out of a curse. Vasilisa is then imprisoned by Koschey the Invincible, another stock Russian character. It is only with the help of Baba Yaga that Ivan tricks the terrible demon and breaks the curse on Vasilisa. Gennady Spirin's stunningly beautiful illustrations lend a wonderful sense of the old Imperial Russia to this complex tale.

[18]See the vivid description of one classroom's discovery of patterns when a teacher presented them with versions of "Baba Yaga" tales in Joy F. Moss's *Focus on Literature: A Context for Literacy Learning* (Katonah, N.Y.: Richard C. Owen, 1990), pp. 49–62.

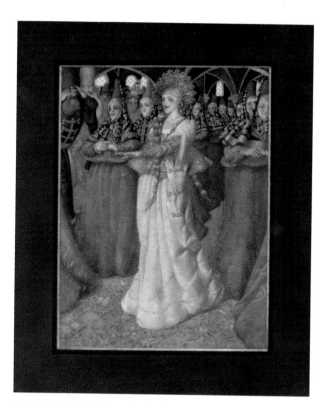

Gennady Spirin's elegant paintings recreate the grandeur of old Russia in J. Patrick Lewis's *The Frog Princess*.
From *The Frog Princess* by J. Patrick Lewis, illustrated by Gennedy Spirin. Copyright © 1994 by Gennady Spirin on illustrations. Used by permission of Dial Books for Young Readers, a division of Penguin Books USA Inc.

Not all Russian folktales are dark and complex. The theme of cooperation is addressed in Katherine Milhous and Alice Dalgliesh's *The Turnip*. Dedoushka plants a turnip seed, which grows so big that he needs to call his wife, Baboushka, to help by pulling him as he pulls. Eventually they are able to pull up the turnip with the help of their daughter Mashenka, a dog, a cat, and finally a mouse. This humorous story would make a good primary drama.

The theme of beauty being in the eye of the beholder is presented in another story. A child lost in the wheatfields, separated from her mother, sobs and proclaims her mother's beauty in Becky Reyher's *My Mother Is the Most Beautiful Woman in the World*. After the townsfolk assemble all of the local beauties for Varya's inspection, a large toothless woman pushes through the crowd and mother and child are reunited.

Jan Brett's *The Mitten* is a Ukrainian tale in which animals small and large accumulate in Nicki's dropped mitten. Jan Brett divides the pages with a birchbark window through which the increasingly stuffed mitten can be seen. A mitten-shaped panel on the left depicts Nicki's busy day; on the right, the next animal who will try to squeeze into the mitten is shown. Alvin Tresselt's version features different animals and reads aloud as if it

were a reminiscence. Both Yaroslava, the illustrator of this version, and Jan Brett have included traditional Ukrainian details, costumes, and patterns.

Carolyn Croll carefully researched Russian architecture, furnishings, toys, and clothing before illustrating a story set at Christmas, *The Little Snowgirl*. An old couple who wish for a child are delighted when the little girl the husband has made from snow comes to life. Caterina loves the snowgirl but cannot bear to let her stay outside on Christmas Eve. In the morning, all the two find is a small puddle by the fireplace, but a soft laugh reveals that the little snowgirl has been granted one wish by Baboushka, who gives good children what they want most on that special night. Reading aloud Charles Mikolaycak's *Baboushka*, about a woman who is destined to wander the world forever bestowing gifts on children, would forge a compelling link in the chain of Russian folklore.

In the Russian story in Samuel Marshak's *The Month-Brothers*, a girl is given an impossible task by her stepmother: to go out in the winter snow and not return until she has gathered snowdrops. However, she luckily comes upon the twelve months of the year gathered about a fire in the forest. January and February agree to give the youngest month-brother, March, one hour to create a forest floor dappled with snowdrops, and the girl is able to complete her task. However, the greedy stepmother next sends her own spoiled daughter into the snow to demand special summertime food to sell in the wintertime market. The rude girl accosts the men and is frozen in snow by old January. The greedy mother also perishes while searching for her daughter. The "generous person/greedy person" motif accompanies this personification and explanation of the changing seasons. In Diane Stanley's lovely watercolors, March is represented as a young boy, reflecting rural people's belief that the year of growing truly begins in March. In Beatrice Schenk de Regniers's retelling, *Little Sister and the Month Brothers*, Margot Tomes adds a touch of humor and whimsy through her illustrations.

Jewish Folktales

Jewish tales have a poignancy, wit, and ironic humor unmatched in any other folklore. Many of them have been preserved by the masterful writing of Isaac Bashevis Singer, who has retained the flavor of both the oral tradition and the Yiddish origin. Singer's warm, humorous stories in *Zlateh the Goat* and *When Shlemiel Went to Warsaw* are based on tradition and his own childhood memories. The amiable fools of Chelm (that fabled village where only fools live), lazy shlemiels, and shrewd poor peasants who outwit rich misers are familiar characters in Singer's tales. In Chelm the wise elders are the most foolish of all, and their "solutions" to people's problems make for some hilarious stories. One night they plan to gather the pearls and diamonds of the sparkling snow so the jewels can be sold for money. Worried about how they can prevent the villagers from trampling the snow, they decide to send a messenger to each house to tell the people to stay inside. But the "wise elders" realize the messenger's feet will spoil the snow, so they have him carried on a table supported by four men so that he will not make any footprints as he goes from house to house!

In *It Could Always Be Worse*, Margot Zemach tells the familiar tale of the poor farmer whose house is so crowded that he seeks the rabbi's advice. Following the rabbi's wise counsel, the farmer brings one animal after another into the house until the noise and confusion become unbearable. The rabbi then advises their removal, and the house appears to be very large and peaceful. Zemach has created a humorous version of this tale with large robust pictures that seem to swarm with squalling children, rambunctious animals, and horrified adults. Joanna Cole retells this story in a simpler style in *It's Too Noisy*. Kate Duke's cheerful cartoonish illustrations place this peasant family less clearly in the Jewish tradition than does Zemach.

Phoebe Gilman's *Something from Nothing* is a gentle tale about a boy whose grandfather makes him a precious blanket. As Joseph grows older the blanket is made into smaller and smaller pieces of clothing, first a jacket, then a vest, a handkerchief, and finally a button. When he loses the button, the boy is told, "You can't make something from nothing." But Joseph does—he writes a story about his blanket. Gilman's illustrations set the story in the villages of the old country, and her patterned text will please young audiences. Susan Gaber's pictures for Steve Sanfield's *Bit by Bit*, another version, have a more modern setting, but they still capture the flavor of Jewish culture and the lighthearted yet poignant tone of the Jewish folktale style.

Isaac Singer retells a Hebrew legend in *Elijah the Slave*, which is magnificently illustrated by Antonio Frasconi. In this story Elijah, a messenger from God, sells himself as a slave in order to help a poor, faithful scribe. The pictures appear to be woodcut prints cut out and pasted on radiant backgrounds. The effect is breathtaking and reminiscent of medieval art.

The Diamond Tree, by Howard Schwartz and Barbara Rush, is a collection of fifteen Jewish tales from around the world. Here readers meet the giant Og, the fools of Chusham, King Solomon, and even a Jewish Thumbelina, Katanya. Uri Shulevitz illustrated most of these tales with brilliant paintings.

Folktales from the Middle East and India

Folktales from Middle Eastern countries and from India would take several books, for these areas are the cradle of civilization and the birthplace of many of our stories. Unfortunately, these tales are not as well known in the United States as they deserve to be. Rather than describe many unfamiliar stories available only in out-of-print collections, this section discusses only available tales or books that might serve as an introduction. Nonny Hogrogian's *One Fine Day* is an Armenian cumulative story that begins when an old woman catches a fox licking up her pail of milk and cuts off his tail. She agrees to sew it back on only when he replaces the milk, which proves to be a difficult task. The simplicity of Hogrogian's drawings is perfect for the rustic humor and setting of this circular tale.

Scheherazade's Arabian Nights tales have provided stories for generations since they were first published in 1712. Sir Richard Burton's translation made them available to English speakers and has been used as the basis for such collections such as Neil Philip's lavishly illustrated *The Arabian Nights*. Deborah Nourse Lattimore selected three of the stories to retell in *Arabian Nights*: the well-known "Aladdin," "The Queen of Serpents," and "The Lost City of Brass." In this last tale, Scheherazade describes how three men—a storyteller, a wise man, and a ruler—travel to find the lost city of Ubar in order to find the ancient brass bottles in which King Solomon imprisoned all the evil Jinn of the earth. Despite many terrible impediments along the way, the three are righteous men, praising Allah, doing good deeds, and thinking good thoughts. They reach the lost city and finally retrieve one of Solomon's bottles. In an author's note Lattimore tells that the remains of this ancient city, which was long thought to be mythical, have recently been unearthed. The city had disappeared into a sinkhole sometime between A.D. 200 and A.D. 400, and it now seems that Scheherazade's story was rooted in fact.

Andrew Lang retold Burton's version in *Aladdin*, and Errol Le Cain depicted it in pictures that resemble Persian miniature paintings. Details, ornate borders, and patterned surfaces lend an authenticity to the story. Carol Carrick's straightforward *Aladdin and the Wonderful Lamp* relies on Donald Carrick's richly hued paintings for romance and drama. Eric Kimmel's *The Tale of Aladdin and the Wonderful Lamp* is a more inclusive story whose text captures some of the flavor of the told tale. Ju-Hong Chen's warmly colored, impressionistic paintings evoke the textured surfaces of desert landscapes and ancient cities of the story's origin.

Readers will recognize recurring folktale motifs in several other tales from the Middle East. *Rimonah of the*

Aladdin finds happiness with the royal princess in Deborah Nourse Lattimore's *Arabian Nights: Three Tales.*
Illustration copyright © 1995 by Deborah Nourse Lattimore. Used by permission of HarperCollins Publishers, New York, NY.

Flashing Sword, a retelling by Eric Kimmel, has its origins in North Africa but contains many elements of "Snow White." When Rimonah's mother dies, her father is tricked into marriage by an evil sorceress. Instead of a magic mirror to answer her questions, however, Rimonah's wicked stepmother has a magic bowl. When her stepmother orders a huntsman to take her into the desert and kill her, Rimonah escapes and is taken in by a tribe of Bedouins. Later she lives with forty thieves. In this version Rimonah is not at all passive. When her prince awakens her from her enchanted sleep, she takes charge and leads her friends in battle against the wicked sorceress.

In Kimmel's *The Three Princes*, three cousins hope to win the hand of a wise and beautiful princess. Realizing that she loves Moshen, the youngest and poorest of the three, the princess sets the cousins the difficult task of finding the greatest wonder in the world. After a year's journey the three meet and compare their treasures. Prince Fahad has found a crystal ball, Prince Muhammed has obtained a magic carpet, and Prince Moshen has been given an orange. When the crystal ball tells them that the princess is dying, they climb aboard the magic carpet to return to the palace. Moshen feeds his orange to the princess and saves her life, but the princess's councilors cannot decide whose gift was the most wondrous. The princess declares that Fahad and Muhammed both still have their treasures but since Moshe gave up everything for her, he is the one she will marry. Leonard

Everett Fisher's boldly colored and textured paintings add a sense of visual magic to this tender story.

Other rich sources of stories are the Hodja stories, known throughout the Mediterranean countries, Turkey, the Balkans, and Greece. Nasredden Hodja was thought to have lived several hundred years ago in Turkey, where he served as a religious teacher or judge when the occasion demanded. The wisdom of the Hodja is seen in the way he settles disputes. One day he watches a man cut wood while his companion rests nearby but groans helpfully each time the man swings his axe (see Barbara Walker's *Watermelons, Walnuts, and the Wisdom of Allah*). When the woodcutter finally sells his wood at the bazaar, the companion demands half the pay. The Hodja listens to both sides, takes the coins, and drops them one by one on a stone. He awards the sound to the companion and the coins to the woodcutter.

Indian folklore tradition has its share of wise men, too. "The Sticks of Truth" in George Shannon's collection *Stories to Solve* tells of an Indian judge asked to determine who stole a gold ring. He gives each suspect a stick and says that only the stick of the thief will grow in the night. In the morning, he is able to accuse the one with the shortest stick of the thievery. Why? In this collection of short pieces, the reader is invited to guess before turning the page to discover the answer. In this case, the girl trims her stick in an effort to hide its growth, thereby proving her guilt.

The Jataka (birth) stories found in India tell of the previous reincarnations of the Buddha and are known to have existed as early as the fifth century A.D. Many of these tales are moralistic or religious in nature. In Margaret Hodges's *Hidden in the Sand,* a caravan of traders becomes lost in the desert and is in danger of dying of thirst. A young boy finds a small plant growing in the sand and urges the men to dig for water. When they have dug a deep hole and found only hard rock, they ridicule the boy. But the youngster won't give up and climbs down into the hole. When he strikes the rock with a hammer, it bursts in two, and cool clean water gushes out. This story of faith and persistence is typical of many of the early Jakata tales but has few other elements of traditional folktales. Later, beast tales were drawn from this collection to form the *Panchatantra,* stories that were used to instruct young princes in morality. When these stories are translated into English, their morals and teaching verses are usually eliminated. The resulting Indian tales sound more like folktales.

Rafe Martin retells an ancient ancestor of "Henny Penny" or "Chicken Little" in the Jataka tale *Foolish Rabbit's Big Mistake.* Rabbit hears an apple fall from a tree and wonders if the earth is breaking up. He panics and arouses a chain of animals who thoughtlessly run with him until a wise lion stops the stampede. He carries the silly rabbit back to the scene, proves it was only an apple that fell from the tree, and finally defends the rabbit from the anger of his friends by pointing out that they, too, ran without trying to find out the true cause of the alarm. Ed Young's large-scale paintings depict the action in dramatic close-ups and vibrant explosions of color.

In vigorous woodcuts, Marcia Brown illustrates the fable *Once a Mouse,* which must have warned young princes about the folly of pride in one's origins. Seeing a mouse about to be eaten by a crow, a hermit rescues it. But a cat stalks the pet, so the hermit changes the mouse into a bigger cat. Each change results in new dangers, until finally the meek mouse is transformed into a huge tiger. But he "peacocked about the forest" until the hermit reminds him that he was once a mouse. When the tiger threatens the hermit, the hermit reduces it to its original shape of a mouse.

Pam Newton's retelling of the traditional Indian tale *The Stonecutter* shares a similar theme with the previous story as well as with the German "The Fisherman and His Wife." A circular tale, it demonstrates how people end up as they started when they cannot control their greed and dissatisfaction. A poor stonecutter sees the house of a rich man when he comes to repair a wall and wishes that he, too, could be wealthy. The spirit of the mountain grants his wish and soon he is a rich merchant guiding a caravan to market. But he soon wants to be king. Even as king he is nearly overpowered by the sun's rays and so wishes to be the sun. A cloud obscures the sun, the wind blows away the cloud, and the stonecutter becomes each. But as the wind, he cannot blow down the mountain, so he becomes the mountain. Then a stonecutter chips away at this surface and the first stonecutter realizes his mistake. Newton's use of gold and yellow tones plays off the gray mountain stone of this magical world. Gerald McDermott, in his spare telling of a Japanese version in *The Stonecutter,* used handpainted paper cut into collages for his stylized illustrations.

The lesson in *The Story of Wali Dad,* a retelling by Kristina Rodanas, is captured with gentle humor as a poor grasscutter decides to spend his hoard of coins on something beautiful. The bracelet he buys seems to be worthy of a princess, so he asks a merchant friend to present it to the one who is most beautiful. The Princess of Khaistan accepts the gift and sends back a camel load of fine silks. But poor Wali Dad passes these on to the young Prince of Nekabad. As the size of the gifts escalates, Wali Dad is kept busy until he is horrified by the news that the Princess will visit her gracious admirer. But when Wali Dad arranges a meeting of the Prince and Princess, they fall in love. The generous and simple matchmaker is the happiest of all at the wedding, for he recognizes on the bride's arm the small gold bracelet that started it all.

While these tales represent but a small portion of stories from the Middle Eastern countries and India, they are indicative of a rich source on which children's literature has yet to draw fully. Perhaps the next decades will provide a greater number of single-tale editions of stories such as these so that children might become more familiar with this important literary tradition.

Folktales from Asia

Although fewer folktales are available from Asia, there are increasing numbers of outstanding, well-illustrated single-tale editions of the folktales from Japan, China, Korea, and Vietnam.

Ai-Ling Louie's *Yeh-Shen* is one of the oldest written variants of "Cinderella," predating European versions by a thousand years. Left in the care of a stepmother and stepsister, Yeh-Shen is made to do the heaviest chores. Her only friend is a fish, which she feeds and talks with each day until the stepmother kills and eats it. However, its magical power lives on in the bones. Through it, Yeh-Shen is able to go to a festival dressed in a gown, a cloak made of kingfisher feathers, and gold slippers. There, the suspicious stepsister causes the girl to run away and lose a slipper. Immediately Yeh-Shen's fine clothes turn to rags. But the king, struck by her beauty, places the slipper in a roadside pavilion and hides to wait for the girl who will reclaim it. When Yeh-Shen creeps, under cover of darkness, to retrieve the slipper, they are united, and later they marry. As in the German version of the Cinderella story, however, the stepsister and mother are punished, "crushed to death in a shower of flying stones." Ed Young's depictions of costumes and footwear reflect his research into textiles, costuming, and festivals of the ancient Hmong people. In addition, each shimmering pastel and watercolor illustration reminds us in shape or shadow of the contours of the magic fish. A much longer but similar version of the tale is the title story in Lynette Dyer Vuong's *The Brocaded Slipper and Other Vietnamese Tales*.

Young's Caldecott Medal book *Lon Po Po* tells a tale that comes from an ancient oral tradition and is thought to be over a thousand years old. Child readers will recognize similarities between this story and "Red Riding Hood." However, this wolf perishes by falling from the gingko tree as a result of three children's trickery and resourceful teamwork. Combining Chinese panel format with contemporary pastel and watercolors, Young creates a mysterious nighttime setting illuminated by candles, moonlight, and the shining eyes of the wolf.

One of the most popular stories in the Chinese storytelling tradition is recounted in Margaret Mahy's *The Seven Chinese Brothers*. Each brother looks like the others but has one unique feature, such as unusual strength, amazing eyesight, acute hearing, bones that will not break, or unhappy tears that will flood an entire village. When Third Brother is imprisoned by the Emperor, the other brothers use their talents to bring about the Emperor's downfall. The carefully researched details of Jean and Mou-Sien Tseng's watercolors reflect our contemporary concerns with authenticity in illustration as well as text. This version contrasts with Claire Huchet Bishop's simpler retelling and Kurt Weise's black-line stereotyped illustrations from an earlier era for *The Five Chinese Brothers*.

Caring for one's parents or others above oneself is also a theme of Chinese folktales. In Rosalind Wang's *The Fourth Question*, Yee-Lee, the son of a poor woman, sacrifices his own desires to help others and finds that his greatest dreams come true. In Demi's *The Magic Tapestry*, as well as in Marilee Heyer's *The Weaving of a Dream*, a poor woman's weaving comes to life due to her youngest son's efforts and sacrifices. In Carol Kendall's *The Wedding of the Rat Family*, a proud rat's desire is to get power by marrying into the powerful cat family. His greed has dire but predictable results for the proud rat clan. However, the poor, hardworking rat cousins who were not invited to the wedding triumph by inheriting the foolish rat clan's wealth. In Doreen Rappaport's *The Long-Haired Girl*, the heroine, Ah-mei, is willing to sacrifice her life for her fellow villagers.

In *The Long-Haired Girl* by Doreen Rappaport, a girl is willing to sacrifice her life for her neighbors, a common theme in Asian folktales.
From *The Long-Haired Girl* by Doreen Rappaport. Pictures by Yang Ming-Yi. Copyright © 1995 by Doreen Rappaport. Pictures copyright © 1995 by Yang Ming-Yi. Used by permission of Dial Books for Young Readers, a division of Penguin Books USA Inc.

When a drought threatens the lives of her people, she climbs up into the mountains and discovers the secret stream of Lei-gong, the God of Thunder. He warns her not to tell of her discovery, on pain of death, and at first Ah-mei obeys. However, keeping her terrible secret causes her long, beautiful hair to turn white. Finally, moved by the awful suffering of an old man, she decides to sacrifice her life and leads the villagers to the hidden spring. In return for her goodness, the old man helps her to outwit Lei-gong, using her white hair as bait. The hair eventually becomes a beautiful waterfall, and Ah-mei returns safely to her people. Yang Ming-Yi's beautiful woodcuts, printed on rice paper and then painted with watercolor, capture the story's mood and reflect its theme.

Pride is the downfall of a village magistrate in Margaret Leaf's *Eyes of the Dragon*. When an artist paints a dragon's likeness on the walls of a village, the magistrate refuses to pay him the agreed-upon sum because he has not painted in the dragon's eyes. Reluctantly, and with a warning, the artist paints in the eyes, quickly retrieves his money, and departs. As he rides away, the dragon comes to life and departs for heaven while the wall surrounding the village crumbles away.

Lily Toy Hong's *Two of Everything* is a lighthearted farce that contains elements of many magical pot stories. When poor old Mr. Haktak finds a brass pot in his field, he brings it home to his wife. They discover that this pot duplicates anything that they put into it, even Mrs. Haktak, who has fallen in by accident. In his consternation over his two identical wives, the farmer trips and falls in, too. Now there are two Mr. Haktaks and two Mrs. Haktaks. The clever solution will appeal to younger children, who might also discover the concept of multiplication.

Japanese folktales contain miniature people, monsters called *oni*, and, like Chinese tales, themes of gentleness toward animals and other people, the value of hard work, and respect for the elderly.

In *Momotaro, the Peach Boy*, Linda Shute recounts what is said to be the most popular folktale in Japan. Momotaro is held up to children as an example of kindness, courage, and strength. In Shute's retelling, a tiny boy who has stepped out of a huge split peach must fight the *oni*, who are robbing and attacking the people. With the help of three companions, Momotaro storms the stronghold of the blue-bodied, horned *oni*. He returns victorious, bringing home all the gold and silver the *oni* had stolen from the people. In an informative source note, Shute includes a glossary of Japanese words and explains the significance of symbols in her lively illustrations that draw on the style of Japanese narrative picture scrolls. Ed Young has used vivid pastel chalks to illustrate a Chinese version in his *Little Plum*. Little Plum, a boy no bigger than a plum seed, promises his parents to fight the evil lord who is terrorizing the people of his village and return their stolen goods. He outwits the lord through trickery, and when his parents realize that Little Plum "was as big as his promise," they are no longer troubled by his tiny size.

Another well-known Japanese story is retold in Sumiko Yagawa's *The Crane Wife*, a tale of the results of succumbing to poor advice and greed. Yohei, a poor peasant, removes an arrow from a wounded crane and dresses the injury. Later, a beautiful young woman appears at his door and asks to be his wife. To help pay for the extra mouth to feed, the woman offers to weave cloth but warns Yohei that he must never look at her as she works. One day, forgetting the warning, he looks in on her, only to see a crane plucking feathers from her own breast in order to weave the beautiful cloth. No longer wishing to remain in human form, she flies away. Suekichi Akaba applied water-thinned ink to textured paper to create haunting and beautiful illustrations. It would be interesting for children to compare Molly

Bang's literary use of the tale in *Dawn*, which is set in nineteenth-century New England. The alert reader may spot clues to Dawn's true identity, such as pieces of eggshell under her bed when she gives birth to a daughter, and the quilt pattern she is piecing called "Wild Geese Flying."

Diane Snyder's *The Boy of the Three-Year Nap* is a humorous realistic folktale involving trickery. A poor widow, tired of supporting her son Taro, who is "lazy as a rich man's cat," pesters him to go to work for a rich rice merchant. Declining to work, the boy tricks the merchant into betrothing him to his daughter. Taro's mother works her own ruse, however, and in the end Taro is caught in his own tricks. Allen Say's precise watercolor illustrations reflect the Japanese love of order. The expressive faces of both the tricksters and the duped make readers laugh at the humorous situations.

Katherine Paterson's *The Tale of the Mandarin Ducks* presents a Japanese tale of a greedy lord who captures a magnificently plumed drake so as to have a beautiful caged bird. Shozo, a former mighty samurai who has lost an eye in battle, warns the lord that the wild bird will surely die in captivity, but the lord shuns his advice. When Yasuko, a kitchen maid, takes pity on the bird and frees him, the lord blames Shozo, strips him of his rank, and puts him to work in the kitchen, where he falls in love with Yasuko. The jealous and vindictive lord sentences them to death by drowning for releasing the duck. On their way to be executed, the condemned couple are rescued and taken to a hut in the forest. In the morning, they wish to thank their saviors but find instead the mandarin duck and his mate, who seem to bow before flying away. Shozo and Yasuko live on for many years in their forest hut in great happiness, for they had learned that "trouble can always be borne when it is shared." Leo and Diane Dillon studied *ukiyo-e*, a Japanese art movement that depicted the everyday life of common people, before creating their lovely watercolor and pastel illustrations for the story that suggest the natural beauty of a simple life.

Some Korean folktales, such as Nami Rhee's *Magic Spring*, deal with themes of hard work, loyalty, and greed; others have a wonderful sense of playful humor. In Holly Kwon's *The Moles and the Mireuk*, a story that has elements of "The Stonecutter," a mole father searches for the most powerful husband in all the universe for his daughter. He asks the sky, the sun, the clouds, and the wind who is the most powerful. The wind finally sends him to the Mireuk, a stone statue in his garden, because the statue is the one thing the wind cannot disturb. The Mireuk tells the mole father that there is only one thing he fears, the moles who dig away

Yumi Heo's stylistic illustrations help establish the magical setting and lighthearted mood in *The Rabbit's Escape* by Suzanne Crowder Han.

From *The Rabbit's Escape* by Suzanne Crowder Han, illustrated by Yumi Heo. Illustration copyright © 1995 by Yumi Heo. Reprinted by permission of Henry Holt and Co., Inc.

the earth beneath his feet. The mole father happily chooses a young mole from his neighborhood for his daughter, proud to have such a powerful husband for his perfect child.

Rabbit is a familiar character in Korean folktales and often appears in the role of a clever trickster who also might be petty and vain. In *The Rabbit's Escape,* a retelling by Suzanne Crowder Han and illustrated by Yumi Heo, the Dragon King of the East Sea is told that he needs a rabbit's liver to cure his sickness. Unwilling to leave his watery kingdom, the king sends Turtle to bring him a rabbit from the land. Turtle lures a curious rabbit back to the sea kingdom, but when the rabbit discovers what his fate is to be, he tells the king that he has left his liver at home and must return to land to get it. Turtle takes the rabbit home, where he promptly runs away. Discovering that he has been tricked, Turtle weeps bitterly, and a god takes pity on him, giving him a piece of ginseng root. The king is cured, and from that day ginseng has been used to treat all sorts of illnesses. Han and Heo also collaborated on *The Rabbit's Judgment.* Both of these books are bilingual, printed in English and Han-gul, the Korean alphabet. Heo's abstracted paintings, with their strong linear designs, seem to mirror the Korean letter forms and recall the fantasy paintings of artist Paul Klee. They add a wonderfully light and humorous touch to these delightful tales.

The many beautiful single-tale editions of folktales from Asia have made these old and magical tales more widely available to an English-speaking audience. Often illustrated in the pictorial style of a particular period of Asian art, these stories can educate a child's artistic eye.

Folktales from Africa

Children today are the fortunate recipients of a rich bounty of African folktales collected by folklorists such as Harold Courlander. Many of these tales have been retold in single editions by authors like Verna Aardema and Ashley Bryan. More recent Caldecott awards have been given to African folktales than to tales from any other cultural tradition. The trickster tale of Anansi the spider told in *A Story, a Story* by Gail Haley won a Caldecott Medal, as did Aardema's pourquoi story *Why Mosquitoes Buzz in People's Ears* with illustrations by Leo and Diane Dillon. Caldecott Honor Books have included two other African pourquoi stories, Elfinstone Dayrell's *Why the Sun and the Moon Live in the Sky* with Blair Lent's distinguished illustrations, and *The Village of Round and Square Houses* by Ann Grifalconi; a second story of the trickster, *Anansi, the Spider* illustrated by Gerald McDermott; and John Steptoe's tale of a greedy and a generous sister, *Mufaro's Beautiful Daughters.*

Storytelling is a highly developed art in Africa, particularly in West Africa. These tales have an aural cadence found in no other stories of the world. They come from the oral tradition and are frequently written in the storyteller's voice. Short sentences, frequent use of parallel constructions, repetition, and dialogue characterize the style of many of the African tales. In Ashley Bryan's rhythmical tale from the Antilles, *The Dancing Granny,* Granny can't resist the song of Spider Ananse, who lures her to dance far out of sight while he raids her vegetable plot. The story sings with rhythmic prose and repeated refrains. Bryan's *The Story of Lightning and Thunder,* a story from Southern Nigeria, is filled with similar word music. It begins,

A long time ago, I mean a long, long time ago, if you wanted to pat Lightning or chat with Thunder, you could do it. Uh huh, you could! (unpaged)

This tale of how thunder and lightning went to live in the sky is accompanied by Bryan's sparkling paintings, which, with their colorful abstracted patterns, seem to flash with a special lightning all their own.

Many similar African tales are about personified animals, including those tricksters Anansi the spider, a rabbit, and a tortoise. In Gerald McDermott's *Zomo the Rabbit,* Zomo asks the Sky God for wisdom. The Sky God agrees but sets the rabbit three difficult tasks. This speedy trickster accomplishes the tasks but wreaks havoc in the jungle, angering Big Fish, Wild Cow, and Leopard. Sky God gives him the wisdom he has asked for, but warns him that he might have a lot of courage, a little good sense, but no caution whatsoever. Therefore, warns the Sky God, he better learn to run very very fast. Gerald McDermott's illustrations recall the patterned designs of African textiles and bring Zomo's tricky character to life.

Verna Aardema has retold a West African tale in *Why Mosquitoes Buzz in People's Ears*. In this cumulative story the mosquito tells the iguana a tall tale, setting off a chain reaction that ends in disaster for a baby owl. Until the animals can find the culprit who is responsible for the owlet's death, Mother Owl refuses to hoot and wake the sun. King Lion holds a council and listens to everyone's excuse until the blame comes to rest on the mosquito. The white outline of the stylized watercolors gives a cool but brilliant atmosphere to this story. Leo and Diane Dillon won the Caldecott Medal for their beautiful illustrations of this story and also illustrated Aardema's humorous Masai tale *Who's in Rabbit's House?* as a play featuring masked actors.

Verna Aardema has retold many other folktales from Africa. *Misoso*, her collection of "once upon a time tales," is a delightful literary tour of the continent. In addition to a map showing each tale's place of origin, every story is introduced with a glossary and pronunciation guide and followed with notes about the tale and its place in African folklore. Accompanied by beautiful stylized illustrations by Reynold Ruffins, this book is a superb introduction to serious study of African folklore for older children.

Many other African stories may also be described as pourquoi stories. Aardema's *How the Ostrich Got Its Long Neck*, Michael Rosen's *How the Giraffe Got Such a Long Neck . . . and Why Rhino Is So Grumpy*, and Ashley Bryan's wonderful retelling of "How the Animals Got Their Tails" in his *Beat the Story Drum, Pum-Pum* tell of the origins of characteristic features of African animals. Gail Haley's *A Story, a Story* explains the origins of a different type of tale—how humans got their stories. Ann Grifalconi's *The Village of Round and Square Houses* explains why, in a particular Cameroon village located at the base of a volcano, the women live in round huts while the men live in square ones, and the way in which people came to be farmers is explained in Mary-Joan Gerson's *Why the Sky Is Far Away*.

A play on words is a favored form of humor in some African tales. In *The Cow-Tail Switch*, Harold Courlander and George Herzog retell the story of the very wealthy man named Time. Change of fortune reduces him to a beggar, and persons remark, "Behold, Time isn't what it used to be!" (p. 77). The same collection has a story about the young hunters who try to capture "The One You Don't See Coming," which is their name for sleep. In another Anansi story in this collection, there is a character named Nothing. Anansi kills him, and all the villagers "cry for nothing!"

Tololwa Mollel's *The King and the Tortoise* is another humorous story in which a king who considers himself the cleverest one in the world challenges the creatures of his kingdom to make him a robe of smoke. A tortoise agrees to make the robe on the condition that the king gives him seven days and provides any materials he needs. The tortoise returns on the day the robe is promised and explains that he must have a thread of fire to finish the robe of smoke. The king, realizing that he has been tricked and thinking fast, tells the tortoise that he doesn't really want the robe anymore. "You have proven to me that you are clever enough to make one, and that is all I really wanted to know." He declares that two cleverest creatures in the world live in his kingdom, "You and I."

Frequently an African tale will present a dilemma and then the storyteller will invite the audience to participate in suggesting the conclusion. The problem of which son should be given the cow-tail switch as a reward for finding his lost father is asked in the title story *The Cow-Tail Switch* in the collection by Courlander and Herzog. The boys undertake the search only after the youngest child learns to speak and asks for his father. Each of the sons has a special talent he uses to help restore his father to life. It is then that the storyteller asks who should receive the father's cow-tail switch.

A more serious dilemma is presented in Nancy Day's *The Lion's Whiskers*, an Ethiopian tale about a stepmother whose stepson refuses to accept her as his new mother. After trying every kindness, she visits a medicine man, who tells her that she must bring back three whiskers of a lion. She is terrified but, loving her stepson, she sets out into the desert. Over the course of several months she patiently feeds a lion, getting closer and closer until she is able to pluck three hairs from his snout. When she returns to the wise man, he tells her she does not need the whiskers anymore, she has learned what she needs to know. "Approach your stepson as you did the lion and you will win his love." Indeed, when she returns home, it is her quiet and loving patience that finally draws her stepson into the circle of her arms. Ann Grifalconi's inventive photocollages embrace African symbols and objects and give this story an unusual but warm visual setting.

While searching for an African variant of "Cinderella," John Steptoe came upon the story he retells in *Mufaro's Beautiful Daughters*, turning it into a strikingly

A kind stepmother faces fearsome danger in order to win her stepson's love in Nancy Raines Day's *The Lion's Whiskers: An Ethiopian Folktale.*

Illustration by Ann Grifalconi from *The Lion's Whiskers: An Ethiopian Folktale* by Nancy Raines Day. Illustrations copyright © 1995 by Ann Grifalconi. Reprinted by permission of Scholastic Inc.

illustrated tale about conflict and contrast. Manyara, the bad-tempered, selfish sister, predicts that one day she will be queen and her sister will be a servant. Nyasha, the humble and hardworking sister, is happy to work in her garden and care for their father. When a message arrives from the king inviting all the worthy daughters in the land to appear before him so that he can choose a bride, Manyara hurries on ahead, thinking to beat her sister to the king's palace. Along the way she meets a hungry boy with whom she haughtily refuses to share her food, and she ignores the advice of an old woman. The next day, however, Nyasha shares her food with both people. When her sister arrives, Manyara comes running from the palace in hysterics because she has seen a five-headed serpent on the throne. But Nyasha bravely approaches and is relieved to find a little garden snake that transforms itself into the king. He reveals that he had also taken the shape of the little boy and the old woman and thus knows that she is the most beautiful daughter in the land, worthy to be his wife. Steptoe's careful research creates an accurate picture of the region. The intensely colored plants and animals living in the forest, architectural details from the

actual ruined city of Zimbabwe, and a pair of crowned cranes that symbolize the royal couple all contribute authenticity to this Caldecott honor winner.[19]

Obviously there is no dearth of folk literature from Africa, where oral tradition has been maintained. Children who hear these tales will become familiar with other cultures and the rhythmical chord of ancient African storytellers. They will learn of a land where baobab trees grow and people fear lions, leopards, droughts, and famines. More importantly, they will learn something about the wishes, dreams, hopes, humor, and despair of other peoples. They may begin to see literature as the universal story of humankind.

Folktales of North America

When the early settlers, immigrants, and slaves came to North America, they brought their folktales with them from Europe, China, and West Africa. As they repeated their folktales, some of the tales took on an unmistakable North American flavor. Indigenous to the continent are folktales told by Native Americans and tall tales that developed from the pioneer spirit of the young American country.

In a discussion of folktales of North America, it is impossible to describe any one body of folklore such as the Grimms discovered in Germany. However, the folklore of North America may be sorted into four large categories:

1. Native American, Eskimo, and Hawaiian tales that were originally here
2. Tales that came from other countries, primarily from West Africa, and were changed in the process to form the basis of African American folktales
3. Tales that came primarily from Europe and were modified into new variants
4. Tall tales, legends, and other Americana that developed here

Virginia Haviland's collection *North American Legends*[20] presents tales from each of these categories and gives a broad overview of folklore in the United States. *From Sea to Shining Sea,* Amy Cohn's extensively researched collection of American folklore and folk songs, offers children a stirring journey into an America that consists of many cultures, many stories, and many songs. Fourteen Caldecott Medal–winning artists provide the

[19]Darcy Bradley, "John Steptoe: Retrospective of an Imagemaker," *New Advocate* 4, no. 1 (winter 1991): 21.

[20]Virginia Haviland, *North American Legends,* illustrations Ann Strugnell (New York: Collins, 1979).

visual map for this marvelous exploration. A glossary, extensive footnotes, and suggested readings add to the book's value as a classroom resource.

Other notable collections include Laurence Yep's *The Rainbow People* and *Tongues of Jade*, tales Chinese immigrants told not only to remind themselves of home but to show how a wise person could survive in a strange new land. Paul Yee's *Tales from Gold Mountain* draws on the wellspring of stories told by the Chinese who settled in Vancouver's Chinatown. African Americans are represented in such fine collections as Virginia Hamilton's *The People Could Fly* and *Her Stories*. Both collections have been illustrated by Leo and Diane Dillon in their distinctive style. Native American tales have been assembled in thematic collections, such as Maria Brusca and Tona Wilson's *When Jaguars Ate the Moon and Other Stories About Animals and Plants of the Americas*, and in tribal collections such as Joseph Bruchac's *The Boy Who Lived with the Bears and Other Iroquois Stories*. Increasingly, readers will find that many other well-written collections and beautifully illustrated tales represent the many colorful threads that make up America's rich tapestry of story.

Native American Folktales

To try to characterize all the folklore of the various Native American tribes as one cohesive whole is as unreasonable as it would be to lump all of the folklore of Europe together. Variations in Native American dwellings, such as pueblos, longhouses, and teepees, or in the symbolic artwork of totem poles, beading, story skins, and carvings are mirrored in the variations of Native American folktales. The Resources for Teaching box "Some Native American Folktales by Region" is a useful grouping of tales for those wishing to study Native American folktales, specifically of a particular geographical area. However, there are some common characteristics among the various tribes and between the folklore of Native Americans and that of northern Europeans.

Many Native American tales might be categorized as mythology, for they include creation myths and sacred legends. Jean Monroe and Ray Williamson's *They Dance in the Sky* is a collection of Native American star myths that includes stories of the origin of the Pleiades, the Big Dipper, and other constellations. Manitonquat's *The Children of the Morning Light* brings together creation myths and other legends from the Wampanoag people of southeastern Massachusetts. Some myths attempt to explain religious beliefs while telling people about tribal customs and how to act. Some of these tales were told as separate stories, but as with Greek or Roman mythology, they were heard by insiders who understood these tales within the context of a large interlocking set of stories.

Native American tales, when originally told, were loosely plotted rather than highly structured like European fairy tales. Thomas Leekley, who retold some of the stories of the Chippewa and Ottawa tribes in his *The World of Manobozho*, says:

> Indian folklore is a great collection of anecdotes, jokes, and fables, and storytellers constantly combined and recombined these elements in different ways. We seldom find a plotted story of the kind we know. Instead, the interest is usually in a single episode; if this is linked to another, the relationship is that of two beads on one string, seldom that of two bricks in one building. (pp. 7–8)

The very act of storytelling was considered to be of ceremonial importance in various tribal groups. Storytelling took place at night and, in certain tribes, such as the Iroquois, it was permitted only in the winter. Men, women, and children listened reverently to stories, some of which were "owned" by a teller and could not be told by any other person. The sacred number four is found in all Indian tales, rather than the pattern of three common to other folktales. Four hairs might be pulled and offered to the four winds; or four quests must be made before a mission will be accomplished.

Many Native American tales are nature myths, pourquoi stories that explain how animals came to earth or why they have certain characteristics. Jane Yolen's retelling in *Sky Dogs* captures perfectly the amazement and uncertainty with which a small tribe of Piegans might have greeted the first horses. Paul Goble tells a similar story in *The Gift of the Sacred Dog*, in which the gift is the Great Spirit's attempt to help the Plains tribes hunt the buffalo more efficiently.

In William Toye's *The Loon's Necklace*, the loon receives his markings as a reward for his kindness in restoring the sight of a blind old man. Elizabeth Cleaver created stunning collage illustrations for this picture-book story of the origin of the "necklace." In *How Turtle's Back Was Cracked*, Gayle Ross recounts how Turtle, who used to have a smooth shell, became so full of himself that he annoyed a group of wolves who heard his bragging. They determine to kill him, but Turtle tricks them into throwing him in the river, where they think he'll drown. Instead of landing in the water, however, he falls on a large boulder and his shell cracks in a dozen places. Being a good healer, Turtle fixes his shell, but today if you look closely you can still see where his back was cracked. Marvin Jacob's paintings, executed in natural earth tones with patterned borders, nicely capture the story's Cherokee origin. Ashley Wolff's appealing linoleum block prints illustrate Gerald Hausman's *How Chipmunk Got Tiny Feet*, a collection of seven Native American animal origin stories.

Resources for Teaching
Some Native American Folktales by Region

Plains

Emery Bernhard, *Spotted Eagle and the Black Crow: A Lakota Legend*

Caron Lee Cohen, *The Mud Pony* (Pawnee)

Paul Goble, *Iktomi and the Berries: A Plains Indians Story* (Lakota Sioux)

Jamie Oliviero, *The Fish Skin,* (Cree)

Kristina Rodanas, *Dance of the Sacred Circle: A Native American Tale* (Blackfoot)

John Steptoe, *The Story of Jumping Mouse: A Native American Legend*

Nancy Van Laan, *Buffalo Dance: A Blackfoot Legend*

Jane Yolen, *Sky Dogs* (Siksika)

Woodland

John Bierhorst, ed., *The White Deer and Other Stories Told by the Lenape*

Barbara Juster Esbensen, *Ladder to the Sky* (Ojibwa)

———, *The Star Maiden* (Ojibwa)

Virginia Hamilton, "Divine Woman the Creator" (Huron), in *The Beginning: Creation Stories from Around the World*

Rafe Martin, *The Rough-Face Girl* (Algonquin)

Howard Norman, *How Glooscap Outwits the Ice Giants and Other Tales of the Maritime Indians*

Robert D. San Souci, *Sootface: An Ojibwa Cinderella*

William Toye, *How Summer Came to Canada* (Micmac)

Southwest

Byrd Baylor, ed., *And It Is Still That Way*

Shonto Begay, *Ma'ii and Cousin Horned Toad* (Navajo)

John Bierhorst, *Doctor Coyote: A Native American Aesop's Fables*

Tomie de Paola, *The Legend of the Bluebonnet: An Old Tale of Texas* (Comanche)

Gerald Hausman, *Coyote Walks on Two Legs: A Book of Navajo Myths and Legends*

Gerald McDermott, *Arrow to the Sun* (Pueblo)

———, *Coyote* (Zuni)

Kristina Rodanas, *Dragonfly's Tale* (Zuni)

Michael Rosen, *Crow and Hawk: A Traditional Pueblo Indian Story*

Nancy Wood, *The Girl Who Loved Coyote: Stories of the Southwest*

Northwest

Gerald McDermott, *Raven: A Trickster Tale from the Pacific Northwest*

Jean Guard Monroe and Ray A. Williamson, "How Coyote Arranged the Night Stars" (Wasco), in *They Dance in the Sky: Native American Star Myths*

Susan Hand Shetterly, *Raven's Light: A Myth from the People of the Northwest Coast* (Haida)

William Toye, *The Loon's Necklace* (Tsimshian)

Southeast

Joseph Bruchac, *The First Strawberries: A Cherokee Story*

———, *The Great Ball Game: A Muskogee Story* (Creek)

Beatice Orcutt Harrell, *How Thunder and Lightning Came to Be* (Choctaw)

Gretchen Will Mayo, "Ice Man Puts Out the Big Fire" (Cherokee), in *Earthmaker's Tales: North American Indian Stories from Earth Happenings*

Jean Guard Monroe and Ray A. Williamson, "What the Stars Are Like" (Cherokee), in *They Dance in the Sky*

Susan Roth, *The Story of Light* (Cherokee)

Joanna Troughton, *How Rabbit Stole the Fire* (Creek)

Eskimo

Emery Bernhard, *How Snowshoe Hare Rescued the Sun: A Tale Told from the Arctic* (Yuit)

Dale De Armond, *The Seal Oil Lamp*

Virginia Hamilton, "Raven the Creator," in *In the Beginning: Creation Stories from Around the World*

James Houston, *The White Archer: An Eskimo Legend*

Teri Slote, *The Eye of the Needle*

Perhaps one of the best known stories of explanation, which combines religious beliefs, how-and-why explanations, and references to Indian custom, is "Star Boy," which has many versions. Paul Goble retells this tale in *Star Boy* with beautiful illustrations drawn from careful references to Blackfoot artistic traditions. In this story, Star Boy, expelled from the sky world with his mother and marked with a mysterious scar because of her disobedience, becomes known as Scarface. In order to marry, he must make a journey to the Sun, who removes the scar. To commemorate and honor the Sun's gesture, the Blackfeet have a sacred Sun Dance each summer. In

Murv Jacob's color scheme and his use of Cherokee designs add authenticity to *How Turtle's Back Was Cracked* by Gayle Ross.

From *How Turtle's Back was Cracked* by Gayle Ross, illustrated by Murv Jacob. Copyright © 1995 Murv Jacob on illustrations. Used by permission of Dial Books for Young Readers, a division of Penguin Books USA Inc.

Goble's version, Star Boy becomes another star and joins his father, Morning Star, and his mother, Evening Star.

Another version of this story forms the skeleton of Jamake Highwater's novel *Anpao*. In the tradition of "beads on a string" rather than "bricks in a building," Highwater lets Anpao meet many traditional Indian characters, like Coyote, Grandmother Spider, Raven, and the Mouse People, as he journeys to ask the Sun for the removal of his scar. Parts of this novel are very humorous and would be fun to read aloud to middle schoolers familiar with the outline of the tale.

The heavens hold special significance for native peoples, as can be seen in such tales as Joseph Bruchac and Gayle Ross's *The Story of the Milky Way*, a Cherokee tale; Paul Goble's *Her Seven Brothers*, a Cheyenne myth about the origin of the Big Dipper; and Goble's *The Lost Children*, a Blackfoot story about the origin of the Pleiades. Beatrice Harrell's *How Thunder and Lightning Came to Be* is set closer to earth and is a humorous story from the Choctaw about two birds who agree to help the Great Sun Father warn the people when a bad storm is coming. Their silly attempts only amuse the people, however, until one day when Helotha's eggs roll off the

clouds creating a great thumping and bumping. When her husband, Melatha, races to catch them, sparks fly from his heels. The Sun Father was pleased with the effect this made. Now every time Helotha lays her eggs and Melatha chases them, Sun Father sends wind and rain to the earth. Susan Roth's textured collages capture the essence of the story's motifs and reflect the rich and varied patterns of Native American stories.

Almost all Native American folklore traditions contain a trickster figure who mediates between the sky world and earth. The woodland tribes tell tales of Manabozho, a kind of half god, half superpower among the eastern tribes. The Great Plains trickster Coyote snatches fire from the burning mountain in Margaret Hodges's *The Fire Bringer*, illustrated by Peter Parnall with clean lines and an economy of color. To this day, says the legend, Coyote's fur is singed and yellow along his sides where the flames blew backward as he ran down the mountain carrying the burning brand. A version of this story can be found in Gerald Hausman's *Coyote Walks on Two Legs*, a collection of Navajo myths and legends about this well-known trickster that includes a version of the Great Flood. Paintings by Floyd Cooper lend the poetic text a sense of the glowing warmth of the deserts of the Southwest. Navajo artist and storyteller Shonto Begay has retold another coyote tale in *Ma'ii and Cousin Horned Toad*. In this case Ma'ii (Ma'ii is the Navajo name for coyote) is the one who is tricked—by Horned Toad, who makes life so miserable when Ma'ii swallows him that to this day all coyotes keep their distance from their rough-skinned cousins.

Paul Goble has illustrated many tales from the Plains tribes, including several about the Plains trickster, Iktomi. Amusing stories that often have moral lessons within, they were to be told only after the sun had set. These stories were meant to elicit audience participation, and Goble has incorporated this in an inviting way. Asides like "It looks like the end of Iktomi, doesn't it?" and Iktomi's often self-serving remarks would make this very funny as a shared reading. Alert readers will spot, too, the watchful coyote as he moves closer to his dinner. *Iktomi and the Boulder*, *Iktomi and the Buffalo Skull*, *Iktomi and the Berries*, *Iktomi and the Buzzard*, and *Iktomi and the Ducks* are five tales about this Plains Indian trickster. Goble's illustrations for other titles, such as his *The Great Race of the Birds and the Animals* and *Buffalo Woman*, are filled with patterns of flowers, trees, birds, and other animals indigenous to the prairie. Goble received the Caldecott Medal for his stunning illustrations for *The Girl Who Loved Wild Horses*. All of Goble's work draws on Native American artistic traditions as well.

The trickster of the Pacific Northwest is Raven. While he is a wily, crafty being who loves to get the better of others, he is also a friend to humankind. *Raven's*

Light by Susan Shetterly tells how Raven created the earth from a stone and populated it with people and animals drawn from a sack around his neck. He then stole light for his world from the Kingdom of Day so that humans could see the world in its glory. Gerald McDermott's version of this story, *Raven: A Trickster Tale from the Pacific Northwest,* is illustrated in watercolors but Raven in his many guises wears the more abstract and solidly colored patterns of Northwest tribal art. Other Raven stories tell of how he brought salmon to the people (Gail Robinson, *Raven the Trickster*) and, in an Eskimo version, how he created the first human from a peavine (Virginia Hamilton, *In the Beginning*).

The stories of many tribes often revolved around a cultural hero like the woodland character Gluskap, Glooscap, or Gluskabe. This hero accomplished great deeds and often served as helper to the Great Spirit. In Joseph Bruchac's *Gluskabe and the Four Wishes,* Gluskabe has retired across the big water to take a rest after making the world a better place for his children. Four Abenaki men decide to undertake a difficult journey to ask Gluskabe for their hearts' desires. Impressed by the difficulties they have faced to get to him, Gluskabe gives them each a pouch but warns them not to look inside until they get home. The first three men cannot resist a peek and are justly punished. The fourth man, who only asked to be a good hunter to provide food for his people, resists temptation, but when he returns home he finds the pouch is empty. As he is about to despair, however, he hears the voices of the animals, who speak to him of the proper ways to prepare for the hunt and how to show respect for the animals. "From that day on he was the best hunter among the people. He never took more game than was needed, yet he always provided enough to feed his people." Perhaps this is one of the "Glooskabe" stories Attean told to Matt as the two boys survived the long winter in Speare's *Sign of the Beaver* (see Chapter 10).

Other, more human, heroes can be found in many Native American stories. Rafe Martin's *The Rough-Face Girl* is a retelling of an Algonquin story and has many elements of the Cinderella tales. In this version, Rough Face is the youngest of three sisters and has become scarred from sitting too close to the fire in order to feed the flames. Although her sisters both hope to be the ones to marry the Invisible Being, Rough Face is the only one who can see his face in the beauty of the world around her. When she has passed the tests set her, the Invisible Being appears and sees her true beauty. Then she is sent to bathe in the lake and her physical scars disappear, revealing her true form to all. David Shannon's carefully modeled paintings bring the characters in the story to life.

San Souci's *Sootface* is an Ojibwa story that is very similar to many other Native American versions of this tale. In this variant Sootface, the youngest sister, is only dirty with the soot from the fire rather than physically scarred. When she goes to meet the invisible warrior, she dresses in a gown of birch bark and wears a crown of wildflowers on her head. Daniel San Souci's realistic illustrations are based on thoroughly researched details of mid-1700s Ojibwa life.

Rafe Martin's poignant *The Boy Who Lived with the Seals* is based on a Chinook legend and tells of a boy who is torn between the world of The People and the undersea world of the seals. Although he does not transform physically into a seal as do the Selkies of North Atlantic legend, he eventually chooses to live in their kingdom, returning only once a year to leave a beautiful carved canoe for the humans he has left behind.

The character of Mouse Woman figures prominently in Dale De Armond's *The Seal Oil Lamp,* another story about a child caught between two worlds. Because Allegua was blind and Eskimo tribal law stated that no child may live if it cannot grow up to support itself, his family sadly left him behind when they moved to the summer fish camp. But the 7-year-old had fed a starving mouse that winter, so the Mouse Woman and her family take care of Allegua and he comes to know and love their world.

> They told him wonderful stories about the mouse world and about the owls and foxes and eagles who try to catch them, and how the mouse people outwit their enemies. They told him about Raven and the magic that lives under the earth and in the sky country. And the mouse people sang their songs for him and did their dances on the back of his hand so he could feel how beautiful their dances were. (p. 20)

De Armond's stylized wood engravings suggest dramatically the powerful beauty of Eskimo artwork.

Although survival themes are constant in Indian tales, they are particularly strong in Eskimo stories. James Houston, who spent many years among the Inuit, is especially sensitive to authentic depictions of Eskimo art and culture. His illustrations often look like renderings of Eskimo carvings. In his *Tikta Liktak,* a legendary hunter is isolated when an ice pan breaks away. In a dream, he gains courage, kills a seal, and is able to find his way home. *The White Archer* is a tale of a revengeful hunter who finally succumbs to the kindness and wisdom of an Eskimo couple.

The Resources for Teaching box "A Study of Folktales by Culture" provides a start for comparing characteristics, characters, collectors, and typical tales representative of specific areas around the world.

Resources for Teaching
A Study of Folktales by Culture

Cultures and Collectors	Typical Tales, Author	Characters	Characteristics
British Folktales			
Joseph Jacobs (1854–1916)	*The Three Little Pigs* (Rounds) *The Little Red Hen* (Galdone, M. Zemach) *Tam Lin* (Yolen) *The Selkie Girl* (Cooper) *Jack and the Beanstalk* (Cauley) *Tattercoats* (Jacobs)	Talking beasts Lazy Jack Giants "Wee folk" Dick Whittington	Cumulative tales for youngest children Beast tales Droll humor Transformations Giant killers
German Folktales			
The Grimm brothers Jacob (1785–1863) Wilhelm (1786–1859)	*Little Red Cap* (Grimm brothers) *Rumpelstiltskin* (Sage) *Hansel and Gretel* (Grimm brothers) *The Frog Prince* (Grimm brothers) *Snow-White and the Seven Dwarfs* (Grimm brothers) *The Elves and the Shoemaker* (Grimm brothers)	Tom Thumb Rumpelstiltskin Hansel and Gretel Red Riding Hood Witches, elves, dwarfs Bears, wolves Snow White King Thrushbeard	Somber stories Children as characters Harsh punishments Romances Transformations
Scandinavian Folktales			
Peter Christian Asbjørnsen (1812–1885) Jorgen E. Moe (1813–1882) Translated into English by George Webbe Dasent (1817–1896)	*The Three Billy Goats Gruff* (Galdone, Rounds) "The Lad Who Went to the North Wind," in *East o' the Sun and West o' the Moon* (Asbjørnsen and Moe) *East o' the Sun and West o' the Moon* (Dasent) *The Little Old Woman and the Hungry Cat* (Polette) *Tatterhood and the Hobgoblins* (Mills) *Boots and His Brothers* (Kimmel)	Trolls, Tomte Many-headed giants Youngest sons or "Boots" North Wind White bears Salmon Cats Reindeer, elk	Tongue-in-cheek humor Helpful animals Magical objects Magical enchantments Many trials and tasks Poor boy succeeds
French Folktales			
Charles Perrault (1628–1703)	*Puss in Boots* (Perrault) *Cinderella* (Perrault) *The White Cat* (San Souci) *Beauty and the Beast* (de Beaumont) *The Sleeping Beauty* (Perrault) *Stone Soup* (Brown)	Fairy godmothers Jealous stepsisters Royalty Talking cats Unselfish youngest daughter	Traditional fairy tale Romance Wicked enchantments Long sleep
Russian Folktales			
Alexander Afanasyev (1855–1864)	*The Firebird* (Demi) *Baba Yaga* (Kimmel) *Baba Yaga and Vasilisa* (Mayer) *The Frog Princess* (Lewis) *The Fool of the World and His Flying Ship* (Ransome) *Salt* (H. Zemach)	Vasilissa, beautiful and wise Ivan, youngest brother Baba Yaga, the witch Wolves, bears Firebird Koschey the Deathless	Peasants outwit tsars Many tasks Quest for firebird Dire punishments Helpful animals Fool or youngest triumphs

Resources for Teaching
A Study of Folktales by Culture (concluded)

Cultures and Collectors	Typical Tales, Author	Characters	Characteristics
Japanese Folktales	*The Boy of the Three-Year Nap* (Snyder) *The Crane Wife* (Yagawa) *Momotaro, the Peach Boy* (Shute) *The Inch Boy* (Morimoto) *The Funny Little Woman* (Mosel) *Three Strong Women* (Stamm) *Bamboo Hats and Rice Cakes* (Tompert) *The Wise Old Woman* (Uchida)	Inch Boy Momotaro Wicked *oni*, ogres Trickster badger Urashima Taro Poor farmers, fisherman	Transformation to birds Childless couples have "different" children Respect for elderly Self-sacrifice
African Folktales Harold Courlander and other present-day collectors	*Mufaro's Beautiful Daughters* (Steptoe) *Rabbit Makes a Monkey of Lion* (Aardema) *A Story, a Story* (Haley) *The Cow-Tail Switch* (Courlander and Herzog) *How Many Spots Does a Leopard Have?* (Lester) *Traveling to Tondo* (Aardema) *A Promise to the Sun* (Mollel) *Zomo the Rabbit* (McDermott)	Anansi, trickster spider Zomo, trickster rabbit Various animals	Pourquoi stories Talking-beast tales Animal tricksters "Why" humor Onomatopoeia Wordplay
Native American Folktales Henry Rowe Schoolcraft (1820s–1850s)	*Gluskabe and the Four Wishes* (Bruchac) *Star Boy* (Goble) *How Rabbit Stole the Fire* (Troughton) *Raven's Light* (Shetterly) *The Gift of the Sacred Dog* (Goble) *Ladder to the Sky* (Esbensen) *Iktomi and the Buzzard* (Goble) *The Eye of the Needle* (Slote) *The Dark Way* (Hamilton)	Gluskap, Gluskabe Manabozho, the Hare Coyote Raven Iktomi Sky People Mouse Woman	Nature myths Tricksters Transformation tales Pattern of four Pourquoi stories Interaction with spirit world

European Variants in the United States

Richard Chase collected and published *The Jack Tales* and *Grandfather Tales*, which are American variations of old stories brought to this country by English, Irish, and Scottish settlers in the seventeenth and eighteenth centuries. They are as much a part of Americana as the Brer Rabbit stories. In some respects Jack is an equivalent to Brer Rabbit. He is a trickster hero who overcomes his opponent through quick wit and cunning, rather than through the strength that triumphs in the tall tales that originated in the United States. All of these variants come from the mountain folk of the southern Appalachians. Cut off from the mainstream of immigration and changing customs, these people preserved their stories and songs in the same way that they continue to weave the Tudor rose into their fabrics.

Kindergarten children retold and illustrated their favorite fairy tales. Notice Rapunzel's long yellow braids hanging out the window and the title of "The Three Bears" story with its picture of three porridge bowls.
Martin Luther King, Jr., Laboratory School, Evanston Public Schools, Evanston, Illinois. Esther Weiss, teacher.

The Jack Tales is a cycle of stories in which Jack is always the central figure. You'd expect to find him playing this role in "Jack in the Giant's Newground" and "Jack and the Bean Tree." However, he shows up again in "Jack and the Robbers," which is a variant of "The Bremen Town Musicians." The delightful aspect of these tales is Jack's nonchalance about his exploits and the incongruous mixing of the mountaineer dialect with unicorns, kings, and swords. Yet another version is Gail Haley's *Jack and the Bean Tree*, cast as an Appalachian story told by Poppyseed, a character who is based on Haley's grandmother.

In *Moss Gown*, William H. Hooks retells an old story from North Carolina that melds elements of "Cinderella" with motifs from *King Lear*. Rejected by her father and banished from home by her two sisters, Candace meets a gris-gris woman who gives her a shimmering gown that will change back into Spanish moss when the morning star sets. Candace finds work in the kitchen of a plantation where the Young Master is about to give a ball. Calling on the gris-gris woman for help, Candace goes to each of the three balls and falls in love with the Young Master. When Candace finally reveals herself, the Young Master has come to know her through conversation and, it is implied, to love her for more than her beauty. Although the moss gown has magic to help her, Candace is more similar in spirit to Princess Furball and The Rough-Face Girl than to the Disney and Perrault Cinderellas, for it is her own

intelligence and spirit that wins her a husband, a home, and her father's love once again.

Others continue to Americanize European folktales. Hooks has also written an Appalachian *The Three Little Pigs and the Fox* that depends on local detail, colloquial language, and mountain customs for flavor. In it, Hamlet rescues her two pig brothers from a "drooly-mouth fox" and comes home in time for Sunday dinner. In *The Soup Stone*, Iris Van Rynbach illustrates and retells the French folktale in a post–Revolutionary War New England setting, while Susan Patron gives the story a mountain locale in *Burgoo Stew*. Barry Moser has set the Rumpelstiltskin story in modern-day Appalachia in *Tucker Pfeffercorn*. While purists might object, borrowing a tale from one tradition and retelling it in another is time honored, and these modern retellings will most likely be "found" in some other collection years from now.

African American Folktales

Africans who were brought to America as slaves continued to tell the tales they remembered, particularly the talking-beast tales. Some of these stories took on new layers of meaning about the relationship between the slaves and their masters. In the late 1800s, Joel Chandler Harris, a Georgia newspaperman, recorded these tales in a written approximation of the Gullah dialect in which the tales were told to him. In his *Uncle Remus: His Songs and His Sayings*, Harris invented

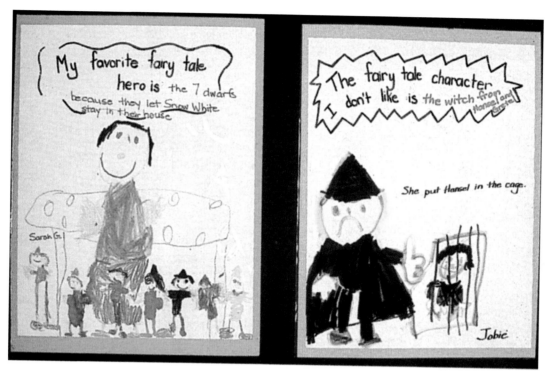

Kindergarten children illustrated their favorite fairy-tale characters and the one they disliked the most. They gave reasons for their choices.
Martin Luther King, Jr., Laboratory School, Evanston Public Schools, Evanston, Illinois. Deborah Kaplan, teacher.

Uncle Remus, an elderly plantation slave who told these talking-beast tales to a little white boy (see Harris's *The Complete Tales of Uncle Remus*). Harris was later criticized for his portrayal of the Old South, but the "Brer Rabbit" stories live on in retellings by other people.

Two excellent series have adapted these stories for today's children. In *Jump Again!* Van Dyke Parks and Malcolm Jones present "The Wonderful Tar-Baby Story," in which Brer Fox sets up a sticky contraption and then, "Brer Fox, he lay low." When Brer Rabbit is finally stuck, Brer Fox saunters forth and laughs threateningly, showing "his teeth all white and shiny, like they were brand-new." Of course, Brer Rabbit pleads with the fox to do anything but throw him into a briar patch, and the gullible fox is tricked once again into sparing the rabbit's life, for Brer Rabbit was "bred and born in a briar patch" (p. 9). In contrast, Julius Lester's "Brer Rabbit and the Tar Baby" from his *Complete Tales of Uncle Remus* is a more rambunctious version that sounds as if it is being told directly to the reader. Asides, contemporary allusions, creative figurative language, and interjections are characteristic of this storyteller. Lester describes Brer Rabbit as strutting "like he owned the world and was collecting rent from everybody in it" (p. 11). But by the time the poor rabbit is stuck, Brer Fox saunters out "as cool as the sweat on the side of a glass of ice tea" (p. 14).

Full-colored watercolors by Jerry Pinkney depict incidents in the story. Julius Lester's foreword for his three collections dispel many of the myths surrounding the "Brer Rabbit" stories, discuss the nature of storytelling, and reflect on the role of the trickster figure in valuing a little disorder in today's society. Lester has also included several talking-beast tales in *The Knee-High Man and Other Tales*.

The Talking Eggs by Robert D. San Souci is a Creole folktale that seems to have its roots in European tales like those in Robert Bender's *Toads and Diamonds*. A poor widow and her two daughters live on a farm that looks like "the tail end of bad luck." Blanche, who has to do all the work, runs into the forest one day and meets a strange old woman who gives her the gift of special eggs, which will turn into riches when she throws them over her shoulder. But she is warned to take only the ones that say "Take me." Blanche follows this advice even though the ones she leaves are jewel-encrusted. When she arrives home with fancy clothes and a carriage, her mother plots to steal Blanche's things and send Rose for more. But Rose steals the jeweled eggs and is paid for her greediness by the release of whip snakes, wasps, and a cloud of bad things that chase her home. Jerry Pinkney's rich and colorful illustrations magically evoke the forest and swamp settings of this Louisiana "generous person/greedy person" tale.

San Souci has retold another tale in *Sukey and the Mermaid*, a longer version of a short tale from the Sea Islands of South Carolina. In this story, Sukey has a mean stepfather who works her from dawn to dusk. Mama Jo, a mermaid, befriends her and gives her a gold coin whenever she calls her to the shore. Sukey's stepfather eventually discovers the mermaid's existence and tries to capture her for her gold. Sukey is led on several journeys between the world of the sea and that of her home on land, but eventually she decides to give up the mermaid's treasure for the love of a simple man. Her greedy stepfather, who has caused her so much trouble and pain, drowns as he tries to escape with Mama Jo's gold. Brian Pinkney's scratchboard illustrations help shape this wonderfully textured and complex story.

Virginia Hamilton is responsible for two superior collections of stories representing African American folktales. In *The People Could Fly*, she has collected twenty-four stories, including animal tales, stories with motifs of transformation and trickery, Jack tales and a tale of John de Conquer, and slave tales of freedom, including one handed down in the author's own family. In *Her Stories*, Hamilton follows a similar organizational format, but these tales have their roots in the history and folklore of African American women. They include animal stories, fairy tales, stories of the supernatural, and stories about real-life heroines. Hamilton has preserved the individual voices of the storytellers from whom the stories were collected. Some are in Gullah or plantation dialect, and others include African words whose meanings are lost to us today. Excellent classroom resources, these collections contain author notes and extensive bibliographies. Bold black-and-white illustrations by Leo and Diane Dillon evoke the humor, beauty, and liveliness of these traditional stories.

According to Steve Sanfield's introduction to his *The Adventures of High John the Conqueror*, the High John stories were popular among slaves but for obvious reasons were never shared with white people. Although John was a slave, he spent his time doing as little slaving as possible, tricking the Old Master out of a roasting pig or a few hours of rest. Sanfield prefaces eight of the sixteen tales with notes explaining historical context or giving background. In "Tops and Bottoms," titled after a motif found in many tales, John asks Boss which half of the planting he wants. Thinking that High John will plant cotton, Boss chooses the top. But John has planted sweet potatoes. Each of the next three years, Boss is tricked by John. Finally, he chooses *both* tops and bottoms, which leaves High John the middle. But John, no fool, plants corn, and Boss is left with a heap of tassels and stalks while High John takes the corn. Virginia

Hamilton extended the adventures of this sometimes mythical hero into a folktale-like novel, *The Magical Adventures of Pretty Pearl*.

Tall Tales

Ask any visitors to the United States what they have seen, and they are apt to laugh and reply that, whatever it was, it was the "biggest in the world"—the longest hot dog, the highest building, the largest store, the hottest spot. This is the land of superlatives, "the best." Many countries have tall tales in their folklore, but only the United States has developed so many huge legendary heroes. Perhaps the vast frontier made settlers seem so puny that they felt compelled to invent stories about superheroes. Whatever the reasons, North American tall tales contain a glorious mixture of the humor, bravado, and pioneer spirit that was needed to tame a wilderness.

Paul Bunyan was a huge lumberjack who bossed a big gang of lumbermen in the North Woods of Michigan, Minnesota, and Wisconsin. Paul's light lunch one day was "three sides of barbecued beef, half a wagon load of potatoes, carrots and a few other odds and ends," Glenn Rounds reports in *Ol' Paul, the Mighty Logger* (p. 28). Rounds asserts, as do most chroniclers of Paul's doings, that he worked for Paul and was the biggest liar ever in camp. By switching from past to present tense, Rounds gives these eleven tales special immediacy. Steven Kellogg synopsizes Paul Bunyan's life in his humorously illustrated picture-book version, *Paul Bunyon*. Tidy endpapers depict Paul's New England seacoast beginnings and a map of the States highlights Paul's feats. This action-packed version serves as an introduction to Bunyan's exploits, but the extended text of the other versions fleshes out individual tall tales and makes them better choices for reading aloud.

Kellogg's *Pecos Bill* tells the tale of a Texan who, as a child, fell out of his parents' wagon as they moved west and was raised by coyotes. Bill's exploits include squeezing the poison from a rattler to create the first lasso, and inventing cattle roping. He also bred cattle with shorter legs on the uphill side so that they could graze steep pinnacles without falling off. His taming of a wild horse eventually won him a bride, Slue-Foot Sue. Kellogg's depiction of this exuberant tall-tale hero is full of humor, exaggeration, and boundless energy. Ariane Dewey's *Pecos Bill* follows the same story line in easy-reader format with attractive but less active and less colorful pictures.

Of all the heroes, only Johnny Appleseed was a gentle, tame person who lived to serve others. His real name was John Chapman, and he grew up in the Connecticut Valley before setting out for Pennsylvania,

Ohio, and Indiana. Kathy Jakobsen's full-page folk-art paintings for Reeve Lindbergh's *Johnny Appleseed* capture the changing face of the land as settlers moved west in this poetic retelling. Steven Kellogg's *Johnny Appleseed*, in contrast, focuses on the more rollicking incidents that grew around the tales Chapman told to settlers and their own embellishments of these stories. Both authors include notes that help readers see how storytellers select events to shape into tales.

Industry has its heroes, too. "Joe Magarac," in Adrien Stoutenberg's *American Tall Tales*, tells of a man of steel who came to Hunkietown. The word *magarac* means "jackass" (which to steelworkers was a term of admiration), and Joe Magarac worked and ate like one. He finally melted himself down to become part of a new steel mill. Ariane Dewey's *Gib Morgan, Oilman* tells about a real oilman whose tall tales chronicle the rise of the American oil business. John Henry was a powerful African American who swung his mighty hammer in a contest with a steam drill to build the transcontinental railroad. Jerry Pinkney won a Caldecott Honor Medal for his sparkling watercolor illustrations for Julius Lester's robust retelling in *John Henry*. Steve Sanfield's illustrated short story *A Natural Man* also chronicles John Henry's life from childhood to his death after defeating the steam drill. Ezra Jack Keats created bold figures to depict this legendary hero in his picture book *John Henry*. "The Working of John Henry," in William J. Brooke's *A Telling of the Tales*, is a variation in which the steel-driving man triumphs by changing with the times and learning to use the newfangled machine.

Mary Pope Osborne tells the stories of nine heroes in *American Tall Tales*. In the tradition of nineteenth-century storytellers, she uses figurative language easily and has combined, edited, and added her own touches to these stories. Michael McCurdy's watercolor-washed bold wood engravings of Pecos Bill, John Henry, and Stormalong perfectly suit the exaggerated language of the tall tale.

In *Cut from the Same Cloth*, Robert San Souci has assembled a marvelous multicultural collection of tall tales with women heroines. Illustrated by Brian Pinkney, the stories are arranged by region and include such characters as Sal Fink, wife of the famous Mike; Annie Christmas, an African American heroine; and Otoonah, a member of the Sugpiaq people of the Aleutian Islands. Although not all of these stories can be strictly defined as tall tales, they do feature women who are tall in courage and strong in will. Anne Isaacs has surely based *Swamp Angel*, her original tall tale, on these wonderful heroines. (See Chapter 5.)

The Resources for Teaching box "Some American Tall-Tale Heroes" outlines some of the characteristics of

Jerry Pinkney portrays a magnificent American tall-tale hero in Julius Lester's retelling of *John Henry*.
From *John Henry* by Julius Lester, illustrated by Jerry Pinkney. Copyright © 1994 by Jerry Pinkney on illustrations. Used by permission of Dial Books for Young Readers, a division of Penguin Books USA Inc.

eight of these legendary heroes. Others whom children might research and add to the list include Casey Jones, Old Stormalong, Slue-Foot Sue, Febold Feboldson, Tony Beaver, and Mike Fink.

Folktales from Central and South America

Each year a little more of the rich story heritage of Central and South America becomes available. Many stories from this area appear in excellent collections of folktales, myths, or fables edited by John Bierhorst. *The Monkey's Haircut and Other Stories Told by the Maya* includes stories collected in Guatemala and southeastern Mexico from Mayan Indians since 1900. Some are obvious variations of European tales, and other are *ejemplos* (explanatory myths). Robert Andrew Parker's gray-washed drawings and Bierhorst's informative introduction both contribute appeal for middle-grade readers. (See the sections "Fables" and "Myths" in this chapter for other Bierhorst titles.) Nicholasa Mohr's *The Song of el Coqui and Other Tales of Puerto Rico* includes stories with Taino, African, and

Resources for Teaching
Some American Tall-Tale Heroes

Hero and Tales	Occupation/Locale	Characteristics
Johnny Appleseed (John Chapman) (1774–1845) *Johnny Appleseed* (Kellogg, Lindbergh) "Johnny Appleseed," in *American Tall Tales* (Osborne) "Rainbow Walker," in *American Tall Tales* (Stoutenberg)	Born in Massachusetts, wanderer in Pennsylvania, Indiana, and Ohio; planter of apple trees	Selfless; friend to animals; dressed in rags with cook pot for hat
Paul Bunyan *Ol' Paul, the Mighty Logger* (Rounds) *Paul Bunyan* (Shephard, Kellogg) "Sky Bright Axe," in *American Tall Tales* (Stoutenberg) "Paul Bunyan," in *American Tall Tales* (Osborne)	Lumberjack; North American woods; created the Great Lakes, St. Lawrence Seaway, and Grand Canyon	Huge; strong even as a baby; Babe the Blue Ox was the pet; inventive problem solver
Joe Magarac "Steelmaker," in *American Tall Tales* (Stoutenberg)	Steel worker; Pittsburgh, or "Hunkietown"	Made of steel; works and eats like a mule; born from an ore pit; stirs steel with bare hands
Pecos Bill *Pecos Bill* (Kellogg, Dewey) "Coyote Cowboy," in *American Tall Tales* (Stoutenberg) "Pecos Bill," in *American Tall Tales* (Osborne) "Slue-Foot Sue and Pecos Bill" (San Souci)	Cowboy; first rancher; Texas panhandle and the Southwest	Raised by coyotes; Widowmaker was his horse; Slue-Foot Sue was his wife; invented lasso, six-shooter, cattle roping
Sally Ann Thunder Ann Whirlwind Crockett *Sally Ann Thunder Ann Whirlwind Crockett* (Cohen) *Sally Ann Thunder Ann Whirlwind Crockett* (Kellogg)	Kentucky, Mississippi River	Could outwrestle, outrun, and outfish her brothers even as a child. Rescued Davy Crockett, then married him
John Henry *John Henry* (Keats, Lester) *A Natural Man* (Sanfield) "Hammerman," in *American Tall Tales* (Stoutenberg) "John Henry," in *American Tall Tales* (Osborne) "The Working of John Henry," in *A Telling of the Tales* (Brooke) John Henry the Steel Driving Man," in *Larger Than Life* (San Souci)	Railroad man; West Virginia west to the Mississippi	African American wanderer, exceedingly strong even as a baby; Polly Ann was his wife; companion was Little Willie
Davy Crockett (1786–1836) "Davy Crockett," in *American Tall Tales* (Osborne) "Frontier Fighter," in *American Tall Tales* (Stoutenberg)	Frontiersman; Tennessee	Tall; good hunter and fighter; Betsy was his rifle; tamed a bear; wore coonskin cap
Alfred Bulltop Stormalong "Five Fathoms Tall," in *American Tall Tales* (Stoutenberg) "Stormalong," in *American Tall Tales* (Osborne) "Old Stormalong: The Deep Water Sailor," in *Larger Than Life* (San Souci)	Sailor whaler, ship's captain; Massachusetts and northern coasts	Giant man, huge appetite; ship called the Tuscarora; made the White Cliffs of Dover with soap

Spanish origins and is indicative of the rich interweaving of cultures that contributed to the folklore of this vast region.

In Verna Aardema's Mexican tale *Borreguita and the Coyote*, a crafty "little lamb" outwits a coyote. Petra Mathers's stylish watercolor paintings feature bright saturated colors and primitive figures reminiscent of Henri Rousseau. Harriet Rohmer's *The Invisible Hunters* is a Nicaraguan Miskito Indian folktale about an isolated tribe's first contact with the outside world when a magic vine bestows the gift of invisibility on three brother hunters. In *Brother Anansi and the Cattle Rancher*, a folktale from Nicaragua, James de Sauza tells a bilingual tale of the exploits of the trickster spider found throughout the Caribbean countries and West Africa. When Tiger wins the lottery, Anansi outwits him and becomes a partner in a cattle ranch.

Ellen Alexander's *Llama and the Great Flood* is a Quechua story from Peru. Llama foresees the future ruin of the tribe when the sea overflows, and he warns his owner. He and his wife flee to the top of the highest mountain in the Andes with all the other animals of the world. After five days of flooding, the waters recede and the world can be inhabited again. Alexander's note links this story to other flood myths worldwide. Emery and Durga Bernhard's *The Tree That Rains* is a more complex story from the Huichol Indians of Mexico that has the great flood as one of its episodes. In this version Great-Grandmother Earth warns the hardworking Nakawe that the great flood is coming, and he escapes with his faithful dog in a canoe he has made out of his fig tree. He sails the floodwaters for five years and when the flood recedes he plants the seeds he has brought and prays for rain to grow them. He awakes the next morning to find a full-grown fig tree that gushes water to nourish his crops. Now every year the Huichol people remember this story at the Festival of the New Corn.

Pourquoi stories are as common in Central and South America as they are in other cultures. Mary-Joan Gerson's *How Night Came from the Sea* is a Brazilian story with African roots that explains how night and day originated, and how the Goddess Lemanja gave three gifts to the world to signal the return of day. Lois Ehlert's *Moon Rope* is a bilingual retelling of a Peruvian tale in which Mole and Fox try to climb to the moon on a grass rope. Mole falls off the rope and is so embarrassed by the other animals' teasing that he goes to live underground. As for Fox, Lois Ehlert's illustrations, adapted from Peruvian folk arts, show his face, just visible in the silvery moon. Two pourquoi stories tell different versions of how birds became brightly colored. "Humming-Bird and the Flower" appears in Charles Finger's *Tales from Silver Lands*, a collection of South American stories, illustrated with woodcuts, that won a Newbery Medal in 1925. The story attributes the hummingbird's colors to

Emery and Durga Bernhard use traditional Indian motifs to illustrate their version of a Mexican flood myth in *The Tree That Rains*.

clay, jewels, the color of the sunset, and the greens of the forests, which Panther helped the bird to gather after it helped restore Panther's eyesight. Flora's *Feathers Like a Rainbow* explains how the Amazonian birds received their own bright colors by stealing poor Hummingbird's pot of colors, which she gleaned as she kissed the flowers. Colorful paintings depict the vegetation and birds of the Amazon River basin.

Colorful Amazonian birds decorate the endpapers of Beatriz Vidal's *The Legend of El Dorado*. The name *El Dorado* symbolized for the Spanish conquistadors everything related to the search for gold in the unexplored jungles of South America. But El Dorado, "the gilded man," comes from a story first recorded in Colombia. A tribal king loses his wife and son to a serpent who has lured them to his watery kingdom. The serpent promised to reunite the family if the king ruled his kingdom wisely. To remind the serpent of its promise, each year the king oiled his body, covered it with gold, and then threw treasures to the serpent. Finally the king was accepted into the serpent's world to join his family, but to this day the treasures of the gilded king, El Dorado, are locked in the depths of Lake Guatavita.

With the changing population of North America, we need more editions of traditional folktales, myths, and legends that reflect South and Central American cultural heritage. Small publishers have begun to feature folktales of the region, and teachers will need to be persistent in finding these sources.

The "Folktales" web on page 311 suggests the rich possibilities inherent in a study of this genre of literature. It provides for a serious look at the types of folktales and certain motifs found in the tales that would appeal to younger children. A study of more-complex tales or myths or a cross-cultural study could be planned for older children.

Fables

Fables are usually associated with Aesop, a Greek slave who is supposed to have been born in Asia Minor about 600 B.C. Some scholars doubt his actual existence and believe that his works were the product of several storytellers. We know that some of the fables appeared in Greek literature two centuries before Aesop's birth, and in India and Egypt before that. The first written fables were in Greek, translated into Latin and again into English by William Caxton, and printed in 1484.

Other sources for fables, as we have seen, were the Jataka tales—animal stories that told of the previous births of the Buddha—and the *Panchatantra*, which was written for the purpose of instructing the young princes of India. These stories, longer than Aesop's fables, have moralistic verses interspersed throughout. When these are removed, the tales are closer to folktales. (See the earlier section "Folktales.")

A third common source for fables is the work of La Fontaine, a French poet, who wrote his fables in verse form. However, he drew largely on the collections of Aesop's fables that were available in the seventeenth century.

Characteristics of Fables

Fables are brief, didactic tales in which animals, or occasionally the elements, speak as human beings. Examples of these might be the well-known race between the hare and the tortoise or the contest between the sun and the north wind. Humans do appear in a few fables, such as "The Country Maid and the Milk Pail" or "The Boy Who Cried Wolf." The characters are impersonal, with no name other than "fox," rabbit," or "cow." They do not have the lively personalities of Anansi the spider or Raven the trickster of folktale fame. The animals are merely representative of different aspects of human nature—the lion stands for kingliness, the fox for cunning, the sheep for innocence and simplicity, and so on. Fables seldom have more than three characters, and the plots are usually based on a single incident. Fables were primarily meant to instruct. Therefore, all of them contain either an implicit or an explicit moral.

Because of their brevity, fables appear to be simple. However, they convey an abstract idea in relatively few words, and for that very reason they are highly complex. In selecting fables, then, it is wise to look at the quality of both language and illustrations. Compare the following two beginnings for "The Town Mouse and the Country Mouse." The first is Lisbeth Zwerger's, in her *Aesop's Fables:*

🐜 A Town Mouse went to visit his cousin in the country. This Country Mouse lived simply, and he was not rich, but he brought out all that he had to feed and entertain his honored guest. (unpaged)

Contrast Heidi Holder's:

🐜 An honest, plain, sensible Country Mouse invited her city friend for a visit. When the City Mouse arrived, the Country Mouse opened her heart and hearth in honor of her old friend. There was not a morsel that she did not bring forth out of her larder—peas and barley, cheese and parings and nuts—hoping by quantity to make up for what she feared was wanting in quality, eating nothing herself, lest her guest should not have enough. (p. 5)

Holder's illustrations for her *Aesop's Fables* are framed with borders suggesting medieval embellishments; Zwerger's illustrations feature a simple picture of two mice conversing on a hillside. These reflect some of the unique and various treatments given to Aesop's stories for today's readers.

Editions

Younger children might appreciate some fables, but they are not usually able to extract a moral spontaneously until about second or third grade. Eve Rice's *Once in a Wood* is a collection of ten well-known fables in easy-reader format with rhyming morals. Fulvio Testa's *Aesop's Fables* recounts its fables concisely, with morals concealed in the conversation rather than appended. Testa's use of crisp line and bright borders makes this version especially useful in reading aloud to larger groups.

Tom Paxton's lively verses in his *Aesop's Fables* are a rhythmical delight. Robert Rayevsky's illustrations, which have the look of richly tinted hand engravings, show animals and humans in medieval dress. In *A Sip of Aesop*, Jane Yolen has also used rhymes to retell thirteen of the fables, including "The Dog in the Manger" and "Counting Your Chickens." Her amusing introduction sets the tone for these decidedly modern retellings.

Folktales

Types of Tales

Cumulative Tales
The Gingerbread Boy (Galdone)
One Fine Day (Hogrogian)
The Turnip (Milhous and Dalgliesh)
The Mitten (Brett)
Make a chart of what accumulates.
Make a flannelboard story.
Make a circular map of the action.
Write your own version.

Pourquoi or "Why" Tales
The Cat's Purr (Bryan)
Why Ducks Sleep on One Leg (Garland)
Make a collage picture.
The Great Race (Goble)
The Village of Round and Square Houses (Grifalconi)
How Night Came from the Sea (Gerson)
Write your own nature "why" tale.

Wonder Tales
Ali Baba and the Forty Thieves (McVitty)
Momotaro, the Peach Boy (Shute)
Tam Lin (Cooper)
Snow White (Grimm)
Baba Yaga (Kimmel)
Puss in Boots (Perrault)
Make a catalog of magical objects.
Make a wanted poster for a villain.
Make a chart of transformation from/to.

Beast Tales
The Three Billy Goats Gruff (Asbjørnsen)
The Three Bears (Rockwell)
Traveling to Tondo (Aardema)
The Little Red Hen (M. Zemach)
The Bremen-Town Musicians (Grimm/Plume)
Make a "book of threes."
Bake Red Hen's bread.
Put on a play of Tondo or Billy Goats.
Make paperbag puppets and retell a story.

Actions

Folktale Party
Dress as a character from a tale.
Invite others.
Serve folktale fare:
Gingerbread cookies
Strega Nona's pasta (De Paola)
Stone Soup (Stewig)
Anasi's baked yams from *A Story, a Story* (Haley)
Snow White's unpoisoned apples
Conduct tours of the Folktale Museum.

Surveys
Favorite folktale character
Best-illustrated version of one story
Most disliked character
Parent's best-remembered tale
Favorite folktale food

Pulling It Together
Make a mural of houses from folktales (Gretel's witch's candy house; Baba Yaga's stilted house).
Assemble a museum of things important to folktales (Princess's pea; Hansel's chicken bone; Wiley's rope; Beauty's rose), and write labels for each one.
Make a "Photograph Album"; draw snapshots from a tale.
Locate these tales on a wall map of the world and place a label and string to the country of origin. What do you notice?

Motifs

Transformations
The Crane Wife (Yagawa)
The Princess and the Frog (Isadora)
The Story of Jumping Mouse (Steptoe)
The Little Snowgirl (Croll)
List real-life transformations (ice/water; jello; caterpillar/butterfly).
Group by what causes transformation (love, disloyalty, magic, etc.).
Retell from transformed one's point of view.

Trickery
The Boy of the Three-Year Nap (Snyder)
Puss in Boots (Perrault)
The Tales of Uncle Remus (Lester)
The Tale of Rabbit and Coyote (Johnston)
Write the tricky plans for a character.
Make a "bad guy" out of stuffed construction paper.
Interview the trickster for television.

Comparing Versions and Variants

Henny Penny (Butler)
Foolish Rabbit's Big Mistake (Martin)
Chicken Little (Kellogg)

Little Red Riding Hood (Grimm/Hyman)
Lon Po Po (Young)

List similarities and differences for each grouping.
Compare wolf illustrations.
Write another story from the wolf's point of view.

Yeh-Shen (Louie)
The Egyptian Cinderella (Climo)
Cinderella (Perrault/Le Cain)
Compare the three stories.
Write a "found" ad and make a picture for a girl who owns the shoe.
How many years separate these versions?
Why do you think they are so similar?
Write a modern version of Cinderella.

MORAL:
You may not have time
For a final correction.
Don't open your mouth
Without proper reflection.

Karen Barbour's lively illustrations add to the appeal of Jane Yolen's retellings in *A Sip of Aesop.*

Illustration by Karen Barbour from *A Sip of Aesop* by Jane Yolen. Illustrations copyright © 1995 by Karen Barbour. Reprinted by permission of Scholastic Inc.

Brightly colored paintings by Karen Barbour recall the work of Henri Matisse and are vivid reminders of the timeliness of the stories. Eric Carle, in *Twelve Tales from Aesop,* took some liberties in retelling, so that in "The Grasshopper and the Ant," instead of being left out in the cold as a result of his lack of foresight, the grasshopper is invited into a second house as an honored musician.

In *The Exploding Frog and Other Fables from Aesop,* John McFarland retells more than thirty fables with a contemporary flair. Cheerfully humorous illustrations by James Marshall add much to these fables, and because the morals are omitted, this collection may challenge children to add their own. A reissue of *The Caldecott Aesop* shows how Randolph Caldecott applied the moral of a fable to a contemporary (for Caldecott) setting. Each fable has two pictures—one, a literal animal scene, and the second, a human one. The title character of "The Ass in the Lion's Skin" impresses the other animals until the disguise blows off. In Caldecott's satiric

second interpretation, a pompous art critic is discovered to know nothing. In *Aesop & Company,* Barbara Bader has sandwiched nineteen of Aesop's fables between an introduction to the origins of the stories and an afterword that retells the legends that surround Aesop's life. Detailed etchings by Arthur Geisert add visual complexity to the brief fables and provide a nice feel of timelessness.

John Bierhorst, a distinguished collector and editor of Native American literature, discovered that Aesop's fables had been recorded by the Aztecs in the sixteenth century. His *Doctor Coyote* is a collection of these stories, translated from the Aztec manuscript, in which the main character of each fable became Coyote, a Native American trickster. Bierhorst's cohesive collection of twenty fables weaves one story into the next and shows Coyote getting a little wiser with each "lesson." With ample use of blues and roses, Wendy Watson's full-color illustrations warmly depict the desert and mountain settings of New Mexico.

Like the many other books by Mitsumasa Anno, *Anno's Aesop* challenges readers both visually and verbally. Little Freddy Fox finds a book of fables, which he asks his father to read to him. Readers see the original fable with a literal or enigmatic illustration on the top three-quarters of the page. At the bottom, Mr. Fox spins out his version of the story, which might be humorous, parallel, crazily imaginative, or part of a longer story he weaves from picture to picture. Older readers recognize Anno's trademark optical illusions, puzzles, allusions, and inclusions.

Other illustrators have chosen fewer tales for interpretation. Paul Galdone's *Three Aesop Fox Fables* includes two stories in which the same fox is outsmarted and one in which he triumphs. Galdone has also illustrated a Jataka tale, *The Monkey and the Crocodile,* as did Marcia Brown in *Once a Mouse.* Startling close-ups heighten the drama of "little and big" in Ed Young's black-and-white illustrations for *The Lion and the Mouse.* By contrast, Young's vividly colored collages for the Indian fable *Seven Blind Mice* highlight the patchwork nature of understanding that these mice bring to their definition of an elephant. La Fontaine based many of his fables on Aesop, and Brian Wildsmith illustrated La Fontaine's *The Miller, the Boy and the Donkey, The Hare and the Tortoise,* and *The Lion and the Rat* in his familiar splashes of color.

Older children might enjoy comparing treatments of several of these fables. In this way they would become familiar with the spare language, the conventional characters, and the explicit or implied morals of fables. They might appreciate modern writers of fables, such as Leo Lionni, whose *Frederick* is similar to Carle's version of "The Grasshopper and the Ant," or William Steig, whose *Amos & Boris* mirrors "The Lion and the Mouse."

After such comparisons, discussions, and readings, they would then be well prepared to write their own fables and variations.

Myths

Mythology evolved as primitive peoples searched their imaginations and related events to forces, as they sought explanations of the earth, sky, and human behavior. These explanations moved slowly through the stages of a concept of one power or force in human form, who controlled the phenomena of nature; to a complex system in which the god or goddess represented such virtues as wisdom, purity, or love; to a worshiping of the gods in organized fashion. Gods took the forms of men and women, but they were immortal and possessed supernatural powers.

Myths deal with human relationships with the gods, with the relationships of the gods among themselves, with the way people accept or fulfill their destiny, and with people's struggles with good and evil forces both within themselves and outside themselves. The myths are good stories, too, for they contain action, suspense, and basic conflicts. Usually each story is short and can be enjoyed by itself, without deep knowledge of the general mythology.

Types of Myths

Many myths can be characterized by the type of explanation they offer about the beginnings of the world or about some natural phenomenon. Other myths might focus on difficult tasks or obstacles to be overcome by the hero or heroine.

Creation Myths

Every culture has a story about how the world began, how people were made, how the sun and the moon got into the sky. These are called creation myths, or origin myths; they give an explanation for the beginnings of things. Deborah Nourse Lattimore based *Why There Is No Arguing in Heaven* on myths found in the Mayan codices, books painted on bark or deerskin and preserved from invading Spaniards. In this creation story, Hunab Ku spits in a jar of rainwater and pours out the world. Two other gods, Lizard House and Moon Goddess, compete to create a being worthy of worshiping the gods. But it is the watchful Maize God who is finally successful in creating men and women and is allowed to take his place beside Hunab Ku. Lattimore's illustrations resemble the Mayan stonework and paintings found in Guatemala and parts of Mexico.

John Bierhorst's *The Woman Who Fell from the Sky* is an Iroquois creation story in which First Woman falls from her home in the sky and lands on Turtle's back, creating the world. She soon gives birth to two boys, Sapling and Flint. Sapling busies himself creating gifts for the people who are soon to come. Flint, whose heart is hard, injects difficulties into every gift. Then Flint invents terrible troubles for people, but Sapling mediates and makes these easier to bear. Finally Sapling takes some earth and makes human beings, teaching them to make houses and light fires. Then he and Flint return to the sky, each taking a separate path that becomes the Milky Way. Their mother leaps into a campfire and rises with the smoke into the air. To this day the people give her their thanks as smoke rises from their fires. Robert Andrew Parker's flowing watercolor illustrations bring a sense of magic and mystery to this lovely story.

Virginia Hamilton chose creation stories from around the world for her collection *In the Beginning*.

> These myths from around the world were created by people who sensed the wonder and glory of the universe. Lonely as they were, by themselves, early people looked inside themselves and expressed a longing to discover, to explain who they were, why they were, and from what and where they came. (p. xi)

Barry Moser's watercolor portraits and representations are mysterious and dramatic accompaniments to these tales. An Eskimo story tells how Raven the Creator made a pea pod from which humans sprang. A Chinese story explains how Phan Ku burst from a cosmic egg to create the world. A California Indian legend, "Turtle Dives to the Bottom of the Sea," begins with a sea turtle that dives underwater to bring up enough earth to make dry land.

John Bierhorst's expertise in Aztec literature is the basis for his *Mythology of Mexico and Central America*. This book traces twenty basic myths and explains how they functioned among the ancient Aztec and Maya people and how they survive today. This volume, as well as its two companions, *The Mythology of South America* and *The Mythology of North America*, would give teachers and older students the background needed to understand these creation stories. Bierhorst's *The Hungry Woman: Myths and Legends of the Aztecs* is for a younger audience and includes reproductions of early Aztec paintings that functioned as a way of preserving stories.

Children who compare myths may marvel at the human imagination and see the world in a different way. Comparing myths also often raises interesting questions for children about the similarities, connections, and migrations of early peoples.

Nature Myths

The nature myths include stories that explain seasonal changes, animal characteristics, earth formations, constellations, and the movements of the sun and earth. Many Native American nature myths are easier for young children to comprehend than are the creation myths. Some of these myths have been previously discussed in the section "Native American Folktales."

The Greek story of Demeter and Persephone explains the change of seasons. Hades, god of the underworld, carried Persephone off to the underworld to be his bride, and Demeter, her mother, who made plants grow, mourned so for her daughter that she asked Zeus to intercede. It was granted that the girl might return if she had eaten nothing in Hades. Since she had eaten four seeds of a pomegranate, she was compelled to return to Hades for four months each year, during which time the earth suffered and winter came. In *Daughter of Earth*, Gerald McDermott tells the Roman version of the myth, visually contrasting the cool greens of earth above with the smoke reds of the underworld. In *Persephone*, Warwick Hutton retells the Greek version with a more substantial text. The character of Hades is more fully developed, and he becomes a figure of sympathy in his lonely existence. Hutton's transparent watercolor illustrations are lighter in tone than McDermott's, although he manages to create a smoky darkness in the scenes set in the underworld.

Hero Myths

The hero myths, found in many cultures, do not attempt to explain anything at all. These myths have some of the same qualities as wonder stories—the hero is given certain tasks or, in the case of Heracles, labors, to accomplish. Frequently the gods help (or hinder) a particular favorite (or disliked) mortal. Monsters, such as gorgons, hydras, and chimeras, are plentiful in the Greek stories, but these provide the hero with a challenge. Characteristic of the hero role is that he or she accepts all dangerous assignments and accomplishes his quest or dies in one last glorious adventure.

Greek Mythology

The myths with which we are most familiar are those of the ancient Greeks collected by the poet Hesiod sometime during the eighth century B.C. The Roman versions of these myths were adapted by the poet Ovid during the first century B.C. in his well-known *Metamorphoses*. This has caused some confusion, in that the Roman names for the gods are better known than the Greek, even though the stories originated with the Greeks. However,

the more recent versions of these myths are using Greek names. In working with children, it is best to be consistent in your choice of names, or they will become confused. You might wish to reproduce the Resources for Teaching box "Some Gods and Goddesses of Greek and Roman Mythology" for their reference. Leonard Everett Fisher's *The Olympians* provides an introduction to the pantheon. Each double-page spread features a painting as well as a paragraph about a particular god or goddess, and lists both Greek and Roman names, parentage, and the symbols representing that deity.

Greek mythology is composed of many stories of gods and goddesses, heroes, and monsters. The Greeks were the first to see their gods in their own image. As their culture became more sophisticated and complex, so too did their stories of the gods. These personified gods could do anything that humans could do, but on a much mightier scale. The gods, although immortal, freely entered into the lives of mortals, helping or hindering them, depending on their particular moods. Their strength was mighty and so was their wrath. Many of the myths are concerned with the gods' conflicts and loves. Their jealousy and their struggles for power often caused trouble for humans. (Some of the stories concerning the loves and quarrels of the immortals are inappropriate for children.)

Greek mythology includes the creation story that Earth and Sky were the first gods. Their children were the giant Cyclopes and the Titans, one of whom was Cronus, who drove his father away with a scythe (the source of the traditional picture of Father Time). Cronus swallowed his children so they would not usurp his place, but his wife gave him a stone in place of her last child, Zeus. Of course, Zeus overthrew his father and made him disgorge his brothers and sisters, who were still alive. Zeus married the jealous Hera, who caused all kinds of trouble. Prometheus was a Titan who defied the other gods in order to give fire to humankind. Zeus punished his disobedience by chaining him to Mount Caucasus, where each day his liver was devoured by an eagle but each night it was renewed. Zeus also sent Pandora and a box of trouble to punish Prometheus and humankind (see "Pandora" in Virginia Hamilton's *In the Beginning*). Warned not to open the box, Pandora was so curious that she could not help herself. All the evils of the world were released, but hope remained in the box and gave humans the ability to endure.

Another story concerned Zeus's punishment of the greedy King Midas (see the versions by Alice Low and Neil Philip). Midas's curse was that everything he touched, including his little daughter, turned to gold. Children who have a good background in folktales will find that many of the same elements are present in the Greek myths. In the *D'Aulaires' Book of Greek Myths*

Resources for Teaching
Some Gods and Goddesses of Greek and Roman Mythology

Greek	Roman	Title	Relationship
Zeus	Jupiter or Jove	Supreme Ruler, Lord of the Sky	
Poseidon	Neptune	God of the Sea	Brother of Zeus
Hades or Pluto	Pluto	God of the Underworld	Brother of Zeus
Hestia	Vesta	Goddess of the Home and Hearth	Sister of Zeus
Hera	Juno	Goddess of Women and Marriage	Wife and sister of Zeus
Ares	Mars	God of War	Son of Zeus and Hera
Athena	Minerva	Goddess of Wisdom	Daughter of Zeus
Apollo	Apollo	God of Light and Truth, the Sun God	Son of Zeus and Leto
Aphrodite	Venus	Goddess of Love and Beauty	Daughter of Zeus, wife of Hephaestus
Hermes	Mercury	Messenger of the Gods	Son of Zeus and Maia
Artemis	Diana	Goddess of the Moon and Hunt	Twin sister of Apollo
Hephaestus	Vulcan	God of Fire	Son of Hera
Eros	Cupid	God of Love	Son of Aphrodite (in some accounts)
Demeter	Ceres	Goddess of Grain	Daughter of Cronus and Rhea
Dionysus or Bacchus	Bacchus	God of Wine	Son of Zeus and Semele
Persephone	Proserpine	Maiden of Spring	Daughter of Demeter

the story of King Midas is economically told in two pages with a bold stone lithograph illustration. The d'Aulaires' collection presents a well-woven selection of tales ranging from the birth of Cronus's children to the stories of the mortal descendants of Zeus.

The gods could not tolerate human pride, which the Greeks called *hubris.* Arachne was transformed into a spider because of her pride when she foolishly challenged the goddess Athena to a weaving contest. Bellerophon slew the monster Chimaera, defeated the Amazons, and rode Pegasus. But when he boasted that he would fly to Olympus, the offended Zeus caused a gadfly to sting Pegasus, who bucked and tossed Bellerophon to his death.

Other stories of the disastrous results of *hubris* include the myths of Daedalus and Phaethon. In Jane Yolen's *Wings*, Daedalus is presented as a proud Athenian inventor who is banished for inadvertently killing a nephew. Exiled to Crete, he designs and builds a labyrinth for King Minos but years later gives the Athenian Theseus the key to its maze. In punishment for this, Daedalus and his young son Icarus are imprisoned in a high tower. Using candle wax, Daedalus makes a framework of wings from bird feathers. As they are about to escape, he warns his son not to fly too high or the sun will melt the wax, but Icarus does not heed his father's warning and falls to his death in the ocean. In italics, Yolen's text provides a Greek chorus, or commentary by the gods, who give approval, observe, laugh, or listen gravely. Dennis Nolan's illustrations show the faces of the gods hidden in the clouds, looking on, mourning, but doing nothing to prevent Icarus's death.

Descended from the sun god Helios, Phaethon desires to drive the sun chariot to prove his parentage to his friends. When his father is finally tricked into agreeing, Phaethon cannot control the sun chariot and nearly burns up the earth. Zeus saves humankind by killing Phaethon with a thunderbolt. Alice Low retells both of these stories and many others in *The Macmillan Book of Greek Gods and Heroes.* An excellent, insightfully illustrated collection of stories that feature more dialogue than the d'Aulaire versions, Low's book also includes hero tales of Perseus, Heracles, Jason, Theseus, and Odysseus.

Pride is also the downfall of Atalanta, a young woman who is a skillful hunter and the swiftest of runners in Shirley Climo's *Atalanta's Race.* Reluctant to marry and give up her life of freedom, Atalanta finally agrees to wed the man who can beat her in a foot race. Melanion, a suitor whom she has admired, is given three golden apples by Aphrodite, who is angered by Atalanta's lack of reverence for the gods. As the two race side by side, Melanion throws an apple in Atalanta's path, distracting her so that he can win the race. The two marry and live relatively happily for many years, but because they have ignored the gods, Aphrodite punishes the two by changing them into lions. Alexander

In Shirley Climo's *Atalanta's Race,* the race is interrupted by an angry Aphrodite, who gives three golden apples to Atalanta's rival.

Illustration from *Atalanta's Race* by Shirley Climo. Illustration copyright © 1995 by Alexander Koshkin. Reprinted by permission of Clarion Books/Houghton Mifflin Company. All rights reserved.

Kohskin's painted illustrations are set in Corinthian columns and resemble the murals found in Greek and Roman dwellings.

Margaret Hodges retells the story of Eros (or Cupid) and Psyche in *The Arrow and the Lamp.* Eros, who has been sent by the jealous Aphrodite to find a horrible mate for the beautiful Psyche, instead falls in love with her. Invisible, Eros woos Psyche, and she falls in love with him sight unseen. When Psyche's sisters talk her into lighting a lamp in order to see her husband, Eros flees. To win him back, Psyche must perform difficult tasks, and the last one kills her. Eros carries her to Olympus, where the gods honor her for her steadfastness by making her immortal. Donna Diamond's delicate paintings, like beautiful hand-tinted old photographs, give readers a glimpse of a time long gone. Children will be struck by the similarity of patterns in this tale with the folktales in *East o'the Sun and West o'the Moon* (see the versions by Asbjørnsen and Moe, and the Hagues).

Doris Gates has written a series of books each of which features the stories related to one god or goddess.

These provide a continuing theme and avoid the fragmentation in books that attempt to give complete coverage of the myths. *Lord of the Sky: Zeus* includes the lovely "Baucis and Philemon," a story of a poor couple who were willing to share all that they had with the stranger who stopped at their humble hut, never dreaming that he was Zeus. The longer stories of Theseus and Daedalus are well written, as are the other books in the series: *The Warrior Goddess: Athena, The Golden God: Apollo,* and *Two Queens of Heaven: The Story of Demeter and Aphrodite.* These would be fine stories to read aloud to 10- to 12-year-olds.

Older children who have been introduced to Greek mythology through the simpler stories will be ready for the longer hero tales of Perseus, the gorgon-slayer; Theseus, killer of the minotaur; Heracles and his many labors; Jason and his search of the golden fleece; and the wanderings of Odysseus. Fortunately, several of these stories are now published in single-tale editions. Leonard Everett Fisher's *Jason and the Golden Fleece* is told in spare prose with dramatic paintings to underscore Jason's trials in overcoming Harpies, avoiding the crashing rocks of the Symplegades, and numerous other tasks. Jason wins the fleece with the help of Medea, sails home victoriously, but then betrays his wife, finally coming to a lonely end. Fisher has also illustrated and retold *Theseus and the Minotaur.*

Warwick Hutton has also undertaken a series of Greek myths, including *Persephone, Perseus,* and *The Trojan Horse.* His *Theseus and the Minotaur* is more poetic and evocative of an Aegean setting than Fisher's version. Theseus promises his father that he will go with the fourteen youths sacrificed each year to King Minos's monster, the Minotaur. There, with the help of Ariadne, who has fallen in love with him and gives him a cord to follow to find his way out again, he is able to find his way into the labyrinth and kill the evil creature. Theseus's tragedy is that he must abandon Ariadne to the god Dionysus and in his misery he forgets to change the sail of his boat from black to white to indicate to his father that he is alive. Seeing the black sail, the grief-stricken King Aegeus hurls himself into the sea, from whence comes its name—the Aegean Sea. Theseus later becomes king of Athens, but he is never truly happy and finally steps down. Hutton's artwork reflects designs and motifs of Minoan architecture, clothing, and artifacts.

Doris Orgel has told this myth from Ariadne's point of view in the short chapter book *Ariadne, Awake!* illustrated by Barry Moser. The first-person narrative has an exciting immediacy as Ariadne, a sheltered teenager, tells of falling in love with the beautiful but callow Theseus. After he has used her to gain his own ends, his abandonment of her is especially heart-rending. Left alone on the island of Naxos, Ariadne is visited by the

Barry Moser's paintings provide a romantic realism for Doris Orgel's retelling of Theseus's betrayal of Ariadne in *Ariadne, Awake!*

From *Ariadne, Awake!* by Doris Orgel, illustrated by Barry Moser. Copyright © 1994 by Bear Run Publishing, Inc., illustrations. Used by permission of Viking Penguin, a division of Penguin Books USA Inc.

god Dionysus. He comforts her with the thought that even love that ends in pain is merely a stop along the way to greater love. His advice seems to be true, for eventually these two are married and live a long and happy life. This powerfully romantic version will have special appeal for early adolescents.

Bernard Evslin's *Hercules*, part of a series that includes *Jason and the Argonauts*, is told in modern language and allusion, which makes for an exciting and fast-paced narrative. By heightening the action and emphasizing characterization of the villainous Hera or the faithful and brave Iole, Evslin makes Hercules into a hero very much in keeping with the heroes children already know from television and fantasy movies. Evslin also employs modern vernacular in *Heroes and Monsters of Greek Myth*.

Like Evslin, Robert Graves in *Greek Gods and Heroes* utilizes the same rather flippant approach in his telling. This style makes the stories seem more contemporary, but they lose part of their mystery and grandeur. *Tales of the Greek Heroes* by Roger Lancelyn Green is a somewhat more difficult but well-written collection.

Norse Mythology

A mythology derives its characteristics from the land and peoples of its origin. The land of the Norse was a cold, cruel land of frost, snow, and ice. Life was a continual struggle for survival against these elements. It seems only natural that Norse mythology was filled with gods who had to battle against huge frost giants, also. These were heroic gods who, unlike the immortal Greek gods safe in their home on sunny Mount Olympus, knew that they and their home on Asgard would eventually be destroyed. And in a way their prophecy was fulfilled, for Christianity all but extinguished talk of the old gods, except in Iceland. There, in the thirteenth century, Snorri Sturluson—a poet, scholar, and historian—collected many of the Norse myths and legends into a book called the *Prose Edda*. Much of his writing was based on an earlier verse collection called the *Poetic Edda*. These two books are the primary sources for our knowledge of Norse mythology.

It is too bad that children do not know these myths as well as they know those of the Greeks. In some ways the Norse tales seem more suited to children than the highly sophisticated Greek tales. These stories appeal to the child's imagination, with their tales of giants and dwarfs, eight-legged horses and vicious wolves, magic hammers and rings. Primarily they are bold, powerful stories of the relationships among the gods and their battles against the evil frost giants. Odin is the serious protector of the humans he created, willingly sacrificing one of his eyes to obtain wisdom that would allow him to see deep into their hearts. The largest and the strongest of the gods is Thor, owner of a magic hammer that will hit its mark and then return to his hands. And Balder, the tragic god of light, is the most loved by all the other gods.

Some of the stories are amusing. Seven- and 8-year-olds would enjoy the picture-book versions of the story of Thor's stolen hammer by Ann Pyk and Shirley Climo. In *The Hammer of Thunder*, the enormous Thor, the god of Thunder, is dressed as a bride and goes with Loki, who is his "bridesmaid," to trick the giant Thrym into returning Thor's magic hammer. Loki is a puzzling character who seems a likable mischief maker in the beginning of the tale but becomes increasingly evil. Finally, he is responsible for the death of Balder. He guides the hand of Hoder, Balder's blind brother, who shoots a fatal arrow made of mistletoe, the only object that could harm Balder. The gods impose a cruel punishment on Loki that reminds one of the punishment of Prometheus. One of the best collections of these myths is the classic *The Children of Odin* by Padraic Colum.

If children have time to become acquainted with only one mythology, they should know the Greek stories (or their Roman adaptations). No other tales have so influenced the literature and art of the Western world. Norse mythology, too, has left its marks on Western culture, as in the names *Thursday* ("Thor's day") and *Friday* ("Freya's day"). Also, these tales have a special appeal for children. However, there are many other important mythologies that might be sampled as a part of the study of a culture or simply be enjoyed as literature.

Epic and Legendary Heroes

An epic is a long narrative or a cycle of stories clustering around the actions of a single hero. Epics grew out of myths or along with them, since the gods still intervene in earlier epics like the *Iliad* and the *Odyssey*. Gradually, the center of action shifted from the gods to human heroes, so that in tales like "Robin Hood" the focus is completely on the daring adventures of the man himself.

The epic hero is a cultural or national hero embodying all the ideal characteristics of greatness in his time. Thus Odysseus and Penelope, his wife, represented the Greek ideals of intelligence, persistence, and resourcefulness. Odysseus survived by his wit rather than his great strength. Both King Arthur and Robin Hood appealed to the English love of justice and freedom: King Arthur and his knights represented the code of chivalry; Robin Hood was the champion of the commoner—the prototype of the "good outlaw." The epics, then, express the highest moral values of a society. A knowledge of the epics gives children an understanding of a particular culture; but more importantly, it provides them with models of greatness through the ages.

The *Iliad* and the *Odyssey*

According to tradition, a blind minstrel named Homer composed the epic poems the *Iliad* and the *Odyssey* about 850 B.C.; but, scholars generally believe that parts of the stories were sung by many persons and that they were woven into one long narrative before they were written. The *Iliad* is an account of the Trojan War fought over Helen, the most beautiful woman in the world. When Helen is kidnapped by Paris, a Trojan, her Greek husband, King Menelaus, enlists the Greeks in a ten-year siege of Troy that is led by the Greek warriors Agamemnon and Achilles. The complex story is long and difficult to understand, although specific incidents, such as the final defeat of the Trojans by the cunning device of the Trojan Horse, do intrigue some children (see Warwick Hutton's version, *The Trojan Horse*).

The *Odyssey* is the story of the hazardous ten-year journey of Odysseus (called Ulysses by the Romans) from Troy to his home in Ithaca, following the end of the war. Odysseus has one terrifying experience after another, which he manages to survive by his cunning. For example, he defeats the horrible one-eyed Cyclops by blinding him and then strapping his men to the undersides of sheep, which were allowed to leave the cave. His ship safely passes between the whirlpool of Charybdis and the monster Scylla, but later is shipwrecked and delayed for seven years. A loyal servant and his son aid the returned hero in assuming his rightful throne and saving his wife; Penelope has had a difficult time discouraging the many suitors who wished to become king. While children or teachers might be acquainted with episodes from the story, it is the total force of all his trials that presents the full dimensions of this hero.

Barbara Picard's excellent retelling, *The Odyssey of Homer Retold*, emphasizes character development. Padraic Colum's *The Children's Homer* keeps the essence of the traditional poem, and Pogany's illustrations distinguish this book from others.

The *Ramayana*

The *Ramayana* is the great epic tale of India that tells how the noble Rama, his devoted brother, and his beautiful, virtuous wife Sita manage to defeat the evil demon Ravana. Heir to the throne, Rama is banished from his home through the trickery of his stepmother. Prince Rama, his brother, and the devoted Sita spend fourteen years in wandering and adventure. One day Sita vanishes, kidnapped by Ravana. Rama searches for her unsuccessfully and then turns to a tribe of monkeys for help. Finally Sita is found, and with the help of an entire army of monkeys, Rama rescues her. To be cleansed from her association with the demon, Sita must withstand a trial by fire. Her faithfulness proved, she is united with her beloved Rama. Peace and plenty prevail during Rama's reign.

Composed in India by the sage Vlamiki during the fourth century B.C., the *Ramayana* represented some 24,000 couplets that were memorized and repeated. It constitutes part of the gospel of Hindu scripture, for Rama and his wife are held as the ideal man and woman. Rama is believed to be an incarnation of the god Vishnu come to earth in human form.

Elizabeth Seeger created a prose-version *Ramayana* that reads smoothly as one long and exciting narrative. Joseph Gaer relates the story for children in *The Adventures of Rama*. Surely Western children should know something of this epic hero who is so important to a large part of the world.

Heroes of the Middle Ages

Some historians believe there was a King Arthur who became famous around the sixth century. Defeated by the invading Saxons, his people fled to Wales and Brittany and told stories of his bravery and goodness. Other stories became attached to these, and the exploits of Tristram, Gawaine, and Lancelot were added to the Arthurian cycle. The religious element of the quest for the Holy Grail, the cup used by Christ at the Last Supper, was also added. Whether or not the chalice actually existed, it remains as a symbol of purity and love. In the fifteenth century, Sir Thomas Malory's *Morte d'Arthur* was one of the first books printed in England and became a major source of later versions.

In the short novel *The Dragon's Boy*, Jane Yolen tells of the boyhood of Arthur, here called Artos. Artos has been raised by Sir Ector in a small castle. One day while searching for a prized dog he discovers a cave in which a dragon dwells. Both fascinated and terrified, Artos agrees to seek wisdom from the dragon when he is not doing his work at the castle. Children will find this a compelling introduction to the Arthur legends as they sympathize with the lonely boy who confronts his fears to discover the truth about the supposed dragon, his own parentage, and his future as the great King Arthur.

Other illustrated books about Arthur and Merlin will also introduce children to these stories. In Robert D. San Souci's *Young Merlin*, Merlin, whose parentage was thought to be half human and half fairy, is dragged before Vortigern, King of Britain, to be sacrificed to save Vortigern's defense tower. Merlin instead is able to see that underneath the tower's foundation, a red dragon fights a white one. When the dragons are freed, the tower will stand. Merlin foretells the victory of Uther Pendragon over Vortigern as well, and is taken into the new king's household. Daniel Horne depicts the magician's childhood in paintings fittingly lit by eerie yellows and diffused by mists and smoke. In *Young Guinevere*, San Souci presents a courageous and resourceful heroine who explores the magical kingdoms around her father's palace and faces a terrible monster to bring Arthur to her castle to relieve a siege. When Arthur falls in love with her, she overhears Merlin warn him that she will prove to be his downfall. However, she finally agrees to the marriage when Merlin tells her that without her love Arthur will die all the sooner. Hudson Talbott's *King Arthur: The Sword in the Stone* recounts a single episode in Arthur's life, and his vivid watercolors reflect the romance of the tale. T. H. White's *The Sword in the Stone* is an imaginative retelling of Arthur's boyhood and growth under Merlin's tutelage. Middle-school readers enjoy this novel for its humor.

Arthur narrates his own adventures in Michael Morpugo's *Arthur, High King of Britain.*

Illustration from *Arthur: High King of Britain* by Michael Morpugo, illustrations copyright © 1994 by Michael Foreman, reproduced by permission of Harcourt Brace & Company.

Arthur himself is the narrator of nine episodes of his life in Michael Morpugo's *Arthur, High King of Britain.* The book begins in modern times when a small boy is trapped on an offshore island and is rescued by an old man who claims to be Arthur Pendragon. In telling the boy his story, Arthur provides a poignant and honest portrayal of a youth grown to manhood, a man with faults as well as strengths. When Arthur finishes his tale, he gives the boy an acorn from Merlin's tree in the courtyard at Camelot. Arthur urges him to plant it and remember him. This beautifully complex retelling will ensure that older readers do, indeed, remember these ancient tales.

Rosemary Sutcliff brings thirteen stories from the Arthurian cycle to life in *The Sword and the Circle.* Beginning with the events surrounding Arthur's accession to the throne, she weaves other stories into the text in separate chapters. "Tristan and Iseult," "Beaumains, the Kitchen Knight," "Sir Gawain and the Green Knight," and "Gawain and the Loathly Lady" are but a few of the tales included. Two other volumes, though concerning important parts of Arthurian legend, deal with less adventurous or romantic aspects of the story and might be of less interest to middle-grade readers. *The Light Beyond the Forest: The Quest for the Holy Grail* details the wanderings of Lancelot, Galahad, Percival, and others in search of the Grail but also in search of their own salvation. *The Road to Camlann* tells of the sad end of Arthur and the Round Table fellowship. Sutcliff has also retold the romantic *Tristan and Iseult* in a full-length novel by that title. The language has a lyrical quality reminiscent of the old storytellers:

> It was young summer when they came to the hidden valley; and three times the hawthorn trees were rusted with berries and the hazelnuts fell into the stream. And three times winter came and they huddled about the fire in the smoky bothie and threw on logs from the wood-store outside. (p. 90)

Sidney Lanier's *The Boy's King Arthur*, which first appeared in 1880, and Howard Pyle's *The Story of King Arthur and His Knights*, which was published as a four-volume work between 1902 and 1910, are classic works told in a stately mode.

Children who wish to learn more about the legendary King Arthur would appreciate *Quest for a King: Searching for the Real King Arthur*. Here, Catherine M. Andronik presents the various legends connected with King Arthur and carefully explores the historical facts behind them.[21]

Several stories set in King Arthur's time and retold with pictorial conventions of the Middle Ages are available in picture storybook format. In *Sir Gawain and the Loathly Lady* by Selina Hastings, King Arthur is caught without his sword, Excalibur, and to save his life must answer a riddle: What is it that women most desire? On the way home, a despairing Arthur meets a Loathly Lady (rendered in truly horrible detail by Juan Wijnegaard) who offers him the riddle's answer if he will marry her to one of his knights. Arthur agrees but is heartbroken when valiant Sir Gawain offers himself. Alone in their bedchamber after they are married, the Lady turns into a beautiful young woman who gives her new husband a choice. Will she be beautiful by day and ugly by night, or the opposite? When Gawain cannot bear to make the decision, he answers, "You must decide whichever you prefer." This breaks the spell and is also the key to the

riddle. What every woman desires is to have her own way. This exquisitely illuminated story features bordered and decorated illustrations full of medieval detail and suffused with light. The story is a companion to Hastings's *Sir Gawain and the Green Knight*.

Margaret Hodges retells the first part of "The Tale of Sir Gareth of Orkney," taken from Malory's *Le Morte D'Arthur*, in *The Kitchen Knight*. In this story, Gareth, who is a nephew of King Arthur, wishes to earn his knighthood by deeds, not by birthright. So he becomes a kitchen lad in Arthur's castle and accepts a quest that no other knight will undertake, that of saving the beautiful Linette's sister, Linesse, from imprisonment in the castle of the Knight of the Red Plain. He vanquishes the Red Knight, but it takes extra effort to win the gratitude of Linette and the acceptance of the highly selective Lady Linesse, whom he has rescued. Trina Schart Hyman researched weaponry, enabling her to accurately depict a leather rather than metal shield and an early horned helmet that was discovered recently in the Thames River.

Hyman also conducted painstaking research to produce accurate illustrations for Hodges's *Saint George and the Dragon*, set in fourth-century England. She studied ancient lore of wildflowers and herbs in order to use them symbolically in the borders of each picture. For example, when Saint George engages the dragon in battle, agrimony, which was a charm against serpents, appears in the borders. The fourth century was a time in which Christianity and ancient beliefs competed, so red-winged angels and pale fairies are both part of the borders. A pre-Norman sailing vessel appears in small pictures as a symbol of the hero's progress. Children are appropriately awed and thrilled by the truly terrible dragon, which Hyman drew after a long siege she had with a snapping turtle in her New Hampshire pond. While the story of St. George has little to do with King Arthur, it shares similar time, theme, and conventions with other tales told in the Middle Ages.

All of these books contribute to a child's knowledge of the mystique that surrounds the story of King Arthur. Students seldom discover these tales on their own, but once introduced to them, they delight in taking their place at that round table of adventure.

Another legendary hero who captures children's imagination is Robin Hood. Scholars have been unable to agree over whether there was indeed a medieval outlaw by the name of Robin Hood or whether he was really a mythical character derived from festival plays that took place in France at Whitsuntide. But by the fifteenth century, May Day celebrations in England were called "Robin Hood's Festivals," and the story of Robin Hood had become a legend for all time.

[21]See Barbara Elleman's annotated list of other books that relate to King Arthur: "The Days of Camelot," *Book Links* 1, no. 1 (September 1991): 23–27.

Children love this brave hero who lived in Sherwood Forest, outwitted the Sheriff of Nottingham, and shared his stolen goods with the poor. Others in the band included the huge Little John, Friar Tuck, the minstrel Alan-a-Dale, and Robin's sweetheart, Maid Marian. These characters can be found in Howard Pyle's classic, *The Merry Adventures of Robin Hood.* Ann McGovern retells this familiar legend in clear, direct language; a few words, such as *perchance* and *thou,* retain the spirit of the medieval language without making her *Robin Hood of Sherwood Forest* too difficult to read.

Robin McKinley's *The Outlaws of Sherwood* presents a Robin Hood for modern times. Robin is not much of a shot, but others in his band do the hunting while Robin broods over how to manage, shelter, and feed his ever-growing group. McKinley fleshes out the emotions of Little John, Robin Hood, Maid Marian, and others while exploring various dimensions of heroism. Theresa Tomlinson tells Marion's story in *The Forestwife.* In this version Marian runs away to the forest with her nurse Agnes in order to escape an unwanted marriage. As she and Agnes provide aide to other poor refugees, Marion meets Agnes's son Robert, who, falsely accused of murder, has also made the forest his home. Older readers who understand loyalty and appreciate the romance of a good tale will find these stories rewarding and compelling.

The Bible as Literature

The Bible has an important and rightful place in any comprehensive discussion of traditional literature because it is a written record of people's continuing search to understand themselves and their relationships with others and their creator. It makes little sense to tell children the story of Jack the Giant Killer but to deny them the stories about David and Goliath or Samson. They read of the wanderings of Odysseus, but not those of Moses. They learn that Gilgamesh built an ark and survived a flood, but do not know the story of Noah. Our fear should not be that children will know the Bible; rather it should be that they will *not* know it. Whatever our religious persuasion or nonpersuasion, children should not be denied their right to knowledge of the traditional literature of the Bible. Children cannot fully understand other literature unless they are familiar with the outstanding characters, incidents, poems, proverbs, and parables of this literature of the Western world of thought.

We must clarify the difference between the practice of religious customs and indoctrination in one viewpoint and the study of the Bible as a great work of literature. In 1963 the Supreme Court asserted that "religious exercises" violated the First Amendment, but the Court also encouraged study of the Bible as literature:

In addition, it might well be said that one's education is not complete without a study of comparative religion or the history of religion and its relationship to the advancement of Civilization. It certainly may be said that the Bible is worthy of study for its literary and historic qualities.[22]

The literary scholar Northrop Frye believes it is essential to teach the Bible, for it presents humans in all their history. "It's the *myth* of the Bible that should be the basis of literary training, its imaginative survey of the human situation which is so broad and comprehensive that everything else finds its place inside it."[23] Some critics will be disturbed by the use of the term *myth* unless they understand its larger literary context as the human search for and expression of truth and meaning.

Collections of Bible Stories

When a school staff agrees that children should have an opportunity to hear or read some of the great stories from the Bible, it faces the task of selecting material. Walter de la Mare's introduction to his *Stories from the Bible* provides an excellent background for understanding the problems of translation. He compares versions of the story of Ruth in the Geneva Bible (1560), the Douai Bible (1609), and the Authorized Version (1611). The old form of spelling is used in his quotations from Wycliffe of 1382, John Purvey of 1386, and Miles Coverdale of 1536. He clearly explains the differences between the literal, allegorical, oral, and analogical meanings of given words and phrases. This book presents the Creation, the Flood, and the stories of Moses, Joseph, Samson, Samuel, Saul, and David. The text combines modern descriptive imagery with a biblical style of narration. For example: "As Joseph grew older, and in all that he was and did showed himself more and more unlike themselves, jealousy gnawed in their hearts like the fretting of a cankerworm."[24]

---

[22]Quoted by Betty D. Mayo, "The Bible in the Classroom," *Christian Science Monitor,* 30 September 1966, p. 9.

[23]Northrop Frye, *The Educated Imagination* (Bloomington: Indiana University Press, 1964), p. 111.

[24]Walter de la Mare, *Stories from the Bible,* illustrated by Edward Ardizzone (New York: Knopf, 1961), p. 62.

In *Moses' Ark,* a collection ranging from Genesis through Kings, Alice Bach and J. Cheryl Exum retain the spirit of the original stories as they expand the narration with subtle details. Conversation, based on archaeological and anthropological research, and borrowings from other parts of the Bible enrich our understanding. In *Miriam's Well* these authors focus on the role of women in the Old Testament. In both books stunning illustrations by Leo and Diane Dillon depict the stories of familiar Biblical figures.

In *Does God Have a Big Toe?* Marc Gellman, a rabbi, follows a long-held Jewish tradition of telling *midrashim,* stories about stories in the Bible. These involve readers with their humorous, contemporary tellings. For instance, Noah doesn't have the heart to tell his friends what God has told him, so he hints: "You know, Jabal, this might be a very good time for you to take those swimming lessons you have been talking about for so long" (p. 31). A more serious undertaking is *The Bible Story,* written by Philip Turner and illustrated by Brian Wildsmith. Presented in chronological order, stories from both the Old Testament and the New Testament are told with dignity and illustrated with colorful flair.

Single Bible Stories

Many individual picture books based on individual stories from the Bible are especially useful to introduce children to this literature. *Light* by Sarah Waldman is a simple retelling of the story of creation brought vividly to life through Neil Waldman's glowing impressionistic paintings. Leonard Everett Fisher also told this story in his adaptation, *The Seven Days of Creation,* and used bold colorful paintings to excite readers' imagination. Fisher followed this book with retellings of two other Old Testament stories in *David and Goliath* and *Moses.* Several illustrators, including Warwick Hutton, Charles Mikolaycak, and Tomie de Paola, have also contributed beautiful editions of single Bible stories. Hutton's *Adam and Eve* is illustrated with quietly powerful watercolors depicting the Garden of Eden in all its splendor. A snake encircles the final illustration of two people walking away.

Hutton's *Moses in the Bulrushes* is more intimate in scale. Hutton uses close-up views of Moses being cared for by his mother and the Pharaoh's daughter discovering him as she bathes in a gossamer bathing dress. This version ends with a short paragraph and an illustration of the resolute Moses followed by his people as they leave Egypt. Miriam Chaikin's *Exodus* reveals what happened from the time Moses arrived in the Pharaoh's palace until his final march across the desert; among the scenes portrayed in Charles Mikolaycak's dramatic illustrations bordered in weathered browns are Moses confronting the Pharaoh as he conveys God's words "Let my people go," the plagues that were visited on the Egyptians, Moses receiving the Ten Commandments, and the Israelites' march toward the Promised Land. A contrast in artistic styles, these two books show how two different illustrators can depict the same story in unique but equally compelling ways.

Mikolaycak has illustrated two New Testament stories adapted by Elizabeth Winthrop. His illustrations for Winthrop's *A Child Is Born* give a more active and protective role to Joseph. In Winthrop's *He Is Risen,* he portrays the central events of the Easter story in strong diagonals and a muted palette of rusts, browns, and reds. As in all of his illustrations of stories from the Bible, Mikolaycak's authentic depiction of textile patterns, everyday details, armor, and headgear are based on research he conducted in places like the Metropolitan Museum of Art in New York.

The Christmas story has been retold in words and pictures many times. Among the traditional tellings, Maud and Miska Petersham's *The Christ Child* has long been a favorite. Isabelle Brent's *The Christmas Story* resembles medieval manuscripts with its burnished gold, illuminated capitals, patterned backgrounds, and embellishments. Jan Pienkowski also uses gilt for the borders in his exquisite *Christmas: The King James Version.* Detailed black silhouettes against softly colored backgrounds give this telling the look of a pageant. Jacqueline Rogers's *The Christmas Pageant,* on the other hand, is a real modern-day version. While the text is from the traditional King James version, the pictures humorously and lovingly depict contemporary families gathering in a country meeting house to see the children's annual play. Julie Vivas also used the King James text for her exuberantly childlike vision of the Christmas story, *The Nativity.* Mary is shown in a cosy tête-à-tête with the angel Gabriel, and her look of surprise and delight as she tells Joseph his news is priceless. After she gives birth, Mary leans exhaustedly against Joseph, who lovingly cradles the baby Jesus. These glowing pictures must surely present the story as seen through the innocent eyes of a child. John Bierhorst recounts an Aztec version in *Spirit Child;* Barbara Cooney's beautiful paintings portray the story against a background of Central American mountains abloom with yucca and poinsettia.

Told from Mary's point of view, Cecil Bødker's *Mary of Nazareth* is an insightful narrative of Mary's life from the time she receives the bewildering news from an angel until her son begins to learn the carpenter's trade. This psychological portrait of a young woman is illustrated in richly detailed watercolors depicting

Neil Waldman's lovely paintings convey a sense of dignity and wonder in Sarah Waldman's *Light,* a retelling of the Genesis creation story.

Illustration from *Light* retold by Sarah Waldman, illustrations copyright © 1993 by Neil Waldman, reproduced by permission of Harcourt Brace & Company.

everything from quiet evenings in outdoor courtyards to the busy work of a shipyard. The everyday life of people two thousand years ago is richly realized. Tomie de Paola's *Mary, the Mother of Jesus* reflects the stately power of Early Renaissance frescoes yet has the warm and earthy reality of de Paola's other books.

Many legends are associated with the Christmas story as well. *The Cobweb Curtain* by Jenny Koralek tells how a friendly spider wove a web across a cave where Mary and Joseph hid from soldiers. Mikolaycak's *Babushka* presents the Russian story of the old woman too busy sweeping to follow the three wise men and so is destined to wander the world forever. Tomie de Paola's Italian version is *The Legend of Old Befana.* His *The Story of the*

Three Wise Kings begins with a historical note about how this story has developed over the centuries. It would make a good companion to either of the previous stories, as would Ruth Robbins's *Baboushka and the Three Kings.* The stories concerning Befana would be ripe for reading on 6 January, or Twelfth Night, the traditional Feast of the Three Kings.

The Bible, myths and legends, fables, and folktales represent literature of people through the ages. Folk literature has deep roots in basic human feelings. Through this literature, children can form a link with the common bonds of humanity from the beginnings of recorded time, as well as form a foundation for much of their future reading.

Learning Experiences

1. Choose one motif, such as transformations, wishes, or magical objects, and see how many different tales you can find, and how many different cultures or countries your collection represents.

2. Read folktales and myths from one country or one geographical or cultural region. Assume that these stories provide your only basis for understanding the country. Chart what you might derive from these tales, using categories like climate, food, animals, typical occupations, customs, geography, values, expressions, and story conventions.

3. Find as many different editions as you can of well-known stories like "Cinderella," "Hansel and Gretel," "Sleeping Beauty," "Noah's Ark," or "Puss in Boots." Chart or compare both the language of the retellings and the illustrations.

4. Find as many variations as you can on a particular theme, such as "helpful companions," "Jack and the Beanstalk," or "Cinderella." Bring them to class and share them in small groups.

5. Select one folktale that you think you would like to learn to tell. Prepare it and tell it to four or five members of your class or to a group of children. What suggestions do they or you have for improving your presentation?

6. Beginning with a moral chosen from one of the fable collections, write a modern fable. Use present-day animals, people, or objects.

7. Collect advertisements and references that show our use of words from the myths: for example, *Ajax* cleanser, *Mercury* as a floral delivery symbol, or *Atlas* tires. Using a collection of myths, determine the story behind the reference and decide why the advertiser might wish consumers to connect this reference with their product.

8. On the basis of your knowledge of the characteristics of an epic, what do you think the hero of a North American epic might be like? Consider personal qualities, obstacles, achievements, and so forth.

9. Develop a simple inventory of names from folktales, myths, legends, and the Bible. Give it to your class or ask to give it to a group of children. How well known is traditional literature today?

Related Readings

Bettelheim, Bruno. *The Uses of Enchantment.* New York: Knopf, 1976.

This noted child psychologist maintains that fairy tales have a unique place in children's development, satisfying many of their deepest emotional needs. He offers detailed analysis of several individual tales to show how they enable children to cope with their emotions and their world.

Bosma, Betty. *Fairy Tales, Fables, Legends, and Myths: Using Folk Literature in Your Classroom.* 2nd ed. New York: Teachers College Press, 1992.

This practical handbook provides a brief overview and rationale for using folktales, then lists classroom activities for exploring this genre with children. The emphasis is on reading, writing, and oral language activities, but suggestions also include responding to these stories with puppetry, art, drama, and music. An annotated bibliography is included.

Caduto, Michael J., and Joseph Bruchac. *Keepers of the Earth: Native American Stories and Environmental Activities for Children.* Foreword by N. Scott Momaday. Illustrated by John Kahionhes and Carl Wood. Golden, Col.: Fulcrum, 1989.

This is a collection of Native American folktales grouped under such headings as Creation, Fire, Earth, and Life/Death/Spirit, retold and illustrated with black-line drawings. Stories are followed by discussion and many far-ranging activities for the elementary-age child. The map of Native American tribes and cultural boundaries is a helpful organizer for teachers. See also, by the same authors, *Keepers of the Animals*, illustrated by John K. Fadden (Fulcrum, 1991); *Keepers of Life*, illustrated by John K. Fadden (Fulcrum, 1994); and *Keepers of the Night*, illustrated by John K. Fadden (Fulcrum, 1994).

Campbell, Joseph, and Bill Moyers. *The Power of Myth*. New York: Doubleday, 1988.

Campbell, a preeminent teacher and scholar of mythology, converses with Moyers about myth in the modern world, the first storytellers, the power of myth in our lives, and mythical themes across cultures.

Dundes, Alan, ed. *Cinderella: A Casebook*. New York: Wildman Press, 1983.

This is a collection of scholarly essays spanning the history of folklore research on the Cinderella theme. Of special interest to teachers and librarians are the essay "Cinderella in Africa," the Jungian approach in the essay "The Beautiful Wassilissa," and Jane Yolen's look at Cinderella in the mass market in "America's Cinderella."

Favat, André. *Child and Tale: The Origins of Interest*. NCTE Research Report No. 19. Urbana, Ill.: National Council of Teachers of English, 1977.

Favat traces parallels between the components of traditional fairy tales and the concepts of reality as held by children 6 to 8 years of age, the period of peak interest in fairy tales.

Frye, Northrop. *The Great Code: The Bible in Literature*. San Diego: Harcourt Brace Jovanovich, 1982.

The eminent literary critic develops a theory of literature based on patterns found in the Bible.

Hamilton, Edith. *Mythology*. New York: New American Library, 1953.

The introduction to this literary standard summarizes the emergence of Greek ideas, followed by a readable presentation of Creation, Stories of Love and Adventure, and Heroes of the Trojan War. Genealogical tables are helpful inclusions.

Hearne, Betsy. *Beauty and the Beast: Visions and Revisions of an Old Tale*. Chicago: University of Chicago Press, 1989.

This book presents an analysis of versions of one of our culture's most persistent tales, in chronological order from 1740 to Warwick Hutton's version in 1985. Hearne's comparisons of versions told by women with those told by men is especially provocative.

Moss, Joy F. *Focus on Literature: A Context for Literacy Learning*. Katonah, N.Y.: Richard C. Owen, 1990.

With classroom examples, Moss presents ten "focus units" developed around such themes as "Baba Yaga Tales," "Cat Tales," "Magic Object Tales," and "Bird Tales." Units involve traditional and other genres of literature, thoughtful discussions of children's learning and curriculum development, and excellent bibliographies. This is a valuable teacher resource and a companion volume to Moss's *Focus Units in Literature* (Urbana, Ill.: National Council of Teachers of English, 1984).

Opie, Iona, and Peter Opie. *The Classic Fairy Tales*. New York: Oxford University Press, 1974.

This volume presents twenty-four of the best-known fairy tales as they first appeared in print in English. Pictures are gleaned from two centuries of illustrators. An invaluable source of information on primary sources is the Opies' introductory essay for each tale.

Schmidt, Gary D., and Donald R. Hettinga, eds. *Sitting at the Feet of the Past: Retelling the North American Folktale for Children*. Westport, Conn.: Greenwood Press, 1992.

This collection of essays focuses on tales told in the context of a North American setting and raises issues of concern to authors, illustrators, critics, and teachers. Authors of selections include Paul Goble, Patricia McKissack, William H. Hooks, and Steven Kellogg.

Thompson, Stith. *The Folktale*. New York: Holt, Rinehart & Winston, 1951.

Various theories of the origins of folktales and folktale themes are presented in a thorough manner in this book.

Yolen, Jane. *Touch Magic: Fantasy, Faerie and Folklore in the Literature of Childhood*. New York: Philomel, 1981.

In short, lively essays the author, herself a writer of fantasy and literary tales, discusses the history of folklore and its role in the social, emotional, and intellectual growth of the child.

Children's Literature

Except where obvious from the title, the country or culture of origin follows each entry in parentheses. Modern stories with strong folktale roots are referred to as "Modern Literary." The notation (S) stands for single-tale edition. Dates in square brackets are original publication dates.

Children's Literature

Folktales

Aardema, Verna. *Bimwili & the Zimwi*. Illustrated by Susan Meddaugh. Dial, 1985. (S)(Africa, Zanzibar)

———. *Borreguita and the Coyote*. Illustrated by Petra Mathers. Knopf, 1991. (S)(Mexico)

———. *How the Ostrich Got Its Long Neck*. Illustrated by Marcia Brown. Scholastic, 1995. (S)(Africa)

———. *Misoso: Once Upon a Time Tales from Africa*. Illustrated by Reynold Ruffins. Applesoup/Knopf, 1994. (S)

———. *Rabbit Makes a Monkey of Lion*. Illustrated by Jerry Pinkney. Dial, 1989. (S)(Africa, Tanzania)

———. *Traveling to Tondo: A Tale of the Nkundo of Zaire*. Illustrated by Will Hillenbrand. Knopf, 1991. (S)

———. *Who's in Rabbit's House?* Illustrated by Leo and Diane Dillon. Dial, 1977. (S)(West Africa)

———. *Why Mosquitoes Buzz in People's Ears*. Illustrated by Leo and Diane Dillon. Dial, 1975. (S)(Africa, Kenya)

Ada, Alma Flor. *The Rooster Who Went to His Uncle's Wedding*. Illustrated by Kathleen Kuchera. Putnam, 1993. (S)(Cuba)

Afanasyev, Alexander Nikolayevich. *The Fool and the Fish*. Retold by Lenny Hort. Illustrated by Gennady Spirin. Dial, 1990. (S)(Russia)

Alexander, Ellen. *Llama and the Great Flood: A Folktale from Peru*. Crowell/Harper & Row, 1989. (S)

Arkhurst, Joyce Cooper. *The Adventures of Spider: West African Folk Tales*. Illustrated by Jerry Pinkney. Little, Brown, 1964.

Arnold, Katya. *Knock, Knock, Teremok!* North-South, 1994. (S)(Russia)

Aruego, Jose, and Ariane Dewey. *Rockaby Crocodile*. Greenwillow, 1988. (S)(Philippines)

Asbjørnsen, Peter Christian, and Jorgen E. Moe. *East o' the Sun and West o' the Moon*. Translated by George Webbe Dasent. Dover, 1970 [1842–1843]. (Norway)

———. *The Three Billy Goats Gruff*. Illustrated by Marcia Brown. Harcourt Brace, 1957. (S)(Norway)

Bang, Molly. *Dawn*. Morrow, 1983. (S)(United States)

Baylor, Byrd. *And It Is Still That Way*. Scribner's, 1976. (Native American)

Begay, Shonto. *Ma'ii and Cousin Horned Toad*. Scholastic, 1992. (S)(Navajo)

Bender, Robert. *Toads and Diamonds*. Lodestar, 1995. (S)(France)

Bernhard, Emery. *The Girl Who Wanted to Hunt*. Illustrated by Durga Bernhard. Holiday House, 1994. (S)(Siberia)

———. *How Snowshoe Hare Rescued the Sun: A Tale Told from the Arctic*. Illustrated by Durga Bernhard. Holiday House, 1993. (S)(Yuit)

———. *Spotted Eagle and the Black Crow: A Lakota Legend*. Illustrated by Durga Bernhard. Holiday House, 1993. (S)(Lakota)

———. *The Tree That Rains: The Flood Myth of the Huichol Indians of Mexico*. Illustrated by Durga Benhard. Holiday House, 1994. (S)

Bierhorst, John, ed. *The Monkey's Haircut and Other Stories Told by the Maya*. Illustrated by Robert Andrew Parker. Morrow, 1986. (Central American)

———. *The White Deer and Other Stories Told by the Lenape*. Morrow, 1995.

Birdseye, Tom. *A Song of Stars: An Asian Legend*. Illustrated by Ju-Hong Chen. Holiday House, 1990. (S)(China/Japan)

Bishop, Claire Huchet. *The Five Chinese Brothers*. Illustrated by Kurt Wiese. Coward-McCann, 1938. (S)

Bishop, Gavin. *Chicken Licken*. Oxford University Press, 1984. (S)(England)

Brett, Jan. *The Mitten*. Putnam, 1989. (S)(Ukrainian)

Briggs, Raymond. *Jim and the Beanstalk*. Coward-McCann, 1970. (Modern Literary)

Brooke, William J. *A Telling of the Tales: Five Stories*. Illustrated by Richard Egielski. HarperCollins, 1990. (Modern Literary)

Brown, Marcia. *Dick Whittington and His Cat*. Scribner's, 1950. (S)(England)

————. *Once a Mouse*. Scribner's, 1961. (S)(India)

————. *Stone Soup*. Scribner's, 1947. (S)(France)

Bruchac, Joseph. *The Boy Who Lived with the Bears and Other Iroquois Stories*. Illustrated by Murv Jacob. HarperCollins, 1995.

————. *The First Strawberries: A Cherokee Story*. Illustrated by Anna Vojtech. Dial, 1993. (S)

————. *Gluskabe and the Four Wishes*. Illustrated by Christine Nyburg Shrader. Cobblehill, 1995. (S)(Native American)

————. *The Great Ball Game: A Muskogee Story*. Illustrated by Susan L. Roth. Dial, 1994. (S)(Native American)

Bruchac, Joseph, and Gayle Ross. *The Story of the Milky Way*. Illustrated by Virginia Stroud. Dial, 1995. (S)(Cherokee)

Brusca, Maria Christina, and Tona Wilson. *When Jaguars Ate the Moon and Other Stories About Animals and Plants of the Americas*. Illustrated by Maria Christina Brusca. Holt, 1995.

Bryan, Ashley. *Beat the Story-Drum, Pum-Pum*. Atheneum, 1980. (Africa)

————. *The Cat's Purr*. Atheneum, 1985. (S)(Antilles)

————. *The Dancing Granny*. Atheneum, 1977. (S)(Antilles)

————. *The Story of Lightning and Thunder*. Atheneum, 1993. (S)(West Africa)

Butler, Stephen. *Henny Penny*. Tambourine, 1991. (S)(England)

Carrick, Carol. *Aladdin and the Wonderful Lamp*. Illustrated by Donald Carrick. Scholastic, 1989. (S)(Middle East)

Cauley, Lorinda Bryan. *Jack and the Beanstalk*. Putnam, 1983. (S)(England)

————. *Puss in Boots*. Harcourt Brace, 1986. (S)(France)

Chase, Richard. *Grandfather Tales*. Houghton Mifflin, 1973 [1948]. (United States)

————. *The Jack Tales*. Illustrated by Berkeley Williams, Jr. Houghton Mifflin, 1993 [1943]. (United States)

Climo, Shirley. *The Egyptian Cinderella*. Illustrated by Ruth Heller. Crowell/Harper & Row, 1989. (S)

————. *The Korean Cinderella*. Illustrated by Ruth Heller. HarperCollins, 1993. (S)

Cohen, Caron Lee. *The Mud Pony*. Illustrated by Shonto Begay. Scholastic, 1988. (S)(Native American)

————. *Sally Ann Thunder Ann Whirlwind Crockett: A Tall Tale*. Illustrated by Ariane Dewey. Greenwillow, 1993. (United States)

Cohn, Amy. *From Sea to Shining Sea*. Illustrated by various artists. Scholastic, 1993.

Cole, Brock. *The Giant's Toe*. Farrar, Straus & Giroux, 1988. (S)(Modern Literary)

Cole, Joanna. *Bony-Legs*. Illustrated by Dirk Zimmer. Four Winds, 1983. (S)(Russia)

————. *It's Too Noisy*. Illustrated by Kate Duke. Crowell/Harper & Row 1989. (S)(Jewish)

Cooper, Susan. *The Selkie Girl*. Illustrated by Warwick Hutton. McElderry, 1986. (S)(Scotland)

————. *The Silver Cow: A Welsh Tale*. Illustrated by Warwick Hutton. McElderry, 1983. (S)

————. *Tam Lin*. Illustrated by Warwick Hutton. McElderry, 1991. (S)(Scotland)

Courlander, Harold, and George Herzog. *The Cow-Tail Switch and Other West African Stories*. Illustrated by Madye Lee Chastian. Holt, 1947.

Croll, Carolyn. *The Little Snowgirl*. Putnam, 1989. (S)(Russia)

Dasent, George. *East o'the Sun and West o'the Moon*. Illustrated by Gillian Barlow. Philomel, 1988. (S)(Norway)

Day, Nancy Raines. *The Lion's Whiskers: An Ethiopian Folktale*. Illustrated by Ann Grifalconi. Scholastic, 1995. (S)

Dayrell, Elphinstone. *Why the Sun and the Moon Live in the Sky*. Illustrated by Blair Lent. Houghton Mifflin, 1968. (S)(Africa)

De Armond, Dale. *The Seal Oil Lamp*. Sierra Club/Little, Brown, 1988. (S)(Eskimo)

de Beaumont, Mme. *Beauty and the Beast*. Illustrated by Jan Brett. Houghton Mifflin, 1989. (S)(France)

————. *Beauty and the Beast*. Retold and illustrated by Mordicai Gerstein. Dutton, 1989. (S)(France)

———. *Beauty and the Beast*. Illustrated by Michael Hague. Holt, 1988. (S)(France)

———. *Beauty and the Beast*. Retold and illustrated by Warwick Hutton. Atheneum, 1985. (S)(France)

De Felice, Cynthia, and Mary DeMarsh. *Three Perfect Peaches*. Illustrated by Irene Trias. Orchard, 1995. (S)(France)

Demi. *The Empty Pot*. Holt, 1990. (S)(China)

———. *The Firebird*. Holt, 1994. (S)(Russia)

———. *The Magic Tapestry*. Holt, 1994. (S)(China)

de Paola, Tomie. *The Legend of the Bluebonnet: An Old Tale of Texas*. Putnam, 1983. (S)(Comanche)

———. *Strega Nona*. Prentice Hall, 1975. (S)(Italy)

de Regniers, Beatrice Schenk. *Little Sister and the Month Brothers*. Illustrated by Margot Tomes. (S)(Russia)

de Sauza, James. *Brother Anansi and the Cattle Rancher*. Illustrated by Stephen Von Mason. Children's Book Press, 1989. (S)(Nicaragua)

Dewey, Ariane. *Gib Morgan, Oilman*. Greenwillow, 1987. (S)(United States)

———. *Pecos Bill*. Greenwillow, 1983. (S)(United States)

Duff, Maggie. *Rum Pum Pum: A Folk Tale from India*. Illustrated by Jose Aruego and Ariane Dewey. Macmillan, 1978. (S)

Ehlert, Lois. *Moon Rope/Un Lazo de la Luna*. Harcourt Brace, 1992. (S)(South America)

Esbensen, Barbara Juster. *Ladder to the Sky*. Illustrated by Helen K. Davie. Little, Brown, 1989. (S)(Native American)

———. *The Star Maiden*. Illustrated by Helen K. Davie. Little, Brown, 1988. (S)(Native American)

Esterl, Arnica. *The Fine Round Cake*. Translated by Pauline Hejl. Illustrated by Andrej Dugin and Olga Dugina. Four Winds, 1991. (S)(England)

Finger, Charles. *Tales from Silver Lands*. Illustrated by Paul Honore. Doubleday, 1924. (Central and South America)

Flora. *Feathers Like a Rainbow: An Amazon Indian Tale*. Harper & Row, 1989. (S)

Freedman, Florence B. *Brothers: A Hebrew Legend*. Illustrated by Robert Andrew Parker. Harper & Row, 1985. (S)

Galdone, Paul. *The Gingerbread Boy*. Clarion, 1984 [1968]. (S)(England)

———. *The History of Mother Twaddle and the Marvelous Achievements of Her Son Jack*. Seabury, 1974. (S)(England)

———. *The Little Red Hen*. Clarion, 1979. [1974]. (S)(England)

———. *The Magic Porridge Pot*. Clarion, 1979 [1976]. (S)(France)

———. *Puss in Boots*. Clarion, 1979 [1976]. (S)(France)

———. *Rumpelstiltskin*. Houghton Mifflin, 1985. (S)(Germany)

———. *The Three Billy Goats Gruff*. Clarion, 1979 [1970]. (S)(Norway)

———. *The Three Little Pigs*. Clarion, 1981 [1973]. (S)(Norway)

Garland, Sherry. *Why Ducks Sleep on One Leg*. Illustrated by Jean and Mou-Sien Teng. Scholastic, 1993. (S)(Vietnam)

Gerson, Mary-Joan. *How Night Came from the Sea: A Story from Brazil*. Illustrated by Carla Golembe. Little, Brown, 1994. (S)

———. *Why the Sky Is Far Away*. Illustrated by Carla Golembe. Joy Street, 1992. (S)(Nigeria)

Gerstein, Mordicai. *The Seal Mother*. Dial, 1986. (S)(Scotland)

Gilman, Phoebe. *Something from Nothing*. Scholastic, 1992. (S)(Jewish)

Goble, Paul. *Buffalo Woman*. Bradbury, 1984. (S)(Plains Indian)

———. *The Gift of the Sacred Dog*. Bradbury, 1980. (S)(Plains Indian)

———. *The Girl Who Loved Wild Horses*. Bradbury, 1978. (S)(Plains Indian)

————. *The Great Race of the Birds and the Animals*. Bradbury, 1985. (Plains Indian)

————. *Her Seven Brothers*. Bradbury, 1988. (S)(Native American)

————. *Iktomi and the Berries: A Plains Indian Story*. Orchard, 1989. (S)

————. *Iktomi and the Boulder: A Plains Indian Story*. Orchard, 1988. (S)

————. *Iktomi and the Buffalo Skull: A Plains Indian Story*. Orchard, 1991. (S)

————. *Iktomi and the Buzzard*. Orchard, 1994. (S)(Native American)

————. *Iktomi and the Ducks: A Plains Indian Story*. Orchard, 1990. (S)

————. *The Lost Children*. Bradbury, 1993. (S)(Blackfoot)

————. *Star Boy*. Bradbury, 1983. (S)(Plains Indian)

Grifalconi, Ann. *The Village of Round and Square Houses*. Little, Brown, 1986. (S)(West Africa, Cameroon)

Grimm brothers. *The Bremen-Town Musicians*. Retold and illustrated by Ilse Plume. Doubleday, 1980. (S)

————. *Cinderella*. Illustrated by Nonny Hogrogian. Greenwillow, 1981. (S)

————. *The Devil with the Three Golden Hairs*. Illustrated by Nonny Hogrogian. Knopf, 1983. (S)

————. *The Elves and the Shoemaker*. Illustrated by Bernadette Watts. North-South, 1986. (S)(Germany)

————. *The Fisherman and His Wife*. Translated by Randall Jarrell. Illustrated by Margot Zemach. Farrar, Straus & Giroux, 1980. (S)

————. *The Fisherman and His Wife*. Retold by John Warren Stewig. Illustrated by Margot Tomes. Holiday House, 1988. (S)

————. *The Frog Prince*. Retold by Jan Ormerod and David Lloyd. Illustrated by Jan Ormerod. Lothrop, Lee & Shepard, 1990. (S)

————. *Hansel and Gretel*. Illustrated by Anthony Browne. Knopf, 1988 [1981]. (S)

————. *Hansel and Gretel*. Translated by Elizabeth D. Crawford. Illustrated by Lisbeth Zwerger. Morrow, 1979. (S)

————. *Hansel and Gretel*. Illustrated by Paul Galdone. McGraw-Hill, 1982. (S)

————. *Hansel and Gretel*. Retold by Rika Lesser. Illustrated by Paul O. Zelinsky. Dodd Mead, 1984. (S)

————. *Household Stories of the Brothers Grimm*. Translated by Lucy Crane. Illustrated by Walter Crane. Dover, n.d. [1886].

————. *The Juniper Tree and Other Tales from Grimm*. Translated by Lore Segal and Maurice Sendak. Illustrated by Maurice Sendak. Farrar, Straus & Giroux, 1973.

————. *Little Red Cap*. Translated by Elizabeth D. Crawford. Illustrated by Lisbeth Zwerger. Morrow, 1983. (S)

————. *Little Red Riding Hood*. Illustrated by Trina Schart Hyman. Holiday House, 1983. (S)

————. *Mother Holly*. Retold and illustrated by Bernadette Watts. North-South, 1988. (S)

————. *The Princess and the Frog*. Illustrated by Rachel Isadora. Greenwillow, 1989. (S)

————. *Princess Furball*. Retold by Charlotte Huck. Illustrated by Anita Lobel. Greenwillow, 1989. (S)

————. *Rapunzel*. Retold by Barbara Rogasky. Illustrated by Trina Schart Hyman. Holiday House, 1982. (S)

————. *Rumpelstiltskin*. Illustrated by Paul Galdone. Clarion, 1985. (S)

————. *Rumpelstiltskin*. Retold and illustrated by Paul O. Zelinksy. Dutton, 1986. (S)

————. *The Seven Ravens*. Translated by Elizabeth D. Crawford. Illustrated by Lisbeth Zwerger. Morrow, 1981. (S)

————. *The Sleeping Beauty*. Retold and illustrated by Trina Schart Hyman. Little, Brown, 1974. (S)

————. *Snow White*. Translated by Paul Heins. Illustrated by Trina Schart Hyman. Little, Brown, 1974. (S)

————. *Snow White and Rose Red*. Illustrated by Barbara Cooney. Delacorte, 1991 [1965]. (S)

————. *Snow White and Rose Red*. Illustrated by Gennady Spirin. Philomel, 1992. (S)

————. *Snow White and the Seven Dwarfs*. Translated by Randall Jarrell. Illustrated by Nancy Ekholm Burkert. Farrar, Straus & Giroux, 1972. (S)

————. *The Table, the Donkey, and the Stick*. Illustrated by Paul Galdone. McGraw-Hill, 1976. (S)

———. *Thorn Rose or the Sleeping Beauty*. Illustrated by Errol Le Cain. Bradbury, 1975. (S)

———. *Twelve Dancing Princesses*. Illustrated by Errol Le Cain. Bradbury, 1975. (S)

Hague, Kathleen, and Michael Hague. *East of the Sun and West of the Moon*. Illustrated by Michael Hague. Harcourt Brace, 1980. (S)(Norway)

Haley, Gail E. *Jack and the Bean Tree*. Crown, 1986. (S)(United States)

———. *A Story, a Story*. Atheneum, 1970. (S)(Africa)

Hamilton, Virginia. *The Dark Way: Stories from the Spirit World*. Illustrated by Lambert Davis. Harcourt Brace, 1990. (Native American)

———. *Her Stories: African American Folktales*. Illustrated by Leo and Diane Dillon. Blue Sky. 1995. (S)(African American)

———. *In the Beginning: Creation Stories from Around the World*. Illustrated by Barry Moser. Harcourt Brace, 1988.

———. *The Magical Adventures of Pretty Pearl*. Harper & Row, 1983. (African American)

———. *The People Could Fly*. Illustrated by Leo and Diane Dillon. Knopf, 1985. (African American)

Han, Suzanne Crowder. *The Rabbit's Escape*. Illustrated by Yumi Heo. Holt, 1995. (S)(Korea)

———. *The Rabbit's Judgment*. Illustrated by Yumi Heo. Holt, 1994. (S)(Korea)

Harrell, Beatrice Orcutt. *How Thunder and Lightning Came to Be*. Illustrated by Susan L. Roth. Dial, 1995. (S)(Native American)

Harris, Joel Chandler. *The Complete Tales of Uncle Remus*. Compiled by Richard Chase. Illustrated by Arthur Frost and others. Houghton Mifflin, 1955. (African American)

Hausman, Gerald. *Coyote Walks on Two Legs: A Book of Navajo Myths and Legends*. Illustrated by Floyd Cooper. Putnam, 1994.

———. *How Chipmunk Got Tiny Feet: Native American Animal Origin Stories*. Illustrated by Ashley Wolff. HarperCollins, 1995.

Heyer, Marilee. *The Girl, the Fish and the Crown: A Spanish Folktale*. Viking, 1995.

———. *The Weaving of a Dream: A Chinese Folktale*. Penguin, 1986. (S)

Highwater, Jamake. *Anpao*. Illustrated by Fritz Scholder. Lippincott/Harper & Row, 1977. (Modern Literary)

Hodges, Margaret. *The Fire Bringer: A Paiute Indian Legend*. Illustrated by Peter Parnall. Little, Brown, 1972. (S)

———. *Hidden in the Sand*. Illustrated by Paul Birling. Scribner's, 1994. (S)(Middle East)

———. *The Little Humpbacked Horse*. Illustrated by Chris Conover. Farrar, Straus & Giroux, 1980. (S)(Russia)

———. *The Wave*. Illustrated by Blair Lent. Houghton Mifflin, 1964. (S)(Japan)

Hogrogian, Nonny. *One Fine Day*. Macmillan, 1971. (S)(Armenia)

Hong, Lily Toy. *Two of Everything*. Whitman, 1993. (S)(China)

Hooks, William. *Moss Gown*. Illustrated by Donald Carrick. Clarion, 1987. (United States)

———. *The Three Little Pigs and the Fox*. Illustrated by S. D. Schindler. Macmillan, 1989. (S)(United States)

Houston, James. *Tikta Liktak: An Eskimo Legend*. Harcourt Brace, 1965. (S)

———. *The White Archer: An Eskimo Legend*. Harcourt Brace, 1967. (S)

Isaacs, Anne. *Swamp Angel*. Illustrated by Paul O. Zindel. Dutton, 1994. (Modern Literary)

Ishii, Momoko. *The Tongue-Cut Sparrow*. Translated by Katherine Paterson. Illustrated by Suekichi Akaba. Dutton, 1982. (S)(Japan)

Jacobs, Joseph. *The Story of the Three Little Pigs*. Illustrated by Lorinda Bryan Cauley. Putnam, 1980. (S)(England)

———. *Tattercoats*. Illustrated by Margot Tomes. Putnam, 1989. (S)(England)

Jeffers, Susan. *Wild Robin*. Dutton, 1976. (S)(Scotland)

Johnston, Tony. *The Tale of Rabbit and Coyote*. Illustrated by Tomie de Paola. Putnam, 1994. (S)(Mexico)

Karlin, Barbara. *Cinderella*. Illustrated by James Marshall. Little, Brown, 1989. (S)(France)

Keats, Ezra Jack. *John Henry: An American Legend*. Pantheon, 1965. (S)(African American)

Kellogg, Steven. *Chicken Little*. Morrow, 1988. (S)(United States)

———. *Jack and the Beanstalk*. Morrow, 1991. (S)(England)

———. *Johnny Appleseed*. Morrow, 1988. (S)(United States)

———. *Paul Bunyan*. Morrow, 1986. (S)(United States)

———. *Pecos Bill*. Morrow, 1986. (S)(United States)

———. *Sally Ann Thunder Ann Whirlwind Crockett*. Morrow, 1995. (S)(United States)

Kendall, Carol. *The Wedding of the Rat Family*. Illustrated by James Watt. McElderry, 1988. (S)(China)

Kimmel, Eric A. *Baba Yaga: A Russian Folktale*. Illustrated by Megan Lloyd. Holiday House, 1991. (S)

———. *Boots and His Brothers*. Illustrated by Kimberly Bulken Root. Holiday House, 1992. (S)(Norway)

———. *I Know Not What, I Know Not Where*. Illustrated by Robert Sauber. Holiday House, 1994. (S)(Russia)

———. *Iron John*. Illustrated by Trina Schart Hyman. Holiday House, 1994. (S)(German)

———. *Rimonah of the Flashing Sword*. Illustrated by Omar Rayyan. Holiday House, 1995. (S)(Middle East)

———. *The Tale of Aladdin and the Wonderful Lamp*. Illustrated by Ju-Hong Chen. Holiday House, 1992.
(S)(Middle East)

———. *The Three Princes*. Illustrated by Leonard Everett Fisher. Holiday House, 1995. (S)(Middle East)

———. *Three Sacks of Truth: A Story From France*. Illustrated by Robert Rayevsky. Holiday House, 1993.
(S)(France)

Knutson, Barbara. *Sungura and the Black Leopard: A Swahili Trickster Tale*. Little, Brown, 1993. (S)(Tanzania)

Kurtz, Jane. *Fire on the Mountain*. Illustrated by E. B. Lewis. Simon & Schuster, 1994. (S)(Ethiopia)

Kwon, Holly. *The Moles and the Mireuk*. Illustrated by Woodleigh Hubbard. Houghton Mifflin, 1993. (S)(Korea)

Lang, Andrew. *Aladdin*. Illustrated by Errol Le Cain. Viking, 1981. (S)(Middle East)

Langton, Jane. *The Hedgehog Boy: A Latvian Tale*. Illustrated by Ilse Plume. Harper & Row, 1985. (S)

Lattimore, Deborah Nourse. *Arabian Nights: Three Tales*. HarperCollins, 1995. (S)(Middle East)

Leaf, Margaret. *Eyes of the Dragon*. Illustrated by Ed Young. Lothrop, Lee & Shepard, 1987. (S)(China)

Lester, Julius. *How Many Spots Does a Leopard Have? and Other Tales*. Illustrated by David Shannon. Scholastic,
1989. (Africa)

———. *John Henry*. Illustrated by Jerry Pinkney. Dial, 1994. (S)(African American)

———. *More Tales of Uncle Remus: Further Adventures of Brer Rabbit, His Friends, Enemies, and Others*. Illustrated
by Jerry Pinkney. Dial, 1988. (African American)

———. *The Knee-High Man and Other Tales*. Illustrated by Ralph Pinto. Dial, 1972. (African American)

———. *The Last Tales of Uncle Remus*. Illustrated by Jerry Pinkney. Dial, 1994. (African American)

———. *The Tales of Uncle Remus: The Adventures of Brer Rabbit*. Illustrated by Jerry Pinkney. Dial, 1987. (African
American)

Lewis, J. Patrick. *The Frog Princess*. Illustrated by Gennady Spirin. Dial, 1994. (S)(Russia)

Lindbergh, Reeve. *Johnny Appleseed*. Illustrated by Kathy Jakobsen. Little, Brown, 1990. (S)(United States)

Louie, Ai-Ling. *Yeh-Shen: A Cinderella Story from China*. Illustrated by Ed Young. Philomel, 1982. (S)

Mahy, Margaret. *The Seven Chinese Brothers*. Illustrated by Jean and Mou-Sien Tseng. Scholastic, 1990. (S)

Manitonquat. *The Children of the Morning Light: Wampanoag Tales*. Illustrated by Mary F. Arguette. Macmillan,
1994. (Native American)

Marshak, Samuel. *The Month-Brothers: A Slavic Tale*. Translated by Thomas P. Whitney. Illustrated by Diane
Stanley. Morrow, 1983. (S)(Russia)

Marshall, James. *Goldilocks and the Three Bears*. Dial, 1988. (S)(England)

———. *Red Riding Hood*. Dial, 1987. (S)(Germany)

———. *The Three Little Pigs*. Dial, 1989. (S)(England)

Martin, Rafe. *The Boy Who Lived with the Seals*. Illustrated by David Shannon. Putnam, 1993. (S)(Native American)

———. *Foolish Rabbit's Big Mistake*. Illustrated by Ed Young. Putnam, 1985. (S)(India)

———. *The Rough-Face Girl*. Illustrated by David Shannon. Putnam, 1992. (S)(Native American)

Mayer, Marianna. *Baba Yaga and Vasilisa the Brave*. Illustrated by K. Y. Craft. Morrow, 1994. (S)(Russia)

———. *The Twelve Dancing Princesses*. Illustrated by Kinuko Y. Craft. Morrow, 1989. (S)(France)

Mayo, Gretchen Will. *Earthmaker's Tales: North American Indian Stories from Earth Happenings*. Walker, 1989.

McCurdy, Michael. *The Devils Who Learned to Be Good*. Little, Brown, 1987. (S)(Russia)

McDermott, Gerald. *Anansi the Spider*. Holt, 1972. (S)(Africa)

———. *Arrow to the Sun*. Viking, 1974. (S)(Native American)

———. *Coyote: A Trickster Tale from the American Southwest*. Harcourt Brace, 1994. (S)(Native American)

———. *Raven: A Trickster Tale from the Pacific Northwest*. Harcourt Brace, 1993. (S)(Native American)

———. *The Stonecutter: A Japanese Folk Tale*. Penguin, 1975. (S)

———. *Zomo the Rabbit: A Trickster Tale from West Africa*. Harcourt Brace, 1992. (S)

McVitty, Walter. *Ali Baba and the Forty Thieves*. Illustrated by Margaret Early. Abrams, 1989. (S)(Middle East)

Mikolaycak, Charles. *Babushka: An Old Russian Folktale*. Holiday House, 1984. (S)

Milhous, Katherine, and Alice Dalgliesh. *The Turnip*. Illustrated by Pierr Morgan. Philomel, 1990.

Mills, Lauren. *Tatterhood and the Hobgoblins*. Little, Brown, 1993. (S)(Norway)

Minard, Rosemary, ed. *Womenfolk and Fairy Tales*. Illustrated by Suzanne Klelin. Houghton Mifflin, 1975.

Mohr, Nicholasa. *The Song of el Coqui and Other Tales of Puerto Rico*. Illustrated by Antonio Martorell. Viking, 1995. (S)

Mollel, Tololwa. *The King and the Tortoise*. Illustrated by Kathy Blankley. Clarion, 1993. (S)(Africa, Cameroon)

———. *The Orphan Boy*. Illustrated by Paul Morin. Clarion, 1991. (S)(Africa, Maasai)

———. *A Promise to the Sun*. Illustrated by Beatriz Vidal. Little, Brown, 1992. (S)(Native American)

Monroe, Jean Guard, and Ray A. Williamson. *They Dance in the Sky: Native American Star Myths*. Illustrated by Edgar Stewart. Houghton Mifflin, 1987. (Native American)

Moody, Fiona. *The Boy and the Giants*. Farrar, Straus & Giroux, 1993. (S)(Scotland)

Morimoto, Junco. *The Inch Boy*. Viking, 1986. (S)(Japan)

Mosel, Arlene. *The Funny Little Woman*. Illustrated by Blair Lent. Dutton, 1972. (S)(Japan)

Moser, Barry. *Tucker Pfeffercorn*. Little, Brown, 1994. (S)(United States)

Namioka, Lensey. *The Loyal Cat*. Illustrated by Aki Sogabe. Browndeer, 1995. (S)(Japan)

Ness, Evaline. *Tom Tit Tot*. Scribner's, 1965. (S)(England)

Newton, Pam. *The Stonecutter*. Putnam, 1990. (S)(India)

Norman, Howard. *How Glooscap Outwits the Ice Giants and Other Tales of the Maritime Indians*. Illustrated by Michael McCurdy. Little, Brown, 1989.

Oliviero, Jamie. *The Fish Skin*. Illustrated by Brent Morrisseau. Hyperion, 1993. (S)(Cree/Native American)

Osborne, Mary Pope. *American Tall Tales*. Illustrated by Michael McCurdy. Knopf, 1991.

Oxenbury, Helen. *The Helen Oxenbury Nursery Story Book*. Knopf, 1985.

Parks, Van Dyke. *Jump Again! More Adventures of Brer Rabbit*. Illustrated by Barry Moser. Harcourt Brace, 1987. (African American)

———. *Jump on Over! The Adventures of Brer Rabbit and His Family*. Illustrated by Barry Moser. Harcourt Brace, 1989. (African American)

Parks, Van Dyke, and Malcolm Jones. *Jump! The Adventures of Brer Rabbit*. Illustrated by Barry Moser. Harcourt Brace, 1986. (African American)

Paterson, Katherine. *The Tale of the Mandarin Ducks*. Illustrated by Leo and Diane Dillon. Lodestar, 1990. (S)(Japan)

Patron, Susan. *Burgoo Stew*. Illustrated by Mike Shenon. Orchard, 1991. (S)(United States)

Perrault, Charles. *Cinderella*. Illustrated by Marcia Brown. Scribner's, 1954. (S)(France)

———. *Cinderella, or the Little Glass Slipper*. Illustrated by Errol Le Cain. Bradbury, 1973. (S)(France)

———. *Puss in Boots*. Translated by Malcolm Arthur. Illustrated by Fred Marcellino. Farrar, Straus & Giroux, 1990. (S)(France)

———. *Puss in Boots*. Retold by Lincoln Kirstein. Illustrated by Alain Vaës. Little, Brown, 1992. (S)(France)

———. *The Sleeping Beauty*. Illustrated by Margaret Early. Abrams, 1993. (S)(France)

Phelps, Ethel Johnston. *The Maid of the North: Feminist Folk Tales from Around the World*. Illustrated by Lloyd Bloom. Holt, 1981.

Philip, Neil. *The Arabian Nights*. Illustrated by Sheila Moxley. Orchard, 1994. (S)(Middle East)

Polette, Nancy. *The Little Old Woman and the Hungry Cat*. Illustrated by Frank Modell. Greenwillow, 1989. (S)(Norway)

Ransome, Arthur. *The Fool of the World and the Flying Ship*. Illustrated by Uri Shulevitz. Farrar, Straus & Giroux, 1968. (S)(Russia)

Rappaport, Doreen. *The Long-Haired Girl*. Illustrated by Yang Ming-Yi. Dial, 1995. (S)(China)

Reyher, Becky. *My Mother Is the Most Beautiful Woman in the World*. Illustrated by Ruth Gannett. Lothrop, Lee & Shepard, 1945. (S)(Russia)

Rhee, Nami. *Magic Spring: A Korean Folktale*. Putnam, 1993. (S)(Korea)

Richard, Francoise. *On Cat Mountain*. Adapted by Arthur A. Levine. Illustrated by Anne Buguet. Putnam, 1994. (S)(Japan)

Robinson, Gail. *Raven the Trickster*. Atheneum, 1982. (Native American)

Rockwell, Anne. *The Old Woman and Her Pig and Ten Other Stories*. Crowell/Harper & Row, 1979.

———. *The Three Bears & Fifteen Other Stories*. Crowell/Harper & Row, 1975.

Rodanas, Kristina. *Dance of the Sacred Circle: A Native American Tale*. Little, Brown. 1994. (S)(Blackfoot/Native American)

———. *Dragonfly's Tale*. Clarion, 1991. (Zuni/Native American)

———. *The Story of Wali Dad*. Lothrop, Lee & Shepard, 1988. (S)(India)

Rohmer, Harriet. *The Invisible Hunters*. Illustrations by Joe Sam. Children's Book Press, 1987. (S)(Nicaragua)

Rosen, Michael. *Crow and Hawk: A Traditional Pueblo Indian Story*. Illustrated by John Clementson. Harcourt Brace, 1995.

———. *How the Giraffe Got Such a Long Neck . . . and Why Rhino Is So Grumpy*. Illustrated by John Clementson. Dial, 1993. (S)(East Africa)

Ross, Gayle. *How Turtle's Back Was Cracked*. Illustrated by Marvin Jacob. Dial, 1995. (S)(Native American)

Ross, Tony. *Stone Soup*. Dial, 1990. (S)(Modern Literary)

———. *The Three Pigs*. Pantheon, 1983. (S)(England)

Roth, Susan. *The Story of Light*. Morrow, 1990. (S)(Native American)

Rounds, Glen. *Ol' Paul, the Mighty Logger*. Holiday House, 1949. (S)(United States)

———. *The Three Billy Goats Gruff*. Holiday House, 1993. (S)(Norway)

———. *Three Little Pigs and the Big Bad Wolf*. Holiday House, 1992. (S)(England)

Rubalcaba, Jill. *Uncegila's Seventh Spot: A Lakota Legend*. Illustrated by Irving Toddy. Clarion, 1995.

Sage, Alison. *Rumpelstiltskin*. Illustrated by Gennady Spirin. Dial, 1991. (S)(Germany)

Sanfield, Steve. *The Adventures of High John the Conqueror*. Illustrated by John Ward. Orchard, 1989. (African American)

———. *Bit by Bit*. Illustrated by Susan Gaber. Philomel, 1995. (S)(Jewish)

———. *A Natural Man*. Illustrated by Peter J. Thornton. Godine, 1986. (S)(African American)

San Souci, Robert D. *Cut from the Same Cloth: American Women of Myth, Legend and Tall Tale*. Illustrated by Brian Pinkney. Philomel, 1993. (United States)

———. *Larger Than Life: The Adventures of American Legendary Heroes*. Illustrated by Andrew Glass. Doubleday, 1991. (United States)

———. *Sootface: An Ojibwa Cinderella*. Illustrated by Daniel San Souci. Doubleday, 1994. (S)

———. *Sukey and the Mermaid*. Illustrated by Brian Pinkney. Four Winds, 1992. (S)(African American)

———. *The Talking Eggs*. Illustrated by Jerry Pinkney. Dial, 1989. (S)(African American)

———. *The White Cat*. Illustrated by Gennady Spirin. Orchard, 1990. (S)(France)

Sawyer, Ruth. *Journey Cake, Ho!* Illustrated by Robert McCloskey. Viking, 1953. (S)(United States)

Schwartz, Howard, and Barbara Rush. *The Diamond Tree: Jewish Tales from Around the World*. Illustrated by Uri Shulevitz. HarperCollins, 1991.

Schroeder, Alan. *Lily and the Wooden Bowl*. Illustrated by Yoriko Ito. Doubleday, 1994. (S)(Japan)

Scott, Sally. *The Three Wonderful Beggars*. Greenwillow, 1987. (S)(Russia)

Shannon, George. *More Stories to Solve: Fifteen Folktales from Around the World*. Illustrated by Peter Sis. Greenwillow, 1990.

———. *Stories to Solve: Folktales from Around the World*. Illustrated by Peter Sis. Greenwillow, 1985.

Shephard, Esther. *Paul Bunyan*. Illustrated by Rockwell Kent. Harcourt Brace, 1924. (United States)

Sherlock, Philip M. *Anansi the Spider Man: Jamaican Folk Tales*. Illustrated by Marcia Brown. Crowell/Harper & Row, 1954.

Sherman, Josepha. *Vassilisa the Wise: A Tale of Medieval Russia*. Illustrated by Daniel San Souci. Harcourt Brace, 1988. (S)

Shetterly, Susan Hand. *Raven's Light: A Myth from the People of the Northwest Coast*. Illustrated by Robert Shetterly. Atheneum, 1991. (S)(Native American)

Shulevitz, Uri. *Soldier and Tsar in the Forest: A Russian Tale*. Translated by Richard Lourie. Farrar, Straus & Giroux, 1972. (S)

Shute, Linda. *Clever Tom and the Leprechaun*. Lothrop, Lee & Shepard, 1988. (S)(Ireland)

———. *Momotaro, the Peach Boy*. Lothrop, Lee & Shepard 1986. (S)(Japan)

Singer, Isaac Bashevis. *Elijah the Slave*. Translated by the author and Elizabeth Shub. Illustrated by Antonio Frasconi. Farrar, Straus & Giroux, 1970. (S)(Jewish)

———. *Mazel and Shlimazel, or the Milk of a Lioness*. Illustrated by Margot Zemach. Farrar, Straus & Giroux, 1967. (S)(Jewish)

———. *When Shlemiel Went to Warsaw and Other Stories*. Translated by the author and Elizabeth Shub. Illustrated by Margot Zemach. Farrar, Straus & Giroux, 1968. (Jewish)

———. *Zlateh the Goat, and Other Stories*. Translated by the author and Elizabeth Shub. Illustrated by Maurice Sendak. Harper & Row, 1966. (Jewish)

Slote, Teri. *The Eye of the Needle*. Dutton, 1990. (S)(Native American)

Snyder, Diane. *The Boy of the Three-Year Nap*. Illustrated by Allan Say. Houghton Mifflin, 1988. (S)(Japan)

Stamm, Claus. *Three Strong Women: A Tall Tale from Japan*. Illustrated by Jean and Mou-Sien Tseng. Viking, 1991 [1962]. (S)

Steptoe, John. *Mufaro's Beautiful Daughters: An African Tale*. Lothrop, Lee & Shepard, 1987. (S)(Zimbabwe)

———. *The Story of Jumping Mouse: A Native American Legend.* Morrow, 1984. (S)

Stewig, John Warren. *Stone Soup.* Illustrated by Margot Tomes. Holiday House, 1991. (S)(France)

Stobbs, William. *The House That Jack Built.* Oxford University Press, 1983. (S)(England)

Stoutenberg, Adrien. *American Tall Tales.* Illustrated by Richard M. Powers. Penguin, 1976.

Tompert, Ann. *Bamboo Hats and Rice Cakes.* Illustrated by Demi. Crown, 1993. (S)(Japan)

Toye, William. *How Summer Came to Canada.* Illustrated by Elizabeth Cleaver. Walck, 1969. (S)(Native American)

———. *The Loon's Necklace.* Illustrated by Elizabeth Cleaver. Oxford University Press, 1977. (S)(Native American)

Tresselt, Alvin. *The Mitten.* Illustrated by Yaroslava. Lothrop, Lee & Shepard, 1964. (S)(Ukrainian)

Troughton, Joanna. *How Rabbit Stole the Fire.* Bedrick/Blackie, 1986. (S)(Native American)

Uchida, Yoshiko. *The Dancing Kettle and Other Japanese Folk Tales.* Illustrated by Richard C. Jones. Harcourt Brace, 1949.

———. *The Magic Purse.* Illustrated by Keiko Narahasi. McElderry, 1993. (S)(Japan)

———. *The Wise Old Woman.* Illustrated by Martin Springetti. McElderry, 1994. (S)(Japan)

Van Laan, Nancy. *Buffalo Dance: A Blackfoot Legend.* Illustrated by Beatriz Vidal. Little, Brown, 1993. (S)

———. *The Legend of El Dorado.* Illustrated by Beatriz Vidal. Knopf, 1991. (S)(Colombia)

Van Rynbach, Iris. *The Soup Stone.* Greenwillow, 1988. (S)(United States/Modern Literary)

Vuong, Lynette Dyer. *The Brocaded Slipper and Other Vietnamese Tales.* Illustrated by Vo-Dinh Mai. HarperCollins, 1991.

Walker, Barbara. *Watermelons, Walnuts, and the Wisdom of Allah and Other Tales of the Hoca.* Illustrated by Harold Berson. Parents Magazine Press, 1967. (Middle East)

Wang, Rosalind C. *The Fourth Question: A Chinese Tale.* Illustrated by Ju-Hong Chen. Holiday House, 1991. (S)

Wilson, Barbara Ker. *Scottish Folk-Tales and Legends.* Illustrated by Joan Kiddell-Monroe. Walck, 1954.

Winthrop, Elizabeth. *Vasilissa the Beautiful.* Illustrated by Alexander Koshkin. HarperCollins, 1991. (S)(Russia)

Wolkstein, Diane. *The Magic Orange Tree and Other Haitian Folktales.* Illustrated by Elsa Henriquez. Knopf, 1978.

———. *Oom Razoom, or Go I Know Not Where, Bring Back I Know Not What.* Illustrated by Dennis McDermott. Morrow, 1991. (S)(Russia)

Wood, Nancy. *The Girl Who Loved Coyote: Stories of the Southwest.* Illustrated by Diana Bryer. Morrow, 1995.

Yagawa, Sumiko. *The Crane Wife.* Translated by Katherine Paterson. Illustrated by Suekichi Akaba. Morrow, 1981. (S)(Japan)

Yee, Paul. *Tales from Gold Mountain.* Illustrated by Simon Ng. Macmillan, 1990. (Chinese American)

Yep, Laurence. *The Man Who Tricked a Ghost.* Illustrated by Isadore Seltzer. Bridgewater, 1993.

———. *The Rainbow People.* Illustrated by David Wiesner. Harper & Row, 1989. (Chinese American)

———. *The Star Fisher.* Morrow, 1991.

———. *Tongues of Jade.* Illustrated by David Wiesner. HarperCollins, 1991. (Chinese American)

Yolen, Jane. *Greyling.* Illustrated by David Ray. Philomel, 1991. (S)(Shetland Islands)

———. *Sky Dogs.* Illustrated by Barry Moser. Harcourt Brace, 1990. (S)(Native American)

———. *Tam Lin.* Illustrated by Charles Mikolaycak. Harcourt Brace, 1990. (S)(Scotland)

Young, Ed. *Little Plum.* Philomel, 1994. (S)(China)

———. *Lon Po Po: A Red Riding Hood Story from China.* Philomel, 1989. (S)

Zemach, Harve. *Duffy and the Devil.* Illustrated by Margot Zemach. Farrar, Straus & Giroux, 1973. (S)(England)

———. *Nail Soup.* Adapted from the text of Nila Djurklo. Illustrated by Margot Zemach. Farrar, Straus & Giroux, 1964. (S)(Sweden)

————. *Salt: A Russian Tale*. Illustrated by Margot Zemach. Follett, 1965. (S)

Zemach, Margot. *It Could Always Be Worse*. Farrar, Straus & Giroux, 1977. (S)(Jewish)

————. *The Little Red Hen*. Farrar, Straus & Giroux, 1983. (S)(England)

————. *The Three Wishes: An Old Story*. Farrar, Straus & Giroux, 1986. (S)(England)

Zwerger, Lisbeth. *The Merry Pranks of Till Eulenspiegel*. Picture Book Studio, 1990. (Germany)

Fables

Anno, Mitsumasa. *Anno's Aesop: A Book of Fables by Aesop and Mr. Ox*. Orchard, 1987.

Bader, Barbara. *Aesop & Company*. Illustrated by Arthur Geisert. Houghton Mifflin, 1991.

Bierhorst, John. *Doctor Coyote: A Native American Aesop's Fables*. Illustrated by Wendy Watson. Macmillan, 1987.

Brown, Marcia. *Once a Mouse*. Scribner's, 1961. (S)

Caldecott, Randolph. *The Caldecott Aesop*. Doubleday, 1978 [1883].

Carle, Eric. *Twelve Tales from Aesop*. Putnam, 1980.

Galdone, Paul. *The Monkey and the Crocodile*. Seabury, 1969. (S)

————. *Three Aesop Fox Fables*. Seabury, 1971.

Holder, Heidi. *Aesop's Fables*. Viking, 1981.

La Fontaine. *The Hare and the Tortoise*. Illustrated by Brian Wildsmith. Oxford University Press, 1982. (S)

————. *The Lion and the Rat*. Illustrated by Brian Wildsmith. Oxford University Press, 1986.

————. *The Miller, the Boy and the Donkey*. Illustrated by Brian Wildsmith. Oxford University Press, 1984.

Lionni, Leo. *Frederick*. Pantheon, 1967. (S)(Modern Literary)

McFarland, John. *The Exploding Frog and Other Fables from Aesop*. Illustrated by James Marshall. Little, Brown, 1981.

Paxton, Tom. *Aesop's Fables*. Illustrated by Robert Rayevsky. Morrow, 1988.

Rice, Eve. *Once in a Wood: Ten Tales from Aesop*. Greenwillow, 1979.

Steig, William. *Amos & Boris*. Farrar, Straus & Giroux, 1971. (S)(Modern Literary)

Testa, Fulvio. *Aesop's Fables*. Barron's, 1989.

Yolen, Jane. *A Sip of Aesop*. Illustrated by Karen Barbour. Blue Sky, 1995.

Young, Ed. *The Lion and the Mouse*. Doubleday, 1980.

————. *Seven Blind Mice*. Philomel, 1992. (S)

Zwerger, Lisbeth. *Aesop's Fables*. Picture Book Studios, 1989.

Myths and Epics

Bierhorst, John. *The Hungry Woman: Myths and Legends of the Aztecs*. Morrow, 1984.

————. *The Mythology of Mexico and Central America*. Morrow, 1990.

————. *The Mythology of North America*. Morrow, 1985.

————. *The Mythology of South America*. Morrow, 1988.

————. *The Woman Who Fell from the Sky*. Illustrated by Robert Andrew Parker. Morrow, 1993. (S)

Climo, Shirley. *Atalanta's Race*. Illustrated by Alexander Koshkin. Clarion, 1995. (S)

————. *Stolen Thunder*. Illustrated by Alexander Koshkin. Clarion, 1994. (S)

Colum, Padraic. *The Children of Odin*. Illustrated by Willy Pogany. Macmillan, 1920.

————. *The Children's Homer: The Adventures of Odysseus and the Tale of Troy*. Illustrated by Willy Pogany. Macmillan, 1962.

D'Aulaire, Ingri, and Edgar Parin d'Aulaire. *D'Aulaires' Book of Greek Myths*. Doubleday, 1962.

Evslin, Bernard. *Hercules*. Illustrated by Joseph A. Smith. Morrow, 1984.

————. *Jason and the Argonauts*. Illustrated by Bert Dodson. Morrow, 1986.

Evslin, Bernard, Dorothy Evslin, and Ned Hoopes. *Heroes and Monsters of Greek Myth*. Illustrated by William Hunter. Scholastic, 1970.

Fisher, Leonard Everett. *Jason and the Golden Fleece*. Holiday House, 1990. (S)

————. *The Olympians*. Holiday House, 1984.

————. *Theseus and Minotaur*. Holiday House, 1988. (S)

Gaer, Joseph. *The Adventures of Rama*. Illustrated by Randy Monk. Little, Brown, 1954.

Gates, Doris. *The Golden God: Apollo*. Illustrated by Constantinos Coconis. Viking, 1973.

————. *Lord of the Sky: Zeus*. Illustrated by Robert Handville. Viking, 1972.

————. *Two Queens of Heaven: The Story of Demeter and Aphrodite*. Illustrated by Trina Schart Hyman. Viking, 1974.

————. *The Warrior Goddess: Athena*. Illustrated by Don Bolognese. Viking, 1972.

Graves, Robert. *Greek Gods and Heroes*. Doubleday, 1960.

Green, Roger Lancelyn. *Tales of the Greek Heroes*. Penguin, 1958.

Hamilton, Virginia. *In the Beginning: Creation Stories from Around the World*. Illustrated by Barry Moser. Harcourt Brace, 1988.

Hastings, Selina. *Sir Gawain and the Green Knight*. Illustrated by Juan Wijngaard. Lothrop, Lee & Shepard, 1981. (S)

————. *Sir Gawain and the Loathly Lady*. Illustrated by Juan Wijngaard. Lothrop, Lee & Shepard, 1985. (S)

Hodges, Margaret. *The Arrow and the Lamp: The Story of Psyche*. Illustrated by Donna Diamond. Little, Brown, 1989. (S)

————. *The Kitchen Knight: A Tale of King Arthur*. Illustrated by Trina Schart Hyman. Holiday House, 1990. (S)

————. *Saint George and the Dragon*. Illustrated by Trina Schart Hyman. Little, Brown, 1984. (S)

Hutton, Warwick. *Persephone*. McElderry, 1994. (S)

————. *Perseus*. McElderry, 1994. (S)

————. *Theseus and the Minotaur*. McElderry, 1989. (S)

————. *The Trojan Horse*. McElderry, 1992. (S)

Lanier, Sidney. *The Boy's King Arthur*. Illustrated by N. C. Wyeth. Scribner's, 1989 [1917].

Lattimore, Deborah Nourse. *Why There Is No Arguing in Heaven: A Mayan Myth*. Harper & Row, 1989. (S)

Low, Alice. *The Macmillan Book of Greek Gods and Heroes*. Illustrated by Arvis Stewart. Macmillan, 1985.

McDermott, Gerald. *Daughter of Earth: A Roman Myth*. Delacorte, 1984. (S)

McGovern, Ann. *Robin Hood of Sherwood Forest*. Illustrated by Tracy Sugarman. Scholastic, 1970.

McKinley, Robin. *The Outlaws of Sherwood Forest*. Greenwillow, 1988.

Monroe, Jean Guard, and Ray A. Williamson. *They Dance in the Sky: Native American Star Myths*. Illustrated by Edgar Stewart. Houghton Mifflin, 1987.

Morpugo, Michael. *Arthur, High King of Britain*. Illustrated by Michael Foreman. Harcourt Brace, 1995.

Orgel, Doris. *Ariadne, Awake!* Illustrated by Barry Moser. Viking, 1994. (S)

Philip, Neil. *King Midas*. Illustrated by Isabelle Brent. Little, Brown, 1994. (S)

Picard, Barbara Leonie. *The Odyssey of Homer Retold*. Walck, 1952.

Pyk, Ann. *The Hammer of Thunder*. Illustrated by Jan Pyk. Putnam, 1972.

Pyle, Howard. *The Merry Adventures of Robin Hood*. Scribner's, 1946 [1888].

————. *The Story of King Arthur and His Knights*. Scribner's, 1954.

San Souci, Robert D. *Young Guinevere*. Illustrated by Jamichael Henterly. Doubleday, 1993. (S)

————. *Young Merlin*. Illustrated by Daniel Horne. Doubleday, 1990. (S)

Seeger, Elizabeth. *The Ramayana*. Illustrated by Gordon Laite. Young/Scott, 1969.

Sutcliff, Rosemary. *The Light Beyond the Forest: The Quest for the Holy Grail*. Dutton, 1980.

——. *The Road to Camlann*. Dutton, 1982.

——. *The Sword and the Circle*. Dutton, 1981.

——. *Tristan and Iseult*. Dutton, 1981.

Talbott, Hudson. *King Arthur: The Sword in the Stone*. Morrow, 1991. (S)

Tomlinson, Theresa. *The Forestwife*. Orchard, 1995.

White, T. H. *The Sword in the Stone*. Putnam, 1939.

Yolen, Jane. *The Dragon's Boy*. HarperCollins, 1990.

——. *Wings*. Illustrated by Dennis Nolan. Harcourt Brace, 1991. (S)

Bible

Bach, Alice, and J. Cheryl Exum. *Miriam's Well: Stories About Women in the Bible*. Illustrated by Leo and Diane Dillon. Delacorte, 1991.

——. *Moses' Ark: Stories from the Bible*. Illustrated by Leo and Diane Dillon. Delacorte, 1989.

Bierhorst, John, trans. *Spirit Child: A Story of the Nativity*. Illustrated by Barbara Cooney. Morrow, 1984. (S)(Mexico)

Bødker, Cecil. *Mary of Nazareth*. Translated by Erick Bibb. Illustrated by Bengt Arne Runnerström. R & S Books/Farrar, Straus & Giroux, 1989.

Brent, Isabelle. *The Christmas Story*. Dial, 1989. (S)

Chaikin, Miriam. *Exodus*. Illustrated by Charles Mikolaycak. Holiday House, 1987. (S)

de la Mare, Walter. *Stories from the Bible*. Illustrated by Edward Ardizzone. Knopf, 1961.

de Paola, Tomie. *The Legend of Old Befana*. Harcourt Brace, 1980. (S)

——. *Mary, Mother of Jesus*. Holiday House, 1995. (S)

——. *The Story of the Three Wise Kings*. Putnam, 1983. (S)

Fisher, Leonard Everett. *David and Goliath*. Holiday House, 1993. (S)

——. *Moses*. Holiday House, 1995. (S)

——. *The Seven Days of Creation*. Holiday House, 1981.

Gellman, Marc. *Does God Have a Big Toe? Stories About Stories in the Bible*. Illustrated by Oscar de Mejo. Harper & Row, 1989.

Hutton, Warwick. *Adam and Eve: The Bible Story*. McElderry, 1987. (S)

——. *Moses in the Bulrushes*. McElderry, 1986. (S)

Koralek, Jenny. *The Cobweb Curtain: A Christmas Story*. Illustrated by Pauline Baynes. Holt, 1989. (S)

Mikolaycak, Charles. *Babushka: An Old Russian Folktale*. Holiday House, 1984. (S)

Petersham, Maud, and Miska Petersham. *The Christ Child*. Doubleday, 1931. (S)

Pienkowski, Jan. *Christmas: The King James Version*. Knopf, 1984. (S)

Robbins, Ruth. *Baboushka and the Three Kings*. Illustrated by Nicolas Sidjakov. Parnassus, 1960. (S)

Rogers, Jacqueline. *The Christmas Pageant*. Grosset & Dunlap, 1989. (S)

Turner, Philip. *The Bible Story*. Illustrated by Brian Wildsmith. Oxford University Press, 1987.

Vivas, Julie. *The Nativity*. Harcourt Brace, 1986. (S)

Waldman Sarah. *Light*. Illustrated by Neil Waldman. Harcourt Brace, 1993. (S)

Winthrop, Elizabeth. *A Child Is Born*. Illustrated by Charles Mikolaycak. Holiday House, 1983. (S)

——. *He Is Risen*. Illustrated by Charles Mikolaycak. Holiday House, 1985. (S)

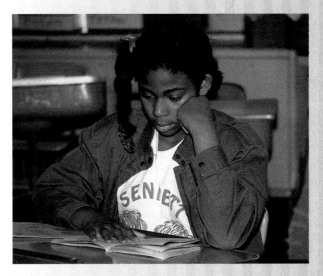

© James L. Shaffer

chapter
seven

Modern Fantasy

Fantasy for Today's Child   341
Modern Fairy Tales   343
The Beginnings of the Modern Fairy Tale   343
Fairy Tales Today   345
Modern Fantasy   346
Evaluating Modern Fantasy   346
*Resources for Teaching: Books That
  Introduce Aspects of Fantasy
  Novels*   347
Animal Fantasy   347
*Guidelines: Evaluating Modern
  Fantasy*   348
*Teaching Feature: Keeping Journals Helps
  Children Understand Fantasy*   352
The World of Toys and Dolls   353
Eccentric Characters and Preposterous
  Situations   355

Extraordinary Worlds   357
Magical Powers   360
Suspense and the Supernatural   361
Time-Shift Fantasy   363
Imaginary Realms   367
High Fantasy   369
The Struggle Between Good and Evil   370
Quests and Adventures   371
Science Fiction   373
Through the Door   374
Visitors to Earth   375
Outer Space and Cyberspace   375
Views of the Future   376
Learning Experiences   379
Related Readings   379
Children's Literature   380

A wonderfully perceptive teacher maintained a diary in which she recorded significant events in her teaching day. These excerpts reveal her students' responses to a reading aloud of the well-known fantasy *Charlotte's Web* by E. B. White:

January 18

A wisp of a girl with dark dreaming eyes, Judy F. sits transfixed, listening to *Charlotte's Web*. When I read aloud, I'm aware of an irreplaceable group feeling. But beyond that, if children aren't read to, how will they see the purpose of such a difficult skill?

February 6

Judy came in glowing.

"We've bought a baby pig. Mother took me to a nearby farm."

"How marvelous. What's his name?"

"Wilbur," she said, in a matter-of-fact voice—as if the name of the pig in *Charlotte's Web* was the only one possible. "He's quite cuddly for a pig. We bathe him every day."

February 20

When I'm alone with Judy, I ask about Wilbur.

"Oh, he's getting along just fine. We bought him a large pink ribbon and only take it off when he goes to bed."

"Where does he sleep?"

"In my bed," said Judy, as if I ought to know.

March 2

Everyone was silent at the end of *Charlotte's Web*. David wept when Charlotte died. Later he asked to borrow the book. It'll be interesting to see how he maneuvers such difficult reading. But there's the motivation they talk about.

April 3

Judy's mother hurried over to me at the P.T.A. meeting.

"What's all this about your pig?" she queried.

"My pig?" I answered incredulously. "You mean your pig; the one you and Judy bought at the farm."

"Come now," said Mrs. F. "This is ridiculous. Judy's been telling me for weeks about the class pig. The one you named for Wilbur in *Charlotte's Web*."

We looked at each other, puzzled, and suddenly the truth dawned upon us.

Wilbur, that immaculately clean pig in his dazzling pink ribbon, belonged to neither Mrs. F. nor me. He was born in dreams—a creature of Judy's wonderful imagination.[1]

A book of fantasy had seemed so real to these children that 7-year-old David had cried at its end, and Judy had continued the story in her imagination, convincing both her teacher and her mother that Wilbur did indeed exist.

[1]Jean Katzenberg, "More Leaves from a Teacher's Diary: On Reading," *Outlook* issue 2 (spring 1974): 28–29. Published by the Mountain View Center for Environmental Education, University of Colorado.

Fantasy for Today's Child

Some educators and parents question the value of fantasy for today's child. They argue that children want contemporary stories that are relevant and speak to the problems of daily living—"now" books about the real world, not fantasies about unreal worlds. Others object to any fantasy at all for children, afraid that reading about goblins, trolls, and witches will lead children to practices of satanism or belief in the occult.[2]

But good fantasy may be critical to children's understanding of themselves and of the struggles they will face as human beings. Lloyd Alexander argues that fantasy is of the utmost value for children.

> We call our individual fantasies dreams, but when we dream as a society, or as a human race, it becomes the sum total of all our hopes. Fantasy touches our deepest feelings and in so doing, it speaks to the best and most hopeful parts of ourselves. It can help us learn the most fundamental skill of all—how to be human.[3]

The great fantasies frequently reveal new insights into the world of reality. Both *Charlotte's Web* and *The Wind in the Willows* detail the responsibilities and loyalties required of true friendship. The fundamental truth underlying Ursula Le Guin's story *A Wizard of Earthsea* is that people are responsible for the evil they create and are free of it only when they face it directly. In a book of realism, such a theme might appear to be a thinly disguised Sunday school lesson; in fantasy it becomes an exciting quest for identity and self-knowledge. Fantasy consistently asks the universal questions concerning the struggle of good versus evil, the humanity of humankind, and the meaning of life and death.

A modern realistic fiction novel can be out of date in five years, but well-written fantasy endures. Hans Christian Andersen's *The Nightingale* speaks directly to this century's adoration of mechanical gadgetry to the neglect of what is simple and real. Lois Lowry's *The Giver* asks how the freedom of an individual can be weighed against the needs of the group. Natalie Babbitt's *Tuck Everlasting* questions whether anything or anyone would wish to live forever.

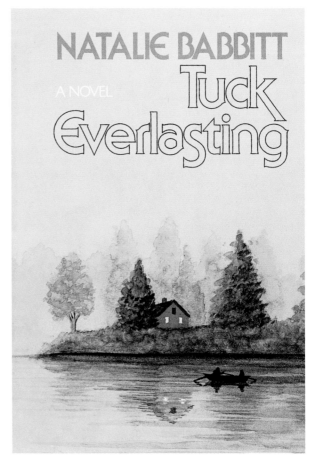

Natalie Babbitt's *Tuck Everlasting* asks children to consider what it means to be mortal.
Jacket from *Tuck Everlasting* by Natalie Babbitt. Copyright © 1975 by Natalie Babbitt. Reprinted by permission of Farrar, Straus & Giroux, Inc.

More importantly, however, fantasy helps the child develop imagination. To be able to imagine, to conceive of alternative ways of life, to entertain new ideas, to create strange new worlds, to dream dreams—these are all skills vital to human survival. Maxine Greene argues that "of all our cognitive capacities, imagination is the one that permits us to give credence to alternative realities."[4]

> It is imagination—with its capacity to both make order out of chaos and open experience to the mysterious and the strange—that moves us to go in quest, to journey where we have never been.[5]

Susan Cooper suggests that because of the heterogeneous mix of cultures in the United States, children

[2]According to the *Newsletter on Intellectual Freedom* (March 1994, p. 54), for example, a group who objected to Lloyd Alexander's classic Prydain Chronicles said that the series "contained religious themes that are pagan in nature and young minds would be drawn to the allure of witchcraft and black magic that runs through the books."

[3]Lloyd Alexander, "Fantasy and the Human Condition," *New Advocate* 1, no. 2 (spring 1983): 83.

[4]Maxine Greene, *Releasing the Imagination: Essays on Education, the Arts, and Social Change* (San Francisco: Jossey-Bass, 1995), p. 3.

[5]Ibid., p. 23.

here have no shared myths to inherit as children in more homogeneous cultures do. She believes that the role of fantasy, with its heroes, struggles, and allegories, becomes even more important because it satisfies our modern-day hunger for myth.[6]

These arguments aside, children themselves have shown that they continue to want books that satisfy this hunger. *Charlotte's Web* is one of the most popular children's books to be published in the past fifty years. C. S. Lewis's Narnia series, Roald Dahl's *Charlie and the Chocolate Factory*, and Madeleine L'Engle's *A Wrinkle in Time* are all fantasies that rank among children's favorite books. And many of the classics, books that have endured through several generations—such as *Winnie-the-Pooh*, *The Wind in the Willows*, and *Alice's Adventures in Wonderland*—are also fantasies. As Molly Hunter suggests, children (and writers of fantasy) are the ones who "never pass a secret place in the woods without a stare of curiosity for the mystery implied . . . who still turn corners with a lift of expectation at the heart."[7] And who still open a book of fantasy with that same sense of anticipation.

The modern literature of fantasy is diverse. We have contemporary fairy tales; stories of magic, talking toys, and other wonders; quests for truth in lands that never were; and narratives that speculate on the future. While these types of stories might seem very different, they do have something in common: they are rooted in earlier sources—in folktales, legends, myths, and the oldest dreams of humankind.

All literature borrows from itself, but the fantastic genre is particularly dependent. The motifs, plots, characters, settings, and themes of new fantasy books often seem familiar. And well they should, for we have met them before, in other, older stories.

Jane Yolen, in an essay on the importance of traditional literature, says:

> Stories lean on stories, art on art. This familiarity with the treasure-house of ancient story is necessary for any true appreciation of today's literature. A child who has never met Merlin—how can he or she really recognize the wizards in Earthsea? The child who has never heard of Arthur—how can he or she totally appreciate Susan Cooper's *The Grey King?*[8]

[6]Susan Cooper, "Fantasy in the Real World," *Horn Book Magazine,* May/June 1990, pp. 304–315.

[7]Molly Hunter, "One World," in *Talent Is Not Enough* (New York: Harper & Row, 1976), p. 77.

[8]Jane Yolen, "How Basic Is Shazam?" in *Touch Magic: Fantasy, Faerie and Folklore in the Literature of Childhood* (New York: Philomel Books, 1981), p. 15.

Many authors borrow directly from the characters and motifs of folklore. The African American folk heroes John de Conquer and John Henry Roustabout enliven the unusual fantasy *The Magical Adventures of Pretty Pearl* by Virginia Hamilton. Mollie Hunter's fantasy books are filled with the magic folk of her native Scotland. There are, among others, worrisome trows; the Selkies, who are seals capable of taking human form on land; and water sprites called kelpies, often seen as horses.

Such shape shifting often occurs in folk and fairy tales, and similar transformations are frequently arranged by authors of modern fantasy. In *The Cat Who Wished to Be a Man*, Lloyd Alexander's wizard transforms his cat Lionel into a young man whose catlike ways wear off only gradually. The wizard himself, of course, is a character drawn from the magician figures of old tales. In the same book, a good-hearted rogue named Tudbelly invites inhospitable townspeople to a feast, promising them a special stew, and then tricks them into furnishing the ingredients themselves. Readers who have had prior experience with folktales may recognize that Alexander's "delicious Pro Bono Publico" stew is made from the same basic recipe as *Stone Soup* in the retelling by Marcia Brown.

In the case of Robin McKinley's *Beauty*, the debt to an earlier source is immediately clear. McKinley recasts the tale of Beauty and the Beast in the form of a novel by exploring character, motive, and the everyday details that do not fit within the frame of a conventional fairy tale. The result is a rich and satisfying book that manages to sustain a sense of anticipation even in readers who know the outcome. Shirley Rousseau Murphy incorporates several variants of the Cinderella story in *Silver Woven in My Hair*, another fully developed fantasy for young readers built on the simpler structure of a familiar tale. In *The Magic Circle*, a powerful tale for older readers, Donna Jo Napoli's healer gives a gripping yet sensitive account of how she came to be bewitched and fled deep into a magic forest so that she might do no harm to humans. Here she lives for years until one day two children named Hansel and Gretel stumble upon her cottage. Although they will prove to be her undoing, they will also be her salvation from the evil powers that have held her in their grip for so many years.

Some bodies of traditional lore have proven to be more popular than others as sources of new stories. Echoes of King Arthur—both the Arthur of the medieval romances (as in Malory's *Le Morte d'Arthur*) and his historic precursor, Arthur the tribal chieftain of early Britain—are found in a great many modern fantasies. William Mayne's *Earthfasts* and Peter Dickinson's *Merlin Dreams* are two books much in Arthur's debt. Susan Cooper's five books that make up the Dark

Is Rising sequence weave together elements of the Arthurian legends and broader themes from Celtic mythology, with its emphasis on ancient powers. Lloyd Alexander's Prydain Chronicles borrow extensively from the Welsh stories known as the "Mabinogion."

Many fantasies are based on multiple sources. Perhaps it is this striking of several familiar notes at once that brings them such enduring popularity. *The Hobbit*, by J. R. R. Tolkien, places the archetypal hero of mythology against a smaller-scale setting more common in folklore. C. S. Lewis's Narnia series puts centaurs and fauns from classical myths in company with modern children fighting medieval battles parallel to those recounted in Christian theology. Madeleine L'Engle draws on a similar array of referents. The volumes of her Time trilogy (*A Wrinkle in Time, A Wind in the Door, A Swiftly Tilting Planet*) explore intriguing possibilities of astrophysics and cellular biology, as befits science fiction, but the books also reflect her knowledge of theology, classical literature, myths, legends, and history.

L'Engle's *A Wrinkle in Time* as well as Robert C. O'Brien's *Mrs. Frisby and the Rats of NIMH* are termed science fiction as well as fantasy. Often fantasies that draw on various sources are difficult to classify. Dennis Hamley's *Hare's Choice* is a multilayered story of an elementary class's need to create a story for a hare they found dead by the roadside. The story the children create is science fiction, but the hare's own story, which alternates in italics, shows how the children's storytelling imbues the hare with mythic powers. Hare may choose a pastoral hare heaven where real rabbits go or the place where animals such as Peter Rabbit, Fiver and Hazel, Stuart Little, and Tom Kitten, who have also been brought to life in stories, now dwell.

No matter how we classify these stories, however, the ultimate taproot of all fantasy is the human psyche. Like the ancient tale-tellers and the medieval bards, modern fantasy writers speak to our deepest needs, our darkest fears, and our highest hopes. Maurice Sendak, for instance, relies on such themes in his picture storybooks and in the singular small volume entitled *Higglety, Pigglety, Pop!* In this book a dog named Jennie sets out on an unspecified quest because "There must be more to life than having everything."[9] Her experiences are childlike and highly symbolic: the comforts of eating, and the fear of being eaten in turn by a lion; the importance of one's own real name; the significance of dreams. Jennie's quest, as it turns out, may be read as the search for maturity and personal identity.

Ursula K. Le Guin conducts a similar psychic adventure for an older audience in *A Wizard of Earthsea*,

where a young magician must learn the power of naming and recognize the Shadow that pursues him as part of himself. Adults may find, in these and similar stories, many of the collective images or shared symbols called archetypes by the great psychologist Carl Jung. Children will simply recognize that such a fantasy is "true." All our best fantasies, from the briefest modern fairy tale to the most complex novel of high adventure, share this quality of truth.

Modern Fairy Tales

The traditional folklore or fairy tale had no identifiable author but was passed on by retellings by one generation to the next. Even though the names Grimm and Jacobs have become associated with some of these tales, they did not *write* the stories; they compiled and edited the folktales of Germany and England. The modern literary fairy tale utilizes the form of the old but has an identifiable author.

The Beginnings of the Modern Fairy Tale

Hans Christian Andersen is generally credited with being the first *author* of modern fairy tales, although even some of his stories, such as *The Wild Swans*, are definite adaptations of the old folktales. (Compare Andersen's *The Wild Swans* with the Grimm brothers' "The Six Swans," for example.) Many of Andersen's stories bear his unmistakable stamp of gentleness, melancholy, and faith in God. Often even his retellings of old tales are embellished with deeper meanings, making them very much his creations.

Some of Andersen's tales are really commentaries on what he saw as the false standards of society. In *The Princess and the Pea*, Andersen laughs at the snobbish desire of a prince to determine the true nature of his intended spouse by means of a dried pea. In *The Emperor's New Clothes*, farce is disclosed by a child who tells the truth—that the Emperor indeed has no clothes. Others of Andersen's tales are thought to be autobiographical commentaries. In *The Ugly Duckling* the jest of the poultry yard became a beautiful swan, just as the gawky Andersen suffered in his youth but was later honored by the Danish king and the world. *The Steadfast Tin Soldier* was rejected by his ballerina love just as Andersen was rejected by the woman he loved.

Andersen was not afraid to show children cruelty, morbidity, sorrow, and even death in his stories. *The Little Match Girl* freezes to death on Christmas Eve while seeing a vision of her grandmother, the only person who

---

[9]Maurice Sendak, *Higglety, Pigglety, Pop!* (New York: Harper & Row, 1967), p. 5.

As Christmas revelers dance in the background, the Tin Soldier gazes longingly at the beautiful ballerina in Fred Marcellino's illustrations for Hans Christian Andersen's poignant story *The Steadfast Tin Soldier*.
Pictures copyright © 1992 by Fred Marcellino. Used by permission of HarperCollins Publishers, New York, NY.

truly loved her, in the flames of her unsold matches. The grandmother carries the girl to heaven. In the long tale of *The Snow Queen*, a glass splinter enters Kai's (or Kay's) eye and stabs his heart. He becomes spiteful and angry with his friend Gerda, who is hurt by the change in his behavior. When he disappears with the Snow Queen, Gerda searches for and finds him, and her tears melt the splinter and dissolve his icy demeanor.

Many of Andersen's stories have been beautifully illustrated in single editions. In her version of *The Snow Queen* Susan Jeffers features close-ups and swirling images of the dreams and snowstorms the two children encounter. Errol Le Cain brings the same story to life with brilliantly colored and ornately patterned surfaces and emphasizes the strangeness of Gerda's journey to find Kai. Nancy Ekholm Burkert's pictures for *The Nightingale* resemble paintings on old Chinese silk screens. Demi's outlined landscapes on golden green silk backgrounds appear in a more decorative version; Lisbeth Zwerger's simple composition and sure sepia line illustrate the story in still another edition. Warwick Hutton's bright watercolors for *The Tinderbox* depict with humor the three large-eyed dogs that help a common soldier win riches and the princess while outwitting her father. In *The Steadfast Tin Soldier* Fred Marcellino's soft

colored-pencil drawings depict in a Victorian Christmas card setting the touch of poignancy in this bittersweet story.

Hans Christian Andersen: The Complete Fairy Tales and Stories presents faithful translations by Erik Haugaard. Here we find the original telling of "The Little Mermaid" and "Thumbelina." Eighteen of these stories, selected for a single volume and illustrated by Michael Foreman, provide children with several of the most popular and well known of Andersen's stories. Many other illustrators, such as Warwick Hutton, Thomas Locker, and Maurice Sendak, have illustrated their own favorite tales from the body of Andersen's work.

Two other early authors of the modern literary fairy tale are Oscar Wilde and George MacDonald. Wilde's *The Happy Prince*, strikingly illustrated both by Jean Claverie and by Ed Young, is the sentimental story of a bejeweled statue who little by little gives his valuable decorations to the poor. His emissary and friend is a swallow who faithfully postpones his winter migration to Egypt to do the prince's bidding, only to succumb to the cold at the statue's feet. When the town councilors melt down the now shabby statue for its lead, all burns except the heart, which is cast on the same ash heap as the body of the dead bird. Together, the two are received in Heaven as the most precious things in the city. Wilde's *The Selfish Giant* has even more religious symbolism.

Many of MacDonald's fairy tales are also religious in nature, including *The Golden Key*, which has been sensitively illustrated by Maurice Sendak. Sendak also illustrated MacDonald's *The Light Princess*, the story of a princess deprived of gravity by an aunt who was angry at not being invited to her christening. It is interesting to compare Sendak's tender yet humorous illustrations for this story with the detailed, amusing, and colorful pictures by William Pène DuBois. MacDonald is also remembered for *At the Back of the North Wind*, published in 1871 and one of the foundation stories of modern fantasy.

Fairy Tales Today

In many instances modern authors have written farcical versions of the old fairy-tale form. The story might be set in the days of kings and queens and beautiful princesses, the language will reflect the manners of the period, and the usual "Once upon a time" beginning and "They lived happily ever after" ending will be present—but the conflict usually has a modern twist. True to all fairy tales, virtue will be rewarded and evil overcome.

James Thurber's *Many Moons*, with new illustrations by Marc Simont, is the story of a petulant princess who desires the moon. The characterizations of the frustrated king, the perplexed wise men, and the understanding jester are well realized. Princess Lenore solves the problem of obtaining the moon in a completely satisfying and childlike manner. Thurber's *Thirteen Clocks* is a more sophisticated folktale for older readers. A cold duke who is afraid of "now" freezes time in Coffin Castle, where he keeps the beautiful Princess Saralinda. A prince in disguise accomplishes impossible tasks set by the duke and thus wins Saralinda's hand. Middle graders thoroughly enjoy this imaginative spoof on folktales.

Jane Yolen writes lyrical tales that make use of modern psychological insights while following the traditional patterns in folk literature. Ed Young's illustrations in the style of Chinese cut-paper artwork grace *The Emperor and the Kite*, in which the youngest daughter rescues her emperor father from imprisonment by means of a kite. In *The Girl Who Loved the Wind*, Yolen tells of the princess Danina who is protected by her father from all the unlovely things of the world by a high wall he has constructed around the palace. But when Danina hears the wind sing a true song of the world, she spreads her cape and off she flies with the wind. Ed Young studied Persian miniatures before designing the richly textured pictures for this beautiful book. A blind Chinese princess learns to "see" from the remarkable vision of a

The sad-faced hero of Laurence Yep's *The City of Dragons* causes the dragon maidens to weep tears of pearls.
Illustration by Jean and Mou-Sien Tseng from *The City of Dragons* by Laurence Yep. Illustrations copyright © 1995 by Jean and Mou-Sien Tseng. Reprinted by permission of Scholastic Inc.

wise blind man in *The Seeing Stick*. Color is used selectively by Remy Charlip and Demetra Maraslis to help the reader see and feel the princess's excitement.

In *Dove Isabeau* by Jane Yolen, the heroine, Dove, is pure of heart, but when her mother dies and her father remarries a witch, Dove is transformed into a terrible dragon. Her destiny is to kill young men beneath her claws and to be cursed by all. While kisses may save Isabeau, the one who bestows them will himself turn to stone. This story of a spirited heroine and faithful love is a fine introduction to many longer fantasy novels.

Several other modern folktales present contrasting characterizations of dragons. Jay Williams suggests in *Everyone Knows What a Dragon Looks Like* that appearances can be deceiving, for no one except a small boy will believe that a small fat man with a long white beard is really a dragon come to defend the city. Laurence Yep also tells a tale about appearances in *The City of Dragons*. In this story a small boy has such a sad face that he is banished from his village. He is employed by a band of merchant Giants who take him to the undersea Dragon Kingdom to trade for silk and pearls. Having heard all the sad stories in the world, however, the dragons who normally weep tears of pearls have not been able to cry. When they see the boy's face, however, they imagine such sad tales that their tears produce baskets of pearls. The boy returns home to find that his neighbors have decided to judge him by his deeds rather than his appearance. Kenneth Grahame's *The Reluctant Dragon* is the droll tale of a peace-loving dragon who is forced to fight Saint George. The dragon's friend, called simply "Boy," arranges a meeting between Saint George and the dragon, and a mock fight is planned. Saint George is the hero of the day, the dragon is highly entertained at a banquet, and Boy is pleased to have saved both the dragon and Saint George. Black-line drawings by Ernest Shepard add to the subtle humor of this book.

A popular fairy tale of our time for adults and children is the haunting story *The Little Prince* by Antoine de Saint-Exupéry. Written in the first person, the story tells of the author's encounter with the Little Prince in the Sahara Desert, where he has made a forced landing with his disabled plane. Bit by bit, the author learns the strange history of the Little Prince, who lives all alone on a tiny planet no larger than a house. He possesses three volcanoes, two active and one extinct, and one flower unlike any other flower in all the galaxy. However, when he sees a garden of roses, he doubts the uniqueness of his flower until a fox shows him that what we love is always unique to us. This gentle story means many things to different people, but its wisdom and beauty are for all.

A study of traditional tales and modern fairy tales can provide children with the framework for reading longer and more complex works of fantasy. The Resources for Teaching box, "Books That Introduce Aspects of Fantasy Novels," lists some of the stories and motifs and themes that connect to some of the novels discussed in the next section.

Modern Fantasy

Fantasy, like poetry, means more than it says. Underlying most of the great books of fantasy is metaphorical commentary on society today. Some children will find deeper meanings in a tale like *The Little Prince*, others will simply read it as a good story, and still others will be put off from reading it altogether because it isn't "real." Children vary in their capacity for imaginative thinking. The literal-minded child finds the suspension of reality a barrier to the enjoyment of fantasy; other children relish the opportunity to enter the world of enchantment. Children's reactions to books of modern fantasy are seldom predictable or mild; they appear to be vehemently either for or against them. Frequently teachers can help children develop a taste for fantasy by reading aloud favorite books, such as Beverly Cleary's *Ralph S. Mouse*, Jean Merrill's *The Pushcart War*, or Sid Fleischman's *The Whipping Boy*.

Evaluating Modern Fantasy

Well-written fantasy, like other fiction, has a well-constructed plot, convincing characterization, a worthwhile theme, and an appropriate style. However, additional considerations must guide the evaluation of fantasy. The primary concern is the way the author makes the fantasy believable. A variety of techniques can be used to create belief in the unbelievable. Many authors firmly ground a story in reality before gradually moving into fantasy. Not until Chapter 3 in *Charlotte's Web* does author E. B. White suggest that Fern can understand the farm animals as they talk. And even then, Fern never talks to the animals; she only listens to them. By the end of the story Fern is growing up and really is more interested in listening to Henry Fussy than to the animals. White's description of the sounds and smells of the barnyard allows readers to experience the setting as well.

Creating belief by careful attention to the detail of the setting is a technique also used by Mary Norton in *The Borrowers*. Her graphic description of the Borrowers' home beneath the clock enables the reader to visualize this domestic background and to feel what it would be like to be as small as the Borrowers.

Having one of the characters mirror the disbelief of the reader is another device for creating convincing fantasy. In *Jeremy Visick*, David Wiseman has portrayed his protagonist, Matthew, as a boy who thinks history is rubbish. Therefore, when even he is persuaded that the past lives again, the reader shares Matthew's terror as he descends to sure disaster within the depths of the Wheal Maid mine. In another well-written fantasy, *The Indian in the Cupboard* by Lynne Reid Banks, the boy Omri so respects the integrity of his toy cowboy and Indian, who have come to life, that the reader also begins to think of them as real. If they did not indeed exist, why should this thoroughly believable child take such pains with them?

The use of appropriate language adds a kind of documentation to fantasy. Underground for nearly two hundred years, the drummer uses such obsolete words as *arfish* for "afraid" in *Earthfasts*, by William Mayne, and his lack of understanding of modern words like *breakfast* seems very authentic indeed.

In *The Fox Busters*, a clever story full of wordplay and puns, Dick King-Smith creates languages for a farm community in which chickens speak Hennish while the foxes speak Volpine. When one of the hens curses, using "fowl language," she tells a fox, "Go fricassee yourself," and calls a human a "stupid scrambled boy." The hens are named after famous farm-implement companies like Massey-Harris or Allis-Chalmers, which adds further authenticity to this delightful fantasy.

The proof of real objects gives an added dimension of truth in books. How can we explain the origin of

Resources for Teaching
Books That Introduce Aspects of Fantasy Novels

Book, Author	Motif, Theme, or Topic	Fantasy Novel
Tam Lin (Yolen) *Wild Robin* (Jeffers) *Tam Lin* (Cooper)	Shape changing	*The Haunted Mountain* (Hunter) *Owl in Love* (Kindl) *The Moorchild* (McGraw)
The Soup Stone (Van Rynbach) *Stone Soup* (Stewig) *Stone Soup* (Brown	"Stone soup" motif	*The Cat Who Wished to Be a Man* (Alexander)
The Tunnel (Browne) *The Snow Queen* (Andersen) *Elizabeth and the Water Troll* (Wangerin) *Beauty and the Beast* (de Beaumont)	Transformation by love	*The Lion, the Witch, and the Wardrobe* (Lewis) *Amy's Eyes* (Kennedy) *A Wrinkle in Time* (L'Engle)
The Seal Mother (Gerstein) *The Selkie Girl* (Cooper) *Greyling* (Yolen)	Selkie legend	*A Stranger Came Ashore* (Hunter) *Seal Child* (Peck)
Rumpelstiltskin (Grimm brothers) *Duffy and the Devil* (Zemach)	Power of naming	*A Wizard of Earthsea* (Le Guin)
Dove Isabeau (Yolen) *St. George and the Dragon* (Hodges) *The City of Dragons* (Yep)	Nature of dragons	*The Hobbit* (Tolkien) *Dragon's Blood* (Yolen) *Dealing with Dragons* (Wrede) *The Dragon of the Lost Sea* (Yep)

Greta's kitten or her father's penknife if not from Blue Cove in Julia Sauer's story *Fog Magic*? In *Tom's Midnight Garden* by Philippa Pearce, it is the discovery of a pair of ice skates that confirms the reader's belief in Tom's adventures.

Another point to be considered when evaluating fantasy is the consistency of the story. Each fantasy should have a logical framework and an internal consistency in the world set forth by the author. For instance, characters should not become invisible whenever they face difficulty unless invisibility is a well-established part of their natures. The laws of fantasy may be strange indeed, but they must be obeyed.

Lloyd Alexander, master of the craft of writing fantasy, explains the importance of internal consistency within the well-written fantasy:

Once committed to his imaginary kingdom, the writer is not a monarch but a subject. Characters must appear plausible in their own setting, and the writer must go along with the inner logic. Happenings should have logical implications. Details should be tested for consistency. Shall animals speak? If so, do *all* animals speak? If not, then which—and how?

Above all, why? Is it essential to the story, or lamely cute? Are there enchantments? How powerful? If an enchanter can perform such-and-such, can he not also do so-and-so?[10]

Finally, while all plots should be original, the plots of fantasy must be ingenious and creative. A contrived or trite plot seems more obvious in a fanciful tale than in a realistic story.

Modern fantasy makes special demands on authors. The Guidelines box "Evaluating Modern Fantasy" summarizes the criteria that need to be considered when evaluating this genre for children.

Animal Fantasy

Children might first be introduced to fantasy through tales of talking animals, toys, and dolls. The young child frequently ascribes powers of thought and speech to pets

[10]Lloyd Alexander, "The Flat-Heeled Muse," in *Children and Literature*, ed. Virginia Haviland (Glenview, Ill.: Scott, Foresman, 1973), p. 243.

Guidelines:
Evaluating Modern Fantasy

The following specific questions might guide an evaluation of modern fantasy.

What are the fantasy elements of the story?

How has the author made the story believable?

Is the story logical and consistent within the framework established by the author?

Is the plot original and ingenious?

Is there a universal truth underlying the metaphor of the fantasy?

How does the story compare to other books of the same kind or by the same author?

or toys and might already be acquainted with some of the Beatrix Potter stories or the more sophisticated tales of William Steig.

A humorous introduction to animal fantasy is *Bunnicula* by Deborah and James Howe. When the Monroe family return from seeing the movie *Dracula* with a small rabbit they found on a theater seat, the family cat, Chester, is immediately suspicious. Evidence mounts up: A note written in an obscure Transylvanian dialect is tied around the rabbit's neck; in the kitchen a white tomato and other vegetables appear drained of their juices; and the rabbit can go in and out of his locked cage. Is Bunnicula a vampire? Chester is convinced of it, and his efforts to protect the Monroes are laconically observed and recounted by Harold, the family dog. Older children can appreciate Harold's clever observations and his very doglike concern for food. There are several pun-filled sequels in this series, including *The Celery Stalks at Midnight* and *Howliday Inn*.

Other introductions to animal fantasy are Beverly Cleary's *The Mouse and the Motorcycle*, *Runaway Ralph*, and *Ralph S. Mouse*. In the first story, Ralph makes friends with a boy who gives him a small toy motorcycle. *Runaway Ralph* continues Ralph's adventures with the motorcycle. In the third story, to escape his jealous mouse relatives, Ralph goes to school in the pocket of his friend Ryan, becomes a class project, and loses his precious motorcycle but gains a sports car. Cleary's excursions into the world of fantasy are as well accepted by children as are her realistic humorous stories of Henry Huggins and Ramona Quimby.

Michael Bond's Paddington series continues to please children who are just discovering the pleasures of being able to read longer books. Bond's first book, *A Bear Called Paddington*, introduces readers to the bear found in a London railway station and taken home by the Brown family. Paddington earnestly tries to help the Browns, but invariably ends up in difficulty. There are many other books in the series, and the numerous

commercial spinoffs from this popular series have made Paddington a household word.

British writer Dick King-Smith introduces Thomas, Richard, and Henry Gray, three intrepid mouse brothers, in *The Terrible Trins*. Their mother is determined that the boys will not meet the same unhappy fate as their father, who was killed at the paws of Bertha the cat. She undertakes a rigorous training schedule, the outcome of which is to produce three guerrilla fighters in the cause of mousedom. In a hilarious sequence of events the trins not only rid the house of cats but also convince Farmer and Mrs. Budge, the human owners, that mice are pretty good companions to have around. The title character of Avi's *Poppy* is an equally fearless mouse heroine who is willing to brave the terrible Mr. Oxcax, an owl bully who has run a protection racket in Dimwood Forest for years. Poppy defeats the owl bully with the help of a grumpy porcupine and finds a desperately needed new home for her large mouse family.

In another mouse story, poet Lilian Moore gives younger readers a chance to think about the art of poetry. In *I'll Meet You at the Cucumbers*, Adam, a country mouse, shares his love for his natural surroundings with his mouse pen-pal friend, Amanda, who lives in the city. When he finally visits Amanda, Adam is nearly overwhelmed by all that the city has to offer. But his best discovery is the library, where Amanda tells him about human story hour and all the wonderful stories humans have written about mice. Amanda finally shows Adam that the thoughts he has written to her are really poems when she reads aloud poetry by Judith Thurman and Valerie Worth. In this gentle and humorous book, Moore skirts the "city mouse/country mouse" issue of which place is best in order to deal with larger themes. She helps readers think about the value of new experiences and new friendships, and the way poetry helps us see the world from a fresh perspective.

Adam and Amanda might have enjoyed the gentle and poignant tale of *The Mousewife* by Rumer Godden, a story of the friendship between an industrious mouse and a caged turtledove. Reminiscent of Hans Christian Andersen tales, this story has been realistically illustrated by Heidi Holder with soft-pencil drawings emphasizing the limited sphere of the mousewife's world.

The same qualities of wonder and tenderness are found in the story of a small brown bat who becomes a poet in Randall Jarrell's *The Bat-Poet.* A perfect story and a commentary on the writing of poetry itself, it features a bat who cannot sleep during the day and makes up poems. The other bats aren't interested, and the mockingbird comments only on the form of his poem. The chipmunk, however, is delighted with his poems and believes them. The fine pen-and-ink drawings by Maurice Sendak are as faithful to the world of nature as are the animals and the poetry in this story.

Unquestionably the most beloved animal fantasy of our time is E. B. White's delightful tale *Charlotte's Web.* While much of our fantasy is of English origin, *Charlotte's Web* is as American as the Fourth of July and just as much a part of our children's heritage. Eight-year-old Fern can understand all of the animals in the barnyard—the geese who always speak in triplicate ("certainly-ertainly-ertainly"), the wise old sheep, and Templeton, the crafty rat—yet she cannot communicate with them. The true heroine of the story is Charlotte A. Cavatica—a beautiful large gray spider who befriends Wilbur, a humble little pig. When the kindly old sheep inadvertently drops the news that as soon as Wilbur is nice and fat he will be butchered, Charlotte promises to save the hysterical pig. By miraculously spinning words into her web that describe the pig as "radiant," "terrific," and "humble," she makes Wilbur famous. The pig is saved, but Charlotte dies alone at the fairgrounds. Wilbur manages to bring Charlotte's egg sac back to the farm so that the continuity of life in the barnyard is maintained. Wilbur never forgets his friend Charlotte, though he loves her children and grandchildren dearly. Because of her, Wilbur may look forward to a secure and pleasant old age:

> Life in the barn was very good—night and day, winter and summer, spring and fall, dull days and bright days. It was the best place to be, thought Wilbur, this warm delicious cellar, with the garrulous geese, the changing seasons, the heat of the sun, the passage of swallows, the nearness of rats, the sameness of sheep, the love of spiders, the smell of manure, and the glory of everything.[11]

A loyal Charlotte spins out her opinion of her friend Wilbur in Garth Williams's illustration for E. B. White's *Charlotte's Web.*
Illustration copyright renewed © 1980 by Garth Williams. Used by permission of HarperCollins Publishers, New York, NY.

This story has humor, pathos, wisdom, and beauty. Its major themes speak of the web of true friendship and the cycle of life and death. All ages find meaning in this most popular fantasy.

Children also enjoy two other animal fantasies by White, *Stuart Little* and *The Trumpet of the Swan.* Neither book has all the strengths of *Charlotte's Web,* but both appeal to children for their curious blend of fantasy and reality.

The English counterpart of Wilbur the pig is Daggie Dogfoot, the runt hero of Dick King-Smith's *Pigs Might Fly.* Saved from the Pigman's club by luck and his own determination, Daggie watches birds and aspires to fly. He discovers instead a talent for swimming that allows him to help rescue all the pigs from a flood. Like E. B. White's barn, the pigyard and pastures here are described in sharp, sensory detail, and the animals' conversation reflects the author's shrewd perceptions about human as well as animal nature. Another pig hero is King-Smith's *Babe: The Gallant Pig,* whose remarkable ability to speak politely to sheep gains him a stunning victory in a sheepdog trial meet. In *Ace: The Very Important Pig,* Babe's great-grandson even manages to communicate with his owner in this joyful and absurd continuation of a barnyard saga.

---

[11] E. B. White, *Charlotte's Web,* illustrations Garth Williams (New York: Harper & Row, 1952), p. 183.

In *Rabbit Hill*, Robert Lawson has written a satisfying and tender story about all the little animals who live on Rabbit Hill. When they discover that new folks are moving into the big house on the hill, they are worried: Will they be planting folks who like small animals, or shiftless, mean people? Although on probation for several days after their arrival, the new folks win approval by putting up a large sign that says: "Please Drive Carefully on Account of Small Animals." *The Tough Winter* is a sequel to *Rabbit Hill*, describing the plight of all the animals when the "Folks" go away for the winter and leave a neglectful caretaker and a mean dog in charge.

The urban counterpart of *Charlotte's Web* and *Rabbit Hill* is *The Cricket in Times Square* by George Selden. A fast-talking Broadway mouse named Tucker and his pal, Harry the Cat, initiate a small country cricket called Chester into the vagaries of city living. Chester spends the summer in New York City, having been transported there in someone's picnic basket. The climax of Chester's summer adventures comes when the cricket begins giving nightly concerts from the Bellinis' newsstand, saving his benefactors from bankruptcy. In several sequels the animal friends reunite for further adventures. In all these warm and witty books, illustrator Garth Williams creates human expressions for the animals to complement their very real personalities.

Garth Williams also illustrated Margery Sharp's series of tongue-in-cheek melodramas about the pure and beautiful white mouse Miss Bianca. The first story, *The Rescuers*, tells of the breathtaking adventure of three mice—Miss Bianca, Bernard, and Nils—as they rescue a Norwegian poet from the grim, windowless Black Castle. *Miss Bianca*, *The Turret*, and *Miss Bianca in the Salt Mines* continue the adventures of these intrepid mice.

In chronicling the year-long survival of a mouse on an island, William Steig firmly establishes himself as a superb author as well as illustrator. *Abel's Island* details the survival of Abel, a very Victorian mouse, who is trapped on an island after being caught in a torrential rainstorm. Left on his own, this rodent Crusoe finds a hollow log and learns to feed off the land. In addition to battling physical elements, he overcomes the psychological fears of loneliness and overwhelming despair. Finally, after almost a year of foraging for himself, Abel is able, and easily swims the distance to shore. Creating more than a mouse melodrama, Steig shows us what qualities help a mouse or person survive. Abel relies on his resourcefulness, but he is kept alive by his love for his wife Amanda, his art, his friendship with a forgetful frog, and his joy of life.

Using the patterns familiar to folktale readers, Steig has also written *Dominic*, the story of an adventuring dog who meets good and evil on his road to happiness, and *The Real Thief*, a tale of a goose wrongly accused.

Abel contemplates his fate from the sheltered branch of his home away from home in William Steig's *Abel's Island.*
Jacket from *Abel's Island* by William Steig. Copyright © 1976 by William Steig. Reprinted by permission of Farrar, Straus & Giroux, Inc.

Children delight in Steig's use of language and his allusions to traditional literature's settings, themes, and characters.[12]

The Warm Place by Nancy Farmer is also an animal survival story. It begins in a game park in Africa, then moves to California and then into a magical netherworld that includes such characters as Gross Green Sea Going Sargasso Snails and a terrible family of demons called the Slopes. When Ruva, a young giraffe, is kidnapped and taken to a zoo in San Francisco, she is determined to escape and find her home, the warm place she can sense in her heart. At the zoo, she makes friends with Nelson, a chameleon, and Troll, a rat; the three escape and manage to stow away on a yacht heading for

[12]See "The Real Thief: Reading Like a Writer" in Joy Moss's *Focus Units on Literature: A Context for Literacy Learning* (Katonah, N.Y.: Richard C. Owen, 1990) for a discussion of this book's classroom use and its impact on older elementary school readers.

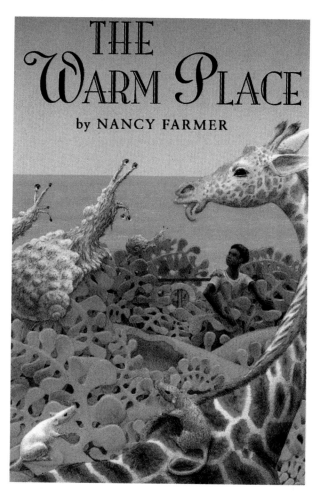

THE WARM PLACE
by NANCY FARMER

Animals and other fantastic characters join a human child named Jabila for marvelous adventures in Nancy Farmer's *The Warm Place.*

From *The Warm Place* by Nancy Farmer. Jacket illustration copyright © 1995 by Matthew Henry. Reprinted by permission of the Publisher, Orchard Books, New York.

Africa. Unfortunately the boat is manned by the entire evil Slope family. Fortunately Rodentus von Stroheim the Third, the Tawny Prince of rats, and a human boy named Jabila are aboard. The group manages to scuttle the ship in the middle of the Sargasso sea, ridding the world of Slopes (or almost all the Slopes) forever. Ruva is returned to her grassland home and the others sail off, perhaps for more adventures. This charming story defies easy classification, but the fast-moving plot and amusing characterization should appeal to middle-grade readers.

What E. B. White did to popularize and humanize spiders, Robert C. O'Brien has accomplished for rats in *Mrs. Frisby and the Rats of NIMH.* Part of the story, which could be categorized either as animal fantasy or as science fiction, concerns the widowed mouse Mrs. Frisby and her efforts to save her family and their cement-block house in the garden from the spring plowing. The

other part gradually reveals the history of a remarkable band of rats who—along with Mrs. Frisby's late husband—were trained to read and write in a laboratory at NIMH (National Institute for Mental Health—although it is never so identified in the story). When Mrs. Frisby meets the rats of NIMH, they are just completing a plan to move to a wilderness preserve where they can establish a self-sufficient community. The rats agree to help move the cement block, thus saving Mrs. Frisby's family, and she returns the favor by warning them about government exterminators who are coming with cyanide gas. Jane Conly, O'Brien's daughter, has written two sequels. In *Racso and the Rats of NIMH,* Mrs. Frisby's son Timothy meets Racso, a cocky and street-wise rat from the city, locates the rat preserve, and cooperates with the rats to thwart the building of a dam that would flood their home. *R-T, Margaret, and the Rats of NIMH* introduces the danger two lost children pose to a nervous rat colony. Short chapters, fast-moving plots advanced frequently by conversation, and memorable characters help make these longer books accessible and exciting to readers. The Teaching Feature on keeping journals shows how journals helped sixth graders respond to *Mrs. Frisby and the Rats of NIMH.*

The well-loved *The Wind in the Willows* by Kenneth Grahame endures even though it is slow-paced, idyllic, and more sentimental than more modern animal fantasy. It is the story of four friends: kindly and gruff old Badger, practical and good-natured Ratty, gullible Mole, and boisterous, expansive, and easily misled Toad. Toad gets into one scrape after another, and the other three loyally rescue their errant friend and finally save his elegant mansion from a band of wicked weasels and stoats. The themes of friendship, the importance of a home place, and the love of nature pervade this pastoral fantasy. Not all children have the experience or patience with words to appreciate this book, but generations of parents have read it aloud a chapter at a time, which is perhaps the best way to introduce the book. One other way would be to share Adrienne Adam's beautifully illustrated picture book of just the first chapter, titled *The River Bank,* or one of two excerpts illustrated by Beverly Gooding, *The Open Road* and *Wayfarers All: From the Wind in the Willows.*

The villainous animals threatening Toad Hall in *The Wind in the Willows* are the same sorts who threaten Redwall Abbey in Brian Jacques's Redwall books. But this series is swiftly told, complexly plotted, and action-packed by comparison. *Redwall* tells of Matthias, a clumsy, young, and peace-loving mouse who galvanizes himself to defeat the evil rat, Cluny the Scourge. Aided by Cornflower the Fieldmouse, Constance the Badger, and Brother Methuselah, Matthias's efforts to fortify the Abbey alternate with chapters of the terrible Cluny

In September, a sixth-grade language arts teacher asked her students to keep a journal and react to Robert C. O'Brien's *Mrs. Frisby and the Rats of NIMH.* She divided the book into about ten parts, and children responded in their journals after reading each assignment. The diversity of children's responses showed how differently individual readers engage with a story.

One girl challenged the believability of this fantasy: "I wonder where Mr. Ages gets the paper for the bags for medicine? . . . I wonder how Mrs. Frisby can hold on to Jeremy's back. She's too small to wrap her 'arms' around it. I also wonder how mice can understand people talk." The teacher acknowledged her concerns and invited her to try to find some answers. She also reminded her that this was an animal fantasy that had its own rules.

Another girl sympathized with Mrs. Frisby's very modern predicament and mused about the humor of the story: "Mrs. Frisby has a lot on her mind being a single parent with four children and one sick in bed with pneumonia. I would feel really pressured like that and Moving Day coming. . . . I like the crow Jeremy. He's funny and stupid. He picked up the string because it was *sparkly.* (That's cute.)" The teacher called attention to the way an author creates believability when she wrote back, "O'Brien has given the crow some human characteristics but has kept the animal habits faithful to the species."

Children asked questions: "I don't understand what the Boniface Estate is," said one. "I still have a question. What does *NIMH* stand for?" asked another. A third lamented,

"All my questions aren't answered yet. I may seem like a bottomless pit of questions." The teacher reassured them that it is fine to have questions, clarified meanings, or referred a child to a classmate or back to a page in the book.

Some children worried about the morality of experimenting on animals: "I am very very very very very mad that they give those poor rats shocks plus giving the rats injections. I think it is very mean." "It made me wonder if given injections, animals are in as much pain as they look." The teacher asked children to talk about the animal experimentation in this story and scientific experimentation in general.

In their final journal entries, some children were dissatisfied with the ending. "I think he should have put more pictures in and made the story a couple of chapters longer. He should have said something about like how Jeremy had a family." "Who died in the rat hole?" Others found the sequels and filled themselves in on what happened next.

Writing journals allowed the children to work out the meaning of the story for themselves. They also revealed themselves to the teacher in ways that would help her plan discussions, choose books, select writing topics, and diversify instruction for the rest of the school year.

Based on journals selected from the sixth-grade language arts class taught by Susan Steinberg, George Mason Elementary School, Alexandria, Virginia

---

subduing woodland creatures to his will. The sinister names of Cluny's band (*Fangborn, Cheesethief, Ragear, Mangefur*) alert young readers to the evil characters. In fact, one of the major appeals of the story is that one never doubts that good will triumph. *Mossflower* and *Martin the Warrior* are prequels to *Redwall* and detail the escapades of the founder of Redwall. In *Mattimeo,* Matthias's son is kidnapped along with other animals and led to the underground rat kingdom of Malkarris. In *Mariel of Redwall,* a feisty mousemaid leads a successful fight to recover the bell her father made for the Abbey. *Salamandastron* is the story of Urthstripe the Strong, a badger who leads his warriors against Ferhago the Assassin in defense of Redwall Abbey and the fortress of Salamandastron. In *The Bellmaker* Mariel and her friend Dandin are locked in combat with the villainous foxwolf, Urgan Nagru, while her father Joseph the Bellmaker sets out by sea with an unlikely band of characters to come to her aid. This series resembles high fantasy (discussed later in this chapter), in that

good and evil battle for possession of the Redwall Abbey world; quests are undertaken; the heroes are small, unprepared, and sometimes unwilling; and courage, truth, wisdom, and goodness are finally rewarded. Even though these books are long, they provide satisfaction to readers who enjoy adventurous quests, humor, and intrigue but are not yet ready for the deeper themes, ambiguous characters, or created worlds of high fantasy.

When *Watership Down* by Richard Adams was first published in England, one reviewer maintained that the "story is what one might expect had *The Wind in the Willows* been written after two world wars, various marks of nuclear bomb, the Korean and Vietnam obscenities and half a dozen other hells created by the inexhaustibly evil powers of man."[13] Published as adult

---

[13]Aidan Chambers, "Letter from England: Great Leaping Lapins!" *Horn Book Magazine,* June 1973, p. 255.

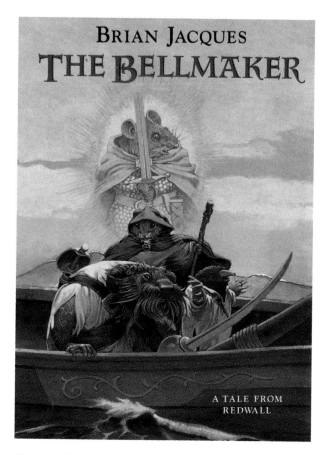

BRIAN JACQUES
THE BELLMAKER

A TALE FROM REDWALL

Mariel and other characters from the world of Redwall Abbey undertake a dangerous quest in Brian Jacques's *The Bellmaker*.

From *The Bellmaker* by Brian Jacques. Copyright © 1995 by The Putnam & Grosset Group, New York, NY. Reprinted by permission.

moving story, a rabbit redeemer braves the palace of death to offer his own life for his people. And at the end of the book, when one of the does tells her little one a new story of El-ahrairah, we know that she is telling a garbled version of the story of the establishment of Watership Down and adding Hazel's accomplishments to those of the legendary rabbit—a comment on the entire process of mythmaking.

The World of Toys and Dolls

As authors have endowed animals with human characteristics, so, too, have they personified toys and dolls. Young children enjoy stories that bring inanimate objects such as a tugboat or a steamshovel to life. Seven-, 8-, and 9-year-olds still like to imagine that their favorite playthings have a life of their own. Hans Christian Andersen appealed to this in "The Steadfast Tin Soldier," "The Fir Tree," and many other stories.

Probably no one has made toys seem quite so much like people as has A. A. Milne in his well-loved Pooh stories. Each chapter contains a separate adventure about the favorite stuffed toys of Milne's son, Christopher Robin. The good companions introduced in *Winnie-the-Pooh* include Winnie-the-Pooh, "a bear of little brain"; Eeyore, the doleful donkey; Piglet, the happy follower and devoted friend of Pooh; and Rabbit, Owl, Kanga, and little Roo. A bouncy new friend, Tigger, joins the group in Milne's second book, *The House at Pooh Corner*. They all live in the "100 Aker Wood" and spend most of their time getting into—and out of—exciting and amusing situations. Eight- and 9-year-olds thoroughly enjoy the humor of the Heffalump story, the self-pity of gloomy Eeyore on his birthday, and kindly but forgetful Pooh, who knocks at his own door and then wonders why no one answers. The humor in these stories is not hilarious but quiet, whimsical, and subtle. Such humor is usually lost on young children but greatly appreciated by third graders. However, younger children might enjoy the Pooh stories when they are read within a family circle. Parents' chuckles are contagious, and soon everyone in the family becomes a Pooh admirer.

Miss Hickory by Carolyn Bailey is the story of a unique country doll whose body is an applewood twig and whose head is a hickory nut. Miss Hickory has all the common sense and forthright qualities that her name implies. She survives a severe New Hampshire winter in the company of her friends—Crow, Bull Frog, Ground Hog, and Squirrel. Rumer Godden also makes the world of toys seem very much alive in several of her books—*The Dolls' House, Fu-Dog, Miss Happiness and Miss Flower,* and *Little Plum.* The idea expressed in all Godden's doll books is stated best by

fiction in the United States, this remarkable story of a rabbit band who cherish their freedom enough to fight for it is presented in a lengthy and complex book inaccessible to many children. Adams has created a complete rabbit civilization including a history, a religion, a mythology, and even a lapine language with a partial set of accompanying linguistic rules. The central character is Hazel, a young buck who leads a little band of bucks away from their old warren that is doomed by a new housing tract. He does so reluctantly but at the urging of his younger and weaker brother, Fiver, who has a form of extrasensory perception. The slow, steady growth of Hazel as a leader is told in this surprisingly unsentimental, even tough, story. It is more realistic than most "realism," because the story is firmly rooted in a world we know: Rabbits mate, make droppings, and talk and joke about both, very much as humans do. They get hurt, bleed, and suffer; they grow ugly with age, and they die. During their storytelling sessions readers learn of El-ahrairah, the great chief rabbit and trickster. In a remarkable creation legend and a deeply

Toddie in *The Dolls' House.* She says: "It is an anxious, sometimes a dangerous thing to be a doll. Dolls cannot choose; they can only be chosen; they cannot 'do'; they can only be done by" (p. 13).

A doll who tries to "do" rather than be "done by" is portrayed in *Caitlin's Holiday* by Helen V. Griffith. Visiting a resale shop, Caitlin trades her old doll for the most perfect doll she has ever seen. But when the doll comes to life, she is rude and self-centered. Holiday, the doll, insists on spending Caitlin's allowance on fancy doll clothes and refuses to play with Caitlin and her friends. After trying to reason with the amoral doll, Caitlin angrily relegates her to the garage, where she scares a would-be intruder and redeems herself.

In the *The Mennyms, The Mennyms in the Wilderness,* and *The Mennyms Under Siege,* Sylvia Waugh has created a family of three generations who have survived after the death of the old woman who made them.

> They were not human you see—at least not in the normal sense of the word. They were not made of flesh and blood. They were just a whole lovely family of life-size ragdolls. They were living and walking and talking and breathing, but they were made of cloth and kapok. They each had a little voicebox, like the sort they put in teddy bears to make them growl realistically. Their frameworks were strong but pliable. Their respiration kept their bodies supplied with oxygen that was life to the kapok and sound to the voices. (p. 17)

These are fully realized characters, doll-like only in that they are made of cloth and stuffing. Otherwise they have the same idiosyncrasies, quarrels, and desires as any other family, and these conflicts are played out in all three tautly paced stories. In *The Mennyms* they are faced with the threat of discovery after successfully hiding their secret for forty years. In trying to avoid this disaster, they discover a new sister hidden in an old trunk in the attic. In *The Mennyms in the Wilderness,* Brocklehurst Grove, the only home they have ever known, is threatened by a superhighway. The ghost of their creator appears to her human nephew and urges him to go to their aid. At first Albert Pond, a shy and lonely professor, is somewhat dazed by their existence. However, he becomes enmeshed in the Mennyms' personalities and problems as he seeks a solution to their dilemma, and he grows to love and appreciate being a part of their unusual world. In the third book in the series, *The Mennyms Under Siege,* the family secret is in danger of being revealed by an impetuous Mennym and a nosy neighbor. The Mennym family members are so beautifully realized that children will be reluctant to close the covers of these imaginative books.

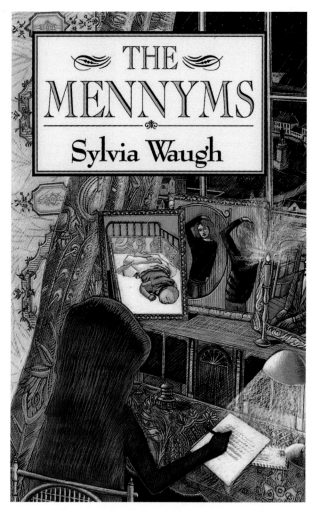

Sylvia Waugh has created a remarkable series about the Mennyms, a family of life-size rag dolls.
Cover of *The Mennyms* by Sylvia Waugh. Jacket illustration by Richard Ross. Jacket illustration copyright © 1994 by James McMullan. By permission of Greenwillow Books, a division of William Morrow & Company, Inc.

In *The Indian in the Cupboard* by Lynne Reid Banks, a toy plastic Indian comes to life when Omri puts it inside a cupboard, locks it, and then unlocks it with a special key. Nine-year-old Omri feels pride and responsibility in caring for "his" Indian, Little Bear, and is quickly involved in providing for his needs. But trouble begins when Omri's friend Patrick places a cowboy in the cupboard. The British author uses stereotypical language in this and the other books in the series ("Little Bear fight like mountain lion. Take many scalps!"), but the characters transcend this in their growing concern for each other's welfare. Banks suggests once again to readers that we are responsible for what we have tamed or brought to life. *The Return of the Indian* carries Omri back to Little Bear's world. *The Secret of the Indian* takes place in a contemporary setting where Omri and the tiny beings frighten "skinhead" robbers away. In *The Mystery of the Cupboard* Patrick unravels the story behind the magic cupboard's origins.

Elizabeth Winthrop's *The Castle in the Attic* also examines responsibility for one's own actions. Although an accomplished gymnast, 10-year-old William lacks confidence in himself. When he hears that Mrs. Phillips, his lifelong friend and live-in baby-sitter, is returning to her native England, he is crushed but determined to find a way to make her stay. Inside her parting gift, a huge model of a castle that has been in her family for generations, William discovers a tiny lead knight that comes to life at his touch. The knight shows William a charm that can be used to miniaturize objects or people, and William uses it to reduce his baby-sitter to toy size and keep her in the castle. Regretting this hasty act, he submits himself to the charm, travels back in time with the knight, and recovers the amulet that will reverse the spell. On this quest William discovers unexpected strengths in himself. He returns victorious, prepared to wish Mrs. Phillips farewell. In *The Battle for the Castle* Mrs. Phillips sends William a magic token for his twelfth birthday; twelve was the age at which a young man could be trained as a squire in the Middle Ages. The token allows William to return to the land of the castle, where further adventures teach him about love, courage, and loyalty. The strong grounding in reality and the elaborately described castle give these fantasies special appeal for upper elementary students.

The inventive plot and memorable characters created by Richard Kennedy in *Amy's Eyes* help sustain reader interest in this lengthy but compelling story. Amy, left at an orphanage by her sailor father, is delighted when her sailor doll comes to life. Pining for her father, she eventually turns into a doll herself, and sets off with her sailor doll on a voyage to hunt for treasure. Together with a decidedly odd crew, they eventually outwit the pirate Goldnose and discover Amy's father, but not without paying a terrible price. The language is unusual, often poetic, and frequent humorous passages move the story to its serious conclusion. While fourth graders have enjoyed hearing the story read aloud, its length, complexity, and numerous philosophical and nautical digressions make it more suitable for older and more proficient readers of fantasy.

Another strangely cruel yet tender tale by Russell Hoban, *The Mouse and His Child*, tells of two windup toys and their efforts to become "self-winding." New and shiny in the toy shop the day before Christmas, the naive little toys end up on the rubbish heap in the cruel clutches of Manny Rat. In their long and tedious journey, they search for a home, a family, and "their territory." The story is not a gentle one. It is filled with images of death and decay, violence and vengeance, tears and laughter. Like *Alice's Adventures in Wonderland*, the complex ideas, satire, and symbolism might appeal more to adults than to children. Yet it is a fantasy that is not easily forgotten.

Eccentric Characters and Preposterous Situations

Many fantasies for children are based on eccentric characters or preposterous situations. Cars or people might fly, eggs might hatch into dinosaurs or dragons, ancient magical beings might come up against modern technology. Often these characters and situations occur in otherwise very normal settings—which allows readers to believe more readily.

Pippi Longstocking, a notoriously funny character created by Astrid Lindgren, has delighted children for more than forty years. Pippi is an orphan who lives alone with her monkey and her horse in a child's utopian world where she tells herself when to go to bed and when to get up! Although she is only 9 years old, Pippi can hold her own with anyone, for she is so strong that she can pick up a horse or a man and throw him into the air. Children love this amazing character who always has the integrity to say what she thinks, even if she shocks adults. Seven-, 8-, and 9-year-olds enjoy her madcap adventures in *Pippi Longstocking* and in the sequels, *Pippi Goes on Board*, *Pippi in the South Seas*, and *Pippi on the Run*.

When the east wind blew the title character of P. L. Travers's *Mary Poppins* into the Bankses' house in London to care for Michael and Jane, it blew her into the hearts of many thousands of readers. Wearing her shapeless hat and white gloves, carrying her parrot-handled umbrella and a large carpetbag, Mary Poppins is as British as tea, yet many children in the United States also love this nursemaid with strange magical powers. Nothing seems impossible for this prim autocrat of the nursery, and she goes serenely on her way through other funny adventures in *Mary Poppins Comes Back*, *Mary Poppins Opens the Door*, and *Mary Poppins in the Park*.

Mr. Popper's Penguins by Richard and Florence Atwater has long been the favorite funny story of many primary-grade children. Mr. Popper is a mild little house painter whose major interest in life is the study of the Antarctic. When an explorer presents Mr. Popper with a penguin, he promptly names him Captain Cook, and he obtains Greta from the zoo to keep Captain Cook company. After the arrival of ten baby penguins, Mr. Popper puts a freezing plant in the basement of his house and moves his furnace upstairs to the living room. The Atwaters' serious account of a highly implausible situation adds to the humor of this truly funny story.

In *James and the Giant Peach* by Roald Dahl, James, one of the saddest and loneliest boys in the world, lives with his wicked aunts in an old, ramshackle house on a high hill in the south of England. Given a bag of green crystals by an old man, James hurries home with them, but he trips and falls, and all of the magic crystals disappear into the ground under an old peach tree. In the enormous peach that grows on the tree, James discovers six amazing creatures who have been waiting for him—a grasshopper the size of a large dog, a giant ladybug, an enormous spider, a centipede, an earthworm, and a silkworm. Early the next morning the centipede gnaws off the stem, the huge peach rolls down the hill, incidentally crushing the aunts, and the marvelous adventure begins. This wonderful spoof on Victorian morality tales features well-drawn characters whose grumbling conversations are very believable. This book is popular with children of all ages. Its short chapters make it a good read-aloud selection for first and second graders, as well as for older children.

Allan Ahlberg's *The Giant Baby* is another book that will delight 7- to 9-year-olds. Alice Hicks desperately wants a baby brother, but her parents insist there's no room in their little house. When late one night thunderous footsteps approach the Hicks house and then fade off into silence, Alice is delighted to discover a big bundle left on the doorstep. Inside is an amazingly large baby. The Hickses are flabbergasted. Feeding the baby is a bit of a problem, and changing nappies is an even bigger difficulty. Pretty soon the giant baby is no secret in the neighborhood. The press gets wind of the story, and this brings onto the scene the Grubbling Brothers, circus people who are down on their luck, and other villains. The giant baby keeps falling into the wrong hands, but Alice and her friends keep rescuing him. Finally the biggest rescue of all occurs when the giant baby's giant mother returns for her "little baby." Alice, who "had wanted a baby brother, got one and lost him," is inconsolable. But happily after all, Mr. and Mrs. Hicks had gotten quite attached to the big baby, so at the very end Alice is invited to the hospital to meet her new and "proper size" baby brother. This is a delightful story told with wit and warm good humor that is given added zest by Fritz Wegner's pen-and-ink illustrations.

Older readers will find similar enjoyment in Patricia Kindl's *Owl in Love*. Owl Tycho is an unusual 14-year-old who belongs to a family of shape shifters, and she has the ability to change into an owl. This causes great distress for her as she tries to fit into the teenage world. She can't eat in the cafeteria because her diet consists of grasshoppers and mice. She can't participate in the science class experiment on blood types because her blood is black. And worst of all she is madly in love with her science teacher and state law says they cannot marry for several more years. This hilarious story finds Owl as troubled and torn as any other youngster trying to deal with the changing body and shifting emotions of adolescence, and her journey to self-understanding is no less poignant because it takes place in a tree in the cool night air as often as at a desk in a brightly lit classroom. Kindl's characterization is flawless and her sense of humor right on target for middle-school readers.

Younger children will fall in love with Hob, a brownie-like creature whose job is to be helpful to humans in William Mayne's *Hob and the Goblins*. "He tidies away abandoned things, like scraps of quarrel, or pieces of spite. He banishes small troubles, makes ghosts happy, soothes tired curtains, charms kettles into singing, and stops milk sulking" (p. 6). He has been out of practice for some time when he adopts a new family. They don't realize that their new house sits atop a crock of gold that is coveted by all manner of dwarfs, witches, gremlins, and a goblin king, but Hob does—and his humble talents are put to the test in a charming tale with a rollicking finale. This endearing character's roots in folklore will be familiar to children who have read "The Elves and the Shoemaker" and other stories about mythical creatures, and who may be delighted to find his relatives in Tolkien's *The Hobbitt*.

The title character of Susan Cooper's *The Boggart* is another ancient sort who must wrestle with the modern world. When a Canadian family inherits an old Scottish castle, they do not realize that the property includes the Boggart, an ancient and mischievous spirit. Trapped in a desk that the family ships back to Canada, the Boggart discovers a new world of technological wonders. His pranks, however, wreak havoc on the Volnik family, who blame each other for the Boggart's tricks. A solution is found only when the Volnick children and the Boggart enter the world of computer "magic" and the Boggart is returned to his familiar world. The beauty of Cooper's story lies as much in the Boggart's thoroughly developed character as in the story's well-paced plot. The Boggart is not simply a naughty spirit but one who has feelings and needs friends and companionship as much as any human child does.

Technology of a different sort is encountered in *The Twenty-One Balloons* by William Pène DuBois. Professor Sherman leaves San Francisco on 15 August 1883 in a hot air balloon, telling reporters that he hopes to be the first person to fly across the Pacific Ocean. He is picked up three weeks later in the Atlantic Ocean clinging to the wreckage of a platform that has been flown through the air by twenty-one balloons. The story, told as the professor's speech to the Explorers' Club, recounts his forced landing on the volcanic island of Krakatoa, where he discovers twenty families who live over the most fabulous diamond mine in the world. The professor describes in graphic detail the inventions and customs of Krakatoans and their escape when the volcano erupts. As usual, DuBois's minute descriptions are matched only by the meticulous perfection of his pen-and-ink drawings.

It seems preposterous to try to raise a dinosaur in a small New Hampshire town. However, that is precisely what Nate Twitchell does in Oliver Butterworth's *The Enormous Egg* when the egg he is taking care of hatches into a baby triceratops. Consulted about the problem, members of Congress attempt to have "Uncle Beazley" (the dinosaur) destroyed, since he is extinct and probably un-American! This satire on U.S. politics is a delightful mixture of humor and truth.

A preposterous situation is presented in one of the few satires really enjoyed by children, Jean Merrill's *The Pushcart War*. The story is presented as a "documented report" of the famous Pushcart War of 1996 (more than thirty years in the future when the book was first published). Believing that we cannot have peace in the world unless people understand how wars start, the "author-historian" proceeds to describe the beginning of the war, between the giant trucks of New York City and the pushcarts, that began when Mack, driver of the Mighty Mammoth, rode down the cart of Morris the Florist. The straight-faced account of the progress of the war and the eventual triumph of the pushcart peddlers provides a funny and pathetic commentary on life today. Children thoroughly enjoy this satire; in fact, when one fifth-grade class returned for report cards on the last day of school, they stayed an extra hour to hear their teacher finish reading the book. Few books can claim such devotion!

Extraordinary Worlds

When Alice followed the White Rabbit down his rabbit hole and entered a world that grew "curiouser and curiouser," she established a pattern for many modern books of fantasy. Starting in the world of reality, they move quickly into a world where the everyday becomes extraordinary, yet still believable. The plausible impossibilities of Lewis Carroll's *Alice's Adventures in Wonderland* include potions and edibles that make poor Alice grow up and down like an elevator. At the famous "Mad Hatter's tea party" no one has the time to drink tea. The Mad Hatter, the Dormouse, and the Rabbit are just a few of the individuals Alice meets in her wanderings. Other characters include the Red Queen, who has to keep running in order to stay "in the same place"; the hurrying White Rabbit, who keeps murmuring that he'll be late yet no one knows where he is going; Humpty Dumpty, whose words mean exactly what he chooses them to mean; and the terrifying Queen of Hearts, who indiscriminately shouts, "Off with her head!" Always the proper Victorian young lady, Alice maintains her own personality despite her bizarre surroundings, and her acceptance of this nonsense makes it all seem believable. She is the one link with reality in this amazingly fantastic world.

The cyclone that blew Dorothy into the Land of Oz continues to blow swirling controversies around this series of books by L. Frank Baum and others. Some maintain that *The Wizard of Oz* is a skillfully written fantasy, a classic in its own right. Others condemn the first book because some of the forty-plus volumes that followed are poorly written. Dorothy and her companions eventually achieve their particular wishes, but the wizardry is what they do for themselves, rather than anything that the Wizard does for them. For the most part this fantasy depends on the strange situations and creatures that Dorothy and her companions meet. Adults never doubt that the four will overcome all odds and achieve their wishes. Even the Wizard holds no terror for practical, matter-of-fact Dorothy. This lack of wonder and awe— the basic ingredients of most fantasy—makes *The Wizard of Oz* seem somewhat pedestrian when compared with other stories of its kind.

For many years the Moomintroll family has delighted the children of Sweden. Strange but endearing creatures that look slightly like hippopotamuses, the Moomin live in a lonely valley with various peculiar friends. Each member of the Moomin family is an individual and remains faithful to his or her characterization throughout the series of books. *Tales from Moominvalley* by Tove Jansson is the first, and perhaps best, of this fantastic series.

Mary Norton tells a fascinating story about tiny people and their miniature world under the grandfather clock in *The Borrowers*. The Borrowers derive their names from their occupation, which is "borrowing" from human "beans," those "great slaves put there for them to use." "Borrowing" is a dangerous trade, for if one is seen by human beings, disastrous things may happen. Therefore, Pod and Homily Clock are understandably alarmed when they learn of their daughter Arrietty's desire to explore the world upstairs. Finally Pod allows Arrietty to go on an expedition with him. While Pod is borrowing fibers from the hall doormat to make a new brush for Homily, Arrietty wanders outside, where she meets the boy. Arrietty's disbelief about the number of people in the world who are the boy's size, compared to those of her size, is most convincing:

"Honestly—" began Arrietty helplessly and laughed again. "Do you really think—I mean, whatever sort of world would it be? Those great chairs . . . I've seen them. Fancy if you had to make chairs that size for everyone? And the stuff for their clothes . . . miles and miles of it . . . tents of it . . . and the sewing! And their great houses, reaching up so you can hardly see the ceilings . . . their great beds . . . the food they eat . . . great smoking mountains of it, huge bags of stew and soup and stuff." (p. 78)

Mary Norton creates a memorable miniature world in *The Borrowers*.
Illustration from *The Borrowers,* copyright © 1953, 1952 by Mary Norton and renewed 1981, 1980 by Mary Norton, Beth Krush and Joe Krush, reproduced by permission of Harcourt Brace & Company.

In the end, the Borrowers are "discovered" and flee for their lives. This surprise ending leads directly to the sequel, *The Borrowers Afield*. Strong characterizations, apt descriptions of setting, and detailed illustrations by Beth and Joe Krush make the small-scale world of the Borrowers come alive. Other titles continue the series.

The story of the Minnipins, mostly sober, sedate, and tradition-bound little folk in the Land Between the Mountains, is told in *The Gammage Cup* by Carol Kendall. When a "best village" contest is announced, the people of Slipper-on-the-Water decide that in order to win the coveted Gammage Cup, all homes must be painted green and all Minnipins must wear green. Muggles is the spokesperson for the nonconforming few who insist on bright doors and orange sashes. The rebellious ones are exiled to the mountains, where by chance they discover a threat to the village from the Minnipins' ancient enemies, the Mushrooms. Muggles and her companions sound the alarm, save the village, and are welcomed back as heroes. This well-written fantasy offers tart commentary on false values in society and the theme of the individual versus the group. Ironically, the gentle Minnipins prove to be surprisingly fierce in their encounter with the Mushrooms.

In *The Minpins*, Roald Dahl relates an illustrated story about tiny people with a similar name who live in the Forest of Sin behind Little Billy's house. One day Little Billy, who has been warned never to go beyond his garden wall, gets fed up with being coddled and heads for adventure in the forest. When he encounters the terrible Gruncher, he climbs a tree and discovers the Minpins, who live in rooms and staircases of the hollow trees.

Riding on the back of a swan, Little Billy lures the Gruncher into the lake, where it dissolves into steam and smoke. He returns home safely but his sheltered life is changed forever. Patrick Benson's charming illustrations make this a perfect read-aloud for younger children and a fine introduction to extraordinary and magical worlds.

One of the most popular fantasies for children is Dahl's tongue-in-cheek morality tale *Charlie and the Chocolate Factory*. Mr. Willie Wonka suddenly announces that the five children who find the gold seal on their chocolate bars will be allowed to visit his fabulous factory. And what an assortment of children win— Augustus Gloop, a greedy fat pig of a boy; Veruca Salt, a spoiled little rich girl; Violet Beauregarde, the world's champion gum chewer; Mike Teevee, a fresh child who spends every waking moment in front of the television set; and Charlie Bucket, a hero, who is honest, brave, trustworthy, obedient, poor, and starving. One by one the children disobey and meet with horrible accidents in the chocolate factory. Nothing, of course, happens to the virtuous Charlie, who by the story's conclusion has brought his poor family to live in the chocolate factory and is learning the business from his benefactor. The 1964 edition of this book was criticized for its stereotypical depiction of the Oompa-Loompas, black pygmies supposedly imported from Africa by Mr. Wonka and exploited as factory workers.[14] In the 1973 edition, Dahl

[14]Lois Kalb Bouchard, "A New Look at Old Favorites: 'Charlie and the Chocolate Factory'," *Interracial Books for Children* 3 (winter/spring 1971): 3, 8.

Little Billy, the sheltered hero of Roald Dahl's *The Minpins,* discovers a secret world in the forbidden forest behind his house.
From *The Minpins* by Roald Dahl, illustrated by Patrick Benson. Copyright © 1991 by Patrick Benson on illustrations. Used by permission of Viking Penguin, a division of Penguin USA Inc.

revised the text so that the Oompa-Loompas were long-haired little people imported from Loompaland. The sequel to this book, *Charlie and the Great Glass Elevator,* lacks the humor and the imaginative sparkle of the first book.

In Norton Juster's *The Phantom Tollbooth,* when Milo goes through a peculiar tollbooth he discovers a strange and curious world indeed—"The Lands Beyond," which include the Foothills of Confusion, the Mountains of Ignorance, and the Sea of Knowledge. Here Milo meets King Azaz the Unabridged, the unhappy ruler of Dictionopolis, the Mathemagician who serves them subtraction stew and increases their hunger, and the watchdog Tock, who keeps on ticking throughout their adventures. The substance of this fantasy is in its play on words rather than its characters or situations. Its appreciation is dependent on the reader's knowledge of the definitions of various words, phrases, and allusions. For this reason children with mature vocabularies particularly enjoy its humor.

Kate Gordon has traveled to a remote area on the coast of Baja California to help her father hunt for a lost Spanish galleon in T. A. Barron's *The Merlin Effect.* Kate's father is distracted by the team's failure to find the treasure ship, and Kate is bored and unhappy. Trying to rescue a trapped whale, she destroys a piece of important equipment, and their relationship is strained even further. When Kate's father is drawn into an undersea kingdom ruled by the evil spirit Nimue, Kate must use all her inner resources to retrieve the treasure of Merlin's horn and rescue her father. Although the plot sometimes seems overly complicated, children familiar with folktales and legends will recognize many elements of the story. In addition, environmental issues that are woven into this and Barron's other books may appeal to the reader who is more scientifically oriented.

In Emily Rodda's *The Pigs Are Flying!* readers are introduced to a world, "Inside," that parallels our own—with a few small differences. Rachel, sick in bed and bored, wishes something would happen and finds herself Inside with a terrible storm about to begin. During these storms, called Grunters, pigs actually do fly. Other strange things also happen during storms, so people keep tethered pigs that float in the sky during storms and thus warn everyone to get inside or risk the consequences. Since Rachel arrives during a "force ten Grunter," an elderly couple takes her in to replace their lost daughter who wandered away in a previous storm. Although people here are kind to her, Rachel longs to return to her own life Outside and finally finds the key in the children's room of the library. Porcine wordplay and funny occurrences are enhanced by Noela Young's clever black-line illustrations. A small mystery of a family friend's identity in real time neatly frames Rachel's suspenseful adventure in this extraordinary world where "pigrise" is a dangerous occasion.

Magical Powers

The children in books of fantasy often possess a magical object, know a magical saying, or have magical powers themselves. In *Half Magic* by Edward Eager, the nickel Jane finds turns out to be a magical charm, or at least half of a magical charm, for it provides half of all the children's wishes, so that half of them will come true. Eager's *Seven-Day Magic* tells of a magical book that the children borrow from the library. When they open the book, they find it is about themselves. Everything they did that morning is in the book, and the rest of the book is shut tight waiting for them to create it. Logic and humor are characteristic of the many books of fantasy that were Eager's legacy of modern magic to today's children.

Frequently, less demanding fantasy relies on magical powers, slight characterization, and fast-moving plots to interest less able readers. Scott Corbett's "trick" books, such as *The Lemonade Trick*, rely on Kirby Maxwell's use of a magic chemistry set belonging to Mrs. Greymalkin, a neighborhood witch. Greedy John Midas suffers the consequences of his newly acquired magical power, *The Chocolate Touch*, in Patrick Skene Catling's new twist on an old story. While none of these stories challenge an accomplished reader, many children come to discover the pleasures of wide reading through books such as these.

The magical object in Jon Scieszka's five Time Warp Trio stories is "The Book." In *Knights of the Kitchen Table*, the Book, a birthday present from his magician uncle, whisks Joe and his friends Fred and Sam back into King Arthur's time. The boys' quick thinking saves them from the Black Knight, a foul-smelling giant, and a fire-breathing dragon before they find their way back to modern time. In *The Not-So-Jolly Roger*, the boys materialize on the island where Blackbeard is about to bury his treasure. In *The Good, the Bad, and the Goofy, Your Mother Was a Neanderthal*, and *2095* the boys travel back to the past and into the future for more adventures. Short chapters, broad humor and gross characters, Lane Smith's quirky line illustrations, a fast-moving plot, and contemporary-sounding dialogue appeal especially to second-, third-, fourth-, and fifth-grade boys.

Jane Langton has created several stories of mystery and magical powers surrounding the Halls, who live in a strange old turreted house in Concord, Massachusetts. In *The Diamond in the Window*, Uncle Freddy had been a world-renowned authority on Emerson and Thoreau until the mysterious disappearance of his younger brother and sister left him slightly deranged. In the tower room two beds are made up in a vain hope for the return of the two children. Edward and Eleanor move to the tower room and search in their dreams for the two missing members of the family.

Peter Sis's fine line drawing depicts the orphan Touch as he escapes on a bundle of straw magically turned into a horse in *The Midnight Horse* by Sid Fleischman.
Illustration from *The Midnight Horse* by Sid Fleischman, illustrated by Peter Sis. Illustration copyright © 1990 by Peter Sis. By permission of Greenwillow Books, a division of William Morrow & Company, Inc.

Another story of the Hall family, *The Fledgling*, centers upon 8-year-old Georgie's desire, and eventual ability, to fly. She is befriended by the Goose Prince, who takes her on his back and teaches her to glide in the air by herself. Although Georgie outgrows her gift and the goose falls prey to a gun, he leaves her with a magical present—a ball that projects an image of the whole world, and the admonition "Take good care of it." Langton's descriptions give the story a warm and comfortable tone; her evocation of flying might make earthbound readers' spirits soar. Another story, *The Summer Birds* by Penelope Farmer, presents child flyers taught by a strange boy who hopes to draw them to his island to restore his birdlike race. However, Farmer's story is darker and its conclusion less hopeful than in *The Fledgling*.

In a much lighter vein, Sid Fleischman sets his fantasy *The Midnight Horse* near the New England town of Cricklewood, New Hampshire: "Population 217. 216 Fine Folks & 1 Infernal Grouch." An orphan comes to claim his inheritance from the infernal grouch, a shady judge who is his great-uncle. Fleischman, in setting the scene, minces no words:

> It was raining bullfrogs. The coach lurched and swayed along the river road like a ship in rough seas. Inside clung three passengers like unlashed cargo.
>
> One was a blacksmith, another was a thief, and the third was an orphan boy named Touch. (p. 1)

When Touch arrives in Cricklewood, Judge Wigglesforth tries to force him to sign for his inheritance, thirty-seven cents. No fool, Touch refuses to sign and escapes to a ramshackle inn. In fast-paced, humorous, short chapters, Touch discovers his real inheritance, saves the inn, and unmasks both the thief and the judge. Fleischman's ear for comic dialogue, his inspired similes, and his ability to strip a tale to its essentials make this a lively story in the same vein as his *The Whipping Boy*.

Older readers with a tolerance for invented worlds and the ability to follow a large cast of characters will enjoy the many books by Diana Wynne Jones. Stories featuring the magician Chrestomanci are a good place to begin. In *Charmed Life*, young Eric Chant (called "Cat" for short) and his conniving sister Gwendolyn are invited to live at Chrestomanci's castle. Cat is unaware of his own magical talents, but his sister has been using minor witchcraft to borrow power from him. Chrestomanci must help Cat realize his own powers while he preserves his household against the evil that assails them from outside the castle walls. *The Lives of Christopher Chant*, a prequel, is about the boyhood of Chrestomanci, who is able to dream himself into strange worlds and bring back from these places what others cannot. Like Eric he is naive about adult motives, an unwitting accomplice to his uncle's wicked plans, and an unwilling heir to the previous Chrestomanci's power. These imaginatively plotted stories reveal the author's wry humor, her love of language, and her ability to balance aspects of time and space in impossible but believable ways.

Suspense and the Supernatural

Interest in the occult and the supernatural, always an adult preoccupation, also captures the imagination of children. They enjoy spooky, scary stories, just as they like being frightened by TV or theater horror stories.[15] This may in part explain the popularity of authors like John Bellairs, whose mysteries, such as *The House with a Clock in Its Walls*, are full of spooky old houses, scary characters, fast-moving plots, and plenty of dialogue. Increasingly, publishers issue finely crafted suspense fantasies that are often superior to the usual ghost story or mystery tale. These well-written tales of suspense and the supernatural deserve attention.

Paul Fleischman's *The Half-a-Moon Inn* has the tone of a folktale and a setting to match. Born mute, 12-year-old Aaron sets off to find his mother when she becomes lost in a great snowstorm. He accidentally stumbles into the Half-a-Moon Inn, where he is imprisoned by the evil Miss Grackle, who needs a boy to tend the bewitched fires none but honest folk can kindle. Aaron's escape, his reunion with his mother, and the folktale-like demise of the witch (she freezes to death beside her unlit fireplace) provide a satisfying conclusion. The narration is lighter than the content, and the well-wrought dialogue makes this a challenging and entertaining choice for reading aloud to 9- and 10-year-olds.

In *The Mermaid Summer*, Molly Hunter explores the ancient legend of a mermaid who was thought to live near the "Drongs" and could lure poor fishermen to their deaths on these rocks. Eric Anderson refuses to believe in the legend until he nearly loses his entire fishing crew to her singing. No one will sail with Eric after that, and he is forced to leave his wife, son, and two grandchildren, named Jon and Anna, and find a place on a large ship leaving for faraway ports. When Anna and Jon trick the vain and deadly mermaid into removing the curse from their grandfather, he is able to return home. Filled with the cadenced language of the storyteller, this tale evokes the rich heritage of Scottish folklore.

Mollie Hunter has based another eerie tale, *A Stranger Came Ashore*, on the old legends of the Shetland Islands that tell of the Selkie Folk, seals who can take on human form. Only young Robbie Henderson and his grandfather are suspicious of the handsome stranger who appears in their midst on the stormy night of a shipwreck. After Old Da dies, Robbie must put together the clues that reveal the real identity of Finn Learson and the sinister nature of his interest in the golden-haired Elspeth, Robbie's sister. Events build to a fearsome climax on a night of ancient magic, when the dark powers of the sea are pitted against the common folk dressed as earth spirits and celebrating the last of the yule festival. Teachers who read aloud *A Stranger Came Ashore* find Jane Yolen's picture book *Greyling* or Susan Cooper's *The Selkie Girl* a good prior introduction to Selkie lore. Children familiar with these stories are much more sensitive to Hunter's use of foreshadowing, folk beliefs, mood, and setting in this finely crafted novel.

---

[15]See Carl M. Tomlinson and Micheal O. Tunnell, "Children's Supernatural Stories: Popular but Persecuted," in *Censorship: A Threat to Reading Thinking and Learning*, ed. John S. Simmons (Newark, Del.: International Reading Association, 1994), pp. 107–113.

Patricia Wrightson, like Mollie Hunter, also mingles long-ago legends in stories with contemporary settings. Wrightson peoples her fantasies with legendary Australian creatures such as Narguns, Ninya, and water spirits. In *The Nargun and the Stars*, men disturb the ancient ones at Wongadilla, a sheep ranch in northern Australia. Simon Brett, a city boy, is awed by the size of the ranch, where he has come to live following the death of his parents. He meets a Potkoorok, a froglike creature who lives in a swamp, and elusive tree spirits called Turongs. But on the night of a terrible storm, Simon is terrified by another, older presence, the ancient Nargun, who has been disturbed by road-building machinery and has emerged from primeval silence to crush everything in its path. Simon and his middle-aged cousin Charlie must bring all their cleverness and ingenuity to bear in trapping the Nargun in a cavern.

In *Balyet*, also by Wrightson, Jo, a 14-year-old girl, inadvertently discovers the power of ancient aboriginal sites to preserve spirits and is almost led to her death when Balyet, the spirit of a young girl banished from her tribe a thousand years ago, lures her to a mountain crag. Wrightson's personification of the ancient mountains, depiction of aboriginal rites, and totally believable blending of contemporary vernacular with old ways are compelling examples of this storyteller's power. For non-Australian readers, the little-known traditions underlying Wrightson's books and their emphasis on magical rather than human characters make unusual demands. However, a dramatic story and the force of Wrightson's language plus the idea of living in harmony with nature make this a compelling book for older readers.

Friendship binds a child from the present with a child from the past in Pam Conrad's *Stonewords*. Zoe, who lives with her grandparents in an old farmhouse while her flighty mother "shows up when she shows up," makes friends with a strange, transparent girl from the past named Zoe Louise, whom only she can see. The ghost girl appears, plays with Zoe, and enigmatically states that she is looking in Zoe's eyes for "the truth." On a rare visit, Zoe's mother points out the memory roses planted for a child who died on the property. When Zoe realizes that her ghost friend is that child, she must find out how her death occurs in order to prevent it from happening. A stack of old newspapers moldering away in the basement provides a clue, and the real Zoe is able to go up the back stairs into the past and change history and the present as well.

In Mary Downing Hahn's *Wait Till Helen Comes*, a ghost child named Helen has perished in a fire and now waits by a pond to drag children to their deaths as play companions. When Molly and Michael's mother remarries, their new father's child joins the family, but Heather is a brat who forever whines about imagined injustices. Nobody believes Heather's stories of the ghostly Helen until Molly begins to develop some sympathy for her stepsister's point of view. In a chilling ending, Molly pieces together the mystery, saves Heather from a sure death, and forges a hopeful beginning of a loving family. Hahn's fast-paced stories consistently win state young-readers awards, showing how much children appreciate a good and scary ghost story.

Betty Ren Wright is another writer who can spin a good ghost story. In *The Ghost Comes Calling*, a ghost comes to call on 9-year-old Chad Weldon, who is a reluctant camper at an old cottage his father is trying to restore. The ghost is old Tim Tapper, who years earlier was wrongly accused of misconduct by the townspeople and went to live in the old cabin as a recluse. When Chad proposes a solution that restores the old man's good name, the ghost can finally rest in peace. In Wright's *Out of the Dark* a ghost appears to 12-year-old Jessica in a nightmare just after she and her family move in to house-sit for her grandmother. Jessie is even more terrified to find that the setting of her nightmare, an old one-room schoolhouse, exists in the middle of a nearby nature preserve and that her grandmother had attended the school as a young girl. The ghost of her dreams begins to appear in various places in and around Gran's house and is obviously trying to harm her. This apparition in white almost succeeds in locking her and a neighbor girl in a metal storage room in the floor of the old school. The mystery of the ghost's identity and Gran's role in a long-ago incident is finally resolved in a riveting conclusion.

Margaret Mahy's *The Haunting* blends a ghost story with deft observations of family interactions. Shy Barney Palmer is receiving unwanted messages from a ghostly relative but is afraid to tell anyone, especially his beloved new stepmother, who is about to have a baby. At a family gathering, writing appears on a page of a book Barney is looking at. Barney soon discovers that on his real mother's side of the family, there is in each generation a magician or psychic. His black-sheep Uncle Cole, holder of the magical power for his generation, is lonesome for other psychics and is trying to possess Barney's mind. In an effort to remain normal, Barney struggles against his uncle's mounting frustration and anger. When the malevolent Uncle Cole finally arrives in Barney's house, different family members come to Barney's aid, revealing individual strengths with surprising results. Mahy's trenchant observations of family communications, her deft and often humorous turns of phrases, and a riveting plot make this an excellent choice for reading aloud to older elementary-school children.

Another restless spirit is found in *The Ghost of Thomas Kempe* by Penelope Lively. Released from a bottle dislodged by workmen refinishing James Harrison's room, the ghost is determined to harass James into being his apprentice. This seventeenth-century poltergeist blows through rooms, causes some small accidents and a near tragedy, and leaves accusing notes in an effort to control James and make his own presence felt in this century. When at last the ghost is returned to his final resting place, James experiences a sense of the layers of time coexisting in his English village. Penelope Lively tells a good story with humor, and readers are left with the feeling of being, like James, in the middle of time that reaches away behind and before us.

The opening paragraph of *Sweet Whispers, Brother Rush* by Virginia Hamilton quickly draws the reader into a remarkable story:

> 🔖 The first time Teresa saw Brother was the way she would think of him ever after. Tree fell head over heels for him. It was love at first sight in a wild beating of her heart that took her breath. But it was a dark Friday three weeks later when it rained, hard and wicked, before she knew Brother Rush was a ghost. (p. 9)

Fourteen-year-old Tree takes care of her older brother Dab while her mother, Viola, works in another city as a practical nurse. Tree painfully accepts her mother's absences and devotes her time to schoolwork and caring for her brother. As Dab's occasional bouts of sickness suddenly become more frequent, Brother Rush appears to Tree and shows her her family's recent past, which until now she has not questioned. Through Brother Rush, Tree begins to understand why her mother has always avoided Dab, the hereditary nature of Dab's sickness, and something about her father. When Dab succumbs to the disease, Tree's experiences with Brother Rush enable her to understand what has happened. But it is her mother's love and the gentle strength of her companion Silversmith that pull Tree through her anger and despair toward an acceptance of her brother's death and the promise of new extended family relationships. Making use of African American cadences and inflections, Hamilton moves surely from narration to dialogue and into Tree's thoughts. She has created complex characters whose steady or fumbling reachings for each other may linger with middle-school readers long past the end of this story.

Time-Shift Fantasy

Probably everyone at one time or another has wondered what it would be like to visit the past. We have looked at old houses and wished they could tell us of their previous occupants; we have held antique jewelry in our hands and wondered about its former owners. Our

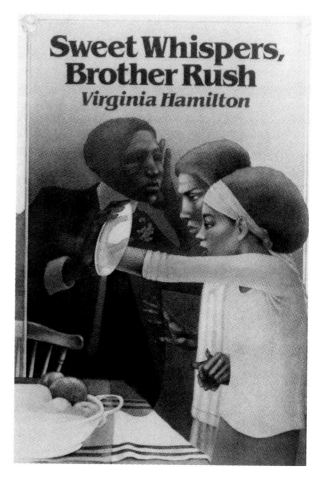

Teresa reaches for images in the mirror held by her uncle's ghost to try to grasp what she has seen but has yet to understand in Leo and Diane Dillon's painting for the jacket of Virginia Hamilton's story *Sweet Whispers, Brother Rush*. From *Sweet Whispers, Brother Rush*, by Virginia Hamilton. Copyright © 1982 by The Putnam & Grosset Group, New York, NY. Reprinted by permission.

curiosity has usually been more than just historical interest; we have wished to communicate, to enter into the lives of the past without somehow losing our own particular place in time.

Recognizing this, authors of books for children have written many fantasies that are based on characters who appear to shift easily from their particular moment in the present to a long-lost point in someone else's past. Usually these time leaps are linked to a tangible object or place that is common to both periods. In *Tom's Midnight Garden* by Philippa Pearce, the old grandfather clock that strikes thirteen hours serves as the fixed point of entry for the fantasy. And in *Playing Beatie Bow* by Ruth Park, Abby slips into the 1870s by virtue of the antique crochetwork she wears on her dress; she cannot return to her own time without it.

Julia Sauer's *Fog Magic* is the tender, moving story of Greta Addington, a young girl of Nova Scotia. One day while walking in the fog, Greta discovers a secret world, Blue Cove, a fishing village that is present only in the fog. Here Greta forms a friendship with a girl her own age, whose mother senses that Greta is from "over the mountain" and quietly reminds her each time the fog is lifting that it is time to go home. On the foggy evening of Greta's twelfth birthday she enters Blue Cove, where her friend's mother gives her a soft gray kitten and quietly wishes her "Safe passage for all the years ahead." Greta senses that this will be the last time that she will be able to visit Blue Cove. She walks slowly down the hill to find her father waiting. As she shows him her kitten, he reaches into his pocket and pulls out an odd little knife that he had received on his twelfth birthday at Blue Cove. This is a hauntingly beautiful story, memorable for its mood and setting. Part of its appeal may come from the underlying view, common in mystical fantasy, that childhood confers special sensibilities that adults can no longer share.

No one is more skillful in fusing the past with the present than L. M. Boston in her stories of Green Knowe, that mysterious old English house in which the author lived. In *The Children of Green Knowe*, the first in this series, Boston tells the story of Tolly, who is sent to live with his great-grandmother. Over the large fireplace in the drawing room hangs a picture of three children who grew up at Green Knowe in the seventeenth century. When Tolly's great-grandmother tells him stories about the children, they seem so real that Tolly is convinced they often play hide-and-seek with him. His great-grandmother believes him, and soon the reader does too. Each story of Green Knowe blends a child of the present with characters and situations from previous centuries while creating for the reader a marvelous sense of place.

One of the finest time fantasies ever written is the mysterious and exciting *Tom's Midnight Garden* by Philippa Pearce. Forced to spend part of a summer with a rather boring aunt and uncle, Tom finds his visit quite dull until he hears the grandfather clock in the hall strike thirteen. Then he is able to slip into the garden and play with Hatty, a child of the past. Tom becomes so absorbed in his midnight visits, when "there is time no longer," that he does not wish to return home. One fateful night Tom opens the back door and sees only the paving and the fences that stand there in daylight—Hatty and her garden have vanished. When Tom meets the real Hatty Bartholomew, a little old lady, he understands why the weather in the garden has always been perfect, why some nights it has been one season and the next night a different one, why Hatty was sometimes young and sometimes older; it all depended on what old Mrs. Bartholomew had been dreaming. Lonely and

bored, Tom joined her in her dreams. This is a fascinating story that should please both boys and girls in the middle grades.

While the characters in most time fantasies slip in and out of the past, the problem in *Tuck Everlasting* is that the Tuck family is trapped forever in the present. Natalie Babbitt's elegant prose leads the reader to expect a quiet Victorian fantasy, but the book holds many surprises—including a kidnapping, a murder, and a jailbreak. The story opens with Winnie Foster, an overprotected 10-year-old, sitting in front of her family's prim touch-me-not cottage on a hot August day talking to a large plump toad. She informs the toad that she wants to do something interesting, something that will make a difference to the world. The very next morning Winnie "runs away" to the nearby woods owned by her parents and sees a young man of 17 (although he first says he is 104 years old) drinking from a spring. When Winnie asks for a drink, Jesse Tuck warns her not to take one. Just at that moment his mother, Mae Tuck, and brother Miles arrive. With all due apologies to Winnie, they bundle her onto their horse to go back to their home to have a talk with Mae's husband, Angus Tuck. On the way, Mae tells Winnie that drinking the spring water has given them everlasting life. Back at the shabby three-room cottage of the Tucks, they gently try to persuade Winnie to guard their secret. In the morning Angus Tuck takes Winnie rowing on the lake and explains to her what it is like to live forever. He longs for a natural conclusion to his life. "I want to grow again, . . . and change. And if that means I got to move on at the end of it, then I want that, too" (p. 63). Although the Tucks intend to let Winnie make her own decision, they do not know that a man in a yellow suit, who has been searching for them for years, has overheard Mae Tuck reveal their secret to Winnie. Caught in the melodrama of the Tucks' lives, Winnie decides to protect and help them, a decision that does indeed change her life. The simplicity of the Tucks and their story belies the depth of the theme of *Tuck Everlasting*. With its prologue and epilogue, the story is reminiscent of a play, a kind of *Our Town* for children.

Many fantasies written in the United States seem more lighthearted than those of the British. For example, Edward Ormondroyd's *Time at the Top* is a refreshingly different time fantasy. It starts out with a windy, wretched day when everything goes wrong until Susan meets and helps a funny little old "Mary Poppins-ish" woman who says she will "give her three." When Susan pushes the elevator button for the top floor where she and her father live, the elevator keeps right on going to the eighth floor—except there is no eighth floor. Susan gets off and finds herself in a different time and different place. How she makes friends with Victoria and her brother Robert and solves their financial difficulties and their widowed mother's marital problems makes for a fast-paced, amusing story.

Mystery is also an important part of the complex fantasy by Eleanor Cameron titled *The Court of the Stone Children*. The story of modern-day Nina, who has a "Museum Feeling" and thinks she would like to be a curator, is intertwined with the story of Dominique, a young noblewoman of nineteenth-century France whose father was executed by Napoleon's regime and whose family possessions are now housed in a French museum in San Francisco. Domi enlists Nina's help in the task of clearing her father's name of the charge of murder. A suspenseful mystery, with telling clues foreshadowed in one of Nina's "real-life" dreams, leads to a painting that serves as evidence of the count's innocence. A Chagall painting, *Time Is a River Without Banks*, which also hangs in the museum, is used throughout the story as a symbol of Nina's unusual interest in the abstract nature of time. This is a profound theme explored by a truly accomplished writer. However, young readers will more likely value the book for its exciting events and for the haunting presence of Domi in her museum domain than for its eloquent abstractions.

Like the "Green Knowe" stories, *A String in the Harp* gains strength from its setting and also from its connection to legend. Nancy Bond tells of an American family's adjustment to living in Wales when their newly widowed father accepts a university post. It is a particularly difficult time for 12-year-old Peter, who is stubborn, lonely, and hateful until he finds a strange object later identified as the harp key of Taliesin, the great sixth-century bard who lived in this part of Wales. When the key draws Peter back in time, his present-day life is adversely affected. Eventually he is able to return the key to its proper place and assume a responsible place in his family. This strongly characterized but lengthy story mingles past and present time in a believable and involving way.

In *Earthfasts* William Mayne also draws on legendary characters to tell his story of three interwoven times. When two boys meet at a swelling in the earth, the ground begins to vibrate with the sound of drumming. Out of the earth emerges a stranger who is beating a drum and clutching a steady, cold white flame. It is Nellie Jack John, who according to local legend went underground two hundred years ago to seek the treasure of King Arthur. Nellie Jack John's disturbance of time causes many bizarre events: ancient stones called "earthfasts" work up in a farmer's field; a family's poltergeist returns after a long absence; and one boy vanishes in what looks like a flash of lightning. Only by restoring

the candle to its proper place because "King Arthur's time has not yet come" can the boys right the imbalance of time. This unforgettable book owes much of its impact to Mayne's use of language and his finely realized setting.

Another story that alludes to King Arthur, *Merlin Dreams* by Peter Dickinson, defies categorizing. Nine highly original short stories or dreams are each prefaced by Merlin's remembrance of some event in his long life. Whether the dreams are of time to come, time that was, or time that never will be is for the reader to decide. In one story, a damsel from the north and a knight use their powers to change into hunting dogs to outwit her greedy uncle, whose other body is that of a wolf. In a humorous story, a basilisk turns on its evil master with predictable results. Between the short stories, Merlin's dreams allude to the many exploits of the famous magician as he helped King Arthur regain and hold his throne. Illustrator Alan Lee contrasts watercolor paintings for the stories and black-line drawings for the dreams. His depiction of the woodland castles and poisoned wells, the threadbare knights, or the needful damsels highlights the subtleties and moods of this remarkable book for middle school readers.

Often time travelers learn to deal with a troubled present through experiences in an equally troubled past. In the Australian prize winner *Playing Beatie Bow*, Ruth Park presents Abigail, a contemporary 14-year-old who has been deeply hurt—first by her father's defection from the family and then by her mother's quick agreement when he wants to come back. In this resentful mood, Abigail follows a strangely dressed child who has been watching a neighborhood street game called "Beatie Bow." The little girl, the original Beatie Bow, leads Abigail through increasingly unfamiliar streets to her home in the Rocks area of Sydney—in the year 1873. Injured in a fall and divested of the dress with antique crochetwork that has made her time passage possible, Abigail is trapped with Beatie's family. She comes to care for them all, especially charming cousin Judah, who is engaged to Beatie's older sister but attracted to Abby as well. Through her courage during a fire in the Bow family candy shop, Abigail earns her return to the twentieth century, where she finds that she is now more tolerant of her father's lapse of affection.

Mary Downing Hahn's *Time for Andrew* is a gripping time-shift mystery. Staying at his great-grandfather's old house for the summer while his parents travel abroad, Drew is a nervous 12-year-old, afraid of bullies, bad storms, and bogeymen. Exploring the attic one day, he finds a bag of marbles that had belonged to Andrew, a distant relative who died of diptheria at the age of 12. Disturbing the marbles has also disrupted time, however, and at the hour of his death Andrew is transported to Drew's bedroom. Andrew begs Drew to change places with him and give him a chance to live. Reluctantly Drew does so, going back to the early 1900s to live as Andrew. Here he must face bullies and frightening situations similar to those he feared in his own time. Most frightening of all, however, is Andrew's growing reluctance to trade places and allow Drew back into his own time. The longer Drew stays in Andrew's time, the more he begins to forget his own. Yet he also finds some of the courage he lacked in the modern world and grows to appreciate the close family life he has never had. Hahn is a master at building tension as the story approaches its resolution, and the question of Drew's and Andrew's futures is brought to a satisfying and wholly believable conclusion.

Self-understanding and better family relationships are also the outcomes for characters in two time-shift fantasies by Canadian authors. In *A Handful of Time* by Kit Pearson, a 12-year-old girl is sent to her cousins' camp on a lake near Edmonton while her parents' divorce becomes final. Patricia is definitely the "city cousin" who knows little about boating or horseback riding and is the constant butt of her cousins' jokes. When she discovers an old watch hidden under the floor of a guest house, she finds herself taken back in time to the same summer cabin where her mother was 12 and equally miserable. In her frequent trips to view the past, Patricia learns much about her short-tempered grandmother and her beautiful but reserved mother. By coming to understand her mother, Patricia moves toward understanding herself.

The Haunting of Frances Rain (published in Canada as *Who Is Frances Rain?*) by Margaret Buffie might well be a script for a Canadian *On Golden Pond* movie. When Lizzie, her egotistical brother, little sister, mother, and new stepfather drive from Winnipeg to a northern lake to see her grandmother, Lizzie thinks the holiday will be a disaster. Then, while exploring deserted Rain Island, she finds a pair of old glasses that enable her to see a log cabin and its inhabitants, a young girl and her mother. Lizzie is haunted by them. Who are they? And who is the fat man who takes the girl away in a canoe while the mother is gone? Slowly she discovers that the young girl is her Gran, now old and confined to bed but remembering the same vivid scenes Lizzie is seeing. This mysterious story is as haunting and memorable as the cry of a loon on northern waters. Both stories feature girls who are in danger of using the past to escape their problems in the present. But when her entry into the past is blocked, each girl faces the present with new resolve.

Welwyn Wilton Katz, another Canadian author, imagines a disastrous future for Earth in *Time Ghost*. In the year 2044, the natural world is far removed from

In *Time Ghost*, Welwyn Wilton Katz raises questions about the future of Earth's environment by sending characters back into the past.
Cover illustration by Martin Springett. Reprinted by permission.

most people who live in large block buildings in crowded cities and rarely venture outdoors for fear of air pollution and ultraviolet radiation. Gwyneth Green, Sara and Karl's grandmother, is an environmental lawyer, determined to protect the last remaining wild areas of the Arctic from oil industry tycoons. Grandma invites 12-year-old Sara, her brother, and their two friends Dani and Josh on a trip to the North Pole to negotiate with a "grey suit" representative of the oil company that wants to drill beneath the arctic ice. Sara, angry at being forced to leave her home, is a reluctant traveler, and once outdoors she is badly stricken with agoraphobia. But Dani is thrilled by the open expanses of the wilderness world and the two boys are pleased to be able to conduct their time experiments. Knowing that all time zones meet at the North Pole, they believe that this is the point that would allow time travel. However, Dani, Sara, and

Mr. Duguay (the "grey suit") are the ones who are sent back in time to central Canada when Sara's twelfth-birthday gift from her grandmother is accidentally broken, repeating an accident that occurred to the same necklace on Grandma's twelfth birthday in 1993. Struggling to figure out a way to return to their own time, the three come to new understandings about themselves, each other, and the beautiful natural world they have lost. The story ends with real growth for these characters and real hope for the little natural wilderness they have left.

In some books where characters are shifted from modern times into specific periods of history, the concern with social and political issues of the past is very strong. Several notable examples serve the purposes of historical fiction as well as fantasy. In *A Chance Child* by Jill Paton Walsh, Creep, a present-day English boy who has been abused and kept locked in a closet, gets out by chance and follows a canal that takes him back to the Industrial Revolution. As a child laborer, he travels from one exhausting and dangerous job to another, eventually losing his grip on the present altogether. His half-brother, the only person with any clue to his disappearance, searches historical documents from the early 1800s and is at last satisfied that Creep has escaped into the past and lived out his life there. The amount of technological information about work in the coal mines, the nailer's forge, the pottery, and the textile mill attests to the research necessary for recreating these settings. Walsh's juxtaposition of the abusive treatment of children in the nineteenth century and Creep's contemporary plight makes a strong statement about children and society.

David Wiseman's *Jeremy Visick* explores the conditions of child laborers in England's nineteenth-century copper mines when Matthew's school assignment leads him into a mine disaster of a previous century. In *A Girl Called Boy* by Belinda Hurmence, an African American girl, Blanche Overtha Yancy ("Boy"), is bored by her father's obvious pride in their African American heritage. But a tiny African soapstone "freedom bird" sends her into the past when her father's ancestors were slaves, and she is taken for a runaway. The author's use of actual slave narratives and plantation records provides the same authenticity of background that would be expected in historical fiction. Using the device of time travel strengthens this story, however, for it allows the interjection of a contemporary perspective to balance the impact of that era's distorted values.

Janet Lunn, American born but now living in Canada, weaves together a haunting tale of a contemporary child, an old Canadian farmhouse, and the American Civil War in her book *The Root Cellar.* When her grandmother dies, Rose is sent to live with her Aunt Nan's family in their country home on the northern shore of Lake Ontario. A shy child who has lived only with adults in New York City, 12-year-old Rose feels desperately lonely in the midst of Aunt Nan's and Uncle Bob's lively family. When she discovers an old root cellar door covered with vines and grass, she opens it and finds herself in a world more than a hundred years past. She is more comfortable in this world and easily makes friends with Susan and Will. When Will runs off to fight in the Civil War and does not return, Rose and Susan set out on a hazardous journey that eventually takes them to an army hospital in Washington, D.C. On the journey Rose discovers a strength and determination she did not know she had that helps her when she returns to her own time.

Imaginary Realms

Many authors of fantasy create believability by setting their stories in an imaginary society where kings and queens rule feudal societies that resemble the Middle Ages. Often lighter in tone than high fantasy, these stories might nonetheless feature some of its attributes—such as a human character's search for identity, a quest, or the struggle against evil—and are good introductions to the more complex and more serious works of high fantasy. Children are often drawn to this kind of fantasy, as it seems so closely related in many ways to folktales and traditional literature.

Two of Natalie Babbitt's stories, *The Search for Delicious* and *Kneeknock Rise,* are set in an imaginary medieval kingdom. In the first story, young Gaylen is sent out as the King's messenger to poll the kingdom as to which food should stand for the word *delicious* in the dictionary the prime minister is compiling. Before he finishes, Gaylen uncovers Hemlock's plot to overthrow the king. With the help of supposedly fictitious creatures such as woldwellers, dwarfs, and Ardis the mermaid, Gaylen is able to foil Hemlock and save his king. In *Kneeknock Rise,* Egan climbs the mountain and finds a perfectly rational explanation for the groaning noises of the mythical Megrimum. When he eagerly relates his findings to the villagers, they refuse to listen to him, and Egan discovers that people do not relinquish their myths easily; harmless monsters may be preferable to facts.

Patricia Wrede's Enchanted Forest Chronicles feature the unconventional Princess Cimorene. In *Dealing with Dragons,* Cimorene runs off to be librarian and cook to the dragon Kazul rather than stay in the palace, sew, and wait for a suitor. Cimorene organizes the dragon's hoard, reads ancient books, and makes friends with neighboring princesses captured by dragons and awaiting rescue. Cimorene's gradual mastery of rudimentary magic and her friendship with the witch Morwen allow her to defeat an evil band of wizards who are trying to influence the choice of the new dragon ruler. Cimorene's further adventures are told in *Searching for Dragons* and *Calling on Dragons*. *Talking to Dragons* finds Cimorene's son Daystar and a feisty fire-witch named Shiara ready for their own adventure with Kazul. All the books make many sly references to folktale and fantasy conventions. While Cimorene and Menolly in Anne McCaffrey's high-fantasy Dragonsinger series (discussed in the next section) are sisters under the skin, the two series differ in tone. Children who enjoy Wrede's unconventional feminine adventurer would appreciate being guided to the works of McCaffrey, as well as those of Robin McKinley and Lloyd Alexander, whose heroines appeal to slightly older readers.

This same audience will appreciate two other writers who have spun series that feature feisty characters who will not stay put in the roles their society has dictated for them. Tamora Pierce's Lioness Quartet is especially popular with early adolescents and follows the career of Alanna, a young girl whose dearest wish is to train as a warrior maiden. In the books *Alanna, In the Hand of the Goddess, The Woman Who Rides Like a Man*, and *Lioness Rampant* she faces many trials and tribulations as she attempts to restore the Dominion Jewel to the King of Tortall and a just peace to the kingdom. *Wild Magic, Wolf Speaker*, and *Emperor Mage* are set in the same imaginary land of Tortall and feature Daine, a heroine whose magical talent is the ability to communicate with animals. In the first book she is a homeless urchin whose abilities are discovered and nurtured by the Mage Numair. In *Wolf Speaker*, Daine is enlisted to help save a beautiful valley from destruction by evil immortals, beings who have been unleashed upon the realm through a breach in the protective wall. Her magical abilities allow her to call on all manner of animals for aid, including wolves, a dragon, and a basilisk named Tkaa. In *Emperor Mage* she joins forces with the animals once again as they seek to negotiate a peace treaty with an evil ruler. All of Pierce's books feature fast-paced adventures for another strong female who can do anything she sets out to do.

Although the orphan Wren is the central character in Sherwood Smith's *Wren to the Rescue, Wren's Quest*, and *Wren's War*, her friends Tess, Connor, and Tyron are strong supporting characters. As the four companions battle the evil wizard-king Andreus, they also struggle with the roles they are expected to play and seek to understand the gifts that are uniquely theirs. In this fully realized imaginary kingdom, Smith's appealing characters have the type of wonderful adventures that are the perfect introduction to the more-complex fantasy worlds of Ursula Le Guin and J. R. R. Tolkien.

William Mayne's remarkable *Antar and the Eagles* takes place in a mountainous kingdom. Antar is plucked by eagles off the steeple of a church where he has perched while disobeying his father. The eagles carry him to their aerie, where they peck and prod him to eat raw meat, to sew feathers on his now-ragged clothes, and to learn to fly. After gradually learning the eagles' language, Antar understands that only he can accomplish the mission to restore the beautiful egg of the next Great Eagle. Wishing only to go home, Antar undertakes this quest, surviving near-burial in an erupting volcano, the weapons of the men, and near-imprisonment by the king. Told with a minimum of dialogue, this riveting story leads readers to consider not only the nature of a majestic bird but also the boundless possibilities of the human imagination.

In Zilpha Keatley Snyder's fast-paced adventure *Song of the Gargoyle*, 13-year-old Tymmon eludes capture when his court-jester father is mysteriously kidnapped. The boy is befriended by a huge and ugly dog, Troff, which he believes is a stone gargoyle come to life. Troff displays a talent for singing along with Tymmon's flute music, and the two are able to make a living as itinerant musicians. As Tymmon searches for his father, he sees the poverty and suffering that peasants endure because of the greed of the nobility, and he takes on responsibility for two homeless children. When the tale of a mysterious old man sends Tymmon to rescue or avenge his father, the boy and dog are thrown into a dungeon. Music again saves boy, dog, and father, who reunite with the two children in an exciting conclusion.

Sid Fleischman sets *The Whipping Boy*, his humorous variation on the prince-and-the-pauper theme, in a time of velvet britches, princely tutors, and robber brigands. Jemmy, the whipping boy for Prince Brat, has taken all the abuse for the prince that he can stand. Each time the bored prince makes mischief and is caught, Jemmy must receive the twenty whacks. But before Jemmy can leave, the prince commands the former street urchin to sneak away from the dull palace with him to see what the world holds. When the boys are kidnapped by two notorious outlaws, Hold-Your-Nose-Billy and Cutwater, one of the boys' identities is given away: Prince Brat had thoughtfully stowed his crown in his picnic basket. But which one is the prince? Since Jemmy had learned to read and write as a tutor futilely labored to teach the prince, the cutthroats consider the whipping boy the one to be ransomed. The exaggerated characters in humorous situations are balanced by the prince's gradual transition into a decent person when he finds that none of his future subjects think much of him. Fleischman's appealing use of colorful figurative language, witty repartee, broadly drawn characters, and clever chapter titles make this a good shared-reading choice for fourth or fifth graders. Peter Sis's quirky drawings and small chapter openings are perfectly suited to this spoof.

Joan Aiken sets her stories within imaginary kingdoms with a nod to history as well. *The Wolves of Willoughby Chase* has all of the ingredients of a nineteenth-century chiller, including wicked wolves without and an outrageously wicked governess within. It takes place in a period of history that never existed—the Stuarts, in the person of good King James III, are on the throne in the nineteenth century. Readers will applaud Aiken's resourceful heroines and hiss the evil villains in all the Wolf Chronicles. Eleven-year-old Dido is the resourceful heroine of *The Wolves of Willoughby Chase*, *Black Hearts in Battersea*, *Nightbirds on Nantucket*, and *The Stolen Lake*. Dido's distant relative, "Is" Twite, has her own hair-raising adventures in *Is Underground* and *Cold Shoulder Road*. In the latter book, Is and her cousin Arun come up against such sinister characters as Dominic de la Twite, Admiral Fishkin, a band of smugglers called The Merry Gentry, and the members of a religious group called the Silent Sect. Strange inventions, hidden treasure, and kidnapped children are other features of this thrilling story. As with all these titles, children will find the books hard to put down.

Lloyd Alexander has a gift for portraying comic adventures in which serious themes lie under a surface of fast action and polished wit. *The Cat Who Wished to Be a Man*, *The Marvelous Misadventures of Sebastian*, and *The Wizard in the Tree* are books of this sort. *The Arkadians* is equally lighthearted, with all the trappings of madcap adventure, but it also includes some serious ideas about the craft of storytelling. Lucian is a young accountant in the court of King Bomios who finds his life threatened when he discovers that Calchas, the king's royal soothsayer, is fiddling with the royal books. He must flee for his life, and his journey to restore his good name takes him throughout the hills and dales of Arkadia. In the company of Fronto, a poet who has been turned into a donkey, he encounters all manner of refugees from Greek myths as well as a charming but spirited young woman named Joy-in-the-Dance. The three sometimes reluctant companions have wonderful adventures before all wrongs are righted and all characters are restored to their original forms. Alexander's books share certain common elements: rich use of language, comic tone, usually a strong-willed female foil to the likable, all-too-human hero, and a setting in an imaginary kingdom.

Older readers find satisfaction with Lloyd Alexander's two series, both of which take place in unmagical but imagined settings. *Westmark* is the story of Theo, a printer's apprentice, who pursues questions of honor, justice, and freedom of the press as he tries to avoid the villainous chief minister of the realm. Theo helps restore his street-urchin friend Mickle to her rightful place as princess, but he also questions the concept of a monarchy: Does anyone have a rightful place on a throne? *The Kestrel* and *The Beggar Queen* are sequels in which Theo

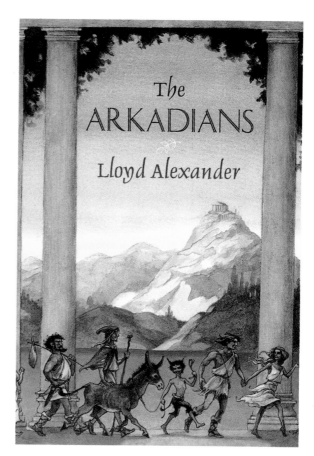

Lloyd Alexander's *The Arkadians* includes a storyteller named Lucian who encounters a cast of characters who might have lived in mythical Greece.
From *The Arkadians* by Lloyd Alexander. Jacket art by Trina Schart-Hyman. Copyright © 1995 by Trina Schart-Hyman. Used by permission of Dutton Children's Books, a division of Penguin USA Inc.

and Mickle, now the "Beggar Queen," prove their worth in battle but learn the cost of personal victory. In a lighter vein, Vesper Holly is the intrepid young woman who, with her guardian Brinnie, embarks on adventures in *The Illyrian Adventure*, *The El Dorado Adventure*, *The Drackenburg Adventure*, *The Jedera Adventure*, and *The Philadelphia Story*. The high-minded heroine and her guardian journey to imaginary places in Europe, Africa, and Central America where they discover treasure, recover important antiquities, foil villains, and narrowly escape all dangers. Told with Alexander's usual wit, these five stories invite middle-grade readers to create their own adventure "movies of the mind."

High Fantasy

Many readers who learn to enjoy popular stories of magic, ghosts, time travel, and the like go on to become fans of a more serious and demanding type of story called high fantasy. These complex narratives, which often extend into sequels, are characterized by certain recurring themes and motifs. For instance, the stories frequently take place in created worlds or imaginary realms. Characters might call on ancient and fundamental powers, for good or ill. The conflict between these opposing forces becomes the focus of many stories. Frequently the protagonists of high fantasy have a quest to fulfill. Finally, although there may be touches of humor, the overall tone of high fantasy is serious, because its purpose is serious. High fantasy concerns itself with cosmic questions and ultimate values: goodness, truth, courage, wisdom.

In accepting the National Book Award for *The Farthest Shore*, Ursula K. Le Guin spoke about the intent of fantasy at this level:

> The fantasist, whether he uses the ancient archetypes of myth and legend or the younger ones of science and technology, may be talking as seriously as any sociologist—and a good deal more directly—about human life as it is lived, and as it might be lived, and as it ought to be lived. For after all, as great scientists have said and as all children know, it is above all by the imagination that we achieve perception, and compassion, and hope.[16]

High fantasy's best audience stretches over a wide age range, from preadolescents to adults. Some of its most enthusiastic readers are the same young people who are devoted to video games of imagined adventures. Many older readers simply call themselves science fiction fans and make little distinction between the two types of books. In fact, much science fiction is also high fantasy; Madeleine L'Engle's *A Wrinkle in Time* is one familiar example. Some stories, like Anne McCaffrey's *Dragonsong*, appear to be science fiction with their extraterrestrial settings and the use of precepts of science (in this case, the bonding of a newborn animal and a mother figure). But *Dragonsong* seems more fantasy than science, since the newborns are traditional dragons and "fire lizards."

Not all critics will agree about the proper categorization of books like these. But it is the book itself, not its label, that matters to the reader. However it might be identified, well-written high fantasy rewards its audience with new understandings as well as a good read.

The Struggle Between Good and Evil

The age-old conflicts between good and evil, light and darkness, life and death are recurring themes in modern fantasy as well as in traditional literature. The setting

for the struggle might be the world as we know it, or an invented land like Narnia, which some children know as well as their own backyards or city blocks. C. S. Lewis, a well-known English scholar and theologian, created seven fantasies about the country of Narnia. The best of the series is the first one published, *The Lion, the Witch, and the Wardrobe*, although it was the second in the sequence according to the history of Narnia. Beginning quite realistically in our time and world, four children find their way into the land of Narnia through the back of a huge wardrobe (or closet) in one of the large rooms of an old English house. The land, blanketed in snow and ice, is under the wicked Snow Queen's spell, which controls the weather so that it is "always winter and never Christmas." The children and the Narnians pit themselves against the evil witch and her motley assortment of ghouls, boggles, minotaurs, and hags. With the coming, sacrifice, and resurrection of the great Aslan the Lion, signs of spring are seen in the land. The children successfully aid the lion king in destroying the evil forces, and he crowns them Kings and Queens of Narnia. Narnia has its own history and time, and in *The Magician's Nephew* the reader is told of the beginnings of Narnia.[17] In the last of the books of Narnia, *The Last Battle*, King Tirian calls on the Earth Children to come to his aid. Narnia is destroyed; yet the real Narnia, the inner Narnia, is not. The children learn that no good thing is ever lost, and the real identity of Aslan is finally revealed to them. These stories are mysterious, intriguing, and beautifully written. Even if children do not always understand their religious allegory, they can appreciate them as wondrous adventures that somehow reveal more than they say.

Susan Cooper has written a series of five books about the cosmic struggle between good and evil. *Over Sea, Under Stone* introduces the three Drew children, who, on holiday in Cornwall, find an ancient treasure map linked to King Arthur. The third book in the series, *Greenwitch*, continues this quest story. Both stories are less complex than the remarkable second book, *The Dark Is Rising*. On Midwinter Day, his eleventh birthday, Will Stanton discovers that he is the last of the Old Ones, immortals dedicated throughout the ages to keeping the world from the forces of evil, the Dark. Will must find the six Signs of Life in order to complete his power and defeat, even temporarily, the rising of the Dark. Strange powers enable him to move in and out of time, where he meets Merriman Lyon, the first of the Old Ones, who becomes his teacher and mentor. While rich in symbolism and allegory, the story is grounded in

---

[16]Ursula K. Le Guin, "National Book Award Acceptance Speech," in *The Language of the Night: Essays on Fantasy and Science Fiction*, ed. Susan Wood (New York: Putnam, 1979), p. 58.

[17]See Brian Sibley's *The Land of Narnia*, with illustrations by Pauline Baynes (New York: HarperCollins, 1990) for help in sorting out the chronology of Narnia, notes on the creation of the series, and a simplified biography of C. S. Lewis.

reality so that both Will's "real" life and his quest in suspended time are distinct, yet interwoven. In the fourth book of the series, *The Grey King,* Will once again must prepare for the coming battle between the Dark and the Light. Special help comes from Bran, a strange albino boy, and his dog, Cafall. Set in Wales, the story works on many levels—with the feud over a sheep-killing dog taking on more significance when Bran's mysterious background is revealed. *Silver on the Tree* draws together characters from the previous four novels for a final assault on the Dark. Much that was hidden in the other tales is made explicit here, and knowledge of the major threads of the first four books is necessary to understand this exciting and fulfilling climax to the saga.

Quests and Adventures

High fantasy is almost always the story of a search—for treasure, justice, identity, understanding—and of a hero-figure who learns important lessons in the adventuring. One of the most famous seekers in all fantasy is J. R. R. Tolkien's Bilbo Baggins in *The Hobbit.* Generally hobbits are very respectable creatures who never have any adventures or do anything unexpected. Bilbo Baggins, however, has an adventure and finds himself doing and saying altogether unexpected things. He is tricked by the dwarfs and the elves into going on a quest for treasure when he would much rather stay at home where he could be sure of six solid meals a day rather than be off fighting dragons. On the way, he is lost in a tunnel and nearly consumed by a ghoulish creature called Gollum, who is "dark as darkness except for his two big round pale eyes." Gradually the hobbit's inner courage emerges, as he struggles on through terrifying woods, encounters with huge hairy spiders, and battles with goblins to a somewhat enigmatic victory over the dragon (a more heroic figure is allowed to slay it). *The Hobbit* gives children an introduction to Middle Earth and its creatures. Later they may pursue this interest in Tolkien's vastly expanded view of Middle Earth in *The Lord of the Rings,* a 1,300-page trilogy that again draws on the author's scholarly knowledge of the myth and folklore of northwestern Europe.

Welsh legends and mythology are the inspiration for the intriguing chronicles of the imaginary land of Prydain as told by Lloyd Alexander. In *The Book of Three* the reader is introduced to Taran, an assistant pigkeeper who dreams of becoming a hero. With a strange assortment of companions he pursues Hen Wen, the oracular pig, and struggles to save Prydain from the forces of evil. The chronicles are continued in the most exciting of all of the books, *The Black Cauldron.* Once again the faithful companions fight evil as they seek to find and destroy the great cauldron in which the dread Cauldron-Born are created, "mute and deathless warriors" made from the stolen bodies of those slain in battle. Taran is proud to be chosen to fight for Lord Gwydion, for he believes he will have more opportunity to win honor than when washing pigs or weeding a garden. His wise and sensitive companion, Adaon, tells him:

> 🐾 I have marched in many a battle host . . . but I have also planted seeds and reaped the harvest with my own hands. And I have learned there is greater honor in a field well plowed than in a field steeped in blood. (p. 43)

Gradually Taran learns what it means to become a man among men—the sacrifice of his gentle Adaon, the final courage of the proud Ellidyr, and the faithfulness of his companions. He experiences treachery, tragedy, and triumph; yet a thread of humor runs throughout to lighten the tension. Good does prevail, and Taran has matured and is ready for his next adventure. In the third book of the series, *The Castle of Llyr,* Taran escorts Princess Eilonwy to the Isle of Mona, where Queen Teleria is expected to teach the temperamental Eilonwy to behave in the manner of a proper princess—not an easy task. In the fourth book, *Taran Wanderer,* Taran searches for his parentage. More important than the identity of his parents, however, is Taran's discovery of who he is and what he dares to become. *The High King,* the masterful conclusion to this cycle of stories about the kingdom of Prydain, received the Newbery Medal. However, the recognition carried praise for all five of these chronicles. Each can be read independently, but together they present an exciting adventure in some of the best-written fantasy of our time.

Lloyd Alexander writes another quest story in *The Remarkable Journey of Prince Jen.* Set in China during the Tang Dynasty, young Prince Jen, heir to the Dragon Throne, starts off to find T'ien-kuo, or the Heavenly Kingdom, the utopia described by a wandering scholar. Jen sets off with six gifts for the ruler of T'ien-kuo, a retinue of soldiers, and a loyal servant. As his journey progresses, he loses everything but gains his manhood, love, and friendship. Filled with excitement and wisdom, this would be a superb story to read aloud to middle-grade students.

Often in high fantasy an unsuspecting or reluctant hero born to be leader, princess, or king accepts her or his true identity in a way that symbolizes each young person's own discovery of the powers and burdens of maturity. In Grace Chetwin's series, which begins with *Gom on Windy Mountain,* Gom Gobblechuck is such a hero. At 11, he can converse with animals but is content to follow in his woodchopper father's footsteps. However, his father tells him about his mother, Harga the Brown, who left her eleven children when Gom was born. Upon his father's death, Gom sets forth from his sequestered valley to find his wizard mother in *The Riddle and the Rune*. Successive novels take Gom deeper beneath his own world and finally out of it into another time and space as he becomes more aware of the evil threatening his land, Ulm. Chetwin's stories feature a familiar earthiness, a celebration of a simple life, and the virtues of a steadfast heart. Readers will identify with Gom's unready demeanor, his hasty actions that cause later difficulties, and his gradual understanding of the dangers of wielding power unwisely. More unexpected is Chetwin's creation of a universe in which this small world exists. Like Sylvia Engdahl in *Enchantress from the Stars* and Ursula K. Le Guin in *A Wizard of Earthsea*, she explores the moral responsibility each person holds to maintain the balance of the universe.

Just as Grace Chetwin's woodcutter Gom and Lloyd Alexander's pigkeeper Taran discover that they have been chosen from the beginning for a high purpose, so does Patricia McKillip's Morgon of Hed find an undreamed-of destiny in the trilogy that begins with *The Riddle-Master of Hed*. Morgon knows he is a prince and a land ruler, but he does not know the significance of the three stars he bears on his forehead. As a student at the College of Riddle-Masters, he comes upon riddles that concern the stars, but he is reluctant to accept the powers that are his to claim. In the second book, *Heir of Sea and Fire*, Morgon disappears into Erlenstar Mountain on a search for the High One, and Raederle, the beautiful girl who is pledged to him, comes into full possession of her own magic. In *Harpist in the Wind*, the two are together once more, and the solution to the riddle of the Star-Bearer is known at last. These are difficult books, dense with allusions to the history and geography of their imaginary setting. Fantasy fans who are proficient readers are easily caught up in the compelling narrative, however. To avoid dissatisfaction with the abrupt endings of the first two books, it may be a good idea to begin this series with all three volumes at hand.

In Robin McKinley's *The Blue Sword*, a book with closer ties to the world as we know it, a young woman called Harry discovers that her heritage has destined her to be a "Lady Hero." A ward of her brother, Harry feels vaguely out of place in the military outpost where he has brought her to live and is strangely drawn by the mountains where Free Hillfolk live. When Corlath the Hill-King comes to ask the Homelanders' cooperation in turning back the Northerners, who have demonic powers in battle, he is rebuffed. But his visionary gift of *kelar* drives him to kidnap Harry. She is treated as an honored captive and is destined to play a part in the Hillfolk's efforts against the hordes of the North. More and more at ease with her abductors, Harry trains for battle and earns the right to be a king's Rider and to bear the treasured Blue Sword, whose special power in her hand must finally stand between the Hillfolk and

their enemies. The girl's poignant relationship with Corlath and his people is put in new perspective by her defiant courage and by her discovery of an ancestral link that proves she is in truth one of them. The story is rich with details of horsemanship, combat, and the romance of a nomadic life. It also speaks directly about women's roles and responsibilities, a message all the more intriguing for being set in a frame of military and desert life, where traditional roles for women are often rigid. *The Hero and the Crown* happens in time before *The Blue Sword* and features many of the same themes. It chronicles the coming of the king's only child, Aerin, into her powers while leaving the reader with the desire to know more of what Aerin's future will bring.

In *Dragonsong*, Anne McCaffrey writes of another young woman, Menolly, whose special power is tied to her remarkable talent for music. Her family denies her dream of becoming a Harper because tradition dictates that the making of music is a man's task. Menolly runs away, taking shelter from her planet's fiery scourge of "Threadfall" in a hollow cliff by the sea. Here she stumbles on a hatching clutch of coveted fire lizards, kin to the great dragons that patrol the skies. Being the first to feed and touch the new creatures, she "bonds" with nine of them, commanding their loyalty for life. Menolly's beautiful lizards help give her the confidence she needs to take up a new life when she is rescued by a dragonrider and brought to the attention of the Master Harper. *Dragonsinger* tells of Menolly's trials and successes as an apprentice at Harper Hall, and *Dragondrums* takes up the story of her fellow student Piemur, who has his own role to play in protecting the kingdom of Pern. Except for the unusual proper names, these books are less complex and easier to read than many of the high fantasies previously discussed. *Dragonsong* in particular has great reader appeal; but it may be worth noting that in comparison to other fantasy protagonists, Menolly pays a small price for getting her heart's desire.

Dragon's Blood by Jane Yolen has some similarity to the McCaffrey books although it embodies a sterner view of the world. On a mythical planet, dragons who fight for sport must be trained from hatchlings by one who has the gift for mind-bonding with them. Yolen tells the story of Jakkin, a bond servant who steals a newly hatched dragon and trains it in the hope of earning his bond price and his freedom. His surprising success is due in part to the help of a girl named Akki, who has distinct ideas about running her own life. In *Heart's Blood*, Jakkin's plans to enter his own dragon in the gaming pits are disrupted when he agrees to infiltrate a treacherous rebel group. *A Sending of Dragons* brings Jakkin and Akki together for the exciting conclusion to the series.

A superior tale against which other novels of high fantasy may be judged is *A Wizard of Earthsea* by Ursula

K. Le Guin. Studying at the School for Wizards, Sparrowhawk is taunted by a jealous classmate to use his powers before he is ready. Pride and arrogance drive him to call up a dreadful malignant shadow that threatens his life and all of Earthsea. Thus begins a chase and the hunt between the young wizard and the shadow-beast across the mountains and the waters of this world. Sparrowhawk, or Ged, his true name known only by his most trusted friends, is a well-developed character who transforms from an intelligent, impatient adolescent into a wise and grateful mage, or wizard. A major theme of the story is the responsibility that each choice carries with it. When Ged asks one of his teachers at the school how transformation of objects can be made permanent, he is answered:

> . . . you will learn it, when you are ready to learn it. But you must not change one thing, one pebble, one grain of sand, until you know what good and evil will follow the act. The world is in Equilibrium. A wizard's power of Changing and of Summoning can change the balance of the world. It is dangerous, that power. It is most perilous. It must follow knowledge, and serve need. To light a candle is to cast a shadow. (p. 57)

The word *shadow* is one of the recurring motifs of the story: Ged's boat bears this name; the evil he releases into the world is called a shadow; and in the end, Ged recognizes this evil as a shadow of himself and his hasty deed. The power of knowing the true name of someone or something, a common motif in traditional literature, is of central importance to this story. So, too, is the value of self-knowledge:

> Ged's ultimate quest . . . had made him whole: a man who knowing his whole true self, cannot be used or possessed by another power other than by himself, and whose life therefore is lived for life's sake and never in the service of ruin, or pain, or hatred, or the dark. (p. 203)

The next story in this quartet of Earthsea is *The Tombs of Atuan*, the sinister tale of a child priestess given at the age of 5 to a cult of darkness and evil. At 15, Tenar discovers Ged trapped in the tombs of Atuan, a place where no man is allowed, and she must decide whether to save him. This more somber story provides important insights into trust and the price of freedom. *The Farthest Shore* in a sense completes the mighty deeds of Ged, as the wizard must use all of his wisdom to defeat evil forces threatening to overcome Earthsea. *Tehanu* returns to Tenar and her attempts to save a child, who has been abused both physically and sexually. Ged returns to these hills entirely spent of his powers and humiliated,

but it is his human act, rather than his powers of wizardry, that saves Tenar and the child, who must herself come into her own powers. This final volume explores the many sources of a woman's strength—hearth, heart, and humanity—that she draws upon to arrive at mature and vital love. The metaphors in all four stories speak clearly and profoundly to today's world.

Science Fiction

The line between fantasy and science fiction has always been difficult to draw, particularly in children's literature. Children are likely to use the label *science fiction* for any book that includes the paraphernalia of science, although critics make finer distinctions. It has been suggested that fantasy (even "science fantasy") presents a world that never was and never could be, whereas science fiction speculates on a world that, given what we now know of science, might just one day be possible. Sylvia Engdahl says that "science fiction differs from fantasy not in subject matter but in aim, and its unique aim is to suggest real hypotheses about mankind's future or about the nature of the universe."[18] Of course, the difficulty comes in deciding what constitutes a "real hypothesis." Are talking cats possible? Plants with a crystalline structure? Spaceships that think and are self-repairing? All these ideas have been put forth by science fiction writers asking themselves "What if . . . ?"

Science fiction is relevant for today's rapidly changing world. Writers must speculate about future technology and how new discoveries will affect our daily lives and thoughts. To do this, they must construct a world in which scientific frontiers of genetic engineering, artificial intelligence, space exploration, or robotics have advanced beyond our present knowledge. As in modern fantasy, detailed descriptions of these "scientific principles" and the characters' acceptance of them make the story believable. H. M. Hoover speaks about the author's responsibility to be consistent with "facts":

> If the story takes place on an alien world, the reader must be able to believe humans can walk there. Everything, from gravity and atmosphere, geology and life forms, must fit and be a part of that world if it is to ring true. . . . If not, somewhere a bright child will say "baloney" or a less polite equivalent, and toss the book aside. Children may be gullible from lack of time to learn, but they're not stupid, and they remember details.[19]

[18]Sylvia Louise Engdahl, "The Changing Role of Science Fiction in Children's Literature," *Horn Book Magazine*, October 1971, p. 450.

[19]H. M. Hoover, "Where Do You Get Your Ideas?" *Top of the News* 39 (fall 1982): 61.

In addition, authors who speak to today's reader about the future must consider the ethical or social implications inherent in the scientific issues they raise.

One of the values of science fiction is its ability to develop children's imagination and intuition as well as exercise their speculative and improvisational abilities. Most literature offers a view of society as it is; science fiction assumes a vastly different society. Madeleine L'Engle suggests that children enter this world of speculation more easily than adults do: "Children have always been interested in these cosmic questions and riddles that adults often attempt to tame by placing into categories fit only for scientists or adults or theologians."[20]

Much science fiction that considers cosmic questions falls within the realm of young adult novels. For instance, Peter Dickinson in *Eva* considers the consequences when the mind of a human girl is transferred from her ruined body to that of a healthy chimpanzee. H. M. Hoover's *Orvis* suggests what might happen if a robot developed human emotions. *The Duplicate* by William Sleator gives a teenage boy the power to be in two places at once, with chilling results. Occasionally, however, older elementary and middle school readers, drawn by a love of science, might read well above what adults consider their usual reading levels. Because newer science fiction tends to emphasize a concern with the complex emotional and physical consequences of technological breakthroughs to the future of humankind rather than the dangers posed by aliens or intergalactic warfare, perhaps science fiction readers will be more compassionate and informed in choosing the future.

Through the Door

Many children come easily to science fiction by way of books that might not fit a purist's definition of the genre but that incorporate some of its trappings, such as robots, spaceships, futuristic settings, or scientific terminology. Eleanor Cameron's *The Wonderful Flight to the Mushroom Planet* begins a series of stories about Mr. Bass, who lives on the planet Basidium. Alfred Slote has written a popular series that begins with *My Robot Buddy*, in which Jack Jameson and his robot Danny One switch places to foil robotnappers. Older readers are often entertained by Isaac Asimov's Norby series about an adolescent boy and his robot. Few of these books tackle weighty themes, but they provide satisfaction to readers who can follow the characters through a series of adventures or who relish the ultimately happy conclusions in a science fiction setting.

[20]Madeleine L'Engle, "Childlike Wonder and the Truths of Science Fiction," *Children's Literature* 10 (1982), 102.

From the porthole of their departing spaceship, two sisters watch as the world diminishes and finally disappears in Lloyd Bloom's illustration from *The Green Book* by Jill Paton Walsh.
Illustration by Lloyd Bloom from *The Green Book* by Jill Paton Walsh. Copyright © 1982 by Lloyd Bloom. Reprinted by permission of Farrar, Straus & Giroux, Inc.

An exceptional book that presents a hopeful view of the future is Jill Paton Walsh's *The Green Book*. A family escapes Earth with others in a preprogrammed spacecraft before the "Disaster." Father tells Joe, Sarah, and Pattie that they can take very little with them but that this includes "one book per voyager." Pattie is ridiculed for wasting her choice on a blank green-covered book. When they arrive at their destination planet, Pattie, as the youngest, has the privilege of naming their new home, a place of red foliage and shimmering silver plains. "We are at Shine, on the first day," says Pattie. Ironically, this shine is produced by the crystalline structure of the plant life on the planet. When the wheat seeds brought from Earth produce a crop of grains like "hexagonal yellow beads, shining like golden glass," it appears that the colony will face starvation. The children secretly grind the glasslike beads, mix and bake the dough, and eat the bread without harm. It is then that Pattie's blank book is needed to keep records, and the story-starved people discover that the green book is now full of the most satisfying story of all—their own. An excellent choice for reading aloud and discussing with third and fourth graders, this brief, high-quality book raises thought-provoking speculations about life and survival on another planet. The writing is vivid and tight, evocative without being obscure, and an interesting twist in the narrative voice neatly brings together the opening and closing sentences. Illustrations by Lloyd Bloom match the solemn tone of the text and are memorable for their rounded shapes softened by the light on Shine.

Visitors to Earth

Television and motion pictures have eased our acceptance of the possibility of visitors from other parts of the universe. Whether the visitor arrives purposefully or inadvertently, young readers today are willing to suspend disbelief and are usually prepared to consider the dilemmas that interactions between visitors and humans present.

Alexander Key presents a visitor to Earth in *The Forgotten Door*, which explores the rights of individuals and challenges readers' assumptions about the nature of human society. Little Jon wakens cold and bruised in a mossy cave and cannot remember who he is or where he came from. He is found by the kindly Bean family, who gradually discover that he is not from this world. Rumors about his strange powers spread, however, and soon the federal government demands custody of Little Jon. Other political groups would like to use Jon's powers, and the Beans are desperate for help. Finally, Jon is able to hear his parents calling him, and he communicates his concern for his friends, the Beans. As various forces close in on their tiny cabin, Jon and the Beans disappear through the Forgotten Door to the world Jon has described to them—a world so simple as to need no laws, leaders, or money, and where intelligent people work together. The fast pace of the story and its substantial characters and challenging themes have made this a good discussion choice for small groups of fourth and fifth graders.

The title character in Dick King-Smith's *Harriet's Hare* is really a visitor from the planet Pars who has been dropped off on Earth for a brief vacation. He assumes the shape of a hare and is discovered by Harriet in the middle of a flattened circle in her father's wheat field. Harriet, a lonely child since her mother's death, is thrilled to have a new friend, whom she names Wiz. The two have a wonderful time exploring the countryside together. Wiz is certainly an extraordinary friend, and because he can communicate with animals he shows Harriet the natural world in a new and magical way. Dreading the end of his vacation, Harriet implores him to stay longer, but he reminds her that he misses his home and must return. He leaves behind several wonderful gifts, however—three little hare offspring and a new mother for Harriet. Although this is a lovely surprise to Harriet, it is no wonder at all to readers who have watched the romance grow between Harriet's father and a children's book author who has moved in nearby. King-Smith spins a warm and gentle tale for younger readers, filled with the wonders of the English countryside and brimming with likable and amusing characters.

In this illustration by Roger Roth for *Harriet's Hare* by Dick King-Smith, Harriet meets Wiz, an alien who has assumed the form of an Earth animal.
From *Harriet's Hare* by Dick King-Smith, illustrated by Roger Roth. Illustrations copyright © 1995 by Roger Roth. Reprinted by permission of Crown Publishers, Inc.

The title-character visitor to this planet in Daniel Pinkwater's *Borgel* moves into Melvin Spellbound's family's guest room as a sort of long-lost uncle. The special occasions when Melvin is invited into Uncle Borgel's room to drink Norwegian vole-moss tea lead to an invitation to travel in time, space, and "the other," a place Borgel compares to a tossed salad. Borgel, Melvin, and the unlovable family dog, Fafnir, who can suddenly speak, are off to outer space to visit a time traveler's root beer stand managed by a Bloboform. There they begin their search for the Great Popsicle, which is a coveted sort of energy bundle. Pinkwater's puns, jokes, and asides and the flip "science" he invents are bound to be traded back and forth by older readers who relish the social aspects of reading a truly funny book.

In Lesley Howarth's *Maphead*, older readers will appreciate the adventures of a half-human, half-alien 12-year-old who has returned to Earth with his father. Their purpose is to meet his mother and to understand his roots so that he can come into his full power. This is as much a coming-of-age story as it is a power trip for Maphead. Like any young adolescent, he longs to know who he really is, aches for friends, and wishes for the love of a mother he has never known. He is also inept and clumsy, able to flash a map of any location on his head but unable to map the vagaries of the human heart. Howarth's wickedly funny descriptions of alien habits, particularly their diet, will appeal to the adolescent's sense of the gross, but good writing and strong characterization make this book more than a run-of-the-mill visit from aliens.

Outer Space and Cyberspace

The technology of the late twentieth century makes visits beyond Earth's surface much more plausible to today's child, and many writers have tapped into the premise that interstellar travel is just around the corner. In Annette Klause's *Alien Secrets*, Robin Goodfellow, nicknamed "Puck," is a troubled 12-year-old expelled from her boarding school and traveling to join her parents on the distant planet of Shoon when she witnesses a murder. On board her spaceship she encounters an alien boy named Hush who has lost the Soo, a treasure of his people that he was entrusted with returning to them. It becomes apparent that, along with a few ghosts, the murderer is on board their spaceship, and that the Soo is at the center of a devious plot. Puck risks her life to help Hush find the treasure but the two make a great team. The mystery is solved, the villains unmasked, and the Soo restored to its rightful place. Both Puck and Hush find their strengths in adversity and also come to accept their faults. This is a thrilling story, interwoven with subtle political themes of oppression and colonization that raise the book far above the level of most outerspace adventures.

Enchantress from the Stars by Sylvia Louise Engdahl centers on the mission of Elana, to save the Andrecians from the Imperialists. Elana belongs to an anthropological service of the future that represents the most advanced humanity in the universe. By contrast, the Andrecians are at a medieval stage of development; people still believe in magic and will reward anyone who can kill the "terrible dragon." The dragon, however, is really an earthmover with which the Imperialists intend to destroy forests and colonize the planet. Eventually the fourth son of an Andrecian woodcutter and Elana defeat the invaders with the values of love, faith, and sacrifice that transcend all levels of material development. The story helps readers see their own world in a different perspective, a function of all good literature. In a somewhat didactic sequel, *The Far Side of Evil*, Engdahl deals with the consequences of misusing nuclear power. *This Star Shall Abide* and *Beyond the Tomorrow Mountains* are other contributions by this major writer of science fiction for young adults.

Although outerspace adventures have been popular since Jules Verne wrote *From the Earth to the Moon*, there is now a growing subgenre of science fiction set in cyberspace. In the hilarious *Lost in Cyberspace* by Richard Peck, Josh Lewis's friend Aaron figures out a way to use his laptop computer to travel through time. The two sixth graders then carry out the ultimate research paper and plan to present their findings at their school's Parents' Night. In *Cyberstorm*, Gloria Skurzynski's 11-year-old heroine, Darcy, escapes into a virtual reality machine in the year 2015. Trying to save her dog, Chip, from the Animal Control Division, Darcy is sent back in time with Mrs. Galloway, an elderly woman who rented the machine to revisit her youth. When the machine malfunctions, the two are caught

in a terrifying world that might be real or surreal. Both books have the type of fast-moving plots that appeal to middle-grade readers, but they also deal with more serious problems that confront families and cut across generations.

Works like Orson Scott Card's *Ender's Game* and Joan Vinge's *Psion*, although published for adult readers, have been discovered by adolescents who are devotees of computer games and steeped in the language of the computer. These readers might have the background to enjoy such young-adult titles as Vivian Vande Velde's *User Unfriendly* and Monica Hughes's *Invitation to the Game*, and they will certainly find Gillian Cross's *New World* accessible. Cross tells a gripping tale in which Miriam, Will, and Stuart, three 14-year-olds unknown to each other, are recruited by a computer company to test a prototype of a new virtual reality game. As each becomes more and more hooked on the game, one of them begins to suspect that there is something sinister behind the fun. In circumstances that become increasingly threatening, the youngsters are forced to face questions about their own identities and the nature of reality itself. In a thought-provoking and chilling scenario Cross manages to address issues such as manipulation, greed, and the lengths young people will go to for excitement.

Views of the Future

Science fiction of the highest level presents the reader with complex hypotheses about the future of humankind. Many of H. M. Hoover's novels raise questions about the organization of society and the nature of the world following a massive ecological disaster. Writers such as John Christopher and Madeleine L'Engle imagine other life-forms and their interactions with our world. William Sleator in *The Green Futures of Tycho* asks how present time can be altered to affect the future; in L'Engle's *A Swiftly Tilting Planet*, the past is altered to change the present and future. Throughout these novels of speculation runs the question of which human qualities and responsibilities will become—or remain—essential in time to come.

A Wrinkle in Time suggests that love and individuality will continue to be important for the future. If there is a classic in the field of science fiction for children, it might be this Newbery Medal award winner by Madeleine L'Engle. The exciting story concerns Charles Wallace, a 5-year-old brilliant beyond his age and time, and Meg, his 12-year-old sister, whose stubbornness later becomes an asset. With the help of Calvin O'Keefe, a 14-year-old on whose stability the two often rely, the children begin a frenzied search for their missing father, a scientist working for the government. They are aided in their search by three women who have supernatural powers—Mrs. Whatsit, Mrs. Who, and Mrs. Which. The children travel by means of a wrinkle in time, or a tesseract, to the evil planet Camazotz. The people of Camazotz, having given up their identities to "It," do everything in synchronization. When Charles Wallace attempts to resist It by reason, he, too, is captured. Though Meg is able to save her father, they must leave Charles Wallace behind. Exhausted and still under the evil influence of It, Meg is slowly nursed back to love and peace by another strange but loving creature, Aunt Beast. When Meg realizes that only she can save Charles Wallace, she returns to confront It with what she knows It does not have or understand—the power of love. This many-layered story can be read for the exciting plot alone or for the themes and the values it espouses.

A *Wind in the Door*, also by L'Engle, is a companion story involving many of the previous characters with new situations and other creatures. The story concerns the fight to save Charles Wallace from a baffling illness. Meg, Calvin, and Mr. Jenkins, the cold, remote principal of the school, are led to a planet in galactic space where size does not exist. Here they are made small enough to enter Charles Wallace's body and help fight the attacking forces of evil, the Echthroi. Only when Meg names them with her own name does she overcome the Echthroi and save Charles. The story emphasizes the importance of every minuscule part of the universe in carrying out its purpose in living. A *Wind in the Door* is more complex than A *Wrinkle in Time*, but L'Engle is capable of conveying her message to perceptive children of 9 or 10 and up.

A *Swiftly Tilting Planet* completes L'Engle's Time Trilogy. Charles Wallace has been saved, first from the dehumanization of It, and second from a rare blood disease. Now, in this story, the reader discovers why Charles Wallace has been twice rescued, for his ultimate mission involves saving the world from total destruction. He must journey back in historical time to change some seemingly small part of past relationships so that a potential world war in the present can be averted. This is by far the most demanding of the three volumes, as there are many characters in several time frames to attend to. The Time Trilogy is a unique and wonderful combination of science fiction, modern fantasy, traditional lore, and religious symbolism by which L'Engle stretches the minds and the spirits of her readers.

The *Ear, the Eye, and the Arm* by Penelope Farmer is a complex, gripping, and funny story set in Zimbabwe in the year 2194. Thirteen-year-old Tendai and his younger brother and sister live in a protected enclave in a society that separates out the haves from the have-nots. Like children in other tales, however, they long for adventure, and when they venture out from behind the electrified fences one day, they get more than they bargained for. Kidnapped by the She Elephant's hooligans, they are taken to a toxic waste dump where this evil old woman holds court. They escape to an idyllic village where technology is banned and the people live in pastoral splendor. But they find that the price for this peace is often death for those who are weak or won't conform. Close behind the three children in their escapades is an unusual trio of detectives—Ear, Eye, and Arm, who have unusual powers because of genetic mutation and have been hired by the children's parents to bring them home. As in all good cliffhangers, however, they discover the children's whereabouts just a fraction too late to rescue them, and the children, particularly Tendai, must take responsibility for themselves. Farmer weaves Shona mythology, science fiction, and a little Hollywood action thriller into a book that has many layers. She raises searching questions about social and political issues without neglecting issues that are closer to the heart of a young boy's coming of age, all in the context of a strapping good yarn.

The White Mountains quartet by John Christopher describes a future world that has been reduced to a primitive society. However, people in this twenty-first-century world are controlled by machine creatures called Tripods. At 14 each human being must be "capped," a ceremony in which a steel plate is inserted into the skull to make the wearer a servant of the state. In *The White Mountains* Will talks to a seemingly crazy Vagrant and finds out that there is a colony of free people living in the White Mountains to the south. Will describes the terrifying journey that he and two other boys make to reach this refuge. In the second book, *The City of Gold and Lead*, Will wins an athletic contest in order to have "the privilege" of serving the master Tripods. Actually, he goes as a spy to learn the secrets of this alien culture. In the third book of the series, *The Pool of Fire*, the Tripods are defeated and humans are free to set up their own government. The reader hopes that Will's plan for world unity will succeed, but realistically Will is forced by quarreling dissident groups to give up his plans for world peace. Christopher explains in an ingenious prequel how the Tripods assumed power in *When the Tripods Came*.

Christopher's second science-fiction series—*The Prince in Waiting, Beyond the Burning Lands*, and *The Sword of the Spirits*—deals with England in the twenty-first century. People measure time since the "Disaster," a period of volcanic activity, earthquakes, and strong radiation from the sun that destroyed all of humanity's technical accomplishments. Amid the ruins, a kind of medieval society has sprung up, with independent city-states not far advanced beyond barbarian tribal life. Religion takes the form of Spiritism in this society, and the use of machines or the pursuit of science is strictly forbidden. These books are much more violent than the White Mountain quartet, which is in keeping with their imagined setting. However, the violence may be justified because it raises the ethical questions of whether violence impersonalized by distance and machine is any different from hand-to-hand violence and whether it is possible to keep "rules" in war. All of John Christopher's books help children consider the problems of the future of humankind, but the themes never overburden the suspense or action of the stories.

Teenager Ann Burden in *Z for Zachariah* by Robert C. O'Brien thinks she is the last living person on Earth, following a nuclear war. She begins to carve out a solitary life, accompanied only by the family dog, when she sees what appears to be smoke from a campfire on the horizon. She finds another survivor, John Loomis. But instead of providing Ann with hoped-for companionship, he becomes more and more possessive. At last she decides on a plan of escape and leaves the valley in hopes that she will find other survivors she has dreamed about. Written in the form of a diary kept by Ann, this story is rich in the details of her survival and growing resolve. Ann relates her doubt and anger about the many choices she must make, but the reader does not doubt that Ann will find the others for whom she searches.

In *Phoenix Rising* by Karen Hesse, Nyle and her grandmother must deal with nuclear threat that is all the more chilling for being so possible. The setting for the story is rural Vermont, where the countryside has been contaminated by a terrible accident at the Cookshire nuclear power plant. Nyle is horrified when her grandmother takes in two survivors from the disaster, 15-year-old Ezra and his mother. Ezra is dying, and Nyle, deeply wounded by the deaths of her mother and grandfather, wants nothing to do with these refugees. She finds she is drawn to the boy, however, and gradually she grows to care deeply for him. In the end, accepting his death means that she accepts life. This lovely coming-of-age story is full of hope, for Nyle is no longer the angry child shut off from those around her, but a mature young woman who clearly sees her responsibility to others and to their future world.

Lois Lowry's *The Giver* imagines a future that at first seems benign and idyllic. Pollution is gone, family life is tranquil, and communities are orderly and peaceful. In this world young Jonas approaches the Ceremony of Twelve with anticipation, for this is when he will be assigned to his life's work. He is stunned when his name is passed over during the ceremony, but then the Chief Elder announces that Jonas has been selected to be the next Receiver of Memory. This is the one person in the

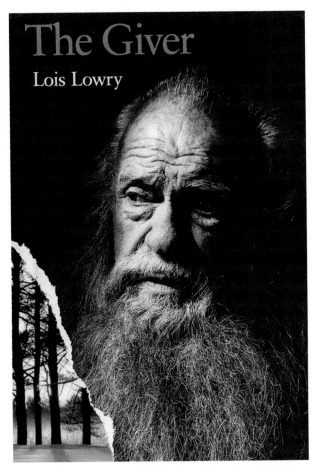

In her Newbery Medal–winning book *The Giver,* Lois Lowry raises fundamental questions about human nature and human society.
Cover from *The Giver.* Copyright © 1993 by Lois Lowry. Reprinted by permission of Houghton Mifflin Company. All rights reserved.

community who holds memories not just of events, but of feelings. As he is instructed by the old Receiver, now the Giver, he comes to understand the fullness of human experience in all its color, joy, and pain. He also begins to see beneath the orderly surface of his existence and to understand the terrible price his people have paid for their serenity. Determined to change the course of the future, Jonas and the Giver plan for his escape. But at the last moment a terrible threat to Gabriel, a foster child about whom Jonas cares deeply, forces a change of plan, and he sets out on a journey that might lead to his end or might bring him full circle to his humanity. *The Giver* is a richly rewarding fantasy, full of subtle clues, connections, and ideas. Lowry has given each reader the wonderful gift that Jonas's community lacked, the gift of choice. This is a book to be read, enjoyed, and understood on an intensely personal level. In her Newbery acceptance speech, Lowry remarked on the interpretation a young reader brought to the book.

The child—as we all do—has brought her own life to a book. She has found a place, a place in the pages of a book, that shares her own frustrations and feelings. . . . Most of the young readers who have written to me have perceived the magic of the circular journey—the truth that we go out and come back, and that what we come back to is changed, and so are we.[21]

[21]Lois Lowry, "Newbery Medal Acceptance," *Horn Book Magazine,* July/August 1994, pp. 420–421.

The ability to change lives is the power of such good writing. Fantasy for children needs no defense. Whether a modern fairy tale like *Many Moons* or *The Little Prince*, modern fantasy like *Charlotte's Web* or *The Dark Is Rising*, or the science fiction of *A Wrinkle in Time* or *The Giver*, these lasting books can speak for our time and the times to come. They stretch children's imaginations, present our own world in a new perspective, and ask readers to consider how present actions might affect Earth's ecological, political, and social future.

Learning Experiences

1. Ask a group of middle graders, or your friends, to list their ten favorite children's books. How many of these could be categorized as modern fantasy?

2. Write a modern fairy tale, fable, or tall tale using the old forms, but with twentieth-century content reflecting today's changing values. For example, you might want to consider reversing the stereotyped sex roles of the prince and princess.

3. Working with children, or your peers, make an illustrated map to show an extraordinary world or imaginary realm that you have discovered in a book. Make a key to locate events of the story.

4. Compare the Chronicles of Narnia by C. S. Lewis with Lloyd Alexander's Prydain Chronicles; or compare two animal fantasies, such as *Charlotte's Web* and *Pigs Might Fly*. In what ways are they alike? How are they different?

5. Choose a book of high fantasy or time fantasy and identify motifs that seem derived from folklore, myth, or legend. Which of these motifs are common in other modern fantasies?

6. Make a display or a chart of the many symbols and their meaning found in *The Dark Is Rising* by Susan Cooper.

7. Think of some family heirloom that might act as a magical amulet that would take you back to the time when your mother or father was 12 years old. How does the heirloom "work"? Where would you be? What might you witness?

8. Ask yourself what might happen to the world of tomorrow if hunger were eliminated, or if robots took over your school, or if hydrogen fusion were made a workable source of energy. Think through the impact of one such scientific advancement.

Related Readings

Anderson, Douglas A. *The Annotated Hobbit.* Illustrated by J. R. R. Tolkien. New York: Houghton Mifflin, 1988.

Fascinating background information on Tolkien's sources for story, choices of names, scholarship, revisions, and illustrations, including many examples from foreign editions.

Cameron, Eleanor. *The Green and Burning Tree.* Boston: Little, Brown, 1969.

The title essay in this fine book of literary criticism is a study of time fantasy. As the author of many fantasies herself, Cameron is in a unique position to evaluate the fantasies in this category.

Campbell, Joseph. *The Hero with a Thousand Faces.* 2nd ed. Princeton, N.J.: Princeton University Press, 1968.

This standard scholarly work on the "monomyth," or the archetypal story of the hero, helps the serious student of high fantasy to see the protagonist of the quest in a universal perspective.

Egoff, Sheila. *Worlds Within: Children's Fantasy from the Middle Ages to Today.* Chicago: American Library Association, 1988.

A study of the development of children's fantasy from its roots in ancient myth and legend to the intense and sometimes violent novels being written today.

Egoff, Sheila, G. T. Stubbs, and L. F. Ashley. *Only Connect: Readings on Children's Literature.* 2nd ed. New York: Oxford University Press, 1980.

All the selections under "Fairy Tales, Fantasy, Animals" would be appropriate reading for this chapter. However, don't miss reading the article by C. S. Lewis, "On Three Ways of Writing for Children," or the fine article by P. L. Travers (creator of Mary Poppins), "Only Connect."

Gose, Elliott. *Mere Creatures: A Study of Modern Fantasy Tales for Children.* Toronto: University of Toronto Press, 1988.

In twelve thoughtful essays Gose focuses on creatures in fantasy, from the "real" rabbits of *Watership Down* to the toy animals in *Winnie-the-Pooh* to mythical creatures in *The Hobbitt* and finds psychological as well as literary underpinnings.

Hunter, Mollie. *Talent Is Not Enough.* New York: Harper & Row, 1975.

A talented author discusses writing for children. In the essay "One World," Hunter maintains that true fantasy so integrates the real and the imagined worlds that it becomes believable. She also acknowledges fantasy's debt to ancient folklore, describing the basis for her own writing of *A Stranger Came Ashore.*

Le Guin, Ursula K. *The Language of the Night: Essays on Fantasy and Science Fiction.* Edited by Susan Wood. New York: Putnam, 1979.

Excellent essays by an outstanding writer of fantasy and science fiction, including "Myth and Archetype in Science Fiction" and "Why Are Americans Afraid of Dragons?"

Mahy, Margaret. "A Dissolving Ghost: Possible Operations of Truth in Children's Books and the Lives of Children." In the ALA *Arbuthnot Lectures 1980–1989.* Chicago: American Library Association, 1990.

Mahy's intriguing essay reveals the transformation of a real-life experience into a fantastic tale. See also Patricia Wrightson's essay "Stones in Pools," in the same volume, in which she discusses the continuity of story from ancient times and the wonder found in fantasy.

May, Jill P. *Lloyd Alexander.* New York: Twayne, 1991.

A twelve-page biographical essay is followed by a critical examination of each of Alexander's books. Among other things, May discusses Alexander's innovative abilities and the diverse sources his books draw on.

Nadelman, Ruth Lynn. *Fantasy Literature for Children and Young Adults: An Annotated Bibliography.* 3rd ed. New York: Bowker, 1989.

A helpful reference tool, especially for the discovery and sorting out of fantasy series.

Tunnell, Michael O. *The Prydain Companion: A Reference Guide to Lloyd Alexander's Prydain Chronicles.* Westport, Conn.: Greenwood, 1989.

Major characters, places, objects, and themes from Alexander's ten Prydain books are examined in encyclopedic fashion. Entries include a pronunciation guide (helpful for Welsh names), a full discussion of the entry as it is found across the books, and information about the topic's roots in Welsh and Celtic folklore.

Children's Literature

The books listed here are recommended, subject to the qualifications noted in the text. Original publication dates appear in square brackets. See Appendix C for publishers' complete addresses.

Adams, Richard. *Watership Down.* Macmillan, 1974.

Ahlberg, Allan. *The Giant Baby.* Illustrated by Fritz Wegner. Viking, 1994.

Aiken, Joan. *Black Hearts in Battersea.* Illustrated by Robin Jacques. Doubleday, 1964.

———. *Cold Shoulder Road.* Delacorte, 1996.

———. *Is Underground.* Dell, 1995.

———. *Nightbirds on Nantucket.* Illustrated by Robin Jacques. Doubleday, 1966.

———. *The Stolen Lake.* Delacorte, 1981.

———. *The Wolves of Willoughby Chase.* Illustrated by Pat Marriott. Doubleday, 1963.

Alexander, Lloyd. *The Arkadians*. Dutton, 1995.

———. *The Beggar Queen*. Dutton, 1984.

———. *The Black Cauldron*. Holt, 1965.

———. *The Book of Three*. Holt, 1964.

———. *The Castle of Llyr*. Holt, 1966.

———. *The Cat Who Wished to Be a Man*. Dutton, 1973.

———. *Coll and His White Pig*. Illustrated by Evaline Ness. Holt, 1965.

———. *The Drackenburg Adventure*. Dutton, 1988.

———. *The El Dorado Adventure*. Dutton, 1987.

———. *The High King*. Holt, 1968.

———. *The Illyrian Adventure*. Dutton, 1986.

———. *The Jedera Adventure*. Dutton, 1989.

———. *The Kestrel*. Dutton, 1982.

———. *The Marvelous Misadventures of Sebastian*. Dutton, 1970.

———. *The Philadelphia Adventure*. Dutton, 1990.

———. *The Remarkable Journey of Prince Jen*. Dutton, 1991.

———. *Taran Wanderer*. Holt, 1967.

———. *The Truthful Harp*. Illustrated by Evaline Ness. Holt, 1971.

———. *Westmark*. Dutton, 1981.

———. *The Wizard in the Tree*. Illustrated by Laszlo Kubinyi. Dutton, 1975.

Andersen, Hans Christian. *The Emperor's New Clothes*. Illustrated by Virginia Lee Burton. Houghton Mifflin, 1949.

———. *The Fir Tree*. Illustrated by Nancy Ekholm Burkert. Harper & Row, 1970.

———. *Hans Christian Andersen: The Complete Fairy Tales and Stories*. Translated by Erik Haugaard. Doubleday, 1974.

———. *The Little Match Girl*. Illustrated by Rachel Isadora. Putnam, 1987.

———. *The Little Match Girl*. Illustrated by Blair Lent. Houghton Mifflin, 1968.

———. "The Little Mermaid." In *Hans Christian Andersen: The Complete Fairy Tales and Stories*, translated by Erik Christian Haugaard. Doubleday, 1974.

———. *The Nightingale*. Translated by Anthea Bell. Illustrated by Lisbeth Zwerger. Picture Book Studio, 1985.

———. *The Nightingale*. Adapted by Anna Bier. Illustrated by Demi. Harcourt Brace, 1985.

———. *The Nightingale*. Translated by Eva Le Gallienne. Illustrated by Nancy Ekholm Burkert. Harper & Row, 1965.

———. "The Princess and the Pea." In *Seven Tales*, translated by Eva Le Gallienne, illustrated by Maurice Sendak. HarperCollins, 1990 [1959].

———. *The Princess and the Pea*. Illustrated by Paul Galdone. Seabury, 1978.

———. *The Snow Queen*. Retold by Amy Ehrlich. Illustrated by Susan Jeffers. Dial, 1982.

———. *The Snow Queen*. Adapted by Naomi Lewis. Illustrated by Errol Le Cain. Viking, 1979.

———. *The Snow Queen*. Retold by Neil Philip. Illustrated by Sally Holmes. Lothrop, Lee & Shepard, 1989.

———. *The Steadfast Tin Soldier*. Retold by Tor Seidler. Illustrated by Fred Marcellino. HarperCollins, 1992.

———. *Thumbelina*. Retold by Amy Ehrlich. Illustrated by Susan Jeffers. Dial, 1979.

———. *The Tinderbox*. Illustrated by Warwick Hutton. McElderry, 1988.

———. *The Ugly Duckling*. Illustrated by Troy Howell. Putnam, 1990.

———. *The Ugly Duckling*. Retold by Marianna Mayer. Illustrated by Thomas Locker. Macmillan, 1987.

———. *The Wild Swans*. Retold by Amy Ehrlich. Illustrated by Susan Jeffers. Dial, 1981.

Asimov, Janet, and Isaac Asimov. *Norby, the Mixed-Up Robot*. Walker, 1983.

Atwater, Richard, and Florence Atwater. *Mr. Popper's Penguins*. Illustrated by Robert Lawson. Little, Brown, 1938.

Avi. *Poppy*. Illustrated by Brian Floca. Orchard, 1995.

Babbitt, Natalie. *Kneeknock Rise*. Farrar, Straus & Giroux, 1970.

———. *The Search for Delicious*. Farrar, Straus & Giroux, 1969.

———. *Tuck Everlasting*. Farrar, Straus & Giroux, 1975.

Bailey, Carolyn Sherwin. *Miss Hickory*. Illustrated by Ruth Gannett. Viking, 1962 [1946].

Banks, Lynne Reid. *The Indian in the Cupboard*. Illustrated by Brock Cole. Doubleday, 1981.

———. *The Mystery of the Cupboard*. Illustrated by Tom Newsom. Doubleday, 1992.

———. *The Return of the Indian*. Illustrated by William Geldard. Doubleday, 1986.

———. *The Secret of the Indian*. Illustrated by Ted Lewin. Doubleday, 1989.

Barron, T. A. *The Merlin Effect*. Philomel, 1994.

Baum, L. Frank. *The Wizard of Oz*. World, 1972 [1900].

Bellairs, John. *The House with a Clock in Its Walls*. Dial, 1973.

Bond, Michael. *A Bear Called Paddington*. Illustrated by Peggy Fortnum. Houghton Mifflin, 1960.

———. *More About Paddington*. Illustrated by Peggy Fortnum. Houghton Mifflin, 1963.

———. *Paddington at Large*. Illustrated by Peggy Fortnum. Houghton Mifflin, 1963.

———. *Paddington Helps Out*. Illustrated by Peggy Fortnum. Houghton Mifflin, 1961.

———. *Paddington Marches On*. Illustrated by Peggy Fortnum. Houghton Mifflin, 1965.

———. *Paddington Takes the Air*. Illustrated by Peggy Fortnum. Houghton Mifflin, 1971.

Bond, Nancy. *A String in the Harp*. Atheneum, 1976.

Boston, L. M. *The Children of Green Knowe*. Illustrated by Peter Boston. Harcourt Brace, 1955.

———. *An Enemy at Green Knowe*. Illustrated by Peter Boston. Harcourt Brace, 1964.

———. *The River at Green Knowe*. Illustrated by Peter Boston. Harcourt Brace, 1959.

———. *The Treasure of Green Knowe*. Illustrated by Peter Boston. Harcourt Brace, 1958.

Brown, Marcia. *Stone Soup*. Scribner's, 1947.

Browne, Anthony. *The Tunnel*. Knopf, 1990.

Buffie, Margaret. *The Haunting of Frances Rain*. Scholastic, 1989 [Published in Canada as *Who Is Frances Rain?* Kids Can Press, 1987].

Butterworth, Oliver. *The Enormous Egg*. Illustrated by Louis Darling. Little, Brown, 1956.

Cameron, Eleanor. *The Court of the Stone Children*. Dutton, 1973.

———. *The Wonderful Flight to the Mushroom Planet*. Illustrated by Robert Henneberger. Little, Brown, 1954.

Card, Orson Scott. *Ender's Game*. Tor, 1985.

Carroll, Lewis [Charles L. Dodgson]. *Alice's Adventures in Wonderland and Through the Looking Glass*. Illustrated by John Tenniel. Macmillan, 1963 [1865, 1872].

Catling, Patrick Skene. *The Chocolate Touch*. Illustrated by Margot Apple. Morrow, 1979 [1952].

Chetwin, Grace. *The Crystal Stair*. Bradbury, 1988.

———. *Gom on Windy Mountain*. Lothrop, Lee & Shepard, 1986.

———. *The Riddle and the Rune*. Bradbury, 1987.

———. *The Starstone*. Bradbury, 1989.

Christopher, John. *Beyond the Burning Lands*. Macmillan, 1971.

———. *The City of Gold and Lead*. Macmillan, 1967.

————. *The Guardians*. Macmillan, 1968.

————. *The Pool of Fire*. Macmillan, 1968.

————. *The Prince in Waiting*. Macmillan, 1970.

————. *The Sword of the Spirits*. Macmillan, 1972.

————. *The White Mountains*. Macmillan, 1967.

————. *When the Tripods Came*. Dutton, 1988.

Cleary, Beverly. *The Mouse and the Motorcycle*. Illustrated by Louis Darling. Morrow, 1965.

————. *Ralph S. Mouse*. Illustrated by Paul O. Zelinsky. Morrow, 1982.

————. *Runaway Ralph*. Illustrated by Louis Darling. Morrow, 1970.

Conly, Jane. *Rasco and the Rats of NIMH*. Illustrated by Leonard Lubin. Harper & Row, 1986.

————. *R-T, Margaret, and the Rats of NIMH*. Illustrated by Leonard Lubin. HarperCollins, 1990.

Conrad, Pam. *Stonewords*. HarperCollins, 1990.

Cooper, Susan. *The Boggart*. McElderry, 1993.

————. *The Dark Is Rising*. Illustrated by Alan E. Cober. Atheneum, 1973.

————. *Greenwitch*. Atheneum, 1974.

————. *The Grey King*. Atheneum, 1975.

————. *Over Sea, Under Stone*. Illustrated by Marjorie Gill. Harcourt Brace, 1966.

————. *The Selkie Girl*. Illustrated by Warwick Hutton. Macmillan, 1986.

————. *Silver on the Tree*. Atheneum, 1977.

————. *Tam Lin*. Illustrated by Warwick Hutton. Macmillan, 1990.

Corbett, Scott. *The Lemonade Trick*. Illustrated by Paul Galdone. Little, Brown, 1972 [1960].

Dahl, Roald. *Charlie and the Chocolate Factory*. Illustrated by Joseph Schindelman. Knopf, 1972.

————. *Charlie and the Great Glass Elevator*. Illustrated by Joseph Schindelman. Knopf, 1972.

————. *James and the Giant Peach*. Illustrated by Nancy Ekholm Burkert. Knopf, 1961.

————. *The Minpins*. Illustrated by Patrick Benson. Viking, 1991.

de Beaumont, Mme. *Beauty and the Beast*. Illustrated by Jan Brett. Houghton Mifflin, 1989.

Dickinson, Peter. *Eva*. Delacorte, 1989.

————. *Merlin Dreams*. Illustrated by Alan Lee. Delacorte, 1988.

DuBois, William Pène. *The Twenty-One Balloons*. Viking, 1947.

Eager, Edward. *Half Magic*. Illustrated by N. M. Bodecker. Harcourt Brace, 1954.

————. *Seven-Day Magic*. Illustrated by N. M. Bodecker. Harcourt Brace, 1962.

Engdahl, Sylvia Louise. *Beyond the Tomorrow Mountains*. Illustrated by Richard Cuffari. Atheneum, 1973.

————. *Enchantress from the Stars*. Illustrated by Rodney Shackell. Atheneum, 1970.

————. *The Far Side of Evil*. Illustrated by Richard Cuffari. Atheneum, 1971.

————. *This Star Shall Abide*. Illustrated by Richard Cuffari. Atheneum, 1972.

Farmer, Nancy. *The Ear, the Eye, and the Arm*. Orchard, 1994.

————. *The Warm Place*. Orchard, 1995.

Farmer, Penelope. *The Summer Birds*. Illustrated by James Spanfeller. Harcourt Brace, 1962.

Fleischman, Paul. *The Half-a-Moon Inn*. Illustrated by Kathy Jacobi. Harper & Row, 1980.

Fleischman, Sid. *The Midnight Horse*. Illustrated by Peter Sis. Greenwillow, 1990.

————. *The Whipping Boy*. Illustrated by Peter Sis. Greenwillow, 1986.

Gerstein, Mordicai. *The Seal Mother*. Dial, 1986.

Godden, Rumer. *The Dolls' House*. Illustrated by Tasha Tudor. Viking, 1962 [1947].

———. *Fu-Dog*. Illustrated by Valerie Littlewood. Viking, 1990.

———. *Little Plum*. Viking, 1987.

———. *Miss Happiness and Miss Flower*. Viking, 1987.

———. *The Mousewife*. Illustrated by Heidi Holder. Viking, 1982 [1951].

Grahame, Kenneth. *The Open Road*. Illustrated by Beverly Gooding. Scribner's, 1980.

———. *The Reluctant Dragon*. Illustrated by Ernest H. Shepard. Holiday House, 1938.

———. *The River Bank: From the Wind in the Willows*. Illustrated by Adrienne Adams. Scribner's, 1977.

———. *The Wind in the Willows*. Illustrated by E. H. Shepard. Scriber's, 1940 [1908].

———. *Wayfarers All: From the Wind in the Willows*. Illustrated by Beverly Gooding. Scribner's, 1981.

Griffith, Helen V. *Caitlin's Holiday*. Illustrated by Susan Condie Lamb. Greenwillow, 1990.

Grimm brothers. *Rumpelstiltskin*. Illustrated by Paul O. Zelinsky. Dutton, 1986.

Hahn, Mary Downing. *Time for Andrew: A Ghost Story*. Clarion, 1994.

———. *Wait Till Helen Comes: A Ghost Story*. Houghton Mifflin, 1986.

Hamilton, Virginia. *The Magical Adventures of Pretty Pearl*. Harper & Row, 1983.

———. *Sweet Whispers, Brother Rush*. Philomel, 1982.

Hamley, Dennis. *Hare's Choice*. Illustrated by Meg Rutherford. Delacorte, 1990.

Hesse, Karen. *Phoenix, Rising*. Holt, 1994.

Hoban, Russell. *The Mouse and His Child*. Illustrated by Lillian Hoban. Harper & Row, 1967.

Hodges, Margaret. *St. George and the Dragon*. Illustrated by Trina Schart Hyman. Little, Brown, 1984.

Hoover, H. M. *Orvis*. Penguin, 1987.

Howarth, Lesley. *Maphead*. Candlewick, 1994.

Howe, Deborah, and James Howe. *Bunnicula*. Illustrated by Leslie Morrill. Atheneum, 1983.

Howe, James. *The Celery Stalks at Midnight*. Illustrated by Leslie Morrill. Atheneum, 1983.

———. *Howliday Inn*. Illustrated by Lynn Munsinger. Atheneum, 1982.

Hughes, Monica. *Invitation to the Game*. Simon & Schuster, 1990.

Hunter, Mollie. *The Haunted Mountain*. Illustrated by Laszlo Kubinyi. Harper & Row, 1972.

———. *The Mermaid Summer*. Harper & Row, 1988.

———. *A Stranger Came Ashore*. Harper & Row, 1975.

Hurmence, Belinda. *A Girl Called Boy*. Clarion, 1982.

Jacques, Brian. *The Bellmaker*. Philomel, 1995.

———. *Mariel of Redwall*. Illustrated by Gary Chalk. Philomel, 1992.

———. *Martin the Warrior*. Philomel, 1994.

———. *Mattimeo*. Illustrated by Gary Chalk. Philomel, 1990.

———. *Mossflower*. Illustrated by Gary Chalk. Philomel, 1988.

———. *Redwall*. Illustrated by Gary Chalk. Philomel, 1987.

———. *Salmandastron*. Philomel, 1993.

Jansson, Tove. *Tales from Moominvalley*. Translated by Thomas Warburton. Walck, 1964.

Jarrell, Randall. *The Bat-Poet*. Illustrated by Maurice Sendak. Macmillan, 1964.

Jeffers, Susan. *Wild Robin*. Dutton, 1976.

Jones, Diana Wynne. *Charmed Life*. Greenwillow, 1989.

———. *The Lives of Christopher Chant*. Greenwillow, 1988.

Juster, Norton. *The Phantom Tollbooth*. Illustrated by Jules Feiffer. Random House, 1961.

Katz, Welwyn Wilton. *Time Ghost*. McElderry, 1995.

Kendall, Carol. *The Gammage Cup*. Illustrated by Erik Blegvad. Harcourt Brace, 1959.

Kennedy, Richard. *Amy's Eyes*. Illustrated by Richard Egielski. Harper & Row, 1985.

Key, Alexander. *The Forgotten Door*. Westminster, 1965.

Kindl, Patricia. *Owl in Love*. Houghton Mifflin, 1993.

King-Smith, Dick. *Ace: The Very Important Pig*. Illustrated by Lynette Hemmant. Crown, 1990.

———. *Babe the Gallant Pig*. Illustrated by Mary Rayner. Crown, 1985.

———. *The Fox Busters*. Illustrated by Jon Miller. Delacorte, 1988.

———. *Harriet's Hare*. Illustrated by Roger Roth. Crown, 1994.

———. *Pigs Might Fly*. Illustrated by Mary Rayner. Viking, 1982.

———. *The Terrible Trins*. Illustrated by Mark Teague. Crown, 1994.

Klause, Annette Curtis. *Alien Secrets*. Delacorte, 1993.

Langton, Jane. *The Diamond in the Window*. Illustrated by Erik Blegvad. Harper & Row, 1962.

———. *The Fledgling*. Harper & Row, 1980.

Lawson, Robert. *Rabbit Hill*. Viking, 1944.

———. *The Tough Winter*. Viking, 1954.

Le Guin, Ursula K. *The Farthest Shore*. Illustrated by Gail Garraty. Atheneum, 1972.

———. *Tehanu: The Last Book of Earthsea*. Atheneum, 1990.

———. *The Tombs of Atuan*. Illustrated by Gail Garraty. Atheneum, 1971.

———. *A Wizard of Earthsea*. Illustrated by Ruth Robbins. Parnassus, 1968.

L'Engle, Madeleine. *A Swiftly Tilting Planet*. Farrar, Straus & Giroux, 1978.

———. *A Wind in the Door*. Farrar, Straus & Giroux, 1973.

———. *A Wrinkle in Time*. Farrar, Straus & Giroux, 1962.

Lewis, C. S. *The Horse and His Boy*. Illustrated by Pauline Baynes. Macmillan, 1962.

———. *The Last Battle*. Illustrated by Pauline Baynes. Macmillan, 1964.

———. *The Lion, the Witch, and the Wardrobe*. Illustrated by Pauline Baynes. Macmillan, 1961.

———. *The Magician's Nephew*. Illustrated by Pauline Baynes. Macmillan, 1964.

———. *Prince Caspian: The Return to Narnia*. Illustrated by Pauline Baynes. Macmillan, 1964.

———. *The Silver Chair*. Illustrated by Pauline Baynes. Macmillan, 1962.

———. *The Voyage of the "Dawn Treader."* Illustrated by Pauline Baynes. Macmillan, 1962.

Lindgren, Astrid. *Pippi Goes on Board*. Translated by Florence Lamborn. Illustrated by Louis S. Glanzman. Viking, 1957.

———. *Pippi in the South Seas*. Translated by Florence Lamborn. Illustrated by Louis S. Glanzman. Viking, 1959.

———. *Pippi Longstocking*. Illustrated by Louis S. Glanzman. Viking, 1950.

———. *Pippi on the Run*. Viking, 1976.

Lively, Penelope. *The Ghost of Thomas Kempe*. Illustrated by Anthony Maitland. Dutton, 1973.

Lowry, Lois. *The Giver*. Houghton Mifflin, 1993.

Lunn, Janet. *The Root Cellar*. Scribner's, 1983.

MacDonald, George. *At the Back of the North Wind*. Garland, 1976 [1871].

———. *The Golden Key.* Illustrated by Maurice Sendak. Farrar, Straus & Giroux, 1967 [1867].

———. *The Light Princess.* Illustrated by William Pène DuBois. Crowell, 1962.

———. *The Light Princess.* Illustrated by Maurice Sendak. Farrar, Straus & Giroux, 1969.

Mahy, Margaret. *The Haunting.* Macmillan, 1982.

Mayne, William. *Antar and the Eagles.* Delacorte, 1989.

———. *Earthfasts.* Dutton, 1967.

———. *Hob and the Goblins.* Illustrated by Norman Messenger. Dorling Kindersley, 1994.

McCaffrey, Anne. *Dragondrums.* Illustrated by Fred Marcellino. Atheneum, 1979.

———. *Dragonsinger.* Atheneum, 1977.

———. *Dragonsong.* Illustrated by Laura Lydecker. Atheneum, 1976.

McGraw, Eloise. *The Moorchild.* McElderry, 1996.

McKillip, Patricia. *Harpist in the Wind.* Atheneum, 1979.

———. *Heir of Sea and Fire.* Atheneum, 1977.

———. *The Riddle-Master of Hed.* Atheneum, 1976.

McKinley, Robin. *Beauty: A Retelling of the Story of Beauty and the Beast.* Harper & Row, 1978.

———. *The Blue Sword.* Greenwillow, 1982.

———. *The Hero and the Crown.* Greenwillow, 1985.

Merrill, Jean. *The Pushcart War.* Illustrated by Ronni Solbert. W. R. Scott, 1964.

Milne, A. A. *The House at Pooh Corner.* Illustrated by Ernest H. Shepard. Dutton, 1928.

———. *Winnie-the-Pooh.* Illustrated by Ernest H. Shepard. Dutton, 1926.

Moore, Lilian. *I'll Meet You at the Cucumbers.* Illustrated by Sharon Wooding. Atheneum, 1988.

Murphy, Shirley Rousseau. *Silver Woven in My Hair.* Illustrated by Alan Tiegreen. Atheneum, 1977.

Napoli, Donna. *The Magic Circle.* Dutton, 1993.

Norton, Mary. *The Borrowers.* Illustrated by Beth and Joe Krush. Harcourt Brace, 1953.

———. *The Borrowers Afield.* Illustrated by Beth and Joe Krush. Harcourt Brace, 1955.

———. *The Borrowers Afloat.* Illustrated by Beth and Joe Krush. Harcourt Brace, 1959.

———. *The Borrowers Aloft.* Illustrated by Beth and Joe Krush. Harcourt Brace, 1961.

———. *The Borrowers Avenged.* Illustrated by Beth and Joe Krush. Harcourt Brace, 1982.

O'Brien, Robert C. *Mrs. Frisby and the Rats of NIMH.* Illustrated by Zena Bernstein. Atheneum, 1971.

———. *Z for Zachariah.* Atheneum, 1975.

Ormondroyd, Edward. *All in Good Time.* Illustrated by Ruth Robbins. Parnassus, 1975.

———. *Time at the Top.* Illustrated by Peggy Bach. Parnassus, 1963.

Park, Ruth. *Playing Beatie Bow.* Atheneum, 1982.

Pearce, Phillipa. *Tom's Midnight Garden.* Illustrated by Susan Einzig. Lippincott, 1959.

Pearson, Kit. *A Handful of Time.* Viking Penguin, 1988.

Peck, Richard. *Lost in Cyberspace.* Dial, 1995.

Peck, Sylvia. *Seal Child.* Illustrated by Robert Andrew Parker. Morrow, 1989.

Pierce, Tamora. *Alanna, the First Adventure.* Atheneum, 1982.

———. *Emperor Mage.* Simon & Schuster, 1995.

———. *In the Hand of the Goddess.* Atheneum, 1984.

———. *Lioness Rampant.* Atheneum, 1988.

———. *Wild Magic.* Atheneum, 1992.

———. *Wolf-Speaker*. Atheneum, 1994.

———. *The Woman Who Rides Like a Man*. Atheneum, 1986.

Pinkwater, Daniel. *Borgel*. Macmillan, 1990.

Rodda, Emily. *The Pigs Are Flying!* Illustrated by Noela Young. Morrow, 1988.

Saint-Exupéry, Antoine de. *The Little Prince*. Translated by Katherine Woods. Harcourt, 1943.

Sauer, Julia. *Fog Magic*. Illustrated by Lynd Ward. Viking, 1943.

Scieszka, Jon. *2095*. Illustrated by Lane Smith. Viking, 1995.

———. *The Good, the Bad, and the Goofy*. Illustrated by Lane Smith. Viking, 1992.

———. *Knights of the Kitchen Table*. Illustrated by Lane Smith. Viking, 1991.

———. *The Not-So-Jolly Roger*. Illustrated by Lane Smith. Viking, 1991.

———. *Your Mother Was a Neanderthal*. Illustrated by Lane Smith. Viking, 1993.

Selden, George. *Chester Cricket's Pigeon Ride*. Illustrated by Garth Williams. Farrar, Straus & Giroux, 1981.

———. *The Cricket in Times Square*. Illustrated by Garth Williams. Farrar, Straus & Giroux, 1960.

———. *Harry Cat's Pet Puppy*. Illustrated by Garth Williams. Farrar, Straus & Giroux, 1974.

———. *Tucker's Countryside*. Illustrated by Garth Williams. Farrar, Straus & Giroux, 1969.

Sendak, Maurice. *Higglety, Pigglety, Pop!* Harper & Row, 1967.

Sharp, Margery. *Miss Bianca*. Illustrated by Garth Williams. Little, Brown, 1962.

———. *Miss Bianca in the Salt Mines*. Illustrated by Garth Williams. Little, Brown, 1967.

———. *The Rescuers*. Illustrated by Garth Williams. Little, Brown, 1959.

———. *The Turret*. Illustrated by Garth Williams. Little, Brown, 1963.

Sibley, Brian. *The Land of Narnia*. Illustrated by Pauline Baynes. HarperCollins, 1990.

Skurzynski, Gloria. *Cyberstorm*. Macmillan, 1995.

Sleator, William. *The Duplicate*. Dutton, 1988.

———. *The Green Futures of Tycho*. Dutton, 1981.

Slote, Alfred. *My Robot Buddy*. Lippincott, 1975.

Smith, Sherwood. *Wren's Quest*. Harcourt Brace, 1993.

———. *Wren's War*. Harcourt Brace, 1995.

———. *Wren to the Rescue*. Harcourt Brace, 1990.

Snyder, Zilpha Keatley. *Song of the Gargoyle*. Delacorte, 1991.

Steig, William. *Abel's Island*. Farrar, Straus & Giroux, 1976.

———. *Dominic*. Farrar, Straus & Giroux, 1972.

———. *The Real Thief*. Farrar, Straus & Giroux, 1973.

Stewig, John. *Stone Soup*. Illustrated by Margot Tomes. Holiday House, 1991.

Thurber, James. *Many Moons*. Illustrated by Marc Simont. Harcourt Brace, 1990.

———. *The Thirteen Clocks*. Illustrated by Marc Simont. Simon & Schuster, 1950.

Tolkien, J. R. R. *The Fellowship of the Ring. The Two Towers. The Return of the King* (the Lord of the Rings trilogy). Houghton Mifflin, 1965.

———. *The Hobbit*. Houghton Mifflin, 1938.

Travers, P. L. *Mary Poppins*. Illustrated by Mary Shepard. Harcourt Brace, 1934.

———. *Mary Poppins Comes Back*. Illustrated by Mary Shepard. Harcourt Brace, 1935.

———. *Mary Poppins in the Park*. Illustrated by Mary Shepard. Harcourt Brace, 1952.

———. *Mary Poppins Opens the Door*. Illustrated by Mary Shepard and Agnes Sims. Harcourt Brace, 1943.

Van Rynbach, Iris. *The Soup Stone*. Greenwillow, 1988.

Vande Velde, Vivian. *User Unfriendly*. Harcourt Brace, 1991.

Vinge, Joan D. *Psion*. Delacorte, 1982.

Walsh, Jill Paton. *A Chance Child*. Farrar, Straus & Giroux, 1978.

———. *The Green Book*. Illustrated by Lloyd Bloom. Farrar, Straus & Giroux, 1982.

Wangerin, Walter. *Elizabeth and the Water Troll*. Illustrated by Deborah Healy. HarperCollins, 1991.

Waugh, Sylvia. *The Mennyms*. Greenwillow, 1994.

———. *The Mennyms in the Wilderness*. Greenwillow, 1995.

———. *The Mennyms Under Siege*. Greenwillow, 1996.

White, E. B. *Charlotte's Web*. Illustrated by Garth Williams. Harper & Row, 1952.

———. *Stuart Little*. Illustrated by Garth Williams. Harper & Row, 1945.

———. *The Trumpet of the Swan*. Illustrated by Edward Frascino. Harper & Row, 1970.

Wilde, Oscar. *The Happy Prince*. Illustrated by Ed Young. Simon & Schuster, 1989.

———. *The Happy Prince*. Illustrated by Jean Claverie. Oxford University Press, 1981.

———. *The Selfish Giant*. Illustrated by Lisbeth Zwerger. Picture Book Studios, 1984.

Williams, Jay. *Everyone Knows What a Dragon Looks Like*. Illustrated by Mercer Mayer. Four Winds, 1976.

Winthrop, Elizabeth. *The Battle for the Castle*. Holiday House, 1993.

———. *The Castle in the Attic*. Holiday House, 1985.

Wiseman, David. *Jeremy Visick*. Houghton Mifflin, 1981.

Wrede, Patricia C. *Calling on Dragons*. Harcourt Brace, 1993.

———. *Dealing with Dragons*. Harcourt Brace, 1990.

———. *Searching for Dragons*. Harcourt Brace, 1991.

———. *Talking to Dragons*. Harcourt Brace, 1993.

Wright, Betty Ren. *The Ghost Comes Calling*. Scholastic, 1994.

———. *Out of the Dark*. Scholastic, 1995.

Wrightson, Patricia. *Balyet*. Macmillan, 1989.

———. *The Nargun and the Stars*. Atheneum, 1979.

Yep, Laurence. *The City of Dragons*. Illustrated by Jean and Mou-Sien Tseng. Scholastic, 1995.

———. *The Dragon of the Lost Sea*. Harper & Row, 1982.

Yolen, Jane. *Dove Isabeau*. Illustrated by Dennis Nolan. Harcourt Brace Jovanovich, 1989.

———. *Dragon's Blood*. Delacorte, 1982.

———. *The Emperor and the Kite*. Illustrated by Ed Young. World, 1967.

———. *The Girl Who Loved the Wind*. Illustrated by Ed Young. Crowell, 1972.

———. *Greyling*. Illustrated by David Ray. Philomel, 1991.

———. *Heart's Blood*. Delacorte, 1984.

———. *The Seeing Stick*. Illustrated by Remy Charlip and Demetra Maraslis. Crowell, 1977.

———. *A Sending of Dragons*. Delacorte, 1987.

———. *Tam Lin*. Illustrated by Charles Mikolaycak. Harcourt Brace Jovanovich, 1990.

Zemach, Harve. *Duffy and the Devil*. Illustrated by Margot Zemach. Farrar, Straus & Giroux, 1986.

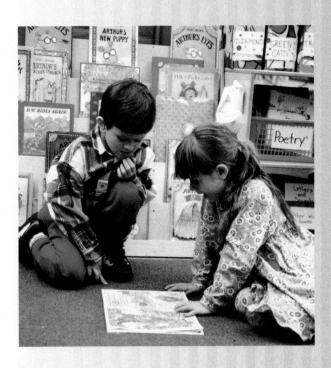

chapter
eight

Poetry

The Meaning of Poetry 390

Poetry for Children 391
The Elements of Poetry 392

Rhythm 393
Rhyme and Sound 394
Imagery 395
Figurative Language: Comparison and Contrast 396
Shape 398
Emotional Force 398
Guidelines: Evaluating Poetry for Children 399

Forms of Poetry for Children 399

Ballads 399
Narrative Poems 400
Lyrical Poetry 401
Limericks 401
Free Verse 401
Haiku 402
Concrete Poetry 402
Selecting Poetry for Children 403

Children's Poetry Preferences 403
Poets and Their Books 404

Humorous Verse 404
Interpreters of the World of Childhood 406
Multicultural Poetry 408
Poets of Nature 409
Versatile Poets 411

Anthologies of Poems for Children 413

Comprehensive Poetry Collections 413

Guidelines: Evaluating Poetry Anthologies 413

Specialized Collections 415
Resources for Teaching: Comprehensive Poetry Anthologies 416

Picture-Book Editions of Single Poems 418
Sharing Poetry with Children 418
Resources for Teaching: Specialized Collections of Poetry 419
Resources for Teaching: Picture-Book Editions of Single Poems 423

Creating a Climate for Enjoyment 424
Web: In Praise of Poetry 425

Finding Time for Poetry 426
Resources for Teaching: Developing Enjoyment of Poetry 427
Resources for Teaching: Connections Between Poetry and Prose 428

Reading Poetry to Children 432
Teaching Feature: Studying Poetry and Nature 433
Involving Children in Poetry 433

Discussing Poetry 433
Writing Poetry 435
Choral Reading 439
Learning Experiences 441
Related Readings 441
Children's Literature 442

A fifth-grade teacher finished reading aloud Katherine Paterson's *Bridge to Terabithia* to her class. This is the well-loved story of friendship between a highly imaginative girl, Leslie, and Jess—middle child in a rural family of five. It was Leslie's idea to create Terabithia, their secret kingdom in the woods that could be approached only by swinging across a stream on a rope. And it was this frayed rope that brought about the tragedy in the story. Following the completion of the story, the group was silent for a moment thinking about Leslie's death and the legacy she had left Jess. Wisely, the teacher respected their silence, recognizing that this book had moved them deeply. They did not discuss it immediately but quietly began to do other work. That evening one of the girls in the class wrote this poem:

As the stubborn stream swirls and pulls out a
    song,
The hillside stands in the cold dark sky.
Over the hillside stands a lonely palace.

Before it shook with joy
But now its queen is dead
So the sour sweet wind blows the tassels of
    the weak rope,
And the tree mourns and scolds the rope,
Saying "Couldn't you have held on a little
    longer?"

> Cheri Taylor
> Highland Park School
> Grove City, Ohio
> Linda Charles, teacher

Poetry was as much a part of this classroom as prose was. The teacher shared some poetry every day, in addition to reading stories. Frequently she read a poem that reflected the same content or feeling as the novel she was reading. So it was natural for Cheri to write a poem in response to her feelings about *Bridge to Terabithia*.

Poetry is the language of emotions. It can encapsulate a deep response in a few words. For Cheri, poetry was the only way to capture her feelings about a book that had moved her as no other had ever done before.

The Meaning of Poetry

There is an elusiveness about poetry that makes it defy precise definition. It is not so much what it is that is important, as how it makes us feel. In her *Poems for Children*, Eleanor Farjeon tells us that poetry is "not a rose, but the scent of the rose . . . Not the sea, but the sound of the sea."* Fine poetry is this distillation of experience that captures the essence of an object, a feeling, or a thought. Such intensification requires a more highly structured patterning of words than prose does. Each word must be chosen with care for both sound and meaning, because poetry is language in its most connotative and concentrated form. Laurence Perrine defines poetry as "a kind of language that says more and says it more intensely than ordinary language."[1]

Poetry can both broaden and intensify experience, or it might present a range of experiences beyond the realm of personal possibility for the individual listener. It can also illuminate, clarify, and deepen an everyday occurrence in a way the reader never considered, making the reader see more and feel more than ever before. For poetry does more than mirror life; it reveals life in new dimensions. Robert Frost said that a poem goes from delight to wisdom. Poetry does delight children, but it also helps them develop new insights, new ways of sensing their world.

Poetry originally appeared in *Sing For Your Supper*. Copyright © 1938 by Eleanor Farjeon; renewed 1966 by Gervase Farjeon. Used by permission of HarperCollins Publishers, New York, NY.

[1]Laurence Perrine, *Sound and Sense: An Introduction to Poetry*, 5th ed. (New York: Harcourt Brace Jovanovich, 1981), p. 3.

Poetry communicates experience by appealing to both the thoughts and the feelings of its reader. It has the power to evoke in its hearers rich sensory images and deep emotional responses. Poetry demands total response from the individual—all the intellect, senses, emotion, and imagination. It does not tell *about* an experience as much as it invites its hearers to *participate in* the experience. Poetry can happen only when the poem and the reader connect. Eve Merriam says this about the process:

 "I," says the poem matter-of-factly,
"I am a cloud,
I am a tree.

I am a city,
I am the sea,

I am a golden Mystery."

But, adds the poem silently,
I cannot speak until you come.
Reader, come, come with me.

> "I, Says the Poem," from *A Sky Full of Poems* by Eve Merriam. Copyright © 1973 by Eve Merriam. All rights reserved by Eve Merriam. Reprinted by permission of Marian Reiner for the author.

Much of what poetry says is conveyed by suggestion, by indirection, by what is not said. As Carl Sandburg put it, "What can be explained is not poetry. . . . The poems that are obvious are like the puzzles that are already solved. They deny us the joy of seeking and creating."[2] A certain amount of ambiguity is characteristic of poetry, for more is hidden in it than in prose. The poet does not tell readers "all," but invites them to go beyond the literal level of the poem and discover its deeper meanings for themselves.

Robert Frost playfully suggested that poetry is what gets lost in translation—and translation of poetry into prose is as difficult as translation of poetry into another language. To paraphrase a poem is to destroy it. Would it be possible to reduce Frost's "Mending Wall" to prose? The scene, the situation, the contrast of the two men's thoughts about the wall they are repairing can be described, but the experience of the poem cannot be conveyed except by its own words.

Poetry for Children

Poetry for children differs little from poetry for adults, except that it comments on life in dimensions that are meaningful for children. Its language should be poetic and its content should appeal directly to children. Bobbi

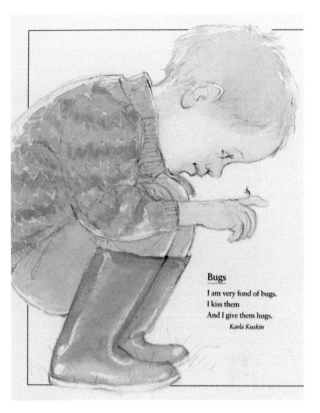

Bugs
I am very fond of bugs.
I kiss them
And I give them hugs.
Karla Kuskin

Anthologies of poetry such as Lilian Moore's *Sunflakes* introduce young children to the delights of poetry. Here Karla Kuskin's "Bugs" and Jan Ormerod's artwork have real child appeal.
Illustration by Jan Ormerod from *Sunflakes*, by Lilian Moore. Illustrations copyright © 1992 by Jan Ormerod. Reprinted by permission of Houghton Mifflin Company. All rights reserved. Poem copyright © 1980 by Karla Kuskin. Used by permission of HarperCollins Publishers, New York, NY.

Katz describes the feel of cat kisses in a way that appeals to children's sensory experiences and helps them think about a cat in a new imaginative way.

 Sandpaper kisses
on a cheek or a chin—
that is the way
for a day to begin!

Sandpaper kisses—
a cuddle, a purr
I have an alarm clock
that's covered with fur.

> Bobbi Katz, "Cat Kisses," in *Tomie de Paola's Book of Poems*. *Cat Kisses* by Bobbi Katz. Copyright © 1974 by Bobbi Katz. Reprinted with the permission of the author.

The comparison of the rough feel of a cat's tongue to sandpaper kisses and a cat's function as an alarm clock are both metaphors that will delight a child. These metaphors are childlike, but not "childish."

The emotional appeal of children's poetry should reflect the real emotions of childhood. Poetry that is cute,

[2]Carl Sandburg, "Short Talk on Poetry," in *Early Moon* (New York: Harcourt Brace, 1930), p. 27.

coy, nostalgic, or sarcastic might be *about* children, but it is not *for* them. Whittier's "The Barefoot Boy" looks back on childhood in a nostalgic fashion characteristic of adults, not children; "The Children's Hour" by Longfellow is an old man's reminiscences of his delight in his children (both poems can be found in Helen Ferris's *Favorite Poems Old and New*). Some poems patronize childhood as a period in life when children are "cute" or "naughty." Joan W. Anglund's poetry is as cute and sentimental as her pictures of "sweet little boys and girls."

Many poems are didactic and preachy. Unfortunately, some teachers will accept moralizing in poetry that they would never accept in prose. Sentimentality is another adult emotion that is seldom felt by children. The poem "Which Loved Best," frequently quoted before Mother's Day, drips with sentiment and morality. Poems that are *about* childhood or aim to instruct are usually disliked by children.

Yet children do feel deep emotions; they can be hurt, fearful, bewildered, sad, happy, expectant, satisfied. Almost all surveys show that adults believe children have a harder time growing up today than their parents did.[3] More and more modern poetry for children reflects the despair of struggling to grow up in America today. Some poets have been successful in capturing the real feelings of troubled children. For example, Elizabeth Smith, an African American poet, describes the mixed feelings of pride and loneliness felt by a latchkey child:

I don't go to daycare
Or a sitter any more.
Now that I am grown-up
I've a key to my front door.

I check my pocket through the day,
Making sure I have my key.
I call my mom when I get home
To tell her all is right with me.

I get a little scared sometimes
When there's no one else at home.
The TV keeps me company—
I'm not all that alone.

I like the grown-up feeling
Of having my own key.
But every now and then I wish
My mom was home with me.

Elizabeth A. Smith, "My Key," from *Through Our Eyes* edited by Lee Bennett Hopkins. Reprinted by permission of the author.

Many of the poems in Myra Cohn Livingston's book *There Was a Place and Other Poems* are written from

[3]Kati Haycock, "Producing a Nation of Achievers," *Journal of Youth Services in Libraries* 4 (spring 1991): 237.

the perspective of children from broken homes and one-parent families. The constant tug-of-war feeling of a child caught in the middle of a divorce is reflected in one of her poems from this book:

Mom
says
she wants me
more than Dad.
How do I ever choose?
Dad
says
he wants me
more than Mom.
Somebody has to lose.

Myra Cohn Livingston, "In the Middle." Reprinted with the permission of Margaret K. McElderry Books, an imprint of Simon & Schuster from *There Was A Place and Other Poems* by Myra Cohn Livingston. Copyright © 1988 Myra Cohn Livingston.

Not only has she described the feelings of a child caught in the middle of a divorce, she has even spaced her words to convey the tension in this household—the constant seesawing back and forth. Poets have many ways to reinforce the meaning of a poem.

The Elements of Poetry

A child responds to the total impact of a poem and should not be required to analyze it. However, teachers need to understand the language of poetry if they are to select the best to share with children. How, for example,

In Lee Bennett Hopkin's *Through Our Eyes,* Jeffrey Dunn's photographs mirror Elizabeth Smith's poem "My Key" and reflect the feelings of many modern children.
Copyright © Jeffrey Dunn.

can you differentiate between real poetry and mere verse? Mother Goose, jump-rope rhymes, tongue twisters, and the lyrics of some songs are not poetry; but they *can* serve as a springboard for diving into real poetry. Elizabeth Coatsworth, who has written much fine poetry and verse for children, refers to rhyme as "poetry in petticoats."[4] Such rhymes may have the sound of poetry, but they do not contain the quality of imagination or the depth of emotion that characterizes real poetry.

It is a difficult task to identify elements of poetry for today's children, for modern poets are breaking traditional molds in both content and form. These poems speak directly to the reader about all subjects. Frequently the words are spattered across pages in a random fashion or they become poem-pictures, as in concrete poetry. As children become more sophisticated through their exposure to films and television, the dividing line between what is poetry for adults and what is poetry for children becomes fainter. It is, however, possible to identify those poems that contain the elements of fine poetry yet still speak to children.

Rhythm

The young child is naturally rhythmical. She beats on the tray of her high chair, kicks her foot against the table, and chants her vocabulary of one or two words in a singsong fashion. She delights in the sound of "Pat-a-cake, pat-a-cake, baker's man," or "Ride a cock-horse to Banbury Cross" before she understands the meaning of the words. She is responding to the monotonous rocking-horse rhythm of Mother Goose. This response to a measured beat is as old as humans themselves. Primitive people had chants, hunting and working songs, dances, and crude musical instruments. Rhythm is a part of the daily beat of our lives—the steady pulse rate, regular breathing, and pattern of growth. The inevitability of night and day, the revolving seasons, birth and death provide a pattern for everyone's life. The very ebb and flow of the ocean, the sound of the rain on the window, and the pattern of rows of corn in a field reflect the rhythm of the world around us.

Poetry satisfies the child's natural response to rhythm. A poem has a kind of music of its own and the child responds to it. The very young child enjoys the rocking rhythm of Mother Goose and expects it in all other poems. Mary Ann Hoberman explores other rhythms in the child's life as she links weather and seasonal patterns to the rhythm of a child's swinging:

> *Hello and good-by*
> *Hello and good-by*
>
> When I'm in a swing
> Swinging low and then high,
> Good-by to the ground
> Hello to the sky.
>
> Hello to the rain
> Good-by to the sun,
> Then hello again sun
> When the rain is all done.
>
> In blows the winter,
> Away the birds fly.
> *Good-by and hello*
> *Hello and good-by.*

Mary Ann Hoberman, "Hello and Good-by," in *Yellow Butter Purple Jelly*. Reprinted by permission of Gina Maccoby Literary Agent. Copyright © 1981 by Mary Ann Hoberman.

This poem could be compared to Robert Louis Stevenson's well-known poem "The Swing" (in *Tomie de Paola's Book of Poems*), which suggests a different meter for the physical sensation of swinging.

In some poems both the rhythm and the pattern of the lines are suggestive of the movement or mood of the poem. The arrangement of these poems forces the reader to emphasize a particular rhythm. For example, the words of Eleanor Farjeon's "Mrs. Peck-Pigeon" (in de Regnier et al., *Sing a Song of Popcorn*) and the repetition of the hard sounds of *b* and *p* help to create the bobbing rhythm of the pigeon herself.

A change of rhythm is indicative of a new element in the poem: a contrast in mood, a warning, or a different speaker, for example. The following poem by Lilian Moore gathers momentum with the sound of all the things the wind blows, and then becomes suddenly quiet when the wind dies down.

> When the wind blows
> the quiet things speak.
> Some whisper, some clang,
> Some creak.
>
> Grasses swish.
> Treetops sigh.
> Flags slap
> and snap at the sky.
> Wires on poles
> whistle and hum.
> Ashcans roll.
> Windows drum.
>
> When the wind goes—
> suddenly
> then,
> the quiet things
> are quiet again.

Lilian Moore, "Wind Song," in *Tomie de Paola's Book of Poems*. "Wind Song" from *I Feel the Same Way* by Lilian Moore. Copyright © 1967 by Lilian Moore. All rights reserved by Lilian Moore. Reprinted with permission of Marian Reiner for the author.

[4]Elizabeth Coatsworth, *The Sparrow Bush*, illus. Stefan Martin (New York: Norton, 1966), p. 8.

Rhyme and Sound

In addition to the rhythm of a poem, children respond to its rhyme—for rhyme helps to create the musical qualities of a poem, and children enjoy the "singingness of words." The Russian poet Kornei Chukovsky maintains that in the beginning of childhood we are all "versifiers," and that it is only later in life that we begin to speak in prose.[5] He is referring to the young child's tendency to double all syllables so that *mother* is first "mama" and *water* "wa-wa." This, plus the regular patterning of such words as *daddy, mommy, granny,* and so on, makes for a natural production of rhyme. The young child's enjoyment of Mother Goose is due almost entirely to the rhyme and rhythm of these verses. This poem by Eloise Greenfield captures the rhythm of the turning rope and the slapping sound of the rope itself:

Get set, ready now, jump right in
Bounce and kick and giggle and spin
Listen to the rope when it hits the ground
Listen to that clappedy-slappedy sound
Jump right up when it tells you to
Come back down, whatever you do
Count to a hundred, count by ten
Start to count all over again
That's what jumping is all about
Get set, ready now,
    jump
       right
          out!

Eloise Greenfield, "Rope Rhyme," in *Honey, I Love and Other Poems.* Text copyright © 1978 by Eloise Greenfield. Used by permission of HarperCollins Publishers, New York, NY.

If children have not heard any poetry or do not know any Mother Goose rhymes, teachers may want to introduce poetry with street rhymes, jump-rope rhymes, or raps through such collections as David Booth's *Doctor Knickerbocker and Other Rhymes.* But children need to be freed from the notion that all poetry must rhyme. They should be introduced to some poetry that doesn't rhyme, such as free verse or haiku, so that they begin to listen to the meaning of a poem as well as the sound of it.

Rhyme is only one aspect of sound; alliteration, or the repetition of initial consonant sounds, is another; assonance, or the repetition of particular vowel sounds, is still another. Jack Prelutsky frequently uses alliteration to create the humor in his verse. For example, read "The Lurpp Is on the Loose" (in his *Rolling Harvey Down the Hill*) and listen to the repetition of the *l* sounds. Younger children delight in the sounds of the mud that "splishes

and sploshes" in Rhoda Bacmeister's well-known poem "Galoshes" (in *Tomie de Paola's Book of Poems*).

The quiet *s* sound and the repetition of the double *o* in *moon* and *shoon* suggest the mysterious beauty of the moon in Walter de la Mare's poem "Silver" (in Helen Ferris's *Favorite Poems Old and New*). The term *onomatopoeia* refers to the use of words that make a sound like the action represented by the word, such as *crack, hiss,* and *sputter*. Occasionally a poet will create an entire poem that resembles a particular sound. David McCord has successfully imitated the sound of hitting a picket fence with a stick in his popular chant:

The pickety fence
The pickety fence
Give it a lick it's
The pickety fence
Give it a lick it's
A clickety fence
Give it a lick it's
A lickety fence
Give it a lick
Give it a lick
Give it a lick
With a rickety stick
Pickety
Pickety
Pickety
Pick

David McCord, "The Pickety Fence," from *One at a Time* by David McCord. Copyright © 1961, 1962 by David McCord. Reprinted by permission of Little, Brown and Company.

Repetition is another way the poet creates particular sound effects in a poem. Certainly, David McCord employed repetition along with onomatopoeia to create "The Pickety Fence." Robert Frost frequently used repetition of particular lines or phrases to emphasize meaning in his poems. The repetition of the last line "miles to go before I sleep" in his famous "Stopping by Woods on a Snowy Evening" (in de Regniers, et al., *Sing a Song of Popcorn*) adds to the mysterious element in that poem.

Children are intrigued with the sound of language and enjoy unusual and ridiculous combinations of words. The gay nonsense of Laura Richards's "Eletelephony" (also in the de Regniers, et. al., anthology) is as much in the sound of the ridiculous words as in the plight of the poor elephant who tried to use the "telephant." Children love to trip off the name "James James Morrison Morrison Weatherby George Dupree" in A. A. Milne's "Disobedience" (*The World of Christopher Robin*). Poets use rhyme, rhythm, and the various devices of alliteration, assonance, repetition, and coined words to create the melody and sound of poetry loved by children.

[5]Kornei Chukovsky, *From Two to Five,* trans. and ed. Miriam Morton (Berkeley: University of California Press, 1963), p. 64.

Imagery

Poetry draws on many kinds of language magic. The imagery of a poem involves direct sensory images of sight, sound, touch, smell, or taste. This aspect of poetry has particular appeal for children, as it reflects one of the major ways they explore their world. The very young child grasps an object and immediately puts it in her mouth. Children love to squeeze warm, soft puppies, and they squeal with delight as a pet mouse scampers up their arms. Taste and smell are also highly developed in the young child.

In our modern society, children are increasingly deprived of natural sensory experiences. One of the first admonitions they hear is "Don't touch." On the endless pavements of our cities, how many children have an opportunity to roll in crunchy piles of leaves? Air pollution laws assure that they will never enjoy the acrid autumn smell of burning bonfires (rightly so, but still a loss). Many also miss the warm yeasty odor of homemade bread or the sweet joy of licking the bowl of brownie batter. Some of our newest schools are windowless, so children are even deprived of seeing the brilliant blue sky on a crisp cold day or the growing darkness of a storm or the changing silhouette of an oak tree on the horizon.

Poetry can never be a substitute for actual sensory experience. A child can't develop a concept of texture by hearing a poem or seeing pictures of the rough bark of a tree; he must first touch the bark and compare the feel of a deeply furrowed oak with the smooth-surfaced trunk of a beech tree. Then the poet can call up these experiences and extend them or make the child see them in a new way.

Because most children are visual-minded, they respond readily to the picture-making quality of poetry. Barbara Esbensen's images of autumn birch trees is perfectly childlike and sure to surprise and delight children:

Why do you think
the birches
tore off their yellow
sweaters
on the windiest coldest day
of all   waved good-bye
and watched them scatter
down the street?

Why do you think
the birches
are standing in our yard
in their underwear?

Barbara Esbensen, "Tell Me," in *Who Shrank My Grandmother's House?* Copyright © 1992 by Barbara Juster Esbensen. Used by permission of HarperCollins Publishers, New York, NY.

Tennyson's description of an eagle is rich in the use of visual imagery. In the first verse the reader can see the eagle perched on the crest of a steep mountain, posed ready for his swift descent whenever he sights his quarry. But in the second verse the poet "enters into" the eagle's world and describes it from the bird's point of view. Looking down from his lofty height, the might of the waves is reduced to wrinkles and the sea seems to crawl:

He clasps the crag with crooked hands;
Close to the sun in lonely lands,
Ringed with the azure world, he stands.

The wrinkled sea beneath him crawls;
He watches from his mountain wall,
And like a thunderbolt he falls.

Alfred, Lord Tennyson, "The Eagle," in *Piping Down the Valleys Wide*, ed. Nancy Larrick.

The lonely, peaceful scene is shattered by the natural metaphor of the final line: "And like a thunderbolt he falls." In your mind's eye you can see, almost feel, the wind on your wings as you plunge down the face of the cliff.

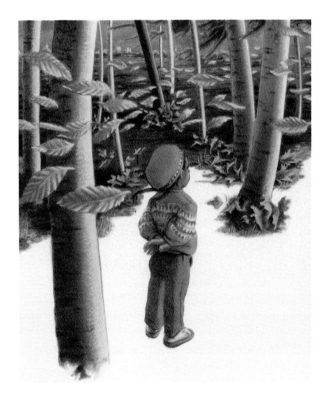

Eric Beddows's illustration helps children understand Barbara Esbensen's delightful imagery in "Tell Me" found in *Who Shrank My Grandmother's House?*

Copyright © 1992 by Eric Beddows. Used by permission of HarperCollins Publishers, New York, NY.

Most poetry depends on visual and auditory imagery to evoke a mood or response, but imagery of touch, taste, and smell is also used. Valerie Worth's poem "Mud" makes fingers tingle with the feel of squishy earth:

Mud mixed
With a stick
To the right
Thickness,
Not too stiff
Nor too full
of rain,

Can then
Be picked up
In the hand,
Soft, still cold
As a stone,
And squeezed
Until it strains

Out between the fingers—
Warmed a bit,
But still heavy
With earth's
Rich grit and grain.

"Mud" from *All the Small Poems and Fourteen More*, by Valerie Worth. Copyright © 1994 by Valerie Worth. Reprinted by permission of Farrar, Straus & Giroux, Inc.

Psychologists tell us that some of children's earliest memories are sensory, recalling particularly the way things smell and taste. Most children have a delicate sense of taste that responds to the texture and smell of a particular food. In "Hard and Soft," in his *Eats: Poems*, Arnold Adoff contrasts the crunch of eating a carrot with the quiet sound of swallowing raisins. In "A Matter of Taste," in her *Jamboree*, Eve Merriam relates the way food tastes to the way it feels and sounds when being chewed. Rose Rauter captures both the feel of a fresh-picked peach and its delicious taste in this poem:

Touch it to your cheek and it's soft
as a velvet newborn mouse
who has to strive
to be alive.
Bite in. Runny
honey
blooms on your tongue—
as if you've bitten open
a whole hive.

Rose Rauter, "Peach," from X. J. Kennedy and Dorothy M. Kennedy, *Knock At a Star: A Child's Introduction to Poetry*, Little, Brown & Company, 1982.

Certain smells can recapture a whole experience that may have happened years earlier. Joanna Cole contrasts the smells of the road with the smells of the beach in her poem "Driving to the Beach" (in *By Myself*, ed. Lee Hopkins). Constance Levy's "Greensweet," in her *A Tree Place*, evokes the summer smells of newly mown grass.

Figurative Language: Comparison and Contrast

Because the language of poetry is so compressed, every word must be made to convey the meaning of the poem. Poets do this by comparing two objects or ideas with each other in such a way that the connotation of one word gives added meaning to another.

In "Peach," Rose Rauter compared the soft fuzzy feel of a peach to a velvety newborn mouse; its sweet taste made her think of a whole hive of honey. X. J. Kennedy portrays the observations of a passenger who is riding backward on a speeding train:

Squeezing round a bend, train shrieks
Like chalk on gritty blackboards.

People talk or read or stare.
Street names pass like flashcards.

Hope this train keeps going on
Flying uptown backwards.

X. J. Kennedy, "Flying Uptown Backwards." Reprinted with the permission of Margaret K. McElderry Books, an imprint of Simon & Schuster from *The Forgetful Wishing Well* by X. J. Kennedy. Copyright © 1985 X. J. Kennedy.

When writers compare one thing with another, using such connecting words as *like* or *as*, they are using a *simile*. Using two similes that call up common school experiences, Kennedy compares the shrieking sound of the train with the piercing shriek of chalk on a blackboard and the quickly passing street names with the use of old-fashioned flashcards. In a *metaphor* the poet speaks of an object or idea as if it *were* another object. In recent years we have paid little attention to the difference between these two techniques, referring to both as examples of metaphorical or figurative language.

It is not important that children know the difference between a simile and a metaphor. It is important that they know what is being compared and that the comparison is fresh and new and helps them view the idea or object in a different and unusual way. Two well-known poems containing metaphors that help children see their world afresh are Vachel Lindsay's "The Moon's the North Wind's Cooky" (in Jack Prelutsky's *Random House Book of Poetry for Children*) and the first line of Dorothy Aldis's "On a Snowy Day" (in her *All Together*), which describes fenceposts as wearing marshmallow hats. Perhaps the reason these poems have endured is that they also reveal a true understanding of a child's point of view.

Some figurative language is so commonplace that it has lost its ability to evoke new images. Language and verse are filled with clichés like "it rained cats and dogs," "a blanket of snow," "quiet as a mouse," or "thin as a rail." In her poem "Cliché," in *It Doesn't Always Have to Rhyme*, Eve Merriam describes a cliché as what lazy people use in their writing. Her poem "Metaphor Man" (in *Out Loud*) also pokes fun at such expressions as *drives a hard bargain, stands four square,* and *flies off in a rage.*

Valerie Worth received the NCTE Award for Excellence in Poetry for Children for her Small Poems books. These have been combined and added to in her *All the Small Poems and Fourteen More.* Her simple free verse contains vivid metaphors that describe ordinary objects like chairs, earthworms, or a safety pin:

Closed, it sleeps
On its side
Quietly,
The silver image
Of some
Small fish

Opened it snaps
Its tail out
Like a thin shrimp
And looks
At the sharp
Point with a
Surprised eye

"Safety Pin" from *All the Small Poems and Fourteen More* by Valerie Worth. Copyright © 1994 by Valerie Worth. Reprinted by permission of Farrar, Straus & Giroux, Inc.

Some poets sustain a metaphor throughout the poem. Most children are intrigued with the subject of dinosaurs and readily respond to Charles Malam's poem that compares a steam shovel with those enormous beasts.

The dinosaurs are not all dead.
I saw one raise its iron head
To watch me walking down the road
Beyond our house today.
Its jaws were dripping with a load
Of earth and grass that it had cropped.
It must have heard me where I stopped,
Snorted white steam my way,
And stretched its long neck out to see,
And chewed, and grinned quite amiably.

Charles Malam, "Steam Shovel," in *Reflections on a Gift of Watermelon Pickle*, ed. Stephen Dunning et al. From *Upper Pastures: Poems* by Charles Malam. Copyright © 1930 and 1958 by Charles Malam. Reprinted by permission of Henry Holt and Co., Inc.

Personification is a way of speaking about inanimate objects and animals as though they were persons. Human beings have always personified inanimate objects. Young children personify their toys; adolescents and adults name their computers, their cars and boats. Poetry simply extends this process to a wider range of objects. In "Flashlight" (in *Go with the Poem*), Judith Thurman compares a flashlight to a hound straining on his leash. James Stephens's well-known poem "The Wind" (in *Wider than the Sky*, ed. Scott Elledge) personifies the wind as a person who will "kill, kill." Diane Siebert personifies the desert in her book *Mojave* and the Sierra Nevada Mountains in *Sierra*. Debra Chandra sings winter's song with a mother's voice in this poem:

The leaves are gone,
The world is old,
I hear a whisper from the sky—
The dark is long,
The ground's grown cold,
I hear the snow's white lullaby.

She breathes it softly
Through the air,
While with her gown of flakes she sweeps
The sky, the trees, the ground grown cold,
Singing hush
   Now hush.
     Now hush,
       Hush
       Sleep.

"Snowfall" from *Balloons and Other Poems* by Deborah Chandra. Copyright © 1988, 1990 by Deborah Chandra. Reprinted by permission of Farrar, Straus & Giroux, Inc.

Another way of strengthening an image is through contrast. Elizabeth Coatsworth employs this device in much of her poetry. Her well-known "Poem of Praise" (in *Reflections on a Gift of Watermelon Pickle*, ed. Stephen Dunning et al.) contrasts the beauty of swift things with those that are slow and steady. Marci Ridlon presents two points of view concerning life in the city in her poem "City City" (in *The Random House Book of Poetry for Children*, ed. Jack Prelutsky). By contrasting a view of a bridge by day and by night, Lilian Moore gives us two images, one of strength and one of lacy lightness in her poem "The Bridge" (in *Something New Begins*). In the following poem Marcie Hans compares the launching of a man-made rocket with the miraculous growth of a seedling pushing its way through the earth. The first feat receives much acclaim; the second goes virtually unnoticed. There seems to be no doubt in the poet's mind which is the greater event, for she has even shaped her poem to resemble half of a tree:

Fueled
by a million
man-made
wings of fire—
the rocket tore a tunnel
through the sky—
and everybody cheered.
Fueled
only by a thought from God—
the seedling
urged its way
through the thickness of black—
and as it pierced
the heavy ceiling of the soil—
and launched itself
up into outer space—
no
one
even clapped.

Marcie Hans, "Fueled," in *Reflections on a Gift of Watermelon Pickle*, ed. Stephen Dunning et al. "Fueled" from *Serve Me A Slice of Moon*, copyright © 1965 by Marcie Hans and renewed 1993 by Ernestine Hans. Reprinted by permission of Harcourt Brace & Company.

Even though all children know about rockets and seeds, they might not be able to see the connection between the two images that the poet has created. Among one group of educationally and economically advantaged 8-year-olds, not one child saw both of these ideas; yet 11-year-olds in the same school easily recognized them. This suggests the importance of knowing the developmental level of a group before selecting poetry for them.

Shape

The first thing children notice about reading a poem is that it looks different from prose. And usually it does. Most poems begin with capital letters for each line and have one or more stanzas.

Increasingly, however, poets are using the shape of their poems to reinforce the image of the idea. In "The Grasshopper," in his *One at a Time*, David McCord describes the plight of a grasshopper that fell down a deep well. As luck would have it, he discovers a rope and up he climbs one word at a time! The reader must read up the page to follow the grasshopper's ascent. Eve Merriam's "Windshield Wiper" (in *Knock at a Star*, ed. X. and D. Kennedy) not only sounds like the even rhythm of a car's wiper but has the look of two wipers (see p. 403). Lillian Morrison's poem about a sidewalk racer describes the thrill of the rider at the same time as it takes the shape of a skateboard and strengthens her image.

Skimming
an asphalt sea
I swerve, I curve, I
sway; I speed to whirring
sound an inch above the
ground; I'm the sailor
and the sail, I'm the
driver and the wheel
I'm the one and only
single engine
human auto
mobile

Lillian Morrison, "The Sidewalk Racer," in *Knock at a Star*, ed. X. and D. Kennedy. "The Sidewalk Racer" from *The Sidewalk Racer and Other Poems of Sports and Motion* by Lillian Morrison. Copyright © 1977 by Lillian Morrison. All rights reserved by Lillian Morrison. Reprinted with permission of Marian Reiner for the author.

Children enjoy mounting their own poems on a piece of paper shaped in the image of their poem, such as a verse about a jack-o'-lantern on a pumpkin shape or a poem about a plane mounted on the silhouette of a plane. Later the words themselves may form the shape of the content, as in concrete poetry.

Emotional Force

We have seen how sound, language, and the shape of a poem can all work together to create the total impact of the poem. Considered individually, the rhyme scheme, imagery, figurative language, and appearance of the poem are of little importance unless all of these interrelate to create an emotional response in the reader. The craft of the poem is not the poem.

In the following poem a modern poet writes of the way two children feel when caught in the vortex of their parents' quarrel:

Listening to grownups quarreling,

standing in the hall against the
wall with my little brother, blown
like leaves against the wall by their
voices, my head like a pingpong ball
between the paddles of their anger:
I knew what it meant
to tremble like a leaf.

Cold with their wrath, I heard
the claws of the rain
pounce. Floods
poured through the city,
skies clapped over me,
and I was shaken, shaken
like a mouse
between their jaws.

Ruth Whitman, "Listening to Grownups Quarreling," in *Knock at a Star*, ed. X. and D. Kennedy. "Listening To Grownups Quarreling" from *The Marriage Wig and Other Poems*, copyright © 1968 by Ruth Whitman. Reprinted by permission of Harcourt Brace & Company.

Guidelines:
Evaluating Poetry for Children

How does the rhythm of the poem reinforce and create the meaning of the poem?

If the poem rhymes, does it sound natural or contrived?

How does the sound of the poem add to the meaning? Does the poem use alliteration? onomatopoeia? repetition?

Does the poem create sensory images of sight, touch, smell, or taste? Are these related to children's delight in their particular senses?

What is the quality of imagination in the poem? Does the poem make the child see something in a fresh, new way, or does it rely on tired clichés?

Is the figurative language appropriate to children's lives? Are the similes and metaphors ones that a child would appreciate and understand?

What is the tone of the poem? Does it patronize childhood by looking down on it? Is it didactic and preachy? Does it see childhood in a sentimental or nostalgic way?

Is the poem appropriate for children? Will it appeal to them, and will they like it?

How has the poet created the emotional intensity of the poem? Does every word work to heighten the feelings conveyed?

Does the shape of the poem—the placement of the words—contribute to the poem's meaning?

What is the purpose of the poem? To amuse? To describe in a fresh way? To comment on humanity? To draw parallels in our lives? How well has the poet achieved this purpose?

A teacher could destroy the total impact of this poem for children by having them count the number of metaphors in it, looking at their increasing force and power. Children should have a chance to hear it, comment on it if they wish, or compare it with Myra Cohn Livingston's poem "In the Middle" (see p. 392) or Debra Chandra's "The Argument" (see p. 412). All elements of these poems work together to create the feeling of being overpowered by a quarrel between those you love most.

Good poetry has the power to make the reader moan in despair, catch the breath in fear, gasp in awe, smile with delight, or sit back in wonder. For poetry heightens emotions and increases one's sensitivity to an idea or mood.

Teachers need to be able to identify the characteristics of good poetry in order to make wise selections to share with children. They need to know the various kinds of poetry and the range of content of poetry for children. Then they can select poetry that will gradually develop children's appreciation and sense of form. The questions listed in the Guidelines box "Evaluating Poetry for Children" would not be appropriate to use for every poem. However, they can serve as a beginning way to look at poetry for children.

Forms of Poetry for Children

Children are more interested in the "idea" of a poem than in knowing about the various forms of poetry. However, teachers will want to expose children to various forms of poetry and note their reactions. Do these children like only narrative poems? Do they think all poetry must rhyme, or will they listen to some free verse? Are they ready for the seemingly simple, yet highly complex, form of haiku? Understanding of and appreciation for a wide variety of poetry grow gradually as children are exposed to different forms and types of poems.

Ballads

Ballads are narrative poems that have been adapted for singing or that give the effect of a song. Originally, they were not made or sung for children but were the literature of all the people. Characteristics of the ballad form are the frequent use of dialogue in telling the story, repetition, marked rhythm and rhyme, and refrains that go back to the days when ballads were sung. Popular ballads have no known authors, as they were handed down from one generation to the next; the literary ballad, however, does have a known author. Ballads usually deal with heroic deeds and include stories of murder, unrequited love, feuds, and tragedies.

Children in the middle grades enjoy the amusing story of the stubborn man and his equally stubborn wife in "Get Up and Bar the Door" (in *The Oxford Book of Poetry for Children*, ed. Edward Blishen) or the story of the "Wraggle Taggle Gypsies" (in *Wider than the Sky*, ed. Scott Elledge), in which the newlywed wealthy lady leaves her lord to run off with gypsies. (For discussions of the Scottish ballad "Tam Lin," see Chapters 6 and 7.)

American ballads frequently were popular songs, such as "On Top of Old Smoky" (in the Kennedys' *Knock at a Star*) and "The Foggy Foggy Dew" (in *Wider than the Sky*, ed. Scott Elledge). Few literary ballads are being written today. One, "Ballad of Birmingham" (in *Wider than the Sky*) by Dudley Randall, is a civil rights ballad about the tragic death of a child in the bombing of a church in Birmingham, Alabama, in 1963. When a young girl begs to go to the freedom march in the streets of Birmingham, her mother tells her it is too dangerous. Instead the mother sends the girl off to the children's choir, where she thinks she will be safe. That day the church is bombed and the daughter is killed. Ballads frequently have this ironic twist to their stories.

Narrative Poems

The narrative poem relates a particular event or episode or tells a long tale. It may be a lyric, a sonnet, or free verse; its one requirement is that it must tell a story. Many of children's favorite poems are these so-called story poems. One of the best-known narrative poems is Robert Browning's *The Pied Piper of Hamelin.* First illustrated by Kate Greenaway in 1888, it continues to be published with new illustrators, such as Terry Small.

The most popular narrative poem in this country is Clement Moore's *The Night Before Christmas* (or *A Visit from St. Nicholas*). Every artist from Grandma Moses to Tasha Tudor to Tomie de Paola and Wendy Watson has illustrated this Christmas story. Presently there are nearly forty editions of *The Night Before Christmas*.

One of young children's favorite narrative poems is the simple story of the parents who lovingly pretend to look for their child in the poem "Hiding" by Dorothy Aldis (in her *All Together*). A. A. Milne's narrative poems are favorites of many young children. They love his story of a lost mouse in "Missing" and the disappearing beetle in "Forgiven." Six-, 7-, and 8-year-olds delight in Milne's "The King's Breakfast" and "King John's Christmas," poems about petulant kings, one of whom wants a "bit of butter" for his bread and the other of whom wants a big red India-rubber ball (all of these poems are in *The World of Christopher Robin*). Other favorite story poems for this age group are Karla Kuskin's ridiculous tale "Hughbert and the Glue" and her loving story about a plush toy, "Bear with Golden Hair" (both in *Dogs & Dragons, Trees & Dreams*). The long narrative tale "Custard the Dragon" by Ogden Nash, in *The Tale of Custard the Dragon*, has been illustrated by Lynn Munsinger.

Without a doubt the all-time favorite narrative poems of children today are the outrageously funny ones in Shel Silverstein's *Where the Sidewalk Ends* and *The Light in the Attic.* Some of their favorite story verses include Shel Silverstein's "Sick," in which Peggy Ann McKay claims to have every known symptom of dreadful diseases until she realizes it is Saturday; the sad tale "Sarah Cynthia Sylvia Stout Who Would Not Take the Garbage Out," and the man who is slowly being

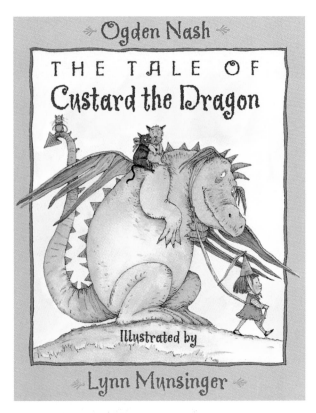

Ogden Nash's well-loved *The Tale of Custard the Dragon* is made even more appealing by Lynn Munsinger's droll illustrations.
Cover of the *Tale of Custard the Dragon* by Ogden Nash. Reprinted by permission of Little, Brown and Company.

swallowed alive in "Boa Constrictor" (all are in Silverstein's *Where the Sidewalk Ends*).

Children also enjoy Jack Prelutsky's story verse, particularly his collection of poems about the bully Harvey and the children's ultimate revenge on him, *Rolling Harvey Down the Hill*. Middle graders delight in Prelutsky's macabre tales in *Nightmares* and *The Headless Horseman*, enriched by Arnold Lobel's grisly black-and-white illustrations.

Not all narrative poems for children are humorous. Older children, for example, respond to the pathos of Eve Merriam's poem "To Meet Mr. Lincoln" (in *Sing a Song of Popcorn*, ed. de Regniers et al.). They are stirred by the galloping hoofbeats in Longfellow's *Paul Revere's Ride*, recently illustrated with vibrant moonlit pictures by Ted Rand. A favorite romantic tale is the dramatic *Highwayman* by Alfred Noyes, which has been portrayed in three stunning picture-book editions, illustrated by Charles Mikolaycak, Charles Keeping, and Neil Waldman.

One of the best ways to capture children's interest in poetry is to present a variety of narrative poems. Teachers will want to build a file of story poems appropriate to the interests of the children in their classes to use to introduce poetry to the children.

Lyrical Poetry

Most of the poetry written for children is lyrical. The term *lyrical* derives from the word *lyric* and means poetry that sings its way into the minds and memories of its listeners. It is usually personal or descriptive poetry, with no prescribed length or structure other than its melody.

Much of William Blake's poetry is lyrical, beginning with the opening lines of his introductory poem to *Songs of Innocence:* "Piping down the valleys wild/Piping songs of pleasant glee" (in *Piping Down the Valleys Wide,* ed. Nancy Larrick). Robert Louis Stevenson's poems have a singing quality that makes them unforgettable. Everyone knows his poems "The Swing" and "The Wind" (both in *A Child's Garden of Verses*). Equally popular is his mysterious "Windy Nights," which compares the sound of the wind to a galloping horseman:

> Whenever the moon and stars are set,
>   Whenever the wind is high,
> All night long in the dark and wet,
>   A man goes riding by.
> Late in the night when the fires are out,
> Why does he gallop and gallop about?
>
> Whenever the trees are crying aloud,
>   And ships are tossed at sea,
> By, on the highway, low and loud,
>   By at the gallop goes he.
> By at the gallop he goes, and then
> By he comes back at the gallop again.

Robert Louis Stevenson, "Windy Nights," in Sing a Song of Popcorn, ed. Beatrice de Regniers et al.

Eleanor Farjeon's lovely "The Night Will Never Stay" (in *Wider than the Sky,* ed. Scott Elledge) is another thoughtful lyrical poem. Masefield's well-known poem "Sea Fever" (in *Favorite Poems Old and New,* ed. Helen Ferris) would be a good one to read *after* sharing *The True Confessions of Charlotte Doyle* by Avi. Children always respond to the sound of the internal rhyme of "The Lone Dog" (in Ferris's *Favorite Poems Old and New*) by Irene Rutherford McLeod, which begins with "I'm a lean dog, a keen dog, a wild dog and lone." Lyrical poetry is characterized by this lilting use of words that gives children an exhilarating sense of melody.

Limericks

A nonsense form of verse that is particularly enjoyed by children is the limerick. This is a five-line verse in which the first and second lines rhyme, the third and fourth rhyme, and the fifth line rhymes with lines 1 and 2 and usually is a surprise or humorous statement. Freak spellings, oddities, and humorous twists characterize this form of poetry. David McCord, in his book *One at a Time,* suggests that "a limerick, to be lively and successful, *must* have *perfect* riming and *flawless*

rhthm." He gives several suggestions on how to write a limerick, using the limerick form itself. He also describes the shape of a limerick in this poem:

> A limerick shapes to the eye
> Like a small very squat butterfly,
>   With its wings opened wide
>   Lots of nectar inside,
> And a terrible urge to fly high.

David McCord, from "Write Me a Verse," from One at a Time by David McCord. Copyright © 1952 by David McCord. Reprinted by permission of Little, Brown & Company.

Other modern poets who continue to produce limericks include William Jay Smith and Myra Cohn Livingston. John Ciardi's collection *The Hopeful Trout and Other Limericks* offers limericks on a variety of themes from families to outer space. Arnold Lobel's *The Book of Pigericks* is a most humorous book of limericks, with verses about different pigs from various cities in the United States. His illustrations of humanized pigs are as funny as the limericks.

Children in the middle grades enjoy writing limericks, whether based on nursery rhymes, pigs, or their own names. It is certainly a far easier form for them to write than the highly abstract haiku.

Free Verse

Free verse does not have to rhyme but depends on rhythm or cadence for its poetic form. It may use some rhyme, alliteration, and pattern. It frequently looks different on a printed page, but it sounds very much like other poetry when read aloud. Children who have the opportunity to hear this form of poetry will be freed from thinking that all poetry must rhyme. Many of Valerie Worth's deceptively simple poems in *Small Poems* are written in free verse. Sylvia Cassedy's *Roomrimes* characterizes various rooms such as an attic, a closet, or a very proper parlor. *Zoomrimes* follows a similar A-to-Z format with things that move—from the ark to zeppelins. Not all these vehicles are traditional means of transportation:

> One day each spring
> and I never know
> which day it will be,
> the tree outside my window
> fills with a wind
> all its own,
> swells like a giant
> silk parasol,
> lets fall
> a wondrous storm
> of helicopters,
> pale, pale green.

Sylvia Cassedy, "Helicopters," in Zoomrimes. Copyright © 1993 by Sylvia Cassedy. Used by permission of HarperCollins Publishers, New York, NY.

Children would enjoy writing their own room or zoom descriptions in free verse after hearing these. While much of Eve Merriam's poetry rhymes, she has also written free verse. Her well-known poem "How to Eat a Poem" (in *It Doesn't Always Have to Rhyme*) is written in free verse. Langston Hughes's melodic "April Rain Song" (in *The Dream Keeper*) is another example of the effective use of free verse. Probably one of the best-known poems of our day is Carl Sandburg's "Fog" (in *Rainbows Are Made*, ed. Lee Bennett Hopkins). This metaphorical description of the fog characterized as a cat is written in free verse.

Haiku

Haiku is an ancient Japanese verse form that can be traced back to the thirteenth century. There are only seventeen syllables in the haiku; the first and third lines contain five syllables, the second line seven. Almost every haiku can be divided into two parts: first, a simple picture-making description that usually includes some reference, direct or indirect, to the season; and second, a statement of mood or feeling. A relationship between these two parts is implied, either a similarity or a telling difference.

The greatest of haiku writers, and the one who crystallized the form, was Basho. In his lifetime Basho produced more than eight hundred haiku. In the following poem the negative emotion expressed in the first line is reversed in the surprisingly pleasing image left by the last line. This image of black on white maintains the contrast of the two emotions that sustain the poem.

    Detestable crow!
Today alone you please me—
blurb black against the snow.

Basho, in *Red Dragonfly on My Shoulder*, trans. S. Cassedy and K. Suetake. Text copyright © 1992 by the estate of Sylvia Cassedy and Kunihiro Suetake. Used by permission of HarperCollins Publishers, New York, NY.

Three collections of haiku feature illustrations that lend subtle meaning to the poems. Molly Bang's found-object collages for Sylvia Cassedy and Kunihiro Suetake's *Red Dragonfly on My Shoulder* reflect the interrelationships that the poems seek to represent. Ezra Jack Keats created stunning pictures featuring silhouettes projected against marbleized paper for Richard Lewis's *In a Spring Garden*. Lewis has written his own collection of haiku in *Black Swan/White Crow*. His thirteen poems are given visual expression by Chris Manson's lovely woodcuts, which subtly enhance images in the poems and recall the classic prints of Japanese artist Hokusai.

The meaning of haiku is not expected to be immediately apparent. The reader is invited to add his or her

Molly Bang uses natural materials to create the illustrations for the haiku poetry in *Red Dragonfly on My Shoulder*, translated by Sylvia Cassedy and Kunihiro Suetake.
Illustration copyright © 1992 by Molly Bang. Used by permission of HarperCollins Publishers, New York, NY.

own associations and meanings to the words, thus completing the poem in the mind. Each time the poem is read, new understandings will develop. Haiku is deceiving in that the form appears simple yet it requires much from its reader. Unless children have reached the Piagetian level of formal operations in their thinking, haiku might be too abstract a form of poetry for them to fully understand. The common practice of asking young children to write haiku suggests that teachers do not understand its complexity. In this case, short is not simple!

Concrete Poetry

Many poets today are writing picture poems that make the reader see what they are saying. The message of the poem is presented not only in the words (sometimes just letters or punctuation marks) but in the arrangement of the words. Meaning is reinforced, or even carried, by the shape of the poem. We have seen how Lillian Morrison formed her poem "The Sidewalk Racer" into the shape of a skateboard (p. 398) and how "Fueled" by Marcie Hans was shaped to resemble half a tree (p. 398).

Eve Merriam uses concrete poetry to create the image of a windshield wiper while her words imitate its sound:

<table>
<tr><td>fog smog</td><td>fog smog</td></tr>
<tr><td>tissue paper</td><td>tissue paper</td></tr>
<tr><td>clear the blear</td><td>clear the smear</td></tr>
<tr><td></td><td></td></tr>
<tr><td>fog more</td><td>fog more</td></tr>
<tr><td>splat splat</td><td>downpour</td></tr>
<tr><td>rubber scraper</td><td>rubber scraper</td></tr>
<tr><td>overshoes</td><td>macintosh</td></tr>
<tr><td>bumbershoot</td><td>muddle on</td></tr>
<tr><td>slosh through</td><td>sloth through</td></tr>
<tr><td></td><td></td></tr>
<tr><td>drying up</td><td>drying up</td></tr>
<tr><td>sky lighter</td><td>sky lighter</td></tr>
<tr><td>nearly clear</td><td>nearly clear</td></tr>
</table>

clearing clearing veer
clear here clear

Eve Merriam, "Windshield Wiper," in *Knock at a Star*, ed. X. and D. Kennedy. "Windshield Wiper" from *Out Loud* by Eve Merriam. Copyright © 1973 by Eve Merriam. All rights reserved by Eve Merriam. Reprinted by permission of Marian Reiner for the author.

Steve Scott has created attractive graphic forms for Joan Bransfield Graham's poems about water in *Splish, Splash*. Robert Froman's pictures and words provide an innovative way of seeing in *Seeing Things*. His "A Seeing Poem" is drawn in the shape of a light bulb. He suggests that concrete poetry helps children turn on a light in their minds.

Once children have been exposed to concrete poetry, they invariably want to try creating some of their own. However, some children become so involved in the picture-making process, they forget that the meaning of the poem is carried by both words and arrangement. If emphasis is placed on the meaning first, then the shaping of the words will grow naturally from the idea of the poem.

Selecting Poetry for Children

Before they enter school, children seem to have a natural enthusiasm for the sounds and rhythms of language. Schoolteachers and librarians will want to select poems and poets that will build upon these inclinations and that appeal to children's interests. They will also want to find ways to extend and deepen children's initial preferences into a lifelong love of poetry.

Children's Poetry Preferences

Starting in the early 1920s, children's interest in poetry has been the subject of many research studies. The interesting fact about all these studies is the similarity of

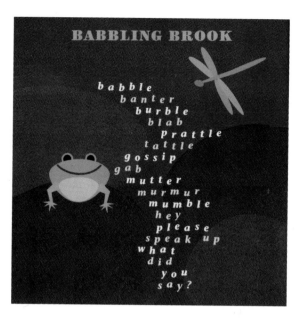

Art and words combine to create watery poems in Joan Graham's book of concrete poetry, *Splish, Splash*, with illustrations by Steve Scott.
Illustration by Steve Scott from *Splish, Splash* by Joan Bransfield Graham. Illustration copyright © 1994 by Steve Scott. Reprinted by permission of Houghton Mifflin Company/Ticknor & Fields Books for Young Readers. All rights reserved.

their findings and the stability of children's poetry preferences over the years. According to Ann Terry, these studies suggest the following:

1. Children are the best judges of their preferences.
2. Reading texts and courses of study often do not include the children's favorite poems.
3. Children's poetry choices are influenced by (1) the poetry form, (2) certain poetic elements, and (3) the content, with humor and familiar experience being particularly popular.
4. A poem enjoyed at one grade level may be enjoyed across several grade levels.
5. Children do not enjoy poems they do not understand.
6. Thoughtful, meditative poems are disliked by children.
7. Some poems appeal to one sex more than the other; girls enjoy poetry more than boys do.
8. New poems are preferred over older, more traditional ones.
9. Literary merit is not necessarily an indication that a poem will be liked.[6]

Terry also reports that in her study of children in grades 4 through 6, narrative poems, such as John

[6]Ann Terry, *Children's Poetry Preferences: A National Survey of the Upper Elementary Grades* (Urbana, Ill.: National Council of Teachers of English, 1974, 1984), p. 10.

Ciardi's "Mummy Slept Late and Daddy Fixed Breakfast" (in *You Read to Me, I'll Read to You*), and limericks, including both modern and traditional, were the children's favorite forms of poetry. Haiku was consistently disliked by all grade levels. Elements of rhyme, rhythm, and sound increased children's enjoyment of the poems, as evidenced by their preference for David McCord's "The Pickety Fence" (in *Every Time I Climb a Tree*) and "Lone Dog" (in *Favorite Poems Old and New*, ed. Ferris). Poems that contained much figurative language or imagery were disliked. Children's favorite poems at all three grade levels contained humor or were about familiar experiences or animals. All children preferred contemporary poems containing modern content and today's language more than the older, more traditional poems.

Carol Fisher and Margaret Natarella[7] found similar preferences among first, second, and third graders, as did Karen Kutiper[8] among seventh, eighth, and ninth graders. However, the younger children enjoyed poems about strange and fantastic events, such as Prelutsky's "The Lurpp Is on the Loose" (in *The Snopp on the Sidewalk*) and Nash's "Adventures of Isabel" (in *The Adventures of Isabel*), while the older children opted for more realistic content. Younger children also appeared to like traditional poems more than the older children did. They insisted that poetry must rhyme, and all of the traditional poems did, so they could have been selecting on the basis of rhyme rather than content. However, one consistent finding of these studies was that adults cannot accurately predict which poems children will like.

How then can we most effectively select poetry for children? Certainly a teacher will want to consider children's needs and interests, their previous experience with poetry, and the types of poetry that appeal to them. A sound principle to follow is to begin where the children are. Teachers can share poems that have elements of rhyme, rhythm, and sound, such as Rhonda Bacmeister's "Galoshes" (in *Sing a Song of Popcorn*, ed. Beatrice de Regniers et al.) or David McCord's "The Song of the Train" (in *One at a Time*). They can read many narrative verses and limericks and look for humorous poems and poems about familiar experiences and animals. They should share only those poems that they really like themselves; enthusiasm for poetry is contagious. However, teachers will not want to limit their sharing only to poems that they know children will like. For taste needs to be developed, too; children

should go beyond their delight in humorous and narrative poetry to develop an appreciation for variety in both form and content. We want children to respond to more poetry and to find more to respond to in poetry.

It may well be that the consistency in children's poetry preferences over the years simply reflects the poverty of their experience with poetry. We tend to like the familiar. If teachers only read traditional narrative poems to children, then these children will like narrative poems. Or having had little or no exposure to fine imaginative poetry, children might not have gone beyond their natural intuitive liking for jump-rope rhymes or humorous limericks. In brief, the results of the studies of children's interests in poetry may be an indictment more of the quality of their literature program than of the quality of their preferences. We need to ascertain children's poetry preferences *after* they have experienced a rich, continuous exposure to poetry throughout the elementary school years. It is hoped that as children have increased experience with a wide range of quality poetry by various poets, they will grow in appreciation and understanding of the finer poems.

Poets and Their Books

Recent years have seen an increase in the number of writers of verse for children and the number of poetry books published for the juvenile market. Poetry itself has changed, becoming less formal, more spontaneous, and imitative of the child's own language patterns. The range of subject matter has expanded with the tremendous variation in children's interests. It is difficult to categorize the work of a poet on the basis of the poems' content, for many poets interpret various areas of children's experience. However, an understanding of the general subject matter of the works of each poet will help the teacher select poems and make recommendations to children.

Humorous Verse

In every preference study that has been done, children prefer narrative rhyme and humorous verse. Today the popularity of the verse of Shel Silverstein and Jack Prelutsky attests to this. The use of imaginative symbols and vivid imagery and metaphor mark the difference between real poetry and verse. The versifiers provide instant gratification but leave the reader with little to ponder. However, because children begin here in their enjoyment of poetry, it seems appropriate to start this section with writers of humorous verse.

Almost all poets have written some humorous verse, but only a few have become noted primarily for this form. In the nineteenth century the names of Edward Lear and Lewis Carroll became almost synonymous with

[7]Carol J. Fisher and Margaret A. Natarella, "Young Children's Preferences in Poetry: A National Survey of First, Second and Third Graders," *Research in the Teaching of English* 16 (December 1982): 339–353.

[8]Karen Sue Kutiper, "A Survey of the Adolescent Poetry Preferences of Seventh, Eighth and Ninth Graders," (Ed.D. dissertation, University of Houston, 1985).

humorous nonsense poems. Lear's limericks, alphabet rhymes, and narrative poems have been compiled into one book, *The Complete Nonsense Book*. Each absurd verse is illustrated by the poet's grotesque drawings, which add greatly to Lear's humor. Artist Fred Marcellino has collected three of Lear's narrative poems in *The Pelican Chorus and Other Nonsense*. In addition to the title poem, Marcellino's watercolor paintings add zest and humor to "The Owl and the Pussycat" and "The New Vestments."

Several of our modern poets are following in the tradition of Lear. William Jay Smith included limericks, rhyming ABCs, and imaginary dialogue in much of his nonsense verse. The best of his poetry has been reissued in a new *Laughing Time* illustrated with amusing pictures by Fernando Krahn. One of the best of Smith's poems is the well-known "Toaster," which compares that kitchen utensil to a dragon. J. Patrick Lewis writes wonderfully funny verse in his books *A Hippopotamusn't*, *Ridicholas Nicholas*, and *The Fat Cats at Sea*. Victoria Chess illustrates all these poems with most amusing pictures of dumpy-looking creatures and fat, nautically natty cats. The puns in the poem "Tom Tigercat" in *A Hippopotamusn't* are reminiscent of the work of Ogden Nash and John Ciardi.

Ogden Nash's sophisticated light verse and limericks are mostly out of print. However, a new edition of his long narrative verse about the cowardly dragon has been illustrated by Lynn Munsinger in *The Tale of Custard the Dragon*. Quentin Blake created the pictures for Custard's story and some eighty-four other Nash poems under the title *Custard & Company*. "The Adventures of Isabel," about a girl who eats a bear, continues to be one of children's favorite story-poems. Maurice Sendak illustrates this poem in the fine collection titled *Sing a Song of Popcorn* edited by Beatrice de Regniers and others. James Marshall's illustrations for Nash's legendary Isabel, in *The Adventures of Isabel*, are outrageously funny. Isabel might wear hair bows and nail polish, but she is as tough as the bear she encounters.

Many of Douglas Florian's rhymes in *Beast Feast* are reminiscent of Nash's animal sketches in their brevity and their sense of playfulness:

Just when you think you know the boa
There's moa and moa and moa and moa.

"Boa" from *Beast Feast*, copyright © 1994 by Douglas Florian.
Reprinted by permission of Harcourt Brace & Company.

Florian's witty artwork adds to the delight in *Beast Feast* and *Bing Bang Bong*, a second collection of his nonsense verse.

John Ciardi's light verse for children is enjoyed by girls and boys with enough sophistication to appreciate his tongue-in-cheek humor. One particular favorite is "The Cat Heard the Cat Bird" (in *I Met a Man*), which tells the story of "Thin-Grin Cat" who became a fat cat when the catbird disappeared! His "Mummy Slept Late and Daddy Fixed Breakfast" (in *Piping Down the Valleys Wild*, ed. Nancy Larrick) was the most popular poem of the children in the fourth, fifth, and sixth grades in the Terry study (see p. 403). A former poetry editor for the *Saturday Review*, Ciardi could write serious verse as well as light verse. His "How to Tell the Top of the Hill" (in *The Reason for the Pelican*) and "The River Is a Piece of the Sky" (in Larrick's *Piping Down the Valleys Wild*) are both proof of this. Over the years, he wrote over a dozen books of poetry for children, and his last, *Mummy Took Cooking Lessons and Other Poems*, was published posthumously. Ciardi was an early winner of the NCTE Poetry Award.

X. J. Kennedy has a wonderfully weird sense of humor. Most of his poetry is pure nonsense and delights children. His poem "Wildlife Refuge," in which he describes "a reindeer in rain gear," is just one example of his talent for wordplay. "A Stupendous Pincushion" tells about a pincushion not only for pins but for rolling pins and bowling pins besides. In "Backyard Volcano," Uncle Jack delights in swimming in the volcano in the backyard and Mother props her feet up on it to keep them warm. These three poems are all in *Ghastlies, Goops and Pincushions*. His other books include *Brats*, *Fresh Brats*, *Drat Those Brats*, and *The Forgetful Wishing Well*.

Douglas Florian's "Boa" is one of many brightly colored paintings and poems that will delight young readers in *Beast Feast*.

Illustration from *Beast Feast*, copyright © 1994 by Douglas Florian, reproduced by permission of Harcourt Brace & Company.

Much of what children consider funny is frequently sadistic and ghoulish. Colin McNaughton's *Making Friends with Frankenstein* is a collection that ranges from the stomach-turning "Cockroach Sandwich" to the mournful satire of "The Doom Merchant," with much pure silliness in between. McNaughton's bizarre illustrations add humor and clarify his wordplay, as when we see Frankenstein's feet, head, and other body parts sprouting angel wings ("may he rest in pieces"). Jack Prelutsky's macabre poems in *Nightmares* and *The Headless Horseman* and Arnold Lobel's black-and-white illustrations are splendidly terrifying. One seventh-grade teacher of children in the inner city maintained that this book got her through her first year of teaching! Prelutsky is also a master at creating such zany imaginary creatures as the "Wozzit," who is hiding in the closet, and the "Grobbles," who quietly wait to gobble someone up. Both of these poems are in *The Snopp on the Sidewalk*. He creates more appealing creatures in *The Baby Uggs Are Hatching*, including the "Sneezy-Snoozer," the "Dreary Dreeze," and the "Sneepies." *The Dragons Are Singing Tonight* includes a dragon whose cold is cured with a dose of turpentine and one whose fire is doused in a bout with a thunderstorm.

All ages enjoy Prelutsky's large collection (more than a hundred poems) titled *The New Kid on the Block*, which includes humorous realistic poems such as "I'm Disgusted with My Brother" and "My Sister Is a Sissy," plus many funny characters and more zany creatures. *Something Big Has Been Here* is another large collection of amusing poems. Children love to listen to "The Wumpaloons, Which Never Were" and then draw what they think the Wumpaloons looked like according to the description in the poem. They also enjoy creating their idea of the animal that left the huge footprints in the title poem of this collection.

Prelutsky has written some lighthearted realistic verse for younger children about special holidays and seasons. These include some useful poems in *It's Halloween* and *It's Thanksgiving* and some very amusing ones in *Rainy Rainy Saturday*, and *It's Snowing! It's Snowing!* His books *Ride a Purple Pelican* and *Beneath a Blue Umbrella* are filled with Mother Goose–type verses that appeal to preschoolers. Garth Williams has made large, handsome, colored illustrations for each of these joyous poems that play with place names—such as "Grandma Bear from Delaware" and "Cincinnati Patty" (both in *Ride a Purple Pelican*).

Shel Silverstein's *Where the Sidewalk Ends* was on the *New York Times* best-sellers list for three years. It is the one poetry book that all teachers, children, and parents seem to know. Librarians complain that they can't keep the book on the shelf, no matter how many copies they have. Here you meet a boy who turns into a TV set, a

Peter Sis creates the imaginative pictures for Jack Prelutsky's humorous collections *The Dragons Are Singing Tonight* and *Monday's Troll*.
Illustration from *The Dragons Are Singing Tonight* by Jack Prelutsky, illustrated by Peter Sis. Illustration copyright © 1993 by Peter Sis. By permission of Greenwillow Books, a division of William Morrow & Company, Inc.

king who eats only a "Peanut-Butter Sandwich," and those three characters "Ickle Me, Pickle Me, Tickle Me Too." Much of the humor of these poems is based on the sounds of words, the preposterous characters, and amusing situations. While some verses are slightly unsavory, others surprise you with their sensitivity, such as "Invitation," "Listen to the Mustn'ts," and the title poem, "Where the Sidewalk Ends." *The Light in the Attic* and *Falling Up* provide more of the same fun.

Poetry is neglected in our schools today, but there is no dearth of humorous verse. Children take to it as they do to a hamburger, fries, and a shake. And like a fast-food meal, it is enjoyable but not the only food to include in a balanced diet.

Interpreters of the World of Childhood

Robert Louis Stevenson was the first poet to write of childhood from the child's point of view. *A Child's Garden of Verses,* published in 1885, continues to be popular today. Stevenson was himself a frail child and spent much of his early life in bed or confined indoors. His poetry reflects a solitary childhood, but a happy one. In "Land of Counterpane" and "Block City," he portrays a resourceful, inventive child who can create his own amusement. He found playmates in his shadow, in his dreams, and in his storybooks. The rhythm of Stevenson's "The Swing," "Where Go the Boats," and "Windy Nights" appeals to children today as much as it did to the children of a century ago. Currently, some eighteen illustrated editions of *A Child's Garden of Verses* are in print. They range in interpretation from Tasha Tudor's quaint pastels, which portray Stevenson as a young child, to Brian Wildsmith's edition, a brilliant kaleidoscope of color. Ted Rand has created a stunning picturebook edition of Stevenson's *My Shadow*, expanding the meaning of this poem to incorporate children from all over the world. Ashley Wolff's illustrations extend Stevenson's *Block City* from a story about a boy building with blocks at home to creating an elaborate landscape that seems to come alive. Such picture books make fine introductions to Stevenson's poems.

Perhaps the best loved of British children's poets is A. A. Milne. Some of his poems, such as "Halfway Down" and "Solitude," show perceptive insight into the child's mind. "Happiness" captures a child's joy in such delights as new waterproof boots, a raincoat, and a hat. Told in the first person, "Hoppity" reveals a young child's enjoyment of the state of perpetual motion. Most of Milne's poems are delightfully funny. The poetry from both of Milne's poetry books has now been collected into one volume, titled *The World of Christopher Robin*. Illustrations by Ernest Shepard seem to belong with Milne's poetry as much as Pooh belongs with Christopher Robin; it is hard to imagine one without the other.

Another well-loved British poet for children is Eleanor Farjeon. Her knowledge and understanding of children's thoughts and behavior are reflected in her book *Eleanor Farjeon's Poems for Children*. The simple poem "New Clothes and Old" tells of a child's preference for old things. "Over the Garden Wall" is a hauntingly beautiful poem that makes the reader feel as lonely as the child who is left out of the ball game on the other side of the wall. This poet also wrote the lovely nature poem "The Night Will Never Stay" and the graphically descriptive "Mrs. Peck-Pigeon."

Before her death in 1965 Eleanor Farjeon had received notable recognition for her poetry and prose. She was the first recipient of the international Hans Christian Andersen Medal and she received the Regina Medal for her life's work. A prestigious British award "for distinguished services to children's books" that bears the name of this well-known poet and writer is given annually. No other poet who has written exclusively for children has received such recognition.

Dorothy Aldis was one of the first American poets to celebrate children's feelings and everyday experiences with simple childlike verses. With rhyme and singsong meter, she captures the child's delight in the ordinary routines of home life, as in "After My Bath" and "Going to Sleep." Aldis is particularly sensitive to the emotions of childhood in "Bad," "Alone," and "No One Heard Him Call." Family relationships are lovingly portrayed in "Little," "My Brother," and "Hiding." Poems from the first four books by Dorothy Aldis were collected in a single volume entitled *All Together*, which can still be found in most library collections.

Mary Ann Hoberman writes lively rhythmical verse for young children. The poems in the collection *Yellow Butter Purple Jelly Red Jam Black Bread* range from such delightful nonsense as "The Llama Who Had No Pajama" to the swinging rhythm of "Hello and Goodbye." The poem "Brother" (in *Sing a Song of Popcorn*, ed. Beatrice de Regniers et al.), about a boy who is a bit of a bother to everyone, is a favorite with children and could well be shared as an introduction to books on sibling rivalry. Hoberman wrote the poems for *A Fine Fat Pig* after Malcah Zeldis created brilliant folk-art paintings of various animals. Each poem captures the uniqueness of the animals described, from the giraffe to the walrus. Primary children also enjoy the long, sustained poem in Hoberman's picture book *A House Is a House for Me*. In this book she plays with the concept of houses, including regular houses and animals' houses, and then looks at other possibilities, such as a glove becoming a house for a hand and a pocket as a house for pennies. Once children hear this poem, they like to make up their own "house" poems. All of Hoberman's poetry is distinguished by its fast-paced rhymes and marked rhythms.

Karla Kuskin also sees with the eyes of a child as she creates her well-known poems. Her book *Dogs & Dragons, Trees & Dreams* includes many of her best-known narrative poems, such as "I Woke Up This Morning," which tells of a child who feels she/he hasn't done anything right since "quarter past seven," or "Lewis Has a Trumpet," or "The Bear with the Golden Hair." She can write mysterious poems, such as the haunting "Where Would You Be?" or play with the sounds of words, as in "The Full of the Moon." Her book *Any Me I Want to Be* is written from the point of view of the subject. Instead of writing how a cat or the moon or a pair of shoes appear to her, the poet tries to get inside the object and be its voice. Children then enjoy guessing what the verse is about. In *Near the Window Tree* the poet attaches a note to each of her poems explaining what prompted her to write it. This was in response to the number of letters she receives from children asking her where she gets her ideas. Many of her poems contain both humor and wisdom, as in this quizzical one:

🎵 People always say to me
"What do you think you'd like to be
When you grow up?"
And I say "Why,
I think I'd like to be the sky
Or be a plane or train or mouse
Or maybe a haunted house
Or something furry, rough and wild . . .
Or maybe I will stay a child."

Karla Kuskin, "The Question," in *Dogs & Dragons,
Trees & Dreams*. Copyright © 1980 by Karla Kuskin. Used by
permission of HarperCollins Publishers, New York, NY.

Kuskin's *Soap Soup and Other Verses* and *Something Sleeping in the Hall* are collections of easy-to-read poems. Six- and 7-year-olds would like to write about the pets, big or small, that might be "sleeping in their halls" after reading about all kinds of pets in the latter book. Karla Kuskin illustrates all her own poetry books with tiny, precise pen-and-ink drawings. She designed the artwork for the NCTE Poetry Award and then was the third recipient of that coveted prize.

Multicultural Poetry

Long before the experiences of African Americans became recognized in literature, Pulitzer Prize–winner Gwendolyn Brooks wrote poignant poetry about African American children living in the inner city. *Bronzeville Boys and Girls* contains some thirty-four poems, each bearing the name, thoughts, and feelings of an individual child. There is "John, Who Is Poor"; "Michael," who is afraid of the storm; "Beulah," who has quiet thoughts at church; and "Luther and Breck," who have a make-believe dragon fight. Unfortunately, this poet has written only one volume of poetry for children.

Langston Hughes was the first African American to write poems of black protest and pride, such as "What Happens to a Dream Deferred?" *The Dream Keeper and Other Poems* is a handsome new collection of his poems illustrated by Brian Pinkney. "Dreams" and "April Rain Song" and "Mother to Son" are among the sixty-six poems that show the full range of this poet's powerful voice. The title poem reflects the lyrical beauty of Hughes's imagination.

🎵 Bring me all of your dreams,
You dreamers
Bring me all of your
Heart melodies
That I may wrap them
In a blue cloud cloth

Away from the too rough fingers
Of the world.

From *The Dream Keeper and Other Poems* by Langston Hughes.
Copyright © 1932 and renewed 1960 by Langston Hughes.
Reprinted by permission of Alfred A. Knopf, Inc.

Honey, I Love is by Eloise Greenfield, who has a great capacity for speaking in the voice of a young African American child. This joyous little book of sixteen poems includes a chant, the jump-rope rhyme (see p. 394), and thoughtful observations on experiences like dressing up ("I Look Pretty") or thinking about a neighbor who left her a nickel ("Keepsake") before she died. The Dillons' illustrations are as sensitive as these poems that celebrate the rich content of a child's world.

Greenfield portrays a slightly older child in the eighteen first-person poems in *Nathaniel Talking*. Nathaniel gives us his "philosophy" of life in these poems. Some are bittersweet memories; others look to the future. Sharp, clear pencil drawings by Jan Spivey Gilchrist help to make this a distinguished book of poetry. Gilchrist also illustrated the eighteen poems in Greenfield's *Night on Neighborhood Street*, poems about family, friends, and neighbors. Greenfield has written poems to go with Amos Ferguson's Bahamian folk-art paintings in *Under the Sunday Tree*.

Nikki Giovanni is well known for her adult poetry, but she has also written for children. *Spin a Soft Black Song* has been reissued with new illustrations. "Poem for Rodney" expresses both a child's point of view and an adult's. Rodney is tired of everyone asking him what he is going to do when he grows up; his reply is simply that he'd like to grow up. Giovanni's *Knoxville, Tennessee* has been published in a picture book lushly illustrated with paintings by Larry Johnson. The brief but evocative text singles out the special summer pleasures of childhood—barbecue and buttermilk at the church picnic, okra and greens from daddy's garden, and the warmth of a close family.

Sing to the Sun, by noted artist and storyteller Ashley Bryan, is a collection of poems that are as vibrant as the paintings that decorate the book's pages. While there is poignancy in poems such as "Leaving," there are also strong rhythms and bright images that fulfill the promise of the sunny title and evoke the warmth of Caribbean culture. Bryan's special magic is present in the "Storyteller," about a storyteller whose stories were pieced together with bird song, and in "Artist," about an artist who can transform sorrow.

Monica Gunning's *Not a Copper Penny in Me House* captures the everday life and special celebrations of her Jamaican childhood. Frané Lessac's folk-art paintings illustrate island scenes like the little country church that Nana walks three miles to every Sunday in "Walking to Church" and the classes that Miss Zettie holds when the weather turns too hot to stay indoors ("Classes Under the Tree").

Arnold Adoff writes strong poems about the inner thoughts and feelings of a girl born of a mixed-race

"The Storyteller," in Ashley Bryan's *Sing to the Sun,*
captures the warmth of the Caribbean culture portrayed in
Bryan's poems and paintings.
Copyright © 1992 by Ashley Bryan. Used by permission of HarperCollins
Publishers, New York, NY.

marriage. In *All the Colors of the Race,* as in his other work,
he shapes each poem to balance the semantic and rhythmic lines of force. He wants his words to sing as well as
say. His poem "The way I see any hope for later" is one
that everyone should read and heed. His story-poem *Black
Is Brown Is Tan* describes a biracial family growing up
happy in a house full of love:

> Black is brown is tan
> is girl   is boy
> is nose   is face
> is all the colors
> of the race
> is dark   is light
> singing songs
> in singing night
> kiss big woman   hug big man
> black   is brown   is tan

Copyright © 1973 by Arnold Adoff. Used by permission of the
author and HarperCollins Publishers, New York, NY.

These poems not only reflect Arnold Adoff's love for his
own family but celebrate diversity and individuality.
While many of his poems are about caring and friendship
between races, others are about seasons and eating. *In for
Winter, Out for Spring* is a journal of poems of the changing seasons, capturing the joy of everything from the first
snowflake in winter to pumpkins in late October. Adoff
creates vivid images in these poems of people and seasons. His *Street Music: City Poems* presents the vigor of

city life, its clangor and its vibrancy. *Eats* and *Chocolate
Dreams* celebrate the poet's passion for tasty treats, particularly sweets. Adoff is also a 1988 recipient of the prestigious NCTE Poetry Award for Excellance in Children's
Literature.

The poems by Cynthia Rylant in her book *Waiting to
Waltz* capture the essence of growing up in a small town
in Appalachia. Her vivid images chronicle the minor
crises that make up a childhood: the day the girl's
mother runs over the black dog down the road ("Little
Short Legs"); the time the girl loses the spelling bee;
and her dismay at being reprimanded for swearing. The
most poignant poem of all, "Forgotten," describes her
mixed feelings when she hears that her long-absent father has died. Stephen Gammell's soft-pencil drawings
are as sensitive as these poems, each picturing a fleeting
moment of childhood that suddenly is gone.

Gary Soto has several collections of poetry for older
students that capture the Latino experience. *Neighborhood Odes* sings the praises of everything from tortillas
to tennis shoes. In "Ode to Senor Leal's Goat" a goat
amuses the chickens and shocks Senor Leal when he
runs away with his smoking pipe. "Ode to My Library"
touches upon the rich life in, and out of, books that the
library provides a young dreamer.

Charlotte Pomerantz is not Latina, but she and her
husband and two children spend winters in Puerto Rico.
This experience encouraged her to write poetry in two
languages, English and Spanish. She does this so skillfully in her poems in *The Tamarindo Puppy* that the
child easily learns words in both languages while reading and hearing these poems. Illustrations by Byron Barton also help indicate meaning. In another collection, *If
I Had a Paka: Poems in Eleven Languages,* Pomerantz
builds the child's cross-cultural vocabulary by repeating
a key word in a different language, such as Swahili.
With the help of English-language clues and the clear
pictures by Nancy Tafuri, young children can easily
guess the meaning of the words and poems.

In My Mother's House by Ann Nolan Clark was a
breakthrough book when it was first published in 1941.
Now reissued, it contains poems describing a close-knit
farming community of Pueblo Indians. Based on stories
told by Pueblo children, it was the first book to represent
a Native American point of view. Velino Herrera did
the beautifully clear pictures for this fine book of poems.

There are many multicultural voices that are beginning to be heard through some of the fine collections of
poetry that are now being published. Many of these
anthologies are discussed in the section "Specialized
Collections" later in this chapter.

Poets of Nature

Like poets, children are very attuned to the world around
them. They are fascinated by the constant changes in

nature and enjoy poems that communicate their delight in the first snow, their sense of wonder when they touch a pussy willow or hear a foghorn or see a deer.

Aileen Fisher is adept at observing both nature and children. She views the natural world through the eyes of the child, preserving a remarkable sense of wonder. Her poems are filled with sensory imagery, as in this verse:

> Close your eyes
> and do not peek
> and I'll rub Spring,
> across your cheek—
> smooth as satin,
> soft and sleek—
> close your eyes
> and do not peek.

"Pussy Willows" from *Always Wondering* by Aileen Fisher. Reprinted by permission of the author.

Fisher's comparisons are simple and fresh, very much within the experience of a child. Some of Aileen Fisher's favorite poems appear in her book *Always Wondering*. Included are such popular nature poems as "Bird Talk," "Pussy Willow," and "I Like Fall," as well as poems about children's interests, such as "First Day of School" and "When It's Thanksgiving." Aileen Fisher was the second recipient of the Award for Excellence in Poetry for Children given by the National Council of Teachers of English.

Lilian Moore describes the changing moods and seasons of both the city and the country in her short-line free verse. Her poems frequently appeal to the senses, as she talks about the moaning of foghorns or the "tree-talk" or "wind-swish" of the night. Of her poems in *Something New Begins*, "Encounter" tells of a "heart-stopping" meeting with a deer, "Wind Song" describes the flapping and snapping noise the wind makes as it blows flags and ashcans, and "Snowy Morning" speaks of waking to a hushed morning of snow in the city. Her poem "Until I Saw the Sea" (in de Regniers, et al., *Sing a Song of Popcorn*) provides a fresh new image of the "wrinkled sea." A former teacher, reading specialist, and editor who lived in the city, Lilian Moore now lives on a farm in the country. Her poetry reflects her knowledge of what children enjoy and her close observations of her surroundings. Many of her poems from her earlier books have been included in *Something New Begins*. Moore is also a recipient of the NCTE Poetry Award.

J. Patrick Lewis includes seventeen poems in *Earth Verses and Water Rhymes*. He begins with poems about the fall and progresses through the seasons. Among these poems' fresh images is his description of trees as "Earth umbrellas." Robert Sabuda's handcut linoleum block prints in soft muted colors seem just right for the contemplative tone of these poems.

Byrd Baylor writes story-length prose poems that reflect her appreciation for nature and the beauty of the landscape of the Southwest. In *The Other Way to Listen*, an older man tells a young girl how you can hear wildflower seeds burst open or a rock murmuring or hills singing—of course, it takes practice! *Your Own Best Secret Place, Everybody Needs a Rock,* and *I'm in Charge of Celebrations* are fine poetry workshop starters, as they inspire children to describe their secret places or plan special celebrations. Peter Parnall incorporates the text as part of his bold illustrations.

Constance Levy has written two volumes of poetry that make strong connections to children's experiences with nature. In *I'm Going to Pet a Worm Today* she muses in "The Color Eater" about how night laps up the sunset, and wonders about bees in "The Business of Bees" and about butterflies in "Questions to Ask a Butterfly." The poems in *A Tree Place* introduce creatures like the black snake who can write his name, in "S Is for Snake," or the inchworm:

> A little green inchworm
> dropped from a tree,
> and rode in my hair
> unknown to me,
> till I looked in the mirror.
> "Aha!" I said,
> "What is this green thing on my head?"
>
> And the worm must have wondered
> seeing me,
> "What is this funny looking tree?"

Constance Levy, "Inchworm." Reprinted with the permission of Margaret K. McElderry Books, an imprint of Simon & Schuster from *A Tree Place and Other Poems* by Constance Levy. Copyright © 1994 Constance Levy.

Two unusually fine picture books of nature poems are Marilyn Singer's *Turtle in July* and Charles Norman's *The Hornbeam Tree and Other Poems*. In *Turtle in July*, Singer writes from the point of view of the animal, fish, or insect. She includes a different animal for each month of the year, describing, for example, a deer who runs over the hard-packed January snow or the beavers in November who add mud and more mud, sticks and more sticks, to their winter homes. Jerry Pinkney's clear watercolors portray each creature in its natural habitat. In the nineteen poems in *The Hornbeam Tree*, Norman describes the characteristics of creatures as small as a snail and as large as a polar bear, as common as a squirrel and as exotic as the duck-billed platypus. Ted Rand's vibrant watercolor illustrations for this book capture the dive of a kingfisher and the drumming of a woodpecker.

While Carl Sandburg is noted for his sage commentary on people, he did make two collections of poetry

Arithmetic is where numbers fly like pigeons
in and out of your head.

Ted Rand's anamorphic artwork reflects Carl Sandburg's numerical enigma in a picture-book edition of Sandburg's poem *Arithmetic*.

From *Arithmetic*, copyright 1950 by Carl Sandburg and renewed 1978 by Margaret Sandburg, Janet Sandburg, and Helga Sandburg Crile. Illustrations copyright © 1993 by Ted Rand. Reproduced by permission of Harcourt Brace & Company.

with young people in mind, *Early Moon* and *Wind Song*. Only *Early Moon* is still available, in paperback. Lee Bennett Hopkins has made a handsome new edition of selected poems of Carl Sandburg titled *Rainbows Are Made*, illustrated with six of Fritz Eichenberg's wood engravings—themselves as powerful as some of Sandburg's poetry. This collection includes selections from *The People, Yes* and poems about nature, people, the seasons, the sea, and the stars. Ted Rand has illustrated a picture-book version of the old favorite by Sandburg, *Arithmetic*, using anamorphic, or distorted, pictures that must be viewed with a special mylar cylinder or by holding the book at a special angle. These two handsome books will introduce children to the thoughtful, quizzical nature of Carl Sandburg's poetry.

Many poems by Robert Frost are both simple enough for a child to understand and complex enough for graduate study. Before his death, Frost selected some of his poems to be read to, or by, young people. Interestingly, the title of this collection, *You Come Too*, was taken from a line of "The Pasture," the first poem in this book and the introductory poem of the very first book Frost ever published. Upon initial reading, this poem seems no more than a literal invitation to join someone as he cleans the pasture spring. However, the poem takes on more meaning when viewed in the context of its placement; the trip to the pasture to clean the spring might well be an invitation to the enjoyment of poetry itself— "you come too!" By reading *You Come Too*, children can enjoy "The Runaway," "Dust of Snow," "The Last Word of a Bluebird," and "The Pasture," poems on their level of understanding. Older children will begin to comprehend the deeper meanings in "Mending Wall," "The Road Not Taken," and "The Death of the Hired Man."

Versatile Poets

It is almost impossible to characterize the wide variety of poems produced by certain poets. David McCord's poetry, for example, ranges in subject matter from poems about everyday experiences to nature poems to verses about verse. He plays with sound in "The Pickety Fence" and "Song of the Train"; with form, including couplets, quatrains, limericks, and triolets, in "Write Me a Verse"; and with words and their meanings in many of his poems, including "Glowworm," "Ptarmigan," and "Goose, Moose and Spruce." He can write with a lively wit or quietly enter the serious inner world of the child.

McCord's *Every Time I Climb a Tree* was one of the first poetry books to be illustrated by the well-known picture-book illustrator Caldecott Medal-winning Marc Simont. All of David McCord's poetry was collected in a single volume titled *One at a Time*. It is appropriate that this book was published in the same year that McCord received the first NCTE Award for Excellence in Poetry for Children.

Eve Merriam's poetry has a lilt and bounce that will capture the most disinterested child's attention, beginning with her narrative poems "Alligator on the Escalator" and "Teevee" (both in *Jamboree*), the story of a married couple who watched so much TV they became strangers to each other. Her books for primary children—*You Be Good & I'll Be Night*, *A Poem for a Pickle*, *Blackberry Ink*, and *Higgle Wiggle*—contain bouncy jump-rope rhymes such as "Jump, Jump," the rhythmical "Swing Me Swing Me," and the loving "You're My Turtle." *Fresh Paint* contains lovely fresh images of new snow, and of spring and sunset in "The First Day of Spring" and "Sunset." Older students, once they have read her "A Throw of Threes," might like to try writing three things that they think go together. *Chortles* is full of wordplay, including "Gazinta," "Whodunnit," and "A Token of Unspoken." Here, too, students can find "Windshield Wiper" (see p. 403). *The Singing Green* contains poems about indoors and outdoors, and one called "The Poem as a Door." Many of Merriam's most popular poems—including "Satellite, Satellite," "To Meet Mr. Lincoln," "A Commercial for Spring," and "A Yell for Yellow"—all appear in the paperback edition of *Jamboree*. It seems obvious that such a versatile poet received the NCTE Poetry Award.

Another NCTE Poetry Award winner is Myra Cohn Livingston, a prolific and versatile writer of poetry for children of all ages. She handles a variety of styles and forms masterfully, including rhymes, free verse, limerick, triolet, haiku, concrete poems, and others. Her first books of poetry appealed more to the younger child and included such well-known poems as "Whispers," "The Night," and "Bump on My Knee." Many of these poems for younger children have been gathered together in a small-size book, *A Song I Sang for You*, illustrated with Margot Tomes's appropriately naïve black-and-white illustrations. In *Worlds I Know*, Livingston echoes the emotions of slightly older children. Here she talks about the aunts and uncles who people a child's world, as well as relatives they'll never meet ("The Grandfather I Never Knew"). In *Flights of Fancy* the poems range from a flight of imagination to images seen on a real airplane flight. Livingston gets inside older children's thoughts in poems like "Lonesome," "I'm Sorry," and "Poor" in *The Way Things Are and Other Poems*. Her poems in *There Was a Place* are remarkable for reflecting how children from broken homes and one-parent families feel (see "In the Middle," p. 392).

Livingston has also combined her poetry with the artwork of Leonard Everett Fisher to produce such striking books as *A Circle of Seasons*, *Sky Songs*, *Earth Songs*, *Sea Songs*, *Space Songs*, and *Up in the Air*. In *Celebrations* both the art and the poems present a moving panorama of sixteen holidays, including Martin Luther King Day, Columbus Day, Presidents' Day, and all birthdays. *Festivals* includes poems and pictures to celebrate Chinese New Year, Kwanza, and Ramadan. Not only is Myra Cohn Livingston a versatile poet, but she is also a well-known anthologist and teacher of creative writing to children.

Deborah Chandra has been awarded the International Reading Association/Lee Bennett Hopkins Promising Poet Award for two volumes of poetry, *Balloons* and *Rich Lizard*. Many of her poems, such as "Snowfall" (in *Balloons and Other Poems*) and "The Wild Wood" (in *Rich Lizard*) focus on the natural world. Other poems show her ability to uncover fresh images in the everyday concerns of children. In "Bubble" (in *Balloons*) a child discovers "*my breath*—wrapped in a

quivering skin, . . . so marble round and glistening." The following poem leaves a memorable image of angry words hanging in an empty room:

> Her words rose, swarming round,
> Ugly, stinging shapes of sound,
> Circling the foe.
>
> His words bristled, black with warning,
> Arched and stiff, they met the swarming,
> Hissing low
>
> They sprang and clawed and stung in space,
> But shaped as words, they left no trace
> Of fur or fang around the place

"The Argument" from *Rich Lizard and Other Poems* by Deborah Chandra. Copyright © 1993 by Deborah Chandra. Reprinted by permission of Farrar, Straus & Giroux, Inc.

Barbara Esbensen, a well-known writer of fiction and nonfiction, is a recent winner of the NCTE Poetry Award for poems about such varied topics as dance, discoveries, and animals. In *Who Shrank My Grandmother's House?* she discovers something new in "Doors" and "Pencils" and invites children to make science connections through such poems as "Sand Dollar," "Geode," and "Prism in the Window." *Dance with Me* includes poems about movement

In Barbara Esbensen's *Dance with Me,* Megan Lloyd's illustrations capture the energy and flow of physical movement.

Illustration copyright © 1995 by Megan Lloyd. Used by permission of HarperCollins Publishers, New York, NY.

What is the age-level appeal of this book?

How many poems are included?

What types of poems are included?

How many poets are represented?

What is the quality of the poetry?

Are there contemporary poems as well as old favorites?

What is the subject matter of the poems?

How are the poems arranged and organized?

How adequate are the indexes in helping the reader find a poem?

How helpful are the introduction and commentaries?

Has the compiler achieved the stated or implied purpose of the collection?

Are the illustrations and format appropriate for the poems and age appeal of the collection?

---

and invites children to imagine dances with their bodies as well as in their heads. *Words with Wrinkled Knees* is a collection of poems in which she examines the images in the letters of animal names. The title poem shows the imaginative scope of her poet's ear and eye.

The word is too heavy
to lift   too cumbersome to
lead through a room filled with
relatives or small
glass trinkets

E L E P H A N T

He must have invented it
himself. This is a lumbering
gray word   the ears of it
are huge and flap like loose
wings   a word with
wrinkled knees and toes
like boxing gloves

This word   E L E P H A N T
sways toward us   bulk
and skull-bones filling up
the space   trumpeting
its own wide name
through its nose!

Barbara Esbensen, "Elephant," in *Words with Wrinkled Knees.* Text copyright © 1986 by Barbara Juster Esbensen. Used by permission of HarperCollins Publishers, New York, NY.

Anthologies of Poems for Children

Today poetry anthologies do not stay in print as long as they used to because time limits are usually placed on permissions to use certain poems. This has meant the publication of fewer large anthologies and the proliferation of many specialized collections containing fewer than twenty poems. For this reason only a selected number of anthologies are reviewed here; others will be found in the Resources for Teaching box on pp. 416–417.

Comprehensive Poetry Collections

Every family with children will want to own at least one excellent anthology of poetry for children. Teachers will want to have several, including some for their personal use and some for the children's use. In selecting a general anthology of poetry, consider the criteria listed in the Guidelines box "Evaluating Poetry Anthologies."

Sing a Song of Popcorn, edited by Beatrice Schenk de Regniers and others, is a stunning collection of poetry for all children. The poems were first selected for a popular paperback called *Poems Children Will Sit Still For* (now out of print, this Scholastic title sold over a quarter of a million copies). The selection of poetry for *Sing a Song of Popcorn* has been updated and is now illustrated in full color by nine Caldecott Medal–winning artists. The volume contains over 128 poems that had to meet the criterion of captivating children. The represented poets range from Mary Ann Hoberman to Emily Dickinson. Included are such well-known poems as "Galoshes," "Eletelephony," "Brother," and "Stopping by Woods on a Snowy Evening." If a teacher or parent could only have one collection, this would be the one to buy.

Tomie de Paola's Book of Poems is also a handsome anthology. Emily Dickinson's poem "There is no frigate like a book" is used to symbolically unite the cover, title page, introduction, and final page. These eighty-six well-chosen poems include classics like Stevenson's "Land of Counterpane" and contemporary poems like Myra Cohn Livingston's "Secret Door" and Eve Merriam's funny

"Alligator on the Escalator." A unique addition is some poems in Spanish.

Jack Prelutsky has produced two very popular anthologies. *Read-Aloud Rhymes for the Very Young* contains over two hundred of the most popular poems for very young children, including a few Mother Goose and jump-rope rhymes, Dennis Lee's "Dreadful Doings of Jelly Belly," and Milne's "Halfway Down." Lively illustrations by Marc Brown emphasize the fun and nonsense of some of these verses.

Many parents and teachers will be attracted to the large *Random House Book of Poetry*, with its 572 poems selected by Jack Prelutsky and profusely illustrated with Arnold Lobel's lively pictures. For children who have known only Shel Silverstein's and Prelutsky's humorous verse, this is a good place to begin. Though much of the book is dominated by humorous verse (including some thirty-eight poems by Prelutsky himself), fine poems by Robert Frost, Eve Merriam, Eleanor Farjeon, Emily Dickinson, Myra Cohn Livingston, Dylan Thomas, and others are interspersed with them. Arnold Lobel's humorous full-color illustrations also draw children to this anthology.

Two other anthologies for parents and teachers of young children are Lillian Moore's *Sunflakes*, illustrated by Jan Omerod, and X. J. and Dorothy Kennedy's *Talking Like the Rain*, illustrated by Jane Dyer. Both collections contain a mixture of old and new poems that have the kind of sound and word play that is particularly appealing to younger children. *Talking Like the Rain* contains 123 poems, ranging from Robert Louis Stevenson's "The Swing" to Myra Cohn Livingston's "Working with Mother." *Sunflakes* is a good introduction to some of the best modern poets for children as well as to Mother Goose and Christiana Rosetti. It includes such favorites as Aileen Fisher's "I Like It When It's Mizzly" and Dennis Lee's "The Muddy Puddle."

David Booth's *Til All the Stars Have Fallen* is an exciting collection of over seventy Canadian poems for children ages 8 and up. These include poems by such well-known poets as Dennis Lee and Jean Little and some wonderful new voices such as Duke Redbird, A. M. Klein, Lois Simmie, and George Swede. Kady Denton has echoed the poetic imagery of many of these poems in her expressive watercolors and collage illustrations.

Knock at a Star: A Child's Introduction to Poetry, compiled by the well-known adult poet and anthologist X. J. Kennedy and his wife, Dorothy, is a memorable collection of poetry for children 8 years old and up. The poets represented range widely, from adult poets like James Stephens, Emily Dickinson, Robert Frost, and William Stafford to children's poets Aileen Fisher, David

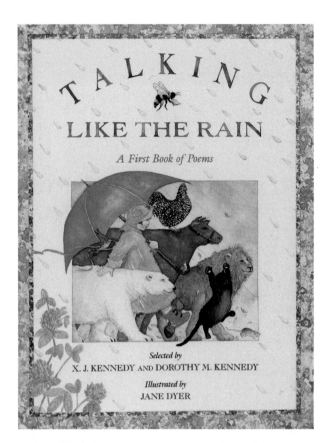

X. J. and Dorothy Kennedy's poetry selection and Jane Dyer's lovely illustrations provide an inviting introduction to poetry for young children in *Talking Like the Rain*.

Cover of *Talking Like the Rain* by X. J. and Dorothy M. Kennedy. Reprinted by permission of Little, Brown and Company.

McCord, and Lillian Morrison. Many familiar poems are here, but most of them are new and fresh to children's collections. The three section headings in this book also are addressed to children and provide an understanding of how poetry does what it does: (1) "What Do Poems Do?" (make you laugh, tell stories, send messages, share feelings, start you wondering); (2) "What's Inside a Poem?" (images, word music, beats that repeat, likenesses); and (3) "Special Kinds of Poems." Teachers, librarians, and parents as well as children can learn from this wise book, which teaches at the same time as it develops enthusiasm for poetry.

Another unique anthology that provides insight into how some thirty-nine poets work and feel about their poems is Paul Janesczko's *The Place My Words Are Looking For*. Here Jack Prelutsky, X. J. Kennedy, Myra Cohn Livingston, and others talk about how they create their poetry, by providing personal comments and examples of their poems. Pictures of the poets accompany each section so children can see what their favorite poet looks like. Lillian Morrison comments on how she wrote "The Sidewalk Racer" (see p. 398), for example:

🏃 Writing poems can be a way of pinning down a dream (almost); capturing a moment, a memory, a happening; and, at the same time, it's a way of sorting out your thoughts and feelings. Sometimes words tell you what you didn't know you knew.[9]

One of the most enduring current anthologies is *Reflections on a Gift of Watermelon Pickle and Other Modern Verses*, edited by Stephen Dunning and others. Illustrated with superb black-and-white photographs surrounded by much space, this anthology appeals to the eye as well as the ear of older students in middle school. They will take delight in "Sonic Boom" by John Updike, "Ancient History" by Arthur Guiterman, "Dreams" by Langston Hughes, and "How to Eat a Poem" by Eve Merriam. They will appreciate the honesty and realistic viewpoint of "Husbands and Wives," in which Miriam Hershenson tells of couples who ride the train from station to station without ever speaking to each other. For descriptions of some other anthologies that are not discussed in the text, see the Resources for Teaching box "Comprehensive Poetry Anthologies."

Specialized Collections

As poetry permissions become more expensive and more difficult to obtain for long lengths of time, anthologists have turned to making small specialized collections. Most of these are organized for a particular age level or around certain subjects, such as dogs or seasons. Some are related to the ethnic origin of the poems, such as poetry of Native Americans or poems that celebrate the experiences of African Americans. An increasing number of specialized collections contain stunning illustrations. Some of the best of these are noted in the text; others are listed in the Resources for Teaching box on pp. 419–422.

Nancy Larrick's books *Cats Are Cats* and *Mice Are Nice* are superbly illustrated with Ed Young's charcoal and pastel pictures. Each book contains some twenty-five well-chosen poems. The illustrations for *Cats Are Cats* were quickly drawn on brown wrapping paper, but they make a stunning book. Lee Bennett Hopkins is a prolific anthologist, collecting poems on subjects as varied as his books; *Weather, Dinosaurs*, and a superb collection of poems about enjoying reading, *Good Books,*

[9]Lillian Morrison, in *The Place My Words Are Looking For,* by Paul B. Janeczko (New York: Bradbury Press, 1990), p. 11.

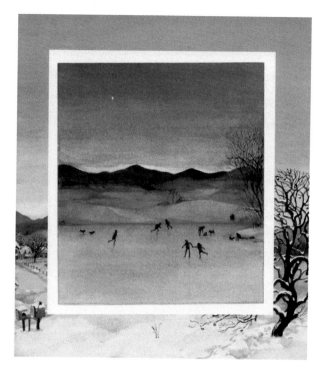

Trina Schart Hyman has created dazzling landscapes to accompany Barbara Rogasky's *Winter Poems.*
Illustration by Trina Schart Hyman from *Winter Poems* edited by Barbara Rogasky. Illustrations copyright © 1995 by Trina Schart Hyman. Reprinted by permission of Scholastic Inc.

Good Times! Myra Cohn Livingston not only writes fine poetry for children but she creates excellent anthologies for them, such as her five collections of poems about various members of families and her collection about small things, *Animal, Vegetable, Mineral.*

Children will find imaginative connections to themes such as "Time" or "Animals" and to subjects as varied as American history, music, and science through many of these anthologies. Barbara Rogasky's collection *Winter Poems*, beautifully illustrated by Trina Schart Hyman, recreates a cycle of time from late autumn to the first buds of spring with poems like Melville Cane's "Snow Toward Evening," Elizabeth Coatsworth's "Cat on a Night of Snow," and Robert Frost's "A Patch of Old Snow" to fill up the long winter. Cows have never been more appealing than in the fifteen poems in Alice Schertle's *How Now, Brown Cow?* Schertle ruminates on various topics in "The Cow's Complaint" (the grass is always greener) and "The Bull" (the title character wonders if the cows can see him bellowing, blowing, and striking a pose). Schertle's imaginative *Advice for a Frog* is a collection of poems about animals found in the wild, including "Black Rhino," "Iguana," and "Secretary Bird."

Several collections invite children to move to the beat and sing with the music of poetry. Michael R. Strickland

Resources for Teaching
Comprehensive Poetry Anthologies

Title	Age Level	Compiler	Description
Sunflakes	3–9	Lilian Moore	See text.
Talking Like the Rain	3–9	X. J. Kennedy and Dorothy M. Kennedy	See text.
Tomie de Paola's Book of Poems	6–10	Tomie de Paola	See text.
Side by Side	6–10	Lee Bennett Hopkins	Fifty-seven poems ranging from traditional to poems by such modern poets as McCord, Kuskin, Lilian Moore, Robert Frost, and Lewis Carroll.
Sing a Song of Popcorn	6–12	Beatrice Schenk de Regniers et al.	See text.
Read-Aloud Rhymes for the Very Young	7–12	Jack Prelutsky	See text.
The Random House Book of Poetry	7–12	Jack Prelutsky	See text.
Piping Down the Valleys Wild	8–12	Nancy Larrick	A distinctive collection of some 250 poems ranging from traditional to poems by such modern poets as Kuskin, Milne, Merriam, and Livingston, plus favorites by Frost and Sandburg.
To the Moon and Back	9 and up	Nancy Larrick	A fresh collection of 66 poems, including poems by such well-known poets as X. J. Kennedy, Lucille Clifton, and Lillian Morrison, and some fine Native American and Eskimo poems.
Til All the Stars Have Fallen	8–12	David Booth	See text.
Knock at a Star	9–12	X. J. Kennedy and Dorothy M. Kennedy	See text.
This Delicious Day	12 and up	Paul Janeczko	Sixty-five poems with fresh new images. The title refers to various "meals" for the eye and mind that each day provides.
Reflections on a Gift of Watermelon Pickle and Other Modern Verses	12 and up	Steve Dunning, Edward Lueders, and Hugh Smith	See text.
Favorite Poems Old and New	8–12	Helen Ferris	First published in 1957, when there was no time limit on poetry permissions, this collection has over 700 poems! Now in paperback, it is still an excellent source for teachers.
The Oxford Book of Poetry for Children	8–12	Edward Blishen	This collection of poems by traditional poets, such as Lear, Carroll, de la Mare, Stevenson, and even Shakespeare and Shelley, has been beautifully illustrated in a kaleidoscope of color by Brian Wildsmith.

Resources for Teaching
Comprehensive Poetry Anthologies (concluded)

Title	Age Level	Compiler	Description
Wider than the Sky	10 and up	Scott Elledge	Over 200 poems, mostly written by traditional English poets. Most of the poems are appropriate for children, however. First prepared for Elledge's 10-year-old niece, this is a fine source of traditional poetry.
This Same Sky	12 and up	Naomi Shihab Nye	Here 129 poets from 68 countries look at the world in poems rich with images and feeling. This is an international collection with universal connections.
Peeling the Onion	12 and up	Ruth Gordon	Gordon has chosen poets from around the world, such as Octavio Paz and Boris Pasternak, in a collection that invites children to peel back the layers of a poem and discover the feelings at its heart.

has chosen fifty poems and songs about music and music makers, dancers and dance in *Poems That Sing to You*. In *Singing America*, Neil Philip has collaborated with artist Michael McCurdy to tell America's history through the voices of Walt Whitman, Emily Dickinson, Gwendolyn Brooks, Woodie Guthrie, and seventy other poets. This handsome volume includes poems from many Native American tribes, traditional ballads, and Shaker anthems.

Collected African American poetry can be found in such attractive editions as Tom Feelings's *Soul Looks Back in Wonder*, a winner of the Coretta Scott King Award for illustration. Feelings has chosen selections from thirteen poets that celebrate African American heritage and sing of African pride. Wade Hudson's collection *Pass It On*, illustrated by Floyd Cooper, is broader in scope. It includes poems like Nikki Giovanni's "Prickled Pickles Don't Smile" and Henry Dumas's "Peas," which are light in tone, as well as more serious reflections such as Lucille Clifton's "Listen Children." Both volumes include well-known poets and introduce newer voices. Eleven Caribbean-born poets, including James Berry, are represented in *A Caribbean Dozen*, edited by John Agard and Grace Nichols. Poems like Valerie Bloom's "Chicken Dinner" and Faustin Charles's "Steel Band Jump Up" capture the structure and rhythm of island cultures, while others, like David Campbell's "Corn and Potatoes," praise contributions of native people. A picture and short biographical paragraph precedes each of the poet's works.

Hettie Jones's *The Trees Stand Shining* represents Native American poets of the past century. These short

Artist Amanda Schaffer creates unique personalities for the bovines in Alice Schertle's collection of poetry, *How Now, Brown Cow?*

Illustration from *How Now, Brown Cow?* by Alice Schertle, illustrations copyright © 1994 by Amanda Schaffer, reproduced by permission of Harcourt Brace & Company.

song-poems are accompanied by Robert Andrew Parker's impressionistic watercolor paintings that evoke the Native American reverence for the sun and moon, the eagle and owl. Stephen Gammell illustrates *Dancing Teepees*, edited by Virginia Driving Hawk Sneve, with sensitive full-color watercolors. This is a handsome

Tom Feelings's striking artwork accompanies his selections of poetry by African Americans in *Soul Looks Back in Wonder*.
Cover from *Soul Looks Back in Wonder* by Tom Feelings. Copyright © 1993 by Tom Feelings, illustrations. Used by permission of Dial Books for Young Readers, a division of Penguin Books USA Inc.

book of some twenty poems chosen from various tribes. John Bierhorst also emphasizes humanity's close relationship to nature in his anthology *In the Trail of the Wind: American Indian Poems and Ritual Orations*. This authentic collection includes poems of the Aztec, Maya, and Eskimo as well as North American Indians. It is more appropriate for older students.

We can be grateful for the reissue of *. . . I Never Saw Another Butterfly*, edited by Hana Volavkova. This book contains poems and pictures created by children in the Terezin concentration camp from 1942 to 1944. These drawings and poems are all that are left of the fifteen thousand children who passed through this camp on their way to Auschwitz. They are an eloquent statement of their courage and optimism in the midst of despair. For descriptions of some collections not discussed in this section, see Resources for Teaching, "Specialized Collections of Poetry."

Picture-Book Editions of Single Poems

It was inevitable that poetry should also follow the trend to single-poem editions already established by the many beautifully illustrated editions of single fairy tales and folk songs.

The first book of poetry to be presented with the Newbery Medal was *A Visit to William Blake's Inn* by Nancy Willard. In the same year, the illustrators for this book, Alice and Martin Provensen, received a Caldecott Honor Award. Inspired by Blake's work, Nancy Willard created a book of magical poems about life at an imaginary inn run by William Blake himself. Each poem

creates a story of all the activities going on in this remarkable place. Children ages 8 and up will be intrigued by the detailed pictures of the inn and its guests.

Susan Jeffers has illustrated two well-known poems in picture-book format. Her pictures for Frost's *Stopping by Woods on a Snowy Evening* evoke the quiet stillness of the forest in contrast to the staid New England village. In *Hiawatha*, she pictures the romantic Indian in keeping with Longfellow's poem and time. Lovely pictures of Nokomis and a growing Hiawatha hold children's interest. The artist is not always consistent in portraying the age of the Iroquois lad, however; he seems older, then younger, before he reaches manhood and leaves the tribe.

In some instances these stunning picture books may create new interest in a poem like *Hiawatha* or *Paul Revere's Ride*. It is generally a good idea to read the poem through once before sharing the pictures, because turning the pages to look at the illustrations interrupts the flow of the poem. Many of these picture/poetry books provide the text of the complete poem at the end of the book. Since poetry is the most concentrated and connotative use of language, it needs to be shared several times anyway. The Resources for Teaching box "Picture-Book Editions of Single Poems" lists some of the picture/poetry books available for children.

Sharing Poetry with Children

Very young children respond spontaneously to the sensory-motor action of "Ride a Cock Horse" or "Peas porridge hot/Peas porridge cold." They enjoy the damp adventures of poor old Dr. Foster, and they delight in the misfortune of the "Three Blind Mice." Children in the primary grades love to pantomime "Hiding" by Dorothy Aldis or join in the chant of Eve Merriam's "Cheers" (in *Jamboree*). The young child naturally delights in the sound, rhythm, and language of poetry.

However, at some time toward the end of the primary grades, children begin to lose interest in poetry. The poet William Jay Smith comments: "How natural and harmonious it all is at the beginning; and yet what happens along the way later to make poetry to many children the dullest and least enjoyable of literary expressions?"[10] Studies have consistently reported a decreasing interest in poetry as children progress through the middle grades.[11] These findings suggest that rather than develop enjoyment of poetry, many teachers might actually destroy children's natural liking for this form of literature.

[10]Virginia Haviland and William Jay Smith, *Children and Poetry* (Washington, D.C.: Library of Congress, 1969), p. iv.

[11]George W. Norvell, *What Boys and Girls Like to Read* (New York: Silver Burdett, 1958), p. 26; and Terry, *Children's Poetry Preferences*, p. 29.

Resources for Teaching
Specialized Collections of Poetry

Compiler, Poet	Title	Age Level	Description
Children's Everyday Experiences			
Myra Cohn Livingston	Dilli Dilli Piccalilli	6–10	An appealing selection of 55 poems for young children, ranging from Edward Lear to Karla Kuskin, Eve Merriam, and Clyde Watson.
Nancy Larrick	The Merry-Go-Round Poetry Book	6–10	Black-and-white sketches by Karen Gundersheimer add to the appeal of these nearly 60 lively poems for youngsters.
Lee Bennett Hopkins	Extra Innings	10–12	These poems about baseball will invite fans of the sport as well as nonfans to enjoy the runs and the rhythms of the game.
Lee Bennett Hopkins	Surprises and More Surprises	6–8	With unerring taste for good poetry and what children enjoy, Hopkins has selected poems that children can read independently.
Lee Bennett Hopkins	It's About Time!	9–12	Poems by noted children's poets portray one day's activities through a child's perspective.
Lee Bennett Hopkins	Through Our Eyes: Poems and Pictures About Growing Up	8–12	A collection of poems depicting children of various backgrounds—their thoughts, hopes, lifestyles. Full-color photographs help make these voices come alive.
Bobbye S. Goldstein	Inner Chimes	8 and up	Twenty poems that celebrate poetry. A perfect introduction to poetry for children and adults.
Myra Cohn Livingston	I Like You, If You Like Me	10 and up	Nearly a hundred poems that celebrate friends and comradeship. Some are funny, others are sad or lonesome.
Myra Cohn Livingston	Animal, Vegetable, Mineral	9–12	Poems about small things, categorized as animal, vegetable, or mineral.
Night Poems			
Helen Plotz	A Week of Lullabies	3–6	Fourteen goodnight poems, containing childlike illustrations by Marisabina Russo. The colored borders of the pictures create a cozy feeling.
Lee Bennett Hopkins	Still as a Star: A Book of Nighttime Poems	5–8	Many well-known and some fresh goodnight poems.
Nancy Larrick	When the Dark Comes Dancing: A Bedtime Poetry Book	5–8	Some forty-five poems by well-known poets like Aileen Fisher and Karla Kuskin, plus songs and familiar nursery rhymes.
Nancy Larrick	Bring Me All Your Dreams	10 and up	A wide range of exciting poems by many contemporary poets. Dreams include daydreams, wishes, night dreams.
John Bierhorst	On the Road of Stars	5–8	Native American night poems and sleep charms.
Families			
Myra Cohn Livingston	Poems for Fathers	5–8	Well-chosen poems that avoid typical stereotypes of father roles.
Myra Cohn Livingston	Poems for Mothers	5–8	A collection that provides a good balance between humor and affection; also avoids stereotyping mothers.

Resources for Teaching
Specialized Collections of Poetry (continued)

Compiler, Poet	Title	Age Level	Description
Myra Cohn Livingston	*Poems for Brothers, Poems for Sisters*	5–8	Nineteen poems about siblings; some are humorous, others serious.
Myra Cohn Livingston	*Poems for Grandmothers*	5–8	Eighteen poems about grandmothers, great-grandmothers, and a stepgrandmother, of various races, ages, and economic backgrounds.
Dorthy and Michael R. Strickland	*Families: Poems Celebrating the African American Experience*	5–8	Poems celebrating African American family life.

Poetry of Nature and Seasons

Lee Bennett Hopkins	*The Sky Is Full of Song*	6–8	A jewel of a book. Poems about the seasons described from a young child's point of view. Illustrated with small colored linocuts by Dirk Zimmer.
Lee Bennett Hopkins	*The Sea Is Calling Me*	7–10	Over 20 poems about the ocean, seashore, lighthouses, seashells, and sand castles.
David Booth	*Voices on the Wind: Poems for All Seasons*	6–9	Over 20 poems from a wide range of poets, from William Blake to John Ciardi. Lovely full-page acrylic paintings by Michele Lemieux.
Josette Frank	*Snow Toward Evening*	7–10	Thirteen poems, one for each month plus an introductory poem. Thomas Locker has painted a full-page oil landscape for each poem.
Myra Cohn Livingston	*If the Owl Calls Again*	9 and up	Over 70 owl poems by poets ranging from Shakespeare to Eve Merriam and David McCord. Nursery rhymes and poems from the Navajo and Chippewa are included.
Barbara Rogasky	*Winter Poems*	9 and up	See text.

Animal Poems

Laura Whipple	*Eric Carle's Animals Animals*	5–9	See text.
Nancy Larrick	*Cats Are Cats*	5–9	See text.
Nancy Larrick	*Mice Are Nice*	5–9	See text.
Myra Cohn Livingston	*Cat Poems*	5–9	Over 20 poems about cats. Stylish black-and-white illustrations by Trina Schart Hyman.
Myra Cohn Livingston	*Dog Poems*	5–9	Some 20 poems, contemporary and traditional, illustrated by Leslie Morrow.
Bobbye S. Goldstein	*Bear in Mind*	5–8	Nearly 30 poems about bears—live ones and teddy bears. Wonderful full-color pictures by William Pène DuBois.
Lee Bennett Hopkins	*Dinosaurs*	8 and up	Eighteen poems, including "The Last Dinosaur" and "How the End Might Have Been." Good for discussion and dinosaur units.
Laura Whipple	*Eric Carle's Dragons Dragons & Other Creatures That Never Were*	8 and up	See text.

Resources for Teaching
Specialized Collections of Poetry (continued)

Compiler, Poet	Title	Age Level	Description
Humorous Poetry			
Emma Chichester Clark	*I Never Saw a Purple Cow*	4–9	A superb collection of 117 nonsense rhymes, including verses by Carroll, Lear, and Hilaire Belloc. Action-packed watercolors add to the appeal.
Jack Prelutsky	*For Laughing Out Loud: Poems to Tickle Your Funnybone*	5–10	Over 130 of the funniest poems. Lively colored illustrations by Marjorie Priceman add to the humor.
Jack Prelutsky	*Poems by A. Nonny Mouse and A. Nonny Mouse Writes Again*	5–10	The first volume contains over 70 of the silliest poems attributed by publishers to "anonymous." The sequel contains some 50 more poems that are short, silly, and fun to recite.
Dorothy Kennedy	*I Thought I'd Take My Rat to School*	5–10	A year's worth of silly poems about school.
William Cole	*Oh, What Nonsense! Oh, How Silly! Oh, That's Ridiculous!*	7–12	These collections contain some of Shel Silverstein's verses and other favorites of children.
William Cole	*Poem Stew*	6–12	A hilarious feast of poems about food. Children love this collection.
Sara Brewton et al.	*Of Quarks, Quasars, and Other Quirks: Quizzical Poems for the Supersonic Age*	10 and up	Lighthearted poems that are both humorous and scientific.
Holiday Collections			
Lee Bennett Hopkins	*Hey-How for Halloween*	6–9	Some 20 poems celebrating one of children's favorite holidays.
Lee Bennett Hopkins	*Ragged Shadows*	5–10	Poems about Halloween night.
Myra Cohn Livingston	*Christmas Poems Easter Poems Halloween Poems Thanksgiving Poems Valentine Poems Poems for Jewish Holidays New Year's Poems*	6–9	Each of these illustrated books contains a fine collection of approximately 20 poems. Some are well-known favorites; others are new, commissioned for these books.
Myra Cohn Livingston	*Why Am I Grown So Cold? Poems of the Unknowable*	10 and up	Some 150 ghostly poems. Some are appropriate for Halloween, many can be read throughout the year. Children would enjoy comparing the four poems about haunted houses.
Lee Bennett Hopkins	*Ring Out Wild Bells*	8–12	Here are poems to read around the calendar. Arranged in chronological order, they include special holiday poems and more general seasonal topics.
Multiethnic Poetry Collections			
Arnold Adoff	*My Black Me*	8 and up	A collection of contemporary poems that mixes black pride with power and protest. Brief biographical notes on each of the poets add interest.

Resources for Teaching
Specialized Collections of Poetry (concluded)

Compiler, Poet	Title	Age Level	Description
Arnold Adoff	*I Am the Darker Brother: An Anthology of Modern Poems by Black Americans*	10 and up	Contains some of the best-known poetry of Langston Hughes, Gwendolyn Brooks, and Countee Cullen, as well as some modern poets.
Ann Nolan Clark	*In My Mother's House*	6–10	See text.
Virginia Driving Hawk Sneve	*Dancing Teepees*	8–12	See text.
Hettie Jones	*The Trees Stand Shining*	5–9	See text.
John Bierhorst	*In the Trail of the Wind*	12 and up	See text.
John Agard and Grace Nichols	*A Caribbean Dozen*	5–9	See text.
Lori M. Carlson	*Cool Salsa*	12 and up	Bilingual poems about growing up Latino in the United States.
Wade Hudson	*Pass It On*	5–9	See text.
Tom Feelings	*Soul Looks Back in Wonder*	5–9	See text.

There are several ways in which teachers have alienated children from poetry. Poor selection of poetry is one of the most common mistakes made by both teachers and textbook publishers. A study by Chow Loy Tom found that teachers in the middle grades usually read traditional poems rather than contemporary ones that would be more suited to the modern child's maturity, experiences, and interests.[12] Sentimental poems or poems that are *about* childhood rather than *for* children will turn today's young people away from poetry very quickly. Poems that are too difficult, too abstract for children to understand, will also be rejected.

Several studies have indicated teachers' neglect of poetry. Ann Terry found, for example, that over 75 percent of the teachers in the middle grades read poetry to their children only once a month or less.[13] Children can hardly be expected to develop a love of poetry when they hear it less than nine times a year! It is also possible to hear too much poetry, particularly at one time. Teachers who read poetry for an hour or have every child read a poem on a Friday afternoon are contributing to children's dislike of poetry as much as those who simply neglect it. This also happens when we relegate poetry to a "Poetry Week" in the spring. Poetry needs to be shared naturally every day by a teacher who loves it.

Another way to create distaste for poetry is by requiring memorization of certain poems, usually selected by the teacher. When everyone has to learn the same poem, it is especially dull. Many children do enjoy memorizing favorite poems, provided they can do it voluntarily and can select the poem. But choosing to commit a certain poem to memory is quite different from being required to do so.

Too-detailed analysis of every poem is also detrimental to children's enjoyment of poetry. An appropriate question or comment to increase meaning is fine; but critical analysis of every word in a poem, every figure of speech, and every iambic verse, is lethal to appreciation. Jean Little captures one student's reaction to too much analysis in this poem:

> I used to like "Stopping by Woods on a Snowy Evening,"
> I liked the coming darkness,
> The jingle of harness bells, breaking—and adding to—the stillness,
> The gentle drift of snow . . .
>
> But today, the teacher told us what everything stood for.
> The woods, the horse, the miles to go, the sleep—
> They all have "hidden meanings."
> It's grown so complicated now that,
> Next time I drive by,
> I don't think I'll bother to stop.

Jean Little, "After English Class," in *Hey World, Here I Am!*
Text copyright © 1986 by Jean Little.

---

[12]Chow Loy Tom, "Paul Revere Rides Ahead: Poems Teachers Read to Pupils in the Middle Grades," *Library Quarterly* 43 (January 1973): 27–38.

[13]Terry, *Children's Poetry Preferences*, p. 53.

Resources for Teaching
Picture-Book Editions of Single Poems

Poem, Poet	Illustrator	Age Level	Description
Block City (Robert Louis Stevenson)	Ashley Wolff	5–8	See text.
My Shadow (Robert Louis Stevenson)	Ted Rand	5–8	See text.
General Store (Rachel Field)	Nancy Winslow Parker	5–8	A little girl dreams of having a general store like the old-fashioned ones of the 1920s. Clear, childlike pictures.
The Tale of Custard the Dragon (Ogden Nash)	Lynn Munsinger	5–8	See text.
The Cataract of Lodore (Robert Southey)	Mordecai Gerstein David Catrow	6–9	Southey's wonderfully rhythmic descriptive poem is brought to life through the different visions of two fine illustrators.
The Owl and the Pussy Cat (Edward Lear)	Jan Brett	5–8	A dapper owl and a demure cat set off in their boat *Promise* to find a paradise in the Caribbean. Lush colors and intricate detail in the pictures extend this poem.
The Quangle Wangle's Hat (Edward Lear)	Janet Stevens	5–8	A cast of amazing characters decide to nest on the mysterious Quangle Wangle's beribboned hat.
The Adventures of Isabel (Ogden Nash)	James Marshall	5–8	See text.
The Scroobious Pip (Edward Lear and Ogden Nash)	Nancy Ekholm Burkert	7 and up	Delicate line drawings and jewel-like watercolors and pastels illustrate this long nonsense poem.
Hist Whist (e.e. cummings)	Deborah K. Ray	7 and up	Ray's illustrations create a spooky Halloween story from this poem.
A Visit to William Blake's Inn (Nancy Willard)	Alice and Martin Provensen	8 and up	See text.
Mr. Mistoffelees with Mungojerrie and Rumpelteazer (T. S. Eliot)	Errol Le Cain	8 and up	Le Cain has given us precise, detailed pictures of this "conjuring cat," plus pictures of a notorious couple of cats with bad reputations. The pictures are as clever as the poems.
Arithmetic (Carl Sandburg)	Ted Rand	5–9	See text.
Barbara Frietchie (John Greenleaf Whittier)	Nancy Winslow Parker	5–9	Parker uses detail and her signature style as well as extra information to bring this Civil War poem alive.
Casey at the Bat (Ernest Thayer)	Wallace Tripp	8 and up	These humorous illustrations portray the Mudville team as animals who are in deep despair when Casey strikes out.
Casey at the Bat (Ernest Thayer)	Barry Moser	8 and up	A centennial edition with an afterword by Donald Hall discussing the poem's history. Moser's watercolors look almost like photos of baseball players.
Paul Revere's Ride (Henry Wadsworth Longfellow)	Nancy Winslow Parker	6 and up	Provides a foreword on the setting and an illustrated map of both Revere's and Prescott's rides. Pictures are flat-colored wash, painted in much the same way as a child would depict the action.

Resources for Teaching
Picture-Book Editions of Single Poems (concluded)

Poem, Poet	Illustrator	Age Level	Description
Paul Revere's Ride (Henry Wadsworth Longfellow)	Ted Rand	6 and up	Rand's moonlit vision of this famous ride adds to its drama. He provides fresh new perspectives, such as the inside view of the steep belfry chambers where the lanterns are placed. A handsome book.
Hiawatha (Henry Wadsworth Longfellow)	Susan Jeffers	7 and up	See text.
Hiawatha's Childhood (Henry Wadsworth Longfellow)	Errol Le Cain	7 and up	The Indian designs and borders are handsome, but Hiawatha appears as a stereotyped Indian figure.
The Legend of William Tell (Terry Small)	Terry Small	7 and up	The well-known story of William Tell, who must shoot an apple off his son's head, is told in metered beat. Full-color pictures capture the action of this adventure story.
Johnny Appleseed (Reeve Lindbergh)	Kathy Jakobsen	7 and up	The traditional story of Johnny Appleseed is told in verse form. Lively folk-art paintings illustrate his travels.
The Cremation of Sam McGee and *The Shooting of Dan McGrew* (Robert W. Service)	Ted Harrison	10 and up	Glorious illustrations in brilliant colors bring to life these classic poems of the gold rush days.
The Highwayman (Alfred Noyes)	Charles Keeping	10 and up	See text.
The Highwayman (Alfred Noyes)	Charles Mikolaycak	10 and up	See text.
The Highwayman (Alfred Noyes)	Neil Waldman	10 and up	See text.
Birches (Robert Frost)	Ed Young	10 and up	Ed Young never pictures the swinger of birches but leaves that to the reader's imagination. He does portray lovely birches seen from various perspectives. The complete poem is given at the end.
Stopping by Woods on a Snowy Evening (Robert Frost)	Susan Jeffers	10 and up	See text.

Creating a Climate for Enjoyment

There have always been teachers who love poetry and who share their enthusiasm for poetry with students. There are teachers who make poetry a natural part of the daily program of living and learning. They realize that poetry should not be presented under the pressure of a tight time schedule, but should be enjoyed every day. Children should be able to relax and relish the humor and beauty that the sharing of poetry affords. The "In Praise of Poetry" web provides an overview of the experiences with poetry these teachers provide for their children.

Teachers who inspire children to love poetry will provide an abundance of poetry books and not rely on a single anthology that might overpower children with its sheer quantity of poems. Students will be encouraged to buy their own copies of some of the fine paperback collections, such as Eve Merriam's *Jamboree* or Nancy Larrick's *Piping Down the Valleys Wild*. Beautiful poetry books such as Diane Siebert's *Sierra* and *Heartland* or Carl Sandburg's *Arithmetic* could be featured in the science and math centers. In a primary classroom, David McCord's poem "The Shell" (in *One at a Time*) could be displayed with a group of shells, or his poem "Cocoon" (in *Every Time I Climb a Tree*) might be taped to the

In Praise of Poetry

Poetry Cycles
Find and read poems about similar themes
Siblings—"Brother" (Hoberman), "Satellite, Satellite" (Merriam)
Feelings—"Wrong Start" (Chute), "When I Woke Up This Morning" (Kuskin)
Weather—"Fog" (Sandburg), "Fog" (Chandra, *Balloons*)

Poetry and The Arts
Imaginary Gardens (Sullivan)
Families, Children, Seascapes (Roalf)
Collect reproductions of paintings based on a theme and choose poems that match each painting.
Poems That Sing to You (Strickland)
Select poems about a topic. Choose music that matches the mood, rhythm, or theme of the poems. Put together a poetry reading to music.

Poetry Corner
Hailstones and Halibut Bones (O'Neill)
Everybody Needs a Rock (Baylor)
These Small Stones (Faber and Livingston)
Establish a rotating display around special topics such as "Small Things" or "Color." Display poems, artwork, and artifacts that fit the theme.

Sensory Explorations
"Mud" (Worth), "Peach" (Rauter), "Greensweet" (Levy, *A Tree Place*)
Blindfold group members. Have them touch, taste, or smell objects. List words or phrases they use to describe sensory impressions. Compare these to ways that poets have compared similar experiences.

Poetry Models
Poetry from A to Z (Janeczko)
Prayers from the Ark (Bernos de Gaztold)
A House is a House For Me (Hoberman)
Words With Wrinkled Knees (Esbensen)
Use poems as spring boards to try your own forms.
Quiet Please (Merriam)
City Noise (Kuskin)
Make a collection of quiet or noisy phrases.

Hailstones and Halibut Bones (O'Neill), *Fresh Paint* (Merriam)
Think of a favorite color. Write color poems or color phrases.
"Cliché" (Merriam)
Think of other ways to say "warm as toast" or "snug as a bug in a rug."
"Throws of Threes" (Merriam)
Create your own patterns of threes.

Poetry/Prose Connections
Find poems to match the mood, theme, etc., of favorite books.
"Until I Saw the Sea" (Moore)/ *Time of Wonder* (McCloskey)
"Mother To Son" (Hughes)/ *Scorpions* (Myers)

Poetry Celebrations
I'm In Charge of Celebrations (Baylor)
Find something simple and special ways to celebrate every day.
Compile a class list of special celebrations.
Hold a Poetry Celebration Day.
Invite parents and other special people to read or recite favorite poems.
Display class poetry collections.
Eats (Adoff)
Poem Stew (Cole)
Chocolate Dreams (Adoff)
"Rah, Rah, Peas" (Levy, *I'm Going…*)
"Spaghetti" (Silverstein)
Have a class feast inspired by poems about food.

Reading Aloud
The Poetry Troupe (Wilner)
"Harriet Tubman" (Greenfield)
Read poems together in one voice.
Bam Bam Bam (Merriam)
Read poems and create hand or body movements to accompany yourselves.
"The Grobbles" (Prelutsky)
"The Song of the Train" (McCord)
Plan choral reading with single and many voices, loud and soft sounds, high and low pitch.
I Am Phoenix (Fleischman)
Joyful Noise (Fleischman)
Read poems in two, three, or four, voices. Write your own poems for several voices.

Patterned Poems
Splish, Splash (Graham)
Seeing Things (Froman)
Write a poem about a concrete object like a tree, waterfall, or popsicle. Change it into a visual art form.

Haiku
In a Spring Garden (Lewis)
Black Swan/White Crow (Lewis)
Red Dragonfly on My Shoulder (Cassedy and Suetake)—
Illustrate your haiku with collage or prints.

Limericks
The Hopeful Trout and Other Limericks (Ciardi)
The Book of Pigericks (Lobel)
Make a class book of limericks on a theme or topic.

screen cage where a cocoon awaits spring hatching. Evidence of enjoyment of poetry should not be limited to one time or place. The Resources for Teaching box "Developing Enjoyment of Poetry" lists some suggestions for how to lead children to a lifelong enthusiasm for poetry.

The book center should contain many poetry books. One fifth- and sixth-grade class that really makes poetry central to their curriculum has more than two hundred poetry books in the classroom. They also have a listening area where children can hear poets reading from their own works on tapes or recordings. A bulletin board displays a list of children's current favorite poems, along with paintings and copies of their own poetry work. Many teachers and children have enjoyed setting up displays of real objects and pictures of a predominant color to highlight their favorite poem from *Hailstones and Halibut Bones* by Mary O'Neill.

The writing center should have all kinds of shapes, sizes, and colors of paper available, including long skinny adding-machine rolls, wide storybook paper, pastel-colored papers for pages, blank books in different shapes, and large or small index cards. Then children can choose what fits their poems the best. Art materials and bookbinding supplies should be nearby for when children are ready to illustrate their poems and publish their poetry books or personal anthologies.

A brief visit to a classroom, library, or school will reveal whether poetry is "alive and well" in that place or sadly neglected and dying. Faculty might evaluate their own school by determining where they would place themselves on the continuum presented in Resources for Teaching, "Developing Enjoyment of Poetry." Teachers might also evaluate their own practices.

Finding Time for Poetry

Teachers who would develop children's delight in poetry will find time to share it with them sometime each day. They know that anytime is a good time to read a poem to children, but they will especially want to capitalize on exciting experiences like the first snow, a birthday party, or the arrival of a classmate's new baby brother. Perhaps there has been a fight on the playground and someone is still grumbling and complaining—that might be a good time to share poetry about feelings. The teacher could read Eve Merriam's "Mean Song" (in *Jamboree*) or Karla Kuskin's "I Woke Up This Morning" (in *Dogs & Dragons*), and then everyone could laugh the bad feelings away. Poetry can also be thought of as a delicious snack to nibble on during transition times between going out to recess or the last few minutes of the day. Anytime is a good time for a poetry snack!

Inspiring teachers frequently read poetry cycles, three or four poems with the same theme. One teacher capitalized on children's interest in "special places." She shared Byrd Baylor's poetic story *Your Own Best Secret Place* and Charlotte Huck's specialized collection of poems about *Secret Places* with a group of third graders. Later the children wrote about their own secret places in both prose and poetry. Children also enjoy selecting a particular subject and creating their own poetry cycles from anthologies in the library or classroom.

One way to be sure to share poetry every day is to relate children's favorite prose stories to poetry. One teacher who keeps a card file of poems always slips one or two cards into the book that is to be read aloud that day. For example, after sharing *Whistle for Willie* by Ezra Jack Keats, Jack Prelutsky's "Whistling" (in *Read-Aloud Rhymes for the Very Young*) and Dorothy Aldis's "Where Is It?" (in *All Together*) could be read. Teachers in the middle grades could read Byrd Baylor's *Hawk, I'm Your Brother* or Jean George's *On the Far Side of the Mountain*. Then they could share Joseph Bruchac's "Birdfoot's Grampa" (in Lilian Moore's *Go with the Poem*) with the class and talk about how freeing a hawk or a peregrine falcon was similar to Grampa's caring for toads. Librarians and teachers will want to make their own poetry/prose connections. We hope that Resources for Teaching, "Connections Between Poetry and Prose," will get you started.

Other subjects and activities in the curriculum can be enriched with poetry. A "science discovery walk" could be preceded by reading Florence McNeil's "Squirrels in My Notebook" (in *Til All the Stars Have Fallen*, ed. David Booth), in which a child records his observations of a squirrel, including the fact that he couldn't repeat what the squirrel said to him! Older children would enjoy Moffitt's well-known poem "To Look at Anything" (in *Reflections on a Gift of Watermelon Pickle*, ed. Stephen Dunning et al.). A math lesson might be introduced with Carl Sandburg's "Arithmetic" (in his *Arithmetic*). Many poems can enhance social studies, including Neil Philip's *Singing America* and Rosemary and Stephen Vincent Benét's *Book of Americans*, which includes the well-known poems "Nancy Hanks," "Abraham Lincoln," and "Western Wagons." The first poem in their collection is "Christopher Columbus," but the second one is "The Indians," about the people who were here first. In *Celebrations*, Myra Cohn Livingston has the poems "Martin Luther King Day" and "Columbus." Eve Merriam's paperback *Jamboree* includes "Which Washington?" and "To Meet Mr. Lincoln."

Several volumes pair poetry and art in unique ways. Charles Sullivan's *Imaginary Gardens* makes such matches as a Grandma Moses painting with Lydia Child's

Resources for Teaching
Developing Enjoyment of Poetry

Teachers can lead children toward an enjoyment of poetry

by selecting modern contemporary poems	instead of selecting only traditional poems
by beginning with students' interests—nonsense verse, narrative verse, jump-rope rhymes, song lyrics	instead of selecting "appropriate poems" approved by adults
by working with children and discovering and enjoying poetry together	instead of neglecting and fearing poetry
by daily sharing of poetry	instead of reading poetry only once a month or less
by *experiencing* a poem	instead of *studying* a poem
by asking questions that contribute to the meaning and enjoyment of the poem	instead of dissecting and analyzing the poem
by using many poetry books, records, and cassette tapes of poets reading their own works; student-recorded tapes with appropriate backgrounds of music, or sound; slides, filmstrips, and pictures	instead of the teacher presenting poetry from a single anthology
by relating poetry to children's experiences, classroom activities, favorite books, art, music, and drama	instead of presenting poetry in isolation
by inviting children to voluntarily memorize poems they select by themselves	instead of requiring memorization of assigned poems
by encouraging children to keep a poetry journal	instead of assigning the writing of poetry
by letting students select what they want to write about	instead of assigning a topic for writing a poem
by listening to other students' critiques, and by self-evaluations, along with teacher conferences	instead of teacher evaluation of every poem

"Over the River and Through the Woods" and "Afternoon on a Hill" by Edna St. Vincent Millay and "Spring" by Marjorie Frost Fraser with Andrew Wyeth's painting of "Christina's World." This last pairing is pure genius. The repeated phrase *to tangled grass I cling* is so right for Christina, who must pull her crippled body back to that bleak house on the hill. Norma Panzer has created similar matches with American art and poetry in *Celebrate America*. This attractive volume includes works and images that represent the many cultures in American life both past and present. These are books that middle graders would enjoy looking at and reading over and over again. In addition, books like these might inspire children to make their own connections between art and poetry.

Children will also be delighted with two excellent poetry books on sports: Lee Bennet Hopkins's *Extra Innings*, and *American Sports Poems* selected by R. R. Knudson and May Swenson. They also enjoy the superb tension captured by Hoey's basketball poem "Foul Shot" (in *Reflections on a Gift of Watermelon Pickle*, ed. S. Dunning et al.). Every taut move of the player is felt as he prepares to make the free throw that can win the game. "Base Stealer" by Robert Francis (in the same anthology) is another poem that combines sports with poetry. All areas of the curriculum can be enhanced with poetry; teachers should realize that there are poems on *every* subject, from dinosaurs to quasars and black holes.

Finding the right poem for the right moment requires preparation and planning. Many teachers make their own collection of poems either on cards or in a notebook. These can be categorized in ways the teachers find the most appropriate for their own styles of teaching. Finding several poems on the same subject or developing cycles of poems gives students an opportunity to compare and contrast different points of view. The Teaching Feature "Studying Poetry and Nature" shows how one teacher found connections between poetry and the natural world.

Resources for Teaching
Connections Between Poetry and Prose

Subject/Theme	Age Level	Poems	Prose
Be yourself	6–8	"Changing" by Mary Ann Hoberman, in *Yellow Butter* "Everybody Says" by Dorothy Aldis, in *All Together* "The Question" by Karla Kuskin, in *Dogs & Dragons, Trees & Dreams* "Who Am I?" by Felice Holman, in *To The Moon and Back*, ed. Larrick "When I Am Me" by Felice Holman, in *By Myself*, ed. Hopkins	*Alexander and the Wind-Up Mouse* (Leo Lionni) *Dandelion* (Don Freeman) *Elmer* (David McKee) *Leo, the Late Bloomer* (Robert Kraus)
Bears	5–7	"Algy Met a Bear," Anon., in *I Never Saw a Purple Cow*, ed. E. Clark "The Bear with Golden Hair" by Karla Kuskin, in *Dogs & Dragons, Trees & Dreams* "Oh, Teddy Bear" by Jack Prelutsky, in *New Kid on the Block* "Grandpa Bear's Lullaby" by Jane Yolen, in *Sing a Song of Popcorn*, ed. de Regniers et al. "Koala" by Karla Kuskin, in *Dogs & Dragons, Trees & Dreams* *Bear in Mind*, Bobbye Goldstein *The Three Bears Rhyme Book*, Jane Yolen	*The Bear's Toothache* (David McPhail) *Corduroy* (Don Freeman) *Ira Sleeps Over* (Bernard Waber) *Where's My Teddy?* (Jez Alborough) *Koala Lou* (Mem Fox) *Goldilocks and the Three Bears* (Jan Brett) *Jamberry* (Bruce Degen)
Bedtime/dreams	5–7	"Bedtime" by Eleanor Farjeon, in *Wider than the Sky*, ed. Elledge "Conversation" by David McCord, in *One at a Time* "The Middle of the Night" by Karla Kuskin, in *Dogs & Dragons, Trees & Dreams* "The Llama Who Had No Pajama" by Mary Ann Hoberman, in *By Myself*, ed. Hopkins "Going to Sleep" by Lilian Morrison, in *Whistling the Morning In* *When the Dark Comes Dancing*, Nancy Larrick	*The Boy and the Cloth of Dreams* (Jenny Koralek) *Bedtime for Frances* (Russell Hoban) *The Quilt* (Ann Jonas) *The Napping House* (Audrey Wood) *There's a Nightmare in My Closet* (Mercer Mayer) *What's Under My Bed?* (James Stevenson) *Why Do Grown-Ups Have All the Fun?* (Marisabina Russo) *Is Your Mama a Llama?* (Deborah Guarino)
Color	5–7	"Yellow" by Deborah Guarino, in *One at a Time*, ed. David McCord "A Yell for Yellow" by Eve Merriam, in *Jamboree* "Lullaby" by Eve Merriam, in *Jamboree* "Winter Carnival" by Lilian Moore, in *Something New Begins* *Hailstones and Halibut Bones*, Mary O'Neill *My Head Is Red and Other Riddle Poems*, by Myra Cohn Livingston	*Color Dance* (Ann Jonas) *Color Farm* (Lois Ehlert) *Color Zoo* (Lois Ehlert) *Little Blue and Little Yellow* (Leo Lionni) *The Mixed-Up Chameleon* (Eric Carle) *Freight Train* (Donald Crews) *Brown Cow, Green Grass, Yellow Mellow Sun* (Ellen Jackson)

Resources for Teaching
Connections Between Poetry and Prose (continued)

Subject/Theme	Age Level	Poems	Prose
Death/loss	7–8	"For a Bird" by Myra Cohn Livingston, in *A Song I Sang to You* "Skipper" by Gwendolyn Brooks, in *Bronzeville Boys and Girls* "For a Dead Kitten" by Sara Henderson Hay, in *Reflections on a Gift of Watermelon Pickle*, ed. Stephen Dunning et al. "Poem" by Langston Hughes, in *The Dream Keeper*	*The Accident* (Carol and Donald Carrick) *Mustard* (Charlotte Graeber) *The Tenth Good Thing About Barney* (Judith Viorst) *Blow Me a Kiss, Miss Lilly* (Nancy W. Carlstrom) *Granpa* (John Burningham) *The Very Best of Friends* (Margaret Wild)
Family	5–7	"Little" by Dorothy Aldis, in *Tomie de Paola's Book of Poems* "My Brother" by Marci Ridlon, in *The Random House Book of Poetry for Children*, ed. Jack Prelutsky "My Father's Words" by Claudia Lewis, in *Poems for Fathers*, ed. Myra Cohn Livingston "All Kinds of Grands" by Lucille Clifton, in *Sing a Song of Popcorn*, ed. Beatrice Shenk de Regniers et al. "I Never Hear" by Dorothy Aldis, in *Morning, Noon and Nighttime, Too*, ed. Lee Hopkins "Happy" by Stacy Jo Crossen and Natalie Anne Crovell, in *Morning, Noon and Nighttime, Too*, ed. Lee Hopkins	*Aunt Nina, Good Night* (Franz Brandenberg) *A Chair for My Mother* (Vera Williams) *Dogger* (Shirley Hughes) *Mr. Rabbit and the Lovely Present* (Charlotte Zolotow) *The Whales' Song* (Dyan Sheldon) *The Stories Julian Tells* (Ann Cameron)
Feelings	6–8	"When I Woke Up This Morning" by Karla Kuskin, in *Dogs & Dragons, Trees & Dreams* "When I Was Lost" by Dorothy Aldis, in *The Random House Book of Poetry for Children*, ed. Jack Prelutsky "Wrong Start" by Marchette Chute, in *The Random House Book of Poetry for Children*, ed. Jack Prelutsky "A Small Discovery" by James Emannuel, in *Tomie de Paola's Book of Poetry* "I'm in a Rotten Mood" by Jack Prelutsky, in *The New Kid on the Block*	*Alexander and the Terrible, Horrible, No Good, Very Bad Day* (Judith Viorst) *Dinah's Mad, Bad Wishes* (Barbara M. Joosse) *The Hating Book* (Charlotte Zolotow) *Lost in the Museum* (Miriam Cohen) *Will I Have a Friend?* (Miriam Cohen) *Osa's Pride* (Ann Grifalconi)
Folktales	7–8	"Look Cinderella" by Myra Cohn Livingston, in *A Song I Sang to You* "The Gingerbread Man" by Rowena Bennett, in *Sing A Song of Popcorn*, ed. Beatrice Shenk de Regniers et al. "The Troll Bridge" by Lilian Moore, in *Something New Begins* "In Search of Cinderella" by Shel Silverstein, in *Where the Sidewalk Ends* "Spaghetti" by Shel Silverstein, in *A Light in the Attic* "The Builders" by Sara Henderson Hay, in *Reflections on a Gift of Watermelon Pickle*, ed. Stephen Dunning et al.	*Cinderella* (Charles Perrault) *The Gingerbread Boy* (Paul Galdone) *The Frog Prince* (Edith H. Tarcov) *The Frog Prince Continued* (Jon Scieszka) *The Three Little Pigs* (James Marshall) *The True Story of the 3 Little Pigs* (Jon Scieszka) *Strega Nona* (Tomie de Paola)

Resources for Teaching
Connections Between Poetry and Prose (continued)

Subject/Theme	Age Level	Poems	Prose
Secret places	7–8	"Hideout" by Aileen Fisher, in *Tomie de Paola's Book of Poems* "Secret Place" by Dorothy Aldis, in *All Together* "Tree House" by Shel Silverstein, in *A Light in the Attic* *Secret Places,* Charlotte Huck	*Your Own Best Secret Place* (Byrd Baylor) *The Little Island* (Golden MacDonald) *Come Away from the Water, Shirley* (John Burningham) *Dawn* (Uri Shulevitz) *When I Was Young in the Mountains* (Cynthia Rylant)
Sibling rivalry	5–7	"Brother" by Mary Ann Hoberman, in *Tomie de Paola's Book of Poems* "I'm Disgusted with My Brother" by Jack Prelutsky, in *New Kid on the Block* "For Sale" by Shel Silverstein in *A Light in the Attic* "Satellite, Satellite" by Eve Merriam, in *Jamboree* "Moochie" by Eloise Greenfield, in *Honey, I Love*	*A Baby Sister for Frances* (Russell Hoban) *Julius, the Baby of the World* (Kevin Henkes) *She Come Bringing Me That Little Baby Girl* (Eloise Greenfield) *Peter's Chair* (Ezra Jack Keats) *Titch* (Pat Hutchins) *Noisy Nora* (Rosemary Wells)
Vacations	7–8	"Driving to the Beach" by Joanna Cole, in *By Myself,* ed. Lee Hopkins "Until I Saw the Sea" by Lilian Moore, in *Sing a Song of Popcorn,* ed. Beatrice Shenk de Regniers et al. "Pretending to Sleep" by Judith Thurman, in *By Myself,* ed. Lee Hopkins "Encounter" by Lilian Moore, in *Something New Begins* "Picnic" by Dorothy Aldis, in *All Together* "July" by Fran Newman, in *Til All the Stars Have Fallen,* ed. David Booth "Leavetaking" by Eve Merriam, in *The Sky Is Full of Song,* ed. Lee Hopkins	*Dawn* (Uri Shulevitz) *Time of Wonder* (Robert McCloskey) *Arthur's Family Vacation* (Marc Brown) *Up North at the Cabin* (Marsha W. Chall) *Sleep Out* (Carol and Donald Carrick) *Stringbean's Trip to the Shining Sea* (Vera B. Williams) *The Lost Lake* (Allen Say)
Change	10–12	"Running Away" by Karla Kuskin, in *Near the Window Tree* "Long-Ago Days" by Myra Cohn Livingston, in *There Was a Place* "Olive Street" by Myra Cohn Livingston, in *There Was a Place* "The Visit" by Barbara Esbensen, in *Who Shrank My Grandmother's House?*	*The Stone-Faced Boy* (Paula Fox) *From the Mixed-Up Files of Mrs. Basil E. Frankweiler* (E. L. Konigsburg) *Tuck Everlasting* (Natalie Babbitt) *Staying Nine* (Pam Conrad) *Maniac Magee* (Jerry Spinelli) *Anastasia Krupnik* (Lois Lowry) *Flip-Flop Girl* (Katherine Paterson)
Courage and pride	10–12	"Mother to Son" by Langston Hughes, in *The Dream Keeper* "I Too Sing America" by Langston Hughes, in *The Dream Keeper* "Which Washington?" by Eve Merriam, in *Jamboree* "Otto" by Gwendolyn Brooks, in *Bronzeville Boys and Girls* *. . . I Never Saw Another Butterfly,* ed. Hana Volavkova	*Sounder* (William Armstrong) *Roll of Thunder, Hear My Cry* (Mildred Taylor) *The Most Beautiful Place in the World* (Ann Cameron) *The Wednesday Surprise* (Eve Bunting) *Number the Stars* (Lois Lowry) *Lyddie* (Katherine Paterson) *The Land I Lost: Adventures of a Boy in Vietnam* (Quang Nhuong Huynh)

Resources for Teaching
Connections Between Poetry and Prose (continued)

Subject/Theme	Age Level	Poems	Prose
Decisions	11–12	"The Way Things Are" by Myra Cohn Livingston, in *The Way Things Are* "The Road Not Taken" by Robert Frost, in *You Come Too* "An Easy Decision" by Kenneth Patchen, in *To the Moon and Back*, ed. Nancy Larrick "In the Middle" by Myra Cohn Livingston, in *There Was a Place*	*The Cry of the Crow* (Jean George) *Sarah, Plain and Tall* (Patricia MacLachlan) *Jacob Have I Loved* (Katherine Paterson) *Homecoming* (Cynthia Voigt) *Tuck Everlasting* (Natalie Babbitt)
The environment	12–13	"To Look at Anything" by Robert Francis, in *Reflections on a Gift of Watermelon Pickle*, ed. Stephen Dunning et al. "Birdfoot's Grampa" by Joseph Bruchac, in *Go With the Poem*, ed. Lilian Moore "Hurt No Living Thing" by Christina Rossetti, in *The Random House Book of Poetry for Children*, ed. Jack Prelutsky "Ecology" by Lilian Moore, in *Something New Begins* "Recycled" by Lilian Moore, in *Something New Begins* "Quest" by Eve Merriam, in *Fresh Paint* *Sierra*, by Diane Siebert "Tree Coming Up" by Constance Levy, in *I'm Going to Pet a Worm Today*	*Window* (Jeannie Baker) *On the Far Side of the Mountain* (Jean George) *Who Really Killed Cock Robin?* (Jean George) *One Day in the Tropical Rain Forest* (Jean George) *Hawk, I'm Your Brother* (Byrd Baylor) *The Way to Start a Day* (Byrd Baylor) *The Year of the Panda* (Miriam Schlein) *The Great Kapok Tree* (Lynne Cherry) *Ancient Ones* (Barbara Bash)
Friendship	10–12	"Poem" by Langston Hughes, in *The Dream Keeper* *Hey World, Here I Am!* by Jean Little "Friendship" by Shel Silverstein, in *A Light in the Attic* *I Like You, If You Like Me* by Myra Cohn Livingston	*Bridge to Terabithia* (Katherine Paterson) *The Sign of the Beaver* (Elizabeth Speare) *Look Through My Window* (Jean Little) *Kate* (Jean Little) *Other Bells for Us to Ring* (Robert Cormier)
Holocaust/war	11–12	*. . . I Never Saw Another Butterfly*, ed. Hana Volavkova "Earth" by John Hall Wheelock, in *Relections on a Gift of Watermelon Pickle*, ed. Stephen Dunning et al. "War" by Dan Roth, in *Sing a Song of Popcorn*, ed. Beatrice Shenk de Regniers et al. "Inside" by Kim Chiha, in *This Same Sky*, ed. Naomi Nye	*Anne Frank: Diary of a Young Girl* (Anne Frank) *Hiroshima No Pika* (Toshi Maruki) *Rose Blanche* (Christophe Gallaz and Roberto Innocenti) *Number the Stars* (Lois Lowry) *The Wall* (Eve Bunting) *Year of Impossible Goodbyes* (Sook Choi)

Resources for Teaching
Connections Between Poetry and Prose (concluded)

Subject/Theme	Age Level	Poems	Prose
The future	11–12	"Where Will We Run To?" by X. J. Kennedy, in *The Forgetful Wishing Well* "Neuteronomy" by Eve Merriam, in *The Poetry Troupe,* ed. Isabel Wilner "I'm Sorry Says the Machine," by Eve Merriam, in *Chortles* "A New Song for Old Smokey" by Eve Merriam, in *Poem for a Pickle* "Southbound on the Freeway" by May Swenson, in *Reflections on a Gift of Watermelon Pickle,* ed. Stephen Dunning et al. "The Forecast" by Dan Jaffe, in *Reflections on a Gift of Watermelon Pickle,* ed. Stephen Dunning et al.	*The Green Book* (Jill Paton Walsh) *Z for Zachariah* (Robert C. O'Brien) *When the Tripods Came* (John Christopher) *Eva* (Peter Dickinson) *The Green Futures of Tycho* (William Sleator) *The Lake at the End of the World* (Caroline MacDonald) *The Ear, the Eye, and the Arm* (Penelope Farmer)

Students also can be encouraged to find poems that they think complement particular books. One fifth grader chose Felice Holman's poem "Who Am I?" (in *To the Moon and Back,* ed. Nancy Larrick) to go with the Prydain Chronicles by Lloyd Alexander because he felt the person in the poem was searching for her identity in the same way Taran was searching for who he was and how he fit in the world. Students have to read many poems in order to find one that connects with a book. It is a useful assignment, however, for it requires them to think of the main theme of both the poem and the story.

Children also need time to share and read poetry, and to write in their poetry journals, a kind of "poetry workshop" time. One middle-grade group reserves fifteen to twenty minutes a day when everyone reads poetry. Frequently children work in pairs, for once they have found a poem they particularly like, it is only natural that they want to share it. Children also enjoy making their own personal anthologies of favorite poems.

Reading Poetry to Children

Children need to be immersed in poetry from the very first day of school. Some lucky ones will have come from poetry-loving families and will have heard Mother Goose rhymes or some poems before they enter school, but increasingly teachers tell us that this group is very small. One kindergarten teacher reported only two children of her class of thirty-two knew any nursery rhymes.

Teachers need to find out what children do know, however. Try reading some of the street rhymes in Joanna Cole and Stephanie Calmenson's *Miss Mary Mack* and see which ones they recognize. Or read some nonsense poetry like Ogden Nash's *The Adventures of Isabel.* Recite some popular Mother Goose rhymes, such as "Jack and Jill" or "Mary Had a Little Lamb." Let children move to Jack Prelutsky's poem "Holding Hands" (in *Read-Aloud Rhymes for the Very Young*), which describes the heavy way that elephants walk. The trick is to read a variety of poems to children and find out what they do like. Read or recite the verses several times and encourage them to join in on the refrains. Let them clap or move to the rhythm of a poem if that seems appropriate.

Poetry should be read in a natural voice with a tone that fits the meaning of the poem. Generally, the appropriate pace for reading poetry is slower than for reading prose. It is usually recommended that a poem be read aloud a second time, perhaps to refresh children's memories, to clarify a point, or to savor a particular image. Most poetry, especially good poetry, is so concentrated and compact that few people can grasp its meaning in one exposure. Following the reading of a poem, discussion should be allowed to flow. In certain instances discussion is unnecessary or superfluous. Spontaneous chuckles might follow the reading of Kaye Starbird's "Eat-It-All Elaine" (in *The Random House Book of Poetry for Children,* ed. Prelutsky), while a thoughtful silence might be the response to Robert P. Tristram Coffin's "Forgive My Guilt" (in *Reflections on a Gift of Watermelon Pickle,* ed. S. Dunning et al.). It is not necessary

Teaching Feature — Studying Poetry and Nature

Linda Woolard combines poetry and nature study with her fifth-grade class on their visits to the school's William E. Miller Land Lab in Newark, Ohio. The students explore the land lab's trails on a wooded hillside by the school. Each student has selected a favorite spot and returns there each season. They usually spend the first ten minutes in silence to better use all their senses. They observe the woods carefully, sketching and recording their observations. They may list their sightings using books to identify wildflowers, rocks, animals, or other special finds. Linda encourages them to record their thoughts and feelings also.

Before they visit the wooded area, Linda reads to them from books and poems, such as Jean George's My Side of the Mountain, Jim Arnosky's books on sketching nature in different seasons and his Secrets of a Wildlife Watcher, John Moffitt's poem "To Look at Anything" (in Reflections on a Gift of Watermelon Pickle, ed. S. Dunning et al.), Marcie Hans's "Fueled" (in the same anthology), Lew Sarrett's "Four Little Foxes" (in Piping Down the Valleys Wild, ed. Nancy Larrick), and many more.

The children bring back their notebooks, nature specimens, such as interesting fossils, leaf rubbings, and sketches, lists of bird sightings and wildflowers, and so on. These are placed on a special bulletin board. Poems are reread, reference books consulted, and pictures mounted. Many of the careful observations now become part of poems. Two that came from these trips follow:

The Woods Are So Still

Still
Still
The woods are very
Still;
Water dripping, dripping
Off the trees.
Nothing moves
It all stays very
Still.

Katie Hopkins

Eagle

Soaring high
   Soaring low
From mountain to hill
   And back
Wind whispering under his
magnificent wings
   gently falling
climbing
   falling
      climbing
      then he lands.

Brian Dove

Linda writes poetry at the same time as her students do, and she is brave enough to ask them to make suggestions on how she can improve! Obviously, this is another classroom where a love of poetry is nurtured by much sharing of poetry, relating it to children's experiences, and modeling the joy of writing it by the teacher herself.

Miller Elementary School
Newark, Ohio
Linda Woolard, teacher

to discuss or do something with each poem read, other than enjoy it. The most important thing you as a teacher or librarian can do when you are reading poetry is share your enthusiasm for the poem.

If you feel uncomfortable reading poetry, try taping it and see how you sound. There are also many tapes of poets reading their own poems aloud to help you find out how the authors themselves thought it should be read. The more you read poetry, the more comfortable you will become. Recordings may supplement the teacher's presentation, but they should never substitute for it. There is no substitute for a teacher's reading and enthusiastically sharing poetry with a class.

Involving Children in Poetry

Assuming that the goal of teachers and librarians is not only to introduce poetry to children but to develop a love of poetry in them, how should they do it? The first principle, as we have seen, is to immerse children in poetry from kindergarten onward. Read it to them every day. Read several poems with the same theme, and contrast them. Combine poetry and prose. Make poetry a part of every content area. Provide many poetry books in the classroom, along with time to read them and share them. Teachers need to convey enthusiasm for poetry by reading it well and often. Only then will poetry become alive and grow in our schools.

However, teachers want to know more; they want to know what to do with poetry that is positive. They want to know how to involve children in poetry.

Discussing Poetry

After teachers or librarians have shared a poem with children, they frequently will discuss it. They may want to link it to other poems children have read, comparing and contrasting how the poet dealt with the concept. Suppose a second-grade teacher reads the picture book *The Accident* by the Carricks to children. She or he may want to follow that book with Sarah Henderson Hay's "For a Dead Kitten" (in *Reflections on a Gift of Watermelon Pickle*, ed. S. Dunning et al.) or

Myra Cohn Livingston's "For a Bird" (in *Poem Stew*, ed. William Cole). Children could then compare how the person in the poems felt about the cat and the little bird. Were they as hurt by their loss as Christopher was when Bodger was struck by a truck? How much detail can an author and artist give? How much can a poet give? With many such discussions children will eventually see how poetry has to capture the essence of a feeling in very few words and how important each of the words must be. Starting then with the content (children will want to tell of their experiences of losing pets—and they should have a chance to link these real-life experiences with literature), the teacher can gradually move into a discussion of the difference between prose and poetry. Discussion should center on meaning and feelings first. Only after much exposure to poetry does a teacher move into the various ways a poet may create meaning.

Children might help each other to find meaning in a poem by meeting in small discussion groups, or the teacher might lead a whole class discussion. In the following class discussion, the teacher had read aloud this short poem by Nikki Giovanni:

Daddy says the world
Is a drum
Tight and hard
And I told him
I'm gonna beat out my own rhythm.

"The Drum" from *Spin a Soft Black Song* by Nikki Giovanni. Copyright © 1971, 1985 by Nikki Giovanni. Reprinted by permission of Farrar, Straus & Giroux, Inc.

This fifth- and sixth-grade group of children had heard and discussed many poems, so they were eager to talk about the meaning of this one with their teacher, Sheryl, and offered the following opinions in answer to her question, "What do you think about this poem?"

"Well, when Mike said about when the father was telling what the world was going to be like—he said the world is a tight drum. He said it is, not it will be," Aaron answered, seemingly intent on examining each word carefully so he understood the poet's message.

"Yes," agreed Sheryl. "Why did the father say the world is a drum, tight and hard. Why did he say it *is* instead of it *will be*?"

"Because it is right now," answered many voices.

"Because he is the one that has to pay all the taxes and make a living," said Stacie.

"Why does the father know that and the girl doesn't," Sheryl asked again, intent on helping them delve as far into the poem as they could.

Many voices again responded: "Because he's out in the world." "He knows about life." "He's lived longer." And similar comments were offered. . . .

Carrie had an interesting observation. "This reminds me of that poem by . . . I forget . . . the one you read yesterday to us about the crystal stairs." She was referring to Langston Hughes's moving poem "Mother to Son," in which a black mother gives advice to her child about not giving up in the face of adversity. "The part . . . when he said the part about the drum, is tight," she continued, "that's the part that reminded me of the [Hughes] poem because it talks about nails and spots without any boards and no carpet. That sounded the same."

"That is an interesting connection because Langston Hughes and Nikki Giovanni could well have had similar experiences growing up," answered Sheryl. "Do people who heard 'Mother to Son' see any relationship between these poems?"

Jennifer had an idea. "They're both talking about how life is or was. Like the mother was talking about how hard hers was and the dad—he is talking about how hard his life was."

"It also seems like they're alive and it could happen," added Aaron.

"Like my dad," said Deon. "My mom and dad . . . he always says things like you can't get your own way—just like that poem."

"All right," responded Sheryl.

"I think that in both poems—that this one and the one we're comparing it to—that they're warning their children of what life will be and they should be ready for it," said Jennifer.

"And in 'The Drum,' how is the child responding to that?" Sheryl asked the group.

"She's gonna beat her own rhythm," answered Stacie and Deon together.

"Is it okay to do that?" Sheryl wanted to know. Many children shook their heads no. "If you didn't, what would you be like?"

"Boring," said Stacie, wrinkling up her nose in distaste.

"You would be the same as everybody else," added Mike.

"Or at least the same as what?" asked Sheryl. "Do you think the father was telling her she *had* to live her life in a certain way?"

Her question was greeted by a strong chorus of "No."

"She chose to live that way," added Angela.

"But he is trying to warn her what life is going to be like. Nevertheless she is going to try—just like the mother in Langston Hughes's poem, she is going to climb her stairs," said Sheryl.[14]

[14]Amy A. McClure, Peggy Harrison, and Sheryl Reed, *Sunrises and Songs: Reading and Writing Poetry in an Elementary Classroom* (Portsmouth, N.H.: Heinemann Educational Books, 1990), pp. 61–62.

Not only did the children understand the meaning of this poem, they connected it with their own lives and with another poem. Notice that the teacher did not tell them the meaning of the poem but let them discover the meaning for themselves. In the total discussion, she reread the poem twice. By comparing this poem with the Langston Hughes poem "Mother to Son" (in *The Dream Keeper*), the children extended their understanding of both poems. They also considered the idea of creating their own individual lives—beating their own rhythms.

Writing Poetry

Children need to hear much poetry and discuss it before attempting to write it themselves. Teachers can invite children to write poetry by providing them with poetry models and by developing a workshop approach to writing that helps children to understand that writing poetry takes time and effort.

Using Models from Literature

Children's early efforts at writing poetry are usually based on the false notion that all poetry must rhyme. Acting on this assumption, beginning efforts might be rhyme-driven and devoid of meaning. One third-grade teacher, in an effort to avoid this rhyming trap, read her children Aileen Fisher's poem "All in a Word" (in *Always Wondering*), which is a Thanksgiving acrostic based on the word *thanks*. She also shared William Smith's poem "Elephant" (in *Laughing Time*), which is

laid out in the shape of that animal. One child created an acrostic "Winter Is" and another one did a shaped poem about a mouse. These were then included in a bound book of class poems for all to read. The mouse poem shows the influence of hearing Mary O'Neill's well-loved poems about color in *Hailstones and Halibut Bones*. The first time children try to write their own takeoffs on these poems, they are apt to make a kind of grocery list of all the objects that are a particular color. By returning to the book they can begin to appreciate the craft of the poems, realizing that all lines do not begin in the same way. They see that the poems contain objects that are that color but also describe the way the color made the poet feel, smell, and taste. One sixth grader made several revisions of her poem before she was satisfied with it:

 MY RED MOOD

Red is the heat from a hot blazing fire,
A soft furry sweater awaiting a buyer.
Red is the sweet smell of roses in the spring,
Red are my cheeks that the winter winds sting.
Red is a feeling that rings deep inside
When I get angry and want to hide.
Red is a sunset waving good-bye.
Red is the sunrise shouting "Surprise!"

Treeva
Ridgemont Elementary School
Mt. Victory, Ohio
Sheryl Reed, Peggy Harrison, teachers

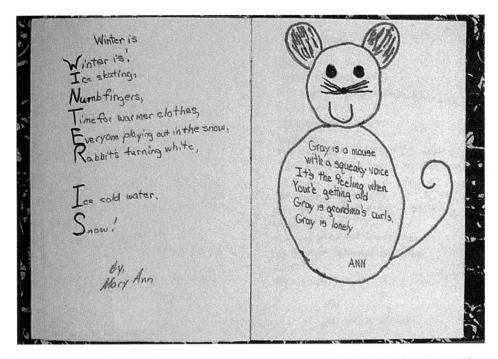

A class poetry book includes third graders' poems that are expressed in both visual and written form.
Greensview School, Upper Arlington Public Schools, Upper Arlington, Ohio. Susan Lee, teacher.

After their teacher read aloud from Mary Ann Hoberman's *A House Is a House for Me,* 5- and 6-year-olds dictated and illustrated their ideas of other things that could be houses.
Martin Luther King, Jr., Lab School, Evanston, Illinois. Esther Weiss, teacher.

Looking at the way other poets have described color can extend children's thinking. Examples are Rossetti's well-known poem "What Is Pink?" (in *The Random House Book of Poetry for Children,* ed. J. Prelutsky), Lilian Moore's "Red" (in *Something New Begins*), David McCord's "Yellow" (in *One at a Time*), and Eve Merriam's "A Yell for Yellow" (in *Jamboree*).

One group of 5- and 6-year-olds responded to Mary Ann Hoberman's long picture-book poem *A House Is a House for Me* by creating pictures and ideas of other possible houses.

In Chapter 4 we saw how another kindergarten/first-grade group adapted the pattern in *Brown Bear Brown Bear* by Bill Martin, Jr., to fit their study of bugs. In New Zealand, a group of primary children visited a park and also used the patterned sentence *Brown bear, brown bear, what do you see?* as a model for their group poem "Trees." The poem was then made into a big book and illustrated with the children's glorious tissue-paper collages:

> Trees
> We walked to the park
> And what did we see?
>   Big trees, small trees,
>   Fat trees, tall trees
>   And trees with coloured leaves.

We looked at the trees and what did we find?

Trees with branches, Trees with trunks

While kindergarten children used *Brown Bear, Brown Bear, What Do You See?* as their model for a book on trees, they looked closely at the bark, the texture, and the shape of trees. This is reflected in their glorious tissue paper collage illustrations for their "Big Book of Trees."
Mt. Eden Normal School, Auckland, New Zealand. Jo Massam-Windsor, teacher.

We looked at the trees
And what did we find?
   Trees with branches,
   Trees with trunks,
   Rough bark, smooth bark
   And tiny little twigs.

Sun shining on the trees
What does it show?
   Shiny leaves, tiny buds
   Big branches, wide trunks
   And giant shadows that
   Grow and grow and grow . . .

K–2 Children
Mt. Eden Normal School
Auckland, New Zealand
Jo Massam-Windsor, teacher

Many children have been inspired to be the voice of an animal and write its prayer after hearing Rumer Godden's translation of Carmen Bernos de Gasztold's *Prayers from the Ark*. One 10-year-old composed this poem about a worm:

God, I am but a wiggling worm.
Who sees beauty in me?
I am brown and squishy,
   and they feed me to the fish.
Is it because of *that*; they say I have no beauty?
They laugh and scream and run away.
I ask nothing of you
   but that you consider my humble plea.
Dress me in riches!
Feed me apples!
So that people will not say "worm holes" in disgust
   or fear that I might still be there.
I am just a worm,
   your creation to plow the earth
     So why do I bother?

Lisa Schiltz, age 10
Martin Luther King, Jr., Lab School
Evanston, Ill.
Barbara Friedberg, teacher

Another student wrote a poem based on Jean George's *The Cry of the Crow* and Robert P. Tristram Coffin's poem "Forgive My Guilt" (in *Reflections on a Gift of Watermelon Pickle*, ed. S. Dunning et al.). While the work was his own, he carefully acknowledged the sources of his ideas:

The Cry of the Crow
I sat in a tree
Waiting for a bird.
That day I sighted
Three large crows.

I sighted them with my gun,
I squeezed the trigger,
One wing pulled
From a bird's body.
I still hear
The cry of that crow.
As it haunts me forever.

Thoughts about this poem came from *Cry Of the Crow* and "Forgive My Guilt" by Jean Craighead George and Robert P. Tristram Coffin.

Matt Jennings
Ridgemont Elementary School
Mt. Victory, Ohio
Sheryl Reed, Peggy Harrison, teachers

Different forms of poetry can offer poetic structures to children and serve as models for creative poetry writing. We have seen how shaped poetry can get children started. Concrete poetry is another gateway. Using Robert Froman's *Seeing Things* or Joan Graham's *Splish, Splash*, children could try creating their own concrete poems. Again the emphasis should be on the meaning of the poem first, then its shape.

Haiku frequently helps children lose their insistence upon rhyme and focus on the idea of the poem. However, this form of poetry has been overused with students too immature to understand the beauty of its concise thought and high level of abstraction. Despite their brevity of form, haiku are not easy to write. Only when children are ready for the formal discipline imposed by haiku should they try it. Some middle graders are challenged by it; others are only confused. Certainly, primary-grade children who are still at the cognitive level of concrete operations should not be asked to try anything so abstract and foreign to their way of thinking. The examples here illustrate two 12-year-olds' success in writing haiku:

The cabin is small
in the vast whiteness. Only
the smoke reveals it.

Carole Bartlett
Boulder Public Schools, Colorado
Allaire Stuart, teacher

The leaves on a tree
Rustle, impatient, restless,
Waiting to fall off.

Patti Krog
Boulder Public Schools, Colorado
Allaire Stuart, teacher

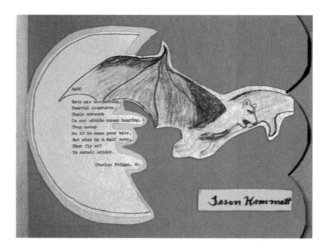

Two sixth graders worked together to create this book of poems titled *Bats and Owls*. Charles Phipps, Jr., created the poetry while his friend Jason Hammet drew the illustrations. Notice how the pages are scalloped like the wings of owls. Ridgemont Elementary School, Mt. Victory, Ohio. Sheryl Reed and Peggy Harrison, teachers.

Poetry Workshop

Using models can be a way to get children started in writing poetry. It provides the opportunity to "write like a poet," and the given structures usually help the child produce an acceptable poem. In no way does this approach help a child *think* like a poet. That will happen only after much sustained writing and revisions.

In a small rural school in Ohio, two teachers, Sheryl Reed and Peggy Harrison, began a year-long poetry program with their combined group of fifth and sixth graders. Amy McClure spent a year studying this poetry program and then writing an ethnographic research report on it.[15] Still later this study was rewritten for a fine book for teachers on how to include poetry in the classroom.[16]

These teachers begin their poetry workshop with reading poetry aloud several times a day. The classroom collection of over two hundred poetry books is extensive. Children read poetry for ten or fifteen minutes a day and keep poetry journals in which they write every day. They do not have to produce a poem a day—they can list possibilities, revise a poem they have been working on, or invite one of their friends to critique a poem. Frequently they illustrate one of their best poems, or they make anthologies of their own poetry or create personal anthologies of their favorite poems from various books. This requires that the child read a wide variety of poetry and then decide on the organizing feature. Is it to be a book of animal poems or, as one child titled his, "deep feeling poems"?

One student wrote over four hundred poems in the two years he was in this class. He created an anthology with all the poems he had written about bats and owls, an interest that developed from his teacher's reading of Randall Jarrell's story of *The Bat-Poet*. He then asked one of his friends in the class who was known for his artistic ability to illustrate it with detailed black-and-white pencil drawings. These pictures were mounted on black, tan, and gray pages cut with scalloped edges to imitate the shape of an owl's wing. Their finished book reflected the subject as well as the carefully crafted poems. Here is one of the poems from their book:

 A Bat

A bat
Feeds lavishly
On moths
And beetles
Flies loops
And twirls
Catches bugs
From behind
When the sun
Rises faintly
The bat
Retires to rest

Charles Phipps, Jr.
Ridgemont Elementary School
Mt. Victory, Ohio
Sheryl Reed, Peggy Harrison, teachers

In New York City, Georgia Heard, a published poet herself, also encourages children to write what they know and what they feel when she conducts poetry workshops with all age groups. In conferring with

[15]Amy A. McClure, "Children's Responses to Poetry in a Supportive Literary Context," (Ph.D. dissertation, Ohio State University, Columbus, 1984).

[16]McClure, Harrison, and Reed, *Sunrises and Songs*.

children, she frequently asks them to close their eyes and visualize their topic. Jason had written a first draft of a poem about cats:

Cats are cats
Cats are great
Cats can't be beat

After reading his poem, Georgia Heard writes:

The old me wants to evaluate Jason's poem. The researcher, the curious me, notices what Jason knows about poetry. There's some rhythm in his poem, repetition, and a little rhyme; it sounds like a chant or a cheer. He definitely knows the difference between a poem and a story. I tell him what I notice about his poem, but I also want to know why he chose cats as his subject.[17]

When she discovered that Jason owned a cat, she asked him to close his eyes again and visualize his cat. Slowly, he told her what he saw. She repeated his words back to him, and Jason wrote his poem again:

My Cat

My cat is black and white
I pretend he is my son
I love him.
His feet smell like popcorn.[18]

At another time, this child might want to play with the order of his lines. However, because he is just beginning to write poems, Georgia Heard wisely let his second draft stand. He has specifically described *his* cat and how he feels about him in this poem, a far cry from his first generic poem about all cats.

Children's poems do not have to be perfect. One of the reasons for having them write poetry is to increase their enjoyment of poetry; it is not necessary to produce poets. In critiquing children's poems, it is important to evaluate improvement. In Georgia Heard's evaluation conferences, she asks students to bring all of their poems to her, and then they spread them out on the floor. Here are some of the questions she offers as guidelines:

What things do you usually write about?
    What kind of poems do you tend to write? Rhyming poems, long, short, narrative, lyric?

What kind of lines do you usually work with? Long or short?
What are you really good at? Titles, images, interesting words, repetition, rhyme?
What are you not so good at? How would you like to improve?
Do you revise? How do you do it? Do you change or add a word or overhaul the whole poem?
What is the hardest part of writing a poem for you? Where do you get stuck?
Are there any new things you'd like to learn?[19]

This process enables the child, rather than the teacher, to be the evaluator. It is a learning process for both of them, however. Children who hear poetry every day, who read poetry every day, and who write it every day develop a deep love for poetry. Writing honest poems that reflect their own thoughts and feelings helps children develop a real appreciation for poetry.

Choral Reading

The reading and sharing of poetry through choral speaking is another way to foster interest in poetry. Choral speaking or reading is the interpretation of poetry by several voices speaking as one. At first, young children *speak* it as they join in the refrains. Middle-grade children may prefer to *read* their poems. They are not always read in unison; in fact, this is one of the most difficult ways to present a poem.

Four types of choral speaking are particularly suited for use in the elementary school. In the first, the "refrain" type, one person (teacher or child) reads the narrative and the rest of the class joins in the refrain, or "echo" as Nancy Larrick calls it.[20] In her book *Let's Do a Poem,* Larrick suggests using the well-known folk poem that begins "In a dark, dark wood there was a dark dark house" and letting children join in on the "dark darks." She also recommends David McCord's "Windshield Wipers' Song" (in *Knock at a Star,* ed. X. and D. Kennedy) and Vachel Lindsay's poem "The Mysterious Cat" (in *Cats Are Cats,* ed. N. Larrick) as good echo poems to try. Both of these poems are included in her book.

Another way to do a group reading, called antiphonal, is to divide the class into two groups. For example, in reading Rosy Fyleman's "Witch, Witch" (in *The Poetry Troupe,* ed. Isabel Wilner), one group can ask the witch the questions and the other group can give her answers. An effective approach with young children is the "line-a-child" arrangement, where different children

[17]Georgia Heard, *For the Good of the Earth and Sun: Teaching Poetry* (Portsmouth, N.H.: Heinemann Educational Books, 1989), pp. 40–41.

[18]Ibid., p. 41.

[19]Ibid., p. 53.

[20]Nancy Larrick, *Let's Do a Poem* (New York: Delacorte Press, 1991), pp. 45–47.

say, or read, individual lines, with the class joining in unison at the beginning or end of the poem. "One, Two, Buckle My Shoe" is a good rhyme to introduce this type of choral reading. The dialogue of David McCord's "At the Garden Gate" (in *One at a Time*) lends itself to this approach for children in the middle grades. A more difficult and formal version of this method is part speaking. Groups are divided according to the sound of their voices into high, middle, and low parts. The poem is then interpreted much as a song might be sung in parts. This is usually done with mature groups and is the method utilized by verse-speaking choirs. Another difficult method is to have children say the whole poem in unison, giving just one interpretation.

Many variations to these approaches will be used by creative teachers and children. A certain sound that complements both the rhythm and the meaning of the poem may be an accompaniment, such as "clickety clack" for David McCord's "The Song of the Train" (in *One at a Time*). One group might repeat this phrase as another group says the words of the poem. Another poem that provides an interesting sound is Arthur Guiterman's "What the Gray Cat Sings" (in *The Poetry Troup*, ed. Isabel Wilner). Alternate groups or solo voices could say the verses, with the entire class joining in on the cat's weaving song. This would be a wonderful poem to share after reading Ashley Bryan's West Indian folktale *The Cat's Purr*.

Eve Merriam's "Bam Bam Bam" (in *Jamboree*) has also been published in a picture book illustrated by Dan Yaccarino. There is so much sound as well as movement in this poem that children will enjoy pantomiming the poem as well as accompanying the "bams," "zams," and "zowies" with musical instruments (preferably in a sound-proof room). Children can also plan how to read Jack Prelutsky's "The Grobbles" (in *The Snopp on the Sidewalk*). One child can be the innocent soul walking through the woods, while others can each give a line describing the grobbles. Then the poem can grow with scary intensity as the person walks closer to the grobbles:

The grobbles are gruesome	(Child 1)
The grobbles are green	(Child 2)
The grobbles are nasty	(Child 3)
The grobbles are mean	(All)
The grobbles hide deep	(Child 4)
in a hollowy tree	
just waiting to gobble	(All)
whomever they see	
I walk through the woods	(Solo)
for I'm quite unaware	
that the grobbles are waiting	
to gobble me there	

they suddenly spring	(Children 1–4)
from their hollowy tree	
Oh goodness! the grobbles	(Solo)
are gobbling m . . .	

"The Grobbles" from *The Snopp on the Sidewalk*, by Jack Prelutsky. Copyright © 1987, 1977 by Jack Prelutsky. By permission of Greenwillow Books, a division of William Morrow & Company, Inc., New York, NY.

This interpretation of how to read "The Grobbles" is only one of many that could be developed. After you have worked with children in choral reading, they will suggest variations of different ways to interpret poems. Try these out and see which ones are the most pleasing to the ear and the most appropriate for the meaning of the poem. More serious poetry can also be read effectively by a group. Lew Sarett's "Four Little Foxes," Elizabeth Coatsworth's "Sea Gull," and Eve Merriam's "Neuteronomy" all lend themselves beautifully to choral speaking. All three are in Isabel Wilner's useful book *The Poetry Troupe*, which gives more suggestions.

Older children particularly enjoy practicing reading Paul Fleischman's poems for two voices found in his Newbery Medal book *Joyful Noise* and in his *I Am Phoenix*. All of the poems in *Joyful Noise* are about insects. In *I Am Phoenix*, all of the poems are about birds. With two columns of words placed side by side, sometimes each reader reads alone and at other times the readers are reading in unison or sometimes in opposition. The result is a wonderful image of each bird or insect that results as much from the sound of the reading as from the meaning of the words.

The values of children reading poetry together are many. They derive enjoyment from learning to respond as a group to the rhythm and melody of the poem. They learn much about the interpretation of poetry as they help plan various ways to read the poem. Shy children forget their fears when participating with the group, and all children learn to develop cooperation as they work together with a leader to present a poem. It is necessary to remember that the process of choral reading is much more important than the final product. Teachers must work for the enjoyment of poetry, not perfection of performance. Too frequently choral reading becomes a "stunt" or a quick way to entertain a PTA group. If teachers and children are pressured into a "production," interpretation of poetry will be exploited for unnatural ends.

Boys and girls should have many opportunities to share poetry in interesting and meaningful situations, if they are to develop appreciation for the deep satisfactions that poetry brings. Appreciation for poetry develops slowly. It is the result of long and loving experience with poetry over a period of years. Children who are fortunate enough to have developed a love of poetry will always be the richer for it.

Learning Experiences

1. Begin a poetry collection for future use with children. Make your own filing system. What categories will you include? Indicate possible uses for some poems, possible connections with prose, ways to interpret poems.

2. Make a study of one poet. How would you characterize her or his work in style and usual content? What can you find out about her or his background? How are these experiences reflected in the poetry?

3. Make a cycle of poems about one particular subject—for example, friends, secret places, the city, loneliness. Share these with the class.

4. Bring your favorite children's poem to present to the class or to tape-record. Invite class members to comment on both your selection and your presentation.

5. Select three different kinds of poems and read them to a group of children. Record their responses. What poems had the greatest appeal? Why?

6. Select one or two poems that contain figurative language. Share them with children at different developmental stages. When do children appear to understand the metaphors being used? One way to link into their understanding is to ask them to draw a picture of the images they see.

7. Find a poem to go with a passage in a book or with your favorite picture book.

8. Compare two general anthologies of poetry, using criteria suggested in the text.

9. Select several poems you think would lend themselves to choral reading. Work with a group of children or classmates in planning ways to present one of these poems. If possible, tape-record these interpretations.

10. Make a survey of the teachers in an elementary school to see how often they read poetry to their students, what their favorite poems are, what their favorite sources for poetry are. Make a visual presentation of your results.

11. Listen to some recordings of poetry read by authors and by interpreters. Contrast the presentations and appropriateness of the records for classroom use. Share these with children. Which ones do they prefer?

12. Try writing some poetry yourself. You may want to use some experimental verse forms, such as concrete poetry or found poetry.

Related Readings

Chatton, Barbara. *Using Poetry Across the Curriculum: A Whole Language Approach.* Phoenix: Oryx Press, 1993.

An indispensible classroom resource for any classroom teacher, this book will enable teachers to immerse children in poetry throughout the school day. Chapters include suggestions for making connections to all the content areas, including science, mathematics, and social studies. Also included are thematic units that are filled with poems, multicultural resources, and ideas for sharing poetry with children.

Chukovsky, Kornei. *From Two to Five.* Translated and edited by Miriam Morton. Berkeley: University of California Press, 1963.

This is a classic review of the young child's delight in poetry. Written by a well-known Russian poet, it emphasizes that poetry is the natural language of little children.

Cullinan, Beatrice, Marilyn C. Scala, and Virginia C. Schroeder. *Three Voices: An Invitation to Poetry Across the Curriculum.* York, Maine: Stenhouse, 1995.

This practical book includes thirty-three detailed strategies for using poetry with children and provides three hundred additional brief suggestions. Teachers describe the classroom poetry activities in which their children were involved and include examples of student work.

Heard, Georgia. *For the Good of the Earth and Sun: Teaching Poetry.* Portsmouth, N.H.: Heinemann Educational Books, 1989.

A published poet describes her methods of teaching elementary children in New York City schools to enjoy poetry, to read poetry, and to write poetry. She describes the many poetry workshops she does with children from kindergarten through sixth grade. Filled with practical suggestions, this book offers the reader help and inspiration for ways to teach poetry to children.

Hopkins, Lee Bennett. *Pass the Poetry, Please*. Rev. ed. New York: Harper & Row, 1987.

This revised edition of a well-known book presents a wealth of ideas for making poetry come alive in the classroom. It contains suggestions for sparking children's interest in writing poetry. It also includes interviews with more than twenty contemporary poets.

Larrick, Nancy. *Let's Do a Poem*. New York: Delacorte Press, 1991.

Nancy Larrick's enthusiasm for poetry is obvious in this wonderfully useful book, which suggests that children should be introduced to poetry through listening, singing, chanting, impromptu choral reading, body movement, dance, and drama.

Livingston, Myra Cohn. *Climb into the Bell Tower: Essays on Poetry*. New York: HarperCollins, 1990.

A noted poet and anthologist, Myra Cohn Livingston offers a collection of her own essays, articles, and speeches on poetry for children published between 1967 and 1987. This book brings together her insights into teaching and writing poetry for children, her sharp criticism, and praise for those who create poetry. A stimulating collection from someone courageous enough to take a stand for quality in children's literature.

————. *The Child as Poet: Myth or Reality?* Boston: Horn Book, 1984.

————. *Poem-Making: Ways to Begin Writing Poetry*. New York: HarperCollins, 1991.

In the first text, Livingston disputes the widely believed statement that the child is a natural poet. She reacts strongly to some techniques used in teaching children to write poetry. In the second book, she provides positive help for middle-grade students or teachers who want to learn more about the form and elements of poem making. She clearly presents the process of writing poetry and gives many poems as examples. Teachers will find this a very useful book.

Janeczko, Paul. *Poetry from A to Z: A Guide for Young Writers*. Bradbury, 1994.

Janeczko includes seventy-two poems that can serve as models and fourteen poetry-writing exercises that invite children to poetry in engaging, nonthreatening ways. The A-to-Z format is meant to show children that they can write poetry about anything. The exercises include patterns such as acrostics and haiku and themes such as prayer poems, memory poems, and opposites.

McClure, Amy A., Peggy Harrison, and Sheryl Reed. *Sunrises and Songs: Reading and Writing Poetry in an Elementary Classroom*. Portsmouth, N.H.: Heinemann Educational Books, 1990.

This book has been rewritten for teachers from McClure's dissertation. The research voice is exchanged for an almost poetic description of one year in a classroom where poetry was the heart of the curriculum. This is a text middle-grade teachers should not miss.

Children's Literature

Poetry

Adoff, Arnold. *All the Colors of the Race*. Illustrated by John Steptoe. Lothrop, Lee & Shepard, 1982.

————. *Black Is Brown Is Tan*. Illustrated by Emily McCully. Harper & Row, 1973.

————. *Chocolate Dreams*. Illustrated by Turi MacCombie. Lothrop, Lee & Shepard, 1988.

————. *Eats: Poems*. Illustrated by Susan Russo. Lothrop, Lee & Shepard, 1979.

————. *In for Winter, Out for Spring*. Illustrated by Jerry Pinkney. Harcourt Brace, 1991.

————. *Street Music: City Poems*. Illustrated by Karen Barbour. HarperCollins, 1995.

————, ed. *I Am the Darker Brother: An Anthology of Modern Poems by Black Americans*. Macmillan, 1970.

————, ed. *My Black Me: A Beginning Book of Black Poetry*. Dutton, 1994 [1974].

Agard, John, and Grace Nichols. *A Caribbean Dozen: Poems from Caribbean Poets*. Illustrated by Cathie Felstead. Candlewick, 1994.

Aldis, Dorothy. *All Together*. Illustrated by Marjorie Flack, Margaret Frieman, and Helen D. Jameson. Putnam [1925, 1952; out of print].

Benét, Stephen Vincent, and Rosemary Benét. *A Book of Americans*. Illustrated by Charles Child. Henry Holt, 1984.

Bernos de Gasztold, Carmen. *Prayers from the Ark*. Translated by Rumer Godden. Illustrated by Barry Moser. Viking, 1992.

Bierhorst, John, ed. *In the Trail of the Wind: American Indian Poems and Ritual Orations*. Farrar, Straus & Giroux, 1971.

————. *On the Road of Stars: Native American Night Poems and Sleep Charms*. Illustrated by Judy Pedersen. Macmillan, 1994.

Blishen, Edward, ed. *The Oxford Book of Poetry for Children*. Illustrated by Brian Wildsmith. Bedrick Books, 1984 [1963].

Booth, David, ed. *Doctor Knickerbocker and Other Rhymes*. Illustrated by Marilyn Kovalski. Ticknor & Fields, 1993.

———. *Til All the Stars Have Fallen: Canadian Poems for Children*. Illustrated by Kady MacDonald Denton. Kids Can Press, 1989.

———. *Voices on the Wind: Poems for All Seasons*. Illustrated by Michele Lemieux. Morrow, 1990.

Brewton, Sara, et al., eds. *Of Quarks, Quasars, and Other Quirks: Quizzical Poems for the Supersonic Age*. Illustrated by Quentin Blake. Harper & Row, 1977.

Brooks, Gwendolyn. *Bronzeville Boys and Girls*. Illustrated by Ronni Solbert. Harper & Row, 1965.

Browning, Robert. *The Pied Piper of Hamelin*. Illustrated by Kate Greenaway. Random House, 1993 [1889].

———. *The Pied Piper of Hamelin*. Illustrated by Terry Small. Harcourt Brace, 1988.

Bryan, Ashley. *Sing to the Sun*. HarperCollins, 1992.

Carlson, Lori M., ed. *Cool Salsa: Bilingual Poems on Growing Up Latino in the United States*. Holt, 1994.

Cassedy, Sylvia. *Roomrimes*. Illustrated by Michele Chessare. Crowell, 1987.

———. *Zoomrimes: Poems About Things That Go*. Illustrated by Michele Chessare. HarperCollins, 1993.

Cassedy, Sylvia, and Kinihiro Suetake, trans. *Red Dragonfly on My Shoulder*. Illustrated by Molly Bang. HarperCollins, 1992.

Chandra, Deborah. *Balloons and Other Poems*. Illustrated by Leslie Bowman. Farrar, Straus & Giroux, 1990.

———. "Fog." In *Balloons and Other Poems*, illustrated by Leslie Bowman. Farrar, Straus & Giroux, 1990.

———. *Rich Lizard and Other Poems*. Illustrated by Leslie Bowman. Farrar, Straus & Giroux, 1993.

Chute, Marchette. "Wrong Start." In *The Random House Book of Poetry for Children*, edited by Jack Prelutsky, illustrated by Arnold Lobel. Random House, 1983.

Ciardi, John. *The Hopeful Trout and Other Limericks*. Illustrated by Susan Meddaugh. Houghton Mifflin, 1992.

———. *I Met a Man*. Illustrated by Robert Osborn. Houghton Mifflin, 1961.

———. *Mummy Took Cooking Lessons and Other Poems*. Illustrated by Merle Nacht. Houghton Mifflin, 1990.

———. *The Reason for the Pelican*. Illustrated by Dominic Catalano. Boyds, 1994.

———. *You Read to Me, I'll Read to You*. Illustrated by Edward Gorey. Lippincott, 1962.

Clark, Ann Nolan. *In My Mother's House*. Illustrated by Velno Herrera. Viking, 1991 [1941].

Clark, Emma Chichester, ed., illus. *I Never Saw a Purple Cow and Other Nonsense Rhymes*. Little, Brown, 1991.

Cole, Joanna, and Stephanie Calmenson. *Miss Mary Mack and Other Children's Street Rhymes*. Illustrated by Alan Tiegreen. Morrow, 1990.

Cole, William, ed. *Oh, How Silly*. Illustrated by Tomi Ungerer. Viking, 1970.

———, ed. *Oh, That's Ridiculous*. Illustrated by Tomi Ungerer. Viking, 1972.

———, ed. *Oh, What Nonsense*. Illustrated by Tomi Ungerer. Viking, 1966.

———, ed. *Poem Stew*. Illustrated by Karen Ann Weinhaus. Lippincott, 1981.

cummings, e. e. *Hist Whist*. Illustrated by Deborah Kogan Ray. Crown, 1989.

de Paola, Tomie, ed. *Tomie de Paola's Book of Poems*. Putnam, 1988.

de Regniers, Beatrice Schenk, et al., eds. *Sing a Song of Popcorn*. Illustrated by nine Caldecott Medal artists. Scholastic, 1988.

Dunning, Stephen, Edward Lueders, and Hugh Smith. *Reflections on a Gift of Watermelon Pickle and Other Modern Verses*. Lothrop, Lee & Shepard, 1966.

Eliot, T. S. Mr. *Mistoffelees with Mungojerrie and Rumpelteazer*. Illustrated by Errol Le Cain. Harcourt Brace, 1991.

Elledge, Scott, ed. *Wider than the Sky: Poems to Grow Up With*. HarperCollins, 1990.

Esbensen, Barbara. *Dance with Me*. Illustrated by Megan Lloyd. HarperCollins, 1995.

———. *Who Shrank My Grandmother's House?* Illustrated by Eric Beddows. HarperCollins, 1992.

————. *Words with Wrinkled Knees*. Illustrated by John Stadler. Harper & Row, 1986.

Faber, Norma, and Myra Cohn Livingston, eds. *These Small Stones*. Harper & Row, 1987.

Farjeon, Eleanor. *Eleanor Farjeon's Poems for Children*. Lippincott, 1985 [1951].

Feelings, Tom. *Soul Looks Back in Wonder*. Dial, 1993.

Ferris, Helen, ed. *Favorite Poems Old and New*. Illustrated by Leonard Weisgard. Doubleday, 1957.

Field, Rachel. *General Store*. Illustrated by Nancy Winslow Parker. Greenwillow, 1988.

Fisher, Aileen. *Always Wondering*. Illustrated by Joan Sandin. HarperCollins, 1992.

Fleischman, Paul. *I Am Phoenix: Poems for Two Voices*. Illustrated by Ken Nutt. Harper & Row, 1985.

————. *Joyful Noise: Poems for Two Voices*. Illustrated by Eric Beddows. Harper & Row, 1988.

Florian, Douglas. *Beast Feast*. Harcourt Brace, 1994.

————. *Bing Bang Bong*. Harcourt Brace, 1994.

Frank, Josette, ed. *Snow Toward Evening*. Illustrated by Thomas Locker. Dial, 1990.

Froman, Robert. *Seeing Things*. Crowell, 1974.

Frost, Robert. *Birches*. Illustrated by Ed Young. Henry Holt, 1988.

————. *Stopping by Woods on a Snowy Evening*. Illustrated by Susan Jeffers. Dutton, 1978.

————. *You Come Too*. Illustrated by Thomas W. Nason. Henry Holt, 1959.

Giovanni, Nicki. *Knoxville, Tennessee*. Illustrated by Larry Johnson. Scholastic, 1994.

————. *Spin a Soft Black Song: Poems for Children*. Illustrated by George Martins. Hill & Wang, 1985 [1971].

Goldstein, Bobbye S., ed. *Bear in Mind*. Illustrated by William Pène DuBois. Viking, 1989.

————. *Inner Chimes: Poems on Poetry*. Illustrated by Jane Breskin Zalben. Birdsong/Boyds, 1992.

Gordon, Ruth, ed. *Peeling the Onion: An Anthology of Poems*. HarperCollins/Zolotow, 1993.

Graham, Joan. *Splish, Splash*. Illustrated by Steve Scott. Ticknor & Fields, 1994.

Greenfield, Eloise. "Harriet Tubman." In *Honey I Love: And Other Poems*, illustrated by Leo and Diane Dillon. Harper & Row, 1978.

————. *Honey, I Love: And Other Poems*. Illustrated by Leo and Diane Dillon. Harper & Row, 1978.

————. *Nathaniel Talking*. Illustrated by Jan Spivey Gilchrist. Black Butterfly Children's Books, 1988.

————. *Night on Neighborhood Street*. Illustrated by Jan Spivey Gilchrist. Dial, 1991.

————. *Under the Sunday Tree*. Illustrated by Amos Ferguson. Harper & Row, 1988.

Gunning, Monica. *Not a Copper Penny in Me House: Poems from the Caribbean*. Illustrated by Frané Lessac. Boyds Mills/Word Song, 1993.

Hoberman, Mary Ann. *A Fine Fat Pig*. Illustrated by Malach Zeldis. HarperCollins, 1991.

————. *A House Is a House for Me*. Illustrated by Betty Fraser. Penguin, 1982.

————. *Yellow Butter Purple Jelly Red Jam Black Bread*. Illustrated by Chaya Burstein. Viking, 1981.

Hopkins, Lee Bennett, ed. *By Myself*. Illustrated by Glo Goalson. Harper & Row, 1980.

————, ed. *Dinosaurs*. Illustrated by Murray Tinkelman. Harcourt Brace, 1987.

————, ed. *Extra Innings: Baseball Poems*. Illustrated by Scott Medlock. Harcourt Brace, 1993.

————, ed. *Good Books, Good Times!* Illustrated by Harvey Stevenson. HarperCollins, 1990.

————, ed. *Hey-How for Halloween!* Illustrated by Janet McCaffrey. Harcourt Brace, 1974.

————, ed. *It's About Time!* Illustrated by Matt Novak. Harcourt Brace, 1993.

————, ed. *More Surprises*. Illustrated by Megan Lloyd. Harper & Row, 1987.

————, ed. *Morning, Noon and Nighttime, Too*. Illustrated by Nancy Hannans. Harcourt Brace, 1980.

————, ed. *Ragged Shadows: Poems of Halloween Night*. Illustrated by Giles Laroche. Little, Brown, 1993.

————, ed. *Rainbows Are Made: Poems by Carl Sandburg*. Illustrated by Fritz Eichenberg. Harcourt Brace, 1984.

————, ed. *Ring Out, Wild Bells: Poems About Holidays and the Seasons*. Illustrated by Karen Baumann. Harcourt Brace, 1992.

————, ed. *The Sea Is Calling Me*. Illustrated by Walter Gaffney-Kessell. Harcourt Brace, 1986.

————, ed. *Side by Side: Poems to Read Together*. Illustrated by Hilary Knight. Simon & Schuster, 1988.

————, ed. *The Sky Is Full of Song*. Illustrated by Dirk Zimmer. Harper & Row, 1983.

————, ed. *Still as a Star: A Book of Nighttime Poems*. Illustrated by Karen Milone. Little, Brown, 1989.

————, ed. *Surprises*. Illustrated by Megan Lloyd. Harper & Row, 1984.

————, ed. *Through Our Eyes: Poems and Pictures About Growing Up*. Photography by Jeffrey Dunn. Little, Brown, 1992.

————, ed. *Weather*. Photographs by Melanie Hale. HarperCollins, 1994.

Huck, Charlotte, ed. *Secret Places*. Illustrated by Lindsay Barrett George. Greenwillow, 1993.

Hudson, Wade, ed. *Pass It On: African American Poetry for Children*. Illustrated by Floyd Cooper. Scholastic, 1993.

Hughes, Langston. *The Dream Keeper and Other Poems*. Illustrated by Brian Pinkney. Knopf, 1992 [1932].

————. "Mother to Son." In *The Dream Keeper and Other Poems*, illustrated by Brian Pinkney. Knopf, 1992 [1932].

Janeczko, Paul B., ed. *The Place My Words Are Looking For*. Bradbury, 1990.

————. *This Delicious Day*. Orchard, 1987.

————. *Poetry from A to Z*. Bradbury, 1994.

Jones, Hettie, ed. *The Trees Stand Shining: Poetry of the North American Indians*. Dial, 1993.

Kennedy, Dorothy, ed. *I Thought I'd Take My Rat to School: Poems for September to June*. Illustrated by Abby Carter. Little, Brown, 1993.

Kennedy, X. J. *Brats*. Illustrated by James Watts. Atheneum, 1986.

————. *Drat Those Brats*. Illustrated by James Watts. Atheneum, 1993.

————. *The Forgetful Wishing Well: Poems for Young People*. Illustrated by Monica Incisa. Atheneum, 1985.

————. *Fresh Brats*. Illustrated by James Watts. Atheneum, 1990.

————. *Ghastlies, Goops and Pincushions*. Illustrated by Ron Barrett. Atheneum, 1989.

Kennedy, X. J., and Dorothy M. Kennedy, compilers. *Knock at a Star: A Child's Introduction to Poetry*. Illustrated by Karen Ann Weinhaus. Little, Brown, 1982.

————. *Talking Like the Rain*. Illustrated by Jane Dyer. Little, Brown, 1992.

Knudson, R. R., and May Swenson. *American Sports Poems*. Orchard, 1988.

Kuskin, Karla. *Any Me I Want to Be*. Harper & Row, 1972.

————. *City Noise*. Illustrated by Renée Flower. HarperCollins, 1994.

————. *Dogs & Dragons, Trees & Dreams: A Collection of Poems*. Harper & Row, 1980.

————. *Near the Window Tree*. Harper & Row, 1975.

————. *Soap Soup and Other Verses*. HarperCollins, 1992.

————. *Something Sleeping in the Hall*. Harper & Row, 1985.

Larrick, Nancy, ed. *Bring Me All of Your Dreams*. Photographs by Larry Mulvehill. M. Evans, 1980.

————. *Cats Are Cats*. Illustrated by Ed Young. Philomel, 1988.

————. *The Merry-Go-Round Poetry Book*. Illustrated by Karen Gundersheimer. Delacorte, 1989.

————. *Mice Are Nice*. Illustrated by Ed Young. Philomel, 1990.

————. *Piping Down the Valleys Wild*. Illustrated by Ellen Raskin. Delacorte, 1985 [1968].

————. *To the Moon and Back*. Illustrated by Catherine O'Neill. Delacorte, 1991.

————. *When the Dark Comes Dancing*. Illustrated by John Wallner. Philomel, 1983.

Lear, Edward. *The Complete Nonsense Book*. Dodd, Mead, 1946.

————. *The Owl and the Pussycat*. Illustrated by Jan Brett. Putnam's, 1991.

————. *The Pelican Chorus and Other Nonsense*. Illustrated by Fred Marcellino. HarperCollins, 1995.

————. *The Quangle Wangle's Hat*. Illustrated by Janet Stevens. Harcourt Brace, 1988.

Lear, Edward, and Ogden Nash. *The Scroobious Pip*. Illustrated by Nancy Ekholm Burkert. Harper & Row, 1968.

Levy, Constance. *I'm Going to Pet a Worm Today and Other Poems*. Illustrated by Ron Himler. Macmillan, 1991.

————. *A Tree Place and Other Poems*. Illustrated by Robert Sabuda. Macmillan, 1994.

Lewis, J. Patrick. *Black Swan/White Crow*. Illustrated by Chris Manson. Atheneum, 1995.

————. *Earth Verses and Water Rhymes*. Illustrated by Robert Sabuda. Atheneum, 1991.

————. *The Fat Cats at Sea*. Illustrated by Victoria Chess. Apple Soup/Knopf, 1994.

————. *A Hippopotamusn't*. Illustrated by Victoria Chess. Dial, 1990.

————. *In a Spring Garden*. Illustrated by Ezra Jack Keats. Dial, 1989 (1964).

————. *Ridicholas Nicholas: More Animal Poems*. Illustrated by Victoria Chess. Dial, 1995.

Lindbergh, Reeve. *Johnny Appleseed*. Illustrated by Kathy Jakobsen. Little, Brown, 1990.

Little, Jean. *Hey World, Here I Am!* Illustrated by Sue Truesdell. Harper & Row, 1986.

Livingston, Myra Cohn. *Animal, Vegetable, Mineral: Poems About Small Things*. HarperCollins, 1994.

————. *Cat Poems*. Illustrated by Trina Schart Hyman. Holiday House, 1987.

————. *Celebrations*. Illustrated by Leonard Everett Fisher. Holiday House, 1985.

————, ed. *Christmas Poems*. Illustrated by Trina Schart Hyman. Holiday House, 1985.

————. *A Circle of Seasons*. Illustrated by Leonard Everett Fisher. Holiday House, 1982.

————, ed. *Dilly Dilly Piccalilli: Poems for the Very Young*. Illustrated by Eileen Christelow. McElderry, 1989.

————, ed. *Dog Poems*. Illustrated by Leslie Morrill. Holiday House, 1990.

————. *Earth Songs*. Illustrated by Leonard E. Fisher. Holiday House, 1986.

————, ed. *Easter Poems*. Illustrated by John Wallner. Holiday House, 1985.

————. *Festivals*. Illustrated by Leonard Everett Fisher. Holiday House, 1996.

————. *Flights of Fancy and Other Poems*. McElderry, 1994.

————, ed. *Halloween Poems*. Illustrated by Stephen Gammell. Holiday House, 1989.

————, ed. *If the Owl Calls Again: A Collection of Owl Poems*. Illustrated by Antonio Frasconi. McElderry, 1990.

————, ed. *I Like You, If You Like Me: Poems of Friendship*. McElderry, 1987.

————. *My Head Is Red and Other Riddle Poems*. Illustrated by Tere Lo Prete. Holiday House, 1990.

————, ed. *New Year's Poems*. Illustrated by Margot Tomes. Holiday House, 1987.

————, ed. *Poems for Brothers, Poems for Sisters*. Illustrated by Jean Zallinger. Holiday House, 1991.

————, ed. *Poems for Fathers*. Illustrated by Robert Assilla. Holiday House, 1989.

————, ed. *Poems for Grandmothers*. Illustrated by Patricia Cullen-Clark. Holiday House, 1990.

————, ed. *Poems for Jewish Holidays*. Illustrated by Lloyd Bloom. Holiday House, 1986.

————, ed. *Poems for Mothers*. Illustrated by Deborah K. Ray. Holiday House, 1988.

————. *Sea Songs*. Illustrated by Leonard E. Fisher. McElderry, 1986.

————. *Sky Songs*. Illustrated by Leonard E. Fisher. McElderry, 1984.

————. *A Song I Sang to You: A Selection of Poems*. Illustrated by Margot Tomes. Harcourt Brace, 1984.

————. *Space Songs*. Illustrated by Leonard E. Fisher. McElderry, 1988.

————, ed. *Thanksgiving Poems*. Illustrated by Stephen Gammell. Holiday House, 1985.

————. *There Was a Place and Other Poems*. McElderry, 1988.

————. *Up in the Air*. Illustrated by Leonard E. Fisher. McElderry, 1989.

————, ed. *Valentine Poems*. Holiday House, 1987.

———. *The Way Things Are and Other Poems*. Illustrated by Jenni Oliver. Atheneum, 1974.

———, ed. *Why Am I Grown So Cold? Poems of the Unknowable*. Atheneum, 1984.

———. *Worlds I Know*. Illustrated by Tim Arnold. McElderry, 1985.

Lobel, Arnold. *The Book of Pigericks*. Harper & Row, 1983.

Longfellow, Henry Wadsworth. *Hiawatha*. Illustrated by Susan Jeffers. Dial, 1983.

———. *Hiawatha's Childhood*. Illustrated by Errol Le Cain. Farrar, Straus & Giroux, 1984.

———. *Paul Revere's Ride*. Illustrated by Nancy Winslow Parker. Greenwillow, 1985.

———. *Paul Revere's Ride*. Illustrated by Ted Rand. Dutton, 1990.

McCord, David. *Every Time I Climb a Tree*. Illustrated by Marc Simont. Little, Brown, 1967.

———. *One at a Time*. Illustrated by Henry B. Kane. Little, Brown, 1977.

———. "The Song of the Train." In *One at a Time*, illustrated by Henry B. Kane. Little, Brown, 1977.

McNaughton, Colin. *Making Friends with Frankenstein: A Book of Monstrous Poems and Pictures*. Candlewick, 1994.

Merriam, Eve. *Bam Bam Bam*. Illustrated by Dan Yaccarino. Holt, 1995.

———. *Blackberry Ink*. Illustrated by Hans Wilhelm. Morrow, 1985.

———. *Chortles*. Illustrated by Sheila Hamanaka. Morrow, 1981.

———. "Cliché." In *A Skyful of Poems*, illustrated by Walter Gaffney-Kessell. Dell, 1986.

———. *Fresh Paint*. Illustrated by David Frampton. Macmillan, 1986.

———. *Higgle Wiggle: Happy Rhymes*. Illustrated by Hans Wilhelm. Morrow, 1994.

———. *It Doesn't Always Have to Rhyme*. Illustrated by Malcom Spooner. Atheneum, 1964.

———. *Jamboree: Rhymes for All Times*. Illustrated by Walter Gaffney-Kassell. Dell, 1984.

———. *Out Loud*. Illustrated by Harriet Sherman. Atheneum, 1973.

———. *A Poem for a Pickle*. Illustrated by Sheila Hamanaka. Macmillan, 1989.

———. *Quiet Please*. Illustrated by Sheila Hamanaka. Simon & Schuster, 1993.

———. "Satellite, Satellite." In *Jamboree: Rhymes for All Times*, illustrated by Walter Gaffney-Kassell. Dell, 1984.

———. *The Singing Green: New and Selected Poems for All Seasons*. Illustrated by Kathleen Collins Howell. Morrow, 1992.

———. "Throws of Threes." In *Fresh Paint*, illustrated by David Frampton. Macmillan, 1986.

———. *You Be Good & I'll Be Night*. Illustrated by Karen Lee Schmidt. Morrow, 1988.

Milne, A. A. *The World of Christopher Robin*. Illustrated by E. H. Shepard. Dutton, 1958.

Moore, Clement C. *The Night Before Christmas*. Illustrated by Tomie de Paola. Holiday House, 1980.

———. *The Night Before Christmas*. Illustrated by Grandma Moses. Random House, 1962.

———. *The Night Before Christmas*. Illustrated by Tasha Tudor. Macmillan, 1975.

———. *The Night Before Christmas*. Illustrated by Wendy Watson. Clarion, 1990.

Moore, Lilian, ed. *Go with the Poem*. McGraw-Hill, 1979.

———. *Something New Begins*. Illustrated by Mary J. Dunton. Atheneum, 1982.

———. *Sunflakes: Poems for Children*. Illustrated by Jan Ormerod. Clarion, 1992.

———. "Until I Saw the Sea." In *Sing A Song of Popcorn*, edited by Beatrice Shenk de Regniers et al., illustrated by nine Caldecott Medal artists. Scholastic, 1988.

Morrison, Lillian. *Whistling the Morning In*. Illustrated by Joel Cook. Wordsong/Boyds, 1992.

Nash, Ogden. *The Adventures of Isabel*. Illustrated by James Marshall. Little, Brown, 1991.

———. *Custard & Company*. Selected and illustrated by Quentin Blake. Little, Brown, 1980.

———. *The Tale of Custard the Dragon*. Illustrated by Lyn Munsinger. Little, Brown, 1995.

Norman, Charles. *The Hornbeam Tree and Other Poems*. Illustrated by Ted Rand. Henry Holt, 1988.

Noyes, Alfred. *The Highwayman*. Illustrated by Charles Keeping. Oxford University Press, 1981.

———. *The Highwayman*. Illustrated by Charles Mikolaycak. Lothrop, Lee & Shepard, 1983.

———. *The Highwayman*. Illustrated by Neil Waldman. Harcourt Brace, 1990.

Nye, Naomi Shihab. *This Same Sky: A Collection of Poems from Around the World*. Four Winds, 1992.

O'Neill, Mary. *Hailstones and Halibut Bones: Adventures in Color*. Illustrated by John Wallner. Philomel, 1989 [1961].

Panzer, Nora, ed. *Celebrate America: In Poetry and Art*. Hyperion, 1994.

Philip, Neil. *Singing America: Poems That Define a Nation*. Illustrated by Michael McCurdy. Viking, 1995.

Plotz, Helen, ed. *A Week of Lullabies*. Illustrated by Marisabina Russo. Greenwillow, 1988.

Pomerantz, Charlotte. *If I Had a Paka: Poems in Eleven Languages*. Illustrated by Nancy Tafuri. Greenwillow, 1993 [1982].

———. *The Tamarindo Puppy and Other Poems*. Illustrated by Byron Barton. Greenwillow, 1993 [1980].

Prelutsky, Jack, ed. *A. Nonny Mouse Writes Again*. Illustrated by Marjorie Priceman. Knopf, 1993.

———. *The Baby Uggs Are Hatching*. Illustrated by James Stevenson. Greenwillow, 1982.

———. *Beneath a Blue Umbrella*. Illustrated by Garth Williams. Greenwillow, 1990.

———. *The Dragons Are Singing Tonight*. Illustrated by Peter Sis. Greenwillow, 1993.

———, ed. *For Laughing Out Loud: Poems to Tickle Your Funnybone*. Illustrated by Marjorie Priceman. Knopf, 1991.

———. *The Headless Horseman: More Poems to Trouble Your Sleep*. Illustrated by Arnold Lobel. Greenwillow, 1977.

———. *It's Halloween*. Illustrated by Marylin Hafner. Greenwillow, 1977.

———. *It's Snowing! It's Snowing!*. Illustrated by Jeanne Titherington. Greenwillow, 1984.

———. *It's Thanksgiving*. Illustrated by Marylin Hafner. Greenwillow, 1982.

———. *Monday's Troll*. Illustrated by Peter Sis. Greenwillow, 1996.

———. *The New Kid on the Block*. Illustrated by James Stevenson. Greenwillow, 1984.

———. *Nightmares: Poems to Trouble Your Sleep*. Illustrated by Arnold Lobel. Greenwillow, 1976.

———, ed. *Poems by A. Nonny Mouse*. Illustrated by Henrik Drescher. Knopf, 1989.

———. *Rainy Rainy Saturday*. Illustrated by Marylin Hafner. Greenwillow, 1980.

———, ed. *The Random House Book of Poetry for Children*. Illustrated by Arnold Lobel. Random House, 1983.

———. *Read-Aloud Rhymes for the Very Young*. Illustrated by Marc Brown. Knopf, 1986.

———. *Ride a Purple Pelican*. Illustrated by Garth Williams. Greenwillow, 1986.

———. *Rolling Harvey Down the Hill*. Illustrated by Victoria Chess. Greenwillow, 1980.

———. *The Snopp on the Sidewalk and Other Poems*. Illustrated by Byron Barton. Greenwillow, 1977.

———. *Something Big Has Been Here*. Illustrated by James Stevenson. Greenwillow, 1990.

Rauter, Rose. "Peach." In *Knock at a Star: A Child's Introduction to Poetry*, edited by X. J. and Dorothy M. Kennedy, illustrated by Karen Ann Weinhaus. Little, Brown, 1982.

Rogasky, Barbara. *Winter Poems*. Illustrated by Trina Schart Hyman. Scholastic, 1994.

Rylant, Cynthia. *Waiting to Waltz: A Childhood*. Illustrated by Stephen Gammell. Bradbury, 1984.

Sandburg, Carl. *Arithmetic*. Illustrated by Ted Rand. Harcourt Brace, 1993.

———. *Early Moon*. Illustrated by James Daugherty. Harcourt Brace, 1930.

———. "Fog." In *The Random House Book of Poetry for Children*, edited by Jack Prelutsky, illustrated by Arnold Lobel. Random House, 1983.

———. *The People, Yes*. Harcourt Brace, 1936.

Schertle, Alice. *Advice for a Frog*. Illustrated by Norman Green. Lothrop, Lee & Shepard, 1995.

———. *How Now, Brown Cow?* Illustrated by Amanda Schaffer. Browndeer/Harcourt Brace, 1994.

Service, Robert W. *The Cremation of Sam McGee*. Illustrated by Ted Harrison. Greenwillow, 1987.

————. *The Shooting of Dan McGrew*. Illustrated by Ted Harrison. Godine, 1988.

Siebert, Diane. *Heartland*. Illustrated by Wendell Minor. Crowell, 1989.

————. *Mojave*. Illustrated by Wendell Minor. Crowell, 1988.

————. *Sierra*. Illustrated by Wendell Minor. Crowell, 1991.

Silverstein, Shel. *Falling Up*. HarperCollins, 1996.

————. *A Light in the Attic*. Harper & Row, 1981.

————. *Where the Sidewalk Ends: Poems and Drawings*. Harper & Row, 1974.

Singer, Marilyn. *Turtle in July*. Illustrated by Jerry Pinkney. Macmillan, 1989.

Small, Terry. *The Legend of William Tell*. Bantam, 1991.

Smith, William Jay. *Laughing Time*. Illustrated by Fernando Krahn. Delacorte, 1990 [1980].

Sneve, Virginia Driving Hawk. *Dancing Teepees*. Illustrated by Stephen Gammell. Holiday House, 1989.

Soto, Gary. *Neighborhood Odes*. Illustrated by David Diaz. Harcourt Brace, 1992.

Southey Robert. *The Cataract of Lodore*. Illustrated by David Catrow. Holt, 1992.

————. *The Cataract of Lodore*. Illustrated by Mordecai Gerstein. Dial, 1991.

Stevenson, Robert Louis. *Block City*. Illustrated by Ashley Wolff. Dutton, 1988.

————. *A Child's Garden of Verses*. Illustrated by Tasha Tudor. Oxford University Press, 1947 [1885].

————. *A Child's Garden of Verses*. Illustrated by Brian Wildsmith. Oxford University Press, 1966 [1885].

————. *My Shadow*. Illustrated by Ted Rand. Putnam, 1990.

Strickland, Dorothy S., and Michael R. Strickland. *Families: Poems Celebrating the African American Experience*. Illustrated by John Ward. Boyds Mills/Wordsong, 1994.

Strickland, Michael R. *Poems That Sing to You*. Illustrated by Alan Leiner. Boyds Mills/Wordsong, 1993.

Sullivan, Charles, ed. *Imaginary Gardens: American Poetry and Art for Young People*. Abrams, 1989.

Thayer, Ernest. *Casey at the Bat: A Ballad of the Republic, Sung in the Year 1888*. Illustrated by Wallace Tripp. Putnam, 1980.

————. *Casey at the Bat: A Centennial Edition*. Illustrated by Barry Moser. Godine, 1988.

Viorst, Judith. *If I Were in Charge of the World and Other Worries*. Illustrated by Lynne Cherry. Atheneum, 1982.

Volavkova, Hana, ed. . . . *I Never Saw Another Butterfly: Children's Drawings and Poems from Terezin Concentration Camp, 1942–1944*. Schocken, 1992.

Whipple, Laura, ed. *Eric Carle's Animals Animals*. Philomel, 1989.

————, ed. *Eric Carle's Dragons Dragons & Other Creatures That Never Were*. Philomel, 1991.

Whittier, John Greenleaf. *Barbara Frietchie*. Illustrated by Nancy Winslow Parker. Greenwillow, 1992.

Willard, Nancy A. *A Visit to William Blake's Inn*. Illustrated by Alice and Martin Provensen. Harcourt Brace, 1981.

Wilner, Isabel, compiler. *The Poetry Troupe: An Anthology of Poems to Read Aloud*. Scribner's, 1977.

Worth, Valerie. *All the Small Poems*. Illustrated by Natalie Babbitt. Farrar, Straus & Giroux, 1987.

————. *All the Small Poems and Fourteen More*. Illustrated by Natalie Babbitt. Farrar, Straus & Giroux, 1994.

————. "Mud." In *All the Small Poems and Fourteen More*, illustrated by Natalie Babbitt. Farrar, Straus & Giroux, 1994.

————. *Small Poems*. Illustrated by Natalie Babbitt. Farrar, Straus & Giroux, 1972.

Yolen, Jane. *The Three Bears Rhyme Book*. Illustrated by Jane Dyer. Harcourt Brace, 1987.

Prose

Alborough, Jez. *Where's My Teddy?* Candlewick, 1992.

Armstrong, William H. *Sounder*. Illustrated by James Barkley. Harper & Row, 1969.

Arnosky, Jim. *Secrets of a Wildlife Watcher*. Lothrop, Lee & Shepard, 1983.

Avi. *The True Confessions of Charlotte Doyle*. Orchard, 1990.

Babbitt, Natalie. *Tuck Everlasting*. Farrar, Straus & Giroux, 1975.

Baker, Jennie. *Window*. Greenwillow, 1991.

Bash, Barbara. *Ancient Ones: The World of the Old Growth Firs*. Sierra Club, 1994.

Baylor, Byrd. *Everybody Needs a Rock*. Illustrated by Peter Parnall. Scribner's, 1974.

———. *Hawk, I'm Your Brother*. Illustrated by Peter Parnall. Scribner's, 1976.

———. *I'm in Charge of Celebrations*. Illustrated by Peter Parnall. Scribner's, 1986.

———. *The Other Way to Listen*. Illustrated by Peter Parnall. Scribner's, 1978.

———. *The Way to Start a Day*. Illustrated by Peter Parnall. Scribner's, 1978.

———. *Your Own Best Secret Place*. Illustrated by Peter Parnall. Scribner's, 1979.

Brandenberg, Franz. *Aunt Nina, Goodnight*. Illustrated by Aliki. Greenwillow, 1989.

Brett, Jan. *Goldilocks and the Three Bears*. Dodd, Mead, 1987.

Brown, Marc. *Arthur's Family Vacation*. Joy Street, 1993.

Bryan, Ashley. *The Cat's Purr*. Atheneum, 1985.

Bunting, Eve. *The Wall*. Illustrated by Ronald Himler. Clarion, 1990.

———. *The Wednesday Surprise*. Illustrated by Donald Carrick. Clarion, 1989.

Burningham, John. *Come Away from the Water, Shirley*. Harper & Row, 1977.

———. *Granpa*. Crown, 1985.

Cameron, Ann. *The Most Beautiful Place in the World*. Illustrated by Thomas B. Allen. Knopf, 1988.

———. *The Stories Julian Tells*. Illustrated by Ann Strugnell. Knopf, 1981.

Carle, Eric. *The Mixed-Up Chameleon*. Crowell, 1984.

Carlstrom, Nancy W. *Blow Me a Kiss, Miss Lilly*. Illustrated by Amy Schwartz. HarperCollins, 1990.

Carrick, Carol, and Donald Carrick. *The Accident*. Seabury, 1976.

———. *Sleep Out*. Seabury, 1973.

Chall, Marsha Wilson. *Up North at the Cabin*. Illustrated by Steve Johnson. Lothrop, Lee & Shepard, 1992.

Cherry, Lynne. *The Great Kapok Tree*. Harcourt Brace. 1990.

Choi, Sook Nyul. *Year of Impossible Goodbyes*. Houghton, 1991.

Christopher, John. *When the Tripods Came*. Dutton, 1988.

Cohen, Miriam. *Lost in the Museum*. Illustrated by Lillian Hoban. Greenwillow, 1979.

———. *Will I Have a Friend?* Illustrated by Lillian Hoban. Macmillan, 1967.

Conrad, Pam. *Staying Nine*. Illustrated by Mike Wimmer. Harper & Row, 1988.

Cormier, Robert. *Other Bells for Us to Ring*. Illustrated by Deborah Kogan Ray. Delacorte, 1990.

Crews, Donald. *Freight Train*. Greenwillow, 1978.

Degen, Bruce. *Jamberry*. Harper & Row, 1983.

de Paola, Tomie. *Strega Nona*. Prentice Hall, 1975.

Dickinson, Peter. *Eva*. Delacorte, 1989.

Ehlert, Lois. *Color Farm*. Lippincott, 1990.

———. *Color Zoo*. Lippincott, 1989.

Farmer, Penelope. *The Ear, the Eye, and the Arm*. Orchard, 1994.

Fox, Mem. *Koala Lou*. Illustrated by Donald A. Mackay. Bradbury, 1968.

Fox, Paula. *The Stone-Faced Boy*. Illustrated by Donald A. Mackay. Bradbury, 1968.

Frank, Anne. *Anne Frank: Diary of a Young Girl*. Doubleday, 1952.

Freeman, Don. *Corduroy*. Viking, 1968.

———. *Dandelion*. Viking, 1964.

Galdone, Paul. *The Gingerbread Boy*. Clarion, 1979.

Gallaz, Christophe, and Roberto Innocenti. *Rose Blanche*. Illustrated by Roberto Innocenti. Creative Education, 1985.

George, Jean Craighead. *The Cry of the Crow*. Harper & Row, 1980.

———. *One Day in the Tropical Rain Forest*. Illustrated by Gary Allen. Crowell, 1990.

———. *On the Far Side of the Mountain*. Dutton, 1990.

———. *Who Really Killed Cock Robin?* HarperCollins, 1991 [1971].

Graeber, Charlotte. *Mustard*. Illustrated by Donna Diamond. Macmillan, 1982.

Greenfield, Eloise. *She Come Bringing Me That Little Baby Girl*. Illustrated by John Steptoe. Lippincott, 1974.

Grifalconi, Ann. *Osa's Pride*. Little, Brown, 1990.

Guarino, Deborah. *Is Your Mama a Llama?* Illustrated by Steven Kellogg. Scholastic, 1989.

Henkes, Kevin. *Julius, the Baby of the World*. Greenwillow, 1990.

Hoban, Russell. *A Baby Sister for Frances*. Illustrated by Lillian Hoban. Harper & Row, 1970.

———. *Bedtime for Frances*. Illustrated by Garth Williams. Harper & Row, 1960.

Hughes, Shirley. *Dogger*. Lothrop, Lee & Shepard, 1988.

Hutchins, Pat. *Titch*. Macmillan, 1971.

Huynh, Quang Nhuong. *The Land I Lost: Adventures of a Boy in Vietnam*. Illustrated by Vo-Dinh Mai. Harper & Row, 1982.

Jackson, Ellen. *Brown Cow, Green Grass, Yellow Mellow Sun*. Illustrated by Victoria Raymond. Hyperion, 1995.

Jarrell, Randall. *The Bat-Poet*. Illustrated by Maurice Sendak. Macmillan, 1964.

Jonas, Ann. *Color Dance*. Greenwillow, 1989.

———. *The Quilt*. Greenwillow, 1984.

Joosse, Barbara M. *Dinah's Mad, Bad Wishes*. Illustrated by Emily Arnold McCully. Harper & Row, 1989.

Keats, Ezra Jack. *Peter's Chair*. Harper & Row, 1967.

———. *Whistle for Willie*. Viking, 1964.

Konigsburg, Elaine. *From the Mixed-Up Files of Mrs. Basil E. Frankweiler*. Atheneum, 1967.

Koralek, Jenny. *The Boy and the Cloth of Dreams*. Illustrated by James Mayhew. Candlewick, 1994.

Kraus, Robert. *Leo, the Late Bloomer*. Illustrated by Jose Aruego. Harper & Row, 1987 [1971].

Lionni, Leo. *Alexander and the Wind-Up Mouse*. Pantheon, 1969.

———. *Little Blue and Little Yellow*. Astor-Honor, 1959.

Little, Jean. *Kate*. Harper & Row, 1971.

———. *Look Through My Window*. Illustrated by Joan Sandin. Harper & Row, 1970.

Lowry, Lois. *Anastasia Krupnik*. Houghton Mifflin, 1979.

———. *Number the Stars*. Houghton Mifflin, 1989.

MacDonald, Caroline. *The Lake at the End of the World*. Dial, 1989.

MacDonald, Golden. [Margaret Wise Brown]. *The Little Island*. Illustrated by Leonard Weisgard. Doubleday, 1946.

MacLachlan, Patricia. *Sarah, Plain and Tall*. Harper & Row, 1985.

Marshall, James. *The Three Little Pigs*. Dial, 1989.

Martin, Bill, Jr. *Brown Bear, Brown Bear, What Do You See?* Illustrated by Eric Carle. Henry Holt, 1983.

Maruki, Toshi. *Hiroshima No Pika* (The Flash of Hiroshima). Lothrop, Lee & Shepard, 1980.

Mayer, Mercer. *There's a Nightmare in My Closet*. Dial, 1968.

McCloskey, Robert. *Time of Wonder*. Viking, 1957.

McKee, David. *Elmer*. Lothrop, Lee & Shepard, 1989 [1968].

McPhail, David. *The Bear's Toothache*. Little, Brown, 1972.

Myers, Walter Dean. *Scorpions*. Harper & Row, 1988.

O'Brien, Robert. *Z for Zachariah*. Atheneum, 1975.

Paterson, Katherine. *Bridge to Terabithia*. Illustrated by Donna Diamond. Crowell, HarperCollins, 1977.

———. *Flip-Flop Girl*. Lodestar, 1994.

———. *Jacob Have I Loved*. Crowell, 1980.

———. *Lyddie*. Dutton, 1991.

Perrault, Charles. *Cinderella*. Retold by May Ehrlich. Illustrated by Susan Jeffers. Dial, 1985.

Roalf, Peggy. *Children*. Hyperion, 1993.

———. *Families*. Hyperion, 1992.

———. *Seascapes*. Hyperion, 1992.

Russo, Marisabina. *Why Do Grown-Ups Have All the Fun?* Greenwillow, 1987.

Rylant, Cynthia. *When I Was Young in the Mountains*. Illustrated by Diane Goode. Dutton, 1982.

Say, Allen. *The Lost Lake*. Houghton Mifflin, 1989.

Schlein, Miriam. *The Year of the Panda*. Illustrated by Kam Mak. Crowell, 1990.

Scieszka, Jon. *The Frog Prince Continued*. Illustrated by Steve Johnson. Viking, 1991.

———. *The True Story of the 3 Little Pigs!* Illustrated by Lane Smith. Viking, 1989.

Sheldon, Dyan. *The Whales' Song*. Illustrated by Gary Blythe. Dial, 1991.

Shulevitz, Uri. *Dawn*. Farrar, Straus & Giroux, 1974.

Sleator, William. *The Green Futures of Tycho*. Dutton, 1981.

Speare, Elizabeth. *The Sign of the Beaver*. Houghton Mifflin, 1983.

Spinelli, Jery. *Maniac Magee*. Little, Brown, 1990.

Stevenson, James. *What's Under My Bed?* Greenwillow, 1983.

Tarcov, Edith H. *The Frog Prince*. Illustrated by James Marshall. Scholastic, 1987.

Taylor, Mildred. *Roll of Thunder, Hear My Cry*. Dial, 1976.

Viorst, Judith. *Alexander and the Terrible, Horrible, No Good, Very Bad Day*. Illustrated by Ray Cruz. Atheneum, 1972.

———. *The Tenth Good Thing About Barney*. Illustrated by Erik Blegvad. Atheneum, 1971.

Voigt, Cynthia. *Homecoming*. Atheneum, 1983.

Waber, Bernard. *Ira Sleeps Over*. Houghton Mifflin, 1972.

Walsh, Jill Paton. *The Green Book*. Illustrated by Lloyd Bloom. Farrar, Straus & Giroux, 1982.

Wells, Rosemary. *Noisy Nora*. Dial, 1973.

Wild, Margaret. *The Very Best of Friends*. Illustrated by Julie Vivas. Harcourt Brace, 1990.

Williams, Vera B. *A Chair for My Mother*. Greenwillow, 1982.

Williams, Vera B., and Jennifer Williams. *Stringbean's Trip to the Shining Sea*. Greenwillow, 1988.

Wood, Audrey. *The Napping House*. Illustrated by Don Wood. Harcourt Brace, 1984.

Zolotow, Charlotte. *The Hating Book*. Illustrated by Ben Shecter. Harper & Row, 1969.

———. *Mr. Rabbit and the Lovely Present*. Illustrated by Maurice Sendak. Harper & Row, 1962.

chapter nine

Contemporary Realistic Fiction

Realism in Contemporary Children's Literature 454

The Value of Contemporary Fiction 454

Issues Relating to Realistic Fiction 456

What Is Real? 456

How Real May a Children's Book Be? 456

Bias and Stereotyping 457

The Author's Background 458

Categorizing Literature 459

Becoming One's Own Person 459

Living in a Family 459

Family Relationships 460

Extended Families 461

Families in Transition 464

Living with Others 466

Finding Peer Acceptance 466

Making Friends 467

Growing Toward Maturity 468

Developing Sexuality 468

Finding Oneself 470

Survival Stories 472

Coping with Problems of the Human Condition 475

Physical Disabilities 475

Developmental and Learning Disabilities 476

Mental Illness 477

Aging and Death 478

Aging 478

Death and Dying 480

Living in a Diverse World 482

Appreciating Racial and Ethnic Diversity 483

African American Experiences in Books for Children 483

Guidelines: Evaluating Multicultural Literature 484

Books About Other Minorities 486

Understanding Various World Cultures 488

Popular Types of Realistic Fiction 491

Teaching Feature: Teachers Discuss Literature by and About Minorities 492

Humorous Stories 492

Resources for Teaching: "To Be Continued"—Popular Series Books for Children 493

Animal Stories 496

Sports Stories 498

School Stories 499

Mysteries 501

Learning Experiences 503

Related Readings 504

Children's Literature 505

Gilly in Me

I think I am a lot like Gilly in some ways. One way is everything somebody says I can't do, I have to show them that I can do it or something like it. I think Gilly and I feel the same way about foster parents. If I had foster parents, I probably would feel that my mother would come and get me; but I wouldn't run away or steal money.

In school I don't act like she does, going to the principal or slipping notes in teacher's books. It seems she doesn't like to be with her friends. I like to be around with my friends. I don't like to be by myself. I think Gilly gets mad easy. I get mad easy like getting called names. I always have to call them a name back.

Amy Kauffman, seventh grade
Delaware Public Schools, Ohio
Christy Slavik, teacher

A small group of seventh graders read Katherine Paterson's *The Great Gilly Hopkins* in their in-depth reading group. One of their options when they finished the book was to write about ways they were like Gilly and different from Gilly. Obviously, Amy had identified with the character of Gilly Hopkins. By contrasting her perception of herself with Gilly, she learned more about Gilly and developed insight into her own personality.

A well-written contemporary story should do more than just mirror modern life. It should take children inside a character and help them understand the causes of behavior; at the same time it should take them outside themselves to reflect on their own behavior. *The Great Gilly Hopkins* had opened a window of understanding for Amy and let her view herself and the world with slightly changed perception.

Realism in Contemporary Children's Literature

Realistic fiction may be defined as imaginative writing that accurately reflects life as it was lived in the past or could be lived today. Everything in such a story can conceivably happen to real people living in our natural physical world, in contrast to fantasy, where impossible happenings are made to appear quite plausible even though they are not possible. Historical fiction (see Chapter 10) portrays life as it may have been lived in the past; contemporary realism focuses on the problems of living today. Though other genres in children's literature, such as fantasy, are popular, children consistently are found to prefer realistic fiction. The books discussed in this chapter can be categorized as contemporary realistic fiction for children. Many of these are stories about growing up today and finding a place in the family, among peers, and in modern society. In addition, aspects of coping with the problems of the human condition may be found in contemporary literature for children. Books that are humorous or reflect special

interests—such as animal or sports stories and mysteries—are also classified as realistic literature and so are included in this chapter.

The content of contemporary realism for children has changed dramatically in the past thirty years. These changes have provoked controversy among writers, critics, librarians, teachers, and parents. For this reason we give attention to some of the values of contemporary realism for children and some of these issues.

The Value of Contemporary Fiction

Realistic fiction serves children in the process of understanding and coming to terms with themselves as they acquire "human-ness." Books that honestly portray the realities of life help children gain a fuller understanding of human problems and human relationships and, thus, a fuller understanding of themselves and their own potential. In describing her purpose in writing for children, Nina Bawden states:

If a children's writer presents his characters honestly and is truthful about their thoughts and their feelings, he is giving his readers "a means to gain a hold on fate" by showing them that they can trust their thoughts and their feelings, that they can have faith in themselves. He can also show them a bit of the world, the beginning of the path they have to tread; but the most important thing he has to offer is a little hope and courage for the journey.[1]

This is not a function unique to contemporary realism. Other types of books can show children a slice of the world. Some fantasy is nearer to truth than realism; biography and autobiography frequently provide readers with models of human beings who offer "hope and courage for the journey." The ability to maintain one's humanity and courage in the midst of deprivation is highlighted in *Number the Stars*, Lois Lowry's story about Danish efforts to save Jewish citizens in World War II. Personal bravery and responsible behavior under dire circumstances is also one of the themes of the high fantasy *A Wizard of Earthsea* by Ursula Le Guin. However, most children appear to identify more readily with characters in books of contemporary realism than with those of historical fiction or fantasy.

Realistic fiction helps children enlarge their frames of reference while seeing the world from another perspective. For example, human rights abuses in Haiti are strongly realized in Frances Temple's *Taste of Salt*, and children who are repelled by elderly people might come to understand them as real people through Janet Hickman's *Jericho*. Stories like these help young people develop compassion for and an understanding of human actions.

Realistic fiction also reassures young people that they are not the first in the world to have faced problems. In Marion Dane Bauer's *A Question of Trust* they read of other children whose parents have divorced; in Betsy Byars's *The Burning Questions of Bingo Brown*, they read about someone concerned about relationships with the opposite sex. They gain some solace from recognizing the problems a ghetto environment poses for Jamal in Walter Dean Myers's *Scorpions*. This knowledge that they are not alone brings a kind of comfort to child readers. James Baldwin recognized the power of books to alleviate pain:

You think your pain and your heartbreak are unprecedented in the history of the world, but then you read. It was books that taught me that the things that tormented me the most were the very things that connected me with all the people who were alive, or who had ever been alive.[2]

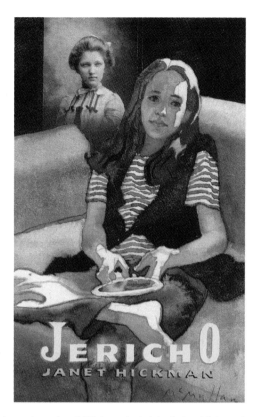

Books such as Janet Hickman's *Jericho* help children view contemporary problems from many perspectives.
Cover of *Jericho* by Janet Hickman. Jacket illustration by James McMullan. Jacket illustration copyright © 1994 by James McMullan. By permission of Greenwillow Books, a division of William Morrow & Company, Inc.

Realistic fiction can also illuminate experiences that children have not had. A child with loving parents whose only chore consists of making a bed may have a deeper need to read Marilyn Sachs's *The Bears' House* than a child of poverty whose life may more nearly be reflected in the story. A child who takes school for granted might gain much from Ann Cameron's poignant *The Most Beautiful Place in the World*, about a Guatemalan who desperately wants an education. Realistic fiction can be a way of experiencing a world we do not know.

Some books also serve as a kind of preparation for living. Far better to have read Katherine Paterson's *Bridge to Terabithia* or Cynthia Voigt's *Dicey's Song* than to experience firsthand at age 10 or 12 the death of your best friend or your mother. For many years, death was a taboo subject in children's literature. Yet, as children face the honest realities of life in books, they are developing a kind of courage for facing problems in their own lives. Madeleine L'Engle, whose *Meet the Austins* was among the first works of modern children's literature to treat the subject of death, maintained that "to pretend there is no darkness is another way of extinguishing light."[3]

[1]Nina Bawden, "Emotional Realism in Books for Young People," *Horn Book Magazine*, February 1980, p. 33.

[2]James Baldwin, "Talk to Teachers," *Saturday Review*, 21 December 1963, pp. 42–44, 60.

[3]Madeleine L'Engle, in a speech before the Florida Library Association, May 1965, Miami.

Realistic fiction for children does provide many possible models, both good and bad, for coping with problems of the human condition. As children experience these stories, they may begin to filter out some meaning for their own lives. This allows children to organize and shape their own thinking about life as they follow, through stories, the lives of others.

Issues Relating to Realistic Fiction

More controversy surrounds the writing of contemporary realistic fiction for children than perhaps any other kind of literature. Everyone is a critic of realism, for everyone feels he or she is an expert on what is real in today's world. But realities clash, and the fact that "what is real for one may not be real for another" is a true and lively issue. Some of the questions that seem uniquely related to contemporary realism in writing for children need to be examined.

What Is Real?

The question of what is "real" or "true to life" is a significant one. C. S. Lewis, the British author of the well-known Narnia stories (see Chapter 7) described three types of realistic content:

🐾 But when we say, "The sort of thing that happens," do we mean the sort of thing that usually or often happens, the sort of thing that is typical of the human lot? Or do we mean "The sort of thing that might conceivably happen or that, by a thousandth chance, may have happened once?"[4]

Middle graders reading the Narnia series know that these stories are fantasy and couldn't happen in reality. However, middle graders might read stories like Vera and Bill Cleaver's *Where the Lilies Bloom* or Gary Paulsen's *Hatchet* and believe that children can survive any hardship or crisis if only they possess determination. These well-written books cast believable characters in realistic settings facing real problems. But an adult reader might question whether this is the sort of thing that "by a thousandth chance, may have happened once."

How Real May a Children's Book Be?

Controversy also centers on how much graphic detail may be included in a book for children. How much violence is too much? How explicit may an author be in describing bodily functions or sexual relations? These

are questions that no one would have asked thirty-five years ago. But there are new freedoms today. Childhood is not the innocent time we like to think it is (and it probably never was). Although youth might not need protection, they do still need the perspective that literature can give. A well-written book makes the reader aware of the human suffering resulting from inhumane acts by others, whereas television and films are more apt to concentrate on the acts themselves.

The TV newscasts of the local Saturday-night killings or the body count in the latest "peacekeeping" effort seldom show the pain and anguish that each death causes. The rebuilding of human lives is too slow and tedious to portray in a half-hour newscast. Even video games are based on violence. The winner of the game is the one who can eliminate or destroy the "enemy." Reasons or motivations are never given, and the aftereffects are not a part of the game.

By way of contrast to the media world, a well-written story provides perspective on the pain and suffering of humankind. In a literary story the author has time to develop the characters into fully rounded human beings. The reader knows the motives and pressures of each individual and can understand and empathize with the characters. If the author's tone is one of compassion for the characters, if others in the story show concern or horror for a brutal act, the reader gains perspective.

A story that makes violence understandable without condoning it is Suzanne Fisher Staples's *Shabanu, Daughter of the Wind*. In the Pakistani desert culture in which 12-year-old Shabanu lives, obedience to rules has enabled many tribes to live in peace in an environment that offers little material comfort. When Shabanu runs away to avoid an arranged marriage to a middle-aged man, she discovers her favorite camel has broken its leg. In choosing to remain with the camel, Shabanu tacitly agrees to the rules of her clan. Her father catches up with her and beats her severely. But she is soaked with his tears as he does what he must, and the reader realizes both are trapped in roles their society has defined for them.

James Giblin, a former children's book editor, suggests that a book can be realistic without being overly graphic.

🐾 For instance, if the young detective in a mystery story was attacked by a gang of bullies, I wouldn't encourage an author to have them burn his arms with a cigarette to get him to talk (although that might conceivably happen in an adult mystery). However, I would accept a scene in which the gang *threatened* to do so: that would convey the reality and danger of the situation without indulging in all the gory details.[5]

---

[4]C. S. Lewis, *An Experiment in Criticism* (Cambridge: Cambridge University Press, 1961), p. 57.

[5]James Cross Giblin, *Writing Books for Young People* (Boston: The Writer, 1990), p. 73.

Giblin maintains that very few subjects are inappropriate in themselves; it is all in how the author treats them. The facts of a situation, ugly as they may be, can be presented with feeling and depth of emotion, which carry the reader beyond the particular subject.

The same criteria are appropriate for evaluating explicitness about sex and bodily functions in books for children. Betty Miles raises this issue in *Maudie and Me and the Dirty Book*. When seventh grader Kate Harris teams up with a classmate to read aloud to first graders, one of her choices—a story about a puppy being born—triggers a discussion among the 6-year-olds about human birth and conception. While Kate handles the discussion with poise, a parent complaint eventually brings about a town meeting concerning what is appropriate in the elementary classroom curriculum. Miles treats the topics of conception, birth, and censorship in an open and forthright way.

Bias and Stereotyping

Children's books have always reflected the general social and human values of a society, so it is not surprising they are also scrutinized for implied attitudes or biases of that society. Contemporary realistic fiction is examined for racism, cultural inaccuracies, sexism, ageism, and treatment of people with physical or mental impairments. Because consciousness generally has been raised in the world of children's book publishing, there are now more books that present diverse populations positively and fairly.

The political and social activism of the 1960s contributed to an awareness of racism in children's books. (See the section "Appreciating Racial and Ethnic Diversity" later in this chapter.) In the 1980s and 1990s, children have been able to find fully realized African American characters in books such as Virginia Hamilton's *Cousins*, Jacqueline Woodson's *I Hadn't Meant to Tell You This*, Walter Dean Myers's *Darnell Rock Reporting*, and Jerry Spinelli's *Maniac Magee*; these characters exist in their own right and not so that a white main character may "find" herself or himself. Still, adults need to be alert to reissues of books from an earlier era—such as the 1945 Newbery Honor Book *The Silver Pencil*,[6] which has many racist descriptions of people in Trinidad. Books like this help us recognize the gains of recent decades.

Because feminists in the 1970s made us more aware of the subtle ways in which literature has perpetuated stereotypes, contemporary realistic fiction now does a much better job of portraying women in a variety of roles. Capable working mothers; caring female role models outside of a child's family; characters who fight sexism; intelligent, independent, and strong girls and women; and romance as a consequence of strong friendship are all found in realistic fiction of the present decade.

Decrying a work of historical realistic fiction as sexist has its own problems. Elizabeth George Speare's *The Witch of Blackbird Pond* has been criticized for depicting the heroine as someone whose greatest problem is deciding who to marry. But in 1688, Kit had little other choice. Again, there is no point in denouncing fairy tales for their sexist portrayal of evil stepmothers, nagging wives, or beautiful young girls waiting for the arrival of princes. Such stories reflect the longings and beliefs of a society long past. To change the folktales would be to destroy our traditional heritage. A book should not, then, be criticized for being historically authentic or true to its traditional genre. However, we have every right to be critical when such stereotyped thinking is perpetuated in contemporary literature.

Boys have also been subtly victimized by the stereotypes of the past. They have been consistently reminded that men and boys don't cry, for example. But more-modern realistic fiction shows that everyone may cry as they grieve, as do a boy and his father following the drowning of a friend in *On My Honor* by Marion Dane Bauer or following the death of a beloved old cat in *Mustard* by Charlotte Graeber. Boys have also been frequently stereotyped in animal stories as having to kill an animal they have loved as an initiation rite. In Marjorie Kinnan Rawlings's *The Yearling*, for instance, Jody is ordered to shoot his pet deer because it is destroying the family crops: "He did not believe he should ever again love anything, man or woman or his own child, as he loved the Yearling. He would be lonely all his life. But a man took it for his share and went on" (p. 400). In Fred Gipson's *Old Yeller*, after the boy shoots his possibly rabid dog, his father tells him to try to forget and go on being a man. Stories such as these cause us to question the way some of our best literature conditions boys to be hard and strong.

People with mental or physical impairments have in the past been depicted as "handicapped" or "disabled." A more enlightened view suggests that the person in front of the impairment is more important than the impairment; one can be differently abled without necessarily being disabled. Older people (and other adults) in children's literature have often been dismissed to an irrelevant position in a young person's life, as ineffectual in contrast to the vibrancy of young spirits, or as unable to do certain things because of their age. (See the section "Coping with Problems of the Human Condition" later in this chapter.) High-quality contemporary realistic fiction stories depict adults and the elderly in many ways—as mentors to a young person, for instance, and as having their own romances, problems, and triumphs.

---

[6]Alice Dalgliesh, *The Silver Pencil* (New York: Puffin, 1991 [1944]).

Illustrator Ann Strugnell portrays a likable African American family in *More Stories Julian Tells* by Ann Cameron.
From *More Stories Julian Tells* by Ann Cameron, illustrated by Ann Strugnell. Illustrations copyright © 1986 by Ann Strugnell. Reprinted by permission of Alfred A. Knopf, Inc.

Children's books have made great gains in the depiction of our changing society. However, today's books need to continue to reflect the wide ranges of occupations, education, speech patterns, lifestyles, and futures that are possible for all, regardless of race, gender, age, or belief.

The Author's Background

Another controversy swirls around authors' racial backgrounds. Must an author be black to write about African Americans, or Native American to write about Native Americans? As Virginia Hamilton states:

> It happens that I know Black people better than any other people because I am one of them and I grew up knowing what it is we are about. . . . The writer uses the most comfortable milieu in which to tell a story, which is why my characters are Black. Often being Black is significant to the story; other times, it is not. The writer will always attempt to tell stories no one else can tell.[7]

It has been generally accepted that an author should write about what she or he knows. But Ann Cameron, the white author of *The Stories Julian Tells*, *More Stories Julian Tells*, and other books about an African American family, maintains a different point of view:

> It seems to me that the people who advise "write about what you know" drastically underestimate the human capacity for imagining what lies beyond our immediate knowledge and for understanding what is new to us. Equally, they overestimate the extent to which we know ourselves. A culture, like a person, has blind spots. . . . Often the writer who is an outsider—an African writing about the United States, an American writing about China—sees in a way that enriches him as an observer, the culture he observes, and the culture he comes from.[8]

The hallmark of fine writing is the quality of imagining it calls forth from us. Imagination is not the exclusive trait of any race or gender but is a universal quality of all fine writers. No authors or artists want to be limited to writing about or portraying only the experiences of persons of a single race or cultural background, nor should they be. We need to focus on two aspects of every book: (1) What is its literary merit? and (2) Will children enjoy it?

[7]Virginia Hamilton, "Writing the Source: In Other Words," *Horn Book Magazine*, December 1978, p. 618.

[8]Ann Cameron, "Write What You Care About," *School Library Journal* 35, no. 10 (June 1989): 50.

Categorizing Literature

Reviewers, educators, and curriculum makers often categorize books according to their content. Categorizing serves textbook authors by allowing them to talk about several books as a group. It serves educators who hope to group books around a particular theme for classroom study. While one person might place Paterson's *Bridge to Terabithia* in a group of books about "making friends," it could just as easily be placed in other groups, such as books about "growing up" or "learning to accept death," or "well-written books." It is a disservice to both book and reader if, in labeling a book, we imply that this is all the book is about. Readers with their own purposes and backgrounds will see many different aspects and strengths in a piece of literature. It is helpful to remember that our experiences with art occur at many different, unique, and personal levels. Even though teachers might wish to lead children to talk about a particular aspect of a book, they will not want to suggest that this is the only aspect worth pursuing. Author Jean Little argues that teachers need to trust children to find their own messages in books.

Individual readers come to each story at a slightly different point in their life's journey. If nobody comes between them and the book, they may discover within it some insight they require, a rest they long for, a point of view that challenges their own, a friend they may cherish for life. If we, in the guise of mentor, have all the good messages listed or discussed in small groups . . . the individual and vitally important meeting of child and story may never happen.[9]

A second issue in the categorizing of literature is age-appropriateness. Realistic fiction is often categorized as being for upper elementary or middle-grade and junior high or young-adult (YA) readers. Yet anyone who has spent time with 9- to 14-year-old readers has surely noticed the wide ranges of reading interests, abilities, and perceptions present. Betsy Byars's *The Pinballs* and Judy Blume's *Are You There, God? It's Me, Margaret* have challenged and entertained readers from fourth grade through high school. To suggest that these titles are only "for 10- to 12-year-old readers" would ignore the ages of half of the readership of these popular authors.

In this chapter, books are arranged according to categories based on theme and content merely for the convenience of discussion. They could have been arranged in many other ways. The ages of main characters are noted, where appropriate, as a clue to potential readership. In some instances we have also noted, with references to actual classroom teachers' experiences, at which grade levels certain titles seem to have the greatest impact.

Becoming One's Own Person

The story of every man and every woman is the story of growing up, of becoming a person, of struggling to become one's own person. The kind of person you become has its roots in your childhood experiences—how much you were loved, how little you were loved; the people who were significant to you, the ones who were not; the places you've been, and those you did not go to; the things you had, and the things you did not get. Yet a person is always more than the totality of these experiences; the way a person organizes, understands, and relates to those experiences makes for individuality.

Childhood is not a waiting room for adulthood but the place where adulthood is shaped by one's family, peers, society, and, most importantly, the person one is becoming. The passage from childhood to adulthood is a significant journey for each person. It is no wonder that children's literature is filled with stories about growing up in our society today.

Living in a Family

The human personality is nurtured within the family; here the growing child learns of love and hate, fear and courage, joy and sorrow. The first "family life" stories tended to portray families without moments of anger and hurt, emphasizing only the happy or adventurous moments. Today the balance scale has tilted in the other direction, and it is often more difficult to find a family story with well-adjusted children and happily married parents than it is to find a story about family problems.

Children still enjoy series such as Eleanor Estes's pre-television-era books *The Moffats*, *The Middle Moffat*, and *Rufus M*, or Sidney Taylor's All-of-a-Kind Family series, which recreates family life in a Lower East Side Jewish home in the 1930s, and adults often point to them as evidence of the pleasures of a less fast-paced life. However, many young readers prefer stories about today's children, those they might meet in the neighborhood, the shopping center, a playground, or the classroom. More recent books include adults with both strengths and weaknesses and show children interacting with them, although formula stories might depict

[9]Jean Little, "A Writer's Social Responsibility," *New Advocate* 3 (spring 1990): 83

parents and adults as completely inept and unable to cope with or understand their children. If children are to see life wholly and gain some perspective from their reading, educators must help children balance their reading choices.

Family Relationships

Episodic stories centered comfortably in a warm family setting are often the first chapter-book stories younger children read independently. Young readers who more readily follow episodic rather than complicated plots find Johanna Hurwitz's Russell and Elisa stories satisfying reading. Chapters alternate between 4-year-old Elisa and her older brother, Russell, who is 7. Hurwitz portrays character through authentic dialogue and description of the small tensions that make up many children's lives. Sibling rivalry, an older child's scorn for the younger one and the younger one's revenge, and exasperated but patient parents who set limits and warn of consequences are familiar to most readers.

Beverly Cleary's perennially popular and humorous stories about Ramona are enjoyed both by 7- to 9-year-olds who identify with Ramona's problems, and by 10- and 11-year-olds who remember "how I used to be." Cleary's stories concern "the problems which are small to adults but which loom so large in the lives of children, the sort of problems children can solve themselves."[10] In *Ramona the Pest*, Ramona can hardly wait for kindergarten to begin so that she can share her doll with the green hair, named "Chevrolet" after her aunt's car. The green hair is a result of the doll's encounter with soap and Dutch Cleanser. In *Ramona and Her Mother*, Ramona worries that her mother doesn't love her as much as she loves Beezus, her older sister. In *Ramona and Her Father*, Ramona is able to be with her father more often now that she returns from school to find him waiting for telephone calls about jobs he has applied for. In *Ramona Forever*, Ramona's favorite aunt marries, the family's pet cat dies, and Mrs. Quimby expects a new baby. Still a third grader, but a more mature, *older* sister now, Ramona continues to be her irrepressible dramatic self. Ramona and her family are people worth knowing.

In Lois Lowry's *Anastasia Krupnik*, Anastasia is the only girl in fourth grade whose name will not fit on the front of a sweatshirt. To top off the list of "Things I Love/Things I Hate" that Anastasia keeps, one of the things she is sure she is going to hate is the arrival of a new baby brother. In an effort to appease her, Anastasia's parents let her choose the baby's name, and she

considers the worst ones possible. But the death of her grandmother gives Anastasia some thoughts about the importance of family and of memories—and the new baby is named Sam after her grandfather, whom Anastasia knows only through the reminiscences of her grandmother. Each succeeding novel in the Anastasia series chronicles some new quandary—a move to the Boston suburbs, a stint as a maid, a growing need to talk to someone who understands, and managing the household while her mother is away. In Lowry's stories, the Krupnik parents treat Anastasia and her brother with openness, humor, and respect; they are both literate and concerned parents whose careers as artist and English teacher do not interfere with their interactions with Anastasia. Lowry has a gift for natural-sounding dialogue and situational humor, anchored by keen observations of human nature and family relationships. She has also told baby brother Sam's story in the hilarious *All About Sam* and *Attaboy, Sam*.

A very different family life is portrayed by Paula Fox in *The Stone-Faced Boy*. Gus, a middle child, has learned to keep an expressionless face when his brothers and sisters tease him, thus earning himself the nickname "Stone-Face." During a snowstorm, his visiting great-aunt gives him a geode. That night Gus is talked into rescuing a stray dog that his sister has found in a fox trap. Although Gus is terrified, he does rescue the dog, and the experience changes him so that when his brother goads him to break open the geode, he refuses:

> He knew how the stone would look inside, but he didn't choose to break it open yet. When he felt like it, he would take the hammer and tap the geode in such a way that it would break perfectly. (p. 106)

For behind Gus's stone face lies a personality as intact and as perfect as the crystals of the geode.

No book has revealed the complexities of sibling rivalry with as much depth as Katherine Paterson's challenging Newbery Medal–winning story *Jacob Have I Loved*. Louise is convinced that she lives in her twin sister's shadow. Caroline, her beautiful, blond, delicate sister, is the talented one, who leaves their island home of Rass each week to take piano lessons. Louise, or "Wheeze," the hated name Caroline has given her, believes her sister has stolen everything from her: her parents' affection, her friends Call and the Captain, and her chance for an education. Her half-crazed Bible-quoting grandmother recognizes her burning resentment of Caroline and taunts her with the quote "Jacob have I loved but Esau have I hated."

Paterson has skillfully woven the Bible story of Esau, firstborn, who was tricked into giving up his birthright to Jacob, the younger of the twin brothers, into this modern novel of sibling rivalry. Only maturity and a

---

[10]Beverly Cleary, "The Laughter of Children," *Horn Book Magazine*, October 1982, p. 557.

family of her own can help Louise to put her hatred and resentment of her sister to rest. The novel ends on a theme of reconciliation as Louise, now a midwife in a mountain community, fights to save the life of the weaker second-born baby of a pair of twins. In her Newbery acceptance speech for *Jacob Have I Loved*, the author, herself the middle child of five, said: "among children who grow up together in a family there run depths of feeling that will permeate their souls for good and ill as long as they live."[11]

Adolescence also seems to be a time for sometimes bitter conflicts between parents and children. In Keven Henkes's *Protecting Marie*, 12-year-old Fanny finds it difficult to deal with her temperamental father's inconsistencies at the same time as she is thrust into the inconsistencies of early adolescence. When her artist father presents her with the puppy she has longed for all her life and then gives it away because it interferes with his painting, Fanny is devastated. Although her father repents and brings home Dinner, an older, better-trained dog, Fanny finds that she cannot trust him, and their alienation increases. When the dog disappears one afternoon, Fanny is sure Henry has given this one away, too. When Henry returns home with Dinner, Fanny reveals her fear of him. "You don't understand me sometimes," she whispered, her voice changing sharply as her emotions rose. "I'm always worrying that you're going to take something away from me" (p. 177). In response Henry reveals something of his own vulnerabilty. There are strong enough bonds of love in this family that, with the stabilizing element of Fanny's mother, there is a final promise of an improved relationship for Fanny and Henry and a permanent home for Dinner.

Several books for older readers examine complex mother-daughter relationships and the conflicts between two generations that seem to intensify during adolescence. In Maude Casey's *Over the Water*, Mary, a 14-year-old Irish Catholic girl living with her family in London, is isolated from friends by her own anger and her mother's fear and bitterness at having had to leave her beloved Irish farm. When the family returns to the farm for the summer, Mammy's strictness gets even worse and Mary's resentment deepens. But over the course of the visit, as her grandmother and Aunt Nuala act as buffers between the two, Mary comes to appreciate the strong community that exists in the Irish countryside and to revel in its quiet beauty after the grimy, gray city landscape of London. There is no easy resolution to the conflict between Mary and her mother, but at the end Mary begins to understand something of her mother's sacrifices. On the night before they are to leave, Mammy breaks down in Nuala's arms and weeps bitterly at the thought of returning to the city. Mary thinks,

This is the first time I've ever seen her cry, but I know she must have felt sorrow before . . . after Dadda [Grandfather] died for instance. Has she always done her crying away from us, in secret, then? Doesn't she think we could help her? Oh, Mammy! I close my eyes and squeeze them to stop my tears from falling. Will I be able to help her in England? Or am I a stranger to her, this daughter of hers who was born in a foreign land? (p. 238)

Mary resolves to learn how to open doors for her mother as she hopes to open them for herself, "instead of standing lonely, with my eyes closed behind them." This is not a pat ending with a grand reconciliation. Instead Casey has painted excruciatingly painful pictures of real people as they exist in complex family relationships within a society that is less than ideal.

Canadian writer Budge Wilson has two collections of exquisitely written short stories that explore parent-child relationships and other conflicts of adolescence. *The Leaving*, which won the Canadian Library Association Young Adult Book Award, explores the painful, sometimes funny journeys of nine girls moving into the adult world. "The Pen Pal" holds a wonderfully funny surprise ending, but the other eight stories are more poignant, told by adult women looking back on their youth but never losing the adolescent's point of view. Wilson's *The Dandelion Garden* is told from a similar perspective but is broader in the scope of relationships it examines and the tenor of the stories. "The Canoe Trip" is the tale of a father who is determined not to be like his own demanding father yet falls into the same patterns on a canoe trip with his young son. The title story is a modern-day fable about adult expectations and how quickly they can kill a child's imagination. The quality of Wilson's writing makes these stories wonderful choices for middle school read-alouds, but adolescents will also want to take time to savor, in response journals and small-group discussions, the accuracy of the author's perceptions about youth and her beautiful writing.

Extended Families

The extended family of grandparents, uncles, aunts, cousins, and so on, often plays a significant role in a child's developing perception of the world. Children's literature presents other adults, and sometimes even children, acting in the place of absent or incapacitated parents.

---

[11]Katherine Paterson, "Newbery Medal Acceptance," in *Gates of Excellence* (New York: Elsevier/Nelson Books, 1981), p. 118.

I See the Moon by C. B. Christiansen is written in the form of a letter to a young niece by her Aunt Bitte. At 12, Bitte is thrilled at the news that she is to become an aunt and imagines all of the things she will do with and for the baby when it arrives. She is shocked to find out that her unmarried 15-year-old sister is planning to give the baby up and has met the childless couple she has chosen as the parents. Bitte goes on a campaign to change Kari's mind and is finally sent to stay with her favorite uncle and aunt until after the baby is born. Changes have also come to these two, for Bitte finds that Aunt Minna is in a nursing home, ill with Alzheimer's disease. When Bitte begins to menstruate, Uncle Axel helps her to accept these changes, and to leave behind her unrealistic childish daydreams. She meets Jacob and Hope, her niece's adoptive parents, and when they come to the hospital to take the baby home, she is able to let go. She understands finally that "love is a circle, full as the moon," and that, separate but linked together, she, her family, Jacob, Hope, and the baby are part of the same constellation.

Patricia MacLachlan's *Arthur for the Very First Time* chronicles the summer of a 10-year-old boy. From the moment his parents drop him off at the farm of idiosyncratic Uncle Wrisby and Aunt Elda, Arthur begins to change. His aunt and uncle speak French to a pet chicken, sing to a pig, and allow Arthur to check off the foods he doesn't like to eat. His new friend Moira is bothered by Arthur's introspective nature. Refusing to call Arthur anything but "Mouse," she accuses him of spending so much time writing in his journal that he doesn't really see what is going on around him. When Arthur saves a piglet from dying and protects its mother from the rain with Moira's help, however, she excitedly tells everyone "Arthur did it . . . Arthur really *did* it." She has called him "Arthur" for the very first time. MacLachlan's story is full of warmth, humor, and quirky characters, both human and animal.

MacLachlan's *Journey* is the story of an 11-year-old boy named Journey who is devastated and angered when his mother leaves him with his grandparents. He cannot accept the fact that his mother is gone—not for the summer, but for good. His loving grandparents, a cat named Bloom, and his grandfather's photographs finally help him to accept the loss of his mother. His grandfather has told him that "sometimes pictures show us what is really there," and later his sister explains that the collection of photographs his grandfather has taken represent his grandfather's efforts to give him back everything that his mother took away. Journey understands then that his grandparents, unlike his mother, have given him the family he has longed for. MacLachlan's writing respects readers' intelligence, and these two books suggest that what is important or real is often at first difficult to see.

In Betsy Byars's *The House of Wings*, Sammy's parents leave him behind with his aged grandfather, a recluse in an old run-down house, while they go ahead to find a place to stay in Detroit. When Sammy refuses to believe his parents have left and tries to follow them, the old man runs after the furious boy. But in the midst of the chase he calls him to come and look at a wounded crane. Together the two of them catch the crane and care for it. Suddenly the boy desperately wants his grandfather to know him the way he knows birds:

🐛 He wanted his grandfather to be able to pick him out of a thousand birds the way he could pick out the blackbird, the owls, the wild ducks. . . . He said, "My name's Sammy." (p. 141)

His grandfather looks at Sammy and then, instead of calling him "Boy," calls him "Sammy," and the relationship is sealed. This is one of Betsy Byars's best books. Her two characters are well drawn: the eccentric old man, more interested in birds than in his grandson; the boy Sammy, furious at being left, uncertain of himself, and desperately wanting to love and be loved.

Several books frame family history by setting it in the present. In Kathryn Lasky's *The Night Journey*, old Nana Sashie wants to talk about her family's escape from Russia in the early 1900s. She tells her granddaughter Rachel how, at age 9, she and her family fled from Russian czarist persecution of the Jews. *The Night Journey* is told in alternate chapters; one is set in the present and details Rachel's contemporary trials over a school drama production, and the next is part of Nana Sashie's continuing story about the family's flight from Russia disguised as Purim players, itinerant actors who recreate the ancient story of Queen Esther's saving of her people. Readers who might not readily be interested in historical fiction are gently moved in that direction, as is Rachel. Trina Schart Hyman's bold black-and-white drawings help children visualize places, characters, and possessions like the family samovar, which plays an important role in both past and present time. This is an excellent story to read aloud to fifth or sixth graders in conjunction with a study of family history.

Another story that looks back on the past from the present is Pam Conrad's *My Daniel*. More complex in the telling than the previous novel, it concerns the pilgrimage of 80-year-old Julia Creath Summerwaite to a natural history museum where lie the bones of a dinosaur her brother once discovered. In the course of a day, Julia takes her grandchildren, Ellie and Stevie, to the museum and tells them bits about her brother Daniel, silently recalls other moments, and gradually reveals to the children how he died. This powerful story about Julia's life on the prairie and her love for her brother also captures

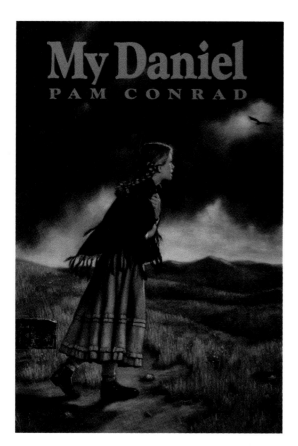

In *My Daniel,* Pam Conrad weaves together the past and present for a grandmother and her two grandchildren.

Cover of *My Daniel* by Pam Conrad. Jacket art by Darryl S. Zudeck. Copyright © 1989. Used by permission of HarperCollins Publishers, New York, NY.

the time when the discovery of dinosaur bones was beginning to suggest to humankind the evolution of life on this planet. Some readers will classify this novel, like time-slip fantasies, as historical fiction.

Thirteen-year-old Jan Tucker, the title character of *The Outside Child* by Nina Bawden, has lived differently than other people. Instead of being in a proper family, she has lived with her two loving but eccentric aunts for as long as she can remember. But when she discovers a photograph of two other children while visiting her father's ship, she learns of Annabel and George, the children of her father's second marriage. With her best friend, an asthmatic outsider named Plato Jones, Jane locates the family on the other side of London, spies on them, and finally meets them without telling her aunts. Jane's plan has near-tragic results when her stepmother recognizes the melody a gift music box plays and realizes that this now grown child is the one she refused to raise ten years ago. Even though Jane repairs her relationship with her aunts and her father's wife apologizes for her outbursts, at the end of the novel Jane sees the adult world and her own family a little less idealistically. Like Katherine Paterson, Nina Bawden suggests that what

people most often wish for is not necessarily what is best for them. In a second book, *The Real Plato Jones,* Jane's friend Plato travels to Greece to confront his own ancestry. As his grandfather lies dying, Plato becomes involved in a mystery about the old man's past and finally begins to understand the complex heritage that has made him who he is.

Among Virginia Hamilton's many books are those that draw on her family experiences as part of the fifth generation of free African Americans to have lived in southern Ohio. On one level, *Cousins* is the story of 10-year-old Cammy, who is consumed with jealousy for her beautiful and probably bulimic cousin, Patty Ann. During a summer camp outing, Patty Ann disappears in a sinkhole of a fast-moving river after saving another cousin from drowning, and Cammy is convinced the death is her fault for having hated this perfect cousin so much. But on a deeper level *Cousins* is a story about how interconnected tensions, complex relationships, and surprising discoveries can nurture and sustain each member of an extended family. Hamilton's *Zeely,* another story set in Ohio, concerns 11-year-old Geeder Perry's need to make a Watusi queen out of Zeely Taber, a herder of pigs. It is Zeely who convinces Geeder that real beauty comes from accepting yourself and others for what they are.

Cynthia Voigt's saga about the Tillerman family spans at least six novels as it fills in the events of several families' lives in a small Chesapeake Bay town. *Homecoming* introduces 13-year-old Dicey Tillerman, who, along with her two younger brothers and a younger sister, was abandoned in the parking lot of a Connecticut shopping mall by her mentally ill mother. Dicey decides the children must walk south along the Connecticut shoreline to Bridgeport to live with an aunt. But the aunt has died and her daughter, Cousin Eunice, wants to divide the family into foster homes. From Eunice, Dicey discovers that they have a grandmother living in Maryland. Determined to keep her family together, Dicey manages against all odds to reach her grandmother's home on the Chesapeake Bay, only to find an eccentric, independent, and angry old lady. The children try to keep up the huge run-down house and garden and quickly grow to love the place. But they are less sure about their prickly grandmother. This believable survival story ends with a tentative understanding formed between Gram and the children. In the sequel, *Dicey's Song,* Dicey must learn to let her family change, accept her own move toward maturity, and acknowledge her feelings for others. It is the growing warmth the Tillermans take on as they learn to be a family that lets the children, and the reader, accept their mother's death at the story's end.

Other stories in the Tillerman saga include *A Solitary Blue,* the story of Jeff Green, a minor character in

Dicey's Song. Two young-adult novels, *The Runner* and *Seventeen Against the Dealer,* continue the story. In all of her novels about the Tillerman family, Voigt explores love in its many forms—love that can't be expressed, learning to love, manipulative love, and family love.

Families in Transition

The 1990 U.S. census report found that one-fourth of American children live in single-parent families; although a majority of suburban children live with married parents, as many as two-thirds of city children do not. Nearly one out of every two marriages now ends in divorce. It is only natural, then, that books acknowledge children's attempts to deal with the disruption and confusion or pain and anger that often result from divorce, death, and other family upsets.

Beverly Cleary won the Newbery Medal for *Dear Mr. Henshaw,* the story of Leigh Botts, a child of divorce. The plot is skillfully revealed through a series of letters to an author, Mr. Henshaw. Required to write a letter to his favorite author, sixth grader Leigh writes Mr. Henshaw and asks for an immediate answer to ten questions. Mr. Henshaw responds with ten questions of his own. In the process of answering these questions (his mother says he has to), Leigh reveals how much he misses his truck-driver father and Bandit, his dog; his concern over who is stealing food from his lunch box; and his many attempts to write a prize story for the yearbook. While not as humorous as some of Beverly Cleary's other books, this one is more thoughtful and certainly presents an honest picture of a child living in a single-parent home. Leigh learns that there are some things he can't control (like his parents' getting back together again), but he does figure out a way to scare away the lunch box thief and receives not first place but honorable mention for his story "A Day on Dad's Rig." Cleary's ear for the way children think and speak is remarkably true.

Cleary's *Strider,* a buoyant sequel, begins four years later. Leigh is a high school student, a track runner, and still writes in his diary. When he and his best friend, Barry, discover an abandoned dog on the beach, they name it Strider and agree to have "joint ownership." Leigh's hurt over his father's abandonment is also lessened by his new friend, a redheaded girl hurdler, and his success in school. But Leigh's special bond with the new dog causes him to have a falling-out with Barry before the two reach a new agreement. Middle schoolers will enjoy this sequel, but Paul O. Zelinsky's many blackline illustrations seem designed to appeal to even younger readers.

Phyllis Reynolds Naylor's entertaining series about Alice, beginning with *The Agony of Alice,* is not about life after divorce but is instead about making one's own way toward adulthood without a mother's guidance. Alice, an 11-year-old whose mother died when she was 4, is searching for a female role model. Her father and 19-year-old brother are no help when it comes to buying jeans or bras, and she longs for a mother to help explain what being a teenager is all about. Like Anastasia Krupnik, Alice keeps lists of her successes and failures as she casts around for someone on whom to model her life. Realistic dialogue, humor, and the message that most people have to work out for themselves the answers to important questions give the stories about Alice high reader appeal.

Vinnie Matthews is the title character in Katherine Paterson's *Flip-Flop Girl,* about a family devastated by a father's death and their forced move from the Washington suburbs to their grandmother's crowded house in rural Virginia. Nine-year-old Vinnie is miserable in her new home and isolated in her new school except for one very strange little girl named Lupe, who wears orange flip-flops to school and lives in a shack in the middle of a pumpkin patch. Vinnie's mother is distracted by her own grief and her younger brother Mason's refusal to talk. Vinnie displaces all the longing she feels for her absent father onto her fourth-grade teacher, who takes extra time with her. When she learns that Mr. Clayton is going to be married, she feels betrayed and lashes out at him by vandalizing his car and then blaming Lupe. Her self-hatred leads her to drive Mason away; when he cannot be found, Lupe comes to her aid. They find Mason when they hear him calling for his father. Stuck high above ground on an old railroad trestle, his fear has finally given him back his voice. This incident also gives Vinnie the words to express her pain to her mother and to tell the truth to Mr. Clayton. The family begins to heal as Vinnie takes responsibility for her actions and accepts the new role she must play in her altered family.

In *Baby* Patricia MacLachlan tells of a family that is in transition following the death of an infant son. When baby Sophie is left in their driveway, she becomes a foil for their grief and deflects their unspoken inner pain in their efforts to care for her. But eventually Sophie's real mother returns to claim her and the family cannot hide from their sorrow any longer. Byrd, a 70-year-old friend, insists that they need to find the words for their grief. "If we talk about Sophie, we can talk about Larkin's brother who died. The Baby she never saw. The Baby with no name" (p. 122). Slowly her mother and father begin to describe the baby's blue eyes and his "long serious thoughtful look," and the infant, now finally named Michael, is given a proper funeral service. MacLachlan's beautiful story of healing is filled with wonderful characters and interwoven with a subtle message about the healing power of poetry and music.

The words of a storyteller also prove healing in Sharon Creech's *Walk Two Moons*. Salamanca Tree Huddle has found it difficult to reconcile herself to the changes in her family's situation. Living in suburban Cleveland, she longs for the family's beautiful Kentucky farm, but most of all she desperately misses her mother, who went West to find herself following the death of her newborn baby. Sal is convinced that if she can only get to her mother in Idaho in time for her birthday, she can bring her home. Her grandparents agree to undertake the long journey, and in the car Salamanca regales them with stories of her friend Phoebe Winterbottom, Phoebe's mother's disappearance, a kidnapping, and an ax murder that the two girls set out to solve. Interwoven with this story and the ongoing story of their trip are Salamanca's memories of her mother and their life in Kentucky. Her grandparents, wonderfully warm and funny characters, give her the help she needs to accept the truth about her family. Sal comes to understand the purpose that these stories have served for her.

   🐾 It seems to me that we can't explain all the truly awful things in the world like war and murder and brain tumors, and we can't fix these things so we look at the frightening things that are closer to us and we magnify them until they burst open. Inside is something that we can manage, something that isn't as awful as it had at first seemed. (p. 277)

Walk Two Moons is a complex narrative peopled by quirky yet fully realized characters. As the plot evolves, Salamanca's stories to herself burst open to involve and surprise the reader in a story that has all the action of a great read yet all the depth of great literature.

Betsy Byars frequently writes about children who live in single-parent families and are often left on their own. Even though adult intervention eventually helps allay a crisis, Byars's main characters generally work things out for themselves while realizing a "little moment of growth." In *Cracker Jackson*, 11-year-old Cracker suspects that his much loved former baby-sitter Alma is being abused by her husband. With the help of his best friend, Goat, he tries to drive his mother's car and take Alma to a shelter. In a response that is classic for battered women, Alma backs out and returns home. Cracker seeks help from his flight attendant mother, but it is nearly too late to save Alma's life. *The Night Swimmers* is about three children who sneak into neighbors' pools under cover of darkness. They are raising themselves while their father tries to pursue a career as a country western singer. Retta cares for her two younger brothers but is having trouble letting them become more self-reliant. Only when the youngest nearly drowns does she realize that things can't go on as they have been. A keen ear for dialogue and humor and an accurate eye for the memorable incidents of childhood typify the novels by Betsy Byars.

The Pinballs, also by Byars, deals with three children who have been placed in a foster home. Carlie is a tough, likable 12-year-old girl who has repeatedly been beaten up by her third stepfather. She endures her world by watching television and making caustic comments. Harvey comes to the Masons' in a wheelchair because his alcoholic father accidentally ran him over and broke both his legs. The third child in this mismatched group is Thomas J., an 8-year-old boy going on 80. Elderly twin spinsters had tried to raise him without notifying the authorities, so Thomas J. had never gone to school. Carlie maintains that they are all "just like pinballs. Somebody put in a dime and punched a button and out we come, ready or not, and settled in the same groove" (p. 29). By the end of the story, Carlie has learned that life is determined not only by blind chance but also by initiative, for it is her creative planning that finally breaks through Harvey's depression and gives him some reason to live. Carlie's change, from being a defensive, self-centered person into becoming a compassionate human being, is gradual and believable, and she never loses her comical perspective on life. Middle-grade students enjoy hearing this story read aloud and meeting this fine cast of characters.

In Katherine Paterson's *The Great Gilly Hopkins*, Gilly is not nearly the likable character that Carlie is. When Gilly arrives at her next foster home, she can't bear the huge, semiliterate Maime Trotter and her "retard" 7-year-old ward. So she sends a letter to her beautiful mother in California greatly exaggerating her situation. When she steals over a hundred dollars of Trotter's foster-care money and tries to buy a ticket to California, she is stopped by the police. Finally she understands the real love and trust that Trotter has for her as she refuses to let the social worker move Gilly to yet another home. It is too late, however, as Gilly receives an answer to her letter in the form of a visit from her grandmother, who she never knew existed. Desperately sad about leaving Trotter, Gilly learns then that one has to accept responsibility for one's own actions. One of the consistent themes in Paterson's writings is that main characters always get their wishes—but not in the way they expected.[12] At the end of the story Gilly's wish for a real home comes true, but it is a home with her grandmother, not with Courtney, the beautiful idealized mother she has created in her dreams. However, life with Maime Trotter, in which she had learned to accept and give love for the first time, made her ready for her

---

[12]Christy Richards Slavik, "The Novels of Katherine Paterson: Implications for the Middle School" (Ph.D. dissertation, Ohio State University, 1983).

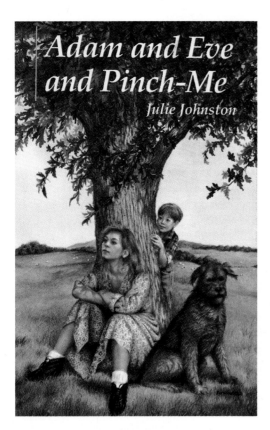

Sara Moon is a foster child who is determined to isolate herself from others in Julie Johnston's *Adam and Eve and Pinch-Me*.

Cover of *Adam and Eve and Pinch-Me* by Julie Johnston. Reprinted by permission of Little, Brown and Company.

real family. The reader knows that Gilly is capable of healing the hurt in Nonnie's life and that her own will be healed in the process. These larger-than-life characters are superbly drawn and most believable. Children delight in the swearing, self-sufficient young Gilly, but they admire the more mature Gilly who has to learn her lessons the hard way.

Sara Moon, in Julie Johnston's *Adam and Eve and Pinch-Me*, could be an older Gilly, an adolescent who has been passed around from one foster home to another. At 15, however, she'll soon be able to be on her own, and there is nothing this isolated teen wants more than to be left alone. Like the computer that she types her thoughts into, Sara is a cold machine, unable to show emotions to the outside world. And just as her computer is without a printer, she is without the ability to reveal her thoughts to anyone. Impinging on this isolation are the Huddlestons, her new foster parents, their two other foster children, and a mysterious stranger who is in town looking for her long-lost daughter. Their problems soon draw Sarah into the middle of a suspenseful and somewhat complicated plot. The ending is not quite what Sara, or the reader, expected, but the

"Queen of Cool" finds the warm and loving home she has needed all along and the courage to finally put her words into printed form.

In Cynthia Rylant's Newbery Medal book *Missing May*, Summer has finally found a family only to lose its heart. Following her mother's death Summer had been bounced around from one relative to another until her Aunt May and Uncle Ob showed up and took her home with them. Home was only a trailer in the West Virginia hills, but it was heaven to the little 6-year-old, and May was its center.

> May was the best person I ever knew. Even better than Ob. She was a big barrel of nothing but love and while Ob and me were off in our dreamy heads, May was there in this trailer seeing to it there was a good home for us when we were ready to land. She understood people and she let them be whatever way they needed to be. She had faith in every single person she ever met, and this never failed her, for nobody ever disappointed May. Seems people knew she saw the very best of them and they'd turn that side to her to give her a better look. (pp. 15–16)

Summer is 12 when May dies, and she and Ob cannot seem to find their way without her. *Missing May* is about the grieving that people need to do and the healing that comes with time, with love, and with a little help from Summer's strange friend Cletus, a dead medium named Miriam Young, and perhaps a guardian angel named May. And while Summer, Ob, and Cletus set out on a real journey to cure their pain, it is the journey of the spirit that finally brings them home, ready to be a family to each other with May's memory at the center.

Living with Others

Three- and 4-year-olds show momentary concern for their sandbox companions, but it is usually only when children go to school that the peer group becomes important. By the time children approach the middle of elementary school, what other children think is often more significant than what parents, teachers, or other adults think. By the time children reach middle school or junior high school, the peer group and making friends are all-important.

Finding Peer Acceptance

A classic example of children's cruelty to others who are "different" is the well-known, somewhat didactic story *The Hundred Dresses* by Eleanor Estes. Wanda, a poor Polish girl, attempts unsuccessfully to win a place in the group by telling of the hundred dresses she owns. It is only after she moves away, and the hundred dresses—all drawings—are displayed, that her peers understand that their cowardice in not befriending Wanda and their meanness have deprived them of both a friend and their own self-respect.

Louise Fitzhugh's *Harriet the Spy* has also achieved the status of a modern classic. It is the story of a precocious child who finds it difficult to relate to either her parents or her peers. Harriet tells her own story, interspersed with her notes about people she observes at school and after school. Her baby-sitter, Ole Golly, has been Harriet's consistent source of security, and when she leaves, Harriet's loneliness is compounded when her classmates find her journal. The underlying theme of this 30-year-old story is still relevant today. It contains serious statements about how children respond to teachers, to cliques, and to each other.

Other books, such as Walter Dean Myers's *Scorpions* and Jan Slepian's *Risk 'n Roses,* examine the serious consequences of peer pressure. In Dennis Haseley's *Getting Him,* sixth grader Donald is furious at his weird neighbor Harold for causing a terrible injury to Donald's dog. When a group of older boys invite him into their club with a chance to get back at Harold, Donald is flattered. As he spies on Harold in order to concoct a scheme that will utterly humiliate the boy, Donald begins to feel some sympathy for the boy and to see the cruelty behind the other boys' pranks. He cannot find the courage to back out of their plan, however, and the boys humiliate Harold in a terrible hoax. When Donald sees the consequences of his actions, he finally accepts responsibility, and turning his back on his heroes he tentatively reaches out to Harold in apology. This is a book that will speak to any child who has longed to be part of the "in group" or wished for revenge. Donald's dilemma and Harold's behavior will raise important questions for older children who are faced with similar issues.

In two books by Mary Stolz, the same characters and events are examined from different points of view. In the first story, *A Dog on Barkham Street,* Edward is frightened of Martin, the bully next door, who threatens him each day. When his uncle comes with his collie dog to visit the family, he helps Edward learn how to handle a bully. When he leaves, he gives Edward what he has always wanted, his own dog. In the other book, *The Bully of Barkham Street,* the reader learns that Martin Hastings had once had a dog but that his parents had given it away when Martin had failed to care for it. Then the reader knows why Martin is so resentful of Edward and his collie dog. Martin, now 13 years old and an ex-bully, struggles to lose his old reputation in *The Explorer of Barkham Street.* His teacher has introduced him to the joys of reading (and daydreaming) about explorers. Old problems continue to plague Martin, but he begins to understand that he can be an explorer, and

the discovery will be his own real self. Although there are touching scenes and a satisfying end, there is little action or suspense. Instead, this book may be enjoyed for its characters, vivid imagery, and lively dialogue. A rich discussion could center on Martin's fears and dreams, how these changed, and why.

Making Friends

The theme of building friendships is often a part of realistic fiction. Stories about life in families often include one child's relationship with someone outside the home. Popular fiction traces the ups and downs of friendships in the classroom. Other stories, such as Nina Bawden's *The Outside Child,* Lois Lowry's *Rabble Starkey,* Ann Cameron's *Julian's Glorious Summer,* or Beverly Cleary's depiction of Ramona and her friends, have multiple themes besides the tentative ways boys and girls form important friendships.

Two fifth-grade friendships are presented in Betsy Byars's *The Cybil War;* the first is a long-standing one between Simon Newton and Cybil Ackerman, and the other is a rocky one between Simon and his boastful, lying friend Tony Angott. While both boys vie for Cybil's attention, Tony tricks her into going out on a first date with him. However, his scheme backfires, for Cybil recognizes Tony's true nature. Simon's triumphant bicycle ride with Cybil provides a satisfying conclusion to this lighthearted tale of friendship.

In Ellen Conford's novel *Anything for a Friend,* Wallis Greene has moved too many times and hates the prospect of trying to make friends in her new suburban neighborhood where all the streets are named for flowers and the houses all look alike. Wallis would do anything to have a friend. She finally does make friends, including an unwanted one, only to discover that the family is to move again. Wallis is angry and disappointed until she begins to realize that if she has made friends here, she can do it again in a new place. Frequently, authors like Conford, Judy Blume, and Paula Danziger have included the development of peer relationships and friendships as one of the themes in their popular novels about and for 10- to 14-year-olds.

Emily Blair is an only child until the summer when she and her parents move into an eighteen-room house and her four cousins come to stay with them. Not only does Emily have an instant family, but she discovers Kate, a very special person who writes poetry, as Emily does. In *Look Through My Window,* Jean Little has created the life that an only child might hope for. This is an affectionate story with real characters who come alive. Passages that are serendipitous for book lovers are Emily and Kate's rapt discussions about the books they love. In *Kate,* a sequel, the difficulties of friendship is one theme; Kate's search for her identity through her father's Jewish background becomes another. Kate also reveals her thoughts in poetry and prose in *Hey World, Here I Am!*

Characters in Zilpha Keatley Snyder's books are often intelligent children from differing backgrounds who develop strong friendships. In *The Egypt Game*, six young children in a Berkeley, California, neighborhood set up in an abandoned storage yard an imaginary game based on their research into the ceremonies and culture of ancient Egypt. When one of the game players is attacked and another neighborhood child is murdered, the children's outdoor play is curtailed. In this mystery, Snyder leads readers to believe that a junk dealer/professor who owns the storage yard is the murderer. But he is instrumental in apprehending the criminal, which forces the children to reconsider their appraisal of him. The children continue their friendship, this time with a game based on gypsies.

Snyder's *Libby on Wednesday* is about an 11-year-old who, because of her home schooling by well-educated adults, is placed in the eighth grade. Her actress mother, away in New York, thinks Libby needs to be "socialized." But Libby hates school because she is ridiculed for her height and intelligence. When she wins a writing competition and is placed in a five-person writers group, she retreats to her Victorian treehouse where she writes in her journal about the others in her group: Alex, a brilliant parodist with cerebral palsy; Wendy, whose clichéd writing reflects her concern for clothes and boyfriends; Tierney, angry because she did not inherit her family's good looks; and G. G., whose searing sarcasm and angry comments cover his fear of an alcoholic father. As Libby finds the courage to share herself, beginning with a tour of the run-down family mansion and the treehouse her eccentric-author grandfather built, her views of those in her writing group begin to change. Like Madeleine L'Engle, Snyder creates exceptional and gifted child characters whose intelligent thoughts and actions often lead older readers to reflect more widely on their own lives.

In Katherine Paterson's Newbery Medal book *Bridge to Terabithia*, imaginary play is the basis for a friendship that develops between 10-year-old Jess Aarons, an artistic boy who is a misfit in his family, and Leslie Burke, a newcomer who is a misfit at school. Her parents, both writers, have moved to rural Virginia in pursuit of a simpler lifestyle. These two lonely children invent an imaginary realm based on Leslie's image of Narnia and other fantasy worlds in literature. Their "Terabithia" is a real place, however, a private hideout in the woods reached by swinging on a rope across a dry creek bed. On a day when spring rains turn the creek into a torrent, Leslie goes alone to their meeting place, falls off the rope swing, and drowns. As Jess works through his complex feelings of grief, he comes to see a more supportive side of his usually unsympathetic family and realizes that

Leslie's gifts to him—a wider perspective and confidence in his own imaginative powers—are gifts that last and can be shared.

> Now it occurred to him that perhaps Terabithia was like a castle where you came to be knighted. After you stayed for a while and grew strong you had to move on. . . . Now it was time for him to move out. She wasn't there, so he must go for both of them. It was up to him to pay back to the world in beauty and caring what Leslie loaned him in vision and strength. (p. 126)

With lumber given him by Leslie's father, Jess builds a bridge to Terabithia, a safe entry for his younger sister, May Belle, as he leads her into the shining realm with the unspoken hope that her world, like his own, will grow. By asking fourth and fifth graders if there are any other "bridges" in this story, teachers have allowed children to discuss the many emotional or metaphorical bridges portrayed in Paterson's beautifully written book.

Growing Toward Maturity

In building a concept of self, each person begins to answer questions like "What kind of person am I?" "How am I changing?" "What do others think of me?" "What are my roles in society?" Based on their experiences, children begin to see themselves as worthy and successful people who can give and receive love and respect.

As children move toward adulthood, they may experience brief moments of awareness of this growth process. A conversation, an event, or a literary experience might give a child the sudden realization that he or she has taken a step toward maturity. The step might be toward understanding complex human emotions, acknowledgment of sexuality, or acceptance of responsibility for one's actions. This process of becoming is never easy or painless. In modern realistic fiction, there are models of ordinary boys and girls who find the courage to grow and change, or to stand up for their beliefs.

Developing Sexuality

The first story to discuss menstruation, *The Long Secret* by Louise Fitzhugh, was published in 1965. In it, a girl explains menstruation to her friend in a matter-of-fact manner to correct misinformation the friend's grandmother had given her. None of the girls are pleased with the prospect, but they take some satisfaction in the fact that when they have their periods, they'll be able to skip gym. By way of contrast, Margaret, in the story *Are You There, God? It's Me, Margaret* by Judy Blume, prays for her period because she doesn't want to be the last of her secret club to start menstruating. She regularly does exercises that she hopes will increase her size-28 bust, and she practices wearing a sanitary napkin. Mixed with her desire for physical maturation is a search for a meaningful relation with God. Adults find this book very funny and reminiscent of their own preadolescence, but it is extremely serious for 10- and 11-year-old girls who share Margaret's concern for their own physical maturation.

Judy Blume has also written a book about the physical and emotional maturing of a boy, *Then Again, Maybe I Won't*. One strand of the story concerns the sexual awakening of Tony, a 13-year-old boy who is embarrassed and concerned about erections and nocturnal emissions. The other concerns the conflicts that Tony feels about his family's sudden adoption of a new lifestyle when they move from a cramped two-family house in Jersey City to an acre of land on Long Island. The title conveys the same ambiguity as the direction of Tony's life. There is no doubt that Tony has achieved physical maturation, but will he be able to sustain his personal values in the difficult task of growing toward psychological and emotional maturity?

In Brock Cole's remarkable novel *The Goats*, a boy and girl are stripped of their clothes and left on an island in the night as a summer camp prank. Angry and humiliated, the two outcasts, or "goats," decide not to return to camp and instead to escape from the island. They float ashore holding on to a floating log, and break into a cabin and find some clothes, crackers, and ginger ale. Then, penniless, they begin an aimless journey, finding food, coping with various new problems (including the arrival of the girl's period), and making do until the Saturday when the girl's mother plans to visit camp. As a friendship gradually develops between them, the two become awkwardly aware of each other and more self-aware. When they cleverly figure out a way to stay in a motel at someone else's expense, a suspicious cleaning woman accuses them of "spending the afternoon in the same bed." Ironically, it is the adult suspicion of sexual activity, rather than the thievery of clothes, food, or a motel room, that leads to the two fugitives' being caught. The girl and boy, nameless to each other until the final chapter, are reunited with the girl's mother and other adults who will straighten things out. But Laura and Howie are different now: more self-reliant, able to form real friendships based on their own inner sense of themselves, and unlikely ever again to be gullible victims of peer cruelty or thoughtlessness. Emotionally gripping and thought provoking, this story leads individual young-adult readers to consider what it means to be alienated from one's peers and what it means to have a trusted friend.

Jacqueline Woodson's *I Hadn't Meant to Tell You This* is a powerfully moving story that deals with sexual

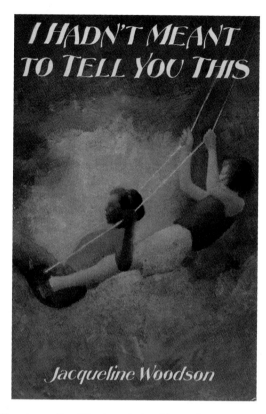

Author Jacqueline Woodson deals with sensitive issues of abuse in the moving *I Hadn't Meant to Tell You This*.
From *I Hadn't Meant To Tell You This* (jacket cover) by Jacqueline Woodson. Designed by Joseph Run. Used by permission of Delacorte Press, a division of Bantam Doubleday Dell Publishing Group, Inc.

abuse in the context of larger social issues. The town of Chauncey, Ohio, is divided along racial lines but in an unexpected way. Poor white families live on one side of town and prosperous middle-class African Americans on the other. Twelve-year-old Marie is from the latter group, a confident, popular black girl who is somehow drawn to the new white girl, Lena Bright, perhaps because they have both lost their mothers. Marie is isolated from her unemotional professor father, who seems even more distant since her mother left him. Marie wonders why he never touches her. Lena has the opposite problem—her father touches her in the wrong ways. She confides in Marie but exacts a promise that she will tell no one; caught in a social service system that has not served her well, Lena is afraid that if she reports the abuse she will be taken away from her younger sister again, the only loving connection she has had since her mother died. Marie must struggle with her own hurt at the same time as she desperately tries to protect Lena without violating her confidence. This is not a typical problem novel, nor is it a book that provides easy answers. Rather, Woodson raises critical questions about class, race, prejudice, and loyalty in the context of this beautifully realized friendship.

First published in 1969, John Donovan's sensitively told story *I'll Get There, It Better Be Worth the Trip* was the first book for young readers to confront questions of homosexuality. Davy Ross and his 13-year-old friend Altschuler are playing with Davy's dog and, impelled by an "unusual" feeling, the two exchange a kiss. After that, they pretend to box, "like tough guys." A later incident causes Davy's divorced mother to call his father to come and have a talk with Davy. When Davy and Altschuler eventually cool their friendship, and Davy's dog dies, Davy seems to have lost more than he has gained—a move toward a future that, as the book's title says, had better be worth the trip.

In Kate Walker's *Peter,* the title character, at 15, wants to fit in with his macho Australian classmates but has always felt an outsider. He is alarmed at being pushed to have sex and a bit afraid of the girls in his class. When he finds himself attracted to David, the gay friend of his college-age brother, he is more than confused. He tentatively reaches out to him, and David gently tells him that at Peter's age its not unusual not to know who or what he is. David tells him, "You've got nothing to lose by giving yourself more time" (p. 168). It is not the answer Peter thought he would hear, but in the end it is the answer that gives him the wisdom to be himself and the patience to find out who that self might really be.

Perhaps because of groundbreaking books such as these, authors are now able to incorporate aspects of a child's acknowledgment of sexuality into stories with other themes as well.

Finding Oneself

Most of the stories about physical maturing also suggest a kind of emotional growth or coming to terms with oneself. The process of becoming a mature person is a lifelong task that begins in the latter stages of childhood and continues for as long as a person lives. Many stories in children's literature chronicle the steps along the way to maturity.

In Pam Conrad's short novel *Staying Nine,* Heather wishes in the week before her tenth birthday that she "could stay just the same for millions of years." She doesn't like change, and she especially doesn't want to lose the ability to edge up to the ceiling by way of the kitchen doorway. So Heather decides not to have a birthday party, to wear the same clothes for her school picture that she wore last year, and to stay the passing of time by ignoring it. Her mother wisely agrees to an unbirthday party, but it is Rose Rita, her uncle's young girlfriend, who sympathetically and humorously conveys to Heather that growing up just might be fun and that her wall-climbing skills won't atrophy with age. Conrad's depiction of a week in the life of a child who has trouble accepting changes is both humorous and poignant.

Lois Lowry's memorable title character of *Rabble Starkey,* a 12-year-old, tells her own story of accepting growth and change, "about all kinds of loving, and about saying good-bye. And about moving on to where more things are in store" (p. 191). Rabble (short for Parable Ann) lives with her mother Sweet Hosanna above the Bigelow family's garage, where they take care of two children whose mother is hospitalized for depression. Veronica Bigelow and Rabble are like sisters; Mr. Bigelow even buys both girls new dresses, treating Rabble as if he were the father she has never known. She feels she finally has a family. Her mother, Sweet-Ho, an abandoned wife at 14, is also trying to grow as she acknowledges she doesn't want to be a housekeeper or a waitress forever. Rabble is a sympathetic character, a clear-eyed and unsentimental observer, a lover of words, and a person who initially has trouble accepting her mother's decision to start college when Mrs. Bigelow returns to the family. But the strength of the story is its quiet assurance that while it is all right to be wary of change, love and a plan make growth not only bearable but rewarding.

Another aspect of growing up is accepting people as they are, including their small pretenses and idiosyncrasies. This is one of the themes of E. L. Konigsburg's *Journey to an 800 Number,* in which highly proper prepschool student Maximilian Stubbs must come to terms with his father, Woody, a camel keeper who moves through the Southwest giving rides at shopping centers, state fairs, and conventions. Konigsburg's first-person narrative is sharp, humorous, and insightful. The gradual revelation to Max of the strange and wonderful possibilities in a world outside prep school suggests to him new definitions of "normal" and "first class."

In Virginia Euwer Wolff's *Make Lemonade,* when 14-year-old LaVaugn takes a job baby-sitting for a teenage mother, she's interested only in the extra money to put into her college account. But 17-year-old Jolly is as much a child as her two children Jilly and Jeremy, and LaVaugn is soon so involved with this family that she begins to neglect her studies. As she tries desperately to give Jolly the kind of moral support that her own mother has given her, LaVaugn must also struggle with being a mother to the two children. With LaVaugn's help, Jolly begins to pull her life together. When she finally takes responsibility for herself and her family, however, LaVaugn is hurt because she's not at the center of their lives anymore.

 It's all completely different now.
I been broken off,
like part of her bad past.
I was the one that knew the saddest parts of Jolly,
  I guess. (p. 198)

The experience has tempered her own maturing and she emerges more sure about her future plans and more at peace with her own past. Each of these young women has learned to "make lemonade" from whatever lemons life hands her. Virginia Euwer Wolff tells the story in LaVaugn's voice, placing the words like poetry on the page in phrasing that rings of the rhythms of speech patterns. This lends a sense of immediacy to the telling and underscores the important truths in this coming-of-age story.

A sixth grader who is facing problems in growing up is Sara in Jan Slepian's *The Broccoli Tapes*. While her father completes a term as a visiting professor in Hawaii and her mother is distraught over the medical condition of her own mother, Sara and her older brother Sam are left on their own. Sara has agreed to send tape-recorded messages back to her class in Boston while she is in Hawaii. At first, the messages are about an injured wild cat she and her brother free from its trap in the rocks. Later messages record Sara's feelings about her grandmother's impending death, her brother's inability to face this, and her growing attachment to the cat, which the two have named Broccoli because of its fondness for the vegetable scraps they bring to it. In private tapes that Sara erases, she records her feelings for a boy named Eddie and the moments of understanding that lead to her first kiss. In the five months in which the story takes place, Sara begins to realize that love has both risks and rewards, that nothing is gained from protecting yourself from caring, and that friends are where you find them. Slepian uses the word *click* to remind readers that Sara is now recording for her teacher and friends. This serves to place readers squarely in Sara's group of Boston friends as they listen to her tell her story.

Gilly Ground is also a loner, torn between his desire for freedom and his longing for peace and security. In Julia Cunningham's *Dorp Dead,* Kobalt's house seems a haven of peace compared to the orphanage where Gilly first lived. But gradually Gilly realizes that while Kobalt provides clothing, good food, and shelter, he is cruel and evil. Gilly has begun to acquire the same dull and unresponsive look he had first noticed in Kobalt's beaten dog. When Gilly finally gathers the courage to escape, a mysterious hunter provides the human contact Gilly needs to choose freedom. As a last act of defiance, he scrawls on Kobalt's door the message "Dorp dead." This intense and allegorical novel deals with the problems all youth face in accepting some amount of insecurity while searching for love and freedom.

Another psychologically complex novel, *One-Eyed Cat* by Paula Fox, begins when 11-year-old Ned Willis receives from his favorite uncle an unexpected birthday present—an air rifle. But Ned's minister father banishes the gun to the attic until Ned is older. Longing to shoot just once, Ned steals into the attic at night, points the gun out the window, and fires toward something moving near a shed. He is immediately guilt-stricken. Was it an animal? As he broods on his disobedience, he begins to lie, and each lie "makes the secret bigger." He can't confide in his mother, who is wheelchair-bound by arthritis, or in the temperamental housekeeper Mrs. Scallop, or in his preoccupied father. As he carries his uncomfortable secret, Ned seems most at ease at the house of an elderly neighbor, Mr. Scully, for whom he does household chores and odd jobs after school. There he and the old man see a sickly one-eyed cat that they feed and observe during the winter. When Mr. Scully suddenly suffers a stroke and is taken to the hospital, Ned is afraid he has lost both his friend and the cat. Finally, on a visit to the home where Mr. Scully, unable to speak, resides, Ned gathers enough courage to tell his guilty secret to his friend. This release brings a change in Ned and enables him to repair the pains of separation. Although Mr. Scully dies, the cat returns in the spring with its own family, and his mother is able to ease her pain somewhat with a new treatment. Ned's rich interior monologues contrast with his own inability to talk to anyone; this motif of being unable to speak about some of life's most important moments recurs throughout the story. Paula Fox's carefully chosen images, such as "people aging the way trees do, getting gnarled and dried out" or "the gun was a splinter in his mind" lend real depth to this perceptive and well-written story. Although it is set in 1935, children are likely to see the book not as historical fiction but rather as a story of one person's moral dilemmas that spiral around as a result of his disobedience and lying.

Readers know that Ned has made it through a difficult time; they are not so sure that 12-year-old Joel will be able to do the same in the powerful story *On My Honor* by Marion Dane Bauer. Goaded by his friend Tony, Joel asks his father if the two boys can ride to the bluffs outside of town and is surprised when his father gives permission. Joel promises on his honor to be careful, but when the two boys come to a bridge across a swiftly moving river, they agree to stop for a swim. When they reach the fast current, Tony, who can't swim, is swept away and drowned. Joel, horrified, doesn't know what to do. When he reaches his home, he can't tell anyone what has happened and withdraws to his bed. Finally, the arrival of the police at Tony's house and the anguish of the adults forces Joel to tell his story. He angrily blames his father and himself. In a moving scene by Joel's bedside, his father says: "We all made choices today, Joel. You, me, Tony. Tony's the only one who doesn't have to live with his choice" (p. 88). His father's admission of partial responsibility frees Joel to cry and begin to grieve. While for some children the book ends abruptly, it is not a story of dealing with the death of a friend. Instead, it is a story about facing the tragic consequences of your own actions with the help of a loving family. After reading this story, fifth graders are anxious to discuss honor, conscience, and parental obligations versus self-responsibility. They are also eager to predict a hopeful future for Joel.

Two differing novels by Katherine Paterson are concerned with similar themes of growing up. In *Come Sing, Jimmy Jo*, James struggles to reconcile his singing talent and his growing love of performance in his Appalachian family's country western band with his need for the quiet security of his grandmother and her country life. His friendship with an African American classmate, Eleazer Jones, who is uncowed by adults, helps him acknowledge his real father as he confronts his feelings about his stepfather. James finds support for his growth from both inside and outside his family. The boy in Paterson's *Park's Quest* journeys from his home near Washington, D.C., to the home where his dead father once lived in rural Virginia. Like James, Park is trying to discover who he is, and his family both supports and interferes with his desire to know more. Park's father died in Vietnam, and his mother wants nothing to do with Park's grandfather, who has suffered a stroke and cannot speak. When he visits his ancestral home, Park finally has a glowing moment of understanding and communication with the old man. He also forms a prickly friendship with a girl on the farm called Thanh, her Vietnamese mother, and the mother's husband, but the reader realizes who this girl is long before Park does. Like the characters in *Bridge to Terabithia*, Park loves books, especially the story of King Arthur. Paterson's many allusions reinforce points in the story where Park demonstrates heroism as he seeks to know about his parents and their past, himself, and his future.

His real name is Jeffrey Lionel Magee but the kids of Two Mills call the homeless boy who became a legend "Maniac Magee." Jerry Spinelli's Newbery Medal book *Maniac Magee* is more a tale of a modern-day superman than it is realistic fiction. There is nothing Maniac can't do. He beats a kid called Mars Bar in a race running backward; he hits home runs, scores touchdowns; he teaches old Mr. Grayson to read and gets the famous McNab twins to go to school. Most importantly, he brings together the town, which is racially divided. Yet Maniac continues running. He finds many shelters for himself, but no home. He lives for a while with the Beals, a kind African American family, and later with the McNabs, who are racist whites. He is happiest with Mr. Grayson, a locker room attendant at the YMCA who lives with him under a band shell. But when Grayson dies, Maniac is running again. Only when Amanda Beal goes to the zoo where Maniac is now

spending his nights and forces Maniac to listen does he finally know that someone is calling him home. Maniac is bigger than life, a legend in his own world. Short chapters, punchy dialogue, and nonstop action make this a book that readers will not want to put down.

In *Scorpions* by Walter Dean Myers, 12-year-old Jamal reluctantly takes his brother's place as leader of a Harlem gang, the Scorpions, after his brother is sent to prison. His best friend, Tito, constantly counsels him not to get involved with the gang, while his long-suffering mother and his uppity sister, Sassy, fear that he might follow in his brother's footsteps. When Jamal is given the gang's gun, he briefly displays it to get away from a school bully. On his way to a meeting with dissatisfied older boys in the gang, Tito and Jamal reflect on their lives:

"I don't like this park, man," Tito spoke under his breath to Jamal.

"How come?"

"You got guys laying on the ground, you got guys laying on the grass, you even got some women laying around in here."

"They either winos or crackheads," Jamal said.

"They look like they thrown-away people," Tito said. "That makes me scared, because I don't want to be no thrown-away guy."

"That's why we got to be like this"—Jamal held up two fingers close together—"So we don't let nobody throw us away." (p. 161)

But in a nighttime encounter with two older boys in the gang, Jamal is beaten and Tito, who is holding the gun, shoots the assailants. Both boys are stunned by the incident but Tito worries and finally goes to the police. Because he is a minor, he may return to Puerto Rico to avoid prosecution. The novel leaves readers to wonder if Jamal, who has lost his best friend and his innocence, is strong enough to follow his own conscience and resist becoming a "thrown-away guy" himself.

Survival Stories

Survival stories have powerful appeal to children in middle grades. Numerous stories in all genres portray an individual child or a small group of children, without adults, in situations that call for ingenuity, quick thinking, mastery of tools and skills, and strength of character. Survivors return to civilization or their former lives knowing that they have changed as a result of their experiences. In primitive societies, surviving a hazardous experience often marked the transition from childhood to adulthood. Today, we have forms of this in "survival training" conducted in schools, camps, or juvenile homes. Children in middle grades avidly read survival stories and wonder, "Could I do it? How? What would I do in this same situation?"

Armstrong Sperry's quintessential survival story *Call It Courage* begins and ends in the manner of a story told in the oral tradition:

> It happened many years ago, before the traders and the missionaries first came into the South Seas, while the Polynesians were still great in numbers and fierce of heart. But even today the people of Hikueru sing this story in their chants and tell it over the evening fires. It is the story of Mafatu, the Boy Who Was Afraid. (p. 7)

Taunted for his fears, Mafatu sets out to conquer his dread of the water by sailing to some other island, accompanied only by his pet albatross and his dog. On a distant island his character gradually develops as he proves his courage to himself: He defies a taboo, steals a much-needed spear from an idol, fights dangerous animals, and escapes from cannibals. These heroic deeds, which represent the many faces of courage, build his self-esteem. As in so many survival stories, having proven to himself that he can carve out an existence, Mafatu is ready to return to his former life as a changed person who knows his own worth. The first paragraph of the book is repeated at the end—only the last sentence is left off.

Jean George's well-loved *My Side of the Mountain* is about a city boy who chooses to spend a solitary winter in the Catskills on family land. Armed with knowledge from reading, he makes a home in a hollow tree, tames a falcon, sews buckskin clothing, and lays up stores for the winter. In his journal, he records his observations as he goes about the business of living. When a reporter discovers him in the spring, Sam realizes he is ready to be found. Thirty years after the publication of this story, George wrote a bittersweet but worthy sequel, *On the Far Side of the Mountain*, which picks up the plot immediately following the first story. Sam allows his younger sister Alice to become his neighbor while he continues to enrich his environment and his life in the wild. But a criminal posing as a conservation officer steals Sam's falcon and his sister vanishes. In both books George expresses concern about our relationship to the natural world and our responsibility to preserve it.

Another exciting story of survival is George's Newbery Medal novel *Julie of the Wolves*. Miyax, the Eskimo heroine of this beautiful story, finds herself alone on the Alaskan tundra. She realizes that her salvation or her destruction depends on a nearby pack of wolves. Julie (Miyax is her Eskimo name) watches the wolves carefully and gradually learns to communicate with them by

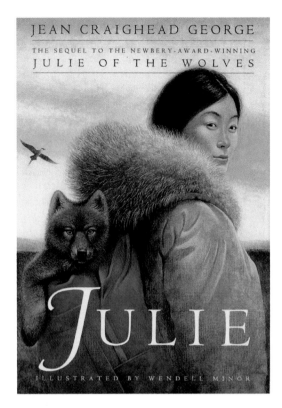

Wendell Minor creates a beautiful portrait of Julie for the cover of *Julie*, Jean Craighead George's sequel to *Julie of the Wolves*.
Illustration copyright © 1994 by Wendell Minor. Used by permission of HarperCollins Publishers, New York, NY.

glance, movement, and caress until Amaroq, their leader, acknowledges her as a friend. Because of the wolves Julie survives and finds her way back to civilization. But civilization kills Amaroq, as white hunters wantonly shoot him down from a plane for the "sport" of killing. Much of the story is based on research on wolves conducted at the Arctic Research Laboratory.[13] In the sequel *Julie*, Julie has returned to her father's home near Point Barrow and finds she must deal with the changes in the community as well as a new stepmother. Her father, concerned about the fledgling herd of musk oxen that is to become part of a new native industry, insists he will kill any wolf that attacks the herd. Julie is frantic to protect her beloved pack, and in an exciting climax she leads them away from the village and out on the tundra in search of a herd of caribou. Once again George weaves a complex story of cultures in the middle of change, a young girl in the midst of becoming a woman, and a natural world in danger of disappearing forever.

---

[13]See Jean Craighead George's Newbery award acceptance speech, *Horn Book Magazine*, August 1973, pp. 337–347.

Canadian author James Houston has based his survival story *Frozen Fire* on the actual survival experiences of a boy in the Canadian Arctic. Two boys, Matthew Morgan and his Inuit friend Kayak, set forth on a snowmobile to search for Matthew's prospector father, whose plane has been downed by a snowstorm. Carelessness in securing the cap of the gas can leaves them stranded seventy miles from Frobisher Bay. Kayak is able to use the skills taught him by his grandfather and helps both boys eventually walk out on the ice, where they are seen and rescued. They discover that Matthew's father has also been saved. Houston's crisp telling and cliff-hanger chapter endings make this a fast-paced story. Where the strengths of George's book lies in her naturalist's knowledge of wolf behavior, Houston spent twelve years among the Inuit people and he is able to weave aspects of a changing Eskimo culture and folk wisdom into the text.

Gary Paulsen's survival story *Hatchet* also begins with a crash of a bush plane. On his way to meet his father when the pilot suffers a heart attack, Brian Robeson manages to land the plane in a lake in the Canadian wilderness and swim to shore. Alone, 13-year-old Brian lets self-pity and anxiety over his parents' impending divorce distract him from the immediate needs of survival, and he is soon sick and frightened. But gradually he begins to act intelligently, building a shelter, finding ripe berries, fending off a bear, and discovering respect for a cow moose that nearly kills him. A hatchet his mother had given him as a parting gift becomes essential to his survival. When a huge storm disturbs the plane enough to raise its tail in the water, Brian ventures out to seek the survival kit all pilots carry with them. But his carelessness when he loses his hatchet in the water and his horror of what he might find when he dives to the cockpit nearly prevents him from retrieving the kit. Ironically, Brian is cooking a delicious meal of trail food in a real pot and has survived for over two months when he is finally spotted from the air by a mapping plane. In *Brian's Winter*, Paulsen speculates on what it might have been like had Brian been forced to spend the winter in the wilderness. In *The River*, Brian is once again pitted against the elements when he agrees to make a film to teach survival techniques to the military. But the man recording Brian's experiences is struck by lightning and will die unless Brian can build a raft and navigate himself and Derek downriver to a trading post. Other survival stories by Paulsen include *Dogsong*, which is partially based on the author's own experiences of training sled dogs for the Iditarod trail race, and *The Voyage of the Frog*, which reveals the courage of a boy who ventures out on the ocean to scatter his dead uncle's ashes and is caught unprepared in a sudden storm.

Vera and Bill Cleaver's *Where the Lilies Bloom* is a well-known survival story set in Appalachia. The torturous death of Roy Luther from "worms in the chest" puts the full responsibility for the survival of the family on Mary Call, his 14-year-old daughter. She and Romey, her younger brother, bury him secretly so the "county people" will not find out that they are orphaned and separate them. Then Mary Call strives to keep her "cloudy-headed" older sister, Devola, and her two younger siblings alive through the winter. Mary Call's fierce pride gives her fortitude to overcome a severe winter, a caved-in roof, and the constant pretense that Roy Luther still lives. At 14, Mary Call's strength and responsibility have made her mature beyond her years, but she pulls the family through the crisis:

> My name is Mary Call Luther, I thought, and someday I'm going to be a big shot. I've got the guts to be one. I'm not going to let this beat me. If it does, everything else will for the rest of my life. (p. 144)

Mary Call and her family do survive, through wildcrafting on the mountains, scheming, and pure grit. The authors have captured the beauty of the Smokies and of this memorable family who live in what an old hymn calls the land "Where the Lilies Bloom So Fair." Mary Call's story is continued in *Trial Valley*, a sequel that is more contrived and less believable.

This story's tone stands in sharp contrast to that in E. L. Konigsburg's *From the Mixed-Up Files of Mrs. Basil E. Frankweiler*, in which two children decide to run away from home and live in comfort in the Metropolitan Museum of Art. Claudia, feeling unappreciated at home and bored with the sameness of her straight-A life, wants to do something that is different and exciting. She chooses her brother Jamie to go along with her because he has the money they need. Claudia is a good organizer, and the two of them take up residence in the museum. They take baths in the museum's fountain, eat meals at the automat and the museum's cafeteria, and join tour groups for their education. Their adventure grows more exciting when Claudia becomes involved in the mystery surrounding the statue of a little angel. The children's research finally takes them to the home of Mrs. Basil E. Frankweiler, who arranges for Claudia to return home the way she had hoped she would—different in some aspect. Now she is different because she knows the secret of the angel. In return for this knowledge the two children tell Mrs. Frankweiler the details of their survival; she carefully records it and then writes their story. This story-within-a-story is a sophisticated and funny account of two very resourceful survivors.

Two other survival stories set in New York City take place in much grimmer circumstances. In Felice Holman's *Slake's Limbo*, Slake is a 13-year-old nearsighted orphan who lives with his aunt and thinks of himself as a worthless lump. Slake has no friends; his vision makes him a poor risk for any gang, and a severe reaction to smoke and drugs makes him useless in other ways. Hunted and hounded for sport, Slake takes refuge in the subway, staying for 121 days. He earns a little money re-selling papers he picks up on the trains and makes his home in a hidden cave in the subway wall. One day when the subway repair crew comes through, Slake real-izes that his "home" will be destroyed. He becomes ill and is taken to the hospital, where he is given nourish-ment and proper eyeglasses. Later he slips out of the hospital. His first reaction is to return to the subway, but when he hears a bird sing he looks up and decides he could perhaps exist on the roofs of some of the build-ings: "He turned and started up the stairs and out of the subway. Slake did not know exactly where he was going but the general direction was up" (p. 117).

A more hopeful story is told in Paula Fox's *Monkey Island*. Eleven-year-old Clay Garrity is abandoned by his despondent and pregnant mother, and not wishing to let his neighbor in the New York welfare hotel report him to the social worker, Clay runs away. On the street, he manages to survive because two homeless men share with him their place in a park, a box where they sleep. Calvin and Buddy become his family, sharing their food and their life stories. Clay learns to wear all his clothes at once, where to find food, and how not to attract at-tention during the day. One terrifying November night, a street gang destroys the makeshift shelters of the homeless people living in the park, Calvin disappears, and Clay catches pneumonia. Realizing his friend needs help, Buddy makes the choice of taking him to a hospi-tal even though it means Clay will lose his freedom. But in a hopeful conclusion, Clay, his mother, and his new baby sister are reunited. Paula Fox's story prompts read-ers to consider the causes of homelessness and to con-sider what may happen. Clay's dangerous journey is made at least partially bearable by the dog-eared copy of *Robinson Crusoe* he carries from the welfare hotel. Later, it is a copy of *David Copperfield* whose story of a life out-side a lost family lends Clay some courage. Paula Fox creates memorable characters in an unsentimental but hopeful survival story in which the social services of a large city, as well as caring individuals who take action, are able to do well for at least one boy and one family.

There are intriguing patterns in stories of survival. Many deal with questions and themes basic to hu-mankind. Some survival stories suggest that surviving with another person provides comforting benefits as well as difficulties. Questions readers might ask while comparing survival stories of all genres include these: What qualities make one able to survive? How does sur-viving an ordeal change a person's outlook? After basic wants are satisfied, what other needs do survivors seem to have? Which is more difficult, physical survival or emotional survival? What role does art or beauty play in the survivor's ability to endure?

Coping with Problems of the Human Condition

People in all times and places must cope with problems of the human condition—birth, pain, and loneliness; poverty, illness, and death. Children do not escape these problems, but literature can give them windows for looking at different aspects of life, show them how some characters have faced personal crises, and help them ask and answer questions about the meaning of life.

In discussing the portrayal of emotionally significant themes in children's literature, Mollie Hunter points out:

> A broken home, the death of a loved person, a di-vorce between parents—all these are highly charged emotional situations once considered unsuitable for children's reading, but which are nevertheless still part of some children's experience; and the writer's success in casting them in literary terms rests on the ability to create an emotional frame of reference to which children in general can relate.[14]

David Elkind, a psychologist, warns that we might nonetheless be overburdening our children with the ills of society before they have an opportunity to find them-selves. He says:

> This is the major stress of the literature of young children aimed at making them aware of the prob-lems in the world about them before they have a chance to master the problems of childhood.[15]

Certainly teachers and librarians should balance the reading of "problem books" with those that emphasize joy in living.

Physical Disabilities

Good stories about people with physical disabilities serve two purposes. They provide positive images with which disabled youngsters may identify, and they may help physically unimpaired children to develop a more intelligent understanding of some of the problems that disabled persons face. In stories, disabilities should be

[14]Mollie Hunter, *Talent Is Not Enough* (New York: HarperCollins, 1990), p. 20.

[15]David Elkind, *The Hurried Child: Growing Up Too Fast Too Soon* (Reading, Mass.: Addison-Wesley, 1981), p. 84.

neither exaggerated nor ignored, neither dramatized nor minimized, neither romanticized nor belittled.[16] It is particularly important that stories of disabilities be well written, not sentimental or maudlin. They should not evoke pity for what children with disabilities cannot do, but respect for what they *can* do. As in all well-written stories, characters should be multidimensional persons with real feelings and frustrations. The author should be honest in portraying the condition and future possibilities for the character. Illustrations should also portray disabilities in an honest and straightforward manner.

Literary treatment of disabilities may rely on time-honored themes: a disabled person has special powers, grace, or a predetermined destiny; a disabled person serves as a catalyst in the maturation of others; a disability is a metaphor for society's ills, such as a blind person who can "see" what others do not choose to acknowledge or are too insensitive to see. Occasionally, disabilities are somewhat misleadingly portrayed as something that can be overcome with determination, faith, and grit,[17] but in the hands of a fine writer, themes like these avoid becoming clichés and can present the reader with fresh insight into coping with the human condition.

Older stories have depicted children with cerebral palsy and families who deal courageously with this illness. The theme "what kind of help and how much" is evident in Jean Little's *Mine for Keeps.* When Sally, who has cerebral palsy, returns from a special school to live at home, she attends regular school and faces several problems. But a dog that may be hers "for keeps" helps her gain physical skill and the emotional courage to help another child who has been ill.

In *The Alfred Summer,* Jan Slepian presents a 14-year-old boy with cerebral palsy who also chafes resentfully at the strings that he feels bind him to his overprotective mother and ignoring father. Lester describes himself self-mockingly as a walking "perpetual motion machine." One day he makes a friend of Alfred, a retarded boy he sees collecting tinfoil from the gutters. Alfred's total acceptance of him frees Lester, and the two discover a third friend in Myron. As the three friends make a boat, each accomplishes something he thought he could not do and gains some self-respect. When the boat is finally launched, it sinks, but Myron and Lester realize that what they have built over the summer is much more important than a leaky old boat. By using Lester as a narrator in several chapters, Slepian injects humor and insight into this well-characterized, compassionate story.

[16]Barbara H. Baskin and Karen H. Harris, *More Notes from a Different Drummer: A Guide to Juvenile Fiction Portraying the Disabled* (New York: Bowker, 1984).

[17]Baskin and Harris, *More Notes from a Different Drummer,* chap. 2.

Rowena Batts, the heroine of Australian writer Morris Gleitzman's *Blabber Mouth,* has been born, as she puts it, with "some bits missing from my throat." She is mainstreamed into a regular classroom after her special school is shut down, and like any middle-grade child, she wants to fit in and find friends. She stumbles a bit at first, but her ability as a runner brings her a new friend named Amanda who had learned rudimentary sign language for a community service project. Her real problem, as she sees it, is her quirky father, who dresses in wild cowboy clothes and sings country western at the top of his lungs. He is constantly embarrassing her in front of her new classmates. Then Ro is terribly hurt when she finds that Amanda is planning to use her as this year's community service project. But they work through the problem and Rowena speaks for all differently abled people when she signs to an auditorium full of people and Amanda translates.

> "I'm just like all of you," I said. . . .
> "I've got problems making word sounds," I said. "Perhaps you've got problems making a living or a sponge cake or number twos."
> Amanda said it all, even the bit about number twos. The hall was still silent.
> "You can feel sympathy for me if you want," I continued, "and I can feel sympathy for you if I want. And I do feel sympathy for any of you who haven't got a true friend."
> I looked over at Amanda. (pp. 79–80)

This upbeat story of how Ro and her father make peace and how Ro makes it in her new environment is moving and funny and incidentally provides a positive picture of a child who is differently abled but not dis-abled. In the sequel, *Sticky Beak,* Rowena gets a new mother, a new baby sister, a new cockatoo, and a new friend, formerly the class bully. This likable heroine can take her place alongside Anastasia Krupnik and other popular middle-grade characters for her gutsy stick-to-it-iveness and wry good humor.

Developmental and Learning Disabilities

The opening line of *Take Wing* by Jean Little reads: "James had wet the bed again." As usual, 7-year-old James calls on his sister Laurel to help him, rather than on his mother, because Laurel has a special way and a special love for this younger brother who is "different." Laurel has always tried to hide her fear that he isn't quite normal. Her mother won't talk about him and her father is too busy to notice how slow and unsure his son is. When Laurel's mother breaks her hip, and her Aunt

Jessica comes to stay at their house, she recognizes that Laurel is carrying too much responsibility in having to care for James. Finally an appointment is made for him to have an examination at the medical clinic. Their findings confirm Laurel's fears that her brother is retarded, but he is also educable. This is as much Laurel's story as James's. By refusing to face the facts of James's disability, the family had overburdened his older sister. The title, *Take Wing*, symbolizes Laurel's freedom to begin to have a childhood of her own, to make friends, and to grow.

Betsy Byars won a Newbery Medal for her story about an adolescent girl and her retarded brother in *The Summer of the Swans*. Sara feels very much like the ugly duckling in her difficult fourteenth summer. She weeps over her big feet, her skinny legs, and her nose, even over her gross orange sneakers. But when her brother is lost in the woods, her tears vanish in the terror she feels for Charlie. In her anguish Sara turns to Joe Melby—whom she had despised the day before—and together they find Charlie. It is the longest day of the summer and Sara knows that she will never be the same again. Like the awkward flight of the swans with their "great beating of wings and ruffling of feathers," Sara is going to land with a long, perfect glide. Sara's love for her brother and concern for his safety help her break through her shell of adolescent moodiness.

In Jan Slepian's *Risk 'n Roses*, a novel set in the Bronx just after World War II, it seems to 11-year-old Skip that her parents have been having the same argument forever. How responsible is Skip supposed to be for her older and mentally retarded sister, Angela? The family has moved to a new neighborhood so that Angela can be closer to a special school, and Skip is desperate for a friend. Then she meets the compelling Jean Persico, who "didn't care about feelings or laws or being good so far as Skip could tell. She wasn't like the rest. She was untamed. Wonderful" (p. 107). Jean forms a club, the Dares, in which she cruelly preys on each member's weakness, getting each girl to do things such as shoplifting or disrupting an ice cream store by dropping a cockroach in it. Angela makes friends with a reclusive neighbor, Mr. Kaminsky, whose precious roses have all been named for family and friends he believes have been exterminated by Hitler. But Jean has targeted him for malice, and her final act of cruelty, enticing Angela to cut down his prize roses, is her way of paying Angela back for inadvertently reporting on one of Jean's cruel jokes. Jean's manipulation of her sister shocks Skip into realizing that her desire for a friend has blinded and trapped her. But her realization and her actions show the reader she has changed. This is as much a story of peer pressure and the desire for friendship as it is a story of accepting a sibling for herself and not for what one wishes she were. Like Dennis Haseley's *Getting Him* and

Marion Dane Bauer's *On My Honor*, *Risk 'n Roses* is also about taking responsibility for one's own actions.

The ambivalent feelings of a rebellious 15-year-old toward her retarded 11-year-old brother are examined with compassion in Colby Rodowsky's novel *What About Me?* It seems to Dorrie that her own life is swallowed up in the family's constant concern for Fred. Her frustration and anger boil to the surface as expressions of hatred for her brother; yet when she is left alone with him and his heart condition becomes critical, she finds herself caring for him, loving him, just as her parents have always done. In the story's poignant resolution Fred dies and, like Dorrie, the reader is left to consider what it means to grow up in a family that includes a retarded child.

In *All Together Now* Sue Ellen Bridgers portrays an important summer in 12-year-old Casey Flanagan's life. Casey, whose mother works at two jobs while her father is away fighting in the Korean War, has come to spend the summer with her grandparents in a small southern town. There she meets Dwayne Pickens, a retarded man who is her father's age. Dwayne has the mind of a 12-year-old and a passion for baseball. Their friendship grows when Dwayne, who dislikes girls but mistakes Casey for a boy, includes her in his endless baseball sessions, often with Casey's feisty Uncle Taylor playing, too. Casey contracts what may be polio, and her anxious family sits with her through several terrible August days. Having forgiven Casey for being a girl, Dwayne faithfully visits during the long convalescence that follows and keeps her spirits up. By summer's end, Casey has grown in awareness of herself and the nature of friendship. "Having responsibility made people responsible. Having someone to love gave you a chance to be loved yourself" (p. 229). Humorous and sometimes poignant subplots involving Casey's observations and interactions with adults make this a complex and richly characterized novel. In this well-crafted story for middle school readers, Bridgers reveals the characters' thoughts and feelings with a shifting viewpoint, allowing readers to consider the potential of human relationships.

Mental Illness

Few stories about mental illness have been written for the elementary school child. In the title of the book (*George*), E. L. Konigsburg has let the name with parentheses stand for Ben's alter ego, a real and constant companion. Ben manages to keep his schizophrenic symptoms to himself until he enters sixth grade. Then, because of his fear that he might be sent away to live with his father and stepmother and the pressure of knowing that his lab partners are stealing equipment from chemistry class to make LSD, George begins to speak out loud. Part of this story is very witty, as is typical of Konigsburg's stories, but part is very serious. George and Ben finally become one again, and the book ends on a cheerful note of recovery. In a more demanding and serious book, *3 NBs of Julian Drew* by James Deem, 15-year-old Julian has been traumatized and abused both physically and mentally. Writing in a code he invents as a way of escaping his pain, he keeps a series of notebooks, which this book is named after. Deem has told the story through this cryptic code, mirroring Julian's mental state in a way conventional spelling could not. Thus the book is for mature and accomplished readers who will be intrigued by the device and moved by Julian's struggle to escape the tyranny of his home and the prison of his disturbed mind.

Thirteen-year-old Carrie Stokes, in Zibby Oneal's *The Language of Goldfish*, does not like what is happening to her. She wishes her family could return to the days when they lived in a cramped Chicago apartment rather than in an affluent suburb. If only things hadn't changed, she would still be close to her sister, Moira, and they would share all that they had as children. Instead, Carrie is under pressure from her mother and sister to wear more appropriate and stylish clothes, to go to school dances, and, somehow, be someone Carrie feels she is not. When she attempts suicide by overdosing on pills, her mother still avoids dealing with the real Carrie. Gradually, as Carrie mends, she is better able to understand her mother's denial. She is helped in this by a therapist, a trusted art teacher, and a new friend, a neighbor boy. Finally she learns to accept changes in others and herself while those closest to her display various ways in which they, too, cope with mental illness.

While there are few books about mentally ill children, there are several that present a child or children dealing with a mentally ill adult. Voigt's *Homecoming* and *Dicey's Song*, for instance, portray the aftereffects of a depressed mother's abandonment of her children. Paula Fox's *The Village by the Sea* concerns a girl's two-week stay with a mentally ill aunt. Bruce Brooks, in *The Moves Make the Man*, shows through the eyes of a compassionate and articulate boy narrator how the mental breakdown of his friend's mother nearly brings about the breakdown of the friend as well.

In Kristine L. Franklin's *Eclipse*, sixth grader Trina must deal with the changes in her father's mental state following an accident that disabled him. As she looks forward to the birth of a sibling the family has wanted for years, her normally outgoing father either sleeps all the time or lashes out irrationally at Trina. Trina is troubled by his behavior and the fear that the new baby may be born retarded because of her mother's age. Her mother tries to protect her from the truth but finally admits to Trina that her father has attempted suicide. When the baby is born prematurely, her father cannot seem to cope and, refusing to take his medication, falls further into depression. On the night of a lunar eclipse, in a tremendously tense and painful conclusion, he takes a rifle into their barn and a shot rings out just as Trina and her mother realize what his calm goodnight must have meant. The consequences to families of mental illness are painfully clear in this moving yet ultimately hopeful story.

Jocelyn Riley's *Only My Mouth Is Smiling* follows 13-year-old Merle Carlson as she moves with her psychotic mother and two siblings first to camp in Wisconsin and then into a small rented house in town. Merle enjoys making friends until her mother's increasingly erratic behavior becomes more difficult to conceal. Eventually Merle realizes that she and her family cannot cope alone and a social worker intervenes. The story ends with hope, although the family will have to learn to live with their mother's illness. Merle's story is continued in *Crazy Quilt*. Sue Ellen Bridgers's *Notes for Another Life* portrays the effects of a father's incurable mental illness and a mother's inability to cope with 13-year-old Wren and her older brother. With the help of memorable grandparents, it is up to Wren to make important decisions about her future in this young-adult novel.

Aging and Death

In the early part of this century the aging and death of loved ones were accepted as a natural part of a child's firsthand knowledge. However, most modern children are removed from any such knowledge of senility and death. Few grandparents live with their families anymore, and many relocate to apartments or retirement communities. When older relatives become ill, they are shunted off to hospitals and nursing homes. Few people die at home today, and many children have never attended a funeral. Seldom is death discussed with children. Contemporary authors realize that there is enough genuine mystery about death, without hiding it under this false cloak of secrecy.

Today, realistic fiction for children reflects society's concern for honesty about aging and dying. We have moved from a time when the subject of death was one of the taboos of children's literature to a time when it is being discussed openly and frankly.

Aging

Many recent picture books have portrayed young people learning to accept older people as they are or to recall them fondly as they were (see Chapter 5). Realistic fiction portrays older people in all their rich variety, as treasured grandparents, as activists or as passive observers, as senile or vitally involved in events around them, and as still-valuable contributors to a society they have helped to build.

The Hundred Penny Box, written by Sharon Bell Mathis and illustrated by Leo and Diane Dillon, tells of the love between Great-Great-Aunt Dew, an aged African American woman, and Michael, a young boy. Aunt Dew is 100 years old and she keeps a box full of pennies, one for each year of her life. Michael loves to count them out while Aunt Dew tells him the story behind each one, relating it to life and historical events. Michael's mother wants to give the old box away, but Michael plans a special hiding place for it. This story is remarkable for presenting perspectives on aging from the viewpoints of three different persons: Aunt Dew, who is content to sing her long song and recall the past with her pennies; Michael's mother, who has to take care of her; and Michael, who loves her but in his child-like way also wants to be entertained by her storytelling.

Told from the point of view of its 10-year-old narrator, who is unnamed in the story, Bruce Brooks's novel *Everywhere* depicts the love of the sensitive boy narrator for his grandfather who may be dying from a heart attack. In order to save his life, the boy and Dooley, nephew of his grandfather's African American nurse, decide to try a "soul switch," which Dooley has read about in a comic book about Native Americans. Dooley finds a turtle that they plan to kill to "give the souls a chance to fly by each other in the sky." As the boy climbs the porch to see when his grandfather's soul is leaving, he witnesses another heart attack. Shocked, he cries out, which somehow calls his grandfather back from what seems to be the verge of dying. Whether Dooley actually kills the turtle isn't discovered until the final chapters, when the boy and his grandfather are out in the garage working on a summer project before Dooley returns to his family and school. Brooks has written a beautiful short novel filled with nuances, ambiguities, and depth. It will challenge sixth and seventh graders to wonder about the power of love and the gifts that friends may share with each other.

The title character of Peter Härtling's *Old John* is an independent, cantankerous, lovable, and opinionated 75-year-old when he comes to live with Laura and Jacob's family. One of his prized possessions is a poster of Albert Einstein sticking out his tongue, a comment on Old John's belief that people should give themselves the freedom to put people on a little bit. While each person in the family must cope with exasperation over the old man's habits, each loves him and learns from him. Old John finds raucous companions in the small German village where he now lives, paints and decorates his bedroom to his own tastes, picks up his former profession as a dyer, and even falls in love. However, he suffers a stroke, and as the next year passes he becomes progressively more disoriented and crotchety. But the

family rallies to care for him and he dies peacefully at home. Härtling lets incidents speak for themselves, leaving the reader to observe what life with an older person can be like for one family. While Old John will "never be there again" on his favorite corner of the couch, the reader knows that he will be there in the minds of Jacob and Laura, who are richer people for having known their grandfather so well.

In Janet Hickman's *Jericho,* Angela's great-grandmother, Grandmin, is also old and disoriented. When her family decides to spend the summer helping to fix up the old woman's house, Angela resents having to leave home and her friend Tessa. She is repulsed by the old woman's physical needs and angry that Grandmin cannot remember who she is. But in her mind Grandmin *is* remembering; she has gone back to the time when she was a young girl like Angela. As Angela's summer progresses, Min's story runs parallel to hers, and as we experience Angela's frustration and adolescent longing, we see Min's even more clearly. This is a lovely story about the gulf that often separates generations. Although she never learns Min's story, after Min's death Angela is looking at some old photographs and comes across one of her great-grandmother as a young woman. "For that first speechless moment she feels a sense of connection so strong and so unsettling that she thinks she cannot bear it" (p. 135). Looking at the picture is like looking in a mirror. Grandmin is Angela in ways that go deeper than the flat surface of an old photograph.

There are also books that portray older people as active, lively, and engaging. British author Nina Bawden portrays vital and energetic older people in many of her books. In the humorous *Granny the Pag,* Catriona Brooke's beloved Granny is a psychiatrist who tools around town on her Harley-Davidson motorcycle. In the witty and often poignant *Tiger, Tiger, Burning Bright* by Ron Koertge, Pappy, Jesse's grandfather, is also an independent spirit. When Pappy reports that he has seen a tiger in the hills surrounding their desert home, Jesse is afraid that this vital, funny man may be getting senile as his mother believes. Jesse gradually comes to accept the normal processes of aging and to understand that he cannot pretend that his grandfather is not changing. But Pappy also proves to be more alert than anyone had realized, and although he may need some extra help, he still isn't ready for a nursing home. Jesse's mother acknowledges, "Neither one of us ever had it right about Pappy. So now I think we just take it one day at a time" (p. 174).

In Lois Lowry's *Anastasia Again,* Anastasia devises a scheme for involving her grouchy neighbor with a group of lively older people at a local senior citizen center. In Eth Clifford's *The Rocking Chair Rebellion,* 14-year-old "Opie" (short for Penelope) is volunteering at the Maple Ridge Home for the Aged when a former neighbor takes up residence there. Opie eventually is instrumental in helping several of the residents to leave and set up their own group home in her neighborhood. Although events are somewhat improbable, both Lowry and Clifford present older people as diverse, intelligent, active, and interesting as potential friends.

Another book that suggests that different generations have much to offer each other is Angela Johnson's *Toning the Sweep*. Fourteen-year old Emily and her mother have traveled to the desert Southwest to bring her sick grandmother back to Cleveland. Grandma Ola has built a rich life for herself in this desert land she loves so much, and the summer visit is the opportunity for Emily to discover her grandmother's present and her own past. She undertakes a video project and interviews Ola, her mother, and the people who make up her grandmother's community. The story that emerges includes the awful facts about her grandfather's death in Alabama and the painful truth that her grandmother is coming home to die. But this story is not about dying. Rather, it is a celebration of a remarkable woman who has lived a full, if unconventional, life. Emily's project becomes a fitting way to "tone the sweep" for her, the opportunity to ring her soul to heaven as her ancestors in South Carolina might have done in previous generations.

Death and Dying

A child's first experience with death is frequently the loss of a pet. While picture books for younger children portray this experience with younger protagonists, several longer books have depicted slightly older children dealing with the death of a pet. In *The Growing Time* by Sandol Stoddard Warburg, Jamie's old collie dog King dies and Jamie is desolate. Eventually the family buys Jamie a puppy, but he doesn't even want to look at it. In the middle of the night, however, the new pup cries and needs someone to love it. Jamie comes downstairs to comfort and claim him.

Charlotte Graeber's *Mustard* tells the story of a beloved old cat's eventual death from a series of strokes. Eight-year-old Alex stubbornly refuses to believe that his cat is dying. His father says, "I wish I could tell you Mustard will be okay, but we can only hope." After the sympathetic veterinarian puts Mustard to sleep, Alex tearfully helps his father bury the cat in the backyard. When he and his father go to the animal shelter to donate some of Mustard's things, they both agree that it is hard to consider another new cat. Alex thinks that maybe next Easter they will come back to the shelter. "But now he only had room for remembering Mustard." Emotions are portrayed honestly: both adults shed tears over their 14-year-old cat's death, and Alex isn't ready yet to accept another pet. Donna Diamond's soft charcoal drawings portray family members and Mustard with warmth and truth.

Other children's first experience with death is the loss of a grandparent. Two warmly illustrated short stories show a child coping with the death of one grandparent while continuing a rewarding relationship with the remaining one. In Mavis Jukes's *Blackberries in the Dark*, Austin spends the summer on the farm with Grandma and everywhere around him are reminders of his grandfather: the tire swing he built, his fishing reel hanging in the barn, and his treasured old fishing knife now strangely out of place in the dining room cupboard. Grandpa had promised to teach him how to fish this summer, and with him gone, there's no one to teach him or to help him pick blackberries at night. After Grandma and Austin recall the past summer, however, Austin starts out to pick blackberries on his own, only to have his grandmother follow, complete with her husband's fishing gear, so the two of them can teach each other to fish. Readers can almost feel the two resolve to move on from grief to new challenges, and the decision is neatly punctuated by Grandma's gift of Grandpa's fishing knife to Austin. Thomas B. Allen's black-and-white soft-pencil illustrations capture poignancy, accept the pleasant loneliness of the farm, and depict the humor of Austin's story.

Marcia Sewall's full-color pastel and fine line illustrations reaffirm in a contrasting way that life goes on in the midst of one extended family's funeral gathering in *Saying Good-Bye to Grandma* by Jane Resh Thomas. Seven-year-old Suzie and her parents return to the small town where Mother grew up. While the many cousins play, the adults reminisce and occasionally weep as they fix meals and make arrangements. The narrator, Suzie, shares her concerns about not knowing what is going to happen at the funeral, her fears that she might not recognize Grandma in her casket, and her small guilt over "not being sad enough" because she played with her cousins. Parents reassure her, and Mom even says that funerals are for saying good-bye but also for saying hello to family and friends.

A *Taste of Blackberries* by Doris Smith is a believable story of the sudden death of a young boy. Jamie and his friends are catching Japanese beetles for Mrs. House when Jamie shoves a slim willow limb down a bee hole. The bees swarm out and Jamie is stung. Allergic to bee stings, Jamie screams and gasps and falls to the ground. His best friend thinks Jamie is just showing off, until the ambulance arrives. Jamie is dead by the time he arrives at the hospital. His friend goes to the funeral, and the author graphically describes his reaction to seeing Jamie:

> There was Jamie. He was out straight with one hand crossed over his chest. He didn't look like he was asleep to me. Jamie slept all bunched up. Jamie looked dead. (p. 34)

After the funeral Jamie's friend picks blackberries because the two of them had planned to do so together. He shares the berries with Jamie's mother, who is very loving toward him. Because the story is told in the first person, the reader views death through a child's eyes. Simple, yet direct, this story seems very real. Paterson's *Bridge to Terabithia* and Bauer's *On My Honor,* which were discussed earlier in this chapter, are each about a child who suffers after the death of a friend.

In *A Family Project* by Sarah Ellis, 11-year-old Jessica is delighted when her parents announce that Mum is pregnant. She embarks on a class project of researching babies with her best friend, Margaret. Baby Lucie's arrival creates the expected chaos but also provides Jessica with special moments of love and appreciation. One night when Jessica is at a friend's slumber party, Lucie dies suddenly of sudden infant death syndrome. Following the funeral and a large gathering of friends and relatives, each member of the family grieves. Mum withdraws, Dad is frenetically busy, her brother Simon is curt, and Jessica feels as if her life will never be joyous or whole again. Margaret acknowledges her friend's grief, saying that while time will help her feel less sad, she will always have a small sad spot in her memory for this baby sister. Weeks pass, and it is finally Simon and Jessica who help each other accept their sister's death. Ellis creates a totally believable contemporary family whose grief over the sudden death of a baby will be healed by their love for each other.

Several other stories deal with the process of grieving the death of a brother or sister. Barbara Park's *Mick Harte Was Here* begins after the bike accident that killed thirteen-year-old Phoebe's younger brother, Mick. As she remembers this lively boy and deals with her guilt at the petty quarrels they had, Phoebe learns that her mother and father are struggling under the burden of their own guilt. The family members finally acknowledge the "if onlys" each of them has carried silently. When Phoebe cries, "If only I had ridden his bike home Mick would still be here" (p. 84), her father sits her down and makes a list of all the other "if onlys" the family has used to blame themselves. Bringing these out into the open signals a new and healthier stage in their grieving. *Beat the Turtle Drum* by Constance Greene is narrated by 13-year-old Kate and tells of the summer that Joss had saved her money, rented a horse, and finally, in an accidental fall from a tree, was killed. Readers who have come to know the two sisters feel, along with Kate and her parents, the tragedy of Joss's death. *A Summer to Die* by Lois Lowry presents two sisters who quarrel constantly until the older one contracts leukemia. Lowry juxtaposes the celebration of birth with the sadness of a death, and Meg moves through the stages of dealing with her sister's death, but the other two stories seem more compelling.

Crescent Dragonwagon's *Winter Holding Spring* is a simple poetic story with complex ideas about death, time, hope, and love. It begins as 11-year-old Sarah and her father can tomatoes just as her mother used to before she died. Both adult and child find it difficult to talk about their feelings, but they observe, as a yellow leaf falls, that the season of summer holds fall. As the seasons progress, the two go about the daily chores of living, and Sarah uses the idea of a future embedded in the present to give herself hope and courage. This eventually allows Sarah to talk with her father about the small reminders of her mother: a twirly skirt she wore, the way she loved basil, and how much Sarah still misses her. As father and daughter talk, Sarah realizes that her mother's love will always remain with her. The elegant telling, the symbolism, and the philosophical discussion of death in the midst of life are grounded realistically for child readers in the ordinary events of Sarah's everyday life.

Another story that tells of a boy's emotional reconciliation following the death of a parent from cancer is told in Jean Little's *Mama's Going to Buy You a Mockingbird.* Eleven-year-old Jeremy and his little sister spend an uneasy summer at their cottage with an aunt while their father has an operation in a nearby Canadian city. When his father returns, weak and pale, Jeremy refuses to accept his father's impending death. One evening his father and he share a sighting of two owls, and his father commemorates the event by giving Jeremy a gift of a small carved owl. Later in the fall, when his father has died, Jeremy is unable to look at the owl and hides it on his bookshelf. He thinks,

Forgetting *was* the easiest way. When he forgot Dad was dead, when he forgot Dad altogether and concentrated on other things, then life was easier. When something made him think of his father—birds flying south, a song the two of them had liked coming over the radio, the sight of Dad's name written in the front of a book—he felt so mixed-up, lonely and scared that he wished with all his heart that he had not been made to remember. (p. 151)

His new but tentative friendship with lanky classmate Tess and a move to a new apartment where he adopts a grandfather helps cheer him. It is only when he begins to think of the feelings of others that he can finally hold the small owl and realize the "more difficult" joy that remembering brings. Jean Little crafts an extraordinary story out of richly observed detail, humor, and the emotions of this loving family's reconciliation with their loss. The many references to other novels and poems with which Jeremy and his sister are familiar are a plus for readers. Another fine story, *Home from Far,* also by Jean Little, portrays a girl's resentment and anger following the death of her twin brother.

Two books face the issue of AIDS and the death of a parent from this disease. In Teresa Nelson's *Earthshine*, Slim McGranahan's father is an out-of-work actor who is being cared for by his friend Larry when Slim leaves her mother and stepfather and moves in with the two. As Mack McGranahan deals with his sickness in his own indomitable way, Slim attends a support group for children and meets Isaiah, whose mother has the AIDS virus. Isaiah convinces Slim to take a pilgrimage to a healer as her father moves closer to death. Their strange journey does not bring a cure to her father, but it lifts the burden of anger and guilt from her own spirit. Gillian is the feisty, somewhat eccentric central character in Barbara Ann Porte's *Something Terrible Happened*. When her mother dies of AIDS, Gillian is sent to her deceased father's family in Tennessee. Gillian is angry that she could not stay with her grandmother and still grieving at losing her mother. But being with her father's family gives her a part of herself that this biracial child had not known, and brings her a stable family structure that is just what she needs to work through her grief. Porte tells the story through an unusual point of view: The unknown narrator recounts events as they were pieced together from multiple sources—eyewitness accounts, Gilly's letters, and the wonderful folktales that feature in Gilly's heritage.

Previously discussed books deal with a child who recovers from the death of a friend, sibling, parent, or grandparent. *Hang Tough, Paul Mather* tells a memorable story of a boy who is anticipating his own death. Alfred Slote writes of Paul, a Little Leaguer who develops leukemia. The family moves from California to Michigan to be close to the university hospital where Paul will have special treatments. He is not supposed to play baseball, but the neighborhood team needs a pitcher for their big game. Paul slips out without his parents' knowledge, forges the permission slip, and pitches a great game. However, he injures himself and endures a long stay in the hospital. There, a young doctor becomes his friend. Their discussion of death is one of the most honest in children's literature. Paul leaves the hospital in his wheelchair, at least long enough to watch and help win another game. While Paul sounds hopeful at the end of the story, he is back in the hospital and his condition has worsened.

Two books for older readers discuss the impact of an awareness of death on life's possibilities. Mollie Hunter's compelling autobiographical novel *A Sound of Chariots* is the story of a young Scottish girl coming to terms with her father's death. Living with her nightmares about her father, Bridie finally faces the real meaning of death when her brother's pet rabbit dies. She makes her brother touch the cold, stiff rabbit so he will finally know what dead means. Suddenly she is aware of her physical surroundings as if she could feel "the shape of the smallest stones on her feet . . . through all her senses she was filtering into their component parts the whole vast complex of smells and sounds, shapes, colors and textures through which she moved" (p. 135). At last Bridie knows she is alive, and despite her fear of death, she recognizes the present for the miracle it is.

Another powerful story that asserts that coming to terms with death can be an affirmation of life and hope is Madeleine L'Engle's *A Ring of Endless Light*. Vicky Austin, whom readers met in *Meet the Austins*, begins her sixteenth summer at graveside services for a family friend who has suffered a heart attack after rescuing a spoiled teenager from an attempted suicide. While Vicky is already grieving for the impending death of her beloved grandfather, she tries to understand what mortality and immortality mean. She also deals with the attentions of three different young men. Zachary, the boy who attempted suicide, is rich, impulsive, and exciting; Leo, whose father had tried to save Zachary, is plain and awkward but reliable and candid; and Adam, a marine biologist studying dolphin communication, is warm, kind, and intensely eager to involve Vicky in his research after he sees her natural ability to communicate with dolphins. When the death of a child numbs Vicky, it is her experience with the dolphins that brings her back to an emotional present. Throughout the story shines the "ring of endless light" that her grandfather has been leading her to see. He tells Vicky, in the depths of her grief and denial:

"You have to give the darkness permission. It cannot take over otherwise. . . . Vicky, do not add to the darkness. . . . This is my charge to you. You are to be a light-bearer. You are to choose the light." (p. 318)

Living in a Diverse World

In a true pluralistic society it is essential that we learn to respect and appreciate cultural diversity. Books can never substitute for firsthand contact with other people, but they can deepen our understanding of different cultures. Rather than falsely pretend that differences do not exist, children need to discover what is unique to each group of persons and universal to the experience of being human.

Appreciating Racial and Ethnic Diversity

The civil rights movement of the 1950s led to the publication of many books about integration (see Chapter 3). These books tended to emphasize similarity of groups rather than unique racial, cultural, or ethnic identities. Increasing activism in the 1960s further influenced the publication of books that featured Native Americans, Hispanic Americans, and African Americans. However, many of these titles went out of print rapidly when federal funds for schools and libraries diminished. We continue to need high-quality literature that reflects many ethnicities and the changing population of our schools. All readers should be able to find their own cultural heritage reflected in the literature they read. It is still necessary, however, to evaluate literature about minority people according to not only its general literary value but also the image of the minority group presented by the text and illustrations. The Guidelines "Evaluating Multicultural Literature" introduce some of the general criteria that teachers and librarians should keep in mind when reading literature written about other cultures.

African American Experiences in Books for Children

In the last decades many fine books have been published that reflect the social and cultural traditions associated with growing up as an African American child in America. This "culturally conscious fiction," says Rudine Sims, has certain recurring features that offer all children, but especially African American children, a unique perspective in fiction. In culturally conscious fiction there often appear references to distinctive language patterns and vocabulary; relationships between a young person and a much older one; extended or three-generational families; descriptions of skin shades, including positive comparisons, such as "dark as a pole of Ceylon ebony"; and acknowledgment of African American historical, religious, and cultural traditions.[18]

Today, there is an increasing number of picture books and folktales, by authors and illustrators such as Lucille Clifton, the late John Steptoe, Eloise Greenfield, Pat Cummings, Jerry Pinkney, and others, that portray an African American experience for younger readers (see Chapters 5 and 6). There is also an increasing but still small number of chapter books for younger

[18]Rudine Sims Bishop, *Shadow and Substance: Afro-American Experience in Contemporary Children's Fiction* (Urbana, Ill.: National Council of Teachers of English, 1982), pp. 49–77.

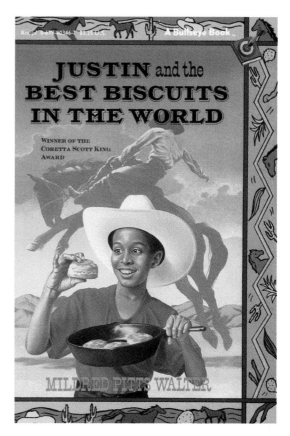

In *Justin and the Best Biscuits in the World* Mildred Pitts Walter interweaves the story of a contemporary African American boy with information about African American cowboys in the old West.
Cover of *Justin and the Best Biscuits in the World* by Mildred Pitts Walker, illustrated by Paul Tankersley. Copyright © 1991. Reprinted by permission of Alfred A. Knopf, Inc.

readers. For instance, Ann Cameron's Julian series, such as *Julian, Dream Doctor*, portrays a small-town family consisting of a soft-spoken mother, a stern but fun-loving father, and two brothers. Another chapter book children aged 7 or 8 can read easily is Lucille Clifton's *The Lucky Stone*. In four short chapters, Clifton traces the path of a black stone with a letter scratched on it as it is passed from generation to generation of African Americans, from slave times to now.

Mildred Pitts Walter's *Justin and the Best Biscuits in the World* draws on information about African American cowboys on the American frontier in the late 1800s while telling a contemporary story. Tired of his family of sisters and his mother, 10-year-old Justin is relieved when his grandfather invites him to stay at his Missouri ranch. From Grandpa, Justin learns family history and how to clean fish, keep his room in order, and cook. When he goes home, Justin has developed self-confidence and his family is more appreciative of his talents. Walter's

Guidelines:
Evaluating Multicultural Literature

While the emphasis should be placed on selecting high-quality literature, the following guidelines may be useful in evaluating literature that depicts minorities or other cultures. More-detailed guidelines can be found in Augusta Baker, *The Black Experience in Children's Books* (New York: New York Public Library, 1984); and Rudine Sims, *Shadow and Substance: Afro-American Experience in Contemporary Children's Fiction* (Urbana, Ill.: National Council of Teachers of English, 1982).

1. *Diversity and range of representation.* In the portrayal of any minority group, a collection of books should show a wide range of representation of that particular race or ethnic group. Some African Americans live in city ghetto or rural settings; others live in middle-class suburbs and small towns. Some Hispanic Americans make a living in migrant camps; most hold jobs that have nothing to do with seasonal crops. Only when a collection of books about a particular group offers a wide spectrum of occupations, educational backgrounds, living conditions, and lifestyles will we honestly be moving away from stereotyping in books and offering positive images about minorities.

2. *Avoidance of stereotyping.* Literature must depict the varieties of a particular culture or ethnic group. Illustrations should portray the distinctive yet varied characteristics of a group or race so that readers know they are looking at a people of, for example, Sioux, Jamaican, or Vietnamese descent. The portrayal of stereotypical articles should be avoided, such as the sombrero and poncho, a feathered headdress and moccasins, or the "pinkaninny with a watermelon" so often pictured in children's books from earlier decades. Literature should avoid implying that specific occupations (such as computer expert), recreational pastimes (such as soccer), family organizational structure, or values are descriptive of any particular race or ethnic group. (For further discussion of stereotypes, see the sections "Picture Books" in Chapter 5 and "Informational Books" in Chapter 11.)

3. *Language considerations.* Derogatory terms for particular racial groups should not be used in stories about minorities unless these are essential to a conflict or used in historical context. Even then, it should be made clear that the use of these unacceptable terms casts aspersion on the speaker, not the one spoken about or to. Another consideration is the use of dialect or "broken English." Some recent books about African Americans make a conscious effort to reproduce the cadence and syntax of certain language patterns without resorting to phonetically written spellings or stereotypical dialect. Books that incorporate the language of a minority group, such as Spanish, do not need to translate a word if context defines it. Children need to understand that all languages adequately serve their speakers and that no one language is better than another.

4. *The perspective of the book.* In evaluating a book about a minority group, we need to ask if it truly represents that minority's experience. This is a difficult guideline to define because we don't want to suggest there is only one sort of African American experience, for example. Who solves the problems in stories? Do minority characters take the initiative in problem solving or are solutions provided by paternalistic whites? Are racial pride and positive self-image apparent in the story? How authentic are the details of the story to the experience of the represented minority?

No one is free from his or her own particular bias or background. Teachers or librarians in specific school settings may want to add other criteria to this list as they select books for children. It is essential to provide books about minorities for *all* children and to choose variety, not merely reflect the minority population a specific school serves. Books can help develop children's appreciation for our ever-changing pluralistic society.

---

digressions about African Americans in the old West, under the guise of books read by Justin, might send some children to the library for further research. Another book by Walter, *Have a Happy . . .* , traces an 11-year-old boy's feelings as he tries to earn money to help out his family during the Christmas season. His participation in the events of Kwanza is presented so that even readers unfamiliar with this modern African American holiday can visualize the celebration and understand its significance.

In *Sister,* using the device of a secret diary about her "special days," Eloise Greenfield has presented an intimate picture of Doretha, called "Sister" by her family. The diary begins when Doretha is 10, and details the sudden death of her father while they are all attending a picnic. At 11 Doretha learns the family's story of her freedom-fighting ex-slave ancestor. When she is 12 she records her tears and her mother's disappointment when her mother's friend jilts her. Throughout the book Doretha worries about her alienated sister, but gradually

Doretha emerges from the pages of her book and from her role as sister to become a very real person in her own right.

A four-time winner of the Coretta Scott King Award, Walter Dean Myers sets many of his stories in Harlem, but he portrays a less grim, and even humorous, city existence in some of his stories. *The Mouse Rap*, which alternates between poetry and prose, is written in the vernacular and slang of jive-talking, rapping, 14-year-old Mouse Douglas, boy "hoop" player. Mouse's parents are separated but his father wants to rejoin the family, and Mouse and his best friend Styx like the same girl. In addition, Mouse and his friends know an old man who used to be part of Tiger Moran's gang. The old fellow says there is money from a 1930s bank robbery hidden in an abandoned Harlem building. In an exciting and humorous conclusion, Mouse cleverly uses a television news reporter who is in the neighborhood covering a dance contest he and his friends have entered to gain a chance to explore the abandoned building. Myers also relies on the keen observations of an intelligent boy narrator in his *Fast Sam, Cool Clyde, and Stuff*, a story of the interdependence of a group of basketball-playing boys who inadvertently become involved with drugs while trying to help a former addict. The author's lighter books also show boys coping successfully with urban life.

In 1975, Virginia Hamilton became the first African American to win the Newbery Medal, with *M. C. Higgins, the Great*. Like *Cousins*, it is set in southern Ohio where 13-year-old Cornelius Higgins and his family live on old family property just beneath a slag heap created by strip miners. M. C. dreams of moving his family away from the slow-moving heap that threatens to engulf their home. His place of refuge from which he surveys the world is a 40-foot steel pole. From there M. C. sees a "dude" who he imagines will make his mother a singing star and enable them to move. Another outsider, Lurhetta, who is hiking through this section of Appalachia, awakens M. C.'s initiative and makes him see that he is never going to solve his problems by daydreaming about them. M. C. is finally moved to a small but symbolic action. (Mildred Taylor in 1977 was the second African American author to win the Newbery Medal. Her books are discussed in Chapter 10.)

Hamilton has also written *The Planet of Junior Brown*, which is really a story about three complementary "planets." The first planet is a huge mass added to a model solar system that Mr. Poole, the custodian, and Buddy have set up in the school basement. Like the 300-pound Buddy, the planet is larger than anything else in its area. The second is a set of sanctuaries for homeless boys throughout the forgotten places of New York City, held together by boys like Junior Brown who act as leaders of children who do not have homes or

families. The final planet is the one that readers see as possible if people like Junior Brown could lead us there. This planet could be a place where everyone belongs, where people respect each other, and where all value themselves as well. Hamilton's books celebrate the uniqueness of an African American experience in elegant and approachable prose. Her books speak to all readers, encouraging young people to take risks on behalf of others, to love all members of their immediate or extended or adopted families, and to do their best to act responsibly and honorably, for all of these actions will improve a small part of humankind.

Several books look at middle-class African Americans and the special pressures they face as they try to succeed in an often hostile white world. Jacqueline Woodson's Margaret and Maizon are best friends growing up in Brooklyn when Maizon wins a scholarship to a mostly white private school. Her struggles to fit into a world that is alien and alienating are detailed in *Maizon at Blue Hill*. Margaret's own year apart from Maizon is related in *Last Summer with Maizon*. The two are reunited in *Between Madison and Palmetto* when Maizon drops out of Blue Hill and returns home to Madison Street. In all these books the girls confront difficult issues of race and class, but first and foremost these are stories about real young people whose friendship is strengthened through a variety of trials.

The Willis family in Andrea Davis Pinkney's *Hold Fast to Dreams* must confront similar issues when they move to suburban Connecticut from urban Baltimore. Dee's father has been promoted to vice president of sales at the Kentwood Corporation. Dee has a hard time fitting into the all-white environment of Wexford Middle School and misses her close friends in Baltimore. Eventually she finds that everyone in the family has had to confront some form of racism. She has had to deal with muffled whispers and "beady eyed" stares of classmates who know nothing of her world. Her sister has responded to her private-school classmates by "trying to act white" but is humiliated by her lacrosse teammates. Her father is harassed by a security guard at work, and her mother is trying desperately to pretend everything is fine. Mr. Willis admits his own problems and tells the girls that he finally had to stand up to the guard,

When white folks stare and wonder and show disrespect, it's best to kindly—but firmly—let them know that you won't stand for it. Then you've just got to go on about your business. I figure if they don't have anything better to do than watch every blink I make, then boo-*hoo* for *them*. (p. 82)

His actions serve as a model for each of the girls to find a way to deal honorably with her own situation. Dee wins acceptance at an important all-school talent

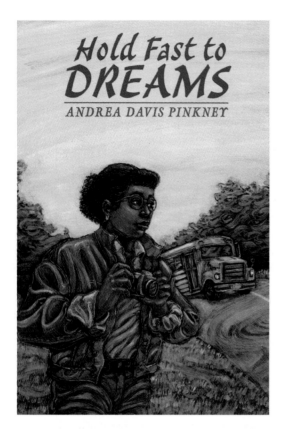

In Andrea Davis Pinkney's *Hold Fast to Dreams,* Dee Willis is a middle-class African American girl who must face an all-white environment when her family moves to the suburbs.

Illustration from the cover of the book *Hold Fast to Dreams* copyright © 1995 by Brian Pinkney. Written by Andrea Davis Pinkney. Published by William Morrow & Company. All rights reserved. Used with permission.

assembly when she presents her photographs and a reading of Langston Hughes's poems. She also accepts something of the realities of the new world her family must live in and comes to value the loyalty and good humor of a new white friend.

Books About Other Minorities

For some years there have been far better quality and range in novels about African Americans than there are for other minorities. Informational books, folktales, biographies, and picture books have done a much better job of reflecting the multicultural society in which we now live. In older books about Hispanic Americans, for instance, forced stories and thin characterizations tended to perpetuate stereotypes rather than dispel them. Other titles, such as *Felita* by Nicolasa Mohr, suggest that "stick to your own kind" is the only way 9-year-old Felita and her family can cope with prejudice from their new neighbors. They return to the ghetto rather than stay in an apartment building where they have no friends. In *Going Home,* Felita, now a sixth grader, spends a summer in Puerto Rico and recognizes

the universality of prejudice when her friendliness and artistic talents cause jealousy from her Puerto Rican peers.

In striking contrast, Gary Soto's *Baseball in April and Other Stories* and *Local News* are inspired collections of short stories that depict a variety of Hispanic children in daily life. In *Baseball in April* Fausto longs for a guitar but his scheme to raise the money to buy one makes him feel so guilty that he finally gives the money to a church. His honorable behavior is amply rewarded when he becomes the owner of his grandfather's *guitarron.* In other stories one girl becomes marbles champ while another learns that it may be more painful to stay home when your family goes on vacation than it is to endure their company. *Local News* includes the wonderfully funny "School Play" and the sweetly gentle "New Year's Eve." Soto's portrayal of these central-Californian youngsters, through description and dialogue, reflects a sympathy for the universal experiences of growing up. Soto's fine novels explore these experiences further. In *Taking Sides,* Lincoln Mendoza finds that he has divided loyalties when he moves from a barrio school to a suburban junior high school and competes in basketball against his former teammates. In *Pacific Crossing,* Lincoln and his friend Tony travel to Japan for a summer exchange program and find a further mixture of culture. *Crazy Weekend* and *Summer on Wheels* follow the adventures of Hector and Mando, two teenage friends, and in *Boys at Work* and *The Pool Party* 10-year-old Rudy Herrera is the main character. In all his books Soto writes gentle stories of family and friends that are infused with the rhythms and images of Mexican American culture. Glossaries in the books help those readers who cannot use context to translate the Spanish words and phrases that flow naturally through the story.

An older story of a boy of Spanish descent is Joseph Krumgold's *. . . And Now Miguel.* Miguel is the middle brother of a Hispanic family living on a New Mexico sheep ranch. Pedro, the younger brother, seems satisfied with what he has, but Miguel thinks his 19-year-old brother Gabriel not only can do everything but also has everything. Miguel has one all-consuming desire, and that is to be able to go with the men when they take the sheep to the Sangre de Cristo Mountains. His prayers are answered, but not as Miguel wished. Because Hispanics are one of the fastest growing groups of immigrants to the United States, we still urgently need more contemporary realistic fiction that reflects Hispanic culture.

Asian Americans are among the most rapidly growing minority groups in North America. Many of the excellent stories set in this country that include children from countries in Asia are historical fiction titles such as Yoshiko Uchida's books that build on her experiences in the 1930s and in relocation camps for Japanese

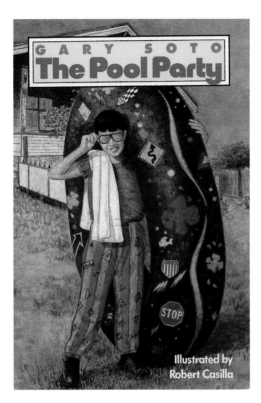

When a fancy invitation arrives from beautiful Tiffany, 10-year-old Rudy Herrera gets all decked out for a party in *The Pool Party* by Gary Soto.

From *The Pool Party* by Gary Soto. Illustrated by Robert Casilla. Copyright © 1993 by Gary Soto. Illustrations © 1993 by Robert Casilla. Used by permission of Bantam Doubleday Dell Books for Young Readers.

Americans in World War II. Jean Fritz's *Homesick: My Own Story* and Bette Bao Lord's *In the Year of the Boar and Jackie Robinson* are also in the past.

Notable exceptions are Laurence Yep's fine contemporary novels. *Child of the Owl* is the story of a Chinese American girl who finds herself and her roots when she goes to live with Paw Paw, her grandmother, in San Francisco's Chinatown. At first Casey doesn't like the narrow streets and alleys or the Chinese schools. But Paw Paw tells her about Jeanie, the mother Casey never knew, about her true Chinese name, and the story of the family's owl charm. Gradually she comes to appreciate it all and to realize that this place that has been home to Paw Paw, Jeanie, and Barney is her home, too. *Child of the Owl* is as contemporary as the rock music that Paw Paw enjoys and as traditional as the owl charm, but Casey and Paw Paw are true originals. *Thief of Hearts* follows Casey's daughter Stacy on her own journey to understanding. Set in contemporary suburbia south of San Francisco, the book explores more subtle issues of prejudice and belonging. A mixed-race child, Stacy has her father's blond hair and her mother's Chinese eyes. She is a confident adolescent, at home in her multiethnic middle school, until her mother urges a new

friend upon her. Hong Ch'un and her family are newly arrived from China and the girl is aloof and critical of American society. She and Stacy do not hit it off at all. When Hong Ch'un is accused of theft, however, Stacy stands up for her and finds that friends whom she has trusted hold her mixed-race status against her. Suddenly she sees her world in a different light.

> All my life I thought I had lived in a safe warm secure world where I was just like everyone else, but it had only been my little fantasy. I looked too Chinese. And yet, even if I learned Chinese and the culture, I looked too American. (p. 45)

Fortunately Paw Paw is there to set things right. Now called Tai-Paw, Stacy's great-grandmother, the wonderful old woman, has moved in with the family. She, too, has lost her familiar world, and this becomes even clearer when she and Stacy return to Chinatown to solve the mystery regarding Hong Ch'un. The Chinatown that existed when she raised Stacy's mother is almost unrecognizable and many of her old friends are dead. But the old woman is as wise as ever and she helps heal some of Stacy's hurt at the same time as she smooths a growing rift between Stacy and her mom. Well written, with fully developed, likable characters and a wonderful story, *Thief of Hearts* is a worthy sequel to *Child of the Owl*.

In *Later, Gator* Yep writes for a slightly younger audience and takes a lighter tone to tell the story of Teddy and his annoyingly perfect younger brother, Bobby. When Teddy's mother nags him to get a really nice birthday present for Bobby, she has a quiet turtle in mind. Instead, Teddy comes home with an alligator, and both he and his family are in for a big surprise. Lensey Namioka also addresses a younger audience in *Yang the Youngest and His Terrible Ear*. Nine-year-old Yingtao Yang would rather play baseball than practice the violin with his musical siblings. His American friend Matthew has the opposite problem. Unlike Yingtao, he has quite an ear for music and would love to have violin lessons. With the help of Third Sister everyone gets to play the instrument of his or her choice. Third Sister, Yingmei, has her own problems to deal with in *Yang the Third and Her Impossible Family*. Both of these warm, amusing books tell of a Chinese immigrant family and their attempts to fit in with the people and customs of their new country.

Jamie Gilson's novel *Hello, My Name Is Scrambled Eggs* takes its name from the stick-on labels Harvey Trumble uses to teach Vietnamese refugee Tuan Nguyen to speak English while Tuan, his father, and his grandmother are staying with Harvey until their own home is ready. But 12-year-old Tuan, eager to please, is nonetheless his own person, too, and he decides that although he will be American, he will also keep his Vietnamese

Yingtao Yang would rather be playing with a baseball than a violin in Lensey Namioka's *Yang the Youngest and His Terrible Ear.*
From *Yang the Youngest and His Terrible Ear* by Lensey Namioka. Text copyright © 1992 by Lensey Namioka. Illustration copyright © 1992 by Kees de Kiefte. By permission of Little, Brown and Company.

name. Gilson allows Tuan to reveal parts of his harrowing boat escape from Vietnam, and a classmate's current-events report fills in other details. Like Barbara Cohen's historical story *Molly's Pilgrim,* this novel culminates symbolically in a Thanksgiving celebration. Both would be excellent catalysts for discussing the many reasons, including political repression, that have caused people to emigrate to the United States.

Novels about Native American minorities are also scarce. The following books with geographically diverse settings, all depict adolescents involved in survival who must draw on their Native American heritage in various ways.

In Kirkpatrick Hill's well-crafted survival story *Toughboy and Sister,* the title characters are suddenly on their own at the family summer fish camp in Canada's Yukon Territory after their widowed father, an alcoholic, literally drinks himself to death. Eleven-year-old Toughboy, an Athabascan Indian, and his sister expect to be rescued in a few days because their father's boat with his corpse in it will float downriver by their village. But when no one comes, the two must work together to cook, fish, make bread, deal with a pesky bear, and keep their clothes and cabin clean. The trials of these two resourceful children don't compare to those in many other stories in the survival genre, which usually feature greater dangers and deprivations. However, this story does provide fourth- and fifth-grade readers with a sympathetic glimpse into the life of two self-reliant and strong Native American children.

In Jean Craighead George's *The Talking Earth,* Billy Wind, a Seminole Indian girl who has been to school at the Kennedy Space Center, scoffs at the legends of her ancestors. As punishment, she is sent to stay in the Everglades for one night and two days to see if she then

will believe in talking animals and little people who live under the ground. In the company of a baby panther, a pet otter, and a turtle, she survives a swamp fire, a hurricane, and a tidal wave; after twelve weeks in the wilderness, she arrives home convinced that the animals do indeed know the earth as she and others do not. As in *Julie of the Wolves* (discussed previously in this chapter), George states a powerful ecological message.

Bearstone by Will Hobbs tells the story of 14-year-old Cloyd Atcitty, a Ute Indian who has lived resentfully in a group home in Durango, Colorado, for much of his life. Cloyd is placed for the summer on a ranch where he will work for an old widower named Walter. Angry, Cloyd runs off after he is driven to the remote ranch in the Colorado/Utah mountain country. Taking refuge in a small cave, he discovers a small carved stone bear, an animal important to Ute tribal beliefs. Adopting this bear as his totem, Cloyd decides to give Walter and ranch life a try. While Cloyd and Walter develop respect for each other, Cloyd finds respect for himself. More important, in this excellent coming-of-age story, Cloyd's knowledge of his people's ways finally gives him the power to control his own life. *Beardance* continues Cloyd's story.

Understanding Various World Cultures

Despite the increasing number of fine books of nonfiction and folklore and picture books from and about other countries, there are fewer novels that attempt to portray the lives of modern children and their families living in other places. Yet, as children study Australia or the countries of South America, Europe, or Africa, it is critical that they also be made aware of the stories that reveal the feelings of people in those countries. Children will find descriptions of Australian culture in books by such fine writers as Ivan Southall, Colin Thiele, Patricia Wrightson, Ruth Park, Emily Rodda (see Chapter 7), and Robin Klein. In addition, the American Library Association annually gives the Batchelder Award to the publisher of the most outstanding book of that year originally published in a foreign language in a foreign country. These books are excellent firsthand accounts of life in other countries (see Appendix A). However, children might need to be reminded that no single book can convey a complete picture of a country and its people. To make this point clear, one might ask students to consider what book, if any, they would like to have sent to other countries as representative of life in the United States.

One of the few novels that reflect urban life in a Central American country is Ann Cameron's *The Most Beautiful Place in the World,* which tells of 7-year-old Juan who lives in Guatemala. His young mother has remarried, but her new husband can't support Juan, so he

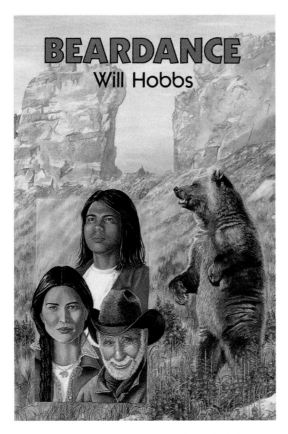

Native American Cloyd Atcitty almost loses his life in an attempt to save two grizzly bear cubs in Will Hobb's exciting *Beardance*.
From *Beardance* by Will Hobbs, 1993.

moves in with his grandmother. His grandmother makes her living by selling *arroz con leche* in the market every day, and she puts Juan to work helping her in the marketplace. As he waits for customers, he practices reading on scraps of newspaper, produce signs, and other print that comes his way. When Juan asks to go to school, his grandmother tries to enroll him, but they are nearly turned away until Juan shows that he has learned to read. When his grandmother explains why she never went to school, Juan realizes how important an education could have been to her. He might live in the most beautiful place in the world, as the travel poster says, but he knows that truly the best place is where there is someone like his grandmother who loves him. Thomas B. Allen's black-line drawings capture the warmth of Juan's life, yet the artist also reveals the cold realities of the boy's poverty and abandonment. Third- or fourth-grade children who read this story learn something of the geography of Guatemala, the distant volcanoes and the cornfields, the customary stroll through the streets in the evening, and what a marketplace is like. However, they learn nothing about the political realities or the pervasive military influence in this country.

In contrast, one child's discovery of political realities is the focus of several books about South Africa. In Beverley Naidoo's *Journey to Jo'burg*, 13-year-old Naledi is forced to face the terrible realities of apartheid when she must journey from her sheltered village to Johannesburg. On the way, Naledi contrasts her own family's values and lifestyle with those of the white families and begins to question the political system that divided South Africa. In a sequel for older readers, *Chain of Fire*, Naledi learns that the people of her village are to be relocated to a "homeland." A peaceful student demonstration is violently terminated by police, some of Naledi's neighbors betray their own people, and homes are bulldozed. The move will eventually transpire, but not before Naledi and others unify to fight injustice.

Sheila Gordon's *The Middle of Somewhere* depicts the effects on two families of relocating their village. Nine-year-old Rebecca's family refuses to leave, and when Rebecca's father is arrested in a demonstration, the family must struggle to survive without him. Outside observers at his trial help gain his release at the time when Nelson Mandela is also released. This story of a family helping itself through difficult times is written for a younger reader than Gordon's earlier *Waiting for the Rain*, which also captures a feel for the geography, the people, and the language of South Africa. Happily these books can now be read as historical fiction but they give young readers a powerful glimpse of human rights abuses that continue in other parts of the world.

Such issues are still very much at the center of many countries in the Western hemisphere, and several excellent novels for middle school readers provide a powerful glimpse of what it is like to live in poverty and fear. In Frances Temple's *Taste of Salt*, two voices retell events in recent Haitian history as Djo, one of Father Jean-Bertrand Aristide's street boys, lies near death from a fire bombing by Aristide's enemies. Jeremie, a Haitian girl, has been sent to record Djo's story and perhaps to give him reason to live. At first Djo's voice, full of the rhythms of the native Creole, remembers his childhood in the streets and alleys of Port-au-Prince, the harshness of his life, and the political realities of Haiti. When Djo slips into a coma, Jeremie's distinctive voice takes up the narrative. Born into poverty like Djo, she has been fortunate to fall under the protection of Catholic nuns and to be educated at the same time as she has been sheltered from important truths. As she reflects on her own and Djo's stories, she is faced with difficult choices about the future. The title *Taste of Salt* comes from the books that one of the priests is using to teach Djo and others to read. The term is taken from the belief that giving a zombie a taste of salt will open his true eyes and he will become free of his master. It is a powerful hope to give an oppressed people.

The story of a young Haitian girl, Paulie, and a small group of refugees desperately trying to escape to the United states is told in Temple's *Tonight, by Sea*, while her *Grab Hands and Run* follows the journey of a family from El Salvador who must flee government soldiers after the father disappears. Their journey on a modern-day underground railroad to freedom in Canada is full of danger, despair, and betrayal. Temple's books give vivid and compelling accounts of the human yearning for freedom and security, and the terrible price that some must pay to obtain the rights too many of us take for granted.

Other books give readers a glimpse of the environments and cultures of Asian and South Asian countries. In *The Year of the Panda* by Miriam Schlein, Lu Yi rescues a starving baby panda against his father's wishes and names it Su Lin. The pandas are moving down from the high ground, where their food source, bamboo, has died out as it does every seventy years. Their needs conflict with those of the people in Su Lin's village, and the government urges the villagers to relocate so that their land can be made into a refuge for wild pandas. His family refuses to move, and Lu Yi agrees to accompany his pet by helicopter to a panda rescue center. There he witnesses what American and Chinese scientists are doing to save the giant pandas. His sadness at leaving Su Lin behind is tempered by the center's invitation for him to be a student aide the following year. Schlein's notes at the end of the story satisfy third and fourth graders' need to know "what happened next" while her research suggests the ways countries work together to save endangered species.

In Emily Cheney Neville's story *The China Year*, 14-year-old Henrietta Rich spends a year in Beijing while her father is a "foreign expert" at the university. Through Henri's eyes, readers see modern Chinese city living just before the Chinese army drove into Tienanmen Square. The story unfolds in a variety of ways: Henri writes to friends back home, completes assignments for her correspondence courses, tells a 6-year-old American friend stories, and talks with a Chinese friend, Minyuan, and others about the differences between Chinese and Americans. Cheney's slow-moving story both mirrors Henri's pace as she struggles to understand Chinese culture and subtly allows readers to absorb and visualize details of life in China in the early 1990s.

The Land I Lost: Adventures of a Boy in Vietnam by Quang Nhuong Huynh is a series of portraits remembered from the author's home village in the central highlands of Vietnam. Although it is "endless years of fighting" that make his homeland lost, his reminiscences barely mention war. Instead, his stories focus on people: farmers, hunters, bandits, his karate-expert grandmother, his older cousin who could capture pythons and train birds to sing popular tunes. Each

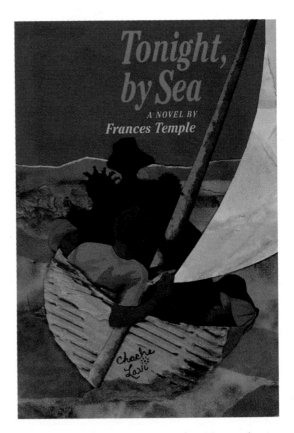

Francis Temple tells a moving story of Haitians trying to escape from their country's brutality in *Tonight, by Sea*.
From *Tonight, By Sea* by Frances Temple. Jacket illustration copyright © 1995 by Frances Temple. Reprinted by permission of the Publisher, Orchard Books, New York.

episode is sparely told, often humorous, and infused with the elusive meanings of folklore. *The Land I Lost* personalizes the Vietnamese people and can help children become acquainted with what has so often been represented as an alien land.

A Vietnamese girl comes to terms with the trauma of escaping from her country without knowing what has happened to the rest of her family in Diana Kidd's brief *Onion Tears*. In first-person narrative, Nam reveals her life with Auntie and another refugee called Chu Minh who cooks in Auntie's restaurant. As time passes, Nam is able to shed real tears over the sickness of her teacher instead of the onion tears she sheds as she helps in Auntie's kitchen. Instead of being a lonely survivor, she is now a part of a school and a neighborhood community. Based on interview accounts of girls who journeyed from Southeast Asia to Australia, this story has many gaps that readers must fill in by inference. Children might be misled by Lucy Montgomery's line drawings, which misrepresent the characters' ages. This book would be a good small-group choice for its excellent discussion possibilities about Nam and the qualities she possesses that make her, too, a survivor.

Several excellent books about countries in the Middle East provide young people with insights into social and political issues at the same time as they involve readers with compelling characters in exciting stories. Elizabeth Laird's *Kiss the Dust* follows the journey of 13-year-old Tara and her family of middle-class Kurds. They have a comfortable home in Iraq, but because the father has been involved with the Kurdish resistance movement, the family is forced to flee. They journey first to the mountains of northern Iraq, where they experience rural Kurdish culture, and then they are forced into a refugee camp in Iran. Finally they are able to emigrate to England, but their lives are drastically altered by the events that have taken place. In Gaye Hiçyilmaz's *Against the Storm*, 12-year-old Mehmet and his family try to escape the circumstances of poverty. When they leave their beautiful country village to move to Ankara, their previously close family is torn apart by the crowded and dehumanizing conditions of the city. Only Mehmet seems to have the energy to fight against this storm and seek a better life. Vedat Dalokay's view of Turkey is more benign in *Sister Shako and Kolo the Goat*. Suitable for a younger audience, this evocative memoir centers on an old woman whose family has been killed in a vendetta and who moves into a deserted stable on the narrator's father's land. Kolo is the unusual and somewhat miraculous goat who appears at Sister Shako's door one day. This "Guest of God," as Sister calls her, becomes the leader of the village flock and the perpetrator of some funny and strangely supernatural incidents. The book is memorable not so much for its facts about Turkish life but for its sense of a Turkish culture, which is conveyed through the cadences of the prose and the images in the writing.

The Cholistan desert area of modern Pakistan is the setting for the coming-of-age story *Shabanu: Daughter of the Wind*, Suzanne Fisher Staples's riveting portrait of a young girl in a family of nomadic camel herders. Shabanu, nearly 12, knows that she must accept an arranged marriage in the next year following the wedding of her older sister Phulan. However, as the time of Phulan's marriage draws near, the two girls are accosted by a rich landowner's hunting guests, who threaten to abduct and rape the pair. In seeking revenge, Phulan's intended husband is killed. Phulan is quickly married to her sister's betrothed, and Shabanu is promised against her will to an older man as his fourth wife. Shabanu struggles to reconcile her own independent spirit with her loyalty to her family. An aunt offers support, saying, "Keep your wits about you. Trust yourself. Keep your inner reserves hidden." Shabanu chooses to run away, but when a much loved camel she has raised breaks his leg in the desert, she decides to stay with him and accept the beating she knows will follow when her father finds her. She will accept her marriage, too, but she vows to herself that no one can ever unlock the secrets of her heart. Telling her compelling story in present tense, Shabanu faces giving up her life as a camel herder, discovers and accepts her sexuality, and finds a place in the adult world. Vivid details of camel behavior, camel-trading fairs, feasts and celebrations, the differing roles of men and women, and the ever-changing desert are brilliantly evoked for older readers. It is difficult for Western readers to imagine that this story takes place today. Reading *Shabanu* and its sequel *Haveli* would certainly lead readers to discuss women's roles in other countries as well as in their own.

Many young-adult novels also deal with contemporary life in other lands. *The Honorable Prison* by Lyll Becerra de Jenkins depicts the internment of Marta's family in an Andean Mountain village when her father's political opinions fall out of favor. In *The Forty-Third War* by Louise Moeri, 12-year-old Uno is conscripted into the army and forced, like the reader, to learn of the harsh realities of a Central American military state. *The Return* by Sonia Levitin is a survival story of Ethiopian Jews trying to escape to Jerusalem. Minfong Ho's *Rice Without Rain* presents the class struggles for land reform in Thailand in the 1970s as seen by 17-year-old Jinda. While some middle schoolers may be ready for the complex political and emotional scopes of young-adult novels such as these, teachers should first read any of these titles before introducing them into the classroom.

All children deserve a chance to read about the lives of children in other lands. As modern technology reduces the distances between cultures, books such as these contribute to a deeper, richer, more sympathetic and enduring communication between people.

The Teaching Feature "Teachers Discuss Literature by and About Minorities" shows how three teachers began an effort to introduce their district to some of the many books that represent the cultures of their community and the children of the world.

Popular Types of Realistic Fiction

Certain categories of realistic fiction are so popular that children ask for them by name. They want a good animal story, usually about a dog or horse; a sports book; a "funny" book; or a good mystery. Each decade seems to have a popular series, as well, that lingers on the bookshelves. From Gertrude Chandler Warner's Boxcar Children to Ann Martin's Baby-Sitters Club series, from Nancy Drew and the Hardy Boys to Patricia Reilly Giff's Kids of Polk Street School series, children read one volume of a series and demand the next. Many of these books are not high-quality literature, and we would hope that children would not read these titles to the exclusion

Teaching Feature

Teachers Discuss Literature by and About Minorities

Three curriculum specialists in the Fairfax County Public Schools in northern Virginia were concerned that teachers were not incorporating books by and about minorities into their classroom reading programs. With a significant and growing population of minorities, the school system needed to modify its choices of assigned reading. The specialists noted that while they provided annually updated book lists and library media specialists added multicultural titles to school collections, these titles did not then become a part of classroom study. They concluded that teachers would not work recent books into their curriculum unless they had read and discussed the books. Providing book lists was not enough to change teacher behaviors.

A modest sum of grant money was available for programs that would "improve minority achievement." So they invited teachers in grades 4 through 12 to hold book discussion groups. Groups of at least three teachers agreed to discuss one book per month for a three-, four-, or five-month period. In-service credits could be earned for time spent in discussion. They supplied a list of paperback books (purchased with grant and other money) that could be checked out from a central office location and were available in multiple copies. Titles included Gary Soto's *Baseball in April*, *El Chino* by Allen Say, *The Talking Earth* by Jean Craighead George, Virginia Hamilton's *Cousins*, Diana Kidd's *Onion Tears*, and Mildred Taylor's *The Friendship*.

They were overwhelmed by the response. Over three hundred administrators and teachers in all subject areas formed groups in 35 of the 37 schools in their area. The three facilitators drew up charts of which schools needed which books and shipped them via interoffice mail. The facilitators' advice to discussion leaders was to talk about the book. "Talk about whatever you want. Did you like it? Was it good? And save the inevitable question of how you would use it in the classroom for the very last." The groups began to meet.

As a result of these discussions, teachers discovered many books that were new to them and also read beyond the book list to find additional titles to add to it. Their book evaluation skills increased. They became risk takers as they ventured opinions and discovered how others' responses meshed with, illuminated, or conflicted with their own. In fact, in evaluating the program, teachers indicated that what was most important to them was the experience of discussing books with their peers. Many of the books are now in children's hands. A grant provided some extra funding so that participating schools could purchase literature featuring minorities. The discussion groups are still meeting and continuing to add new books to their classroom reading plans.

This could happen anywhere, couldn't it? What it takes is some planning, some seed money to purchase multiple paperbacks of selected titles, and the belief that teachers are willing to change if given support.

This program was designed and carried out by Joan Lewis, Shirley Bealor, and Patricia M. Williams, Curriculum Specialists in Area II of the Fairfax County Public Schools.

---

of other books. Yet many of these stories do serve the useful function of getting children hooked on books so that they will move on to better literature.[19] Children also develop fluency and reading speed as they quickly read through popular books or a series. Teachers and librarians need to identify and evaluate these popular books. Knowing and honoring the books children like increases an adult adviser's credibility, while also allowing him or her to recommend other titles that can broaden children's reading choices. Resources for Teaching, " 'To Be Continued'—Popular Series Books for Children," lists some of the popular series books for children.

[19]See Margaret Mackey's "Filling the Gaps: *The Baby-Sitters Club*, the Series Book, and the Learning Reader," *Language Arts* 67, no. 5 (September 1990): 484–489 and *Bookbird* 33, no. 3/4, special issue "Bad Books, Good Reading" (fall/winter 1995–1996).

Humorous Stories

Children like to laugh. The humorous verses of contemporary poets like Shel Silverstein and Jack Prelutsky are some of children's favorite poetry (see Chapter 8). Collections of jokes and riddles circulate at all levels of the elementary school. Humorous realistic fiction often presents characters involved in amusing or exaggerated predicaments that are solved in clever or unique ways. Often these stories are episodic in plot structure—each chapter might stand alone as a complete story.

Beverly Cleary's stories about Ramona have probably made more real readers than any basal reading series has. Cleary has written another genuinely funny series of books about a very normal boy, starting with *Henry Huggins*. In this first book Henry's problems center on a stray dog named Ribsy and Henry's efforts to keep him.

Resources for Teaching
"To Be Continued"—Popular Series Books for Children

Author	Titles	Description	Grade Level
Betsy Byars	*Bingo Brown, Gypsy Lover* and others	A funny look at a young adolescent boy's problems as he grows up.	4–8
Betsy Byars	*The Dark Stairs* *Tarot Says Beware*	Mysteries starring Herculeah Jones and her friend Meat.	4–6
Betsy Byars	*Wanted . . . Mud Blossom* and others	The continuing adventures of the wacky Blossom family.	3–6
Ann Cameron	*The Stories Julian Tells* and others	Easy-reading adventures of a young African American boy.	1–4
Eleanor Cameron	*Julia and the Hand of God* and others	A well-written series that chronicles the growing up of a young California girl in the years after World War I.	4–8
Judith Caseley	*Harry and Arney* and others	A funny series that centers on Harry and the everyday occurrences in his Jewish family.	1–3
Matt Christopher	*Dirt Bike Racer, Skateboard Tough,* and others	A long list of titles by Christopher that center on the thrill of the play and action of a sport.	3–7
Ilene Cooper	*Choosing Sides* and others	The Kids from Kennedy Middle School series, which treats middle school themes both humorously and seriously.	5–8
Helen Cresswell	*Ordinary Jack* and other titles in the Bagthorpe saga	The hilarious adventures of a brillantly talented, if somewhat eccentric, British family.	4–7
Paula Danzinger	*Amber Brown Goes Fourth* and others	A feisty heroine gives an appealing first-person account of her trials and tribulations.	2–4
Walter Farley	*The Black Stallion* and others	Popular horse and dog adventures.	3–7
Patricia Reilly Giff	*The Beast in Ms. Rooney's Room* and others	Adventures of the Kids of Polk Street School through second grade.	1–3
Jamie Gilson	*Hobie Hanson, Greatest Hero of the Mall* and others	A fourth grader's antics in and out of school.	2–4
Sheila Greenwald	*Rosy Cole, She Walks in Beauty* and others	The ups and downs of an indomitable grade school girl.	2–5
Carolyn Haywood	*"B" is for Betsy* and others	A classic series about Betsy and Eddie that provides a safe, predictable experience for fledgling readers.	1–3
Marguerite Henry	*Misty of Chincoteague* and others	Well-researched, well-written, and well-loved horse stories.	3–6
James Howe	*Dew Drop Dead* and others	Sebastian Barth mysteries, which develop situations and characters to a depth seldom found in a mystery series.	4–6
Johanna Hurwitz	*Aldo Applesauce* and others	Humorous stories featuring fifth grader Aldo and his friend DeDe.	2–5
Johanna Hurwitz	*Busybody Nora* and others	Episodic family stories featuring Elisa, Russell, Nora, and her brother Teddy, who all live in the same apartment building.	1–3
Rebecca Jones	*Germy Blew It* and others	A hilarious series centering on Jeremy Bluett and life in the sixth grade.	3–6

Resources for Teaching
"To Be Continued"—Popular Series Books for Children (concluded)

Author	Titles	Description	Grade Level
Suzy Kline	*Orp Goes to the Hoop* and others	Sports stories with a middle school hero.	5–8
Janet Taylor Lisle	*The Gold Dust Letters* and others	Well-written books featuring "Investigators of the Unknown," friends who solve mysteries that might or might not involve the supernatural.	2–4
Maude Hart Lovelace	*Betsy-Tacy* and others	A popular series, originally published in the 1940s, that details the adventures of two best friends.	2–5
Lois Lowry	*Anastasia Krupnik* and others	Sensitive, funny, and well-written books with a strong-minded heroine.	4–7
Christine McDonnell	*Don't Be Mad, Ivy* and others	Books that follow the friendships of a group of first graders.	1–2
Claudia Mills	*Dynamite Dinah* and others	A well-written series that follows an intrepid middle grader through the trials and tribulations of childhood.	4–8
Phyllis Reynolds Naylor	*Alice In-Between* and others	Growing up female in an all-male household.	4–8
Peggy Parrish	*Amelia Bedelia* and others	A longtime favorite easy-to-read series that features the literal-minded maid of the Rogers family.	1–3
Robert Newton Peck	*Soup* and others	Boys especially enjoy following the antics of Soup and friends.	4–8
Cynthia Rylant	*Henry and Mudge* and others	An easy-to-read series about likable Henry and his lovable dog.	1–3
Louis Sachar	*Marvin Redpost: Why Pick on Me?* and others	Hilarious misadventures of Marvin and his classmates in an easy-to-read format.	1–4
Louis Sachar	*Wayside School Gets a Little Stranger* and others	Crazy misadventures at the thirty-story Wayside School.	2–5
Marjorie Wiseman Sharmat	*Nate the Great*	Entertaining detective stories for beginning readers.	1–4
Janice Lee Smith	*Serious Science* and other Adam Joshua stories	A funny series that follows Adam Joshua and his friends through the trials and tribulations of elementary school.	1–4
Zilpha Keatly Snyder	*Libby on Wednesday* and others	A gifted child and her adventures in middle school.	4–8

In *Henry and Beezus*, Henry's major interest is in obtaining a new bicycle. At the opening of the Colossal Market he is delighted when he wins one of the door prizes but then horrified to find out it is fifty dollars' worth of Beauty Shoppe services. Cleary's intimate knowledge of boys and girls is evident as she describes their problems, adventures, and hilarious activities.

The opening chapter of Barbara Park's *Skinnybones* is also hilarious. The self-acclaimed funniest person in the sixth grade is telling his story about trying to enter a cat food commercial contest. In addition, Alex (also known as "Skinnybones") has been a size "small" in Little League for six years, never is able to catch the ball or make a hit, and is the butt of the class bully's jokes. The bully wins the baseball trophy, but Alex wins, too, in this story of a wisecracker with a knack for getting into trouble.

Peter Hatcher's endless problems with his brother begin in Judy Blume's *Tales of a Fourth Grade Nothing*. In this story, 2-year-old Fudge, whose real name is Farley Drexel Hatcher, eats Peter's pet turtle but the long-suffering Peter earns a pet dog. In *Superfudge*, Peter narrates further complications in his life—his new baby sister Tootsie, new school, and new friends—when his family moves to New Jersey. Fudge begins kindergarten much to Peter's embarrassment and dismay. Dialogue and plot unfold like television situation comedies in these entertaining stories appealing to children in second through fifth grades.

How to Eat Fried Worms by Thomas Rockwell begins with a dare and a fifty-dollar bet. To win it, Billy plans to eat fifteen worms in fifteen days. They are fried, boiled, and smothered with catsup, horseradish, and other toppings. Each ingestion becomes more bizarre the closer Billy comes to winning his bet. The brief chapters, extensive and amusing dialogue, and plot make this a favorite story of less-able middle-grade readers.

One of the funniest books to be published for children is Barbara Robinson's *The Best Christmas Pageant Ever*. The six Herdman children are the terror of the public school, so it is not surprising that they extend their reign of terror to Sunday school and take over the Christmas pageant. The poor unsuspecting substitute teacher cannot understand why only the Herdmans volunteer for parts in the pageant, unaware that they have threatened to stuff pussy willows down the ears of any other children who raise their hands to volunteer. The Herdmans have never heard the Christmas story before, and their interpretation is contemporary, humorous, and surprisingly close to the true meaning of Christmas. The Herdmans return for more laughs in *The Best School Year Ever*.

Several books have a more sophisticated brand of humor that will appeal particularly to middle school audiences. Gary Paulsen takes a break from his more serious and intense stories in *Harris and Me*. In a memorable and riotously funny voice, Paulsen's narrator recalls a summer spent with relatives on a farm in the Midwest in the 1950s and the many hilarious adventures that revolved around his cousin Harris, who at age 9 was a wicked combination of Huck Finn and Holden Caulfield. This city-boy narrator, who had been shuffled from relative to relative because of alcoholic parents, knew nothing of farm life or of loving family relationships. By the end of the summer he became an expert in agricultural science, but, even more important, he discovered what it means to belong to a loving, if slightly wacky, family.

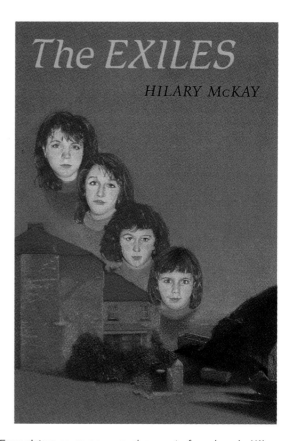

Four sisters cause an unusual amount of mayhem in Hilary McKay's hilarious story *The Exiles*.
From *The Exiles* by Hilary McKay, 1992.

In *The Exiles*, a funny novel by British writer Hilary McKay, the four Conroy sisters, Ruth, Naomi, Rachel, and Phoebe, ranging in age from 6 to 13, don't mean to be difficult, they just gravitate to trouble the way rain ends up in puddles. They hold races with their father's fishing maggots. They collect cast-off school projects and attract disorder and disaster. Their parents are driven by frustration and the happy circumstance of a house-remodeling job to send the girls to imposing Big Grandma's house in the country for the summer, and they become "the exiles." Big Grandma looks on their visit as an opportunity to instill discipline, fresh air and exercise, and a little hard work. Moreover, Big Grandma thinks they read too much, so she hides all her books away in a locked room. The girls, starved for reading materials, discover adventures outside the covers of books (some that Big Grandma wishes they hadn't). The outcome of this family conflict is poetic *and* hilarious. There are lessons to be learned by everyone and more than one surprise in store for all concerned, including the reader. Their adventures continue in *The Exiles at Home* when Ruth, in a burst of good cheer, sends her Christmas money to support an African child and then has to scramble, beg, and otherwise improvise to come up with the continuing payments.

There are certainly many other books in which humor plays a part. The fantasies of Roald Dahl and Daniel Pinkwater, for instance, often portray absurd situations that children find funny. The animal antics in stories by Farley Mowat or Nina Bawden cause readers to laugh out loud. The snappy retorts of Carlie in Betsy Byars's *The Pinballs* or the accurate and humorous observations about everyday school situations in *The Burning Questions of Bingo Brown* give readers a smile of recognition. The Magic School Bus series by Joanna Cole and Bruce Degen is an example of nonfiction packaged in child-appealing humorous asides and funny conversation balloons. Humorous books need no justification other than that they provide pure enjoyment. They are a healthy contrast to a reading diet that might be over-burdened with contemporary social problems. Funny stories also beg to be shared with other readers in the classroom and are powerful reading catalysts. Children who laugh with books are building a love of reading in which enjoyment is the foundation.

Animal Stories

Stories about animals provide children with the vicarious experience of giving love to and receiving devotion and loyalty from an animal. Frequently these animal tales are really stories of the maturing of their major characters. For example, the well-loved story *The Yearling* by Marjorie Kinnan Rawlings is as much the story of Jody's growth and realization of the consequences of giving love as it is the story of a boy's discovery and raising of a pet deer. Sterling North's *Rascal: A Memoir of a Better Era* presents a boy who shares happy outings with his father, worries about his older brother serving in World War I, builds a canoe in the living room, and raises a crow and a raccoon as pets. But Sterling gradually and painfully realizes that his beloved companion raccoon, Rascal, will survive only in the wild.

Using the setting of Wales, where her family moved to avoid the World War II bombings of London, Nina Bawden tells a humorous autobiographical tale about their pet squirrel in *Henry*. Shot out of a tree as a baby and adopted immediately, Henry sleeps in the sleeve of a jacket, makes nests or dreys from dirty laundry, swears "vut, vut, vut," eats nuts, apple "pips," or things he finds in the children's pockets, and generally intoxicates the family with his antics. Like Bawden's *The Peppermint Pig*, this novel is more than an animal story as the perceptive 12-year-old narrator reflects on rural life, the wartime absence of her father, the death of an elderly neighbor, and her own inadvertent release of Henry, which readers are alerted to on the first page of the story.

Like Nina Bawden, Jean Craighead George draws on her own experiences with animals to provide fascinating information and many humorous anecdotes about crows as part of her novel *The Cry of the Crow*. Mandy is accustomed to roaming the piney woods surrounding her family's Florida strawberry farm and rescues a fledgling crow shot from its nest. Naming it Nina Terrance, she secretly raises it over the summer, learns to recognize crow calls, and teaches it to make some human speech sounds. Torn between letting the maturing crow go with the flock and keeping it as a pet, she opts to keep the crow. But crows have been known to seek revenge, and when Mandy, and finally Nina Terrance, discover that it was Mandy's brother who shot at the crow's nest, she must face the consequences of having kept a wild animal as a pet when the crow attacks her brother. Jean George's careful research is skillfully woven into this story of the difficult choices people must make as they grow to maturity.

Koby Easten befriends a slightly more exotic animal in Ben Mikaelsen's exciting story *Stranded*. Twelve-year-old Koby lost a foot when her bike was hit by a car, and she is trying to adjust to her prosthesis and her mother's overprotectiveness. Her own problems haven't helped her parents' marriage, and they are on the verge of separating. The only place where Koby feels at home is in the water; she spends hours slipping around the Florida Keys in her dinghy. Heading home at sunset one day, she almost runs into a pilot whale that has been caught in a fishing net and badly injured. Koby jumps in to free her and also witnesses the birth of her calf. Because the whale is too weak to help her calf, Koby has to help it to the surface to take its first breath. The next day Koby comes upon the two again, but this time they are stranded on a sandbar. Koby waits through the night with them until help arrives. Then, because of her special bond with the animals, she becomes part of a team of scientists who attempt to nurse the whales back to health and return them to their ocean home. In this fast-moving and fascinating story Koby learns something about her own needs and strengths as well as those of the whales.

Dogs respond to human affection and return it warmly. This bond of love is one of the themes in Sidney's Taylor's *The Trouble with Tuck*, based on a true story. Helen lacked self-confidence until she became involved in raising Tuck, a beautiful golden Labrador retriever given to her by her parents. Tuck once saved Helen from drowning and is devoted to her. By the time Helen reaches 13, Tuck has grown totally blind. Rejecting the advice of the veterinarian to give Tuck to the university for research or have him put to sleep, Helen finds an alternative—she obtains a seeing-eye dog for Tuck. Jealous and confused, Tuck refuses to accept this stranger until Helen's patient and innovative training methods teach Tuck to follow the guide dog. As the two dogs parade before Helen and her proud family, the reader rejoices in both canine and human triumphs. In a sequel, *Tuck Triumphant*, the focus shifts from Tuck to a Korean boy the family adopts.

In Jane Resh Thomas's *The Comeback Dog*, Daniel must decide if he is once again going to risk his love on a dog who has already rejected him. While 9-year-old Daniel is still grieving for the loss of his old dog, Captain, he discovers a starved and nearly drowned English setter in the culvert near his family's Michigan farm. He brings the dog home, names her Lady, and nurses her back to health, assuming that she will return his love in the same way Captain did. But Lady, who has been mistreated, cringes at Daniel's touch and refuses to wag her tail for him. One day, in anger at her lack of affection, Daniel releases Lady from her chain, and she bounds away over the fields. She is gone, only to return a week later bristling with porcupine quills. Sympathetic parents who show their love finally help Daniel show his. Troy Howell's frequent illustrations, the believable dialogue, and short chapters make this book easily approachable by independent 8- and 9-year-old readers.

The same age group will enjoy Karen Hesse's *Sable*, which is also about a stray dog. Tate is determined to keep Sable when she turns up one day in the family's yard, even though her mother is afraid of dogs. An uneasy compromise is arrived at and Sable is allowed to stay on the property. But the dog keeps roaming and causing trouble with the neighbors. When Sable is given to a family friend, Tate is heartbroken but determined to prove she is responsible enough to take care of a dog. After much reading and planning, she builds a fence to keep Sable out of trouble, but when she goes to bring Sable home she finds that the dog has run away. Her parents are impressed with her hard work and softened by her devotion to the dog, so that when Sable finally turns up weeks later, skinny and torn, they accept the fact that they have a dog in the family.

Meindert DeJong's moving story *Hurry Home, Candy* tells of another dog's search for love and security. Candy had first been owned by two children and punished with a broom by their impatient mother. In a storm Candy is separated from the family, and fear of a broom across the ditch prevents him from crossing to them. Alone, hungry, lost, and sorrowful, he at last finds shelter with a lonely old man, a retired captain turned artist. One night, the artist interrupts some thieves, and the news story brings Candy's original owners. But the children want only the reward, not the small dog. Candy hides again, but is drawn to the house by hunger. Once more, a broom stands between the dog and love and security. The captain discovers the source of the dog's fear; at the same time he gains understanding of his own. The big

In Karen Hesse's moving book *Sable*, a dog is without a home until Tate tries to convince her parents to let her keep him.
From *Sable* by Karen Hesse, illustrated by Marcia Sewall. Illustration copyright © 1994 by Marcia Sewall. Reprinted by permission of Henry Holt and Co., Inc.

man tosses the broom aside, and the dog edges his way to food, to love, and home.

In Phyllis Reynolds Naylor's Newbery Medal-winning *Shiloh*, Marty Preston befriends a cringing stray beagle that surrounds the boy with joy. The dog, however, belongs to a neighbor known for abusing his animals; Marty, reluctantly but obedient to his father, returns the puppy. When the half-starved dog later slinks back to the field by the Preston home, Marty decides to hide the dog in the woods of his West Virginia mountain hollow. He deceives his family until a crisis forces him to fight for his principles and confront the owner of the dog, whom he has named Shiloh. Well-drawn characters, a strongly realized setting, and a quick-paced plot are woven into this first-person narrative. Marion Dane Bauer's *A Question of Trust* raises similar problems for Brad and his brother, who are hurt and angered by their parent's divorce. Although their father, with whom they are living, forbids them to have any pets, Brad comes across a stray mother cat and her two newborn kittens. He is determined to care for them even though he risks losing his father's trust. However, he finds that he is in over his head when things go dreadfully wrong with one of the kittens. Like Bauer's *On My Honor*, these two stories ask upper elementary students to think about what constitutes honorable and responsible behavior when rebelling against parents and their beliefs.

Heroic dogs who overcome obstacles are the subject of popular animal stories for children. Sheila Burnford's *The Incredible Journey* recounts the odyssey of courage and endurance of three runaway pets, a young Labrador retriever, an old bull terrier, and a Siamese cat. Left with a friend of their owner, the animals try to reach their home more than 250 miles away. Hunger, storms, dangerous river crossings, and fights are the nearly insurmountable problems of these three animals. Their survival and care for each other make a remarkable story.

A sled dog named Searchlight and his owner, little Willy, are the heroes of John Reynolds Gardiner's well-loved *Stone Fox*. Little Willy needs five hundred dollars to pay off the back taxes on his grandfather's farm or it will be taken from them. So the two enter a dogsled race. But among the contestants is the legendary Indian Stone Fox with his five Samoyed sled dogs. Willy nearly wins the race, but Searchlight's heart gives out in a final burst of speed just before the finish line. In the moving conclusion, Stone Fox and his team halt just short of the finish while Willy carries his dog across the line to win the race and save his farm. This short story, an excellent read-aloud choice, causes fourth- and fifth-grade readers to ask for tissues and more animal stories.

Where the Red Fern Grows by Wilson Rawls is a heartwarming sentimental tale of the love between two hound dogs and their master. Young Billy trains his two dogs, Old Dan and Little Ann, to be the finest hunting team in the Cherokee country of the Ozarks in northeastern Oklahoma. Twenty-five sets of hounds are entered in the big coon hunt. After five nights of hunting, catching raccoons, skinning them, and turning in the hides, Billy's hounds win three hundred dollars and the first-place cup. During the hunt Old Dan and Little Ann nearly freeze to death after getting lost during an unexpected blizzard. When the family decides to move, Billy plans to remain behind with his beloved grandfather and the two dogs. But when the dogs die, one defending Billy against a mountain lion attack and one pining away, he regretfully departs with his family. Billy's decision is reaffirmed when a legendary red fern springs up at the dogs' gravesite. This story is memorable to 10-, 11-, and 12-year-olds because of its warmth and its strong portrayal of devotion between humans and animals.

Occasionally books intended for an adult audience become part of the reading of older children. Jack London's *The Call of the Wild* was written for adults but is read by some gifted middle-grade students. The men in the story are ruthless, and the dog Buck returns to the wildness of nature just as the men revert to force and cruelty to survive. Jim Kjelgaard communicates a love of wilderness through exciting dog stories like *Big Red*, a tale of an Irish setter groomed for championship showing who, along with his 17-year-old trainer, faces the bear Old Majesty. Farley Mowat's *The Dog Who Wouldn't Be* tells of his boyhood on the Saskatchewan prairie in the company of his Prince Albert retriever, Mutt, and a score of other animal pets. In his shorter novel *Owls in the Family*, Mowat recounts in hilarious detail his adventures in acquiring and training two pet great-horned owls, the intrepid Wol and his timid companion, Weeps.

Sports Stories

Sports fiction for children reflects their energetic participation and interest in a variety of individual and team sports. Recent fiction includes books about team sports, like baseball, football, soccer, and basketball, and popular individual sports like tennis, running, gymnastics, dirt-bike racing, skateboarding, and swimming. Fiction, biography, and informational books about sports extend and enrich the personal experiences of the child who participates in or observes sports.

It is difficult to find well-written sports stories. Most of the characters are flat, one-dimensional figures. The dialogue tends to be stilted, and the plots predictable. Nevertheless, children continue to select these stories because they are so personally involved and interested in the activities. Series like Dean Hughes's Angel Park All-Stars series and the Rookies series, by various authors, cater to sports fans.

Even though there are now many more stories that feature girls in sports, there are still few female athletes in formula sports fiction. The same clichés—making the team through hard work or overcoming fear and triumphing over pain—are prevalent in both stories for boys and stories for girls. One important change, however, is that girls on boys' sports teams are no longer greeted with disbelief and protest.

A serious story that portrays characters of real depth and understanding is *Thank You, Jackie Robinson* by Barbara Cohen. Though the story takes place in 1947–1948, it is written in the first person and told as a reminiscence to a contemporary child. Sam Green is the only son of a Jewish widow who runs an inn in New Jersey. He doesn't care much about sandlot ball, but he can recite the batting order and play-by-play for every Dodgers game since the time he became a fan. Sam's best friend is the inn's African American cook, Davy, who takes Sam to his first Dodgers game. The two see other games together, and the hero of all the games for both of them is Jackie Robinson. In midseason Davy has a heart attack. Sam gathers his courage, buys a baseball, and goes alone to a Dodgers game, where he asks Jackie Robinson to autograph the ball for Davy. Then Davy's son-in-law, Elliott, helps Sam sneak into the hospital in a laundry cart so he can personally present the ball to Davy. This book succeeds at many levels: as a warm and understanding consideration of friendship across ages and races, as a realistic presentation of death, and as a retrospective look at Jackie Robinson and the Brooklyn Dodgers during the height of their baseball fame. Peter Golenbock's nonfiction *Teammates* would help children further understand Robinson's courageous entry into major league baseball.

Another book that succeeds on many levels is Alfred Slote's *The Trading Game*. Andy Harris, who loves to play baseball and collect baseball cards, receives the cards his deceased father had bequeathed to him. Among them is a precious 1953 Mickey Mantle card worth over two thousand dollars. But the card Andy truly wants is Ace 459, the card of his grandfather, a former major league player, whom he idolizes. Greedy Tubby Watson owns the card and won't part with it unless Andy will trade the Mickey Mantle card. When Grampa comes to visit, it is clear to Andy that the cards his father collected are of no importance to the old man and that Grampa has not reconciled himself to his son's death. Andy eventually realizes that friendships and the memories the cards represent are more important than winning and the money the cards are worth. Slote's books, many of which are told in first person, capture the emotions, actions, and conversation of typical fifth- and sixth-grade boys.

Upper elementary school students have laughed at the antics of Orp, or Orville Rudemeyer Pygenski, Jr. In one story in the series by Suzy Kline, *Orp Goes to the Hoop*, the seventh grader is trying to make the basketball team of his Connecticut middle school. With a mother who was a free-throw champion and a father with a terrific lay-up, Orp has great advice. While Orp's story is one of near-continuous successes both on the court and in the social arena, readers will appreciate Orp's long pass to a teammate for the winning basket.

Other stories depict the blurring of the lines between traditionally all-male and all-female teams. Mel Cebulash's fictional speculation about the first woman to break into major league baseball is chronicled in several stories. *Ruth Marini, Dodger Ace* and *Ruth Marini of the Dodgers* both relate Ruth's difficulties in becoming accepted for what she can do for the team, not for who she is or what she represents.

Middle schoolers ready to move into more-complex novels that use sports to explore other subjects might be guided to Ilene Cooper's *Choosing Sides*, Bruce Brooks's *The Moves Make the Man*, Robert Lipsyte's *The Contender*, Virginia Euwer Wolff's *The Mozart Season*, or Chris Crutcher's *Stotan!* Sports fiction at its best provides readers with the vicarious satisfactions of playing the sport as well as struggling with the problems and issues that arise in practice, in play, and at home.

School Stories

Stories that take place in school offer children the solace of the familiar. All schoolchildren recognize settings furnished with desks and lockers; characters like the friendly custodian or principal, the class bully, the understanding teacher, the hatchet-faced teacher, the cheating student; and situations such as the looming deadline for a project or paper, misunderstandings between friends, and seasonal celebrations. Books like these do not always encourage readers to stretch their abilities, but they do provide a kind of support for horizontal growth as children learn to read faster with more satisfaction. Unfortunately (or fortunately for the readers), many of these stories are part of a numbered series and children want to read them in order. This challenges teachers and parents to help children find other books while they are "waiting for number 7 of the series."

Susan Shreve's school story *The Flunking of Joshua T. Bates* is about being held back. Joshua hasn't mastered reading, but through the thoughtful tutoring and friendship of his new teacher he is able to pass a test at Thanksgiving and join his old class. Adults will wince as Joshua vents his frustration by threatening to move to East Africa or become a custodian in Japan, and they might find unrealistic the implication that children can be promoted after two months of tutoring. But children applaud the subduing of the bully in Joshua's former class and the satisfying happy ending.

Beverly Cleary, Jamie Gilson, and Johanna Hurwitz make use of the humor of school situations for third and fourth graders. In Cleary's *Ramona Quimby, Age 8*, Ramona arrives in third grade, where she enjoys her teacher's "Dear" (Drop Everything and Read) time. She also stages a hilarious parody of a cat food commercial for her book report, makes a friend of "Yard Ape," and realizes that her teacher likes her. In *Class Clown*, Hurwitz introduces Lucas Cott, the most obstreperous boy his third-grade teacher has ever seen. Lucas finally settles down when he stands in for a sick classmate to become the ringmaster of the class circus. Gilson's *4-B Goes Wild* and *Thirteen Ways to Sink a Sub* and her Hobie Hansen books are also popular school tales. Gilson's stories are fast-moving and full of pranks and funny dialogue, with reasonable adults who remain very much in the background.

Authors have not neglected the school as a setting for older readers. In Walter Dean Myers's *Darnell Rock Reporting*, Darnell is a normal underachieving middle school student who spends as much time in the principal's office as he does in a classroom. To get the principal off his back, he mentions that he is thinking of joining the school newspaper, and this is the delaying tactic he needs to keep his parents ignorant of his little problems. As he attends staff meetings, Darnell's interest is

Alan Tiegreen's illustration shows Ramona Quimby tackling her bicycle in the same way she takes on the third grade in Beverly Cleary's *Ramona Quimby, Age 8.*

Illustration from *Ramona Quimby Age 8* by Beverly Cleary, illustrated by Alan Tiegreen. Copyright © 1981 by Beverly Cleary. By permission of Morrow Junior Books, a division of William Morrow & Company, Inc.

piqued and he begins to get involved. When he sets out to interview Seebie, a homeless man, he begins to see the man as a human being and takes on his cause. At the same time his success at writing begins to have an effect on the way he sees himself. Trying to establish a community garden for the homeless, Darnell makes a speech to the town council and draws this analogy:

🐾 If you're a kid who isn't doing so good, people start off telling you what you should be doing, and you know it, but sometimes you still don't get it done and mess up some more. Then people start expecting you to mess up, and then *you* start expecting you to mess up. (p. 156)

Darnell realizes that being on the newpaper has changed how he sees himself and also made people look at him differently. Believing that the garden is a way of helping them become self-sufficient, he is asking the same chance for Seebie and the other homeless people in the area. Myers writes with a keen understanding of adolescent concerns and creates funny, likable characters. In this case he shapes to perfection a picture of an

underachieving middle-class boy, and mirrors a segment of the population who don't often see themselves reflected in books.

Anne Fine zeroes in on the same group of young teens in her very funny, but ultimately very poignant, *Flour Babies*. Room 8 at St. Boniface's School is a teacher's nightmare, the classroom where the "Sads and the Bads" end up. It is time for the school science fair, and in an effort to avoid repeating previous disasters, Mr. Cassidy presents the boys with some pretty tame choices. In a glorious misunderstanding, Simon Martin, a "clumsy young giant," convinces his classmates to choose the child development experiment, eighteen days of caring for flour sacks as if they were babies. Simon believes that the boys will be allowed to explode the sacks at the end of the experiment. But before this end occurs, Simon finds he has grown quite attached to his sack. He paints eyes on it and confides his innermost thoughts to it. Not only does the experiment teach the boys the weighty responsibilities of parenting, but it also gives Simon, whose own father skipped out when he was 6 weeks old, some important insights about fathering. Simon gets his explosive ending, but he also ends up knowing that "if keeping what you care for close and safe counts for any thing" (p. 127), he'll make a better father than most.

Other authors also set their stories for older readers within the cozy confines of a school. Gordon Korman's private school Macdonald Hall has been the setting for many of his slapstick stories. The characters of the popular Sweet Valley High and Sweet Valley Twins paperback series (created by Francine Pascal but written by a stable of authors) use school as a backdrop for their interactions. A giant step up from these series is Ilene Cooper's Kids from Kennedy Middle School series, in which deeper themes and situations are treated both humorously and seriously. In *Choosing Sides,* for instance, sixth grader Jonathan Rossi is trying to be the basketball player his father wants him to be and his older brother already is. But Jonathan's heart isn't in it. His friend Ham Berger purposely gets cut from the team, but Jon continues to put up with pressure and lessons from his father. When his teacher Mrs. Volini asks the class to write about "moral dilemmas," Jon suddenly sees that his is not how to skip basketball practice but how to reconcile his own feelings with his father's unreasonable demands. *Queen of the Sixth Grade* introduces readers to Jon's friend Robin, who suddenly becomes a class outcast when she rebels against the cruel Veronica's jokes. Each of Cooper's stories deals with a major theme against the backdrop of everyday school concerns, such as what to do at a first sixth-grade coed dance, peer groups and making friends of both sexes, dealing with bad and good teachers, or handling difficult school assignments.

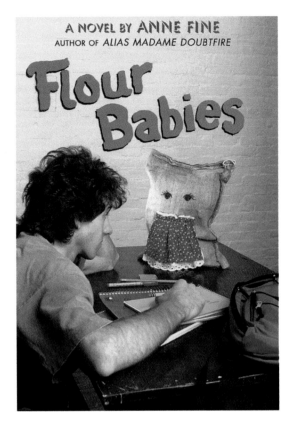

In Ann Fine's comical *Flour Babies* a class of misfits chooses "child care" as their class project.
Cover of *Flour Babies* by Anne Fine. Reprinted by permission of Little, Brown and Company.

Mysteries

Most children enjoy mystery stories during some period in their lives. James Howe, author of the popular Sebastian Barth mysteries, has said that in adult mysteries "Who done it?" is the question to be answered but in children's mysteries the question is more likely to be "What's going on here?"[20] Children enjoy figuring out the "rules of the game" in a mystery, and they are proud to be masterful solvers of the problem. They enjoy the order of a mystery's universe, where loose ends are tied up, everything is explained, and evil is punished. They like escapist reading just as much as adult mystery fans do.

Even first- and second-grade readers demand mysteries. Whole series, such as the Something Queer books by Elizabeth Levy, the Miss Mallard and Sherlock Chick animal detective stories by Robert Quackenbush, Crosby Bonsall stories, or Patricia Reilly Giff's Polka Dot Private Eye books, satisfy a child's need to keep reading.

Slightly older children usually become enmeshed in the Nancy Drew or Hardy Boys series. These formula books have predictable plots, one-dimensional characters, stilted dialogue, and cliché-ridden prose. Although most librarians and teachers do not order these books, they continue to sell well. Rather than discount mystery stories in general because of popular series, teachers and librarians should look for better-written mysteries and other books that contain the elements of mystery, such as "suspense and supernatural fantasy" (see Chapter 7), to expand children's interests.

Two popular mystery series give the reader a chance to match wits with clever boys. Both boys and girls enjoy the Encyclopedia Brown stories by Donald Sobol. In *Encyclopedia Brown Takes a Case*, Mr. Brown, chief of police of Idaville, brings home all the cases his detectives cannot solve. At dinner he describes them to his son, Encyclopedia Brown, who usually solves them before it is time for dessert. Each Encyclopedia Brown book presents ten cases whose solutions are included in the back of the book. Seymour Simon, author of many nonfiction titles, also features short mysteries in his Einstein Anderson series. In *Einstein Anderson Lights Up the Sky*, the brainy Einstein applies his knowledge of science to show that mysterious UFOs are really spotlights reflected off low nighttime clouds, and he "solves" another nine problems. While each series features both consistent format and a continuing case of characters, Einstein's incidental jokes, puns, and riddles and the scientific observations give this series extra appeal and depth.

Attics in two mystery stories hold clues to the past and keys to the future for two horse-loving girls. In Rumer Godden's *The Rocking Horse Secret*, 8-year-old Tibby discovers a rocking horse in the attic playroom of the old Pomeroy mansion. When the horse's tail falls off and a piece of paper falls out, she repairs the damage and hopes no one will notice. But the paper proves to be a will that holds the secret of the old house, and Tibby is the one who solves the mystery and saves the house. *The Horse in the Attic* by Eleanor Clymer is a story about an old painting that, when restored, proves to be an important work of a long-dead local artist. When 12-year-old Caroline tracks down the painting's "bloodlines," she changes her family's future. Both Clymer and Godden create memorable characters and provide satisfying endings sure to delight middle elementary mystery and horse lovers.

The House of Dies Drear by Virginia Hamilton is a compelling story of the weird and terrifying happenings that threaten and mystify an African American professor and his family when they rent a house that was a former underground railway station. The brooding old house holds many secrets for Thomas Small and his family, who are threatened by dangers from outside as well as inside the house. The treasure of fleeing slaves that is discovered by Thomas in this title becomes one of the problems in a sequel, *The Mystery of Drear House*. Now the Small family must help determine the fate of the abolitionist's house and the disposal of the goods. Hamilton's finely crafted plot, elegant prose, and well-developed characters provide gripping reading.

Philippa Pearce's *The Way to Sattin Shore* is the satisfying story of a girl's longing to understand the mystery surrounding the disappearance of her father the day she was born. Her mother and her grandmother both tell her that he is dead. Kate believes them until she discovers that the tombstone in the cemetery is her uncle's, not her father's as she had thought. The clues to the mystery ebb and flow like the tide in which she learns her uncle drowned. The tension rises between her mother and her disagreeable grandmother, and her older brother reveals they had once lived somewhere else—at Sattin Shore. Kate rides her bicycle alone to the shore and discovers a grandmother she didn't know she had. Through her own determination and initiative she does find her father and brings about a reunion with her mother. While the plot provides suspense, it is the author's skill in creating believable relationships among the characters and a haunting sense of place that the reader admires. The eerie loneliness of the shore is as threatening as Kate's dark, unhappy home. It is up to Kate to discover what happened on that beach the day she was born and solve the mystery that has engulfed them all.

In Ellen Raskin's *The Westing Game* millionaire Sam Westing cut out the words to the song "America the Beautiful" and distributed them among his heirs as clues to his murderer.[21] At the reading of his will the sixteen characters are presented with a directive to discover the identity of his murderer and other clues cleverly hidden within the will. The characters, all with their own physical, moral, or emotional imperfections, play in pairs. They include a judge, a Chinese restaurateur, a dressmaker, a track star, a 15-year-old palsied boy, a reluctant bride-to-be, and a 13-year-old terror, Turtle Wexler. It is Turtle who begins to link clues and discover patterns as she and readers piece together Westing's amazing game. In a tightly constructed story divided into many short sections, Raskin piles detail upon detail; rereading shows that what appears to be insignificant always proves otherwise. Warmly realized characters interrelate and grow in this Newbery Medal winner, but it is Turtle who, unbeknownst to any of the other players, quietly solves the puzzle and bikes up to the Westing house to receive her prize in the satisfying ending.

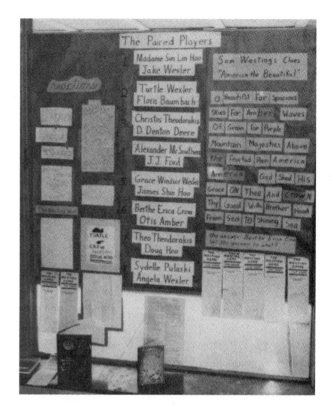

Fourth graders keep track of Ellen Raskin's intricate mystery *The Westing Game* by listing character pairs, assembling cut-up clues, and making predictions.
Barrington Road Elementary School, Upper Arlington Public Schools, Ohio. Pat Enciso, teacher.

Popular mystery writer Vivien Alcock skirts the fantastic in novels such as *The Mysterious Mr. Ross*, in which 12-year-old Felicity suspects that the man she has saved from drowning, Albert Ross, may well be the human incarnation of an injured albatross. Readers are kept in suspense, however, as this young, gullible girl on the edge of adolescence moves through sympathy, doubt, anger, and remorse before defending Mr. Ross from nosy seacoast villagers. Alcock's numerous other titles, such as *The Monster Garden* and *The Stonewalkers*, venture into supernatural and science fiction territory and appeal to middle schoolers for their mixture of mystery, fantasy, and adolescent awareness of the adult world.

Joan Lowery Nixon's riveting story *The Other Side of Dark* won the Edgar Allan Poe Mystery Writer's Award for its distinctive portrayal of a girl who, after witnessing the murder of her mother and being shot herself, loses her memory for four years. At 17, Stacy McAdams regains some of her memory and is adjusting to being an adolescent. When publicity suggests that she might remember the face of the killer, Stacy is again in danger and she attempts to identify the killer before he kills her. The plot is complicated when it appears that new friends might not be what they seem. Stacy's first-person

[21]See Ellen Raskin, "Newbery Medal Acceptance," *Horn Book Magazine*, August 1979, pp. 385–391.

narrative reveals her desire for revenge, her confusion over who she is, and her growth toward adulthood in this thriller. Another of Nixon's thrillers, *A Candidate for Murder*, concerns Cary and the crank calls she begins to receive when her father runs for governor of Texas. Cary has unknowingly witnessed something that places her in the midst of political intrigue and danger. Older readers enjoy Nixon's compelling mysteries for their skilled combination of human emotions, suspense, romance, and terror with a fast-moving plot and cliff-hanger chapters.

Like Nixon, Lois Duncan writes about high school students who inadvertently stumble into mysteries. *The Twisted Window*, for instance, is the story of high school junior Tracy Lloyd who believes Brad Johnson when he says his stepfather has stolen his little sister from his mother's house. Three days later she is involved in a kidnapping, a case of mistaken identity, and a dangerous game with a disturbed boy. Middle school girl readers pass Duncan's young-adult mysteries from hand to hand.

Popular fiction should be evaluated with the same criteria used to consider all fiction, with the recognition that its major appeals are fast action, contemporary characters in familiar settings, straightforward plot development, humor, and suspense. Children develop the skills of rapid reading, vocabulary building, and prediction and the ability to notice relevant details when they read popular fiction. They develop a love of reading with popular novels, and skillful teachers can extend and diversify readers' choices with all that realistic fiction has to offer.

Contemporary realistic fiction is diverse. It has moved away from the problem novels of the 1960s and 1970s to serious fiction balanced with characters less prone to despair. Contemporary novels encompass diverse themes and writing styles. While paperback series and popular novels continue to attract readers, these selections are now counterbalanced by many well-written and compelling stories. The diverse cultures of the United States and many other world cultures are represented in literature for children, and the number of titles available continues to grow. Contemporary realistic fiction, the most popular genre among child readers, continues to thrive in this decade.

Learning Experiences

1. Find books about a specific minority group. Look for poetry, biography, fiction, picture storybooks, and nonfiction that would extend these books in a classroom. What kinds of books were the easiest to find, and which were the most difficult to find?

2. Select a current subject in realistic fiction, such as single-parent families, foster children, immigration, or disability, and create an annotated bibliography. Find some nonfiction that can be grouped with the fiction.

3. Compare the treatment of a topic, such as the death of a pet, a child, or a grandparent, in a picture book, a novel, poetry, and informational books.

4. Select several books from various decades that portray a particular minority group. Do you find stereotypes? What themes prevail?

5. Compare several humorous stories. Where does the humor lie? (Slapstick? Exaggeration? Puns or wordplay? Situations? Satire?) How would you rank these titles from lesser to greater sophistication?

6. Discuss with peers or a small group of children a novel such as Lowry's *Rabble Starkey*, MacLachlan's *Arthur for the Very First Time*, Creech's *Walk Two Moons*, Paterson's *Flip-Flop Girl*, or Bawden's *The Outside Child*. How is the main character influenced by other characters in the book? When the child character becomes an adult, which of these other characters might he or she want to thank? Why?

7. Compare the relationships of parents and children in several titles discussed in the section of this chapter entitled "Living in a Family."

8. Compare several survival stories discussed in this chapter. After basic wants are satisfied, what else does the surviving person seem to need? What qualities does each person possess or develop in order to survive? How does (or might) surviving change a person?

Related Readings

Baskin, Barbara H., and Karen H. Harris. *More Notes from a Different Drummer: A Guide to Juvenile Fiction Portraying the Disabled*. New York: Bowker, 1984.

> Annotations and analysis of more than three hundred books published between 1976 and 1981, plus two introductory chapters that provide context, background, and excellent evaluative criteria. This supplements *Notes from a Different Drummer* (New York: Bowker, 1977), which covered titles published from 1940 to 1975.

Bernstein, Joanne E., and Marsha K. Rudman. *Books to Help Children Cope with Separation and Loss*. 3rd ed. New York: Bowker, 1988.

> This book-selection guide summarizes six hundred recent fiction and nonfiction titles grouped by such topics such as divorce, mental illness, moving, tragic loss, and disabilities.

Bishop, Rudine Sims, ed. *Kaleidoscope: A Multicultural Booklist for Grades K–8*. Urbana, Ill.: National Council of Teachers of English, 1994.

> This annotated bibliography includes a discussion of criteria and a list of resources pertaining to multicultural literature. Titles are grouped by genre or theme.

Bishop, Rudine Sims. *Shadow and Substance: Afro-American Experience in Contemporary Children's Fiction*. Urbana, Ill.: National Council of Teachers of English, 1982.

> The author surveys 150 books published between 1965 and 1979 that portray contemporary African American experience. She categorizes images portrayed in three sections: fiction with a social conscience, "melting pot" fiction that essentially assumes a cultural homogeneity, and "culturally conscious fiction." Five African American authors are discussed against a backdrop of other contemporary authors.

Bishop, Rudine Sims. *Presenting Walter Dean Myers*. New York: Twayne, 1990.

> A discussion and criticism of Myers's books about young urban African Americans, including an analysis of humor, theme, characterization, and other patterns found in Myers's work. Other titles in this critical series discuss works by authors such as Sue Ellen Bridgers, Robert Cormier, Richard Peck, and Judy Blume.

Dreyer, Sharon Spredeman. *The Bookfinder: A Guide to Children's Literature About the Needs and Problems of Youth Aged 2–15*. Vol. 1–4. Circle Pines, Minn.: American Guidance Service, 1981, 1985, 1989.

> Titles are indexed and annotated under headings that suggest a range of problems in growing up: responsibility, parental absence, disabilities, friendship, and so on. The introductory essay discusses ways parents and teachers might plan thematic studies to develop children's understandings.

Harris, Violet J., ed. *Teaching Multicultural Literature: Grades K–8*. Norwood, Mass.: Christopher Gordon, 1992.

> An indispensible guide to issues surrounding the teaching of multicultural literature. In addition, various chapters provide criteria and titles for choosing African American, Asian Pacific, Native American, Puerto Rican, Mexican American, and Carribbean children's books.

Hunter, Mollie. *The Pied Piper Syndrome*. New York: HarperCollins, 1992.

> A collection of speeches and essays that shows how Scotland's best-known children's author sees her craft. Because Hunter's first language is not English, her essay "Writing from a Minority Literature" rings true. In an earlier collection, *Talent Is Not Enough* (New York: Harper & Row, 1976, 1990), Hunter reflects on the challenges and demands of writing for children.

Lass-Woodfin, Mary Jo, ed. *Books on American Indians and Eskimos: A Selection Guide for Children and Young Adults*. Chicago: American Library Association, 1978.

> An annotated bibliography of some 750 titles that identifies the understandings and information available from each story. Ratings for quality and reading level are included.

Paterson, Katherine. *The Spying Heart: More Thoughts on Reading and Writing Books for Children*. New York: Dutton, 1989.

> A collection of essays, speeches, and book reviews that develop the author's views on three themes: story, imagination, and hope. See also an earlier companion volume by Paterson, *Gates of Excellence: On Reading and Writing Books for Children* (New York: Elsevier/Nelson, 1981).

Rees, David. *Painted Desert, Green Shade: Essays on Contemporary Writers of Fiction for Children and Young Adults*. Boston: Horn Book, 1984.

> Rees critiques the work of thirteen American and British writers, focusing on such authors as Betsy Byars, Katherine Paterson, Jan Mark, Robert Westall, Virginia Hamilton, and John Rowe Townsend. See also the companion volume, *Marble in the Water: Essays on Contemporary Writers of Fiction for Children and Young Adults* (Boston: Horn Book, 1980.)

Williams, Hazel. *Books by African American Authors and Illustrators for Children and Young Adults*. Chicago: American Library Association, 1991.

An annotated bibliography of over twelve hundred works of fiction and nonfiction written or illustrated by African Americans. The section on illustrators categorizes their styles and mentions their artistic media.

Children's Literature

The books listed here are recommended, subject to the qualifications noted in this chapter. See Appendix C for publishers' complete addresses. References to books of genres other than realism are noted in parentheses. Original publication dates are in square brackets.

Alcock, Vivien. *The Monster Garden*. Delacorte, 1988. (Fantasy)

———. *The Mysterious Mr. Ross*. Delacorte, 1987.

———. *The Stonewalkers*. Delacorte, 1983. (Fantasy)

Bauer, Marion Dane. *On My Honor*. Houghton Mifflin, 1986.

———. *A Question of Trust*. Houghton Mifflin, 1994.

Bawden, Nina. *Granny the Pag*. Clarion, 1996.

———. *Henry*. Illustrated by Joyce Powzyk. Lothrop, Lee & Shepard, 1988.

———. *The Outside Child*. Lothrop, Lee & Shepard, 1989.

———. *The Peppermint Pig*. Lippincott, 1975. (Historical fiction)

———. *The Real Plato Jones*. Clarion, 1993.

Blume, Judy. *Are You There, God? It's Me, Margaret*. Bradbury, 1970.

———. *It's Not the End of the World*. Bradbury, 1972.

———. *Superfudge*. Dutton, 1980.

———. *Tales of a Fourth Grade Nothing*. Illustrated by Roy Doty. Dutton, 1972.

———. *Then Again, Maybe I Won't*. Bradbury, 1971.

Bridgers, Sue Ellen. *All Together Now*. Knopf, 1979.

———. *Notes for Another Life*. Knopf, 1981.

Brooks, Bruce. *Everywhere*. HarperCollins, 1990.

———. *The Moves Make the Man*. Harper & Row, 1984.

Bunting, Eve. *Is Anybody There?* Lippincott, 1988.

Burnford, Sheila. *The Incredible Journey*. Illustrated by Carl Burger. Little, Brown, 1961.

Byars, Betsy. *Bingo Brown, Gypsy Lover*. Viking, 1990.

———. *The Burning Questions of Bingo Brown*. Viking, 1988.

———. *Cracker Jackson*. Viking, 1985.

———. *The Cybil War*. Illustrated by Gail Owens. Viking, 1981.

———. *The Dark Stairs*. Viking, 1994.

———. *The House of Wings*. Illustrated by Daniel Schwartz. Viking, 1972.

———. *The Night Swimmers*. Delacorte, 1980.

———. *The Pinballs*. Harper & Row, 1977.

———. *The Summer of the Swans*. Illustrated by Ted CoConis. Viking, 1970.

———. *Tarot Says Beware*. Viking, 1995.

———. *Wanted . . . Mud Blossom*. Delacorte, 1991.

Cameron, Ann. *Julian, Dream Doctor*. Illustrated by Ann Strugnell. Random House, 1990.

———. *Julian's Glorious Summer*. Illustrated by Dora Leder. Random House, 1987.

———. *More Stories Julian Tells*. Illustrated by Ann Strugnell. Knopf, 1986.

———. *The Most Beautiful Place in the World*. Illustrated by Thomas B. Allen. Knopf, 1988.

———. *The Stories Julian Tells*. Illustrated by Ann Strugnell. Knopf, 1981.

Cameron, Eleanor. *Julia and the Hand of God*. Illustrated by Gail Owens. Dutton, 1977.

Caseley, Judith. *Harry and Arney*. Greenwillow, 1994.

Casey, Maude. *Over the Water*. Holt, 1994.

Cebulash, Mel. *Ruth Marini, Dodger Ace*. Lerner, 1983.

———. *Ruth Marini of the Dodgers*. Lerner, 1983.

Christiansen, C. B. *I See the Moon*. Atheneum, 1994.

Christopher, Matt. *Dirt Bike Racer*. Illustrated by Barry Bomzer. Little, Brown, 1979.

———. *Fighting Tackle*. Little, Brown, 1995.

Cleary, Beverly. *Dear Mr. Henshaw*. Ilustrated by Paul O. Zelinsky. Morrow, 1983.

———. *Henry and Beezus*. Illustrated by Louis Darling. Morrow, 1952.

———. *Henry Huggins*. Illustrated by Louis Darling. Morrow, 1950.

———. *Ramona and Her Father*. Illustrated by Alan Tiegreen. Morrow, 1977.

———. *Ramona and Her Mother*. Illustrated by Alan Tiegreen. Morrow, 1979.

———. *Ramona Forever*. Illustrated by Alan Tiegreen. Morrow, 1984.

———. *Ramona the Pest*. Illustrated by Louis Darling. Morrow, 1968.

———. *Ramona Quimby, Age 8*. Illustrated by Alan Tiegreen. Morrow, 1981.

———. *Strider*. Illustrated by Paul O. Zelinsky. Morrow, 1991.

Cleaver, Vera, and Bill Cleaver. *Trial Valley*. Lippincott, 1977.

———. *Where the Lilies Bloom*. Illustrated by James Spanfeller. Lippincott, 1969.

Clifford, Eth. *The Rocking Chair Rebellion*. Houghton Mifflin, 1978.

Clifton, Lucille. *The Lucky Stone*. Illustrated by Dale Payson. Delacorte, 1979.

Clymer, Eleanor. *The Horse in the Attic*. Illustrated by Ted Lewin. Bradbury, 1983.

Cohen, Barbara. *Molly's Pilgrim*. Illustrated by Michael J. Deraney. Lothrop, Lee & Shepard, 1983. (Historical fiction)

———. *Thank You, Jackie Robinson*. Illustrated by Richard Cuffari. Lothrop, Lee & Shepard, 1974.

Cole, Brock. *The Goats*. Farrar, Straus & Giroux, 1987.

Conford, Ellen. *Anything for a Friend*. Little, Brown, 1979.

Conrad, Pam. *My Daniel*. Harper & Row, 1989.

———. *Staying Nine*. Illustrated by Mike Wimmer. Harper & Row, 1988.

Cooper, Ilene. *Choosing Sides*. Morrow, 1990.

———. *Queen of the Sixth Grade*. Morrow, 1988.

Creech, Sharon. *Walk Two Moons*. HarperCollins, 1994.

Cresswell, Helen. *Ordinary Jack*. Macmillan, 1977.

Crutcher, Chris. *Stotan!* Greenwillow, 1986.

Cunningham, Julia. *Dorp Dead*. Illustrated by James Spanfeller. Pantheon, 1965.

Dalokay, Vedat. *Sister Shako and Kolo the Goat*. Translated by Güner Ener. Lothrop, Lee & Shepard, 1994.

Danziger, Paula. *Amber Brown Goes Fourth*. Illustrated by Tony Ross. Putnam, 1995.

Deem, James. *3 NBs of Julian Drew*. Houghton Mifflin, 1994.

de Jenkins, Lyll Becerra. *The Honorable Prison*. Dutton, 1988.

DeJong, Meindert. *Hurry Home, Candy*. Illustrated by Maurice Sendak. Harper & Row, 1953.

Donovan, John. *I'll Get There, It Better Be Worth the Trip*. Harper & Row, 1969.

Dragonwagon, Crescent. *Winter Holding Spring*. Illustrated by Ronald Himler. Macmillan, 1990.

Duncan, Lois. *The Twisted Window*. Delacorte, 1987.

Ellis, Sarah. *A Family Project*. Macmillan, 1988.

Enright, Elizabeth. *The Saturdays*. Holt, 1941.

Estes, Eleanor. *The Hundred Dresses*. Illustrated by Louis Slobodkin. Harcourt, 1944.

———. *The Middle Moffat*. Illustrated by Louis Slobodkin. Harcourt, 1942.

———. *The Moffats*. Illustrated by Louis Slobodkin. Harcourt, 1941.

———. *Rufus M*. Illustrated by Louis Slobodkin. Harcourt, 1943.

Farley, Walter. *The Black Stallion*. Illustrated by Keith Ward. Random House, 1944.

Fine, Anne. *Flour Babies*. Little, Brown, 1994

Fitzhugh, Louise. *Harriet the Spy*. Harper & Row, 1964.

———. *The Long Secret*. Harper & Row, 1965.

Fox, Paula. *Monkey Island*. Orchard, 1991.

———. *One-Eyed Cat*. Bradbury, 1984.

———. *The Stone-Faced Boy*. Illustrated by Donald A. MacKay. Bradbury, 1968.

———. *The Village by the Sea*. Orchard, 1988.

Franklin, Kristine L. *Eclipse*. Candlewick, 1995.

Fritz, Jean. *Homesick: My Own Story*. Illustrated by Margot Tomes. Putnam, 1982. (Historical fiction)

Gardiner, John Reynolds. *Stone Fox*. Illustrated by Marcia Sewall. Crowell, 1980.

George, Jean Craighead. *The Cry of the Crow*. Harper & Row, 1980.

———. *Julie*. Illustrated by Wendell Minor. HarperCollins, 1994.

———. *Julie of the Wolves*. Illustrated by John Schoenherr. Harper & Row, 1972.

———. *My Side of the Mountain*. Dutton, 1959.

———. *On the Far Side of the Mountain*. Dutton, 1990.

———. *The Talking Earth*. Harper & Row, 1983.

Giff, Patricia Reilly. *The Beast in Ms. Rooney's Room, #1*. Dell, 1985.

Gilson, Jamie. *4-B Goes Wild*. Illustrated by Linda S. Edwards. Lothrop, Lee & Shepard, 1983.

———. *Hello, My Name Is Scrambled Eggs*. Illustrated by John Wallner. Lothrop, Lee & Shepard, 1985.

———. *Hobie Hanson, Greatest Hero of the Mall*. Illustrated by Anita Riggio. Lothrop, Lee & Shepard, 1989.

———. *Hobie Hanson, You're Weird*. Illustrated by Elise Primavera. Lothrop, Lee & Shepard, 1987.

———. *Thirteen Ways to Sink a Sub*. Illustrated by Linda S. Edwards. Lothrop, Lee & Shepard, 1982.

Gipson, Fred. *Old Yeller*. Illustrated by Carl Burger. Harper & Row, 1956.

Gleitzman, Morris. *Blabber Mouth*. Harcourt Brace, 1995.

———. *Sticky Beak*. Harcourt Brace, 1995.

Godden, Rumer. *The Rocking Horse Secret*. Illustrated by Juliet S. Smith. Viking, 1978.

Gordon, Sheila. *The Middle of Somewhere: A Story of South Africa*. Orchard, 1990.

———. *Waiting for the Rain*. Orchard, 1987.

Graeber, Charlotte. *Mustard*. Illustrated by Donna Diamond. Macmillan, 1982.

Greene, Constance C. *Beat the Turtle Drum*. Illustrated by Donna Diamond. Viking, 1976.

Greenfield, Eloise. *Sister*. Crowell, 1974.

Greenwald, Sheila. *Rosy Cole, She Walks in Beauty*. Little, Brown, 1994.

Hamilton, Virginia. *Cousins*. Philomel, 1990.

———. *The House of Dies Drear*. Illustrated by Eros Keith. Macmillan, 1968.

———. *M. C. Higgins, the Great*. Macmillan, 1974.

———. *The Mystery of Drear House*. Greenwillow, 1987.

———. *The Planet of Junior Brown*. Macmillan, 1971.

———. *Zeely*. Illustrated by Symeon Shimin. Macmillan, 1967.

Härtling, Peter. *Old John*. Translated by Elizabeth D. Crawford. Lothrop, Lee & Shepard, 1990.

Haseley, Dennis. *Getting Him*. Farrar, Straus & Giroux, 1994.

Haywood, Carolyn. *"B" Is for Betsy*. Harcourt, 1956.

Henkes, Keven. *Protecting Marie*. Greenwillow, 1995.

Henry, Marguerite. *Misty of Chincoteague*. Illustrated by Wesley Dennis. Macmillan, 1947.

Hesse, Karen. *Sable*, Illustrated by Marcia Sewall. Holt, 1994.

Hickman, Janet. *Jericho*. Greenwillow, 1994.

Hiçyilmaz, Gaye. *Against the Storm*. Joy Street, 1990.

Hill, Kirkpatrick. *Toughboy and Sister*. McElderry, 1990.

Ho, Minfong. *Rice Without Rain*. Lothrop, Lee & Shepard, 1988.

Hobbs, Will. *Beardance*. Atheneum, 1993.

———. *Bearstone*. Atheneum, 1989.

Holman, Felice. *Slake's Limbo*. Scribner's, 1974.

Houston, James. *Frozen Fire*. Atheneum, 1977.

Howe, James. *Dew Drop Dead: A Sebastian Barth Mystery*. Atheneum, 1990.

———. *What Eric Knew: A Sebastian Barth Mystery*. Atheneum, 1985.

Hunter, Mollie. *A Sound of Chariots*. Harper & Row, 1972.

Hurwitz, Johanna. *Aldo Applesauce*. Illustrated by John Wallner. Morrow, 1979.

———. *Busybody Nora*. Illustrated by Susan Jeschke. Morrow, 1976.

———. *Class Clown*. Illustrated by Sheila Hamanaka. Morrow, 1987.

———. *Russell and Elisa*. Illustrated by Lillian Hoban. Morrow, 1989.

Huynh, Quang Nhuong. *The Land I Lost: Adventures of a Boy in Vietnam*. Illustrated by Vo-Dinh Mai. Harper & Row, 1982.

Johnson, Angela. *Toning the Sweep*. Orchard, 1993.

Johnston, Julie. *Adam and Eve and Pinch-Me*. Little, Brown, 1994.

Jones, Rebecca. *Germy Blew It*. Dutton, 1987.

———. *Germy Blew It Again*. Holt, 1988.

———. *Germy Blew "the Bugle."* Arcade, 1990.

Jukes, Mavis. *Blackberries in the Dark*. Illustrated by Thomas B. Allen. Knopf, 1985.

Kidd, Diana. *Onion Tears*. Illustrated by Lucy Montgomery. Orchard, 1991.

Kjelgaard, Jim. *Big Red*. Illustrated by Bob Kuhn. Holiday House, 1956.

Klein, Robin. *Hating Alison Ashley*. Viking Kestrel, 1987.

Kline, Suzy. *Herbie Jones*. Illustrated by Richard Williams. Putnam, 1985.

———. *Orp*. Putnam, 1989.

———. *Orp Goes to the Hoop*. Putnam, 1991.

Koertge, Ron. *Tiger, Tiger, Burning Bright*. Orchard, 1994.

Konigsburg, E. L. *From the Mixed-Up Files of Mrs. Basil E. Frankweiler*. Atheneum, 1967.

———. *(George)*. Atheneum, 1970.

———. *Journey to an 800 Number*. Atheneum, 1982.

Korman, Gordon. *This Can't Be Happening at Macdonald Hall*. Scholastic, 1978.

Krumgold, Joseph. *. . . And Now Miguel*. Illustrated by Jean Charlot. Crowell, 1953.

Laird, Elizabeth. *Kiss the Dust*. Dutton, 1992.

Laskey, Kathryn. *The Night Journey*. Illustrated by Trina Schart Hyman. Warne, 1981.

Le Guin, Ursula K. *A Wizard of Earthsea*. Illustrated by Ruth Robbins. Houghton Mifflin, 1968. (Fantasy)

L'Engle, Madeleine. *Meet the Austins*. Dell, 1981 [1960].

———. *A Ring of Endless Light*. Farrar, Straus & Giroux, 1980.

———. *A Wrinkle in Time*. Farrar, Straus & Giroux, 1962. (Fantasy)

Levitin, Sonia. *The Return*. Atheneum, 1987.

Lipsyte, Robert. *The Contender*. Harper & Row, 1967.

Lisle, Janet Taylor. *The Gold Dust Letters*. Orchard, 1994.

———. *Looking for Juliette*. Orchard, 1994.

———. *A Message from the Match Girl*. Orchard, 1995.

Little, Jean. *Hey World, Here I Am!* Illustrated by Sue Truesdell. Harper & Row, 1989.

———. *Home from Far*. Illustrated by Jerry Lazare. Little, Brown, 1965.

———. *Kate*. Harper & Row, 1971.

———. *Look Through My Window*. Illustrated by Joan Sandin. Harper & Row, 1970.

———. *Mama's Going to Buy You a Mockingbird*. Viking, 1984.

———. *Take Wing*. Little, Brown, 1968.

London, Jack. *The Call of the Wild*. Illustrated by Charles Pickard. Dutton, 1968 [1903].

Lord, Bette Bao. *In the Year of the Boar and Jackie Robinson*. Illustrated by Marc Simont. Harper & Row, 1984. (Historical fiction)

Lovelace, Maude Hart. *Betsy-Tacy*. Illustrated by Lois Lensky. Harper & Row, 1940.

Lowry, Lois. *All About Sam*. Houghton Mifflin, 1988.

———. *Anastasia Again!* Illustrated by Diane de Groat. Houghton Mifflin, 1981.

———. *Anastasia Krupnik*. Houghton Mifflin, 1979.

———. *Attaboy, Sam*. Illustrated by Diane de Groat. Houghton Mifflin, 1992.

———. *Number the Stars*. Houghton Mifflin, 1989. (Historical fiction)

———. *Rabble Starkey*. Houghton Mifflin, 1987.

———. *A Summer to Die*. Illustrated by Jenni Oliver. Houghton Mifflin, 1977.

MacLachlan, Patricia. *Arthur for the Very First Time*. Illustrated by Lloyd Bloom. Harper & Row, 1980.

———. *Baby*. Delacorte, 1993.

———. *Journey*. Delacorte, 1991.

Martin, Ann. *Kristy's Great Idea: The Baby-Sitters Club, #1*. Scholastic, 1986.

Mathis, Sharon Bell. *The Hundred Penny Box*. Illustrated by Leo and Diane Dillon. Viking, 1975.

McDonnell, Christine. *Don't Be Mad, Ivy*. Illustrated by Diane de Groat. Dial, 1981.

McKay, Hilary. *The Exiles*. McElderry, 1992.

———. *The Exiles at Home*. McElderry, 1994.

Mikaelsen, Ben. *Stranded*. Hyperion, 1995.

Miles, Betty. *Maudie and Me and the Dirty Book*. Knopf, 1980.

Mills, Claudia. *Dynamite Dinah*. Macmillan, 1990.

Moeri, Louise. *The Forty-Third War*. Houghton Mifflin, 1989.

Mohr, Nicolasa. *Felita*. Illustrated by Ray Cruz. Dial, 1979.

———. *Going Home*. Dial, 1986.

Mowat, Farley. *The Dog Who Wouldn't Be*. Little, Brown, 1957.

———. *Owls in the Family*. Little, Brown, 1961.

Myers, Walter Dean. *Darnell Rock Reporting*. Delacorte, 1994.

———. *Fast Sam, Cool Clyde, and Stuff*. Viking, 1975.

———. *The Mouse Rap*. HarperCollins, 1990.

———. *Scorpions*. Harper & Row, 1988.

Naidoo, Beverley. *Chain of Fire*. Illustrated by Eric Velasquez. Lippincott, 1990.

———. *Journey to Jo'burg*. Illustrated by Eric Velasquez. Lippincott, 1986.

Namioka, Lensey. *Yang the Third and Her Impossible Family*. Illustrated by Kees de Kiefte. Little, Brown, 1995.

———. *Yang the Youngest and His Terrible Ear*. Illustrated by Kees de Kiefte. Little, Brown, 1992.

Naylor, Phyllis Reynolds. *The Agony of Alice*. Atheneum, 1985.

———. *Alice In-Between*. Atheneum, 1994.

———. *Shiloh*. Atheneum, 1991.

Nelson, Theresa. *Earthshine*. Orchard, 1994.

Neville, Emily Cheney. *The China Year*. HarperCollins, 1991.

Nixon, Joan Lowery. *A Candidate for Murder*. Delacorte, 1991.

———. *The Other Side of Dark*. Delacorte, 1986.

North, Sterling. *Rascal: A Memoir of a Better Era*. Illustrated by John Schoenherr. Dutton, 1963.

Oneal, Zibby. *The Language of Goldfish*. Viking, 1980.

Parish, Peggy. *Amelia Bedelia*. Illustrated by Fritz Siebel. Harper & Row, 1963.

Park, Barbara. *Mick Harte Was Here*. Apple Soup, 1995.

———. *Skinnybones*. Knopf, 1982.

Paterson, Katherine. *Bridge to Terabithia*. Illustrated by Donna Diamond. Crowell, 1977.

———. *Come Sing, Jimmy Jo*. Dutton, 1985.

———. *Flip-Flop Girl*. Lodestar, 1994.

———. *The Great Gilly Hopkins*. Crowell, 1978.

———. *Jacob Have I Loved*. Harper & Row, 1980.

———. *Park's Quest*. Dutton, 1988.

Paulsen, Gary. *Brian's Winter*. Delacorte, 1996.

———. *Dogsong*. Bradbury, 1985.

———. *Harris and Me*. Harcourt Brace, 1993.

———. *Hatchet*. Bradbury, 1987.

———. *The River*. Delacorte, 1991.

———. *The Voyage of the Frog*. Bradbury, 1989.

Pearce, Philippa. *The Way to Sattin Shore*. Ilustrated by Charlotte Voake. Greenwillow, 1983.

Peck, Robert Newton. *Soup*. Illustrated by Charles Gehm. Knopf, 1974.

Pinkney, Andrea Davis. *Hold Fast to Dreams*. Morrow, 1995.

Porte, Barbara Ann. *Something Terrible Happened*. Orchard, 1994.

Raskin, Ellen. *The Westing Game*. Dutton, 1978.

Rawlings, Marjorie Kinnan. *The Yearling*. Illustrated by Edward Shenton. Scribner's, 1938.

Rawls, Wilson. *Where the Red Fern Grows*. Doubleday, 1961.

Riley, Jocelyn. *Crazy Quilt*. Morrow, 1983.

———. *Only My Mouth Is Smiling*. Morrow, 1982.

Robinson, Barbara. *The Best Christmas Pageant Ever*. Illustrated by Judith Gwyn Brown. Harper & Row, 1972.

———. *The Best School Year Ever*. HarperCollins, 1994.

Rockwell, Thomas. *How to Eat Fried Worms*. Watts, 1973.

Rodowsky, Colby F. *What About Me?* Watts, 1976.

Rylant, Cynthia. *Henry and Mudge:The First Book of Their Adventures*. Illustrated by Suçie Stevenson. Bradbury, 1987.

———. *Missing May*. Orchard, 1992.

Sachar, Louis. *Marvin Redpost: Why Pick on Me?* Illustrated by Neal Hughes. Random House, 1993.

———. *Wayside School Gets a Little Stranger*. Illustrated by Joel Schick. Morrow, 1995.

Sachs, Marilyn. *The Bears' House*. Illustrated by Louis Glanzman. Doubleday, 1971.

Schlein, Miriam. *The Year of the Panda*. Illustrated by Kam Mak. Crowell, 1990.

Sharmat, Marjorie Wiseman. *Nate the Great*. Illustrated by Marc Simont. Putnam, 1986.

Shreve, Susan. *The Flunking of Joshua T. Bates*. Illustrated by Diane de Groat. Knopf, 1984.

Simon, Seymour. *Einstein Anderson Lights Up the Sky*. Illustrated by Fred Winkowski. Viking, 1982.

Slepian, Jan. *The Alfred Summer*. Macmillan, 1980.

———. *The Broccoli Tapes*. Putnam, 1989.

———. *Risk 'n Roses*. Philomel, 1990.

Slote, Alfred. *Hang Tough, Paul Mather*. Lippincott, 1973.

———. *The Trading Game*. Lippincott, 1990.

Smith, Doris Buchanan. *A Taste of Blackberries*. Illustrated by Charles Robinson. Crowell, 1973.

Smith, Janice Lee. *Serious Science: An Adam Joshua Story*. Illustrated by Dick Gackenbach. HarperCollins, 1993.

Snyder, Zilpha K. *The Egypt Game*. Illustrated by Alton Raible. Atheneum, 1967.

———. *Libby on Wednesday*. Delacorte, 1990.

Sobol, Donald. *Encyclopedia Brown Takes a Case*. Illustrated by Leonard Shortall. Nelson, 1973.

Soto, Gary. *Baseball in April and Other Stories*. Harcourt Brace, 1990.

———. *Boys at Work*. Delacorte, 1995.

———. *Crazy Weekend*. Scholastic, 1995.

———. *Local News*. Harcourt Brace, 1993.

———. *Pacific Crossing*. Harcourt Brace, 1992.

———. *The Pool Party*. Delacorte, 1993.

———. *Summer on Wheels*. Scholastic, 1995.

———. *Taking Sides*. Harcourt Brace, 1991.

Speare, Elizabeth George. *The Witch of Blackbird Pond*. Houghton Mifflin, 1958. (Historical fiction)

Sperry, Armstrong. *Call It Courage*. Macmillan, 1968.

Spinelli, Jerry. *Maniac Magee*. Little, Brown, 1990.

Staples, Suzanne Fisher. *Haveli*. Knopf, 1993.

————. *Shabanu: Daughter of the Wind*. Knopf, 1989.

Stolz, Mary. *The Bully of Barkham Street*. Illustrated by Leonard Shortall. Harper & Row, 1963.

————. *A Dog on Barkham Street*. Illustrated by Leonard Shortall. Harper & Row, 1960.

————. *The Explorer of Barkham Street*. Illustrated by Emily A. McCully. Harper & Row, 1985.

Taylor, Mildred. *The Friendship*. Illustrated by Max Ginsburg. Dial, 1987. (Historical fiction)

Taylor, Sidney. *More All-of-a-Kind Family*. Illustrated by Mary Stevens. Follett, 1954.

————. *The Trouble with Tuck*. Doubleday, 1981.

————. *Tuck Triumphant*. Doubleday, 1991.

Temple, Frances. *Grab Hands and Run*. Orchard, 1993.

————. *Taste of Salt*. Orchard, 1992.

————. *Tonight, by Sea*. Orchard, 1995.

Thomas, Jane Resh. *The Comeback Dog*. Illustrated by Troy Howell. Houghton Mifflin, 1981.

Voigt, Cynthia. *Dicey's Song*. Atheneum, 1983.

————. *Homecoming*. Atheneum, 1981.

————. *The Runner*. Atheneum, 1985.

————. *Seventeen Against the Dealer*. Atheneum, 1985.

————. *A Solitary Blue*. Atheneum, 1984.

Walker, Kate. *Peter*. Houghton Mifflin, 1993.

Walter, Mildred Pitts. *Have a Happy . . .* Lothrop, Lee & Shepard, 1989.

————. *Justin and the Best Biscuits in the World*. Illustrated by Catherine Stock. Knopf, 1986.

Warburg, Sandol Stoddard. *The Growing Time*. Illustrated by Leonard Weisgard. Harper & Row, 1969.

Wilson, Budge. *The Dandelion Garden*. Philomel, 1995.

————. *The Leaving*. Philomel, 1992.

Wolff, Virginia Euwer. *Make Lemonade*. Holt, 1993.

————. *The Mozart Season*. Holt, 1991.

Woodson, Jacqueline. *Between Madison and Palmetto*. Delacorte, 1993.

————. *I Hadn't Meant to Tell You This*. Delacorte, 1994.

————. *Last Summer with Maizon*. Delacorte, 1990.

————. *Maizon at Blue Hill*. Delacorte, 1992.

Yep, Laurence. *Child of the Owl*. Harper & Row, 1977.

————. *Later, Gator*. Hyperion, 1995.

————. *Thief of Hearts*. HarperCollins, 1995.

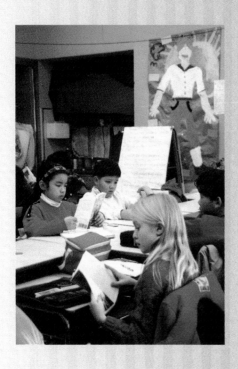

chapter
ten

Historical Fiction

Historical Fiction for Today's Child **514**

The Value of Historical Fiction   515
Types of Historical Fiction   516
Criteria for Historical Fiction   517
**Guidelines: Evaluating Historical
   Fiction** **520**
Stories of Prehistoric Times **520**
Stories of the Old World **521**

Ancient Times   521
Tales of Early Britain   521
Medieval Times and Tales   521
The Emergence of the Modern World   523
Stories of the New World **524**

Colonial America   524
Teaching Feature: The Sign of the Beaver—
   A World of Possibilities **526**

The Revolutionary Era   528

Native Americans   529
The American Frontier   531
The Civil War Era   533

Slavery   533
The Civil War   535
**Resources for Teaching: Recurring Themes
   in Historical Fiction** **536**
Into the Twentieth Century **536**

Immigrants   536
African Americans   537
The World at War   538

Escape and Resistance   539
The Impact of World War II in the Americas   542
War Continues   543
Learning Experiences **544**
Related Readings **544**
Children's Literature **545**

The author of a historical novel visited a public library's after-school program to meet with a group of children. In her talk she described the research she had done to establish an authentic Civil War background for her book. To make these efforts more concrete for the children, she had brought along many examples of source material: maps, reproductions of nineteenth-century photographs, books and pamphlets, and a three-ring binder bulging with notes. One 10-year-old girl regarded this display with a troubled expression, and when time came for questions quickly raised her hand.

"You found out a lot of things that you didn't put in the book, didn't you?" she asked. The author agreed, and the girl smiled. "Good!" she said. "If you had put all *that* stuff in, there wouldn't have been any room for the imagining!"

This child intuitively knew that historical fiction must draw on two sources, fact and imagination—the author's information about the past and her or his power to speculate about how it was to live in that time.

Biography for children also draws on both sources (see Chapter 11). Although biography is by definition a nonfiction genre, its success depends as much on its imaginative presentation of facts as on accuracy. Both biography and historical fiction have narrative appeal. By personalizing the past and making it live in the mind of the reader, such books can help children understand both the public events that we usually label "history" and the private struggles that have characterized the human condition across the centuries.

Historical Fiction for Today's Child

Historical fiction is not as popular with readers today as it was a generation ago. Children generally select realistic fiction, the so-called "I" stories with modern-day characters and settings. Even so, children have more historical fiction available now than in the 1980s.

Publishers have capitalized on children's interest in series books by developing collectible sets of historical fiction titles. The American Girl books offer five different series, each chronicling the adventures of a girl in a particular time. These books, along with the expensive dolls and period costumes that go with them, have been phenomenally successful.

Other publishers, influenced by public debate about children's need to know their heritage, have also targeted the 7-to-11 age range. Viking's Once Upon America books, written by many different authors, vary widely in quality. However, they offer an unusually wide range of settings, such as the Oklahoma land rush (*Beautiful Land* by Nancy Antle) and the polio epidemic of 1952 (*Close to Home* by Lydia Weaver).

Another noticeable trend in historical fiction is the number of picture storybooks that portray the life of a particular period. For example, children can sail on the Mayflower through picture books like Jean Van Leeuwen's *Across the Wide Dark Sea*; Thomas B. Allen's impressionistic pastel drawings help them visualize details of seventeenth-century life. In Eve Bunting's *Dandelions* they can travel across the prairie, helped by Greg Shed's textured paintings to experience the vast distances and huge skies of a land in which the closest neighbors were three hours away. They can walk among the tenements of an immigrant community in New York City in Elisa Bartone's *Peppe the Lamplighter*. Here Ted Lewin's flowing watercolors will light their way through the frightening darkness of city streets and overwhelming demands of a new land and a new culture.

The increased use of books across the curriculum has created a demand for more historical fiction and biography in the social studies curriculum. Many books that were written in the 1950s—such as Eloise McGraw's *Moccasin Trail* and William Steele's *Winter Danger*, *The Buffalo Knife*, and *Flaming Arrows*—have been reissued in paperback in the 1990s. These are still exciting,

Greg Shed's illustration represents the isolation of life on the prairie in Eve Bunting's *Dandelions.*

Illustration from *Dandelions* by Eve Bunting, illustrations copyright © 1995 by Greg Shed, reproduced by permission of Harcourt Brace & Company.

Ted Lewin received a Caldecott Honor Medal for his dramatic illustrations of immigrant life in Elisa Bartone's *Peppe the Lamplighter.*

Illustration from *Peppe the Lamplighter* by Elisa Bartone, illustrated by Ted Lewin. Illustration copyright © 1993 by Ted Lewin. By permission of Lothrop, Lee & Shepard Books, a division of William Morrow & Company, Inc.

well-written stories of frontier living and will capture children's interest. *On to Oregon!* by Honoré Morrow is an almost unbelievable tale of the courage of the six Sager children, who, after their parents' deaths, walked over a thousand miles by themselves through the wilderness until they reached the Whitman missionary station. First published in 1926, then again in 1946 and 1954, and now in paperback in the 1990s, this novel proves the lasting quality of a true survival story.

While many books of American historical fiction are being reissued, many fine books, such as Rosemary Sutcliff's books about early Britain, have been allowed to go out of print. Except for an increase in the number of titles about the Holocaust, we have fewer books of historical fiction about other lands. This is a loss, indeed, in a world in which we are all becoming increasingly interdependent. We need to know our history *and* the history of other countries.

The Value of Historical Fiction

Historical novels for children help a child to experience the past—to enter into the conflicts, the suffering, the joys, and the despair of those who lived before us. There is no way that children can feel the jolt of a covered wagon, the tediousness of the daily trek in the broiling sun, or the constant threat of danger unless they take an imaginative journey in books like Jean Van Leeuwen's *Bound for Oregon* or *Beyond the Divide* by Kathryn Lasky. Well-written historical fiction offers young people the vicarious experience of participating in the life of the past.

Historical fiction encourages children to think as well as to feel. Every book set in the past invites a comparison

with the present. In addition, opportunities for critical thinking and judgment are built into the many novels that provide conflicting views on an issue and force characters to make hard choices. Readers of *My Brother Sam Is Dead* by the Colliers can weigh Sam's patriot fervor against his father's Tory practicality as young Tim tries to decide which one is right. Readers will question Will Page's dislike of his uncle because he refused to fight the Yankees in Carolyn Reeder's *Shades of Gray.* And yet there have been conscientious objectors to every war that this nation has participated in. Mary Downing Hahn deals with the same issue in *Stepping on the Cracks,* a story set during World War II.

An historical perspective also helps children see and judge the mistakes of the past more clearly. They can read such books as *Ajeemah and His Son* by James Berry, *Hide and Seek* by Ida Vos, or *Under the Blood-Red Sun* by Graham Salisbury and realize the cruelty that people are capable of inflicting on each other, whether by slavery, persecution, or the internment of Japanese Americans in "relocation centers." Such books will quicken children's sensibilities and bring them to a fuller understanding of human problems and human relationships. We hope that our children will learn not to repeat the injustices of the past. Many years ago George Santayana cautioned: "Those who cannot remember the past are condemned to repeat it."

Stories of the past help children see that times change, nations do rise and fall, but universal human needs have remained relatively unchanged. All people need and want respect, belonging, love, freedom, and security, regardless of whether they lived during the period of the Vikings or the pioneers or are alive today. It matters not how many different "Little Houses" the Ingalls family lived in as long as Pa's fiddle sang a song of love and security in each one. Children today living in tenements, trailers, or suburban homes seek the same feeling of warmth and family solidarity that Laura Ingalls Wilder portrayed so effectively in her Little House series.

Historical fiction also enables children to see human interdependence. We are all interconnected and interrelated. We need others as much as Matt needed Attean and Saknis in Elizabeth George Speare's *The Sign of the Beaver* or Ellen Rosen needed Annemarie Johansen's family in order to escape the Nazis in Lois Lowry's award-winning book *Number the Stars*. Such books also dramatize the courage and integrity of the thousands of "common folk" who willingly take a stand for what they believe. History does not record their names, but their stories are frequently the source of inspiration for books of historical fiction.

Children's perceptions of chronology are inexact and develop slowly. Even so, stories about the past can develop a feeling for the continuity of life and help children to see themselves and their present place in time as part of a larger picture. Bonnie Pryor's *The House on Maple Street* provides this sense for younger elementary students. Lost objects from early times are unearthed in a contemporary child's yard. Paintings by Beth Peck link past and present, showing changes that came to that specific setting over the intervening centuries. Reading historical fiction is one way children can develop this sense of history and begin to understand their place in the sweep of human destiny.

Types of Historical Fiction

The term *historical fiction* can be used to designate all realistic stories that are set in the past. Even though children tend to see these in one undifferentiated category (since all the action happened "in the olden days" before they were born), students of literature will want to keep in mind that various distinctions can be made on the basis of the author's purpose and the nature of the research and writing tasks required.

In the most obvious type of historical fiction, an author weaves a fictional story around actual events and

Illustrator Beth Peck shows a Native American father burying an arrowhead that will be found years later in *The House on Maple Street* by Bonnie Pryor.

Illustration from *The House on Maple Street* by Bonnie Pryor, illustrated by Beth Peck. Illustration copyright © 1987 by Beth Peck. By permission of Morrow Junior Books, a division of William Morrow & Company, Inc.

people of the past. *Johnny Tremain* by Esther Forbes, the story of a fictional apprentice to Paul Revere, is a novel of this sort. The author had previously written a definitive adult biography of Revere and had collected painstakingly accurate details about life in Boston just before the Revolutionary War: the duties of apprentices, the activities of the Committee for Public Safety, and much, much more. Johnny Tremain's personal story, his development from an embittered boy into a courageous and idealistic young man, is inextricably connected with the political history and way of life of his place and time.

In other stories of the past, fictional lives are lived with little or no reference to recorded historical events or real persons. However, the facts of social history dictate the background for how the characters live and make their living; what they wear, eat, study, or play; and what conflicts they must resolve. Rachel Anderson's *Black Water* is of this type. Set in Victorian England, the book focuses on the problems of Edward, a child with epilepsy in a time when such conditions were little understood. As he grows toward adulthood, the boy learns to accept his limitations but also to understand that his talents hold hope for a rich and fulfilling life. While the details of nineteenth-century life enrich the story and shape the action, the book's theme and the character's development could be placed in any time period. Authors who write within this generalized frame of social history have more freedom to imagine their story, because they are not bound to the chronology of specific historical events.

If we look at the author's task in another way, we can see that some authors deliberately reconstruct, through research, the life and times of a period long past. Others recreate, largely from memory, their own personal experiences of a time that is "history" to their child audience. The Little House books for example, are all based on actual childhood experiences in the life of their author, Laura Ingalls Wilder, or those of her husband. Such books require searching the memory for details and then the sorting and imaginative retelling of significant events, but extensive research is seldom done.

In other instances, a purely contemporary story about a significant event might endure until it acquires historical significance. *Snow Treasure* by Marie McSwigan is the exciting story of Norwegian children who heroically strapped gold bullion under their sleds and slid downhill to the port past the watchful Nazi commandant. Written as realism in 1942, this book is read by children today as historical fiction.

Some essentially historical stories defy commonly accepted classifications. A few authors tell stories of the past in the guise of another genre to draw the hesitant reader in more quickly. Jane Yolen's devastating story of the Holocaust, *The Devil's Arithmetic*, begins in the present when Hannah, bored with all the remembering of the Passover Seder, opens the door to welcome symbolically the prophet Elijah and finds herself in the unfamiliar world of a Polish village in the 1940s. In Lois Ruby's *Steal Away Home*, 12-year-old Dana Shannon finds a skeleton in a closet after her family moves into an old house in Kansas. A small black diary found with the skeleton helps Dana to discover that the skeleton is that of Lizbeth Charles, who had died 130 years earlier. In addition, alternate chapters take the reader back to the 1850s, when the house was owned by a Quaker family and was part of the underground railroad. Other devices are used to transport the main character (and the reader) from the present day to a carefully researched past in books like Janet Lunn's *The Root Cellar* (see Chapter 7).

Cynthia De Felice's *Lostman's River* is an exciting adventure set in the Florida Everglades in the early 1900s. Children will learn more about the fragile ecology of the Everglades than they will about historical details, but the story is based on real events—particularly the murder of an Audubon Society game warden hired to protect the rookeries of birds who were being wiped out for their feathers. E. L. Konigsburg's unique story of

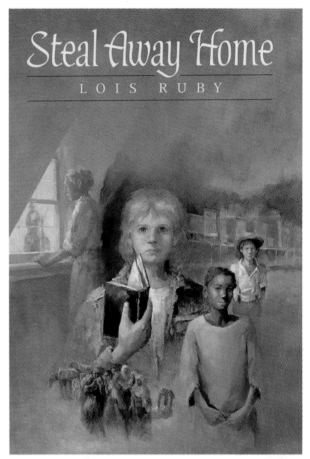

Lois Ruby weaves together a modern-day mystery with historical fiction in *Steal Away Home.*
Cover of *Steal Away Home* by Lois Ruby, illustrated by Ron Himler. Copyright © 1994 by Ron Himler. Reprinted by permission.

Eleanor of Aquitaine, *A Proud Taste for Scarlet and Miniver,* combines fantasy, historical fiction, and biography. Categorizing books like these is far less important than bringing them to the attention of children, for they all tell good stories and make their subjects memorable.

No type of historical story is intrinsically better than another. However, the type of story might influence a teacher's selection process when choosing books for specific classroom purposes. And in applying the criteria for evaluating historical fiction, which are described in the following section, standards of authenticity must be applied most rigorously to stories that give a prominent place to real people and real events.

Criteria for Historical Fiction

Books of historical fiction must first of all tell a story that is interesting in its own right. The second, and unique, requirement is balancing fact with fiction.

Margery Fisher maintains that fact must always be subordinated to the story:

> For the more fact he [the author] has to deal with, the more imagination he will need to carry it off. It is not enough to be a scholar, essential though this is. Without imagination and enthusiasm, the most learned and well-documented story will leave the young reader cold, where it should set him on fire.[1]

Historical fiction does have to be accurate and authentic. However, the research should be thoroughly digested, making details appear as an essential part of the story, not tacked on for effect. Mollie Hunter, a well-known Scottish writer of fine historical fiction for children, maintains that an author should be so steeped in the historical period of the book that "you could walk undetected in the past. You'd wake up in the morning and know the kind of bed you'd be sleeping in, . . . even to the change you'd have in your pocket!"[2] The purpose of research, she said, is

> to be able to think and feel in terms of a period so that the people within it are real and three-dimensional, close enough to hear the sound of their voices, to feel their body-warmth, to see the expression in their eyes.[3]

Although fictional characters and invented turns of plot are accepted in historical novels, nothing should be included that contradicts the actual record of history. If President Lincoln was busy reviewing Union troops in Virginia on a given day in 1863, an author cannot "borrow" him for a scene played in New York City, no matter how great the potential dramatic impact. It breaks the unwritten contract between author and child reader to offer misinformation in any form.

Stories must accurately reflect the spirit and values of the times, as well as the events. Historical fiction can't be made to conform to today's more enlightened point of view concerning women or minorities or medical knowledge. You can't save George Washington with a shot of penicillin any more than you can have the African American mother in William Armstrong's *Sounder* become a militant in the 1890s. Characters have to act in accordance with the values and beliefs of the time. In Carol Ryrie Brink's *Caddie Woodlawn*, Caddie's father allowed her to be a tomboy while she was growing up in the Wisconsin backwoods, but she had to become a "proper lady" during the Victorian era; there was no other choice. Avi's *The True Confessions of Charlotte Doyle* is a dramatic sea adventure story in the manner of Robert Louis Stevenson's *Kidnapped*. In 1832, 13-year-old Charlotte Doyle boards the *Seahawk* to sail from Liverpool, England, to Providence, Rhode Island. Fresh from her proper boarding school experience in England, Charlotte is dismayed to find that she is the only passenger and the only female on the ship. Within hours of her arrival onboard, the ship's cook gives her a dagger for her protection. And that is just the beginning of this exciting sea yarn. Charlotte is a strong female character, yet some of her adventures stretch credibility as tightly as the full-blown sails that she climbs. Despite the many awards this book has received, we cannot help wondering if it wasn't written with today's values in mind rather than the New England of the early 1830s.

The historian Christopher Collier, who has collaborated with his brother James Lincoln Collier on several novels set during the era of the American Revolution, maintains that authors should pay careful attention to historiography, "that is, the way that professional historians have approached and interpreted the central episode of the story."[4] Collier believes that authors should weigh opposing views on the causes or meaning of a conflict and decide which should be predominant in the story, but also find a way to include the other significant interpretations. One way is to have different characters espouse different points of view. In *Bull Run* Paul Fleischman overcomes this problem by telling the story of this early battle of the Civil War through the voices of sixteen different characters, northerners and southerners, male and female, civilian and military, slave and free. However, fiction that draws the reader into the thoughts and feelings of a central character cannot be truly impartial. In the middle of a massacre scene, a bleeding settler who cries "But the Indians are only fighting for what is theirs!" will sacrifice the story's credibility. Many other fine books, like Carolyn Reeder's *Shades of Gray* and Avi's *The Fighting Ground*, do let the reader feel more than one side of an issue. But for a more inclusive viewpoint, teachers and librarians will want to provide a variety of books, each with its own approach to the topic.

The authenticity of language in historical fiction should be given careful attention. We have no recordings of the speech of people from much earlier times, but the spoken word in a book with an historical background should give the flavor of the period. However,

[1]Margery Fisher, *Intent upon Reading: A Critical Appraisal of Modern Fiction for Children* (New York: Watts, 1962), p. 225.

[2]Mollie Hunter, lecture, Columbus, Ohio, November 1968.

[3]Mollie Hunter, "Shoulder the Sky," in *Talent Is Not Enough* (New York: Harper & Row, 1976), pp. 43–44.

[4]Christopher Collier, "Criteria for Historical Fiction," *School Library Journal* 28 (August 1982): 32.

too many *prithees* and *thous* will seem artificial and may discourage children's further reading. Some archaic words can be used if they are explained in the content. For example, the book *The Cabin Faced West* notes that George Washington "bated" at the Hamiltons. The author, Jean Fritz, makes it very clear by the action in the story that "bated" meant "stopped by for dinner."

Some words commonly used in earlier times are offensive by today's standards. Authors must consider whether or not it would be misleading to omit such terms entirely and how necessary such language is for establishing a character. In Graham Salisbury's *Under the Blood-Red Sun*, "haoles," or white Hawaiians, refer to the Japanese as "Japs." It would have defeated the purpose and ruined the tensions of the story to have these people use more acceptable language.

Well-written historical fiction also makes use of figurative language that is appropriate for the times and characters in the story. For example, in Katherine Paterson's powerful story *Lyddie*, about a farm girl who goes to work in the fabric mills of Lowell, Massachusetts, in the 1840s, all allusions and metaphors are those of an uneducated rural girl. In the very beginning of the story a bear gets into their farm cabin and Lyddie stares him down while the other children climb the ladder to the loft. Finally she herself backs up to the ladder, climbs it, and pulls it up behind her. Throughout the book Lyddie alludes to "staring down the bears." She thinks of the huge machines as "roaring clattering beasts . . . great clumsy bears" (p. 97). And when she throws a water bucket at the overseer to get him to let go of a young girl, she laughs as she imagines she hears the sound of an angry bear crashing the oatmeal bucket in the cabin. Everything about this book works together to capture Lyddie's view of the world. At the same time, the long thirteen hours a day of factory work, life in the dormitories, the frequency of TB, and the treatment of women all reflect the spirit and the values of the times. More important than the authenticity of the writing is the fast-paced story and Lyddie's grit, determination, and personal growth.

A book of historical fiction should do even more than relate a good story of the past authentically and imaginatively. It should illuminate today's problems by examining those of other times. The themes of many historical books are basic ones about the meaning of freedom, loyalty and treachery, love and hate, acceptance of new ways, closed minds versus questing ones, and, always, the age-old struggle between good and evil. Many tales of the past echo recent experience. Books like *Catherine, Called Birdy* by Karen Cushman, *Lyddie* by Katherine Paterson, and *Prairie Songs* by Pam Conrad could well be used in a discussion of the history of women's roles. All these books can shed light and understanding on today's problems.

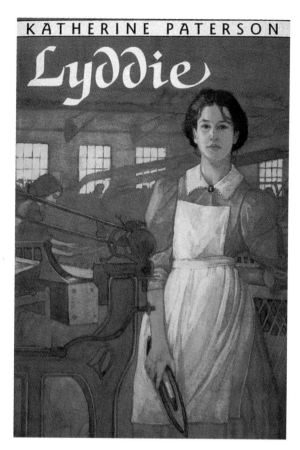

The cover of Katherine Paterson's *Lyddie* introduces a main character whose fortitude is written on her face.
From *Lyddie* by Katherine Paterson, jacket illustration by Debbi Chabrian. Copyright © 1991 by Katherine Paterson. Used by permission of Lodestar Books, an affiliate of Dutton Children's Books, a division of Penguin USA Inc.

To summarize, historical fiction must first meet the requirements of good writing, but it demands special criteria beyond that. In evaluating historical fiction the reader will want to consider whether the story meets these specialized needs.

Historical fiction can dramatize and humanize the facts of history that can seem sterile in so many textbooks. It can give children a sense of participation in the past and an appreciation for their historical heritage. It should enable the child to see that today's way of life is a result of what people did in the past and that the present will influence the way people live in the future. For some of the most important criteria to keep in mind, see Guidelines, "Evaluating Historical Fiction."

One way to approach historical fiction is to look at common topics or themes as they are presented in different settings across the centuries; the Resources for Teaching box later in this chapter groups titles by such themes. Another approach is to discuss books chronologically, according to the periods and settings they represent; the following sections are organized in this fashion.

Guidelines:
Evaluating Historical Fiction

Does the book tell a good story?

Is fact blended with fiction in such a way that the background is subordinate to the story?

Is the story as accurate and authentic as possible?

Does the author avoid any contradiction or distortion of the known events of history?

Are background details authentic, in keeping with accurate information about the period?

Does the story accurately reflect the values and spirit of the times?

Are different points of view on the issues of the time presented or acknowledged?

Is the dialogue constructed so as to convey a feeling of the period without seeming artificial? Does it reflect character as well as setting?

Is the language of the narrative appropriate to the time, drawing figures of speech from the setting?

Does the theme provide insight and understanding for today's problems as well as those of the past?

Stories of Prehistoric Times

Anthropologists and geologists are slowly uncovering scientific data that make it possible to imagine what life in prehistoric times might have been like. Authors and their readers have been fascinated with trying to reconstruct the minds and feelings of primitive people. How did they discover that there were others living in the world? Were all the tribes at the same level of development, or did different groups mature ahead of others? What happened when two groups met? These and other questions have provided the stimulus for some remarkably fine stories.

In *Time of the Bison*, Ann Turner creates a story of the cave painters. Who were they? What did their pictures mean to them? Scar Boy hates his name and longs for the time when he will find his real name, his inner name. One night he dreams of a great stallion. The next day at the river he makes a remarkable red clay statue of the horse in his dreams. His father is astonished and decides he must take Scar Boy on a journey to see the Painter of the Caves, a wise man who belongs to his mother's tribe. When Scar Boy is allowed to visit the cave, he discovers the true meaning of his gift and what his real name will someday be.

T. A. Dyer's *A Way of His Own* deals with early people of North America, a small band of hunters and gatherers on an inland prairie. According to their way, they abandon young Shutok because he cannot keep up and because they believe his crippled back houses an evil spirit responsible for all their misfortunes. But Shutok, a well-developed character with great determination, does

not die as expected. He is joined by the escaped slave girl Uita, and together the two outcasts kill the fearsome jaguar that invades their cave, struggle against bitter cold and hunger, and live to reclaim a position of worth with Shutok's people. The story is fast-paced, with lively dialogue.

Seth of the Lion People by Bonnie Pryor also tells the story of a boy crippled from birth. At first it was thought that Seth would follow in his father's footsteps and become the clan's storyteller, the one who kept their history alive. But the new leader's son is cruel and measures a man's worth only by his hunting and fighting skills. Seth, his best friend Esu, and the loyal Dog he has tamed set off across the mountains to see if it is really true that people there tend crops, domesticate animals, and live in warm huts. After a long and treacherous journey they discover that all they had heard is true. They return to their tribe just in time to save them from an erupting volcano. Because of all he learned from the other tribe, Seth is chosen leader over the cruel Nar.

J. H. Brennan's *Shiva* relates the warlike meeting of two groups of prehistoric peoples: the Neanderthals, called "ogres" by Cro-Magnon people, who in turn were called "The Weakling Strangers" by the Neanderthals. One group kept to the forests and caves; the other was nomadic and hunted. No ogre had been seen for many years, and it was assumed they had all died, until Shiva, an orphan Cro-Magnon girl, wanders too far from camp and is attacked by wolves. To her amazement, she is saved by a young ogre boy who jumps on the wolf and kills him. Her cries attract her own tribe, who promptly capture the young ogre. Shiva frees him.

This is a complex story of the distrust felt by one group toward another group who look different. Only Shiva can see the humanity of both tribes.

Stories of the Old World

Children in the United States are often more interested in stories of the American frontier, the Civil War, or World War II than they are in fiction about ancient or medieval days. However, there is some fine historical fiction about the Old World.

Ancient Times

The ancient world of Egypt with all of its political intrigue provides a rich background for Eloise McGraw's *Mara, Daughter of the Nile*. Mara, the mistreated slave of a wealthy jewel trader, is bought by a mysterious man who offers her luxury in return for her services as a spy for the queen. On a Nile riverboat Mara meets Lord Sheftu, who employs her as a spy for the king. In this exciting and sinister story of espionage and counterespionage, the transformation of Mara from a selfish, deceitful slave into a loyal and courageous young woman is made slowly and believably. Eloise McGraw has written another exciting, complex story of this period of ancient history titled *The Golden Goblet*, which has recently been reissued in paperback.

In Elizabeth George Speare's *The Bronze Bow*, Daniel Bar Jamin has one all-consuming purpose in life, to avenge the cruel death of his father and mother by driving the Romans out of his land, Israel. First with an outlaw band, and then with a group of boy guerrillas, Daniel nurses his hatred and waits for the hour to strike. He takes comfort in the verse from 2 Samuel 22:35: "He trains my hands for war, so that my arms can bend a bow of bronze." A bronze bow is a symbol for what no one can do. *The Bronze Bow* is the story of Daniel's tormented journey from blind hatred to his acceptance and understanding of love. Only after he has nearly sacrificed his friends and driven his sister, Leah, deeper into mental darkness, does he seek the help of Simon's friend, Jesus. After he pours out his troubles and hatred, Jesus tells him:

> It is hate that is the enemy, not men. Hate does not die with killing. It only springs up a hundred-fold. The only thing stronger than hate is love. (p. 224)

The healing strength of Jesus cures Leah, and at that moment Daniel can forgive the Romans. He understands at last that only love can bend the bow of bronze. Each character stands out in this startling story of conflict between good and evil.

Tales of Early Britain

No one has surpassed Rosemary Sutcliff in her ability to recreate the life and times of early Britain. In books such as *Sun Horse, Moon Horse* and *Warrior Scarlet*, she vividly portrays the Iron and Bronze Age peoples of Britain, of which there is no written record. Equally remarkable, she writes of the native peoples of Britain and of the Roman occupation forces with equal skill and sympathy.

Sutcliff's *The Eagle of the Ninth*, *The Silver Branch*, and *The Lantern Bearers* form a trilogy that describes the period when Britain was ruled by Romans. In the third book, the last of the Roman auxiliaries set sail in their galleys and abandon Britain to internal strife and the menace of invasion by Saxons. At the final moment, one Roman officer decides that his loyalties lie with Britain rather than with the legions. Aquila returns to his family villa, only to see all that he loves destroyed by the Saxons. His father is killed, his sister is captured, and he is enslaved by a band of invaders. Three years later he escapes his thralldom, but it is many years before he can rid himself of the black bitterness of his sister's marriage to a Saxon.

In *The Shining Company*, Sutcliff tells of the king's betrayal of his war host of three hundred young men sent to fight the invading Saxons. Among them is his own son, Gorthyn, and his shieldbearer, Prosper. Set in A.D. 600, the story is based on *The Gododdin*, the earliest surviving North British poem. It is a story of adventure and heroism, loyalty and betrayal.

Medieval Times and Tales

In the Dark Ages, the chivalrous deeds of the knights were a window to the light. Young children of 7 and 8 are intrigued with stories of the days of knighthood. Some of them will be able to read Clyde Bulla's *The Sword in the Tree*, the story of a boy who saved his father and Weldon Castle by bravely going to King Arthur. Through treachery, Shan's uncle makes his own brother a captive and takes control of the castle. Remembering where he hid his father's sword in a tree, Shan establishes his identity as the rightful owner of Weldon Castle. This is an easy-reading book with excitement on every page. It has more than just a lively plot, however, for it presents an interesting picture of the justice of the time.

Medieval entertainers were minstrels, whose special way of life provides a natural frame for journey or chase stories. Thirteenth-century England is the setting for the Newbery Medal winner *Adam of the Road* by Elizabeth Janet Gray. It is the story of Adam, his minstrel father, Roger, and Adam's devoted dog, Nick. Nick is stolen on their way to the great Fair of St. Giles, and in the frantic chase that follows, Adam is separated from his father. It takes him a whole long winter to find both Nick and Roger again. Adam has many adventures and some disasters, but he learns that the road is home to the minstrel and that people generally are kind.

Marguerite de Angeli has written many books, but her finest is *The Door in the Wall*, a Newbery Medal winner. Setting the book in fourteenth-century England, de Angeli painted in words and pictures the dramatic story of Robin, son of Sir John de Bureford. Robin is to become a page to Sir Peter de Lindsay. He becomes ill with a strange malady, however, and is taken to the monastery by Brother Luke. There, Robin learns many things: to whittle, to swim, to read, to write, and above all to have patience—all "doors in the wall," according to Brother Luke:

> Whether thou'lt walk soon I know not. This I know. We must teach thy hands to be skilled in many ways, and we must teach thy mind to go about whether thy legs will carry thee or no. For reading is another door in the wall, dost understand, my son? (p. 28)

Eventually Robin is reunited with his father and mother. Robin's rebellion, final acceptance, and then challenge to live a rich life *with* his handicap should provide inspiration for children today.

Frances Temple's *The Ramsey Scallop* centers upon Eleanor and Thomas, two youngsters who have been betrothed by their families but have grown up with little knowledge of one another. Fourteen-year-old Eleanor is frightened of marriage and the burdens that will be placed upon her as an adult woman. Thomas, just returned from the Crusades, is sick at heart and in spirit, and he doesn't think much of marriage either. Father Gregory, their village priest, proposes a pilgrimage of penance to the shrine of Saint James in Spain. The journey of these two young people (who promise chastity as part of their penance) takes them from England to France and Spain, and gives Temple the opportunity for rich descriptions of life in the Middle Ages. At the same time, however, she never loses sight of Eleanor and Thomas, and she skillfully tells the story of their coming of age and their gaining of faith. Their pilgrimage successfully accomplished, they return home committed to each other and to the future of their community.

Author Karen Cushman has given us two memorable heroines whose experiences provide insights into women's roles in the Middle Ages. The title character of *Catherine Called Birdy* is the daughter of a minor baron whose schemes to marry her off to one appalling husband after another form the center of the plot. Catherine, called "Birdy" because of the birds she keeps as pets, wishes desperately for the freedom to move about the countryside and beyond the limitations placed upon her. The birds' cages represent her own constraints, and although she escapes from confinement long enough to have an adventure with a dancing bear, she must return to her cage like this performing animal and step into the role she has been given. The outcome is not tragic, however, for Catherine escapes marriage with the worst of her ancient suitors and ends up with a husband who can match her wit and independent spirit. Told in the form of Catherine's journal, the book is earthy and funny. The wonderfully descriptive and often obscure Saints Days that mark each diary entry, as well as her descriptions of the more vulgar aspects of medieval life, lend Catherine's voice an unusual ring of truth that will appeal especially to middle school readers.

Cushman's *The Midwife's Apprentice* strikingly contrasts the lot of a midwife's apprentice with Catherine's more privileged life. In fact, this young girl cannot get much farther from a castle keep than the midden heap into which she crawls for warmth at the book's beginning. She has little memory of her origins, and none of her name, and so she is called "Brat" by the urchins who tease and torment her, "Dung Beetle" by the sharp-tongued midwife who takes her in, and "Midwife's Apprentice" by the people in the community to which she has come. As she finds companionship with a stray cat and kindness from some of the people she meets, she also begins to discover her identity. At St. Swithin's Day Fair, she is given a comb, a wink, and a compliment and then is mistaken for a woman named Alyce who knows how to read, and her experiences lead her to stop and examine her reflection in a horse trough as she heads for home.

> "And this is me Beetle." She stopped. Beetle was no name for a person, no name for someone who looked like she could read.
>
> Frowning she thought a minute, and then her face shone as though a torch were fired inside her. "Alyce," she breathed. Alyce sounded clean and friendly and smart. You could love someone named Alyce. She looked back at the face in the water. "This then is me Alyce." It was right.
>
> So the newly called Alyce shifted the pack on her shoulders, and with her head back and bare feet solid on the ground, she headed back to the midwife's cottage and never noticed when it grew cold and dark, for the heat and light within her. (pp. 31–32)

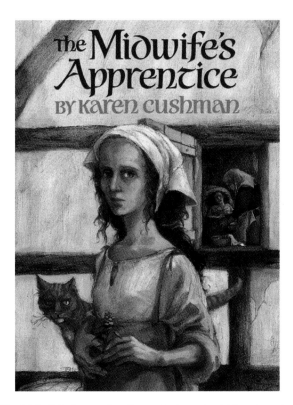

The Midwife's Apprentice, Karen Cushman's vivid portrayal of life in the Middle Ages, reflects the dreams and difficulties of modern-day adolescents.

Cover, from *The Midwife's Apprentice* by Karen Cushman. Jacket illustration copyright © 1995 by Trina Schart Hyman. Reprinted by permission of Clarion Books/Houghton Mifflin Company. All rights reserved.

This does not end Alyce's story but begins the real tempering-through-adversity that is at the heart of a good book. This Newbery Medal–winning story is almost heartbreakingly beautiful in its portrait of a child who comes to a full understanding of her true self. Cushman's writing captures the speech patterns of a medieval village and the rhythms of life in a different age, but her character and theme speak to all that is universal in human longing for identity.

In *The King's Shadow* by Elizabeth Alder, it is the year 1053 and Evyn, a young Welsh boy, loses rather than finds his name. He must also give up his dreams of being a "storiawr" (storyteller) when, in revenge for his uncle's misdeed, his tongue is cut out and he is sold into slavery to Lady Ealdgyth, the consort of the Saxon leader, Harold Godwinson. Evyn is called "Shadow" because of his black hair, and his bitterness at his fate is just as dark. Yet Lady Ealdgyth is kind to him, and when he breaks his arm she sends him to Lewys, a Welsh monk, who teaches him how to read and write. This ability opens up new doors for him. When he finally accepts the identity fate has handed him, he finds a greater destiny than he had ever imagined. Shadow eventually becomes the squire and then the foster son of

Harold Godwinson and witnesses events leading up to the Battle of Hastings. When Harold is defeated and killed by William the Conqueror, Shadow is rescued at the point of death. Nursed back to health by Lewys, he spends his remaining days writing his eyewitness account of these momentous events, an account that will become part of the Anglo-Saxon Chronicle.

The Emergence of the Modern World

Fifteenth-century Eastern Europe is vividly portrayed as the background of Eric Kelly's Newbery Medal winner *The Trumpeter of Krakow.* This is a complex tale of the quest for the shimmering Great Tarnov Crystal, coveted by a Tartar chieftain for its supposed magical powers and zealously guarded by the ancestral oath of a Ukrainian family.

In *Bartholomew Fair,* Mary Stolz weaves the story of six persons of varying stations of life, from the aging Queen Elizabeth down to Will Shaw, a starveling apprenticed to a stonemaker, who are attending the last day of Bartholomew Fair. As the day progresses, we see into the lives of these six fair-goers, all but one of whom return home that night. Mary Stolz has created a vivid tapestry of sixteenth-century life.

The Renaissance and the centuries that followed were particularly remarkable for the flowering of art and architecture that occurred in Europe. Several books have given us glimpses of what life might have been like for the young people who inhabited the world of the great masters. In *The Second Mrs. Giaconda,* E. L. Konigsburg hypothesizes the true identity of the Mona Lisa through the point of view of a young apprentice to Leonardo da Vinci. Set in a later time period, Elizabeth Borton de Trevino's *I, Juan de Pareja* is the fictionalized account of the real apprentice of Spanish master Diego Velázquez. Pilar Molina Llorente's *The Apprentice,* winner of the Batchelder Award, is the story of a Florentine boy whose greatest wish is to become a painter. His father, who is one of the finest tailors in the city, is against this, but he agrees to give Arduino one chance at success in the workshop of Cosimo di Forli. Arduino discovers that the life of an apprentice is tedious at best, and that his new master is mean-spirited and worse. Jealous of the talents of Donato, his head assistant, Cosimo has imprisoned him in an attic room. Arduino discovers this secret and befriends Donato, sneaking to his prison late at night, where Donato gives him drawing lessons and talks about painting. When de Forli falls ill and cannot complete a commission, Arduino convinces him to give Donato the chance. Although somewhat melodramatic, the story provides a vivid picture of a time in history that is not often addressed in children's books.

Flame-Colored Taffeta is Rosemary Sutcliff's exciting eighteenth-century story about smugglers on the Sussex Coast and an emissary of Bonnie Prince Charlie. Two young children find a wounded man; with the help of the Wise Woman, who is a healer, they hide and care for him. Students will love this adventure story in which the young girl, Damaris, and Peter play the major role in hiding Tom and arranging for his escape. In her quiet conversations with him, Damaris reveals her desire to someday have a flame-colored taffeta petticoat. Four years after his escape, Tom sends her one as a wedding present for her marriage to Peter.

Stories in English about life in China and Japan during this period are rare. Notable exceptions are Katherine Paterson's stories of feudal Japan, *The Sign of the Chrysanthemum, Of Nightingales That Weep,* and *The Master Puppeteer.* Lensey Namioka has set two stories, *The Coming of the Bear* and *Island of Ogres,* in the same time period with young samurai warriors as heroes. Malcolm Bosse's *The Examination* is a fascinating look at life in China during the late sixteenth century. The examination is one that Chen, a brilliant scholar, decides to undertake. If he passes, his future will be assured. But as the poor and unworldly son of a disgraced father, he faces many obstacles on the road to Beijing, where the exam will be given. His younger brother Hong, who makes up in quick wit for what he lacks in intellectual abilities, decides to travel with his brother to keep him safe. This long and complexly plotted novel is demanding yet has enough excitement to maintain interest. The picture Bosse presents of this period in Chinese history will have mature readers hungry for more details.

Stories of the New World

Although recorded history in the Americas is relatively brief in comparison to European and Asian chronicles, the years from the fifteenth century to the present have been of interest to many writers of historical fiction. Many of these books show how the past has shaped present events in the United States and in the world.

Colonial America

The varied settings and conflicts of colonial America have inspired an unusually large number of books about this period. *A Lion to Guard Us* by Clyde Bulla tells of three motherless London children who sail to Jamestown in hopes of finding their father, who has gone ahead to the new colony. When the ship is wrecked in a storm near Bermuda, the children manage to save their own treasure from home, a lion's head

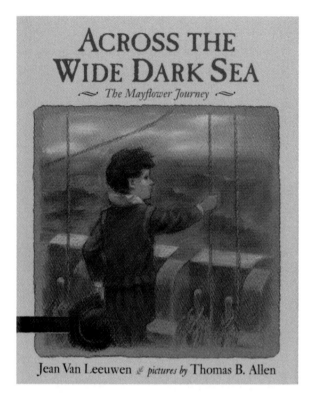

Thomas B. Allen's pastel drawings provide a lovely accompaniment to Jean Van Leeuwen's *Across the Wide Dark Sea,* a story based on William Bradford's diary.
From *Across The Wide Dark Sea* by Jean Van Leeuwen, pictures by Thomas B. Allen. Copyright © 1995 by Thomas B. Allen, pictures. Used by permission of Dial Books for Young Readers, a division of Penguin Book USA Inc.

doorknocker. They eventually make it to Virginia, where they find their father, weak and ill, one of the few who survived the Starving Time of 1609–1610. Young Jemmy hangs the lion's head on a peg above the door latch, a symbol of home. The carefully limited historical detail and simple writing style make this book accessible to readers as young as 8 or 9.

Many informational books tell us what the Pilgrims did, but there are few records that tell how they felt about what they did. Jean Van Leeuwen based *Across the Wide Dark Sea* on entries in William Bradford's diary and tells the story in the imagined voice of 9-year-old Love Brewster, who was aboard the ship. *The Thanksgiving Story* by Alice Dalgliesh details the life of one family on the *Mayflower,* including their hardships on the voyage and during their first winter. It tells, too, of joy in the arrival of their new baby, of spring in their new home, of planting, harvest, and giving thanks. *The Pilgrims of Plimoth,* written and illustrated with full-color illustrations by Marcia Sewall, provides a descriptive text that discusses the travels of the Pilgrims and their way of life at the settlement. Using George Ancona's black-and-white photographs of the reconstructed settlement at Plymouth Plantation, Joan Anderson presents her concept of the first Thanksgiving in *The First Thanksgiving Feast*. The text includes dialogue based on historical accounts from the era. All these picture books are appropriate for children in grades 2 and up. They can serve to celebrate Thanksgiving or as an introduction to a serious study of the Pilgrims.

One of the liveliest stories about the Pilgrims is *Constance: A Story of Early Plymouth* by Patricia Clapp. Written in the form of a diary, the story of Constance Hopkins, daughter of Stephen Hopkins, begins in November 1620 on the deck of the *Mayflower* and ends seven years later with her marriage in Plymouth to Nicholas Snow. Constance describes the grim first winter at Plymouth—the fear of Indians, the deaths of many of the colonists, and difficulties with the English backers of the settlement. The device of a diary allows the author to use first-person narrative, which promotes the reader's immediate identification with Constance. An excellent romance, it is all the more fascinating for being the story of real people.

The Puritans soon forgot their struggle for religious freedom as they persecuted others who did not follow their beliefs or ways. Older students will thoroughly enjoy the superb story *The Witch of Blackbird Pond* by Elizabeth Speare. Flamboyant, high-spirited Kit Tyler is a misfit in the Puritan household of her aunt and stern-faced uncle. Her colorless cousins are as different from Kit as the bleak barren shoreline of Wethersfield, Connecticut, is from the shimmering turquoise bay of Barbados that had been Kit's home for sixteen years. The only place Kit feels any peace or freedom is in the meadows near Blackbird Pond. Here she meets the lonely, bent figure of Quaker Hannah, regarded as a witch by the colonists. Here, too, Kit meets Nathaniel Eaton, the sea captain's son, with his mocking smile and clear blue eyes. Little Prudence, a village child, also comes to the sanctuary in the meadows. One by one, outraged townspeople draw the wrong conclusions, and the result is a terrifying witch hunt and trial. The story is fast-paced and the characters are drawn in sharp relief against a bleak New England background.

Although the subject is the same, the tone of *Tituba of Salem Village* by Ann Petry is as forbidding as the rotten eggs found on the parsonage steps the day Reverend Samuel Parris, his family, and slaves, John and Tituba, arrive in Salem Village in 1692. Tituba, too, is from sunny Barbados but has been sold as a slave to the self-seeking, pious minister. The fact that Tituba is both a slave and a black makes her particularly vulnerable to suspicion and attack from the obsessed witch hunters in Salem. A sense of foreboding, mounting terror, and hysteria fills the story of great evil done in the name of God.

A different look at the Salem witch trials is provided by Patricia Clapp in *Witches' Children*. The first-person narrator is Mary Warren, a bond servant and one of ten girls who are "possessed." Mary admits to herself that the ravings began as "sport," a way to vent boredom and high spirits, and grew into group hysteria. When she tries to explain, she is not believed and is herself accused. In spite of the grim subject, the story moves at a fast and readable pace. A comparison of *Tituba of Salem Village* with *Witches' Children* would provoke much critical thinking by mature readers, especially in considering the two characterizations of Tituba.

During the eighteenth century, colonists pushed farther and farther into the wilderness. Many favorite stories have been set against this background. Jean Fritz has written the poignant story of lonely 10-year-old Ann Hamilton, who was the only girl in the wilderness of early eastern Pennsylvania. The title of this book, *The Cabin Faced West*, expresses Ann's father's attitude toward the family's new adventure. They were not to look back to the past, but forward; and so he built the cabin facing west. Someday Ann will have books to read; someday they will have windows in the cabin; and someday there will be a special occasion to use the linen tablecloth and the lavender flowered plates. All the "somedays" seem so very far away to Ann. At last, however, a special occasion does arise: George Washington stops at the Hamilton cabin for dinner. Ann wears ribbons in her hair and sets the table in the way she has longed to do. This final episode is based on fact and really happened to Ann Hamilton, who was the author's great-great-grandmother.

Another lonely girl has been immortalized for children of 7 and 8 by Alice Dalgliesh in her popular book *The Courage of Sarah Noble*. This is the true and inspiring story of 8-year-old Sarah, who accompanies her father into the wilderness to cook for him while he builds a cabin for their family. Many times Sarah has to remind herself of her mother's final words to her when she left home: "Keep up your courage, Sarah Noble!" Sarah has reason to remember when she hears the wolves howl, but she faces the real test of her courage when her father tells her that he must leave her with Tall John, a friendly Indian, while he returns to Massachusetts for the rest of the family. Symbolic of Sarah's courage is the cloak that Sarah's mother had fastened around her just before she left home. When her family are finally reunited in their new home in the wilderness, Sarah is secure in the knowledge that she has "kept up her courage."

The situation in *The Sign of the Beaver* by Elizabeth George Speare is much like that in Sarah Noble's story, as young Matt is left to tend the new cabin in Maine territory while his father goes back to Massachusetts for

The Sign of the Beaver
by Elizabeth George Speare
A World of Possibilities

Book Connections

Clash of White and Native American Cultures in Colonial Times

The Double Life of Pocahontas (Fritz)
The Light in the Forest (Richter)
Saturnalia (P. Fleischman)
King Philip, the Indian Chief (Averill)
Thunder from the Clear Sky (Sewall)
Guests (Dorris)

Other Books by Speare
Calico Captive
Compare portrayal of Native American characters with Attean and family.
The Witch of Blackbird Pond
The Bronze Bow
How are Speare's other books alike and different? Compare characters, themes.

Setting

Map the trip that Matt's father made from Maine to Massachusetts and back.
Make a time line showing events during Matt's long wait. How many ways could you represent time passing?
Make an illustrated catalog of items that would have been familiar to Matt but are not common today. Consider tools, household items, clothing; see *Colonial Living* (Tunis). Arrange a display of artifacts (or make your own reproductions) of colonial life or the northeast Native Americans.
Build a model of Matt's cabin, or Attean's village. Compare and discuss—what differences in lifestyles are dictated by shelter and its surroundings?

Style and Technique

Use of Language

Notice descriptions that are comparisons (simile and metaphor). Compile a list, and suggest others of your own.
Why would the author say that the gun was smooth as a silk dress rather than shiny as a no-wax floor?
How does the author make Attean's speech different from Matt's? What problems do you think an author has in deciding how people might have talked more than 200 years ago?
Write a story about Matt's family. How might they have felt about being separated from Matt?

Foreshadowing

What bits of warning does the author give that there might be trouble from a bear? That something might happen to Matt's father's gun?
Can you find early clues for other events?

Predictions

What does the cover make you think the book will be about?
Read and predict from chapter endings what might happen in the following chapter.
Make up your own chapter titles.

Pace of Plot

How long are the chapters?
What kinds of things happen as the chapters end?
How do "cliff-hangers" help to keep the reader interested?

Motifs

Gifts and Exchanges

What gifts are given in this story by Matt? By the Abenaki Indians? Think of some that are not material things.
What gifts would you have to share with a friend like Matt or Attean?
What gifts did Matt make for his family? What does that show you about how he felt?

Animals

How are animals important to this story?
Make a chart picturing the animals. Describe their role in the story's events; explain what that shows about setting, character, or theme.

Signs and Symbols

What makes *The Sign of the Beaver* a good title?
How many examples of signs and symbols can you find in the book? Which are Abenaki signs? signs of the white man? animal signs?

Freedom

Who is more free, Matt or Attean?
As winter sets in, Matt's snowshoes "set him free." What other things gave him more freedom?

Changing Relationships

Trace the development of friendship between Matt and Attean. What events or passages from the story show a change in ideas about each other's culture?
Think about Matt and Attean as teacher and student. How did Matt become a better teacher? How would you teach someone to read? What did Attean teach Matt? How did he conduct the lessons?
Discuss the changes in the balance between the Beaver clan's existence and the coming of white settlers.
What other changes do you see in characters' attitudes toward one another?

Themes

The Value of Stories

What does this book have to say about the importance of stories and storytelling?
How might Matt tell his story when he is a grandfather?
What books does Matt's family own? Can you find any parallels between *The Sign of the Beaver* and *Robinson Crusoe* (Defoe)?
What stories did Attean's family tell?
What traditional tales might they have known? Read folktales of the Northeastern Indians: *The Talking Stone* (deWit); *North American Legends* (Haviland); *The Winter Wife* (Crompton); *Gluskabe and the Four Wishes* (Bruchac).

Survival

What survival skills did Matt develop? Which did he learn by observation?
Without the Indians, what might have happened to Matt?
Read other stories of survival: *My Side of the Mountain* (George); *The Talking Earth* (George); *Toughboy and Sister* (Hill); *Hatchet* (Paulson).
How does the predicament of the main character in any of these books compare to Matt's?
Try out some of Matt's survival skills. What did he cook? What were common foods in colonial times? Make johnnycake.

Growing Up

How does Attean mark his preparation for manhood? What tests must he pass?
What does Matt do that shows he is a man? Which of his actions earn the respect of Attean's people?
Keep a journal for Matt that shows his feelings about passing events.

The Heritage Sampler (Hopple)
Slumps, Grunts and Snickerdoodles (Perl)

Based on *The WEB: Wonderfully Exciting Books*, Charlotte Huck and Janet Hickman, eds. Columbus: The Ohio State University, vol. 8, no. 2 (winter 1984).

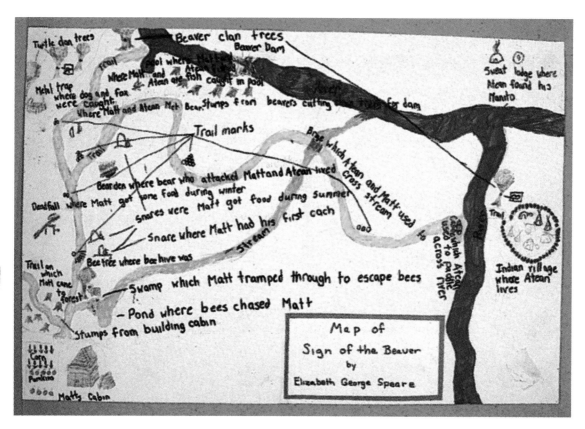

One of the projects that grew out of an in-depth study of Elizabeth George Speare's *The Sign of the Beaver* was this imaginary map of the places in the story.
Barrington Road School, Upper Arlington, Ohio. Marlene Harbert, teacher.

the rest of the family. Matt eventually learns essential survival skills from Attean, grandson of the chief of the Beaver clan. The story explores their growing friendship, their changing attitudes, and the shifting balance between their two cultures. In this fine book Speare has included carefully researched details of colonial life, and she has also considered some of the ethical questions that may have faced the early settlers. The web "*The Sign of the Beaver*—A World of Possibilities" shows the many possibilities for study and extensions inherent in this book and the connections teachers might make to other books and other events in colonial history.

Other books, like *The Matchlock Gun* by Walter D. Edmonds, show that the differences between white and Native American people could not always be bridged. This book, based on the experiences of a Dutch family living in the Hudson Valley in 1756, focuses on the terror as well as the courage of settlers who were victims of fierce Indian raids. This is much more than an exciting adventure story in which a child kills three marauders to protect his baby sister and wounded mother. The characters are very real and true to life. Readers sense the parents' anxiety when they hear of the Indian raid and can share the fear that seems to fill the silence in the

tiny cabin. This story, which won the Newbery Medal in 1942, has since been criticized for presenting Native Americans as bloodthirsty savages and for having a child shoot them. Obviously, this account of events is told from the colonists' point of view.

An Indian point of view is given in *Saturnalia*, Paul Fleischman's complex story of life in colonial Boston in 1681. Six years earlier the militia had attacked and nearly wiped out a Narragansett village, bringing back a few of the survivors as servants. Fourteen-year-old William is apprenticed to kindly Mr. Currie, a printer who has the boy taught Greek and Latin and the Bible and treats him as a member of his family. Each night William roams the streets after curfew, searching for his brother by playing an Indian melody on his bone flute. He never finds him, but one night he does find a cousin and uncle, now servants of a cruel eyeglass maker. William goes to see them regularly in order to give them food and to learn of his own Narragansett past. Meanwhile, William's nighttime activities are observed by Mr. Baggot, the tithing-man whose grandsons were killed by Indians and who yearns to entrap William as his revenge. When the eyeglass maker is killed, his Indian servants are accused, but William saves them.

Then Baggot focuses his accusations on William. The dark side of this novel is lightened by the story of a wig maker's romantic and humorous pursuit of a wealthy widow. Paul Fleischman weaves these many stories of good and evil persons in colonial Boston back and forth like a musical fugue. Only William is a part of all worlds: night and day, servant and family, Indian and Colonial, educated and nonliterate. His is the melody that holds this many-layered novel together.

The Revolutionary Era

One of the best-known stories of the American Revolution for children is *Johnny Tremain* by Esther Forbes. Johnny Tremain is a silversmith's apprentice, a conceited, cocky young lad who is good at his trade and knows it. The other apprentices are resentful of his overbearing manner and are determined to get even with him. Their practical joke has disastrous results, and Johnny's hand is maimed for life. Out of a job and embittered, Johnny joins his new friend Rab and becomes involved in pre-Revolutionary activities. As a dispatch rider for the Committee of Public Safety he meets such men as Paul Revere, John Hancock, and Samuel Adams. Slowly, Johnny regains his self-confidence and overcomes his bitterness. Rab is killed in the first skirmish of the Revolution, and Johnny is crushed but not defeated. Somehow, this greatest of blows makes him a man of fortitude and courage, a new man of a new nation.

For Johnny Tremain, the decision to join the Patriot cause was clear. In many other books, because the Loyalist tradition and point of view are presented in a more compelling way, the characters are perceived to have a more difficult choice. In *John Treegate's Musket* by Leonard Wibberly, the title character is a solid citizen of Boston who has fought for his king at the Battle of Quebec. Not until he sees hundreds of troops marching through a peaceful countryside to seize two men does he arm himself and join his son Peter to fight the British at the Battle of Bunker Hill. In *Early Thunder* by Jean Fritz, 14-year-old Daniel adopts his father's loyalty to the king. Daniel hates the rowdy Liberty Boys who creep up on Tory porches and distribute their "Liberty Gifts" of manure, but he becomes equally disillusioned by the British attitudes. Daniel's struggle to sort out his loyalties will help children see that issues in war are seldom clear-cut.

My Brother Sam Is Dead by the Colliers tells of conflicting loyalties within a family and the injustices that are always inflicted on the innocent in time of war. Sam is the only member of his Connecticut family who is fighting for the rebel cause. Ironically, it is Sam who is falsely accused of stealing his own cattle and is executed as an example of General Putnam's discipline. No one will believe the real facts of the case, for despite Sam's excellent war record, his family are Tories. This story takes on special poignancy because it is told by the younger brother, Tim, who loves and admires Sam.

Some of the same dreams of glory that drew Sam into the Patriot army plague 13-year-old Jonathan in *The Fighting Ground* by Avi. In 1778, near Trenton, Jonathan desperately wants to be in on the "cannons and flags and drums and dress parades. . . . O Lord, he said to himself, make it something *grand!*" (p. 9). Sent to find if the tolling bell at the tavern means bad news, Jonathan agrees to go with a few volunteers to head off a small band of approaching enemy soldiers. Caught up in a real battle and captured by Hessians who seem no worse than the Patriot corporal who enlisted his aid, Jonathan does not know which way to turn. The action takes place in little more than one day, with the text divided into many short segments labeled by the hour and minute. This makes the book look simpler than it is, for although the print is not dense on the page, the story makes strong emotional demands on the reader.

The title character in Scott O'Dell's *Sarah Bishop* hates war, and with good reason. Her father, a British Loyalist, dies after being tarred and feathered by Patriot sympathizers. Her brother dies on a British prison ship, and Sarah herself is arrested on a false pretense. She escapes and flees to the Connecticut wilderness, where she struggles against the elements instead of soldiers. Her biggest battle is with herself, however, as she brings herself to face the world of towns and people once again. This story is based on the experiences of a real Sarah Bishop during the Revolutionary period.

Another little-known story of the American Revolution is that of a spunky young girl named Tempe Wick, who hid her horse in her bedroom for three days to save it from Revolutionary soldiers looting the countryside around their New Jersey camp. Finally, when a soldier demanded to search the house, the feisty Tempe threw him out in the snow. This humorous legend of the Revolutionary War is told by Patricia Lee Gauch in a brief book, *This Time, Tempe Wick?* A fuller characterization of this heroine is given in Ann Rinaldi's novel for older readers, *A Ride into Morning.*

Few stories are available about the role of African Americans during the Revolutionary era. The Collier brothers have featured black characters in several books, however, including a trilogy that deals with the wartime problems of blacks in the northern colonies and their futile hope for a guarantee of liberty under the new government. In *Jump Ship to Freedom*, the memory of the late Jack Arabus, who had won his freedom in the courts as a result of his service in the Continental army, serves as inspiration for his son Dan. The boy's first problem is keeping the soldiers' notes earned by Jack to buy his family's freedom. Even if the notes can be saved, they might be worth nothing under the terms of the new Constitution just being written. Exciting action brings Dan as a messenger to the site of the Constitutional Convention. Because he is bringing important word about the slavery compromise (which will, ironically, set up a fugitive slave law), he gets to meet George Washington, Alexander Hamilton, and other statesmen. A strong theme of this book is Dan's growing belief in himself and his abilities. The other titles in this trilogy are *War Comes to Willy Freeman* and *Who Is Carrie?* Each features a young African American woman as the central character. In all their books, the Colliers provide detailed authors' notes to explain their background sources. For this series the notes also explain their choice of language, including the liberal use of the term "nigger" in dialogue.

Novels about Revolutionary America offer an intriguing variety of viewpoints. Individual books will help children feel the intense emotions of the time, but the impact of several read for comparison and contrast will be much greater. Children can also increase their knowledge of details about a time period in this way. Knowing more background each time, they will read each succeeding book with greater ease.

Native Americans

Too often in historical fiction, Native Americans have been portrayed as cruel, bloodthirsty savages attacking small groups of helpless settlers. The provocations for the attacks are seldom explained. Thus, in Walter Edmonds's story *The Matchlock Gun*, the reader can only guess the Indians' reasons for wounding Edward's mother and burning their cabin. In Rachel Field's *Calico Bush*, the Indians seem equally cruel as they burn the settler's house.

More recently, Native American author Michael Dorris has written two beautiful works of historical fiction that begin to balance the picture of Native American cultures that children have seen in books. In *Morning Girl* Dorris gives us an almost ethereal portrait of an island culture and two children who are the central members of a loving family unit. Morning Girl and Star Boy tell their stories in alternate chapters, providing insights into their own personalities as well as details of their day-to-day life on the island. A terrible storm, their mother's miscarriage, and Star Boy's running away are events that emerge in a circular pattern characteristic of Native American storytelling. One day, curious to know what people see when they look at her, Morning Girl asks her mother and her brother, but their answers

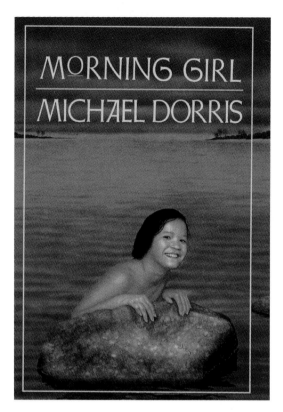

Michael Dorris provides a different perspective on European settlement in the Americas in *Morning Girl*.
From *Morning Girl* by Michael Dorris. Text copyright © 1992 Michael Dorris. Jacket illustration copyright © 1992 Kam Mak. Reprinted by permission of Hyperion Books for Children.

do not satisfy her. Finally her father motions her to stand beside him. He kneels down beside Morning Girl and tells her to look into his eyes. She explains,

I leaned forward, stared into the dark brown circles, and it was like diving into the deepest pools. Suddenly I saw two tiny girls looking back. Their faces were clear, their brows straight as canoes, and their chins as narrow and clean as lemons. As I watched their mouths grew wide. They were pretty.

"Who are they?" I couldn't take my eyes off those strange new faces. "Who are these pretty girls who live inside your head?"

"They are the answer to your question," Father said. "And they are always here when you need to find them." (p. 36)

It is through such evocative reflecting, rather than through the relating of particular facts, that we learn most about these people. The ending, an excerpt from Christopher Columbus's journal describing Morning Girl's people, is all the more powerful because we have come to know them with such intimacy.

Dorris's *Guests* visits another unnamed people who are preparing to share their yearly harvest meal with some strange outsiders. Young Moss is angered that this special time will be ruined by ignorant people who don't know how to behave properly. He runs off into the forest, hoping to learn his true identity during a special coming-of-age event, but he really discovers that the world is much more complicated than he had first considered. In *Guests* Dorris helps the reader with a similar lesson and enlarges understandings of an event that has long been portrayed from a European point of view.

Other fine books that relate historical events from a Native American perspective include Scott O'Dell's *Sing Down the Moon* and Jamake Highwater's *Legend Days,* two stories that provide the shocking details of whites' destruction of the Indians' way of life. O'Dell's title *Sing Down the Moon* takes on tragic significance when compared to the southwestern Indians' creation myths that tell of "singing up the mountains." O'Dell's book describes the "Long Walk," the disastrous three-hundred-mile march the Navajo were forced to make from their canyon homes to Fort Sumner. The Navajo were held as virtual prisoners from 1863 to 1865, and more than fifteen hundred of them died—and many others lost the will to live. This moving story is told from the point of view of Bright Morning, who somehow maintains her hope for a better future. Tall Boy, the proud and handsome youth who is to become her husband, was once wounded by a Spaniard's bullet, but being held in the American fort causes an even greater injury to his spirit. Only through Bright Morning's urging does he make the effort to escape. The young couple return to a cave in their familiar canyon to begin a new life with their new son. This is a haunting story for older readers, told in spare prose that reflects the dignity of the Navajo people.

Jamake Highwater brings a strong cultural perspective and gift for vivid language to a powerful novel of the Northern Plains Indians, *Legend Days,* the first book of the Ghost Horse Cycle. The central character, Amana, is a girl who attains adolescence and young adulthood while the buffalo herds dwindle and her people are no longer able to withstand white traders, settlers, soldiers, government, or the hideous smallpox that kills almost everyone in the winter camp. This grim story is infused with the spiritual strength of Amana and her people. The characters' visionary experiences are not set apart from the other events of their lives. This lack of separation between the spiritual and the material embodies a Native American point of view.

Several books are based on accounts of Indians' capture of white settlers. *Calico Captive* by Elizabeth Speare is for more mature readers. Based on real people and events, this is a fictionalized account of the experiences of young Miriam Willard, who had just been to her first dance when she was captured by Indians. Her sister, brother-in-law, three children, and a neighbor are captured with her, taken to Montreal, and sold as slaves. Their hardships and ordeals are taken from a diary kept by a real captive in 1754. Speare tells this story with her usual fine characterizations and attention to authentic detail.

In *Moccasin Trail* by Eloise McGraw, Jim Heath is rescued from a grizzly bear by Crow Indians and brought up to think and feel like an Indian. Eventually reunited with his younger sister and brothers, Jim begins to long for the sensible Indian ways. Everything he does seems to be wrong. He steals a horse as a gift for Jonnie—the grandest present a Crow Indian can give—and is rebuffed in front of the other settlers and made to return the horse. A loner, Jim decides to leave. Little Daniel is heartbroken and runs away, only to be captured by the Umpqua Indians, who keep slaves. Jim rescues him but knows that for his sake and his brother's he must forsake the moccasin trail forever. He symbolically cuts his braids and is at peace with himself and his family at last.

Jenny of the Tetons by Kristiana Gregory is the fictionalized account of an Englishman called "Beaver Dick" and his Shoshone wife, Jenny. When an Indian attack leaves Carrie Hill wounded and alone, she decides to join Beaver Dick and help care for his family. She is horrified when she finds that he is married to a Native American. But gradually she learns to respect this gentle person who carefully tends her wound. Later it is Carrie's responsibility to care for Jenny and her family when they get smallpox. She rides to a neighbor's house through a blizzard to obtain medicine, but it's too late. Jenny and all her children die, leaving only Beaver Dick alive. This is a moving story of changing relationships.

One of the most popular stories about Indians is Scott O'Dell's Newbery Medal book *Island of the Blue Dolphins.* Based on fact, the story concerns Karana, an Indian girl who lived alone on an island off the coast of California for some eighteen years. Following an attack by Aleuts who had come to kill otters, all of Karana's people leave their island home by boat. When Karana realizes that her younger brother has been left on the island, she jumps overboard and returns to him. Within a few hours the boy is killed by wild dogs, and memories of the tribe are all Karana has left. Despite her despair when she realizes the boat will not return, Karana creates a life for herself. She makes a house and utensils, and fashions weapons, although in so doing she violates a tribal taboo against women making weapons. Eventually she makes friends with the leader of the dog pack, and thereafter enjoys his protection and companionship. When Spanish priests "rescue" Karana, she leaves in sadness. The reader may question whether she will find as much happiness at the mission with human companionship as she had known alone on the island. The question is answered in a sequel, *Zia*, in which Karana's last days are witnessed through the eyes of her niece.

Mature readers will also enjoy the highly fictionalized biography *Ishi, Last of His Tribe* by Theodora Kroeber. Most of the Yahi Indians of California had been killed or driven from their homes by the invading gold seekers and settlers during the early 1900s. A small band resisted their fate by living in concealment; but everywhere it seemed that Saldu (white people) had come. One by one, Ishi's family dies, and at last he is the lone survivor of his tribe. Hungry and ill, he allows himself to be found. Haltingly, he tells his story to an anthropologist who takes him to live at the University of California's museum. Here he dwells happily for five years, helping to record the language and ways of the Yahi world.

The American Frontier

No other period in U.S. history has been more dramatized in films and television than that of the westward movement of the American pioneers. Because civilization grows with a ragged edge, nineteenth-century frontier stories are set in widely scattered locations. Some settlers moved with the wilderness, like Pa Ingalls in what might be the best loved of all American historical fiction, the nine Little House books by Laura Ingalls Wilder. These stories describe the growing up of the Ingalls girls and the Wilder boys. In the first book of the series, *Little House in the Big Woods*, Laura is only 6 years old; the last three books—*Little Town on the Prairie*, *These Happy Golden Years*, and *The First Four Years*—tell of Laura's teaching career and her marriage. Based on the author's own life, these books portray the hardships and difficulties of pioneer life in the 1870s and 1880s and describe the fun and excitement that was also a part of daily living in those days. Throughout the stories the warmth and security of family love run like a golden thread that binds the books to the hearts of their readers. There are floods, blizzards, grasshopper plagues, bears, Indians, droughts, and the fear of starvation, but also the wonderful Christmas when Laura receives her rag doll, a new house with real windows, trips to town, and dances. Best of all, there are the long winter evenings of firelight and the clear singing of Pa's fiddle. These mean love and security, whether the home is in Wisconsin, in the wild Kansas country as described in *Little House on the Prairie*, in the Minnesota of *On the Banks of Plum Creek*, or in Dakota Territory as in *By the Shores of Silver Lake*. The last book of the series, *The First Four Years*, describes the years immediately following Laura and Manley's marriage in 1885. The manuscript for this story was found among Laura's papers after her death in 1957. Garth Williams illustrated a uniform edition of all the books in the series. His black-and-white pictures capture the excitement and terror of many of the episodes in the books, but they also convey the tenderness, love, amusement, and courage that were necessary in the life of the early settlers.[5]

Another favorite book of pioneer days is *Caddie Woodlawn* by Carol Ryrie Brink. This story takes place in the Wisconsin wilderness of the 1860s, but it is primarily the story of the growing up of tomboy Caddie. Caddie had been a frail baby, and so her father persuaded her mother to allow her to be reared more freely than her older sister, Clara, who was restricted by the rules of decorum for young ladies. Caddie was free to run about the half-wild Wisconsin frontier with her two brothers. Their escapades and adventures read like a feminine *Tom Sawyer*. Caddie is a self-willed, independent spirit who is assured a memorable place in children's literature.

The Texas frontier has provided a distinctive setting for many exciting stories. One of the best known is Fred Gipson's *Old Yeller*, the story of a boy's integrity and love for his dog on an early Texas homestead. Patricia Beatty's *Wait for Me, Watch for Me, Eula Bee* takes place at the time of the Civil War, when the absence of men who had joined the Confederate army made West Texas homesteads especially vulnerable to Indian attack. Lewallen's mother, brother, and uncle are killed by Comanches, but he and his 3-year-old sister, Eula Bee, with her bouncy red curls that fascinate the warriors, are taken captive. When Lewallen manages at last to escape, he vows to return for his sister. Many months later he makes good his promise, but Eula Bee has forgotten him and has to be carried away, kicking and struggling. Long after they have reached safety, she is won to remembrance by the chance hearing of a song, the popular tune "Lorena," which Lewallen had whistled over and over during their captivity to assure her he was near.

Following the Civil War, Sam White and his family leave the safety and security of their grandparents' white house in Kentucky and head for Dakota Territory. In *The Grasshopper Summer*, Ann Turner details the hardships faced by this determined southern family. After staking their claim, they built a sod house facing south and planted their first crops; then the grasshoppers came, eating everything green in sight. Sam's younger brother, Bill, said, "They ate up all the pretty things and left all the ugly things" (p. 134). Their neighbors, the Grants, give up and go back home, but the Whites meet the challenge of the harsh land and decide to stay on in their sod house. *Dakota Dugout*, also by Ann Turner, is the perfect picture storybook to read either before or after *Grasshopper Summer*. The black-and-white illustrations

[5]See Michael Dorris, "Trusting the Words," *Booklist* 89 (1 & 15 June 1993): pp. 1820–1822, for the perspective of a Native American parent.

by Ronald Himler show both the beauty and the ruggedness of living in a sod house sandwiched between the wide prairie and the endless sky.

By the mid-nineteenth century, the far western frontier was in California and Oregon. *On to Oregon!* by Honoré Morrow and Jean Van Leeuwen's *Bound for Oregon* are based on the accounts of real people who braved the Oregon Trail and make fascinating reading for middle graders. *Trouble for Lucy* by Carla Stevens uses information from first-person accounts of a journey in 1843 to set the scene for each of its brief chapters. Appropriate for 8- and 9-year-old readers, the story focuses on Lucy's efforts to keep her fox terrier puppy from being a nuisance to the oxen and drivers. When he gets lost in a storm and Lucy follows, she and the pup are rescued by friendly Pawnees. Lucy's mother is too busy to scold her, however; she is having a baby in the family's covered wagon, which has been drawn out of the line of march and sits alone on the prairie. There is no pretending here that the pioneers' way was easy, yet the story is more concerned with the universal feelings of childhood than it is with hardship.

Kathryn Lasky's *Beyond the Divide* is a dramatic story for mature readers about an Amish father and daughter bound for the California gold rush. The plain ways of Meribah Simon, 14, are thought peculiar by some of her fellow travelers, but she makes many friends among them. The author creates a community of characters who bring very different pasts and problems to the challenging journey they share. Because they do seem like a community, it is all the more shocking that they should decide to abandon Will Simon along the trail when his wagon is disabled and he seems too weak to continue. Angry and disillusioned, Meribah elects to stay with her father. From that point the story hinges on her efforts to save him and then herself. She is forced to shoot a mountain man who is about to attack her and fights off vultures to get food from the carcass of a deer. With help from a mapmaker who had traveled with the wagon train and from the gentle Indians of Mill Creek who feed her and take her in, Meribah does survive to choose for herself what sort of life she wants.

Another vivid story for older readers is *Prairie Songs* by Pam Conrad. It contrasts two points of view of homesteading in the new lands, that of the Downing family, who had settled in a "soddy," and that of the beautiful, cultured wife of the new doctor in Howard County, Nebraska, who has come to live in the next soddy. The story is told by young Louisa Downing and reflects her wonder at the back-East world of wealth and learning that Mrs. Emmeline Berryman represents. But when the doctor's wife loses her premature baby after a long and difficult labor, Louisa is shocked by the gradual changes in her behavior. Always distraught, Mrs. Berryman is

terrified out of all reason one winter day by the visit of two Indians. It is shy little Lester who later finds her where she has fled, sitting in the snow, frozen to death. Louisa's narration is vivid, and her casual acceptance of life in a soddy points up the irony of Mrs. Berryman's inability to cope. The woman Louisa had admired could not match her own mother in strength of spirit or the special kind of beauty that made Louisa feel good inside.

Moving westward and settling the frontier was a major force in the life of many Americans throughout the nineteenth century. Farming the vast mid-American prairies put special demands on families. In *Sarah, Plain and Tall*, a beautifully written short novel by Patricia MacLachlan, motherless Anna and Caleb are delighted when Papa's advertisement for a mail-order bride brings Sarah to their prairie home. Sarah comes from the coast of Maine, with mementos of the sea she loves, her gray cat Seal, a moon shell for Caleb, and a round sea stone for Anna. She has agreed only to a month's visit, and the children, who quickly learn to love her lively, independent ways, are afraid that they will lose her. On the day Sarah goes to town for colored pencils to add the blue, gray, and green of the ocean to the picture she has drawn of the prairie, they realize that she will stay. She misses the sea, she tells them, but she would miss them more. The rhythm and lyrical simplicity of the writing are especially effective when read aloud. MacLachlan continues the story in *Skylark*, an equally well written sequel. In *Three Names*, a slice-of-life picture book that would make a good companion piece for the two books, MacLachlan tells of her great-grandfather when he went to a one-room schoolhouse on the prairie with his dog, Three Names. Alexander Pertzoff's lovely watercolors show the beauty and spaciousness of the wide-open prairie.

Not all stories of this period take place in the West, however. Although set in the early 1900s, Mary Riskind's *Apple Is My Sign* is less an historical novel than a story of a 10-year-old deaf child learning to live among the hearing with his disability. Harry Berger, called "Apple" because of his family's orchards, is sent to a school for the deaf in Philadelphia. His whole family is deaf, but Harry is the first one to go away, and his early days at the school are difficult and lonely. During the fall, however, Harry discovers many doors opening for him, learns a new game called football, and makes new friends. He tells his family that he thinks he'd like to be a teacher, but a family friend signs "Hearing best teacher." His mother, however, reassures Harry: "I-f you want teach deaf, must try. That's-all. Never know, i-f never try. In head must think can. Brave" (p. 119). Riskind conveys the rapidity of signed talk by approximating its actual meanings, eliminating the little words or word endings, as signers do, and spelling out meanings for which there are no signs. Through Harry's story, readers may come to realize that opportunities for people with disabilities have changed over the years.

The Civil War Era

Attention to American history in the nineteenth century often seems to be centered on the Civil War. The events leading up to the war and those that followed also need to be considered if children are to have an accurate picture of this volatile period.

Slavery

The country was involved and concerned with the issue of slavery long before the Civil War. *Nettie's Trip South* by Ann Turner is a picture book based on the real diary of the author's great-grandmother. When Nettie is 10 years old, she goes with her older brother, a reporter, and her 14-year-old sister on a trip from Albany, New York, to Richmond, Virginia. As Nettie writes to her friend Addie, she remembers all of the things she saw in that prewar city, including Tabitha, a black slave, in the hotel, who had no last name, and the slave auction where two children clasping hands were bought by different masters. Ronald Himler illustrated this moving account of a young girl's horror at her first exposure to slavery.

That cruelty is viewed from a variety of perspectives in several fine books for older children. In smoky tones of gray and black Tom Feelings's powerful *The Middle Passage* presents vivid images of the slaves' journey across the Atlantic. The pictures are preceded by a lengthy introduction that provides background about Feelings's work and provides details about the slave trade. The artwork is presented without words, however, because no written text could express the horror that these pictures convey.

Two fine novels, Joyce Hansen's *The Captive* and James Berry's *Ajeemah and His Son,* give readers an understanding of the lives their characters lived in Africa prior to their enslavement. At the beginning of Hansen's *The Captive,* Kofi, the 12-year-old son of an Ashanti chief, is attending a ceremony honoring Ashanti kings. When Kofi's father is murdered in a plot to weaken the Ashanti tribes, Kofi is captured and eventually placed aboard a "water house" bound for Boston. Kofi is sold to a white merchant and must adjust to his master's cruelties and the terrible bleakness of New England winters, but he never gives up his dreams of returning home. When he runs away, he is helped by Paul Cuffe, a free black merchant sea captain. Because the importing of slaves is illegal in Massachusetts, a judge declares that Kofi cannot be held as a slave and he

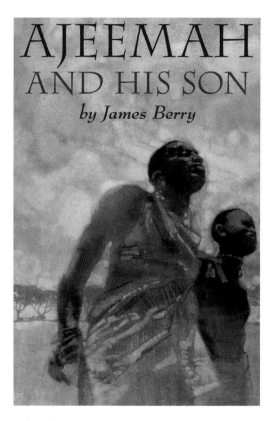

Ajeemah and His Son, by James Berry, shows how one family was affected by the brutality of the slave trade.
Jacket copyright © 1991 by Bernie Fuchs. Jacket copyright © 1991 by HarperCollins Publisher. Used by permission of HarperCollins Publishers, New York, NY.

is given into Paul Cuffe's custody. In Cuffe's caring home Kofi comes of age and eventually joins Cuffe in fighting slavery. In Berry's *Ajeemah and His Son,* Ajeemah and his son, Atu, are on their way to present the dowry for Atu's bride when they are captured and sent aboard a slaver to Jamaica. There the two are separated, and parallel chapters portray their experiences of slavery in moving detail. Atu is killed in an escape attempt, but Ajeemah is freed in 1838 when the British outlawed slavery. Although he creates a new family for himself, Ajeemah forever misses Atu and the loved ones he left behind in Africa.

Gary Paulsen's *Nightjohn* is a graphic and emotionally wrenching account of the terrible cruelties of slavery. Sarny, a young slave on the Waller plantation, narrates the story of Nightjohn, who is brought to the plantation in a most inhumane way by owner Clel Waller. Although he has been brutally used, that night in the slave quarters Nightjohn offers Sarny a wonderful gift in exchange for a bit of tobacco. He gives her the first three letters of the alphabet and begins to teach her to read and write. When Waller discovers Sarny writing a letter in the dirt, Nightjohn pays a terrible price. Waller informs Nightjohn that it is against the law for slaves to learn to read and that punishment "according to the law, is removal of an extremity." Even the loss of two toes does not defeat this heroic figure, however, and Nightjohn runs away only to return later to teach Sarny and other slaves to read and write.

Mary Lyons's *Letters from a Slave Girl* is a fictionalized account of Harriet Jacob's early life as a slave in North Carolina. The letters, addressed to her dead or absent relatives, provide a moving account of her growing-up years, her longing for freedom, and her love for her family. Although not as horrifying as in those in Paulsen's book, Harriet's experiences still portray the dehumanizing effects of slavery, particularly on women. After hiding for seven years in an attic storeroom, Harriet escapes, and later her memoir becomes important to the abolitionist movement. In Sandra Forrester's *Sound the Jubilee*, Maddie is not as horribly treated as Sarny or Harriet but she still bears witness to the cruelties of human bondage on her North Carolina plantation. When the war breaks out, she and her family manage to escape to Roanoke Island, where the Union army provides sanctuary for runaway slaves. Forrester shows that mistreatment of African Americans was not limited to southerners, however, as Union promises of land and education are withdrawn with the end of the war.

In *The Slave Dancer* by Paula Fox, Jessie Bollier is a 13-year-old white boy who is shanghaied in New Orleans and made to join the crew of a slave ship. In this grim story, Jessie is forced to play his fife and "dance the slaves" so their muscles will remain strong and they will bring a higher price on the slave market. Jessie is young, innocent, and still capable of feeling shock. Everyone else on board the ship is so hardened that they have become indifferent to human suffering. And this is the real message of the story—the utter degradation that eventually engulfs everyone connected with slavery, including the captain, the black Portuguese broker, the depraved Ben Stout, and even Jessie himself. In one of the most compelling and symbolic scenes in the book, Jessie is forced into the hold of the ship to look for his fife. Here he must touch, literally step on, the bodies of the captives, who were so crowded together that there was no room to walk. Jessie's descent into that hold somehow represents the descent of the whole of humankind.

Many stories of the pre–Civil War period relate to slavery and the activities of the underground railroad, when people faced the moral issue of breaking laws out of their compassion for other human beings. F. N. Monjo titled his easy-reading book *The Drinking Gourd* after the "code song" that the slaves sang. The song was used to point the direction for escape by following the North Star, using the Big Dipper as a guide. The words

to the song are included in this short story of how a young mischievous boy helps a family on their way to freedom.

In *Brady*, Jean Fritz tells the story of a very believable boy who discovers that his father is an agent for the underground railway. His parents had not told him of their forbidden activities, for Brady just cannot keep a secret. However, Brady discovers the secret for himself when his father suffers a broken leg during a fire in the barn and Brady must carry out the plan for moving a fugitive slave.

A fugitive slave whom Catherine never meets brings changes to her life in *A Gathering of Days: A New England Girl's Journal, 1830–32* by Joan Blos. Catherine and her friend Cassie agonize over a plea for help slipped into her writing book when she leaves it in the woods. They have heard about slavery and the abolitionist movement from their teacher, yet their activities are circumscribed by strict but loving families. Finally compassion and a sense of justice outweigh their respect for authority, and they leave food and a quilt where the fugitive will be sure to find them. Much later a packet arrives from Canada with a cryptic message and two bits of lace as a thank-you; the runaway is safe and free.

Paul Fleischman tells the moving story of Georgina Lott's life in *The Borning Room*. In one of the episodes, Georgina recalls hiding a runaway slave in the barn loft. Later, when her mother is giving birth and they cannot get the midwife, Georgina goes out to the barn and brings in Cora to help her mother. When her father comes home that night, he drives Cora by moonlight to the home of Mr. Reedy, a Quaker. Georgina's mother says:

> It's been a day of deliverance, . . . Cora brought Zeb here out of the womb. And we helped deliver her from slavery. . . . We must continue with that work, Georgina. (p. 33)

A runaway slave is also a part of the many-layered *Lyddie* by Katherine Paterson. When Lyddie's mother abandoned their farm, she hired out 13-year-old Lyddie to a hotel for fifty cents a week. On a visit home, Lyddie finds that the Quakers next door have hidden a runaway slave there. At first Lyddie, who is desperate for money to pay off the mortgage, thinks about the one hundred dollar reward for turning in a slave. But the more she talks with Ezekiel, the more she sees that she could never turn him in. In fact she gives him all the money she has and wishes him a safe journey. He in turn hopes she will find her freedom. This is something Lyddie thinks about frequently, as she realizes she is no more than a slave at the hotel where she works and later at the textile mills that enslaved cheap labor in the rapidly industrializing Northeast.

Patricia Beatty's *Jayhawker* is the story of Lije Tulley, a Kansas 12-year-old who joins in his family's abolitionist activities. Lije rides in his dead father's place in raids to free slaves across the border in Missouri. As war begins, he becomes a spy to serve the cause, posing as a supporter of the South while working on a Missouri farm. Courage, loneliness, and conflicting loyalties are highlighted in this well-crafted story with a dramatic conclusion.

The Civil War

There are many fine stories for children about the Civil War itself. Most of these describe the war in terms of human issues and suffering, rather than political issues. Two books focus on very different adventures of young drummer boys in the Civil War. *Charley Skedaddle*, written by Patricia Beatty, tells the story of 13-year-old Charley Quinn, a tough kid from the New York Bowery who, after his older brother is killed at Gettysburg, enlists in the Union army as a drummer boy. When the horrors of war become a reality to him, he runs away to the Blue Ridge Mountains. Here he must prove his courage in a different way. Charley's gradual change from a boy filled with bravado into one who shows real bravery is made very believable in this fast-paced story.

Ransom Powell is not as lucky as Charley Skedaddle, for two years after joining the Tenth West Virginia Regiment as a drummer boy for the Union army, he is captured with eighteen others and sent to Andersonville Prison. Well loved by his company for his humor, helpfulness, and red cap, Powell beat taps on his drum for every member of his group. G. Clifton Wisler has told Ransom Powell's story in *Red Cap*, based on authentic records and other men's reminiscences. This is the only Civil War story for children that details the horrors of Andersonville Prison.

In *Thunder at Gettysburg*, Patricia Lee Gauch tells the story of Tillie Pierce, a little girl caught in the midst of battle. She had gone out to a farm for safety and to help a neighbor with her children. The farm was right by Little Round Top, and for three days battle roared around them. Tillie carried water and helped with the wounded. The high drama of this three-day battle is also the focus of a story for older readers, *The Slopes of War* by N. A. Perez. Buck Summerhill returns to Gettysburg, his home town, as a soldier in the Army of the Potomac and loses his leg in the fight for Little Round Top. His sister Bekah cares for a wounded Union officer, Captain Waite, upstairs in the family's home while injured rebels are taken into the parlor. Bekah's 12-year-old brother Leander sees enough of this fighting and its terrible aftermath to convince him that war is not the glorious thing he had anticipated. Captain Waite tells him,

"that's what war is all about, Leander . . . an accumulation of *little* deaths that piles up into enormous grief" (p. 138). *The Slopes of War* is packed with authentic information about real officers and battle strategies, as well as several threads of fictional story line. The Resources for Teaching box "Recurring Themes in Historical Fiction" lists books about other times that carry a similar message.

The effect of the war on a frontier family in Illinois has been told by Irene Hunt in the fine historical novel *Across Five Aprils*. Jethro Creighton is only 9 years old at the outbreak of the war that at first seemed so exciting and wonderful. But one by one Jethro's brothers and cousins and his beloved schoolteacher enlist in the Union army. His favorite brother, Bill, after a long struggle with his conscience, joins the South. As the war continues, Jethro learns that it is not glorious and exciting, but heartbreaking and disruptive to all kinds of relationships. This book makes difficult reading because the device of letter writing is used to carry the action of the story to different places and provide historical detail; but it is beautifully written and thought provoking.

Rifles for Watie by Harold Keith tells of the life of a Union soldier and spy engaged in fighting the western campaign of the Civil War. Jefferson Davis Bussey, a young farm boy from Kansas, joins the Union forces and becomes a scout and, quite accidentally, a member of Stand Watie's Cherokee Rebels. Jeff is probably one of the few soldiers in the West to see the Civil War from both sides. This vibrant novel is rich in detail, with fine characterizations.

With Every Drop of Blood by James and Christopher Collier is the first-person narrative of 14-year-old Johnny. After his father is killed fighting for the Confederate army, Johnny is desperately worried that he cannot keep his family alive. He is lured into transporting food for Confederate troops despite his promise to his family to stay out of the fighting. He is captured by Cush, an African American Union soldier, but as the war disintegrates into chaos, the two find that their dependence on each other overrides their enmity. Their bond of friendship grows as their questions about the war and its savagery deepen. At the war's end, the two have survived, but they wonder about the future in a world that is so full of meanness and hate. Patricia Polacco's *Pink and Say* is a moving picture book that deals with a similar friendship, this one between two Union soldiers (see Chapter 5).

In Patricia Beatty's *Turn Homeward, Hannalee*, the story of 12-year-old Hannalee Reed from Roswell, Georgia, Hannalee, her little brother Jem, and hundreds of other young millworkers in Yankee-occupied Georgia are branded as traitors for making cloth and rope for the Confederacy. They are sent north by Sherman's soldiers

Resources for Teaching
Recurring Themes in Historical Fiction

Theme	Title, Author	Setting
The clash of cultures	*The Lantern Bearers* (Sutcliff)	Fifth-century England
	The Sign of the Beaver (Speare)	Maine Territory, 1760s
	The Man from the Other Side (Orlev)	Poland, World War II
	Year of Impossible Goodbyes (Choi)	North Korea, 1940s
The human cost of war	*My Brother Sam Is Dead* (Collier and Collier)	American Revolution
	The Slopes of War (Perez)	U.S. Civil War
	After the Dancing Days (Rostkowski)	World War I
	The Eternal Spring of Mr. Ito (Garrigue)	Canada, World War I
In quest of freedom	*Jump Ship to Freedom* (Collier and Collier)	United States, 1780s
	The Captive (Joyce Hansen)	United States, 1840s
	North to Freedom (Holm)	Europe, 1940s
	The Clay Marble (Ho)	Cambodia, 1980s
Overcoming handicaps	*A Way of His Own* (Dyer)	Prehistoric America
	The King's Shadow (Alder)	Medieval England
	Door in the Wall (de Angeli)	Medieval England
	Black Water (Anderson)	Victorian England
	Apple Is My Sign (Riskind)	United States, early 1900s

to work in mills in Kentucky and Indiana or hired out as servants to northern families. Hannalee runs away disguised as a boy, and with her brother makes her way home to burned-out Roswell. There is great pride and family feeling built into Hannalee's character. Although she learns that there are good Yankees and bad Yankees, her loyalties are firmly in the South. This book emphasizes the point that few southerners were slaveholders, and it forces readers to consider the war's effects on the common people of the South—a good balance to the many books that present northerners' views. The sequel to this story is *Be Ever Hopeful, Hannalee*, which tells of the family's struggle to survive the aftermath of the war.

Shades of Gray by Carolyn Reeder is also a story about the aftermath of the Civil War. Twelve-year-old Will Page blames the Yankees for the loss of his entire family. He is sent to live with his aunt and uncle out in the Virginia Piedmont. He can endure living in the country, but he finds it hard to accept the hospitality of his uncle, who had refused to fight the Yankees because he did not believe in war. It is even more difficult for Will to hang on to his resentment because his uncle is so fair and kind and can do everything well. Gradually Will begins to understand the courage it took for his uncle to stand up for his beliefs. When his uncle shelters a wounded Yankee on his way home to Pennsylvania, Will learns that there were good men fighting on both sides of the war. Well plotted, this is an exciting story that will make readers think of the many "shades of gray" that surround all prejudices.

Into the Twentieth Century

The twentieth century has been a period of new hopes for many people and of broken dreams for others. As we prepare to look back on this century from a new millennium, we can see how many different stories have shaped our world.

Immigrants

Immigrants who came to North America in the nineteenth and early twentieth centuries had many different origins and destinations. Still, they shared common dreams of a better life and faced similar difficulties in making a place for themselves in a new country.

In story and pictures, *Immigrant Girl* by Brett Harvey tells what it was like to live in a Jewish family in the Lower East Side of New York in 1910. Becky and her large family of nine move from the Russian countryside to squeeze into only three rooms above a grocery store. Illustrations by Deborah Kogan Ray depict the crowded conditions, the sweatshop where Becky's Aunt Sonia

Otter, a young Chinese boy, travels to the Sierra Nevada Mountains to join the Chinese laborers building the transcontinental railroad in Laurence Yep's *Dragon's Gate*. Illustration copyright © 1993 by Charles Lilly. Used by permission of HarperCollins Publishers, New York, NY.

makes shirtwaists, and the large union meeting at Cooper Square where her aunt speaks out for a strike. Despite their struggles, they maintain the Jewish Sabbath and holidays, the very reason they came to this country.

Laurence Yep's *Dragon's Gate* begins in China, where Otter and his community have welcomed Otter's father and Uncle Foxfire home from "Gold Mountain," the United States. There they have earned money that has been sent back to support the family and help the people of the Middle Kingdom drive out the hated Manchus. When the two men return to America to work on the railroad, Otter begs to go with them, but he has been trained as a scholar and his mother talks him into staying in China. Then he is held responsible for the death of a Manchu soldier and must be sent to America. Otter arrives in the Sierra Nevada Mountains in February of one of the worst winters on record, and he finds the Chinese engaged in a brutal battle to tunnel through mountains that seem made of iron. The story of how they accomplished this, their tremendous contributions to the building of the transcontinental railroad, and the unfairness of their treatment by the white bosses is told in the remainder of the book, with

Otter, his father, and his uncle as the central characters. As in his earlier books—*Dragonwings*, *The Serpent's Children*, and *Mountain Light*—Yep weaves fascinating cultural and historical details into a story that is both gripping and emotionally satisfying.

Set some sixty years later, Yep's *The Star Fisher* is lighter in tone and describes the trials of a Chinese American family who move from Ohio to Clarksburg, West Virginia, in 1927. The father, who thinks of himself as a scholar, is proud and stubborn. He moves his family into a converted schoolhouse and attempts to run a new laundry business. The mother, who was the youngest in her family, never learned to cook. They first meet Miss Lucy, their landlady, when Mama sets fire to the dinner the night of their arrival. With a mixture of humor and real emotion, the family realizes that their laundry has no customers in this narrow-minded town that cannot accept outsiders. Only when they conquer their pride and allow Miss Lucy to help them by teaching Mama how to make apple pie, do they finally become a part of the community. The Chinese folktale "The Star Fisher," which the oldest daughter tells to the youngest, becomes an extended metaphor throughout this fine story of adjustment to a new life.

African Americans

The history of African Americans from the late 1800s to the middle of the twentieth century is a bitter record of high hopes brought low by others' prejudice, hatred, and greed. Because novels that explore these situations examine issues that are still sensitive today, critics with a sociological point of view sometimes disagree about the merits of these books. Some question the authenticity or appropriateness of portraying racist attitudes for today's children. Others point to the inherent drama of the stories and their intended themes of tolerance and understanding. In the books we will discuss in this section, memorable characters face the uncertain future common to African Americans in the South during the first half of this century.

Mildred Taylor, one of the first African American authors to win a Newbery Medal, has written with understanding about the experiences of African Americans in rural Mississippi during the 1930s. *Roll of Thunder, Hear My Cry* is the story of the Logan family, their pride in the land they have owned since Reconstruction, and their determination not to let injustice go unchallenged. The crucial action in the narrative is the conflict that 9-year-old Cassie observes in the adult world around her: night riders who terrorize the black community; her mother's teaching job gone as a result of her efforts to organize a boycott of the store whose white owners are among those night riders; and her father's dramatic part in rescuing a black teenager, T. J., from a lynch mob. The grim nature of the events is off-set by the portrayal of the family caught up in them, the warmth of their concern for one another, the strength of their pride, and their courage.

A direct sequel, *Let the Circle Be Unbroken*, follows the tragic trial of T. J. and carries Cassie's family saga into 1935. Cassie continues to be a witness to the victimization of poor sharecroppers, both black and white, the beginnings of unionization, and the first attempts at black voter registration. It is the family that sustains all through these difficult times, made more difficult by her older brother Stacey's running away to find work. The complex social issues and human relationships in this book make it better suited to middle school or junior high school readers. A younger audience could be introduced to the Logan family in Taylor's *Song of the Trees*, which has the format of a short illustrated book.

Taylor has written several shorter stories of the Logan family. In *Mississippi Bridge*, blacks and whites meet briefly at the Wallace store while they wait for the weekly bus. Jeremy Simms, a 10-year-old white boy and would-be friend of the Logan children, watches as the bus splashes through a heavy rainstorm to stop at the store. When it is fully loaded, Jeremy is dismayed to see the bus driver order the black passengers off to make room for late-arriving white passengers. In the next few minutes the bus skids off the bridge and all are drowned. In *The Well*, a drought has dried up the water sources for all of the Logans' neighbors, and they freely share their own well water with both black and white families. The Simmses, white sharecroppers, cannot accept this gift gracefully, however, and animosity builds between David's older brother Hammer and the Simms boy Charlie, with near-tragic results. Both books portray the terrible effects of prejudice and the fear that was a daily part of life in rural Mississippi in the 1930s.

Another story about this time period is the Newbery Medal winner *Sounder* by William Armstrong. This is the stark tale of a black sharecropper and his family who endure cruel injustice with dignity and courage. The father is thrown into jail for stealing a ham for his starving family. Years later, crippled from a dynamite blast in the prison quarry, the father comes home to die. The story would be one of deep despair except for the fact that during the boy's long searches to find where his father is imprisoned, he meets a kind schoolmaster who enlarges his world by educating him and offering some hope for the future. This is a family that has the courage and faith to endure within a setting so inhumane that they seem to be nameless, in contrast to their dog. They do not fight back because they cannot fight back—not in the rural South near the end of the nineteenth century.

In Ouida Sebestyen's compelling *Words by Heart*, black Ben Sills has moved his family to an all-white community in the West and taken a job as hired hand to rich Mrs. Chism. The hatred and resentment of her tenant farmer, Mr. Haney, and his son Tater grow as Ben proves himself to be honest and hardworking, which the Haneys are not. Ben's oldest child, Lena, also proves herself to be an eager, keen-minded student; her ability to recite Bible verses by heart wins a contest at the book's opening. Even though the family begins to settle in and make progress against their neighbors' uneasiness, the Haneys' animosity remains. When Tater shoots Ben as he works, he is nearly killed in a fall from his horse. Lena finds them and loads both into the wagon—her dying father and the injured boy he has struggled to keep alive. This is a stunning act of mercy, in keeping with the characterization of Ben Sills as a man of faith and strength. However, it does perpetuate the stereotype of a minority character serving the dominant race to the ultimate degree of self-sacrifice.

In the prejudiced climate of tidewater North Carolina in the 1930s, children were expected to acquire bigotry as part of their growth into adulthood. At 11 years old, however, Harrison Hawkins, who is white, and Kitty Fisher, who is black (and a boy), can still be best friends. In *Circle of Fire* by William H. Hooks, these two join forces to help a band of Irish tinkers camped on the Hawkins property escape the wrath of the Ku Klux Klan. The theme of the horrors of intolerance is doubled in force by having two sets of victims, the tinkers, who are actually harassed and beaten, and the African Americans, whose fate is implied in every threat made by the Klan. This story has a dramatic climax that seems real and immediate.

The World at War

Unfortunately, much of the history of the twentieth century is the story of a world at war. Many books for young people chronicle its horrors. In these stories the common enemy is war itself. While most of them depict people's inhumanity to each other, they also show many individual acts of humanity and extreme courage.

Oddly enough, very few books for children about World War I have been published. *Goodbye Billy Radish* by Gloria Skurzynski tells the story of Hank, aged 11 when America enters the war. He sees the war from the distant but no less painful perspective of a child working in the factories that feed the war machine. In an unusual touch, black-and-white photographs introduce each chapter, lending a sense of reality to this story of a time many modern children know little about. *After the Dancing Days* by Margaret I. Rostkowski is a moving story of the aftermath of that war for those who were wounded. Annie's father is a doctor in one of the veterans hospitals, and despite her mother's disapproval,

Annie goes to visit the soldiers with her father. There she meets Andrew, a bitter, withdrawn young veteran with a disfigured face. In time, Annie no longer sees his face as horrible and begins to draw him out of his shell. At the end of the summer Andrew is beginning to heal both physically and psychologically and Annie has matured while confronting the ironies of war.

The majority of the war stories are about World War II and the Holocaust. Several picture storybooks might be used to introduce the topic or as companion books to longer stories. *Rose Blanche* by Christophe Gallaz and Roberto Innocenti is the story of a girl of about 10 who observes the actions of the Nazis and one day follows a van out to a concentration camp. Later she visits the camp and slips food to the inmates. Her actions would not actually have been possible, but they symbolize all of the little efforts made by people who resisted the war in small ways. The very name *Rose Blanche* was derived from a group of young German citizens who protested the war. They were all killed, as is the Rose Blanche in this story. *Let the Celebrations Begin!* by Margaret Wild is the poignant story of a group of Polish women in the Belsen concentration camp who are determined to make toys for the children in the camp to have on the day of their liberation. So out of scraps of materials, rags, buttons, and pockets, they secretly make stuffed elephants, owls, and other toys. Based on a reference to a small collection of toys found at the Belsen concentration camp, this is a moving testament to all that is good in humankind.

Hiroshima No Pika (The Flash of Hiroshima) by Toshi Maruki, *Sadako* by Eleanor Coerr, Tatsuharu Kodama's *Shin's Tricycle*, and *My Hiroshima* by Junko Morimoto record in pictures and stories the horror of the atomic bomb. All these picture storybooks (see Chapter 5) are for older children and could well serve as an introduction to units on World War II or units on peace.

Escape and Resistance

Some of the most popular war stories are about families who escaped to freedom or endured long years of hiding from the Nazis. *Journey to America* by Sonia Levitin tells of a German Jewish family who become refugees when Hitler comes to power. Pap goes ahead to the United States, but Mama and the girls must wait in Switzerland. There Mama is an alien and cannot work, and other living arrangements are made for the children. After a difficult separation, the family are all reunited in America. Simple language and the emphasis on family solidarity and mutual love make this story appealing for 8- to 10-year-olds.

Along with its intriguing title, *When Hitler Stole Pink Rabbit* by Judith Kerr also has the validity of solid detail that comes from personal experience. This is the story

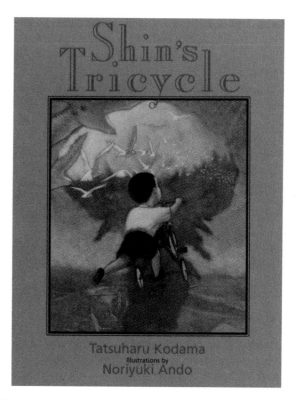

Illustrations such as those by Noriyuki Ando in *Shin's Tricycle* by Tatsuharu Kodama add an emotional impact to stories about war.
Cover, from *Shin's Tricycle* by Tatsuharu Kodama, illustrated by Noriyuki Ando. Copyright © 1995 by Walker Publishing Co., New York, NY. Reprinted by permission.

of another family's escape to Switzerland and their trials in trying to earn a living there, then in France, and finally in England. Again, this is a prewar story taking place in the 1930s. It is a happier account than Levitin's *Journey to America*; yet as they leave France for England, Anna wonders if they will ever really belong anywhere.

Others made their escape by hiding for the duration of the war. *Anne Frank: The Diary of a Young Girl* is the classic story of hiding from the Nazis. Autobiographical, this is a candid and open account of the changes wrought upon eight people who hid for two years in a secret annex of an office building in Amsterdam and were ultimately found and imprisoned by the Nazis. Anne's diary reveals the thoughts of a sensitive adolescent growing up under extraordinary conditions. No one who lived in the annex survived the war except Anne's father. He returned to their hiding place and found Anne's diary. When it was published, it became an immediate best-seller and was translated into many languages. Its popularity continues today, an appropriate tribute to Anne Frank's amazing spirit.

The Upstairs Room by Johanna Reiss is a moving account of the author's own experiences when she and her sister were hidden by a farm family, the Oostervelds.

The girls spent most of the time in an upstairs room so that they wouldn't be seen. The greatest excitement occurs when German soldiers make the Oosterveld house their temporary headquarters. Mostly, however, this is a story of the reactions of all the characters in close confinement and secrecy—the irritability, tension, and fear. The real delight of the book is the Oosterveld family with their plain-folks values, salty language, and generosity. Annie's story is continued in *The Journey Back*, which shows the aftereffects of war on her family and her difficulties with a perfectionist stepmother.

In *Hide and Seek* Ida Vos tells the story of one Jewish family in the Netherlands after the arrival of the German army. Rachel is bewildered by the constant change of laws, the confiscation of the family's bicycles, the yellow stars that must be sewn on coats, the disappearances of friends and relatives. The first day Rachel must wear her yellow star, she feels very self-conscious. As she boards the tram the driver calls out to them:

> "It really is springtime in my tram now. All these children with yellow daffodils on their coats. I wish I could wear one." (p. 18)

Rachel and her sister eventually go into hiding, sheltered by various "uncles" and "aunts" who are willing to risk their lives to hide the girls. At the end of the story the children are reunited with their parents, but 105 of her parents' family members have been killed. More than a hundred thousand Dutch Jews were killed in German concentration camps.

Uri Orlev's *The Island on Bird Street* takes the reader into an almost deserted Polish ghetto where Alex, not yet 12, has an ingenious hiding place high in the ruins of building No. 78. His mother, a Zionist, has disappeared, and his father is taken away by the Germans along with the last workers cleared from the ghetto. But Alex's instructions are to wait for his return at No. 78—for a day, a week, or even a year, if necessary. As the months pass he proves to be a clever and courageous survivor, avoiding detection even when German soldiers come to blast open a secret bunker under the cellar. The story ends as Alex and his father, now a part of the underground, are miraculously reunited. The author's confident tone comes from experience; he spent two years in hiding in the Warsaw ghetto as a child. Orlev's *The Man from the Other Side* is also set in Warsaw. In this Batchelder Award–winning book, Marek is a young Polish boy who must help his stepfather smuggle food into the ghetto for monetary rather than altruistic reasons. These activities give him access to the ghetto through the sewers and bring him into the middle of the ghetto uprising. When he finds out that his real father was Jewish, he reflects on his own attitude toward the Jews, and he begins to examine the anti-Semitism that is so prevalent in Polish society. Based on the experiences of a Polish journalist, this is an exciting story that raises important questions about community attitudes and the terrible consequences of prejudice.

One of the best survival stories is *The Endless Steppe* by Esther Hautzig. This is the author's own account of growing up in a slave labor camp in Siberia. The Rudomins, a wealthy Jewish family, live in Vilna, a city in Poland. The Russians occupy Vilna and confiscate the family business; then one day they arrest the whole family as "capitalists and therefore enemies of the people." They are shipped in filthy, stiflingly hot cattle cars across Siberia—the barren flat land that is to be their home for five endless years. Despite the poverty and privation, Esther manages to satisfy her adolescent needs and find hope in a hopeless situation. During the time the Rudomins are in Siberia, the Nazis enter Poland and kill all their Jewish relatives and friends; in retrospect they consider themselves supremely lucky to have been deported to "The Endless Steppe." The ending of this story is less grim than that of *Anne Frank*, but both stories are a tribute to the courage of the human spirit.

Many refugees were helped to flee or hide from authorities by common folk who did what they could to resist the Nazis. Many stories relate the roles that children played in helping these resisters. Two stories of enduring popularity with young readers are Claire Bishop's *Twenty and Ten*, in which French orphans manage to hide ten Jewish children during a Nazi investigation, and Marie McSwigan's *Snow Treasure*, which tells how a brave group of Norwegian children helped to smuggle gold out of the country to keep it from the Nazis.

Lois Lowry tells the dramatic story of the Danish Resistance as they successfully smuggled nearly seven thousand Jews across the sea to Sweden. In *Number the Stars*, she details the story of how one family saved the lives of the Rosens, their friends. Perhaps the most exciting scene is when the German soldiers come to the house where Ellen Rosen is staying and pretending to be a member of the family. She still wears her Star of David necklace and Annemarie hisses to her to take it off. She is unable to get it unclasped, so Annemarie yanks it off just before the Nazis enter the room. When they leave,

> Annemarie relaxed the clenched fingers of her right hand, which still clutched Ellen's necklace. She looked down, and saw that she had imprinted the Star of David into her palm. (p. 49)

Only through the cooperation and extraordinary bravery of the common people were the Danes able to save most of their Jewish population.

Lisa's War by Carol Matas tells of the part two Jewish young people played in the Danish Resistance. Rather than being saved by others, they are actively involved in the rescue effort. Finally it becomes too dangerous for them to continue their work and they are persuaded to go to Sweden.

Another story of a dramatic rescue of Jewish children by a whole French town is told in *Waiting for Anya* by Michael Morpurgo. A reclusive widow's farm set high in the hills close to Spain is the perfect escape point for Jewish children. Benjamin, the widow's son-in-law, is waiting for the arrival of his own daughter, Anya, but when German soldiers start patrolling the borders, he and Jo, a young boy in the village, form a plan to help a group of children escape. The plan works, but Benjamin is captured with Leah, a young child who refused to leave him at the border, and they are sent to Auschwitz. Ironically, the war is over in a few weeks and Anya comes home at last. This is a moving story of uncommon bravery by the small village of Vichy, France.

Some of the most dramatic stories about young people who lived through the conflict in Europe are autobiographical. However, they employ many of the techniques of fiction, including the creation of dialogue.

In *Touch Wood*, Renée Roth-Hano uses a diary format to record her story of life in occupied France. This Jewish family flees Alsace and lives a precarious existence in Paris until Renée and her sister escape to the shelter of a Catholic women's residence in Normandy. In the end they are caught in crossfire but manage to traverse a minefield to safety.

Ilse Koehn's *Mischling, Second Degree* describes her childhood of active participation in the Hitler Youth movement, made ironic by the secret kept even from her at the time: Her father's mother was Jewish, and Ilse would have been classified as an enemy of the Third Reich had that fact been known. In Emma Macalik Butterworth's *As the Waltz Was Ending*, an autobiographical account of growing up in Vienna, 8-year-old Emmy auditions for and is accepted by the selective Vienna State Ballet School, but the fairy-tale quality of her life is shattered by the ugliness of politics and the crush of war. Her childhood pains with the barre exercises pale beside her adolescent struggles to survive air raids, food shortages, and kidnap and rape by Russian soldiers. Aranka Siegal's own story of her Hungarian childhood, *Upon the Head of the Goat*, is filled with dread, for the Davidowitz family is Jewish. The final scene is emotionally shattering, as Piri, her mother, brother, and two sisters are forced to board a train for a destination with a name that is unfamiliar to them— Auschwitz. Books like these are really for adolescents, but they require maturity of their readers, whatever their age level.

Children in Asia also suffered during the war years. *The House of Sixty Fathers* by Meindert DeJong is an example of a book that does not glorify war. It clearly, vividly tells of the horror of being in a rain of bullets and the pains of hunger. DeJong's descriptions of Tien Pao's fear, loneliness, and hunger are starkly realistic but couched in terms that even 9- or 10-year-olds can well understand. The Chinese boy and his family flee before the Japanese invasion, but they are separated. Clutching his pet pig, Tien Pao struggles on, not knowing where to go. He finds a U.S. flier who helps him survive. The boy is taken to the barracks and becomes a mascot of the soldiers, his sixty fathers. Although it seems impossible, he continues to believe his parents will be found. In a rather contrived but satisfying ending he does identify his mother from a plane as she is working on the construction of an airfield.

A few Western children, mainly those of missionary parents, were trapped in Asia during World War II. In *The Bombers' Moon* Betty Vander Els tells the story of Ruth and her little brother, Simeon, who must go to an emergency boarding school as the Japanese invaders come closer to their home in China. They endure falling bombs, a terrifying airlift over the Himalayas to India, and one new "home" after another before being reunited with their parents. In Joan Manley's exciting, if somewhat melodramatic, *She Flew No Flags*, Janet and her missionary family have been evacuated from India in 1944 and are aboard a ship heading for the United States. Always in danger of attack by the Japanese, the people onboard must also contend with storms, mysterious secrets, and their own emotions.

Many authors from England have written about children's experiences there at the time of the bombing raids. Susan Cooper's *Dawn of Fear* and Robert Westall's *The Machine Gunners* are frequently read by young adolescents. One of the best selections for elementary readers is Nina Bawden's *Carrie's War*, about three children who are evacuees living in a Welsh mining town. Nick and Carrie, brother and sister, are sent to live with stern Mr. Evans and his sister, Auntie Lou. The story moves ahead on two levels—the family's feud with Mr. Evans's older sister, Dilys, and the children's involvement in it. The characters are seen from a child's-eye view, with a child's perception of adults. This is a remarkable story that tells much more of the personal wars of living, both for children and for adults, than of the war of bombs and blitzes.

An unusual story that concerns itself with the aftermath of a war is *North to Freedom* by Anne Holm. A boy named David is given a chance to escape from the prison camp in eastern Europe where he has been imprisoned for most of his 12 years. He has no knowledge of his own background or of the world at large, and no feeling about people except that no one can be trusted. Although David is able to read and has learned seven languages from the other prisoners, much of his learning has been without the essential experience that brings meaning. He finds it difficult to relate to the world, avoids people, and makes only tentative gestures toward others. Slowly his trust in human beings grows, and with it the desire to live and be part of the world of sunshine, beauty, and color that is in such contrast to the drabness of the prison camp. David's change from an imprisoned creature completely shut off from normal human feelings into a responsive and responsible boy makes for a remarkable story.

The Impact of World War II in the Americas

Thousands of American families lost sons, fathers, and husbands in World War II, but we never endured the physical horror of war in North America. For this reason, perhaps, we have fewer stories about the impact of the war in the West.

Two popular stories tell of the English children who were sent to Canada for the duration of the war. *Searching for Shona* by Margaret Anderson is more about trading identities than it is about the war, but it could not have happened except for the children's evacuation. In *The Sky Is Falling* by Kit Pearson, Norah and her younger brother Gavin are sent to live with a rich woman and her sister in Toronto. This story details the difficult adjustment of the children, particularly since "Aunt Florence" obviously prefers Gavin to Norah. This well-written story tells a believable tale of the gradual change in relationships between 10-year-old Norah and her sponsor.

The Cay by Theodore Taylor is a story of both war survival and overcoming prejudice. Shipwrecked following a German attack on his ship, Phillip finds himself cast up on a small, barren Caribbean island with an old black man named Timothy. Blinded during the incident, Phillip is totally dependent on the old man. Both the prejudiced white Virginian and the unschooled West Indian are products and prisoners of their backgrounds. This story of a color-conscious white boy and a self-sacrificing man of color does not provide a model for multicultural living today; what it does do is present an exciting account of survival in the Caribbean in 1942, emphasizing human interdependence in time of crisis.

The Summer of My German Soldier by Bette Greene is the story of 12-year-old Patty Bergen, who is Jewish and the awkward elder daughter of a small-town Arkansas department-store owner. Except for the real love of Ruth, the Bergens' African American cook, Patty lives in a loveless situation. Perhaps this explains her compassion for a handsome, well-educated German

prisoner of war named Anton who lives in a prison camp near town and comes to her father's store. Patty begins to think of him as her friend, and later, when she sees him running down the railroad tracks, she offers him the safety of her special hideout room over the garage. Only after Anton has gotten away and is captured elsewhere is Patty's role in his escape uncovered. She is arrested and sent to a reform school, clinging to the knowledge that one day she will be free to leave her family and become a "person of value," a term Anton had used.

Two authors have written children's books about the aftermath of the Holocaust. In Myron Levoy's *Alan and Naomi*, Alan Silverman does not want to have to make friends with crazy-acting Naomi Kirshenbaum, but at the insistence of his parents he visits her. Her haunted face and her horrifying experiences during the war in France challenge him, and by acting silly with his puppet, he gets her to laugh and speak. When Alan gets into a bloody fight with the school bully, however, Naomi is traumatized and retreats again into her shell. Alan and his father go to visit her at a nursing home, but it is of no use. Alan cannot reach her. His father assures him that she will be all right in time, but Alan thinks Hitler has destroyed her. The impact of the war had come home. The outcome of Ida Vos's *Anna Is Still Here* is more hopeful though no less painfully achieved. Anna was a hidden child in Holland during the war, and at the war's end she is struggling to overcome her fears and come to terms with the guilt of being a survivor. Reunited with her parents and helped by Mrs. Neuman, another adult survivor who is looking for her daughter, Anna's rage and grief eventually are tempered by the rebuilding of community.

Citizens of the United States can take no pride in the treatment of Japanese Americans at the beginning of the war against Japan. Graham Salisbury's *Under the Blood-Red Sun* vividly recreates the paranoia that occurred in Hawaii following the attack on Pearl Harbor. Until that time Tomi was a typical eighth grader, more interested in baseball than in his studies, and eager to help out on his father's fishing boat. But the attack turns his world upside down. His father's boat is scuttled and his father imprisoned. Tomi is further torn between his need to fit in with his "haoli" (white) friends, and his loyalty to his grandfather, who cannot give up his Japanese identity. In *Journey to Topaz*, Yoshiko Uchida has given a fictionalized account of her family's evacuation and internment in a relocation camp. Yuki's father, a businessman, is taken away from his family on the very day of Pearl Harbor. Taken first to a temporary center at an old race track, Yuki and her mother and older brother eventually end up in the "permanent" camp in Topaz, Utah. The author writes the story with restraint

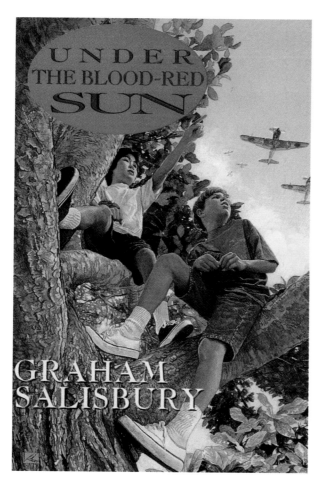

The lives of two friends are unalterably affected by the bombing of Pearl Harbor in Graham Salisbury's *Under the Blood-Red Sun*.

From *Under the Blood-Red Sun* (jacket cover) by Graham Salisbury. Copyright © 1994 by Graham Salisbury. Used by permission of Delacorte Press, a division of Bantam Doubleday Dell Publishing Group, Inc.

and no bitterness. The quiet courage, dignity, and loyalty with which this Japanese family endures their unjust internment makes its own statement to the reader. Citizens of Japanese descent in Canada were subjected to similar treatment. Sheila Garrigue's *The Eternal Spring of Mr. Ito* helps the reader experience the passionate anti-Japanese feeling along the Pacific Coast even as it demonstrates the blamelessness of those who were shunned, jeered, vandalized, and interned.

War Continues

Unfortunately war did not end with World War II but continued in other conflicts, such as those in Korea, Vietnam, Iraq, and Bosnia. Sook Nyul Choi writes a poignant story of her childhood in northern Korea in the 1940s in *Year of Impossible Goodbyes*. As the war rages, 10-year-old Sookan, her mother, her brother, and

Aunt Tiger endure the cruelties of the Japanese occupation. Her father is a resistance fighter in Manchuria and her brothers have been taken to Japanese labor camps. When the war is over in 1945, the Koreans hope for a permanent peace, but then communist Russian troops come. By now Sook Choi and her family have lost everything dear to them. They decide to escape to the Americans at the 38th parallel, but their guide double-crosses them and their mother is taken into custody. Left alone, Sook Choi and her little brother escape after a terrifying dash through barbed wire. The two children finally make it to the Red Cross center and are later reunited with their parents. This is a story that emphasizes that all the so-called victors of a war always make the people of a country their victims. Again it relates the uncommon courage of the common people.

Set in a similar time period, *So Far from the Bamboo Grove* by Yoko Kawashima Watkins is also a true story that tells of a Japanese family living in northern Korea at the close of the war. Fleeing from the Korean communists, 11-year old Yoko, her older sister Ko, and her mother head south, hoping their brother, Hideyo, and their father will catch up with them on their journey. Their nightmarish trip is described in harrowing detail, and when they reach Japan they find a country devastated by the war and all their relatives killed. Their mother places the two girls in school, but when she dies suddenly they must struggle to survive, selling cloth toys, shining shoes, and picking food from garbage cans. Eventually Hideyo finds them in Kyoto and this unforgettable story ends on a note of hope. Watkins continues their story of survival in the equally moving *My Brother, My Sister, and I*.

The Clay Marble by Minfong Ho tells of 12-year-old Dara and her family, who are among the thousands forced to flee from their villages in war-torn Cambodia during the early 1980s. In the refugee camp, there is peace and plenty of food, and Dara makes a new friend, Jantu. Then the shells and bombs start falling again, this time in the middle of camp. In the chaos, Dara is separated from her family and from Jantu. Alone, she must find the strength to reunite her family. When she finally finds them, her brother wants to enlist in the army rather than go home to help them plant their rice crop. Listening to the propaganda over the loudspeaker, Jantu says:

"They all say the same thing. They seem to think it's a game. . . . They take sides, they switch sides, they play against each other. Who wins, who loses, whose turn it is to kick next—it's like an elaborate soccer game. Except they don't use soccer balls. They use us." (p. 141)

The author grew up in Thailand and worked as a nutritionist with an international relief organization on the Thai-Cambodian border in 1980. Dara and Jantu's story is the story of every child in that refugee camp.

Well-written historical fiction like that reviewed in this chapter can enable children to see the continuity of life and their own places in this vast sweep of history. The power of good historical fiction can give children a feeling for a living past. History can become an extension of their own personal experiences, rather than a sterile subject assigned to be studied in school. Such books can offer children new perspectives by which they come to realize that people make and shape their destinies through their own decisions and actions. The events that are happening today do become the history of tomorrow.

Learning Experiences

1. Read four or five books about one particular period or place and chart the references to kinds of food, clothing, houses, transportation, language, and so on. Which books give the most authentic picture?

2. Prepare a decorated portfolio or box of materials of a particular event or period of time to help children build a background for selected books of historical fiction. You might want to include copies of newspaper clippings, artifacts, an annotated bibliography, copies of appropriate paperback books, and examples of art, music, and handicrafts. Plan activity cards for children's use and extension of these materials. (See the description of jackdaws in Chapter 14.)

3. Work with classmates or middle-grade students in role-playing dramatic confrontations in historical fiction. Some possible choices would be the witch trial of Kit Tyler in *The Witch of Blackbird Pond* by Speare or Sam Meeker's argument with his father about going to war in *My Brother Sam Is Dead* by the Colliers.

4. Collect examples of dialogue and descriptive language from several books of historical fiction. You might want to include something by Patricia Beatty, Paul Fleischman, or Rosemary Sutcliff in this sample. What techniques do the authors use to indicate the setting?

5. Compare the values and attitudes of the heroine of *Lyddie* by Katherine Paterson with those of a young heroine in a contemporary novel, such as Dicey in *Dicey's Song* by Cynthia Voigt. What are their hopes and expectations? How do they express themselves? How are their priorities different or alike?

6. Compare a picture storybook such as *Rose Blanche* by Christophe Gallaz and Roberto Innocenti, a fantasy such as *The Devil's Arithmetic* by Jane Yolen, and a realistic adventure like *Hide and Seek* by Ida Vos. What does each genre do that is unique? How much information do you receive from each? Chart the differences and similarities.

Related Readings

Collier, Christopher. "Johnny and Sam: Old and New Approaches to the American Revolution." *Horn Book Magazine*, April 1976, pp. 132–138.

   One of the coauthors of popular novels about the American Revolution discusses three historiographic interpretations of that conflict and contends that modern historical fiction should not present historical events in simple or one-sided terms.

Haugaard, Erik Christian. " 'Before I Was Born': History and the Child." *Horn Book Magazine*, October 1979, pp. 514–521.

   The author writes of the relationship between history and truth and makes an eloquent case for the value of history in showing that people always have choices.

Hunter, Mollie. "Shoulder the Sky." In *Talent Is Not Enough* (pp. 31–56). New York: Harper & Row, 1976.

> A fine writer reveals her sense of history as human drama while discussing several issues critical to historical fiction, including the portrayal of violence and the relationship of contemporary attitudes to those of the past.

Levstik, Linda S. "Research Directions: Mediating Content Through Literary Texts." *Language Arts* 67 (December 1990): 848–853.

> This article looks at the connection between historical literature and children's ability to think carefully about history's moral and interpretive issues. It is based on a series of studies with children and provides good evidence of the role historical fiction can play in content learning.

Rudman, Masha K., and Rosenberg, Susan P. "Confronting History: Holocaust Books for Children." *New Advocate* 4 (summer 1991): 163–177.

> This practical article discusses several aspects of Holocaust literature for young people. Specific books are grouped by categories, such as survivors, rescuers, group responsibility, and Jewish rescuers and resistance.

Segel, Elizabeth. "Laura Ingalls Wilder's America: An Unflinching Assessment." *Children's Literature in Education* 25 (summer 1977): 63–70.

> Segel examines the values portrayed in the Little House series, particularly *Little House on the Prairie,* and points out that Wilder, through the character of Laura, not only presented the attitudes and beliefs of nineteenth-century America but also questioned them.

Stanley, Diane. "Picture Book History." *New Advocate* 1 (fall 1988): 209–220.

> The author and illustrator of several picture-book biographies of historical figures describes the difficulties of providing accurate pictures. The background details about *Shaka, King of the Zulus* are interesting to children as well as adults.

Children's Literature

Alder, Elizabeth. *The King's Shadow*. Farrar, Straus & Giroux, 1995.

Anderson, Joan. *The First Thanksgiving Feast*. Photographs by George Ancona. Clarion, 1983.

Anderson, Margaret J. *Searching for Shona*. Knopf, 1989 [1979].

Anderson, Rachel. *Black Water*. Holt, 1995.

Antle, Nancy. *Beautiful Land: A Story of the Oklahoma Land Rush*. Illustrated by John Gampert. Viking, 1994.

Armstrong, William H. *Sounder*. Illustrated by James Barkley. Harper & Row, 1969.

Averill, Esther. *King Philip: The Indian Chief*. Illustrated by Vera Belsky. Linnet, 1993 [1950].

Avi [Avi Wortis]. *The Fighting Ground*. Lippincott, 1984.

———. *The True Confessions of Charlotte Doyle*. Orchard, 1990.

Bartone, Elisa. *Peppe the Lamplighter*. Illustrated by Ted Lewin. Lothrop, Lee & Shepard, 1993.

Bawden, Nina. *Carrie's War*. Illustrated by Colleen Browning. Lippincott, 1973.

Beatty, Patricia. *Be Ever Hopeful, Hannalee*. Morrow, 1988.

———. *Charley Skedaddle*. Morrow, 1987.

———. *Jayhawker*. Morrow, 1991.

———. *Turn Homeward, Hannalee*. Morrow, 1984.

———. *Wait for Me, Watch for Me, Eula Bee*. Troll, 1986.

Berry, James. *Ajeemah and His Son*. HarperCollins, 1992.

Bishop, Claire Huchet. *Twenty and Ten*. As told by Janet Jolly. Illustrated by William Pène DuBois. Viking, 1964.

Blos, Joan W. *A Gathering of Days: A New England Girl's Journal, 1830–32*. Scribner's, 1979.

Bosse, Malcolm. *The Examination*. Farrar, Straus & Giroux, 1994.

Brennan, J. H. *Shiva: An Adventure of the Ice Age*. Lippincott, 1989.

Brink, Carol Ryrie. *Caddie Woodlawn*. Illustrated by Kate Seredy. Macmillan, 1936.

———. *Caddie Woodlawn*. Illustrated by Trina Schart Hyman. Macmillan, 1973.

Bruchac, Joseph. *Gluskabe and the Four Wishes*. Illustrated by Christine Nyburg Shrader. Cobblehill, 1995.

Bulla, Clyde Robert. *A Lion to Guard Us*. Illustrated by Michelle Chessare. Harper Trophy, 1990 [1981].

———. *The Sword in the Tree*. Illustrated by Paul Galdone. Crowell, 1956.

Bunting, Eve. *Dandelions*. Illustrated by Greg Shed. Harcourt Brace, 1995.

Butterworth, Emma Macalik. *As the Waltz Was Ending*. Four Winds, 1982.

Choi, Sook Nyul. *Year of Impossible Goodbyes*. Houghton Mifflin, 1991.

Clapp, Patricia. *Constance: A Story of Early Plymouth*. Lothrop, Lee & Shepard, 1968.

———. *Witches' Children*. Lothrop, Lee & Shepard, 1982.

Coerr, Eleanor. *Sadako*. Illustrated by Allen Say. Philomel, 1993.

Collier, James Lincoln, and Christopher Collier. *Jump Ship to Freedom*. Delacorte, 1981.

———. *My Brother Sam Is Dead*. Four Winds, 1974.

———. *War Comes to Willy Freeman*. Delacorte, 1983.

———. *Who Is Carrie?* Delacorte, 1984.

———. *With Every Drop of Blood*. Delacorte, 1994.

Conrad, Pam. *Prairie Songs*. Illustrated by Darryl Zudeck. Harper & Row, 1985.

Cooper, Susan. *Dawn of Fear*. Illustrated by Margery Gill. Harcourt Brace, 1970.

Crompton, Anne Eliot. *The Winter Wife*. Illustrated by Robert Andrew Parker. Little, Brown, 1975.

Cushman, Karen. *Catherine, Called Birdy*. Clarion, 1994.

———. *The Midwife's Apprentice*. Clarion, 1995.

Dalgliesh, Alice. *The Courage of Sarah Noble*. Illustrated by Leonard Weisgard. Scribner's, 1954.

———. *The Thanksgiving Story*. Illustrated by Helen Sewell. Scribner's, 1954.

de Angeli, Marguerite. *The Door in the Wall*. Doubleday, 1949.

De Felice, Cynthia. *Lostman's River*. Macmillan, 1994.

Defoe, Daniel. *Robinson Crusoe*. Edited by Angus Ross. Penguin, 1966.

DeJong, Meindert. *The House of Sixty Fathers*. Illustrated by Maurice Sendak. Harper & Row, 1956.

de Trevino, Elizabeth Borton. *I, Juan de Pareja*. Farrar, Straus & Giroux, 1965.

de Wit, Dorothy, ed. *The Talking Stone: An Anthology of Native American Tales and Legends*. Illustrated by Donald Crews. Greenwillow, 1984.

Dorris, Michael. *Guests*. Hyperion, 1994.

———. *Morning Girl*. Hyperion, 1992.

Dyer, T. A. *A Way of His Own*. Houghton Mifflin, 1981.

Edmonds, Walter D. *The Matchlock Gun*. Illustrated by Paul Lantz. Dodd, Mead, 1941.

Feelings, Tom. *The Middle Passage: White Ships/Black Cargo*. Introduction by Dr. John Henrik Clarke. Dial, 1995.

Field, Rachel. *Calico Bush*. Illustrated by Allen Lewis. Macmillan, 1931.

Fleischman, Paul. *The Borning Room*. HarperCollins, 1991.

———. *Bull Run*. HarperCollins, 1993.

———. *Saturnalia*. HarperCollins, 1990.

Forbes, Esther. *Johnny Tremain*. Illustrated by Lynd Ward. Houghton Mifflin, 1946.

Forrester, Sandra. *Sound the Jubilee*. Lodestar, 1995.

Fox, Paula. *The Slave Dancer*. Illustrated by Eros Keith. Bradbury, 1973.

Frank, Anne. *Anne Frank: The Diary of a Young Girl*. Rev. ed. Translated by B. M. Mooyart. Introduction by Eleanor Roosevelt. Doubleday, 1967.

Fritz, Jean. *Brady*. Illustrated by Lynd Ward. Coward-McCann/Penguin, 1987 [1960].

———. *The Cabin Faced West*. Illustrated by Feodor Rojankovsky. Coward-McCann, 1958.

———. *The Double Life of Pocahontas*. Illustrated by Ed Young. Putnam, 1983.

———. *Early Thunder*. Illustrated by Lynd Ward. Coward-McCann, 1967.

Gallaz, Christophe, and Roberto Innocenti. *Rose Blanche*. Illustrated by Roberto Innocenti. Creative Education, 1985.

Garrigue, Sheila. *The Eternal Spring of Mr. Ito*. Bradbury, 1985.

Gauch, Patricia L. *This Time, Tempe Wick?* Illustrated by Margot Tomes. Putnam, 1974.

———. *Thunder at Gettysburg*. Illustrated by Stephen Gammell. Putnam, 1990 [1975].

George, Jean. *My Side of the Mountain*. Dutton, 1975.

———. *The Talking Earth*. Harper & Row, 1983.

Gipson, Fred. *Old Yeller*. Illustrated by Carl Burger. Harper & Row, 1956.

Gray, Elizabeth Janet. *Adam of the Road*. Illustrated by Robert Lawson. Viking, 1942.

Greene, Bette. *The Summer of My German Soldier*. Bantam, 1984 [1973].

Gregory, Kristiana. *Jenny of the Tetons*. Harcourt Brace, 1989.

Hahn, Mary Downing. *Stepping on the Cracks*. Clarion, 1991.

Hansen, Joyce. *The Captive*. Scholastic, 1994.

Harvey, Brett. *Immigrant Girl: Beck of Eldridge Street*. Illustrated by Deborah K. Ray. Holiday House, 1987.

Hautzig, Esther. *The Endless Steppe: Growing Up in Siberia*. Crowell, 1968.

Haviland, Virginia, ed. *North American Legends*. Putnam, 1979.

Highwater, Jamake. *Legend Days*. Harper & Row, 1984.

Hill, Kirkpatrick. *Toughboy and Sister*. McElderry, 1990.

Ho, Minfong. *The Clay Marble*. Farrar, Straus & Giroux, 1991.

Holm, Anne. *North to Freedom*. Translated by L. W. Kingsland. Harcourt Brace, 1965.

Hooks, William H. *Circle of Fire*. Atheneum, 1984.

Hoople, Cheryl. *The Heritage Sampler: A Book of Colonial Arts and Crafts*. Dial, 1975.

Hunt, Irene. *Across Five Aprils*. Follett, 1964.

Keith, Harold. *Rifles for Watie*. Crowell, 1957.

Kelly, Eric P. *The Trumpeter of Krakow*. Rev. ed. Illustrated by Janina Domanska. Macmillan, 1966 [1928].

Kerr, Judith. *When Hitler Stole Pink Rabbit*. Coward-McCann, 1972.

Kodama, Tatsuharu. *Shin's Tricycle*. Translated by Kazuko Hokuman-Jones. Illustrated by Noriyuki Ando. Walker, 1995.

Koehn, Ilse. *Mischling, Second Degree: My Childhood in Nazi Germany*. Greenwillow, 1977.

Konigsburg, E. L. *A Proud Taste for Scarlet and Miniver*. Atheneum, 1973.

———. *The Second Mrs. Giaconda*. Macmillan, 1978.

Kroeber, Theodora. *Ishi, Last of His Tribe*. Illustrated by Ruth Robbins. Parnassus, 1964.

Lasky, Kathryn. *Beyond the Divide*. Macmillan, 1983.

Levitin, Sonia. *Journey to America*. Illustrated by Charles Robinson. Atheneum, 1970.

Levoy, Myron. *Alan and Naomi*. Harper Trophy, 1987 [1977].

Llorente, Pilar Molina. *The Apprentice*. Translated by Robin Longshaw. Illustrated by Juan Ramón Alonso. Farrar, Straus & Giroux, 1993.

Lowry, Lois. *Number the Stars*. Houghton Mifflin, 1989.

Lunn, Janet. *The Root Cellar*. Macmillan, 1983.

Lyons, Mary E. *Letters from a Slave Girl: The Story of Harriet Jacobs*. Scribner's, 1992.

MacLachlan, Patricia. *Sarah, Plain and Tall*. Harper & Row, 1985.

————. *Skylark*. HarperCollins, 1994.

————. *Three Names*. Illustrated by Alexander Pertzoff. HarperCollins, 1991.

Manley, Joan. B. *She Flew No Flags*. Houghton Mifflin, 1995.

Maruki, Toshi. *Hiroshima No Pika* (The Flash of Hiroshima). Lothrop, Lee & Shepard, 1980.

Matas, Carol. *Lisa's War*. Scribner's, 1987.

McGraw, Eloise Jarvis. *The Golden Goblet*. Viking Penguin, 1986 [1961].

————. *Mara, Daughter of the Nile*. Viking Penguin, 1985 [1953].

————. *Moccasin Trail*. Viking Penguin, 1986 [1952].

McSwigan, Marie. *Snow Treasure*. Illustrated by Alexander Pertzoff. HarperCollins, 1991.

Monjo, F. N. *The Drinking Gourd*. Illustrated by Fred Brenner. Harper & Row, 1970.

Morimoto, Junko. *My Hiroshima*. Viking, 1987.

Morpurgo, Michael. *Waiting for Anya*. Viking, 1990.

Morrow, Honoré. *On to Oregon!* Beech Tree, 1991 [1946].

Namioka, Lensey. *The Coming of the Bear*. HarperCollins, 1992.

————. *Island of Ogres*. Harper & Row, 1989.

O'Dell, Scott. *Island of the Blue Dolphins*. Houghton Mifflin, 1960.

————. *Sarah Bishop*. Houghton Mifflin, 1980.

————. *Sing Down the Moon*. Houghton Mifflin, 1970.

————. *Zia*. Illustrated by Ted Lewin. Houghton Mifflin, 1976.

Orlev, Uri. *The Island on Bird Street*. Translated from the Hebrew by Hillel Halkin. Houghton Mifflin, 1984.

————. *The Man from the Other Side*. Translated by Hillel Halkin. Houghton Mifflin, 1991.

Paterson, Katherine. *Lyddie*. Dutton, 1991.

————. *The Master Puppeteer*. Harper & Row, 1975.

————. *Of Nightingales That Weep*. Harper & Row, 1974.

————. *The Sign of the Chrysanthemum*. Harper & Row, 1973.

Paulsen, Gary. *Hatchet*. Bradbury, 1987.

————. *Nightjohn*. Delacorte, 1993.

Pearson, Kit. *The Sky Is Falling*. Viking, 1989.

Perez, N. A. *The Slopes of War*. Houghton Mifflin, 1984.

Perl, Lila. *Slumps, Grunts and Snickerdoodles: What Colonial America Ate and Why*. Illustrated by Richard Cuffari. Clarion, 1979.

Petry, Ann. *Tituba of Salem Village*. Crowell, 1964.

Polacco, Patricia. *Pink and Say*. Philomel, 1994.

Pryor, Bonnie. *The House on Maple Street*. Illustrated by Beth Peck. Morrow, 1987.

————. *Seth of the Lion People*. Morrow, 1988.

Reeder, Carolyn. *Shades of Gray*. Macmillan, 1989.

Reiss, Johanna. *The Journey Back*. Crowell, 1976.

————. *The Upstairs Room*. Crowell, 1972.

Richter, Conrad. *The Light in the Forest*. Illustrated by Warren Chappell. Knopf, 1966.

Rinaldi, Ann. *A Ride into Morning*. Harcourt Brace, 1991.

Riskind, Mary. *Apple Is My Sign*. Houghton Mifflin, 1981.

Rostkowski, Margaret I. *After the Dancing Days*. Harper & Row, 1986.

Roth-Hano, Renée. *Touch Wood: A Girlhood in Occupied France*. Viking Puffin, 1989.

Ruby, Lois. *Steal Away Home*. Macmillan, 1994.

Salisbury, Graham. *Under the Blood-Red Sun*. Delacorte, 1994.

Sebestyen, Ouida. *Words by Heart*. Little, Brown, 1979.

Sewall, Marcia. *The People of the Breaking Day*. Atheneum, 1986.

———. *The Pilgrims of Plimoth*. Atheneum, 1986.

———. *Thunder from the Clear Sky*. Atheneum, 1995.

Siegal, Aranka. *Upon the Head of the Goat: A Childhood in Hungary, 1939–1944*. Farrar, Straus & Giroux, 1981.

Skurzynski, Gloria. *Goodbye Billy Radish*. Bradbury, 1992.

Speare, Elizabeth George. *The Bronze Bow*. Houghton Mifflin, 1961.

———. *Calico Captive*. Illustrated by W. T. Mars. Houghton Mifflin, 1957.

———. *The Sign of the Beaver*. Houghton Mifflin, 1983.

———. *The Witch of Blackbird Pond*. Houghton Mifflin, 1958.

Steele, William O. *The Buffalo Knife*. Illustrated by Paul Galdone. Harcourt Brace, 1952.

———. *Flaming Arrows*. Illustrated by Paul Galdone. Harcourt Brace, 1957.

———. *Winter Danger*. Illustrated by Paul Galdone. Harcourt Brace, 1954.

Stevens, Carla. *Trouble for Lucy*. Illustrated by Ronald Himler. Clarion, 1979.

Stolz, Mary. *Bartholomew Fair*. Greenwillow, 1990.

Sutcliff, Rosemary. *The Eagle of the Ninth*. Illustrated by C. W. Hodges. Walck, 1954.

———. *Flame-Colored Taffeta*. Farrar, Straus & Giroux, 1986.

———. *The Lantern Bearers*. Illustrated by Charles Keeping. Walck, 1959.

———. *The Shining Company*. Farrar, Straus & Giroux, 1990.

———. *The Silver Branch*. Illustrated by Charles Keeping. Walck, 1959.

———. *Sun Horse, Moon Horse*. Dutton, 1978.

———. *Warrior Scarlet*. Walck, 1958.

Taylor, Mildred. *Let the Circle Be Unbroken*. Dial, 1981.

———. *Mississippi Bridge*. Illustrated by Max Ginsburg. Dial, 1990.

———. *Roll of Thunder, Hear My Cry*. Illustrated by Jerry Pinkney. Dial, 1976.

———. *Song of the Trees*. Illustrated by Jerry Pinkney. Dial, 1975.

———. *The Well*. Dial, 1995.

Taylor, Theodore. *The Cay*. Doubleday, 1989 [1969].

Temple, Frances. *The Ramsey Scallop*. Orchard, 1994.

Tunis, Edwin. *Colonial Living*. Crowell, 1976.

Turner, Ann. *Dakota Dugout*. Illustrated by Ronald Himler. Macmillan, 1985.

———. *Grasshopper Summer*. Macmillan, 1989.

———. *Nettie's Trip South*. Illustrated by Ronald Himler. Macmillan, 1987.

———. *Time of the Bison*. Illustrated by Beth Peck. Macmillan, 1987.

Uchida, Yoshiko. *Journey to Topaz*. Illustrated by Donald Carrick. Scribner's, 1971.

Van Leeuwen, Jean. *Across the Wide Dark Sea*. Illustrated by Thomas B. Allen. Dial, 1995.

———. *Bound for Oregon*. Illustrated by James Watling. Dial, 1994.

Vander Els, Betty. *The Bombers' Moon*. Farrar, Straus & Giroux, 1985.

Vos, Ida. *Anna Is Still Here*. Translated by Terese Edelstein and Inez Smidt. Houghton Mifflin, 1994.

———. *Hide and Seek*. Translated by Terese Edelstein and Inez Smidt. Houghton Mifflin, 1991.

Watkins, Yoko Kawashima. *My Brother, My Sister, and I*. Bradbury, 1994.

———. *So Far from the Bamboo Grove*. Lothrop, Lee & Shepard, 1986.

Weaver, Lydia. *Close to Home: A Story of the Polio Epidemic*. Illustrated by Aileen Arrington. Viking, 1993.

Westall, Robert. *The Machine Gunners*. Greenwillow, 1976.

Wibberley, Leonard. *John Treegate's Musket*. Farrar, Straus & Giroux, 1959.

Wild, Margaret. *Let the Celebrations Begin!* Illustrated by Julie Vivas. Orchard, 1991.

Wilder, Laura Ingalls. *By the Shores of Silver Lake*. Illustrated by Garth Williams. Harper & Row, 1953 [1939].

———. *The First Four Years*. Illustrated by Garth Williams. Harper & Row, 1971.

———. *Little House in the Big Woods*. Illustrated by Garth Williams. Harper & Row, 1953 [1932].

———. *Little House on the Prairie*. Illustrated by Garth Williams. Harper & Row, 1953 [1935].

———. *Little Town on the Prairie*. Illustrated by Garth Williams. Harper & Row, 1953 [1932].

———. *On the Banks of Plum Creek*. Illustrated by Garth Williams. Harper & Row, 1953 [1937].

———. *These Happy Golden Years*. Illustrated by Garth Williams. Harper & Row, 1953 [1943].

Wisler, G. Clifton. *Red Cap*. Dutton, 1991.

Yep, Laurence. *Dragonwings*. Harper & Row, 1977.

———. *Dragon's Gate*. HarperCollins, 1993.

———. *Mountain Light*. Harper & Row, 1985.

———. *The Serpent's Children*. Harper & Row, 1984.

———. *The Star Fisher*. Morrow, 1991.

Yolen, Jane. *The Devil's Arithmetic*. Viking Penguin, 1990.

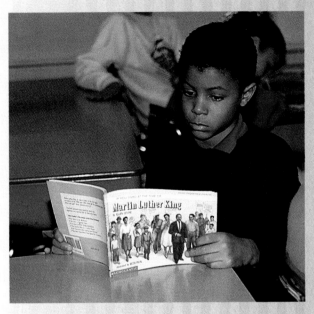

© James L. Shaffer

chapter eleven

Biography

Biography for Today's Child   552
Criteria for Juvenile Biography   554
Choice of Subject   554
Accuracy and Authenticity   554
Style   556
Characterization   556
Teaching Feature: Thinking Critically
   About Biographies   557
Theme   557
Guidelines: Evaluating Juvenile
   Biography   558
Types of Presentation and Coverage   559

Picture-Book Biographies   559
Simplified Biographies   562
Partial Biographies   563
Complete Biographies   564
Collective Biographies   567
Autobiographies and Memoirs   569
Resources for Teaching: Author
   Autobiographies   570
Learning Experiences   571
Related Readings   571
Children's Literature   571

Following a classroom study of biographies, a fourth-grade teacher asked her students to reflect on their experiences in their response journals. Nicholas, age 10 wrote:

Reading about the lives of other people could be very interesting. Each person has his unique life experiences. You can learn about when and where he was born, how he was raised, what kind of family did he come from. You can also learn about where he went to school and what kind of student he was when he went to school. Most of all, you can learn about his dreams and how he fulfilled his dreams. For example if I happened to be reading a book about Michael Jordan, I would be very interested to know how he trained himself to be a great basketball star. Also why did he all of a sudden switch his career as basketball player to become a baseball player. I would want to know who was his role model when he was young like me. How did he become interested in basketball games? What kind of advice would he give to young people who have the same kind of dream to become a basketball star?

Nicholas Lee, fourth grade
PS 124, Manhattan
Mary S. Gallivan, teacher

Elementary and middle school students are in the process of becoming themselves, and reading about real people can provide glimpses of the kinds of lives they might choose to live. For children like Nicholas, biographies can answer questions that are important to young readers and raise questions about how their futures might unfold.

Biography for Today's Child

In children's literature, biography often bridges the gap between historical fiction and informational books. A life story might read like fiction, but, like nonfiction, it will center on facts and events that can be documented. In the past, writers of biography for children have been allowed more freedom in the use of fictional techniques than those who write for adults. As a result, children's biographies over the years have shown a wide range of factual orientations, from strict authenticity to liberal fictionalization. The trend today, however, is clearly toward authenticity.

Authentic biography follows many of the same rules as serious scholarly works written for adults. A book of this type is a well-documented, carefully researched account of a person's life. Only statements that are known to have been made by the subject are included in the conversation. Jean Fritz was one of the first authors to demonstrate that biographies for children could be authentic as well as lively and readable. Her writing helped to set a new standard. Her books about famous figures of the American Revolution—including *And Then What Happened, Paul Revere?* and *Will You Sign Here, John Hancock?*—are based on detailed research. The same is true of her more recent, longer books, such as *You Want Women to Vote, Lizzie Stanton?* Natalie S. Bober's *Abigail Adams: Witness to a Revolution* and Russell Freedman's *Eleanor Roosevelt* are other excellent examples of authentic biography.

Fictionalized biography is grounded in thorough research, but the author dramatizes certain events and personalizes the subject, in contrast to the straight reporting of authentic biography. Fictionalized biography makes use of the narrative rather than the analytical approach. Children come to know the character of the subject as portrayed through actions, deeds, and conversations. In fictionalized biography the author may invent dialogue and even ascribe unspoken thoughts to the subject. These conversations might be based on actual facts taken from diaries, journals, or other period sources.

Mary Lyons used this technique in *Letters from a Slave Girl* (discussed in Chapter 10). Basing her story on Harriet Jacobs's autobiography and other documents about life and language at that time, Lyons constructed letters that Harriet might have written during her childhood. F. N. Monjo used a similar technique in *Letters to Horseface: Young Mozart's Travels in Italy*. The author drew on research about Mozart's 1769 tour to "reconstruct" what the young genius might have reported if he had written home to his sister Nannerl (nicknamed "Horseface"). The factual details are essentially true; their presentation in Mozart's voice is imagined.

Not everyone agrees where to the draw the line between fictionalized biography or memoirs and historical fiction. When Jean Fritz wrote about her childhood in China and her much-longed-for trip to the United States in *Homesick: My Own Story*, she found that her "memory came out in lumps" and finally chose not to worry about exact sequence. She telescoped events of all her childhood into a two-year span:

> but they are all, except in minor details, basically true. The people are real people; the places are dear to me. But most important, the form I have used has given me the freedom to recreate the emotions that I remember so vividly. Strictly speaking, I have to call this book *fiction*, but it does not feel like fiction to me. It is my story, told as truly as I can tell it. (foreword)

The library cataloging information in the front of the book designates it as fiction, but many readers will think of it as the autobiography of Jean Fritz. The inclusion of a section of family photographs from their days in China strengthens the book's claim to authenticity. Fritz's humor, her depth of feeling, and her vivid portrayal of the turmoil in China during the 1920s make *Homesick* worth reading, regardless of the label that is put on it. Older readers and adults may enjoy a sequel, *China Homecoming*, that is clearly nonfiction.

Publishers of biography for children have been quick to capitalize on trends in the social studies curriculum as well as shifts in children's interests. In the mid 1970s, many biographies about leaders in the American Revolution appeared in connection with the Bicentennial. Likewise, dozens of new books about Christopher Columbus came out in time for the quincentennial observation in 1992. As attention to multicultural education has grown, more stories about women, African Americans, and other underrepresented groups have also been written.

In the 1980s, new biographies of popular-culture celebrities and other contemporary figures outnumbered those of historical subjects as publishers recognized children's tremendous interest in sports and entertainment personalities. Although such books tend to be objective and almost journalistic in their approach, many are superficial in scholarship and poorly written. A great number of these and other biographies are published as parts of series, and the result is often life stories that are tailored to fit certain format specifications rather than explored in all their uniqueness.

Russell Freedman has received many awards for his well-written biographies. This photo from *Eleanor Roosevelt: A Life of Discovery* shows Eleanor with her younger brother.
Franklin D. Roosevelt Library

In spite of all these cautions, we should remember that children's biography, like historical fiction, offers more to choose from today than it did a decade ago. A rekindled interest in the lives of historical figures, the appearance of many autobiographies by children's authors, and the growing use of photographs and picture-book formats have all had significant impact. It is true that many mediocre biographies are still being published, but the number of high-quality books has grown. Biographies have received several prestigious awards in recent years. Russell Freedman won the Newbery Medal in 1988 for *Lincoln: A Photobiography* and Newbery Honor designations for *The Wright Brothers: How They Invented the Airplane* in 1992 and *Eleanor Roosevelt: A Life of Discovery* in 1993; Jean Fritz's *The Great Little Madison* was the first-ever winner of the Orbis Pictus Award for nonfiction; and *Bill Peet: An Autobiography* was named a Caldecott Honor Book in 1990. Not all good books win awards, of course. Teachers and librarians still need to be able to decide for themselves which biographies are distinctive and deserving of attention.

Criteria for Juvenile Biography

The criteria for evaluating biographies for boys and girls differ somewhat from those established for juvenile fiction. They also diverge from generally accepted patterns for adult biography. Children read biography as they read fiction—for the story, or *plot*. Children demand a fast-moving narrative. In biography, events and actions become even more exciting because "they really happened." Thus, children like biography written as a story with continuity; they do not want just a collection of facts and dates. An encyclopedia gives them facts in a well-organized fashion. Biography, to do more than this, must help them to *know* the person as a living human being.

Choice of Subject

Formerly, most biographies for children were about familiar figures of the past in the United States, particularly those whose lives offered the readiest action material, such as Daniel Boone or Abraham Lincoln. Now the range of subjects is much broader, including artists and intellectuals as well as soldiers and presidents, plus world figures whose presence suggests the widened concerns of our pluralistic society. Biographies of contemporary figures in the worlds of sports and entertainment continue to reflect the influence of the mass media.

For many years biography for children was limited to subjects whose lives were considered worthy of emulation. This is no longer true. There are books about people remembered for their misdeeds, like *Traitor: The Case of Benedict Arnold* by Jean Fritz. Controversial persons like Fidel Castro, Ho Chi Minh, and Lenin have all been subjects of juvenile biographies. As long as the biographies are objective and recognize the various points of view concerning the subjects, these books can serve a useful purpose in presenting a worldview to boys and girls.

Biographies of less well-known figures or subjects whose accomplishments are highly specialized also have value for children. Diane Stanley's *The True Adventures of Daniel Hall* is the story of a young New England boy who sailed aboard a whaling ship in 1856. Abused by a cruel captain, he escaped when the boat was off the coast of Siberia. With the help of some local villagers, he managed to survive the awful Siberian winter until he was rescued the following June. Marshall Taylor, a champion cyclist at the turn of the century when bicycle racing was a popular sport, was the first black person to ride in integrated races. Mary Scioscia's *Bicycle Rider*

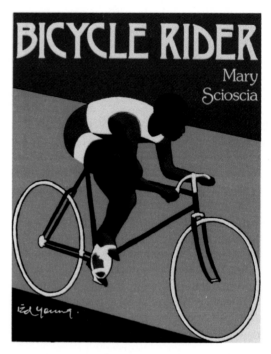

In *Bicycle Rider,* Mary Scioscia tells the little-known story of African American cyclist Marshall Taylor.
Cover of *Bicycle Rider* by Mary Scioscia, illustrated by Ed Young. Copyright © 1983. Used by permission of HarperCollins Publishers, New York, NY.

tells the story of his first victory, focusing on family values and pride of accomplishment. *El Chino* by Allen Say introduces readers to Bong Way "Billy" Wong, a Chinese American who longed to be a great athlete and found his niche as a bullfighter.

A sense of discovery is added to the satisfaction of a good story where children read about intriguing but little-known lives. Children have a right to read biographies about a wide range of subjects—famous persons, great human beings who were not famous, and even antiheroes.

Accuracy and Authenticity

Accuracy is the hallmark of good biographical writing, whether it is for adults or for children. More and more writers of juvenile biography are acknowledging primary sources for their materials in either an introductory note or an appended bibliography. Conscientious authors of well-written children's biographies frequently travel to the locale of the setting in order to get a "feeling" for a place. They visit museums to study actual objects that were used by their subjects; they spend hours poring over original letters and documents. Much of this research might not be used in the actual biography, but its effect will be evident in the author's true insight into the character of the subject and in the accuracy of the historical detail.

The same kind of careful research should be reflected in the accuracy of the illustrations that convey the time, place, and setting. The dress of the period, the interiors of the houses, the very utensils that are used must be authentic representations. Many books, such as Rhoda Blumberg's *The Remarkable Adventures of Captain Cook* and Albert Marrin's *The Sea King: Sir Francis Drake and His Times*, make use of reproductions of maps, letters, and artwork of the period to authenticate the subject matter.

But most difficult of all, perhaps, is the actual portrayal of the subject. There are many drawings and paintings of most historical figures, but an accurate likeness is problematical, particularly for subjects who lived before the advent of photography. In their book *Christopher Columbus: The Great Adventure and How We Know About It*, Delno and Jean West point out:

> There are hundreds of paintings, engravings, woodcuts, and statues of Christopher Columbus, but they were all made after he died by people who never saw him. (p. 13)

Several of these competing portraits are reproduced in their book. They also quote Columbus's son, Ferdinand, who described his father's long face, light eyes, big nose, and red hair, so that readers have a basis for reacting to the illustrations.

Photographs provide authentic illustrations for many biographical accounts of recent subjects, such as Russell Freedman's highly acclaimed photobiographies, *Jesse Jackson: A Biography* by Patricia McKissack, and Ruud van der Rol and Rian Verhoeven's *Anne Frank Beyond the Diary*. Photographs play a special role in *Prairie Visions: The Life and Times of Solomon Butcher* by Pam Conrad. Butcher was a pioneer photographer on the Nebraska prairie; his pictures, reproduced in generous numbers to illustrate the book, described his work and help to define his character. At the same time they provide authentic details about the time in which he lived. The author shows us that not even photographs are completely trustworthy, however, by describing how Butcher retouched some of his photographs with invented details like a swarm of locusts in a cornfield or a turkey perched on the roof of a soddy.

An authentic biography must be true in every detail. A fictionalized biography must also be true to the factual record, and any invented dialogue or background detail must be plausible and true to the times. Yet the

Pam Conrad's inclusion of photographs and other primary source materials in *Prairie Visions: The Life and Times of Solomon Butcher* helps bring the past alive for young readers. Cover of *The Life and Times of Solomon Butcher* by Pam Conrad, illustrated by David Saylor. Copyright © 1991. Used by permission of HarperCollins Publishers, New York, NY.

truth of what is included in a biography does not quite answer the entire question of its accuracy. Sometimes what is left out is just as important as what goes in.

Formerly, authors of biographies for children avoided writing about certain aspects of the lives of their subjects. Serious criticism has been leveled at biographies of Washington and Jefferson that did not include the fact that they owned many slaves. More-recent biographies, even those for younger children, do include this information. In the note appended to the end of the biography of Jefferson titled *Grand Papa and Ellen Aroon*, F. N. Monjo points out that Jefferson's will did provide for freeing his personal slaves, but because all of his property (including slaves) was mortgaged and he was in debt, most of his slaves were not freed. The book also credits Jefferson with prohibiting slavery in the Northwest Territory and indicates his distress at the fact that his condemnation of slavery was struck from the original draft of the Declaration of Independence.

Certain biographers when writing for younger children might present only a portion of a person's life. In planning their picture book *Abraham Lincoln*, the D'Aulaires deliberately omitted his assassination and closed the book with the end of the Civil War. The authors' purpose was to present the greatness of the man as he lived, for too frequently, they believed, children remember only the manner of Lincoln's death. There is a danger, however, that omissions might over-simplify and thereby distort the truth about a person's life. The critic Jo Carr has argued that it is better not to offer biography to young children at all than to present them with unbalanced portraits distorted by flagrant omissions.[1]

For many years it was thought that children were interested only in reading about the childhoods of great men and women and not about the complexities of their adult activities. For this reason many earlier biographies focused primarily on childhood pranks and legends that suggested future accomplishments, but neglected or rushed through the real achievements of later life. The current emphasis on authentic biography has reversed this trend, since it is much more difficult to find primary source material about a subject's childhood than about his or her adult life. Increasingly, the best authors respect children's right to read honest, objective biographies that tell more of the truth and document their writing with source notes or a bibliography. The Teaching Feature "Thinking Critically About Biographies" shows how one teacher asked his students to compare biographies of the same subjects in order to help them think more critically about authors' objectivity and accuracy.

Style

The author's language is especially important to biography because it bears the burden of making the subject seem alive and sound real. Documented quotes should be woven smoothly into the narrative. When dialogue is invented, it should have the natural rhythms of speech, regardless of the period it represents, because stilted writing makes characters seem wooden.

In today's authentic biography, the author's way with words makes all the difference between a dull and a lively book. The opening paragraph of Jean Fritz's *Harriet Beecher Stowe and the Beecher Preachers* shows how the writer can choose and present detail in a way that engages the reader:

Harriet Beecher had always understood that, along with her sisters, she was second best in her family. On June 14, 1811, when she'd been born, her father had grumbled to a neighbor, "Wisht it had been a boy!" Of course her father was disappointed. He was Lyman Beecher, a minister in Litchfield, Connecticut, and he was collecting boys. (p. 7)

The narrator's tone always pervades the presentation, but a dispassionate point of view usually is used for authentic biography. Whatever the form or viewpoint, the

background materials should be integrated into the narrative with smoothness and proportion. The judicious use of quotes from letters or journals may support the authenticity of biography, but it should not detract from the absorbing account of the life of the subject. Children enjoy a style that is clear and vigorous. The research must be there, but it should be a natural part of the presentation. Russell Freedman's *Eleanor Roosevelt* and Jean Fritz's *Harriet Beecher Stowe and the Beecher Preachers* provide masterful demonstrations of this kind of clarity.

The choice of narrator, or point of view, is also an important consideration in the style of a biography. Rather than write about the childhood of a famous person, some authors choose to tell the story from the point of view of a child who was close to the adult character. F. N. Monjo was particularly successful with this approach when writing about Franklin's visit to France with his grandsons in *Poor Richard in France* and in seeing Jefferson through the eyes of his granddaughter in *Grand Papa and Ellen Aroon*. Such a point of view allows the reader to see greatness through the loving eyes of a grandchild. These are joyful, childlike, fictionalized biographies that present authentic facts from a perspective that will capture the imaginations of 7- to 9-year olds.

Characterization

The characterization of the subject of a biography must be true to life, neither adulatory nor demeaning in tone. The reader should have the opportunity to know the person as a real human being with both shortcomings and virtues. To emphasize the worthiness of their subjects, juvenile biographers sometimes portray them as too good to be true.

Jean Fritz is one author who manages to create vivid portraits of great figures without according them pseudo-sainthood. She has presented Paul Revere as a busy and sometimes forgetful human being in her humorous yet authentic picture-book biography *And Then What Happened, Paul Revere?* He didn't always meet his deadlines, once producing a hymnbook some eighteen months after he had promised it! A dreamer, he even left one page in his "Day Book" simply for doodling. The author does not debunk her character; she simply makes him come alive by admitting his foibles, as well as describing his accomplishments.

Comparing two or more biographies of the same subject is one way of understanding the importance of characterization. Doris Faber's *Eleanor Roosevelt, First Lady of the World* and Maryann Weidt's *Stateswoman to the World: A Story About Eleanor Roosevelt* are similar in length and coverage. Both are generally suitable for grades 3 to 5. While both books emphasize the young Eleanor's growing desire for independence, they provide

---

[1]Jo Carr, "What Do We Do About Bad Biographies?" in *Beyond Fact: Nonfiction for Children and Young People* (Chicago: American Library Association, 1982), pp. 119–129.

Teaching Feature   Thinking Critically About Biographies

At Hilltonia Middle School in Columbus, Ohio, Richard Roth put his students in groups of four to consider which of two biographies was the better book. Some groups read about Abraham Lincoln, using *Lincoln: A Photobiography* by Russell Freedman and *True Stories About Abraham Lincoln* by Ruth Belov Gross. Other groups read *Bully for You, Teddy Roosevelt!* by Jean Fritz and a second biography of Roosevelt. Still others read two selections about Leonardo da Vinci.

First, students read the books individually and noted their reactions to the cover, chapter titles, pictures, and content (facts, bias, writing style), and rated its usefulness. Groups needed only two copies of each book, since each student could read one title and then trade with a partner. Sharing copies also encouraged students to take good notes, including page numbers for reference.

When the students had read both books, the teacher gave each student a blank chart with space for rating each book on the same items, with the following directions: "Rate the categories for each book from 1 to 10: 10 is excellent, 5, average, and 1, poor. As a group, decide what score each book deserves for each category. Then total the scores and determine which book the group thought best overall." The final step was to work as a group to compose a recommendation of their top book for other students to read.

Although not all the groups chose the book that the teacher (or critics) would have chosen, the students gained valuable experience in exercising their own judgment. The teacher planned this study because he wanted all his students to have the opportunity to take stock of their own responses and share them with classmates. He also knew that his students would participate more fully in discussion if they first had a chance to formulate their ideas and write them down. In retrospect, he reported that this process really did encourage critical thinking. There were meaningful group discussions with healthy disagreements about which book was superior. Moreover, students were able to rethink their own first impressions and make comparisons in the interest of fairness and accuracy. In the class discussion that followed the completion of small-group work, the teacher gave the students still more to think about by contributing his own perspectives on the books they had read.

Like in most middle schools, this teacher has many students and a limited time with them each day. One of the advantages of this biography study was that it gave him new insight into their responses and the factors that contribute to their reading interests. It also confirmed his thinking that it is important for students to work through their own responses as they develop ways to appreciate literature.

Richard Roth
Hilltonia Middle School
Columbus City Schools, Ohio

---

somewhat different views of the childhood experiences that helped shape her determination and sense of duty.

Jean Fritz's characterization of the famed explorer in *Where Do You Think You're Going, Christopher Columbus?* emphasizes both his courage and his huge pride. The author's sense of irony and her wry humor guard against overdramatizing Columbus's greatness. Alongside the reports of his impressive discoveries are the reminders that he was consistently mistaken about them and fierce in protecting his own personal interests:

Indeed, Colba [Cuba] *had* to be China, just as this *had* to be the Indies. Columbus had been born to find the Indies. His whole life couldn't be a mistake: God couldn't be wrong. But in case anyone disagreed with him, Christopher Columbus had his entire crew sign an oath, swearing that Colba was part of a continent. The crew was told that if any of them ever denied this, he would have his tongue cut out. (p. 54)

Asking students to describe what kind of person Columbus seems to be at various points during the reading of this book can help them appreciate the complexities of his character.

Biography must not degenerate into mere eulogy; reexamining should not become debunking. The background of subjects' lives, their conversations, their thoughts, and their actions, should be presented as faithfully to the facts as possible. The subject should also be seen in relation to her or his times, for no person can be "read" in isolation.

Theme

Underlying the characterization in all biography—whether it be authentic, fictionalized, or biographical fiction—is the author's interpretation of the subject. No matter how impartial an author might be, a life story cannot be written without some interpretation. An author's selection of facts can limit the dimensions of the

Guidelines:
Evaluating Juvenile Biography

• Choice of subject
Does the subject's life offer interest and meaning for today's child?
Will knowing this historical or contemporary figure help children understand the past or the present?
Can the subject's experiences widen children's views on the possibilities for their own lives?

• Accuracy and Authenticity
Do the text and illustrations reflect careful research and consistency in presentation?
Does the author provide notes about original source material, a bibliography, or other evidence of documentation?
Are there discrepancies of fact in comparison with other books?
Are there significant omissions that result in a distorted picture of the subject's life?

• Style
Are quotations or dialogue used in a way that brings the subject to life?
For a fictionalized biography, does the choice of narrator's point of view add to the story?
Is the author's style clear and readable, with background material included naturally?

• Characterization
Is the subject presented as a believable, multidimensional character, with both strengths and weaknesses?
Does the author avoid both eulogizing and debunking?

• Theme
Does the author's interpretation of the subject represent a fair and balanced approach?
Does the author avoid oversimplifying or manipulating the facts to fit the chosen theme?

portraiture or highlight certain features. In this context every author walks a thin line between theme and bias. Time usually lends perspective and objectivity, but contemporary biography might tend more toward bias. Teachers and librarians need to help children realize that all biographies have a point of view determined by their authors. Again, a comparison of several biographies of the same person will help children discover this fact.

Frequently in juvenile biography the theme will be identified in the title, as in *Martin Luther King: The Peaceful Warrior* by Ed Clayton or *I'm Nobody! Who Are You? The Story of Emily Dickinson* by Edna Barth. Both of these titles contain double meanings and point up the theme of the books. The title of the Dickinson biography reflects the retiring attitude of the New England poet who in later life became a recluse. It is also, however, the first line of one of Dickinson's well-known poems.

In picture-book biographies, illustrations as well as the story title reveal the theme. Author/illustrator Peter Sis offers an artist's interpretation of Christopher Columbus in *Follow the Dream: The Story of Christopher Columbus*. Sis grew up in Czechoslovakia, a country surrounded by a political "wall" known as the Iron Curtain. He relates his background to Columbus's by emphasizing the many forces that walled Columbus in. He

describes the ancient maps that showed the known world surrounded by a high wall. One such map is drawn on the book's endpapers; the title page shows a small boy peering out through a small doorway in the wall to the unknown. The wall motif appears consistently throughout the book, always countered by an opening or archway through which Columbus can follow his dream. Although this book ends with the arrival of Columbus in 1492 and says nothing about his character as a leader or his later cruelty to the native people, the theme of breaking down the wall surrounding the old world is a fresh insight. A close examination of the last picture and its border, however, suggests that Sis questions whether civilization was much of a "gift" to the New World.

There is a danger in oversimplifying and forcing all facts to fit a single mold. An author must not re-create and interpret a life history in terms of one fixed picture, particularly in a biography that covers the full scope of a subject's life. The most common people have several facets to their personalities; the great are likely to be multidimensional. The perceptive biographer concentrates on those items from a full life that helped to mold and form that personality. It is this selection and focus that create the theme of the biography. The Guidelines "Evaluating Juvenile Biography" summarizes the criteria we have discussed in this section.

Types of Presentation and Coverage

Writers of adult biography are by definition bound to try to re-create the subject's life as fully as possible, with complete detail and careful documentation. Writers of children's biography, however, may use one of several approaches. The resulting types of biography need individual consideration, for each offers to children a different perspective and a different appeal. Keep in mind, however, that a single book might fit into more than one of the following categories.

Picture-Book Biographies

A biography cast in a picture-book form might span the subject's lifetime or a part of it; it might be directed to a very young audience or to a somewhat older one; it may be authentic or fictionalized. Whatever the case, it remains for the pictures to carry a substantial part of the interpretation, as Leonard Marcus points out:

🐟 Illustrations, then, contribute more to a picture book biography than occasional picture-equivalents of the author's words. They traffic to some degree in unnameable objects, states and feelings. . . . Along with what it tells us about the values, temperament and concerns of a biography's central character, fine illustration also puts us in contact with an individuality—and a form of praise—that is esthetic.[2]

This sense of heightened perception comes with the illustrations by Alice and Martin Provensen for their Caldecott Medal winner *The Glorious Flight: Across the Channel with Louis Blériot, July 25, 1909*. Papa Blériot carries himself with intrepid grace in his unsuccessful attempts to fly, and the pictures that show him above the channel use contrast and perspective to convey the elation and danger of flight. Many historical and background details appear in the illustrations without being mentioned in the text, inviting speculation, inferences, and discussion. Even the hardcover front of this book contains new picture material that will contribute to children's feeling for the time and place.

Ingri d'Aulaire and Edgar Parin d'Aulaire were among the first to create beautifully illustrated picture-book

Michael Dooling's illustrations for James Giblin's *Thomas Jefferson: A Picture Book Biography* show this American hero in a warm and sympathetic light.

Illustration by Mike Dooling from *Thomas Jefferson* by James Cross Giblin. Illustrations copyright © 1994 by Mike Dooling. Reprinted by permission of Scholastic Inc.

biographies for children. As new citizens of this country, they were fascinated with American heroes, and the biographies they wrote include *George Washington, Abraham Lincoln, Pocahontas, Benjamin Franklin,* and *Columbus*. Their charming but idealized pictures sometimes made their subjects seem larger than life.

James Cross Giblin has taken similar American heroes as a focus for picture-book biographies. In *Thomas Jefferson* and *George Washington*, he approaches his subjects with the same meticulous research he applies to his many informational books (see Chapter 12). He writes of Jefferson's ambivalence about slavery,

🐟 Thomas also favored the end of the slave trade. Hadn't he written that 'all men are created equal'? And didn't he believe that slavery was wrong? Yes, but he also knew that estates like his beloved Monticello could not be run without slave labor. Thomas went back and forth, back and forth about slavery. What could be done about it? He could not make up his mind. (p. 20)

---

[2]Leonard S. Marcus, "Life Drawings: Some Notes on Children's Picture Book Biographies," *The Lion and the Unicorn* 4 (summer 1980): 17.

Giblin's portraits of Jefferson and Washington are brief enough to serve as excellent introductions for younger children and detailed enough that readers of all ages come away with a profound admiration for these complex and exceptional human beings. In both books, Michael Dooling's oil paintings recreate the vitality of the subject and the details of a way of life long past.

In Jean Fritz's *What's the Big Idea, Ben Franklin?* the droll pictures by Margot Tomes emphasize a particular side of Franklin's character—his ingenuity. Trina Schart Hyman's illustration of Samuel Adams thumbing his nose at the British flag helps set the tone for Fritz's biography *Why Don't You Get a Horse, Sam Adams?* The same illustrator and author highlight their subject's vanity and penchant for flourishes in *Will You Sign Here, John Hancock?* Tomie de Paola's pictures for *Can't You Make Them Behave, King George?* emphasize Fritz's humor as she helps readers think of the unpopular English monarch in a new way.

Other biographies have established the heroic struggles of many African Americans. David Adler, who has provided many fine biographies for younger readers, tells of the life of an important figure in the fight against slavery and for human rights in *A Picture Book of Sojourner Truth*. In *Dear Benjamin Banneker* Andrea Davis Pinkney and Brian Pinkney have collaborated to tell the story of an African American scientist and inventor who was an important contributor to the development of the United States in its earliest beginnings. Malcah Zeldis's vibrant folk art illustrations for Rosemary L. Bray's *Martin Luther King* are the perfect accompaniment for this story about a man of the people, while Floyd Cooper's realistic oil paintings bring the same sense of flowing warmth to *Coming Home: From the Life of Langston Hughes* that this writer's poems brought to his listeners.

The mood or tone of a biography can be quickly established by its pictures. Rocco Baviera's richly textured oil paintings provide a dark and brooding underpinning to Joseph Bruchac's *A Boy Called Slow: The True Story of Sitting Bull*. Brian Pinkney's scratchboard pictures add a sense of vigorous movement to Andrea Davis Pinkney's biography *Alvin Ailey*. Max Ginsburg's paintings capture the high drama of Robert D. San Souci's *Kate Shelley: Bound for Legend*. Kate was a 15-year-old growing up on a farm in Iowa in 1881 when a terrible storm washed away the trestle bridge over Honey Creek. Realizing that the Midnight Express with hundreds of passengers was due, she set off in the storm to give the warning. Ginsburg's vivid paintings convey a sense of mounting tension as the storm builds. The wild fury of the storm and Kate's terrifying struggle to cross the Des Moines River Bridge to reach help is brought to life, and the illustrations underscore the danger and magnify Kate's courage in facing the elements.

Malcah Zeldis captures the essence of African American culture and the energy of the civil rights movement in his illustrations for Rosemary Bray's *Martin Luther King*.
Illustration from *Martin Luther King* by Rosemary Bray, illustrated by Malcah Zeldis. By permission of Greenwillow Books, a division of William Morrow & Company, Inc.

Joe Lasker's pictures illustrate the military feats of a classic hero in *The Great Alexander the Great*. Because these were real battles that became legendary, it seems appropriate that the art depicts both intense human drama and the hovering presence of the mythical gods of Greece. Another book with lively pictures is *The Heroine of the Titanic: A Tale Both True and Otherwise of the Life of Molly Brown* by Joan Blos. Tennessee Dixon's illustrations have a slapdash quality and display a cheerful clutter of material possessions that help characterize this controversial turn-of-the-century celebrity. Vivid language and a mixture of narrative and rhyme add appeal to this entertaining biography.

Diane Stanley and Peter Vennema, her husband, have collaborated in writing several complete biographies in picture-book format with exquisitely detailed paintings by Diane Stanley. *Cleopatra* is an example of their fine work. It tells the story of Cleopatra's life from the age of 18 until her death, and shows a woman who was not the siren of movie legend but a bright and intellectually vigorous leader. She had great dreams for her people and hoped to see these realized through alliances with Julius Caesar and Mark Anthony. The mosaic portrait of Cleopatra on the cover suggests her

Max Ginsburg's illustration foretells the tense drama that will unfold in Robert D. San Souci's *Kate Shelley: Bound for Legend*, a picture-book biography of a young American heroine.
From *Kate Shelley: Bound for Legend* by Robert D. San Souci; paintings by Max Ginsburg. Copyright © 1995 by Max Ginsburg. Used by permission of Dial Books for Young Readers, a division of Penguin Books, USA Inc.

Greek ancestry, and motifs of Greek art are found throughout the book. No book as brief as this can do full justice to a complex subject, but the authors do succeed in portraying Cleopatra's strengths as a leader and in providing an intriguing invitation to further study.

These same authors collaborated in writing *Shaka: King of the Zulus*; *Good Queen Bess: The Story of Elizabeth I of England*; *Charles Dickens: The Man Who Had Great Expectations*; and *Bard of Avon: The Story of William Shakespeare*. Diane Stanley both wrote and illustrated *Peter the Great*. Fay Stanley, Diane Stanley's mother, wrote *The Last Princess: The Story of Princess Ka'iulani of Hawai'i*. Clear, almost primitive paintings by Diane Stanley help to tell the poignant story of the betrayal of Hawaii by Americans and the sad death of Hawaii's last princess at age 23.

Several picture-book biographies have been written about Mozart. In Julie Downing's *Mozart Tonight*, the composer rides with his wife in a rented carriage to the opening of his opera *Don Giovanni*. As he reviews his life with his much-loved Constanza, he confides his hopes that this opera will be a huge success. The illustrations capture the drama of this particular night,

conveying the artist's own enthusiasm and love for Mozart's music. In a long note at the end, she tells the reader of the research she did and that the detail and dialogue in the scenes are based on letters written by and about the Mozart family. Catherine Brighton's picture biography *Mozart: Scenes from the Childhood of the Great Composer* is told by Nannerl, his talented sister. The two children toured Europe together, giving many concerts, until Nannerl turned 16 and became a teacher of pianoforte. Her brother, however, was already composing and continued to tour with his father. Lisl Weil's *Wolferl: The First Six Years in the Life of Wolfgang Amadeus Mozart, 1756–1762* takes its title from the nickname that Nannerl gave to her little brother. These last two books are partial biographies that do not attempt to go beyond the childhood of this amazing musical genius.

In *The King's Day: Louis XIV of France*, Aliki presents only one day in the life of Louis XIV. Yet a single day in the life of the splendid Sun King reveals much about the man. Louis loved ceremony, and his entire day was planned, from the special getting-up ritual called the *Lever* (which lasted for two hours) to the going-to-bed ceremony called the *Coucher*. Sometimes the public was allowed to watch the king as he dined alone on a menu that might include "four soups, a stuffed pheasant, a partridge, a duck, some mutton, sliced ham, three salads, boiled eggs, a dish of pastry, fruit, and compotes." Aliki always includes details that intrigue children, but in so doing provides insight into the way her subjects lived.

The last several years have seen an increased interest in biographies of artists. Jeanette Winter's paintings in Jonah Winter's *Diego* bring rich color and meaning to this brief book about the life of the famous Mexican artist Diego Rivera. The small pictures construct scenes from his early years, full of a magical sense of celebrations and play, as well as times of turmoil that were reflected in the huge murals Rivera painted as an adult.

Robyn Montana Turner has published well-written biographies of artists, including *Rosa Bonheur*, *Mary Cassatt*, *Frida Kahlo*, *Dorothea Lange*, and *Georgia O'Keefe*. Illustrated with photographs and many reproductions of each artist's work, these books offer insights into the artist's approach to her work as well as details about her life. Mary Lyons has developed a fine series of books about African American artists, including painters Bill Traylor and Horace Pippin, quilt maker Harriet Powers, and woodworker and carpenter Tom Day. Through words and pictures Lyons gives readers glimpses of social history, fascinating details about the lives of these fine artists, and information about the links each of them had to their African heritage.

Several series for older children focus on a subject's work and philosophy rather than her or his life. In books like Barbara Braun's *A Weekend with Diego Rivera* and Rosabianca Skira-Venturi's *A Weekend with Van Gogh,* the Weekend with the Artist series (Rizzoli) has artists speak directly to readers as if they were spending several days on a visit to their homes. Ernest Raboff's Art for Children series presents commentary and full-color reproductions of the work of great artists, along with brief biographical sketches. Paul Klee, Marc Chagall, and Pablo Picasso are among the subjects.

Milton Meltzer reminds us that biography is more than the personal history of one person:

> If biography is well done, it is also social history. [As a biographer] I must tell the story of my subject's time and of the people who lived through that time.[3]

This approach usually calls for a complete biography of the subject. In the case of picture-book biographies, it suggests the sharing of several titles with different points of view. Together, they may provide the range of information that sets a subject in context. David Adler's *A Picture Book of Christopher Columbus* portrays a beneficent leader passing out trinkets on the beach at San Salvador and states that he had "found" the New World. Vicki Liestman's *Columbus Day* tries to present a more balanced picture of Columbus's accomplishments. In her note at the beginning of the book, she mentions the A.D. 1000 landing of Leif Eriksson on the coast of North America. She also includes the fact that Columbus forcibly loaded some five hundred natives onto ships bound for Spain. To prevent children from getting the impression that Columbus was the only excellent navigator of his time, share Leonard Everett Fisher's distinguished picture-book biography *Prince Henry, the Navigator.* In this story, the author shows how Prince Henry's school of navigation prepared the way for Columbus, for Bartholomeu Dias's trip around Cape Hope, and for Vasco da Gama's famous trip to India via the Cape. Henry himself never sailed on his ships, but his school designed the faster caravels and a more accurate compass, improvements that significantly affected all later explorers. Accomplishments like those of Christopher Columbus can be understood only when viewed in the context of their time.

Simplified Biographies

Not all children who have an interest in biographical information are in full command of the skills of reading. Some of these children are beginning readers; some

read independently but are not ready for a long or complex text; some are older children with specialized interests but low skill levels. Various kinds of simplified biographies, usually short and with many illustrations, have been published in response to the needs of these children.

Many picture-book biographies, of course, are written in simple language that many primary-grade readers can handle on their own. David Adler's *A Picture Book of Thomas Jefferson* and *A Picture Book of Benjamin Franklin* provide straightforward accounts of highlights from the lives of these two founding fathers. Companion books are available about George Washington, Abraham Lincoln, and John F. Kennedy as well as other well-known figures, such as Jackie Robinson and Rosa Parks. The advantage of these books is their readability and the support provided by their illustrations. The disadvantage is that, to increase readability, the author had to leave out many of the complexities of character and accomplishment that make these subjects memorable.

Aliki also writes and illustrates easy-vocabulary picture biographies. In *The Story of Johnny Appleseed*, she has captured the humor and simplicity of the legendary pioneer. Similar in simplicity is *A Weed Is a Flower: The Life of George Washington Carver.* Again, Aliki has made meaningful for the youngest reader the inspiring story of a man who was born a slave but lived to become one of the greatest research scientists in the United States. Another picture biography by the same author is *The Many Lives of Benjamin Franklin.*

There are a number of biographies for newly independent readers that are not quite picture books but do have many illustrations as well as limited vocabularies. One of the disadvantages of this kind of writing, however, is that it frequently sounds stilted. Often the sentences are set up line by line for ease of reading, rather than in paragraph form. Unfortunately, this often creates a choppy effect.

Few writers can produce a book that is both easy to read and admirable for its style. F. N. Monjo did it in his I Can Read History book *The One Bad Thing About Father.* "Father" is Theodore Roosevelt, and the one bad thing about him, in his son Quentin's eyes, is that he is President of the United States and thus the whole family—including irrepressible sister Alice—must live in the White House.

> Some man once asked Father why
> he didn't do something about Alice.
> Father said, "I can do one of two things.
> I can be President of the United States.
> Or I can control Alice.
> I cannot possibly do both." (p. 38)

[3]Milton Meltzer, "Selective Forgetfulness: Christopher Columbus Reconsidered," *New Advocate* 5 (winter 1992): 1.

Many simple biographies are not just for beginning readers but are directed toward an 8- or 9-year-old audience. One account that is simply told but difficult to put down is Ann McGovern's *The Secret Soldier: The Story of Deborah Sampson.* Dressed as a man, Deborah Sampson fought in the American Revolution, managing to escape detection for more than a year. Newly proficient readers will appreciate the detail about Deborah's childhood as well as the format that breaks the text into manageable parts.

Several books that are directed at 7- to 10-year-olds emphasize contemporary figures and those from minority populations. These include *Cesar Chavez* by Ruth Franchere, *Mary McLeod Bethune* by Eloise Greenfield, and *Malcolm X* by Arnold Adoff. In *Rosa Parks,* Eloise Greenfield tells the story of the African American woman whose refusal to move to the back of a bus in Montgomery, Alabama, triggered events that grew into the civil rights movement. These books are characterized by brief text enhanced by many pictures.

A series that aims at the 7- to 10-year-old audience is the Women of Our Time series from Viking. These biographies are complete in that they cover the subject's life span (up to the time of writing, for those subjects still living). Written by many different authors, they include some fine examples of lively language and thoughtful characterization. However, the books are all about the same length (fifty to sixty pages) with short chapters and several black-and-white drawings. These constraints prevent the authors from examining any subject in great depth or detail, so the format works to simplify the story. *Sandra Day O'Connor: Justice for All* by Beverly Gherman, *Margaret Mead: The World Was Her Family* by Susan Saunders, and *Astrid Lindgren: Storyteller to the World* by Johanna Hurwitz are just a few of the many titles in this series.

Some simplified biographies fall into the high-interest/low-reading-level category, where the most popular subjects seem to be from the sports and entertainment worlds. The text in these books might be very brief, and illustrations or photographs might be used very liberally. In short, the books are designed to catch and keep the eye of the reluctant or less-able older reader. Unfortunately the writing in some of these books is heavily influenced by the tendency to "hype" a subject. Even though children have a great appetite for personal close-ups of celebrities, it is difficult to find books of this type that are written with perspective and produced with care.

Partial Biographies

One of the liberties allowed writers of biographies for juveniles is the freedom to write about only part of the subject's life. Authors are able to focus, if they wish, on

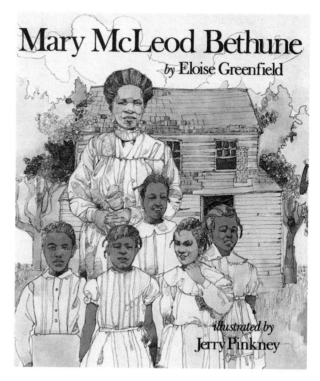

Younger readers will enjoy simplified biographies such as Eloise Greenfield's *Mary McLeod Bethune* with illustrations by Jerry Pinkney.

Illustration copyright © 1977 by Jerry Pinkney. Used by permission of HarperCollins Publishers, New York, NY.

a time of high drama and let the demands of constructing a good story help set the time frame for the book. William Miller has chosen the picture-book format to recount critical moments in the lives of two African Americans. In *Frederick Douglass, The Last Days of Slavery* Miller tells of Douglass's childhood experiences that led to his rebellion against slavery. Miller's *Zora Hurston and the Chinaberry Tree* highlights Zora's important relationship with her mother and her fascination with the folklore and songs of her African American heritage. By highlighting these events, Miller shows how these experiences became influential in the life's work of Douglass and Hurston.

David Kherdian deals with only a portion of the life of Veron Dumehjian, his mother, in *The Road from Home: The Story of an Armenian Girl.* What is central to the story is her family's suffering in the massacre and dispersal of Armenians by the Turks. If those events had been related as only a small part of her life experiences, their impact and historical significance might have been less perceptible. Kherdian chose to assume his mother's first-person point of view, which adds passion and immediacy to this fictionalized biography.

Some partial biographies do furnish information about the subject's entire life but focus on a few incidents that are particularly memorable. Virginia Hamilton has written a complex story in *Anthony Burns: The Defeat and Triumph of a Fugitive Slave.* By creating a fictional narrative about Burns's early life from documents about his later life, she interweaves historical fiction with true biography. Born a slave in Virginia, Anthony Burns was 20 when he escaped to Boston. For a few short months he lived as a free man, until his former owner came to Boston and invoked the Fugitive Slave Act, demanding him back. Thousands of abolitionists rioted and Richard Dana defended him without charge. Yet it was to no avail. Burns was sent back to Virginia, where he was shackled and imprisoned in a tiny room for the next four months. Finally news of his whereabouts reached two ministers in Boston, who raised money to purchase him. He was freed and sent to Canada, where he became a minister. He died when he was only 28 years old, from the dreadful treatment he had received while in jail. Students in middle school interested in pursuing the meaning of the Fugitive Slave Act could do no better than to read this compelling story of the last slave ever seized on Massachusetts soil.

Other biographies are incomplete for the simple reason that a full treatment of the subject's complex life would make a book too long and unwieldy for young readers. There have been several such biographies of Abraham Lincoln, for instance. Carl Sandburg wrote a partial biography for children titled *Abe Lincoln Grows Up.* It was made from the first twenty-seven chapters of the first volume of the longest and most definitive biography of Lincoln for adults, Sandburg's *Abraham Lincoln: The Prairie Years.* For his juvenile biography Sandburg included Lincoln's birth and boyhood until he was 19 and "grown up." In singing prose that begs to be read aloud, the author describes Lincoln's desire for knowledge:

> And some of what he wanted so much, so deep down, seemed to be in books. Maybe in books he would find the answers to dark questions pushing around in the pools of his thoughts, and the drifts of his mind. (p. 135)

A partial biography of Washington is titled *George Washington Wasn't Always Old.* Author Alice Fleming pulls together what is known of her subject's childhood and young adulthood, up to his appointment as Major Washington of the Virginia militia when he was not quite 21. This book takes the perspective that Washington "wasn't anybody special" when he was a boy because no one knew how famous and important he would become, an idea with great appeal for children.

Biographical works about real young people in history can serve to provide a limited but interesting view of famous figures who were close to them. Barbara Brenner's *On the Frontier with Mr. Audubon* is technically a partial biography of apprentice painter Joseph Mason. As a young teenager he accompanied John James Audubon on an expedition down the Mississippi River to collect and make life drawings of birds. Mason painted some of the backgrounds for Audubon's *Birds of America,* although his name did not appear on the finished paintings. Brenner used Audubon's diary to reconstruct the activities of their trip, then recreated the story as a journal that the apprentice might have kept, focusing on Audubon's obsession with his work.

Ruud van der Rol and Rian Verhoeven have produced an unusual form of biography in *Anne Frank Beyond the Diary: A Photographic Remembrance.* The authors, both staff members of the Anne Frank House in Amsterdam, have gathered together a variety of materials including photographs from Otto Frank's widow, Elfriede, and Miep Gies, the woman who helped hide the Frank family. In this powerful photobiography, captioned photographs provide a brief introduction to Anne's childhood before the war and events surrounding Hitler's rise, but the book concentrates mainly on the days following Anne's thirteenth birthday and the gift of her diary. Interspersed with explanatory narrative, the family photographs, maps, diagrams, journal excerpts, and interviews broaden the context for Anne's diary and help readers visualize the setting for her brief life. This documentation helps deepen the power of Anne's words and further strengthens her memory.

Complete Biographies

Complete biography spans the subject's lifetime. It may be relatively simple or difficult, authentic or fictionalized, but the reader should expect a view that has some depth, some balance, some sense of perspective. Among types of biographies, this category has traditionally been the largest, although in recent years trends have favored other kinds of presentations.

Russell Freedman's *Franklin Delano Roosevelt* is an example of a biography that is complete and authentic. The inherent drama of the subject, the clarity of the writing, and the generous use of photographs all contribute to the book's appeal for readers age 10 and up. His fine biography sketches out Roosevelt's major achievements as a politician and statesman, but its real strength lies in the detailed information it provides about his personal life. Freedman probes the facade of a man who managed to be a very private person in spite of having the very public job of being President of the United States. Students are fascinated by the lengths to

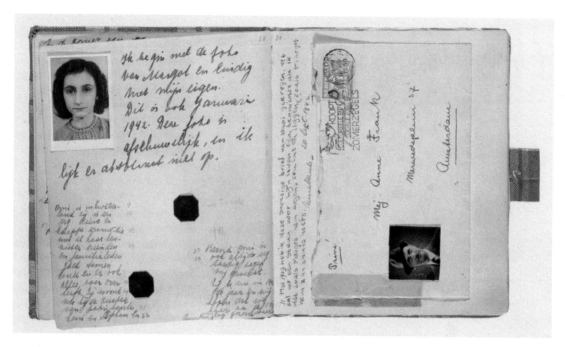

In *Anne Frank Beyond the Diary* by Ruud van der Rol and Rian Verhoeven, Anne's life is documented by family pictures, maps, letters, and excerpts from her diary.
From *Beyond the Diary: A Photographic Remembrance.* Copyright © AFF/AFS, Amsterdam, The Netherlands.

which Roosevelt went in order to camouflage his paralysis. He was hardly ever photographed in a wheelchair, but Freedman does provide one such picture. Freedman's *Eleanor Roosevelt* is a wonderful companion book. By highlighting Eleanor's insecurities, as well as her great accomplishments, Freedman presents an inspiring portrait for children awash in modern-day media blitzes that seem to worship glamour and triviality over courage and inner strength.

Barbara Harrison and Daniel Terris's *A Twilight Struggle* is the honest account of the life of another complex American president, John F. Kennedy. The authors describe the contrasts in the man:

> He set highest standards for himself and for his country even while he encouraged the excesses of competition. He sought peace, and he brought the nation to the brink of war. He was full of wit and energy and life, and yet he was preoccupied with tragedy and death. (p. 133)

The authors' candid account of his failings as well as his accomplishments does not diminish Kennedy's place in history but instead broadens our understanding of a man who faced personal and world problems and endured physical and emotional pain to follow his vision for America.

Some of Jean Fritz's picture-book biographies could be classified as complete because they deal with the subject's entire life span, but she has also written longer books about American figures, such as James Madison in *The Great Little Madison*, Theodore Roosevelt in *Bully for You, Teddy Roosevelt!* and General Thomas J. Jackson in *Stonewall*. All three deal with complex characters in an evenhanded way. In *Stonewall*, for instance, Fritz contrasts the general's heroic Civil War battlefield behavior against his personal idiosyncrasies. The man who kept his line "standing like a stone wall" at Manassas prescribed unusual diets for himself (stale bread and lean meat, or lemons to suck) and lived by arbitrary, self-imposed rules for posture, prayer, and every other form of human conduct. In *Harriet Beecher Stowe and the Beecher Preachers* and *You Want Women to Vote, Lizzie Stanton?* Fritz turns her talents to two important female subjects. Both of these women were born into ages that expected little of them, and both rose above these limitations to contribute to the fight for human rights and women's rights. In all her books Fritz gives us authentic narrative enlivened by personal observations and quotes from contemporaries. Her lists of sources and bibliographies demonstrate her high standards for careful scholarship as well as vivid writing.

The increased interest in biographies of women can be seen in other fine books, such as Patricia and Frederick McKissack's *Sojourner Truth*, Doris Faber's *Calamity Jane*, and Polly Schoyer Brooks's *Cleopatra*. Through

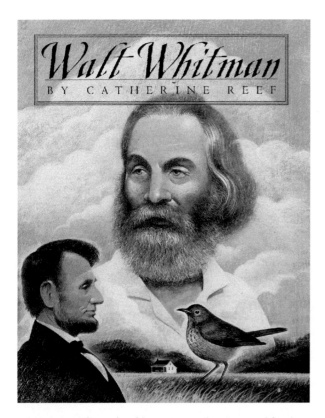

Catherine Reef's *Walt Whitman* is a well-written and frank account of this well-known poet's life.

scrupulous research and captivating narration these authors manage to tackle larger-than-life heroines and turn them into real people without diminishing the significance of their achievements. Natalie S. Bober's *Abigail Adams: Witness to a Revolution* is as fascinating for its inside look at a critical period of American history as it is for its portrait of an intelligent and independent woman who took her role as loving wife and mother very seriously. Using Adams's letters as her main source (over a thousand of them remain), Bober creates a compelling voice for this extraordinary woman and brings the years of America's beginnings to life. Becoming immersed in this thorough biography is like being a long-term guest in Abigail's home. Rather than being put off by its length, older children will close the book and return to their own time only with the greatest reluctance.

Historian Albert Marrin has chosen two well-known figures and documents their times as well as their lives. In *The Sea King* Marrin explores the world of Sir Francis Drake. In the compelling prologue Drake has returned to England aboard the *Golden Hind* after sailing around the world. The Spanish Ambassador insists that Drake

be executed as "the master thief of the unknown world," and at a court banquet Queen Elizabeth addresses Drake:

> 🔖 "Master Drake," she said solemnly, a slight frown on her face. "The King of Spain has asked for your head, and we have a weapon here with which to remove it."
>
> One of the court gentleman gave her a gilded sword, which she handed to a visiting French nobleman. "We shall ask Monsieur . . . to be the headsman. (p. 7)

With that command the Frenchman tapped Drake upon his right shoulder and the Queen addressed him, "Arise, Sir Francis Drake." This beginning is indicative of the exciting story that is about to unfold as Marrin provides a highly readable account of a significant historical period and a man who was a central figure in critically important events. Marrin weaves the same attention to detail and good storytelling into *Unconditional Surrender: U.S. Grant and the Civil War*. Both books are illustrated with maps and reproductions of primary source materials and include footnotes and a list of additional readings.

Children, particularly those who are avid readers or writers, will enjoy reading about well-known creators of favorite books. Beverly Gherman, who has written fine biographies of Agnes DeMille and Georgia O'Keefe for older readers, uncovers the essence of the gentle and shy creator of *Charlotte's Web* in *E. B. White: Some Writer*. In *Ezra Jack Keats: A Biography with Illustrations*, Dean Engel and Florence B. Freedman have used interviews with Ezra Jack Keats and Keats's essays to form the basis of their loving portrait of this children's author and illustrator, who overcame a variety of obstacles to create a world of pleasure for children. Many of Keats's own drawings are used to illustrate his life and to make the connections between his own experiences and those of his characters.

Older readers familiar with Walt Whitman's poetry will enjoy Catherine Reef's *Walt Whitman*, an honest portrayal of this great American poet. The biography includes mention of his homosexuality and focuses on Whitman's generous spirit and his democratic idealism. Accounts of his life, particularly his involvement in the Civil War as a battlefield nurse, are interspersed with quotes from his poetry and enlivened by photographs of Whitman's times and his works. This same audience will also benefit from the broad perspective presented in Clinton Cox's *Mark Twain*. The subtitle of this book is, appropriately, *America's Humorist, Dreamer, Prophet*. Told in lively prose, Cox's biography is filled with quotes from Twain's writing.

In addition we come to see him not merely as a fine storyteller but also as someone haunted by the injustices of racism and committed to the rights of the common people.

The Cherokee leader Sequoyah had unique gifts as a writer and shared these with his people in the form of a whole system of writing, the Cherokee alphabet, which is still used today. Born in the late 1700s, Sequoyah was more than a teacher and author, however. He was a wise and talented leader who strove to unite his people in spite of their betrayal by the United States government. Janet Klausner's fine biography *Sequoyah's Gift* chronicles his life within the context of the broader events surrounding the emerging nation in the early 1800s and the tragedy of the Trail of Tears.

Among the many complete biographies for children are a few that have been awarded the Newbery Medal. One of these is the story of a little-known black pioneer of freedom. *Amos Fortune, Free Man* by Elizabeth Yates is the moving account of a common man who lived simply and greatly. Born free in Africa, he was sold as a slave in North America. In time he purchased his own freedom and that of several others. When he was 80 years old, Amos Fortune purchased twenty-five acres of land in the shadow of his beloved mountain, Monadnock—"the mountain that stands alone." Like Monadnock, Fortune stood alone, a rock of strength and security for all those he loved.

Frequently biographers choose subjects who are credited with unique achievements, whatever the field. Most authors would be dubious about writing an interesting biography for children about a mathematician, but Jean Lee Latham was challenged. She studied mathematics, astronomy, oceanography, and seamanship. Then she went to Boston and Salem to talk with descendants of Nathaniel Bowditch and to do research on the geographical and maritime backgrounds of her story. The result of all this painstaking preparation was the Newbery Medal winner *Carry On, Mr. Bowditch*, the amazing story of Nat Bowditch, who had little chance for schooling but mastered the secrets of navigation and wrote a textbook that was used for more than a hundred years.

A more recent Newbery Medal winner is Russell Freedman's *Lincoln: A Photobiography*. One of the great accomplishments of this book is its groundbreaking use of archival photographs, not just to break up and decorate the text but to seriously extend the reader's understanding of the subject. Yet the text stands as an accomplishment in its own right as a comprehensive, insightful, and readable account of a complex person living in a complicated time. It is very difficult to bring fresh perspective, as Freedman has done, to a story that has been told so often.

Collective Biographies

Many children looking for biographical information want brief material about specific people or about specific endeavors. Many collective biographies have been published to meet this need. In scope and difficulty they run the gamut—some have one-paragraph sketches of many subjects, others have long essays on just a few. Like other books, collective biographies must be judged on more than title and appearance.

Russell Freedman's *The Wright Brothers: How They Invented the Airplane* is an outstanding biography of two people whose lives and work were so closely intertwined that it would be difficult to choose just one to write about. Using archival photographs as he has done in other books, Freedman reconstructs the engrossing story that led to Kitty Hawk and many years of achievement thereafter. In the process he illuminates the character and commitment of Wilbur and Orville Wright.

Collective biographies are an ideal format for highlighting the contributions of more ordinary people whose lives might not bring with them the documentation that lends itself to the writing of full biographies. Brandon Marie Miller's *Buffalo Gals: Women of the Old West* and Penny Colman's *Rosie the Riveter: Women Working on the Home Front in World War II* provide glimpses of two periods in American history when women stepped beyond the usual restraints of their roles. The American West of the 1800s provided the space for women of all races to challenge perceptions of the weaker sex. In this century World War II opened up the world of industry and commerce to women as the government actively encouraged women to do their patriotic duty and go to work. Colman's book also chronicles the harassment these modern-day pioneers faced, their dilemmas in finding child care, and the difficulties they faced when the war was over. Both groups of women served to open the door to equality for the generations of women that followed.

Collective biographies seldom deal with subjects whose stories can be woven together as smoothly as *The Wright Brothers* or *Rosie the Riveter*. Most have many brief entries about individuals whose interests or accomplishments are similar. Women have not been slighted in such collections and books as *Inspirations: Stories About Women Artists* and *Visions: Stories About Women Artists*, both by Leslie Sills, and *Focus: Five Women Photographers* by Sylvia Wolf. Excellent introductions to the stories of women who excelled in the arts, both books feature names that many children will recognize, but they also highlight the achievements of less well-known figures from diverse cultures. These include artists Alice Neel and Betye Saar and photographers Flor Garduño and Sandy Skoglund.

Kathryn Hewitt's droll caricature of Hans Christian Andersen includes details about his stories in this picture from *Lives of the Writers: Comedies, Tragedies, (and What the Neighbors Thought)* by Kathleen Krull.

Illustration from *Lives of the Writers: Comedies, Tragedies (and What the Neighbors Thought)* by Kathryn Krull, illustrations copyright © 1994 by Kathryn Hewill, reproduced by permission of Harcourt Brace & Company.

Kathleen Krull and Kathryn Hewitt have collaborated on three highly entertaining collections of anecdotes about famous artists, writers, and musicians. In *Lives of the Artists: Masterpieces, Messes (and What the Neighbors Thought)* Kathe Kollwitz is shown as a passionate antiwar activist who cared little about her appearance. Artist Marcel Duchamp had a wonderful sense of humor, ate spaghetti with butter and cheese for dinner every night, and let his apartment accumulate several inches of dust to use in his paintings. Although these aren't necessarily the facts found in the usual reference books, they help to highlight the uniqueness of the artist. These books also prove to children that heroes and heroines are not always perfect and sometimes are perfectly awful. The visual portraits by Kathryn Hewitt provide summaries of each artist's work and life.

Pat Cummings has provided similar insights into the lives of illustrators of children's books in two volumes of *Talking with Artists*. Illustrators such as Floyd Cooper, Lois Ehlert, Denise Fleming, Brian Pinkney, and Vera B. Williams respond to Cummings's questions and reflect upon their current work as well as their childhood memories. Each profile is accompanied by examples of the artist's childhood art and current work.

Mary Lyons has chosen to examine the childhood diaries of seven women writers of the nineteenth century, and she shapes a narrative of their lives around these private journals. In the musings of Louisa May Alcott, Kate Chopin, Sarah Jane Foster, and others, Lyons identifies the barriers of gender and race that these independent spirits had to face, yet she also reveals that they had the same longings, frustrations, and joys of today's adolescents. Her account of their struggles as young women forges an important link across the centuries. Peter Burchard has also used the diaries of Charlotte Forten, one of Lyon's subjects, as the basis for a longer biography of this courageous teacher and abolitionist.

Sports figures are also included in collective biographies such as *Champions* by Bill Littlefield. Ten well-written portraits of champions like jockey Julie Krone and baseball player Roberto Clemente read like short stories as Littlefield highlights the contributions of men and women athletes, some who have changed the face of their sport. In *Leagues Apart* Lawrence Ritter highlights the lives of twenty-two African Americans who played in the Negro Leagues. This collection not only reveals the important contributions of these men but also portrays the racial bigotry and often humiliating conditions under which they played.

Take a Walk in Their Shoes by Glennette Tilley Turner introduces fourteen African Americans who played a part in the struggle for racial equality. An unusual feature is the inclusion of brief dramas that can be performed by children to highlight each subject's contribution. Martin Luther King, Jr., Rosa Parks, Arthur Schomburg, Leontyne Price, Frederick Douglass, and "Satchel" Paige are a few of the prominent African Americans featured in this book.

The Great Lives series offers well-written accounts of achievers in many fields. Doris and Harold Faber are the authors of *Great Lives: Nature and the Environment,* which includes twenty-five biographical sketches spanning almost two centuries. Read individually, each sketch is clear and furnishes the context necessary for understanding its subject. Read as a whole, the book provides excellent perspective on our changing ideas about our relationship to our environment. Some of the other titles in this series are *Great Lives: American Government,* also by Doris and Harold Faber; *Great Lives: Exploration* by Milton Lomask; *Great Lives: Sports* by George Sullivan; and *Great Lives: Human Rights* by William Jay Jacobs.

Autobiographies and Memoirs

Life stories are often recalled and written down by the subjects themselves, as autobiographies or memoirs. Some children's books based on autobiographical material have been discussed earlier in Chapter 10 as historical fiction. Autobiography has advantages and disadvantages similar to those of informational books of eyewitness history—the warmth and immediacy of personal detail, but a necessarily limited perspective. The criterion of objectivity is reversed here; it is the very subjectivity of this sort of biography that has value. But children do need to be aware of the inherent bias in autobiographies, and they can be encouraged to look to other sources for balance.

Autobiographies by creators of children's books provide an easy introduction to this specialized form of writing. Children who are familiar with books illustrated by Trina Schart Hyman should be able to pick out motifs and characters from them that also appear in *Self-Portrait: Trina Schart Hyman*. The tone of the text, as well as the art, provides clues to character; the writing is sometimes breezy, sometimes intense.

The fine photobiographies in the Meet the Author series, published by Richard C. Owen, show each author at home with family and pets; clear maps locate where they live. Each author tells something about his or her childhood and provides personal insights into their writing process. Included in the series are Eve Bunting's *Once Upon a Time*, Lee Bennett Hopkins's *The Writing Bug*, Margaret Mahy's *My Mysterious World*, Rafe Martin's *A Storyteller's Story*, and Cynthia Rylant's *Best Wishes*.

Other popular writers provide longer life stories. In *The Moon and I*, a humorous memoir, Betsy Byars tells about realizing her childhood dream of having a pet snake and reveals much about herself. Some authors focus on their work, explaining the process of writing a book and adding advice for students who dream of writing for publication. *How I Came to Be a Writer* by Phyllis Reynolds Naylor reveals the same wit as her realistic novels. *Chapters: My Growth as a Writer* is Lois Duncan's account of her early successes and later development. Roald Dahl in *Boy: Tales of Childhood* recounts stories of his early family life and incidents from his boarding school days, including one that became a scene in one of his own novels.

Beverly Cleary's memoir *A Girl from Yamhill: A Memoir* speaks to adults who have read her books, as well as to older students. Careful readers will catch many glimpses of her popular character Ramona Quimby in

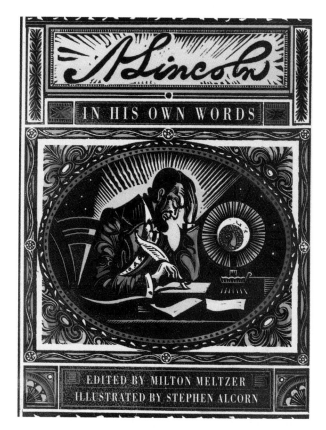

In *Lincoln: In His Own Words,* Milton Meltzer has used excerpts from Lincoln's writings to tell his life story. Stephen Alcorn's moving linocut illustrations represent critical experiences in Lincoln's life.

Cover illustration from *Lincoln: In His Own Words* by Milton Meltzer, illustrations copyright © 1993 by Stephen Alcorn, reproduced by permission of Harcourt Brace and Company.

Cleary's own childhood. The portrayal of her difficult relationship with her mother is particularly good for generating discussion. Cleary's story of her college years and her adult life is told in *My Own Two Feet*.

Resources for Teaching, "Author Autobiographies," lists the titles of a few of the memoirs by authors for children. Most of the books for primary grades are not complete autobiographies but are based on a single incident.

Other memoirs in the form of personal journals and letters can bring the voices of times past vividly to life. Milton Meltzer has based several fine informational books, such as *The American Revolutionaries: A History in Their Own Words*, on such primary sources. In *Lincoln: In His Own Words* and *Frederick Douglass: In His Own Words* Meltzer uses a similar technique, framing selections from the writings and speeches of these two great Americans with commentary that explains the

Resources for Teaching
Author Autobiographies

Author	Title	Grade Level
Brent Ashabrenner	*The Times of My Life: A Memoir*	5 and up
Clyde Bulla	*A Grain of Wheat: A Writer Begins*	2–6
Beverly Cleary	*A Girl from Yamhill: A Memoir*	5 and up
Donald Crews	*Bigmama's*	1–4
Roald Dahl	*Boy: Tales of Childhood*	5 and up
Tomie de Paola	*The Art Lesson*	1–4
Lois Duncan	*Chapters: My Growth as a Writer*	5 and up
Michael Foreman	*War Boy: A Country Childhood*	4–6
Jean Fritz	*Homesick: My Own Story*	5 and up
Trina Schart Hyman	*Self-Portrait: Trina Schart Hyman*	2–5
Jean Little	*Little by Little: A Writer's Childhood*	5 and up
Milton Meltzer	*Starting from Home: A Writer's Beginnings*	5 and up
Phyllis Reynolds Naylor	*How I Came to Be a Writer*	5 and up
Gary Paulsen	*Woodsong*	5 and up
Richard Peck	*Anonymously Yours*	5 and up
Bill Peet	*Bill Peet: An Autobiography*	3 and up
James Stevenson	*Higher on the Door*	2–5
	When I Was Nine	2–5
Yoshiko Uchida	*The Invisible Thread*	5 and up
Laurence Yep	*The Lost Garden*	5 and up

progression of their ideas in the context of their time. Stephen Alcorn's handsome linocut illustrations capture his subjects' lives through compelling visual symbols. Scratchboard illustrations by Michael McCurdy also frame a shorter version of Douglass's words in *Escape from Slavery: The Boyhood of Frederick Douglass in His Own Words*. McCurdy's illustrations lend a similar dignity to Lillian Schisse's adaptation of Amelia Knight's *The Way West: Journal of a Pioneer Woman*. Joseph Plumb Martin's *Yankee Doodle Boy*, edited by George Scheer, is the lively firsthand account of a fifteen-year-old Connecticut farmer who served with Washington's Continental army. While the somewhat archaic speech patterns of previous centuries require some editing, these memoirs do not lose their powerful effect for modern audiences under the skillful handling of Meltzer, Schisse, and Scheer.

Biographies of all types give children a glimpse into other lives, other places, other times. The best of them combine accurate information and fine writing in a context that children enjoy—the story that really happened. Good biographies serve to put facts into a frame of human feeling. Children can come to know about historical events or contemporary figures from textbooks, but literature that touches this content will bring them a different quality of knowing—more intimate and more memorable. All children deserve to have such books as part of their experience.

Learning Experiences

1. Look at the selection of biographies in a school library. Make a checklist of how many biographies are about men, how many about women. What people have been the subject of many biographies? few biographies? one biography? What contemporary figures are presented in these biographies?

2. Gather several picture-book biographies or simplified biographies with many illustrations. What information appears in the pictures but not the text? How do the illustrations help create focus and characterization?

3. Select several biographies of one subject, such as Christopher Columbus. Make a chart to compare information, omissions, author's point of view, and the extent of documentation. *Christopher Columbus: The Great Adventure* by Delno and Jean West, *Christopher Columbus: Voyager to the Unknown* by Nancy Smiler Levinson, and *Where Do You Think You're Going, Christopher Columbus?* by Jean Fritz are good possibilities. Read related informational books or historical fiction that would extend the focus, such as *I, Columbus: My Journal—1492–1493* edited by Peter and Connie Roop, *If You Were There in 1492* by Barbara Brenner, or *Pedro's Journal* by Pam Conrad. Consider the ways a broader range of information makes you a more discriminating reader.

Related Readings

Fritz, Jean. "The Very Truth." In *Celebrating Children's Books,* ed. Betsy Hearne and Marilyn Kaye, pp. 81–86. New York: Lothrop, Lee & Shepard, 1981.

One of the very best writers of juvenile biography addresses the issue of censorship and discusses the necessity for telling all the truth.

The Lion and the Unicorn 4, no. 1 (summer 1980).

This entire issue is devoted to biography for young people. Of special interest are Elizabeth Segel's article about a biography of Beatrix Potter, Leonard Marcus's comments on picture-book biographies for children, and an interview with Milton Meltzer by Geraldine DeLuca and Roni Natov.

Meltzer, Milton. "Selective Forgetfulness: Christopher Columbus Reconsidered." *New Advocate* 5 (winter 1992): 1–9.

A writer of fine complete biographies discusses the dark side of the story of Columbus, namely, his treatment of Indians. He quotes letters and Columbus's own journal as documentation. These are included in his biography *Columbus and the World Around Him* (Franklin Watts, 1990).

Zarnowski, Myra. *Learning About Biographies: A Reading-and-Writing Approach for Children.* Urbana, Ill.: National Council of Teachers of English and the National Council on Social Studies, 1990.

Teachers of upper elementary and middle school students will find many resources here for helping children understand the tasks and responsibilities of a biographer. Discussion of the genre, guides for classroom work, and a bibliography are included.

Children's Literature

Adler, David A. *A Picture Book of Abraham Lincoln.* Illustrated by John and Alexandra Wallner. Holiday House, 1989.

———. *A Picture Book of Benjamin Franklin.* Illustrated by John and Alexandra Wallner. Holiday House, 1990.

———. *A Picture Book of Christopher Columbus.* Illustrated by John and Alexandra Wallner. Holiday House, 1991.

———. *A Picture Book of George Washington.* Illustrated by John and Alexandra Wallner. Holiday House, 1990.

———. *A Picture Book of Jackie Robinson.* Illustrated by Robert Casilla. Holiday House, 1994.

————. *A Picture Book of John F. Kennedy*. Illustrated by John and Alexandra Wallner. Holiday House, 1990.

————. *A Picture Book of Martin Luther King, Jr*. Illustrated by Robert Casilla. Holiday House, 1989.

————. *A Picture Book of Rosa Parks*. Illustrated by Robert Casilla. Holiday House, 1993.

————. *A Picture Book of Sojourner Truth*. Illustrated by Gershom Griffith. Holiday House, 1994.

————. *A Picture Book of Thomas Jefferson*. Illustrated by John and Alexandra Wallner. Holiday House, 1990.

Adoff, Arnold. *Malcolm X*. Illustrated by John Wilson. Harper Trophy, 1988 [1970].

Aliki. [Aliki Brandenberg]. *The King's Day: Louis XIV of France*. Crowell, 1989.

————. *The Many Lives of Benjamin Franklin*. Simon & Schuster, 1988 [1977].

————. *The Story of Johnny Appleseed*. Prentice Hall, 1987 [1963].

————. *A Weed Is a Flower: The Life of George Washington Carver*. Simon & Schuster, 1988 [1965].

Ashabrenner, Brent. *The Times of My Life: A Memoir*. Dutton, 1990.

Barth, Edna. *I'm Nobody! Who Are You? The Story of Emily Dickinson*. Illustrated by Richard Cuffari. Clarion, 1979.

Blos, Joan. *The Heroine of the Titanic: A Tale Both True and Otherwise of the Life of Molly Brown*. Illustrated by Tennessee Dixon. Morrow, 1991.

Blumberg, Rhoda. *The Remarkable Adventures of Captain Cook*. Bradbury, 1991.

Bober, Natalie S. *Abigail Adams: Witness to a Revolution*. Atheneum, 1995.

Braun, Barbara. *A Weekend with Diego Rivera*. Rizzoli, 1994.

Bray, Rosemary L. *Martin Luther King*. Illustrated by Malcah Zeldis. Greenwillow, 1995.

Brenner, Barbara. *If You Were There in 1492*. Bradbury, 1991.

————. *On the Frontier with Mr. Audubon*. Coward, 1977.

Brighton, Catherine. *Mozart: Scenes from the Childhood of the Great Composer*. Doubleday, 1990.

Brooks, Polly Schoyer. *Cleopatra*. HarperCollins, 1995.

Bruchac, Joseph. *A Boy Called Slow: The True Story of Sitting Bull*. Illustrated by Rocco Baviera. Philomel, 1994.

Bulla, Clyde. *A Grain of Wheat: A Writer Begins*. Godine, 1985.

Bunting, Eve. *Once Upon a Time*. Owen, 1995.

Burchard, Peter. *Charlotte Forten: A Black Teacher in the Civil War*. Crown, 1995.

Byars, Betsy. *The Moon and I*. Messner, 1991.

Clayton, Ed. *Martin Luther King: The Peaceful Warrior*. Illustrated by David Hodges. Minstrel, 1986 [1968].

Cleary, Beverly. *A Girl from Yamhill: A Memoir*. Morrow, 1988.

————. *My Own Two Feet: A Memoir*. Morrow, 1995.

Colman, Penny. *Rosie the Riveter: Women Working on the Home Front in World War II*. Crown, 1995.

Conrad, Pam. *Pedro's Journal: A Voyage with Christopher Columbus*. Boyds Mill, 1991.

————. *Prairie Visions: The Life and Times of Solomon Butcher*. HarperCollins, 1991.

Cooper, Floyd. *Coming Home: From the Life of Langston Hughes*. Philomel, 1994.

Cox, Clinton. *Mark Twain: America's Humorist, Dreamer, Prophet*. Scholastic, 1995.

Crews, Donald. *Bigmama's*. Greenwillow, 1991.

Cummings, Pat, ed. *Talking with Artists*. Vol. 1. Bradbury, 1992.

————. *Talking with Artists*. Vol. 2. Simon & Schuster, 1995.

Dahl, Roald. *Boy: Tales of Childhood*. Farrar, Straus & Giroux, 1984.

d'Aulaire, Ingri, and Edgar Parin d'Aulaire. *Abraham Lincoln*. Rev. ed. Doubleday, 1957.

————. *Benjamin Franklin*. Zephyr, 1987 [1950].

————. *Columbus*. Zephyr, 1987 [1955].

————. *George Washington*. Doubleday, 1936.

————. *Pocahontas*. Doubleday, 1985 [1949].

de Paola, Tomie. *The Art Lesson*. Putnam, 1989.

Downing, Julie. *Mozart Tonight*. Bradbury, 1991.

Duncan, Lois. *Chapters: My Growth as a Writer*. Little, Brown, 1982.

Engel, Dean, and Florence B. Freedman. *Ezra Jack Keats: A Biography with Illustrations*. Silver Moon, 1995.

Faber, Doris. *Calamity Jane: Her Life and Legend*. Houghton Mifflin, 1992.

————. *Eleanor Roosevelt, First Lady of the World*. Illustrated by Donna Ruff. Viking, 1985.

Faber, Doris, and Harold Faber. *Great Lives: American Government*. Scribner's, 1988.

————. *Great Lives: Nature and the Environment*. Scribner's, 1991.

Fisher, Leonard Everett. *Prince Henry, the Navigator*. Macmillan, 1990.

Fleming, Alice. *George Washington Wasn't Always Old*. Illustrated by Bert Dodson. Simon & Schuster, 1991.

Foreman, Michael. *War Boy: A Country Childhood*. Arcade, 1990.

Franchere, Ruth. *Cesar Chavez*. Illustrated by Earl Thollander. Harper Trophy, 1988 [1970].

Freedman, Russell. *Eleanor Roosevelt: A Life of Discovery*. Clarion, 1993.

————. *Franklin Delano Roosevelt*. Clarion, 1990.

————. *Lincoln: A Photobiography*. Clarion, 1987.

————. *The Wright Brothers: How They Invented the Airplane*. Holiday House, 1991.

Fritz, Jean. *And Then What Happened, Paul Revere?* Illustrated by Margot Tomes. Coward, 1973.

————. *Bully for You, Teddy Roosevelt!* Illustrated by Mike Wimmer. Putnam, 1991.

————. *Can't You Make Them Behave, King George?* Illustrated by Tomie de Paola. Coward, 1982.

————. *China Homecoming*. Putnam, 1985.

————. *The Great Little Madison*. Putnam, 1989.

————. *Harriet Beecher Stowe and the Beecher Preachers*. Putnam, 1994.

————. *Homesick: My Own Story*. Illustrated by Margot Tomes. Putnam, 1982.

————. *Stonewall*. Illustrated by Stephen Gammell. Putnam, 1979.

————. *Traitor: The Case of Benedict Arnold*. Putnam, 1981.

————. *What's the Big Idea, Ben Franklin?* Illustrated by Margot Tomes. Coward, 1982.

————. *Where Do You Think You're Going, Christopher Columbus?* Illustrated by Margot Tomes. Putnam, 1980.

————. *Why Don't You Get a Horse, Sam Adams?* Illustrated by Trina Schart Hyman. Coward, 1982.

————. *Will You Sign Here, John Hancock?* Illustrated by Trina Schart Hyman. Coward, 1982.

————. *You Want Women to Vote, Lizzie Stanton?* Putnam, 1995.

Gherman, Beverly. *Agnes DeMille, Dancing Off the Earth*. Atheneum, 1990.

————. *E. B. White: Some Writer*. Atheneum, 1992.

————. *Georgia O' Keeffe: The "Wideness and Wonder" of Her World*. Atheneum, 1988.

————. *Sandra Day O'Connor: Justice for All*. Illustrated by Robert Masheris. Viking, 1991.

Giblin, James Cross. *George Washington: A Picture Book Biography*. Illustrated by Michael Dooling. Scholastic, 1992.

————. *Thomas Jefferson: A Picture Book Biography*. Illustrated by Michael Dooling. Scholastic, 1994.

Greenfield, Eloise. *Mary McLeod Bethune*. Illustrated by Jerry Pinkney. Crowell, 1977.

————. *Rosa Parks*. Illustrated by Gill Ashby. HarperCollins, 1995 [1973].

Gross, Ruth Belov. *True Stories About Abraham Lincoln*. Illustrated by Jill Kastner. Lothrop, Lee & Shepard, 1989.

Hamilton, Virginia. *Anthony Burns: The Defeat and Triumph of a Fugitive Slave*. Knopf, 1988.

Harrison, Barbara, and Daniel Terris. *A Twilight Struggle: The Life of John Fitzgerald Kennedy*. Lothrop, Lee & Shepard, 1992.

Hopkins, Lee Bennett. *The Writing Bug*. Owen, 1992.

Hurwitz, Johanna. *Astrid Lindgren: Storyteller to the World*. Illustrated by Michael Dooling. Viking, 1989.

Hyman, Trina Schart. *Self-Portrait: Trina Schart Hyman*. Harper & Row, 1989 [1981].

Jacobs, William Jay. *Great Lives: Human Rights*. Scribner's, 1990.

Kherdian, David. *The Road from Home: The Story of an Armenian Girl*. Greenwillow, 1979.

Klausner, Janet. *Sequoyah's Gift: A Portrait of the Cherokee Leader*. HarperCollins, 1993.

Knight, Amela. *The Way West: Journal of a Pioneer Woman*. Adapted by Lillian Schisse. Illustrated by Michael McCurdy. Simon & Schuster, 1993.

Krull, Kathleen. *Lives of the Artists: Masterpieces, Messes (and What the Neighbors Thought)*. Illustrated by Kathryn Hewitt. Harcourt Brace, 1995.

———. *Lives of the Musicians: Good Times, Bad Times (and What the Neighbors Thought)*. Illustrated by Kathryn Hewitt. Harcourt Brace, 1993.

———. *Lives of the Writers: Comedies, Tragedies (and What the Neighbors Thought)*. Illustrated by Kathryn Hewitt. Harcourt Brace, 1993.

Kuskin, Karla. *Thoughts, Pictures, Words*. Owen, 1995.

Lasker, Joe. *The Great Alexander the Great*. Puffin, 1990 [1983].

Latham, Jean Lee. *Carry On, Mr. Bowditch*. Illustrated by John O'Hara Cosgrave II. Houghton Mifflin, 1955.

Levinson, Nancy Smiler. *Christopher Columbus: Voyager to the Unknown*. Lodestar/Dutton, 1990.

Liestman, Vicki. *Columbus Day*. Illustrated by Rick Hanson. Carolrhoda, 1991.

Little, Jean. *Little by Little: A Writer's Beginnings*. Penguin, 1988.

Littlefield, Bill. *Champions: Stories of Ten Remarkable Athletes*. Little, Brown, 1993.

Lomask, William. *Great Lives: Exploration*. Scribner's, 1988.

Lyons, Mary E. *Deep Blues: Bill Traylor, Self-Taught Artist*. Scribner's, 1994.

———. *Keeping Secrets: The Girlhood Diaries of Seven Women Writers*. Holt, 1995.

———. *Letters from a Slave Girl: The Story of Harriet Jacobs*. Scribner's, 1992.

———. *Master of Mahogany: Tom Day, Free Black Cabinetmaker*. Scribner's, 1994.

———. *Starting Home: The Story of Horace Pippin*. Scribner's, 1993.

———. *Stitching Stars: The Story Quilts of Harriet Jacobs*. Scribner's, 1993.

Mahy, Margaret. *My Mysterious World*. Owen, 1995.

Marrin, Albert. *The Sea King: Sir Francis Drake and His Times*. Atheneum, 1995.

———. *Unconditional Surrender: U.S. Grant and the Civil War*. Atheneum, 1994.

Martin, Joseph Plumb. *Yankee Doodle Boy*. Edited by George Scheer. Illustrated by Victor Mays. Holiday House, 1995 [1964].

Martin, Rafe. *A Storyteller's Story*. Photos by Jill Krementz. Owen, 1992.

McCurdy, Michael, ed. *Escape from Slavery: The Boyhood of Frederick Douglass in His Own Words*. Knopf, 1994.

McGovern, Ann. *The Secret Soldier: The Story of Deborah Sampson*. Illustrated by Ann Grifalconi. Four Winds, 1987 [1975].

McKissack, Patricia C. *Jesse Jackson: A Biography*. Scholastic, 1989.

McKissack, Patricia C., and Frederick McKissack. *Sojourner Truth: Ain't I a Woman?* Scholastic, 1992.

Meltzer, Milton. *The American Revolutionaries: A History in Their Own Words*. Crowell, 1987.

———. *Frederick Douglass: In His Own Words*. Illustrated by Stephen Alcorn. Harcourt Brace, 1995.

———. *Lincoln: In His Own Words*. Illustrated by Stephen Alcorn. Harcourt Brace, 1994.

———. *Starting from Home: A Writer's Beginnings*. Penguin, 1988.

Miller, Brandon Marie. *Buffalo Gals: Women of the Old West*. Lerner, 1995.

Miller, William. *Frederick Douglass: The Last Days of Slavery*. Illustrated by Cedric Lucas. Lee & Low, 1995.

———. *Zora Hurston and the Chinaberry Tree*. Illustrated by Cornelius Van Wright and Ying-hwa Hu. Lee & Low, 1994.

Monjo, F. N. *Grand Papa and Ellen Aroon*. Illustrated by Richard Cuffari. Dell, 1990 [1974].

———. *Letters to Horseface: Young Mozart's Travels in Italy*. Illustrated by Don Bolognese and Elaine Raphael. Puffin, 1991 [1975].

———. *The One Bad Thing About Father*. Illustrated by Rocco Negri. Harper & Row, 1987 [1970].

———. *Poor Richard in France*. Illustrated by Brinton Turkle. Dell, 1990 [1973].

Naylor, Phyllis Reynolds. *How I Came to Be a Writer*. Aladdin, 1987 [1978].

Paulsen, Gary. *Woodsong*. Bradbury, 1990.

Peet, Bill. *Bill Peet: An Autobiography*. Houghton Mifflin, 1989.

Pinkney, Andrea Davis. *Alvin Ailey*. Illustrated by Brian Pinkney. Hyperion, 1993.

———. *Dear Benjamin Banneker*. Illustrated by Brian Pinkney. Gulliver, 1994.

Provensen, Alice, and Martin Provensen. *The Glorious Flight: Across the Channel with Louis Blériot, July 25, 1909*. Viking, 1983.

Raboff, Ernest. *Marc Chagall*. Lippincott, 1988 [1968].

———. *Pablo Picasso*. Lippincott, 1988 [1968].

———. *Paul Klee*. Lippincott, 1988 [1968].

Reef, Catherine. *Walt Whitman*. Clarion, 1995.

Ritter, Lawrence S. *Leagues Apart: The Men and Time of the Negro Baseball Leagues*. Morrow, 1995.

Roop, Peter, and Connie Roop, eds. *I, Columbus: My Journal—1492–1493*. Illustrated by Peter E. Hanson. Walker, 1990.

Rylant, Cynthia. *Best Wishes*. Photos by Carlo Ontal. Owen, 1992.

Sandburg, Carl. *Abe Lincoln Grows Up*. Illustrated by James Daugherty. Harcourt Brace, 1975 [1926].

San Souci, Robert D. *Kate Shelley: Bound for Legend*. Illustrated by Max Ginsburg. Dial, 1995.

Saunders, Susan. *Margaret Mead: The World Was Her Family*. Illustrated by Ted Lewin. Viking, 1988.

Say, Allen. *El Chino*. Houghton Mifflin, 1990.

Scioscia, Mary. *Bicycle Rider*. Illustrated by Ed Young. Harper & Row, 1983.

Sills, Leslie. *Inspirations: Stories About Women Artists*. Edited by Ann Fay. Albert Whitman, 1989.

———. *Visions: Stories About Women Artists*. Edited by Leslie Sills and Abby Levine. Albert Whitman, 1993.

Sis, Peter. *Follow the Dream: The Story of Christopher Columbus*. Knopf, 1991.

Skira-Venturi, Rosabianca. *A Weekend with Van Gogh*. Rizzoli, 1994.

Stanley, Diane. *Peter the Great*. Four Winds, 1986.

———. *The True Adventures of Daniel Hall*. Dial, 1995.

Stanley, Diane, and Peter Vennema. *Bard of Avon: The Story of William Shakespeare*. Illustrated by Diane Stanley. Morrow, 1992.

———. *Charles Dickens: The Man Who Had Great Expectations*. Illustrated by Diane Stanley. Morrow, 1993.

———. *Cleopatra*. Illustrated by Diane Stanley. Morrow, 1994.

———. *Good Queen Bess: The Story of Elizabeth I of England*. Illustrated by Diane Stanley. Four Winds, 1990.

———. *Shaka: King of the Zulus*. Illustrated by Diane Stanley. Morrow, 1988.

Stanley, Fay. *The Last Princess: The Story of Princess Ka'iulani of Hawai'i*. Illustrated by Diane Stanley. Four Winds, 1991.

Stevenson, James. *Higher on the Door*. Greenwillow, 1987.

———. *When I Was Nine*. Greenwillow, 1986.

Sullivan, George. *Great Lives: Sports*. Scribner's, 1988.

Turner, Glennette Tilley. *Take a Walk in Their Shoes*. Illustrated by Elton C. Fax. Cobblehill/Dutton, 1989.

Turner, Robyn Montana. *Dorothea Lange*. Little, Brown, 1994.

———. *Frida Kahlo*. Little, Brown, 1993.

———. *Georgia O'Keefe*. Little, Brown, 1991.

———. *Mary Cassatt*. Little, Brown, 1992.

———. *Rosa Bonheur*. Little, Brown, 1991.

van der Rol, Ruud, and Verhoeven, Rian. *Anne Frank Beyond the Diary: A Photographic Remembrance*. Translated by Tony Langham and Plym Peters. Viking, 1993.

Weidt, Maryann N. *Stateswoman to the World: A Story About Eleanor Roosevelt*. Illustrated by Lydia M. Anderson. Carolrhoda, 1991.

Weil, Lisl. *Wolferl: The First Six Years in the Life of Wolfgang Amadeus Mozart, 1756–1762*. Holiday House, 1991.

West, Delno, and Jean West. *Christopher Columbus: The Great Adventure and How We Know About It*. Atheneum, 1991.

Winter, Jonah. *Diego*. Illustrated by Jeannette Winter. Translation by Amy Prince. Knopf, 1991.

Wolf, Sylvia. *Focus: Five Women Photographers*. Albert Whitman, 1994.

Yates, Elizabeth. *Amos Fortune, Free Man*. Illustrated by Nora S. Unwin. Dutton, 1967 [1950].

© James L. Shaffer

chapter twelve

Informational Books

Trends in Informational Books 578

Increased Quantity and Quality 578
A New Focus on the Very Young 579
The Growing Importance of Illustration 580
Unconventional Formats and Approaches 580
Specialized Topics 581
Recognition and Awards 581

Criteria for Evaluating Informational Books 581

Accuracy and Authenticity 581
The Author's Qualifications 582
Factual Accuracy 582
Being Up-to-Date 582
Inclusion of All the Significant Facts 582
Avoiding Stereotypes 583
Using Facts to Support Generalizations 584
Making the Distinction Between Fact and Theory 584
Avoiding Anthropomorphism 584

Content and Perspective 585
Purpose 585
Intended Audience 585
Adequate Coverage 585
Demonstration of Scientific Method 586
Interrelationships and Implications 587

Style 588
Clarity and Directness 588
Level of Difficulty 588
Reader Involvement 588
Vivid Language 589

Organization 589
Structure 589
Reference Aids 590

Illustrations and Format 590

Clarification and Extension of Text 591
Suitability of Media 592
Captions 592
Format 593

Types of Informational Books 593

Concept Books 593
Guidelines: Evaluating Informational Books 594
Informational Picture Storybooks 594
Photographic Essays 596
Identification Books 598
Life-Cycle Books 598
Experiment and Activity Books 598
Documents and Journals 599
Survey Books 600
Specialized Books 601
Craft and How-to Books 602

Using Literature Across the Curriculum 602

Informational Books in the Classroom 602
Teaching Feature: Helping Children Evaluate Informational Books 604
Choosing Informational Books for the Classroom 604
Integrating Fact and Fiction 605
Resources For Teaching: Fact and Fiction: Books to Use Together 606
Learning Experiences 607
Related Readings 608
Children's Literature 609

We know a 6-year-old who loves to go to the school library because there he can choose any book he wants. At story time he listens eagerly to picture storybooks and other fiction, but the books he chooses to check out, to keep for a time and to pore over at home, are informational. His favorites are about airplanes, rockets, space travel, and complex machinery. He often chooses books far above his level of understanding (once it was an encyclopedia of space facts so big that he could barely carry it by himself). Part of his fun is looking at the illustrations over and over again, but he also wants an adult to "read" these difficult books to him. In this case he means reading the picture captions and talking through main ideas or intriguing details in response to his many questions. He joins in the reading by looking for words he knows or can figure out in the boldface headings or diagram labels.

We call attention to this common scenario because it demonstrates so much about the special role of nonfiction literature in children's lives. The audience for informational books is broad, including young children as well as older students. Adult ideas about what is appropriate for a given age level are often less important than a child's desire to know about a particular topic. A reader's approach to an informational book might not be to read pages in order from first to last, as fiction demands. In this type of reading, illustration plays a vital part by focusing interest and clarifying or extending information. Most of all, our example shows how informational literature can provide powerful motivation to read and to enjoy experiences with books. Children are curious about the world and how it works, and they develop passionate attachments to the right books at the right time. They deserve teachers and librarians who can help them discover this particular kind of satisfaction in reading.

Trends in Informational Books

New worlds and new interests lie waiting for children between the covers of informational books. The secrets of animal intelligence, mummies, and doll making have all been revealed in attractive and inviting formats. For proof, have a look at Margery Facklam's *What Does the Crow Know?*, Patricia Lauber's *Tales Mummies Tell*, and Susan Kuklin's *From Head to Toe: How a Doll Is Made*. Informational books also offer children new perspectives on familiar topics as can be found in Jan Adkins's *String* or in Cathryn Falwell's *The Letter Jesters*. Some informational books, like *Inside and Outside Spiders* by Sandra Markle, have tremendous eye appeal and invite browsing. Others are designed to reward sustained attention, like James Cross Giblin's explanation of the unraveling of an ancient mystery in *The Riddle of the Rosetta Stone*. Informational books for children are more numerous, more various, and

more appealing than ever. Only recently have they begun to receive the critical recognition and classroom attention that they have long deserved. We begin here by looking briefly at some of these changes and the current trends in informational books for today's child.

In many ways the current trends mirror recent changes in the larger world of children's books. The following overview covers the more obvious developments of recent years.

Increased Quantity and Quality

More trade book publishers are producing informational books—and more attractive ones—than ever before. New companies and new imprints have been created to keep up with the demand generated by more teachers using literature in the classroom and more people buying books in retail stores. Some publishers' catalogs that previously offered nonfiction only rarely now show many new titles on a regular basis. Frequently these titles are edited, designed, and produced with the same care that was once reserved for picture books. Jean George's *Everglades*, with illustrations by Wendell Minor, is one example. The result is a stunning array of informational books from which teachers, librarians, and children of all ages can choose.

Informational books such as Susan Kuklin's *From Head to Toe: How a Doll Is Made* offer children fascinating details about familiar objects.

From *From Head To Toe: How A Doll Is Made* by Susan Kuklin. Text and photographs copyright © 1994 Susan Kuklin. Reprinted by permission of Hyperion Books for Children.

A New Focus on the Very Young

Part of the increased production of informational books can be attributed to a growing awareness of a new market. In keeping with the recent emphasis on the importance of early childhood education, there is a new focus on the preschool and early primary audience for informational books. Concept books and identification books that provide the names of objects have long been a popular type of informational picture book for young children (see Chapter 4). Recently, however, many types of informational formats have been offered for the very young. Books in the See How They Grow series (published by Dorling Kindersley) use clear photos and minimal text to show how baby animals change in the first few weeks of life. Angela Royston's *Insects and Crawly Creatures*, a book in the Eye-Openers series, focuses on naming and identification but adds information about each insect and close-up drawings of significant details. Both series are printed on extra-heavy stock to allow for hard wear by preschoolers. Both also originate in England and share some of the visual characteristics of the popular Eyewitness Books series for older readers and their simpler counterparts in the Eyewitness Juniors series (published by Knopf).

The photo essay is another format sometimes directed now to a very young audience, as in Ron Hirschi's gentle commentaries on the seasons in *Spring*, *Summer*, *Fall*, and *Winter*. Even experiment books, usually the province of older students, may be appropriate

Wendell Minor's lovely illustrations for *Everglades* by Jean Craighead George help create an informational book that is also aesthetically pleasing.

Illustration copyright © 1995 by Wendell Minor. Used by permission of HarperCollins Publishers, New York, NY.

Many informational books for the very young child feature attractive photographs, like these in Angela Royston's *Insects and Crawly Creatures*.

Reprinted with the permission of Little Simon, an imprint of Simon & Schuster from *Eye Openers—Insects and Crawly Creatures* by Angela Royston, illustrations by Jane Cradock-Weston and Dave Hopkins. Copyright © 1992 Dorling Kindersley Limited, London.

for younger classes if they are as simple and inviting as Neil Ardley's *The Science Book of Weather*. Although informational series for young children account for many of the new titles, some authors and illustrators do produce fine informational picture books that are one of a kind. Byron Barton's *I Want to Be an Astronaut* and *Bones, Bones, Dinosaur Bones* fit this category.

The Growing Importance of Illustration

Another feature of informational books that has changed in recent years is the increased reliance on illustration, especially photography. In our media-conscious society, both children and adults have become more visually oriented, more likely to expect pictures in magazines, newspapers, and other print materials. At the same time, technological improvements in making and reproducing pictures have made it possible to satisfy the demand for color, close-ups, and novel perspectives.

Informational books for all ages often sell themselves, and their topic, on the basis of sophisticated photography or ingenious illustration. A picture postscript in Bianca Lavies's *Wasps at Home* shows how the author/photographer lay on her back—"camera in hand and strobe lights at the ready"—to photograph paper wasps in their nest through a glass enclosure at her studio

window. Richard Platt's Incredible Cross Sections books are full of facts, but the real fascination of these books lies in Stephen Beisty's intricate illustrations.

Unconventional Formats and Approaches

A related trend in informational books today is enthusiasm for unconventional approaches, including experimental formats and combinations of fact and fiction. Pop-ups and lift-the-flap books are part of this trend. Nancy Willard's pop-up book *Gutenberg's Gift* allows children to get an idea of how the first printing press worked. Scholastic's First Discovery books, such as Pascale de Bourgoing's *Under the Ground*, have clear plastic overlays that help children visualize important concepts. The text of Sheila Hamanaka's distinguished book *The Journey: Japanese Americans, Racism, and Renewal* is organized around a mural painted by the author; each segment of text accompanies and describes one or two details of the larger painting.

Other books that look like conventional picture books might be innovative in the ways they deliver information, often using a fictitious story as the vehicle or at least borrowing from the techniques of fiction. *The Magic School Bus Inside a Hurricane* and other books in this series by Joanna Cole and Bruce Degen could be classified as fantasy picture books, with their miniaturized school bus and impossible field trips led by the intrepid teacher, Ms. Frizzle. Student dialogue is presented in speech balloons borrowed from the comics and a wisecracking tone reminiscent of television situation comedy. Yet the books are clearly designed to present information, both in the details of the bus's journey and in the student "reports" displayed as insets in almost every illustration.

Specialized Topics

During the last decade, more informational books have been published about highly specialized topics. There have always been specialized books, but today there are more and more books that reflect very specific interests. They might report personalized perspectives, give detailed information about a narrowly defined topic, or cut across subject matter in a new way. For instance, Hana Machotka focuses on single features of animal anatomy in such books as *What Neat Feet!*, *Breathtaking Noses*, and *Terrific Tails*. There are books about special topics like sitting down (James Cross Giblin's *Be Seated: A Book About Chairs*), adjectives (Ruth Heller's *Many Luscious Lollipops*), and special zoos for insects (*Insect Zoo* by Susan Meyers). Although students might not identify these topics as something they want or need to read about, the books frequently create interest in the topics.

Recognition and Awards

Many of the trends we have looked at here indicate that informational books are innovative and creative. They carry the unique perspective of individual authors and of artists free to experiment with formats and media. It is not surprising, then, that informational books for children are finally being recognized for their aesthetic qualities as literature. In the past, nonfiction books have not earned their fair share of critical attention and recognition. In 1981, author Betty Bacon pointed out that nonfiction books had won the Newbery Medal only six times in fifty-eight years, and those winners were from history or biography, in which the chronological narrative form is very much like fiction.[1] This is quite a contrast to literature for adults, where authors like John McPhee and Tracy Kidder regularly win critical acclaim for their work and nonfiction frequently dominates the best-sellers lists.

More recently, works of nonfiction, such as Russell Freedman's *Lincoln: A Photobiography*, *The Wright Brothers*, and *Eleanor Roosevelt: A Life of Discovery*, and Patricia Lauber's *Volcano: The Eruption and Healing of*

Mt. St. Helens, have been honored by the Newbery Committee. The Boston Globe–Horn Book Awards have included a nonfiction category for many years. Some of the books recognized in this category have been Natalie S. Bober's *Abigail Adams: Witness to a Revolution*, Robie H. Harris's *It's Perfectly Normal: A Book About Changing Bodies, Growing Up, Sex, and Sexual Health*, and Jim Murphy's *The Great Fire*.

In 1990 the National Council of Teachers of English established the Orbis Pictus Award for Outstanding Nonfiction for Children. Its name commemorates what is thought to be the first book of facts produced for children, dating back to the seventeenth century. Recent winners include Barbara Bash's *Ancient Ones: The World of the Old-Growth Douglas Fir* and Jim Murphy's *Across America on an Emigrant Train*. In general, biography continues to win more awards than other types of nonfiction, but now at least there are opportunities for all kinds of informational books to receive the acclaim they deserve.

Criteria for Evaluating Informational Books

One critic who has given close attention to informational books for children is Jo Carr.[2] Teachers and librarians who want to choose the very best books available can be guided by her view that a nonfiction writer is first a teacher, then an artist, and should be concerned with feeling as well as thinking, passion as well as clarity. Specific criteria can be used to help identify this level of achievement. Being familiar with these criteria and with the types of books in which information is presented will make it easier to choose the best books at the right time. The individual reviewer must judge the relative value of the various criteria in terms of particular books. Sometimes a book's strengths in one or two categories may far outweigh its weakness in others (see the Guidelines box later in this chapter).

Accuracy and Authenticity

Accuracy is of primary importance in informational books for children. No one wants inaccurate information, no matter how well it is presented, especially because many children believe anything printed in a book is true. The author's qualifications, the way in which the author presents facts and generalizations, the correctness of the illustrations, and many other factors

---

[1]Betty Bacon, "The Art of Nonfiction," *Children's Literature in Education* 12 (spring 1981): 3.

[2]Jo Carr, "Writing the Literature of Fact," in *Beyond Fact: Nonfiction for Children and Young People* (Chicago: American Library Association, 1982), pp. 3–12.

need to be considered in evaluating a book's accuracy and authenticity.

The Author's Qualifications

Informational books are written by people who are authorities in their fields, or they are written by writers who study a subject, interview specialists, and compile the data. A few, like naturalist Jean Craighead George, are both specialists and writers. It is always a good idea to check the book's jacket copy, title page, introduction, or "About the Author" page at the back for information about the author's special qualifications, often expressed in terms of professional title or affiliation. Expertise in one field does not necessarily indicate competency in another, however, so we expect a high degree of authenticity only if the author has limited the book to what appears to be his or her specialty.

If a book is written not by an expert in the field but by a "writer," facts can be checked by authorities and the authority cited. For example, the book *Get the Message: Telecommunications in Your High-Tech World* was written by Gloria Skurzynski, a writer better known for fiction than for information. However, the acknowledgments name a long list of experts she interviewed and consulted, corporations that provided materials and information, and experts who reviewed her manuscript. Photo credits show that the illustrations were furnished by companies and universities on the cutting edge of this technology. The record of sources and research provided here gives assurance that the book is accurate.

A number of authors have earned the reputation of writing dependably good informational books. When in doubt, teachers and librarians are likely to turn first to writers who have proved their integrity with facts—Vicki Cobb, James Cross Giblin, Russell Freedman, Milton Meltzer, Laurence Pringle, Seymour Simon, and Helen Roney Sattler, among others. But authorship, while it may be a valuable rule of thumb, is a dangerous final criterion. Each book must be evaluated on its own merits.

Factual Accuracy

Fortunately, many of the errors of fact in children's informational books are minor. Children who have access to a variety of books on one topic should be encouraged to notice discrepancies and pursue the correct answer, a valuable exercise in critical reading.

Errors that teachers and children recognize are less distressing than those that pass for fact because the topic is unfamiliar or highly specialized; then the reader must depend on a competent review to identify inaccuracies. Ideally, a book with technical information should be reviewed by someone with expertise in that field. *Appraisal: Children's Science Books* is a periodical that offers paired reviews, one by a science professional, and one by a teacher or librarian. *Science Books and Films* includes reviews by specialists in the field. The *Horn Book Magazine* singles out science books for special reviewing efforts, although other nonfiction is included. The *School Library Journal* often provides helpful criticism. *Social Education* and *Science and Children* magazines also give some attention to appropriate books, and both publish a list of outstanding books in their respective fields each year. Generally speaking, science books are more likely to be challenged by experts than are those about history or other topics in the humanities.

Being Up-to-Date

Some books that are free of error at the time of writing become inaccurate with the passage of time, as new discoveries are made in the sciences or as changes occur in world politics. Books that focus on the past are less likely to be rapidly outdated, although new discoveries in archaeology or new theories in history and anthropology call for a reevaluation of these materials also. On the other hand, books that focus on subjects on which vigorous research and experimentation are being done, such as viruses and disease or space technology, are quickly outdated. It is worth noting, however, that the latest trade books are almost always more up-to-date than the latest textbooks or encyclopedias.

It is also difficult, but important, to provide children with current information about other countries where national governments are emerging or where future political developments are uncertain. Current events that generate an interest in books about a particular country also call attention to the fact that those books might be out-of-date. Just months after the publication of Laurie Dolphin's *Georgia to Georgia: Making Friends in the U.S.S.R.*, the record of an Atlanta family's trip to Tbilisi, violent changes broke apart the Soviet Union. This does not invalidate the personal and cultural information in the book, but it does mean that statements about the government, the economy, and peace efforts are not accurate for today.

Books about minority cultures also need to include material on contemporary experience, as well as heritage. Books like *Apache Rodeo* and *Cherokee Summer*, both by Diane Hoyt-Goldsmith, show families who take pride in continuing their traditions but also are clearly people of today's world. Being up-to-date is one of the ways that books of this kind can combat stereotypes.

Inclusion of All the Significant Facts

Though the material presented in a book might be current and technically correct, the book cannot be totally accurate if it omits significant facts. Thirty years ago science books that dealt with animal reproduction

Bridget, a Native American girl, is interested in her tribe's history but is also comfortable in the modern world in Diane Hoyt-Goldsmith's *Cherokee Summer.*
Copyright © Lawrence Migdale.

frequently glossed over the specifics of birth or mating. In Robert McClung's *Possum,* the process was explained like this: "All night long the two of them wandered through the woods together. But at dawn each went his own way again. Possum's babies were born just twelve days later."[3] Fortunately, changing social mores that struck down taboos in children's fiction also encouraged a new frankness in informational books. For instance, close-up photographs and a forthright text in *My Puppy Is Born* by Joanna Cole show the birth and early development of a terrier's litter. *Egg to Chick* by Millicent Selsam pictures the mating of a rooster and a hen.

Human reproduction and sexuality have so often been distorted by omissions that books with accurate terminology and explicit information are particularly welcome. An attractive book designed for parents to share with young children is Sara Stein's *Making Babies,* which deals openly with questions that adults often find difficult to answer. After suggesting an uncomplicated way to explain the mechanics of intercourse, the author says: "It is sensible and honest to add that, because it feels nice, people make love together even when they are not starting a baby" (p. 38). A more recent book that speaks of conception with comparable candor is *How I Was Born* by Marie Wabbes. Older children will find that Robie H. Harris's *It's Perfectly Normal: A Book About Changing Bodies, Growing Up, Sex, and Sexual Health* is a thorough and frank guide to adolescent and adult sexuality. Michael Emberley's detailed illustrations

add a wonderful touch of humor to what is often a touchy subject for this age group.

The honest presentation of all information necessary for understanding a topic is just as important in historical or cultural accounts as in the sciences. This may be difficult to achieve because social issues are complex and writing for a young audience requires that the author be brief. Judging whether a book does include all the significant facts can also be difficult, for deciding what really counts is a matter of interpretation, often dependent on the book's intended audience. A. P. Porter's *Kwanzaa,* a book designed for early elementary readers, does an admirable job of explaining in simple terms the purpose and symbolism of this seven-day African American holiday. The historical context, however, might be more helpful if it were more complete. How does Kwanza reflect a heritage that predates slavery? Was the origin of Kwanza related to changes brought about by the civil rights movement? Is Kwanza recognized and celebrated by a large percentage of African Americans? If a book leaves important questions unanswered, it has not included all the significant facts.

Avoiding Stereotypes

A book that omits significant facts tells only part of the truth; a book that presents stereotypes pretends, wrongly, to have told the truth. One very common sort of stereotyping is by omission. If we never see women or minorities in science books, for instance, we are left with the incorrect impression that all scientists must be white males. In recent years, fortunately, some authors, illustrators, and publishers have made conscious efforts to represent the great variety of roles that women and minorities play in science and the world of work. Harlow Rockwell's *My Doctor* was a leader in portraying a woman physician in a book for the very young, and Gail Gibbons has made many similar contributions, including a woman surveyor on the work crew of *New Road!* This no-fanfare approach helps combat stereotypes because it encourages children to accept the contributions of all as a matter of course.

Books about countries around the world and those that describe life in a minority culture are the most likely to include stereotypes. Children can be taught to watch for sweeping general statements and for unwarranted claims about what "everybody" thinks or does. However, all readers need to realize that it is almost impossible to portray a country or region completely in *all* its diversity of people, terrain, industry, lifestyles, and the like. When the region is large and the book is limited in length, it is good if the author deliberately highlights differences rather than generalizing too freely. John Chiasson's *African Journey* focuses one-by-one on six specific locations in the midsection of Africa. This book illuminated

[3]Robert McClung, *Possum* (New York: Morrow, 1963), p. 41.

contrasts in geographical conditions and resulting variation in lifestyles through distinguished color photographs and a clear, detailed text.

Another way that authors try to avoid stereotyping is by relating the story of one individual within a community. Diane Hoyt-Goldsmith's books about Native Americans focus on one tribe and then on a particular child's family, school, and community experiences. Readers associate the facts in these books with specific persons and places. Consequently, they will be less likely to assume that this description of Native American life represents the way *all* people of Native American heritage live.

Using Facts to Support Generalizations

To be distinguishable from stereotype or simple opinion, a proper generalization needs facts for support. Ron Roy begins his book *Move Over, Wheelchairs Coming Through!* in this way:

> Thousands of kids are wheelchair users. These young people are disabled, but in most cases their disabilities have not stopped them from doing the things they want to do. (p. 1)

The entire book is organized to support this point. Seven young wheelchair users were photographed and interviewed; essays about each one show their mobility and determination.

Laurence Pringle says in *Vanishing Ozone: Protecting Earth from Ultra Violet Radiation* that the ozone layer in the atmosphere is shrinking as a result of chemicals released into the atmosphere. He explains how scientists proved that the ozone layer was being depleted and then offers evidence to support the role of chemicals such as CFCs in this phenomenon. Critical readers need to be aware of generalizations and judge for themselves whether adequate facts are offered for support.

Making the Distinction Between Fact and Theory

Careful writers make careful distinctions between fact and theory; but even so, children need guidance in learning to recognize the difference. Often the distinction depends on key words or phrases—such as *scientists believe, so far as we know,* or *perhaps.* Consider the importance of the simple phrase *may have* in this description of a prehistoric reptile: "Pterodactyls lived near the shores of prehistoric seas and may have slept hanging from tree branches by their feet, like bats."[4] Some

discussion of different kinds of possible evidence might be in order as children are led to see that one-half of this statement is presented as fact, the other as theory.

Books about the disappearance of the dinosaurs make good material for helping children sort out the difference between fact and theory, because the problem is dramatic and the evidence provides for legitimate disagreement among scientists. Franklin Branley's *What Happened to the Dinosaurs?* does a particularly good job of helping primary-age children understand what a theory is.

Although it is important to distinguish between fact and theory in all of the sciences, including the social sciences, the matter receives most attention in books dealing with evolution and human origins. In some communities this is a very sensitive topic, but it would seem that children everywhere have a right to information about scientists' discoveries and theories regarding our origins. *Traces of Life* by Kathryn Lasky, a book for older readers, presents "the origins of humankind" in terms of particular fossil discoveries and the sometimes differing interpretations that scientists have made of these. In contrast, David Peters's *From the Beginning: The Story of Human Evolution* fails to acknowledge the process by which ideas about evolution have become accepted in the scientific community.

Avoiding Anthropomorphism

In poetry and fiction, the assignment of human feelings and behavior to animals, plants, or inanimate objects is called *personification*—an accepted literary device that can be used with great effect. In science, however, this device is unacceptable and is known as *anthropomorphism.* Science writer Millicent Selsam addressed the problem of interpreting what animals do in one of her early books on animal behavior:

> It is hard to keep remembering that animals live in a different kind of world from our own. They see, hear, smell, and taste things differently. And they do not have human intelligence or emotions, so we must avoid interpreting their behavior in terms of our own feelings and thoughts. For example, it looks to us as though parent birds are devoted to their young in the same way that human parents are devoted to theirs. But only experimental work can show whether this interpretation is true.[5]

Knowing that young children perceive new things in terms of their experiences and feelings, however, writers have often given names to their animal subjects or

---

[4]David C. Knight, *Dinosaurs That Swam and Flew,* illustrated by Lee J. Ames (Englewood Cliffs, N.J.: Prentice Hall, 1985), p. 39.

[5]Millicent Selsam, *Animals as Parents,* illustrated by John Kaufmann (New York: 1965), p. 16.

expressed animal behavior in childlike terms. Many books with these anthropomorphic touches are still in print. Newer informational books are doing a much better job of reporting only observable animal behavior in a straightforward way. In *To the Top of the World: Adventures with Arctic Wolves*, Jim Brandenburg names the wolves he observes after one of his relatives (Buster), their role in the pack (Mom) or their physical characteristics (Scruffy, Midback). This is not anthropomorphism, just good reporting and clear writing.

Closely related to anthropomorphism is another error called *teleological* explanation of phenomena. Briefly, teleology attempts to account for natural phenomena by assigning a purpose to the plants, animals, or forces involved. Science books should not suggest that leaves turn toward the light in order to bask in the sun or that Mother Nature, capitalized and personified, is at work carving the walls of canyons. While such a description has a certain poetic effect, it also conveys a basically unscientific attitude.

Content and Perspective

Consideration of the purpose of a book, its intended audience, and the objectivity of its author can help readers evaluate an informational book's content and perspective. A good informational book should also foster reflective inquiry in children and enable them to see relationships across disciplines.

Purpose

It is futile to try to pass judgment on the content of an informational book without first determining the purpose for which the book was designed. Identifying the scope of the book lets us know what we can reasonably expect. A quick look at Vicki Cobb's *Why Can't You Unscramble an Egg?* reveals a fascinating collection of questions and explanations for browsing, whereas both the title and the appearance of Helen Sattler's *The New Illustrated Dinosaur Dictionary* indicate a comprehensive treatment of the topic. Titles can be misleading, particularly those that promise to tell "all about" a subject but offer limited coverage instead. At best, titles indicate the scope of the book's content and pique the reader's curiosity, as do the titles of two of James Cross Giblin's books, *The Truth About Unicorns* and *Be Seated: A Book About Chairs*. More about the scope and purpose of informational books can be found in the section "Types of Informational Books" later in this chapter.

Intended Audience

Before evaluating content, we have to know not just for what the book was intended, but for whom. Book jackets and book reviews often indicate an age range according to reading level or interest. It is difficult to know whether one or both of these factors are reflected in the age recommendation. Generally, a book's reading level is not as important as its content in relation to the reader's actual interest in a subject. Older students and adults might turn to children's informational books for introductory material on an unfamiliar topic. In using informational books, children will read "beyond their abilities" when reading for particular facts. Children will frequently turn to difficult books if they contain many pictures or useful diagrams. At the same time, vocabulary, sentence length, size of type, and the organization of the book are factors to be considered. Children might reject a book that contains useful information if they see crowded pages, relatively small type, and few pictures.

The choice of topic, then, is an important factor in determining whether a book will be suitable for its intended audience. Books for young children most often reflect their basic egocentric concerns and their curiosity about themselves and other living things; it is a mistake to assume that they will not be interested in other subjects, however. Many early primary children enjoy browsing through the widely diverse titles of the Eyewitness series, such as Theresa Greenaway's *Jungle*, or *Pyramid* by Jane McIntosh, even though these books are designed for an older audience. On the other hand, books that look like picture books are frequently aimed at upper-grade children. Jon Scieszka's *Math Curse* requires readers to keep track of some complex mathematical concepts while they follow the ins and outs of the visual and verbal narrative.

Examples chosen by an author to clarify concepts are related to the level of cognitive ability needed to get the most out of a book. In *Sarah Morton's Day*, Kate Waters caters to a young child's need to approach historical understanding through concrete details. One double spread of sequenced color photos shows Sarah, the pilgrim girl, getting dressed in her overgarments. First comes the petticoat, then stockings, garters, two more petticoats, a waistcoat, coif, apron, "pocket," and shoes—a clear contrast to sweatsuits and sneakers!

Adequate Coverage

Recognizing the purpose of a book and its intended level, the reader has a basis for deciding if the author has said too much about the topic or too little. Stan Hoig's book for older readers, *A Capital for the Nation*, provides 125 pages of information about the history of the Capitol, the White House, and various monuments and memorials in Washington, D.C. The focus is limited but the treatment is detailed. As a matter of fact, it is hard to imagine any young reader being interested in all the background facts

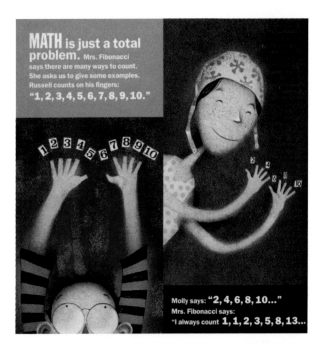

Lane Smith's illustrations and Jon Scieszka's text provide older readers with a nonthreatening foray into math in *Math Curse*.

From *Math Curse* by Jon Scieszka, illustrated by Lane Smith. Copyright © 1995 by Jon Scieszka, text. Copyright © 1995 by Lane Smith, illustrations. Used by permission of Viking Penguin, a division of Penguin Books USA Inc.

and sidelights that are included. For information about present-day Washington, readers might turn to Shirley Climo's simpler *City! Washington, D.C.*, which has color photos, a travelogue flair, and some basic historical information as well. It is worth noting, though, that neither book's title reveals it purpose or scope.

Broader topics, like the history or culture of a nation, might require many pages in order to give even brief attention to all the significant material. History textbooks have earned particularly harsh criticism for faulty coverage,[6] and good trade books help to fill in perspectives that the textbooks omit. A generation ago, Gerald Johnson expressed the need for careful writing in the introduction to his book *America Is Born:*

🐌 Part of the story is very fine, and other parts are very bad, but they all belong to it, and if you leave out the bad parts you never understand it all. (viii–ix)

Authors who fail to acknowledge more than one viewpoint or theory fail to help children learn to examine issues. Even young children should know that authorities do not always agree, though the context might be simple. It is far more common, though, and certainly

[6]See Frances FitzGerald, *America Revised* (Boston: Atlantic/Little, Brown, 1979).

more necessary, for books about complex issues to deal with varying points of view. Laurence Pringle's *Nuclear Energy: Troubled Past, Uncertain Future* outlines efforts for and against a "second nuclear era" and identifies proponents of both sides. Anything less would have been inadequate coverage of the topic.

Demonstration of Scientific Method

Because we are concerned about *how* as well as *what* children learn, it is important to note what kind of thinking a book encourages, as well as the body of facts it presents. Informational books should illustrate the process of inquiry, the excitement of discovery. Children in the upper elementary grades are fascinated by the dramatic account of Frank and John Craighead's groundbreaking wildlife research in *Operation Grizzly Bear* by Marian Calabro. Laurence Pringle's *Bearman: Exploring the World of Black Bears* provides a similar but less detailed treatment of the work of naturalist Lynn Rogers. Both of these books give readers a good idea of the problems scientists try to solve and the kind of day-to-day work that is involved.

While these are fine accounts of the scientific method at work, the reader's involvement is still vicarious. Some books are designed to give children more-direct experience with the skills of inquiry. Millicent Selsam's *How to Be a Nature Detective* encourages children to ask "What happened, who was here, and where did he go?" in order to learn how to read animal tracks. At each step of the process Marlene Donnelly's illustrations help children follow this sequence as if they were actually outdoors tracking various animals. Sandra Markle's guides for observing ants in *Exploring Autumn* provide simple directions (no pictures needed), ask questions that direct attention to important features like the relation between the size of an ant's burden to its body, and give background information that helps children interpret what they see.

The photographs in Patricia Lauber's *Dinosaurs Walked Here and Other Stories Fossils Tell* are chosen and placed to help children make their own observations about the fossil record. A photo of a present-day horseshoe crab beside the fossil print of its 140-million-year-old ancestor allows readers to conclude that these creatures have scarcely changed over time; a companion picture lets us discover how beavers have shrunk in the past fifteen thousand years. All of Lauber's books demonstrate this commitment to presenting scientific evidence in such a way that children can confirm some conclusions for themselves.

The scientific method applies to the social sciences, too. Jean Fritz has illustrated techniques of historical research in a fictionalized account that children like very much—*George Washington's Breakfast*. The story illustrates the role of perseverance and good luck in

It is the remembered smell of its home stream that tells a salmon when its journey is over. Its nostrils quiver as it recognizes the smell. Its body quickens. At last it is home again. Where it finally comes to a stop may be only yards from its birthplace, or, in the case of the Jackson School salmon, from the spot where it was released into the creek.

But not all salmon migrating from stream to ocean will return.

Many smolt-size salmon are gobbled up almost as soon as they enter the sea. Water birds such as mergansers, kingfishers, sea gulls, and great blue herons feed on the tiny fish. Whales, seals, and sea lions eat larger salmon, as do eagles and

GROWING UP IN THE OCEAN

All species of Pacific salmon leave their home streams to feed and to grow to maturity in the salty waters of the Pacific Ocean. But different species of Pacific salmon stay in the ocean for different lengths of time. A Coho, or "Silver," usually lives in the ocean for about one and a half to two years before returning to its home stream to spawn. However, some early-maturing Cohos, known as "Jacks," return from the ocean after less than a year.

The Pacific salmon that stays in the ocean the longest is the Chinook. This "king of salmons" sometimes grows to more than a hundred pounds (while a fully grown Coho usually weighs no more than twelve pounds). No other species grows as big. The Chinook may take four years or more of feeding in the ocean to reach its immense size.

During their life in the ocean, Chinook and Coho salmon may journey as far north as Baranof Island, Alaska, and as far south as the coast of northern California. Pacific salmon generally travel in a counterclockwise direction until the time comes for them to begin their race toward their home streams.

ALASKAN BROWN BEARS ARE EXPERTS AT FISHING.

THE JOURNEY   35

Molly Cone's *Come Back Salmon* provides facts about Pacific salmon alongside the story of fifth graders who restored salmon spawning grounds.

Text copyright © 1992 by Molly Cone from *Come Back, Salmon.* Used by permission of Sierra Club Books for Children. Photo copyright © Jim Nilsen.

problem solving. After young George, who is trying to find out what George Washington customarily ate for breakfast, has asked questions, exhausted library resources, and gone on a futile fact-finding trip to Mt. Vernon, he happens to find the answer in an old book about to be discarded from his own attic. *The Riddle of the Rosetta Stone: Key to Ancient Egypt* by James Cross Giblin and Kathy Pelta's *Discovering Christopher Columbus: How History Is Invented* demonstrate how historians study evidence and develop hypotheses. Intermediate children can also find out about using primary sources for studying personal history in *The Great Ancestor Hunt* by Lila Perl.

Interrelationships and Implications

A list of facts is fine for an almanac, but informational books should be expected to put facts into some sort of perspective. After all, linking facts in one way or another transforms information into knowledge. Thomas Locker's *Sky Tree* shows how the same tree changes through the seasons and how it interacts with the animals, the earth, and the sky around it throughout the

year. *Come Back Salmon* by Molly Cone intersperses information about Coho salmon, the watershed, and water pollution in a story about a class of fifth graders who cleaned up a dead stream near their school and saw the salmon return to spawn there.

Interrelationships of a different sort are pointed out in Barbara Brenner's *If You Were There in 1492.* This book helps readers see the cultural context in which a major event, Columbus's first voyage, took place. The author describes the world as it would have been known to ordinary people in Spain in terms of food, clothing, education, books, the arts, crime, ships, and many other aspects. The vivid presentations of the 1492 expulsion of Jews from Spain and the everyday life of the Lucayan people on the island where Columbus would land are especially good for prompting discussion about the relationship of one culture to another.

Intertwining science and technology with modern culture has become crucial, and many recent informational books have taken this issue as a focus. *Going Green: A Kid's Handbook to Saving the Planet* by John Elkington and others is a popular catalog of information about the effects of daily decisions on the environment.

Even books not specifically designed to call attention to the related social problems of science and technology ought to acknowledge that such problems exist. Where the uses of science have serious implications for society, the relationships should be made clear. (See the discussion of the study theme "Stewards of the Earth" in Chapter 13 for more about this issue.)

Style

The style of an informational book can be crucial in attracting children to the book and in helping them to understand the concepts presented there. The clarity of presentation and the appropriateness of the language for its intended audience are important matters to consider in evaluating a book's style. In addition the writing should involve readers in the topic and provide them with an absorbing and vivid learning experience.

Clarity and Directness

It is difficult to list all of the criteria that influence clarity. The use of precise language and specific detail is one important factor. Nothing is vague in Miriam Schlein's description of a vampire bat's dinner in *Billions of Bats*. She names the animals that are likely prey ("a horse, a cow, a donkey, or even chicken"), describes the approach and the bite ("only about a tenth of an inch long"), and goes on to explain how the bat curves its tongue into a funnel shape and sucks in blood ("for about a half hour"). The language is simple and direct, giving the reader a clear picture of the process.

In earlier decades we could say with some certainty that information presented in the guise of fiction was confusing and ought to be avoided. A few recent books, however, have offered skillful combinations of fact and fiction in which information is clearly presented. One of these is Joe Lasker's *A Tournament of Knights*. The fictional frame for this story in picture-book format provides names, feelings, and family connections for two jousting knights. Still, the center of interest is the book's information about the tournament itself—how it was organized, what weapons and armor were required, and how the assembled lords and ladies responded as per custom to the action. The story element in books like this can help children understand facts that might otherwise seem too distant. On the other hand, not every author is this successful in making the combination; some fail to do a very good job of entertaining or of informing. Each book must be judged on its own merits.

Level of Difficulty

Although the vocabulary does have to be within the child's range, books for primary-grade children need not be restricted to a narrow list of words. New terms can be explained in context. In *Follow the Water from Brook to Ocean*, Arthur Dorros provides a two-paragraph description of the effects of moving water before introducing the word *erosion*. He also gives helpful context through examples and illustrations for the words *meanders* and *reservoir*. Context does not serve to explain everything, however; a writer aware of the background of the intended audience takes pains to make new words clear.

Words that look unpronounceable are another stumbling block for most children. A glossary is helpful, but youngsters who are intent on a book's content might not take time to look in the back. In some cases authors provide pronunciation guides in parentheses for daunting words. Such is the case in Caroline Arnold's *Dinosaurs Down Under: And Other Fossils from Australia* and Miriam Schlein's *Discovering Dinosaur Babies*.

Reader Involvement

Authors use many different techniques to engage readers' attention and help them stay involved with a book's subject matter. David Getz's *Frozen Man*, about a five-thousand-year-old man found frozen in the ice in the Alps, begins with this enticing statement: "Nobody knew what stories the body could tell." Jim Arnosky's *All About Alligators* and *All About Owls* asks questions that alert readers to important information in the text.

Nonfiction authors also use direct address—sentences that speak to the reader as "you." Sometimes an author asks direct questions to claim a bond of communication with the reader. Paul Showers hooks the primary audience for *How Many Teeth?* with a variety of rhymes interspersed throughout the text to ask "How many teeth have you?"

Children may be more quickly drawn into an informational book by a sense of immediacy in the writing. The use of present tense sometimes serves this purpose. *Chimney Sweeps* by James Giblin begins with a present-tense account of a modern chimney sweep at work. Parts of the book are cast in past tense to provide facts about chimneys and sweeps, but the author returns to present tense and second person to describe a typical day in the life of a "climbing boy" in 1800. He invites the reader to participate:

> Then imagine that you are one of three climbing boys working for a master sweep. You are eleven years old and have been cleaning chimneys ever since you were six, when your parents sold you to the master.
>
> It is 4:30 in the morning when the master comes down into the cellar to wake you. (p. 17)

Children reward the author's efforts with this book by becoming deeply involved in the unusual topic.

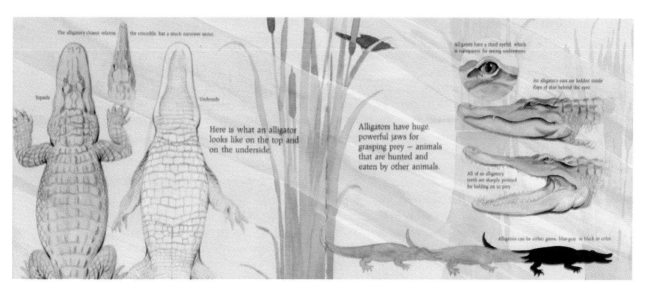

All About Alligators, by Jim Arnosky, engages readers' attention through engaging questions and enthralling pictorial details.
From *All About Alligators* by Jim Arnosky. Copyright © 1994 by Jim Arnosky. Reprinted by permission of Scholastic Inc.

Vivid Language

The writer of informational books uses the same techniques as the writer of fiction to bring a book to life, although the words must be accurate as well as attractive. Imagery is used to appeal to the senses, as in Barbara Bash's *Ancient Ones: The World of the Old-Growth Douglas Fir:*

🌿 Walking into an old-growth forest, you enter a strangely silent world. The Earth feels moist and springy underfoot, and the air is thick with the fragrance of decomposing needles. (p. 7)

Metaphorical language, since it is based on comparison, can be used to contribute to clarity in nonfiction. Carol Carrick's *Octopus* helps the reader visualize the octopus's underwater existence through similes: "the octopus floated down over the lobster like a sinister parachute"; "she crept spider-like over the bottom of the sea." Older readers appreciate the vivid comparisons in *Predator!* by Bruce Brooks. In describing killer whales after a large prey, Brooks says:

🌿 two of them will taunt a large baleen whale by cruising alongside one to a side, nipping and nudging and poking, like two hoods in stock cars hassling a stern old gent riding in a Cadillac between them. (p. 23)

This book's frequent references to sport and to the contemporary scene present the world of nature in an unusually appealing way, especially for young adolescents.

Children probably will not be able to describe an author's style, but they certainly will respond to it. They know that a well-written informational book somehow does not sound the same as an encyclopedia essay, and they enjoy the difference.

Organization

Even if a book is vividly written, accurate, and in command of its topic, children will not find it very useful unless it also furnishes a clear arrangement of information. The way in which a book's content is structured and the reference aids that it includes should help readers find and then understand key concepts and facts.

Structure

Every author must choose a structure, or organizing principle, as a basis for presenting facts. Sometimes an author uses a very obvious principle, such as organizing a collection of facts alphabetically. This format allows Seymour Simon to introduce older readers to important understandings about the global ecosystem in *Earth Words: A Dictionary of the Environment.* In this book, as in others, the alphabet device makes a good format for browsing and is easily understood by children, although it pays less attention to the relationship among facts.

The question-and-answer approach has become more widely used in recent years. For very young children, questions and pictured answers can change a concept book into an engaging guessing game. Several of Margaret Miller's books such as *Guess Who?* repeat a question and suggest four silly answers; turn the page and discover a word or phrase and the photographs of the correct answer. One of the many question books for older readers is *Why Do Volcanoes Erupt?* by Philip

Whitfield with the Natural History Museum. This book presents interesting detail about many earth science topics, but the loose structure makes this volume more appropriate for browsing than for reference.

Another structure closely related to questions and answers is the true/false approach that states common myths or misconceptions and then offers corrected or updated information. One of the best of these books is Patricia Lauber's *The News About Dinosaurs*, with its meticulous but not too technical updates on the latest scientific interpretations of information about the dinosaurs. Children can use this book to check for distortions and misinformation in volumes with older copyright dates, a good application of critical reading and thinking skills.

A common and sensible arrangement for many books, especially about history or biological processes, is based on chronology. Sylvia Johnson's *A Beekeeper's Year* follows the seasons from spring to winter to relate information about the partnership between bees and beekeepers. *Cactus Hotel* by Brenda Guiberson reveals both history and science in its account of the two-hundred-year growth of a giant saguaro cactus.

Regardless of its topic, a general-survey type of book should have a system of headings that help the reader get an overview of the content, unless the book is very brief and has pictures that serve as graphic guides for skimming. The longer the book and the more complex its topic, the greater the need for manageable division. Paul Fleischman's *Townsend's Warbler* gives an account of the difficult cross-country journey of naturalist John Townsend in 1834. Within chapters, extra space between paragraphs indicates changes in the direction of the discussion. A tiny drawing of a bird indicates the switch to parallel information about the journey of the warbler that would come to bear Townsend's name. Subheadings, however, are more helpful as indicators of structure, especially for less-practiced readers.

Reference Aids

With the exception of certain simple and special types, factual books should offer help at both front and back for the reader who needs to locate information quickly. It is important for children to develop reference skills early, so a table of contents and an index should be included in any book whose structure warrants it. Two of Ann Morris's concept books for younger children, such as *Weddings* and *Shoes, Shoes, Shoes*, provide visual indexes with additional information about each of the countries that she has visited in photographs in the books. A map identifies each of the countries shown in the pictures. This is a good way to introduce younger readers to indexes and other reference aids.

For older children an index will be truly useful only if it is complete and has necessary cross-references. It is difficult to think of all the possible words children might use to look up a topic or to answer a question, yet writers should consider as many possibilities as seem reasonable. Lila Perl's *From Top Hats to Baseball Caps, from Bustles to Blue Jeans: Why We Dress the Way We Do* provides the kind of cross-references that readers might need. *Blue jeans, denims, jeans,* and *Levi's* are separate index entries that all lead to the same section of the book; *high-heeled shoes* is cross-referenced with the contemporary variant *heels*.

Other helpful additions to a book are glossaries, bibliographies, suggestions for further reading, and informational appendixes. Picture glossaries are on the increase with the growing number of informational picture books. Nancy Winslow Parker and Joan Richards Wright include illustrated glossaries that summarize growth patterns and add detail about anatomy in their joint productions *Bugs* and *Frogs, Toads, Lizards, and Salamanders*. Either book would be good for demonstrating to children the use of reference aids, because both have touches of humor that add appeal as well as a full range of devices for locating and extending information.

If children are to understand methods of inquiry, they need to learn that a writer uses many sources of information. James Giblin's bibliography for *Be Seated: A Book About Chairs* lists over forty references, including people he interviewed. Suggestions for further reading by children are most helpful if separated from the adult's more technical resources (Giblin uses an asterisk). Many recent informational books include bibliographies, but unfortunately, annotated entries are still the exception rather than the rule.

Appendixes are used to extend information in lists, charts, or tabulations of data that would seem cumbersome in the text itself. *Commodore Perry in the Land of the Shogun*, Rhoda Blumberg's award-winning account of the opening of Japanese harbors to American ships, seems all the more credible because of the documents and lists presented in the appendixes. Having read that lavish gifts were exchanged during the negotiations, children can discover in an appendix that the emperor was offered more than thirty items, including two telegraph sets, a copper lifeboat, champagne, tea, muskets, swords, and two mailbags with padlocks.

Illustrations and Format

In our visually oriented culture, readers of all ages demand that a book's illustrations make it more interesting and attractive. In an informational book, the illustrations and design must do that, and much more.

The photographs and computer-generated images in Helen Roney Sattler's *Our Patchwork Planet* help children understand the concept of plate tectonics.

Illustration from *Our Patchwork Planet* by Helen Roney Sattler, illustrated by Giulio Maestro. Illustration copyright © 1995 by Giulio Maestro. By permission of Lothrop, Lee & Shepard Books, a division of William Morrow & Company, Inc. Photo © American Museum of Natural History, Department of Library Services.

Clarification and Extension of Text

One of the basic functions of illustrations is to clarify and extend the text. *Our Patchwork Planet* by Helen Roney Sattler has photographs of Earth taken from space, photos of nature features on Earth, and computer-generated images that show Earth's shifting surface. It also has drawings and diagrams by Guilio Maestro that help make complicated ideas about plate tectonics more understandable. Cutaway views and clear labeling are other good features of the pictures in this book.

The more abstract the topic, the more important it is that pictures help children "see" explanations. Latitude, longitude, and other mapping concepts, for instance, are often hard for children to grasp, so it is especially important that they be illustrated clearly, as Harriet Barton has done for Jack Knowlton's introductory book *Maps and Globes*. These big, bright pictures use color to focus attention on the equator, contour lines, and other specific aspects of simplified maps.

Illustrations are especially important in clarifying size relationships. Paul Facklam's illustrations for Margery Facklam's *The Big Bug Book* show the actual

Paul Facklam's drawing of a Goliath beetle shows its size in relation to familiar objects in Margery Facklam's *The Big Bug Book*.

From *The Big Bug Book* by Margery Facklam. Text copyright © 1994 by Margery Facklam; illustrations copyright © 1994 by Paul Facklam. By permission of Little, Brown and Company.

size of really big bugs and then places them with familiar objects to help children visualize just how large they really are. Not many topics lend themselves to life-size portrayals, of course, and that makes it important for artists to find other ways to be clear. Photographs and drawings often show magnified parts or wholes, and often some information about actual size is needed. When the reader has no frame of reference for the size of an object, comparison with something familiar is effective. If it weren't for the human hands holding the "Brazilian princess" topaz pictured in *Earth Alive!* by Sandra Markle, most readers would fail to appreciate its tremendous size.

In many books the illustrations add detail and extend the information of the text; in others the illustrations themselves provide the bulk of the information, or become the subject of the text. In Vicki Cobb's *For Your Own Protection: Stories Science Photos Tell*, the subtitle confirms this approach. In addition to thermograms of a child's hands, this book shows a balloon popping in a photo made with a stroboscope, a scanning electron micrograph of plaque bacteria magnified thirty-one thousand times, and other remarkable pictures. The text functions here to clarify and extend the pictures rather than the other way around. When illustrations are this important to a book, they need to have substantive content, high-quality reproduction, and a logical presentation or layout. For other good examples of effective presentation, look at Seymour Simon's books about the planets or Patricia Lauber's *Volcano: The Eruption and Healing of Mt. St. Helen's*.

Suitability of Media

Illustrations in any medium can be clear and accurate, but one medium might be more suitable than another for a given purpose. Three-dimensional illustrations are used for clarity and interest in some informational books. People of all ages are fascinated by the paper engineering in Jonathan Miller's *The Human Body*, designed by David Pelham. This goes beyond the entertainment value of a pop-up book; its movable parts reveal more about anatomy than flat pictures can possibly do. For instance, one double spread of the torso allows the reader to flip back the muscular diaphragm, spread the rib cage to reveal the lungs, and open the lungs to study their connection to the heart.

Diagrams and drawings have an impact of their own and also have many uses especially appropriate to science books. Diagrams can reduce technological processes to their essentials or show astronomical relationships that represent distances too great to be photographed. Diagrams are also fine for giving

directions, and they can be charming as well as clear. This is true of Byron Barton's work for Seymour Simon's popular *The Paper Airplane Book*, where scenes are interspersed with how-to drawings to enliven the text.

Sometimes the perception of a graphic artist is vital to the purpose of a book. David Macaulay's *Ship* traces the modern-day discovery of a sixteenth-century wreck and then takes the reader back in time to watch its construction. Using various color schemes to indicate changes in time and place, Macaulay intersperses realistic drawings with sketches, diagrams, letters, and other documents to show how archaeologists painstakingly research and reconstruct the Spanish caravelle *Magdelena*. Then through a "newly" discovered diary from archives in Seville he reveals how the ship was built and launched. The same standard of excellence, attention to detail, and touches of humor can be found in Macaulay's *The Way Things Work, Cathedral, City, Castle, Pyramid, Underground,* and *Mill*.

In spite of the range of media available for informational books, the medium of choice is now photography. Photographs help establish credibility for real-life stories like *Mom Can't See Me* by Sally Hobart Alexander, an account of living in a family with a blind but very active mother. Photographs reveal the natural world in its astonishing variety, recording minute detail in an instant. The photos by Art Wolfe for James Martin's *Chameleons: Dragons in the Trees* reveal marvels of skin textures, colors, and patterns that would be difficult to reproduce with complete accuracy in a painting.

Photographs in informational books furnish more than technical accuracy, however. Photographers can be artists as well as recorders of information. Ken Robbins uses hand-tinted photographs in *Air* and other books in his Elements series. In *A Flower Grows,* he shows the sequence of stages in the life of a flower, from brown bulb to green stem to pink amaryllis blooms to dying flowers and fat seedpods. Sometimes artistry results not from a single photographer's work but from the careful choice of pictures to accompany an informational text. The photographs that illustrate Seymour Simon's many books come from a variety of sources, but in such books as *Spring Across America* and *Galaxies* their effect is breathtaking.

Captions

Children need to be able to look at an illustration and know what they are seeing, and that requires a wise use of captions and labels. Many writers use the text itself, if it is brief, to explain the pictures, eliminating the need for additional captions. Patricia Lauber's words and Jerome Wexler's photographs are combined in this way for *Seeds: Pop Stick Glide*, a handsome book that explains how plant life spreads. The arrangement of the text on the page and occasional references like "As you can see . . ." or "In this photo, . . ." help readers get maximum information from the illustrations as well as from the writing.

Sometimes it is helpful to have labels or other text printed within the illustration itself. In *Maps: Getting from Here to There* by Harvey Weiss, many drawings and diagrams include labels and arrows to show specifically where items like "a south latitude" or "an east longitude" are represented on the globe. Explanation within the pictures also helps to identify contour lines and the features of a marine chart. Only occasionally does Weiss use a conventional caption to refer to an entire illustration. However an author chooses to use captions, they should be clear.

Format

The total look of a book is its *format*, involving type size, leading, margins, placement of text and pictures, and arrangement of front and back matter—these include title and copyright pages in the front and indexes, bibliographies, and other aids at the back. *Mummies Made in Egypt* by Aliki incorporates hieroglyphic writing on the dedication and half-title pages, and many of the illustrations are arranged like the friezes that decorated the tombs of antiquity. This author frequently arranges sequences of pictures on the page in a comic strip or storyboard variation.

There are no absolute rules for format; the look of a book should be responsive to its purpose and its content. The broad coverage of topic intended in the Eyewitness series published by Knopf makes the busy layout of its pages seem rich rather than crowded. *Think of an Eel* by Karen Wallace is aimed at younger audiences and has wide margins, uncluttered page layouts, and simple captions that give the book an attractive and inviting look.

Even a book that is sparingly illustrated can be notable for its overall design. Spacious margins and tastefully ornamented headings can make a long text seem less forbidding. The format of an informational book is an asset if it contributes to clarity or if it makes the book more appealing to its audience.

The Guidelines box "Evaluating Informational Books" summarizes the key criteria to consider when evaluating informational books.

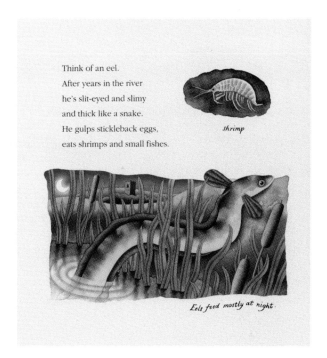

Mike Bostock's illustrations and page designs for Karen Wallace's *Think of an Eel* are particularly inviting to young readers.

Think of an Eel text copyright © 1993 by Karen Wallace; illustration copyright © 1993 by Mike Bostock. Reproduced by permission of Walker Books Ltd, London. Published in the U.S. by Candlewick Press, Cambridge, MA.

Types of Informational Books

Anyone who chooses informational books for children soon notices several subgenres or recognizable types with common characteristics. Knowing about these types helps the teacher and librarian provide balanced and rich resources for learning as they choose particular books for particular purposes.

Concept Books

Concept books explore the characteristics of a class of objects or of an abstract idea. Most of the informational books intended for very young children are of this type. Typically they cover such concepts as size, color, shape, spatial relationships, self, and family. Concept books for this age are discussed at length in Chapter 4. For school-age children, concept books begin with what is already familiar and move toward the unfamiliar, some by showing new ways to consider well-known materials, others by furnishing new and different examples or perspectives. Such books are often useful as idea sources for classroom experiences and discussion.

Guidelines:
Evaluating Informational Books

- Accuracy and Authenticity

Is the author qualified to write about this topic? Has the manuscript been checked by authorities in the field?

Are the facts accurate according to other sources?

Is the information up-to-date?

Are all the significant facts included?

Do text and illustrations reveal diversity and avoid stereotypes?

Are generalizations supported by facts?

Is there a clear distinction between fact and theory?

Do text and illustrations omit anthropomorphism and theleological explanations?

- Content and Perspective

For what purpose was the book designed?

Is the book within the comprehension and interest range of its intended audience?

Is the subject adequately covered? Are different viewpoints presented?

Does the book lead to an understanding of the scientific method? Does it foster the spirit of inquiry?

Does the book show interrelationships? Do science books indicate related social issues?

- Style

Is information presented clearly and directly?

Is the text appropriate for the intended audience?

Does the style create the feeling of reader involvement?

Is the language vivid and interesting?

- Organization

Is the information structured clearly, with appropriate subheadings?

Does the book have reference aids that are clear and easy to use, such as table of contents, index, bibliography, glossary, appendix?

- Illustrations and Format

Do illustrations clarify and extend the text or speak plainly for themselves?

Are size relationships made clear?

Are media suitable to the purposes for which they are used?

Are illustrations explained by captions or labels where needed?

Does the total format contribute to the clarity and attractiveness of the book?

One good book for discussion is Peter Spier's *People*, an oversize picture book that appeals to many different ages as it celebrates the possibilities for variation among the several billion human beings who live on Earth. Spier's drawings include many shapes and colors of ears, eyes, and noses; costumes, shelters, and pastimes from around the world; architecture, alphabets, and foods. Although the author emphasizes the uniqueness of individual appearances and preferences, the concept of cultural differences is implicit in the book. Concept books about culture always raise the issue of stereotyping. Help children think about the author's choice of representative images for this book. Primary students might compare Spier's drawings with the photographs in *Faces* by Shelley Rotner and Ken Kreisler or *Two Eyes, a Nose and a Mouth* by Roberta Intrater.

A beautiful but difficult concept book is *The View from the Oak* by Judith and Herbert Kohl. In leisurely, readable prose, the authors examine the concept of

umwelt, or the world of a living thing as experienced by that creature in terms of its own unique sensory limits. Fascinating bits of information about such diverse animals as wood ticks and oryx antelopes can be found here, as well as an ethological perspective. This is the first nonfiction book for children that received the National Book Award.

Informational Picture Storybooks

As earlier sections of this chapter show, more and more informational books *look* more and more like picture storybooks—that is, they are lavishly illustrated or published in picture-book format. Books such as Barbara Esbensen's *Playful Slider: The North American River Otter*, illustrated by Mary Brown, or Carol Carrick's *Whaling Days*, with woodcuts by David Frampton, present information through conventional, well-written

Mary Barrett Brown's paintings for Barbara Esbensen's *Playful Slider* show details of river otters and their relations.
From *Playful Slider* by Barbara Esbensen. Text copyright © 1993 by Barbara Juster Esbensen; illustrations copyright © 1993 by Mary Barrett Brown. By permission of Little, Brown and Company.

expository text, but the beautiful illustrations and elegant design of these books add to our aesthetic pleasure as well as to our understanding of the topics they present. Other picture books are anything but conventional in their ways of combining fact with fiction. Some books, such as *From Pictures to Words: A Book About Making a Book* by Janet Stevens, have invented characters and a story that is imaginative and satisfying in its own right, but such a narrative framework provides so many facts and understandings about the wider world (places, events, processes) that we consider it a natural choice for sharing information.

One of the first modern picture storybooks, *Pelle's New Suit* by Elsa Beskow, came to this country from Sweden more than sixty years ago. This story shows a little boy getting wool from his pet lamb, then having it carded, spun, dyed, woven, and finally taken to the tailor for a new suit. Compare this classic with *"Charlie*

Needs a Cloak" by Tomie de Paola, which also presents, as a story, basic information about making wool into cloth. The saga of Charlie's cloak is enhanced by humor, and the illustrations serve to emphasize the steps in the cloth-making process. Tomie de Paola was a leader in combining narrative, humor, and attractive pictures to make books that are both good stories and informational resources.

Two beautiful picture books about the medieval period present informational detail and the ambiance of the times even more effectively in their illustrations than in the text. Joe Lasker's *Merry Ever After: The Story of Two Medieval Weddings* contrasts the world of the nobility with that of the peasants by focusing on two typical couples betrothed as children and married as teenagers. Readers must consult the pictures as well as the story to get the full description of the two lifestyles. Aliki's *A Medieval Feast* shows the nobility of a manor

Attractive woodcut illustrations by David Frampton evoke the time and place of Carol Carrick's *Whaling Days*.

Illustration from *Whaling Days* by Carol Carrick. Illustration copyright © 1993 by David Frampton. Reprinted by permission of Clarion Books/Houghton Mifflin Company. All rights reserved.

house and their serfs preparing for a visit from the king and queen and their large entourage. A flurry of hunting, fishing, and harvesting is followed by scenes in the great kitchen and then the banquet presentation of such foods as a roast peacock reassembled with its feathers and a castle molded of pastry. Both of these picture books are standouts for their glowing, jewel-like colors and the use of decorative symbols and designs from the medieval period.

The most popular informational picture books of recent years, and some of the most innovative, are the Magic School Bus stories by Joanna Cole and Bruce Degen. *The Magic School Bus Inside the Earth* was followed by other popular titles, including *The Magic School Bus in the Time of the Dinosaurs*, *The Magic School Bus on the Ocean Floor*, and *The Magic School Bus Inside a Hurricane*. All of these fantastic field trips are presided over by Ms. Frizzle, a memorable teacher, and endured by a group of children who develop recognizable personalities. Characterization, humor, and fantasy allow the creators of these books to approach science from a

child's point of view, incorporating feelings ("Yuck," says one student participating in the digestive tract tour) as well as facts. Moreover, they bring all the information home, both literally and figuratively, to the classroom as each book ends.

Many informational picture books for older readers tell good stories about places or things, although they might not have the central human characters that bring warmth to fiction. Books like David Macaulay's *Ship* and William Kurelek's *Lumberjack* are examples of this type. Two volumes by the Swiss artist Jörg Müller, *The Changing City* and *The Changing Countryside*, are really portfolios rather than books. In each, a series of foldout paintings show the many ways in which so-called progress affects the environment. Lynne Cherry's *A River Ran Wild* traces the changing effects of civilization on the Nashua River in New Hampshire. Nadia Wheatley and Donna Rawlin's *My Place* visits the same neighborhood in Australia back through many decades to a time before the Europeans arrived. On each double-page spread a new child narrator draws a map of the place and describes life in the neighborhod that is "my place." The book ends in 1788 as a child explains, "My name is Barangaroo. I belong to this place." Cultural, sociological, and environmental concepts in books like these are particularly good springboards for discussion with older children who have some prior knowledge of history and can explore similar issues in their own communities.

Photographic Essays

With the increased use of photography in children's books today, the photo essay is an increasingly popular form. However, only some of the books that use photographs are photographic essays. Although the books by Dorothy Hinshaw Patent about various animal species (such as *Gray Wolf, Red Wolf*) depend on photographs by William Muñoz on almost every page, they are not photographic essays. The essay relies on the camera in different ways: to particularize general information, to document emotion, to assure the reader of truth in an essentially journalistic fashion.

Sensitivity and vitality in George Ancona's photographs make *Handtalk: An ABC of Finger Spelling and Sign Language* by Remy Charlip and Mary Beth Miller more than a specialized ABC book. Inspired by the language of the deaf, this is a unique volume about communication, made memorable by the expressive photo demonstrations of the language in action. This documentation of life in the language of the deaf is continued in *Handtalk Birthday* by Charlip and Miller,

In *From Pictures to Words,* Janet Stevens carries on an imaginary dialogue with animal characters to show children how books are created.

Handtalk Zoo by George Ancona and Mary Beth Miller, and *Handtalk School* by Miller and Ancona.

George Ancona is known for his carefully considered photographic essays in other books such as *Fiesta U.S.A.* and *Earth Keepers. Riverkeeper* is a description of the work of one man, John Cronin of the Hudson River Fishermen's Association, and allows the author to bring a fresh perspective to the timely topic of efforts against pollution.

In *Koko's Kitten* by Francine Patterson, Ronald Cohn's photographs serve to assure the reader of truth, for the story of this lowland gorilla who learned sign language and grieved for the death of her companion kitten might be dismissed as fiction by a careless reader. These full-color photos also document the emotion of the story as they show the huge primate cuddling her tiny companion and later signing her distress when the kitten dies. The arrival of a new kitten some months

later provides a happy ending. *Koko's Story* tells more about this intriguing experiment.

Numerous photographic essays present to children a glimpse of life in other lands. Two recent books set in Russia are examples. *On Their Toes: A Russian Ballet School* by Ann Morris and Ken Heyman is an eloquent description of a culture within a culture. Readers believe what the author says about the rigor of the young Soviets' training because they can see it. They will also believe the statement that the young dancers "prefer dancing to anything else in the world" because that message is confirmed in the joyful faces in the photos. *Friendship Across Arctic Waters* by Claire Murphy and Charles Mason is a photojournalistic account of the visit of eleven Cub Scouts from Nome, Alaska, to a counterpart group of Young Pioneers across the Bering Strait in Provideniya. The mix of landscapes, action shots, and revealing close-ups of the participants is similar to that found in feature magazines. The difference, of course, is the focus on children's activities and details of special interest to them, like visiting a school and shopping for toys.

Identification Books

In its simplest form an identification book is a naming book, and this may well be the first sort of book that a very young child sees. *Tool Book* by Gail Gibbons shows simple drawings of common tools in bright colors, with appropriate labels. A phrase or two describes the common function of all the tools displayed on a double spread. This is information for the youngest child. But just as children grow in their ability to discriminate and classify, so do identification books become more detailed, precise, and complex. It is hard to imagine any book more thorough or more technically correct than Helen Rony Sattler's updated volume *The New Illustrated Dinosaur Dictionary*. Students who want to match dinosaur names with further description find plenty of help in this book.

When a child brings a stone or a leaf to school and asks, "What kind is it?" the teacher or librarian has a built-in opportunity to introduce books to help that child discover the answer. Millicent Selsam and Joyce Hunt have written a series that is useful in teaching younger children how to examine a specimen and pick out the features that will be important in making an identification. Harriet Springer's line drawings show basic shapes and textures but eliminate the confusion of variable detail. *A First Look at Seashells*, *A First Look at Insects*, and *A First Look at Bats* are three of the many titles in this outstanding process-oriented series.

Life-Cycle Books

A fascination with animals is one of the most general and durable of children's interests, beginning very early and often continuing through adolescence into adulthood. There is always an audience for factual books that describe how animals live, with an emphasis on the inherent story element. These books cover all or some part of the cycle of life, from the birth of one animal to the birth of its progeny, or the events of one year in the animal's life, or the development of one animal throughout its lifetime.

In Barbara Juster Esbensen's *Great Northern Diver: The Loon*, artist Mary Barrett Brown uses double-spread pages and the book's horizontal shape to emphasize the sweep of northern lakes where the loons live from April to September. The choice of setting dictates the part of the loons' life cycle that will be shown. One pair of birds is the focus, but they are given no names.

While an animal subject can sometimes be given a name, it may not be given powers of speech or human emotions. Even so, an accounting of authentic behavior often produces the effect of characterization; thus children frequently read these books as "stories" rather than as references. Holling C. Holling's beautifully illustrated classics *Minn of the Mississippi* and *Pagoo*, which trace the life histories of a turtle and a crawfish, are unique survival stories. The longer life-cycle stories are often stories of survival against the elements and enemies in the environment. The early books by John and Jean George, such as *Vison the Mink* and *Vulpes the Red Fox* (now out of print), remain outstanding examples of this type. Very few books of this sort are published today.

Charles Micucci's attractively designed and thorough books about apples and bees are every bit as intriguing as these life-cycle stories about animals. *The Life and Times of the Apple* details the growth of apples, how they are cross-fertilized and grafted, and how they are harvested and marketed. Micucci also includes information about types of apples, their history, and the legend of Johnny Appleseed. *The Life and Times of the Honeybee* is equally informative and includes a honeybee calendar and a honeybee flower menu.

Experiment and Activity Books

To some children the word *science* is synonymous with *experiment*, and certainly experience is basic to scientific understandings. Many basic informational books suggest a few activities to clarify concepts; in contrast, experiment books take the activities themselves as content. The appearance of a supplementary experiment or activity, frequently as a final note in a book, is quite common today. For instance, Gail Gibbons includes numbered and illustrated directions for a project on raising bean plants at the end of her *From Seed to Plant*, for primary readers. However, new books dedicated just to experiments have gone through a period of short supply.

For very young children, experiments and directions for simple observation are usually presented in a picture-book context with illustrations that show interest and enjoyment as well as proper procedure. Seymour Simon's *Soap Bubble Magic*, illustrated by Stella Ormai, is a book of this kind. Many experiment books for older children also focus on one subject or one material. *The Science Book of Weather* and others by Neil Ardley are appropriate for grades 1 to 4. These books, British imports, are among the first to take advantage of full-color photography and high-artistry layouts in a book of directed experiments. Bernie Zubrowski's books, including *Shadow Play* and *Wheels at Work*, are produced in conjunction with the Boston Children's Museum and emphasize children discovering their

Charles Micucci provides a detailed account in *The Life and Times of the Honeybee.*

own results. Another outstanding book that provides experiments to help students understand one topic is Irwin Math's *Wires and Watts: Understanding and Using Electricity.*

Some of the most engaging books of science experiments are those by Vicki Cobb. An interesting approach to chemistry is found in her *Science Experiments You Can Eat*, a book that is fun for children old enough to handle various cooking procedures safely. *Chemically Active! Experiments You Can Do at Home* is arranged so that one experiment leads directly to the next. All the books by Cobb are designed with a commentary to link the experiments so that they can be read straight through for information as well as used to guide the actual procedures.

Some books that suggest experiments also include experiences of other kinds, along with collections of interesting facts, anecdotes, or other material. These books that encourage children to explore a topic through a broad range of activities have gained popularity in recent years. *Good for Me! All About Food in 32 Bites* by Marilyn Burns is a compilation of facts, learning activities, experiments, and questions that can lead to further investigation. This is one of many titles from the Brown Paper School Books series, which consistently use this format.

Books like these make good browsing and are a source of possible projects for individual study or for activities that might be tried and discussed in class. Teachers as well as students appreciate the variety and creativity of the ideas. However, it is important to remember that activity books are not designed for reference. There is seldom an index, and headings might have more entertainment value than clarity. For easy access to specific information, other types of books are required.

Documents and Journals

A small but important contribution to literature for children in recent years has been the publication of books based on original documents and journals. Milton Meltzer uses letters and other primary sources in such fine books as *Voices from the Civil War*. Julius Lester's extraordinary *To Be a Slave*, a Newbery Honor Book in 1969, provides reproductions of primary sources as a background for the study of African American history. The author combines the verbatim testimony of former slaves with his own strong commentary:

🐝 To be a slave was to be a human being under conditions in which that humanity was denied. They were not slaves. They were people. Their condition was slavery. (p. 28)

A more recent work that focuses on a broader sweep of history is *Now Is Your Time! The African American Struggle for Freedom* by Walter Dean Myers. Period photographs and reproductions of lists and documents are an important part of this compelling book.

In *Kids at Work: Lewis Hine and the Crusade Against Child Labor,* Russell Freedman shows how photographs were instrumental in changing child labor laws.
From *Lewis W. Hine Collection.* United States History, Local History & Genealogy Division. The New York Public Library. Astor, Lenox and Tilden Foundations.

Firsthand accounts are also the base for Jim Murphy's *The Boys' War: Confederate and Union Soldiers Talk About the Civil War.* On both sides, many soldiers were underage boys who had gone off to war looking for something more adventuresome than routine farm chores. The author quotes a Wisconsin boy who wrote of his experiences at Shiloh:

"I want to say, as we lay there and the shells were flying over us, my thoughts went back to my home, and I thought what a foolish boy I was to run away and get into such a mess as I was in. I would have been glad to have seen my father coming after me." (p. 33)

Books like this lend authenticity to the picture of conflict that students get in historical fiction such as Patricia Beatty's *Charley Skedaddle.*

Russell Freedman frequently uses photographs from archival sources to document his historical books as well as his biographies. *Immigrant Kids* includes reproductions of photos of passengers on the steerage deck of an immigrant liner in 1893, street scenes from New York City's Lower East Side in 1898, and school scenes. In *Kids at Work* he uses photographs by Lewis Hine, who worked to reform child labor laws in the United States in the early part of the twentieth century. *Children of the Wild West* furnishes photographs from a time and place where cameras were scarce. Children interested in the westward movement in the United States can study the pictures as well as the text of this book for information.

Photos of families with their covered wagons clearly show modes of dress and meager possessions. Log cabins, sod houses, and schoolrooms can be compared and described. The pictures of Native American children in tribal dress and at government boarding schools are particularly interesting.

Laura Ingalls Wilder fans will be interested in *West from Home: Letters of Laura Ingalls Wilder, San Francisco 1915.* The letters were written to the author's husband while she was visiting her daughter Rose and attending the 1915 Panama Pacific International Exposition. The firsthand detail provides personal insights as well as a measure of the country during that year. There is similar documentary value in Wilder's *The First Four Years,* a journal-like account discovered as a handwritten manuscript among the author's posthumous papers. In this book, which tells of the first years of the Wilders' married life on a claim that had to be made into a farm, the reader can see the problems, the attitudes, and some of the philosophies of another time. Information presented without an intermediary is the unique contribution of documentary literature.

A much older journal has been excerpted and edited by Peter and Connie Roop to help elementary students form some understanding of the complexities of the man Columbus and his discoveries. *I, Columbus: My Journal—1492–1493* shares simple selections from the log of the explorer's first voyage. Usually shelved with biography for the insights it provides into personality, this stands also among the intriguing documents of history.

Survey Books

The purpose of a survey book is to give an overall view of a substantial topic and to furnish a representative sampling of facts, principles, or issues. Such a book emphasizes balance and breadth of coverage, rather than depth.

The Book of Eagles by Helen Roney Sattler offers a chapter of general introduction plus chapters on eagles as hunters, courting and nesting habits, baby eagles, and eagles' relationships with humans. Additional information is presented in list form and in an extensive picture glossary. However, a child looking for in-depth information on a specific genus, like the bald eagle, might need to go on to other sources. The survey book furnishes an authoritative introduction to a topic but not necessarily all the information a student could want.

Philip M. Isaacson's *A Short Walk Around the Pyramid and Through the World of Art* is an entertaining and beautifully written introduction to the visual arts. Included along with painting and sculpture is information about the arts of photography and architecture and such useful things as furniture making and automobile design. This broad survey allows Isaacson to show how the elements of art can convey an emotional impact that enhances our visual experience no matter what the subject or the medium.

A few books attempt to give children a survey of the important people, places, and events in the history of the world. Hendrik Van Loon's *The Story of Mankind* was the first book to interpret world history to children in an interesting and informational fashion. This book, a pioneer in the field and the winner of the first Newbery Medal, in 1922, is now available in a revised edition.

Historical surveys today are more likely to adopt a particular perspective, an "angle" on history that makes wide-ranging content more manageable. In *Food, Houses,* and *Clothing,* Italian artist Piero Ventura looks at history through these familiar lenses that also convey concepts about basic human needs. A similarly successful book for older readers is Suzanne Jurmain's *Once Upon a Horse: A History of Horses—and How They Shaped Our History.* Horse lovers and history browsers alike will find many leads to follow in this lively narrative.

Survey books are available at many different levels of complexity and reading difficulty. A teacher or librarian may need to help children skim to find those that are most appropriate for their use.

Specialized Books

Specialized books are designed to give specific information about a relatively limited topic. These books satisfy particular interests; they are more likely to be used intensively than extensively, on a onetime basis rather than as a frequent reference. James Giblin's many books such as *When Plague Strikes, Chimney Sweeps, The Truth About Unicorns,* and *Let There Be Light: A Book About Windows* illustrate how thorough research and good writing can illuminate the most mundane of topics. With their vivid language and highly involving organization, Jim Murphy's *Across America on an Emigrant Train,* the story of Robert Louis Stevenson's trip across the continent in 1879, and *The Great Fire,* about the Chicago fire of 1871, read like suspense novels and are every bit as hard to put down.

Many specialized books provide extensions of content areas that are frequently part of the elementary social studies curriculum. Jerry Stanley's *Children of the Dust Bowl* tells how educator Leo Hart started a special school for children of migrant workers who had come to California from drought-stricken Oklahoma in the 1930s. The book also provides information about the climatic and the economic changes that caused this great migration. Howard Greenfeld's *The Hidden Children* details the efforts of the many brave people who risked their lives to hide Jewish children from the Nazis.

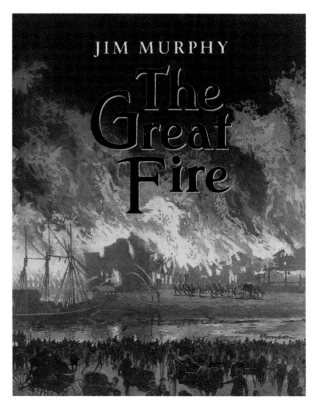

In *The Great Fire*, Jim Murphy's exhaustive research and his lively writing style engage the reader in an exciting account of the 1871 Chicago fire.
From *The Great Fire* by Jim Murphy. Copyright © 1995 by Jim Murphy. Reprinted by permission of Scholastic Inc.

Teachers and librarians have noted that specialized books today are more specialized than ever, covering narrow topics and unique interests. These books can be of high quality and of great appeal to children, but they might not be discovered on the library shelf unless they are introduced. Readers do not deliberately seek a book on a topic that they do not know exists. For that reason, an adult might need to point out Suzanne Haldane's *Helping Hands: How Monkeys Assist People Who Are Disabled,* the fascinating account of a program in which capuchin monkeys are trained to perform crucial tasks for quadriplegics.

Many specialized books are geared to the personal interests of children. *Money Money Money* by Nancy Winslow Parker provides fascinating details about the art and symbols on U.S. currency and will have budding financiers taking a second and third look in their wallets. *What Has Ten Legs and Eats Corn Flakes?* by Ron Roy is about acquiring and caring for three small pets that would be reasonably easy to keep in close quarters. This book has good advice for classroom pet keeping as well as for apartment dwellers or others with limited space. There are books about playing soccer, collecting stamps, losing weight, learning ballet. Whatever the child's interest, it is likely that a specialized book can be found to extend it.

Craft and How-to Books

A fascinating array of craft and activity books give directions for making and doing. Pride of accomplishment is emphasized in Harlow Rockwell's *I Did It,* a just-right combination of easy words and simple directions for primary-grade children. The six activities range in difficulty from making grocery-bag masks to baking bread. Another book geared to younger children is Marc Brown's *Your First Garden Book,* with directions for windowsill, backyard, and sidewalk gardens, plus bright pictures full of good humor.

Cookbooks for children ought to have sparkling, clear directions and adequate warnings about the safe use of tools and equipment. A popular character who has inspired a cookbook is Peter Rabbit. The illustrations in Arnold Dobrin's *Peter Rabbit's Natural Foods Cookbook* are from the original Beatrix Potter books, complementing the theme of simple goodness from nutritional recipes. Another literature-based recipe collection is Barbara Walker's *The Little House Cookbook: Frontier Foods from Laura Ingalls Wilder's Classic Stories.*

Clear directions are usually clearer if appropriately illustrated. *Painting Faces* by Suzanne Haldane shows children applying face paint according to different traditions around the globe. Some of the color photographs are sequentially arranged, so that would-be face painters can easily see what areas of paint should be applied first, as well as what the finished product should look like. Line drawings make appropriate pictures to demonstrate the steps in *How to Make Pop-Ups* and *How to Make Super Pop-Ups* by Joan Irvine. This book has a high success rate with students; they are able to make quite complex-looking paper designs in three dimensions with a minimum of adult help. For those who prefer simpler books, Gwenyth Swain's *Bookworks* will guide them through the process of making books by hand.

Some craft books deal so specifically with approaches and techniques common to the activity-centered classroom that it is likely they will be used as much by teachers as by individual children. Helen Roney Sattler's *Recipes for Art and Craft Materials* will prove indispensable to teachers. Included are recipes for a variety of basic substances that children can make for their own use—such as paste, modeling and casting compounds, papier-mâché, inks, and dried-flower preservatives. See the section "Making Things" in Chapter 14 for ways to incorporate cookbooks and craft books with other literature.

Using Literature Across the Curriculum

One of the important components of a literature program (see Chapters 13 and 14) is using literature across the curriculum. If children are to become real readers, they should meet good books, not only at reading time, but also as they study history, science, the arts—all subject areas. Outstanding informational books, those that might qualify as what author John McPhee calls "the literature of fact," are the most obvious places to begin in choosing titles to use in the content areas.

Informational Books in the Classroom

Like books of any other genre, the best informational books should be appreciated for their artistry. Good writing, fine illustration, and high-quality bookmaking all have intrinsic aesthetic value. And like fiction, informational books can provide satisfaction and delight for interested readers. Informational books are a bit different, however. They also fulfill special teaching functions that need to be considered in planning classroom materials and activities.

The information in trade books is a major content resource for the curriculum. Elementary school textbooks are frequently overgeneralized or oversimplified in the attempt to keep them reasonably short and readable. A selection of informational books can provide the depth and richness of detail not possible in textbook coverage of the same topic. The latest informational books are also likely to be more up-to-date than textbooks, since the process of producing and choosing textbooks can take many months or even years. The adopted series then might not be revised, or replaced, for quite some time. However, new trade books on popular or timely topics appear every year.

Many teachers would use an up-to-date informational book like *Orion the Hunter* by Necia Apfel to supplement the science textbook. Others might completely bypass the textbook and assemble many books about space and the solar system (probably including such titles as Seymour Simon's *Comets, Meters, and Asteroids* and Patricia Lauber's *Journey to the Planets*) to provide information much richer than the text could offer.

The availability of several informational books on a single topic is important for teachers to consider because this presents ready-made opportunities to encourage critical reading. When children's information

Tigers swim to get out of the heat.

Linda Capus Riley's *Elephants Swim,* with collages by Steve Jenkins, introduces young children to concepts about animal behavior.
Illustration by Steve Jenkins from *Elephants Swim* by Linda Capus Riley. Illustration copyright © 1995 by Steve Jenkins. Reprinted by permission of Houghton Mifflin Company. All rights reserved.

all comes from one source, they are likely to accept the author's selection and interpretation of facts without question. The use of two or more books provides a built-in comparison. Bruce Brooks's *Making Sense: Animal Perception and Communication* and Margery Facklam's *Bees Dance and Whales Sing: The Mysteries of Animal Communication* are both fine books, with some differences in coverage and emphasis. Encouraging children to ask themselves questions about these differences helps them make practical and critical judgments about what they are reading.

At the prereading level, children can compare books read aloud by the teacher, look critically at the illustrations, and decide which ones give them needed information. A kindergarten teacher who shared several books about tools with her children asked them to decide which book's pictures did the best job of showing how the tools worked. To check their judgment, they took turns at the classroom workbench, and under adult supervision, trying out the tools.

Most teachers or librarians who encourage the critical comparison of books find that helping children construct a chart of similarities and differences is an aid to clear thinking. As older children are introduced to techniques of inquiry, such as using a table of contents, finding information in indexes, and conducting a library search, they can also be encouraged to develop a list of criteria that they would apply to informational books. Such activities help children become more critical readers of informational books and more careful

writers of their own materials. The Teaching Feature "Helping Children Evaluate Informational Books" shows how a school librarian and a group of fourth graders developed a list of questions that helped them evaluate informational books.

Authors of fine informational books approach their material in interesting ways that can easily be adapted for the classroom. Although it's more usual to find good books that support a lesson, it's also possible for a good book to suggest a lesson.

Lila Perl's *The Great Ancestor Hunt* offers good suggestions for collecting family folklore at holiday get-togethers as well as tips for using public records. Investigations begun with Perl's book could be extended through books like David Weitzman's *My Backyard History Book* and lead to a class study of immigration.

For young children, concept books often lead to ideas for good classification activities. Linda Riley's *Elephants Swim*, with its attractive collages by Steve Jenkins, presents information about animal behavior in water. Children are introduced to words like *paddle, wade, glide, dive,* and *plunge* and to the concept that, unlike humans, many animals take naturally to water. The format of the book invites children to extend their understanding of animal behavior in other environments. Other concept books, such as Hana Machotka's *Outstanding Outsides* or Sandra Markle's *Inside and Outside Spiders,* present excellent opportunities for developing spatial relationships as well as for exploring structures of animal bodies.

Teaching Feature   Helping Children Evaluate Informational Books

When Rebecca Thomas, a school librarian in Shaker Heights, Ohio, introduced *Storms* by Seymour Simon to a group of fourth graders, she covered up most of the front jacket. With only the title visible, she asked them to think what might be included in a book about storms. Their first response was to name the kinds of storms they knew—thunderstorms, snowstorms, tornadoes, and hurricanes. They also suggested other topics that could be in such a book: winds, thunder and lightning, the damage storms can cause, and how scientists know about storms. They decided that a book about storms should be illustrated with high-quality photographs that really picture storms and their actions.

With the librarian's help, they then began to develop some questions they would use to decide if the book was a good one:

Does the book cover the subject?

How good are the pictures?

Who will be able to understand the book?

How much actual information is included?

Does it set information straight (correct mistaken ideas)?

By the time this brief discussion was finished, the children were eager to see if Seymour Simon's book met their expectations, and of course they registered immediate approval when she showed them the front jacket. As she read aloud, she encouraged students to note whether their questions had been answered. She stopped frequently so they could discuss particular pictures and the clarity of the writing based on their question "Who will be able to understand the book?"

These students used the criteria they had developed in question form to measure the success not only of *Storms* but also of other titles on the same topic as they completed a classroom unit on weather. The librarian's introduction engaged the children's interest in one book as it set the stage for their reading of other nonfiction titles. Helping children focus on the possibilities and strengths of specific books encourages them to develop understandings about genre and the broader world of literature.

Rebecca Thomas, Librarian
Fernway School
Shaker Heights, Ohio

Choosing Informational Books for the Classroom

Children do not find the most exciting informational books by chance. Some of these books need to be singled out for prominent attention in the school library, but generally the books we most want children to discover should be brought directly to the classroom and made readily available for browsing, reference, and in-depth study. This requires an investment of time by the teacher for tracking down and selecting titles. Unfortunately, textbooks and curriculum materials give few hints about children's books available in their topic areas. Librarians can direct teachers to standard reference sources and bibliographies, but it is also important for the teacher to watch for new books with particular potential for the classroom.

Two annual book lists prepared by content-area specialists in cooperation with the Children's Book Council identify the best of the new books for the sciences and for social studies. The "Outstanding Science Trade Books for Children" list is published each year in *Science and Children* magazine; the "Notable Children's Trade Books in the Field of Social Studies" list appears annually in *Social Education*. Another source that many

teachers find helpful is *The Kobrin Letter*,[7] a newsletter published ten times a year. Each issue reviews new informational books alongside older ones on several topics— books about train travel, for instance, or wild cats or dealing with divorce. *Book Links*, a periodical of the American Library Association, is geared to those who want to make connections among all kinds of books for units or theme studies. Lists that mix fiction and nonfiction appear alongside short feature articles in this helpful resource (see Appendix B).

Choosing books to serve the purposes of both teachers and children is just as important as selecting for quality. Much of the planning and selecting should be done before beginning a study, although children will raise questions and develop interests along the way that require new resources. This kind of preplanning, especially at the upper-grade levels, eliminates the frustrations of children who are asked to research a topic only to find that books are not available to answer their questions. Cooperation and communication between

---

[7]*The Kobrin Letter*, Beverly Kobrin, Editor, 732 N. Greer Road, Palo Alto, CA 94303.

the teacher and the librarian are *essential* in order to make the right books accessible at the right time.

Regardless of the topic to be studied, teachers might need to consider common purposes and the functions of informational books so that their choices will represent a wide range of possibilities. The following checklist can be used as a reminder of what to look for:

- Books to attract attention to the topic
- Books for browsing and exploring content
- Books with read-aloud possibilities
- Books for independent reading at varying levels of difficulty
- Basic reference books
- Books with enough information for in-depth study
- Books with a limited focus for very specific interests
- Books to guide activities and experiments
- Books that can be readily compared
- Books that introduce new perspectives or connections
- Books to accommodate new and extended interests

A selection of quality informational books representing these categories supports children's growth in reading and appreciation for good writing as well as their development of understandings within the content area.

Integrating Fact and Fiction

Using literature across the curriculum may begin with informational books, but it certainly does not have to end there. Many picture books, poems, traditional stories, novels, and biographies are natural choices for extending children's interest or knowledge base in a subject area. However, literature should never be distorted to fulfill the purposes of an informational lesson. One student participant from a university read Taro Yashima's *Crow Boy* to a class of 9- and 10-year-olds. When she finished the book she told the children that the story took place in Japan and asked them if they knew where Japan was. There was a mad dash for the globe to see who could be the first to locate Japan. Then the participant went on to ask what Japan was, finally eliciting the answer she wanted—"an island." Next she asked what appeared to be a very unrelated question: "Why did Chibi have a rice ball wrapped in a radish leaf for his lunch instead of a hamburger?" The children were baffled. Finally, the participant gave them a brief but erroneous geography lesson in which she told them that because Japan was an island, it was very wet and flat, so the Japanese people could only raise rice, not beef for hamburgers! The student's university supervisor finally stepped in to save the day by helping the children talk about the real strengths of the book, Chibi's loneliness and the artist's use of space and visual symbols.

Scholar Louise Rosenblatt[8] warns against this way of "using" fiction, saying that teachers have a responsibility not to confuse children about the predominant stance or attitude appropriate for a particular reading purpose. The purpose we most want to encourage for works of *fiction* is reading for pleasure and insight (what Rosenblatt calls "aesthetic" reading). The carrying away of factual material ("efferent" reading) is more properly used in reading informational books.

Using literature across the curriculum does not mean forcing connections between fact and fiction, as the student in our example attempted to do. Nor does it mean reading a nature poem for literal information about a bird's habitat or using sentences from a favorite story as the basis for language drill or diagramming sentences. It does mean recognizing that some pieces of literature have a strong background of fact and provide a unique human perspective on historical, scientific, and technological subjects. Works like Jean George's *Julie*, Lois Lowry's *Number the Stars*, and Eve Bunting's *Dandelions* give readers a perspective that allows them to know facts in another way. It is especially important for children to confirm what they are learning from informational sources by meeting similar ideas in the more human frame of fiction.

Pulling together fiction and nonfiction selections that work well together is an ongoing process for most teachers. A record of titles should be kept so that these books can be shelved or displayed together when appropriate. A few sample groupings are shown in the Resources for Teaching box "Fact and Fiction."

Combining fact and fiction resources on a large scale can lead to the creation of an integrated theme unit encompassing learning in all subjects. The focus topic may be taken from the sciences (color, for example), from history or social studies (colonial life or houses), or from language and the arts (signs and symbols), but it must be broad enough to allow students to develop in many skill areas as they work through a wide range of interrelated content, using trade books and other materials. Textbooks are used as reference resources, if at all. This challenging but satisfying way of teaching requires a thorough knowledge of children's literature. (See Chapter 13 for more information about planning units of study.)

Fine informational books and related books of fiction are important to the curriculum whether they serve as the major resource or as supplements to formal instructional materials. Enthusiastic teachers who have learned to recognize the best and to chose wisely for a variety of purposes will put children in touch with an exciting and satisfying way to learn.

---

[8]Louise Rosenblatt, "Literature—S.O.S.!" *Language Arts* 68 (October 1991): 444–448.

Resources for Teaching
Fact and Fiction: Books to Use Together

Eggs (Grades K–2)

Egg (Burton)	Informational
Chickens Aren't the Only Ones (Heller)	Informational
A Nestful of Eggs (Jenkins)	Informational
A Chick Hatches (Cole)	Informational
The Talking Eggs (San Souci)	Traditional
Chicken Man (Edwards)	Picture Book
Hilda Hen's Search (Wormell)	Picture Book
The Extraordinary Egg (Lionni)	Picture Book
Just Plain Fancy (Polacco)	Picture Book
Big Fat Hen (Baker)	Counting Book

Wet Weather (Grades 1–3)

The Science Book of Weather (Ardley)	Informational
A Rainy Day (Markle)	Informational
Flash, Crash, Rumble and Roll (Branley)	Informational
Storms (Simon)	Informational
Llama and the Great Flood (Alexander)	Traditional
The Tree That Rains (Bernhard)	Traditional
The Storm (Rockwell)	Picture Book
Peter Spier's Rain (Spier)	Picture Book
Come a Tide (Lyon)	Picture Book

Bugs (Grades 2–3)

Bugs (Parker and Wright)	Informational
Ladybug (Bernhard)	Informational
Monarch Butterfly (Gibbons)	Informational
The Big Bug Book (Facklam)	Informational
Flit, Flutter, Fly (Hopkins)	Poetry
Demi's Secret Garden (Demi)	Poetry
Joyful Noise (Fleischman)	Poetry
When the Woods Hum (Ryder)	Picture Book
James and the Giant Peach (Dahl)	Fantasy

Native Americans on the Plains (Grades 3–5)

An Indian Winter (Freedman)	Informational
Indian Chiefs (Freedman)	Informational
Buffalo Hunt (Freedman)	Informational
. . . If You Lived with the Sioux Indians (McGovern)	Informational
The Tipi (Yue and Yue)	Informational
Iktomi and the Boulder (Goble)	Traditional
The Lost Children (Goble)	Traditional
The Fish Skin (Oliviero)	Traditional
Dancing with the Indians (Medearis)	Picture Book

Once Upon the Prairie (Grades 3–6)

Sod Houses on the Prairie (Rounds)	Informational
Children of the Wild West (Freedman)	Informational
Prairie Visions (Conrad)	Biography
Dandelions (Bunting)	Picture Book
Dakota Dugout (Turner)	Picture Book
Three Names (MacLachlan)	Picture Book
My Prairie Christmas (Harvey)	Picture Book
Sarah, Plain and Tall (MacLachlan)	Fiction
Prairie Songs (Conrad)	Fiction
My Daniel (Conrad)	Fiction

Slavery and Freedom (Grades 4–6)

Escape from Slavery (Rappaport)	Informational
To Be a Slave (Lester)	Informational
Christmas in the Big House, Christmas in the Quarters (McKissack)	Informational
Lincoln: A Photobiography (Freedman)	Biography
Frederick Douglass: The Black Lion (McKissack and McKissack)	Biography
Harriet Beecher Stowe and the Beecher Preachers (Fritz)	Biography
Anthony Burns: The Defeat and Triumph of a Fugitive Slave	Biography
Nettie's Trip South (Turner)	Picture Book
The Middle Passage (Feelings)	Picture Book
Pink and Say (Polacco)	Picture Book
Lessons from a Slave Girl (Lyons)	Fiction
The Captive (Hansen)	Fiction
Steal Away Home (Ruby)	Fiction
The House of Dies Drear (Hamilton)	Fiction
Jayhawker (Beatty)	Fiction
With Every Drop of Blood (Collier and Collier)	Fiction
Ajeemah and His Son (Berry)	Fiction

Resources for Teaching
Fact and Fiction: Books to Use Together (concluded)

Difficult Journeys (Grades 5–8)

World War II, Asian American

I Am an American (Stanley)	Informational
The Journey (Hamanaka)	Informational
Baseball Saved Us (Mochizuki)	Picture Book
The Bracelet (Uchida)	Picture Book
Journey to Topaz (Uchida)	Fiction
Under the Blood-Red Sun (Salisbury)	Fiction

World War II, Europe and Asia

The Hidden Children (Greenfeld)	Informational
Rescue (Meltzer)	Informational
Rose Blanche (Gallaz and Innocenti)	Picture Book

The Lily Cupboard (Oppenheim)	Picture Book
Number the Stars (Lowry)	Fiction
The Endless Steppe (Hautzig)	Fiction
Year of Impossible Goodbyes (Choi)	Fiction
So Far from the Bamboo Grove (Watkins)	Fiction

Modern-Day Refugees

Where the River Runs (Graff)	Informational
How Many Days to America? (Bunting)	Picture Book
Kiss the Dust (Laird)	Fiction
Grab Hands and Run (Temple)	Fiction
Tonight, by Sea (Temple)	Fiction

Learning Experiences

1. Talk to a group of children to find what special interests or hobbies they have. Make a survey of nonfiction to see what informational books might enrich these interests. Plan a display of some of these books for a classroom or library interest center.

2. Select several informational books on one topic—such as ecology, the solar system, or China. Evaluate them, using the criteria in this chapter. Plan activity cards or questions that would interest children in the books and help them use the books more effectively.

3. Working with one child or a small group of children, select a craft or activity book that seems suited to their age level. Watch carefully as children follow the directions given. What difficulties do they have? What questions do they ask? Could you make the directions clearer, safer, or more imaginative?

4. Working with a small group of your peers, locate informational books published within a single year. Review and discuss these to select one or more "award winners." What criteria would you use? What categories would you establish? What issues arise as you discuss what makes a high-quality informational book?

5. Work with a group of children in writing an informational book modeled after one of the documentary accounts or a photo essay using their own snapshots. What kinds of research and choices are involved in following the form?

6. Choose one informational book with potential for interconnections in many subject areas, such as Aliki's *Mummies Made in Egypt*. Plan questions and activities; choose other literature to help children explore some related topics, such as building the pyramids, writing with hieroglyphics, using preservatives, or the art of ancient Egypt.

7. Develop and use with children a learning activity that will encourage critical reading of informational books. Focus on identifying authors' points of view, comparing authenticity of sources, verifying facts, and the like.

8. Begin a file of book combinations that could be used in science, social studies, the arts, or language study. Consider the different perspectives that children will draw from each.

Related Readings

"Aspects of Children's Informational Books." Guest editor John Donovan. *Wilson Library Bulletin* 49, no. 2 (October 1974): 145–177.

Almost the entire issue of this well-known periodical is devoted to an analysis of children's informational books. Timeless in their insights, the articles include Zena Sutherland's excellent "Information Pleases—Sometimes," which gives criteria for evaluating informational books and takes issue with some of Margery Fisher's criteria in *Matters of Fact.* Olivia Coolidge describes the process of writing authentic biography in her article "My Struggle with Facts." In the essay "To Each Generation Its Own Rabbits," Dennis Flanagan, editor of *Scientific American,* shows how *Watership Down* by Richard Adams embraces the two worlds of science and literature. Other articles relevant to this chapter are included in this fine special issue.

Cleaver, Betty P., Barbara Chatton, and Shirley Vittum Morrison. *Creating Connections: Books, Kits, and Games for Children.* Chicago: Garland, 1986.

This resource guide emphasizes the integration of materials across the curriculum, including the connections to be made between fact and fiction. Six topics of study—Appalachia, bodies, cities, monsters, oceans, and sound—are outlined in detail, with an annotated list of books, kits, and games.

Fisher, Margery. *Matters of Fact: Aspects of Non-fiction for Children.* New York: Crowell, 1972.

This authoritative book by an English author provides criteria for judging and selecting nonfiction books for children. Chapters take an in-depth look at books about particular themes—such as bread, cowboys, honeybees, and atoms. This work has become a standard in the field.

Freeman, Evelyn B., and Diane Goetz Person. *Using Nonfiction Trade Books in the Elementary Classroom.* Urbana, Ill.: National Council of Teachers of English, 1992.

This collection of essays includes a section by authorities such as Russell Freedman and James Cross Giblin that extends understandings about trends and issues in informational books. Subsequent chapters provide many practical suggestions for integrating informational books throughout the curriculum in primary through middle school classrooms.

Giblin, James Cross. "The Rise and Fall and Rise of Juvenile Nonfiction, 1961–1988." *School Library Journal* 48 (October 1988): 27–31.

A distinguished editor and author of informational books provides a firsthand account of nearly three decades of trends and changes in nonfiction for children.

Graves, Donald H. *Investigate Nonfiction.* Portsmouth, N.H.: Heinemann, 1989.

Through its insights into children's efforts to create nonfiction, this slim volume provides new ways of thinking about and teaching about the genre.

"Informational Books for Children." Edited by Geraldine DeLuca and Roni Natov. *The Lion and the Unicorn* 6 (1982).

This theme-centered issue features Patricia Lauber's essay "What Makes an Appealing and Readable Science Book?" and interviews with science writers Seymour Simon and Anne Ophelia Dowden. The interview with Dowden is one of the few to offer insight into the process of illustrating a science book. Other articles and reviews of professional books are also of interest.

Kobrin, Beverly. *Eyeopeners II: Children's Books to Answer Children's Questions About the World Around Them.* New York: Viking, 1995.

Enthusiastic and practical, this review of more than five hundred nonfiction books offers teaching tips for "parents, grandparents, and other educators." The emphasis on linking specific books and activities and an easy-to-read format combine to make a handy classroom reference.

"Nonfiction, Language Learning, and Language Teaching." Edited by William H. Teale. *Language Arts* 68, no. 6 (October 1991).

This themed issue has articles by Louise Rosenblatt on stances toward fiction and nonfiction in the classroom; by Christine Pappas on young children's readings of informational text; and by Lynne Putnam on dramatizing nonfiction. Evelyn Freeman writes about informational books as models for student reports, and Sylvia Vardell explains the selection criteria for the Orbis Pictus Award.

Pappas, Christine C., Barbara Z. Kiefer, and Linda S. Levstik. *An Integrated Language Perspective in the Elementary School: Theory into Action.* 2nd ed. White Plains, N.Y.: Longman, 1992.

The approaches described in this comprehensive text show literature as one of the aspects of language to be integrated throughout the content areas. The specific examples of teaching strategies and of solving problems of classroom logistics are especially helpful.

Children's Literature

Informational Books

Adkins, Jan. *String*. Houghton Mifflin, 1992.

Alexander, Sally Hobart. *Mom Can't See Me*. Photographs by George Ancona. Macmillan, 1990.

Aliki [Aliki Brandenberg]. *A Medieval Feast*. Crowell, 1983.

————. *Mummies Made in Egypt*. Crowell, 1979.

Ancona, George. *Fiesta U.S.A.* Lodestar, 1995.

————. *Riverkeeper*. Macmillan, 1990.

Ancona, George, and Mary Beth Miller. *Handtalk Zoo*. Photographs by George Ancona. Four Winds, 1989.

Anderson, Joan. *Earth Keepers*. Photographs by George Ancona. Harcourt Brace, 1993.

Apfel, Necia H. *Orion the Hunter*. Clarion, 1995.

Ardley, Neil. *The Science Book of Air*. Gulliver/Harcourt Brace, 1991.

————. *The Science Book of Electricity*. Gulliver/Harcourt Brace, 1991.

————. *The Science Book of Motion*. Gulliver/Harcourt Brace, 1992.

————. *The Science Book of Weather*. Gulliver/Harcourt Brace, 1992.

Arnold, Caroline. *Dinosaurs Down Under: And Other Fossils from Australia*. Photographs by Richard Hewett. Clarion, 1990.

Arnosky, Jim. *All About Alligators*. Scholastic, 1994.

————. *All About Owls*. Scholastic, 1995.

Barton, Byron. *Bones, Bones, Dinosaur Bones*. HarperCollins, 1990.

————. *I Want to Be an Astronaut*. Crowell, 1988.

Bash, Barbara. *Ancient Ones: The World of the Old-Growth Douglas Fir*. Sierra Club, 1994.

Bernhard, Emery. *Ladybug*. Illustrated by Durga Bernhard. Holiday House, 1992.

Blumberg, Rhoda. *Commodore Perry in the Land of the Shogun*. Lothrop, Lee & Shepard, 1985.

Bober, Natalie S. *Abigail Adams: Witness to a Revolution*. Atheneum, 1995.

Brandenburg, Jim. *To the Top of the World: Adventures with Arctic Wolves*. Walker, 1993.

Branley, Franklin. *Flash, Crash, Rumble and Roll*. Illustrated by Barbara and Ed Emberley. Rev. ed. Crowell, 1985.

————. *What Happened to the Dinosaurs?* Illustrated by Marc Simont. Crowell, 1989.

Brenner, Barbara. *If You Were There in 1492*. Bradbury, 1991.

Brooks, Bruce. *Making Sense: Animal Perception and Communication*. Farrar, Straus & Giroux, 1993.

————. *Predator!* Farrar, Straus & Giroux, 1991.

Brown, Marc. *Your First Garden Book*. Little, Brown, 1981.

Burns, Marilyn. *Good for Me! All About Food in 32 Bites*. Little, Brown, 1978.

Burton, Richard. *Egg: A Photographic Story of Hatching*. Photographs by Kim Taylor and Jane Burton. Dorling Kindersley, 1994.

Calabro, Marian. *Operation Grizzly Bear*. Four Winds, 1989.

Carrick, Carol. *Octopus*. Illustrated by Donald Carrick. Clarion, 1978.

————. *Whaling Days*. Illustrated by David Frampton. Clarion, 1993.

Charlip, Remy, and Mary Beth Miller. *Handtalk: An ABC of Finger Spelling and Sign Language*. Photographs by George Ancona. Four Winds, 1980.

————. *Handtalk Birthday: A Number and Story Book in Sign Language*. Photographs by George Ancona. Four Winds, 1987.

Cherry, Lynne. *A River Ran Wild*. Gulliver, 1992.

Chiasson, John. *African Journey*. Bradbury, 1987.

Climo, Shirley. *City! Washington, D.C.* Photographs by George Ancona. Macmillan, 1991.

Cobb, Vicki. *Chemically Active! Experiments You Can Do at Home*. Illustrated by Theo Cobb. Lippincott, 1985.

———. *For Your Own Protection: Stories Science Photos Tell*. Lothrop, Lee & Shepard, 1989.

———. *Science Experiments You Can Eat*. Illustrated by Peter Lippman. Lippincott, 1972.

———. *Why Can't You Unscramble an Egg? And Other Not Such Dumb Questions About Matter*. Illustrated by Ted Enik. Lodestar, 1990.

Cole, Joanna. *A Chick Hatches*. Morrow, 1976.

———. *The Magic School Bus at the Waterworks*. Illustrated by Bruce Degen. Scholastic, 1988.

———. *The Magic School Bus in the Time of the Dinosaurs*. Illustrated by Bruce Degen. Scholastic, 1994.

———. *The Magic School Bus Inside a Hurricane*. Illustrated by Bruce Degen. Scholastic, 1995.

———. *The Magic School Bus Inside the Earth*. Illustrated by Bruce Degen. Scholastic, 1987.

———. *The Magic School Bus Inside the Human Body*. Illustrated by Bruce Degen. Scholastic, 1989.

———. *The Magic School Bus Lost in the Solar System*. Illustrated by Bruce Degen. Scholastic, 1990.

———. *The Magic School Bus on the Ocean Floor*. Illustrated by Bruce Degen. Scholastic, 1993.

———. *My Puppy Is Born*. Photographs by Margaret Miller. Mulberry, 1991.

Cone, Molly. *Come Back Salmon*. Photographs by Sidnee Wheelwright. Sierra Club, 1992.

de Bourgoing, Pascale. *Under the Ground*. Illustrated by Danielle Bour. Scholastic, 1995.

de Paola, Tomie. *"Charlie Needs a Cloak."* Simon & Schuster, 1974.

Dobrin, Arnold. *Peter Rabbit's Natural Foods Cookbook*. Warne, 1977.

Dolphin, Laurie. *Georgia to Georgia: Making Friends in the U.S.S.R.* Photographs by E. Alan McGee. Tambourine, 1991.

Dorros, Arthur. *Follow the Water from Brook to Ocean*. HarperCollins, 1991.

Elkington, John, et al. *Going Green: A Kid's Handbook to Saving the Planet*. Illustrated by Tony Ross. Viking, 1990.

Esbensen, Barbara Juster. *Great Northern Diver: The Loon*. Illustrated by Mary Barrett Brown. Little, Brown, 1990.

———. *Playful Slider: The North American River Otter*. Illustrated by Mary Barrett Brown. Little, Brown, 1993.

Facklam, Margery. *Bees Dance and Whales Sing: The Mysteries of Animal Communication*. Illustrated by Pamela Johnson. Sierra Club, 1992.

———. *The Big Bug Book*. Illustrated by Paul Facklam. Little, Brown, 1994.

———. *What Does the Crow Know?* Illustrated by Pamela Johnson. Sierra Club, 1994.

Falwell, Cathryn. *The Letter Jesters*. Ticknor & Fields, 1994.

Feelings, Tom. *The Middle Passage: White Ships/Black Cargo*. Introduction by Dr. John Henrik Clarke. Dial, 1995.

Fleischman Paul. *Townsend's Warbler*. HarperCollins, 1992.

Freedman, Russell. *Buffalo Hunt*. Holiday House, 1988.

———. *Children of the Wild West*. Clarion, 1983.

———. *Eleanor Roosevelt: A Life of Discovery*. Clarion, 1993.

———. *Immigrant Kids*. Dutton, 1980.

———. *Indian Chiefs*. Holiday House, 1987.

———. *An Indian Winter*. Holiday House, 1992.

———. *Kids at Work: Lewis Hine and the Crusade Against Child Labor*. Clarion, 1994.

Fritz, Jean. *George Washington's Breakfast*. Illustrated by Paul Galdone. Coward-McCann, 1969.

George, Jean Craighead. *Everglades*. Illustrated by Wendell Minor. HarperCollins, 1995.

George, John, and Jean George. *Vison the Mink*. Dutton, 1949.

———. *Vulpes the Red Fox*. Dutton, 1948.

Getz, David. *Frozen Man*. Illustrated by Peter McCarty. Holt, 1994.

Gibbons, Gail. *From Seed to Plant*. Holiday House, 1991.

———. *Monarch Butterfly*. Holiday House, 1989.

———. *New Road!* Crowell, 1983.

———. *Tool Book*. Holiday House, 1982.

Giblin, James Cross. *Be Seated: A Book About Chairs*. HarperCollins, 1993.

———. *Chimney Sweeps: Yesterday and Today*. Illustrated by Margot Tomes. Crowell, 1982.

———. *Let There Be Light: A Book About Windows*. Harper & Row, 1988.

———. *The Riddle of the Rosetta Stone: Key to Ancient Egypt*. Crowell, 1990.

———. *The Truth About Unicorns*. HarperCollins, 1991.

———. *When Plague Strikes: The Black Death, Smallpox, AIDS*. Illustrated by David Frampton. HarperCollins, 1995.

Graff, Nancy Price. *Where the River Runs: Portrait of a Refugee Family*. Photographs by Richard Howard. Little, Brown, 1993.

Greenaway, Theresa. *Jungle*. Photographs by Geoff Dan. Knopf, 1994.

Greenfeld, Howard. *The Hidden Children*. Ticknor & Fields, 1993.

Guiberson, Brenda Z. *Cactus Hotel*. Illustrated by Megan Lloyd. Holt, 1991.

Haldane, Suzanne. *Helping Hands: How Monkeys Assist People Who Are Disabled*. Dutton, 1991.

———. *Painting Faces*. Dutton, 1988.

Hamanaka, Sheila. *The Journey: Japanese Americans, Racism, and Renewal*. Orchard, 1990.

Harris, Robie H. *It's Perfectly Normal: A Book About Changing Bodies, Growing Up, Sex, and Sexual Health*. Illustrated by Michael Emberley. Candlewick, 1994.

Heller, Ruth. *Chickens Aren't the Only Ones*. Grosset & Dunlap, 1981.

———. *Many Luscious Lollipops: A Book About Adjectives*. Grosset & Dunlap, 1989.

Hirschi, Ron. *Fall*. Photographs by Thomas D. Mangelsen. Cobblehill/Dutton, 1991.

———. *Spring*. Photographs by Thomas D. Mangelsen. Cobblehill/Dutton, 1990.

———. *Summer*. Photographs by Thomas D. Mangelsen. Cobblehill/Dutton, 1991.

———. *Winter*. Photographs by Thomas D. Mangelsen. Cobblehill/Dutton, 1990.

Hoig, Stan. *A Capital for the Nation*. Cobblehill/Dutton, 1991.

Holling, Holling C. *Minn of the Mississippi*. Houghton Mifflin, 1951.

———. *Pagoo*. Houghton Mifflin, 1957.

Hoyt-Goldsmith, Diane. *Apache Rodeo*. Photographs by Lawrence Migdale. Holiday House, 1995.

———. *Cherokee Summer*. Photographs by Lawrence Migdale. Holiday House, 1993.

Intrater, Roberta Grobel. *Two Eyes, a Nose and a Mouth*. Scholastic, 1995.

Irvine, Joan. *How to Make Pop-Ups*. Illustrated by Barbara Reid. Morrow, 1988.

———. *How to Make Super Pop-Ups*. Illustrated by Linda Hendry. Morrow, 1992.

Isaacson, Philip M. *A Short Walk Around the Pyramids and Through the World of Art*. Knopf, 1993.

Jenkins, Priscilla Belz. *A Nestful of Eggs*. Illustrated by Lizzy Rockwell. HarperCollins, 1995.

Johnson, Gerald. *America Is Born*. Illustrated by Leonard Everett Fisher. Morrow, 1959.

Johnson, Sylvia A. *A Beekeeper's Year*. Photographs by Nick Van Ohlen. Little, Brown, 1994.

Jurmain, Suzanne. *Once Upon a Horse: A History of Horses—and How They Shaped Our History*. Lothrop, Lee & Shepard, 1989.

Knowlton, Jack. *Maps and Globes*. Illustrated by Harriett Barton. Crowell, 1985.

Kohl, Judith, and Herbert Kohl. *The View from the Oak*. Illustrated by Roger Bayless. Little, Brown, 1988.

Kuklin, Susan. *From Head to Toe: How a Doll Is Made*. Hyperion, 1994.

Kurelek, William. *Lumberjack*. Houghton Mifflin, 1974.

Lasker, Joe. *Merry Ever After: The Story of Two Medieval Weddings*. Viking, 1976.

———. *A Tournament of Knights*. Crowell, 1986.

Lasky, Kathryn. *Traces of Life: The Origins of Humankind*. Illustrated by Whitney Powell. Morrow, 1989.

Lauber, Patricia. *Dinosaurs Walked Here and Other Stories Fossils Tell*. Bradbury, 1987.

———. *Journey to the Planets*. Crown, 1993 [1982].

———. *The News About Dinosaurs*. Bradbury, 1989.

———. *Seeds: Pop Stick Glide*. Photos by Jerome Wexler. Crown, 1981.

———. *Tales Mummies Tell*. Crowell, 1985.

———. *Volcano: The Eruption and Healing of Mt. St. Helens*. Bradbury, 1986.

Lavies, Bianca. *Wasps at Home*. Dutton, 1991.

Lester, Julius. *To Be a Slave*. Illustrated by Tom Feelings. Dial, 1968.

Locker, Thomas, with Candance Christiansen. *Sky Tree*. HarperCollins, 1995.

Macaulay, David. *Castle*. Houghton Mifflin, 1977.

———. *Cathedral: The Story of Its Construction*. Houghton Mifflin, 1973.

———. *City: The Story of Roman Planning and Construction*. Houghton Mifflin, 1974.

———. *Mill*. Houghton Mifflin, 1983.

———. *Pyramid*. Houghton Mifflin, 1975.

———. *Ship*. Houghton Mifflin, 1993.

———. *Underground*. Houghton Mifflin, 1976.

———. *The Way Things Work*. Houghton Mifflin, 1988.

Machotka, Hana. *Breathtaking Noses*. Morrow, 1992.

———. *Oustanding Outsides*. Morrow, 1993.

———. *Terrific Tails*. Morrow, 1994.

———. *What Neat Feet!* Morrow, 1991.

Markle, Sandra. *Earth Alive!* Lothrop, Lee & Shepard, 1991.

———. *Exploring Autumn: A Season for Science Activities, Puzzles, and Games*. Atheneum, 1991.

———. *Exploring Spring*. Atheneum, 1990.

———. *Exploring Summer*. Atheneum, 1987.

———. *Exploring Winter*. Atheneum, 1984.

———. *Inside and Outside Spiders*. Bradbury, 1994.

————. *A Rainy Day*. Illustrated by Cathy Johnson. Orchard, 1993.

Martin, James. *Chameleons: Dragons in the Trees*. Photographs by Art Wolfe. Crown, 1991.

Math, Irwin. *Wires and Watts: Understanding and Using Electricity*. Illustrated by Hal Keith. Scribner's, 1988.

McClung, Robert. *Possum*. Morrow, 1963.

McGovern, Ann. . . . *If You Lived with the Sioux Indians*. Scholastic, 1976.

McIntosh, Jane. *Pyramid*. Photographs by Geoff Brighting. Knopf, 1994.

McKissack, Patricia C., and Frederick McKissack. *Christmas in the Big House, Christmas in the Quarters*. Illustrated by John Thompson. Scholastic, 1994.

Meltzer, Milton. *Rescue: The Story of How Gentiles Saved Jews in the Holocaust*. Harper & Row, 1988.

————. *Voices from the Civil War: A Documentary History of the Great American Conflict*. Harper & Row, 1989.

Meyers, Susan. *Insect Zoo*. Photographs by Richard Hewett. Lodestar, 1991.

Micucci, Charles. *The Life and Times of the Apple*. Orchard, 1992.

————. *The Life and Times of the Honeybee*. Ticknor & Fields, 1994.

Miller, Jonathan. *The Human Body*. Book design by David Pelham. Viking, 1983.

Miller, Margaret. *Guess Who?* Greenwillow, 1994.

Miller, Mary Beth, and George Ancona. *Handtalk School*. Photographs by George Ancona. Four Winds, 1991.

Morris, Ann. *On Their Toes: A Russian Ballet School*. Photographs by Ken Heyman. Atheneum, 1991.

————. *Shoes Shoes Shoes*. Lothrop, Lee & Shepard, 1995.

————. *Weddings*. Lothrop, Lee & Shepard, 1995.

Müller, Jörg. *The Changing City*. Atheneum, 1977.

————. *The Changing Countryside*. Atheneum, 1977.

Murphy, Claire Rudolf. *Friendship Across Arctic Waters*. Photographs by Charles Mason. Lodestar, 1991.

Murphy, Jim. *Across America on an Emigrant Train*. Clarion, 1993.

————. *The Boys' War: Confederate and Union Soldiers Talk About the Civil War*. Clarion, 1990.

————. *The Great Fire*. Scholastic, 1995.

Myers, Walter Dean. *Now Is Your Time! The African American Struggle for Freedom*. HarperCollins, 1991.

Parker, Nancy Winslow. *Money, Money, Money: The Meaning of the Art and Symbols on United States Paper Currency*. HarperCollins, 1995.

Parker, Nancy Winslow, and Joan Richards Wright. *Bugs*. Illustrated by Nancy Winslow Parker. Greenwillow, 1987.

————. *Frogs, Toads, Lizards, and Salamanders*. Illustrated by Nancy Winslow Parker. Greenwillow, 1990.

Patent, Dorothy Hinshaw. *Gray Wolf, Red Wolf*. Photographs by William Muñoz. Clarion, 1990.

Patterson, Francine. *Koko's Kitten*. Photographs by Ronald Cohn. Scholastic, 1985.

————. *Koko's Story*. Photographs by Ronald Cohn. Scholastic, 1987.

Pelta, Kathy. *Discovering Christopher Columbus: How History Is Invented*. Lerner, 1991.

Perl, Lila. *From Top Hats to Baseball Caps, from Bustles to Blue Jeans: Why We Dress the Way We Do*. Illustrated by Leslie Evans. Clarion, 1990.

————. *The Great Ancestor Hunt: The Fun of Finding Out Who You Are*. Clarion, 1989.

Peters, David. *From the Beginning: The Story of Human Evolution*. Morrow, 1991.

Platt, Richard. *Stephen Beisty's Cross Sections: Castle*. Illustrated by Stephen Beisty. Dorling Kindersley, 1994.

————. *Stephen Beisty's Cross Sections: Man-of-War*. Illustrated by Stephen Beisty. Dorling Kindersley, 1993.

———. *Stephen Beisty's Incredible Cross Sections.* Illustrated by Stephen Beisty. Dorling Kindersley, 1992.

Porter, A. P. *Kwanzaa.* Illustrated by Janice Lee Porter. Carolrhoda, 1991.

Pringle, Laurence. *Bearman: Exploring the World of Black Bears.* Photographs by Lynn Rogers. Scribner's, 1989.

———. *Nuclear Energy: Troubled Past, Uncertain Future.* Macmillan, 1989.

———. *Vanishing Ozone: Protecting Earth from Ultra Violet Radiation.* Morrow, 1995.

Rappaport, Doreen. *Escape from Slavery: Five Journeys to Freedom.* Illustrated by Charles Lilly. HarperCollins, 1991.

Riley, Linda Capus. *Elephants Swim.* Illustrated by Steve Jenkins. Houghton Mifflin, 1995.

Robbins, Ken. *A Flower Grows.* Dial, 1990.

———. *Air: The Elements.* Holt, 1996.

Rockwell, Harlow. *I Did It.* Macmillan, 1974.

———. *My Doctor.* Macmillan, 1973.

Roop, Peter, and Connie Roop, eds. *I, Columbus: My Journal—1492–1493.* Illustrated by Peter E. Hanson. Walker, 1990.

Rotner, Shelley, and Ken Kreisler. *Faces.* Photographs by Shelley Rotner. Macmillan, 1994.

Rounds, Glen. *Sod Houses on the Prairie.* Holiday House, 1995.

Roy, Ron. *Move Over, Wheelchairs Coming Through!* Photographs by Rosmarie Hausherr. Clarion, 1985.

———. *What Has Ten Legs and Eats Corn Flakes?* Illustrated by Lynn Cherry. Clarion, 1982.

Royston, Angela. *Insects and Crawly Creatures.* Photographs by Jerry Young. Illustrations by Jane Cradock-Watson and Dave Hopkins. Aladdin, 1992.

Sattler, Helen Roney. *The Book of Eagles.* Illustrated by Jean Day Zallinger. Lothrop, Lee & Shepard, 1989.

———. *The New Illustrated Dinosaur Dictionary.* Illustrated by Jean Day Zallinger. Lothrop, Lee & Shepard, 1989.

———. *Our Patchwork Planet: The Story of Plate Tectonics.* Illustrated by Guilio Maestro. Lothrop, Lee & Shepard, 1995.

———. *Recipes for Art and Craft Materials.* Lothrop, Lee & Shepard, 1987 [1973].

Schlein, Miriam. *Billions of Bats.* Illustrated by Walter Kessel. Lippincott, 1982.

———. *Discovering Dinosaur Babies.* Illustrated by Margaret Colbert. Four Winds, 1991.

Scieszka, Jon. *Math Curse.* Illustrated by Lane Smith. Viking, 1995.

Selsam, Millicent. *Egg to Chick.* Illustrated by Barbara Wolff. Harper Trophy, 1987.

———. *How to Be a Nature Detective.* Illustrated by Marlene Hill Donnelly. HarperCollins, 1995 [1958].

Selsam, Millicent, and Joyce Hunt. *A First Look at Bats.* Illustrated by Harriet Springer. Walker, 1991.

———. *A First Look at Insects.* Illustrated by Harriet Springer. Walker, 1974.

———. *A First Look at Seashells.* Illustrated by Harriet Springer. Walker, 1983.

Showers, Paul. *How Many Teeth?* Illustrated by True Kelley. HarperCollins, 1991.

Simon, Seymour. *Comets, Meteors, and Asteroids.* Morrow, 1994.

———. *Earth Words: A Dictionary of the Environment.* Illustrated by Mark Kaplan. HarperCollins, 1995.

———. *Galaxies.* Morrow, 1988.

———. *The Paper Airplane Book.* Illustrated by Byron Barton. Viking, 1971.

———. *Soap Bubble Magic.* Illustrated by Stella Ormai. Lothrop, Lee & Shepard, 1985.

———. *Storms.* Morrow, 1989.

———. *Spring Across America.* Hyperion, 1996.

Skurzynski, Gloria. *Get the Message: Telecommunications in Your High-Tech World.* Bradbury, 1993.

Spier, Peter. *People*. Doubleday, 1980.

Stanley, Jerry. *Children of the Dust Bowl: The True Story of the School at Weedpatch Camp*. Crown, 1992.

———. *I Am an American: A True Story of the Japanese Internment*. Crown, 1994.

Stein, Sara Bonnett. *Making Babies*. Photographs by Doris Pinney. Walker, 1974.

Stevens, Janet. *From Pictures to Words: A Book About Making a Book*. Holiday House, 1995.

Swain, Gwenyth. *Making Books by Hand*. Carolrhoda, 1995.

Van Loon, Hendrik W. *The Story of Mankind*. Rev. ed. Liveright, 1985 [1921].

Ventura, Piero. *Clothing*. Houghton Mifflin, 1994.

———. *Food*. Houghton Mifflin, 1994.

———. *Houses*. Houghton Mifflin, 1994.

Wabbes, Marie. *How I Was Born*. Tambourine, 1991.

Walker, Barbara M. *The Little House Cookbook: Frontier Foods from Laura Ingalls Wilder's Classic Stories*. Illustrated by Garth Williams. Harper & Row, 1979.

Wallace, Karen. *Think of an Eel*. Illustrated by Mike Bostock. Candlewick, 1993.

Waters, Kate. *Sarah Morton's Day: A Day in the Life of a Pilgrim Girl*. Photographs by Russ Kendall. Scholastic, 1989.

Weiss, Harvey. *Maps: Getting from Here to There*. Houghton Mifflin, 1991.

Weitzman, David. *My Backyard History Book*. Illustrated by James Robertson. Little, Brown, 1975.

Wheatley, Nadia, and Donna Rawlins. *My Place*. Kane Miller, 1992.

Whitfield, Philip, Dr., with the Natural History Museum. *Why Do Volcanoes Erupt?* Viking, 1990.

Wilder, Laura Ingalls. *The First Four Years*. Illustrated by Garth Williams. Harper & Row, 1971.

———. *West from Home: Letters of Laura Ingalls Wilder, San Francisco 1915*. Edited by Roger McBride. Harper & Row, 1974.

Willard, Nancy. *Gutenberg's Gift: A Book Lover's Pop-up Book*. Illustrated by Bryan Leister. Harcourt Brace, 1995.

Yue, Charlotte, and David Yue. *The Tipi: A Center of Native American Life*. Knopf, 1984.

Zubrowski, Bernie. *Shadow Play*. Illustrated by Roy Doty. Morrow, 1995.

———. *Wheels at Work*. Illustrated by Roy Doty. Morrow, 1986.

Other References

Alexander, Ellen. *Llama and the Great Flood: A Folktale from Peru*. Crowell, 1989.

Baker, Keith. *Big Fat Hen*. Harcourt Brace, 1994.

Beatty, Patricia. *Charley Skedaddle*. Morrow, 1987.

———. *Jayhawker*. Morrow, 1991.

Bernhard, Emery, and Durga Bernhard. *The Tree That Rains: The Flood Myth of the Huichol Indians of Mexico*. Holiday House, 1994.

Berry, James. *Ajeemah and His Son*. HarperCollins, 1992.

Beskow, Elsa. *Pelle's New Suit*. Harper & Row, 1929.

Bunting, Eve. *Dandelions*. Illustrated by Greg Shed. Harcourt Brace, 1995.

———. *How Many Days to America? A Thanksgiving Story*. Illustrated by Beth Peck. Ticknor & Fields, 1988.

Choi, Sook Nyul. *Year of Impossible Goodbyes*. Houghton Mifflin, 1991.

Collier, James Lincoln, and Christopher Collier. *With Every Drop of Blood*. Delacorte, 1994.

Conrad, Pam. *My Daniel*. Harper & Row, 1989.

———. *Prairie Visions: The Life of Solomon Butcher*. HarperCollins, 1991.

———. *Prairie Songs*. Illustrated by Darryl Zudeck. Harper & Row, 1985.

Dahl, Roald. *James and the Giant Peach*. Illustrated by Nancy Burkert. Knopf, 1962.

Demi. *Demi's Secret Garden*. Holt, 1993.

Edwards, Michelle. *Chicken Man*. Lothrop, Lee & Shepard, 1991.

Fleischman, Paul. *Joyful Noise: Poems for Two Voices*. Illustrated by Eric Beddows. Harper & Row, 1988.

Freedman, Russell. *Lincoln: A Photobiography*. Clarion, 1987.

———. *The Wright Brothers*. Holiday House, 1991.

Fritz, Jean. *Harriet Beecher Stowe and the Beecher Preachers*. Putnam, 1994.

Gallaz, Christophe, and Roberto Innocenti. *Rose Blanche*. Illustrated by Roberto Innocenti. Creative Education, 1985.

George, Jean Craighead. *Julie*. HarperCollins, 1995.

Goble, Paul. *Iktomi and the Boulder*. Orchard, 1988.

———. *The Lost Children*. Bradbury, 1993.

Hamilton, Virginia. *Anthony Burns: The Defeat and Triumph of a Fugitive Slave*. Knopf, 1988.

———. *The House of Dies Drear*. Illustrated by Eros Keith. Macmillan, 1968.

Hansen, Joyce. *The Captive*. Scholastic, 1994.

Harvey, Brett. *My Prairie Christmas*. Illustrated by Deborah Kogan Ray. Holiday House, 1990.

Hautzig, Esther. *The Endless Steppe: Growing Up in Siberia*. Crowell, 1968.

Hopkins, Lee Bennett. *Flit, Flutter, Fly!* Illustrated by Peter Palagonia. Doubleday, 1992.

Laird, Elizabeth. *Kiss the Dust*. Dutton, 1992.

Lionni, Leo. *The Extraordinary Egg*. Knopf, 1994.

Lowry, Lois. *Number the Stars*. Houghton Mifflin, 1989.

Lyon, George Ella. *Come a Tide*. Illustrated by Stephen Gammell. Orchard, 1990.

Lyons, Mary E. *Letters from a Slave Girl: The Story of Harriet Jacobs*. Scribner's, 1992.

MacLachlan, Patricia. *Sarah, Plain and Tall*. Harper & Row, 1985.

———. *Three Names*. Illustrated by Alexander Pertzoff. HarperCollins, 1991.

McKissack, Patricia, and Frederick McKissack. *Frederick Douglass: The Black Lion*. Children's Press, 1987.

Medearis, Angela Shelf. *Dancing with the Indians*. Illustrated by Samuel Byrd. Holiday House, 1991.

Mochizuki, Ken. *Baseball Saved Us*. Illustrated by Dom Lee. Lee & Low, 1993.

Oliviero, Jamie. *The Fish Skin*. Illustrated by Brent Morrisseau. Hyperion, 1993.

Oppenheim, Shulamith Levy. *The Lily Cupboard*. Illustrated by Ronald Himler. HarperCollins, 1992.

Polacco, Patricia. *Just Plain Fancy*. Bantam/Doubleday, 1990.

———. *Pink and Say*. Philomel, 1994.

Reeder, Carolyn. *Shades of Gray*. Macmillan, 1989.

Rockwell, Anne. *The Storm*. Illustrated by Robert Sauber. Hyperion, 1994.

Ruby, Lois. *Steal Away Home*. Macmillan, 1994.

Ryder, Joanne. *When the Woods Hum*. Illustrated by Catherine Stock. Morrow, 1991.

Salisbury, Graham. *Under the Blood-Red Sun*. Delacorte, 1994.

San Souci, Robert D. *The Talking Eggs*. Illustrated by Jerry Pinkney. Dial, 1989.

Spier, Peter. *Peter Spier's Rain*. Doubleday, 1982.

Temple, Frances. *Grab Hands and Run*. Orchard, 1993.

———. *Tonight, by Sea*. Orchard, 1995.

Turner, Ann. *Dakota Dugout*. Illustrated by Ronald Himler. Macmillan, 1985.

———. *Nettie's Trip South*. Illustrated by Ronald Himler. Macmillan, 1987.

Uchida, Yoshiko. *The Bracelet*. Illustrated by Joanna Yardley. Philomel, 1993.

———. *Journey to Topaz*. Illustrated by Donald Carrick. Scribner's, 1971.

Watkins, Yoko Kawashima. *So Far from the Bamboo Grove*. Lothrop, Lee & Shepard, 1986.

Wormell, Mary. *Hilda Hen's Search*. Harcourt Brace, 1994.

Yashima, Taro. *Crow Boy*. Viking, 1955.

part three

❋ *Developing a Literature Program*

chapter thirteen

Planning the Literature Program

Purposes of the Literature Program 622

Discovering Delight in Books 622
Linking Literature to Life 623
Developing Literary Awareness 623
Literary Genres 623
The Elements of Literature 624
The Place of the Classics 624
Knowing Authors and Illustrators 624

Developing Appreciation 625

Different Plans for Literature Programs 625

Literature with a Basal Reading Program 625
Literature Programs Using Real Books 626
Making the Transition to a Literature-Based Approach 627
Resources for Teaching: Approaches to Reading Instruction **628**

The Components of a Literature Program 629

An Enthusiastic Teacher 629
The Classroom Book Collection 630
Creating a Classroom Reading Center 630
Display Techniques 631

Sharing Literature with Children 632

Reading to Children 632

Selecting Books to Read Aloud 633
Techniques for Reading Aloud 634

Storytelling 634
Resources for Teaching: Effective Practices for Reading Aloud **635**

Selecting Stories to Tell 635
Guidelines for Telling Stories 635

Using Props and Felt Boards 636
Resources for Teaching: Suggested Stories for the Felt Board **637**

Book Talks 637

Providing Time to Read Books 637
Talking About Books with Children 638

Guided Discussion 639

Asking Good Questions 639
Children's Questions 640
Teaching Feature: Interviewing Fictional Characters **641**

Working in Small Groups 641

Literature and the Writing Program 642

Helping Children Write About Books 643
Teaching Feature: Using Dialogue Journals **644**

Helping Children Become Authors 645

Guiding the In-Depth Study of Books 645

Making and Using Guides 645
Resources for Teaching: A Guide for Galimoto **646**

Webbing Curriculum Possibilities 646

Web: A Framework for Webbing 647

Studying a Theme: Stewards of the Earth—Ecology 648

The School and the Community 648

The Whole-School Program 648

Web: Stewards of the Earth—Ecology 650

Teaching Feature: A Whole-School Study of One Book 652

Involving Administrators 652
Planning Author/Illustrator Visits 652
The School Library Media Center 653
The Library Media Specialist 654
Selecting Materials 655
Selection versus Censorship 656
Resources for Teaching: The Library Bill of Rights 657

Dealing with Censorship 657
Guidelines: Dealing with a Demand for Censorship 658
Working with Parents and the Community 658
Working with the Public Library 659
Learning Experiences 660
Related Readings 660
Children's Literature 661

tudents in a fifth- and sixth-grade class unanimously agreed that *The Pinballs* by Betsy Byars was their favorite book. Their teacher then asked them to discuss the book, telling what it was that made them like it so much. Part of their discussion follows:

Lenny says, "This is the best book I've ever read. I'd like to know Harvey because I'd like to cheer him up." He decides that "he shows real courage because he has two broken legs." Barb adds, "All the kids do because they have to go to a foster home." "So does Thomas J. because the twins are going to die and he has to go to the hospital to see them," says Will.

Jack talks about Carlie, saying, "She's really funny because she's so rude." The teacher suggests that a book that is "basically serious can have funny elements." Tom says, "You know that Carlie is really tough."

Then Tom goes on to explain the title by saying, "Carlie thinks they're pinballs because they are always being thrown around like pinballs."

By April of that year, eighteen of the class had read *The Pinballs*. They also were reading other Betsy Byars books; thirteen had read

The Summer of the Swans, eight *Good-bye, Chicken Little*.[1]

Individual children had read many books (from 24 to 122 over the year), yet they singled out *The Pinballs* as their favorite. While it is still difficult for them to articulate why they like the story, they have moved beyond the usual circular kind of statement, "I liked it because it was good." They are beginning to recognize the importance of character development and readily identify with Carlie and Harvey. Lenny, who was not a particularly good reader and had read few books, empathizes with Harvey to the point of wanting to comfort him. As suburban children, they have extended their horizons to imagine the courage it would require to live in a foster home away from their family and to have to visit people who are dying in the hospital. Tom attempts a rough statement of the meaning of the title without any prompting.

In this class, book discussions occurred every day during the last fifteen minutes of an hour-long period for sustained silent reading. The children readily supported each other in

[1]Based on children's comments recorded by Susan Hepler in "Patterns of Response to Literature: A One-Year Study of a Fifth and Sixth Grade Classroom" (Ph.D. dissertation, Ohio State University, 1982).

their selection of books and in their evaluations; they exemplify what we have referred to as a "community of readers." It is obvious from their discussion that they were gaining a greater sense of form and were beginning to see more in books than just story.

It takes time for reading and literature to grow in a classroom. The children in this classroom had, for the most part, been exposed to good literature throughout their school attendance. The teacher had been working on a literature-based reading program over a period of several years. Her major goal was to develop children who could read and who loved reading. From this base she added a growing appreciation for and understanding of good literature.

Purposes of the Literature Program

Each school staff will want to develop its own literature program in terms of the background and abilities of the children it serves. Teachers need to know both their children and the potential of their material and have an understanding of the structure of literature; then they will be free to make the right match between child and book. This chapter can suggest guidelines and give examples, but it cannot prescribe *the* literature program that would work with all children.

Discovering Delight in Books

One of the major purposes of any literature program is to provide children with the opportunity to experience literature, to enter into and become involved in a book. The title *Hooked on Books* by Daniel N. Fader comes close to describing this goal.[2] A literature program must get children excited about reading, turned on to books, tuned in to literature.

What if the goal of all reading programs was not only to teach children to learn to read but to help them learn to love reading, to discover joy in reading? Their every activity, every assignment, would have to pass this test: "Will this increase children's desire to read? Will it make them want to continue reading?" Story has always motivated children to want to learn to read. Real books are far more interesting than selections from books.

One of the best ways to interest children in books is to surround them with many of the finest. Give them

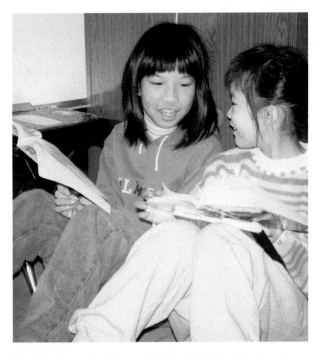

Two fourth-grade girls reveal their delight in literature by sharing some "book talk."
PS 124, New York, New York. Mary S. Gallivan, teacher.

time to read and a teacher who regularly reads to them. Expose them to a wide variety of literature—prose and poetry, realism and fantasy, contemporary and historical fiction, fiction and nonfiction. Provide time for children to talk about books, to share them with others, and to interpret them through various creative activities. Let them see that adults enjoy books, too. One 6-year-old and his teacher were reading Arnold Lobel's *Frog and Toad Are Friends* together. When they came to the part where Toad is experiencing his "sad time of day" (waiting for the mail that he never receives), the

[2]See Daniel Fader, *The New Hooked on Books: Tenth Anniversary Edition* (New York: Berkley, 1976).

teacher burst out laughing. The 6-year-old looked up at her and said: "I didn't know grownups liked books!" If children are to like books, they must be with adults who enjoy them.

The first step in any literature program is to discover delight in books. This should be the major purpose of the literature program in the elementary school and should not be hurried or bypassed. Delight in books only comes about through long and loving experiences with them.

Linking Literature to Life

As children search for meaning in books, they naturally link what they are reading to their own lives. Kindergarten children listen to *Ira Sleeps Over* by Bernard Waber and talk about their own bears and the decisions they had to make about taking them on vacations or overnights. One 6-year-old when listening to the story "The Little Red Hen" linked his experience of watching his mom bake cookies with that of the little red hen watching her cake bake. He lifted his head and sniffed, saying, "Just smell that delicious smell!"

When children become engrossed in a book, they are usually trying on different roles, living the experience. When asked why Jean George's *My Side of the Mountain* was his favorite book, one student replied, "I just always thought I could do what Sam Gribley did." He then went on to make a comparison chart between what he considered to be Sam's qualities and his own. His list showed good understanding of Sam's character and excellent self-understanding.

Books illuminate children's own perceptions of their lives and provide a window through which they can observe, or try on, so to speak, the lives of others. Michelle Landsberg maintains:

> Books let us see how other people grow towards conclusions and solve dilemmas. More than that they make us *feel* every step of the way; it's as though we could live a dozen lives simultaneously, and draw on the wealth of all of them to help shape our own selves.[3]

One of the major purposes of using real books for a reading program is to help children connect literature with their own lives. As teachers and librarians, we want to encourage children to discover personal meaning in books in order to better understand their lives and to extend their perceptions of other lives.

[3]Michelle Landsberg, *Reading for the Love of It* (New York: Prentice Hall, 1987), p. 127.

Developing Literary Awareness

Children in the elementary school can't help but develop some literary awareness. However, their knowledge about literature should be secondary to their wide experiencing of literature. Too frequently, we have substituted the study of literary criticism for the experience of literature itself. Attention to content should precede consideration of form. However, some literary understanding increases children's enjoyment of books. Some 7- and 8-year-olds are excited to discover the different variants of "Cinderella," for example. They enjoy comparing the various beginnings and endings of folktales and like to write their own. Obviously, some of this delight has been derived from knowledge of folklore. Teachers need to know something of the structure of literature in order to provide children with a frame of reference to direct their insights. Children should be led to discover these literary elements gradually, however, and only as these elements help children to understand the meaning of the story or poem. Knowledge of the structure of a discipline frees a teacher in his approach to teaching. Knowing literature, he may tune in to where the children are and extend their thinking and understandings. The teacher does not have to rely on the questions in a literary reader; she is free to ask questions directly related to the needs of the children in the class.

Literary Genres

During the time children are in elementary school, they develop some understanding about types of literature or various genres. The primary child can usually differentiate between prose and poetry, between fiction and nonfiction, between realism and fantasy. Young children will not use those words, nor is it important for them to do so. They probably will tell you that Eric Carle's *The Very Busy Spider* "tells a story," while Claudia Schnieper's book *Amazing Spiders* with its close-up photos by Max Meier "tells you real facts about spiders." This represents a beginning step in the development of a useful classification system. Later as children begin to use the library, they learn that nonfiction includes informational books and biography. They discover that poetry and traditional literature—including folktales, legends, and myths—have their own classifications.

A framework for thinking about literature develops gradually as children consider what kinds of stories they particularly like or what kinds of information they need for a particular purpose. Such knowledge is also useful when children begin evaluating books. Then they discover, for example, that the characters in fairy tales are usually flat, two-dimensional characters because they represent goodness (the fairy godmother) or wickedness (the stepmother). These are seen in sharp relief to the characters in realistic fiction, who grow and change and are a mixture of good and bad. Again, this kind of understanding is developed over a period of time with much experiencing of a wide range of literature.

The Elements of Literature

Knowledge of the components of literature—such as the traditional constants of plot, characterization, theme, style, setting, and author's point of view—also comes about gradually. Some children are intrigued with knowing about literary devices like symbols, metaphors, imagery, use of flashbacks, and point of view. Such knowledge can be forced and taught superficially without children really understanding the relationship between the use of the device and the author's meaning. Or if teachers are aware of these well-known components, they can be taught at the so-called teachable moment.

For example, one group of fifth graders puzzled over who was telling E. L. Konigsburg's story *From the Mixed-Up Files of Mrs. Basil E. Frankweiler*. At first the children thought Claudia was telling this story of her flight to the Metropolitan Museum of Art in New York City with her brother, Jamie. But when they came to the last paragraph of the first chapter, they stopped. Who was the "I" in the sentence with the parentheses?

> And in the course of those miles Claudia stopped regretting bringing Jamie along. In fact when they emerged from the train at Grand Central into the underworld of cement and steel that leads to the terminal, Claudia felt that having Jamie there was important. (Ah, how well I know those feelings of hot and hollow that come from the dimly lit concrete ramp.) And his money and radio were not the only reasons. Manhattan called for the courage of at least two Kincaids. (p. 27)

This sent them back to the introductory letter by Mrs. Basil E. Frankweiler, but they still didn't know how she was able to tell Claudia and Jamie's story as if she were with them. Only when they reached the final chapter, did they understand the reason E. L. Konigsburg had told the story from Mrs. Frankweiler's point of view. They then had an interesting discussion of what difference it had made in the book. Finally, one student said, "It helped to create the mystery"; another one said, "She gave Claudia the chance to be different." These children learned about point of view in the process of reading this story. More importantly, they understood why the author used this particular literary device. Discussion of literary form should be introduced only where it leads to a richer understanding of a book, and then only after children have had time to respond to it personally.

The Place of the Classics

Some literature programs recommend a sequence of particular books for study at each age level. However, we believe that there is no one book, or twenty books, or one hundred books, that should be read by all children. It would be unfortunate if children missed certain special books, but none should be required of all. Knowledge of certain literary classics of childhood—such as *Alice's Adventures in Wonderland* or *The Wind in the Willows*—is enriching but not absolutely essential to one's development. What is important is that we give children rich experiencing of literature at various stages of development.

Knowledge of time-tested works of prose, and poetry—such as Mother Goose rhymes, fables, myths, and Bible stories—does provide a background for understanding many literary allusions: "Don't count your chicks before they hatch," "sour grapes," "dog in the manger," "Midas touch," "Herculean task," and "a coat of many colors" are all examples. However, the reason they continue to be used is that their meanings still have significance for us today. Teachers who know literature share appropriate literary classics with children because they are still *good stories*, not because they are the source of literary allusions. If children are not ready to "connect" with these stories, then such stories have little meaning for them and are therefore inappropriate.

Knowing Authors and Illustrators

Study of the works of particular authors has traditionally been more characteristic of literature at the secondary level than in the elementary school. Still, even young children enjoy knowing something about authors and illustrators as they read their books. Teachers and librarians should tell children the name of the author and illustrator of a book as they introduce it. They might ask children if they know any other books that this particular person has illustrated or written. Some children delight in being able to recognize the artwork of Tomie de Paola or Leo Lionni or Chris Van Allsburg. Recognizing the style of an artist's work should be encouraged. Middle-grade children frequently discover favorite authors. They want another book by Lois Lowry, another Gary Paulsen, or another Betty Ren Wright. They might be reading series books, and so they ask for another one of the Narnia series (C. S. Lewis), the Prydain series (Lloyd Alexander), or the Little House books (Laura Ingalls Wilder). Some children develop special interests in sports stories or mysteries. These are all ways that children categorize books. They show that children are developing a framework for literature, a way of thinking about books.

Knowledge about particular books, authors, and the craft of writing will come about as children find increasing satisfaction in a range and diversity of works. Such knowledge should not be the primary focus of the literature program. It will occur as a natural result of real experiencing of books.

Developing Appreciation

The long-term goal of a literature program is the development of a lifetime pattern of preference for reading quality literature. James Britton maintained that in a quality reading/literature program "a student should read *more books* with satisfaction . . . [and] he should read books with *more satisfaction*."[4] This emphasis on both wide reading and in-depth reading is characteristic of a literature program that develops fluency and appreciation.

We have seen that even kindergarten children can identify the styles of various artists and can recognize different purposes for different genres of literature. Gradually, as children are introduced to more books on their own, they become interested in the ways authors and illustrators create meaning. This is particularly true as children begin to write and publish their own stories.

All good readers go through a stage when they read series books or nondemanding books by the same author. Such wide reading usually produces fluent readers, who read one book after another without much thought. To develop appreciation for the better written book, teachers can suggest that children compare books by different authors. One fifth-grade teacher read aloud Paula Fox's *One-Eyed Cat* to her class. Then she asked a group of girls who had read Judy Blume's *Blubber* to talk about the two books. They realized that the one-dimensional characters in Blume's book never change, never have doubts about the many cruel ways they are teasing Linda Fischer, and show no remorse. But Ned in *One-Eyed Cat* is filled with guilt and has no one to share it with. For eight months, he carries his burden and then finally tells his mother. The girls understood the difference between showing how a cruel action makes a person feel and just describing the cruelty. Children need to discuss books, compare books, and then talk about what they have learned from reading them. Such in-depth reading develops critical appreciative readers.

If children are exposed to the fine writing of authors such as Paula Fox, Paul Fleischman, Katherine Paterson, and Mollie Hunter and given time to discuss books like *One-Eyed Cat*, *Saturnalia*, *Jacob Have I Loved*, and *A Sound of Chariots*, they will be better able to recognize shallow, one-dimensional stories. Once students have knowledge of a repertoire of fine books that they have responded to in a variety of ways, they will begin to become more discriminating readers.

Most parents and some teachers are so relieved their children are reading that they are reluctant to suggest they could be reading more challenging books. If teachers consistently nurture children's enjoyment of literature by reading aloud exciting, well-selected books, if they give children time to read and discuss books in literature groups, their appreciation for quality literature will grow. One major goal of the literature program should be this development of discriminating critical readers.

Different Plans for Literature Programs

For a good part of this century, reading instruction has been delivered through the medium of basal readers, "a series of sequential, all inclusive instructional materials."[5] However, the growth of literature-based reading programs has been phenomenal in the past fifteen years.[6] No single reason can be given for the expanded role of trade books in the schools; rather, the accumulated weight of evidence of many studies, insights from professional educators, and the success of many teachers who are making literature central to the curriculum seem to be reason enough. (See Chapters 1 and 4 for research that supports literature-based programs.)

Literature with a Basal Reading Program

It should come as no surprise, then, that companies that publish these reading textbooks quickly aligned themselves with the interest in literature and produced basal readers using selections from children's books. These are advertised as "literature-based reading programs," when in reality they are the old basal readers with new content but the same workbooks, teachers' manuals, ditto sheets, and end-of-the-unit tests. The emphasis is still on teaching reading skills, and the greatest amount of time is devoted to filling in the blanks in the workbooks rather than actually reading.

Because the texts are drawn from literature (although frequently abridged), the content is more interesting

---

[4]James Britton, "The Nature of the Reader's Satisfaction," in *The Cool Web: The Pattern of Children's Reading*, ed. Margaret Meek, Aidan Warlow, and Griselda Barton (New York: Atheneum, 1978), p. 110.

[5]Kenneth Goodman, Patrick Shannon, Yvonne Freeman, and Sharon Murphy, *Report Card on Basal Readers* (Katonah, N.Y.: Richard C. Owen, 1988), p. 1.

[6]Bernice Cullinan, "Latching on to Literature: Reading Initiations Take Hold," *School Library Journal* 35 (April 1989): pp. 27–31.

than the "Dick and Jane" type of basal reader. However, children are given no choice of what to read and frequently little time to discuss their responses to the stories. Nor do these short selections prepare children to put in the time it may take to get into a full-length book or to experience the joy of being "lost" in a good book for days.

Evaluation of children's progress in a basal reading program is usually determined by the level of book they can read successfully and their performance on the publishers' tests that accompany the basals. Often any direct teaching that takes place is aimed at these criterion tests rather than being planned around the individual needs of students. Grouping children according to reading level also seems to perpetuate the reading problems of the children in the lowest groups. According to the Report from the Commission on Reading, these children often "receive less instruction and qualitatively different instruction than the child would in a group designated as high ability."[7]

Finally, despite the advertisements heralding this "new" literature-based approach, it is well to remember that the McGuffey readers, the old Elson readers, and some of the basal readers of the 1960s also included literature selections.

Literature Programs Using Real Books

Increasingly schools are moving to programs in which trade books are used for all aspects of reading instruction and for integrating traditional areas of the curriculum. This approach ties in with the *whole language* movement, a term used by Kenneth Goodman to describe curriculums that emphasize learning language (including reading and writing) by using it for a variety of real and functional purposes.[8] Because publishers of basal readers are calling their programs "literature based" or "whole language," in some places these terms mean using basal readers with literature content. In a *true* literature-based or whole language program, classrooms are flooded with books. Funds usually appropriated for the purchase of basal readers and workbooks are used for obtaining large classroom libraries of 400 to 500 books. There are books in an attractive reading corner, sets of paperback books for in-depth study, and a changing collection of books obtained from the school library and public libraries on whatever unit focus is in

progress. Books are displayed along with the children's work. Children's interpretations of books, book surveys, and big books are seen throughout the room. Few commercial charts or pictures are seen, only quantities of children's work with captions, labels, or writing on it.

Knowing the research on the importance of reading aloud in developing concepts about print, a sense of story, prediction of plot, and understanding of characters, teachers read aloud to primary children three and four times a day. They frequently reread favorite stories until children almost know them by heart. Parent aides are encouraged to read aloud to small groups of children. Frequently teachers establish a "buddy system" in which older children read with one or two younger ones.

Rather than work on worksheets or workbook activities, children do a variety of things. Some may be seen reading from the big books, others may be reading individually with the teacher, while still others may be busy reading or writing stories of their own or writing in their literature response journals. Many of the literature extension activities described in Chapter 14 are done during this work time. Quiet talk about books flows as children create murals or map the action of a story.

An independent reading time is provided every day. Frequently, however, children read quietly in pairs. Time for discussion of books almost always follows these periods.

The in-depth study of the books of one author, a genre of books, or one book begins as early as kindergarten. With older children, sets of paperbacks like *The Whipping Boy* by Sid Fleischman, *Island of the Blue Dolphins* by Scott O'Dell, *Strider* by Beverly Cleary, and *A Wrinkle in Time* by Madeleine L'Engle are used for literature study. All children are involved in groups for in-depth reading, but the groups are not formed on the basis of ability. Rather, children choose to join a reading group based on their interest in the book or a topic, and these groups change as the focus of a study changes.

Reading and writing across the curriculum are characteristic of this integrated program. Children do research in informational books on the particular class unit. Units and projects that cut across traditional subject-matter areas might be chosen by a class or a small group of children to study. For example, over the period of a year, one second- and third-grade class studied the topics "Fairy Tales," "Plumbing and Water Sources," and "Immigration to the United States." They also had mini-units on "Books by Pat Hutchins," "Grandparents," and "Dinosaurs."

Library skills are learned in the process of using many books and reference books for children's projects. The library is open all day long for children to use as they research particular topics. Parent assistants may help children in one part of the room to find their materials if the librarian is reading a story or working with others.

[7]Richard C. Anderson et al., *Becoming a Nation of Readers* (Washington, D.C.: National Institute of Education, 1984).

[8]Kenneth Goodman, *What's Whole in Whole Language?* (Portsmouth, N.H.: Heinemann, 1986).

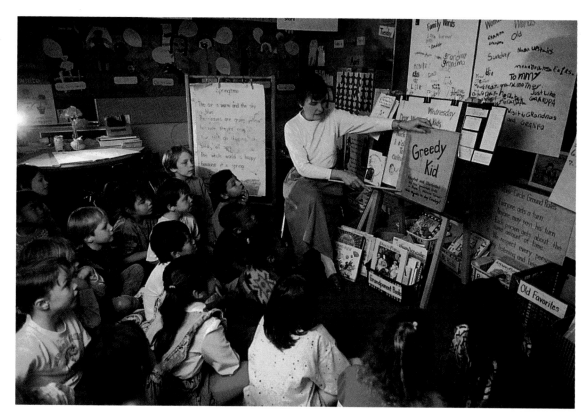

Teacher and children share the reading of the alternative text they created, "Greedy Kid," following the pattern of *Greedy Cat* by Joy Cowley.
Mission School, Redlands Public Schools, Redlands, California. Nancy Anderson, teacher. Photo by Larry Rose.

Children learn strategies for reading many different types of texts through real reading and inquiry. When teachers do direct teaching of such strategies, they are related to children's needs and not isolated drills. No worksheets or workbooks are used. Rather, children write in their response journals, do purposeful reading, and create their own books and group projects.

Teachers and children keep records of children's reading. Each child has a portfolio containing samples of his or her story writing, artwork, and research reports from the beginning of school. These are shared with parents during individual conference times. Book reports are not required, because children are sharing books in a variety of ways. Teachers know what children are reading because they are reading and reacting in their reading journals each week. All children know what others are reading because they discuss their books every day. Children frequently recommend books to others, as they know each other's reading interests. These children become a community of readers as they discuss and recommend particular titles. Books are an essential part of their lives.

The Teaching Resource box "Approaches to Reading Instruction" contrasts some of the major components of basal reading programs and literature-based

reading programs. Literature-based programs that use real books offer a challenge to teachers. They require an in-depth knowledge of children and children's literature. Only when a teacher knows the potential of a child and a book, and is willing to trust the interaction between the two, does learning really occur.

Making the Transition to a Literature-Based Approach

It is not easy to go from reliance on basal readers and teachers' guides, with their careful plans for each lesson, to letting children choose their own books, allowing them to respond in a variety of ways, and helping them plan meaningful activities.

Most teachers in the classroom today had basal readers in their own early schooling. Their teacher-training program might have helped them think of other ways to teach reading, or it might have reinforced their reliance on basal readers. Often their student teaching was with a teacher who used basal readers. So it is little wonder that when teachers first try to use real books they tend to use them like basal readers. They divide children into ability groups and then select what they

Resources for Teaching
Approaches to Reading Instruction

Basal Approach

Medium

A single anthology (usually two per grade level).

Skills

The teacher teaches skills to all children at a particular reading level at the same time.

Prior to reading

The teacher sets the purpose for reading. Children know they will be asked questions about the selection.

Follow-up

Questions from the teacher.

Workbooks and worksheets.

Grouping of students

By ability level.

Reading silently

Ninety-second segments of sustained reading.

Reading aloud

Round-robin reading—children read around a circle.

Assessment

Basal criterion tests.

Goals

High scores on standardized tests.

Literature-Based Approach

Medium

Literature of all genres at a variety of ability levels.

Multiple copies of key books.

Stategies

Strategies are taught as needed by teacher or peers. Strategies are learned in the context of real reading and writing.

Prior to reading

The teacher invites children to read for pleasure and/or links prior experience to the material to be read.

Follow-up

Book discussions.

Response journals.

Authentic responses to books.

Grouping of students

For strategy instruction.

By topic.

By choice.

Social grouping.

Reading silently

Independent reading for a minimum twenty minutes a day and throughout the day as part of authentic learning activities.

Reading aloud

Readers' theater.

Choral reading.

Book sharing.

Buddy reading.

Teacher conferences.

Assessment

Anecdotal records.

Checklists.

Miscue.

Running records.

Response journals.

Response projects.

Retellings.

Goals

Lifelong readers.

Strategic readers.

Reading *more* with satisfaction.

Reading with *more* satisfaction.

think are appropriate titles for each group. They buy teachers' guides for these books that provide comprehension questions, and workbook-like exercises and even black-line masters to duplicate and give to the whole class. Although a few guides do present the strengths of the books and suggest appropriate learning activities (from which teachers may choose), most of them are merely making basal readers out of some of our best children's literature. Such basalization of fine books will never develop a love of reading—in fact, it might kill it altogether.

Teachers who wish to initiate the use of real books in their reading programs may want to visit another school where such a program has already been successfully introduced. They will want to read many professional books describing the process and attend professional meetings where they can talk with teachers who are involved in such a program. It also helps if several teachers in a school support each other in making the change and obtain the support of the administration and parents.

The first task will be to obtain many books for the classroom and to become enthusiastic readers of these good books. Teachers may want to start gradually, by planning time for independent reading and by reading aloud to children each day. If they can obtain four or five sets of paperback titles, teachers could give a brief book talk on each title and let children look at the books to select what they want to read. Then time could be set aside to let children read the books they have selected according to interest groups rather than ability groups.

Record your observations of how children seem to be doing and your reactions to the approach. Share these with your fellow teachers. When a group of teachers who had used real books in their reading programs for over five years were asked, "How have you changed in your teaching?" every one of them said they had become more relaxed about their teaching.[9] At first they wrote questions and planned activities for each book. Later, when they saw children were reading more than they ever had read before, were interpreting books with real insight, and were doing just as well in the testing program, they withdrew their questions and trusted the interaction between the books and the children. Their observations appear to be substantiated by the research on such programs.[10]

[9]Children's Literature '91 conference, Ohio State University, Columbus, Ohio, 24–26 January 1991.

[10]Michael O. Tunnell and James S. Jacobs, "Using Real Books: Research Findings on Literature-Based Reading Instruction," *Reading Teacher* 42 (March 1989):470–477.

The Components of a Literature Program

It is possible to visit any classroom and tell something about the quality of education just by observing what appears to be honored there. If books are honored, they are easily accessible and displayed attractively throughout the classroom. Their covers face outward so children can see them, for example. Each classroom has a comfortable reading corner or loft that provides an inviting quiet place to read. A good classroom collection of books provides children with real reading choices. Children's interpretations of books, both written and artistic, are displayed on bulletin boards. Attractive murals of favorite storybook characters or houses from fairy tales or something about an author might be featured. When you visit, write down what appears to be the most important aspects of this classroom: basal readers or trade books; workbooks or children's own writing; commercial art from teacher stores or children's own artistic interpretations and written work. Are children's seats arranged in ways to encourage talk or in straight rows to discourage it? Are there interesting centers in the room, such as a writing center or science center, that suggest a variety of activities? Can you tell what topic or subject or book the class is working with just by looking at the displays? Each classroom can be as revealing and individual as a teacher's own fingerprints.

An Enthusiastic Teacher

The most important aspect of the classroom environment is the teacher. She or he creates the climate of the classroom and arranges the learning environment. If the teacher loves books, shares them with children, and provides time for children to read and a place for them to read, children will become enthusiastic readers. The teacher who reads to the children every day, talks about books and characters in books as if they were good friends, and knows poems and stories to tell is serving the class as an adult model of a person who enjoys books. One teacher regularly used to read a new children's book while her class was reading. She would keep the book in an old beat-up briefcase that she delighted in carrying. A kind of game she played with her 7- and 8-year-old students was to keep the book hidden from them. Their delight was to find out what book she was reading, so they could read the same one. Of course they always found out, which was what she had in mind in the first place. Walk into any classroom and you can tell if the teacher really respects books. You can look at the teacher's desk or ask the children what books their teacher is reading to them. You can see what provisions have been made to have books in the classroom; you can look at the quality of the books and talk to children about which ones they have read. Enthusiasm for books is contagious; if the teacher has it, so will the children.

The Classroom Book Collection

If we want children to become readers, we will want to surround them with books of all kinds. We know that wide reading is directly related to accessibility; the more books available and the more time for reading, the more children will read and the better readers they will become.

Books should be a natural part of the classroom environment. There should be no argument about whether to have a classroom collection of books or a library media center; both are necessary. Children should have immediate access to books whenever they need them.

The books in the classroom collection will vary from those in the library media center. Many classrooms have an extensive paperback collection (400 to 500 titles). Frequently, there are five or six copies of the same title, so several children can read the same book and have an in-depth discussion of it.

The classroom teacher will also want to provide for a changing collection of books depending on the themes or units the children are studying. The librarian might provide a rolling cart of materials that will enhance children's study of bugs or folktales or the Civil War or explorers. It is important that teachers be thoroughly acquainted with the content of these books so they can help their students use them. If the library media center does not have particular books that the children or the teacher needs, they may be obtained from local public libraries or from a bookmobile. Some state libraries will send boxes of books to teachers in communities that are not serviced by public libraries. An increasing number of teachers are demanding and receiving their share of monies allocated for instructional materials. Teachers using real books as the heart of their curriculum should receive the same amount of money as those using basal readers, workbooks, social studies, science, and other textbooks. We admire the number of teachers who spend their own money to buy tradebooks for their classrooms, but at the same time we question the practice. Do coaches buy the footballs, art teachers the paints and colored paper? Real books are essential to the making of a fluent reader and should be an unquestioned item of every school budget.

Every classroom should have an inviting corner where children can choose and read favorite books.
PS 116, New York, New York. Ilana Dubin-Spiegel, teacher.

Creating a Classroom Reading Center

Most teachers create an inviting reading area where children may go to read. This area should be somewhat secluded and outside the general traffic pattern. It is usually marked off with shelves where trade books are attractively displayed. A rug provides quiet and comfort. Many centers have beanbag chairs, pillows, a rocking chair, and sometimes a comfortable couch for reading. To mark off a reading area, one teacher of 8- and 9-year-olds clipped paperback books to clothespins and hung these by strings suspended from the ceiling. Another group of 7- and 8-year-olds made a quilt of textile crayon squares depicting their favorite stories. This then became a brightly colored divider for their reading center. In a fourth- and fifth-grade classroom, several parents constructed a sturdy loft for the reading area.

Children develop more interest in books when they share in the planning of a reading center. One group of 8-year-olds utilized an unused cloak room for their reading center. With the aid of the teacher and custodian they built and painted bookshelves. Others designed unbleached muslin curtains that were decorated with crayon drawings of their favorite characters from books. A mother provided a hooked rug and a rocking chair to complete the homey aspect of this reading center. Another school changed a storage closet that was between three rooms into a small primary-grade book center. Good lighting, carpeting, and some bookcases made this a quiet, comfortable place for children from several classrooms to meet and share books together.

Inventive teachers and children enjoy planning for and creating their own attractive reading areas.

Display Techniques

Teachers will want to feature particular books by displaying them on top of bookshelves or on the shelves with their covers facing outward, in places that can be easily seen and reached by children. Old, shabby-looking books placed so that only the titles on the spines are visible do not capture children's attention. Books should be constantly and freely available in the classroom.

Department stores feature what they want to sell by arranging interesting displays; teachers could do the same. It takes very little time to collect five or six good Halloween stories and poetry books and place them with a pumpkin on a table that has been covered with a piece of orange or black cloth. All the books by one author or illustrator could be exhibited together, along with a picture of the writer or artist. Children might decide on a "book of the week," which could have a special place of honor. One group of 8- and 9-year-olds moved their favorite books to the windowsills for display. One fifth-grade classroom had books in three places—the reading area, a table of books concerned with whatever focus unit they were studying, and a special place for books they had written and bound themselves. To be effective, displays should be changed frequently.

Trade books should be an integral part of the total environment of the room. For example, Jan Feder's informational book *The Life of a Hamster* might be displayed along with Alan Baker's *Benjamin's Portrait*, a delightful story of a hamster, alongside the cage of the classroom's hamster. Millicent Selsam and Joyce Hunt's *A First Look at Leaves* could accompany a chart of leaves pressed and laminated. If the teacher is reading aloud Jean George's *Julie of the Wolves*, she might display a soapstone sculpture, Dorothy Hinshaw Patent's information book *Return of the Wolf*, or traditional Eskimo tales such as James Houston's *The Falcon Bow, an Arctic Legend*, Dale DeArmond's beautiful story *The Seal Oil Lamp*, or *Toughboy and Sister* by Kirkpatrick Hill, another realistic story. Such book cycles help children make connections with books from other genres about a similar topic. After teachers model this kind of display, children can be encouraged to find books that will go with the read-aloud book or their show-and-tell artifacts.

Whenever possible, teachers should try to involve children in the process of selecting, obtaining, and

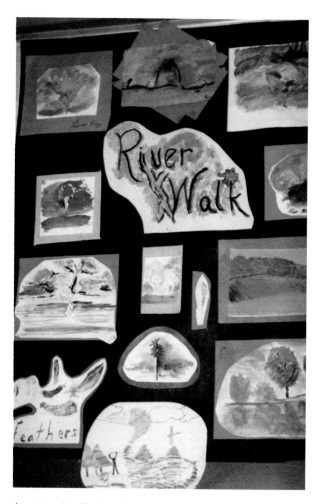

An attractive display of children's work can invite other children to become readers and writers.
Wickliffe Alternative School, Upper Arlington, Ohio.

arranging books for the reading center. Children can review new books and share in their selection. Excitement mounts as they unpack boxes of books, whether they come from the library or directly from the publisher. They can help with book arrangement and display. Three kindergarten children carefully rearranged the books on display in their room into the following categories:

- ABC books and Mother Goose rhymes
- Books by Pat Hutchins
- Fat books
- Little books
- Books with pretty front covers

The teacher was using the first group of books with the class. The second group represented their ongoing study of the work of one illustrator. The last three categories were obviously the children's, but the process of rearranging the books forced them to look at each one, to discuss it, and come to some tentative conclusion about its size or content. Besides their own childlike categories, they learned that books could be classified by type (genre) and author.

In a fifth- and sixth-grade classroom, children decided to display all the books in which the main characters showed courage of some kind. This resulted in much discussion about not only physical courage but also the psychological courage required of the characters in Betsy Byars's *The Pinballs* and in Katherine Paterson's *The Great Gilly Hopkins* and *Lyddie*, her historical fiction about nineteenth-century mill girls.

Sharing Literature with Children

From the time of the earliest primitive fire circle to the Middle Ages—when minnesingers and troubadours sang their ballads—to the modern age of television, people have found delight in hearing stories and poems. Because literature serves many educational purposes in addition to entertainment and enjoyment, teachers should place a high priority on sharing literature with children. Boys and girls of all ages should have the opportunity to hear good literature every day.

Reading to Children

One of the best ways to interest children in books is to read to them frequently from the time they are first able to listen. Preschoolers and kindergartners should have an opportunity to listen to stories three or four times a day. Parent volunteers, high school students, college participants—all can be encouraged to read to small groups of children throughout the day. Children should have a chance to hear their favorite stories over and over again at a listening center. A child from a book-loving family might have heard over a thousand bedtime stories before she ever comes to kindergarten; some children might never have heard one.

One excellent teacher of kindergarten and first-grade children commented on the importance of sharing books with her children.

I read to my children a lot—a whole lot! I'll read anywhere from one to three stories at a time. Sometimes I'll reread a favorite story twice. And I read four to five times a day. I read to the whole group, to small groups of four or five children and to individual children. While I'm reading to the groups I'll encourage them to join in on the refrains. With individuals I may point to words, talk about what a word

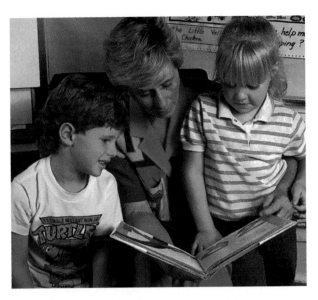

A teacher shares her enthusiasm for books with one or two children as well as the class.
Idyllwild Elementary School, Idyllwild, California. Sharon Schmidt, teacher. Photo by Larry Rose.

is. Sometimes I'll frame a word with my hands or put it on the board. I put songs, poems and refrains on chart paper so children will try to read them by themselves. And I'll read stories over and over again, just the way children hear bedtime stories. It is not unusual for me to read a book twenty times in one month![11]

Teachers accept the idea of reading at least twice a day to the primary-grade child. Increasingly, the daily story time is advocated by almost all authorities in reading. The research done by Cohen, Durkin, Clark, Thorndike, and Wells reported in Chapters 1 and 4 emphasizes the importance of reading aloud to all children, not only for enjoyment but also for their growth in reading skills. Reading to children improves children's reading. Rereading favorite stories is as important as the initial reading.

Unfortunately, daily story times are not as common in the middle grades as in the primary grades, yet we know that they are just as essential there. Reading comprehension is improved as students listen to and discuss events, characters, and motivation. They learn to predict what will happen in exciting tales like Mollie Hunter's *A Stranger Came Ashore*. Their vocabulary increases as they hear fine texts such as Donald Hall's *Ox-Cart Man* or Jane Yolen's poetic *Owl Moon*. Older students can discuss

[11]Interview with Kristen Kerstetter in *The Best of the WEB, 1976–1982*, ed. Susan Hepler (Columbus: Ohio State University, College of Education, The Reading Center, 1982), pp. 2–3.

homelessness and prejudice as they hear Paula Fox's *Monkey Island,* or they can add to their knowledge of Abraham Lincoln's presidency by reading Russell Freedman's remarkable photobiography *Lincoln.* Teachers can take advantage of this time to introduce various genres, such as fantasy, biography, or poetry, that students might not be reading on their own.

Primarily, however, the read-aloud time will cause children to want to read. Once children have heard a good book read aloud, they can hardly wait to savor it again. Reading aloud thus generates further interest in books. Good oral reading should develop a taste for fine literature.

Selecting Books to Read Aloud

Teachers and librarians will want to select read-aloud books in terms of the children's interests and background in literature and the quality of writing. Usually teachers will not select books that children in the group are reading avidly on their own. This is the time to stretch their imaginations, to extend interests, and to develop appreciation of fine writing. If children have not had much experience in listening to stories, begin where they are. Appreciation for literature appears to be developmental and sequential. Six- and 7-year-olds who have had little exposure to literature still need to hear many traditional fairy tales, including "Hansel and Gretel," "Sleeping Beauty," and *The Crane Wife* by Sumiko Yagawa. They delight in such favorite picture storybooks as *Harry the Dirty Dog* by Gene Zion, *Sylvester and the Magic Pebble* by William Steig, and Patricia C. McKissack's *Flossie & the Fox.* Other children of the same age who have had much exposure to literature might demand longer chapter books like *Ramona Forever* by Beverly Cleary, *James and the Giant Peach* by Roald Dahl, or *Ozzie on His Own* by Johanna Hurwitz.

Children tend to enjoy fantasies if they are read aloud. The subtle humor of A. A. Milne's *Winnie-the-Pooh* may be completely lost on a child who is reading alone; but when shared by an appreciative teacher-reader, the awkward but well-meaning "Pooh of Very Little Brain" and the dismal Eeyore become well-loved personages to 7- and 8-year-olds. The mysterious snow-shrouded pictures of *The Polar Express* by Chris Van Allsburg intrigue children of this age. They can discuss the ending of this story and ponder the question of the sound of the Christmas bell. After hearing John Steptoe's *Mufaro's Beautiful Daughters,* children could look for other "generous person/greedy person" stories (see Chapter 6).

Picture storybooks are no longer just for "little kids." There is a real place for sharing some of the beautiful picture books with older children as well as younger ones. *Dawn* by Uri Shulevitz creates the same feeling

It is essential that teachers continue to read aloud to older children. This is the time to introduce books they might miss and get them hooked on reading.
Mission School, Redlands Public Schools, Redlands, California. Joan Schleicher, teacher. Photo by Larry Rose.

visually as one of Emily Dickinson's clear, rarefied poems. It is a literary experience for all ages, but particularly for anyone who has felt "at-oneness" with the world before the sunrise. Older students particularly enjoy Jon Scieszka's *The Stinky Cheese Man and Other Fairly Stupid Tales* and David Macaulay's puzzling four stories in one in *Black and White.*

The teacher should strive for balance in what is read aloud to children. Children tend to like what they know. Introducing a variety of types of books will broaden their base of appreciation. If 11- and 12-year-olds are all reading contemporary fiction, the teacher might read Brian Jacques's powerful fantasy of the fight to save an ancient stone abbey in *Redwall,* or introduce them to Katherine Paterson's indomitable *Lyddie,* the story of a girl who struggles against the unbearable working conditions of factory girls in the Lowell, Massachusetts, mills of the 1840s. The finely honed writing of Patricia MacLachlan's *Sarah, Plain and Tall,* the story of a mail-order bride and the family who longed for a new mother, could be shared with children as young as third grade and as old as fifth. Most of these books are too good for children to miss and should be read aloud to them.

Primary-grade teachers will read many picture books to their children, certainly a minimum of three to four a day. Middle-grade teachers might present parts of many books to their students during book talks or as teasers to interest children in reading the books. But how many entire books will a teacher read in the course of one school year? An educated guess might be that starting with 8-year-olds—when teachers begin to read longer, continuous stories to boys and girls—an average of some six to ten books are read aloud during the year. This means that for the next four years, when children are reaching the peak of their interest in reading, they may hear no more than forty or so books read by their teachers! Today when there are more than ninety thousand children's books in print, read-aloud choices must be selected with care in terms of their relevance for students and the quality of their writing. A list of suggested books to read aloud is included on the endpapers of this book to serve as a beginning guide. Notice that the overlapping of age groups is deliberate. There is no such thing as a book for 5-year-olds or 10-year-olds. Very popular books, such as those by Dr. Seuss or poems by Shel Silverstein, do not appear on our read-aloud lists because children will have read them on their own. Only a teacher who knows the children, their interests, and their background of experience can truly select appropriate books for a particular class.

We note with concern the increasing number of teachers who want to read such complex stories as *Tuck Everlasting* by Natalie Babbitt, *A Wrinkle in Time* by Madeleine L'Engle, or *The Pinballs* by Betsy Byars to 6- and 7-year-olds. While children this age might become involved in the plots of these well-written stories, they will certainly miss much of the deeper meanings reflected in their themes, such as the burden of immortality, the overcoming of evil with love, or the courage of children surviving family rejection and cruelty. Read at the appropriate developmental levels, these books could provide the basis for serious in-depth discussion and study. The number of years when children read literature suited to their age appears to have decreased, as more and more 12- and 13-year-olds begin to read best-sellers and other books written for adults. The inappropriate selection of books for reading aloud by both parents and teachers may contribute to this erosion of childhood.

There is a difference, however, between what parents might choose for family reading and what is appropriate for classroom sharing. Parents have the advantage of knowing all the books that children have enjoyed at home. In a family sharing E. B. White's *Charlotte's Web*, the 5-year-old enjoys the humor of these talking barnyard animals while an 8-year-old might weep at Charlotte's death. The closeness of a family unit helps all members to find enjoyment in a read-aloud story regardless of age level. The teacher, on the other hand, has to consider children's backgrounds in literature, or lack of background, as he or she selects appropriate books to capture their attention.

A read-aloud program should be planned. What books are too good to miss? These should be included in the overall plan. Teachers should keep a record of the books that they have shared with the children they teach and a brief notation of the class's reaction to each title. This enables teachers to see what kind of balance is being achieved and what the particular favorites of

the class are. Such a record provides the children's future teachers with information on the likes and dislikes of the class and their exposure to literature. It also might prevent the situation that was discovered by a survey of one school in which every teacher in the school, with the exception of the kindergarten and the second-grade teachers, had read *Charlotte's Web* aloud to the class! *Charlotte's Web* is a great book, but not for every class. Perhaps teachers in a school need to agree on what is the most appropriate time for reading particular favorites. Teachers and librarians should be encouraged to try reading new books to children, instead of always reading the same ones. But some self-indulgence should be allowed every teacher who truly loves a particular book, because that enthusiasm can't help but rub off on children.

Techniques for Reading Aloud

Effective oral reading is an important factor in capturing children's interest. Some teachers can make almost any story sound exciting; others plod dully through. The storyteller's voice, timing, and intonation patterns should communicate the meanings and mood of the story. Conversation should be read naturally, and volume varied with the content of the story. Humor, mystery, and disgust can all be communicated through the tone of the reader's voice. To read effectively, the teacher should be familiar with the story and communicate his or her enthusiasm for the book. It is good for children to see teachers moved by a story. One teacher of our acquaintance says he has never yet been able to finish *Where the Red Fern Grows* by Wilson Rawls without shedding a tear. Others find White's *Charlotte's Web* or Paterson's *Bridge to Terabithia* equally hard to finish. Literature should communicate feelings, real feelings. A well-read story can move us to tears or laughter.

The Resources for Teaching box "Effective Practices for Reading Aloud" may prove useful. Check the list before selecting and reading a story to a whole class.

Storytelling

A 5-year-old said to his teacher: "Tell the story from your face." His preference for the story *told* by the teacher or librarian instead of the story read directly from the book is echoed by boys and girls everywhere. The art of storytelling is frequently neglected in the elementary school today. There are so many beautiful books to share with children, we rationalize, and our harried life allows little time for learning stories. Yet children should not be denied the opportunity to hear well-told stories. Through storytelling, the teacher helps transmit the literary heritage.

Resources for Teaching
Effective Practices for Reading Aloud

1. Select a story appropriate to the developmental age of the children and their previous exposure to literature.
2. Determine whether you will share the book with the whole class, a small group, or an individual child.
3. Select books that will stretch children's imaginations, extend their interests, and expose them to fine art and writing.
4. Read a variety of types of books to capture the interests of all.
5. Remember that favorite stories should be reread at the primary level.
6. Plan to read aloud several times a day.
7. Select a story that you like so you can communicate your enthusiasm.
8. Choose a story or chapter that can be read in one session.
9. Read the book first so you are familiar with the content.
10. Seat the children close to you so all can see the pictures.
11. Hold the book so children can see the pictures at their eye level.
12. Communicate the mood and meaning of the story and characters with your voice.
13. Introduce books in various ways:

    Through a display

    Through a brief discussion about the author or illustrator

    By asking children to predict what the story will be about through looking at the cover and interpreting the title

    By linking the theme, author, or illustrator to other books children know

14. Encourage older children to discuss the progress of the story or predict the outcome at the end of the chapter.
15. Help children to link the story with their own experiences or other literature.
16. Keep a list of the books read aloud to the whole class that can be passed on to their next teachers.

Storytelling provides for intimate contact and rapport with the children. No book separates the teacher from the audience. The story may be modified to fit group needs. A difficult word or phrase can be explained in context. For example, in telling the story of *The Three Wishes* by Paul Galdone, you could quickly explain that "black pudding" is another word for sausage before continuing the story. Stories can be personalized for very young children by substituting their names for those of the characters. Such a phrase as "and, David, if you had been there you would have seen the biggest Billy Goat Gruff . . ." will redirect the child whose interest has wandered. The pace of the story can be adapted to the children's interests and age levels.

Selecting Stories to Tell

Stories that are to be told should be selected with care. Stories worth the telling have special characteristics, including a quick beginning, action, a definite climax, natural dialogue, and a satisfying conclusion. It is best to select stories with only three or four speaking characters so that listeners can keep the characters straight. Finally, stories with rich literary language

such as Rudyard Kipling's *The Elephant's Child* are best read aloud. Instead, select stories for telling that sound like a "told tale."

Folktales like "The Three Billy Goats Gruff," "The Little Red Hen," and "Cinderella" are particular favorites of younger children. The repetitive pattern of these tales makes them easy to tell. Originally passed down from generation to generation by word of mouth, these tales were polished and embellished with each retelling.

Six-, 7-, and 8-year-olds enjoy hearing longer folktales such as Ashley Bryan's *The Cat's Purr*. They also enjoy some of the tall tales about American folk heroes such as Paul Bunyan, Pecos Bill, and John Henry. Incidents from biographies and chapters from longer books may be told as a way of interesting children in reading them.

Guidelines for Telling Stories

From the time of the early minstrels, storytelling has been considered an art. For this reason many teachers have been afraid to attempt it. However, the classroom teacher is an artist in working with children and should have no fear in telling stories to them. Enjoyment of the

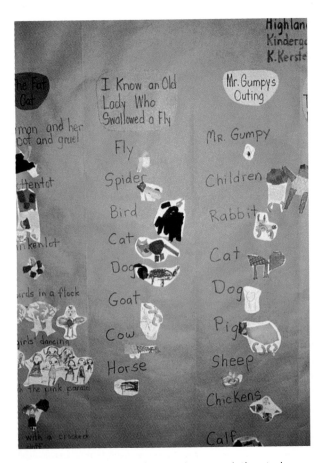

By illustrating this chart about various cumulative stories and songs, children learned to retell the stories in the proper sequence.

Highland Park Elementary School, South-Western City Schools, Grove City, Ohio. Kristen Kerstetter, teacher.

tale and knowledge of children will help to convey enthusiasm and appreciation for the story.

If the teacher knows and enjoys the story, techniques will come naturally. The story should be carefully prepared, however. The teacher needs to be thoroughly familiar with its plot and characters, and with the flavor of its language; but it need not be memorized. In fact, memorization often results in a stilted, artificial presentation. There is also the added danger of being completely confused when forgetting a line. The storyteller should first visualize the setting; imagine the appearance of the characters, their age and costume; and plan an introduction that will set the mood of the story. It may be wise to learn the pattern of some introductions, such as, "Once there was, and once there wasn't. . . ." If there are repeated chants or refrains, these should be memorized. Outline the sequence of events, including major incidents, the climax, and conclusion. Master the structure of a story by reading it from beginning to end several times. Experienced storytellers allow two to three weeks to make a story their own. They learn the story as a whole, not in parts, and practice telling it to themselves, their family, and anyone who will listen.

The good storyteller calls attention not to himself but to the story. He should use a pleasant, low-pitched voice with enough volume to be heard easily. Gestures, if used at all, should be natural for the storyteller and appropriate to the action of the story. The storyteller is not an actor but the channel through which the story is told. Many storytellers believe sound effects should be omitted. If the lion roars, the narrator should not attempt an imitation of a roar, but the idea can be conveyed as the word *roared* is given a deeper tone and increased volume. The *r* sound may be exaggerated—"the lion rrroared." Writers and such well-known storytellers as Bob Barton and Augusta Baker suggest variations in pitch, tone, and volume of voice in accordance with the mood of the story to make it more effective. Well-timed pauses may help listeners anticipate a climax. No amount of study of these techniques will substitute for actual practice. With experience comes assurance and a willingness to experiment.[12]

Using Props and Felt Boards

Storytelling can be varied by using a flannel board, felt board, magnetic board, or simple props that are central to the story. To tell a felt-board story, the scenery or characters of a story can be made of flannel, felt, or paper. As the story is told, the figures are placed in the proper positions on the board. If the figures are made of paper, strips of flannel attached to the reverse side will cause them to adhere to the felt board. Small magnets or magnetic sheets with adhesive backing may be cut and applied directly to the back of characters for use with a magnetic board or blackboard. Gluing felt to the inside of an artist's cardboard portfolio and trimming it with tape is an easy way to make a felt board. Felt boards and magnetic boards can also be purchased, but many classroom blackboards are now magnetic.

Some tales are more suitable for felt-board presentation than others. The stories should be simple and have few characters. Not every incident or scene in the story needs to be included. Detailed settings are too difficult to recreate. While some rapid changes can be portrayed on a felt board, most physical action is better dramatized. A cumulative tale, or one in which elements are added, such as Eric Carle's *The Very Hungry Caterpillar* or Margot Zemach's *It Could Always be Worse*, is usually quite appropriate for a felt-board presentation. For suggestions for felt-board presentations, see the Resources for Teaching box, "Suggested Stories for the Felt Board."

[12]For further assistance see Caroline Feller Bauer's *New Handbook for Storytellers* (Chicago: American Library Association, 1993).

Resources for Teaching
Suggested Stories for the Felt Board

Jan Brett, *The Mitten*

Joanna Cole, *It's Too Noisy*

Roger Duvoisin, *Petunia*

Rebecca Emberley, *Three Cool Kids*

Don Freeman, *Dandelion*

Wanda Gág, *Nothing at All*

Paul Galdone, *The Gingerbread Boy*

Mirra Ginsburg, *Mushroom in the Rain*

Rodney A. Greenblat, *Uncle Wizzmo's New Used Car*

Marilyn Hirsh, *Could Anything Be Worse?*

Nonny Hogrogian, *One Fine Day*

Ann Jonas, *Splash!*

Jack Kent, *The Fat Cat: A Danish Folktale*

Leo Lionni, *Frederick*

———. *Little Blue and Little Yellow*

Megan McDonald, *Is This a House for a Hermit Crab?*

Pierr Morgan, *The Turnip*

Shirley Neitzel, *The Bag I'm Taking to Grandma's*

Joanne Oppenheim, *You Can't Catch Me!*

Charles G. Shaw, *It Looked Like Spilt Milk*

Alvin Tresselt, *The Mitten*

Brinton Turkle, *Do Not Open*

Bernard Waber, *"You Look Ridiculous" Said the Rhinoceros to the Hippopotamus*

Linda Williams, *The Little Old Lady Who Was Not Afraid of Anything*

Audrey Wood, *The Napping House*

Margot Zemach, *It Could Always Be Worse*

———. *The Three Wishes: An Old Story*

Gene Zion, *Harry the Dirty Dog*

Book Talks

Librarians and teachers frequently use a book talk to introduce books to children. The primary purpose of a book talk is to interest children in reading the book themselves. Rather than reveal the whole story, the book talk tells just enough about the book to entice others to read it. A book talk may be about one title; it may be about several unrelated books that would have wide appeal; or it may revolve around several books with a similar theme, such as "getting along in the family" or "courage" or "survival stories."

The book talk should begin with recounting an amusing episode or with telling about an exciting moment in the book. The narrator might want to assume the role of a character in a book, such as Julie in *Julie of the Wolves* by Jean George, and tell of her experience of being lost without food or a compass on the North Slope of Alaska. The speaker should stop before the crisis is over or the mystery solved. Details should be specific. It is better to let the story stand on its own than to characterize it as a "terribly funny" story or the "most exciting" book you've ever read. Enthusiasm for the book will convey the speaker's opinion of it. This is one reason why book talks should be given only about stories the speaker genuinely likes. Children will then come to trust this evaluation. It is best if the book is on hand as it is discussed, so that the children can check it out as soon as the book is finished.

Providing Time to Read Books

One of the primary purposes of giving book talks, telling stories, and reading aloud to children is to motivate them to read. A major goal of every school should be to develop children who not only can read but who *do* read—who love reading and will become lifetime readers.

Unfortunately, schools spend so much of their time teaching the skills of literacy that they fail to develop truly literate persons who read widely and thoughtfully on many diverse subjects. The report of the Commission on Reading titled *Becoming a Nation of Readers* showed how little time students spend reading, both in school and out of school. According to this report, a typical primary class has only 7 or 8 minutes per day for silent reading; middle graders averaged only 15 minutes. In a study of fifth graders' out-of-school reading, 50 percent of the children read books for an average of 4 minutes per day or less, in contrast to the 130 minutes per day spent watching TV. "For the majority of the children, reading from books occupied 1 percent of their free time or less."[13]

To become fluent readers, children need to practice reading from real books that capture their interest and imagination. No one could become a competent

| [13]Anderson et al., *Becoming a Nation of Readers*, p. 77.

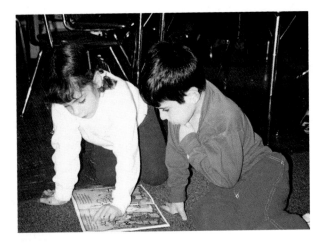

Two first graders share the reading of a picture book and exchange reading strategies.
PS 116, New York, New York. Ilana Dubin-Spiegel, teacher.

swimmer or tennis player by practicing four minutes a day. Schools have little influence on the out-of-school life of their students, but they do control the curriculum in school. If we want children to become readers, we must reorder our priorities and provide time for children to just read books of their own choosing every day.

Recognizing this need, many teachers have initiated a sustained silent reading (SSR) time. The name is somewhat formidable, suggesting more pain than pleasure. Teachers have used other names, such as "Recreational Reading," "Free Reading," or even the acronym DEAR (Drop Everything and Read) used by the teacher in *Ramona Quimby, Age 8* by Beverly Cleary.

One primary teacher called it OTTER (Our Time To Enjoy Reading) time. This certainly comes closer to the goal of such a program than the ominous-sounding "Sustained Silent Reading." Whatever the name, however, this is a time when everyone in the class (in some instances, the entire school) reads, including the teacher. SSR times have been successfully established in kindergarten through middle schools. Usually, a reading period is lengthened gradually from 10 minutes a day to 20, 30, or, in some fifth- and sixth-grade classes, 45 minutes per day. Some teachers allow children to read in pairs, recognizing the social nature of reading.

In classrooms that use real books for teaching reading and studying themes that cut across the curriculum, children are reading and writing throughout the day. Teachers still have a special time each day for children to read the books they have chosen to read for enjoyment. A classroom collection of books supplemented by library books is essential to the organization of this kind of program.

Fourth graders enjoy reading their books during SSR, or independent reading time.
PS 124, New York, New York. Mary S. Gallivan, teacher.

Talking About Books with Children

Equally important as time for wide reading is time to talk about books children are reading. When adults discuss books, we have good conversations about the ones we like, but we seldom quiz each other about character development, themes, or setting of the story. As teachers, we want to show this same respect for children as they share their thoughts about books.

A good time for informal talk about books is after children have had time to read by themselves. In pairs, small groups, or as a class, children may be invited to tell something about a book, show a picture and tell what is happening, read an interesting or powerful paragraph, and so forth. In such discussions, teachers can learn much about what children are reading and how

It is important to give children time to have conversations about books.
PS 124, New York, New York. Mary S. Gallivan, teacher.

leaders were undergraduate education students who were instructed to let meaning emerge from the group rather than solicit it. The results of this study showed that the groups collaborated and built meaning that was deeper and richer than what they attained in their solitary reading. The authors concluded that "Talk helps to confirm, extend, and modify individual interpretations and creates a better understanding of the text."

Teachers do not abdicate any direct teaching about books by holding back questions. Rather, as they listen carefully to children's responses, they can identify teaching possibilities, plan future conversations, or make use of a teachable moment to make a point. When the teacher is an active participant rather than the leader of a group, children more readily collaborate to fill their own gaps in understanding and make meaning together.

Guided Discussion

More structured discussion may occur with the books a teacher chooses to read aloud or to read with small groups. The teacher can play an important role in engendering fruitful discussions by demonstrating the types of responses she hopes children will make. When the teacher introduces the story, she might invite children to recognize the author or illustrator, to notice the dedication, or to speculate on the book's content as they look at the cover. As she gives children time to look at the illustrations in picturebooks, she asks, "How do these pictures make you feel?" "What are you thinking about as you look at these illustrations?" As she reads a chapter book, she asks what might happen next or why a character acts as she does. She might introduce Mollie Hunter's *A Stranger Came Ashore* by reading Mordicai Gerstein's *The Seal Mother* or Jane Yolen's *Greyling* and discussing Selkie lore with the class. She might pause at a chapter's end and ask children how Hunter makes the reader feel that something dreadful is about to happen. She might ask what clues suggest that Finn Learson is not who he pretends to be. She might introduce the term *foreshadowing* and ask them to listen for other examples as she reads. At first the teacher calls attention to aspects such as a well-written passage, an apt chapter heading, or a key moment when a character faces a choice. Later, children will begin noticing the kinds of things the teacher has brought out in these discussions. In this way a teacher models reader behaviors that mature readers practice.

they talk about books. Margaret Meek observes this about talk in the classroom:

> Left to comment on their own, without the stimulus of a question, children often choose to talk about quite other aspects of a tale than those that preoccupy their elders. . . . They create a tissue of collaborative understandings for each other in a way that no single question from an adult makes possible.[14]

Maryann Eeds and Deborah Wells showed how well fifth and sixth graders explored the meaning of novels they were reading through nondirective response groups.[15] The literature discussion groups met two days a week, thirty minutes a day, for four to five weeks. The

Asking Good Questions

Structured book discussions should be aimed at helping children think more widely and deeply about what they

---

[14]Margaret Meek, "What Counts as Evidence in Theories of Children's Literature?" *Theory into Practice* 21, no. 4 (1982): 289.

[15]Maryann Eeds and Deborah Wells, "Grand Conversations: An Exploration of Meaning Construction in Literature Study Groups," *Research in the Teaching of English* 23, no. 1 (1989): 4–29.

Teachers can demonstrate their own responses to books in a community of readers.
Mission School, Redlands Public Schools, Redlands, California. Joan Schleicher, teacher. Photo by Larry Rose.

read. But in a typical classroom, teacher questions often follow the pattern of initiation/response/evaluation. That is, a teacher asks a usually narrow question ("Is this story true?"), a child answers ("No"), and the teacher evaluates the child's answer ("Right. It's just a story") before moving to his next question.[16] Questions like these do nothing to engage children's minds but serve the teacher as a superficial means of evaluating whether a child has "understood" the story. Such interrogations can also dampen children's pleasure in a book. However, there are many ways that teachers, without resorting to inquisition, can use open-ended questions or activities that encourage children to reveal their understandings.

People who discuss questions use different terms. They differentiate between closed and open questions, lower- and higher-level questions, questions that lead the reader into or out of the book, questions that lead to convergent or divergent thought, or chains of questions that march up a hierarchical set of steps. When teachers generate questions from a set of questioning schemas, however, the connection between the book and the reader may get lost rather than enhanced. Good questions ought to arise from a reader's observation of a book's power and strength.

Christenbury and Kelly examined the research on questions and formed these conclusions:

1. Questioning schemas are helpful guidelines rather than rules by which we write questions;
2. It is better to follow a student lead before proceeding to a teacher question;

3. Teachers should be flexible and be prepared to jettison questions if the discussion is progressing fruitfully;
4. Divergent questions elicit better, more complex responses, especially among lower ability students.[17]

Thoughtful questions that provoke good discussions are initially difficult to develop. Teachers need to practice in preparing ones that will open up discussion, enable children to go back to the book for evidence, and help them relate the ideas in books to their own lives.

Teachers can begin planning for discussion by examining their own reactions to a book. Louise Rosenblatt suggested that there are three different strands of response that occur as we read. In one we respond to cues, predict, and synthesize our understandings. In another we experience an emotional reaction such as pleasure or anger, or a sense of approval or disapproval of the work. A third strand may involve our awareness of the author's role and our reaction to the quality of the writing.[18] All these reactions might be present during reading, although they might not occur simultaneously. By becoming aware of these strands of response as we read a book, we can identify areas that will prove fruitful for children to discuss. We might wonder, for example, about the ideal world that seems to exist in Lois Lowry's *The Giver*. "If everything in this society works so well, why do I feel a sense of foreboding?" We feel angry at Jess's father in Katherine Paterson's *Bridge to Terabithia*. "Why can't his father accept Jess's talents? Why would he treat him like that?" We might react to the point of view that William Mayne brings to his character in *Hob and the Goblins*. "I loved the way Hob sees the world so differently from humans—thinking the red bus is a house." By becoming aware of our responses to our own reading and sharing them with children, we can demonstrate ways to think about books and raise interesting questions. These questions or comments can expose the depth of a reader's engagement with a book and improve the quality of the reader's experience with it.

Children's Questions

By demonstrating the types of reactions and questions that readers might bring to books, teachers can help children identify their own responses and develop questions that they might bring to book discussions. One

[16]Courtney Cazden, *Classroom Discourse: The Language of Teaching and Learning* (Portsmouth, N.H.: Heinemann, 1988), p. 55.

[17]A summary of the research on questioning is given in the ERIC report *Questioning: A Path to Critical Thinking* by Leila Christenbury and Patricia P. Kelly (Urbana, Ill.: ERIC Clearinghouse on Reading and Communication Skills and the National Council of Teachers of English, 1983).

[18]Louise Rosenblatt, *The Reader, the Text and the Poem: The Transactional Theory of Literary Work* (Carbondale: Southern Illinois University Press, 1978).

Teaching Feature   Interviewing Fictional Characters

A group of third and fourth graders read their own paperback copies of *Abel's Island* by William Steig. They were encouraged to write questions in the margins of their books and underline favorite passages or particularly descriptive ones in order to make the book theirs through their responses. When they finished the book, they wrote questions to be used in an imaginary interview with Abel by reporters of the "The Mossville News." Their questions were compiled and given to "the reporters" as suggestions for their interview. Some of their questions follow:

Questions from "The Reporters of *The Mossville News*" to Abel

1. Why did you go after Amanda's scarf in a raging storm?
2. In the beginning, how did you try to get back?
3. How did you feel after you realized you were unable to get back?
4. How long did you live on the island?

5. What did you learn on the island?
6. How will your life in Mossville be different now because of your experience on the island?

Questions for Amanda After Abel's Return Home

1. What did you do while Abel was missing?
2. How will your life be different now that Abel has returned?

After the children interviewed Abel, the group discussed the questions themselves. One questioning technique this teacher always uses is to develop one or two questions that cannot be answered in the book. The last question for Abel and the two devised for Amanda require children to continue the story in their imagination.

Third and fourth graders
Martin Luther King, Jr., Laboratory School
Evanston, Illinois, Public Schools
Ellen Esrick, teacher

teacher who regularly uses children's literature as the content of her reading program frequently asks children to write questions when they have finished reading a book. Then she compiles all their questions, and they see if they can answer them in a discussion. Other teachers have given children little Post-it notes to mark pages they want to come back to later. This helps them think about reactions without interrupting the flow of the story. The Teaching Feature "Interviewing Fictional Characters" shows how a middle-grade teacher used role-playing to help children develop questions about William Steig's *Abel's Island*.

Two teachers showed fourth graders how to create open-ended discussion questions. Then children worked in groups of four to develop their own questions for C. S. Lewis's *The Lion, the Witch, and the Wardrobe*. Each group then chose one of their best questions, some of which were these:

1. Why do you think Lucy went with Mr. Tumnus?
2. How do you think the queen felt when she took Edmund? Describe.
3. Why do you think time stopped while Lucy was in the wardrobe?[19]

The teachers reported that children were enthusiastic about this activity and the questions were all discussion generators. This is not time wasted. When children become question makers, they also become question answerers. Good readers continually and unconsciously ask hard questions as they read: Why do people do what they do? What do I think they should do? What's going to happen next and why do I predict that? What does this part mean? How did I know that? What does this story mean to me? How did the author do it? If a teacher encourages children to ask worthwhile questions, she helps them internalize the unconscious question-raising behaviors of good readers.

Working in Small Groups

Although teachers may lead the whole class in some discussions, often children form a group of six or seven to discuss a particular title or topics. They can decide, with the teacher's help, how much they will read prior to the next discussion. They can be encouraged to write down any questions they have, copy a favorite quote, or note anything in their response journals they would like to bring to the next meeting. (See the section "Helping Children Write About Books" later in this chapter.) Teachers might suggest that they begin with open-ended

[19]Regie Routman, *Invitations: Changing as Teachers and Learners K–12* (Portsmouth, N.H.: Heinemann, 1991), pp. 121–122.

Small groups of children need time to discuss books together and time to plan responses to their books.
PS 124, New York, New York. Mary S. Gallivan, teacher.

questions such as "What are you thinking about as you are reading this book?" or focus on a previously raised question such as "What survival problems has Brian [in Gary Paulsen's *Hatchet*] faced and overcome in the chapters we have read so far?"

Small groups can also be formed on the spur of the moment. As she looked for patterns in fifth and sixth graders' reading records, a teacher noted that a group of girls had been reading animal stories. She assembled them at a round table and asked them to discuss titles and patterns in this type of story. They said:

🐛 Usually someone is finding an animal or getting them at the time. They never have them to start with. Usually the animal gets hurt in a lot of stories. The main characters won't accept what their parents say and they're usually very defensive about their animal. Like someone will say "Why don't you get rid of them or kill them?" and they'll say "Not on your life."[20]

A teacher of kindergartners noticed that four children had chosen books to look at that were illustrated in brilliant collage by Lois Ehlert (see *Color Farm* and *Color*

Zoo). She gathered them around her chair to tell them about the pictures. She asked them if they could tell a Lois Ehlert picture from one somebody else had made. One child offered to make a picture "like Lois Ehlert" and created a small collage of bright-colored paper.

In classrooms such as these, where children talk about books, they are free to discover what they think.[21] They may recall or rehearse plots of stories, they may explain, clarify or define meanings for themselves, and they are certainly learning to behave the way readers do.

Literature and the Writing Program

Literature has made a tremendous impact on reading programs, and so too has the writing process approach. Few teachers would consider teaching reading without including writing, because learning in one area means learning in the other. Literature informs both processes. As children become authors, they look at professional

[20]Hepler, "Patterns in Response to Literature," p. 217.

[21]Susan Hepler, "Talking Our Way to Literacy in the Classroom Community," in *Stories and Readers: New Perspectives on Literature in the Elementary School*, ed. Charles Temple and Patrick Collins (Norwood, Mass.: Christopher-Gordon, 1991), pp. 67–85.

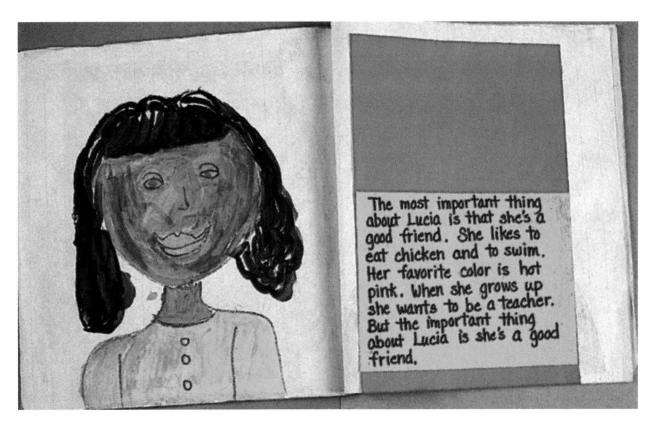

The most important thing about Lucia is that she's a good friend. She likes to eat chicken and to swim. Her favorite color is hot pink. When she grows up she wants to be a teacher. But the important thing about Lucia is she's a good friend.

After interviewing each other, fifth graders painted pictures and wrote biographical sketches following the pattern of *The Important Book* by Margaret Wise Brown, illustrated by Leonard Weisgard.
Esther L. Walter Elementary School, Anaheim Public Schools, Anaheim, California. Janine Batzle, teacher.

authors to see how a book works and sounds. They borrow and improvise on the language, patterns, and format of published books.[22] Young children rewrite their favorite stories (see Chapter 4), particularly when they can use invented spellings and do not have to produce a "correct" copy. Writing and reading go on all day in a classroom where language arts and reading are intertwined and literature is at the heart of the curriculum.

Ideas for writing can come from the child's own life and from the classroom curriculum. They can also be inspired by books. Teachers can read aloud and then display individual books that serve as springboards or provocative formats for children's writing. Margaret Wise Brown's *The Important Book*, Jack Kent's *The Fat Cat*, Katherine Milhous's and Alice Dalgliesh's *The Turnip*, or Vera B. Williams's *Three Days on a River in a Red Canoe* could serve as possible models for children to use. (See the section "Writing from Children's Books" in Chapter 14 for a discussion of many ways children can use literature as starting places for their writing.)

[22]See Frederick R. Burton, "Writing What They Read: Reflections on Literature and Child Writers," in *Stories to Grow On*, ed. Julie M. Jensen (Portsmouth, N.H.: Heinemann, 1989), pp. 97–105.

Helping Children Write About Books

In most schools children are no longer required to write book reports, a particularly inert kind of writing. However, many teachers ask children to write about their reading in other ways. This writing resembles talk, in that a child shares ideas and someone responds to those ideas. Teachers find this is a timesaving idea and can set aside a weekly or biweekly time to react in writing to children's written responses. Some teachers demonstrate supportive responses and let pairs of children react to each other's written work as well. There are various ways a teacher can help children write about their reading.

A *reading log* is a simple record of the title and author of each book a child has read. Needless to say, this is a burden for young children, but it is a source of pride for second graders and older children who like to recall their reading and measure their progress. Teachers might give children six-by-eight-inch cards and let them fill in one side. Then the teacher and child can use these records for generalizing as they talk together about a child's reading. If a child takes her most recent

Teaching Feature Using Dialogue Journals

One teacher of fifth graders asked her class to write a weekly reaction to their reading. Kevin, after weeks of writing two or three sentences about his reading, suddenly wrote a long entry based on his discovery of patterns in the books of Mitsumasa Anno. A partial section read:

> In the Anno books beside putting fairy tale characters in, he puts things like Beethoven playing the piano and Shakespeare making a play. A boy climbs on a fence and there is a lady taking a bath. They also have clocks with four hands and a couple of his books have optical illusions like children throwing rings on top of a church steeple. *Anno's Italy* is the funniest of the bunch. The only one I haven't read is *Anno's Alphabet*. (They are all by

Mitsumasa Anno. He has a foreign name I think.) [Writes his teacher: He is Japanese.] They are really good, really funny, and have super illustrations.

Kevin Carpenter
Barrington Road School
Upper Arlington, Ohio
Lois Monaghan, teacher

The teacher's comments shared his enthusiasm. While this seems like such a small piece of what a teacher does, it sets the teacher up as someone who is interested in what children think about their reading. And it gives a teacher a valuable chance to rejoice, advise, suggest, connect, question, and gently value the efforts children make to become readers.

card to the library, librarians may better help her find a book by seeing what she has enjoyed so far.

In a *response journal* children record their comments as they read a novel. Children respond freely as they think about their reading and write about the things that concern or interest them. A *double-entry draft* is a two-sided journal entry in which the reader copies or paraphrases a quote from the book on the left half of the paper. On the right, the reader comments on the quote. Teachers react to both of these journals and engage in a written dialogue with the reader (thereby creating a *dialogue journal*). Whatever we call it, children's written responses to the books they read provide teachers with another window into understanding how readers teach themselves to read.

When children write about their reading, they follow certain patterns, such as retelling, questioning particular words, clarifying meanings, reacting with like or dislike to a particular part of the story, relating a part of the story to their own lives, or otherwise reflecting. The Teaching Feature "Using Dialogue Journals" shows how teachers can encourage children to elaborate on their responses to books.

Writing about books in the same way every day becomes tedious. Teachers may want to vary the way children can respond. A single dialogue journal might be kept by a group reading the same book. Children can take turns responding. Children might ask their own questions and consider which ones are more interesting to write about. (See the section "Children's Questions" earlier in this chapter.)

Teachers might also ask children to address in their journals a particular question about their wide reading or about a class study book. They might write a journal entry from the point of view of a character in the book they are reading, for instance. During the group reading of a novel, a teacher might ask children to write about some issue prior to a class discussion as a way of rehearsing an idea. A small group who has just read Chapter 5 of *On My Honor* by Marion Dane Bauer, for instance, could write about whether Joel could have prevented Tony's drowning. After finishing this novel, children might discuss how and why the main character changed in the story, or what the story makes them think about. They might consider how this book is like others they have read, thus making links between books.

What teachers need to avoid, however, is overusing written response, or using a journal as a place in which children answer numbers of questions posed by the teacher. The primary power of journals is that the child owns the ideas, not the teacher. The child is director of the reading, and the child reflects on matters of interest to herself. One teacher who compared assigned questions and free-response journals noted, "The thoughtfulness and engagement engendered by the journals results in richer, more complete, elaborate response than I had received when I assigned questions."[23]

[23]J. E. Wollmann-Bonilla, "Reading Journals: Invitations to Participate in Literature," *Reading Teacher* 43, no. 2 (November 1989): 119.

Helping Children Become Authors

The more children read and hear stories, the more they want to write their own books. Teachers need some understanding of the writing process, or writing workshop, if they wish to help children develop their abilities. Once a child has completed a rough draft, she might request a *writing conference*. During this time the teacher and child might discuss the child's opinion of the piece of writing. Certain parts might be read aloud. If a child suggests changes or additions, the teacher might help the child by listening to the child further. Then the child can put the writing in her folder or revise it in preparation for a group sharing.[24]

Some teachers establish an *author's chair*, a special place for children or teachers to sit and share writing as a group. Children sign up for the author's chair, read their stories, and ask the listeners for comments. In this way, children hear the reactions and comments of their immediate audience. Maria, a first grader, sat in the author's chair, and her puzzled teacher noted that it wasn't sharing time yet. Maria explained that she was pretend sharing. "I'm thinking; if I get to share this piece with the kids, what will they ask me?"[25] This first grader has already begun to think about what impact she wants her writing to have on her audience, an important step in revision.

When a child is satisfied that a written piece is the best it can be, it is ready to be *published*. Publishing includes making a final draft and displaying it attractively, whether it is the explanation of the graphed results of a class survey or a modern folktale in bound-book form. Older children often want to put their compositions in the computer for a word-processed copy. Some children may wish to make cloth-covered books of their work. (See "Making Books" in Chapter 14.) Some schools use parents to set up an in-school publishing program complete with a laminator and spiral-binding machines.[26] Whatever methods and whatever the final product, what is important is that publishing makes a child's work into a work of art. It honors children's thinking, gives real reasons for revision and careful presentation, creates a wider audience for children's work, and values the process of writing.

Guiding the In-Depth Study of Books

If children are to have an opportunity to read, discuss widely, and write about books, this activity should be balanced with a time for studying books deeply. Question preparation, activities, and guides all work together to help teachers develop curriculum from literature. Teachers can plan in-depth studies of a single book; books by an author or illustrator; a part of a genre, such as dragon folktales or historical fiction that portrays the colonial period; or a theme that cuts across the curriculum but begins with a subject area such as science.

Making and Using Guides

Many series of commercial guides have been published in response to the increased interest in using literature to teach reading and language arts. Teachers can purchase simple or complex guides. Some include questions for each chapter of a novel; others merely suggest that readers discuss the problem of the novel and the main character's goal. Some have fill-ins, vocabulary study, blank pages for reader responses, and diagrams to copy and complete. Some guides are longer than the picture book whose study they are guiding. Some cost more than a five-book set of the paperback the guide is concerned with. Do teachers need commercial guides?

A good guide can save a teacher time in generating ideas. A guide can be a repository of useful discussion questions, suggestions for activities that send an enthusiastic reader back into the book or out into the world, and a list of other books that might relate to the book under study. Ideally, a good guide causes a reader to say, "I hadn't thought of that!" or to consider a book's depth without losing love for the book. But there is often so much dross in a commercial guide that teachers may have to search longer for the useful nugget than it would take them to consider their own ideas. Teachers can glean some useful ideas from commercial guides. Especially good suggestions might be jotted down on six-by-eight-inch cards and filed by book title. But a good learning experience and a more time- and money-saving way for a group of teachers to have guides is to make them.[27]

The webs in this and previous chapters provide suggestions for discussion topics, activities, and curricular

[24]Thomas Newkirk and Nancie Atwell, eds., *Understanding Writing*, 2nd ed. (Portsmouth, N.H.: Heinemann, 1988), p. 163.

[25]Lucy McCormick Calkins, *The Art of Teaching Writing* (Portsmouth, N.H.: Heinemann, 1986), pp. 20–21.

[26]See "Setting Up an In-School Publishing Process," in *Invitations: Changing as Teachers and Learners* by Regie Routman (Portsmouth, N.H.: Heinemann, 1994), pp. 263–275.

[27]Susan Hepler, "A Guide for the Teacher Guides: Doing It Yourself," *New Advocate* 4, no. 3 (summer 1988): 186–195.

Resources for Teaching
A Guide for *Galimoto*

Williams, Karen Lynn. *Galimoto*. Illustrated by Catherine Stock. Lothrop, Lee & Shepard, 1990.

Summary

Kondi, a resourceful boy from Malawi, finds many ways to get enough wire to make an intricate wire toy.

Before Reading

What can you tell about the story from the front and back cover and from the title page? (Save front note for later.)

Possible Questions for Children

1. What do you like about this story?
2. What words could describe Kondi? What in the story made you think of those words? (Possible word web?)
3. Read the front note and jacket copy. Look at the pages before the story begins. What has the artist shown us? What else do you notice about the artist's work?
4. By reading the pictures, what do you notice about life in this village? Find Malawi on the map; what do you notice?

5. In what ways is Kondi's life like a child's life in our area?

Ideas for Activities for Children

*   Collect wire for several days. Make galimotos. Tell where or how you got a special piece of wire. Be sure toys are three-dimensional and not flat.
*   Write your own directions, or as Kondi might write them, for making a galimoto.
*   Draw and write or tell about a time when you made something all by yourself.
*   Make a list of what we think we know about life in Malawi after reading this book. Find out something more about Malawi.

Related Books: *Steven Caney's Toy Book* and *Tops* (Zubrowski) are useful for making things. Books about other modern African children: *A Country Far Away* (Gray); Jafta series (Lewin); *The Day of Ahmed's Secret* (Heide); *Osa's Pride* (Grifalconi); *Not So Fast, Songololo* (Daly); *At the Crossroads* (Isadora).

---

connections that can serve as models for developing your own guides. Resources for Teaching, "A Guide for *Galimoto*," is a guide for teaching Karen Lynn Williams's *Galimoto*; it suggests a modest and useful format for teachers who want to organize ideas, remember what works, and save the money they would otherwise spend on guides to use in purchasing class sets of paperbacks. Valuable outcomes of writing guides are that teachers get better at phrasing open-ended questions, they match books with a specific school district's curriculum, they learn to evaluate a book for classroom possibilities, they collaborate, and they begin to see what helps readers move ahead and what gets in their way.

Webbing Curriculum Possibilities

One way to begin planning curriculum is to make a web of the many possibilities inherent as a class studies a book, a genre, an author, or a theme. A web is a way of brainstorming and outlining over a period of time. The goal is to get as many ideas and books as possible committed to paper before you shape their use in the classroom.

The Web "A Framework for Webbing" is really a web on the process of webbing. For this reason, it does not contain any specific titles of books, only general activities for children to do that might help you in your planning. For example, you could place any title of a book, a genre, a topic, or an author/illustrator that the class wants to study in the center of this web and quickly see if there are ideas you could use. Webs are based on the strengths of the books and/or topics and the needs of your students. They represent a visual overview of possibilities to be explored rather than a lesson plan set in stone.

A web is usually just a beginning plan. Once you have thought of the many possibilities, you need to choose the ones that would be the most useful to try in your class. If your primary students have not done surveys, then you might decide to highlight that particular activity. If you like the idea of putting them in small groups to compare variants of a tale, you might choose that section. Then you can plan a tentative time line: How to begin the unit? What books will you use to introduce the topic? What activities will get the children intrigued to learn more?

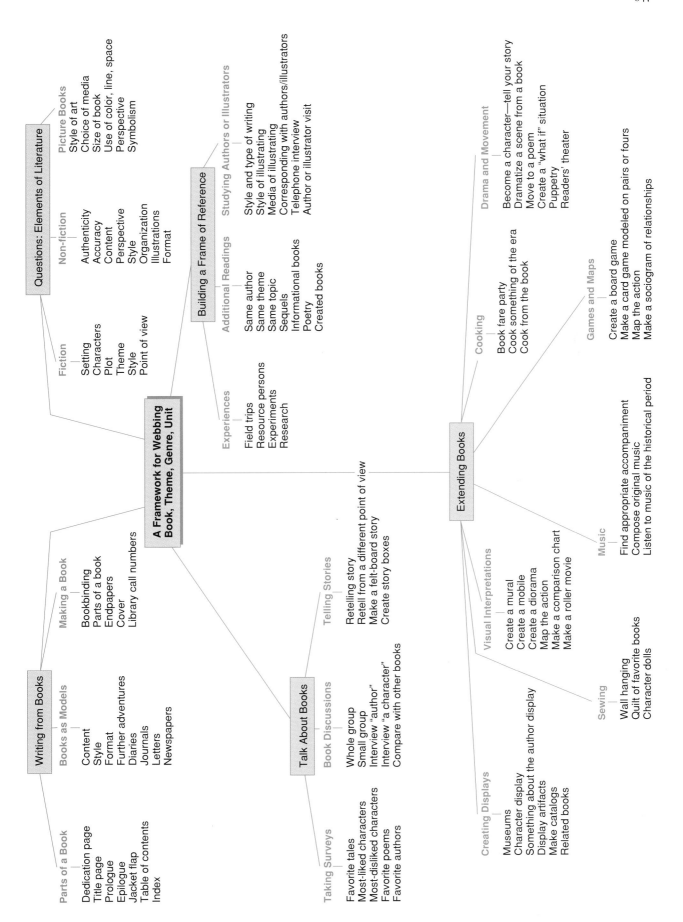

A Framework for Webbing Book, Theme, Genre, Unit

Questions: Elements of Literature

Fiction
- Setting
- Characters
- Plot
- Theme
- Style
- Point of view

Non-fiction
- Authenticity
- Accuracy
- Content
- Perspective
- Style
- Organization
- Illustrations
- Format

Picture Books
- Style of art
- Choice of media
- Size of book
- Use of color, line, space
- Perspective
- Symbolism

Building a Frame of Reference

Experiences
- Field trips
- Resource persons
- Experiments
- Research

Additional Readings
- Same author
- Same theme
- Same topic
- Sequels
- Informational books
- Poetry
- Created books

Studying Authors or Illustrators
- Style and type of writing
- Style of illustrating
- Media of illustrating
- Corresponding with authors/illustrators
- Telephone interview
- Author or illustrator visit

Writing from Books

Parts of a Book
- Dedication page
- Title page
- Prologue
- Epilogue
- Jacket flap
- Table of contents
- Index

Books as Models
- Content
- Style
- Format
- Further adventures
- Diaries
- Journals
- Letters
- Newspapers

Making a Book
- Bookbinding
- Parts of a book
- Endpapers
- Cover
- Library call numbers

Talk About Books

Taking Surveys
- Favorite tales
- Most-liked characters
- Most-disliked characters
- Favorite poems
- Favorite authors

Book Discussions
- Whole group
- Small group
- Interview "author"
- Interview "a character"
- Compare with other books

Telling Stories
- Retelling story
- Retell from a different point of view
- Make a felt-board story
- Create story boxes

Extending Books

Creating Displays
- Museums
- Character display
- Something about the author display
- Display artifacts
- Make catalogs
- Related books

Sewing
- Wall hanging
- Quilt of favorite books
- Character dolls

Visual Interpretations
- Create a mural
- Create a mobile
- Create a diorama
- Map the action
- Make a comparison chart
- Make a roller movie

Music
- Find appropriate accompaniment
- Compose original music
- Listen to music of the historical period

Cooking
- Book fare party
- Cook something of the era
- Cook from the book

Games and Maps
- Create a board game
- Make a card game modeled on pairs or fours
- Map the action
- Make a sociogram of relationships

Drama and Movement
- Become a character—tell your story
- Dramatize a scene from a book
- Move to a poem
- Create a "what if" situation
- Puppetry
- Readers' theater

Examples of webs that explore a book, a genre, or an author can be found in previous chapters. The Web for *The Sign of the Beaver* in Chapter 10 showed the possibilities inherent in this fine book. The "Folk and Fairy Tales" web in Chapter 6 and the "In Praise of Poetry" web in Chapter 8 showed the many different ways children could explore a genre; the "Brian Pinkney" web in Chapter 5 pointed out the ways children might study an author or illustrator. The "Stewards of the Earth" web in this chapter details a unit designed to integrate all areas of the curriculum and could be used across grade levels, but it is particularly aimed at fifth and sixth graders.

Studying a Theme: Stewards of the Earth—Ecology

A thematic unit such as one based on ecology contains many possibilities. With a theme as large as "Stewards of the Earth," it is possible for a whole school to embark on a study of ecology. The "Stewards of the Earth" web begins to focus on what aspects of the earth are endangered, why this is so, and what people are doing about it (see pages 650–651). Some books feature the action of individuals; others show how groups of people form to improve a small part of our ecosystem. Both points are worth making in a study of this magnitude: think globally but act locally; one person can make a difference.

Certain authors are well known for their activist stands on saving the earth. Jean Craighead George, in her novels as well as her nonfiction titles, always addresses interdependence among the living things on the planet. Ron Hirschi, Gail Gibbons, Laurence Pringle, and Helen Roney Sattler are only a few of the many authors of nonfiction who have raised concerns about the environment. Teachers of middle school children might start with futuristic science fiction, such as the titles listed under "Imagine Other Futures," and raise the question: How did humankind become what it is depicted as being in this imagined future? Teachers of fifth or sixth graders might anchor this study with a core novel such as Jean George's *The Talking Earth*, Miriam Schlein's narrative of Chinese and American efforts to save the endangered panda in *The Year of the Panda*, Susan Sharpe's fictional account of a boy's discovery of who was dumping toxic waste in the Chesapeake Bay told in *Waterman's Boy*, or Mary Quattlebaum's story of a boy who becomes involved in a community garden in *Jackson Jones and the Puddle of Thorns*. Other classes might start with endangered birds, creatures of the sea, the way places change and why, or observances of nature.[28]

---

[28]See also Patti Sinclair, *E for Environment: An Annotated Bibliography of Children's Books with Environmental Themes* (New York: Bowker, 1992); Alicia Eames and Daryl Grabarek, "Dreaming Our World," *Book Links* 1, no. 2 (September 1991): 54–58.

In the "Stewards of the Earth" web, activities that begin a topic are suggested as useful overarching concerns developed within the section that follows. Other activities might follow a particular book or culminate that section's content. There are many community resources that should be tapped in a study such as this, such as classroom visits by park rangers and city planners, field trips to preserves or recycling centers, and archives such as the newspaper or interviews with a longtime resident. Books are not the only way to bring the world to the classroom.

Developing a concern for the environment is a lasting topic, and there will always be new problems, new books, and new ways to approach it in the classroom. Even primary children can become interested in the preservation of the earth's natural diversity and interdependence.

The School and the Community

To be successful, a classroom literature program needs an enthusiastic teacher, a good book collection, and students who are eager to read. However, to create a true community of readers, each teacher must also involve other teachers, students, administrators, librarians, and parents in discovering the delights of good books.

The Whole-School Program

Children learn what they live. Increasingly, educators are concerned that the quality of living in a school be equal to the quality of learning in that school. The physical environment of the school provides the context of that learning, but it is only one aspect of it. What teachers really believe in and want for their students will usually be taught.

All teachers and librarians must have a strong commitment to literature. Few children discover books by themselves; in most instances, a parent, teacher, or librarian has served as the catalyst for bringing books and children together. As children grow up seeing significant adults as readers, they become readers. Find a teacher who is enthusiastic about children's books, and you will find a class of children who enjoy reading. Invariably, the teacher who reads, who knows books, and who shares this enthusiasm with students will inspire a love of reading. Many schools have made the development of readers their top priority. As a total school faculty they have met and planned certain activities to promote children's interest in reading. The Teaching Feature "A Whole-School Study of One Book" shows

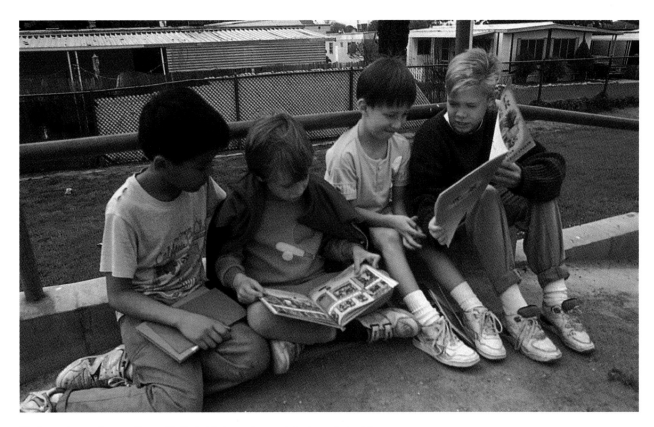

Sixth graders enjoy reading with their kindergarten and first-grade buddies.
Mission School, Redlands Public Schools, Redlands, California. Nancy Anderson, teacher.

how such careful planning created an important bond for readers across grade levels.

Buddy reading involves students from older grades reading with partners in the kindergarten or first grade. Younger children proudly share a book that they can read with their buddies, and the older children then read a book to their partners. Younger children look forward to their buddy time (which is usually once a week), and the older students take a special interest in the progress of their special child. Buddy reading requires cooperation among teachers to establish schedules. Older students must be taught how to select appropriate books to read aloud and the importance of being supportive of the younger reader's efforts to read or tell a story. Teachers who have tried such programs speak of their value for both sets of readers.

One school planned a whole-school unit on traditional literature. Children from kindergarten through sixth grade studied fairy tales, traditional folktales, fables, and myths. They created a Fairy Tale Museum with such objects as "the very pea that disturbed the princess's sleep" and the golden ball that the Frog Prince retrieved for the spoiled princess. Their *Fairy Tale Newspaper* included interviews with Cinderella and the Pied Piper; classified lost-and-found ads, including

an ad for a found glass slipper; a society column; and a sports page describing the race of the Hare and the Tortoise. Older children created their own mythological characters and stories. Different groups dramatized traditional tales like "The Three Billy Goats Gruff" and "Little Red Riding Hood." This whole-school emphasis created a unity among the children and an appreciation for their traditional literary heritage.

Another school offered many minicourses in literature during Book Week. Children made puppets in one course, created a flannel story in another. Many children wrote their own stories in one course. Then, in another, they were introduced to the use of collage, marbleized papers, and ink prints made from plastic foam meat trays. Another course offered bookbinding so that children ended the week with their own bound and illustrated books. Teachers volunteered to offer the various courses. Some gave minicourses on particular genres of books, like folktales or poetry. Others offered drama and choral speaking. In this particular school, children have an opportunity to do these things frequently. However, the minicourses given near the beginning of school focused attention on bookmaking and provided children with skills they used throughout the year.

Developing Respect and a Sense of Wonder

What kinds of experiences fill us with wonder?
Pretend you are a person in one of these stories.
  Tell or write about your moment of wonder.
Dawn (Shulevitz)
Salt Hands (Aragon)
The Lady and the Spider (McNulty)
Owl Moon (Yolen)
The Earth Is Painted Green (Brenner)
Find examples of language that evoke the senses.
  Write your own earth poems.

Heartland; Mojave; Sierra (Siebert)
I Wonder if I'll See a Whale (Weller)
Whales' Song (Sheldon)
The Way to Start a Day (Baylor)
Make up your own way to greet a day.
Write a story of how your perfect day in nature might begin.

The Other Way to Listen (Baylor)
The Listening Walk (Showers)
When the Woods Hum (Ryder)
Take a listening walk. What natural sounds can you hear?

Caring for the Birds

What birds are endangered? Why?
How can people help birds? Why should we?
Bird Watch (Yolen)
The Book of Eagles (Sattler)
Eagles: Lions of the Sky (Bernhard)
Hawk, I'm Your Brother (Baylor)
The Mountain Bluebird (Hirschi)
Saving the Peregrine Falcon (Arnold)
Where Do Birds Live? (Hirschi)
Make a tree on which drawings of local birds are placed.
Let different people count birds at different sites.
How many birds can you count in a half hour?
Which site has the fewest/most birds? Why?

Bird (Burnie)
Find feathers. Determine whether they are wing, pin, down, or some other kind of feather. Mount your collection.

The After-Christmas Tree (Tyler)
Make tree to feed birds, or a feeding station. Observe what comes there.

Pigeons (Schlein)
How have pigeons helped humankind?
Follow a pigeon. Try to describe its movements.
Debate: Are pigeons "rats with wings"?

Do Animals Communicate?

Bees Dance and Whales Sing: The Mysteries of Animal Communication (Facklam)
Koko's Kitten (Patterson)
How do animals communicate?
  Make a list of the types of languages animals use.

How to Talk to Your Dog (George)
Dolphin Adventure (Grover)
How do people communicate with animals? Why is this exciting?
How do people communicate with other species?
What good is it to communicate with other species?
Observe a family pet or other animal for several days.
Write an informational booklet on how this animal communicates.
What do noises mean? Body movements? Expressions?

Caring for the Animals

Which animals are endangered? Why?
What animals are now extinct? Why?
V for Vanishing (Mullins)
Aardvarks Disembark (Jonas)
And Then There Was One: The Mysteries of Extinction (Facklam)

The Year of the Panda (Schlein)
The Vanishing Manatee (Clark)
Saving Our Wildlife (Pringle)
The Crocodile and the Crane (Cutchins & Johnston)
Make a chart of endangered animals; tell why each is endangered; find out what people are doing to help save this animal.
Lost Wild America: The Story of Our Extinct and Vanishing Wildlife (McClung)
What are the threats to wildlife? How has this affected conservation policies?

Imagine Other Futures, Other Worlds

Just a Dream (Van Allsburg)
The Lake at the End of the World (MacDonald)
Z for Zachariah (O'Brien)
When the Tripods Came (Christopher)
The Monster Garden (Alcock)
Eva (Dickinson)
The Ear, the Eye and the Arm (Farmer)
How does each author see our future?
  What kind of world are humans inhabiting?
  What has disappeared? Why?
The Lampfish of Twill (Lisle)
Antar and the Eagles (Mayne)
How do the authors' imagined worlds incorporate environmental messages? How factually based are they?

Stewards of the Earth — Ecology

Saving the Forests

What kinds of actions damage forests?
List individual actions that might help save trees.
Find out what kinds of paper can be recycled.
    Start a recycling spot for school waste paper.
Giants in the Land (Appelbaum)
The Lorax (Seuss)

How does nature maintain a balanced ecology?
Should controlled fires be set to keep forests
    in balance?
Summer of Fire: Yellowstone, 1988 (Lauber)

Deep Dream of the Rain Forest (Bosse)
Locate rain forest areas on a map.
Make a mural of a rain forest from canopy
    to forest floor. Show typical animals
    found in each zone.
One Day in the Tropical Rainforest (George)
The Great Kapok Tree (Cherry)
Rain Forest (Cowcher)
Where the Forest Meets the Sea (Baker)
Rain Forest Secrets (Dorros)
Make a collage of articles that come from
    rain forests. What is yet to be discovered
    in rain forests?

Cleaning Up After Ourselves

Sea Otter Rescue (Smith)
The World That Jack Built (Brown)
Global Warming (Pringle)
Too Much Garbage (Lauber)
Throwing Things Away (Pringle)
Form a playground or neighborhood trash
    pickup. Survey the trash to discover patterns.
    What is the major source of trash? Who is
    responsible? How might you begin an
    anti-litter campaign?
Make a "life-cycle" map of a piece of trash.
    Show where a soda can or cigarette
    butt starts out and where it might end
    up. Write about your map.

Taking Action

How can individual people help? How do groups help?
*Living Treasure: Saving the Earth's Threatened
    Biodiversity* (Pringle)
A River Ran Wild (Cherry)
Come Back Salmon (Cone)
Miss Rumphius (Cooney)
Jackson Jones and the Puddle of Thorns (Quattlebaum)
Going Green: A Kids' Handbook to Saving the Planet
    (Elkington et al.)
Greening the City Streets (Huff)
Fifty Simple Things You Can Do to Save the Earth
    (Earthworks)
The Big Book for Our Planet (Durrell & Paterson)

Take a field trip to a trash-burning power plant; a
    recycling center. Report what you have found, using
    a "Magic School Bus" format.
Interview city council members to find out what long-
    range plans they have for landfills, recycling, creation
    of parks, protection of water, etc.
Trees (Pine)
Plant something and watch it grow.
Beautify the grounds and entrance of your school.
    Take care of the plants.

Protecting the Water

What endangers our water? How can we help?
The Magic School Bus at the Waterworks (Cole)
Waterman's Boy (Sharpe)
Write a news account of the capture of the polluters.
The King's Fountain (Alexander)
Night Ghosts and Hermits (Stolz)
What are the consequences of water pollution?

Then and Now: Changes

Make a "then" and "now" chart for one book.
Pretend you are older and looking back on a special place.
    Write about your memories and feelings for this place
    that has changed.
Debate: Is change good or bad?
Grandpa's Mountain (Reeder)
Toddlecreek Post Office (Shulevitz)
Letting Swift River Go (Yolen)
Shaker Lane (Provensens)

Window (Baker)
Heron Street (Turner)
My Place (Wheatley)
Find old photographs of your city or neighborhood. Find
    out what has changed since those pictures were taken.
Invite a longtime resident to the classroom to talk about
    changes he or she has seen in the place where you live.

Interconnections

Who Really Killed Cock Robin? (George)
The Fire Bug Connection (George)
The Missing Gator of Gumbo Limbo (George)
Make a chart of causes and effects for these mysteries.

Big Friend, Little Friend (Sussman & James)
The Apartment House Tree (Killion)
The Wounded Wolf (George)
What are symbiotic relationships?
Can you name other connected groups?
How do members depend on each other?

What are ecosystems? How are interactions among
    species vital to the environment? How are they put out
    of balance?
The Talking Earth (George)
Everglades (George)
The Story of Rosie Dock (Baker)

Brother Eagle, Sister Sky (Jeffers)
What ideas about the earth are expressed? Do you agree?
All God's Critters Got a Place in the Choir (Staines)
Sing the song. Think about the metaphor.

Teaching Feature   A Whole-School Study of One Book

The Martin Luther King, Jr., Laboratory School in the Evanston, Illinois, public schools frequently has whole-school focus units where the children from kindergarten through grade 8 study one particular subject. This year they decided that all children would hear the same book and then discuss it. *The Lemming Condition* by Alan Arkin was read aloud by all elementary teachers and the homeroom teachers in the sixth, seventh, and eighth grades.

Prior to the reading, a group of teachers met to do some background research on the myth and reality of the lemming condition. For example, the science teacher prepared an information sheet on lemmings, their geographical distribution, what they eat, how long they live, and the so-called lemming run. The teachers formulated a guide with possible questions like these:

- Have you ever felt like a lemming?
- When you plan to do something, do you like to work alone or do what everyone else does?
- What advice did the old lemming give to Bubber?
- If Bubber didn't follow the crowd, he would lose his family and friends. What did it take for him to act alone?
- What heroes do you know who stood by their values and did something that was not popular? (Rosa Parks, Gandhi, Martin Luther King, Jr.)

Forty-two adults in the building, including the administrators, secretaries, and nurse, each agreed to work with a group of about twelve K–8 students for a one-hour discussion of the book. Back in their own classrooms following these discussions, each child created his or her own unique and recognizable picture of a lemming. These were cut out and placed on a very large mural in the school foyer.

The children loved meeting together to discuss a book that had different meanings for each of them. They listened to the little ones' interpretations and encouraged them to speak. Most of their responses were centered on the idea of peer group pressure to do something they did not want to do. The youngest students focused on feelings of loneliness and being left out when they weren't invited to parties, for example.

The bonding together of a K–8 population sharing one book created cohesive and enthusiastic groups. The staff all agreed that it was an experience they wanted to repeat.

Martin Luther King, Jr., Laboratory School
Evanston, Illinois, Public Schools
Vikki Proctor, Ellen Esrick, Ronna Pritikin, coordinating teachers

Involving Administrators

No literature program can be successful without the support of the principal. More and more principals and curriculum coordinators are taking time to read aloud to children. One curriculum coordinator makes it a point to read aloud in one of the classrooms in his school district every day.[29] Children look forward to his coming, and he anticipates their response to his choice of books. Another principal has developed a two-tiered reading program called The Principal's Reading Club. Children from kindergarten through second grade make appointments to read with the principal for fifteen minutes from a book of their choice. Students in grades 3 to 6 select a book from a provided list and after three weeks return to discuss it with the principal. The participants receive a reading certificate, button, and pencil that has "I

Read to the Principal" on it. More importantly, children see the principal as someone interested in them and their reading, and it's a wonderful way for the principal to get to know children and their reading abilities and preferences.

Planning Author/Illustrator Visits

The prospect of having a real live author come for a school visit is exciting and motivates students to read her or his books in anticipation of meeting the author. However, it takes good planning to use a visit to full advantage and make it a learning experience for all students. Sometimes a school may be fortunate enough to have local authors or illustrators who will volunteer to come and talk about their books. Many parent associations aim their fund-raising efforts at bringing well-known children's book authors or illustrators to a school, or teachers write grants to bring such professionals into the classroom. However, increasingly more schools are now budgeting money to pay for such a visit.

[29]James Mitchell, "Sound Bytes, Hamburgers and Billy Joel: Celebrating the Year of the Lifetime Reader," *Reading Today* 9 (August/September 1991): 29.

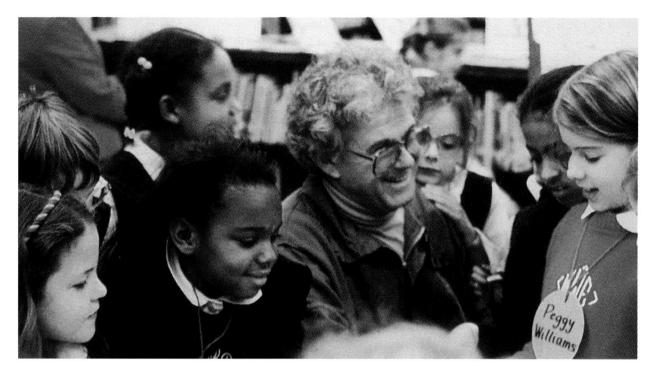

Children are delighted to meet "real live" author/illustrator Tomie de Paola, particularly when they have read his books and prepared for his visit.
Columbus School for Girls, Columbus, Ohio. Marilyn Parker, teacher/librarian.

The usual procedure for contacting an author or illustrator is to call the person in charge of promotion for the publisher and ask about availability, fees, travel arrangements, and so on. Sometimes it is possible to arrange a visit in conjunction with another previously scheduled appearance in your area. This usually cuts down on the major travel expenses, although the author's fee must be paid.

Planning must begin with teachers and children several months before the visit. There is no point in hosting an author or illustrator unless all the children who will be involved know the books. With authors of books for middle graders, this means obtaining many copies of their books, arranging for in-depth discussions of the books, perhaps showing videos or filmstrips about the author. It might be wise to keep a running list of questions to ask the author as children are becoming acquainted with the books.

Several schools got together and invited Tomie de Paola to visit them when he was going to be at a conference in their area. His books were displayed in the learning center and in many of the classrooms. The children made murals of their favorite books, cooked pasta with a parent, and even wove a cloak for *"Charlie Needs a Cloak."* First graders made a list of their expectations of Tomie de Paola based on their knowledge of his books—what he would look like, what he would be

like. Children thus became acquainted with all the books of one artist and had a chance to talk to him about his life and work.

As Marilyn Parker says in describing a visit by Madeleine L'Engle, "the actual event of an author's visit should be something like the tip of an iceberg—the most visible part of something much broader and deeper."[30] It is the preparation for the visit that provides the real learning experiences. As children focus on the work of one author or illustrator and have an opportunity to meet her or him, they have their first-time glimpse into the literary world.

The School Library Media Center

Every school needs a trained librarian and a school library media center. While the name has changed over the years to reflect the inclusion of such nonprint materials as films, videos, tapes, slides, computers, and software as well as books, the purpose of the center is to provide the best services and materials to facilitate learning for children.

[30]Marilyn Parker in *The Best of the WEB, 1976–1982,* ed. Susan Hepler, p. 69. Columbus, Ohio, 1982.

A welcome sign and a large stuffed Strega Nona and Big Anthony hang from the class ceiling to greet Tomie de Paola.
Highland Park Elementary School, South-Western City Schools, Grove City, Ohio. Pam Kesson, teacher. Photo by Barbara Peterson.

A parent helped children make pasta from the magic pasta pot in Tomie de Paola's *Strega Nona*.
Highland Park Elementary School, South-Western City Schools, Grove City, Ohio. Photo by Barbara Peterson.

The library media center should be open all day every day to serve students in its unique way. Flexible scheduling of story hours or lessons on library research may be directed by the librarian in a special area, leaving the rest of the resources free for others to use. Children can learn without the constant presence of a teacher or librarian. A trained aide can help children find relevant books, films, videos, and records. Parents have served most effectively as volunteers in the school media center. Children increase in their ability to do independent study by using a variety of sources. An abundance of materials should be readily and freely available.

Increasingly, new school library media centers have become the focal point of many schools, with classrooms radiating out from them. The space should be as flexible and fluid as possible to allow for growth and change. The environment should encourage free access to materials at all times. Children flow in and out, doing projects, finding resources, making their own books, producing films. As the library media center becomes more closely identified with the total instructional program, it becomes more integrated into the total school environment.

The Library Media Specialist

The library media specialist plays a very important role in the quality of learning and living that takes place in the library media center, the school, and the community.[31] Serving as a full-time contributing faculty member, the librarian works with children, teachers, parents, and volunteer and professional aides. Specialized training provides background knowledge of children's books and all media for instruction, library media procedures, knowledge of children's development and behavior, understanding of various teaching methods, and knowledge of school curriculum needs and organization. Increasingly, the library media specialist is called on to give leadership, not only in providing the materials for instruction, but in shaping the curriculum itself. The library media program should be an integral part of the total school program. Working with teachers, the media specialist needs to be responsive to the curricular and instructional needs of the school. What units of study are the teachers planning to initiate this year? Books, films, and tapes on this subject should be gathered together for the teachers' and children's use. Bibliographies of print and nonprint materials based on units of work should be developed cooperatively with teachers. Book lists and curriculum resources should be shared. The function of the school

[31]The terms *library media specialist* and *librarian* are used interchangeably to denote the person who is responsible for directing the school library media program. It is assumed that such a director would have had training as a school librarian and as a media specialist and in many instances would also have a teaching certificate.

library media center is to provide an information-rich environment where teachers and students become effective users of print and nonprint materials.

In one school, the fifth grade was studying the rather abstract theme of famous "crossings." The children and teacher had webbed possibilities, and then the teacher had made an appointment with the librarian. The two of them filled a rolling cart full of books, films, and videos on such subjects as Columbus, the Pilgrims, the slave trade, crossing the Western Divide, and Hannibal crossing the Alps. There were many more topics, but the abstract concept allowed the children to study many time periods and many famous events. Students chose what aspect of the topic they wished to study and then met in their study groups. The librarian worked with each group to find appropriate materials. The children used the card catalog and the table of contents and index of each book to see what topics were covered. They checked the dates of publications and looked at the authors' qualifications. All of these research skills were taught in the context of a study in which the children wanted to obtain information, rather than an isolated library skills lesson.

Teachers and library media specialists become partners as they work together to help students learn to use information, to be critical of what they read and see, to make judgments about what is authentic and accurate, and to discover meaning. As students share their findings, they learn to question, compare, and combine information. Only such educated students can become contributing citizens to a democratic society.

Selecting Materials

Our children are growing up faster today than twenty years ago. In the limited time children have to be children, we want to give them the very best books available. The adage "The right book at the right time" still holds true. Most children's books have to be read at the appropriate age and developmental stage or they *will never be read*. The 8-year-old does not read *The Tale of Peter Rabbit*; the 12-year-old doesn't want to be seen reading *Ramona Quimby, Age 8*; and the 16-year-old has outgrown *The Sign of the Beaver*. Introduced at the right time, each of these books would have provided a rich, satisfying experience of literature.

The number of books that any one child can read is limited, also. Assuming that a child reads one book every two weeks from the time he is 7 (when independent reading might begin) until he is 13 or 14 (when many young people start reading adult books), he will read about 25 books a year, or some 200 books. Given the number and variety of children's books in print, it is possible that a child may read widely, *yet never read a significant book*. Under these circumstances, the need for good book selection becomes even more imperative.

With the increase of both numbers of books published and objections to the selection of certain books, it is essential that schools develop a selection policy. All professional library groups, and other professional organizations like the International Reading Association and the National Council of Teachers of English, strongly recommend that each school district develop a written statement that governs its selection of material. This policy statement should be approved by the school board and subsequently supported by its members if challenged. Factors to be considered in such a policy would include the following: who selects the materials, the quality of materials, appropriate content, needs and interests of special children, school curriculum needs, providing for balance in the collection, and procedures to follow for censorship and challenged material.

Because the subject matter of contemporary children's books is changing, the need for written criteria of selection has increased. Realism in children's books and young-adult novels reflects the same range of topics that can be seen on TV, at the movies, and in current best-sellers. It makes no sense to "protect" children from well-written or well-presented materials on such controversial subjects as abortion, narcotics, or sexual preferences, when they see stories on the same subjects on TV. Increased sensitivity to sexism, racism, and bias in books and nonbook materials is another area of recent concern that points up the need for a clear statement on selection policies. Some general guidelines to consider when developing policies for book selection include these:

1. **Who Selects the Materials?**
   Teachers, students, and parents may recommend particular titles, but the final selection of materials for the school library should be determined by professionally trained personnel. Reliable reviews of children's books play an important part in the selection of books. Four well-known review journals are *Booklist*, the *Bulletin of the Center for Children's Books*, *Horn Book Magazine*, and the *School Library Journal*. Other sources for reviews are listed in Appendix B.

2. **Quality of Materials**
   Criteria for evaluation and selection of all types of instructional materials should be

established and should be available in written form. Books for the collection should meet the criteria of good literature described in preceding chapters. There may need to be a balance between popular demand and quality literature, but this is a decision that must be made by individual librarians, based on their knowledge of the reading abilities and interests of the children they serve and their own basic philosophy of book selection. A written policy statement of the criteria to be used when purchasing books will help solve this dilemma.

3. **Appropriate Content**
    The content of the materials to be selected should be evaluated in terms of the quality of the writing or presentation. Almost any subject can be written about for children, depending on the honesty and sensitivity of its treatment by the author. We should not deliberately shock or frighten children before they have developed the maturity and inner strength to face the tragedies of life. However, literature is one way to experience life, if only vicariously. In the process, a reader can be fortified and educated.

4. **Children's Needs and Interests**
    Materials should always be purchased in terms of the children who will be using them. This includes materials for children with special needs and books that represent a wide diversity of multicultural experiences. Children from a particular culture should have opportunities to see themselves reflected in books. In a pluralistic society, however, all children should have an opportunity to read about children of different racial, religious, and ethnic backgrounds. Regardless of a child's background, a good selection policy should give children books that provide insight into their own lives but also take them out of those lives to help them see the world in its many dimensions.

5. **School Curriculum Needs**
    Librarians should consider the particular needs of the school curriculum when ordering materials. Particular units in social studies or intensive study of the local region will require additional copies of books about the particular state, industries, and people of the region. The function of the school library media center is to provide a wide range of materials specially chosen to meet the demands of the school curriculum.

6. **Balance in the Collection**
    Every school library needs to maintain a balanced collection. Keeping in mind the total needs of the school, the librarian should consider the following

balances: book and nonbook material (including videotapes, tapes, records, films, discs, filmstrips, and other materials), hardback and paperback books, reference books, and trade books, fiction and nonfiction, poetry and prose, classics (both old and "new"), realistic and fanciful stories, books for younger and older children, books for poor and superior readers at each grade level, books for teachers to read to students and use for enrichment purposes, and professional books for teachers and parents.

Selection versus Censorship

There is a fine line between careful selection of books for children and censorship. The goal of selection is to *include* a book on the basis of its quality of writing and total impact; the goal of censorship is to *exclude* a book in which the content (or even one part) is considered objectionable. Selection policies recommend a balanced collection representative of the various beliefs held by a pluralistic society; censors would impose their privately held beliefs on all.

The American Library Association's "Library Bill of Rights" was adopted in 1948 and amended in 1967, 1969, and 1980. This statement contains six policies relating to censorship of books and the right of free access to the library for all individuals or groups. This statement has been endorsed by the American Association of School Librarians.

Almost every school and each children's librarian in a public library has faced some criticism of the books in the children's collection. Criticism is not necessarily censorship, however. Parents, other faculty members, and citizens have a right to discuss the reasons for the selection of a particular book and to make their own feelings known. Only when they seek to have the book banned, removed from the shelves, restricted in use, or altered are they assuming the role of censors.

In the last decade, censorship increased dramatically throughout the country. Individuals and groups from both the right and left, like the Christian Coalition, religious fundamentalists, members of the feminist movement, and the Council on Interracial Books for Children, have all demanded the removal of certain children's books from libraries for various reasons. Targets of the censor generally include profanity of any kind; sex, sexuality, nudity, obscenity; the "isms," including sexism, racism, ageism; and the portrayal of witchcraft, magic, religion, and drugs.

Award books are objects of censorship as readily as other books. The Caldecott Medal–winning book *Sylvester and the Magic Pebble* by William Steig was

---

Resources for Teaching
The Library Bill of Rights

The American Library Association affirms that all libraries are forums for information and ideas, and that the following basic policies should guide their services.

1. Books and other library resources should be provided for the interest, information, and enlightenment of all people of the community the library serves. Materials should not be excluded because of the origin, background, or views of those contributing to their creation.
2. Libraries should provide materials and information presenting all points of view on current and historical issues. Materials should not be proscribed or removed because of partisan or doctrinal disapproval.
3. Libraries should challenge censorship in the fulfillment of their responsibility to provide information and enlightenment.
4. Libraries should cooperate with all persons and groups concerned with resisting abridgment of free expression and free access to ideas.
5. A person's right to use a library should not be denied or abridged because of origin, age, background, or views.
6. Libraries which make exhibit spaces and meeting rooms available to the public they serve should make such facilities available on an equitable basis, regardless of the beliefs or affiliations of individuals or groups requesting their use.

Source: Information Power: Guidelines for School Library Media Programs (Chicago: American Library Association, 1988), Appendix D.

---

objected to by law enforcement groups because it portrays police as pigs. It made no difference that all the characters in the book are animals, that Sylvester and his family are donkeys, and that other characters besides police are also shown as pigs.

Madeleine L'Engle's Newbery Medal book *A Wrinkle in Time* has been attacked as being non-Christian because of its references to the Happy Medium and Mrs. Who, Mrs. Whatsit, and Mrs. Which, supernatural beings that some have labeled "witches." Madeleine L'Engle is well known for her adult writings on Christianity; ironically, religious literalists have paid no attention to the total message of good overcoming evil in this well-written fantasy, but have seen only "witches." *The Great Gilly Hopkins*, a National Book Award winner written by Katherine Paterson, a minister's wife and twice the winner of the Newbery Medal for excellence in writing, was criticized because Gilly uses an occasional *damn*. Yet surely a foster child who has been in three homes in three years is not likely to be a model of refinement. What is noteworthy about this book is the gradual and believable *change* in Gilly's behavior and character. In Jean Fritz's well-received picture-book biography *And Then What Happened, Paul Revere?* an English Redcoat swears as he apprehends Paul Revere riding to rouse Concord. Fritz was criticized for using *damn*, even though the utterance is a matter of historical record.

Contemporary fiction for older children has come under increasing attack as these books have begun to show the influence of the new freedom allowed in books and films for adults. Such titles as Alvin Schwartz's *Scary Stories to Tell in the Dark*, which recounts tales of horror well-known in folklore, or Judy Blume's *Deenie*, which includes several references to masturbation, have been targets of criticism and censorship attempts.

A more subtle and frightening kind of censorship is the kind practiced voluntarily by librarians and teachers. If a book has come under negative scrutiny in a nearby town, it might be carefully placed under the librarian's desk until the controversy dies down. Or perhaps the librarians and the teachers just do not order controversial books. "Why stir up trouble when there are so many other good books available?" they falsely reason. In-house censorship or closet censorship is difficult to identify. Selection is a positive process; books are added to a collection for their excellence, to meet a curriculum need, to bring balance to the curriculum. Censorship is negative. Whenever books are rejected for nonliterary reasons, for fear of outside criticism, for example, librarians and teachers need to ask themselves whether they are practicing selection or censorship.

Dealing with Censorship

If there is a demand for censorship, how should it be handled? The first rule is to recognize that anyone has the right to question specific selections. The second rule is to be prepared—have an accepted response process. A written selection policy statement should contain a

Guidelines:
Dealing with a Demand for Censorship

1. Do not discuss the issue until you are prepared. Give the person who is seeking to censor a book a form for "reconsideration of a book" and make an appointment to discuss the book.
2. Write out a rationale for choosing and using this book with children if you have not already done so.
3. Make copies of reviews of the questioned book from professional reviewing journals.
4. Notify your principal of the expressed concern. Give her or him copies of the reviews and of your rationale.
5. At your conference, explain the school's selection policy and present copies of the reviews of the book

and the rationale explaining your reasons for selecting it.
6. Listen to the stated concern as objectively as possible.
7. Inform the person that the material will be reconsidered by the selection committee if he or she wishes it to be.
8. Submit the reconsideration form to the book selection committee of librarians, teachers, and parent representatives for their discussion and decision.
9. Inform the person expressing the concern what the committee decided and why.

standardized procedure to follow when materials are challenged and should be part of district policy. The Guidelines "Dealing with a Demand for Censorship" might be useful.

Several Reconsideration of Materials forms are available upon request. The National Council of Teachers of English provides one in their booklet *The Students' Right to Know*.[32] The American Library Association suggests two questions: (1) "What brought this title to your attention?" (2) "Please comment on the resource as a whole, as well as being specific about those matters that concern you."[33] The major consideration, then, is to have a form available when you need it and to make it specific to the book itself and simple enough to fill out.

Generally, if parents or other citizens feel their voices have been heard and that they have been dealt with fairly, they will abide by the decision of the book selection committee. If, however, they represent a group that is determined to impose its values on the schools, they will continue their pressure. This is why it is essential that every library have a selection policy supported by the board and administration. Librarians and teachers also need to be aware of the support they can obtain from organizations like the Office for Intellectual Freedom of the American Library Association, the Freedom

to Read Foundation of ALA, the National Council of Teachers of English, the International Reading Association, the American Civil Liberties Union, and People for the American Way.

Any challenge to a book is a matter to be taken seriously. Ultimately, what is involved is the freedom to learn and freedom of information, both of which are essential to American rights based on our democratic heritage and principles.

Working with Parents and the Community

Many schools have found that by informing and involving parents in school programs and plans, problems such as censorship are headed off or resolved before they can develop into serious discord. Even more important, parent volunteers can be a particularly rich resource for teachers and librarians. Sometimes these volunteers can be parents of students, sometimes they might be volunteers from a senior citizen center. One kindergarten/first-grade teacher has "grandmothers" from a senior citizen center who come once a week for the whole morning. They read stories to small groups of children, even individuals. They help make big books that the teacher uses. Whatever is needed, there is an extra pair of hands to do it.

Parents can also serve as resource persons, depending upon their background of experience. One parent who is an Egyptologist became a tremendous resource for third-grade children who were studying mummies. In preparation for this parent's visit, the teacher read

---

[32]*The Students' Right to Know* (Urbana, Ill.: National Council of Teachers of English, 1982).

[33]"Statement of Concern About Library/Media Center Resources," in *Intellectual Freedom Manual; rev.* (Chicago: American Library Association, 1996), p. 167.

aloud *Mummies Made in Egypt* by Aliki, and the children prepared questions to ask him. He brought Egyptian artifacts and pictures to share with them. Another group of first-grade students were studying about families. They wanted to interview the oldest member of their family about his or her childhood. One grandfather was invited to the class, and children learned how to conduct an interview with him. Wherever possible teachers should draw on the expertise of the community.

Students can also reciprocate by contributing to the community themselves. Junior high school students in the Bronx so loved Katherine Paterson's *Bridge to Terabithia* that they wanted to share it with others. A literature group went out to the local senior citizens' residence and read it aloud to these new friends. Those seniors were invited to keep reading logs and join in the book discussions.[34]

In one school the parents and children created the Book Nook, a tiny paperback bookstore literally made from a broom closet. They decorated it with Maurice Sendak posters and a charming hanging lamp and even turned the old sink into a "trading pot" where children could place a "used" paperback and exchange it for another. The whole school takes justifiable pride in this paperback bookstore. In another school the parents made a large wooden case on wheels that can be opened to create a bookstore anywhere in the building. Closed, it can be pushed flat against a wall. Parents will need help in getting such bookstores started and assuming responsibility for their operation. The librarian, a teacher who knows books, parents, and one or two children could serve as the selection committee to order new books. If teachers and parents support the store in the beginning, it will sustain itself once children know its regular hours and can find the books they want to buy and read.

During Book Week one school had someone scheduled to read aloud every hour of the day in the library. The librarian helped the mayor, the police officer, the superintendent, and others select appropriate books for their story time. Different grades were scheduled to hear stories every day that week.

With good planning the community can be a wonderful resource for schools. The more a community participates, the more the people in that community will begin to take ownership and pride in their schools.

---

[34]Shelley Harwayne, "Reading and Writing for Real-World Reasons" in *The Whole Language Catalog*, ed. Kenneth S. Goodman, Lois Bridges Bird, and Yetta M. Goodman (Santa Rosa, Calif.: American School Publishers, 1991), p. 337.

Working with the Public Library

The school librarian should work closely with the children's librarian of the public library. At the beginning of the year, she might send him a list of the possible study units the school will be undertaking. It is not fair to suddenly deluge the public librarian with requests for books about building houses when he had no warning that the entire third grade would study this topic that year.

Most public librarians are very helpful to teachers who want to supplement their classroom library with particular books. In turn, teachers must see to it that these books are handled carefully and returned to the library on time.

Many public libraries are serving their communities in unique ways. Realizing the importance of reading aloud to young children, they might have a story hour three or four times a week. These are scheduled at various times convenient for working parents. Many libraries hold "pajama" story hours at 8 P.M. on nights when they are open. All the children come in their pajamas, hear several stories, and go home to bed.

Increasingly public libraries are giving outreach service to the many children who do not come to the library. Some librarians are holding story hours in soup kitchens for homeless children; others are going to churches and day schools and holding story hours for the unserved children of the community whose parents never bring them to the library.

Some visionary public librarians are sending a welcome kit to each newborn infant in the community. These kits, funded by a local business, include a brief pamphlet on the importance of reading aloud to the young child. A recommended list of books is part of the kit along with the notation that all titles are available in the library. Two books are included, such as *Goodnight Moon* by Margaret Wise Brown and *Clap Hands* by Helen Oxenbury (see Chapter 4). Along with the books are coupons for two more that may be obtained at the library. These forward-looking librarians know how important it is to read to babies and to develop the library habit early. They know that the future of libraries depends on the development of library users; these are apt to be the very youngsters who learned to love the library at an early age.

When teachers, librarians, and parents concentrate on plans to foster a love of reading in each child, communities become caring, literate places to live in. Only when every child has a library card and uses it, when every preschool group hears stories three and four times a day, when all teachers read aloud, when children have substantial time to read books of their own choosing, when all schools have trained librarians and information-rich media centers—only then will we begin to develop a nation of readers.

Learning Experiences

1. Spend a day in an elementary school. Focus on the environment for learning, the physical environment, the intellectual climate, the emotional climate. Describe the quality of living and learning in the school. Support your descriptions with careful observations.

2. Visit an elementary school and focus on the provisions for a literature program. Does the teacher read to the children? What is read? What are the children reading? What books are available for them to read? How often are these books changed?

3. Spend a day in a school library media center. What does the librarian do? Is she caught up in meeting schedules, or does the center have flexible scheduling?

4. Draw a floor plan of a classroom you would hope to have as a teacher. Plan the reading areas and list what you would have in them.

5. Visit the children's rooms of several different libraries and compare what you see. What books are children reading, taking home? May they check out nonprint materials? Talk with children's librarians. What innovative practices have they initiated? What plans for the future do they have?

6. Examine basal readers, sample kits of literature, and published units on literature. Note the purposes, content, plans of organization, and activities. Analyze the types of questions that have been prepared.

7. Using the framework for webbing, choose a book, genre, or unit to web for a particular age level. If possible, work out some of the planned activities with children.

8. Plan an in-depth study of a book, using the types of questions described in the chapter.

9. Look at several state and local curriculum guides for the elementary school and see what suggestions they give for teaching literature. Literature might be included in the guides for reading or language arts.

10. Interview a librarian and ask to see the current selection policy statement. Ask if the library has had censorship problems and what was done about them.

Related Readings

Atwell, Nancie. *In the Middle: Writing, Reading, and Learning with Adolescents.* Portsmouth, N.H.: Heinemann, 1987.

> A breakthrough book on ways to help middle school students find joy in writing and reading. Much attention is given to dialogue journals, both what students write and how the teacher responds. Reading workshop and mini-lessons are described in this useful book for all teachers.

Barton, Bob, and David Booth. *Stories in the Classroom.* Portsmouth, N.H.: Heinemann, 1990.

> Two well-known Canadian educators talk about the importance of story in a child's life and how we can help engage a child in "storying." They discuss ways to share stories and ways to encourage children to respond and to tell their own.

Bauer, Caroline Feller. *New Handbook for Storytellers.* Chicago: American Library Association, 1993.

> This is one of the most thorough resources on storytelling available. It includes suggestions for choosing and telling stories, and ideas for using film, music, crafts, puppetry, and other story media. Information on storytelling festivals throughout the United States is included.

Green, Ellin. *Books, Babies, and Libraries: Serving Infants, Toddlers, Their Parents, and Caregivers.* Chicago: American Library Association, 1991.

> Green, who is project director and consultant for the New York Public Library's early childhood program, has written a book to prepare librarians to work effectively with infants and toddlers as well as adults.

Hancock, Joelie, and Susan Hill, eds. *Literature-Based Reading Programs at Work.* Portsmouth, N.H.: Heinemann, 1988.

> Twelve teachers and librarians from Australia and New Zealand describe how they made the change from basal reading programs to literature-based programs. The first section presents articles on setting up a literature-based reading program; the second section deals with special-focus programs such as big books, poetry, and biography.

Hansen, Jane. *When Writers Read*. Portsmouth, N.H.: Heinemann, 1987.

One of the most sensible and clearly written books on the relationship between reading and writing. Drawing on her research in the classroom, Hansen explores how a response approach can be used in both writing and reading.

Pappas, Christine C., Barbara Z. Kiefer, and Linda S. Levstik. *An Integrated Language Perspective in the Elementary School*. 2nd ed. White Plains, N.Y.: Longman, 1994.

An excellent text that provides integrated language theory and a wealth of examples from the classroom. Eight detailed units for grades K–6 are featured, along with webs to show their development. Chapters on observation and assessment technique are also included. Literature is shown as central to the curriculum.

Peterson, Ralph, and Maryann Eeds. *Grand Conversations: Literature Groups in Action*. New York: Scholastic, 1990.

A fine discussion of teaching with real books. Both theoretical and practical, the book differentiates between *extensive*, or wide, reading where children just read for enjoyment, and *intensive* reading, where students read and study a book in depth. Highly recommended for any teachers involved in a literature-based reading program.

Reichman, Henry. *Censorship and Selection: Issues and Answers for Schools*. Chicago: American Library Association; Arlington, Va.: American Association of School Administrators, 1988.

This indispensable book examines censorship issues with a rational, low-key approach that respects differences in belief. It suggests specific procedures for establishing selection policies and for dealing with censorship. Appendixes provide documents on intellectual freedom, sample letters, selection policy guidelines, and other helpful reference material for school librarians, administrators, and teachers.

Roser, Nancy L., and Miriam Martinez, eds. *Book Talk and Beyond: Children and Teachers Respond to Literature*. Newark, Del.: International Reading Association, 1995.

A volume of detailed ideas and examples from classrooms where children's talk about literature leads to deepening understanding and appreciation. Sections focus on what teachers need to understand about talk and literature, creating classroom contexts that invite talk, guiding talk, extending talk to dialogue journals, and other responses.

Routman, Regie. *Transitions: From Literature to Literacy*. Portsmouth, N.H.: Heinemann, 1988.

A very popular book with teachers, this details Routman's growth as a whole language primary teacher. Her honesty and practical help are appreciated by teachers in transition themselves. Details of her reading-and-writing program, including many examples of children's work, are given.

Simmons, John S., ed. *Censorship: A Threat to Reading, Thinking, and Learning*. Newark, Del.: International Reading Association, 1994.

Chapters detail examples of censorship in elementary and secondary schools and methods used by censors. Practical information includes how to write rationales for literature selections and ways for teachers, librarians, and administrators to respond to censorship.

Weaver, Constance, with Diane Stephens and Janet Vance. *Understanding Whole Language: From Principles to Practice*. Portsmouth, N.H.: Heinemann, 1990.

An excellent guide to the theory and practice of whole language teaching. Includes theories of language and learning that contributed to the whole language movement, ideas for implementing whole language classrooms, and information on assessment.

Children's Literature

Alcock, Vivien. *The Monster Garden*. Delacorte, 1988.

Alexander, Lloyd. *The Book of Three*. Holt, 1964.

———. *The King's Fountain*. Illustrated by Ezra Jack Keats. Dutton, 1989.

Aliki [Aliki Brandenberg]. *Mummies Made in Egypt*. Harper & Row, 1985.

Amon, Aline. *The Earth is Sore: Native Americans on Nature*. Atheneum, 1981.

Anno, Mitsumasa. *Anno's Alphabet: An Adventure in Imagination*. Harper & Row, 1976.

———. *Anno's Italy*. Philomel, 1984.

Appelbaum, Diana. *Giants in the Land*. Illustrated by Michael McCurdy. Houghton Mifflin, 1993.

Aragon, Jane. *Salt Hands*. Illustrated by Ted Rand. Dutton, 1989.

Arkin, Alan. *The Lemming Condition*. Illustrated by Joan Sandin. Harper & Row, 1976.

Arnold, Caroline. *Saving the Peregrine Falcon*. Photographs by Richard R. Hewett. Carolrhoda, 1985.

Babbitt, Natalie. *Tuck Everlasting*. Farrar, Straus & Giroux, 1975.

Baker, Alan. *Benjamin's Portrait*. Lothrop, Lee & Shepard, 1987.

Baker, Jeannie. *The Story of Rosie Dock*. Greenwillow, 1995.

———. *Where the Forest Meets the Sea*. Greenwillow, 1988.

———. *Window*. Greenwillow, 1991.

Bauer, Marion Dane. *On My Honor*. Clarion, 1986.

Baylor, Byrd. *Hawk, I'm Your Brother*. Illustrated by Peter Parnall. Macmillan, 1976.

———. *The Other Way to Listen*. Illustrated by Peter Parnall. Macmillan, 1978.

———. *The Way to Start a Day*. Illustrated by Peter Parnall. Macmillan, 1978.

Bernhard, Emery. *Eagles: Lions of the Sky*. Illustrated by Durga Bernhard. Holiday House, 1994.

Blume, Judy. *Blubber*. Bradbury, 1974.

———. *Deenie*. Bradbury, 1973.

Bosse, Malcolm. *Deep Dream of the Rain Forest*. Farrar, Straus & Giroux, 1993.

Brenner, Barbara, ed. *The Earth Is Painted Green: A Garden of Poems About Our Planet*. Illustrated by S. D. Schindler. Scholastic, 1993.

Brett, Jan. *The Mitten*. Putnam, 1989.

Brown, Margaret Wise. *Goodnight Moon*. Illustrated by Clement Hurd. Harper & Row, 1947.

———. *The Important Book*. Illustrated by Leonard Weisgard. Harper & Row, 1949.

Brown, Ruth. *The World That Jack Built*. Dutton, 1991.

Bryan, Ashley. *The Cat's Purr*. Atheneum, 1985.

Burnie, David. *Bird*. Knopf, 1988.

Butler, Stephen. *Henny Penny*. Tambourine, 1991.

Byars, Betsy. *Goodbye, Chicken Little*. Harper & Row, 1979.

———. *The Pinballs*. Harper & Row, 1977.

———. *The Summer of the Swans*. Viking, 1970.

Caney, Steven. *Steven Caney's Toy Book*. Workman, 1972.

Carle, Eric. *The Very Hungry Caterpillar*. World, 1968.

———. *The Very Busy Spider*. Philomel, 1984.

Carroll, Lewis [Charles L. Dodgson]. *Alice's Adventures in Wonderland*. Illustrated by John Tenniel. Macmillan, 1963 [1865].

Cherry, Lynne. *The Great Kapok Tree: A Tale of the Amazon Rain Forest*. Harcourt Brace, 1990.

———. *A River Ran Wild: An Environmental History*. Gulliver, 1992.

Christopher, John. *When the Tripods Came*. Dutton, 1988.

Clark, Margaret Goff. *The Vanishing Manatee*. Cobblehill, 1990.

Clearly, Beverly. *Ramona Forever*. Illustrated by Alan Tiegreen. Morrow, 1984.

———. *Ramona Quimby, Age 8*. Illustrated by Alan Tiegreen. Morrow, 1981.

———. *Strider*. Illustrated by Paul O. Zelinsky. Morrow, 1991.

Cole, Joanna. *It's Too Noisy*. Illustrated by Kate Duke. Crowell, 1989.

———. *The Magic School Bus at the Waterworks*. Illustrated by Bruce Degen. Scholastic, 1986.

Cone, Molly. *Come Back Salmon*. Photographs by Sidnee Wheelwright. Little, Brown, 1992.

Cooney, Barbara. *Miss Rumphius*. Penguin, 1982.

Cowcher, Helen. *Rain Forest*. Farrar, Straus & Giroux, 1988.

Cowley, Joy. *Greedy Cat*. Owens, 1988.

Cutchins, Judy, and Ginny Johnston. *The Crocodile and the Crane*. Morrow, 1986.

Dahl, Roald. *James and the Giant Peach*. Illustrated by Nancy Ekholm Burkert. Knopf, 1961.

Daly, Niki. *Not So Fast, Songololo*. McElderry, 1986.

DeArmond, Dale. *The Seal Oil Lamp*. Sierra Club/Little, Brown, 1988.

de Paola, Tomie. *"Charlie Needs a Cloak."* Prentice Hall, 1974.

———. *Strega Nona*. Prentice Hall, 1975.

Dickinson, Peter. *Eva*. Delacorte, 1989.

Dorros, Arthur. *Rain Forest Secrets*. Scholastic, 1990.

Durrell, Ann, Jean Craighead George, and Katherine Paterson, eds. *The Big Book for Our Planet*. Dutton, 1993.

Duvoisin, Roger. *Petunia*. Knopf, 1950.

Earthworks. *50 Simple Things You Can Do to Save the Earth*. Andrews & McNeel, 1991.

Ehlert, Lois. *Color Farm*. Lippincott, 1990.

———. *Color Zoo*. Lippincott, 1989.

Elkington, John, et al. *Going Green: A Kid's Handbook for Saving the Planet*. Illustrated by Tony Ross. Viking, 1990.

Emberley, Rebecca. *Three Cool Kids*. Little, Brown, 1995.

Facklam, Margery. *And Then There Was One: The Mysteries of Extinction*. Illustrated by Pamela Johnson. Sierra Club/Little, Brown, 1990.

———. *Bees Dance and Whales Sing: The Mysteries of Animal Communication*. Sierra Club, 1992.

Farmer, Nancy. *The Ear, the Eye and the Arm: A Novel*. Orchard, 1994.

Feder, Jan. *The Life of a Hamster*. Children's Press, 1982.

Fleischman, Paul. *Saturnalia*. HarperCollins, 1990.

Fleischman, Sid. *The Whipping Boy*. Illustrated by Peter Sis. Greenwillow, 1986.

Fox, Paula. *Monkey Island*. Orchard, 1991.

———. *One-Eyed Cat*. Bradbury, 1984.

Freeman, Don. *Dandelion*. Viking, 1964.

Freedman, Russell. *Lincoln: A Photobiography*. Clarion, 1987.

Fritz, Jean. *And Then What Happened, Paul Revere?* Illustrated by Margo Tomes. Coward-McCann, 1973.

Gág, Wanda. *Nothing at All*. Coward-McCann, 1928.

Galdone, Paul. *The Gingerbread Boy*. Clarion, 1983.

———. *The Three Wishes*. McGraw-Hill, 1961.

Gardiner, John. *Stone Fox*. Illustrated by Marcia Sewall. Harper & Row, 1980.

George, Jean Craighead. *Everglades*. Illustrated by Wendell Minor. HarperCollins, 1995.

———. *How to Talk to Your Dog*. Warner, 1986.

———. *The Fire Bug Connection: An Ecological Mystery*. HarperCollins, 1993.

———. *Julie of the Wolves*. Harper & Row, 1972.

———. *The Missing Gator of Gumbo Limbo: An Ecological Mystery*. HarperCollins, 1992.

———. *My Side of the Mountain*. Dutton, 1975.

———. *One Day in the Tropical Rainforest*. Illustrated by Gary Allen. HarperCollins, 1990.

———. *The Talking Earth*. Harper & Row, 1983.

———. *Who Really Killed Cock Robin? An Ecological Mystery*. HarperCollins, 1991 [1971].

———. *The Wounded Wolf*. Illustrated by John Schoenherr. Harper & Row, 1978.

Gerstein, Mordicai. *The Seal Mother*. Dial, 1986.

Ginsburg, Mirra. *Mushroom in the Rain*. Illustrated by José Aruego and Ariane Dewey. Macmillan, 1974.

Grahame, Kenneth. *The Wind in the Willows*. Illustrated by E. H. Shepard. Scribner's, 1940 [1908].

Gray, Nigel. *A Country Far Away*. Illustrated by Philippe Dupasquier. Orchard, 1989.

Greenblat, Rodney A. *Uncle Wizzmo's New Used Car*. HarperCollins, 1990.

Grifalconi, Ann. *Osa's Pride*. Little, Brown, 1990.

Grover, Wayne. *Dolphin Adventure: True Story*. Illustrated by Jim Fowler. Greenwillow, 1990.

Hall, Donald. *Ox-Cart Man*. Illustrated by Barbara Cooney. Viking, 1979.

Heide, Florence Parry, and Judith Heide Gilliland. *The Day of Ahmed's Secret*. Illustrated by Ted Lewin. Lothrop, Lee & Shepard, 1990.

Hill, Kirkpatrick. *Toughboy and Sister*. McElderry, 1990.

Hirschi, Ron. *The Mountain Bluebird*. Photographs by Galen Burrell. Cobblehill, 1989.

———. *Where Do Birds Live?* Photographs by Galen Burrell. Walker, 1987.

Hirsh, Marilyn. *Could Anything Be Worse?* Holiday House, 1974.

Hogrogian, Nonny. *One Fine Day*. Macmillan, 1971.

Houston, James. *Falcon Bow: An Arctic Legend*. McElderry, 1986.

Huff, Barbara. *Greening the City Streets: The Story of Community Gardens*. Photographs by Peter Ziebel. Clarion, 1990.

Hunter, Mollie. *A Sound of Chariots*. Harper & Row, 1972.

———. *A Stranger Came Ashore*. Harper & Row, 1975.

Hurwitz, Johanna. *Ozzie on His Own*. Johanna Hurwitz. Greenwillow, 1995.

Isadora, Rachel. *At the Crossroads*. Greenwillow, 1991.

Jacques, Brian. *Redwall*. Philomel, 1986.

Jeffers, Susan. *Brother Eagle, Sister Sky: A Message from Chief Seattle*. Dial, 1991.

Jonas, Ann. *Aardvarks Disembark*. Greenwillow, 1990.

———. *Splash!* Greenwillow, 1995.

Kent, Jack. *The Fat Cat: A Danish Folktale*. Parents, 1971.

Killion, Bette. *The Apartment House Tree*. Illustrated by Mary Szilagyi. Harper & Row, 1989.

Kipling, Rudyard. *The Elephant's Child*. Illustrated by Lorinda Bryan Cauley. Harcourt Brace, 1983.

Konigsburg, E. L. *From the Mixed-Up Files of Mrs. Basil E. Frankweiler*. Atheneum, 1967.

Lauber, Patricia. *Summer of Fire: Yellowstone, 1988*. Orchard, 1990.

———. *Too Much Garbage*. Illustrated by Vic May. Garrard, 1974.

L'Engle, Madeleine. *A Wrinkle in Time*. Farrar, Straus & Giroux, 1962.

Lewin, Hugh. *Jafta* (Jafta series). Illustrated by Lisa Kopper. Carolrhoda, 1983.

Lewis, C. S. *The Lion, the Witch, and the Wardrobe* (from the Narnia series). Illustrated by Pauline Baynes. Macmillan, 1950.

Lionni, Leo. *Frederick*. Pantheon, 1967.

———. *Little Blue and Little Yellow*. Astor-Honor, 1959.

Lisle, Janet Taylor. *The Lampfish of Twill*. Orchard, 1991.

Lobel, Arnold. *Frog and Toad Are Friends*. Harper & Row, 1970.

Lowry, Lois. *The Giver*. Houghton Mifflin, 1993.

Macaulay, David. *Black and White*. Houghton Mifflin, 1990.

MacDonald, Caroline. *The Lake at the End of the World*. Dial, 1989.

MacLachlan, Patricia. *Sarah, Plain and Tall*. Harper & Row, 1985.

Mayne, William. *Antar and the Eagles*. Delacorte, 1989.

————. *Hob and the Goblins*. Illustrated by Norman Messenger. Dorling Kindersley, 1994.

McClung, Robert M. *Lost Wild America: The Story of Our Extinct and Vanishing Wildlife*. Linnet, 1994.

McDonald, Megan. *Is This a House for a Hermit Crab?* Illustrated by S. D. Schindler. Orchard, 1990.

McKissack, Patricia C. *Flossie & the Fox*. Illustrated by Rachel Isadora. Dial, 1986.

McNulty, Faith. *The Lady and the Spider*. Illustrated by Bob Marstall. Harper & Row, 1986.

Milhous, Katherine and Alice Dalgliesh. *The Turnip*. Philomel, 1990.

Milne, A. A. *Winnie-the-Pooh*. Illustrated by Ernest H. Shepard. Dutton, 1926.

Mullins, Patricia. *V for Vanishing: An Alphabet of Endangered Animals*. HarperCollins, 1994.

Neitzel, Shirley. *The Bag I'm Taking to Grandma's*. Illustrated by Nancy Winslow Parker. Greenwillow, 1995.

O'Brien, Robert C. *Z for Zachariah*. Macmillan, 1987 [1975].

O'Dell, Scott. *Island of the Blue Dolphins*. Illustrated by Ted Lewin. Houghton Mifflin, 1990 [1960].

Oppenheim, Joanne. *You Can't Catch Me!* Illustrated by Andrew Shachar. Houghton Mifflin, 1986.

Oxenbury, Helen. *Clap Hands*. Macmillan, 1987.

Patent, Dorothy Hinshaw. *Return of the Wolf*. Clarion, 1995.

Paterson, Katherine. *Bridge to Terabithia*. Illustrated by Donna Diamond. Crowell, 1977.

————. *The Great Gilly Hopkins*. Crowell, 1978.

————. *Jacob Have I Loved*. Crowell, 1980.

————. *Lyddie*. Lodestar/Dutton, 1991.

Patterson, Francine. *Koko's Kitten*. Photographs by Ronald H. Cohn. Scholastic, 1985.

Paulsen, Gary. *Hatchet*. Bradbury, 1987.

Pine, Jonathon. *Trees*. HarperCollins, 1995.

Pringle, Laurence. *Global Warming*. Arcade, 1990.

————. *Living Treasure: Saving the Earth's Threatened Biodiversity*. Morrow, 1991.

————. *Saving Our Wildlife*. Enslow, 1990.

————. *Throwing Things Away: From Middens to Resource Recovery*. Crowell, 1986.

Provensen, Alice, and Martin Provensen. *Shaker Lane*. Penguin, 1988.

Quattlebaum, Mary. *Jackson Jones and the Puddle of Thorns*. Delacorte, 1994.

Rawls, Wilson. *Where the Red Fern Grows*. Doubleday, 1961.

Reeder, Caroline. *Grandpa's Mountain*. Macmillan, 1991.

Ryder, Joanne. *When the Woods Hum*. Illustrated by Catherine Stock. Morrow, 1991.

Sattler, Helen Roney. *The Book of Eagles*. Illustrated by Jean Day Zallinger. Lothrop, Lee & Shepard, 1989.

Scieszka, Jon. *The Stinky Cheese Man and Other Fairly Stupid Tales*. Illustrated by Lane Smith. Viking, 1992.

Schlein, Miriam. *Pigeons*. Photographs by Margaret Miller. Crowell, 1989.

————. *The Year of the Panda*. Illustrated by Kam Mak. Crowell, 1990.

Schnieper, Claudia. *Amazing Spiders*. Photos by Max Meier. Carolrhoda, 1987.

Schwartz, Alvin. *Scary Stories to Tell in the Dark*. Illustrated by Stephen Gammell. Harper & Row, 1981.

Selsam, Millicent E., and Joyce Hunt. *A First Look at Leaves*. Illustrated by Harriett Springer. Walker, 1972.

Seuss, Dr. [Theodore S. Geisel]. *The Lorax*. Random House, 1981.

Sharpe, Susan. *Waterman's Boy*. Bradbury, 1990.

Shaw, Charles G. *It Looked Like Spilt Milk*. Harper & Row, 1947.

Sheldon, Dyan. *Whale's Song*. Ilustrated by Gary Blythe. Dial, 1991.

Showers, Paul. *The Listening Walk*. Illustrated by Aliki. HarperCollins, 1991.

Shulevitz, Uri. *Dawn*. Farrar, Straus & Giroux, 1974.

————. *Toddlecreek Post Office*. Farrar, Straus & Giroux, 1990.

Siebert, Diane. *Heartland*. Illustrated by Wendell Minor. Crowell, 1989.

————. *Mojave*. Illustrated by Wendell Minor. Crowell, 1988.

————. *Sierra*. Illustrated by Wendell Minor. Crowell, 1991.

Smith, Roland. *Sea Otter Rescue: The Aftermath of an Oil Spill*. Cobblehill, 1990.

Speare, Elizabeth George. *The Sign of the Beaver*. Houghton Mifflin, 1983.

Staines, Bill. *All God's Critters Got a Place in the Choir*. Illustrated by Margot Zemach. Dutton, 1989.

Steig, William. *Abel's Island*. Farrar, Straus & Giroux, 1976.

————. *Sylvester and the Magic Pebble*. Simon & Schuster, 1969.

Steptoe, John. *Mufaro's Beautiful Daughters: An African Tale*. Lothrop, Lee & Shepard, 1987.

Stolz, Mary. *Night Ghosts and Hermits: Nocturnal Life on the Seashore*. Illustrated by Susan Gallagher. Harcourt Brace, 1985.

Sussman, Susan, and Robert James. *Big Friend, Little Friend: A Book About Symbiosis*. Houghton Mifflin, 1989.

Tresselt, Alvin. *The Mitten*. Illustrated by Yaroslava. Lothrop, Lee & Shepard, 1964.

Turkle, Brinton. *Do Not Open*. Dutton, 1981.

Turner, Ann. *Heron Street*. Illustrated by Lisa Desimini. Harper & Row, 1989.

Tyler, Linda Wagner. *The After-Christmas Tree*. Illustrated by Susan Davis. Viking, 1990.

Van Allsburg, Chris. *Just a Dream*. Houghton Mifflin, 1990.

————. *The Polar Express*. Houghton Mifflin, 1985.

Waber, Bernard. *Ira Sleeps Over*. Houghton Mifflin, 1975.

————. *"You Look Ridiculous," Said the Rhinoceros to the Hippopotamus*. Houghton Mifflin, 1966.

Weller, Frances. *I Wonder if I'll See a Whale*. Illustrated by Ted Lewin. Philomel, 1991.

Wheatley, Nadia. *My Place*. Illustrated by Donna Rawlings. Kane Miller, 1993.

White, E. B. *Charlotte's Web*. Harper & Row, 1952.

Wilder, Laura Ingalls. *The First Four Years*. Illustrated by Garth Williams. Harper & Row, 1971.

————. *Little House in the Big Woods*. Illustrated by Garth Williams. Harper & Row, 1953 [1932].

————. *Little House on the Prairie*. Illustrated by Garth Williams. Harper & Row, 1953 [1935].

————. *Little Town on the Prairie*. Illustrated by Garth Williams. Harper & Row, 1953 [1932].

Wildsmith, Brian. *Professor Noah's Spaceship*. Oxford University Press, 1980.

Williams, Karen Lynn. *Galimoto*. Illustrated by Catherine Stock. Lothrop, Lee & Shepard, 1990.

Williams, Linda. *The Little Old Lady Who Was Not Afraid of Anything*. Illustrated by Megan Lloyd. Crowell, 1986.

Williams, Vera B. *Three Days on a River in a Red Canoe*. Greenwillow, 1981.

Wood, Audrey. *The Napping House*. Illustrated by Don Wood. Harcourt Brace, 1984.

Yagawa, Sumiko. *The Crane Wife*. Translated by Katherine Paterson. Illustrated by Suekichi Akaba. Morrow, 1981.

Yolen, Jane. *Bird Watch*. Illustrated by Ted Lewin. Philomel, 1990.

————. *Greyling*. Illustrated by David Ray. Philomel, 1991.

————. *Letting Swift River Go*. Illustrated by Barbara Cooney. Little, Brown, 1992.

————. *Owl Moon*. Illustrated by John Schoenherr. Philomel, 1987.

Zemach, Margot. *It Could Always Be Worse*. Farrar, Straus & Giroux, 1976.

————. *The Three Wishes: An Old Story*. Farrar, Straus & Giroux, 1986.

Zion, Gene. *Harry the Dirty Dog*. Illustrated by Margaret Graham. Harper & Row, 1956.

Zubrowski, Bernie. *Tops: Building and Experimenting with Spinning Toys*. Illustrated by Roy Doty. Morrow, 1989.

chapter fourteen

Extending and Evaluating Children's Understandings of Literature

Active Learning in the Classroom 669
Exploring Literature Through Art and
   Media 669

Pictures and Collage 670
Murals 671
Media Exploration 671
*Resources for Teaching: Illustrators and
   Their Techniques* 673

Displays, Dioramas, and Museums 674
Story-Retelling Aids 676
Graphic Organizers 677
Videos and Computers 678
*Resources for Teaching: Books About
   Quilts and Stitchery* 680
Making Things 680

Sewing 680
Crafts and Construction 681
*Teaching Feature: Quiltmaking Helps
   Students Review Their Study of
   Mexico* 682
Cooking 682
Games 683
Singing and Movement in the
   Classroom 684

Picture-Book Editions of Single Songs 684
Matching Music and Literature 685
Composing Music 685
Movement and Literature 685
Connecting Literature and Life 686

Artifacts and Collections 686
Maps and Time Lines 686

Jackdaws 687
*Resources for Teaching: Making a
   Jackdaw* 688
Extending Literature Through
   Drama 688

Pantomime 688
Dramatizing Stories 689
Improvisation 690
Readers' Theater 690
Puppetry 691

Selecting Stories 691
Constructing Puppets and Stages 691
Writing from Children's Books 692

Developing Sensitivity to Language 692
Single Books as Springboards 694
Experimenting with Literary Patterns 695

Making Alphabet Books 695
Fooling with Folktales, Fables, and Myths 696
*Resources for Teaching: Fooling with
   Traditional Literature* 698

Experimenting with Poetry 698

Extending Forms of Writing 699

Diaries and Letters 699
Newspapers and Newscasting 700

Expository Writing 700

Directions, Explanations, and Surveys 700
*Resources for Teaching: Books That Serve
   as Writing Models* 701
Nonfiction's Influence on Report Writing 703

Making Books 704

Assessment and Evaluation 704

Determining Children's Literacy Background 705

Record Keeping 706

Ongoing Observations 706
Folders 707
Assessment Portfolios 707

Student and Parent Conferences 707

Evaluating Children's Literary Understandings 708

Evaluating Children's Growth as Readers 709

Evaluating the Literature Program 709
Developing Lifetime Readers 709
Guidelines: Evaluating Children's Growth as Readers 710
Guidelines: Evaluating a Literature Program 711
Learning Experiences 712
Related Readings 713
Children's Literature 714

As part of an all-school theme on Africa, three first-grade teachers immersed children in experiences with literature about the life of African peoples.[1] The children heard and read many stories with African settings. Maps, books, pictures, and things from Africa began to fill the rooms. After hearing Ann Grifalconi's *The Village of Round and Square Houses*, one class discussed "how and why stories" and some children replicated this Cameroon village. The school guidance counselor visited each classroom and read aloud Grifalconi's sequel, *Osa's Pride*, and children compared "good" pride with "bad" pride, giving examples from their own lives.

Others read Joyce Arkhurst's *The Adventures of Spider*, Gail Haley's *A Story, a Story*, and Gerald McDermott's *Anansi the Spider*, all about the trickster of West African lore. Some made attribute charts of Anansi's character ("*Tricky* because he made the tar baby"; "*Proud* when his sons helped him"); others compared two versions of a similar Anansi story in their response logs. Others read John Steptoe's *Mufaro's Beautiful Daughters* and made puppets for a drama of this folktale from Zimbabwe.

[1]This description is based on work accomplished under the direction of Virginia Mears, Joanne Larkin, and Mary Jane McIlwain, all first-grade teachers at George Mason Elementary School in Alexandria, Virginia.

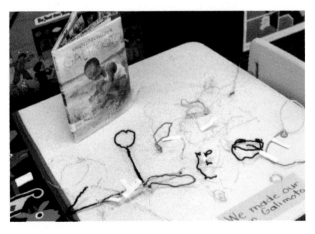

After they heard their teacher read Karen William's *Galimoto*, children created a display that featured the book. George Mason Elementary School, Alexandria City Schools, Alexandria, Virginia. Joanne Larkin, teacher. Photo by Jacki Vawter.

They heard Karen Williams's story *Galimoto*, located the setting of Malawi on their map of Africa, discussed the boy Kondi's skills in bargaining and building, and then made their own wire cars and toys from pipe cleaners. These were labeled and displayed on a table along with the book. Children enjoyed reading Hugh Lewin's South African story *Jafta* and made a class book of American expressions following the similes using African animals found in the book: "When I'm happy, I purr like a lion cub." One teacher shared Muriel Feelings's *Moja Means One* and some children made a wall display depicting East African numbers.

A parent who had been to countries in West Africa brought in slides of large buildings and city life, which surprised some children who thought that most Africans lived in huts in small villages. The parent wore African dress, showed African sculpture and textiles, and passed around money from various African countries, which children located on the map. The children shared their knowledge with the parent as well.

The art teacher displayed pictures from Diane Stanley and Peter Vennema's *Shaka, King of the Zulus* and Shirley Glubok's *The Art of Africa*. Children then made highly patterned miniature Zulu shields. One class made three murals of animals found in the main regions of Africa: the grasslands or plains, the jungle or rain forests, and the desert. To do this, they had to do research in nonfiction, go back to illustrations in the class collection of books, and draw on other sources. Following this three-week study, children's work was displayed along with work from the rest of the school, and parents were invited to celebrate a "Cultural Diversity Night."

What did these teachers do? These first-grade teachers organized the classroom environment so that 6- and 7-year-olds could work with books and ideas in ways that were meaningful to them. They planned multiple experiences so that children could choose; they planned opportunities for children to return to books; they worked closely with the librarian and shared ideas with each other; they informed special-area teachers of their plans so that the music or art could be worked into this thematic study; and they honored children's work by displaying it attractively and letting parents in on the wonderful results.

Active Learning in the Classroom

When children work with books in ways that are meaningful to them—through talk, making things, writing, or drama and music—many things happen. Children have greater satisfaction with, and clarify personal meanings about, what they have read. These activities allow many books to be visible in the classroom. One child's work with a book can dramatically influence another child's willingness to read it. Children working on projects use various skills, exercise more choices, develop planning abilities, and experiment with a variety of learning experiences. In addition, these activities can allow children the opportunity to think more deeply about books and to return to them to explore responses in ways that deepen their understandings.

Teachers who know the children in their classes well recognize the diversity of learning styles this sort of active learning accommodates. They plan diverse activities that enhance children's delight in books, make them want to continue reading more and better books, and cause them to think both more widely and more specifically about what they have read. They know that many options should be open to children and do not expect all children to choose the same book or the same type of response to a book. They consult with children about possibilities for projects and do not assign all children to do the same project; neither do they expect children to do an activity for every book that they read. The activities in this chapter are planned to increase children's enjoyment and understanding of books.

Exploring Literature Through Art and Media

Young children communicate through visual symbols as easily as they communicate through language, yet by the middle grades many children feel very insecure about making art. Children of *all* ages who have the opportunity to transform their responses to books through visual means are learning to be confident creators. In addition, their familiarity with art can increase their visual literacy and their aesthetic understanding.

A fourth grader made a stunning collage of *Anansi the Spider* using colored tissue paper, yarn, and felt.
Martin Luther King, Jr., Laboratory School, Evanston Public Schools, Evanston, Illinois. Barbara Friedberg, teacher.

Pictures and Collage

Too often children are given a box of crayons and a small space at the top of some lined newsprint paper and told to "make a picture" of the story. How much better it is to work with children who are "filled to over-flowing" with knowledge about a book or theme. How much more lively might artwork be if the teacher provided many materials from which to choose instead of the usual crayons and thin newsprint. Chalk, paints, markers, colored tissue papers, yarn, steel wool, cotton, material scraps, wires—anything that might be useful in depicting characters and scenes should be readily accessible. Teachers might provide more interesting paper such as wallpaper samples, construction paper, hand-painted papers, the "second sheets" of computer paper, and remainders from printers. Then when children are asked to make pictures of their favorite part of a story, of a character doing something in the book they have read, or illustrations for their own stories, the results are more exciting.

The teacher's role is to design a rich environment for creativity by providing materials, challenging children's

thinking, and honoring children's work. Teachers can help children think about their stories or poems by asking focusing questions like these:

- What would be the most appropriate material for you to use for your picture?
- What colors do you see when you think of this story?
- How will you portray the main character? How old is he or she? What does he or she wear?
- Where does the story take place? When? How could you show this in your picture?

In follow-up discussions when children show their work to the class, teachers can encourage them to talk about choices and reactions with such questions as these:

- Why did you choose to illustrate this scene or characters?
- Why did you choose those particular materials?
- How did you make that part of your picture?
- Did you discover anything in making this picture?
- How does this help us see the book?

Seven-year-olds create a collage mural of the book, *Hi, Cat* by Ezra Jack Keats.
Barrington Road School, Upper Arlington Public Schools, Ohio. Marlene Harbert, teacher.

In this way, children are encouraged to reflect on or appreciate their own work and that of others. In addition, the teacher gains valuable insight into their thinking.

Some stories suggest children create new visual forms. One teacher gave second graders ink and straws with which to blow a monster shape that could have come out of the magic bottle in Brinton Turkle's *Do Not Open*. Third graders who read stories with nighttime settings, such as Jane Yolen's *Owl Moon*, Donald Crews's *Light*, and Bill Martin, Jr., and John Archambault's *The Ghost-Eye Tree*, made their own crayon-resist pictures by covering crayon drawings with black watercolor wash to produce eerie effects for their own nighttime stories.

Many illustrators' styles invite children to explore a particular medium. Collage artists, for instance, incorporate interesting papers, fabrics, natural objects, and other textures in their work. Jeannie Baker, in *The Story of Rosy Dock*, uses sand, twigs, leaves, and other objects to portray the ecology of central Australia. David Wisniewski works with an X-Acto knife to produce the finely cut paper for his intricate layered illustrations of the Tlingit tale *The Wave of the Sea-Wolf*. Molly Bang, Lois Ehlert, Ezra Jack Keats, Elizabeth Cleaver, Susan Roth, Eric Carle, and Leo Lionni have also worked with collage to illustrate their stories. Children who see the surprising kinds of materials that are used in collages will return to their own artwork with new ideas.

Murals

Murals provide children with opportunities to work and plan together. These collaborative efforts need planning, and teachers might suggest that children make preliminary drawings or sketches before beginning. Lightly chalked areas on the final mural paper help children visualize the overall picture. An easier form of mural is assembled by pasting children's artwork to a background. Older children might discuss how variation in size and shading, or overlapping, creates the illusion of depth.

Murals can be organized around events in one story, a synthesis of children's favorite characters, or a topic or theme of study. One fourth-grade class made individual collage representations of houses from favorite folktales that were later glued in place along a picture of a winding road. Baba Yaga's chicken-footed house from Russian folktales stood between the witch's house from "Hansel and Gretel" and the giant's castle from "Puss in Boots." A written explanation for each house accompanied the mural.

By providing a variety of materials and some organizing assistance, a teacher can help children successfully create eye-catching murals. Backgrounds can be quickly filled in with printing, using sponges dipped in paint for leaves and bushes or potato-printed tree shapes. It is important, both for a writing opportunity and for the many people who will view it, to complete the display of a mural with an explanation of the way it was made.

Media Exploration

A teacher can also make use of a child's desire to replicate an illustrator's way of working by encouraging children to explore various media. Kindergarten children saved their finger-painting pictures, cut them up, and used them to create their own story illustrated in the collage style of three of Eric Carle's stories, *The*

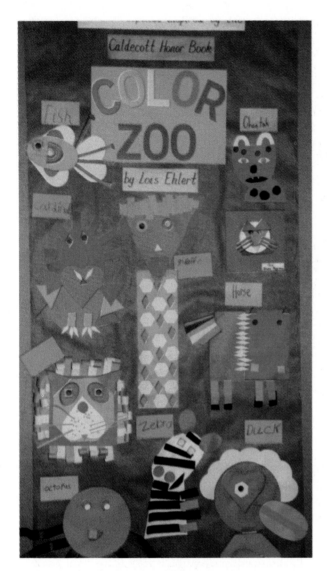

After exploring Lois Ehlert's style, children chose similar shapes and colors to respond to *Color Zoo*.
Emerson and Central College Elementary Schools, Westerville, Ohio. Lisa Dapoz, Joan Fusco, and Jean Sperling, teachers. Photo by Connie Compton.

Very Hungry Caterpillar, *The Very Busy Spider*, and *The Very Quiet Cricket*. (See the Teaching Feature "Creating Big Books with Emergent Readers" in Chapter 4). After seeing Leo Lionni's *Swimmy*, a group of primary children used lace paper doilies and watercolors to make prints creating similar underwater effects. Older children used dampened rice paper, ink, and watercolor to try to capture the look of traditional Japanese artwork used by Anne Buguet in *On Cat Mountain* by Francoise Richard and by Suekichi Akaba in the illustrations for *The Crane Wife* by Sumiko Yagawa. These children were answering for themselves the question "How did the illustrator make the pictures?"

Techniques that easily translate to the elementary classroom include collage, scratchboard, marbleized

paper, many varieties of painting and printing, and stencil prints. By making these materials and processes readily available for children, teachers can extend the ways in which they visualize their world as well as their appreciation for illustrators' works. Resources for Teaching, "Illustrators and Their Techniques," provides an overview of illustrators who work in some of these media and a sampling of books that provide good examples for children.

Though schools can buy commercially prepared scratchboard, similar results can be achieved by crayoning heavily on shiny-surfaced cardboard, then covering the crayon with India ink dabbed on with a cotton ball, and then scratching designs or illustrations through the ink with pin or scissor points after the ink has thoroughly dried. This process is tedious, so the technique is more suited for older children. A simpler "crayon resist" can be done by applying watercolor or black tempera paint over a crayon drawing. It is easy to put several drops of food coloring in water and let children paint this wash over crayon drawings to create sky, forest, or other background.[2]

Marbleized paper has frequently been used in collage and endpapers of well-made books. Children can create marbleized paper, using any paper and one of several kinds of color. Commercial marbleizing kits are available from school art supply catalogs, but binders such as cornstarch added to water achieve satisfactory effects. Fill kitty litterpans or disposable or old baking pans with water and drop the color on the water surface. Acrylic paint works well and does not entail the messy cleanup that enamel paint does. Some types of poster paint and India ink also give good results. Place a piece of paper face down on the water and floating color, being careful not to trap air bubbles between paper and water. Gently lift the paper and hang it to dry. Colored chalk also provides a pleasing effect and poses fewer cleanup problems for younger children. Large sticks of sidewalk chalk may be grated over the water with a small piece of window screen or an old sieve. Results must be sprayed with fixative or hairspray when dry. Marbleized paper may be cut and used in collage or in the making of books as endpapers and covers (see the section "Making Books" later in this chapter).

Printing techniques have been used in book illustration for centuries and are used by many modern illustrators. Young children could create designs for their book responses or book endpapers by printing repeated images. A plate can be made from a cut potato, an image incised on a foam tray, or some other printing medium.

[2]A recipe for preparing scratchboard, including the undercoating over which ink may be brushed, can be found in Helen Roney Sattler's *Recipes for Art and Craft Materials*, illustrated by Marti Shohet (New York: Lothrop, Lee & Shepard, 1987), p. 133.

Resources for Teaching
Illustrators and Their Techniques

Illustrator	Example	Author
Collage		
Holly Meade	*Small Green Snake*	Libba Moore Gray
Georgia Gluback	*Luka's Quilt*	Shirley Gluback
Lois Ehlert	*Mole's Hill*	Lois Ehlert
Scratchboard Drawing		
Leonard Everett Fisher	*Calendar Art*	Leonard Everett Fisher
Michael McCurdy	*Giants in the Land*	Diana Appelbaum
Brian Pinkney	*Wiley and the Hairy Man*	Judy Sierra
Special Papers		
Denise Fleming	*Where Once There Was a Wood*	Denise Fleming
Debra Frasier	*The Animal That Drank Up Sound*	William Stafford
Susan L. Roth	*How the Sky's Housekeeper Wore Her Scarves*	Patricia Hooper
Printmaking		
Carla Golembe	*Why the Sky Is Far Away*	Mary-Joan Gerson
David Frampton	*My Son Jon*	Jim Aylesworth
Ashley Wolff	*Goody O'Grumpity*	Carol Ryrie Brink
Stencil and Airbrush		
Leo and Diane Dillon	*Why Mosquitoes Buzz in People's Ears*	Verna Aardema
Donald Crews	*Sail Away*	Donald Crews
Ed Young	*All of You Was Singing*	Richard Lewis

A reliable plate that will withstand repeated use can be made from pieces of bicycle tire inner tubes. Cement rubber shapes to a wood block using rubber cement, and print as with any other block. This technique takes some careful planning, but such plates can be used to print endpapers for any number of books.

While woodcuts and linoleum block prints are seldom practical or safe for younger elementary children, similar effects can be achieved with printing plates made from the plastic foam trays that grocery stores use to package meat or produce. The trays should be washed to remove all grease. Lines can be incised on the plate with dull pencils or ballpoint pens, and excess foam cut away. Then water-based printing ink is rolled on. It takes time to create these pictures, but children find it very satisfying to work in the same media as an illustrator. In another type of printing process the printing plate is built up by gluing pieces of cardboard, string,

and other materials to a heavy backing. Ink is worked into or rolled onto the plate, and a print is taken or "pulled" off the plate. Often art teachers are happy to be enlisted by the classroom teacher in helping children explore a particular technique such as printing.

A stencil print allows children to apply paint or chalk in ways that resemble art techniques used by many illustrators. Artists like Leo and Diane Dillon often use an art tool called an airbrush to achieve smooth applications of color and clean edges. To make a stencil, a figure is cut from a piece of heavy paper, leaving the figure (the "positive" stencil) and the figure's shape (the "negative" stencil). The stencil is placed on a sheet of paper, and paint can be applied by flicking a brush over a wire screen or simply stippling the tip of the brush on the paper. For a "finger airbrush" technique the edges of either the negative or the positive stencil are heavily chalked and the figure or shape

A group of fourth graders studying New York City made a display of their responses to the books they had read.
PS 124, New York, New York. Mary S. Gallivan, teacher.

is laid on a clean piece of paper. By holding the chalked paper stationary and gently brushing the chalk dust off onto the clean paper, an image shape or its outline is formed. Using different colors of chalk creates surprising shadows and shadings. Even primary children enjoy using this technique to duplicate the fading smoke Donald Crews creates with an airbrush for *Freight Train*.

Eye-catching displays can be assembled when children's efforts at working in the manner of a well-known illustrator are mounted carefully and placed alongside the book that inspired the work. Explanations written by children help clarify for parents and other classroom observers how the work was created. (See Chapter 5 for other examples of media use.)

Displays, Dioramas, and Museums

Displays naturally attract children. While locked glass cases may be appropriate for some materials, it is the inviting hands-on aspect of a table display that entices readers to investigate books and things they might otherwise not discover or to create an inviting exhibit of work in response to a book or theme. Before beginning a study of the beach with kindergartners and first graders, a teacher displayed a child's bathing suit, sand, a souvenir T-shirt from a nearby beach, and some sand toys along with such books as Megan McDonald's *Is This a House for a Hermit Crab?* Douglas Florian's *A Beach Day*, Gail Gibbons's *Beacons of Light: Lighthouse*, and Rebecca Jones's *Down at the Bottom of the Deep Dark*

Sea. The teacher read these stories aloud and children talked about the books and their own beach experiences. Writing topics and research ideas were proposed. Some children brought in seashells and driftwood to add to the display table. As they talked about the shells and attempted to group them, the teacher added Alex Arthur's Eyewitness science book *Shell* to the table. Children began to take the books back to their work spaces, and share information with each other. They found several poems about beaches and shells, sketched their shells using pastel chalks, and wrote poems and reports of their own. The teacher helped them mat their work using colored construction paper, and they created an "At the Beach" exhibition that was hung behind the artifacts and books on display. Soon, the display of books, items, and children's projects and writings spread over two tables and a bulletin board as children became engaged with the topic. The initial display obviously was a catalyst for getting children to talk about and pursue a topic, and the display grew as children's thinking developed.

A diorama, another kind of display, is a three-dimensional scene often including objects and figures. Using cardboard boxes or shoe boxes turned on their sides, children can create a memorable scene from a book. Several fifth and sixth graders might depict Billie Wind and her animal companions as they floated by a Calusa mound in the Everglades in Jean Craighead George's *The Talking Earth*. Using a description of the Clock family's household described by Mary Norton in *The Borrowers*, a child might "borrow" similar materials to furnish a

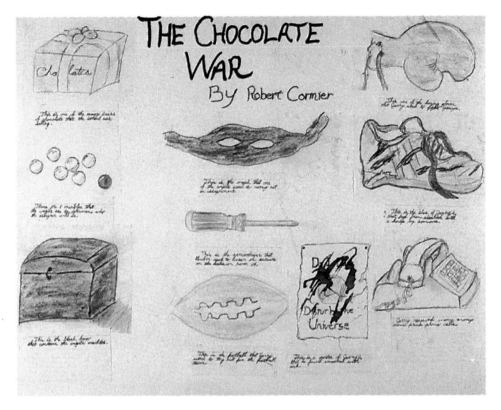

A sixth grader drew objects that could be placed in a museum for *The Chocolate War* by Robert Cormier.
Michael Reukauf, grade 6. George Mason Elementary School, Alexandria City Public Schools, Alexandria, Virginia. Susan Steinberg, teacher.

diorama. A larger box partitioned in two allows a child to contrast two events or settings. For instance, Virginia Lee Burton's *The Little House* could be depicted first in its pastoral setting and next in the city that grew up around it. Older readers might contrast what was important to the beautiful and musically talented Caroline with what was important to the practical and sea-loving Louise in Katherine Paterson's *Jacob Have I Loved*.

Children should be encouraged to make every part of the diorama. Real items such as sheet music or fishing hooks may be appropriate in symbolizing Caroline and Louise's differences, but commercial figurines tend to cheapen a display and decrease the child's involvement. If a teacher emphasizes the importance of accurate details, children must return to the book to check descriptions and facts. Teachers should also ask children to write about their diorama—how it was made, what it shows, and which book it is from. Then observers can appreciate the details, and the child has real authority and real purpose in writing.

A museum is a labeled collection of objects an author included in a story. For a museum based on Arnold Lobel's *Frog and Toad Together*, second graders gathered the string Toad used to tie the box of cookies, a feather dropped by a bird who ate the cookies, Toad's list, and a flower from Toad's garden. These and other items were labeled and explained. One group of 7-year-olds made papier-mâché whales, facsimiles of supplies that accompanied Amos, and models of the good ship *Rodent* as described in William Steig's humorous fable *Amos & Boris*. A folktale museum made by older students included a pea slept on by the princess, a chicken bone Hansel used to fool the witch, and a feather left behind by the Crane Wife. Sixth graders displayed their museum items on posterboard and presented their artwork to the class, explaining why each item pictured was important to the story. A boy who spoke about Robert Cormier's *The Chocolate War* used the pictures to remind him of characters, symbols, themes, plot, and his feelings about the story because he had considered and rehearsed all of this while choosing items for his display. (For other examples, see the section "Artifacts and Collections" later in this chapter.)

Displays, dioramas, and museums have the power to make a book seem more real to readers. Explanatory labels need to be written for each display. If the displays are shared enthusiastically with other classes, some children will surely find books they want to read. In the process of making scenes or visualizing parts of a story, children revisit the book to explore settings, rediscover the author's use of descriptive language, and often are better able to generalize about and discuss a story. These

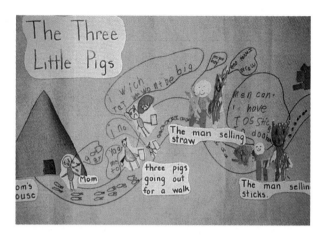

Creating a story map of "The Story of the Three Little Pigs" helped first-grade children to retell the story.
Columbus Public Schools, Columbus, Ohio. Connie Compton, teacher.

collections and the books from which they are taken then become highly visible to children and further invite them to keep reading.

Story-Retelling Aids

Children love to retell stories to each other, and aids help them recall parts of the story or focus on the sequence of events. One skillful kindergarten teacher discovered the power of a story box to turn children into storytellers:

🐾 *October 20:* I sat in front of the class and introduced the cast of characters for Galdone's *The Little Red Hen.* These were all stuffed animal toys and I used an invisible seed, some tall grasses, a tiny bag of white flour, and a loaf of bread for props. At the end of my puppet show I boxed up the cast and props and labeled the box "The Little Red Hen." I put it in the reading corner for anyone who wanted to tell that story. Throughout the morning small groups of children made time to check it all out. Some just fingered the plush toys, examined the bag of flour, and smelled the loaf of unsliced bread. But Allison organized Jamie, Jeffrey, Viviana, and Joey each to be an animal while she spoke the part of the hen. This play was for themselves, not demanding or even needing an audience; the children were unaware of observers. The box is a great idea; there seems to be great ceremony in unpacking and packing up the kit.[3]

Out of the dress-up clothes, one kindergarten teacher gathered men's boots, pants, a shirt, gloves, and a hat

that children manipulated as they retold Linda Williams's *The Little Old Lady Who Was Not Afraid of Anything.* A cardboard pumpkin took the place of a real one, and this collection was boxed and kept in the play corner for the month of October.

Felt boards provide another chance for children to practice telling stories more easily. (See the discussion of felt board stories in Chapter 13.) Once children have seen a teacher tell a story using the felt board, they are eager to use the props or to make their own figures to tell the story. Silhouettes placed on an overhead projector create yet another kind of board story. Where color is important, such as in Leo Lionni's *Little Blue and Little Yellow,* tinted acetate unmounted or mounted behind a cutout shape may be used.

A *roller box movie* is a third retelling aid. Each child draws a different important scene, the pictures are arranged sequentially, taped together, and then mounted on rollers. As each picture passes on the "screen," the child who drew the picture tells that part of the story. Needless to say, roller movies require children to talk through what scenes need to appear, who should present what, and so on. Pictures should be reinforced with masking tape on the back before they are attached to each other. The strip of pictures is then attached and rolled onto two fat dowel rods. The rods are inserted on either side of a decorated box or carton and the movie is scrolled past the audience.

Using story-retelling aids is a special help to young children and students who have heard few stories read aloud. By practicing storytelling, children develop a sense of how stories are supposed to sound and how stories work. The teacher may introduce and demonstrate any of these aids, but it is in the making of their own projects that children utilize the widest variety of skills. They learn to return to the story for information and confirmation, to extract important points, to sequence

[3]Jinx Bohstedt, "Old Tales for Young Tellers," *Outlook* no. 33 (fall 1979): 34.

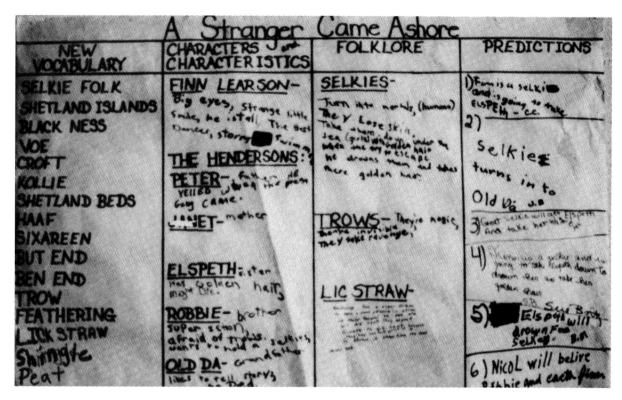

A fifth-grade teacher made a graphic organizer to help fifth graders with the clues, Scottish vocabulary, and folklore of Mollie Hunter's *A Stranger Came Ashore.*
Highland Park Elementary School, South-Western City Schools, Grove City, Ohio. Linda Charles, teacher.

events, to become sensitive to the language of the story-teller, and to "sound like a book." Older children also have the opportunity to practice their skills at summarizing as they negotiate what to tell or depict from longer stories and chapter books.

Graphic Organizers

A graphic organizer is a visual representation of an idea. For example, in Pat Hutchins's *Rosie's Walk*, an unsuspecting hen takes a walk through a farmyard followed by a fox who meets disaster every time he tries to catch Rosie. A map of the action would be a graphic organizer causing children to sequence the plot and discover that Rosie ends her journey in the place where it began.

Older children frequently use this kind of linear thinking to produce board games (see the "Games" section later in this chapter). On a large sheet of paper or posterboard, important events in a story are pictured in the order in which they happen. Seven- and 8-year-olds can map the action of Ron Roy's *Three Ducks Went Wandering* so that the ducks encounter the bull, the foxes, the hawk, and the snake before returning home to their mother. Other books in which the main character completes a journey include many folktales as well as

Colin McNaughton's *Suddenly!* Maurice Sendak's *Where the Wild Things Are*, Beatrix Potter's *The Tale of Peter Rabbit*, and *If You Give a Mouse a Cookie* by Laura Joffe Numeroff.

Semantic maps, attribute webs, or word webs often are used to help children group similar ideas into categories following a brainstorming session and display them to others. In these graphic organizers, a word or idea is placed at the center of a chart with spokes radiating toward related words, attributes, or other examples. One group listed "Outsiders in Literature" at the center of a semantic map and drew lines out to the various characters from novels who seem different from their peers. At the chart's center were clustered words describing insiders. Semantic maps are useful ways to categorize information of what a group knows. Sixth graders who are about to begin Russell Freedman's *Lincoln: A Photobiography* might brainstorm what they already know about Lincoln. Facts are then grouped and categorized on a chart, perhaps as "Early years," "What he looked like," "Famous speeches," "His family," "Assassination," and so forth. Word webs or semantic maps are also useful synthesizing aids for children who are organizing material from a variety of books and sources prior to writing a report. The webs that have been used throughout this book are examples of a kind of semantic mapping.

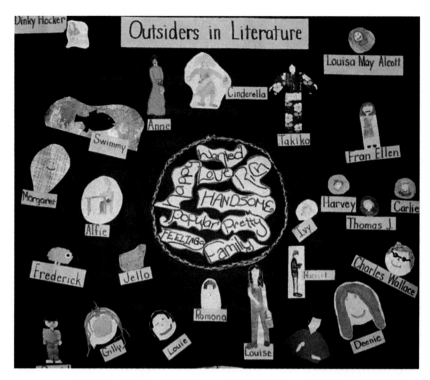

Fifth and sixth graders made a type of sociogram to identify the "outsiders" in various stories. Personality traits that would make you an "insider" were written in the inner circle.
Ridgemont Elementary School, Mt. Victory, Ohio. Sheryl Reed and Peggy Harrison, teachers.

Venn diagrams consisting of two or more intersecting circles can be used in various ways—for instance, to compare different versions of a folktale, to compare two characters that are central to a novel, or to compare two or more books with a similar theme. A more spacious graphic organizer for comparing two things, however, might be a single list of similarities at the top of a chart and a dividing line underneath so that differences can be listed side by side.

Comparison charts have been used as tools for organizing talk and thought, too. One teacher asked a group of children who had read many novels by Betsy Byars to discuss how they are similar. Midway through the conversation children had raised such points as "The parents are never around," "The main character is usually about our age," and "Some big problem is always there." The teacher then helped children generate a chart with the titles of Byars's books, such as *The Night Swimmers*, *Cracker Jackson*, and *The Pinballs*, placed top-to-bottom on the left side of a large sheet of paper. Across the top of the chart, the children generated categories, such as "Where the Parents Are," "About the Main Character," "Big Problems," and "Who Helps and How." Now that the conversation was well under way, the graphic organizer helped children focus and continue the discussion while they filled in the grid they had created on the chart. Later, other Byars books were added, such as *The Summer of the Swans* and *The House of Wings*, which

children also read to see how they fit the pattern. Children created artwork that represented some of the categories and wrote about how the books were alike and different. These were matted and hung next to the comparison chart. This activity helped the children analyze particular stories, synthesize several stories, and evaluate later readings. From the chart, they were able to generalize about the books by one author, a sophisticated skill for 10- and 11-year-olds.

Videos and Computers

Movie making is not an easy task, but video cameras have given more children a chance to experience this art. Choosing what scenes to portray and critiquing the performances give children a chance to look back at a story for important clues to characters' emotions and moods before they take on the roles. Yvonne Anderson's informative book *How to Make Your Own Animated Movies and Videotapes* describes her work with children aged 5 to 18 in creating films. In *Making Your Own Movies*, Harry Helfman gives hints on how to operate a simple, inexpensive movie camera and presents some basic techniques for shooting a film. A description of panning a picture is given, along with ways to vary the length of the shot. Considering the time involved in making movies, a teacher might want to work with someone knowledgeable in the field.

Children created a visual representation of the important events in Bonnie's Pryor's *The House on Maple Street*.
Wickliffe Alternative School, Upper Arlington, Ohio.

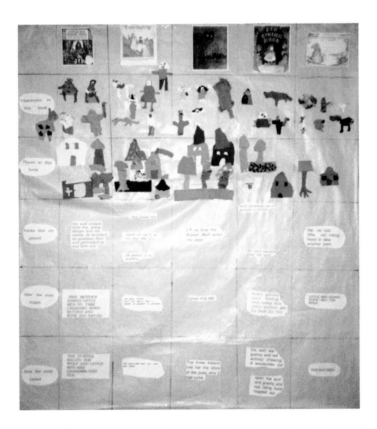

A group of primary children read five folktales and constructed a comparison chart to show similarities and differences among the stories.
Wickliffe Alternative School, Upper Arlington, Ohio.

Resources for Teaching
Books About Quilts and Stitchery

Title, Author	Grade Level	Type/Origin
Dawn (Bang)	1–3	Literary folktale
The Josefina Story Quilt (Coerr)	K–3	American pioneer
Tonight Is Carnaval (Dorros)	1–3	Illustrated with *arpilleras* sewn by the Club de Madres Virgen del Carmen of Lima, Peru
Sam Johnson and the Blue Ribbon Quilt (Ernst)	K–3	American pioneer
The Patchwork Quilt (Flournoy)	1–3	Contemporary African American
Osa's Pride (Grifalconi)	1–4	African (Cameroon)
Luka's Quilt (Gubak)	1–4	Contemporary Hawaiian
Sweet Clara and the Freedom Quilt (Hopkinson)	2–5	African American, pre–Civil War
The Canada Geese Quilt (Kinsey-Warnock)	3–6	Contemporary fiction
The Rag Coat (Mills)	1–4	Appalachian
Eight Hands Round: A Patchwork Alphabet (Paul)	2–6	Nonfiction
The Seasons Sewn (Paul)	2–6	Nonfiction
The Keeping Quilt (Polacco)	1–4	Jewish/family history
Tar Beach (Ringgold)	2–5	African American/family history
Patchwork Tales (Roth and Phang)	1–3	Family history
Sewing Quilts (Turner)	1–4	American pioneer

Computer technology presents children with an ever-increasing variety of ways to respond to books. After reading Zilpha Keatley Snyder's *Cat Running* and Jerry Stanley's *Children of the Dust Bowl* about migrant workers in California during the Great Depression, several fifth-grade children worked with the school's computer specialist to create a documentary that explored the Great Depression. They prepared a CD-ROM program that included pictures of migrant workers, the dust bowl, fruit packing labels, and depression-era songs that served as an important backdrop for understanding some of the books' themes and connected children to larger issues of this era of twentieth-century history.

Making Things

Many stories invite exploration through such activities as stitchery, constructions, games, and cooking. Children take great delight in making things in response to books, and such projects allow them to experience the events and situations in books more intensely.

Sewing

Even very young children are intrigued with stitchery. Once they have mastered a few simple stitches, such as the running stitch or the hem stitch, they are able to sew together outlines of characters from books like David McPhail's *Pig Pig Grows Up* or Tomie de Paola's *Big Anthony and the Magic Ring*. These can be stuffed with newspapers for a large character gallery display. Eve Rice's *Peter's Pockets* presents enterprising Mama who sews six pockets on Peter's pocketless pants and saves the day. Primary children could sew a cloth pocket shape on a construction paper pair of pants or decorate a pair of pants in the dress-up corner as Mama did.

Quiltmaking has long been a way to conserve materials, save the past, and share the making of things. While we often identify quilts with pioneer women, quilts and the art of stitchery appear in many settings.[4] The stories listed in the Resources for Teaching box "Books About Quilts and Stitchery" suggest that children could make small quilts with patterns and materials significant to them. Quilted squares might be displayed with writing that explains the material choice, the pattern choice, or other features. While a bound quilt of squares made by a whole class is a stunning presentation, children do not then get to keep their creations.

In place of stitchery, many teachers let children design quilt blocks drawn on paper with special crayons that transfer when the child's drawing is reversed and ironed onto fabric. Other products such as "liquid embroidery" may be applied directly onto the cloth.

[4]See Mary Lou Burket's article "Quilts" in *Book Links* (May 1991) for an informative annotated bibliography of picture books, fiction, and nonfiction in which quilts play a significant role.

A study of Faith Ringgold's *Tar Beach* led first graders to make a class quilt.
PS 116, New York, New York. Ilana Dubin-Spiegel, teacher.

Crafts and Construction

Press-on interfacing can be used to fix materials to wall hangings or banners, and children can then sew on felt, buttons, lace, beads, or other materials. Quilts, banners, and hangings that reflect a theme the class has studied, such as favorite books, Mother Goose rhymes, "Pioneers," or "Things from the beach," make a unifying end project. Children will then also be able to use the books they have studied for sources of artistic inspiration. The Teaching Feature on quiltmaking shows how a second-grade teacher used quiltmaking to help her students synthesize their understandings in their study of Mexico.

Crafts and Construction

Making things by crafts and construction satisfies a child's natural inclination to be active. Second and third graders read books that feature dragons, such as Kenneth Grahame's *The Reluctant Dragon*, Jane Yolen's *Dove Isabeau*, Jay Williams's *Everyone Knows What a Dragon Looks Like*, Margaret Leaf's *Eyes of the Dragon*, and Margaret Hodges' *Saint George and the Dragon*. They then constructed their own versions of dragons, using such items as egg cartons for spiky spines, juice cans for stocky legs, and spools on a string for a whiplike tail. Once again, as these small groups of children collaborated on making their dragon, they gained valuable language experience in planning, discussion, negotiation, justification, and explication.

Many books that invite extension feature interesting houses. Older children have assembled a cement-block house from Robert C. O'Brien's *Mrs. Frisby and the Rats of NIMH*, a bark-surrounded house in the manner of the one Sam Gribley built in *My Side of the Mountain* by Jean Craighead George, or Baba Yaga's chicken-legged hut of Russian folktale fame. A group of second and third graders created a table on which were displayed three-dimensional houses of folktale characters from around the world. Children's written explanations of the constructions accompanied the display.

Often, making things helps child readers authenticate a book character's experience. Just as 7-year-old Ramona enjoyed making the "longest picture in the

Teaching Feature   Quiltmaking Helps Students Review Their Study of Mexico

A second-grade teacher who planned a short thematic unit on Mexico decided to make a quilt top as a culminating activity. The teacher had provided many experiences for the children to consider as she helped them choose appropriate images. She had read aloud such books as Verna Aardema's *Borreguita and the Coyote*, with illustrations by Petra Mathers, and Harriet Rohmer's *Uncle Nacho's Hat*, with illustrations by Veg Reisberg. From these, children chose a howling coyote and a sombrero. A third-grade expert on pyramids had visited the classroom to share parts of Leonard Everett Fisher's *Pyramid of the Sun—Pyramid of the Moon*. Children made clay pots and noted some of the clay figures in Betsy James's *The Dream Stair*. So clay pots, stepped architecture, and cactus decorated some squares. The rich colors of both Elisa Kleven's collage illustrations for *Abuela* by Arthur Dorros as well as Richard Jesse Watson's vibrant paintings for *The Dream Stair* by Betsy James encouraged children to work in bright and surprising colors.

They decided that the center square should be the Mexican flag and a map of the country. Children had read Jonah and Jeanette Winter's *Diego*, a picture-book biography of artist Diego Rivera. They were struck by the vivid patterned borders of geometric shapes, leaves, flowers, and animals that framed Jeanette Winter's pictures. So the 7-year-olds decided to frame their individual quilt squares with borders.

Each child produced a rough draft that was reviewed by others before she or he began to work on the cotton-and-polyester-blend fabric. Since the supply of fabric markers was small, only a few children could work on their squares at one time. This helped children resist the urge to copy. The teacher taped the fabric square to the table so the child could work without moving the square. Light pencil lines marked the edges of each child's borders so that the frame wouldn't wobble.

When the twenty squares were completed, the teacher asked children how they wanted to arrange them. They decided on three rows and laid out the squares only to discover that two were left over. After much discussion, one child suggested four rows of five squares, which satisfied everyone. Then children discussed whether the arrangement was visually pleasing. Some changed their squares to be by a friend's square; others moved their squares to create better color balance.

A parent volunteered to stitch the twenty squares together with sashing and alternating squares of bright turquoise and magenta print fabric and finished the quilt. It hung in the library media center as a reminder to the children of their study of Mexico. But to the teacher, the quilt was a reminder of her classroom community and of all of the activities that had been forerunners of this marvelous piece of work.

Marci El-Baba, second-grade teacher
George Mason Elementary School
and Rosalind Smith Daniels, quilter, Alexandria, Virginia

world" and old-fashioned tin-can stilts in *Ramona and Her Father* by Beverly Cleary, second graders are eager to replicate Ramona's pleasure by making their own stilts or pictures. Older children have created a memorial of paper-folded cranes to commemorate their reading of *Sadako and the Thousand Paper Cranes* by Eleanor Coerr.

In Ellen Jackson's *Brown Cow, Green Grass, Yellow Sun*, illustrated by Victoria Raymond, and Barbara Reid's *Two by Two*, the illustrations were made from modeling compounds. Children are fascinated with these lively forms and enjoy making pictures, figures for dioramas, and table displays from plasticine or other modeling compounds. While young children use clay as a modeling tool, older children are better able to plan and execute small pictures with this medium.[5]

Cooking

Teachers recognize the value of cooking in the classroom—the math concepts used in doubling a recipe, the reading skills involved in following directions, the social skills of working cooperatively, not to mention children's satisfaction in making something for others to enjoy. Cooking that starts from a book can enrich children's experiences with literature.[6]

Several collections of recipes reflect a literary genre, such as Beatrix Potter's *The Peter Rabbit and Friends Cookbook*. Karen Greene's health-conscious *Once upon a Recipe* alludes to many well-known children's books, with recipes such as "Princess Peas," "Curiouser and Curiouser Casserole," "Mowgli's Tiger Milk," and "Curious George Slush." Kate MacDonald's *The Anne of Green*

[5]See *Playing with Plasticine* by Barbara Reid (New York: William Morrow, 1989) for ideas on how to use this medium with children.

[6]For other ideas, see Jo Osborne, "A Cook's Tour of Children's Cookbooks," *School Library Journal* (February 1986): 28–29.

Gables Cookbook emphasizes Anne's favorite sweets, and each recipe is also accompanied by a quote and illustration. *The Wild, Wild Cookbook* and *Acorn Pancakes, Dandelion Salad, and 38 Other Wild Recipes* by Jean Craighead George tell readers how to prepare wild food as Sam Gribley did in George's *My Side of the Mountain.*

Several cookbooks would augment older children's reading of historical fiction. Barbara Walker's *The Little House Cookbook* features recipes for preparing all of the food that appears in the Laura Ingalls Wilder books. Quotes, historical notes, and Garth Williams's illustrations enliven the pages. In her collections of historical recipes, *Hunter's Stew and Hangtown Fry: What Pioneer America Ate and Why* and *Slumps, Grunts, and Snickerdoodles: What Colonial America Ate and Why,* Lila Perl explains how geography, history, and economics influenced what people ate. While historically authentic, the recipes in these collections use modern ingredients so teachers will not need to find a source for raccoon or skunk meat. All of these books are useful as supplements to American history and social studies as well.

Some books, such as Tomie de Paola's *The Popcorn Book* and *Pancakes for Breakfast* or Benjamin Darling's *Valerie and the Silver Pear,* include recipes at the end of the text. Making a cake with her Russian grandmother helps a little girl be brave during a thunderstorm in Patricia Polacco's *Thunder Cake.* Children would enjoy making their own cake after reading this story. Other books merely suggest to the imaginative reader a possible cooking extension. Young children have made their own sandwiches or soup after hearing Russell Hoban's *Bread and Jam for Frances* and Maurice Sendak's *Chicken Soup with Rice.*

Older students enjoy literary "Book Fares" in which each person brings to the potluck something suggested by a book. Gurgi's "munchings and crunchings" from Alexander's Prydain series, Carlie's "Famous Mayonnaise Cake" from Byars's *The Pinballs,* tea made from an herb that Mary Call Luther might have gathered in the Cleavers' *Where the Lilies Bloom,* and Meg's liverwurst and cream cheese sandwiches from L'Engle's Time Trilogy were some of the offerings at one party.

Cooking things with children based on stories they have read makes books memorable. Cooking gives children a reason to return to a story to check information and a chance to make the book character's experiences a part of their own. Children who follow a recipe practice valuable skills such as following directions, measuring, and doubling a recipe. Teachers can encourage authentic writing experiences as well by suggesting that children explain how something was made, the cooking problems they faced and how they overcame them, and where the idea for the recipe came from and how it was significant to the characters in the story.

Games

Games provide another means of extending children's knowledge of books and authors. In planning games, children return to books—attending to the sequence of events, learning to evaluate these events in terms of progress or setbacks for the characters, and reinterpreting aspects of the story. In creating games, children become problem solvers as they fit their literary knowledge into the pattern of the game or design new game patterns to fit their book choices. In the construction and playing of games, children satisfy a natural inclination to play with something of their own making. Games bring teachers and children together in the mutual enjoyment of books.

Often picture books suggest games children can repeat in their own play. For instance, *The Surprise Party* by Pat Hutchins shows what happens to Rabbit's message, "I'm having a party tomorrow," as it is whispered from animal to animal. Children have delighted in playing this "telephone game" in a circle after hearing this story. *Uncle Elephant* by Arnold Lobel shows his nephew how to pass the time on a trip by counting houses, trees, or telephone poles. This game can save a long class bus trip for tired first graders. The unnamed boy in Margarette S. Reid's *The Button Box* plays games with his grandmother's collections of buttons—sorting them into categories, imagining who used them, lining them up in patterns, and so on. Kindergartners would invent many of these same games if given a large box of buttons to play with. They might list different ways of classifying, such as color, size, and shape. They might discover buttons similar to the one Toad lost and the many his friends found in Arnold Lobel's story "A Lost Button" from *Frog and Toad Are Friends.*

Guessing games are fun for everyone. "Who Am I?" begins a riddle game: "I drive a very small motorcycle by saying Pb-bb-bb. Who am I?" (Ralph, the mouse in Beverly Cleary's *The Mouse and the Motorcycle*). "Twenty Questions" demands astute guessing by increasingly narrowing the field of possibilities. Older children quickly learn to ask selective questions like "Is it a fairy tale?" or "Does it take place in modern times?" before jumping to book titles or characters. Only yes-or-no questions may be asked. Crossword puzzles, if made by children, are also ways to get children to explore the various aspects of a book. However, word searches, even ones made by children, do little to send a reader back to a book and seem more like time-killing workbook exercises.

Children can be encouraged to construct *board games* or table games based on a single title or many titles. The basic game pattern of several players moving along a path toward a goal is familiar to most children. Players move forward by selecting a question card and answering

Children created a board game with rules based on the plot of *Big Anthony and the Magic Ring* by Tomie de Paola. Highland Park Elementary School, South-Western City Schools, Grove City, Ohio.

correctly, by following directions on the board or the card, or by rolling dice or spinning a wheel. The game may be made more interesting by the addition of chance cards or choices of routes to the goal. Part of the fun of game making is choosing the game model, designing the playing pieces, deciding on spinners, cards, or dice for movement, and constructing the playing board.

A group of students created a game from Thomas Rockwell's *How to Eat Fried Worms*. A pot of plastic worms provided penalties for landing on certain squares, and the player who reached the finish with the fewest number of worms won the game. Other children created a game and rules based on the plot of *Big Anthony and the Magic Ring* by Tomie de Paola. It is helpful if game players know the book, so that clues, rewards, and penalties will be understood. However, after playing the game, children unfamiliar with the book are often motivated to read it.

Card games based on the pair pattern of Old Maid or the fours pattern of Go Fish allow children to classify book titles, synthesize information across titles, or extract similar information from individual titles. Pairs of Mother Goose characters ("Bo Peep and her sheep"; "Jack Horner and a Plum") or an author or illustrator and a book title are some of the possibilities for card games. Using folktales, children might make groups of four cards starting with these categories: magical objects, magical people, tales from a particular country, flying things, famous witches, giants, and so forth. Older children might pick a category such as survival stories and include four categories across thirteen titles for a full deck. Categories might include who survives, the book title and author, and two key items or elements from the story. "Brian," "in *Hatchet* by Gary Paulsen," "a hatchet," and "a moose" would be one example.

Children practice many skills in constructing their own games, such as categorizing their reading, recalling facts across a genre, making what they know fit a new pattern, or synthesizing and following through on a complicated set of plans. Games, of course, also need written directions for playing and, if they are displayed, a description of the source of the game or an explanation of how and by whom it was made. It is important for teachers to remember that the purpose of making and playing the games is to stimulate children's thinking and willingness to read, not to hasten mastery of isolated details from literature.

Singing and Movement in the Classroom

Children often enjoy singing to picture-book versions of well-known songs. They can also interpret literature by composing music or creating a dance. These activities help them think more carefully about the mood of a story or poem and to consider their emotional responses to books more thoroughly.

Picture-Book Editions of Single Songs

Among the many values of songbooks in the classroom is their use as predictable and familiar reading material (see Chapter 4). In recent years, there have been numerous fine picture-book interpretations of well-known songs, including *Skip to My Lou*, *The Lady with the Alligator Purse*, and *There's a Hole in the Bucket*, all illustrated by Nadine Bernard Westcott. Music is included in each of Westcott's books. Other musically derived picture books for young children feature familiar counting songs, such as John Langstaff's *Over in the Meadow*. To children who already know the song, the text of these books presents easy and enjoyable reading.

Songs that follow a cumulative pattern challenge singers to remember the order in which events occur. Aliki's *Hush, Little Baby* and Nadine Westcott's *I Know an Old Lady Who Swallowed a Fly* are good candidates for felt board or box-movie storytelling aids. If children help to create these, they are less likely to get lost in the song.

Many familiar folksongs have been researched and presented in authentic historic detail by such illustrators as Peter Spier and Aliki. Spier presents *The Star-Spangled Banner* and *The Erie Canal* with historical background so that the songs almost become an informational book, too. These various editions are a good way to make American history come alive as children are introduced to many folksongs that are a part of the American folk tradition. Aliki's illustrations for *Hush, Little Baby* and *Go Tell Aunt Rhody* reflect early American art in quilt-patterned endpapers and the paint-on-boards method of early limner painters.

In addition to the classroom extensions suggested, children may enjoy making their own book versions of other traditional songs like "Home on the Range," "Where Have All the Flowers Gone," or "Old Dan Tucker." Scott R. Sanders has invented details and told his own stories for twenty folksongs in *Hear the Wind Blow: American Folk Songs Retold.* Some of these long and often funny stories would inspire fifth and sixth graders' imaginations.

Matching Music and Literature

The process of identifying appropriate music to accompany prose and poetry selections helps children appreciate mood and tone in both literature and music. Second graders discussed the kind of music that could accompany the action of Maurice Sendak's *Where the Wild Things Are.* They recognized and created music with increasing tempo and volume, followed by a quiet conclusion of the story. Older children might enjoy reading one of Jack Prelutsky's *Nightmares* poems to music of their own choosing. A teacher might let children listen to Edvard Grieg's "In the Hall of the Mountain King" or Richard Wagner's "Valkyries' Ride" and ask children which of Prelutsky's poems best suit these pieces.

Many themes of subjects featured in literature have counterparts in music. For instance, the quiet awakening of the day in *Dawn* by Uri Shulevitz might be compared to the "Sunrise" movement from the *Grand Canyon Suite* by Ferde Grofé or to Cat Stevens's rendition of Eleanor Farjeon's poem "Morning Has Broken." Teachers can encourage older students to develop their sensitivity to recurring themes in art by juxtaposing literature and music. Other suggestions are given in Chapter 8.

Composing Music

Poetry can be set to music as children create melody and identify the rhythmical elements. One group of talented 7-year-olds composed music to accompany their own sad tale of a princess who was captured during a battle and taken from her palace. Her knight-in-arms wandered the lonely countryside in search of her, while the poor princess grieved for him in her prison tower. The children made up a musical theme for each of the main characters, which they repeated during the various movements of their composition. The story was first told to their classmates and then the song was played on the

autoharp and glockenspiel. Older students composed a three-movement rhythmical symphony for Ged in Ursula K. Le Guin's *A Wizard of Earthsea.* A recorder repeated Ged's theme in appropriate places in this percussion piece. When literature provides the inspiration for children's musical compositions, children's appreciation for both literature and music will be enriched.

Movement and Literature

Increasing attention has been given to children's control of their own body movements. The relationship between thought and movement has received much attention, particularly in England. Basic rhythmical movements might be introduced through Mother Goose rhymes. For example, children could walk to "Tommy Snooks and Bessie Brooks," gallop to "Ride a Cock Horse," jump to "Jack Be Nimble," and run to "Wee Willie Winkie." Nursery rhymes could also motivate dramatic action with such verses as "Hickory Dickory Dock," "Three Blind Mice," and "Jack and Jill."

A favorite poem for young children to move to is "Holding Hands" by Lenore M. Link, which describes the slow ponderous way that elephants walk. By way of contrast, Evelyn Beyer's poem "Jump or Jiggle" details the walk of frogs, caterpillars, worms, bugs, rabbits, and horses. It provides a wonderful opportunity for children to develop diverse movements. Both poems can be found in Jack Prelutsky's *Read-Aloud Rhymes for the Very Young.* In Jean Marzollo's *Pretend You're a Cat,* a longer poem that Jerry Pinkney illustrates as a picture book, Pinkney's watercolors portray twelve animals and, on the facing pages, children pretending to walk, wiggle, or jump like those particular animals. Children also enjoy making the hand motions and sounds for *We're Going on a Bear Hunt* by Michael Rosen, as the adventurous family goes through a river, "Splash, splosh."

As children learn basic movements, they can use them in different areas of space, at different levels, and at different tempos. Swinging, bending, stretching, twisting, bouncing, and shaking are the kinds of body movements that can be made by standing tall, at a middle position, or by stooping low. For example, "A Swing Song" by William Allingham could be interpreted by swinging, pushing motions that vary in speed according to the words in the poem. Other poetry that suggests movement includes "Stop, Go" by Dorothy Baruch, "The African Dance" by Langston Hughes, and "The Potatoes' Dance" by Vachel Lindsay. All of these poems can be found in *Favorite Poems Old and New* by Helen Ferris.

Children who have had this kind of experience are ready to create rhythmical interpretations of a longer story. *May I Bring a Friend?* by Beatrice Schenk de

Regniers, *Where the Wild Things Are* by Maurice Sendak, and *Koala Lou* by Mem Fox are examples of stories that lend themselves to rhythmical interpretations.

Connecting Literature and Life

Children sometimes have difficulty picturing life in other times or places or understanding historical time. They can experience books more completely through making maps and timelines and by compiling special collections. Children who thus ask questions about the details and events in literature are also introduced to methods of inquiry and research.

Artifacts and Collections

Items or artifacts mentioned in books often seem strange to children, even if explained in context. A child who reads that Ma Ingalls cooked prairie dinners in a spider would be puzzled until she could see this three-legged pan in a reference such as *Colonial Life* by Bobbie Kalman. Hefting a modern-day cast-iron replica would give a child a sense of the endurance of these utensils. This object, although a small part of the story, nonetheless connects reader experience with a part of the real world.

A class collection could involve children in assembling book-related artifacts on a large scale. Second graders studying pioneers, for example, made and collected items that pioneers might have taken west with them: such as a wooden spoon, a cornhusk doll, a flour sack, or a wagon wheel. As the teacher read aloud *Trouble for Lucy* by Carla Stevens, children added to the display their facsimiles of the wagon master's log, a bouquet of wildflowers gathered by those who walked beside the moving wagons, and a "letter" from Marcus Whitman detailing his experiences with the wagon train. Labels were made for each article as it was added to the display.

Maps and Time Lines

Often authors of books with historical settings include a geographical map to help the reader locate the story setting. In *Araminta's Paint Box* by Karen Ackerman, a map shows two routes—the route a pioneer girl took to California, and the route her paint box took after she lost it. Other stories make sufficient reference to actual places so that children can infer a story location by carefully comparing the story and a contemporary map. One group of fourth graders found on a road map the probable route Ann Hamilton took in the 1780s when she walked across Pennsylvania in Jean Fritz's *The Cabin Faced West*. The movement of the Wilder family in the Little House books by Laura Ingalls Wilder can be followed on a map. Many fictional and biographical accounts of immigrants can be traced on world maps.

As with many of the previous activities or projects in this chapter, maps, too, can help children look across a genre. The sources of folktales might be identified on a world map. The domains of tall-tale heroes and monsters might be located on a U.S. map. African folktales, fiction, and nonfiction might be located on a map of Africa as a way of differentiating features and regions of that continent. Children need many encounters with maps and their working parts (key, symbols, scale, direction) before they become skilled users of all that a map can reveal.

Older children often enjoy making detailed maps of imaginary "countries of the mind," such as that in Lloyd Alexander's *The Remarkable Journey of Prince Jen* or his Prydain in *The Book of Three*, Ursula K. Le Guin's archipelagos in *A Wizard of Earthsea*, or Brian Jacques's Mossflower Woods surrounding *Redwall*. While fantasy provides ample opportunities for children to design their own maps imaginatively, other genres of books can be mapped as well.

The concept of time is difficult for children to grasp until sometime near the end of the concrete operational stage of thinking or the beginning of formal operations (ages 11 to 12). Prior to this period, time lines may help students organize events in a person's life as represented in a book. Time lines also allow children to represent a synthesis of events in several books. A time line from Jean Fritz's *And Then What Happened, Paul Revere?* might include the date of Paul Revere's birth, the date he took over his father's business, the summer he spent in the army, his famous ride, and his death in 1818. Events in the lives of Revere's contemporaries, such as Benjamin Franklin or George Washington, might be more easily compared if they were placed on a time line of the same scale as Revere's.

Placing book events in the world's time challenges even sophisticated readers to select relevant events in both the book and human history. A three-strand time line allows children to separate groups or types of events from others. While *Friedrich*, Hans Peter Richter's story of a Jewish boy caught in pre–World War II Germany, contains a "chronology" of dates in a reference at the back of the book, students might represent selected governmental decrees on one stratum of a time line. A second stratum might represent the number of Jews living in the Third Reich according to yearly censuses. A third stratum might list important

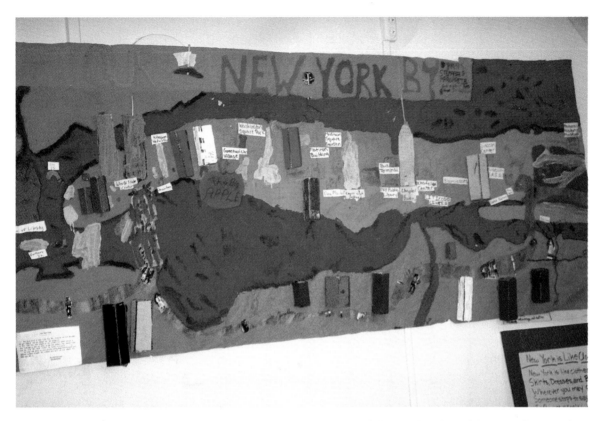

After reading Kathy Jakobsen's *My New York,* fourth graders created a map of the city that showed their own favorite places in the city.
PS 124, New York, New York. Mary S. Gallivan, teacher.

events in Friedrich's life. In this way children could see more clearly the political events against which Friedrich's tragic life was played out.

In making time lines, children need to agree on a scale so that events can be clearly shown—by year or by decade, for instance. Time lines can be made of string from which markers for events and years are hung. If children make time lines on a long roll of paper, entries can be written on cards or Post-it notes and placed temporarily along the line. In this way, corrections or realignments can be made easily.

Jackdaws

The term *jackdaw* comes from the British name for a relative of the crow that picks up brightly colored objects and carries them off to its nest. Commercially prepared jackdaw collections are sometimes available from museums and historical sites. These collections, based on an historical event or period, often include facsimile copies of diaries, letters, newspaper articles, advertisements, and other evidence from the time.

Teachers of elementary school children have modified this concept to suit activities and discussion with younger children. These teacher-made collections assemble resource materials that the teacher and children can handle in discussion, in display, or in actual construction and use. A jackdaw for Yoshiko Uchida's *Journey to Topaz,* for example, might include maps of the western United States on which children could locate the camps in which this Japanese American family was imprisoned in World War II. The jackdaw might also include photocopies of newspaper headlines of the time, relevant articles from that period from magazines such as *Time* and *Colliers,* a facsimile copy of one of the exclusion orders families were handed, and information about the author. Articles and documents that could accompany Laurence Yep's *Dragonwings* include reproductions of photographs of turn-of-the-century San Francisco's Chinatown, photographs of contemporary newspaper accounts of Chinese-built airplanes, a kite like the one Moon Shadow flew, and some green tea. Often sources for the factual material on which an historical fiction title is based are given in an author's note. Some jackdaws can then include copies of these

Resources for Teaching
Making a Jackdaw

Each book will suggest its own specific items or references to collect. Here is a more general list of things that might be included.

- Recipes from the book's time (a typical dinner; a menu for a celebration)
- Price lists of commonly purchased goods then and now (milk, shoes, a dozen eggs, a car)
- A time line of the book's events
- A time line of the period surrounding the book's events
- A map, actual or imagined, of the setting

- A letter, diary, log, or news article that could have been written by or about a book character
- A photocopy of an actual book-related news article or document
- Artwork from the period (painting, architecture, sculpture)
- Songs, music, or dances from the book's setting (sheet music or lyrics, tapes)
- Clothes of characters of the period (paper dolls, catalog format, collage)
- Something about the author of the book
- A list of other fiction or nonfiction references

actual source materials or "facsimiles" can be created by the children. All materials can be placed in an appropriately decorated portfolio or box. The Resources for Teaching box "Making a Jackdaw" suggests some of the items that might be included in a jackdaw. Individual book titles will suggest other artifacts that children could include.

Helping children make connections between literature and their own experiences is an important teacher role. However, teachers need to recognize when enough is enough. After a six-week study of Laura Ingalls Wilder's *Farmer Boy,* one fifth grader said, "I hate this book." If teachers' first priority is to foster children's love of reading, they will be less likely to overburden children with factual inquiry. Teachers who appreciate the child's desire to know as a prior condition of learning can appreciate Louise Rosenblatt's criterion for the usefulness of background information: "it will have value only when the student feels the need of it and when it is assimilated into the student's experience of particular literary works."[7]

Extending Literature Through Drama

Books become more real to children as they identify with the characters through creative drama. Young children begin this identification with others through *dramatic play.* A 5-year-old engaged in impromptu play might become an airplane zooming to the airport built

of blocks; another assumes the role of mother in the playhouse. Sometimes children of this age will play a very familiar story without adult direction. For example, "The Three Billy Goats Gruff" and "The Three Bears" are often favorites. Dramatic play represents this free response of children as they interpret experience.

In schools this type of natural response can find an outlet in activities that are part of a Creative Drama program. Creative Drama is structured and cooperatively planned playmaking, an approach to learning that focuses on processes rather than production. While occasionally a play developed creatively will be shared with others, the value of creative drama lies in the process of playing and does not require an audience. Creative drama activities exist on a continuum from interpretation to improvisation and can include pantomime, story dramatization, improvisation, reader's theater, and puppetry. All of these activities provide important ways for children to reenter the world of a book, to consider the characters, events, problems, and themes that are central in good literature. Such engagement brings children joy and zest in learning and living while broadening their understandings of both literature and life.

Pantomime

Pantomime is a useful form in beginning creative drama. In preparation for acting out Leo Lionni's story *Frederick,* a group of 6-, 7-, and 8-year-olds pantomimed the role of the mice. They scurried and scuttled about the room, busily gathering their winter supplies. Later, the role of Frederick was added, and again all the rest of the children played at being mice. Only after the children had thought about their roles as mice was dialogue included. Children might also pantomime small

A group of 7-year olds dance "The Wild Rumpus" after hearing Sendak's *Where the Wild Things Are*.
West LaFayette Public Schools, Indiana. Nancy Sawrey, teacher.

portions of a scene in order to understand and feel a character more deeply. For example, a group of 9-year-olds pretended they were the evil witch from "Snow White." They pantomimed waking up in the morning and then standing before a mirror to ask the well-known question "Who is the fairest in the land?" Pantomime can be an essential step in the development of believable creative drama with children.

Story Theater is a form of pantomime in which a narrator reads a story aloud while children take the role of characters and act out the unfolding tale. Books that have a lot of action or emotional reaction make the best candidates for story theater. The teacher or librarian might read aloud *The Turnip* by Katherine Milhous and Alice Dalgliesh, while six children pantomime being the old man, the old woman, the little granddaughter, the dog, the calico cat, and the mouse. As the children gain confidence with this kind of drama, the teacher can stop at appropriate points when the old man calls to his wife and invite the designated child to create the dialogue. Moving from pantomime to the extemporaneous dialogue is an easy transition to more complex forms of story reenactment.

Dramatizing Stories

The first step in dramatizing narratives is the selection of a good story to read or tell to children. Children can help decide what characters are essential to the story, what scenes need to be played, and where. Many teachers and librarians have their favorite stories for dramatizing. However, we suggest some titles here as particularly good starters.

Very young children aged 3 through 5 will become involved in dramatic play, but they usually do not have the sustained attention to act out a complete story. They might play a part of a favorite folktale (for example, crossing the bridge as in "The Three Billy Goats Gruff") but they seldom will complete a whole story. And no one should expect them to.

Primary-grade children enjoy playing simple stories such as the funny tale *Nine-in-One Grr! Grr!* by Blia Xiong or *Tricky Tortoise* by Mwenye Hadithi and Adrienne Kennaway. Folktales are also a rich source of dramatization. They are usually short and have plenty of action, a quick plot, and interesting characters. A favorite is *Stone Soup* by Marcia Brown. This is the story of three jovial French soldiers who trick an entire village into providing them with the ingredients for soup, which the soldiers claim to have made from three large stones. The story naturally divides into three parts—the first scene with the soldiers approaching the village; the making of the soup, with the villagers' help of course; and the last scene when the soldiers leave. Children can decide which scenes they want to play first. Usually they like to play the part where the stone soup is made. With some preliminary discussion of the characters of the soldiers and the villagers, the children may decide who will provide certain ingredients for the soup. Discourage them from actually bringing carrots or barley; instead, ask them to describe their contributions so others can almost smell and taste them. If the action lags, the teacher may enter the play and add a particularly nice morsel of beef, for example, telling how she just happened to have found one piece stored in the cellar.

The playing may stop at an agreed-upon signal, such as "I never thought I'd live to see the day when you could make soup out of stones" and the soldiers' reply, "It's all in knowing how!" Following the evaluation period in which the teacher points out some of the good features of the playing (for example, "I liked the way George showed us he was an old man by the way he leaned on his cane" or "How could you tell Ann was cutting carrots?"), the teacher can ask children to tell what they noticed about individual interpretations. Additions to the playing can be discussed and the play then repeated with another group.

Stories from myths, such as "Pandora's Box" or "King Midas' Touch," are fine material for 9- to 11-year-olds to dramatize. Middle-grade children also enjoy presenting parts of books to each other in the form of debates, interviews, or discussions or television talk shows. A group of sixth graders debated one of the issues raised in Alexander Key's science fiction novel *The Forgotten Door:* "Resolved: The boy Jon should be turned over to military intelligence." Three children on either side raised important issues of individual rights and national security in the course of the dialogue. A group of students played the roles of various characters in Natalie Babbitt's *Tuck Everlasting* and were interviewed by another student who took the role of a television talk-show host. They told about their own roles in the events that had taken place and voiced advantages and disadvantages of Winnie's living forever if she chose to drink water from a magic spring. Teachers can help children focus on important and complex issues that characters face in literature by providing these opportunities to explore ideas. This exploration is often a precursor of children's developing ability to discover themes in literature or factors that influence characters to change.

Improvisation

Improvisation takes children beyond a story to the creation of a new situation. For example, in one kindergarten, children heard several versions of "Goldilocks and the Three Bears." The teacher assumed the role of a neighbor reporting that Goldilocks's mother was very concerned because her daughter hadn't come home. The children said they knew where she was and then retold the story. The next day, the teacher became a detective and said she had been hired by Goldilocks's mother because the child still hadn't returned home. In the role of detectives, the children brainstormed what information they would need to create missing-person posters for the lost girl: name, picture, age, and birthday. The children paired up to make their posters. At their third meeting, the children created a map of the forest on which they placed imaginary clues such as an apple

with a bite out of it, or a trail of pebbles, which Goldilocks could have left. The teacher provided a letter saying, "I am looking for a block parent," and a willing parent played the role, saying yes, indeed, Goldilocks had come to her house tired and hungry. But she knew her own phone number, so her mother had come for her and all was well. The next day, there was a thank-you note from Goldilocks to the detectives. The teacher reported that the children extended their play through this drama for weeks.[8]

Improvisation had allowed these children to imagine an event beyond a story and play it out. Improvisation can be used in all curricular areas. It could involve a meeting between Columbus and a native spokesperson, each reacting to the other, for instance. Dorothy Heathcote, a British educator, has been most successful in using improvisation to help children expand their understanding of life experiences, to recreate the past, or to imagine the future.[9] She frequently "frames" a situation, suggesting, for example, that children who are in the midst of studying pioneer life have just been given a large sum of money to establish an outdoor museum devoted to portraying life in a frontier village. The children then must plan what they will exhibit, how to make it authentic, where to obtain artifacts, and so forth. This invariably sends them back to books to find answers to the questions they have posed.

Improvisation also allows children to explore points of view of characters who may be underrepresented in literature. Older children might take on the roles of the Native Americans who appear in several scenes in Pam Conrad's *Prairie Songs.* An improvisation would allow them to create a dialogue with the white settlers, explaining their views and feelings at being displaced by this new culture. The two groups might then come to some understanding about ways to live together peacefully, an outcome that did not occur in reality but that is made possible through creative drama.

Readers' Theater

Teachers who are hesitant to try drama in their classroom might well begin with readers' theater, which involves a group of children in reading a play, a story, or a poem. Children are assigned to read particular parts. After reading through their parts silently, children read the text orally.

---

[8]Jean Sperling, "And She Jumped Out of the Window Never to Be Seen Again," *Literacy Matters* (Ohio State University, Martha L. King Language and Literacy Center) 1, no. 1 (winter 1989): 4–8.

[9]For a greater picture of this educator's influence, see *Dorothy Heathcote: Collected Writings on Education and Drama,* ed. Liz Johnson and Cecily O'Neill (Portsmouth, N.H.: Heinemann, 1984).

Children thoroughly enjoy participating in readers' theater; even though they do not create the dialogue, as they do in improvisation or drama, they do interpret the character's personalities and the mood of the story. They also interact with each other in a kind of play form. The story provides the script, which makes it easy to try in the classroom.

In adapting a story for readers' theater, teachers or students must edit the text to omit phrases like *he said* and *she replied*. A child narrator needs to read the connecting prose between dialogue. Older children can write their own introductions and decide whether to leave out long descriptive passages or summarize them. Many teachers have found it useful to duplicate the parts of the story that children will read. This way, children can highlight their own parts and cross out unnecessary words.

The most effective readers' theater selections contain a lot of dialogue. Folktales are easily adapted for primary children. Some good choices would be Stephen Butler's *Henny Penny*, Paul Galdone's *The Little Red Hen,* or Joanne Oppenheim's *You Can't Catch Me!*— a tale similar to "The Gingerbread Boy." At first the teacher might read the narrator's part and let children take the different roles. When children become more capable readers and have had practice with readers' theater, they can take over the role of narrator.

Older students might use just a chapter of a story for readers' theater. The first chapter of Katherine Paterson's *The Great Gilly Hopkins*, where Gilly is being driven to her fourth foster home by the social worker, makes a wonderful scene for readers' theater. The third chapter of *Sarah, Plain and Tall* by Patricia MacLachlan can be adapted for readers' theater. This is where Caleb and Anna are waiting for the arrival of Sarah. Her actual arrival and her giving the children her gifts from the sea could be included as a second part.

Readers' theater also works for some poetry. Poems that include conversation, such as Karla Kuskin's "Where Have You Been, Dear?" or "The Question," found in her collection *Dogs & Dragons, Trees & Dreams*, have been successfully interpreted in this way. Children reading Mollie Hunter's *The Mermaid Summer* might also wish to read "Overheard on a Saltmarsh," the conversation between a nymph and a goblin about a necklace of green glass beads. This is in Isabel Wilner's collection *The Poetry Troupe*, which includes many poems for choral reading and readers' theater.

Puppetry

Many children will lose themselves in the characterization of a puppet while hidden behind a puppet stage even though they might hesitate to express ideas and feelings in front of the class. Through puppetry, children learn to project their voices and develop facility in varying their voice quality to portray different characters. For example, a rather quiet, shy child might use a booming voice as he becomes the giant in "Jack and the Beanstalk." Puppetry also facilitates the development of skills in arts and crafts. Problems of stage construction, backdrops for scenery, and the modeling of characters provide opportunities for the development of creative thinking. A well-played puppet show extends children's appreciation and interpretation of stories and makes literature a more memorable experience for them.

Beginning in kindergarten with the construction of paper-bag or simple stick figures, children can gain pleasure from their involvement with puppetry. Materials and types of puppets will range from the simple to the complex, depending on age and the child.

The teaching techniques used in creative drama should be followed, as puppet plays are created cooperatively by children and teachers. It is highly recommended that children "play out" stories before using their puppets. Written scripts are not necessary and can prove very limiting. Playing the story creatively allows the child to identify with the characters before becoming involved with the creation and mechanical manipulation of the puppet.

Selecting Stories

The techniques of puppetry are most appropriate for certain stories. For example, a group of 7-year-olds presented a puppet show based on Rudyard Kipling's *The Elephant's Child*. At the appropriate moment the crocodile pulled the elephant's short stocking nose into the familiar elongated trunk. Such action would be nearly impossible for live actors to portray. Another group of 10-year-olds used marionettes to capture the hilarious action of the laughing-gas birthday party described in P. L. Travers's *Mary Poppins*. Again, this scene would be difficult to portray in any other dramatic form. Other stories that lend themselves to interpretation through puppetry are *The Amazing Bone* by William Steig, *The Fat Cat* by Jack Kent, *The Gingerbread Boy* by Paul Galdone, *Rosie's Walk* by Pat Hutchins, and *Frederick* and *Alexander and the Wind-Up Mouse* by Leo Lionni.

Constructing Puppets and Stages

Numerous books are available that tell children how to make puppets, marionettes, and stages. Young children enjoy making simple cardboard figures that can be stapled to sticks or to tongue depressors. Paper bags stuffed with old stockings or newspaper can be tied to represent a puppet head and body. Ears, hair, aprons, and so on, can be attached to create animals or people. By placing a hand in a sock or paper bag, the child can make the puppet appear to talk by moving fingers and thumb.

Finger puppets can easily be made with bodies of finger-sized cylinders stapled at the top. Faces may be glued to the cylinder top or painted on the cylinder itself. These simple puppets make fine storytelling aids for younger children.

A stage can be made by turning a table on its side. The puppeteer sits or kneels behind the tabletop. Another simple stage can be created by hanging curtains so they cover the lower and upper parts of a doorway. A table, cardboard, or side of a large box can also be placed in a doorway. This type of stage is particularly good because children waiting their turns at the side of the stage are hidden from view. Older children or parents can construct a framework for more durable puppet stages. The educational values of planning and creating a puppet show far outweigh the time and effort required to produce it.

Writing from Children's Books

Children's written work should grow out of their own rich experiences, whether with people, places, and things, research and observation, or literature. Children's writing about books may take many forms (see "Literature and the Writing Program" in Chapter 13).

Real possibilities for writing are all around us in the classroom; however, it is literature that gives children a sense of how the written word sounds and looks. Frank Smith suggests that the role of literature in the writing program is central:

> Reading seems to me to be the essential fundamental source of knowledge about writing, from the conventions of transcription to the subtle differences of register and discourse structures in various genres.[10]

When children have a chance to become writers themselves, they begin to notice how other authors work. Literature suggests the many forms that stories, information, or poetry can take; as children experiment with the model, they begin to develop a sensitivity to the conventions of the form. This awareness in turn allows them to bring a wider frame of reference to the reading and writing that follow.

Children in elementary classrooms should have an opportunity to experience a variety of well-written fiction, poetry, and nonfiction. At the same time they can be encouraged to develop an appreciation of language and form through writing. In this way, children develop a sensitivity to language, an increasing control over the power of words, and a diverse writing repertoire.

Developing Sensitivity to Language

Children's appreciation of the writing of others increases as they listen to many fine stories, read widely themselves, and have many opportunities to create their own stories and poems. A teacher can help children develop their skills in descriptive writing by helping them to become aware of the power of words in conveying sensory images. After a story has been finished, the teacher and children might reread and relish particularly enjoyable words, phrases, or paragraphs.

Children's use of sensory language in their writing requires many firsthand experiences of touching and feeling and savoring textures, sounds, colors, shapes, rhythms, and patterns. Literature, too, can sharpen sensitivity to nature, people, and relationships. Rich sensory imagery helps children "see" the world around them in new perspectives.

In George Ella Lyon's *Come a Tide*, the family stands on a bridge and watches parts of the neighbor's gardens, livestock, and household wash away as a spring storm makes the creek rise. When they return to their Kentucky holler, "Soggy furniture and mud-mapped rugs made mountains in front of each house." Lyon describes the noises, sights, and smells as people see their possessions emerging from the muck. When someone asks "What do we do now?" it is Grandma who says, "If it was me, I'd make friends with a shovel." By asking primary children to notice how Lyon's choice of "mud-mapped" and Grandma's pithy statement create pictures in our minds, teachers help children appreciate the ways authors work.

A child's interest in words begins in the cradle and proceeds into adulthood. A 3-year-old memorizes and repeatedly chants "Crash and clang!/Bash and bang! And up in the road the jazz-man sprang!" simply because he loves the way Eleanor Farjeon's words sound.[11] Older children read to each other the outrageous descriptions and wordplay of such Daniel Pinkwater titles as *Borgel* or *The Hoboken Chicken Emergency*.

Teachers can support children's natural fascination with words, wordplay, and word usage in many ways. A third-grade teacher read aloud and discussed William Steig's *Amos & Boris* with the children. Then

[10]Frank Smith, *Writing and the Writer* (New York: Holt, Rinehart & Winston, 1982), p. 177.

[11]Eleanor Farjeon, "Jazz-Man," in *Noisy Poems*, collected by Jill Bennett, illustrated by Nick Sharratt (New York: Oxford University Press, 1987), unpaged.

they wrote diary entries as if they were Amos the mouse or Boris the whale. This was a typical entry on that first day:

🐚 Dear Diary,

It was Tuesday two days after I saved Amos. We are just starting to be getting acquainted. Amos told me all about land, how I wish I could live on land. I wish we could meet sometime again.

by Boris

A participant-observer in the classroom then shared favorite expressions he had copied from the book. They included:

🐚 He loved to hear the surf sounds . . . the bursting breakers, the backwashes with rolling pebbles.

In a few minutes Boris was already in the water, with waves washing at him, and he was feeling the wonderful wetness.

"Amos, help me," said the mountain of a whale to the mote of a mouse.[12]

The next day children wrote a second diary entry. The contrast between their first writing and the second shows the influence of simply calling attention to Steig's rich use of language:

🐚 Dear Diary:

Well it's Tuesday and Amos built a ladder down the great tunnel, well, at least that's what Amos calls it. It really is my spout.

One day we had a feast. We had a fat juicy lobster, some plump juicy sea cucumbers, some meaty clams, and some sand-breaded fish. After that we were so full and tired we talked and talked and finally we went to sleep happy.

Well, Bye. Boris

Barrington Road School, grade 3
Upper Arlington, Ohio
Carolyn Fahrbach, teacher
Roy Wilson, Ohio State University participant-observer

All of the children showed a richer use of language in their second entries. Children seemed to use the first day of writing to master the diary form and to practice taking another point of view. The second day, however, they were ready to consider using language more succinctly and colorfully.

Certain books invite readers to play with language. Kindergartners were eager to make their own two-word rhymes after hearing examples like "Tan man," "Pink drink," and "Stuck truck" from Bruce McMillan's *One Sun: A Book of Terse Verse*. After reading Mary Ann Hoberman's *A House Is a House for Me*, first graders listed other possibilities for houses, including "Arms are houses for hugs" and "Buns are houses for hamburgers." Ruth Heller explores parts of speech in imaginative ways in books like *Many Luscious Lollipops: A Book About Adjectives*, while Jim Arnosky's *A Kettle of Hawks* and Brian Wildsmith's *Birds* call particular attention to collective nouns.

Idioms, similes, and figurative language contribute color to the language. A group of 7-year-olds who were studying the human body traced an outline of a classmate on butcher paper and wrote on this poster idioms about the human body they had collected, such as "broken-hearted," "down in the mouth," and "a green thumb." Marvin Terban explores idioms in two books, *In a Pickle* and *Mad as a Wet Hen*. Other of his titles examine palindromes, homonyms, and double words such as *superduper*. Tom Birdseye's *Airmail to the Moon* is full of the colloquial expressions of Ora Mae Cotton as she describes losing her tooth: she was "popcorn-in-the-pan excited" when it fell out, but when she thought somebody had stolen it, she vowed that if she caught them she would "open up a can of gotcha and send 'em airmail to the moon!" Teachers who expose children to the curious and colorful ways the English language conveys meanings will see children's writing change as they notice the use of colorful language in the books they read.

One fourth-grade teacher asked children to find interesting expressions from Sid Fleischman's *The Midnight Horse*. They made a chart that called attention to Fleischman's masterful wordplay:

The Book Says	*We Might Say*
A face as rough as moldy cheese	He had bad complexion, sort of greenish.
His eyes were drawn to a billfold like a compass needle to true north	He couldn't take his eyes off the billfold
A crying girl's eyes brightened like sudden blue sky when she saw the blacksmith.[13]	She liked him and stopped crying. It was like the sun was shining.

Children who have had experiences that sensitize them to figurative language and rich descriptive writing are much more likely to recognize the way fine writers such as Katherine Paterson, Russell Freedman, Virginia Hamilton, Bruce Brooks, or Nina Bawden use words.

---

[12]Excerpt from *Amos & Boris* by William Steig.

[13]Fleischman, *The Midnight Horse*, pp. 4, 12.

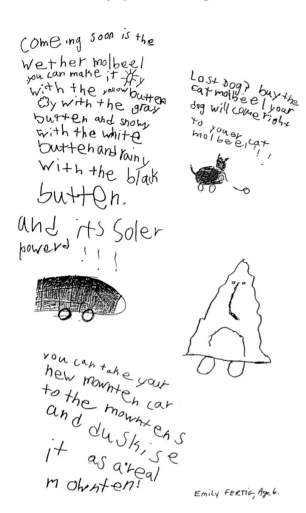

COMEing soon is the
Wether molbeel
you can make it Dy
with the yellowbutten
Cy with the gray
butten and snowy
with the white
butten and rainy
with the black
butten.
and its Soler
powerd ! ! !

Lost Dog? buy the
cat molbeel your
dog will come right
to your
molbeel, cat ! ! !

you can take your
new mownteh car
to the mowntehs
and duskise
it as a real
mownten!

Emily FERTIG, Age 6.

After reading the story *Uncle Wizzmo's New Used Car* by Rodney A. Greenblat, a 6-year-old drew pictures and wrote about other inventive car possibilities.

Single Books as Springboards

Stories with strong organizational patterns often free children from being overwhelmed by the complete set of writers' problems—what to write about and how to begin, organize, sustain an idea, and end. Teachers who invite children to borrow patterns from literature often help especially reluctant writers simply to get started, while they challenge more-able writers to go beyond what an author has created.

In Rodney A. Greenblat's *Uncle Wizzmo's New Used Car*, a used-car lot sells outlandish cars such as the "Fluffy," which looks like a bunny on wheels. This spurred one 6-year-old to design three cars and the advertising to sell them. Using this same book, a group of second graders designed their own mural of a used-car lot, drew cars, and wrote descriptions of what their cars could do.

Judith Viorst's *Alexander and the Terrible, Horrible, No Good, Very Bad Day* has long been a favorite of children from first grade through middle school. Older children especially are masterful portrayers of all that can go wrong in one day. Charlotte Zolotow's ironic *Someday* inspires children to consider the future both seriously and humorously with such ideas as "Someday . . . my brother will introduce me to his friends and say 'This is my sister,' instead of 'Here's the family creep.'" Margaret Wise Brown's *The Important Book* describes what is essential and important about things such as a flower. Young children have written their own definitions of the essence of certain things after hearing this read aloud; older children in fifth grade interviewed each other and wrote descriptions of what they thought was significant about each other. Each illustrated essay was bound in the class's "Important Book."

Byrd Baylor's *The Table Where Rich People Sit* helps readers consider the priceless gifts of the natural world. Children enjoy assigning monetary value to things that money can't buy, such as twenty thousand dollars to "feel the wind and smell the rain an hour before it really rains." Baylor's *Everybody Needs a Rock* gives the reader serious rules to consider in selecting favorite rocks. Children have added their own rules for rock selection, and others might follow the pattern, creating rules for selecting a special tree or shell. Children delight in marking their own special days after reading her *I'm in Charge of Celebrations*. A group of 9-year-olds listened to Baylor's *Your Own Best Secret Place* and talked about the many kinds of secret places people have. After the class discussion, one boy wrote a version of "My Own Best Secret Place" that described how he got to the place, what it felt like to be there, and how it looked:

My Own Best Secret Place

To get to my secret place you have to go down the basment [sic] steps turn right go in the door on the southwall turn left go up the ladder. Crawl in the big hole in the wall and there is my secret place. It feels good to be in my secret place becaus [sic] the cool air washs [sic] away all my troubles into the back of my head. I have a nice soft carpet that I sit on so the hard tough rocks on the floor don't irritate me. When I go in my secret place I turn on my light and read a book with my troubles tucked in the back of my head.

Barrington Road School, Upper Arlington, Ohio Marlene Harbert, teacher

Sometimes a particular book suggests a unique writing experience. When a group of fourth graders finished reading Sid Fleischman's *The Whipping Boy*, they wrote

A third- and fourth-grade group heard Byrd Baylor's story *I'm in Charge of Celebrations* and wrote about special days they wanted to remember.
Mangere Bridge School, Auckland, New Zealand. Colleen Fleming, teacher.

about other practical jokes that Prince Brat could play on his father, the king. One child devised this scheme:

> Prince Brat would get a mouse and put it in the royal soup. First he would hide the mouse in his pocket. Then he would go up to the royal cook and say, "May I smell the soup?" The cook would back away so the prince could smell the soup and slip the mouse into the soup. Then when the soup was served, one unlucky person would get a dead mouse in his or her soup.

Nathaniel Jencks, grade 4
Martin Luther King, Jr., Laboratory School
Evanston, Illinois
Barbara Friedberg, teacher

Tightly patterned or highly formatted stories make it easier for teachers to plan writing extensions. But the example of asking children to invent another of Prince Brat's pranks shows how an alert teacher can plan a writing experience that lets children enter into the mind of a character while at the same time calls attention to a humorous aspect of the story that appeals to children.

Experimenting with Literary Patterns

As children become familiar with many types of literature—folktales, fables, myths, and poetry, for instance—they are able to experiment with these forms in their own writing. A teacher should support writers by exposing children extensively to a well-defined part of a genre, such as alphabet books, pourquoi or wish stories, creation myths, haiku or concrete poetry, before asking children to write their own works.

Making Alphabet Books

One teacher of fifth-grade language arts gave her students fifty alphabet books and asked them to decide which ones were easier, which more difficult, and why. On the second day, they categorized the collection on four large wall charts (see "Alphabet Books" in Chapter 4). The 10-year-olds were surprised to see challenging titles like Jonathan Hunt's medieval informational book *Illuminations*, Max Grover's *Accidental Zucchini*, and Susan Purviance and Marcia O'Shell's alliterative *Alphabet Annie Announces an All-American Album*. When the teacher asked children to make their own 26-letter alphabet books, the results were diverse. There were ABC books of sports, foods, animals, favorite hobbies such as fishing, riddles, lift-the-flap, and hidden-picture ABCs, and alliterative stories. The class was so proud of its work that they held an author party at which children shared their work with parents.

Another class of older children read Brian Jacques's *Redwall*, a fantasy set in a medieval fortress defended by mice. They used an alphabet format and extracted events and things from the book to create their own "A Is for Abbey" book. The annotation for an illuminated *E* read:

> E: Evil is a main part of *Redwall*. Cluny, his hoarde, King Bull Sparra, and Asmodeus are all evil. Cluny's thoughts are filled with evil. Here is an example to show Cluny's evil: " 'Get out of my way, you sniveling little wretch!' he yelled, shoving Friar Hugo away from him."

Grades 4–5
Highland Park Elementary School
Grove City, Ohio
Rhonda L. Dailey-Dickinson, teacher

After a class study of alphabet books, a fifth grader created "An Occupied Alphabet," showing various occupations.
Allison Fraser, grade 5. George Mason Elementary School, Alexandria City Public Schools, Alexandria, Virginia. Susan Steinberg, teacher.

Alphabet books are handy organizers of information from a thematic study. Teachers might use this as a whole-class project on a topic such as ecology, especially if children are encouraged to write a paragraph of information to go with "R is for rain forest," for example.

Fooling with Folktales, Fables, and Myths

Children's literature offers many examples of how authors and illustrators reinterpret traditional literature for new audiences.[14] Some illustrators modify the sense of a well-known tale by preserving the story but changing the setting. Roberto Innocenti took Charles Perrault's "Cinderella" and elegantly placed it in post–World War I Britain. Anthony Browne updated the Grimms's "Hansel and Gretel" by changing the setting to a bleak present-day city.

But many more authors and illustrators take a well-known folktale and change the point of view, mix up the characters, alter the theme, or tell what happened next. Jon Scieszka plays with traditional forms and characters in books like *The Stinky Cheese Man and Other Fairly Stupid Tales* and *The Book That Jack Wrote*. His

The Frog Prince Continued is a sequel in which a dissatisfied prince seeks witches from other folktales who can change him back into a frog. His *The True Story of the 3 Little Pigs by A. Wolf* shifts the story to the wolf's point of view. Babette Cole's *Prince Cinders* and Bernice Myers's *Sidney Rella and the Glass Sneaker* present familiar patterns in new stories, each with a modern boy protagonist, while Ellen Jackson's *Cinder Edna* portrays a take-charge Cinderella. Jane Yolen's *Sleeping Ugly* plays with our expectations about folktales by giving the ugly but kind girl the prince and leaving the beautiful princess asleep to be used as a hat rack.

Children who have been steeped in traditional literature can write wonderful parodies and sophisticated takeoffs. A sixth-grade class studied numerous Greek myths and discussed their characteristics. One boy's story perfectly captures aspects of myth such as a crisp beginning, few characters, the explanation of the origins of an animal, and the often deadly and arbitrary action of the gods:

Princess Skunkina and Olfactor

Olfactor, the goddess of scent, was the sweetest smelling immortal around. She was the goddess who gave everything its scent. Olfactor was very nice and sweet when it came to mortals.

[14]Susan Hepler, "Fooling with Folktales: Updates, Spin-offs, and Roundups," *School Library Journal* 36, no. 3 (March 1990): 153–154.

As part of a study of myths, sixth graders created stories and illustrations describing their own mythological creatures.
George Mason Elementary School, Alexandria City Public Schools, Alexandria, Virginia. Susan Steinberg, teacher.

Princess Skunkina, known as the one with white hair, was very jealous of Olfactor because she thought she smelled better than Olfactor.

Princess Skunkina assembled the town and made an announcement. "I am the new goddess of scent. I am the sweetest smelling person alive. You will now worship me, not Olfactor who smells like a herd of cows in comparison to me."

Of course, Olfactor was enraged. She was so angry she decided she'd pay Princess Skunkina a little visit herself. (She rarely visited mortals.) Olfactor flew down from the heavens and spotted the one with white hair in her garden of trees. Olfactor came up to the princess and cast a spell upon her. "You thought you smelled better than me. I'll see to it that you never dethrone a god or goddess again. . . . Olfactor watched as she was dying and took pity over her. She decided to let her live but not as a mortal, but a putrid-smelling animal with her beautiful white hair in a stripe down her back.

Michael Polson, Grade 6
George Mason Elementary School
Alexandria, Virginia
Susan Steinberg, teacher

Fables also represent a discrete and highly patterned genre of literature that children can experiment with.

Children ought to have many experiences with the original fables by Aesop and La Fontaine before trying their own hands at it. One child heard his teacher read Arnold Lobel's *Fables* aloud in September. Then he read it himself and over the next five weeks produced a total of seven fables. Here's one example:

A Bull Story

One day a bull feeling both strong and mean came down into the valley. To his surprise, there was another bull down there looking as strong and mean as he. They challenged each other to a fight. They killed each other and neither of them carried on a happy life.

Moral: You can't win against an equally equipped opponent.[15]

Working from the moral back to the story, one group of 12-year-olds decided to create other modern versions of fables. They thought of appropriate stories for such

[15]Frederick R. Burton, "The Reading-Writing Connection: A One-Year Teacher-as-Researcher Study of Third-Fourth Grade Writers and Their Literary Experiences" (Ph.D. dissertation, Ohio State University, 1985), p. 166.

Resources for Teaching
Fooling with Traditional Literature

Title, Author	Grade Level	Description
The Jolly Postman or Other People's Letter (Ahlberg and Ahlberg)	1 and up	Letters from one folktale character to another
Jim and the Beanstalk (Briggs)	1–4	Sequel
Teller of Tales (Brooke)	4 and up	Folktales rewritten as short stories
Fanny's Dream (Buehner)	1 and up	Farmgirl "Cinderella" who makes her own magic
The Principal's New Clothes (Calmenson)	1–4	New version of "The Emperor's New Clothes" in a contemporary setting
Prince Cinders (Babette Cole)	3–6	Male character
Princess Smartypants (Babette Cole)	3–6	Feminist variation on "The Frog Prince"
Snow White in New York (French)	4 and up	1920s setting
"The Builders," in *Reflections on a Gift of Watermelon Pickle,* ed. Dunning et al. (Hayes)	3 and up	A poem from the smug point of view of the oldest pig in "The Three Little Pigs"
Fables You Shouldn't Pay Any Attention To (Heide and Van Clief)	2 and up	New morality in an old form
Cinder Edna (Jackson)	2 and up	Feminist outcome to traditional happily-ever-after story
Fables (Lobel)	2 and up	Fresh morals in new stories
Sidney Rella and the Glass Sneaker (Bernice Myers)	1–3	Male character in contemporary setting
Whiff, Sniff, Nibble, and Chew: The Gingerbread Boy Retold (Pomerantz)	K–3	Reworked story with an additional cookie
The Frog Prince Continued (Scieszka)	1 and up	Sequel with a surprise ending
The True Story of the 3 Little Pigs by A. Wolf (Scieszka)	1 and up	Told from the wolf's point of view
The Stinky Cheese Man and Other Fairly Stupid Tales (Scieszka)	2 and up	Familiar tales deconstructed
Somebody and the Three Blairs (Tollhurst)	K–3	Bear intruder in a contemporary apartment
Deep in the Forest (Turkle)	1–3	Bear intruder in a colonial house, the reverse of "The Three Bears"
Sleeping Ugly (Yolen)	1–3	New story with familiar characters

well-known morals as "Beauty is only skin deep" and "Don't cry wolf unless you mean it." (See "Fables" in Chapter 6 for stories suggesting other morals.)

The Resources for Teaching box "Fooling with Traditional Literature" contains selections from the many examples a teacher might use to start children thinking. But nothing is a substitute for exposing children to many examples of traditional literature before asking them to fool with these traditional literary patterns.

Experimenting with Poetry

Poetry provides many opportunities for children's writing. Eve Merriam's *Quiet Please* invites children to imagine quiet sound—"ferns fluttering by the pond" or "invisible writing of butterflies." A group of 7- and 8-year-olds studied Tomie de Paola's *The Comic Adventures of Old Mother Hubbard and Her Dog* and created additional verses such as "She went to the hen house to get him an egg. / But when she got back, he was holding his leg." After reading *The Book of Pigericks* by Lobel, a small group of fourth graders wrote their own "Bugericks." See Chapter 8 for suggestions on other ways to encourage children's writings with poetry.

Extending Forms of Writing

While it is true that most children usually start by writing stories, they should be given many opportunities to write in other forms as well. Writing a character's diary or journal lets a child assume that character's point of view. Reporting a book's events in newspaper-article format allows a child to reshape events in the story. Children can develop practical writing skills as they write directions for a literature-based game or describe how they made a diorama. All levels of writing may spring from a child's involvement with literature, and teachers need to help children discover writing opportunities. Once again we suggest that children need experiences with a form before they are able to take it on in their own writing. Children who have never looked beyond the comics section of the newspaper should not be asked to write "Letters to Ann Landers" or entries for the "obituaries" column without prior experience with the form of today's newspapers.

Diaries and Letters

Once children can assume another point of view, they are able to retell a story in the first person. Authors use letters, journals, and first-person narratives to allow a character to reveal thoughts directly to the reader. Older children are more able developmentally to take on another person's point of view. The books they read often assist in this because many popular stories are written as first-person narratives. Some authors, such as Barbara Park in *Skinnybones* and Walter Dean Myers in *The Mouse Rap*, tell their stories from the main character's point of view. Thus readers see through the eyes of another person as they are immersed in the book. Teachers help children take another point of view when they ask them to write about a book as if they were the main character telling a part of her or his story.

Other authors reveal a character's thoughts by having the character write diary entries or letters. Libby in Zilpha Keatley Snyder's *Libby on Wednesday* is part of a young authors group and keeps a journal; Sam Gribley's journal reveals the story of *My Side of the Mountain* by Jean Craighead George. In thirteenth-century England the title character of Karen Cushman's *Catherine Called Birdy* convinces her mother to let her write a journal

rather than do her spinning. Henri, who spends a year in another culture in Emily Cheney Neville's *The China Year*, writes letters to her teachers and friends back in New York. Fourth grader Anastasia in Lois Lowry's *Anastasia Krupnik* keeps modifying her "Things I love/Things I hate" list as her feelings and thoughts change. Children are quick to notice these narrative conventions if teachers help them.

Several other books use letters to tell the story. Janet and Allan Ahlberg's *The Jolly Postman* includes envelopes containing removable letters to and from various folktale characters that are delivered by a postman. Teachers can supply a variety of envelopes, writing stock, and stamps, and invite children to write a letter as if they were a folktale or picture storybook character.

Vera B. Williams challenges readers to infer the story of *Stringbean's Trip to the Shining Sea* from the backs of the two dozen postcards the boy sends to his family in Kansas. A second-grade teacher asked children to translate this idea to their current topic of study. Children imagined they were visiting the rain forest and wrote a postcard to their parents telling what they had seen there. Some designed clever stamps, as Williams had done in her book.

Judith Caseley's touching *Dear Annie* features some of the letters exchanged between Annie, her mother, and grandfather from the time she is a baby to the time when she shared all eighty-six of them for her grade school show-and-tell. After hearing Caseley's story, children might write their own letters to a treasured older relative or display the letters they have received. Because of their warmth, humor, or innovative formats, books like these are powerful catalysts to children's writing.

Children may create diaries and letters for book characters who never kept them, such as second graders created for William Steig's characters in *Amos & Boris*. In Katherine Paterson's *Lyddie*, the story of a New England mill girl, what might Lyddie have confided to her diary? In Mary Downing Hahn's ghost story *Wait Till Helen Comes*, suppose Molly kept a journal of the strange events leading up to her stepsister's dangerous friendship. How would entries show her gradual change from skepticism to alarm to action?

Imaginary correspondence between characters in one book requires children to maintain two points of view. First graders compared different versions of "Stone Soup" and settled on Tony Ross's *Stone Soup*, a takeoff in which a wolf is bested by a chicken. Children discussed what Mr. Wolf would do with the stone after he stole it; they agreed he would probably be frustrated because the stone didn't work. So they wrote in the person of Mr. Wolf:

🐞 Dear Mrs. Hen,

I tried making the soup and it tasted terrible. Could you be my cook? I promise not to eat you.[16]

Another primary group decided to write letters between Mother Goose characters. This is the one Little Boy Blue received:

🐞 Dear Little Boy Blue:

Never sleep on the job again! The sheep and the crows are eating all the grass and the corn. If you sleep again, you're FIRED!

Sincerely, your boss, the farmer

Barbara Friedberg, teacher
Martin Luther King, Jr., Laboratory School,
Evanston, Illinois

In Carolyn Reeder's *Shades of Gray*, 12-year-old Will Page is forced to move to rural Virginia to live with his uncle, a conscientious objector in the Civil War. Children might write the letters Will never wrote to the friendly doctor who offered to adopt him. Or they might write Will's journal as he wrestles with the problems presented by the hard realities of rural life in Virginia following the war.

Letters written and sent to authors and illustrators can be encouraged rather than assigned if a child or groups of children have read and are enthusiastic about books by that author. Authors appreciate the inclusion of self-addressed, stamped envelopes, or stamps, and they appreciate a child's candor and individuality above a "canned letter" copied from the chalkboard. Requests for pictures or biographical information should be addressed to publishers; letters to authors or illustrators should be addressed to them in care of the publisher. (See Appendix C for publishers' addresses.)

The Resources for Teaching box "Books That Serve as Writing Models" suggests stories teachers might share as examples and incentives for children's own writing efforts.

Newspapers and Newscasting

By putting themselves in the role of reporters from newspapers or television news, children can "cover" the events in a book. An interview with Abel after his year-long stay on an island in *Abel's Island* by William Steig might include his advice on how to survive. A series of news accounts of the events recounted in *The Pushcart War* by Jean Merrill could present amusing battles between the mighty trucks and the puny pushcarts in New York City. Fourth graders created a Camazotz newspaper as part of their activities while the teacher read aloud *A Wrinkle in Time* by Madeleine L'Engle. Their work reflected an awareness of what life might be like on a planet where all persons were required to behave similarly.

As a way of looking across or back on what children know in literature, teachers can help children organize a group newspaper. Sections could include news stories, editorials, announcements, a fashion or society page, sports, lost and found, letters to the editor, advice, obituaries, and so forth. Content could be drawn from a particular genre, such as realistic fiction or folktales. One folktale newspaper, for instance, featured an advertisement for "Big Anthony's Carry-Out Pasta: All You Can Eat!" along with a report on breaking-and-entering at the home of the Three Bears and a review of society doings at Cinderella's ball. It takes time to develop a successful newspaper, as children must sift through what they have to read to recall specific events. If column headings are posted around the classroom, ideas can be noted and children can paste up their rough drafts of articles for reading by the rest of the "newspaper staff." Parents, teacher aides, or high school typing students can often be persuaded to help with typing if the newspapers are to be duplicated for each student.

Expository Writing

Learning expository writing is an essential part of children's literacy development. Literature projects can serve as prewriting activities that help children begin to formulate directions and explanations. In addition, books can offer children models for writing reports, essays, and persuasive papers.

Directions, Explanations, and Surveys

Nearly all of the literature extensions in this chapter have accompanying writing possibilities. Children who write directions for designing and printing from plastic foam trays need to write procedures concisely if others are going to understand the process. Writing directions for a literary game gives children an opportunity to write with clarity and precision. If others can play the game by following what the writer has written, then the directions have succeeded.

Explanations and descriptions help others understand what children have created or accomplished. If

---

[16]Reported by Peggy Compton Moberly in "Children's Choices Make Students Avid Readers," *CBC Features* 44, no. 2 (July/December 1991).

Resources for Teaching
Books That Serve as Writing Models

Title, Author	Grade Level	Type of Writing
The Jolly Postman or Other People's Letters (Ahlberg and Ahlberg)	1 and up	Letters from one folktale character to another
A Gathering of Days: A New England Girl's Journal, 1830–1832 (Blos)	5 and up	Historical fiction in journal form
Dear Mr. Sprouts (Broome)	4–6	Correspondence between two pen pals
The Burning Questions of Bingo Brown (Byars)	5–8	Journal of interesting questions
Dear Annie (Caseley)	1–4	Letters between a girl and her grandfather
Dear Mr. Henshaw (Cleary)	5–7	Story told in letters and journal entries
Strider (Cleary)	6 and up	Journal entries
Catherine Called Birdy (Cushman)	5 and up	Journal entries
Dear Daddy . . . (DuPasquier)	1–3	Letters
Anne Frank: The Diary of a Young Girl (Frank)	5 and up	Historical World War II diary
My Side of the Mountain (George)	4–7	Diary
An Owl in the House: A Naturalist's Diary (Heinrich)		Naturalist's diary
Germy Blows the Bugle (Jones)	5–7	School newspaper
George Shrinks (Joyce)	1–3	Letter
Onion Tears (Kidd)	3–6	Story partially revealed in letters
Hey World, Here I Am! (Little)	4–7	Poetry and journal entries from *Kate*, also a character in Little's books
Anastasia Krupnik (Lowry)	4–6	Lists and poetry
The China Year (Neville)	5–8	Letters
Z for Zachariah (O'Brien)	5 and up	Novel in diary form
Libby on Wednesday (Snyder)	5 and up	Writing group
Cherries and Cherry Pits (Williams)	1 and up	Pictures that serve as prewriting for a child's story
Stringbean's Trip to the Shining Sea (Williams)	2 and up	Story in postcard form
Three Days on a River in a Red Canoe (Williams)	2–5	Journal in words and pictures

students' work is displayed for a wider audience, as in school corridors, lunchrooms, or the library, then children understand the necessity for informative writing to speak clearly for them in their absence. In addition, displays provide a natural encouragement for children to revise and recopy, if necessary, for this public writing. Teachers can help children write longer and more complete descriptions by asking questions like these: How did you do this? What materials did you use? What part of the book is this based on? Why did you choose it? One such discussion produced the following from two second-grade boys:

We made a diorama of Nantucket Harbor. We started with a cardboard box. Then we cut out some houses and then we made the whale and glued the whale on at an angle then we painted the whale black. We were going to make the under ground city but it was to hard to make. We had trouble on the whale we kept making the whale smaller. And we had trouble on the dock. And the sky and clouds because it was very hard. The windows on the houses were hard to. [sic] We painted the clouds 4 times.

FAIRY TALE REVIEW

Gingerbread Man Escapes From Oven

Last Friday at 3:00 p.m a gingerbread man escaped from an oven. As he ran down the road, people who happened to be passing by joined in the chase. It was a long chase because everybody but the gingerbread man was getting tired.

Finally at 3:30 p.m the gingerbread man reached the river where he met a fox. The gingerbread man was last seen being taken across the river by the fox. He was wearing a button coat when last seen. If you have seen him, please notify the local authorities.

Gingerbread man when last seen

Bean Stalks Go Crazy

Two years ago, Jack cut down a bean stalk. Now the bean stalk has grown back and more stalks are sprouting.

The farmers love it because it has so many beans. The stalks have even lifted a few houses off the ground.

A wild bean stalk growing like crazy

Wolf Blows Down Pig's House

Yesterday, after the three little pigs went grocery shopping, the wolf came over and tried to blow down the pig's house. After many attempts, the wolf succeded. Minutes later, the wolf collapsed from loss of breath. When the pigs returned, they called an ambulance and "Hines Lumber and Brick Co." The pigs did not press charges; instead, they made the wolf pay for their new house. The wolf was treated and released from the hospital.

Fourth and fifth graders created a fairy-tale newspaper to sum up their study of these stories.
Martin Luther King, Jr., Laboratory School, Evanston, Illinois Public Schools. Ellen Esrick, reading teacher.

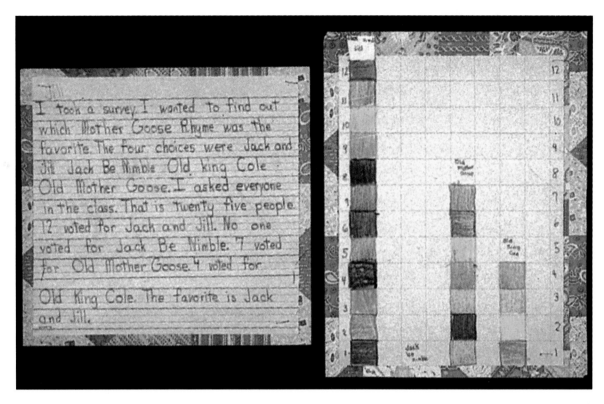

Third graders conducted a survey of the children's favorite Mother Goose rhymes. They then wrote about how they had made the survey and graphed the results.
Columbus Public Schools, Columbus, Ohio. Arleen Stuck, teacher.

A group of first graders responded to *The Biggest House in the World* by Leo Lionni through a variety of media and math activities. They took surveys of children's preferences for color, kind, and size of house (one, two, or three stories). Their concept of the word *house* was enlarged to include the "houses" of a snail and a turtle (shells). A bulletin board displayed the results of these extensions from a single book.

Literary surveys give children experiences with representing their findings in graphs. One group of 11- and 12-year-olds surveyed each other on such topics as "Which Judy Blume books have you read?" "How many books did you read in March?" and "Have you read any books from these series: Baby-Sitters Club, Nancy Drew, the Hardy Boys?" Data were presented in pie and bar graphs, averages, and percentiles in a variety of interesting displays.

Other surveys have been made of how frequently and how long each teacher reads aloud to the class or where and when children like to read. Children doing survey research will learn much about conducting and organizing the results of a survey. In addition, a teacher learns more about the reading profile of the class from these surveys. Teachers can help children state questions clearly so that answers can be categorized and counted. Discussing ways of representing information, such as bar or circle graphs, keys and use of symbols, will help children create more visually interesting survey charts.

Nonfiction's Influence on Report Writing

Contemporary informational books provide numerous examples of how information can be presented in interesting, challenging, humorous, or beautiful fashion. Teachers who help children discover formats in informational writing help them avoid the stilted school writing that begins with "My report is on" and proceeds through copied encyclopedia phrases. Writers like Aliki and Gail Gibbons use a straightforward expository style that is lively and inviting. Their illustrations, with captions or labels, are simple but add to, and extend, the information contained in the words. Seymour Simon's *Animal Fact/Animal Fable* is organized as a guessing game. Statements about animals, such as "Porcupines shoot their quills," are followed on the next page with a related paragraph beginning something like "Fable: Porcupines cannot really shoot their quills." Diane De-Groat's illustrations vary from humorous, to close-up, to straightforward. The useful If series, such as *If You Lived at the Time of the San Francisco Earthquake* by Ellen Levine, is organized in question-and-answer format. Children can arrange some part of nearly any topical report into a true/false, question-and-answer, or guessing-game format.

Children should be exposed to many examples of close-ups, labeled line drawings, processes explained in box-and-arrow arrangements or time lines, and picture captions in such visually stunning books as the Eyewitness series titles *Amazing Birds* or *Amazing Poisonous Animals* by Alexandra Parson. Peter Spier's *Tin Lizzie* and Bernd Heinrich's *An Owl in the House: A Naturalist's Diary* are two examples of treatment of a life cycle, the first of a car and the second of an owl. Children could recast studies of objects or animals in these formats.

Photo essays are wonderful ways to capture children's progress through a project. In *Insect Metamorphosis: From Egg to Adult* Ron and Nancy Goor use clear prose and captioned pictures to portray the stages of insect development. Children who are creating a play from a folktale, making stuffed paper figures for a puppet show, or raising chicks in the classroom could develop a photo essay of the process and the finished product or end point as a way of remembering it.

Teachers who encourage children to notice format and form in informational books and use it in their own reports do much to help children become literate. Understanding the conventions by which information is conveyed, whether it is maps, time lines, charts, photographs, captions, surveys, or graphs, is a part of any literate person's skills.

Making Books

Nothing motivates children to write as much as the opportunity to create, bind, and illustrate a book of their own. Teachers need to learn how to bind books themselves before attempting to teach children. Materials for bookbinding should be made constantly available so that children can make books as the need arises. Most bookmaking materials can be readily purchased, but parents may contribute leftover fabric pieces for book covers to ease classroom budgets.

There are many simple ways to create handmade books in which to "publish" children's writing. However, since bookbinding involves time and some expense, it should be reserved for the publication of carefully planned, written, and illustrated books. Children should look at the way beautiful books are made, the various media used, the carefully designed endpapers or title pages, the placement of the words, and so forth, before they complete their own work. For endpapers children can use marbleized paper or colored construction paper that reflects the mood of their story. They can take as models books with patterned and decorated endpapers,

such as Taro Yashima's endpapers for *Crow Boy*, which depict a butterfly and a blossom, symbols of the main character's growth; or Kathy Jakobsen's endpaper paintings for Reeve Lindbergh's poem of *Johnny Appleseed*, which depict a map of the region where John Chapman wandered. Many children enjoy planning dedications and jacket copy for their books as well. As children create their own books, they learn much about the care and design that have gone into the books they read.

Before binding a book, children can be encouraged to sketch a "dummy" or practice book. The illustrations are roughed out and lines are drawn where text will be written or typed. In *Her Book* by Janet Wolf, the book's dummy is incorporated into the final product as endpapers, and children may wish to compare Wolf's dummy with the more detailed final illustrations as they work on their own books. Aliki's *How a Book Is Made*, Michael Kehoe's *A Book Takes Root*, and Janet Stevens's *From Pictures to Words* give children an excellent overview of the creation and publication of a children's book. *How to Make Pop-Ups* by Joan Irvine suggests ways children can incorporate three-dimensional artwork into their books.

Materials for bookmaking include paper for pages, paper for endpapers, a threaded needle, cover material (such as cotton fabric, wallpaper, or adhesive shelf-liner paper), and cardboard. In addition, an iron and dry-mount tissue (available from photographic supply houses) or white glue and water are needed. Directions for making a simple bound book with dry-mount tissue are shown in the illustration of bookmaking.

Assessment and Evaluation

Assessment and evaluation of children's growth in any area of learning must be consistent with the goals and purposes of the program. As teachers move toward literature-based reading programs that use real books, it makes little sense to evaluate children with tests that are geared to basal readers and hours of workbook practice of filling in blanks, multiple choice, and short-answer questions. What these end-of-the-unit tests evaluate is such a narrow part of the whole process we know as reading that the essential character of one child's reading is lost. Timed multiple-choice tests following the reading of short paragraphs hardly define what a child has learned as a result of all he or she encounters in the course of reading many books. Information gained by these tests does little to help the classroom teacher plan programs that lead students to become more satisfied, more widely adept readers. Evaluation of children's reading should begin with some knowledge of where individual children are starting; observation and evidence of the child's understandings and abilities as revealed by discussion, classroom interactions, solicited and unsolicited

＊ Book Making ＊

① Plan your story and illustrations carefully in a "dummy" or practice book. Decide what size your book should be. Then cut paper for pages that is twice the width" and the same height as the size you want. Cut half as many pieces as pages you need. Remember to allow for the title pages. Cut two pieces of the same or another color or kind of paper for the end papers. Fold the paper to form pages, placing the end papers on the outside. Complete your pages so that they are just the way you want them!

② Fold the completed pages evenly and either hand or machine stitch up the center.

③ Place the open pages on the material that you will use for the cover. Cut the material to a size approximately two inches larger on all sides than the open pages. Press the fabric flat with the iron.

④ Cut two pieces of cardboard, each just slightly larger than a single book page. These will form the support for the cover.

⑤ Cut four large pieces of Dry Mounting Tissue. Make two pieces the size of the cardboard and two pieces the size of a single page. Also, cut several small strips of Dry Mounting Tissue approximately 2" x ½".

⑥ Place the cover material on a flat surface face down. Position the Dry Mounting Tissue (cardboard size) on the material. Now place the cardboard pieces on top. Leave a space between the cardboard pieces to allow for the pages and for the book to open and close.

⑦ With an iron, set on low, carefully press the cardboard. This will mount the material to the cardboard.

⑧ Place the small pieces of Dry Mounting Tissue between the cardboard and the material and use the iron again to adhere the two. Begin with the corners. Then fold the top, bottom and sides until your book cover is completed!

⑨ Place the two remaining pieces of Dry Mounting Tissue on the cardboard side of the book cover. Position the sewn pages in the middle. Press the first and last pages down to form end papers. Use the iron to mount the pages to the cover.

Book making.
Bookbinding directions written by Marilyn Parker, Columbus School for Girls, Ohio.

responses to books; and evidence of changes, or growth, in that child's knowledge, appreciation, understandings, and abilities in reading. Informal tests such as Marie Clay's Concepts of Print or Kenneth Goodman's Modified Miscue Analysis give important information about children's reading abilities.[17] These and other methods of assessment demand that teachers constantly sharpen their observational skills, develop some means of record keeping, and be able to recognize important signs of insight and growth in the learners they teach. The following suggestions focus particularly on the growth and development of literary understandings.

[17]See Marie Clay, *The Early Detection of Reading Difficulties*, 3rd ed. (Portsmouth, N.H.: Heinemann, 1985); and *Reading Miscue Inventory: Alternative Procedures*, ed. Goodman, Yetta, et al., (Katonah, NY: Richard C. Owens, 1987).

Determining Children's Literacy Background

Begin where children are. This maxim applies to literature as well as any other area. In planning a literature program, a staff or teacher must first consider what the children's previous experiences with literature have been. Has the child been fortunate enough to have come from a home where reading is valued, where there are many books? Has a child been read to regularly? Or is school the child's first introduction to books? What have previous teachers read aloud to these children? What common experiences, such as author or illustrator studies or thematic groupings in literature, have these children had?

Teachers should consider beginning the year with an informal interview with each child. Here are some possible questions:

What are your favorite stories?

What kinds of stories do you like?

Who reads with you at home? When?

Do you have some favorite authors or illustrators? Who?

How do you feel about reading?

Why do people read and write?

Are there any TV programs you always watch? What are they?

When do you usually watch TV?

Teachers can develop brief questionnaires and fill them in as they talk with a child or they can tape children's conversations, which frees them to follow up on some of the child's answers.

Older children could meet in groups and discuss some of their favorite books, authors and illustrators, television programs, and after-school activities. These discussions could also be taped as sources for the teacher. The point of these initial interviews is to determine where children are in their literary habits and understandings.

Appreciation for literature seems to be developmental. If children have not had the opportunity to laugh at the antics of *Harry the Dirty Dog* by Gene Zion when they are 5 or 6, they need the experience at 7 or 8. If they have not met "Mother Goose" before they come to school, then early primary grades need to supply this cornerstone of literature. We need research on the sequential stages of appreciating literature, but we have some evidence to show that children must go through the "picture storybook stage," the "nonsense verse stage," even the "series book stage" if they are to become active, involved readers. Knowing where to start, then, is the value of finding what children's exposure to literature has been.

Record Keeping

As a school year begins, it is important to have some record-keeping systems already in place that are simple and consume as little completion time as possible. In this way, records from the very first days of school can be compared as a child progresses, and the teacher will be better able to plan future curriculum.

Ongoing Observations

One of the best kinds of assessment of children's growth are the notes teachers write as they observe children

A teacher listens attentively as a first grader reads "The Three Billy Goats Gruff." She is taking a running record of his oral reading.
Columbus Public Schools, Columbus, Ohio. Connie Compton, teacher.

reading. Many teachers keep a tablet of Post-it notes or sheets of gummed labels on their desk or in other parts of the room where reading is likely to occur. As they observe something significant about a child, they can quickly jot it down. Later the piece of paper can be transferred to a notebook under the child's name or into the child's individual folder. For example, two 7-year-olds loved Patricia Thomas's *"Stand Back," Said the Elephant, "I'm Going To Sneeze!"* Their teacher asked them if it reminded them of another book. Kelly immediately remembered *The Big Sneeze* by Ruth Brown. The children had made comparison charts of variants of folktales, so the teacher suggested that they might want to compare these two books. She gave them a pad of Post-it notes and a large sheet of paper. Then she stood back to see how the girls would proceed. This is the teacher's observation of how they worked together:

April 6

Cindy and Kelly decided to compare *The Big Sneeze* with *"Stand Back," Said the Elephant*. Kelly took charge and made two categories:

Alike/Different
BIG SNEEZE—sneeze
STAND BACK—sneeze   Poetry

As I watched them, C. said quietly, "You know, we need more sections to describe them." "Like what?" said K. C. replied, "Well, one is just the story of a sneeze while the other one is how a mouse stopped the sneeze but then the elephant laughed and it was a disaster. *Its plot is more complicated.*" The girls changed their categories to Story; Characters; Kind of writing; and Funny things that happened.

The teacher's record shows that while Kelly was quick to begin, Cindy's more thoughtful comments helped to shape the comparison.

A kindergarten teacher recorded when Jamie wrote his first complete sentence. Another teacher recorded a child's written definition of a story as "a mindfull of life." A fifth-grade teacher recorded one girl's generalizations about the many animal stories she had read during the year. A sixth-grade teacher noted the first time one boy uncharacteristically read for twenty minutes without looking up from his book.

Each day becomes more exciting as the teacher looks for and records typical moments and peak experiences in a child's reading life. These anecdotes make parent conferences rich with positive comments and evidence of growth that the parent recognizes as real. Each observation should be dated so that a teacher can see the ongoing growth of a student over the course of the school year.

Folders

Most teachers want children to keep their work together. In a classroom where the room is divided into work areas, generally each child has a writing folder or a work folder, and perhaps a reading log or response journal (see Chapter 13). Since teachers look at and respond to these, they must be easily accessible to both the children and the teacher. Clearly designated boxes, shelves, or bookcases should be reserved for whatever record-keeping folders the classroom encompasses.

Assessment Portfolios

At designated times in the year, teachers may ask children to go through their writing and art folders to select their best examples to include in their assessment portfolio. A portfolio of this sort is a year-long collection of a child's work that may be used in various ways by the teacher and child. A child can select from a month of writings the one that should go in the file, for instance. A teacher might honor a child's work by suggesting that it would be a fine addition to her special portfolio. If a student has worked cooperatively with another child— for instance, to produce a research report—copies can be made of their project and placed in each child's portfolio. Photographs as well as written work might be included in the collection. As teachers and children confer about the work in the portfolio, the teacher can ask each child why he or she chose this work and record the child's reasons on a Post-it note. Together they can build criteria for what constitutes good work. In this way, children know what is expected of them because they have helped to establish the standards.

The assessment portfolio belongs to the child. If she leaves the school, she should be allowed to take it with her. It goes home with her at the end of the year. In the meantime, however, it should be shared with her parents at conference time at least twice during the year. Parents and teachers who compare a child's work in the fall with her work in the winter will see their child's progress in a way that no grades on a paper can record. If teachers must give grades, at least they have the evidence (in the portfolio as well as in other records) to show parents what that grade is based on. Children might also include a list of their reading choices for the year.

Some schools maintain permanent records of a child's work that accompany that child through elementary school. This folder of photocopied work comprises a wonderful record that children are proud to note when, as sixth graders, they compare their primary-grade writing samples with ones done later in school.

Student and Parent Conferences

To help their students become part of a community of readers, teachers will want to plan time to communicate with them regularly about their reading. Parents, too, are an integral part of this community, and they will appreciate being informed about the literacy program and their child's progress.

Talking with individual children in a conference takes time. Yet in conferences children frequently reveal their growing edges. Teachers will want to have frequent conferences with children about their reading. It helps if a child brings her reading log or response journal and a current book she is reading to such a conference. Teachers can chat with a child about patterns in her reading selections as evidenced by the log. They can recommend another book that fits the pattern, or suggest a sequel or another book by the child's favorite author. They may ask the child to read aloud from his current SSR book or from a title his small group is reading together. It is helpful to remember that a book conversation with a child may be simply a recounting of plot. Teachers can assist children's thinking by asking such questions as "Could there be any other bridges in Katherine Paterson's *Bridge to Terabithia?*" "Now that you've read three books by Gary Paulsen, how could you recognize one he wrote even if you couldn't see the author and title?" "Since you've read so many mysteries, can you say what makes a book a good mystery?"

In many classrooms, children never have a chance to talk alone with the teacher except in disciplinary situations. Conferences can be exceptionally rewarding to both participants.

Most schools establish time for parent conferences several times a year. Then teachers share the work the

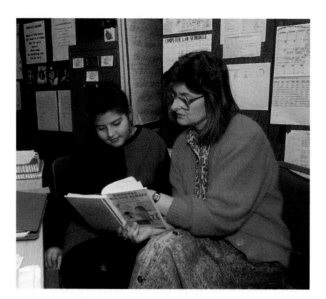

Teachers like to have frequent conferences with children about their reading.
Mission School, Redlands Public Schools, Redlands, California. Myrian Trementozzi, teacher.

child has accomplished or is presently working on. Emphasis should always be placed on what the child knows and is learning. For example, parents of young children who are using developmental spelling may be concerned that words are incorrectly spelled. By reading what the child has written and pointing out what she knows about letters and sounds, a teacher can help a parent appreciate what is taking place in the child's learning processes. A kindergarten child drew a detailed picture of "Rapunzel" in her tower with the witch and bats flying around. On the opposite page she wrote:

🐛 RPNZL
RPNZL
LT DN
U HR.

This is easy to read and the parent can be assured that all emergent writers begin with consonant sounds. The teacher can even share Marie Clay's book *What Did I Write?* to show other patterns emergent writers develop on their way to becoming experienced writers.[18] Older children's writing and projects can be shared with an emphasis on the message of the writing as well as mechanics. By comparing pieces of work written in September with those written in later months, parents can see a child's growing competency with all aspects of writing. Parents want to see their children succeed.

[18]Marie M. Clay, *What Did I Write?* (Portsmouth, N.H.: Heinemann, 1975).

Conferences that emphasize and document growth with writing samples, research and art projects, examples of the kinds of books a child selects, and what the child chooses to notice about those books are very satisfying to both parents and teachers.

Evaluating Children's Literary Understandings

Evaluation of a child's understandings must be seen in light of developmental patterns, as we discussed in Chapter 2. In addition, the teacher must consider a child's understandings as revealed in discussion with the group, in creating products such as murals or imaginary diaries discussed previously, and in some linear sort of way. What did the child start with? What does she know now? What will the child remember long after this moment has passed?

Though the following list of understandings is by no means exhaustive, it may suggest how teachers might look at what children know following a study, for example, of the books of Ezra Jack Keats. Do they notice these things:

- Many books feature a character named Peter. Other characters overlap, too.
- Stories are set in the city, in apartment buildings, in the street.
- Illustrations are often collage, using materials, newspaper, wallpaper, marbleized paper, and some paint.
- There are some ideas here. "Giving up things that you've outgrown is part of growing up" from *Peter's Chair*; "There are many things to do outside when it snows, but you can't save snowballs!" from *The Snowy Day*.

In addition, would children be able to pick out a Keats illustration from ones by Vera B. Williams or Pat Hutchins? Would they remember Keats's name? Insights such as these would not be easily revealed in a multiple-choice test. But as children discuss their choices for materials they used in making a picture "like Ezra Jack Keats did," a teacher will see what children had noticed and remembered. When children go to the media center, a teacher might observe whether they ask the librarian for Keats's books by title or by author. Later a teacher might hear a child say about another book, "That's just like *Peter's Chair*. She gave her little sister something she had outgrown."

Third graders who studied folktales might be expected to recognize the following:

- Some common tales
- Typical characters and settings

- Typical traits of characters
- That there are formal beginnings, endings, refrains, and other characteristics of folktale language
- Basic themes such as "Good is always rewarded" or "Little but honest wins over big," although they may not be able to state them succinctly
- That popular tales such as "Cinderella" exist in many versions and variants
- That some commonly recurring patterns, or motifs, such as magical objects, trickery, or wishes are in many tales

Later, in fourth or fifth grade, when they hear such tales as Susan Cooper's *The Boggart,* Sid Fleischman's *The Whipping Boy,* or Mollie Hunter's *The Mermaid Summer,* can they recognize the folktale elements in these more complex tales?

After older children have read Caroline MacDonald's *The Lake at the End of the World* or Robert C. O'Brien's *Z for Zachariah* and studied some of the informational books from the "Stewards of the Earth" web (see Chapter 13), can they extrapolate a logical future for the world based on their knowledge? Those who predict the world's ecological death could debate their viewpoint with those who predict a continuation of life either on earth or on another planet. Again, the teacher would be looking for the facts on which the children based their imagined futures.

Children's products also reveal understandings and growth. Did the "story map" of "The Gingerbread Boy" include all the important incidents? Could the child maintain Amos's point of view in his diary from *Amos & Boris* by William Steig? Did the child's version of *The Way to Start a Day* suggest a sensitivity to Byrd Baylor's use and arrangement of words? How did the student's two-part diorama reflect the contrasting settings of seashore and prairies in Patricia MacLachlan's *Sarah, Plain and Tall?* What teachers choose to evaluate depends on what they are hoping to have children understand after reading a book or pursuing a thematic study. It is helpful to list some goals and understandings, based on the evaluative criteria for a particular genre or the particular strengths and content of the theme, before evaluating children's literary understandings.

Evaluating Children's Growth as Readers

Throughout this text, we have suggested that children's learning accrues, reorganizes, and reformulates based on their own growth both as children and as readers. While observation and evaluation are daily tasks for teachers, it is the long-range goal of creating

enthusiastic, versatile, and skillful readers that should be the teacher's focus. By becoming documenters of children's encounters with literature, we become better observers. Observations of change, then, provide us with clues to a child's growth. The Guidelines box "Evaluating Children's Growth as Readers" provides a beginning set of questions to guide observations. The most important questions we can ask are often not the easiest to answer. What is a child building? What kind of framework is the child creating based on his or her experiences? How is this sense of literature changing?

Evaluating the Literature Program

It is as easy to identify a school in which literature is an integral part of the curriculum as it is to recognize a home where books are loved and valued. Since we have not recommended any body of content that all children must learn, but rather have suggested that each school should plan its own literature program to include certain categories of experiences with literature, the Guidelines "Evaluating a Literature Program" could serve in two ways. First, it suggests to schools in the planning stages of a literature program what experiences ought to be offered to children. Second, it suggests evaluative criteria for assessing a literature program already in place in an elementary or middle school.

Developing Lifetime Readers

The first goal of all literature programs should be to develop lifetime readers. Since we know children are reading less and less in their free time at home, the school becomes their last best hope, not only for learning how to read, but also for *becoming readers.* Everything we do with books in schools should be measured against these criteria: Will this help children enjoy books? Will this help children become lifetime readers?

We know that children's reading for pleasure drops off when they are faced with added homework and demands of middle school and high school. But if children have learned to love reading before that time, they will continue to read and increase their reading once they leave college. If they have not discovered the joys of reading before high school, they probably never will.

One 12-year-old wrote to her former fifth-grade teacher two years after moving away to tell her of a wonderful book she had just read. Here is her letter:

Dear Miss Woolard:

I just finished the book *A Ring of Endless Light* and I was so excited about it that I just had to write and tell you about it. (It's by Madeleine L'Engle.) She

Guidelines:
Evaluating Children's Growth as Readers

Does the child love one book, many books, reading in general?

Does the child become easily involved or easily distracted in reading a book?

Does the child predict, question, and confirm his way through a book?

Does the child prefer one genre, author, or illustrator over others? Is she aware of her preference? Can she recognize characteristics of genre, author, or illustrator?

Is the child a flexible reader who reads easily in several genres, who reads often and quickly?

Can the child select books that satisfy him? Is he open to suggestions from other readers?

What kinds of understandings and awareness do the child's products reveal?

Does the child visualize, identify with, become involved with, or understand the motives of characters?

Does the child visualize settings?

What connections does the child make between a particular book and others by the same illustrator or author? of the same genre? with the same theme? What patterns does she see?

What kind of thematic statements does the child make? Can he see a book title as a metaphor for a larger idea?

What connection does the child make between literature and life?

What questions does the child's reading raise for her?

What literary elements, such as prologues, unique dedications, interesting chapter titles, language use, or narrative style, does the child notice?

How are these reading patterns changing as the school years progress?

Is the child voluntarily reading more at school? at home?

Is the child responding to a greater range and complexity of work?

---

writes with such description that sometimes the book made me smile, and when the characters were hurt or sad, I was also. On page 308 I wanted to scream along with the characters.

This is by far the *best* book I have ever read. I discovered it at just the right time; it made me enjoy life more. The book really made me think about life, death, happiness, sadness, self-pity, and what kind of person I want to be. If you have not read this book, I suggest you do. Here are some of my favorite passages from the book (she quotes several). I have a lot more passages that I like but these two were my favorites. I have no other news, bye, Love,

Amber[19]

There is no doubt that Amber will be a lifetime reader, discovering just the right book at "just the right time." And because all readers want to share their love of a fine book, Amber will continue to do this. Here, she chose to share her reactions with her former fifth-grade teacher, who loves books and shared her enthusiasm with her students.

A fourth-grade girl chose to reflect on her reading for a 4-H speech contest. Here is the speech she delivered:

🔔 I know what you're thinking. You're thinking: Uh-oh, another fourth grader about to give another dull speech about another stupid subject that's so boring that you won't be able to stay awake for another five minutes.

And, ordinarily, that's what happens. And I'm a pretty ordinary kid. I'm in fourth grade; I have blond hair. I weigh about 68 pounds; I'm about four and a half feet tall. I have a hamster and two hermit crabs that I'm crazy about and I have a brother I'm not so crazy about. But am I ordinary? You decide while you listen to some of the experiences I've had.

For instance, one time I moved to the beach because my dad was fired. My sisters and I found out that our cousin had a boyfriend her parents didn't know about. My mom and dad were going through some hard times. I found out that my mom was going to have a baby. But, in the end, it turned out all right. Am I ordinary?

Another experience I had was when I moved into a boxcar with three other kids to hide from our grandfather. We found stuff to cook with and eat on in a junk pile. The oldest kid in our group got a job. After living like this for awhile, we met our

---

[19]Written to Linda Woolard, Miller Elementary School, Newark, Ohio. Courtesy of Linda Woolard, Miller Elementary School.

Guidelines:
Evaluating a Literature Program

Availability of Books and Other Media

Is there a school library media center in each elementary school building? Does it meet American Library Association standards for books and other media?

Is there a professionally trained librarian and adequate support staff in each building?

Does every classroom contain several hundred paperbacks and a changing collection of hardbacks?

Are reference books easily accessible to each classroom?

May children purchase books in a school-run paperback bookstore?

Do teachers encourage children to order books through various school book clubs?

May children take books home?

Are children made aware of the programs of the public library?

Time for Literature

Do all children have time to read books of their own choosing every day?

Do all teachers read to the children once or twice a day?

Do children have time to discuss their books with an interested adult or with other children every day?

Are children allowed time to interpret books through art, drama, music, or writing?

Do children seem attentive and involved as they listen to stories? Do they ask to have favorites reread?

Is literature a part of all areas, across the curriculum?

Motivating Interest

Do teachers show their enthusiasm for books by sharing new ones with children, reading parts of their favorite children's books, discussing them, and so on?

Do classroom and library displays call attention to particular books?

Are children encouraged to set up book displays in the media center, the halls, and their classrooms?

Does the media specialist plan special events—such as story hours, book talks, sharing films, working with book clubs?

Do teachers and librarians work with parents to stimulate children's reading?

Are special bibliographies prepared by the librarians or groups of children on topics of special interest— mysteries, animal stories, science fiction, fantasy, and so on?

Are opportunities planned for contacts with authors and illustrators to kindle interest and enthusiasm for reading?

Balance in the Curriculum

Do teachers and librarians try to introduce children to a wide variety of genres and to different authors when reading aloud?

Do teachers share poetry as frequently as prose?

Do children read both fiction and nonfiction?

Are children exposed to new books and contemporary poems as frequently as some of the old favorites of both prose and poetry?

Do children have a balance of wide reading experiences with small-group, in-depth discussion of books?

Evaluating Children's Growth as Readers

Do children keep reading logs or records of their free reading?

Do older students (grade 3 and up) keep a response journal of their reading?

Do teachers record examples of children's growth and understanding of literature as revealed in their play, talk, art, or writing?

Do students and teachers together create an assessment portfolio with samples of children's best work?

Are children allowed to respond to books in a variety of ways (art, drama, writing), rather than by required book reports?

Is depth of understanding emphasized, rather than the number of books read?

Are children responding to a greater range and complexity of work?

What percentage of the children can be described as active readers? Has this percentage increased?

Are some children beginning to see literature as a source of lifelong pleasure?

Guidelines:
Evaluating a Literature Program (concluded)

Evaluating Teachers' Professional Growth

Are teachers increasing their knowledge of children's literature?

What percentage of the staff has taken a course in children's literature in the past five years?

Are some staff meetings devoted to ways of improving the use of literature in the curriculum?

Do teachers attend professional meetings that feature programs on children's literature?

Are in-service programs in literature made available on a regular basis?

Are in-service programs, such as administering the running record or the miscue analysis, given regularly?

Are such professional journals as the *New Advocate*, the *Horn Book Magazine*, *Book Links*, and the *School Library Journal* available to teachers and librarians?

Are professional books on children's literature available?

Have the teachers and librarians had a share in planning their literature programs?

Do teachers feel responsible not only for teaching children to read but also for helping children find joy in reading?

---

grandfather and found out that he was actually very nice. Am I ordinary?

Another time I got a plastic Indian from my best friend and a cupboard from my brother. That night I put my Indian in the cupboard and the next morning I heard rapping sounds coming from the cupboard. It was the Indian! The cupboard had turned the Indian into a real human being! I found out that the cupboard turned any plastic object into the real thing. I turned a few other objects real. Do I still sound ordinary?

How would an ordinary kid like me have these experiences? Easy . . . I read. I love to read. I had these experiences in the books *The Jellyfish Season* [Hahn], *The Boxcar Children* [Warner], and *The Indian in the Cupboard* [Banks]. You're probably thinking, she just

read them. But when I'm sitting in front of the fire with my dog on my lap and reading those books, I really am having those experiences. So I guess you were right. I am a pretty ordinary kid, but reading gives me extraordinary experiences. And I suggest it to you, if you are tired of being ordinary.

Susan Komoroske, grade 4
George Mason Elementary School
Alexandria City Public School, Virginia
Susan Steinberg, teacher

It lies within the power of every teacher and librarian to give children a rich experience with literature, to share our enthusiasms for fine books, and to develop readers like Amber and Susan who will find a lifetime of pleasure in the reading of good books.

Learning Experiences

1. Select a book or poem and extend it through one of the activities suggested in this chapter. Work alone or with others. Bring your finished product to class and suggest what value this activity might have for children. What seem to be the advantages of working with others? Of working alone?

2. Write something to go with your activity in question 1. Mount and display your work and writing. What value would this have for children? What other types of writing could you have done after your activity was completed?

3. Write your own version of one of the ideas in "Writing from Books." What observations can you make about your own writing processes? How does this inform your teaching?

Continued

Learning Experiences

4. Ask at least five children to keep a log of titles and authors of books they have read in a month. What do you observe? What does this suggest to you about these children? About next steps as a teacher?

5. Give a literature inventory to a group of children and draw some conclusions about their previous exposure to literature. Plan what you think might be a rich literature program for them.

6. In a small group, choose a book and list scenes or opportunities for drama—interviews, debates, imaginary conversations, and so forth. Which possibilities seem to have the greatest potential for depth? Why?

7. Try an activity suggested in this chapter with children. Evaluate the children's understandings and your role in their learning. What next steps might you take?

8. Working in a small group, choose a chapter book or a picture book and suggest a variety of activities that would extend children's understanding and appreciation of the book. Be prepared to explain how each activity might extend children's thinking or enjoyment.

9. Using the Guidelines "Evaluating a Literature Program," visit an elementary school and evaluate its program. Certain members of the class could be responsible for finding the answers to different sections of the guide. Combine your findings in a report and make recommendations concerning the literature program of that school.

Related Readings

Bauer, Caroline Feller. *Read for the Fun of It: Active Programming with Books for Children.* Illustrated by L. G. Bredeson. New York: H. W. Wilson, 1992.

A lively book that encourages activities that promote joy in reading. The author offers advice on reading aloud and ideas for programs, puppetry, and games. She provides many lists of books on such special topics as dogs, stones, dinosaurs, and trees.

Book Links. American Library Association, 50 East Huron Street, Chicago, IL 60611.

Published six times a year and edited by Barbara Elleman, this invaluable magazine features insider looks at how authors and illustrators work, extended and annotated bibliographies dealing with a particular theme, a column called "Earth Beat," book strategies, and classroom connections. Essential for classroom teachers and the school library media center's teacher resources section.

Cullinan, Bernice E., ed. *Children's Literature in the Reading Program.* Newark, N.J.: International Reading Association, 1987.

Articles by various authors discuss aspects of school reading programs that incorporate children's literature. Numerous boxed teaching ideas are succinct, practical, and classroom tested.

Griffiths, Clyve. *Books You Can Count On: Linking Mathematics and Literature.* Portsmouth, N.H.: Heinemann, 1988.

First published in Australia, this book provides many links with mathematical thinking without distorting the essence of a book. One chapter is devoted to activities based on individual books; others are devoted to counting books and activities based on measuring, classifying, and spatial relationships.

Johnson, Terry D., and Daphne Louis. *Literacy Through Literature.* Portsmouth, N.H.: Heinemann, 1987.

The first chapter elaborates on underlying assumptions about the importance of literature in literacy; the remainder of the book gives practical suggestions on how to make story maps, literary letters, literary sociograms, and newspapers. Drama, readers' theater, and mime are also included.

Johnson, Paul. *A Book of One's Own: Developing Literacy Through Making Books.* Portsmouth, NH: Heinemann, 1993.

The author provides directions for making a variety of books, from simple accordion books to hardcover books. Ideas for involving children in the writing and illustrating process as well as making their own books are included.

McCaslin, Nellie. *Creative Drama in the Classroom*. 5th ed. New York: Longman, 1990.

A well-known drama specialist provides both the theory and the practical help teachers need to initiate a drama program. She includes many suggestions for dramatizing stories and poems, a long section on puppets, and a new one on masks and their importance in drama. A fine revision of a respected book.

Moss, Joy. *Focus on Literature: A Context for Literacy Learning*. Katonah, N.Y.: Richard C. Owen, 1990.

Using twelve focuses, such as "Baba Yaga Tales," "Horse Tales," and a novel, Moss shows how teachers can help children see patterns among books and relate literature to life. Theory, a narrative of events, and children's dialogue are blended in this helpful book.

Raines, Shirley C., and Robert J. Canady. *Story Stretchers*. Mt. Ranier, MD.: Gryphon House, 1989.

Activities (discussion, sand table, dress-up corner, cooking, etc.) suitable for preschool through the early primary grades are suggested for ninety different recent and classic picture books.

Routman, Regie. *Invitations: Changing as Teachers and Learners K–12*. Portsmouth, N.H.: Heinemann, 1994.

An extensive compendium of ways to organize and manage a whole language, literature-based reading and writing program. Journal writing, planning guides, teaching strategies, mini-lessons, evaluation, publishing, and a host of other topics are discussed and illuminated with classroom examples. Helpful bibliographies, both of children's books and of professional references, further extend teachers' thinking.

Swartz, Larry. *Drama Themes: A Practical Guide for Teaching Drama*. Portsmouth, N.H.: Heinemann, 1988.

A Canadian teacher shares many practical suggestions for drama based on thematic exploration of children's literature. Drama suggestions include using nursery rhymes or Chris Van Allsburg's *The Mysteries of Harris Burdick* and improvising from Deborah Nourse Lattimore's Aztec myth *The Flame of Peace*.

Tierney, Robert, Mark A. Carter, and Laura E. Desai. *Portfolio Assessment in the Reading-Writing Classroom*. Norwood, Mass.: Christopher-Gordon, 1991.

A lucid and thorough discussion of the theory and use of portfolios of children's work in the classroom. Examples using elementary and high school students' portfolios, self-assessment by students, and the use of portfolios in parent conferences are included.

Watson-Ellam, Linda. *Start with a Story: Literature and Learning in Your Classroom*. Portsmouth, N.H.: Heinemann, 1991.

Written by a Canadian professor who works extensively with teachers, this useful book contains strategies and activities to help make literature come alive in the classroom with drama, music, art, writing, and bookmaking.

The WEB, Ohio State University, Martha L. King Center for Language, Literature and Reading, Rm. 200 Ramseyer Hall, 29 West Woodruff, Columbus, OH 43210.

Three yearly issues review books and suggest ways they can be used in the classroom. Each issue features a curriculum web of books and teaching suggestions for a particular topic, such as "Dinosaurs and Digs" or "The Wild West," single books, a single author, or a particular theme. Issues alternate focus between primary and older elementary classrooms.

Children's Literature

Aardema, Verna. *Borreguita and the Coyote*. Illustrated by Petra Mathers. Knopf, 1991.

———. *Why Mosquitoes Buzz in People's Ears*. Illustrated by Leo and Diane Dillon. Dial, 1975.

Ackerman, Karen. *Araminta's Paint Box*. Illustrated by Betsy Lewin. Atheneum, 1990.

Ahlberg, Janet, and Allan Ahlberg. *The Jolly Postman, or Other People's Letters*. Little, Brown, 1986.

Alexander, Lloyd. *The Book of Three*. Holt, 1964.

———. *The Remarkable Journey of Prince Jen*. Dutton, 1991.

Aliki [Aliki Brandenberg]. *Go Tell Aunt Rhody*. Macmillan, 1986.

———. *How a Book Is Made*. Crowell, 1986.

———. *Hush, Little Baby*. Prentice Hall, 1968.

Anderson, Yvonne. *How to Make Your Own Animated Movies and Videotapes*. Little, Brown, 1991.

Appelbaum, Diana. *Giants in the Land*. Illustrated by Michael McCurdy. Houghton Mifflin, 1993.

Arkhurst, Joyce. *The Adventures of Spider: West African Folk Tales*. Illustrated by Jerry Pinkney. Little, Brown, 1964.

Arnosky, Jim. *A Kettle of Hawks and Other Wildlife Groups*. Lothrop, Lee & Shepard, 1990.

Arthur, Alex. *Shell*. Photographs by Andreas Einsiedel. Knopf, 1989.

Aylesworth, Jim. *My Son Jon*. Illustrated by David Frampton. Holt, 1994.

Babbitt, Natalie. *Tuck Everlasting*. Farrar, Straus & Giroux, 1975.

Baker, Jeannie. *The Story of Rosy Dock*. Greenwillow, 1995.

Bang, Molly. *Dawn*. Morrow, 1983.

Banks, Lynne Reid. *The Indian in the Cupboard*. Illustrated by Brock Cole. Doubleday, 1985.

Baylor, Byrd. *Everybody Needs a Rock*. Illustrated by Peter Parnall. Scribner's, 1974.

———. *I'm in Charge of Celebrations*. Illustrated by Peter Parnall. Scribner's, 1986.

———. *The Table Where Rich People Sit*. Illustrated by Peter Parnall. Scribner's, 1994.

———. *The Way to Start a Day*. Illustrated by Peter Parnall. Scribner's, 1978.

———. *Your Own Best Secret Place*. Illustrated by Peter Parnall. Scribner's, 1979.

Birdseye, Tom. *Airmail to the Moon*. Illustrated by Stephen Gammell. Holiday House, 1988.

Blos, Joan. *A Gathering of Days: A New England Girl's Journal, 1830–1832*. Scribner's, 1979.

Briggs, Raymond. *Jim and the Beanstalk*. Coward, 1970.

Brink, Carol Ryrie. *Goody O'Grumpity*. Illustrated by Ashley Wolff. North-South, 1994.

Brooke, William J. *Teller of Tales*. HarperCollins, 1994.

Broome, Errol. *Dear Mr. Sprouts*. Knopf, 1993.

Brown, Marcia. *Stone Soup*. Scribner's, 1947.

Brown, Margaret Wise. *The Important Book*. Illustrated by Leonard Weisgard. Harper & Row, 1949.

Brown, Ruth. *The Big Sneeze*. Lothrop, Lee & Shepard, 1985.

Buehner, Caralyn. *Fanny's Dream*. Illustrated by Mark Buehner. Dial, 1996.

Burton, Virginia Lee. *The Little House*. Houghton Mifflin, 1942.

Butler, Stephen. *Henny Penny*. Tambourine, 1991.

Byars, Betsy. *The Burning Questions of Bingo Brown*. Viking Penguin, 1988.

———. *Cracker Jackson*. Viking, 1985.

———. *Goodbye, Chicken Little*. Harper & Row, 1979.

———. *The House of Wings*. Viking, 1972.

———. *The Night Swimmers*. Delacorte, 1980.

———. *The Pinballs*. Harper & Row, 1977.

———. *The Summer of the Swans*. Viking, 1970.

Calmenson, Stephanie. *The Principal's New Clothes*. Illustrated by Denise Brunkus. Scholastic, 1989.

Carle, Eric. *The Very Busy Spider*. Philomel, 1984.

———. *The Very Hungry Caterpillar*. Putnam, 1989 [1969].

———. *The Very Quiet Cricket*. Philomel, 1990.

Caseley, Judith. *Dear Annie*. Greenwillow, 1991.

Cleary, Beverly. *Dear Mr. Henshaw*. Morrow, 1983.

———. *Ramona and Her Father*. Illustrated by Alan Tiegreen. Morrow, 1977.

———. *The Mouse and the Motorcycle*. Illustrated by Louis Darling. Morrow, 1965.

———. *Strider*. Morrow, 1991.

Cleaver, Vera, and Bill Cleaver. *Where the Lilies Bloom*. Harper & Row, 1969.

Coerr, Eleanor. *The Josefina Story Quilt*. Illustrated by Bruce Degen. Harper & Row, 1986.

———. *Sadako and the Thousand Paper Cranes*. Illustrated by Ronald Himler. Putnam, 1977.

Cole, Babette. *Prince Cinders*. Putnam, 1987.

———. *Princess Smartypants*. Putnam, 1987.

Cole, Brock. *The Giant's Toe*. Farrar, Straus & Giroux, 1986.

Conrad, Pam. *Prairie Songs*. Harper & Row, 1985.

Cooper, Susan. *The Boggart*. McElderry, 1993.

Cormier, Robert. *The Chocolate War*. Pantheon, 1974.

Crews, Donald. *Freight Train*. Greenwillow, 1978.

———. *Light*. Greenwillow, 1981.

Cushman, Karen. *Catherine Called Birdy*. Clarion, 1994.

Darling, Benjamin. *Valerie and the Silver Pear*. Illustrated by Dan Lane. Four Winds, 1992.

de Paola, Tomie. *Big Anthony and the Magic Ring*. Harcourt Brace, 1979.

———. *Pancakes for Breakfast*. Harcourt Brace, 1978.

———. *The Comic Adventures of Old Mother Hubbard and Her Dog*. Harcourt Brace, 1981.

———. *The Popcorn Book*. Holiday House, 1978.

de Regniers, Beatrice Schenk. *May I Bring a Friend?* Illustrated by Beni Montresor. Atheneum, 1964.

Dorros, Arthur. *Abuela*. Illustrated by Elisa Kleven. Dutton, 1991.

———. *Tonight Is Carnaval*. Dutton, 1991.

Dunning, Stephen, Edward Lueders, and Hugh Smith. *Reflections on a Gift of Watermelon Pickle and Other Modern Verses*. Lothrop, Lee & Shepard, 1966.

DuPasquier, Philippe. *Dear Daddy . . . .* Bradbury, 1985.

Ehlert, Lois. *Color Zoo*. Lippincott, 1990.

———. *Mole's Hill: A Woodland Tale*. Harcourt Brace, 1994.

Ernst, Lisa Campbell. *Sam Johnson and the Blue Ribbon Quilt*. Lothrop, Lee & Shepard, 1983.

Feelings, Muriel. *Moja Means One: A Swahili Counting Book*. Illustrated by Tom Feelings. Dial, 1971.

Ferris, Helen, comp. *Favorite Poems Old and New*. Illustrated by Leonard Weisgard. Doubleday, 1957.

Fisher, Leonard Everett. *Calendar Art: Thirteen Days, Weeks, Months and Years Around the World*. Four Winds, 1987.

———. *Pyramid of the Sun—Pyramid of the Moon*. Macmillan, 1988.

Fleischman, Sid. *The Midnight Horse*. Illustrated by Peter Sis. Greenwillow, 1990.

———. *The Whipping Boy*. Illustrated by Peter Sis. Greenwillow, 1986.

Fleming, Denise. *Where Once There Was a Wood*. Holt, 1996.

Florian, Doug. *A Beach Day*. Greenwillow, 1990.

Flournoy, Valerie. *The Patchwork Quilt*. Illustrated by Jerry Pinkney. Dial, 1985.

Fox, Mem. *Koala Lou*. Illustrated by Pamela Lofts. Harcourt Brace, 1989.

Frank, Anne. *Anne Frank: The Diary of a Young Girl*. Doubleday, 1952.

Freedman, Russell. *Lincoln: A Photobiography*. Clarion, 1987.

French, Fiona. *Snow White in New York*. New York: Oxford University Press, 1988.

Fritz, Jean. *And Then What Happened, Paul Revere?* Illustrated by Margot Tomes. Putnam, 1973.

———. *The Cabin Faced West*. Putnam, 1958.

Galdone, Paul. *The Gingerbread Boy*. Clarion, 1975.

———. *The Little Red Hen*. Houghton Mifflin, 1979 [1973].

George, Jean Craighead. *Acorn Pancakes, Dandelion Salad and 38 Other Wild Recipes*. Illustrated by Paul Mirocha. HarperCollins, 1995.

———. *My Side of the Mountain*. Dutton, 1988 [1959].

———. *The Talking Earth*. Harper & Row, 1983.

———. *The Wild, Wild Cookbook*. Illustrated by Walter Kessell. Crowell, 1982.

Gerson, Mary-Joan. *Why the Sky Is Far Away: A Nigerian Folktale*. Illustrated by Carla Golembe. Little, Brown, 1992.

Gibbons, Gail. *Beacons of Light: Lighthouse*. Morrow, 1990.

Glubok, Shirley. *The Art of Africa*. Harper & Row, 1965.

Goor, Ron, and Nancy Goor. *Insect Metamorphosis: From Egg to Adult*. Atheneum, 1990.

Grahame, Kenneth. *The Reluctant Dragon*. Illustrated by Ernest Shepard. Holiday House, 1953 [1938].

Gray, Libba Moore. *Small Green Snake*. Illustrated by Holly Meade. Orchard, 1994.

Greenblat, Rodney A. *Uncle Wizzmo's New Used Car*. HarperCollins, 1990.

Greene, Karen. *Once Upon a Recipe*. New Hope Press, 1987.

Grifalconi, Ann. *Osa's Pride*. Little, Brown, 1990.

———. *The Village of Round and Square Houses*. Little, Brown. 1986.

Grimm brothers. *Hansel and Gretel*. Illustrated by Anthony Browne. Knopf, 1988 [1981].

Grover, Max. *Accidental Zucchini: An Unexpected Alphabet*. Harcourt Brace, 1993.

Glubak, Shirley. *Luka's Quilt*. Greenwillow, 1994.

Hadithi, Mwenye. *Tricky Tortoise*. Illustrated by Adrienne Kennaway. Little, Brown, 1988.

Hahn, Mary Downing. *The Jellyfish Season*. Clarion, 1985.

———. *Wait Till Helen Comes*. Houghton Mifflin, 1986.

Hale, Sara Josepha. *Mary Had a Little Lamb*. Illustrated by Tomie de Paola. Holiday House, 1984.

Haley, Gail. *A Story, a Story*. Macmillan, 1970.

Hall, Donald. *Ox-Cart Man*. Illustrated by Barbara Cooney. Viking, 1979.

Hayes, Sara Henderson. "The Builders." In *Reflections on a Gift of Watermelon Pickle*, ed. Stephen Dunning et al. Scott, Foresman, 1966.

Heide, Florence Parry, and Sylvia Worth Van Clief. *Fables You Shouldn't Pay Any Attention To*. Illustrated by Victoria Chess. Dell, 1991 [1978].

Heinrich, Bernd. *An Owl in the House: A Naturalist's Diary*. Adapted by Alice Calaprice. Joy Street, 1990.

Helfman, Harry. *Making Your Own Movies*. Morrow, 1970.

Heller, Ruth. *Many Luscious Lollipops: A Book About Adjectives*. Putnam, 1989.

Hoban, Russell. *Bread and Jam for Frances*. Illustrated by Lillian Hoban. Harper & Row, 1974.

Hoberman, Mary Ann. *A House Is a House for Me*. Illustrated by Betty Fraser. Penguin, 1982.

Hodges, Margaret. *Saint George and the Dragon*. Illustrated by Trina Schart Hyman. Little, Brown, 1984.

———. *The Wave*. Illustrated by Blair Lent. Houghton Mifflin, 1964.

Hogrogian, Nonny. *One Fine Day*. Macmillan, 1971.

Hooks, William H. *The Ballad of Belle Dorcas*. Illustrated by Brian Pinkney. Knopf, 1990.

Hooper, Patricia. *How the Sky's Housekeeper Wore Her Scarves*. Illustrated by Susan L. Roth. Little, Brown, 1995.

Hopkinson, Deborah. *Sweet Clara and the Freedom Quilt*. Illustrated by James Ransome. Knopf, 1993.

Hunt, Jonathan. *Illuminations*. Bradbury, 1989.

Hunter, Mollie. *The Mermaid Summer*. Harper & Row, 1988.

———. *A Stranger Came Ashore*. Harper & Row, 1975.

Hutchins, Pat. *Rosie's Walk*. Macmillan, 1968.

———. *The Surprise Party*. Macmillan, 1969.

Irvine, Joan. *How to Make Pop-Ups*. Illustrated by Barbara Reid. Morrow, 1987.

Jackson, Ellen. *Brown Cow, Green Grass, Yellow Sun*. Illustrated by Victoria Raymond. Hyperion, 1995.

———. *Cinder Edna*. Illustrated by Kevin O'Malley. Lothrop, Lee & Shepard, 1994.

Jacques, Brian. *Redwall*. Illustrated by Gary Chalk. Philomel, 1986.

Jakobsen, Kathy. *My New York*. Little, Brown, 1993.

James, Betsy. *The Dream Stair*. Illustrated by Richard Jesse Watson. HarperCollins, 1990.

Jones, Rebecca C. *Down at the Bottom of the Deep Dark Sea*. Illustrated by Virginia Wright-Frierson. Bradbury, 1991.

———. *Germy Blows the Bugle*. Arcade, 1990.

Joyce, William. *George Shrinks*. Harper & Row, 1985.

Kalman, Bobbie. *Colonial Life*. Crabtree, 1992.

Keats, Ezra Jack. *Hi Cat!* Macmillan, 1970.

———. *Peter's Chair*. Harper & Row, 1967.

———. *The Snowy Day*. Viking, 1962.

Kehoe, Michael. *A Book Takes Root: The Making of a Pic   :* Carolrhoda, 1993.

Kent, Jack. *The Fat Cat: A Danish Folktale*. Scholastic, 1972.

Key, Alexander. *The Forgotten Door*. Scholastic, 1986 [1965].

Kidd, Diana. *Onion Tears*. Illustrated by Lucy Montgomery. Orchard, 1991.

Kinsey-Warnock, Natalie. *The Canada Geese Quilt*. Illustrated by Leslie W. Bowman. Cobblehill, 1989.

Kipling, Rudyard. *The Elephant's Child*. Illustrated by Lorinda Bryan Cauley. Harcourt Brace, 1988.

Kuskin, Karla. *Dogs & Dragons, Trees & Dreams*. Harper & Row, 1980.

Langstaff, John. *Over in the Meadow*. Illustrated by Feodor Rojankovsky. Harcourt Brace, 1957.

Lattimore, Deborah Nourse. *The Flame of Peace: A Tale of the Aztecs*. Harper & Row, 1987.

Leaf, Margaret. *Eyes of the Dragon*. Illustrated by Ed Young. Lothrop, Lee & Shepard, 1987.

Le Guin, Ursula K. *A Wizard of Earthsea*. Illustrated by Ruth Robbins. Parnassus, 1968.

L'Engle, Madeleine. *A Ring of Endless Light*. Farrar, Straus & Giroux, 1980.

———. *A Wrinkle in Time*. Farrar, Straus & Giroux, 1962.

Levine, Ellen. *If You Lived at the Time of the Great San Francisco Earthquake*. Illustrated by Richard Williams. Scholastic, 1987.

Lewin, Hugh. *Jafta*. Illustrated by Lisa Kopper. Carolrhoda, 19

Lewis, C. S. *The Lion, the Witch and the Wardrobe*. Illustrated   Ba   macmillan, 1968.

Lewis, Richard. *All of You Was Singing*. Illustrated by Ed Young.   ian, 1991.

———. *Dreams*. Illustrated by Ezra Jack Keats. Macmillan, 1974.

———. *In a Spring Garden*. Illustrated by Ezra Jack Keats. Dial, 1978.

Lindbergh, Reeve. *Johnny Appleseed*. Illustrated by Kathy Jakobsen. Little, Brown, 1990.

Lionni, Leo. *The Biggest House in the World*. Pantheon, 1968.

———. *Alexander and the Wind-up Mouse*. Pantheon, 1969.

———. *Frederick*. Pantheon, 1966.

———. *Little Blue and Little Yellow*. Astor-Honor, 1959.

———. *Swimmy*. Pantheon, 1963.

Little, Jean. *Hey World, Here I Am!* Illustrated by Sue Truesdell. Harper & Row, 1989.

Lobel, Arnold. *The Book of Pigericks*. Harper & Row, 1983.

———. *Fables*. Harper & Row, 1980.

———. *Frog and Toad Are Friends*. Harper & Row, 1970.

———. *Frog and Toad Together*. Harper & Row, 1972.

———. *Uncle Elephant*. Harper & Row, 1981.

Lowry, Lois. *Anastasia Krupnik*. Houghton Mifflin, 1979.

Lyon, George Ella. *Come a Tide*. Illustrated by Stephen Gammell. Orchard, 1990.

MacDonald, Caroline. *The Lake at the End of the World*. Dial, 1989.

MacDonald, Kate. *The Anne of Green Gables Cookbook*. Illustrated by Barbara DiLella. Oxford University Press, 1987.

MacLachlan, Patricia. *Sarah, Plain and Tall*. Harper & Row, 1985.

Martin, Bill, Jr., and John Archambault. *The Ghost-Eye Tree*. Illustrated by Ted Rand. Holt, 1985.

Marzollo, Jean. *Pretend You're a Cat*. Illustrated by Jerry Pinkney. Dial, 1990.

McDermott, Gerald. *Anansi the Spider: A Tale from the Ashanti*. Holt, 1972.

McDonald, Megan. *Is This a House for a Hermit Crab?* Illustrated by S. D. Schindler. Orchard, 1990.

McMillan, Bruce. *One Sun: A Book of Terse Verse*. Holiday House, 1990.

McPhail, David. *Pig Pig Grows Up*. Dutton, 1980.

Merriam, Eve. *Quiet, Please*. Illustrated by Sheila Hamanaka. Simon & Schuster, 1993.

Merrill, Jean. *The Pushcart War*. Addison-Wesley, 1964.

Milhous, Katherine and Alice Dalgliesh. *The Turnip: An Old Russian Folktale*. Illustrated by Pierr Morgan. Philomel, 1990.

Mills, Lauren. *The Rag Coat*. Little, Brown, 1991.

Myers, Bernice. *Sidney Rella and the Glass Sneaker*. Macmillan, 1985.

Myers, Walter Dean. *The Mouse Rap*. HarperCollins, 1990.

Neville, Emily Cheney. *The China Year*. HarperCollins, 1990.

Norton, Mary. *The Borrowers*. Illustrated by Beth and Jo Krush. Harcourt Brace, 1965.

Numeroff, Laura Joffe. *If You Give a Mouse a Cookie*. Illustrated by Felicia Bond. Harper & Row, 1985.

O'Brien, Robert C. *Mrs. Frisby and the Rats of NIMH*. Illustrated by Zena Bernstein. Atheneum, 1971.

————. *Z for Zachariah*. Atheneum, 1975.

Oppenheim, Joanne. *You Can't Catch Me!* Illustrated by Andrew Shachat. Houghton Mifflin, 1986.

Park, Barbara. *Skinnybones*. Knopf, 1982.

Parson, Alexandra. *Amazing Birds*. Illustrated by Jerry Young. Knopf, 1990.

————. *Amazing Poisonous Animals*. Illustrated by Jerry Young. Knopf, 1990.

Paterson, Katherine. *Bridge to Terabithia*. Illustrated by Donna Diamond. Crowell, 1977.

————. *The Great Gilly Hopkins*. Crowell, 1978.

————. *Jacob Have I Loved*. Crowell, 1980.

————. *Lyddie*. Dutton, 1991.

Paul, Ann Whitford. *Eight Hands Round: A Patchwork Alphabet*. Illustrated by Jeanette Winter. HarperCollins, 1991.

————. *The Seasons Sewn: A Year in Patchwork*. Illustrated by Michael McCurdy. Browndeer, 1996.

Paulsen, Gary. *Hatchet*. Bradbury, 1987.

Perl, Lila. *Hunter's Stew and Hangtown Fry: What Pioneer America Ate and Why*. Illustrated by Richard Cuffari. Houghton Mifflin, 1979.

————. *Slumps, Grunts and Snickerdoodles: What Colonial America Ate and Why*. Illustrated by Richard Cuffari. Houghton Mifflin, 1979.

Perrault, Charles. *Cinderella*. Illustrated by Roberto Innocenti. Creative Education, 1983.

Pinkwater, Daniel. *Borgel*. Macmillan, 1990.

————. *The Hoboken Chicken Emergency*. Prentice Hall, 1977.

Polacco, Patricia. *The Keeping Quilt*. Simon & Schuster, 1988.

————. *Thunder Cake*. Philomel, 1990.

Pomerantz, Charlotte. *Whiff, Sniff, Nibble, and Chew: The Gingerbread Boy Retold*. Illustrated by Monica Incisa. Greenwillow, 1984.

Potter, Beatrix. *The Peter Rabbit and Friends Cookbook*. Frederick Warne, 1994.

————. *The Tale of Peter Rabbit*. Frederick Warne, 1972 [1902].

Prelutsky, Jack. *Nightmares: Poems to Trouble Your Sleep*. Illustrated by Arnold Lobel. Greenwillow, 1976.

———, ed. *Read-Aloud Rhymes for the Very Young*. Illustrated by Marc Simont. Knopf, 1986.

Pryor, Bonnie. *The House on Maple Street*. Illustrated by Beth Peck. Morrow, 1987.

Purviance, Susan, and Marcia O'Shell. *Alphabet Annie Announces an All-American Album*. Illustrated by Ruth Brunner-Strosser. Houghton Mifflin, 1988.

Reeder, Carolyn. *Shades of Gray*. Macmillan, 1989.

Reid, Barbara. *Two by Two*. Scholastic, 1993.

Reid, Margarette S. *The Button Box*. Illustrated by Sarah Chamberlain. Dutton, 1990.

Reinl, Edda. *The Three Little Pigs*. Picture Book, 1983.

Rice, Eve. *Peter's Pockets*. Illustrated by Nancy Winslow Parker. Greenwillow, 1989.

Richard, Francoise. *On Cat Mountain*. Illustrated by Anne Buguet. Putnam, 1994.

Richter, Hans Peter. *Friedrich*. Holt, 1970.

Ringgold, Faith. *Tar Beach*. Crown, 1991.

Rockwell, Thomas. *How to Eat Fried Worms*. Franklin Watts, 1973.

Rohmer, Harriet. *Uncle Nacho's Hat*. Illustrated by Veg Reisberg. Children's Book Press, 1989.

Rosen, Michael. *We're Going on a Bear Hunt*. Illustrated by Helen Oxenbury. Macmillan, 1989.

Ross, Tony. *Jack and the Beanstalk*. Delacorte, 1980.

———. *Stone Soup*. Dial, 1987.

Roth, Susan L., and Ruth Phang. *Patchwork Tales*. Atheneum, 1984.

Roy, Ron. *Three Ducks Went Wandering*. Illustrated by Paul Galdone. Houghton Mifflin, 1979.

Sanders, Scott R. *Hear the Wind Blow: American Folk Songs Retold*. Illustrated by Ponder Goembel. Bradbury, 1985.

Sattler, Helen Roney. *Recipes for Art and Craft Materials*. Illustrated by Marti Shohet. Lothrop, Lee & Shepard, 1987.

Scieszka, Jon. *The Book That Jack Wrote*. Illustrated by Daniel Adel. Viking, 1994.

———. *The Frog Prince Continued*. Illustrated by Steve Johnson. Viking, 1991.

———. *The Stinky Cheese Man and Other Fairly Stupid Tales*. Illustrated by Lane Smith. Viking, 1992.

———. *The True Story of the 3 Little Pigs by A. Wolf*. Illustrated by Lane Smith. Penguin, 1989.

Sendak, Maurice. *Chicken Soup with Rice*. Harper & Row, 1962.

———. *Where the Wild Things Are*. Harper & Row, 1963.

Shulevitz, Uri. *Dawn*. Farrar, Straus & Giroux, 1974.

Sierra, Judy. *Wiley and the Hairy Man*. Illustrated by Brian Pinkney. Lodestar, 1996.

Simon, Seymour. *Animal Fact/Animal Fable*. Illustrated by Diane DeGroat. Crown, 1979.

Snyder, Zilpha Keatley. *Cat Running*. Delacorte, 1994.

———. *Libby on Wednesday*. Delacorte, 1990.

Spier, Peter. *The Erie Canal*. Doubleday, 1970.

———. *The Star-Spangled Banner*. Doubleday, 1973.

———. *Tin Lizzie*. Doubleday, 1978.

Stafford, William. *The Animal That Drank Up Sound*. Illustrated by Debra Frasier. Harcourt Brace, 1992.

Stanley, Diane, and Peter Vennema. *Shaka, King of the Zulus*. Illustrated by Diane Stanley. Morrow, 1988.

Stanley, Jerry. *Children of the Dust Bowl: The Story of the School at Weedpatch Camp*. Crown, 1992.

Steig, William. *Abel's Island*. Farrar, Straus & Giroux, 1976.

———. *The Amazing Bone*. Farrar, Straus & Giroux, 1976.

———. *Amos & Boris*. Farrar, Straus & Giroux, 1971.

Steptoe, John. *Mufaro's Beautiful Daughters: An African Tale*. Lothrop, Lee & Shepard, 1987.

Stevens, Carla. *Trouble for Lucy*. Illustrated by Ronald Himler. Clarion, 1979.

Stevens, Janet. *From Pictures to Words: A Book About Making a Book*. Holiday House, 1995.

Terban, Marvin. *In a Pickle and Other Funny Idioms*. Illustrated by Giulio Maestro. Clarion, 1983.

———. *Mad as a Wet Hen and Other Funny Idioms*. Illustrated by Giulio Maestro. Clarion, 1987.

Thomas, Patricia. *"Stand Back," Said the Elephant, "I'm Going to Sneeze!"* Illustrated by Wallace Tripp. Lothrop, Lee & Shepard, 1990.

Tollhurst, Marilyn. *Somebody and the Three Blairs*. Illustrated by Simone Abel. Orchard, 1990.

Travers, P. L. *Mary Poppins*. Illustrated by Mary Shepard. Harcourt Brace, 1981.

Turkle, Brinton. *Deep in the Forest*. Dutton, 1976.

———. *Do Not Open*. Dutton, 1981.

Turner, Ann. *Sewing Quilts*. Illustrated by Thomas B. Allen. Macmillan, 1994.

Uchida, Yoshiko. *Journey to Topaz*. Illustrated by Donald Carrick. Creative Arts Books, 1985 [1971].

Viorst, Judith. *Alexander and the Terrible, Horrible, No Good, Very Bad Day*. Illustrated by Ray Cruz. Atheneum, 1972.

Walker, Barbara. *The Little House Cookbook*. Illustrated by Garth Williams. Harper & Row, 1979.

Warner, Gertrude Chandler. *The Boxcar Children #1*. Whitman, 1990 [1924].

Westcott, Nadine Bernard. *I Know an Old Lady Who Swallowed a Fly*. Little, Brown, 1980.

———. *The Lady with the Alligator Purse*. Little, Brown, 1988.

———. *Skip to My Lou*. Little, Brown, 1990.

———. *There's a Hole in the Bucket*. Little, Brown, 1990.

Wilder, Laura Ingalls. *Farmer Boy*. Illustrated by Garth Williams. Harper & Row, 1973.

Wildsmith, Brian. *Birds*. Oxford University Press, 1980.

Williams, Jay. *Everyone Knows What a Dragon Looks Like*. Illustrated by Mercer Mayer. Macmillan, 1976.

Williams, Karen Lynn. *Galimoto*. Illustrated by Catherine Stock. Lothrop, Lee & Shepard, 1990.

Williams, Linda. *The Little Old Lady Who Was Not Afraid of Anything*. Illustrated by Megan Lloyd. Harper & Row, 1986.

Williams, Vera. B. *Cherries and Cherry Pits*. Greenwillow, 1986.

———. *Stringbean's Trip to the Shining Sea*. Illustrated by Vera B. Williams and Jennifer Williams. Greenwillow, 1988.

———. *Three Days on a River in a Red Canoe*. Greenwillow, 1981.

Wilner, Isabel. *The Poetry Troupe*. Scribner's, 1977.

Winter, Jonah. *Diego*. Illustrated by Jeannette Winter. Knopf, 1991.

Wisniewski, David. *The Wave of the Sea-Wolf*. Clarion, 1994.

Wolf, Janet. *Her Book*. Harper & Row, 1982.

Xiong, Blia. *Nine-in-One Grr! Grr!* Adapted by Cathy Spagnoli. Illustrated by Nancy Hom. Children's Book Press, 1989.

Yagawa, Sumiko. *The Crane Wife*. Translated by Katherine Paterson. Illustrated by Suekichi Akaba. Morrow, 1981.

Yashima, Taro. *Crow Boy*. Viking, 1955.

Yep, Laurence. *Dragonwings*. Harper & Row, 1977.

Yolen, Jane. *Dove Isabeau*. Illustrated by Dennis Nolan. Harcourt Brace, 1979.

———. *Owl Moon*. Illustrated by John Schoenherr. Philomel, 1987.

———. *Sleeping Ugly*. Illustrated by Diane Stanley. Putnam, 1981.

Zion, Gene. *Harry the Dirty Dog*. Harper & Row, 1956.

Zolotow, Charlotte. *Someday*. Illustrated by Arnold Lobel. Harper & Row, 1965.

appendix a
Children's Book Awards

The John Newbery Medal is named in honor of John Newbery, a British publisher and bookseller of the eighteenth century. He has frequently been called the father of children's literature, because he was the first to conceive the idea of publishing books expressly for children.

The award is presented each year to "the author of the most distinguished contribution to American literature for children." Only books published in the preceding year are eligible, and the author must be an American citizen or a permanent resident of the United States. The selection of the winner is made by a committee of the Association for Library Service to Children (ALSC) of the American Library Association. There are now fifteen members on this committee. The winning author is presented with a bronze medal designed by René Paul Chambellan and donated by Frederick G. Melcher. The announcement is made in January or early February. Later, at the summer conference of the American Library Association, a banquet is given in honor of the award winners.

The following list of books includes the award winners (capitalized and listed first) and the Honor Books for each year. The date is the year in which the award was conferred. All books were published the preceding year.

1922 THE STORY OF MANKIND by Hendrik Van Loon. Boni & Liveright.
The Great Quest by Charles Boardman Hawes. Little, Brown.
Cedric the Forester by Bernard G. Marshall. Appleton.
The Old Tobacco Shop by William Bowen. Macmillan.
The Golden Fleece by Padraic Colum. Macmillan.
Windy Hill by Cornelia Meigs. Macmillan.

1923 THE VOYAGES OF DOCTOR DOLITTLE by Hugh Lofting. Stokes.
(No record of the Honor Books.)

1924 THE DARK FRIGATE by Charles Boardman Hawes. Little, Brown.
(No record of the Honor Books.)

1925 TALES FROM SILVER LANDS by Charles J. Finger. Illustrated by Paul Honoré. Doubleday.
Nicholas by Anne Carroll Moore. Putnam.
Dream Coach by Anne and Dillwyn Parrish. Macmillan.

1926 SHEN OF THE SEA by Arthur Bowie Chrisman. Illustrated by Else Hasselriis. Dutton.
The Voyagers by Padraic Colum. Macmillan.

1927 SMOKY, THE COWHORSE by Will James. Scribner's.
(No record of the Honor Books.)

1928 GAY NECK by Dhan Gopal Mukerji. Illustrated by Boris Artzybasheff. Dutton.
The Wonder-Smith and His Son by Ella Young. Longmans, Green.
Downright Dencey by Caroline Dale Snedeker. Doubleday.

1929 TRUMPETER OF KRAKOW by Eric P. Kelly. Illustrated by Angela Pruszynska. Macmillan.
The Pigtail of Ah Lee Ben Loo by John Bennett. Longmans, Green.
Millions of Cats by Wanda Gág. Coward-McCann.
The Boy Who Was by Grace T. Hallock. Dutton.
Clearing Weather by Cornelia Meigs. Little, Brown.
The Runaway Papoose by Grace P. Moon. Doubleday.
Tod of the Fens by Eleanor Whitney. Macmillan.

1930 HITTY, HER FIRST HUNDRED YEARS by Rachel Field. Illustrated by Dorothy P. Lathrop. Macmillan.
Pran of Albania by Elizabeth C. Miller. Doubleday.
The Jumping-Off Place by Miran Hurd McNeely. Longmans, Green.
A Daughter of the Seine by Jeanette Eaton. Harper & Row.

1931 The CAT WHO WENT TO HEAVEN by Elizabeth Coatsworth. Illustrated by Lynd Ward. Macmillan.
Floating Island by Anne Parrish. Harper & Row.
The Dark Star of Itza by Alida Malkus. Harcourt Brace.
Queer Person by Ralph Hubbard. Doubleday.
Mountains Are Free by Julia Davis Adams. Dutton.
Spice and the Devil's Cave by Agnes D. Hewes. Knopf.
Meggy McIntosh by Elizabeth Janet Gray. Doubleday.

1932 WATERLESS MOUNTAIN by Laura Adams Armer. Illustrated by Sidney Armer and the author. Longmans, Green.
The Fairy Circus by Dorothy Lathrop. Macmillan.
Calico Bush by Rachel Field. Macmillan.
Boy of the South Seas by Eunice Tietjens. Coward-McCann.
Out of the Flame by Eloise Lounsbery. Longmans, Green.
Jane's Island by Marjorie Hill Alee. Houghton Mifflin.
Truce of the Wolf by Mary Gould Davis. Harcourt Brace.

1933 YOUNG FU OF THE UPPER YANGTZE by Elizabeth Foreman Lewis. Illustrated by Kurt Wiese. Winston.
Swift Rivers by Cornelia Meigs. Little, Brown.
The Railroad to Freedom by Hildegarde Swift. Harcourt Brace.
Children of the Soil by Nora Burglon. Doubleday.

1934   INVINCIBLE LOUISA by Cornelia Meigs. Little, Brown.
Forgotten Daughter by Caroline Dale Snedeker. Doubleday.
Swords of Steel by Elsie Singmaster. Houghton Mifflin.
ABC Bunny by Wanda Gág. Coward-McCann.
Winged Girl of Knossos by Erick Berry. Appleton.
New Land by Sarah L. Schmidt. McBride.
Apprentices of Florence by Anne Kyle. Houghton Mifflin.

1935   DOBRY by Monica Shannon. Illustrated by Atanas
Katchamakoff. Viking.
The Pageant of Chinese History by Elizabeth Seeger. Longmans, Green.
Davy Crockett by Constance Rourke. Harcourt Brace.
A Day on Skates by Hilda Van Stockum. Harper & Row.

1936   CADDIE WOODLAWN by Carol Ryrie Brink. Illustrated by
Kate Seredy. Macmillan.
Honk the Moose by Phil Stong. Dodd, Mead.
The Good Master by Kate Seredy. Viking.
Young Walter Scott by Elizabeth Janet Gray. Viking.
All Sail Set by Armstrong Sperry. Winston.

1937   ROLLER SKATES by Ruth Sawyer. Illustrated by Valenti
Angelo. Viking.
Phoebe Fairchild: Her Book by Lois Lenski. Stokes.
Whistler's Van by Idwal Jones. Viking.
The Golden Basket by Ludwig Bemelmans. Viking.
Winterbound by Margery Bianco. Viking.
Audubon by Constance Rourke. Harcourt Brace.
The Codfish Musket by Agnes D. Hewes. Doubleday.

1938   THE WHITE STAG by Kate Seredy. Viking.
Bright Island by Mabel L. Robinson. Random House.
Pecos Bill by James Cloyd Bowman. Whitman.
On the Banks of Plum Creek by Laura Ingalls Wilder. Harper & Row.

1939   THIMBLE SUMMER by Elizabeth Enright. Farrar & Rinehart.
Leader by Destiny by Jeanette Eaton. Harcourt Brace.
Penn by Elizabeth Janet Gray. Viking.
Nino by Valenti Angelo. Viking.
"Hello, the Boat!" by Phyllis Crawford. Holt.
Mr. Popper's Penguins by Richard and Florence Atwater. Little, Brown.

1940   DANIEL BOONE by James H. Daugherty. Viking.
The Singing Tree by Kate Seredy. Viking.
Runner of the Mountain Tops by Mabel L. Robinson. Random House.
By the Shores of Silver Lake by Laura Ingalls Wilder. Harper & Row.
Boy with a Pack by Stephen W. Meader. Harcourt Brace.

1941   CALL IT COURAGE by Armstrong Sperry. Macmillan.
Blue Willow by Doris Gates. Viking.
Young Mac of Fort Vancouver by Mary Jane Carr. Crowell.
The Long Winter by Laura Ingalls Wilder. Harper & Row.
Nansen by Anna Gertrude Hall. Viking.

1942   THE MATCHLOCK GUN by Walter D. Edmonds. Illustrated
by Paul Lantz. Dodd, Mead.
Little Town on the Prairie by Laura Ingalls Wilder. Harper & Row.
George Washington's World by Genevieve Foster. Scribner's.
Indian Captive by Lois Lenski. Stokes.
Down Ryton Water by E. R. Gaggin. Viking.

1943   ADAM OF THE ROAD by Elizabeth Janet Gray. Illustrated
by Robert Lawson. Viking.
The Middle Moffat by Eleanor Estes. Harcourt Brace.
"Have You Seen Tom Thumb?" by Mabel Leigh Hunt. Stokes.

1944   JOHNNY TREMAIN by Esther Forbes. Illustrated by Lynd
Ward. Houghton Mifflin.
These Happy Golden Years by Laura Ingalls Wilder. Harper & Row.
Fog Magic by Julia L. Sauer. Viking.
Rufus M. by Eleanor Estes. Harcourt Brace.
Mountain Born by Elizabeth Yates. Coward-McCann.

1945   RABBIT HILL by Robert Lawson. Viking.
The Hundred Dresses by Eleanor Estes. Harcourt Brace.
The Silver Pencil by Alice Dalgliesh. Scribner's.
Abraham Lincoln's World by Genevieve Foster. Scribner's.
Lone Journey by Jeanette Eaton. Harcourt Brace.

1946   STRAWBERRY GIRL by Lois Lenski. Lippincott.
Justin Morgan Had a Horse by Marguerite Henry. Wilcox & Follett.
The Moved-Outers by Florence Crannell Means. Houghton Mifflin.
Bhimsa, the Dancing Bear by Christine Weston. Scribner's.
New Found World by Katherine B. Shippen. Viking.

1947   MISS HICKORY by Carolyn Sherwin Bailey. Illustrated by
Ruth Gannett. Viking.
The Wonderful Year by Nancy Barnes. Messner.
Big Tree by Mary Buff and Conrad Buff. Viking.
The Heavenly Tenants by William Maxwell. Harper & Row.
The Avion My Uncle Flew by Cyrus Fisher. Appleton.
The Hidden Treasure of Glaston by Eleanore M. Jewett. Viking.

1948   THE TWENTY-ONE BALLOONS by William Pène DuBois.
Viking.
Pancakes-Paris by Claire Huchet Bishop. Viking.
Li Lun, Lad of Courage by Carolyn Treffinger. Abingdon-Cokesbury.
The Quaint and Curious Quest of Johnny Longfoot by Catherine Besterman. Bobbs-Merrill.
The Cow-Tail Switch by Harold Courlander and George Herzog. Holt.
Misty of Chincoteague by Marguerite Henry. Rand McNally.

1949   KING OF THE WIND by Marguerite Henry. Illustrated by
Wesley Dennis. Rand McNally.
Seabird by Holling Clancy Holling. Houghton Mifflin.
Daughter of the Mountains by Louise Rankin. Viking.
My Father's Dragon by Ruth S. Gannett. Random House.
Story of the Negro by Arna Bontemps. Knopf.

1950   THE DOOR IN THE WALL by Marguerite de Angeli.
Doubleday.
Tree of Freedom by Rebecca Caudill. Viking.
Blue Cat of Castle Town by Catherine Coblentz. Longmans, Green.
Kildee House by Rutherford Montgomery. Doubleday.
George Washington by Genevieve Foster. Scribner's.
Song of the Pines by Walter Havighurst and Marion Havighurst. Winston.

1951   AMOS FORTUNE, FREE MAN by Elizabeth Yates.
Illustrated by Nora Unwin. Aladdin.
Better Known as Johnny Appleseed by Mabel Leigh Hunt. Lippincott.
Gandhi, Fighter Without a Sword by Jeanette Eaton. Morrow.
Abraham Lincoln, Friend of the People by Clara I. Judson. Wilcox & Follett.
The Story of Appleby Capple by Anne Parrish. Harper & Row.

1952   GINGER PYE by Elizabeth Chesley Baity. Viking.
Minn of the Mississippi by Holling Clancy Holling. Houghton Mifflin.
The Defender by Nicholas Kalashnikoff. Scribner's.
The Light at Tern Rock by Julia L. Sauer. Viking.
The Apple and the Arrow by Mary Buff. Houghton Mifflin.

1953   SECRET OF THE ANDES by Ann Nolan Clark. Illustrated
by Jean Charlot. Viking.
Charlotte's Web by E. B. White. Harper & Row.
Moccasin Trail by Eloise J. McGraw. Coward-McCann.
Red Sails for Capri by Ann Weil. Viking.
The Bears on Hemlock Mountain by Alice Dalgliesh. Scribner's.
Birthdays of Freedom by Genevieve Foster. Scribner's.

1954 AND NOW MIGUEL by Joseph Krumgold. Illustrated by Jean Charlot. Crowell.
All Alone by Clarie Huchet Bishop. Viking.
Shadrach by Meindert DeJong. Harper & Row.
Hurry Home, Candy by Meindert DeJong, Harper & Row.
Theodore Roosevelt, Fighting Patriot by Clara I. Judson. Follett.
Magic Maize by Buff. Houghton Mifflin.

1955 THE WHEEL ON THE SCHOOL by Meindert DeJong. Illustrated by Maurice Sendak. Harper & Row.
The Courage of Sarah Noble by Alice Dalgliesh. Scribner's.
Banner in the Sky by James Ramsey Ullman. Lippincott.

1956 CARRY ON, MR. BOWDITCH by Jean Lee Latham. Houghton Mifflin.
The Golden Name Day by Jennie D. Lindquist. Harper & Row.
The Secret River by Marjorie Kinnan Rawlings. Scribner's.
Men, Microscopes and Living Things by Katherine B. Shippen. Viking.

1957 MIRACLES ON MAPLE HILL by Virginia Sorensen. Illustrated by Beth Krush and Joe Krush. Harcourt Brace.
Old Yeller by Fred Gipson. Harper & Row.
The House of Sixty Fathers by Meindert DeJong. Harper & Row.
Mr. Justice Holmes by Clara I. Judson. Follett.
The Corn Grows Ripe by Dorothy Rhoads. Viking.
The Black Fox of Lorne by Marguerite de Angeli. Doubleday.

1958 RIFLES FOR WATIE by Harold Keith. Illustrated by Peter Burchard. Crowell.
The Horsecatcher by Mari Sandoz. Westminster.
Gone-Away Lake by Elizabeth Enright. Harcourt Brace.
The Great Wheel by Robert Lawson. Viking.
Tom Paine, Freedom's Apostle by Leo Gurko. Crowell.

1959 THE WITCH OF BLACKBIRD POND by Elizabeth George Speare. Houghton Mifflin.
The Family Under the Bridge by Natalie S. Carlson. Harper & Row.
Along Came a Dog by Meindert DeJong. Harper & Row.
Chucaro by Francis Kalnay. Harcourt Brace.
The Perilous Road by William O. Steele. Harcourt Brace.

1960 ONION JOHN by Joseph Krumgold. Illustrated by Symeon Shimin. Crowell.
My Side of the Mountain by Jean George. Dutton.
America Is Born by Gerald Johnson. Morrow.
The Gammage Cup by Carol Kendall. Harcourt Brace.

1961 ISLAND OF THE BLUE DOLPHINS by Scott O'Dell. Houghton Mifflin.
America Moves Forward by Gerald Johnson. Morrow.
Old Ramon by Jack Schaefer. Houghton Mifflin.
The Cricket in Times Square by George Selden. Farrar.

1962 THE BRONZE BOW by Elizabeth George Speare. Houghton Mifflin.
Frontier Living by Edwin Tunis. World.
The Golden Goblet by Eloise J. McGraw. Coward-McCann.
Belling the Tiger by Mary Stolz. Harper & Row.

1963 A WRINKLE IN TIME by Madeleine L'Engle. Farrar, Straus.
Thistle and Thyme by Sorche Nic Leodhas. Holt, Rinehart & Winston.
Men of Athens by Olivia Coolidge. Houghton Mifflin.

1964 IT'S LIKE THIS, CAT by Emily Neville. Illustrated by Emil Weiss. Harper & Row.
Rascal by Sterling North. Dutton.
The Loner by Ester Wier. McKay.

1965 SHADOW OF A BULL by Maia Wojciechowska. Illustrated by Alvin Smith. Atheneum.
Across Five Aprils by Irene Hunt. Follett.

1966 I, JUAN DE PAREJA by Elizabeth Borten de Treviño. Farrar, Straus.
The Black Cauldron by Lloyd Alexander. Holt, Rinehart & Winston.
The Animal Family by Randall Jarrell. Pantheon.
The Noonday Friends by Mary Stolz. Harper & Row.

1967 UP A ROAD SLOWLY by Irene Hunt. Follett.
The King's Fifth by Scott O'Dell. Houghton Mifflin.
Zlateh the Goat and Other Stories by Isaac Bashevis Singer. Harper & Row.
The Jazz Man by Mary Hays Weik. Atheneum.

1968 FROM THE MIXED-UP FILES OF MRS. BASIL E. FRANKWEILER by E. L. Konigsburg. Atheneum.
Jennifer, Hecate, Macbeth, William McKinley, and Me, Elizabeth by E. L. Konigsburg. Atheneum.
The Black Pearl by Scott O'Dell. Houghton Mifflin.
The Fearsome Inn by Isaac Bashevis Singer. Scribner's.
The Egypt Game by Zilpha Keatley Snyder. Atheneum.

1969 THE HIGH KING by Lloyd Alexander. Holt, Rinehart & Winston.
To Be a Slave by Julius Lester. Dial.
When Shlemiel Went to Warsaw and Other Stories by Isaac Bashevis Singer. Farrar, Straus.

1970 SOUNDER by William H. Armstrong. Harper & Row.
Our Eddie by Sulamith Isk-Kishor. Pantheon.
The Many Ways of Seeing: An Introduction to the Pleasures of Art by Janet Gaylord Moore. World.
Journey Outside by Mary Q. Steele. Viking.

1971 SUMMER OF THE SWANS by Betsy Byars. Viking.
Kneeknock Rise by Natalie Babbitt. Farrar, Straus.
Enchantress from the Stars by Sylvia Louise Engdahl. Atheneum.
Sing Down the Moon by Scott O'Dell. Houghton Mifflin.

1972 MRS. FRISBY AND THE RATS OF NIMH by Robert C. O'Brien. Atheneum.
Incident at Hawk's Hill by Allan W. Eckert. Little, Brown.
The Planet of Junior Brown by Virginia Hamilton. Macmillan.
The Tombs of Atuan by Ursula K. Le Guin. Atheneum.
Annie and the Old One by Miska Miles. Atlantic/Little, Brown.
The Headless Cupid by Zilpha Keatley Snyder. Atheneum.

1973 JULIE OF THE WOLVES by Jean Craighead George. Harper & Row.
Frog and Toad Together by Arnold Lobel. Harper & Row.
The Upstairs Room by Johanna Reiss. Crowell.
The Witches of Worm by Zilpha Keatley Snyder. Atheneum.

1974 THE SLAVE DANCER by Paula Fox. Bradbury.
The Dark Is Rising by Susan Cooper. Atheneum.

1975 M. C. HIGGINS THE GREAT by Virginia Hamilton. Macmillan.
My Brother Sam Is Dead by James Collier and Christopher Collier. Four Winds.
Philip Hall Likes Me, I Reckon Maybe by Bette Greene. Dial.
The Perilous Gard by Elizabeth Pope. Houghton Mifflin.
Figgs & Phantoms by Ellen Raskin. Dutton.

1976 THE GREY KING by Susan Cooper. Atheneum.
Dragonwings by Laurence Yep. Harper & Row.
The Hundred Penny Box by Sharon Mathis. Viking.

1977 ROLL OF THUNDER, HEAR MY CRY by Mildred D. Taylor. Dial.
Abel's Island by William Steig. Farrar, Straus.
A String in the Harp by Nancy Bond. Atheneum.

1978 BRIDGE TO TERABITHIA by Katherine Paterson. Crowell.
Anpao: An American Indian Odyssey by Jamake Highwater. Lippincott.
Ramona and Her Father by Beverly Cleary. Morrow.

1979 THE WESTING GAME by Ellen Raskin. Dutton.
The Great Gilly Hopkins by Katherine Paterson. Crowell.

1980 A GATHERING OF DAYS: A NEW ENGLAND GIRL'S JOURNAL, 1830–32 by Joan W. Blos. Scribner's.
The Road from Home: The Story of an Armenian Girl by David Kherdian. Greenwillow.

1981 JACOB HAVE I LOVED by Katherine Paterson. Crowell.
The Fledgling by Jane Langton. Harper & Row.
Ring of Endless Light by Madeleine L'Engle. Farrar, Straus & Giroux.

1982 A VISIT TO WILLIAM BLAKE'S INN: POEMS FOR INNOCENT AND EXPERIENCED TRAVELERS by Nancy Willard. Illustrated by Alice and Martin Provensen. Harcourt Brace Jovanovich.
Ramona Quimbly, Age 8 by Beverly Cleary. Morrow.
Upon the Head of the Goat: A Childhood in Hungary, 1939–1944 by Aranka Siegal. Farrar, Straus & Giroux.

1983 DICEY'S SONG by Cynthia Voigt. Atheneum.
The Blue Sword by Robin McKinley. Greenwillow.
Doctor De Soto by William Steig. Farrar, Straus & Giroux.
Graven Images by Paul Fleischman. Harper & Row.
Homesick: My Own Story by Jean Fritz. Putnam.
Sweet Whispers, Brother Rush by Virginia Hamilton. Philomel.

1984 DEAR MR. HENSHAW by Beverly Cleary. Morrow.
The Wish-Giver by Bill Brittain. Harper & Row.
A Solitary Blue by Cynthia Voigt. Atheneum.
The Sign of the Beaver by Elizabeth George Speare. Houghton Mifflin.
Sugaring Time by Kathryn Lasky. Photographs by Christopher Knight. Macmillan.

1985 THE HERO AND THE CROWN by Robin McKinley. Greenwillow.
The Moves Make the Man by Bruce Brooks. Harper & Row.
One-Eyed Cat by Paula Fox. Bradbury.
Like Jake and Me by Marvis Jukes. Illustrated by Lloyd Bloom. Knopf.

1986 SARAH, PLAIN AND TALL by Patricia MacLachlan. Harper & Row.
Commodore Perry in the Land of the Shogun by Rhoda Blumberg. Lothrop, Lee & Shepard.
Dogsong by Gary Paulsen. Bradbury.

1987 THE WHIPPING BOY by Sid Fleischman. Greenwillow.
A Fine White Dust by Cynthia Rylant. Bradbury.
On My Honor by Marion Dane Bauer. Clarion.
Volcano by Patricia Lauber. Bradbury.

1988 LINCOLN: A PHOTOBIOGRAPHY by Russell Freedman. Clarion.
After the Rain by Norma Fox Mazer. Morrow.
Hatchet by Gary Paulsen. Bradbury.

1989 JOYFUL NOISE: POEMS FOR TWO VOICES by Paul Fleischman. Harper & Row.
In the Beginning: Creation Stories from Around the World by Virginia Hamilton. Harcourt Brace.
Scorpions by Walter Dean Myers. Harper & Row.

1990 NUMBER THE STARS by Lois Lowry. Houghton Mifflin.
Afternoon of the Elves by Janet Taylor Lisle. Orchard.
Shabanu: Daughter of the Wind by Suzanne Fisher Staples. Knopf.
The Winter Room by Gary Paulsen. Orchard.

1991 MANIAC MAGEE by Jerry Spinelli. Little, Brown.
The True Confessions of Charlotte Doyle by Avi. Orchard.

1992 SHILOH by Phyllis Reynolds Naylor. Atheneum.
Nothing but the Truth by Avi. Orchard.
The Wright Brothers by Russell Freedman. Holiday House.

1993 MISSING MAY by Cynthia Rylant. Jackson/Orchard.
The Dark-Thirty: Southern Tales of the Supernatural by Patricia C. McKissack. Knopf.
Somewhere in the Darkness by Walter Dean Myers. Scholastic.
What Hearts by Bruce Brooks. HarperCollins.

1994 THE GIVER by Lois Lowry. Houghton Mifflin.
Crazy Lady by Jane Leslie Conly. HarperCollins.
Dragon's Gate by Laurence Yep. HarperCollins.
Eleanor Roosevelt: A Life of Discovery by Russell Freedman. Clarion.

1995 WALK TWO MOONS by Sharon Creech. HarperCollins.
Katherine, Called Birdy by Karen Cushman. Clarion.
The Ear, the Eye, and the Arm by Nancy Farmer. Orchard.

1996 THE MIDWIFE'S APPRENTICE by Karen Cushman. Clarion.
What Jamie Saw by Carolyn Coman. Front Street.
The Watson's Go to Birmingham—1963 by Christopher Paul Curtis. Delacorte.
Yolanda's Genius by Carol Fenner. McElderry.
The Great Fire by Jim Murphy, Scholastic.

The Caldecott Medal is named in honor of Randolph Caldecott, a prominent English illustrator of children's books during the nineteenth century. This award is presented each year by an awards committee of the Association for Library Service to children (ALSC) of the American Library Association. It is given to "the artist of the most distinguished American picture book for children." The following list of books includes the medal winners and Honor Books for each year. If the illustrator's name is not cited, the author illustrated the book.

1938 ANIMALS OF THE BIBLE, A PICTURE BOOK. Text selected from the King James Bible by Helen Dean Fish. Illustrated by Dorothy O. Lathrop. Stokes.
Seven Simeons by Boris Artzybasheff. Viking.
Four and Twenty Blackbirds compiled by Helen Dean Fish. Illustrated by Robert Lawson. Stokes.

1939 MEI LI by Thomas Handforth. Doubleday.
The Forest Pool by Laura Adams Armer. Longmans, Green.
Wee Gillis by Munro Leaf. Illustrated by Robert Lawson. Viking.
Snow White and the Seven Dwarfs translated and illustrated by Wanda Gág. Coward-McCann.
Barkis by Clare Turlay Newberry. Harper & Row.
Andy and the Lion by James Daugherty. Viking.

1940 ABRAHAM LINCOLN by Ingri d'Aulaire and Edgar Parin d'Aulaire. Doubleday.
Cock-a-Doodle-Doo by Berta Hader and Elmer Hader. Macmillan.
Madeline by Ludwig Bemelmans. Simon & Schuster.
The Ageless Story by Lauren Ford. Dodd, Mead.

1941 THEY WERE STRONG AND GOOD by Robert Lawson. Viking.
April's Kittens by Clare Turlay Newberry. Harper & Row.

1942 MAKE WAY FOR DUCKLINGS by Robert McCloskey. Viking.
An American ABC by Maud Petersham and Miska Petersham. Macmillan.
In My Mother's House by Ann Nolan Clark. Illustrated by Velino Herrera. Viking.
Paddle-to-the-Sea by Holling Clancy Holling. Houghton Mifflin.
Nothing at All by Wanda Gág. Coward-McCann.

1943   THE LITTLE HOUSE by Virginia Lee Burton. Houghton Mifflin.
Dash and Dart by Mary Buff and Conrad Buff. Viking.
Marshmallow by Clare Turlay Newberry. Harper & Row.

1944   MANY MOONS by James Thurber. Illustrated by Louis Slobodkin. Harcourt Brace.
Small Rain. Text arranged from the Bible by Jessie Orton Jones. Illustrated by Elizabeth Orton Jones. Viking.
Pierre Pidgeon by Lee Kingman. Illustrated by Arnold Edwin Bare. Houghton Mifflin.
Good-Luck Horse by Chih-Yi Chan. Illustrated by Plato Chan. Whittlesey.
Mighty Hunter by Berta Hader and Elmer Hader. Macmillan.
A Child's Good Night Book by Margaret Wise Brown. Illustrated by Jean Charlot. W. R. Scott.

1945   PRAYER FOR A CHILD by Rachel Field. Pictures by Elizabeth Orton Jones. Macmillan.
Mother Goose. Compiled and illustrated by Tasha Tudor. Oxford University Press.
In the Forest by Marie Hall Ets. Viking.
Yonie Wondernose by Marguerite de Angeli. Doubleday.
The Christmas Anna Angel by Ruth Sawyer. Illustrated by Kate Seredy. Viking.

1946   THE ROOSTER CROWS by Maud Petersham and Miska Petersham. Macmillan.
Little Lost Lamb by Margaret Wise Brown. Illustrated by Leonard Weisgard. Doubleday.
Sing Mother Goose. Music by Opal Wheeler. Illustrated by Marjorie Torrey. Dutton.
My Mother Is the Most Beautiful Woman in the World by Becky Reyher. Illustrated by Ruth C. Gannett. Lothrop.
You Can Write Chinese by Kurt Wiese. Viking.

1947   THE LITTLE ISLAND by Golden MacDonald. Illustrated by Leonard Weisgard. Doubleday.
Rain Drop Splash by Alvin R. Tesselt. Illustrated by Leonard Weisgard. Lothrop.
Boats on the River by Marjorie Flack. Illustrated by Jay Hyde Barnum. Viking.
Timothy Turtle by Al Graham. Illustrated by Tony Palazzo. Robert Welch.
Pedro, Angel of Olvera Street by Leo Politi. Scribner's.
Sing in Praise by Opal Wheeler. Illustrated by Marjorie Torrey. Dutton.

1948   WHITE SNOW, BRIGHT SNOW by Alvin Tresselt. Illustrated by Roger Duvoisin. Lothrop.
Stone Soup. Told and illustrated by Marcia Brown. Scribner's.
McElligot's Pool by Theodor S. Geisel [Dr. Seuss]. Random House.
Bambino the Clown by George Schreiber. Viking.
Roger and the Fox by Lavinia R. Davis. Illustrated by Hildegard Woodward. Doubleday.
Song of Robin Hood. Edited by Anne Malcolmson. Illustrated by Virginia Lee Burton. Houghton Mifflin.

1949   THE BIG SNOW by Berta Hader and Elmer Hader. Macmillan.
Blueberries for Sal by Robert McCloskey. Viking.
All Around the Town by Phyllis McGinley. Illustrated by Helen Stone. Lippincott.
Juanita by Leo Politi. Scribner's.
Fish in the Air by Kurt Wiese. Viking.

1950   SONG OF THE SWALLOWS by Leo Politi. Scribner's.
America's Ethan Allen by Stewart Holbrook. Illustrated by Lynd Ward. Houghton Mifflin.

The Wild Birthday Cake by Lavinia R. Davis. Illustrated by Hildegard Woodward. Doubleday.
Happy Day by Ruth Krauss. Illustrated by Marc Simont. Harper & Row.
Henry-Fisherman by Marcia Brown. Scribner's.
Bartholomew and the Oobleck by Theodor S. Geisel [Dr. Seuss]. Random House.

1951   THE EGG TREE by Katherine Milhous. Scribner's.
Dick Whittington and His Cat told and illustrated by Marcia Brown. Scribner's.
The Two Reds by Will [William Lipkind]. Illustrated by Nicolas [Mordvinoff]. Harcourt Brace.
If I Ran the Zoo by Theodor S. Geisel [Dr. Seuss]. Random House.
T-Bone the Baby-Sitter by Clare Turlay Newberry. Harper & Row.
The Most Wonderful Doll in the World by Phyllis McGinley. Illustrated by Helen Stone. Lippincott.

1952   FINDERS KEEPERS by Will [William Lipkind]. Illustrated by Nicolas [Mordvinoff]. Harcourt Brace.
Mr. T. W. Anthony Woo by Marie Hall Ets. Viking.
Skipper John's Cook by Marcia Brown. Scribner's.
All Falling Down by Gene Zion. Illustrated by Margaret Bloy Graham. Harper & Row.
Bear Party by William Pène DuBois. Viking.
Feather Mountain by Elizabeth Olds. Houghton Mifflin.

1953   THE BIGGEST BEAR by Lynd Ward. Houghton Mifflin.
Puss in Boots. Told and illustrated by Marcia Brown. Scribner's.
One Morning in Maine by Robert McCloskey. Viking.
Ape in a Cape by Fritz Eichenberg. Harcourt Brace.
The Storm Book by Charlotte Zolotow. Illustrated by Margaret Bloy Graham. Harper & Row.
Five Little Monkeys by Juliet Kepes. Houghton Mifflin.

1954   MADELINE'S RESCUE by Ludwig Bemelmans. Viking.
Journey Cake, Ho! by Ruth Sawyer. Illustrated by Robert McClosky. Viking.
When Will the World Be Mine? by Miriam Schlein. Illustrated by Jean Charlot. W. R. Scott.
The Steadfast Tin Soldier. Translated by M. R. James. Adapted from Hans Christian Andersen. Illustrated by Marcia Brown. Scribner's.
A Very Special House by Ruth Krauss. Illustrated by Maurice Sendak. Harper & Row.
Green Eyes by Abe Birnbaum. Capitol.

1955   CINDERELLA by Charles Perrault. Illustrated by Marcia Brown. Harper & Row.
Book of Nursery and Mother Goose Rhymes. Compiled and illustrated by Marguerite de Angeli. Doubleday.
Wheel on the Chimney by Margaret Wise Brown. Illustrated by Tibor Gergely. Lippincott.

1956   FROG WENT A-COURTIN' by John Langstaff. Illustrated by Feodor Rojankovsky. Harcourt Brace.
Play with Me by Marie Hall Ets. Viking.
Crow Boy by Taro Yashima. Viking.

1957   A TREE IS NICE by Janice May Udry. Illustrated by Marc Simont. Harper & Row.
Mr. Penny's Race Horse by Marie Hall Ets. Viking.
1 Is One by Tasha Tudor. Oxford University Press.
Anatole by Eve Titus. Illustrated by Paul Galdone. Whittlesey.
Gillespie and the Guards by Benjamin Elkin. Illustrated by James Daugherty. Viking.
Lion by William Pène DuBois, Viking.

1958 TIME OF WONDER by Robert McCloskey. Viking.
Fly High, Fly Low by Don Freeman. Viking.
Anatole and the Cat by Eve Titus. Illustrated by Paul Galdone. Whittlesey.

1959 CHANTICLEER AND THE FOX. Edited and illustrated by Barbara Cooney. Crowell.
The House That Jack Built by Antonio Frasconi. Crowell.
What Do You Say, Dear? by Sesyle Joslin. Illustrated by Maurice Sendak. W. R. Scott.
Umbrella by Taro Yashima. Viking.

1960 NINE DAYS TO CHRISTMAS by Marie Hall Ets and Aurora Labastida. Viking.
Houses from the Sea by Alice E. Goudey. Illustrated by Adrienne Adams. Scribner's.
The Moon Jumpers by Janice May Udry. Illustrated by Maurice Sendak. Harper & Row.

1961 BABOUSHKA AND THE THREE KINGS by Ruth Robbins. Illustrated by Nicolas Sidjakov. Parnassus.
Inch by Inch by Leo Lionni. Obolensky.

1962 ONCE A MOUSE by Marcia Brown. Scribner's.
The Fox Went Out on a Chilly Night by Peter Spier. Doubleday.
Little Bear's Visit by Else Minarik. Illustrated by Maurice Sendak. Harper & Row.
The Day We Saw the Sun Come Up by Alice Goudey. Illustrated by Adrienne Adams. Scribner's.

1963 THE SNOWY DAY by Ezra Jack Keats. Viking.
The Sun Is a Golden Earring by Natalia Belting. Illustrated by Bernarda Bryson. Holt, Rinehart & Winston.
Mr. Rabbit and the Lovely Present by Charlotte Zolotow. Illustrated by Maurice Sendak. Harper & Row.

1964 WHERE THE WILD THINGS ARE by Maurice Sendak. Harper & Row.
Swimmy by Leo Lionni. Pantheon.
All in the Morning Early by Sorche Nic Leodhas. Illustrated by Evaline Ness. Holt, Rinehart & Winston.
Mother Goose and Nursery Rhymes by Philip Reed. Atheneum.

1965 MAY I BRING A FRIEND? by Beatrice Schenk de Regniers. Illustrated by Beni Montresor. Atheneum.
Rain Makes Applesauce by Julian Scheer. Illustrated by Marvin Bileck. Holiday House.
The Wave by Margaret Hodges. Illustrated by Blair Lent. Houghton Mifflin.
A Pocketful of Cricket by Rebecca Caudill. Illustrated by Evaline Ness. Holt, Rinehart & Winston.

1966 ALWAYS ROOM FOR ONE MORE by Sorche Nic Leodhas. Illustrated by Nonny Hogrogian. Holt, Rinehart & Winston.
Hide and Seek Fog by Alvin Tresselt. Illustrated by Roger Duvoisin. Lothrop.
Just Me by Marie Hall Ets. Viking.
Tom Tit Tot. Edited by Joseph Jacobs. Illustrated by Evaline Ness. Scribner's.

1967 SAM, BANGS AND MOONSHINE by Evaline Ness. Holt, Rinehart & Winston.
One Wide River to Cross by Barbara Emberley. Illustrated by Ed Emberley. Prentice Hall.

1968 DRUMMER HOFF by Barbara Emberley. Illustrated by Ed Emberley. Prentice Hall.
Frederick by Leo Lionni. Pantheon.
Seashore Story by Taro Yashima. Viking.
The Emperor and the Kite by Jane Yolen. Illustrated by Ed Young. World Publishing.

1969 THE FOOL OF THE WORLD AND THE FLYING SHIP by Arthur Ransome. Illustrated by Uri Shulevitz. Farrar, Straus.
Why the Sun and the Moon Live in the Sky by Elphinstone Dayrell. Illustrated by Blair Lent. Houghton Mifflin.

1970 SYLVESTER AND THE MAGIC PEBBLE by William Steig. Windmill/Simon & Schuster.
Goggles by Ezra Jack Keats. Macmillan.
Alexander and the Wind-Up Mouse by Leo Lionni. Pantheon.
Pop Corn and Ma Goodness by Edna Mitchell Preston. Illustrated by Robert Andrew Parker. Viking.
The Friend, Obadiah by Brinton Turkle. Viking.
The Judge by Harve Zemach. Illustrated by Margot Zemach. Farrar, Straus.

1971 A STORY, A STORY by Gail E. Haley, Atheneum.
The Angry Moon by William Sleator. Illustrated by Blair Lent. Atlantic/Little, Brown.
Frog and Toad Are Friends by Arnold Lobel. Harper & Row.
In the Night Kitchen by Maurice Sendak. Harper & Row.

1972 ONE FINE DAY by Nonny Hogrogian. Macmillan.
If All the Seas Were One Sea by Janina Domanska. Macmillan.
Moja Means One: Swahili Counting Book by Muriel Feelings. Illustrated by Tom Feelings. Dial.
Hildilid's Night by Cheli Duran Ryan. Illustrated by Arnold Lobel. Macmillan.

1973 THE FUNNY LITTLE WOMAN by Arlene Mosel. Illustrated by Blair Lent. Dutton.
Hosie's Alphabet by Hosea Baskin, Tobias Baskin, and Lisa Baskin. Illustrated by Leonard Baskin. Viking.
When Clay Sings by Byrd Baylor. Illustrated by Tom Bahti. Scribner's.
Snow White and the Seven Dwarfs by the Brothers Grimm. Translated by Randall Jarrell. Illustrated by Nancy Ekholm Burkert. Farrar, Straus.
Anansi the Spider by Gerald McDermott. Holt, Rinehart & Winston.

1974 DUFFY AND THE DEVIL by Harve Zemach. Illustrated by Margot Zemach. Farrar, Straus.
The Three Jovial Huntsmen by Susan Jeffers. Bradbury.
Cathedral by David Macaulay. Houghton Mifflin.

1975 ARROW TO THE SUN. Adapted and illustrated by Gerald McDermott. Viking.
Jambo Means Hello: Swahili Alphabet Book by Muriel Feelings. Illustrated by Tom Feelings. Dial.

1976 WHY MOSQUITOS BUZZ IN PEOPLE'S EARS by Verna Aardema. Illustrated by Leo and Diane Dillon. Dial.
The Desert Is Theirs by Byrd Baylor. Illustrated by Peter Parnell. Scribner's.
Strega Nona. Retold and illustrated by Tomie de Paola.

1977 ASHANTI TO ZULU: AFRICAN TRADITIONS by Margaret Musgrove. Illustrated by Leo and Diane Dillon. Dial.
The Amazing Bone by William Steig. Farrar, Straus & Giroux.
The Contest by Nonny Hogrogian. Greenwillow.
Fish for Supper by M. B. Goffstein. Dial.
The Golem by Beverly Brodsky McDermott. Lippincott.
Hawk, I'm Your Brother by Byrd Baylor. Illustrated by Peter Parnall. Scribner's.

1978 NOAH'S ARK by Peter Spier. Doubleday.
Castle by David Macaulay. Houghton Mifflin.
It Could Always Be Worse by Margot Zemach. Farrar, Straus & Giroux.

1979 THE GIRL WHO LOVED WILD HORSES by Paul Goble. Bradbury.
Freight Train by Donald Crews. Greenwillow.
The Way to Start a Day by Byrd Baylor. Illustrated by Peter Parnall. Scribner's.

1980   OX-CART MAN by Donald Hall. Illustrated by Barbara Cooney. Viking.
Ben's Trumpet by Rachel Isadora. Greenwillow.
The Treasure by Uri Shulevitz. Farrar, Straus & Giroux.
The Garden of Abdul Gasazi by Chris Van Allsburg. Houghton Mifflin.

1981   FABLES by Arnold Lobel. Harper & Row.
The Bremen-Town Musicians by Ilse Plume. Doubleday.
The Grey Lady and the Strawberry Snatcher by Molly Bang. Four Winds.
Mice Twice by Joseph Low. Atheneum.
Truck by Donald Crews. Greenwillow.

1982   JUMANJI by Chris Van Allsburg. Houghton Mifflin.
A Visit to William Blake's Inn: Poems for Innocent and Experienced Travelers by Nancy Willard. Illustrated by Alice and Martin Provensen. Harcourt Brace Jovanovich.
Where the Buffaloes Began by Olaf Baker. Illustrated by Stephen Gammell. Warne.
On Market Street by Arnold Lobel. Illustrated by Anita Lobel. Greenwillow.
Outside over There by Maurice Sendak. Harper & Row.

1983   SHADOW by Blaise Cendrars. Illustrated by Marcia Brown. Scribner's.
When I Was Young in the Mountains by Cynthia Rylant. Illustrated by Diane Goode. Dutton.
A Chair for My Mother by Vera B. Williams. Morrow.

1984   THE GLORIOUS FLIGHT: ACROSS THE CHANNEL WITH LOUIS BLÉRIOT, JULY 25, 1909 by Alice and Martin Provensen. Viking.
Ten, Nine, Eight by Molly Bang. Greenwillow.
Little Red Riding Hood by Trina Schart Hyman. Holiday House.

1985   SAINT GEORGE AND THE DRAGON adapted by Margaret Hodges. Illustrated by Trina Schart Hyman. Little, Brown.
Hansel and Gretel by Rika Lesser. Illustrated by Paul O. Zelinsky. Dodd.
The Story of Jumping Mouse by John Steptoe. Lothrop, Lee & Shepard.
Have You Seen My Duckling? by Nancy Tafuri. Greenwillow.

1986   POLAR EXPRESS by Chris Van Allsburg. Houghton Mifflin.
The Relatives Came by Cynthia Rylant. Illustrated by Stephen Gammell. Bradbury.
King Bidgood's in the Bathtub by Audrey Wood. Illustrated by Don Wood. Harcourt Brace Jovanovich.

1987   HEY AL by Arthur Yorinks. Illustrated by Richard Egielski. Farrar, Straus & Giroux.
Alphabatics by Suse MacDonald. Bradbury.
Rumpelstiltskin by Paul O. Zelinsky. Dutton.
The Village of Round and Square Houses by Ann Grifalconi. Little, Brown.

1988   OWL MOON by Jane Yolen. Illustrated by John Schoenherr. Philomel.
Mufaro's Beautiful Daughters: An African Story. Adapted and illustrated by John Steptoe. Lothrop, Lee & Shepard.

1989   SONG AND DANCE MAN by Karen Ackerman. Illustrated by Stephen Gammell. Knopf.
The Boy of the Three-Year Nap by Dianne Stanley. Illustrated by Allen Say. Houghton Mifflin.
Free Fall by David Wiesner. Lothrop, Lee & Shepard.
Goldilocks and the Three Bears. Adapted and illustrated by James Marshall. Dial.
Mirandy and Brother Wind by Patricia McKissack. Illustrated by Jerry Pinkney. Knopf.

1990   LON PO PO: A RED RIDING HOOD STORY FROM CHINA. Adapted and illustrated by Ed Young. Philomel.
Bill Peet: An Autobiography by Bill Peet. Houghton Mifflin.
Color Zoo by Lois Ehlert. Lippincott.
Herschel and the Hanukkah Goblings by Eric Kimmel. Illustrated by Trina Schart Hyman. Holiday House.
The Talking Eggs by Robert D. San Souci. Illustrated by Jerry Pinkney. Dial.

1991   BLACK AND WHITE by David Macaulay. Houghton Mifflin.
Puss in Boots by Charles Perrault. Translated by Malcolm Arthur. Illustrated by Fred Marcelino. Farrar, Straus & Giroux.
"More More More," Said the Baby by Vera B. Williams. Greenwillow.

1992   TUESDAY by David Wiesner. Clarion.
Tar Beach by Faith Ringgold. Crown.

1993   MIRETTE ON THE HIGH WIRE by Emily Arnold McCully. Putnam.
Seven Blind Mice by Ed Young. Philomel.
The Stinky Cheese Man and Other Fairly Stupid Tales by Jon Scieszka. Illustrated by Lane Smith. Viking.
Working Cotton by Sherley Anne Williams. Illustrated by Carole Byard. Harcourt Brace.

1994   GRANDFATHER'S JOURNEY by Allen Say. Houghton Mifflin.
Peppe the Lamplighter by Elisa Bartone. Illustrated by Ted Lewin. Lothrop, Lee & Shepard.
In the Small, Small Pond by Denise Fleming. Holt.
Owen by Kevin Henkes. Greenwillow.
Raven: A Trickster Tale from the Pacific Northwest by Gerald McDermott. Harcourt Brace.
Yo! Yes? by Chris Raschka. Orchard.

1995   SMOKY NIGHT by Eve Bunting. Illustrated by David Diaz. Harcourt Brace.
Swamp Angel by Paul O. Zelinsky. Dutton.
John Henry by Jerry Pinkney. Dial.
Time Flies by Eric Rohmann. Crown.

1996   OFFICER BUCKLE AND GLORIA by Peggy Rathman. Putnam.
Alphabet City by Stephen T. Johnson. Viking.
Zin! Zin! Zin! A Violin by Lloyd Moss. Illustrated by Marjorie Priceman. Simon & Schuster.
The Faithful Friend by Robert D. San Souci. Illustrated by Brian Pinkney. Simon & Schuster.
Tops and Bottoms by Janet Stephens. Harcourt Brace.

The Batchelder Award, established in 1966, is given by the Association of Library Service to Children (ALSC) of the American Library Association to the publisher of the most outstanding book of the year that is a translation, published in the United States, of a book that was first published in another country. In 1990, honor books were added to this award. The original country of publication is given in parentheses.

1968   THE LITTLE MAN by Erich Kastner, translated by James Kirkup, illustrated by Rick Schreiter. Knopf. (Germany)

1969   DON'T TAKE TEDDY by Babbis Friis-Baastad, translated by Lise Somme McKinnon. Scribner's. (Norway)

1970   WILDCAT UNDER GLASS by Alki Zei, translated by Edward Fenton. Holt. (Greece)

1971   IN THE LAND OF UR by Hans Baumann, translated by Stella Humphries. Pantheon. (Germany)

1972   FRIEDRICH by Hans Peter Richter, translated by Edite Kroll. Holt. (Germany)

1973   PULGA by S. R. Van Iterson, translated by Alison and Alexander Gode. Morrow. (Netherlands)

1974   PETROS' WAR by Aldi Zei, translated by Edward Fenton. Dutton. (Greece)

1975   AN OLD TALE CARVED OUT OF STONE by A. Linevsky, translated by Maria Polushkin. Crown. (Russia)

1976   THE CAT AND MOUSE WHO SHARED A HOUSE by Ruth Hurlimann, translated by Anthea Bell, illustrated by the author. Walck. (Germany)

1977   THE LEOPARD by Cecil Bødker, translated by Gunnar Poulsen. Atheneum. (Denmark)

1978   KONRAD by Christine Nostlinger, illustrated by Carol Nicklaus. Watts. (Germany)

1979   RABBIT ISLAND by Jörg Steiner, translated by Ann Conrad Lammers, illustrated by Jörg Müller. Harcourt Brace. (Germany)

1980   THE SOUND OF THE DRAGON'S FEET by Alki Zei, translated by Edward Fenton. Dutton. (Greece)

1981   THE WINTER WHEN TIME WAS FROZEN by Els Pelgrom, translated by Maryka and Rafael Rudnik. Morrow. (Netherlands)

1982   THE BATTLE HORSE by Harry Kullman, translated by George Blecher and Lone Thygesen-Blecher. Bradbury. (Sweden)

1983   HIROSHIMA NO PIKA by Toshi Maruki. Lothrop, Lee & Shepard. (Japan)

1984   RONIA, THE ROBBER'S DAUGHTER by Astrid Lindgren, translated by Patricia Crampton. Viking. (Sweden)

1985   THE ISLAND ON BIRD STREET by Uri Orlev, translated by Hillel Halkin. Houghton Mifflin. (Israel)

1986   ROSE BLANCHE by Christophe Gallaz and Roberto Innocenti, translated by Martha Coventry and Richard Graglia. Creative Education. (Italy)

1987   NO HERO FOR THE KAISER by Rudolf Frank, translated by Patricia Crampton. Lothrop, Lee & Shepard. (Germany)

1988   IF YOU DIDN'T HAVE ME by Ulf Nilsson, translated by Lone Tygesen-Blecher and George Blecher, illustrated by Eva Eriksson. McElderry. (Sweden)

1989   CRUTCHES by Peter Hätling, translated by Elizabeth D. Crawford. Lothrop, Lee & Shepard. (Germany)

1990   BUSTER'S WORLD by Bjarne Reuter, translated by Anthea Bell. Dutton. (Denmark)

1991   TWO LONG AND ONE SHORT by Nina Ring Aamundsen. Houghton Mifflin. (Norway)

1992   THE MAN FROM THE OTHER SIDE by Uri Orlev, translated by Hillel Halkin. Houghton Mifflin. (Israel)

1993   No Award

1994   THE APPRENTICE by Molina Llorente, translated by Robin Longshaw. Farrar, Straus & Giroux. (Spain)

1995   THE BOYS FROM ST. PETRI by Bjarne Reuter, translated by Anthea Bell. Dutton, 1994. (Denmark)

1996   THE LADY WITH THE HAT by Uri Orlev, translated by Hillel Halkin. Houghton Mifflin. (Israel)

The Laura Ingalls Wilder Award is given to an author or illustrator whose books (published in the United States) have made a substantial and lasting contribution to literature for children. Established in 1954, this medal was given every five years through 1980. As of 1983, it is given every three years by the Association of Library Service to Children (ALSC) of the American Library Association. The following are the award winners thus far.

1954   Laura Ingalls Wilder
1960   Clara Ingram Judson
1965   Ruth Sawyer
1970   E. B. White
1975   Beverly Cleary
1980   Theodor S. Geisel [Dr. Seuss]
1983   Maurice Sendak
1986   Jean Fritz
1989   Elizabeth George Speare
1992   Marcia Brown
1995   Virginia Hamilton

The Hans Christian Andersen prize, the first international children's book award, was established in 1956 by the International Board on Books for Young People. Given every two years, the award was expanded in 1966 to honor an illustrator as well as an author. A committee composed of members from different countries judges the selections recommended by the board or library associations in each country. The following have won the Hans Christian Andersen Prize.

1956   Eleanor Farjeon. Great Britian.
1958   Astrid Lindgren. Sweden.
1960   Eric Kästner. Germany.
1962   Meindert DeJong. United States.
1964   René Guillot. France.
1966   Tove Jansson (author). Finland.
       Alois Carigiet (illustrator). Switzerland.
1968   James Krüss (author). Germany.
       Jose Maria Sanchez-Silva (author). Spain.
       Jiri Trnka (illustrator). Czechoslovakia.
1970   Gianni Rodari (author). Italy.
       Maurice Sendak (illustrator). United States.
1972   Scott O'Dell (author). United States.
       Ib Spang Olsen (illustrator). Denmark.
1974   Maria Gripe (author). Sweden.
       Farshid Mesghali (illustrator). Iran.
1976   Cecil Bødker (author). Denmark.
       Tatjana Mawrina (illustrator). U.S.S.R.
1978   Paula Fox (author). United States.
       Svend Otto (illustrator). Denmark.
1980   Bohumil Riha (author). Czechoslovakia.
       Suekichi Akaba (illustrator). Japan.
1982   Lygia Bojunga Nunes (author). Brazil.
       Zibigniew Rychlicki (illustrator). Poland.
1984   Christine Nostlinger (author). Austria.
       Mitsumasa Anno (illustrator). Japan.
1986   Patricia Wrightson (author). Australia.
       Robert Ingpen (illustrator). Australia.
1988   Annie M. G. Schmidt (author). Netherlands.
       Dusan Kallay (illustrator). Yugoslavia.
1990   Tormod Haugen (author). Norway.
       Lisbeth Zwerger (illustrator). Austria.

1992   Virginia Hamilton (author). United States. Kveta Pacovská
       (illustrator). Czechoslovakia.
1994   Michio Mado (author). Japan.
       Jorg Muller (illustrator). Switzerland.
1996   Uri Orlev (author). Israel.
       Klaus Ensikat (illustrator). Germany.

GENERAL AWARDS

BOSTON GLOBE–HORN BOOK AWARDS

The Horn Book Magazine, 11 Beacon St., Boston, MA 02108.
Currently given for outstanding fiction or poetry, outstanding
nonfiction, and outstanding illustration.

GOLDEN KITE AWARD

Presented annually by the Society of Children's Book Writers to
members whose books of fiction, nonfiction, and picture illustration
best exhibit excellence and genuinely appeal to interests and concerns
of children.

INTERNATIONAL READING ASSOCIATION CHILDREN'S
BOOK AWARD

International Reading Association, 800 Barksdale Rd., Newark, DE
19711. An annual award for first or second book to an author from
any country who shows unusual promise in the children's book field.
Since 1987, the award has been presented to both a picture book and
a novel.

NEW YORK TIMES CHOICE OF BEST ILLUSTRATED
CHILDREN'S BOOKS OF THE YEAR

The New York Times, 229 W. 43rd St., New York, NY 10036. Books
are selected for excellence in illustration by panel of judges.

AWARDS BASED ON SPECIAL CONTENT

JANE ADDAMS BOOK AWARD

Jane Addams Peace Association, 777 United Nations Plaza, New
York, NY 10017. For a book with literary merit stressing themes of
dignity, equality, peace, and social justice.

ASSOCIATION OF JEWISH LIBRARIES AWARDS

National Foundation for Jewish Culture, 122 E. 42nd St., Room 1512,
New York, NY 10168. Given to one or two titles that have made the
most outstanding contribution to the field of Jewish literature for
children and young people. The Sydney Taylor Body of Work Award,
established in 1981, is given for an author's body of work.

CATHOLIC BOOK AWARDS

Catholic Press Association of the United States and Canada, 119 N.
Park Ave., Rockville Centre, NY 11570. Honors selected in five
categories and awarded to books with sound Christian and
psychological values.

CHILD STUDY CHILDREN'S BOOK COMMITTEE AT BANK
STREET COLLEGE AWARD

Bank Street College of Education, 610 W. 112th St., New York, NY
10025. For a distinguished book for children or young people that
deals honestly and courageously with problems in the world.

CHRISTOPHER AWARDS

The Christophers, 12 E. 48th St., New York, NY 10017. Given to works
of artistic excellence affirming the highest values of the human spirit.

EVA L. GORDON AWARD FOR CHILDREN'S SCIENCE
LITERATURE

Helen Ross Russell, Chairman of Publications Committee, ANNS, 44
College Dr., Jersey City, NJ 07305. Given by the American Nature
Study Society to an author or illustrator whose body of work in
science trade books is accurate, inviting, and timely.

JEFFERSON CUP AWARD

Children's and Young Adult Roundtable of the Virginia Library
Association, P.O. Box 298, Alexandria, VA 22313. Presented for a
distinguished book in American history, historical fiction, or
biography.

EZRA JACK KEATS AWARDS

Given biennially to a promising new artist and a promising writer.
The recipients receive a monetary award and a medallion from the
Ezra Jack Keats Foundation.

CORETTA SCOTT KING AWARDS

Social Responsibilities Round Table of the American Library
Association, 50 E. Huron St., Chicago, IL 60611. Given to an African
American author and an African American illustrator for outstanding
inspirational and educational contributions to literature for children.

NATIONAL COUNCIL OF TEACHERS OF ENGLISH AWARD
FOR EXCELLENCE IN POETRY FOR CHILDREN

National Council of Teachers of English, 1111 Kenyon Rd., Urbana,
IL 61801. Given formerly annually and presently every three years to
a living American poet for total body of work for children ages 3–13.

NATIONAL JEWISH BOOK AWARDS

JWB Jewish Book Council, 15 E. 26th St. New York, NY 10010.
Various awards are given for work or body of work that makes a
contribution to Jewish juvenile literature.

NEW YORK ACADEMY OF SCIENCES CHILDREN'S SCIENCE
BOOKS AWARDS

The New York Academy of Sciences, 2 E. 63rd St., New York, NY
10021. For books of high quality in the field of science for children;
three awards are given: Younger Children, Older Children, and the
Montroll Award for a book that provides unusual historical data or
background on a scientific subject.

SCOTT O'DELL AWARD FOR HISTORICAL FICTION

Zena Sutherland, 1418 E. 57th St., Chicago, IL 60637. Honors a
distinguished work of historical fiction set in the New World.

ORBIS PICTUS AWARD FOR OUTSTANDING NONFICTION
FOR CHILDREN

Presented annually by the National Council of Teachers of English to
the outstanding nonfiction book of the previous year.

PHOENIX AWARD

Given to the author of a book published for children twenty years
before that has not received a major children's book award. Sponsored
by the Children's Literature Association.

EDGAR ALLAN POE AWARDS

Mystery Writers of America, 1950 Fifth Ave., New York, NY 10011.
For best juvenile mystery.

WASHINGTON POST/CHILDREN'S BOOK GUILD NONFICTION AWARD

Washington Post, 1150 15th St., NW, Washington, DC 20071. Given to an author or illustrator for a body of work in juvenile informational books.

WESTERN WRITERS OF AMERICA SPUR AWARD

Western Writers of America, Inc., 508 Senter Pl., Selah, WA 98942. For the best western juvenile in two categories, fiction and nonfiction.

CARTER G. WOODSON BOOK AWARD

National Council for the Social Studies, 3501 Newark St., NW, Washington, DC 20016. Presented to outstanding social science books for young readers that treat sensitively and accurately topics related to ethnic minorities.

AWARDS FOR LASTING CONTRIBUTIONS OR SERVICE TO CHILDREN'S LITERATURE

ARBUTHNOT AWARD

International Reading Association, 800 Barksdale Rd., Newark, DE 19714. Named after May Hill Arbuthnot, an authority on literature for children, this award is given annually to an outstanding teacher of children's literature.

ARBUTHNOT HONOR LECTURE

The Association of Library Service to Children (ALSC) of the American Library Association, 50 E. Huron St., Chicago, IL 60611. This free public lecture is presented annually by a distinguished author, critic, librarian, historian, or teacher of children's literature. Both the lecturer and the site for the lecture are chosen by an ALSC committee.

GROLIER FOUNDATION AWARD

American Library Association Awards Committee, 50 E. Huron St., Chicago, IL 60611. Given to a community librarian or a school librarian who has made an unusual contribution to the stimulation and guidance of reading by children and young people.

LANDAU AWARD

Salt Lake County Library System, 2197 E. 7000 S., Salt Lake City, UT 84121. Cosponsored by the Department of Education of the University of Utah and Salt Lake County Library System. The award is given biennially to a teacher of children's literature who has most inspired students to pursue a knowledge of the field.

LUCILE MICHEELS PANNELL AWARD

Awards in the "general store" category and in the "children's specialty bookstore" category are presented annually by the Women's National Book Association to the owners of two bookstores whose innovative programs encourage children's reading.

REGINA MEDAL

Catholic Library Association, 461 West Lancaster Ave., Haverford, PA 19041. For "continued distinguished contribution to children's literature."

UNIVERSITY OF SOUTHERN MISSISSIPPI CHILDREN'S COLLECTION MEDALLION

University of Southern Mississippi Book Festival, USM Library, Hattiesburg, MS 39401. For a writer or an illustrator who has made an "outstanding contribution to the field of children's literature."

For more information about these and other awards, including complete lists of the prizewinners, see *Children's Books: Awards & Prizes*, published and revised periodically by the Children's Book Council, 568 Broadway, New York, NY 10012. Beginning in 1990, each year's *Books in Print* also publishes a listing of the current winners of various prizes.

appendix b
Book Selection Aids

Note: Publishers' addresses may change. For complete and up-to-date information, see the current edition of *Literary Market Place* or *Children's Books in Print*.

COMPREHENSIVE LISTS AND DIRECTORIES

Children's Books in Print. R. R. Bowker, 245 W. 17th St., New York, NY 10011. Annual. $149.95.

A comprehensive listing of children's books currently in print. Includes titles for grades K–12. Titles are arranged alphabetically by author, title, and illustrator. A list of publisher addresses is provided. Also includes children's book awards for the previous ten years.

Children's Media Market Place, 3rd ed. Delores Blythe Jones. Neal-Schuman Publishers, 23 Leonard St., New York, NY 10013. 1988. 397 pp. $45.00, paper.

Annotated list of publishers of books and producers and distributors of nonprint materials, indexed by format, subject, and special interest. Includes a directory of wholesalers, bookstores, book clubs, and children's television sources.

Educational Media and Technology Yearbook. Libraries Unlimited, P.O. Box 263, Littleton, CO 80160. Annual. $60.00.

Includes articles, surveys, and research on various aspects of media administration, creation, and use. Lists organizations, foundations, and funding agencies for media as well as information on graduate programs. Includes an annotated mediography of basic resources for library media specialists.

Fiction, Folklore, Fantasy and Poetry for Children, 1876–1985. R. R. Bowker, 245 W. 17th St., New York, NY 10011. 1986. 2 vols. 2,563 pp. $495.00.

Contains 133,000 entries compiled from a variety of sources and indexed by author, title, illustrator, and awards.

Guide to Reference Books for School Media Centers, 3rd ed. Christine Gehret Wynar. Libraries Unlimited, P.O. Box 263, Littleton, CO 80160. 1986, 407 pp. $36.00.

Includes annotations and evaluations for 2,000 useful reference tools for school media centers. Materials are arranged in order by subject. Also includes a list of sources and selection aids for print and nonprint materials.

Magazines for Children: A Guide for Parents, Teachers, and Librarians, 2nd ed. Selma K. Richardson. American Library Association, 50 E. Huron St., Chicago, IL 60611. 1991. 139 pp. $22.50, paper.

An annotated list of magazines designed especially for children ages 2 to 14; includes descriptions of the publications, age levels of users, and evaluative comments.

Magazines for Young People, 2nd ed. Bill Katz and Kinda Sternberg Katx. R. R. Bowker, 245 W. 17th St., New York, NY 10011. 1991. 250 pp. $49.95.

Evaluates over 1,000 magazines, journals, and newsletters for children and teachers in 60 subject areas.

Reference Books for Children. Carolyn Sue Peterson and Ann D. Fenton. Scarecrow Press, 52 Liberty St., Box 4167, Metuchen, NJ 08840. 1992. 414 pp. $39.50.

Contains annotated entries over a broad range of curriculum areas, collection needs, interests, and reading levels of children. Books are classified by subject. Annotations provide some guidance in making selections for school collections.

Subject Guide to Children's Books in Print. R. R. Bowker, 245 W. 17th St., New York, NY 10011. Annual. $149.95.

A companion volume to *Children's Books in Print.* Arranges all children's titles currently in print using over 6,000 subject headings. Particularly useful for finding and ordering titles on specific subjects; however, titles are not annotated.

GENERAL SELECTION AIDS

Adventuring with Books: A Booklist for Pre-K–Grade 6, 10th ed. Julie M. Jensen and Nancy L. Rosen, eds. National Council of Teachers of English, 1111 Kenyon Rd., Urbana, IL 61601. 1993. 603 pp. $19.95, paper.

Annotates about 1,800 children's titles published from 1988 to 1992. Annotations include summary, age, and interest levels. Contents are arranged by genre, broad subject, and theme. Author, title, and subject indexes.

Award-Winning Books for Children and Young Adults. Betty L. Criscoe. Scarecrow Press, 52 Liberty St., Box 4167, Metuchen, NJ 08840. Annual. $37.50.

Lists books that won awards during the previous year. Includes descriptions of the awards, criteria used for selection, plot synopses of winners, grade levels, and genres.

Best Books for Children: Pre-school Through Grade 6, 5th ed. John T. Gillespie and Corinne J. Naden. R. R. Bowker, 245 W. 17th St., New York, NY 10011. 1994. 1,400 pp. $59.00.

An annotated listing of books that are selected to satisfy recreational needs, curricular needs, and interests of elementary schoolchildren. Books are arranged by broad age groups, subdivided by types of books. Contains author, title, and illustrator as well as subject indexes.

The Best in Children's Books: The University of Chicago Guide to Children's Literature. Zena Sutherland, Betsy Hearne, and Roger Sutton, eds. University of Chicago Press, Chicago, IL 60637. 1991. 616 pp. $37.50.

A selection of reviews that originally appeared in the *Bulletin of the Center for Children's Books.* Reviews are arranged in order by author and are indexed by title, subject, and type of literature.

Bibliography of Books for Children. Helen Shelton, ed. Association for Childhood Education International, 11141 Georgia Ave., Suite 200, Wheaton, MD 20902. 1989. 112 pp. $11.00.

Lists the best books reviewed by the Association for Childhood Education over the previous two years. Books are evaluated for readability and absence of sexism and racism. Entries are annotated and grouped by age levels. Indexed and cross-referenced.

Children's Catalog, 16th ed. H. W. Wilson Co., 950 University Ave., Bronx, NY 10452. 1991. 1,346 pp. $90.00.

A classified (Dewey Decimal System) catalog of about 6,000 recent "best" children's books, including publishing affirmation, grade level, and a brief summary of each title. Also includes alphabetical author, title, subject, and analytical indexes. Contains a list of publishers with addresses. A new edition is issued every five years, with annual supplements in other years.

Choosing Books for Children. Betsy Hearne. Delacorte Press, 1 Dag Hammerskjold Plaza, 245 E. 47th St., New York, NY 10017. 1990. 250 pp. $9.95, paper.

Contains general selection advice for parents, teachers, and librarians, combined with bibliographies.

The Elementary School Library Collection, 19th ed. Laura K. Leer, ed. Brodart Co., 500 Arch St., Williamsport, PA 17705. 1994. 1,150 pp. $99.95.

A basic bibliography of materials, both print and nonprint, for elementary school media center collections. Materials are interfiled and arranged by subject classification (Dewey Decimal System). All entries include bibliographic information, age level, and a brief annotation. Contains author, title, and subject indexes.

More Exciting, Funny, Scary, Short, Different, and Sad Books Kids Like About Animals, Science, Sports, Families, Songs, and Other Things. Frances Laverne Carroll and Mary Meacham. American Library Association, 50 E. Huron St., Chicago, IL 60611. 1992. 192 pp. $18.00, paper.

An annotated bibliography of titles that focuses on subjects and books that have been popular with children in second through fifth grades.

Eyeopeners II. Beverly Kobrin. Scholastic, 555 Broadway, New York, NY 10012. 1995. 305 pp. $6.95, paper.

Over 500 nonfiction titles are arranged in subject categories and annotated with brief summaries and ideas for classroom use. Indexed by author, illustrator, title, and subject.

Fiction for Youth: A Guide to Recommended Books. Lillian L. Shapiro. Neal-Schuman Publishers, 23 Leonard St., New York, NY 10013. 1992. 300 pp. $35.00.

Provides a core collection of titles designed to encourage reading by young people who can read but don't choose to do so.

The Horn Book Guide to Children's and Young Adult Books. Horn Book, Inc., 11 Beacon St., Boston, MA 02108. Semiannual. $50 per annum.

Provides short reviews of children's and young-adult books published in the United States during the prior publishing season with references to longer reviews in *Horn Book Magazine.* Books are given a numerical evaluation from one to six.

New York Times Parents' Guide to the Best Books for Children. Eden Ross Lipson. Times Books/Random House, 201 E. 50th St., New York, NY 10022. 1988. 421 pp. $12.95.

Indexes books by age appropriateness, listening level, author, title, illustrator, and subject. Books are arranged in broad categories, such as wordless books and picture storybooks.

A Parent's Guide to Children's Reading, 5th ed. Nancy Larrick. Westminster/John Knox. 100 Witherspoon St., Louisville, KY 40202-1396. 1983. 284 pp. $12.95.

A handbook for parents that suggests appropriate titles for children's reading at each stage of their development. Contains chapters on television, language development, how reading is taught, poetry, and paperbacks.

Tried and True: 500 Nonfiction Books Children Want to Read. George Wilson and Joyce Moss. R. R. Bowker, 245 W. 17th St., New York, NY 10011. 1992. 300 pp. $34.95.

Lists popular titles arranged by grade level, then by books to be read for pleasure and books to be read for research.

Your Reading: A Booklist for Junior High and Middle School Students. C. Anne Webb, ed. National Council of Teachers of English, 1111 Kenyon Rd., Urbana, IL 61801. 1993. 250 pp. $16.95.

An annotated list of over 2,000 books for grades 5–9, arranged in broad subject categories. Includes author and title indexes.

BOOKLISTS FOR VARIOUS LEVELS OF READERS

The Best: High/Low Books for Reluctant Readers. Marianne Laino Pilla. Libraries Unlimited, P.O. Box 263, Littleton, CO 80160. 1990. 100 pp. $12.50, paper.

Lists books of high literary quality for reluctant readers in grades 3–12. Has brief annotations, reading and interest levels, and popular subject headings.

Beyond Picture Books: A Guide to First Readers. Barbara Barstow and Judith Riggle. R. R. Bowker, 245 W. 17th St., New York, NY 10011. 1989. 354 pp. $39.95.

Annotates 1,600 first readers for ages 4–7, with a plot summary, brief evaluation, and bibliographic information. Indexes by title, illustrator, readability, series, and subject.

Books for Children to Read Alone: A Guide for Parents and Librarians. George Wilson and Joyce Moss. R. R. Bowker, 45 W. 17th St., New York, NY 10011. 1988. 184 pp. $39.95.

Lists books in which concepts and language structures are accessible to beginning readers in the first through third grades. Includes subject index.

Books for the Gifted Child. Volume 1, Barbara Holland Baskin and Karen H. Harris. 1980. 263 pp. $29.95; Volume 2, Paula Hauser and Gail Nelson. 1988. 244 pp. $39.95. R. R. Bowker, 245 W. 17th St., New York, NY 10011.

Each volume critically annotates about 150 titles that would be useful in working with gifted children, ages preschool through 12. They are arranged in alphabetical order with bibliographic information and reading level included. Several chapters on the gifted are included in the book.

Choices: A Core Collection for Young Reluctant Readers, Vol. 3. Sharon Salluzzo. Peg Glisson ed. John Gordon Burke, Publisher. P.O. Box 1492, Evanston, IL 60204-1492. 1994. 272 pp. $45.00.

Annotates books for second through sixth graders reading below grade level, published between 1983 and 1988, with plot summary, interest level, and reading level. Contains author and subject indexes.

Exploring Books with Gifted Children. Nancy Polette and Marjorie Hamlin. Libraries Unlimited, P.O. Box 263, Littleton, CO 80160. 1980. 214 pp. $19.00.

Provides suggested units with activities and lists of books for four primary elements of literature (style, theme, character, setting). Books that stress these elements, or can be used to motivate thinking about them, are included in the lists.

Primary Plots: A Booktalk Guide for Use with Readers 4–8. Rebecca L. Thomas. R. R. Bowker, 245 W. 17th St., New York, NY 10011. 1993. 431 pp. $41.00.

Provides plot summaries for books, organized in eight chapters. For each feature title, includes bibliographic information, suggested use and reading level, thematic material, book talk material and activities, audiovisual adaptations, related title, and information about the author and illustrator. Includes subject index.

BOOKLISTS AND INDEXES FOR PARTICULAR SUBJECTS

PICTURE BOOKS AND CONCEPT BOOKS

A to Zoo: Subject Access to Children's Picture Books, 4th ed. Carolyn W. Lima. R. R. Bowker, 245 W. 17th St., New York, NY 10011. 1993. 1,158 pp. $55.00.

Provides subject access to over 8,000 picture books through 600 subject headings with cross-references and full bibliographic citations. Most titles are useful for children from preschool through second grade. Includes author, illustrator, and title lists.

Alphabet: A Handbook of ABC Books and Activities for the Elementary Classroom. Patricia L. Roberts. Scarecrow Press, 52 Liberty St., Box 4167, Metuchen, NJ 08840. 1984. 220 pp. $32.50.

Reviews over 200 alphabet books and provides about 80 activities to use with children from preschool to grade 6.

Alphabet Books as a Key to Language Patterns: An Annotated Action Bibliography. Patricia L. Roberts. Shoe String Press, P.O. Box 4327, 925 Sherman Ave., Hamden, CT 06514. 1987. 263 pp. $27.50.

Lists over 500 alphabet books that can be used in aiding language development under categories such as alliteration, rhymes and verses, and wordless books.

Counting Books Are More Than Numbers: An Annotated Action Bibliography. Patricia L. Roberts. Shoe String Press, P.O. Box 4327, 925 Sherman Ave., Hamden, CT 06514. 1989. 264 pp. $32.50.

Describes 350 books for preschool through second grades that can be used to encourage early understanding of mathematical concepts.

Picture Books for Children, 3rd ed. Patricia Jean Cianciolo. American Library Association, 50 E. Huron St., Chicago, IL 60611. 1990. 243 pp. $25.00, paper.

An annotated listing of picture books, divided into major subject areas such as "Me and My Family" or "The Imaginative World." Annotations include descriptions of media, age levels, and brief synopses of plot. Material is largely new to this edition, so older editions remain useful.

Wordless/Almost Wordless Picture Books: A Guide. Virginia H. Richey and Katharyn Tuten-Pucket. Libraries Unlimited, P.O. Box 263, Littleton, CO 80160. 1992. 125 pp. $27.50.

Lists books with brief annotations. Includes thematic and subject indexes.

FOLKLORE AND STORYTELLING AND READING ALOUD

Books Kids Will Sit Still For: The Complete Read-Aloud Guide, 2nd ed. Judy Freeman. R. R. Bowker, 245 W. 17th St., New York, NY 10011. 1990. 660 pp. $34.95.

Lists over 2,000 titles recommended for reading aloud, and includes plot summaries, extension ideas, and related titles.

Caroline Feller Bauer's New Handbook for Storytellers. Caroline Feller Bauer. American Library Association, 50 E. Huron St., Chicago, IL 60611. 1993. 550 pp. $30.00, paper.

A thorough guide to telling stories, this book includes ideas for creating puppets, story media, and using music and film in storytelling.

For Reading Out Loud! A Guide to Sharing Books with Children. Margaret Mary Kimmel and Elizabeth Segel. Dell Publishing, 666 Fifth Ave., New York, NY 10103. 1988. 240 pp. $16.95, paper.

Contains suggestions for reading aloud effectively to elementary and middle school students and an annotated list of good titles.

Index to Fairy Tales: Including Folklore, Legends and Myths in Collections, 3rd ed. Joseph W. Sprug, comp. Scarecrow Press, 52 Liberty St., Box 4167, Metuchen, NJ 08840. 1994. 602 pp. $59.50.

Indexes a broad range of collections of folktales and other folk literature by author, compiler, subject of tale (including characters, countries, and so on), and titles of tale. Various editions cover different collections, so the total coverage is quite broad.

The Read-Aloud Handbook, 4th. ed. Jim Trelease. Penguin Books, 375 Hudson St., New York, NY 10014. 1995. 387 pp. $12.95, paper.

Contains a rationale for reading aloud, tips for good presentations, and an annotated list of books recommended for reading aloud.

Stories: A List of Stories to Tell and Read Aloud, 3rd ed. Marilyn B. Iarusso, ed. New York Public Library Publications Office, Fifth Ave. & 42nd St., New York, NY 10018. 1990. 104 pp. $6.00.

Suggests proven stories to tell and read aloud to children. Includes poetry. Entries are briefly annotated.

The Story Vine: A Sourcebook of Unusual and Easy-to-Tell Stories from Around the World. Anne Pellowski. Macmillan, 866 Third Ave., New York, NY 10022. 1984. 160 pp. $14.95; $7.95, paper.

A collection of stories that can be highlighted with simple props such as string figures, picture drawings, musical instruments, or concrete objects.

Storyteller's Sourcebook. Margaret Read MacDonald, ed. Gale Research, 835 Penobscot Bldg., Detroit, MI 48226-4094. 1982. 840 pp. $95.00.

Provides access to folktales and folk literature in 700 collections. Tales are indexed by subject, motif, and title. Index is particularly useful in locating variants of tales.

Storytelling: A Selected Annotated Bibliography. Ellin Greene and George Shannon. Garland, 136 Madison Ave., New York, NY 10016. 1986. 183 pp. $27.00.

Provides bibliographies of stories, telling techniques, stories for different settings, and lists of tellers.

The Storytime Sourcebook: A Compendium of Ideas and Resources for Storytellers. Carolyn M. Cullum. Neal-Schuman Publishers, 23 Leonard St., New York, NY 10013, 1990. 175 pp. $24.95.

Arranged by themes, lists plans for story hour programs including books, films, filmstrips, videocassettes, and toys. Includes activities for 3- to 7-year-olds. Print and nonprint indexes.

HISTORICAL FICTION, HISTORY, AND BIOGRAPHY

American History for Children and Young Adults: An Annotated Bibliographic Index. Vandelia VanMeter. Libraries Unlimited, P.O. Box 263, Littleton, CO 80160. 1990. 324 pp. $32.50.

Books reviewed between 1980 and 1988 are arranged by time periods, subdivided by subject. Indexed by grade level.

Index to Collective Biographies for Young Readers, 4th ed. Karen Breen, ed. R. R. Bowker, 245 W. 17th St., New York, NY 10011. 1988. 494 pp. $44.95.

Indexes biographies in collections by individuals' names and by subject. Biographies are suitable for elementary school through junior high school.

Reading for Young People series:

The Great Plains. Mildred Laughlin. 1985. 168 pp. $12.00, paper.
Kentucky, Tennessee, West Virginia. Barbara Matins. 1985. 157 pp. $12.00, paper.
The Middle Atlantic. Arabelle Pennypacker. 1980. 164 pp. $11.00, paper.
The Midwest. Dorothy Hinman and Ruth Zimmerman. 1979. 250 pp. $11.00, paper.
The Mississippi Delta. Cora Matheny Dorsett. 1983. 157 pp. $15.00, paper.
New England. Elfrieda B. McCauley. 1985. 168 pp. $17.50, paper.
The Northwest. Mary Meachum. 1981. 152 pp. $11.00, paper.
The Rocky Mountains. Mildred Laughlin. 1980. 192 pp. $11.00, paper.
The Southeast. Dorothy Heald. 1980. 174 pp. $11.00, paper.
The Southwest. Dorothy Heald, 1980. 176 pp. $11.00, paper.

The Upper Midwest. Marion Fuller Archer. 1981. 142 pp. $11.00, paper.

All published by the American Library Association, 50 E. Huron St., Chicago, IL 60611.

A series of annotated bibliographies of fiction and nonfiction for primary grades through grade 10 that describe books covering the history and life of various American regions.

Peoples of the American West: Historical Perspectives Through Children's Literature. Mary Hurlbut Cordier. Scarecrow, 52 Liberty St., Box 4167, Metuchen, NJ 08840. 1989. 230 pp. $22.50.

Contains an analysis of historical fiction of the West as a genre and an annotated list of 100 books separated into grades K–3 and 4–9.

Reference Guide to Historical Fiction for Children and Young Adults. Lynda G. Adamson. Greenwood Dr., 88 Post Rd., W., P.O. Box 5007, Westport, CT 06881. 1987. 401 pp. $49.95.

Authors, titles, main characters, and historical events are listed in dictionary format with longer entries under authors that describe their works. Appendixes list books by periods and events and by readability level.

World History for Children and Young Adults. Vandelia VanMeter. Libraries Unlimited, P.O. Box 263, Littleton, CO 80160. 1992. 425 pp. $32.00.

Lists and annotates books about world history by time period and subject. Includes fiction and nonfiction.

CULTURAL AND SEXUAL IDENTITY

Against Borders: Promoting Books for a Multicultural World. Hazel Rochman. American Library Association, 50 E. Huron St., Chicago, IL 60611. 1993. 288 pp. $25.00, paper.

Essays and annotated book lists focus on specific ethnic groups and issues that tie world cultures together through themes.

American Indian Reference Books for Children and Young Adults. Barbara J. Kuipers. Libraries Unlimited, P.O. Box 263, Littleton, CO 80160. 1995. 260 pp. $27.50.

Lists over 200 nonfiction sources of material on Native Americans for grades 3 to 12. Includes strengths and weaknesses of each book as well as curriculum uses. A section of the book deals with general selection criteria to use for these subjects.

Basic Collection of Children's Books in Spanish. Isabel Schon. Scarecrow, 52 Liberty St., Box 4167, Metuchen, NJ 08840. 1986. 230 pp. $17.50.

More than 500 titles for preschool through grade 6 are arranged in Dewey order, with access through author, title, and subject indexes. A list of Spanish language distributors is included.

The Black American in Books for Children: Readings in Racism, 2nd ed. Donnarae MacCann and Gloria Woodward. 1985. 310 pp. $27.50.

Cultural Conformity in Books for Children: Further Readings in Racism. 1977. 215 pp. $20.00. Both published by Scarecrow Press, 52 Liberty St., Box 4167, Metuchen, NJ 08840.

Collections of articles in which the issue of racism in children's books is considered from a variety of points of view. Includes many citations to books of both good and poor quality that reflect positive and negative values.

The Black Experience in Children's Books. Barbara Rollock, selector. New York Public Library Publications Office, Fifth Ave. & 42nd St., New York, NY 10018. 1989. 112 pp. $5.00.

An annotated list that presents titles about the black experience in the United States as well as in other areas of the world. Criteria for selection and inclusion in the list are described.

Books in Spanish for Children and Young Adults: An Annotated Guide. Series 3. Isabel Schon. Scarecrow Press, 52 Liberty St., Box 4167, Metuchen, NJ 08840. 1989. 180 pp. $20.00.

Contains listings of books for preschool through high school that have been published since 1982. The listed books represent diverse Hispanic cultures, including Mexico and Central and South America.

A Guide to Non-Sexist Children's Books: Volume II, 1976–1985. Denise Wilms and Ilene Cooper, eds. Academy Publisher, 213 W. Institute Pl., Chicago, IL 60610. 1987. 240 pp. $17.95; $8.95, paper.

Lists over 600 books in sections by grade level up through twelfth grade, which are then subdivided into fiction and nonfiction. Indexes by author, title, fiction, and nonfiction subjects. Volume 1, which covered books up to 1976, is also available.

Hey Miss! You Got a Book for Me? A Model Multi-Cultural Resource Collection, 2nd ed. Joanna F. Chambers. Austin Bilingual Language Editions, P.O. Box 3864, Austin, TX 78764. 1981. 91 pp. $12.95, paper.

A listing of 350 good multicultural and bilingual books and audiovisual materials. Incudes mainly Spanish-language titles with some materials in Chinese, French, Greek, and Vietnamese.

A Hispanic Heritage: A Guide to Juvenile Books About Hispanic Peoples and Cultures. Series 4. Isabel Schon. Scarecrow Press, 52 Liberty St., Box 4167, Metuchen, NJ 08840. 1991. 173 pp. $22.50.

An annotated subject bibliography of works about the people, history, culture, and politics in the Hispanic countries as well as works about Hispanic people in the United States. The author indicates in the annotations the passages in which cultural bias and stereotyping might appear. Covers grades K–12. Volumes 2 (1985) and 3 (1988) are also available.

Kaleidoscope—A Multicultural Booklist for Grades K–8. Rudine Sims Bishop, ed. National Council of Teachers of English, 1111 W. Kenyon Road, Urbana, IL 61801-1096. 1994. 169 pp. $14.95.

Celebrating cultural diversity with annotations of nearly 400 books, covers a range from poetry to arts to biographies, folktales, and picture books, focusing especially on people of color.

Our Family, Our Friends, Our World: An Annotated Guide to Significant Multicultural Books for Children and Teenagers. Lyn Miller-Lachman. R. R. Bowker, 245 W. 17th St., New York, NY 10011. 1992. 400 pp. $39.95.

Annotated lists of fiction and nonfiction about ethnic and cultural minority groups in the United States and Canada, and about cultures in various parts of the world.

Shadow and Substance: Afro-American Experience in Contemporary Children's Fiction. Rudine Sims Bishop. National Council of Teachers of English, 1111 Kenyon Road, Urbana, IL 61801. 1981. 112 pp. $8.95, paper.

Annotations of 150 children's books published from 1965 to 1979 that present images of African American children. Examines historical context, distortions, and social conscience as expressed in these books and provides some guidelines for teachers and librarians on how to make better-informed selections. Includes bibliographies and a reference list.

OTHER SOCIAL ISSUES

The Aging Adult in Children's Books and Nonprint Media: An Annotated Bibliography. Catherine Townsend Horner. Scarecrow Press, 52 Liberty St., Box 4167, Metuchen, NJ 08840. 1982. 266 pp. $22.50.

A comprehensive list of fiction and nonprint materials about the aging adult. Lists of fiction, arranged according to age levels, include books about relationships, concerns, and activities of older people in relation to children as well as books about illness and death. Nonprint materials are largely factual in approach. No nonfiction book titles are included.

The Bookfinder, Volume 5: When Kids Need Books. Sharon Spredemann Dreyer. American Guidance Service. Publishers' Building, Circle Pines, MN 55014-1796. 1994. 519 pp. $64.95; $29.95, paper.

Subject, author, and title indexes are provided on the top half of the publication, and lengthy reviews that include subject cross-references, age levels, and specific information about the content of the book are on the bottom half. Both fiction and nonfiction are included. The books focus on problems children may experience, feelings, and relationships.

Books to Help Children to Cope with Separation and Loss, 4th Edition. Masha K. Rudman, comp. R. R. Bowker, 245 W. 17th St., New York, NY 10011. 1994. 514 pp. $49.00.

Includes several chapters on bibliotherapy plus annotated lists of titles in such categories as death, divorce, adoption, and foster children, and loss of mental or physical functions. About 600 books are arranged by topic with an annotation evaluation and recommendations for use with children. Age levels from 3 to 16; interest, and reading level are included in each annotation.

Drugs: A Multimedia Sourcebook for Young Adults. Sharon Ashenbrenner, Charles Feldman, and Sari Feldman. Neal-Schuman Publishers, 23 Leonard St., New York, NY 10013. 1980. 200 pp. $27.95.

Contains annotations for fiction and nonfiction as well as nonprint materials about drugs of all kinds. Guidelines for selection are carefully laid out. An appendix lists professional reading and publishers, and there are author, title, and subject indexes.

Portraying Persons with Disabilities: An Annotated Bibliography of Fiction for Children. Debra Robertson. R. R. Bowker, 245 W. 17th St., New York, NY 10011. 1991. 482 pp. $39.95.

Updates *Notes from a Different Drummer* and *More Notes from a Different Drummer*, books that provide annotated lists of titles that portray the disabled in fiction. Includes titles that promote better understanding and acceptance of the disabled.

Portraying Persons with Disabilities: An Annotated Bibliography of Nonfiction for Children. Joan Brest Friedberg, June B. Mullins, and Adelaide Weir Sukiennik. R. R. Bowker, 245 W. 17th St., New York, NY 10011. 1992. 400 pp. $39.50.

Updates *Accept Me as I Am*, listing over 350 nonfiction titles about the disabled. Includes introductory essays about the portrayal of disabilities in literature for children.

CURRICULUM AREAS AND GENRES OF LITERATURE

Anatomy of Wonder: A Critical Guide to Science Fiction. Neil Barron, ed. R. R. Bowker, 245 W. 17th St., New York, NY 10011. 1995. 1,000 pp. $52.00.

Includes a chapter that annotates titles for children and young adults, as well as 3,000 additional titles that would appeal to readers of the genre. Includes discussion of sci-fi poetry, film connections, and a chapter on classroom aids.

Best Science Books and A-V Materials for Children: Selected and Annotated. S. M. O'Connell, V. J. Montenegro, & K. Wolff, eds. American Association for the Advancement of Science, 1333 H. Street NW, 8th Floor, Washington, DC 20005. 1988. 350 pp. $20.00.

An annotated list of high-quality trade books, filmstrips, films, and videos in the sciences that were published or produced between 1982 and 1988.

Celebrations: Read-Aloud Holiday and Theme Book Programs. Caroline Feller Bauer. H. W. Wilson, 950 University Ave., Bronx, NY 10452. 1985. 301 pp. $35.00.

Includes readings and plans for holiday activities for both well-known and Bauer's invented holiday occasions.

E for Environment: An Annotated Bibliography of Children's Books with Environmental Themes. Patti Sinclair. R. R. Bowker, 245 W. 17th St., New York, NY 10011. 1992. 400 pp. $39.95.

Lists 500 books that focus on environmental themes, such as endangered species, pollution, and recycling.

Fantasy Literature for Children and Young Adults: An Annotated Bibliography, 3rd. ed. Ruth Nadelman Lyn. R. R. Bowker, 245 W. 17th St., New York, NY 10011. 1995. 1,150 pp. $52.00.

Annotates about 4,800 fantasy novels for 8- to 17-year-olds in ten chapters arranged by topics. Includes specific subject indexes.

Fun for Kids II: An Index to Children's Craft Books. Marion F. Gallivan. Scarecrow Press, 52 Liberty St., Box 4167, Metuchen, NJ 08840. 1992. 483 pp. $42.50.

An index to several hundred craft books commonly purchased for library collections. Specific craft or art activities are listed with references to books in which plans and directions for the activity can be located.

Health, Illness and Disability: A Guide to Books for Children and Young Adults. Pat Azarnoff. R. R. Bowker Co., 245 W. 17th St., New York, NY 10011. 1983. 259 pp. $34.95.

An annotated list of over 1,000 books about health issues and problems.

Index to Children's Songs: A Title, First Line, and Subject Index. Carolyn Sue Peterson and Ann D. Fento. H. W. Wilson Company, 950 University Ave., Bronx, NY 10452. 1979. 318 pp. $33.00.

Indexes over 5,000 songs in 298 children's songbooks, both single titles and collections. Songs are indexed by title and first line as well as by 1,000 subject headings and cross-references.

Index to Poetry for Children and Young People, 1988–1992. G. Meredith Blackburn, et al. H. W. Wilson Co., 950 University Ave., New York, NY 10452. 1994. 358 pp. $58.00.

Latest in a series of volumes that index collections of poetry by author, title, first line, and subject. Different collections are indexed in each volume. Classifies poems under a wide variety of subjects, making for easy access to poems by their topics.

The Literature of Delight: A Critical Guide to Humorous Books for Children. Kimberly Olson Fakih. R. R. Bowker, 245 W. 17th St., New York, NY 10011. 1993. 269 pp. $40.00.

Lists 1,000 fiction and nonfiction books with humorous presentations. Chapters include books of nonsense, books of satire and parody, poetry, and so on.

Read Any Good Math Lately? Children's Books for Mathematical Learning, K–6. David J. Whitin and Sandra Wilde. 1992. 206 pp. $20.00, paper.
It's the Story That Counts: More Children's Books for Mathematical Learning, K–6. David J. Whitin and Sandra Wilde. 1995. 224 pp. $21.50, paper.

Both published by Heinemann Books, 361 Hanover St., Portsmouth, NH 03801.

The first book discusses basic concepts in mathematics, such as place value, classification, and geometry, and suggests ways to explore these concepts with children's books. The second title highlights children's responses to many of these books and suggests additional titles and ideas, including multicultural perspectives, for exploring mathematics.

Science and Technology in Fact and Fiction: A Guide to Children's Books. DayAnn M. Kennedy, Stella S. Spangler, and Mary Ann Vanderwerf. R. R. Bowker, 245 W. 17th St., New York, NY 10011. 1990. 331 pp. $35.00.

Includes summaries and evaluations for 350 books of both fiction and nonfiction for preschool and elementary students. Indexed by author, title, illustrator, subject, and readability.

INFORMATION ABOUT AUTHORS AND ILLUSTRATORS

Behind the Covers: Interviews with Authors and Illustrators of Books for Children and Young Adults. Jim Roginski. Libraries Unlimited, P.O. Box 263, Littleton, CO 80160. 1985. 249 pp. $23.50.

Interviews 22 authors and illustrators about their work.

Bookpeople: A First Album. 1990. 175 pp. $17.00, paper.
Bookpeople: A Second Album. 1990. 200 pp. $18.00, paper.

Both by Sharon L. McElmeel. Libraries Unlimited, P.O. Box 263, Littleton, CO 80160.

A First Album introduces 41 authors and illustrators of picture books. *A Second Album* introduces authors of intermediate books (grades 3–9). Brief biographies with highlights of life and career and selected bibliographies.

Children's Books and Their Creators. Anita Silvey, ed. Houghton Mifflin, 222 Berkeley St., Boston, MA 02116. 1995. 800 pp. $40.00.

This handsomely designed book includes biographical descriptions of and first-person reflections by important twentieth-century authors and illustrators and critical essays on a range of topics central to the study of children's literature.

The Illustrator's Notebook. Lee Kingman, ed. Horn Book, 11 Beacon St., Boston, MA 02108. 1978. 168 pp. $28.95.

Contains excerpts from articles by artists and illustrators that have appeared in the *Horn Book Magazine.* Articles discuss philosophy of illustration, history, illustration's place in the arts, and their experiences with various techniques of illustration.

Books by African-American Authors and Illustrators for Children and Young Adults. Helen E. Williams. American Library Association, 50 E. Huron St., Chicago, IL 60611. 1991. 270 pp. $39.00.

A comprehensive listing of works by African Americans. Clear, concise annotations are given in three sections divided by reading/interest level: Pre-K–4, 5–8, 9+. Also includes profiles and critical discussion of 53 African-American authors and illustrators.

Illustrators of Children's Books 1744–1945. Bertha E. Mahony, Louise Payson Latimer, and Beulah Formsbee, eds. 1947. 527 pp. $35.95.
Illustrators of Children's Books 1946–1956. Bertha Mahony Miller, RuthHill Viguers, and Marcia Dalphin, eds. 1958. 229 pp. $30.95.
Illustrators of Children's Books 1957–1966. Lee Kingman, Joanna Foster, and Ruth Giles Lontoft, eds. 1968. 295 pp. $30.95.
Illustrators of Children's Books 1967–1976. Lee Kingman, Grace Allen Hogarth, and Harriet Quimbly, eds. 1978. 290 pp. $35.95.

All published by Horn Book, 11 Beacon St., Boston, MA 02108.

All four volumes contain brief biographical and career sketches of artists and illustrators for children who were actively at work in this field during the period covered by the volume. Articles discuss techniques, philosophy, and trends in illustration during the period. Bibliographies are included for each illustrator as well as selected bibliographies covering art and illustration of the period. Volume 4 contains a cumulative index.

The Junior Book of Authors, 2nd rev. ed. Stanley J. Kunitz and Howard Haycraft, eds. 1951. 309 pp. $30.00.
More Junior Authors. Muriel Fuller, ed. 1969. 235 pp. $25.00.
Third Book of Junior Authors and Illustrators. Doris de Montreville and Donna Hill, eds. 1972. 320 pp. $30.00.
Fourth Book of Junior Authors and Illustrators. Doris de Montreville and Elizabeth D. Crawford. 1978. 370 pp. $35.00.
Fifth Book of Junior Authors and Illustrators. Sally Holmes Holtze, ed. 1983. 375 pp. $38.00.

All published by H. W. Wilson Company, 950 University Ave., Bronx, NY 10452.

These volumes provide readable biographies of popular authors for young people that include, generally, a biographical statement by the author or illustrator, a photograph, a brief biography, and a list of that person's works.

The Marble in the Water: Essays on Contemporary Writers of Fiction for Children and Young Adults. David Rees. Horn Book, 11 Beacon St., Boston, MA 02108. 1980. 224 pp. $9.95, paper.

Essays on 18 British and American authors, including Beverly Cleary, Paula Fox, Judy Blume, and Paul Zindel.

Meet the Authors and Illustrators: 60 Creators of Favorite Children's Books Talk About Their Work. Volume I. Deborah Kovacs and James Preller. Scholastic Inc., 730 Broadway, New York, NY 10003. 1991. 142 pp. $19.95.

Two children's book authors have collected information on favorite authors and illustrators from around the world. Each two-page highlight includes information about the author or illustrator, selected titles, pictures, and a "do-it-yourself" activity suggested for children.

Meet the Authors and Illustrators: 60 Creators of Favorite Children's Books Talk About Their Work. Volume II. Deborah Kovacs and James Preller. Scholastic Inc., 730 Broadway, New York, NY 10003. 1993. 142 pp. $19.95.

More profiles of more authors and illustrators for children.

Newbery Medal Books: 1922–1955. Bertha Mahoney Miller and Elinor Whiteney Field, eds. 1955. 458 pp. $22.95.
Caldecott Medal Books: 1938–1957. Bertha Mahony Miller and Elinor Whitney Fields, eds. 1957. 239 pp. $22.95.
Newbery and Caldecott Medal Books: 1956–1965. Lee Kingman, ed. 1965. 300 pp. $22.95.
Newbery and Caldecott Medal Books: 1966–1975. Lee Kingman, ed. 1975. 321 pp. $22.95.
Newbery and Caldecott Medal Books: 1976–1985. Lee Kingman, ed. 1986. 321 pp. $24.95.

All published by Horn Book, 11 Beacon St., Boston, MA 02108.

Each volume contains biographical sketches and texts of the award winners' acceptance speeches as well as general observations of trends in the awards.

Pauses: Autobiographical Reflections of 101 Creators of Children's Books. Lee Bennett Hopkins. HarperCollins, 10 E. 53rd St., New York, NY 10022. 1995. 233 pp. $23.00.

A collection of personal reflections taken from interviews with noted authors and illustrators.

Pipers at the Gates of Dawn: The Wisdom of Children's Literature. Jonathan Cott. Random House, 201 E. 50th St., New York, NY 10022. 1983. $19.45.

Seven essays on authors and illustrators for children that focus both on biographical information and on how these creators fit into the world of literature. Includes essays on Dr. Seuss, Maurice Sendak, William Steig, Astrid Lindgren, Achebe, P. L. Tavers, and the Opies.

A Sense of Story: Essays on Contemporary Writers for Children. John Rowe Townsend. Horn Book, 11 Beacon St., Boston, MA 02108. 1973. 216 pp. $6.95.

Includes essays on 19 English-language authors for children, including brief biographies, notes on their books, critical remarks, and lists of their books. Essays reflect the critical position of the author.

Something About the Author. Anne Commaire. Gale Research, 835 Penobscot Bldg., Detroit, MI 48226-4094. There are over 81 volumes in print, added to periodically. $70.00/vol.

Clear and sizable essays on contemporary authors and illustrators. Updating allows more-recent authors to be included. Contains photographs as well as reproductions from works of the illustrators. Suitable for middle-grade children to use for gathering biographical information.

A Sounding of Storytellers: New and Revised Essays on Contemporary Writers for Children. John Rowe Townsend. Harper & Row, 10 E. 53rd St., New York, NY 10022. 1979. 218 pp. $15.25.

Townsend reevaluates seven of the authors included in his earlier "A Sense of Story," including the new ground they have covered in more-recent works. Several American authors are included in the new selections, including Vera and Bill Cleaver, Virginia Hamilton, and E. L. Konigsburg.

PERIODICALS

Appraisal: Science Books for Young People. Children's Science Book Review Committee, 36 Cummington St., Boston University, Boston, MA 02215. Quarterly. $42.00.

Each issue contains reviews of about 75 children's and young-adult science and technology books. Gives age levels and ratings of quality.

Bookbird. IBBY, The International Board on Books for Young People, P.O. Box 3156, West Lafayette, IN 47906. Quarterly. $30.00.

This excellent journal reflects the international character of children's literature through articles and profiles of authors and illustrators from member countries. Themed issues have included "Children's Poetry," "Southeast Asia," "Girls and Women," and "Philosophy for Children."

Book Links. American Library Association, 50 E. Huron St., Chicago, IL 60611. Six times/year. $20.00.

Originally edited by Barbara Elleman, this publication connects books, libraries, and classrooms. Special features include "book strategies" or guides for teaching a particular book, interviews with authors and illustrators to discover their personal story behind the book, book themes, poetry, and "just for fun," books for children to read and enjoy.

Book Review Digest. H. W. Wilson Co., 950 University Ave., Bronx, NY 10452. Ten times/year. Service basis rates quoted on request.

Evaluates about 4,000 adult and children's books per year. For those books included, provides citations from several reviews that have appeared in other review periodicals.

Booklist. American Library Association, 50 E. Huron St., Chicago, IL 60611. Twice/month. $60.00.

Reviews both adult and children's titles, including both print and nonprint materials. Reviews are annotated and graded by age levels and grades. Includes reviews of new selection tools. Often contains subject lists of good books in particular fields. Lists prizewinning books annually.

Book World. c/o Washington Post, 1150 15th St., NW, Washington, DC 20071. Weekly. $26.00.

A weekly supplement to the *Post* and several other newspapers. Reviews children's books regularly. Issues large special children's book editions in fall and spring.

The Bulletin of the Center for Children's Books. University of Illinois Press, 54 E. Gregory Dr., Champaign, IL 61820. 11 issues. $29.00.

Reviews about 75 current children's books in each issue with negative as well as favorable reviews. Each entry is graded. Annotations stress curricular use, values, and literary merit.

CBC Features. Children's Book Council, 568 Broadway, New York, NY 10012. A one-time $35.00 charge for placement on a mailing list. Twice/year.

A newsletter about children's books, including information about special events, free and inexpensive materials from publishers, and lists of prizewinners, as well as discussion of new books.

CM: Canadian Materials for Schools and Libraries. Canadian Library Association, 200 Elgin St., Ste. 602, Ottawa, Ontario K2P 115. Bimonthly. $42.00.

Reviews English-language materials written by Canadians or published in Canada. Evaluates books, films, filmstrips, games, and periodicals.

Canadian Children's Literature. CC Press, P.O. Box 335, Guelph, Ontario, NIH 6K5, Canada. Quarterly. $28.00.

Literary analysis, criticism, and reviews of Canadian children's literature. A thematic approach for each issue. Predominantly written in English, but some articles are in French or French and English.

Childhood Education. Association for Childhood Education International, 11501 Georgia Ave., Ste. 312, Wheaton, MD 20902. Five times/year. $45.00.

Includes a column on children's books that contains annotated reviews on about 25 books.

Children's Literature in Education. c/o Agathon Press, 233 Spring St., New York, NY 10013. Quarterly. $29.00.

Publishes longer articles on English and American children's literature, including criticism, history, and biographical essays.

Cricket Magazine. Marianne Carus, ed. Carus Corp., 315 Fifth St., Box 300, Peru, IL 61354. Monthly. $29.97.

A literary magazine for children of elementary school age. Includes new stories and poems by well-known children's authors as well as excerpts and serializations of older pieces of literature. Includes children's reviews of books, interviews with authors, and children's writing.

Five Owls. Five Owls, 2004 Sheridan Ave., S., Minneapolis, MN 55405. Bimonthly. $18.00.

Each issue provides an article on a theme or topic and bibliographies that enhance or support it. Includes a signed review section.

Horn Book Magazine. Horn Book, Inc., 11 Beacon St., Boston, MA 02108. Bimonthly. $35.00.

Includes detailed reviews of children's books judged by the editorial staff to be the best in children's literature.

Contains articles about the literature, interviews with authors, and text of important speeches in the field of literature (Newbery and Caldecott acceptance speeches are published in the August issue each year). October issue gives a list of the outstanding books of the previous year.

Journal of Youth Services in Libraries. Association for Library Services to Children and Young Adult Services Division, American Library Association, 50 E. Huron St., Chicago, IL 60611. Quarterly. $40.00.

Formerly *Top of the News.* Provides articles on issues in children's literature and children's librarianship, international news, texts of speeches, and lists of upcoming events of interest in the field. Articles are often annotated bibliographies on subjects of current interest.

Language Arts. National Council of Teachers of English, 1111 Kenyon Rd., Urbana, IL 61801. Monthly September to May. $40.00.

"Books for Children" section features regular reviews of new books. Several issues focus on literature and reading, containing articles on authors, using literature in the classroom, and so on.

The Lion and the Unicorn. Johns Hopkins University Press, 2715 N. Charles St., Baltimore, MD 21218. Annual. $19.00.

Literary criticism, book reviews, and interviews with authors of children's literature. Each issue presents a particular theme or genre around which articles are centered.

The New Advocate. Christopher-Gordon, 480 Washington St., Norwood, MA 02062. Quarterly. $28.00.

Includes articles about authors and illustrators, literary qualities, and classroom uses of children's literature as well as selected book reviews.

The New York Times Book Review. New York Times Co., 229 W. 43rd St., New York, NY 10036. Weekly. $39.00.

Weekly column entitled "For Younger Readers" reviews a few children's books. Two issues in fall and spring are devoted to children's books exclusively. Before Christmas, a list of outstanding books is included.

Publisher's Weekly. R. R. Bowker, 245 W. 17th St., New York, NY 10011. Weekly. $129.00.

Twice a year, in spring and fall, a "Children's Book Number" is published that includes new titles from all major publishers, as well as reviews. Negative reviews are included. Occasionally includes feature articles on children's books and publishing for children.

School Library Journal. P.O. Box 57559, Boulder, CO 80322. Monthly. $74.50.

Reviews most children's books, using librarians, teachers, and critics from around the country as reviewers. Includes both positive and negative reviews. Categorizes reviews by age levels. Also includes feature articles on children's literature, children's library services, technology, and nonprint materials. December issue includes a "Best Books" section.

School Library Media Quarterly. American Association of School Librarians, American Library Association, 50 E. Huron St., Chicago, IL 60611. Quarterly. $40.00.

Official journal of the AASL. Includes articles on book evaluations, censorship, library services, standards of service, and so on.

Science Books and Films. American Association for the Advancement of Science, 1333 H St., NW, Washington, DC 20005. Quarterly. $40.00.

Reviews trade, test, and reference books for students in all grades in both pure and applied sciences. Includes nonprint materials. Indicates level of expertise required to use a piece of material. Books are reviewed by specialists in the field.

Science and Children. National Science Teachers Association, 1201 16th St., NW, Washington, DC 20005. Eight times/year. $37.00.

Includes a monthly column that reviews books and nonprint materials.

Signal: Approaches to Children's Books. Thimble Press, Lockwood Station Rd., South Woodchester, Glos. GL5 5EQ England. Three times/year. $27.00.

Articles of criticism on history of children's literature and on theory and practice of classroom usage. The literature considered is largely British.

Teaching and Learning Literature. Essmont Publishing, P.O. Box 186, Brandon, VT 05733. Five times/year. $29.00.

This journal includes thoughtful essays and critiques on a range of topics and genres in children's literature. Each issue includes a "Workshop" feature, ideas for deepening children's responses and understandings to books.

The WEB: Wonderfully Exciting Books. Ohio State University, The Reading Center, 200 Ramseyer Hall, Columbus, OH 43210. Three times/year. $10.00.

Devoted to helping teachers incorporate children's literature into the curriculum through reviews that emphasize classroom use and through a "web of possibilities" for a major thematic area that is included in each issue. Reviews are written by practicing teachers and librarians.

Wilson Library Bulletin. The H. W. Wilson Co., 950 University Ave., Bronx, NY 10452. Monthly September to June. $52.00.

Includes discussions and reviews of all types of books and materials. Features a monthly column of reviews of children's books, plus articles about authors, a list of awards, and so on. The October issue is devoted to children's books.

appendix c
Publishers' Addresses

Note: Publishers' addresses may change. For complete and up-to-date information, see the current edition of *Literary Market Place* or *Children's Books in Print*.

ABRAMS, 100 Fifth Ave., New York, NY 10010.

ADDISON-WESLEY, 1 Jacob Way, Reading, MA 01867.

ALADDIN BOOKS, see Simon & Schuster.

APPLE SOUP, see Knopf.

ARCADE PUBLISHING, 141 Fifth Ave., New York, NY 10010.

ASTOR-HONOR, 530 Fifth Ave., New York, NY 10036.

ATHENEUM PUBLISHERS, see Simon & Schuster.

ATLANTIC MONTHLY PRESS, 19 Union Square West, New York, NY 10013.

AVON BOOKS, 1350 Avenue of the Americas, New York, NY 10019.

BANTAM DOUBLEDAY DELL, 1540 Broadway, New York, NY 10036.

BLACK BUTTERFLY CHILDREN'S BOOKS, see Writers and Readers Publishing.

BLUE SKY, see Scholastic.

BOYDS MILLS PRESS, 910 Church St., Honesdale, PA 18431.

BRADBURY PRESS, see Simon & Schuster.

BROWNDEER PRESS, see Harcourt Brace.

CAMELOT, see Avon.

CANDLEWICK PRESS, 2067 Massachusetts Ave., Cambridge, MA 02140.

CAROLRHODA BOOKS, INC., 241 First Avenue North, Minneapolis, MN 55401.

CHILDREN'S BOOK PRESS, 6400 Hollis St., Emeryville, CA 94604.

CLARION BOOKS, 215 Park Ave., New York, NY 10003.

COBBLEHILL BOOKS, see Dutton.

COLLIER, see Macmillan.

CREATIVE ARTS BOOKS, 833 Bancroft Way, Berkeley, CA 94710.

CREATIVE EDUCATION INC., 123 S. Broad, Mankato, MN 56001.

CRESTWOOD HOUSE, see Dutton.

THOMAS Y. CROWELL, see HarperCollins.

CROWN PUBLISHERS, see Knopf.

DELACORTE PRESS, see Bantam Doubleday Dell.

DELL PUBLISHING, see Bantam Doubleday Dell.

DIAL, see Penguin USA.

DISNEY PUBLICATIONS, 114 Fifth Ave., 12th Floor, New York, NY 10011.

DK PUBLISHING, INC. (formerly Dorling Kindersley Publishing, Inc.), 95 Madison Ave., 10th Floor, New York, NY 10016.

DOUBLEDAY, see Bantam Doubleday Dell.

DOVER PUBLICATIONS, INC., 180 Varick St., New York, NY 10014.

DUTTON CHILDREN'S BOOKS, see Penguin USA.

FARRAR, STRAUS & GIROUX, INC., 19 Union Square West, New York, NY 10003.

FOUR WINDS PRESS, see Simon & Schuster.

DAVID R. GODINE, PUBLISHERS, INC., 300 Massachusetts Ave., Boston, MA 02115.

GOLDEN BOOKS/WESTERN, 850 Third Ave., New York, NY 10022.

GREEN TIGER PRESS, 435 E. Carmel St., San Marcos, CA 92069.

GREENWILLOW BOOKS, 1350 Avenue of the Americas, New York, NY 10019.

GROSSET & DUNLAP, INC., 200 Madison Ave., New York, NY 10016.

GULLIVER BOOKS, see Harcourt Brace.

HARCOURT BRACE CHILDREN'S BOOKS, 525 B St., Suite 1900, San Diego, CA 92101-4495.

HARPERCOLLINS CHILDREN'S BOOKS, 10 East 53rd St., New York, NY 10022.

HARPER TROPHY PAPERBACKS, see HarperCollins.

HENRY HOLT AND COMPANY, INC., 115 West 18th St., New York, NY 10011.

HOLIDAY HOUSE, 425 Madison Ave., New York, NY 10017.

HOUGHTON MIFFLIN, 222 Berkley St., Boston, MA 02116.

HYPERION BOOKS, 114 Fifth Ave., 12th Floor, New York, NY 10011.

JEWISH PUBLICATION SOCIETY, 60 East 42nd St., Suite 1339, New York, NY 10165.

JOY STREET BOOKS, see Little, Brown.

KANE/MILLER BOOK PUBLISHERS, P.O. Box 8515, La Jolla, CA 92038.

ALFRED A. KNOPF, 201 East 50th St., New York, NY 10022.

LEE & LOW BOOKS INC., 95 Madison Ave., New York, NY 10016.

LERNER PUBLICATIONS COMPANY, 241 First Ave., North, Minneapolis, MN 55401.

LIPPINCOTT JUNIOR BOOKS, see HarperCollins.

LITTLE, BROWN & CO., 34 Beacon St., Boston, MA 02108.

LODESTAR BOOKS, see Dutton.

LOTHROP, LEE & SHEPARD BOOKS, 1350 Avenue of the Americas, New York, NY 10019.

MARGARET K. McELDERRY BOOKS, see Simon & Schuster.

MACMILLAN PUBLISHING CO., see Simon & Schuster.

THE MILLBROOK PRESS, INC., 2 Old New Milford Rd., Brookfield, CT 06804.

MORROW JUNIOR BOOKS, 1350 Avenue of the Americas, New York, NY 10019.

MULBERRY BOOKS, see Morrow.

NATIONAL GEOGRAPHIC PRESS, 1145 17th St. NW, Washington, DC 20036.

NORTH-SOUTH BOOKS, 1133 Broadway, Suite 1016, New York, NY 10010.

ORCHARD BOOKS, see Franklin Watts.

RICHARD C. OWEN, PUBLISHERS, INC., P.O. Box 585, Katonah, NY 10536.

OXFORD UNIVERSITY PRESS, 200 Madison Ave., New York, NY 10016.

PANTHEON, 201 East 50th St., New York, NY 10022.

PARENTS MAGAZINE PRESS, 685 Third Ave., New York, NY 10017.

PARNASSUS PRESS, see Houghton Mifflin.

PENGUIN USA, 375 Hudson St., New York, NY 10014.

PHILOMEL BOOKS, see Putnam.

PICTURE BOOK STUDIO, 2 Center Plaza, Boston, MA 02108.

PLEASANT COMPANY, 8400 Fairway Place, P.O. Box 998, Middleton, WI 53562.

PRENTICE HALL, 115 Columbus Circle, New York, NY 10023.

PUFFIN BOOKS, see Penguin USA.

G. P. PUTNAM'S SONS, 200 Madison Ave., New York, NY 10016.

RAND MCNALLY, P.O. Box 7600, Chicago, IL 60680.

RANDOM HOUSE, 201 E. 50th St., New York, NY 10022.

RIZZOLI INTERNATIONAL PUBLICATIONS, INC., 300 Park Ave., South, New York, NY 10010.

SCHOLASTIC INC., 730 Broadway, New York, NY 10003.

CHARLES SCRIBNER'S SONS, see Simon & Schuster.

SIERRA CLUB BOOKS FOR CHILDREN, 100 Bush St., San Francisco, CA 94104.

SILVER MOON PRESS, 126 Fifth Ave., Suite 803, New York, NY 10011.

SIMON & SCHUSTER BOOKS FOR YOUNG READERS, 1230 Avenue of the Americas, New York, NY 10020.

ST. MARTIN'S PRESS, 257 Park Ave., S., New York, NY 10016.

STEWARD, TABORI & CHANG, INC., 575 Broadway, New York, NY 10012.

TAMBOURINE BOOKS, see Morrow.

TICKNOR & FIELDS, 215 Park Ave., S., New York, NY 10003.

TROLL ASSOCIATES, 100 Corporate Dr., Mahwah, NJ 07430.

TUNDRA BOOKS, 345 Victoria Ave., #604, Montreal Quebec H3Z 2N2 Canada.

VIKING, see Penguin USA.

WALDMAN, 525 N. Third St., Minneapolis, MN 55401.

WALKER & CO., 435 Hudson St., New York, NY 10014.

FREDERICK WARNE & CO., INC., see Penguin USA.

FRANKLIN WATTS, INC., 95 Madison Ave., New York, NY 10016.

WESTERN, see Golden Books.

ALBERT WHITMAN & CO., 6340 Oakton St., Morton Grove, IL 60053.

WRITERS AND READERS PUBLISHING, INC., 625 Broadway, New York, NY 10012.

PAPERBACK BOOK CLUB ADDRESSES

THE TRUMPET BOOK CLUBS, Bantam Doubleday Dell, 1540 Broadway, New York, NY 10036.

THE SCHOLASTIC BOOK CLUBS, [Firefly: Preschool–K; See Saw: K–1; Lucky: Gr. 2–3; Arrow: Gr. 4–6], Scholastic, Inc., 730 Broadway, New York, NY 10003.

THE TROLL BOOK CLUBS, Troll Associates, Inc., 100 Corporate Dr., Mahwah, NJ 07430.

name index

Author, Illustrator, Title

A is for Africa, 159
Aardema, Verna, 673, 682
Aardvarks Disembark!, 155, 158, 650
A, B, See!, 157
ABC Americana from The National Gallery of Art, 155, 159
ABC Bunny, The, 157
Abe Lincoln Grows Up, 564
Abel's Island, 641, 700
Abigail Adams: Witness to a Revolution, 552, 566, 581
Abraham Lincoln, 555, 559
Abraham Lincoln, The Prairie Years, 564
Abuela, 682
Accidental Zucchini: An Unexpected Alphabet, The, 695
Ace: The Very Important Pig, 349
"Achievement and Antecedents of Labelling, The," 12
Ackerman, Karen, 56, 686
Acorn Pancakes, Dandelion Salad and Other Wild Recipes, 683
Across America on an Emigrant Train, 17, 581, 601
Across Five Aprils, 535
Across the Stream, 178
Across the Wide Dark Sea, 514, 524
Ada, Alma Flor, 272
Adam and Eve and Pinch Me, 59, 466
Adam and Eve: The Bible Story, 322
"Adam Joshua" stories, 494
Adam of the Road, 522
Adams, Adrienne, 109, 351
Adams, Harriet Stratemeyer, 107
Adams, Richard, 352, 608
Adel, Daniel, 237
Adkins, Jan, 578
Adler, David A., 560, 562
Adoff, Arnold, 32, 111, 224, 396, 408, 409, 421, 422, 425, 563

"Adult Assistance to Language Development: Scaffolds, Models, and Direct Instruction," 174
"Advantages of a Well-educated Mind," 92
Adventures of High John the Conqueror, The, 306
Adventures of Huckleberry Finn, The, 95, 96, 116
"Adventures of Isabel, The," 404, 405
Adventures of Isabel, The, 404, 423 432
Adventures of Pinocchio, The, 97, 116
Adventures of Rama, The, 318
Adventures of Spider: West African Folk Tales, The, 275, 668
Adventures of Tom Sawyer, 95, 96, 115
Advice for A Frog, 415
Aesop, 310
Aesop & Company, 312
Aesop's Fables, 91, 103, 310
Afanasyev, Alexander Nikolayevich, 279, 302
Africa: Adventures in Eyewitness History, 107
"African Dance, The," 685
African Journey, 583
"After English Class," 422
"After My Bath," 407
After the Dancing Days, 536, 538
After-Christmas Tree, The, 650
"Afternoon on a Hill," 427
Against the Storm, 491
Agard, John, 151, 417, 422
Agony of Alice, 464
Ahlberg, Allen, 45, 52, 150, 221, 237, 243, 356, 698, 699, 701
Ahlberg, Janet, 45, 52, 150, 221, 237, 243, 698, 699, 701
Aïda, 217, 220
Aiken, Joan, 369
Ai-Ling, Louie, 117
Aircraft, 106
Airmail to the Moon, 693
Ajeemah and His Son, 515, 533, 606
Akaba, Suekichi, 294, 672
Aladdin, 277, 279, 290
"Aladdin," 89, 290
Aladdin and the Wonderful Lamp, 290
Alan and Naomi, 57, 542
Alanna, the First Adventure, 368

Albert, Burton, 219
Albert B. Cub and Zebra: An Alphabet Storybook, 157
Alborough, Jez, 428
Alcock, Vivien, 502, 650
Alcorn, Stephen, 569, 570
Alcott, Louisa May, 22, 28, 83, 93, 94, 99, 112, 115, 568
Alder, Elizabeth, 523, 536
Alderson, Brian, 87, 125
Aldhelm, Abbot, 115
Aldis, Dorothy, 110, 396, 400, 407, 418, 426, 428, 429, 430, 431
Aldo Applesauce, 493
Aldrich, Thomas Bailey, 95
Alexander, Ellen, 309, 606
Alexander, Lloyd, 51, 57, 110, 341, 342, 347, 368, 369, 371, 379, 432, 624, 651, 683, 686
Alexander, Martha, 141, 231
Alexander, Sally Hobart, 592
Alexander and the Terrible, Horrible, No Good, Very Bad Day, 55, 233, 429, 694
Alexander and the Wind-up Mouse, 236, 243, 428, 691
Alexander Who Used to Be Rich Last Sunday, 233
Alfie Gets in First, 53, 171, 211
Alfie Gives a Hand, 171
Alfie's Feet, 52, 171
Alfred Summer, 476
Alger, Horatio, 95, 107
"Algy Met a Bear," 428
Ali Baba and the Forty Thieves, 272, 311
"Ali Baba," 89
Alice in Between, 57, 494
Alice the Brave, 58
Alice Through the Looking Glass, 342
Alice's Adventures in Wonderland, 6, 96, 98, 99, 109, 115, 124, 355, 357, 624
Alice's Adventures Underground, 96
Alien Secrets, 376
Aliki (pseudonym Aliki Brandenberg), 52, 53, 142, 167, 181, 221, 429, 561, 562, 593, 595, 684, 685, 686, 703, 704
Alison's Zinnia, 18, 155, 158
All About Alligators, 588, 589
All About Owls, 588
All About Sam, 460
All About Where, 166
All Creatures Great and Small, 6
All God's Critters Got a Place in the Choir, 651
"All in a Word," 435
"All Kinds of Grands," 429
All-of-a-Kind Family, 111
"All-of-a-Kind-Family" series, 459
All of You was Singing, 673
All Pigs are Beautiful, 18, 167
All the Colors of the Race, 409
All the Places to Love, 212
All the Small Poems and 14 More, 396, 397
All Together, 396, 400, 407, 426, 428, 430
All Together Now, 477
Allard, Harry, 55, 238, 244
Allen, Jonathan, 244
Allen, Thomas B., 209, 480, 489, 524, 680
Allen, Virginia, 15
Alligator Arrived with Apples, 154, 157

"Alligator on the Escalator," 411, 414
Allingham, William, 99, 685
Allinson, Beverly, 205
"Alone," 407
Alphabatics, 154, 157
Alphabet Annie Announces an All-American
    Album, 695
Alphabet City, 157
Alphabet of Old Friends and the Absurd ABC, An,
    100
Alphabet Square Book of Animals, 104
Alphabet Tale, The, 157
Alvin Ailey, 219, 560
Always Wondering, 410, 435
Amazing Bikes, 57
Amazing Birds, 704
Amazing Bone, The, 216, 243, 691
Amazing Grace, 55, 232
Amazing Spiders, 623
Amber Brown Goes Fourth, 493
Amelia Bedelia, 40, 55, 116, 494
Amelia Mixed the Mustard and Other Poems, 111
America: Adventures in Eyewitness History, 107
America Revised, 586
American Boy, The, 99
American Girl books, 514
American Is Born, 586
American Picturebooks from Noah's Ark to the
    Beast Within, 104, 125, 198
American Revolutionaries: A History In Their Own
    Words, The, 569
American Sports Poems, 427
American Tall Tales, 56 307, 308
"America's Cinderella," 325
Ames, Lee J., 584
Amos & Boris, 220, 222, 312, 675, 699, 709
Amos Fortune, Free Man, 567
Amy's Eyes, 347, 355
"Analysis of Story Comprehension in Elementary
    School Children, An," 59
"Anansi and Nothing Go Hunting for Wives,"
    273
Anansi the Spider, 109, 275, 281, 295
Anansi the Spider: A Tale from the Ashanti, 668,
    669
Anansi: The Spider Man, 108
Anansi the Spider Man: Jamaican Folk Tales, 279
Anastasia Absolutely, 9
Anastasia Again!, 479
Anastasia Krupnik, 8, 430, 460, 494, 699, 701
"Ancient History," 415
Ancient Ones: The World of the Old-Growth
    Douglas Fir, 431, 581, 588
Ancona, George, 525, 596, 597
And It Is Still That Way, 299
And Now Miguel, 486
"And She Jumped out of the Window Never to
    Be Seen Again," 690
And Then There Was One: The Mysteries of
    Extinction, 650
And Then What Happened, Paul Revere?, 107,
    552, 556, 657, 686
And to Think I Saw It on Mulberry Street, 6, 105,
    116, 239
Andersen, Hans Christian, 16, 92, 97, 99, 103,
    114, 269, 341, 343, 344, 347, 349, 353
Anderson, Douglas A., 379
Anderson, Joan, 525
Anderson, Margaret J., 542
Anderson, Rachel, 516, 536
Anderson, Richard C., 626, 637
Anderson, Yvonne, 678
Ando, Noriyuki, 539
Andrew Shachar, 637

Andrews, Jan, 247, 248
Andrews, Jane, 115
Andronik, Catherine M., 320
"Angel Park All Stars" series, 498
Anglund, Joan W., 392
Angus and the Ducks, 105
Animal Alphabet, 154, 157, 198
Animal Fact Animal Fable, 703
Animal Numbers, 160
Animal That Drank Up Sound, The, 207, 673
Animal, Vegetable, Mineral, 419
Animals as Parents, 584
Animals' Picnic, The, 97
Animals Should Definitely Not Act Like People, 244
Animals Should Definitely Not Wear Clothing, 8,
    244
Anna Is Still Here, 542
Anne Frank Beyond the Diary: A Photographic
    Remembrance, 555, 564, 565
Anne Frank: The Diary of a Young Girl, 117, 431,
    539, 701
Anne of Green Gables, 111
Anne of Green Gables Cookbook, The, 682
Annie and the Old One, 224
Anno, Mitsumasa, 56, 118, 155, 157, 161, 162,
    312, 644
Anno's Aesop: A Book of Fables by Aesop and Mr.
    Ox, 312
Anno's Alphabet, 155, 157
Anno's Alphabet: An Adventure in Imagination,
    644
Anno's Counting Book, 161, 162
Anno's Counting House, 161
Anno's Italy, 644
Anno's Journey, 118
Anno's Math Games III, 56
Annotated Hobbit, The, 379
Annotated Mother Goose, The, 88
Anonymous, 428
Anonymously Yours, 570
Anpao, 300
Anselm, Archbishop, 84, 115
Antar and the Eagles, 368, 650
Anthony Burns: The Defeat and Triumph of a
    Fugitive Slave, 564, 606
Antle, Nancy, 514
Antler, Bear, Canoe: A Northwoods Alphabet Year,
    158
Any Me I Want to Be, 407
Anything for a Friend, 467
Apache Rodeo, 582
Apartment House Tree, The, 651
Apfel, Necia H., 602
Appalachia: The Voices of Sleeping Birds, 212
Appelbaum, Diana, 27, 218, 651, 673
Apple Is My Sign, 536
Apple Pie, A, 101
Applebee, Arthur N., 12, 60, 61, 65, 70
Applebet, 157
Appraisal, 582
Apprentice, The, 523
April, Bubbles, Chocolate: An ABC of Poetry, 158
"April Rain Song," 402, 408
Arabian Nights, The, 89, 108, 290
Arabian Nights: Three Tales, 290, 291
Aragon, Jane, 650
Araminta, 112
Araminta's Paint Box, 686
Arbuthnot Lectures 1980–1989, The, 380
Archambault, John, 54, 154, 207, 224, 671
Ardizzone, Edward, 207, 321
Ardley, Neil, 580, 598, 606
Are You There God? It's Me, Margaret, 25, 45, 57,
    117, 459, 468
"Argument, The," 399, 412

Ariadne, Awake!, 316, 317
Ariès, Philippe, 83, 125
Arithmetic, 411, 423, 426
"Arithmetic," 426
Arkadians, The, 369
Arkhurst, Joyce Cooper, 275, 668
Arkin, Alan, 652
Armed Vision, The, 267
Armstrong, William H., 430, 517, 538
Arnold, Caroline, 588, 650
Arnold, Katya, 272
Arnosky, Jim, 57, 433, 588, 589, 693
Around the World in Eighty Days, 96
Arrow and the Lamp: The Story of Psyche, The,
    266, 285, 316
Arrow to the Sun, 299
Arroz Con Leche: Popular Songs and Rhymes from
    Latin America, 151
Art and Design in Children's Picture Books: An
    Analysis of Caldecott Award Winning
    Illustrations, 252
"Art for Children" series, 562
Art Lesson, The, 570
Art of Africa, The, 669
"Art of Nonfiction, The," 581
Art of Teaching Writing, The, 645
Arthur, Alex, 674
Arthur, High King of Britain, 319
Arthur's Chicken Pox, 238, 244
Arthur's Eyes, 238
Arthur's Family Vacation, 430
Arthur for the Very First Time, 462, 503
Arthur's Halloween, 238
Arthur's Nose, 238
"Arthur" series, 244
Arthur's Valentine, 238
Aruego, Josè, 157, 162, 242, 272, 278, 281
"As I Was Going to St. Ives," 146
As the Waltz Was Ending, 541
Asbjørnsen, Peter Christian, 8, 53, 270, 272,
    281, 285, 302, 311, 316
Ashabranner, Brent, 57, 570
Ashanti to Zulu: African Traditions, 159, 217
Ashley, L. F., 33, 380
Ashworth, Kent P., 15
Asimov, Isaac, 374
Ask Mr. Bear, 105
Asking About Sex and Growing Up: A Question
    and Answer Book for Boys and Girls, 58
Asleep, Asleep, 52
"Aspects of Children's Informational Books," 608
"Ass in the Lion's Skin, The," 312
"Assessing Reading Preferences: A New
    Approach," 40
"Assuming the Spectator Stance: An
    Examination of the Responses of Three
    Young Readers," 60
Astrid Lindgren: Storyteller to the World, 563
At Grammy's House, 221, 232
At the Back of the North Wind, 97, 115, 345
At the Crossroads, 247, 646
"At the Garden," 440
Atalanta's Race, 315, 316
Attaboy, Sam, 460
Atwater, Florence, 355
Atwater, Richard, 355
Atwell, Nancy, 645, 660
Auction, The, 248
Auden, W. H., 6
Aunt Flossie's Hats (and Crab Cakes Later), 227,
    232
Aunt Judy's Magazine, 99
Aunt Nina, Good Night, 429
Averill, Esther, 526

Avi (Avi Wortis), 18, 28, 49, 59, 120, 122, 348, 401, 518, 528
Awakening to Literacy, 185
Away From Home, 155, 158
Away Goes Sally, 107
Aylesworth, Jim, 158, 160, 203, 673
Azarian, Mary, 158

"B" Is for Betsy, 111, 493
"Baba Yaga Tales," 288, 325, 714
Baba Yaga, 288, 302
Baba Yaga: A Russian Folktale, 276, 281, 311
Baba Yaga and Vasilisa the Brave, 288, 302
Babbitt, Ellen, 108
Babbitt, Natalie, 18, 21, 23, 49, 65, 341, 364, 367, 430, 431, 634, 690
"Babbling Brook," 403
Babe the Gallant Pig, 349
Babies, 52, 139
Babies, and Libraries: Serving Infants, Toddlers, Their Parents, and Caregivers, 660
Babies Need Books, 137, 185
Baboushka and the Three Kings, 221, 323
Babushka: An Old Russian Folktale, 289, 323
Baby, 57, 464
Baby, The, 140
"Baby Board Books," 139
"Baby Books," 139
Baby Says, 52, 139
Baby Sister for Frances, A, 53, 184, 430
Baby Uggs Are Hatching, The, 406
Baby's Bouquet, The, 100
Baby's Catalogue, The, 52
"Baby-Sitters Club" series, 32, 108, 491, 703
Baby-Sitters Remember, The, 118
Baby's Opera, The, 100
Bach, Alice, J., 322
"Backyard Volcano," 405
Bacmeister, Rhoda, 394, 404
Bacon, Betty, 581
"Bad," 407
"Bad Books, Good Reading," 492
Bad Day at Riverbend, 241, 245
Bader, Barbara, 33, 104, 125, 198, 252, 312
Bag I'm Taking to Grandma's, The, 637
"Bagthorpe Saga, The," 493
Bailey, Carolyn Sherwin, 353
Baker, Alan, 631
Baker, Augusta, 636
Baker, Jeannie, 118, 205, 221, 248, 431, 650, 651, 671
Baker, Keith, 159, 160, 606
Baker, Olaf, 209, 211
Baldwin, James, 455
Ballad Book, 99
Ballad of Belle Dorcas, The, 219
"Ballad of Birmingham," 399
Balloons and Other Poems, 397, 412, 425
Balyet, 362
Bam Bam Bam, 425
"Bam Bam Bam," 440
Bamboo Hats and Rice Cakes, 303
Bang, Molly, 53, 55, 160, 172, 202, 203, 206, 211, 294, 402, 671, 680
Banks, Lynne Reid, 10, 346, 454, 712
Bannatyne-Cugnet, Jo, 158
Banshee Train, The, 56
Banyai, Istvan, 56, 170
Barbara Frietchie, 423
Barbauld, Mrs., 90
Barbier, Suzette, 160
Barbour, Karen, 312
Bard of Avon: The Story of William Shakespeare, 561
"Barefoot Boy, The," 392

Baring-Gould, Cecil, 88
Baring-Gould, William S., 88
Barlow, Gillian, 285
Barnyard Banter, 179, 207
Barracca, Debra, 53
Barracca, Sal, 53
Barrett, Joyce D., 55
Barrett, Judi, 8, 53, 244
Barrett, Ron, 244
Barrie, J. M., 109, 116
Barron, T. A., 359
Barth, Edna, 558
Bartholomew Fair, 523
Barton, Bob, 636, 660
Barton, Byron, 53, 166, 178, 181, 409, 580, 592
Barton, Griselda, 9, 625
Barton, Harriet, 591
Bartone, Elisa, 514, 515
Baruch, Dorothy, 685
"Base Stealer," 427
Baseball in April and Other Stories, 58, 117, 486, 492
Baseball Saved Us, 607
Bash, Barbara, 431, 581, 588
Basho, 402
Basket Full of White Eggs: Riddle-Poems, A, 56
Baskin, Barbara H., 476, 504
Bat-Poet, The, 349, 438
Battle for the Castle, The, 57, 355
Battle of the Books, 123
"Baucis and Philemon," 316
Bauer, Caroline Feller, 636, 660, 713
Bauer, Marion Dane, 45, 49, 455, 457, 471, 477, 481, 497, 644
Baum, Betty, 112
Baum, Frank L., 109, 116, 357
Baviera, Rocco, 560
Bawden, Nina, 454, 455, 463, 467, 479, 496, 503, 541, 693
Baylor, Byrd, 210, 230, 234, 299, 410, 425, 426, 430, 431, 650, 694, 695, 709
Baynes, Pauline, 370
Bayou, Suzette, 112
Be Ever Hopeful, Hannalee, 536
Be Seated: A Book about Chairs, 581, 585, 590
Be the Best You Can Be, 56
Beach, Richard, 40, 59
Beach Day, A, 674
Beacons of Light: Lighthouse, 674
Bealer, Alex, 107
Bear, The, 216, 221
Bear Called Paddington, A, 348
Bear in Mind, 420, 428
"Bear Went Over the Mountain, A," 148
"Bear with the Golden Hair, The," 400, 407, 428
Beardance, 488, 489
Bearman: Exploring the World of Black Bears, 586
Bears' House, The, 455
Bear's Toothache, The, 235, 242, 428
Bearstone, 58, 488
Beast Feast, 405
Beast in Ms. Rooney's Room, #1, The, 493
Beat the Story-Drum, Pum-Pum, 269, 272, 296
Beat the Turtle Drum, 481
"Beaumains, the Kitchen Knight," 319
Beautiful Land: A Story of the Oklahoma Land Rush, 514
"Beautiful Wassilissa, The," 325
Beauty: A Retelling of the Story of Beauty and the Beast, 342
"Beauty and the Beast," 271, 287

Beauty and the Beast, 272, 275, 277, 279, 302, 347
Beauty and the Beast: Visions and Revisions of an Old Tale, 325
Beaver, Joetta M., 197
Bechtel, Louise Seaman, 105
Becoming a Nation of Readers, 626, 637
"Bed in Summer," 99
Beddows, Eric, 395
"Bedtime," 428
Bedtime for Frances, 242, 428
Bee Tree, The, 54
Beekeeper's Apprentice, or On the Segregation of the Queen, The, 59
Beekeeper's Year, A, 590
Bees Dance and Whales Sing: The Mysteries of Animal Communication, 603, 650
"Before I Was Born: History and the Child," 544
Begay, Shonto, 299, 300
Beggar Queen, The, 369
Behn, Harry, 110
Beims, Gerald, 112
Beims, Lorraine, 112
Beisty, Stephen, 580
Bell, Sharon, 479
Bellairs, John, 361
Bellmaker, The, 57, 352, 353
Belloc, Hillaire, 421
Bells of London, The, 153
Belpré, Pura, 108
Belton, Sandra, 208
Bemelmans, Ludwig, 105, 116, 202
Bender, Robert, 281, 305
Beneath a Blue Umbrella, 406
Benét, Rosemary, 426
Benét, Stephen Vincent, 426
Benjamin Franklin, 559
Benjamin's Portrait, 631
Bennett, Jill, 180
Bennett, Rowena, 429
Benny Bakes a Cake, 171, 181
Beowulf, 84, 115
Berenzy, Alix, 284
Bernhard, Durga, 309, 606
Bernhard, Emery, 281, 299, 309, 606, 650
Bernos de Gasztold, Carmen, 425, 437
Bernstein, Joanne E., 504
Berry, James, 417, 515, 533, 606
Bertrand, Lynne, 46
Beskow, Elsa, 106, 595
Best, Carrie, 225, 226, 231
Best Christmas Pageant Ever, The, 495
Best Friends, 233
Best of the WEB, 1976–1982, The, 632, 653
Best School Year Ever, The, 495
Best Wishes, 569
Betsy-Tacy, 494
Bettelheim, Bruno, 10, 268, 324
Between Madison and Palmetto, 485
"Beulah," 408
Bewick, Thomas, 91, 115
Beyer, Evelyn, 685
Beyond Fact: Nonfiction for Children and Young People, 556, 581
Beyond the Burning Lands, 377
Beyond the Divide, 515, 532
Beyond the High Hills: A Book of Eskimo Poems, 111
Beyond the Tomorrow Mountains, 376
BFG, The, 48
Bible, Authorized Version, 321
Bible, Douai, 321
Bible, Geneva, 321
Bible, King James, 322

Bible, New Testament, 322
Bible, The, 321
"Bible in the Classroom, The," 321
Bible stories, 624
Bible Story, The, 322
Bicycle Rider, 554
Bierhorst, John, 299, 307, 312, 313, 322, 418, 419, 422
Big Alfie and Annie Rose Storybook, The, 171
Big Anthony and the Magic Ring, 680, 684
Big Baby: A Little Joke, The, 214
Big Book for Our Planet, The, 651
Big Bug Book, The, 591, 606
Big Fat Hen, 159, 160, 606
Big Friend, Little Friend: A Book About Symbiosis, 651
Big Red, 498
Big Sneeze, The, 706
Biggest Bear, The, 14, 218
Biggest Boy, The, 173
Biggest House in the World, The, 65, 66, 703
Bigmama's, 570
Biliban, Ivan, 284
Bill Peet: An Autobiography, 570
Billions of Bats, 588
Bimwili & the Zimwi, 274
Binch, Caroline, 232
Bing Bang Bong, 405
Bingham, Jane, 125
Bingo Brown, Gypsy Lover, 493
"Bingo Brown series," 120
"Binker," 110
Birch, Reginald, 99
Birches, 424
Bird Watch, 650
Bird, 650
Bird, Lois Bridges, 659
"Bird Talk," 410
"Birdfoot's Grampa" 426, 431
Birds, 693
Birdseye, Tom, 272, 693
Bishop, Claire Huchet, 293, 540
Bishop, Gavin, 280
Bishop, Rudine Sims (See also Rudine Sims), 123, 504
Bissex, Glenda, 15
Bit By Bit, 290
Blabber Mouth, 476
Black, Charles C., 54
Black and White, 117, 122, 202, 211, 633
Black Beauty, 96
Black Cauldron, The, 371
Black Hearts in Battersea, 369
Black Is Brown Is Tan, 409
Black on White, 139
"Black Rhino," 415
Black Stallion, The, 493
Black Swan, White Crow, 402
Black Water, 516, 536
Blackberries in the Dark, 56, 480
Blackberry Ink, 411
Blake, Quentin, 236, 405
Blake, William, 91, 99, 115, 401, 420
Blanck, Jacob, 95
Blanket, The, 52, 117, 118, 140
Blegvad, Erik, 233
Blishen, Edward, 399, 416
Block City, 423
"Block City," 407
Blood and Thunder Adventures on Hurricane Peak, The, 56
Bloom, Lloyd, 213, 231, 374, 375
Bloom, Valerie, 417

Blos, Joan W., 121, 534, 560, 701
Blow Me a Kiss, Miss Lilly, 229, 233, 429
Blubber, 25, 625
Blue Backed Speller, 91
"Blue Beard," 88
Blue Fairy Book, The, 93, 116
Blue Sword, The, 372
Blue Willow, 111, 116
Blueberries for Sal, 199, 210
Blumberg, Rhoda, 555, 590
Blume, Judy, 25, 33, 45, 57, 113, 117, 120, 123, 124, 458, 467, 468, 469, 495, 504, 625, 657, 703
"Boa, The," 405
"Boa Constrictor," 400
Bobbsey Twins, The, 107
Bober, Natalie S., 552, 565, 566, 581
Bødker, Cecil, 322
Bodkin, Odds, 56
Boggart, The, 356, 709
Bohstedt, Jinx, 676
"Bold Sir Brian," 110
Bombers' Moon, The, 541
Bond, Michael, 348
Bond, Nancy, 365
Bone Stranger, The, 55
Bones, Bones, Dinosaur Bones, 580
Bonsall, Crosby, 501
Bontemps, Arna, 112
Bony-Legs, 276, 288
Book for Boys and Girls, A, 87
Book Links, 120, 604, 713
Book of Americans, A, 425, 426
Book of Curteseye, A, 85, 115
Book of Eagles, The, 600, 650
Book of Nonsense, A, 98, 115
Book of Nursery and Mother Goose Rhymes, The, 152
Book of One's Own: Developing Literacy Through Making Books, A, 713
Book of Pigericks, The, 401, 699
Book of Poetry for Children, The, 416
Book of Three, The, 371, 686
Book Takes Root: The Making of a Picture Book, A, 704
Book Talk and Beyond: Children and Teachers Respond to Literature, 661
Book that Jack Wrote, The, 237, 696
"Book Was Okay, I Love You: Social Aspects of Response to Literature, The," 42
Bookbird, 492
Bookfinder: A Guide to Children's Literature About the Needs and Problems of Youth Aged 2–15, The, 504
Booklist, 655
Bookman, 103
"Books & Boys: Gender Preferences and Book Selection," 71
Books Before Five, 67, 186
Books by African American Authors and Illustrators for Children and Young Adults, 505
"Books in the Classroom," 166
Books on American Indians and Eskimos: A Selection Guide for Children and Young Adults, 504
Books to Help Children Cope with Separation and Loss, 504
Books Without Bias: Through Indian Eyes, 224
Books You Can Count On: Linking Mathematics and Literature, 713
Bookworks, 602
Booth, David, 394, 414, 416, 420, 426, 430, 660
Booth, George, 243
Boots and His Brothers, 286, 302

Borgel, 375, 692
Borning Room, The, 534
Bornstein, Ruth Lercher, 231
Borreguita and the Coyote, 309, 682
Borrowers, The, 346, 358, 674
Borrowers Afield, The, 358
Borrowers Afloat, The, 358
Bosma, Betty, 324
Bosse, Malcolm, 524, 651
Bostock, Mike, 229, 230, 234, 592
Boston, L. M., 364
Bouchard, Lois Kalb, 358
Bound for Oregon, 515, 532
Boundless Grace, 232
Bowen, Betsy, 158
Bowker Annual of Library and Book Trade Information, The, 114, 118
Boxcar Children #1, The, 712
"Boxcar Children" series, 32, 44, 491
Boy, a Dog and a Frog, A, 118, 169
Boy: Tales of Childhood, 569, 570
Boy and the Cloth of Dreams, The, 428
Boy and the Ghost, The, 219
Boy and the Giants, The, 281
Boy Called Slow, A, 560
Boy of the Three-Year Nap, The, 271, 272, 277, 279, 294, 303, 311
"Boy Who Cried Wolf, The," 310
Boy Who Held Back the Sea, The, 209
Boy Who Lived with the Bears and Other Iroquois Stories, The, 290
Boy Who Lived With the Seals, The, 301
Boys at Work, 486
Boy's King Arthur, The, 320
Boys' War, The: Confederate and Union Soldiers Talk About the Civil War, 600
Bracelet, The, 607
Bradley, Darcy, 297
Bradley, Lynette, 146
Brady, 534
Brandenberg, Franz, 429
Brandenburg, Jim, 585
Branley, Franklin, 54, 584, 606
Brats, 405
Braun, Barbara, 562
Brautigan, Richard, 158
Brave Irene, 11, 243
Bray, Rosemary L., 560
Bread and Jam for Frances, 184, 683
Bread, Bread, Bread, 166
Breathtaking Noses, 581
Bremen Town Musicians, The, 210, 214, 272, 311
"Bremen Town Musicians, The," 304
Brennan, J. H., 520
Brenner, Barbara, 564, 571, 587, 650
"Brer Rabbit and the Tar Baby," 305
"Brer Rabbit Gets Even," 275
"Brer Rabbit" stories, 305
"Brer Terrapin," 272
Brett, Jan, 9, 287, 289, 311, 423, 428, 637
Brewton, John E., 421
Brewton, Sara, 421
"Brian Pinkney WEB," 219
Brian Wildsmith's Mother Goose, 153
Brian's Winter, 474
Bridge, Connie A., 174
"Bridge, The," 397
Bridge to Terabithia, 8, 11, 390, 431, 455, 459, 468, 472, 481, 634, 640, 659, 707
Bridgers, Sue Ellen, 477, 478, 504
Briggs, Raymond, 54, 118, 152, 216, 218, 243, 280, 281, 698
Bright April, 112, 117

Brighton, Catherine, 561
Bring Me All Your Dreams, 419
Bringing the Rain to Kapiti Plain, 220
Brink, Carol Ryrie, 107, 116, 518, 531, 673
Brittain, Bill, 57
Britton, James, 10, 60, 64, 625
"Brocaded Slipper, The," 278
Brocaded Slipper and Other Vietnamese Tales, The, 278, 293
Broccoli Tapes, The, 471
Broening, Angela M., 40
Bronze Bow, The, 520
Bronzeville Boys and Girls, 110, 117, 408, 429, 430
Brooke, Leslie, 103, 116, 153
Brooke, William J., 307, 308, 698
Brooks, Bruce, 478, 479, 499, 588, 603, 693
Brooks, Gwendolyn, 110, 117, 408, 417, 429, 430
Brooks, Louise, 116
Brooks, Polly Schoyer, 565
Brooks, Walter, 109
Broome, Errol, 701
"Brother," 407, 413, 430
Brother Anansi and the Cattle Rancher, 309
Brother Eagle, Sister Sky: A Message from Chief Seattle, 651
Brothers: A Hebrew Legend, 272
Brown, Elga, 12
Brown, Marc, 238, 244, 414, 430, 602
Brown, Marcia, 30, 31, 55, 108, 117, 203, 205, 210, 211, 220, 251, 271, 272, 277, 279, 280, 282, 285, 286, 287, 292, 302, 312, 342, 347, 689, 694
Brown, Margaret Wise, 5, 16, 45, 52, 53, 54, 105, 118, 137, 138, 140, 172, 175, 181, 223, 643, 659, 694
Brown, Mary Barrett, 594, 595, 598
Brown, Ruth, 180, 651, 706
Brown Bear, Brown Bear, What Do You See?, 54, 175, 180, 183, 436
Brown Cow, Green Grass, Yellow Mellow Sun, 206, 428, 682
Browne, Anthony, 11, 214, 218, 284, 347, 696
Browning, Robert, 99, 400
Bruce, Bertram, 59
Bruchac, Joseph, 272, 279, 298, 300, 301, 303, 324, 325, 426, 431, 526, 560
Bruner, Jerome, 12, 185
Brunkus, Denise, 243
Brusca, Maria Christina, 298
Bryan, Ashley, 269, 272, 295, 311, 408, 409, 440, 635
Bryant, Peter, 146
"Bubble," 412
Buchanan, Ken, 224
Buehner, Caralyn, 698
Buffalo Dance, A Blackfoot Legend, 299
Buffalo Gals: Women of the Old West, 567
Buffalo Hunt, 606
Buffalo Knife, The, 514
Buffalo Woman, 300
Buffie, Margaret, 366
Bugs, 54, 606
"Bugs," 391
Buguet, Anne, 220, 282, 304, 672
"Builders, The," 429, 698
Building a House, 53
"Bull, The," 415
Bull Run, 518
Bulla, Clyde R., 521, 524, 570
Bullard, Asa, 82
Bulletin for the Center for Children's Books, 655
Bully for You, Teddy Roosevelt!, 557, 565
Bully of Barkham Street, The, 120, 467
"Bump on My Knee," 412

Bundy, B. A., 40
Bunnicula, 56, 348
Bunting, Eve, 8, 30, 55, 117, 210, 214, 231, 247, 248, 250, 251, 430, 431, 514, 515, 569, 606, 607
Bunyan, John, 87, 88, 115
Burchard, Peter, 568
Burgoo Stew, 282, 304
Burke, Carolyn L., 68
Burkert, Nancy Ekholm, 201, 283, 344, 423
Burket, Mary Lou, 680
Burnett, Frances Hodgson, 28, 95, 99, 111, 112, 116
Burnford, Sheila, 65, 498
Burnie, David, 650
Burning Questions of Bingo Brown, The, 8, 57, 455, 493, 496, 701
Burningham, John, 52, 117, 118, 140, 157, 181, 209, 211, 231, 244, 429, 430
Burns, Marilyn, 599
Burress, Lee, 123
Burt Dow, Deep Water Man, 63
Burton, Frederick R., 643, 697
Burton, Marilee Robin, 180
Burton, Richard, 606
Burton, Sir Richard, 290
Burton, Virginia Lee, 53, 105, 116, 220, 240, 245, 675
Bus Stop, The, 180
"Business of Bees, The," 410
Busybody Nora, 493
Butler, Dorothy, 32, 137, 185
Butler, Stephen, 221, 269, 272, 311, 691
Butterfly's Ball and the Grasshopper's Feast, The, 98, 115
Butterworth, Emma Macalik, 541
Butterworth, Oliver, 357
Button Box, The, 683
Buzz Buzz Buzz, 181
By Myself, 55, 396, 428, 430
By the Shores of Silver Lake, 68, 531
Byars, Betsy, 8, 24, 57, 120, 455, 459, 462, 465, 467, 477, 493, 496, 504, 569, 621, 632, 634, 678, 683, 701

C is for City, 155, 156, 158
Cabin Faced West, The, 21, 519, 525, 686
Cactus Hotel, 590
Caddie Woodlawn, 107, 116, 518, 531
Caduto, Michael J., 324, 325
Caines, Jeanette, 231
Caitlin's Holiday, 354
Cake That Mack Ate, The, 178, 181
Calabro, Marian, 586
Calamity Jane, 565
Caldecott, Randolph, 100, 101, 103, 104, 109, 116, 251, 312
Caldecott Aesop, The, 312
"Caldecott Award Acceptance," 221
Calhoun, Mary, 209
Calico Bush, 529
Calico Captive, 526, 530
Calkins, Lucy McCormick, 645
Call It Courage, 27, 473
Call Me Charley, 112, 117
Call of Stories, The: Teaching and the Moral Imagination, 5, 33
Call of the Wild, The, 116, 498
Calling on Dragons, 368
Calmenson, Stephanie, 221, 243, 432, 698
Cameron, Ann, 54, 429, 430, 455, 458, 467, 483, 488, 493
Cameron, Eleanor, 32, 365, 374, 379, 493
Campbell, David, 417
Campbell, Jay, 15

Campbell, Joseph, 266, 325, 380
Campbell, Rod, 52, 180
Camus, 5
Can I Help?, 170
Can I Keep Him?, 223
Can You Guess?, 52, 166
Canada Geese Quilt, The, 680
Canady, Robert J., 714
Candidate for Murder, A, 503
Cane, Melville, 415
Caney, Steven, 646
Canfield, Dorothy, 111
Canterbury Tales, 85, 86
Can't You Make Them Behave, King George?, 560
Capital for the Nation, A, 585
Caps for Sale, 141
Captive, The, 533, 536, 606
Card, Orson Scott, 376
Caribbean Alphabet, 158, 216
Caribbean Canvas, 216
Caribbean Carnival: Songs of the West Indies, 216
Caribbean Dozen: Poems from Caribbean Poets, A, 417, 422
Caribou Alphabet, A, 155, 159
Carigiet, Alois, 114
Carl Goes Shopping, 168
Carle, Eric, 5, 16, 52, 54, 140, 141, 162, 168, 174, 177, 180, 183, 205, 214, 217, 218, 221, 312, 428, 623, 636, 671
Carl's Birthday, 168
Carlsen, G. Robert, 70
Carlson, Lori M., 422
Carlson, Natalie, 112
Carlstrom, Nancy White, 172, 229, 233, 429
Carpenter, Frances, 108, 274
Carpenter, Humphrey, 125
Carpenter, Nancy, 247, 248
Carr, Jo, 556, 581
Carrick, Carol, 228, 233, 290, 429, 430, 433, 588, 594, 596
Carrick, Donald, 117, 212, 228, 231, 233, 290, 429, 430, 433
Carrie's War, 541
Carroll, Kathleen Sullivan, 160
Carroll, Lewis (pseudonym of Charles Dodgson), 5, 6, 96, 97, 98, 115, 357, 416, 421
Carroll, Ruth, 116, 118
Carrot Seed, The, 172, 181
Carry On, Mr. Bowditch, 567
Carson, Rachel, 230
Carter, Mark A., 714
Carter, Polly, 219
"Case of the Uncooked Eggs, The," 272
Caseley, Judith, 5, 24, 55, 220, 231, 232, 493, 699, 701
Casey, Maude, 50, 58, 493
Casey at the Bat, 423
Cassedy, Sylvia, 206, 401, 402, 425
Castle, 592
Castle in the Attic, The, 355
Castle of Llyr, The, 371
Castlemon, Harry (pseudonym of Charles Austin Fosdick), 95
"Cat and the Fiddle, The," 146
"Cat Heard the Cat Bird, The," 405
Cat in the Hat, The, 6, 117, 182, 216
"Cat Kisses," 392
Cat Kong, 238
"Cat on a Night of Snow," 415
Cat on the Mat, The, 178, 181
Cat Poems, 420
Cat Running, 58, 680
Cat Who Wished to Be a Man, The, 342, 347, 369
Cat's Purr, The, 272, 311, 440, 635
Cataract of Lodore, The, 423

Catch Me and Kiss Me and Say It Again, 52
Cathedral: The Story of Its Construction, 592
Catherine Called Birdy, 25, 26, 120, 121, 519, 522, 699
Catling, Patrick Skene, 360
Catrow, David, 423
Cats Are Cats, 420, 425, 439
Cauley, Lorinda Bryan, 144, 153, 236, 270, 278, 281, 286, 302
Caxton, William, 85, 86, 90, 115, 310
Cay, The, 542
Cazden, Courtney B., 12, 174, 640
Cebulash, Mel, 499
Celebrate America: In Poetry and Art, 427
Celebrating Children's Books, 571
Celebrations, 412, 426
Celery Stalks at Midnight, The, 348
Celtic Fairy Tales, 93
Cendrars, Blaise, 205, 220
Censors in the Classroom: The Mind Benders, 123
Censorship, A Threat to Reading, Writing, and Thinking, 361, 661
Censorship and Selection: Issues and Answers for Schools, 661
"Censorship in Ohio: It Is Happening Here," 123
Centuries of Childhood: A Social History of Family Life, 83
Cesar Chavez, 563
Chaikin, Miriam, 322
Chain of Fire, 489
Chair For My Mother, A, 55, 207, 211, 218, 228, 233, 429
Chalk Doll, The, 216, 247
Chall, Marsha W., 430
Chamberlin, Margaret, 122
Chambers, Aidan, 352
Chameleons: Dragons in the Trees, 592
Champions: Stories of Ten Remarkable Athletes, 568
Chance Child, A, 367
Chandra, Deborah, 397, 399, 412, 425
Changes, 214
Changes, Changes, 168
"Changing," 431
Changing City, The, 596
Changing Countryside, The, 596
"Changing Role of Science Fiction in Children's Literature, The," 373
Chanticleer and the Fox, 204
Chapman, Cheryl, 176
Chapters: My Growth as a Writer, 569, 670
Charles, Faustin, 417
Charles Dickens: The Man Who Had Great Expectations, 561
Charley Skedaddle, 535, 600
Charlie and the Chocolate Factory, 342, 358
Charlie and the Great Glass Elevator, 359
Charlie Needs a Cloak, 9, 106, 595, 653
Charlip, Remy, 345, 596
Charlot, Jean, 30
Charlotte's Web, 11, 20, 30, 33, 55, 110, 117, 118, 124, 340, 341, 342, 346, 349, 379, 634
Charm, 99
Charmed Life, 361
Chase, Richard, 275, 281, 303
Chato's Kitchen, 214
Chatton, Barbara, 441, 608
Chaucer, Geoffrey, 85, 115
"Cheers," 418
Chemically Active! Experiments You Can Do at Home, 599
Chen, Ju-Hong, 290
Cherokee Summer, 582

Cherries and Cherry Pits, 701
Cherry, Lynne, 248, 249, 431, 596, 651
Chester's Way, 235, 242
Chetwin, Grace, 371, 372
Chiasson, John, 583
Chick and the Duckling, The, 176, 180, 182
Chick Hatches, A, 606
Chicka Chicka Boom Boom, 54, 154
"Chicken Dinner," 417
Chicken Licken, 235, 243, 280, 311
"Chicken Little," 237
Chicken Man, 247, 606
Chicken Soup with Rice, 177, 181, 683
Chicken World, 105, 106, 116
Chickens Aren't the Only Ones, 606
Chickens! Chickens!, 55
Chiha, Kim, 431
Child, Lydia Maria, 99, 426
Child and His Book, The, 84
Child and Story: The Literary Connection, 33
Child and Tale: The Origins of Interest, 43, 325
Child and the Book: A Psychological and Literary Exploration, The, 71
Child as Poet: Myth or Reality?, The, 442
"Child in the Elementary School: Developmental Trends, The," 45
Child Is Born, A, 322
Child Life, A Collection of Poems, 99
Child of the Owl, 487
Childhood and Society, 50
Childhood of Famous Americans, 107
"Childlike Wonder and the Truths of Science Fiction," 374
Children, 425
"Children, 1990: A Report Card, Briefing Book, and Primer," 45
Children and Adolescents, 47
"Children and Language: They Learn the Same Way All Around the World," 48
Children and Poetry, 418
Children Learning Through Literature, 185
Children of Green Knowe, The, 364
Children of Odin, The, 317
Children of the Dust Bowl, The True Story of the School at Weedpatch Camp, 601, 680
Children of the Morning Light: Wampanoag Tales, The, 298
Children of the Wild West, 600, 606
Children of the Yukon, 217
Children's Books and Their Creators, 126
Children's Books in England, 87, 90, 109
Children's Books in England: Five Centuries of Social Life, 125
Children's Books in England and America in the 17th Century, 86
"Children's Choices Makes Students Avid Readers," 700
Children's Classics, 28
Children's Defense Fund, 45
Children's Homer: The Adventures of Odyseus and the Tale of Troy, The, 318
"Children's Hour, The," 392
Children's Literature in the Reading Program, 713
Children's Minds, 46
Children's Poetry Preferences: A National Survey of the Upper Elementary Grades, The, 403, 418, 422
"Children's Responses to Literature," 71
"Children's Responses to Poetry in a Supportive Literary Context," 438
"Children's Supernatural Stories: Popular But Persecuted," 361
Child's Concept of Story: Ages Two to Seventeen, The, 12, 60, 61, 65, 70

Child's Developing Sense of Theme: Responses to Literature, The, 60, 71
Child's Garden of Verses, A, 99, 116, 401, 406, 407
Childress, Glenda, 41
Chimney Sweeps: Yesterday and Today, 588, 601
China Homecoming, 553
China Year, The, 490, 699, 701
Chinese Mother Goose Rhymes, 151
Chocolate Dreams, 409, 425
Chocolate Touch, The, 360
Chocolate War, The, 675
Choi, Sook Nyul, 431, 536, 543, 607
"Choices 'For Girls'/For Boys': Keeping Options Open," 41
Choosing Books for Children: A Commonsense Guide, 33
Choosing Sides, 493, 499, 500
Chopin, Kate, 568
Chortles, 412, 432
Christ Child, The, 322
Christelow, Eileen, 142, 180
Christenbury, Leila, 640
Christiansen, Bonnie, 154, 157
Christiansen, C. B., 18, 57, 462
"Christina's World," 427
Christmas Alphabet Book, The, 119
Christmas in the Big House, Christmas in the Quarters, 117, 606
Christmas Pageant, The, 322
Christmas Poems, 421
Christmas Story, The, 322
Christmas: The King James Version, 322
Christopher, John, 376, 377, 431, 650
Christopher, Matt, 56, 493
"Christopher Columbus," 426
Christopher Columbus: The Great Adventure and How We Know About It, 555, 571
Christopher Columbus: Voyager to the Unknown, 571
Chrysanthemum, 235, 242
Chukovsky, Kornei, 11, 12, 147, 268, 394, 441
Chute, Marchette, 425, 429
Cianciolo, Patricia, 251
Ciardi, John, 32, 401, 404, 405, 420, 425
"Cincinnati Patty," 406
Cinder Edna, 696, 698
"Cinderella," 10, 266, 269, 271, 282, 285, 296, 304, 324, 623, 635, 696
Cinderella, 103, 108, 210, 267, 279, 281, 286, 302, 311, 429, 696
Cinderella: A Casebook, 325
"Cinderella in Africa," 325
"Cinderella or the Glass Slipper," 88
Cinnamon, Mint and Mothballs: A Visit to Grandmother's House, 206
Cipielewski, Jim, 15
Circle of Fire, 538
Circle of Seasons, A, 412
Circles, Triangles and Squares, 165
City, The Story of Roman Planning and Construction, 592
"City City," 397
City Noise, 425
City of Dragons, The, 345, 347
City of Gold and Lead, The, 377
City of Light, City of Dark: A Comic Book Novel, 122
City Seen from A to Z, 158
City! Washington, D.C., 586
Clap Hands, 139, 140, 659
Clap Your Hands, 141
Clapp, Patricia, 120, 525
Clark, Ann Nolan, 30, 116, 224, 409, 422

Clark, Emma Chichester, 421, 428
Clark, Margaret, 12, 15, 174, 632
Clark, Margaret Goff, 650
Class Clown, 499
"Classes Under the Tree," 408
Classic Fairy Tales, The, 325
Classroom Discourse: The Language of Teaching
    and Learning, 640
Claverie, Jean, 344
Clay, Marie, 138, 186, 705, 708
Clay Marble, The, 536, 543
Clayton, Ed, 558
Cleary, Beverly, 8, 22, 31, 54, 55, 56, 57, 83, 111,
    121, 346, 348, 460, 463, 464, 467, 492,
    499, 500, 570, 626, 633, 638, 682, 683
Cleaver, Betty P., 608
Cleaver, Bill, 113, 117, 456, 457, 683
Cleaver, Elizabeth, 205, 298, 671
Cleaver, Vera, 113, 117, 456, 457, 683
Cleopatra, 56, 565
Clever Bill, 104, 116
Clever Tom and the Leprechaun, 279
Clever Woman of the Family, The, 93
"Cliché," 397, 425
Clifford, Eth, 479
Clifton, Lucille, 416, 417, 429, 483
Climb, The, 213
Climb into the Bell Tower: Essays on Poetry, 442
Climbing Kansas Mountains, 209
Climo, Shirley, 281, 311, 315, 316, 317, 586
Clocks and More Clocks, 53
Close to Home: A Story of the Polio Epidemic, 514
Close Your Eyes, 173
Clothing, 601
Clyde Monster, 245
Clymer, Eleanor, 501
Coatsworth, Elizabeth, 107, 110, 393, 397, 415,
    440
Cobb, Vicki, 582, 585, 592, 599
Cobweb Curtain: A Christmas Story, The, 323
Cochran-Smith, Marilyn, 185
"Cockroach Sandwich," 406
"Cocoon, The," 424
Coerr, Eleanor, 58, 250, 539, 680, 682
Coffin, Robert P. Tristram, 432, 437
Cohen, Barbara, 488, 498, 545
Cohen, Carol Lee, 299, 308
Cohen, Dorothy, 13, 174, 632
Cohen, Leslie B., 44
Cohen, Miriam, 53, 233, 429
Cohn, Amy, 297
Cohn, Ronald, 597
Cold Shoulder Road, 369
Cole, Babette, 698
Cole, Brock, 58, 281, 469, 698
Cole, Joanna, 54, 55, 56, 57, 117, 276, 288, 290,
    396, 430, 432, 496, 580, 583, 596, 606,
    637, 651
Cole, Sheila, 234
Cole, William, 421, 425, 434
Coles, Robert, 5, 33
Collier, Christopher, 17, 117, 120, 515, 518, 528,
    535, 544, 606
Collier, James Lincoln, 17, 117, 120, 515, 518,
    528, 536, 606
Colliers, 687
Collins, Patrick, 642
Collodi, Carlo, 97, 116
Colman, Penny, 567
Colón, Raúl, 213
Colonial Life, 686
Colonial Living, 526
Color Dance, 165, 428
"Color Eater, The," 410
Color Farm, 165, 428, 642

Color Zoo, 165, 428, 642, 672
Colors, 165
Colors Everywhere, 165
Colum, Padraic, 317, 318
Columbus, 559
"Columbus," 426
Columbus and the World Around Him, 571
Columbus Day, 562
Come a Tide, 606, 692
Come Away from the Water, Shirley, 209, 244,
    430
Come Back Salmon, 587, 651
Come In and Other Poems, 110
Come Sing, Jimmy Jo, 472
Comeback Dog, The, 497
Comenius, Johann Amos, 86, 115
Comets, Meteors, and Asteroids, 602
Comic Adventures of Old Mother Hubbard and Her
    Dog, The, 88, 698
Coming Home: From the Life of Langston Hughes,
    208, 560
Coming of the Bear, The, 324
"Commercial for Spring, A," 412
Commodore Perry in the Land of the Shogun, 590
Complete Nonsense Book, The, 405
Complete Tales of Uncle Remus, The, 305
Con Mi Hermano: With My Brother, 224
Concepts About Print, 138
Cone, Molly, 587, 651
Conford, Ellen, 467
"Confronting History: Holocaust Books for
    Children," 545
Conrad, Pam, 19, 57, 58, 240, 245, 362, 430,
    462, 470, 519, 532, 555, 571, 606, 690
Constance: A Story of Early Plymouth, 525
Contemporary Readings in Child Psychology, 48
Contender, The, 499
"Conversation," 428
Cooke, Trish, 140
Cookie's Week, 54, 177, 181
"Cook's Tour of Children's Cookbooks, A," 682
Cool Salsa: Bilingual Poems on Growing Up Latino
    in the United States, 422
Cool Web, The: The Pattern of Children's Reading,
    9, 625
Coolidge, Olivia, 608
Coomer, J. W., 40
Cooney, Barbara, 30, 31, 112, 150, 204, 208,
    215, 218, 219, 228, 232, 234, 322, 651
Cooper, Floyd, 208, 279, 300, 560, 568
Cooper, Ilene, 493, 499, 500
Cooper, James Fenimore, 95
Cooper, Mary, 88
Cooper, Susan, 11, 58, 110, 271, 272, 277, 282,
    283, 302, 311, 342, 347, 356, 361, 370,
    379, 541, 709
Corbett, Scott, 360
Corduroy, 53, 205, 245, 428
Cormier, Robert, 431, 504, 675
"Corn and Potatoes," 417
Cotton, John, 115
Coughlan, Margaret N., 87
Could Anything Be Worse?, 637
Could Be Worse!, 238, 244
Count and See, 160
Country Far Away, A, 247, 646
"Country Maid and the Milk Pail, The," 310
Couple of Kooks and Other Stories About Love, 58
Courage of Sarah Noble, The, 21, 54, 525
Courlander, Harold, 108, 273, 295, 296, 303
Court of the Stone Children, The, 365
Cousins, 19, 57, 457, 463, 485, 492
Cousins, Lucy, 140, 141
Coverdale, Miles, 321
"Cow's Complaint, The," 415

Cow-Tail Switch and Other West African Stories,
    The, 273, 296, 303
Cowcher, Helen, 651
Cowley, Joy, 627
Cox, Clinton, 566
"Coyote Cowboy," 308
Coyote Walks on Two Legs: A Book of Navajo
    Myths and Legends, 299, 300
Cracker Jackson, 465, 678
"Cradle Hymn," 91
Cradock-Watson, Jane, 580
Craft, Kinuko, 287, 288
Crane, Walter, 100, 104, 115
Crane Wife, The, 274, 275, 277, 279, 294, 303,
    311, 633, 672, 675
Crash! Bang! Boom!, 141
Crawford, Elizabeth D., 273
Crazy About German Shepards, 57
Crazy Quilt, 478
Crazy Weekend, 486
Creating Connections: Books, Kits, and Games for
    Children, 608
Creative Drama in the Classroom, 714
Creech, Sharon, 19, 58, 465, 503
Cremation of Sam McGee, The, 424
Cresswell, Helen, 58, 493
Crews, Donald, 53, 161, 166, 179, 181, 428, 570,
    671, 673, 674
Cricket in Times Square, The, 350
"Criteria for Historical Fiction," 518
Critical Handbook of Children's Literature, A, 33
Critical History of Children's Literature, A, 93, 96,
    126
Criticism, Theory, & Children's Literature, 33
Crocodile and the Crane, The, 650
Crocodile Beat, 181, 205
Croco'nile, 217
Croll, Carolyn, 279, 289, 311
Crompton, Anne Eliot, 526
Cross, Gillian, 376
Crossen, Stacy Jo, 429
"Crosspatch," 146
Crovell, Natalie Anne, 429
Crow and Hawk: A Traditional Pueblo Indian
    Story, 299
Crow Boy, 49, 55, 201, 211, 220, 605, 704
Crowe, Robert, 245
"Cruel Boys," 82, 83
Cruikshank, George, 100, 115
Crutcher, Chris, 499
Cruz, Ray, 233
Cry of the Crow, The, 39, 431, 437, 496
Crying for a Vision, The, 58
Cullen, Countee, 422
Cullinan, Beatrice, 441, 625, 713
cummings, e. e., 423
Cummings, Pat, 155, 156, 226, 231, 232, 483,
    568
Cunningham, Julia, 117, 471
Cupboard, The, 52, 118
"Cupid and Psyche," 285
Curious George, 105, 116, 242
Cushla and Her Books, 32
Cushman, Karen, 25, 26, 120, 121, 519, 522,
    523, 699, 701
Custard and Company, 405
Custard the Dragon, 400, 423
"Custard the Dragon," 400
Cut from the Same Cloth: American Women of
    Myth, Legend, and Tall Tale, 219, 276,
    307
Cutchins, Judy, 650
Cyberstorm, 376
Cybil War, The, 467

D'Aulaire, Ingri, 105, 314, 315, 555, 559
D'Aulaires' Book of Greek Myths, 314
D'Aulnoy, Mme., 89
Dad's Back, 139
Daddy, 231
Daddy Is a Monster . . . Sometimes, 231
Daddy-Long-Legs, 111
Dahl, Roald, 48, 56, 342, 358, 359, 496, 569, 570, 606, 633
Daisy Chain, The, 93
Dakota Dugout, 531, 606
Dalgliesh, Alice, 21, 54, 289, 311, 457, 524, 525, 637, 643, 689
Dalokay, Vedat, 491
Daly, Niki, 646
Dame Trot and Her Comical Cat, 100
Dana, Richard Henry, 95
Dance of the Sacred Circle: A Native American Tale, 299
Dance with Me, 412
Dancing Granny, The, 295
Dancing Kettle and Other Japanese Folk Tales, The, 108, 278
Dancing Teepees, 417, 422
Dancing with the Indians, 606
Dandelion, 210, 242, 428, 637
Dandelion Garden, The, 461
Dandelions, 514, 515, 605, 606
Daniel Boone, 107
Danny the Champion of the World, 56
Danzinger, Paula, 476, 493
Dark Dark Tale, A, 180
Dark Is Rising, The, 11, 58, 370, 379
Dark Stairs, The, 493
Dark Thirty: Southern Tales of the Supernatural, The, 219
Dark Way: Stories from the Spirit World, The, 303
Darkness and the Butterfly, 247
Darling, Benjamin, 683
Darnell Rock Reporting, 57, 457, 499
Dartmouth Seminar Papers: Response to Literature, The, 10
Darton, F. J. Harvey, 87, 90, 109, 125
Darwin, Charles, 96
Dasent, Sir George Webbe, 93, 266, 271, 285, 302
Daugherty, James, 107
Daughter of Earth: A Roman Myth, 314
DAulaire, Edgar Parin, 105, 107, 314, 315, 555, 559
David and Goliath, 322
David Copperfield, 475
"Davy Crockett," 308
Dawn, 55, 200, 211, 294, 430, 633, 650, 680, 685
Dawn of Fear, 541
Day, Alexandra, 168
Day, Nancy Raines, 205, 296, 297
Day Jimmy's Boa Ate the Wash, The, 237, 244, 246
Day of Ahmed's Secret, The, 11, 54, 646
Day of Delight, 219
Day with Wilbur Robinson, A, 240, 245
Daydreamer, The, 58
Dayrell, Elphinstone, 272, 295
Days Before Now, The, 54
"Days of Camelot, The," 320
Days with Frog and Toad, 182
De Angeli, Marguerite, 22, 112, 117, 152, 522, 536
De Armond, Dale, 299, 301, 631
de Beaumont, Mme, 272, 275, 277, 279, 287, 302, 347
de Bourgoing, Pascale, 580
de Brunhoff, Jean, 242
De Felice, Cynthia, 28, 287, 517

De Groat, Diane, 703
de Jenkins, Lyll Becerra, 491
de la Mare, Walter, 110, 116, 321, 394, 416
de la Ramee, Louise, 93, 96
De Luca, Geraldine, 608
De Marsh, Mary, 287
de Monvel, Maurice Boutet, 101, 116
de Paola, Tomie, 9, 52, 54, 98, 106, 147, 149, 152, 153, 169, 177, 215, 217, 220, 226, 227, 232, 277, 281, 299, 311, 322, 323, 416, 429, 560, 570, 595, 624, 653, 654, 680, 683, 684, 698
De Regniers, Beatrice Schenk, 53, 55, 244, 277, 289, 393, 394, 400, 401, 404, 405, 410, 413, 416, 428, 429, 431, 685
de Saint-Exupéry, Antoine, 110, 346
de Sauza, James, 309
de Trevino, Elizabeth Borton, 523
Dealing with Dragons, 347, 367
Dear Annie, 232, 699, 701
Dear Benjamin Banneker, 218, 560
Dear Daddy . . . ., 701
Dear Mr. Henshaw, 57, 121, 463, 701
Dear Mr. Sprouts, 701
Dear Zoo, 52, 180
"Death and Burial of Cock Robin, The," 87
"Death of the Hired Man, The," 411
"Deedle, Deedle, Dumpling," 146
Deem, James M., 59, 478
Deenie, 113, 657
Deep Down Underground, 161, 162
Deep Dream of the Rain Forest, 651
Deep in the Forest, 169, 698
"Deer Mouse," 8
Defoe, Daniel, 28, 89, 115, 526
Degas, Edgar, 213
Degen, Bruce, 117, 121, 428, 496, 580, 596
DeJong, Meindert, 30, 47, 497, 541
Delacre, Lulu, 151, 247
DeLuca, Geraldine, 571
Demi, 151, 271, 272, 287, 288, 293, 302, 344, 606
Demi's Secret Garden, 606
Denslow, W. W., 109
Denton, Kady, 414
Denton, Terry, 234
Desai, Laura E., 714
Desimini, Lisa, 248
"Development of a Survey to Ascertain the Reading Preferences of Fourth-, Fifth-, and Sixth-Graders, The," 40
"Development of Moral Character and Moral Ideology," 49
Development of Writing Abilities (11–18) The, 60
"Developmental Factors Influencing Children's Responses to Literature," 43
Developmental Psychology of Jean Piaget, The, 45
Devil with the Three Golden Hairs, The, 283
Devil's Arithmetic, The, 121, 517
Devils Who Learned to Be Good, The, 288
Dew Drop Dead, 493
Dewey, Ariane, 157, 162, 242, 272, 278, 281, 306, 307, 308
deWit, Dorothy, 526
Di Salvo-Ryan, DyAnne, 248
Diamond, Donna, 316
Diamond in the Window, The, 360
Diamond Tree: Tales From Around the World, The, 290
Diaz, David, 30, 214
Dicey's Song, 11, 57, 455, 463, 478
"Dick and His Cat," 280
"Dick and Jane" series, 112, 222, 626
Dick Whittington and His Cat, 109, 271, 272, 280
Dickens, Charles, 5, 92, 93, 100

Dickinson, Emily, 10, 110, 413, 414, 417, 633
Dickinson, Peter, 342, 365, 374, 431, 650
"Diddle Diddle Dumpling," 203
Diego, 561, 682
Dillon, Diane, 30, 109, 117, 159, 217, 220, 270, 294, 295, 296, 298, 306, 322, 363, 408, 479, 673
Dillon, Leo, 30, 109, 117, 159, 217, 220, 270, 294, 295, 296, 298, 306, 322, 363, 408, 479, 673
Dilly Dilly Piccalilli, Poems for the Very Young, 419
Dinah's Mad, Bad Wishes, 429
"Ding, Dong, Bell!," 146
Dinosaur Bob and His Adventures with the Family Lazardo, 240, 245
Dinosaurs, 415, 420
Dinosaurs Down Under: And Other Fossils From Australia, 588
Dinosaurs That Swam and Flew, 584
Dinosaurs Walked Here and Other Stories Fossils Tell, 56, 586
Dirt Bike Racer, 493
Discovering Christopher Columbus, How History Is Invented, 587
Discovering Dinosaur Babies, 588
Disney, Walt, 119
"Disobedience," 394
"Dissolving Ghost: Possible Operations of Truth in Children's Books and the Lives of Children, A," 380
Diverting History of John Gilpin, The, 100, 101, 116
Divine and Moral Songs Attempted in Easy Language for Use of Children, 87, 91, 115
Divine Emblems or Temporal Things Spiritualized, 87
"Divine Woman the Creator," 299
Do Nat Dstrb Gnys At Wrk, 15
Do Not Open, 637, 671
Do You Want to Be My Friend?, 16, 168, 180
Dobrin, Arnold, 601
Dobry, 43
Doctor, The, 92
Doctor Coyote: A Native American Aesop's Fables, 299, 312
Doctor De Soto, 49, 216, 243
Doctor Knickerbocker and Other Rhymes, 394
Dodge, Mary Mapes, 95, 99, 111, 115
Does God Have a Big Toe? Stories About Stories in the Bible, 322
Dog Breath: The Horrible Trouble with Hally Tosis, 238, 244
"Dog in the Manger, The," 310
Dog of Flanders and Other, A, 96
Dog on Barkham Street, A, 120, 467
Dog Poems, 420
Dog Who Wouldn't Be, The, 498
Dogger, 226, 231, 429
Dogs & Dragons, Trees & Dreams, 400, 407, 408, 426, 428, 429, 691
Dogsong, 58, 474
Dogzilla, 238
Doherty, Bertie, 54
Doll Face Has A Party, 240, 245
Dollhouse Murders, The, 56
Dolls' House, The, 353, 354
Dolphin, Laurie, 582
Dolphin Adventure: True Story, 650
Domanska, Janina, 210, 214
Dombey, Henrietta, 12
Dominic, 350
Don Giovanni, 561
Don't Be Mad, Ivy, 494
Don't Fidget a Feather, 49, 50, 235

Don't Tell the Grown-ups: Subversive Children's Literature, 126
Donaldson, Margaret, 46
Donnelly, Marlene Hill, 586
Donovan, John, 113, 470, 608
Dooling, Michael, 559, 560
"Doom Merchant, The," 406
Door in the Wall, The, 22, 522, 526, 530, 536
Doorbell Rang, The, 18, 162, 163
"Doors," 412
Dorothea Lange, 561
Dorothy Heathcote: Collected Writings on Education and Drama, 690
Dorp Dead, 117, 471
Dorris, Michael, 26, 56, 58, 117, 526, 529, 530, 531
Dorros, Arthur, 224, 225, 588, 651, 680, 682
Dorsey-Gaines, Catherine, 185
Dorson, Richard, 267
Double Life of Pochahantas, The, 526
Dove Isabeau, 345, 347, 681
Dowden, Anne Ophelia, 608
Down at the Bottom of the Deep Dark Sea, 674
Down By the Bay: Songs to Read, 181
Downing, Julie, 561
Doyle, Richard, 99
"Dr. Foster," 147, 418
Drackenburg Adventure, The, 369
Dragon of the Lost Sea, The, 345
Dragondrums, 372
Dragonfly's Tale, 299
Dragons, and Kites and Dragonflies: A Collection of Chinese Nursery Rhymes, 151
Dragons Are Singing Tonight, The, 406
Dragon's Blood, 347, 372
Dragon's Boy, The, 319
Dragon's Gate, 120, 537
Dragon's Pearl, The, 121
Dragonsinger, 372
Dragonsong, 58, 372
Dragonwagon, Crescent, 120, 154, 157, 481
Dragonwings, 537, 687
Drama Themes: A Practical Guide for Teaching Drama, 714
Drat Those Brats, 405
Drawing from Nature, 57
"Dreadful Doings of Jelly Belly," 414
"Dream Keeper, The," 408
Dream Keeper and Other Poems, The, 110, 219, 402, 408, 429, 430, 431, 435
Dream Stair, The, 682
"Dreaming Our World," 648
"Dreams," 408, 415
"Dreary Dreeze, The," 406
Dressing, 118, 139
Dreyer, Sharon Spredeman, 504
Drinking Gourd, The, 534
"Driving to the Beach," 396, 430
"Drum, The," 434
Drummer Hoff, 30, 181
Du Bois, William Pène, 117, 345, 357, 420
"Duel, The," 99
Duff, Maggie, 181, 281
Duffey, Betsy, 56
Duffy and the Devil, 276, 278, 282, 347
Duke, Kate, 154, 157, 290
Dumas, Henry, 417
Dumpling Soup, 226, 227, 232
Duncan, Lois, 503, 569, 570
Dundes, Alan, 325
Dunleavey, M. P., 118
Dunn, Fannie Wyche, 40
Dunn, Jeffrey, 392
Dunning, Stephen, 397, 398, 415, 416, 426, 427, 429, 431, 432, 433, 437, 698

Dunrea, Olivier, 161, 162
Dupasquier, Philippe, 247, 701
Duplicate, The, 374
Durkin, Dolores, 12, 632
Durrell, Ann, 650
"Dust of Snow," 411
Dutch Twins, The, 108
Duvoisin, Roger, 105, 116, 117, 229, 234, 242, 637
Dyer, Jane, 414
Dyer, T. A., 520, 536
Dynamite Dinah, 494

E for Environment: An Annotated Bibliography of Children's Books with Environmental Themes, 648
E. B. White: Some Writer, 566
Each Peach Pear Plum, 45, 52, 150
Eager, Edward, 360
"Eagle, The," 395
Eagle Dreams, 212, 213
Eagle Kite, The, 58
Eagle of the Ninth, The, 521
Eagles: Lions of the Sky, 650
Eames, Alicia, 648
Ear the Eye and the Arm, The, 59, 377, 431, 650
Early, Margaret, 286
Early Detection of Reading Difficulties, The, 138, 705
Early Moon, 110, 391
Early Morning in the Barn, 141
Early Thunder, 528
"Earth," 431
Earth Alive!, 592
Earth for Sam, The, 106
Earth Is Painted Green: A Garden of Poems About Our Planet, The, 650
Earth Keepers, 597
Earth Songs, 412
Earth Verses and Water Rhymes, 410
Earth Words: A Dictionary of the Environment, 588
Earthfasts, 342, 346, 365
Earthmaker's Tales: North American Indian Stories from Earth Happenings, 299
Earthshine, 117, 120, 482
Earthworks, 651
East o' the Sun and West o' the Moon, 108, 266, 271, 281, 285, 302, 316
Easter Poems, 421
"Easy Decision, An," 431
Easy Lessons for Children, 90
Eating Fractions, 161
Eating the Alphabet, 53, 154, 158
Eats: Poems, 396, 409, 425
"Eat-it-all Elaine," 432
Ebborn, Caroline, 236
Eclectic Readers, 92
Eclipse, 478
"Ecology," 431
Edible Alphabet, An, 154, 157
Edmonds, Walter D., 527, 529
Educated Imagination, The, 268, 321
Edwards, Michelle, 247, 606
Eeds, Maryann, 639, 661
"Eensy, Weensy Spider," 141
"Effect of Literature on Vocabulary and Reading Achievement, The," 13, 174
Effie, 205
Egg: A Photographic Story of Hatching, 606
Egg to Chick, 583
Egielski, Richard, 245
Egypt Game, The, 468
Egyptian Cinderella, The, 281, 311

Ehlert, Lois, 18, 53, 121, 154, 158, 161, 162, 165, 166, 205, 218, 309, 428, 568, 642, 671, 672, 673
Eichenberg, Fritz, 105, 402, 411
Eight Hands Round: A Patchwork Alphabet, 680
Einstein Anderson Lights Up the Sky, 501
Eisenberg, Lisa, 64
El Chino, 211, 492, 554
El Dorado Adventure, The, 369
Eleanor Farjeon's Poems for Children, 110, 407
Eleanor Roosevelt: A Life of Discovery, 556, 565, 581
Eleanor Roosevelt, First Lady of the World, 552, 553, 556
Elements of Writing About a Literary Work: A Study of Response to Literature, 60
Elements series, 592
"Elephant," 413, 435
Elephant and the Bad Baby, The, 181
Elephant's Child, The, 236, 243, 635, 691
Elephants Swim, 603
Elephant's Wrestling Match, The, 219
"Eletelephony," 394, 413
Elijah the Slave, 290
Eliot, T. S., 423
Elizabeth and the Water Troll, 347
Elkind, David, 47, 70, 475
Elkington, John, 587, 651
Elledge, Scott, 397, 399, 401, 417, 428
Elleman, Barbara, 120, 320, 713
Ellis, Sarah, 481
Elmer, 242, 428
Elsie Dinsmore, 93
"Elson Readers," 626
Elucidarium, 84, 115
Elva S. Smith's History of Children's Literature, 85, 126
Elves and the Shoemaker, The, 283, 302
"Elves and the Shoemaker, The," 92, 356
Emannuel, James, 429
Emberley, Barbara, 30, 181
Emberley, Ed, 30
Emberley, Michael, 48, 583
Emberley, Rebecca, 637
Emeka's Gift: An African Counting Story, 121, 162
Emergent Literacy: Writing and Reading, 186
Emerging Literacy: Helping Young Children Learn to Read and Write, 185
Emily of New Moon, 111
Emma, 228, 234
"Emotional Realism in Books for Young People," 455
Emperor and the Kite, The, 206, 345
Emperor Mage, 368
Emperor's New Clothes, The, 343
"Emperor's New Clothes, The," 92
Empty Pot, The, 272
Empty Schoolhouse, The, 112
Enchantress from the Stars, 372, 376
"Encounter," 410, 430
"Encyclopedia Brown" series, 501
Encyclopedia Brown Takes a Case, 501
Ender's Game, 376
Endless Steppe: Growing Up in Siberia, The, 540, 607
Engdahl, Sylvia Louise, 372, 373, 376
Engel, Dean, 566
Engelbert the Elephant, 216, 244
Engines of Instruction, Mischief, and Magic: Children's Literature in England from Its Beginnings to 1839, 126
English Fairy Tales, 93
Enormous Egg, The, 357
Enright, Elizabeth, 111

"Environmental Assistance to the Child's Acquisition of Grammar," 12

"Envisioning Experience: The Potential for Picture Books," 41

Eric Carle's Animals Animals, 420

Eric Carle's Dragons, Dragons & Other Creatures That Never Were, 420

Erie Canal, 684

Erikson, Erik H., 50

Ernest and Celestine, 11, 242

Ernst, Lisa Campbell, 680

Ernst, Shirley B., 71

Esbensen, Barbara Juster, 32, 299, 303, 395, 412, 413, 425, 430, 594, 595, 598

Escape from Slavery: Five Journeys to Freedom, 606

Escape From Slavery: The Boyhood of Frederick Douglas in His Own Words, 570

Esterl, Arnica, 269, 272

Estes, Eleanor, 83, 116, 117, 459, 466

Eternal Spring of Mr. Ito, The, 536, 543

Etre, Lisa, 160

"Eulogy on Candlelight," 92

Eva, 374, 431, 650

Evans, Eva Knox, 112

Evan's Corner, 231

Evening at Alfie's, An, 171

Everglades, 579, 651

Every Time I Climb a Tree, 404, 411, 424

Everybody Needs a Rock, 230, 234, 410, 425, 694

"Everybody Says," 431

Everyone Knows What a Dragon Looks Like, 345, 681

Everywhere, 479

Evslin, Bernard, 317

Exactly the Opposite, 166

Examination, The, 524

Exiles, The, 57, 495

Exiles at Home, The, 495

Exodus, 322

Experiment in Criticism, An, 456

Exploding Frog and Other Fables from Aesop, The, 312

Explorer of Barkham Street, The, 467

Exploring Autumn: A Season for Science Activities, Puzzles, and Games, 586

"Exploring the Meaning Making Process through the Content of Literature Response Journals," 60

Extra Innings: Baseball Poems, 419, 427

Extraordinary Egg, An, 205, 606

Exum, Cheryl, 322

Eye of the Needle, The, 299, 303

"Eye Openers" series, 579

"Eye Winker," 142

Eye Winker Tom Tinker Chin Chopper, 142

Eyeopeners II Children's Books to Answer Children's Questions About the World Around Them, 608

Eyes of the Dragon, 293, 681

"Eyewitness" books, 579, 585, 593

"Eyewitness Junior" books, 579

"Eyewitness Science" books, 674

Ezra Jack Keats: A Biography with Illustrations, 566

Faber, Doris, 556, 565, 568

Faber, Harold, 568

Faber, Norma, 425

Fables, 243, 698

Fables of Aesop, The, 85, 90, 91, 103, 115

Fables of Aesop and Others, 91

Fables You Shouldn't Pay Any Attention To, 698

Fabulous Histories, 90

Faces, 594

Facklam, Margery, 578, 591, 603, 606, 650

Facklam, Paul, 591, 606

"Factors Influencing Pupils' Reading of Library Books," 40

Facts and Fictions of Minna Pratt, The, 120

Fadden, John K., 325

Fader, Daniel, 622

Fairchild Family, The, 93

"Fairies, The," 99

Fairy Library, 100

Fairy Tales, Fables, Legends, and Myths: Using Folk Literature in Your Classroom, 324

Fairy Tales of Hans Christian Andersen, 103, 109, 115

"Fairy Tales: Poems," 429

Faithful Friend, The, 219

Falcon Bow: An Arctic Legend, The, 631

Fall, 579

Falls, C. B., 104

Falwell, Cathryn, 53, 160, 578

Families: Poems Celebrating the African American Experience, 420, 425

Family, 118, 139

Family Farm, 208

Family Pictures: Cuadros de Familia, 224

Family Project, A, 481

"Family Reading Habits and Children's Progress in Reading," 138

Family Storybook Reading, 186

Fanny's Dream, 698

"Fantasy and the Human Condition," 341

"Fantasy in the Real World," 342

Fantasy Literature for Children and Young Adults: An Annotated Bibliography, 380

Far and Few: Rhymes of Never Was and Always Is, 110

Far Side of Evil, The, 376

Farjeon, Eleanor, 110, 114, 390, 393, 401, 407, 414, 692

Farley, Walter, 493

Farm Book, The, 105, 116

Farmer, Nancy, 59, 350, 357, 360, 377, 650

Farmer Boy, 687

Farmer Duck, 53, 175, 180

Farmer's Alphabet, A, 158

Farquharson, Martha (pseudonym of Martha Farquharson Finley), 93

Farthest Shore, The, 370, 373

Fast Sam, Cool Clyde, and Stuff, 485

Fat Cat, The, 16, 181, 637, 643, 691

Fat Cats at Sea, The, 405

Father Christmas, 216

Father Fox's Pennyrhymes, 148

"Father William," 98

Favat, André, 43, 325

Favorite Poems Old and New, 392, 394, 401, 404, 416, 685

"Fear," 431

Fear Place, The, 57

Feast for Ten, 53, 160

Feathers for Lunch, 121, 166

Feathers Like a Rainbow: An Amazon Indian Tale, 272, 309

Feder, Jan, 631

Feelings, 221

Feelings, Muriel, 158, 160, 668

Feelings, Tom, 158, 160, 417, 418, 422, 533, 606

Felita, 486

Fellowship of the Ring, The, 353

Ferguson, Amos, 408

Ferreiro, Emilia, 186

Ferris, Helen, 392, 394, 401, 404, 416, 685

Festivals, 412

Fiddle-I-Fee, 142, 143

Field, Eugene, 99

Field, Louise Frances Story (Mrs. E. M. Field), 84

Field, Rachel, 110, 423, 529

Fielding, Mrs. Sarah, 90

Fiesta U.S.A., 597

Fifteen Centuries of Children's Literature, 125

Fifty Simple Things You Can Do to Save the Earth, 651

Fighting Ground, The, 518, 528

"Filling the Gaps: *The Baby-Sitters Club*, the Series Book, and the Learning Reader," 492

Fine, Anne, 57, 500, 501

Fine Fat Pig, A, 407

Fine Round Cake, The, 269, 272

Finger, Charles, 108, 309

Fir Tree, The, 353

Fire Bug Connection, 651

Fire on the Mountain, 272

Fire-Bringer: A Paiute Indian Legend, The, 300

Firebird, The, 271, 287, 302

"Firefly and the Apes," 279

"First Day of School," 410

"First Day of Spring, The," 411

First Discovery series, 580

First Four Years, The, 531, 600

First Look at Bats, A, 598

First Look at Insects, A, 598

First Look at Leaves, A, 621

First Look at Seashells, A, 598

First Picture Book: Everyday Things for Babies, 106

First Snow, 169

First Strawberries: A Cherokee Story, The, 299

First Thanksgiving Feast, The, 525

Fish Eyes: A Book You Can Count On, 161, 162, 218

Fish Is Fish, 54, 208

Fish Skin, The, 279, 299, 606

Fisher, Aileen, 32, 110, 410, 414, 419, 430, 435

Fisher, Bobbi, 185

Fisher, Carol J., 404

Fisher, Leonard Everett, 291, 314, 316, 322, 412, 562, 673, 682

Fisher, Margery, 518, 608

"Fisherman and His Wife, The," 292

Fisherman and His Wife, The, 277, 279

FitzGerald, Frances, 586

Fitzhugh, Louise, 6, 113, 117, 467, 468

Five Chinese Brothers, The, 293

"Five Fathoms Tall," 308

Five Little Ducks, 181

Five Little Monkeys Jumping on the Bed, 142, 180

Five Little Peppers, 95

"Five Little Pigs," 141

Five Minutes' Peace, 180

Five Readers Reading, 59

Fix-It, 53

Flack, Marjorie, 105

Flame of Peace: A Tale of the Aztecs, The, 714

Flame-Colored Taffeta, 524

Flaming Arrows, 514

Flanagan, Dennis, 608

Flap Your Wings and Try, 172

Flash, Crash, Rumble and Roll, 606

"Flashlight," 397

"Flat-Heeled Muse, The," 347

Flavell, John, 45

Fledgling, The, 360

Fleischman, Paul, 59, 361, 425, 440, 518, 526, 527, 528, 534, 590, 606, 625

Fleischman, Sid, 346, 360, 361, 368, 626, 693, 694, 709

Fleming, Alice, 564

Fleming, Denise, 179, 180, 207, 568, 673

Fletcher, Ralph, 59
Flights of Fancy, 412
Flip-Flop Girl, 11, 56, 430, 464, 503
Flit, Flutter, Fly!, 606
Floca, Brian, 122
Flood, James, 71
Flora, 272, 309
Florian, Douglas, 405, 675
Flossie & the Fox, 55, 633
Flour Babies, 57, 500, 501
Flournoy, Valerie, 227, 232, 680
Flower Grows, A, 592
Flunking of Joshua T. Bates, The, 499
Fly Away Home, 55, 248
Flying, 166
"Flying Uptown Backwards," 396
Focus: Five Women Photographers, 567
*Focus Units on Literature: A Context for Literacy
    Learning*, 288, 325, 350, 714
"Fog," 402, 425
Fog Magic, 347, 363
"Foggy Foggy Dew, The," 399
"Foghorns," 158
Folk Tales from China, 108
Folktale, The, 325
Follow Me!, 168
*Follow the Dream: The Story of Christopher
    Columbus*, 558
Follow the Water from Brook to Ocean, 588
Food, 601
Fool and the Fish, The, 279
Fool of the World and the Flying Ship, The, 277,
    279, 281, 302
"Fooling with Folktales: Updates, Spin-offs, and
    Roundups," 696
Foolish Rabbit's Big Mistake, 209, 272, 292, 311
"For a Bird," 429, 434
"For a Dead Kitten," 429, 433
*For Laughing Out Loud: Poems to Tickle Your
    Funnybone*, 421
"For Sale," 430
*For the Good of the Earth and Sun: Teaching
    Poetry*, 439, 441
*For Your Own Protection: Stories Science Photos
    Tell*, 592
Forbes, Esther, 117, 516, 528
Ford, Miela, 53
"Forecast, The," 431
Foreman, Michael, 570
Forestwife, The, 321
*Forgetful Wishing Well: Poems for Young People,
    The*, 396, 405, 432
"Forgive My Guilt," 432, 437
"Forgiven," 400
"Forgotten," 409
Forgotten Door, The, 375, 690
Forrester, Sandra, 534
Forty-Third War, 491
Foster, Sarah Jane, 568
"Foul Shot," 427
Foundations of Literacy, The, 138
Founding, The, 228, 233
Four Fur Feet, 181
"Four Little Foxes," 433, 440
4-B Goes Wild, 499
Fourth Question: A Chinese Tale, The, 293
Fox Went Out on a Chilly Night, The, 143
Fox, Mem, 46, 52, 172, 205, 228, 229, 234, 242,
    243, 251, 428, 686
Fox, Paula, 8, 22, 30, 57, 58, 107, 430, 460, 471,
    475, 478, 534, 625, 633
Fox, Sharon, 15
Fox Busters, The, 346
Frames of Mind, 48

Frampton, David, 203, 594, 596, 673
Frances Carpenter, 108
"Frances" series, 184, 222, 242
Franchere, Ruth, 563
Francis, Robert, 427, 431
Frank, Anne, 117, 701
Frank, Josette, 420
Frank on a Gunboat, 95
Franklin, Kristine L., 478
Franklin Delano Roosevelt, 57, 564
Fraser, Debra, 7, 207, 673
Frasier, Marjories Frost, 427
Frazer, Sir James, 267
"Freddy the Pig" stories, 109
Frederick, 236, 243, 312, 637, 691, 688
Frederick Douglass: In His Own Words, 563, 569
Frederick Douglass: The Black Lion, 606
Free Fall, 170
Freedman, Florence B., 272, 566
Freedman, Russell, 57, 117, 119, 525, 535, 555,
    557, 564, 565, 567, 581, 582, 600, 606,
    608, 633, 677, 693
Freeman, Don, 53, 210, 242, 245, 428, 637
Freeman, Evelyn B., 608
Freeman, Yvonne, 625
Freight Train, 53, 166, 428, 674
French, Fiona, 698
Fresh Brats, 405
Fresh Paint, 411, 425
Frida Kahlo, 561
Friedman, Ina, 54, 233
Friedrich, 11, 114, 686
Friends, 118, 139
"Friendship," 431
Friendship, The, 11, 492
Friendship Across Arctic Waters, 597
Fritz, Jean, 21, 31, 33, 56, 58 107, 487, 519, 525,
    526, 528, 534, 552, 553, 554, 556, 557,
    560, 565, 570, 571, 586, 606, 657, 686
Froebel, Friedrich, 141
Frog and Toad All Year, 8, 16, 21, 182
Frog and Toad Are Friends, 8, 16, 21, 182, 622,
    683
"Frog and Toad" series, 8, 15, 21, 182, 222
Frog and Toad Together, 8, 16, 21, 54, 182, 675
Frog Goes to Dinner, 169
Frog Prince, The, 284, 302, 429
Frog Prince Continued, The, 237, 429, 696, 698
Frog Princess, The, 288, 289, 302
Frogs, Toads, Lizards, and Salamanders, 590
*From Dr. Mather to Dr. Seuss: 200 Years of
    American Books for Children*, 126
From Head to Toe: How a Doll is Made, 578, 579
"From Little Black Sambo to Popo and Fifina:
    Arna Bontemps and the Creation of
    African-American Children's
    Literature," 112
From Miss Ida's Front Porch, 208
*From Pictures to Words: A Book About Making a
    Book*, 595, 597, 704
From Rollo to Tom Sawyer, 99
From Sea to Shining Sea, 247
From Seed to Plant, 598
*From the Beginning: The Story of Human
    Evolution*, 584
From the Earth to the Moon, 376
*From the Mixed-Up Files of Mrs. Basil E.
    Frankweiler*, 47, 430, 474, 624
*From Top Hats to Baseball Caps, From Bustles to
    Blue Jeans: Why We Dress the Way We
    Do*, 590
From Two to Five, 11, 12, 147, 268, 394, 441
Froman, Robert, 403, 425, 437
"Frontier Fighter," 308

Frost, Frances, 110
Frost, Robert, 110, 390, 391, 394, 411, 414, 415,
    416, 418, 424, 431
Frozen Fire, 474
Frozen Man, 588
Frye, Northrop, 268, 321, 325
Fudge-a-Mania, 56
Fu-Dog, 353
"Fueled," 398, 402, 433
"Full of the Moon, The," 407
Fungus the Bogeyman, 216
Funny Little Woman, The, 277, 281, 303
Furth, Hans G., 45
Fyleman, Rosy, 439

Gaber, Susan, 290
Gaer, Joseph, 318
Gaffe, Toni, 141
Gág, Wanda, 14, 52, 104, 116, 157, 210, 274,
    637
Galaxies, 592
Galda, Lee, 60
Galdone, Joanna, 8
Galdone, Paul, 14, 16, 109, 142, 178, 180, 181,
    269, 270, 278, 279, 281, 312, 429, 635,
    637, 676, 691
Galimoto, 11, 55, 246, 646, 668
Gallaz, Christophe, 11, 250, 431, 539, 607
"Galoshes," 394, 404, 413
Gammage Cup, The, 358
Gammell, Stephen, 158, 209, 226, 232, 245, 409,
    417
Garden, 139
Garden of Abdul Gasazi, The, 209, 210, 241, 245
Gardiner, John, 8, 56, 498
Gardner, Howard, 48
Garland, Sherry, 272, 311
Garne, S. T., 160
Garrigue, Sheila, 536
Garten, Jan, 157
Garth Pig and the Ice Cream Lady, 243
Garza, Carmen Loma, 224
Gates, Doris, 116, 316
*Gates of Excellence: On Reading and Writing Books
    for Children*, 461, 504
*Gathering of Days: A New England Girl's Journal,
    1830–1832, A*, 121, 534, 701
Gatty, Mrs., 99
Gauch, Patricia L., 528, 535
"Gawain and the Loathly Lady," 319
"Gazinta," 412
Geisert, Arthur, 203, 312
Gellman, Marc, 322
"Gender Gap in the Library: Different Choices
    for Boys and Girls," 41
General Store, 423
Genesis, Book of, 323
"Geode," 412
(George), 113, 477
George, Jean Craighead, 10, 16, 18, 27, 39, 57,
    69, 123, 426, 431, 433, 437, 473, 488,
    492, 496, 526, 598, 579, 582, 598, 605,
    623, 631, 637, 648, 650, 651, 674, 681,
    683, 699
George, John, 598
George and Martha, 238, 244
George and Martha Back in Town, 238, 244
George and Martha Round and Round, 238, 244
"George and Martha" series, 244
George and Martha Tons of Fun, 238, 244
George Shrinks, 239, 245, 701
George Washington, 107, 559
George Washington: A Picture Book Biography, 559
George Washington Wasn't Always Old, 564

George Washington's Breakfast, 56, 586
Georgia Music, 226, 232
Georgia O'Keefe, 561
*Georgia to Georgia: Making Friends in the
    U.S.S.R.*, 582
"Georgie Porgie," 146
Germy Blew It, 493
Germy Blew It Again, 493
Germy Blew "The Bugle," 493, 701
Gerrard, Roy, 217, 218
Gershator, Phillis, 54
Gerson, Mary-Joan, 296, 309, 311, 673
Gerstein, Mordicai, 142, 277, 283, 287, 347, 423,
    639
Gesta Romanorum, 85, 115
*Get The Message: Telecommunications in Your
    High-Tech World*, 582
"Get Up and Bar the Door," 399
Getting Him, 11, 58, 467, 477
Getz, David, 588
Ghastlies, Goops & Pincushions, 405
Gherman, Beverly, 563, 566
Ghost Comes Calling, The, 9, 362
Ghost Horse Cycle, 530
Ghost of Thomas Kempe, The, 362
Ghost-Eye Tree, The, 207, 671
Giant Baby, The, 356
Giants in the Land, 27, 218, 651, 673
Giant's Toe, The, 281, 698
Gib Morgan, Oilman, 307
Gibbons, Gail, 53, 54, 583, 598, 606, 648, 674,
    703
Giblin, James Cross, 456, 559, 578, 581, 582,
    585, 587, 588, 590, 601, 608
Giff, Patricia Reilly, 55, 491, 493, 501
Gift of the Sacred Dog, The, 298, 303
Giganti, Paul Jr., 161
Gilchrist, Jan Spivey, 408
Gilligan, Carol, 49
Gilliland, Judith Heide, 11, 54, 207
Gilman, Phoebe, 272, 290
Gilson, Jamie, 487, 493, 499
Gingerbread Boy, The, 16, 181, 269, 311, 429,
    637, 691
"Gingerbread Boy, The," 46, 691, 709
"Gingerbread Man, The," 173, 429
Ginsburg, Max, 560, 561
Ginsburg, Mirra, 52, 176, 178, 180, 182, 637
Giovanni, Nikki, 406, 417, 434
Gipson, Fred, 457, 531
*Girl, The Fish and the Crown: A Spanish Folktale,
    The*, 279
Girl Called Boy, A, 367
Girl from Yamhill: A Memoir, A, 569, 570
*Girl Who Loved Coyote: Stories of the Southwest,
    The*, 299
Girl Who Loved the Wind, The, 345
Girl Who Loved Wild Horses, The, 221, 300
Girl Who Wanted to Hunt, The, 281
Girls Can Too, 111
Giver, The, 47, 59, 341, 378, 379, 640
Glazer, Tom, 142, 145
Gleitzman, Morris, 476
Glenn, Christine, 59
Global Warming, 651
*Glorious Flight: Across the Channel with Louis
    Blériot, July, The*, 208, 559
Glory Field, The, 59, 120
"Glowworm," 411
Glubok, Shirley, 669, 673
Gluskabe and the Four Wishes, 279, 301, 303, 526
"Go I Know Not Where, Bring Back I Know Not
    What," 288
Go Tell Aunt Rhody, 142, 181, 685

Go With the Poem, 397, 426, 431
Goats, The, 58, 469
Gobble Growl Grunt, 141
Goble, Paul, 217, 221, 269, 298, 299, 300, 303,
    311, 606
Godden, Rumer, 8, 33, 348, 437, 501
Gododdin, The, 521
Goelmann, Hillel, 185
Goggles, 228
*Going Green: A Kid's Handbook to Saving the
    Planet*, 587, 651
Going Home, 486
"Going to Sleep" 407, 428
Going to the Potty, 52
Going Up! A Color Counting Book, 161
Gold Dust Letters, The, 494
Golden Bough, The, 267
Golden Egg Book, The, 16
Golden Goblet, The, 521
Golden God: Apollo, 316
Golden Goose Book, The, 103
Golden Key, The, 345
Goldfield, Beverly, 12
Goldilocks and the Three Bears, 428
"Goldilocks and the Three Bears," 169, 690
Goldsmith, Oliver, 89
Goldstein, Bobbye S., 419, 428, 420
Golem, The, 109
Golembe, Carla, 673
Gom on Windy Mountain, 371
Good Books, Good Times!, 415
Good Dog, Carl, 168
Good for Me! All About Food in 32 Bites, 599
Good Morning, Chick, 180
Good-Night Owl!, 181, 242
*Good Queen Bess: The Story of Elizabeth 1 of
    England*, 561
Good, the Bad, and the Goofy, The, 360
Goodbye, Chicken Little, 621
Goodbye Billy Radish, 538
Goode, Diane, 210, 233
Goodhope, Jeanie, 40
Gooding, Beverly, 351
Goodman, Kenneth, S., 122, 625, 626, 705
Goodman, Yetta M., 68, 185, 659
Goodnight, Teddy Bear, 46
Goodnight Gorilla, 172, 173
Goodnight Moon, 5, 45, 52, 105, 137, 138, 140,
    172, 175, 181, 223, 659
Goodnight Moon Room, 118, 172
Goodrich, Samuel, 92
Goody O'Grumpity, 673
Goody Two Shoes, 89
Goor, Nancy, 704
Goor, Ron, 704
"Goose, Moose and Spruce," 411
"Goose Bumps" series, 108, 118
Gordon, Ruth, 417
Gordon, Sheila, 489
Gorky Rises, 216
Gose, Elliott, 380
Gottlieb, Dale, 225, 226, 231
Governess, The, 90
Grab Hands and Run, 490, 607
Grabarek, Daryl, 648
Graeber, Charlotte, 429, 457, 480
Graff, Nancy Price, 607
Graham, Joan, 403, 425, 437
Graham, S. A., 40
Grahame, Kenneth, 109, 116, 346, 681
Grain of Wheat: A Writer Begins, 570
Gramarky, Hardie, 105, 240
Grand Canyon Suite, 685

"Grand Conversations: An Exploration of
    Meaning Construction in Literature
    Study Groups," 639
Grand Conversations: Literature Groups in Action,
    661
Grand Pap and Ellen Aroon, 555, 556
Grandaddy's Place, 226, 232
"Grandfather I Never Knew, The," 412
Grandfather Tales, 303
Grandfather's Dream, 246
"Grandma Bear from Delaware," 406
"Grandmother" collections, 108
"Grandpa Bear's Lullaby," 428
Grandpa's Mountain, 58, 651
Grandpa's Too-Good Garden, 244
Granfa' Grig Had a Pig, 153
Granfather's Journey, 207
Granger, Neill, 57
Granny the Pag, 479
Granpa, 211, 231, 429
"Grasshopper, The," 398
"Grasshopper and the Ant, The," 312
Grasshopper Summer, 531
Graves, Donald H., 608
Graves, Robert, 317
Gray, Elizabeth Janet, 522
Gray, Libba Moore, 52, 179, 181, 213, 230, 673
Gray, Nigel, 247, 646
Gray Wolf, Red Wolf, 596
Great Alexander the Great, The, 560
*Great Ancestor Hunt: The Fun of Finding Out Who
    You Are, The*, 587, 603
Great Ball Game: A Muskogee Story, The, 272,
    299
Great Code: The Bible in Literature, The, 325
Great Fire, The, 581, 601
Great Gilly Hopkins, The, 5, 24, 25, 39, 58, 454,
    465, 632, 657, 691
*Great Kapok Tree: A Tale of the Amazon Rain
    Forest, The*, 431, 651
Great Little Madison, The, 553, 565
Great Lives: American Government, 568
Great Lives: Exploration, 568
Great Lives: Human Rights, 568
Great Lives: Nature and the Environment, 568
Great Lives: Sports, 568
Great Northern Diver: The Loon, 598
Great Race of the Birds and the Animals, The, 269,
    300
Great White Man-Eating Shark, The, 221, 244
Greedy Cat, 627
Greek Gods and Heroes, 317
Green, Ellin, 660
Green, Lucinda, 56
Green, Roger Lancelyn, 317
Green and Burning Tree, The, 379
Green Book, The, 56, 374, 431, 432
Green Fairy Book, The, 93
Green Futures of Tycho, The, 376, 431
Greenaway, Kate, 100, 104, 116, 152, 400
Greenaway, Theresa, 585
Greenblat, Rodney A., 210, 637, 694
Greene, Bette, 542
Greene, Constance C., 481
Greene, Karen, 682
Greene, Maxine, 341
Greenfeld, Howard, 601, 607
Greenfield, Eloise, 225, 231, 394, 408, 425, 430,
    483, 484, 563
*Greening the City Streets: The Story of Community
    Gardens*, 651
"Greensweet," 396, 425
Greenwald, Sheila, 493
Greenwitch, 370

Gregory, Kristiana, 530
Grey King, The, 371
Grey Lady and the Strawberry Snatcher, The, 211
Greyling, 277, 283, 347, 361, 639
Grieg, Edvard, 685
Griego, Margot C., 150
Grifalconi, Ann, 55, 205, 247, 295, 296, 311, 429, 646, 668, 680
Griffith, Helen V., 226, 232, 354
Griffiths, Clyve, 713
Grimes, Nikki, 155, 156, 158
Grimm Brothers (Jacob and Wilhelm), 16, 92, 108, 208, 210, 211, 214, 267, 268, 269, 272, 273, 276, 277, 278, 279, 281, 282, 283, 284, 286, 297, 302, 311, 343, 347
Grimm's Fairy Tales, 100
Grimm's Popular Stories, 115
"Grobbles, The," 406, 425, 440
Grofé, Ferde, 685
Gross, Ruth Belov, 557
Grouchy Ladybug, The, 54, 182
Grover, 113
Grover, Max, 695
Grover, Wayne, 650
Growing Time, The, 480
Growing Up Literate: Learning from Inner-City Families, 185
Growing Vegetable Soup, 18
Growth of Logical Thinking, The, 45
Guardian of Education, 90
Guarino, Deborah, 178, 181, 428
Guback, Georgia, 680
Gudrun, Thorne-Thomsen, 108
Guess How Much I Love You, 53
Guess Who?, 48, 166, 588
Guests, 56, 117, 526, 530
Guevara, Susan, 214
"Guide for the Teacher Guides: Doing It Yourself, A," 645
Guinagh, Barry J., 138
Guinea Pig ABC, The, 154, 157
Guiterman, Arthur, 415, 440
Gulliver's Travels, 89, 115
Gundersheimer, Karen, 419
Gunning, Monica, 408
Gutenberg's Gift: A Book Lover's Pop-up Book, 580
Guth, Dorothy L., 20
Guthrie, Woodie, 417
Guy of Warwick, 85

Hadithi, Mwenye, 236, 243, 689
Hague, Kathleen, 285, 316
Hague, Michael, 98, 109, 240, 245, 285, 316
Hahn, Mary Downing, 362, 365, 515, 699, 712
Hailstones and Halibut Bones: Adventures in Color, 425, 426, 428, 435
Haldane, Suzanne, 601, 602
Hale, James-Graham, 231
Hale, Lucretia P., 97, 116
Hale, Sarah Josepha, 98, 149, 150, 153, 215
Haley, Gail E., 109, 276, 280, 281, 295, 296, 303, 304, 668
Half Magic, 360
Half-A-Moon Inn, The, 361
"Halfway Down," 407, 414
Hall, Donald, 31, 54, 204, 215, 218, 222, 632
Hall, Katy, 64
Halliday, M. A. K., 48
Halloween Poems, 421
Halperin, Wendy Anderson, 17, 209
Halpern, Shari, 162
Hamanaka, Sheila, 580, 607

Hamilton, Edith, 325
Hamilton, Virginia, 19, 30, 31, 49, 57, 112, 113, 117, 219, 272, 276, 298, 299, 301, 303, 306, 313, 314, 342, 457, 458, 463, 485, 492, 501, 504, 564, 606, 693
Hamley, Dennis, 343
Hammer of Thunder, The, 317
"Hammerman," 308
Han, Suzanne Crowder, 273, 295
Hancock, Joelie, 660
Hancock, Marjorie R., 60
Handbook for Storytellers, 636
Handbook of Research on Teaching the English Language Arts, 71
Handful of Time, A, 366
Handtalk: An ABC of Finger Spelling and Sign Language, 596
Handtalk Birthday: A Number and Story Book in Sign Language, 596
Handtalk School, 597
Handtalk Zoo, 597
Hang Tough, Paul Mather, 482
Hans, Marcie, 398, 402, 433
Hans Brinker, or the Silver Skates, 95, 99, 111, 115
Hans Christian Andersen: The Complete Fairy Tales and Stories, 344
Hansel and Gretel, 217, 273, 284, 302, 671
"Hansel and Gretel," 324, 633, 696
Hansen, Jane, 661
Hansen, Joyce, 533, 536, 606
"Happiness," 407
"Happy," 429
Happy Birthday Sam, 181
Happy Birthday to Me, 170
Happy Birthday, Grampie, 232
Happy Birthday, Martin Luther King, 219
Happy Hippopotami, The, 176
Happy Prince, The, 344
Harbor, 166
"Hard and Soft," 396
Hard to Be Six, 224
Hardy, Barbara, 9
Hardy Boys, The, 107
"Hardy Boys" series, 18, 52, 491, 703
Hare and the Tortoise, The, 312
Hare's Choice, 343
Harpist in the Wind, 372
Harrell, Beatice Orcutt, 299, 300
Harriet Beecher Stowe and the Beecher Preachers, 556, 565, 606
Harriet the Spy, 6, 113, 117, 467
Harriet Tubman, 218
"Harriet Tubman," 425
Harriet's Hare, 375
Harris, Joel Chandler, 93, 116, 270, 275, 304, 305
Harris, Karen H., 476, 504
Harris, Robie H., 58, 581, 583
Harris, Violet J., 112, 504
Harris and Me, 495
Harrison, Barbara, 565
Harrison, Peggy, 434, 438, 442
Harrison, Ted, 158, 217, 424
Harry and Arney, 5, 24, 55, 493
Harry Castlemon: Boys' Own Author, 95
Harry the Dirty Dog, 633, 637, 706
Hart-Hewins, Linda, 185
Härtling, Peter, 479
Harvey, Brett, 536, 606
Harwayne, Shelley, 659
Haseley, Dennis, 11, 58, 467, 477
Hasselriis, Malthe, 274
Hastings, Selina, 320
Hatchet, 20, 23, 57, 456, 474, 526, 642, 684

Hating Book, The, 429
Hattie and the Fox, 205
Hattie and the Wild Waves, 232
Haugaard, Erik Christian, 344, 544
Haunted Mountain, The, 347
Haunting, The, 58, 362, 366
Haunting of Frances Rain, The, 366
Hausman, Gerald, 298, 299, 300
Hautzig, Esther, 540, 607
Have a Happy . . . , 484
Have You Seen My Cat?, 180
Have You Seen My Duckling?, 52, 180
Haveli, 491
Haviland, Virginia, 87, 297, 418, 526
Hawk, I'm Your Brother, 426, 431, 650
Hawkins, Colin, 145, 181
Hawkins, Jacqui, 145, 181
Hawthorne, Elizabeth, 92
Hawthorne, Nathaniel, 92, 93
Haycock, Kati, 392
Hayes, Sara Henderson, 429, 433, 698
Hayes, Sarah, 141, 162, 181
Haywood, Carolyn, 111, 493
He Is Risen, 322
Headless Horseman: More Poems to Trouble Your Sleep, The, 400
Headless Horseman Rides Tonight, The, 123
Hear the Wind Blow: American Folk Songs Retold, 685
Heard, Georgia, 438, 439, 441
Hearne, Betsy, 33, 325, 571
Heart's Blood, 372
Heartland, 424, 650
Hearts in Hiding, 20
Heath, Shirley Brice, 186
Heathcote, Dorothy, 690
Hector Protector and As I Went Over the Water, 149, 153
Hedgehog Boy: A Latvian Tale, The, 279
Heide, Florence Parry, 11, 54, 207, 246, 646, 698
Heidi, 95, 111, 116
Heilman, Robert B., 6
Heinrich, Bernd, 701, 704
Heins, Ethel, 33
Heins, Paul, 201, 284
Heir of Sea and Fire, 372
Helen Oxenbury Nursery Rhyme Book, The, 152
Helen Oxenbury's ABC of Things, 157
Helfman, Harry, 678
"Helicopters," 401
Hellen, Nancy, 144, 180
Heller, Ruth, 581, 606, 693
Hello, My Name is Scrambled Eggs, 487
"Hello and Goodbye," 393, 407
Helping Hands: How Monkeys Assist People Who Are Disabled, 601
Helprin, Mark, 64, 199
Hendershot, Judith, 209
Henkes, Kevin, 5, 53, 173, 218, 230, 242, 430, 464
Hennessy, B. G., 150
Henny Penny, 221, 269, 272, 311, 691
"Henny Penny," 280, 283
Henry, 493, 496
Henry, George, 107
Henry, Marguerite, 118, 493
Henry and Beezus, 494
Henry and Mudge, 182
Henry and Mudge, The First Book of Their Adventures, 494
Henry and Mudge and the Best Day of All, 182, 494
Henry and Mudge and the Happy Cat, 182
"Henry and Mudge" books, 182, 184

Henry and Mudge Take the Big Test, 24, 182
Henry Bear's Park, 235, 242
Henry Huggins, 111, 492
Hentoff, Nat, 33
Henty, George A., 95
Heo, Yumi, 295
Hepler, Susan I., 15, 42, 166, 621, 632, 642, 645, 653, 696
Her Book, 704
Her Seven Brothers, 300
Her Stories: African American Folktales, 276, 298, 306
Hercules, 317
Here and Now Story Book, 105, 116
Here Comes Henny, 176, 180
"Here Is the Church," 142
Heritage Sampler, The, 526
Hero and the Crown, The, 58, 372
Hero with a Thousand Faces, The, 380
Heroes and Monsters of Greek Myth, 317
Heroine of the Titanic: A Tale Both True and Otherwise of the Life of Molly Brown, The, 560
Heron Street, 248, 651
Herrera, Velino, 224, 409, 422
Herriot, James, 6
Hershenson, Miriam, 415
Herstories: African American Folktales, Fairy Tales and True Tales, 219
Herzog, George, 273, 296, 303
Hesse, Karen, 378, 497
Hetherington, E. Mavis, 48
Hettinga, Donald, R., 325
Hewitt, Katherine, 568
Hey Diddle Diddle, 139
"Hey Diddle Diddle," 148
Hey Diddle Diddle Picture Book, 100
Hey World, Here I Am!, 422, 431, 468, 701
Heyer, Marilee, 279, 293
Hey-How for Halloween, 421
Heyman, Ken, 597
Hi, 53
Hi, Pizza Man!, 53
Hi Cat!, 228, 671
Hiawatha, 418, 424
Hiawatha's Childhood, 424
Hickman, Janet, 42, 45, 59, 61, 455, 479
"Hickory Dickory Dock," 146, 150, 685
Hiçyilmaz, Gaye, 491
Hidden Children, The, 601, 607
Hidden in the Sand, 292
Hide and Seek, 515, 540
Hide and Seek Fog, 229, 234
"Hideout," 430
"Hiding," 400, 407, 418
Higgle Wiggle: Happy Rhymes, 411
Higglety, Pigglety, Pop!, 343
High King, The, 371
High Wind in Jamaica, A, 6
Higher on the Door, 570
Highwater, Jamake, 300, 530
Highwayman, The, 400, 424
Hilda Hen's Happy Birthday, 203
Hilda Hen's Search, 203, 606
Hill, Elizabeth Starr, 231
Hill, Eric, 52, 65, 67, 140, 150, 152, 174, 180, 181
Hill, Kirkpatrick, 488, 526, 631
Hill, Mary W., 185
Hill, Susan, 660
Hillenbrand, Will, 237, 243
Himler, Ron, 117, 231, 232, 248, 250, 532, 533
Hindley, Judy, 122
Hine, Lewis W., 107

Hines, Anna Grossnickle, 172, 181
Hippopotamusn't, A, 405
Hiroshima No Pika, 114, 117, 223, 250, 431, 539
Hirschi, Ron, 54, 579, 648, 650
Hirsh, Marilyn, 637
Hist Whist, 423
Histoires ou Contes du Temps Passé; avec des Moralités (Stories or Tales of Times Past, with Morals), 88, 115
History of Cock Robin and Jenny Wren, The, 100
History of Little Goody Two Shoes, The, 89, 115
History of Mother Twaddle and the Marvelous Achievements of Her Son Jack, The, 281
History of Sixteen Wonderful Old Women, The, 88
Historye of Reynart the Foxe, The, 85, 115
Ho, Minfong, 59, 491, 536, 543
Hob and the Goblins, 25, 55, 356, 640
Hoban, Lillian, 233, 430
Hoban, Russell, 53, 184, 222, 242, 355, 428, 430, 683
Hoban, Tana, 44, 45, 52, 53, 107, 139, 156, 157, 160, 161, 165, 179, 181, 198
Hobbit, The, 6, 59, 110, 116, 343, 347, 356, 371, 380
Hobbs, Will, 58, 488, 489
Hoberman, Mary Ann, 393, 407, 413, 425, 428, 430, 431, 436, 693
Hobie Hanson, Greatest Hero of the Mall, 493
Hobie Hanson, You're Weird, 493
"Hobie Hanson" series, 499
Hoboken Chicken Emergency, 692
Hodges, Margaret, 126, 200, 266, 271, 285, 288, 292, 300, 316, 320, 347, 681
Hoey, Mary, 427
Hoff, Rhoda, 107
Hoffman, Dr. Heinrich, 98, 115
Hoffman, Felix, 109
Hoffman, Mary, 55, 232
Hogan, Inez, 112
Hogrogian, Nonny, 30, 109, 272, 283, 290, 311, 637
Hoguet, Susan Ramsay, 153
Hoig, Stan, 588
Hold Fast to Dreams, 485, 486
Holdaway, Don, 138
Holder, Heidi, 310, 349
"Holding Hands," 432, 685
Hole Is to Dig, A, 117, 216
Holland, Kathleen E., 71
Holland, Norman H., 59
Holling, Holling C., 106, 116, 598
Holm, Anne, 536, 541
Holman, Felice, 428, 432, 474
Holme, Bryan, 100
Holmes, Oliver Wendell, 99
Home from Far, 481
"Home on the Range," 585
Home: Where Reading and Writing Begin, 185
Homecoming, 11, 83, 431, 463, 478
Homeplace, 17, 53, 209
Homer, 11, 318
Homer Price, 22, 97, 111, 117
Homesick: My Own Story, 58, 487, 553, 570
Honey, I Love: and Other Poems, 394, 408, 430
Hong, Lily Toy, 279, 294
Honorable Prison, The, 491
Hooks, William H., 209, 219, 277, 279, 281, 304, 538
Hooper, Patricia, 673
Hoover, H. M., 373, 374, 376
Hope, Laura Lee, 126
Hopeful Trout and Other Limericks, The, 401, 425
Hopkins, Dave, 580

Hopkins, Lee Bennett, 55, 111, 158, 392, 396, 401, 402, 411, 412, 415, 416, 419, 420, 421, 425, 427, 428, 430, 431, 442, 569, 606
Hopkinson, Deborah, 680
"Hoppity," 407
Horenstein, Henry, 57
Horn Book Magazine, The, 33, 103, 224, 252, 544, 582, 655
Hornbeam Tree and Other Poems, The, 410
Horning, Kathleen, 123
Horse in the Attic, The, 501
Horton Hatches the Egg, 242
House at Pooh Corner, The, 353
House Is a House for Me, A, 407, 425, 436, 693
House of Dies Drear, The, 501, 606
House of Sixty Fathers, The, 541
House of Wings, The, 462, 678
House on East 88th Street, The, 242
House on Maple Street, The, 54, 516, 679
House That Drac Built, The, 237, 243
"House That Jack Built, The," 220, 237
House That Jack Built, The, 100, 115, 153, 269
House with a Clock in Its Walls, The, 361
"Household Stories," 268
Household Stories of the Brothers Grimm, 108, 268, 283
Houses, 601
Houses and Homes, 166
Houston, Gloria, 228, 234
Houston, James, 299, 301, 474, 631
How a Book Is Made, 704
"How Animals Got Their Tails," 272
"How Basic Is Shazam?," 342
How Chipmunk Got Tiny Feet: Native American Animal Origin Stories, 298
"How Coyote Arranged the Night Stars," 299
"How Doth the Busy Bee," 98
"How Doth the Little Crocodile," 98
How Glooscap Outwits the Ice Giants and Other Tales of the Maritime Indians, 299
"How I Came to Be a Writer*, 569, 570
How I Was Born, 55, 583
"How It Might Have Been," 420
How Many?, 52
How Many Days to America? A Thanksgiving Story, 247, 606, 607
How Many Snails?, 161
How Many Spots Does a Leopard Have? and Other Tales, 303
How Many Teeth?, 588
How Much Wood Would a Woodchuck Chuck," 148
How My Parent's Learned to Eat, 54, 233
How Night Came From the Sea: A Story From Brazil, 309, 311
How Now, Brown Cow? 415, 417
"How Parents Read to Children," 138
How Porcupines Make Love II: Teaching a Response-Centered Literature Curriculum, 71
How Rabbit Stole the Fire, 299, 303
"How Rumpelstiltskin's Name Was Discovered," 280
How Snowshoe Hare Rescued the Sun: A Tale Told From the Arctic, 299
How Summer Came to Canada, 272, 299
How Texts Teach What Readers Learn, 174
"How the Animals Got Their Tails," 269, 296
How the Camel Got Its Hump, 236, 243
How the Giraffe Got Such a Long Neck . . . And Why Rhino is so Grumpy, 296
How the Leopard Got His Spots, 236, 243
How the Ostrich Got Its Long Neck, 296

How the Sky's Housekeeper Wore Her Scarves, 673
How Thunder and Lightning Came to Be, 299, 300
How to Be a Nature Detective, 586
How to be Cool in the Third Grade, 56
"How to Eat a Poem," 402, 415
How to Eat Fried Worms, 495, 684
How to Make Apple Pie and See the World, 245
How to Make Pop-Ups, 602, 704
How to Make Super Pop-Ups, 602
How to Make Your Own Animated Movies and Videotapes, 678
How to Talk to Your Dog, 650
"How to Tell the Top of the Hill," 405
How Turtle's Back Was Cracked, 298, 300
How You Were Born, 55
Howard, Elizabeth Fitzgerald, 227, 232
Howarth, Lesley, 57, 375
Howe, Deborah, 56, 348
Howe, Frederick C., 45
Howe, James, 56, 120, 348, 493, 501
Howitt, Mary, 92, 98, 115
Howliday Inn, 348
Hoyt-Goldsmith, Diane, 582, 584
Hsu-Flanders, Lillian, 226, 227, 232
Huang, Benrei, 161
Huck, Charlotte, 285, 426, 430
Hudson, Wade, 417, 422
Hue Boy, 55
Huff, Barbara, 651
"Hughbert and the Glue," 400
Hughes, Dean, 498
Hughes, Langston, 110, 219, 402, 408, 415, 422, 425, 429, 430, 431, 434, 486, 685
Hughes, Monica, 376
Hughes, Richard, 6
Hughes, Shirley, 52, 141, 171
Human Body, The, 582
"Humming-Bird and the Flower," 309
"Humpty Dumpty," 150
Hundred Dresses, The, 111, 117, 466
Hundred Penny Box, The, 479
Hungerford, Rachael A., 71
Hungry Hyena, 236, 243
Hungry Woman: Myths and Legends of the Aztecs, The, 313
Hunt, Irene, 535
Hunt, Jonathan, 695
Hunt, Joyce, 598, 631
Hunt, Peter, 33, 155, 158
Hunter, Mollie, 10, 342, 347, 361, 362, 475, 482, 504, 518, 545, 625, 632, 639, 677, 691, 709
Hunter's Stew and Hangtown Fry: What Pioneer America Ate and Why, 683
Hunting the White Cow, 209
Huntington, Harriet, 107
Hurmence, Belinda, 367
Hurricane, 234
Hurried Child: Growing Up Too Fast Too Soon, The, 70, 475
Hurry Home, Candy, 47, 497
"Hurt No Living Thing," 431
Hurwitz, Johanna, 56, 493, 499, 563, 633
"Husbands and Wives," 415
Hush Little Baby, 52, 684, 685
Hutchins, Pat, 18, 53, 55, 162, 163, 168, 172, 175, 178, 179, 180, 181, 182, 217, 218, 240, 241, 242, 245, 430, 626, 677, 683, 691, 708
Hutton, Warwick, 217, 282, 283, 287, 314, 316, 318, 322, 325, 344
Huus, Helen, 41
Huynh, Quang Nhuong, 430, 490
Hyman, Stanley E., 267

Hyman, Trina Schart, 200, 201, 208, 211, 273, 284, 311, 320, 415, 420, 462, 569, 570

I, Columbus: My Journal 1492–1493, 571, 600
I, Juan de Pareja, 523
"I, says the poem," 391
I Am an American: A True Story of the Japanese Internment, 607
I Am Phoenix: Poems for Two Voices, 440, 425
I Am the Darker Brother: An Anthology of Modern Poems by Black Americans, 111, 422
I Am Wings: Poems About Love, 59
I Can, 52, 139
I Did It, 602
I Don't Want to Go Back To School, 208
I Hadn't Meant to Tell You This, 59, 117, 120, 457, 469
I Hate to Go to Bed, 53
I Hear, 139
I Heard a Scream in the Street, 111
I Know An Old Lady, 54
I Know an Old Lady Who Swallowed a Fly, 144, 181, 684
"I Know an Old Lady Who Swallowed a Fly," 142
"I Like Fall," 410
"I Like it When It's Mizzly," 414
I Like You, If You Like Me, 419, 431
"I Look Pretty," 408
I Love Guinea Pigs, 54, 167
I Met a Man, 405
"I Never Hear," 429
I Never Saw a Purple Cow, 421
"I Never Saw Another Butterfly," 418, 430, 431
I Never Told and Other Poems, 219
I Play in My Room, 170
I Read Signs, 179, 181
I Read Symbols, 179, 181
I Saw Esau, 152
I See, 139
I See the Moon, 18, 57, 462
"I Spy," 150
I Spy: An Alphabet in Art, 157
I Thought I'd Take My Rat to School, 421
"I Too Sing America," 430
I Touch, 139
I Want to Be an Astronaut, 53, 580
I Went Walking, 175, 180
"I Woke Up This Morning," 407, 426
I Wonder If I'll See a Whale, 650
I'll Get There, It Better Be Worth the Trip, 113, 470
I'll Meet You at the Cucumbers, 348
I'm Deborah Sampson, 120
"I'm Disgusted with My Brother," 406, 430
I'm Going to Pet A Worm Today and Other Poems, 431
"I'm in a Rotten Mood," 429
I'm in Charge of Celebrations, 410, 425, 694, 695
I'm Nobody! Who Are You? The Story of Emily Dickinson, 558
"I'm Sorry," 412
I'm Sorry Says the Machine, 431
"Ice Man Puts Out the Big Fire," 299
"Ickle Me, Pickle Me, Tickle Me, Too," 406
If I Had a Paka: Poems in Eleven Languages, 409
If the Owl Calls Again, 420
If You Give a Mouse a Cookie, 677
If You Lived with the Sioux Indians, 606
If You Were There in 1492, 571, 587
If You Lived at the Time of the Great San Francisco Earthquake, 703, 704
"Iguana," 415

Iktomi and the Berries: A Plains Indian Story, 299, 300
Iktomi and the Boulder, 217, 300, 606
Iktomi and the Buffalo Skull, 300
Iktomi and the Buzzard, 300, 303
Iktomi and the Ducks, 300
Iliad, The, 11, 318
Illuminations, 155, 158, 695
Illyrian Adventure, The, 369
Imaginary Gardens: American Poetry and Art for Young People, 425, 426
Immigrant Girl: Becky of Eldridge Street, 536
Immigrant Kids, 600
Imogene's Antlers, 207
"Impeachment of Warren Hastings," 92
Important Book, The, 643, 694
"In a Dark, Dark Wood," 439
In a Different Voice: Psychological Theory and Women's Development, 49
In a Pickle and Other Funny Idioms, 693
In a Spring Garden, 402, 425
In Adam's Fall/We Sinned All," 154
In Coal Country, 209
In Fairyland, 99
In for Winter, Out for Spring, 409
In My Mother's House, 116, 224, 409, 422
"In Search of Cinderella," 429
In the Beginning: Creation Stories from Around the World, 299, 301, 313, 314
"In the Hall of the Mountain King," 685
In the Hand of the Goddess, 368
"In The Middle," 392, 399, 412, 431
In the Middle: Writing, Reading, and Learning with Adolescents, 660
In the Moonlight, Waiting, 213
In the Night Kitchen, 113, 117, 208, 216, 217
In the Small Small Pond, 179, 207
In the Tall Tall Grass, 179
In the Trail of the Wind: American Indian Poems and Ritual Orations, 418, 422
In the Year of the Boar and Jackie Robinson, 487
Inch Boy, The, 303
"Inchworm," 410
Incredible Cross Sections books, 580
Incredible Journey, The, 65, 498
Indian Chiefs, 606
Indian Fairy Tales, 93
Indian in the Cupboard, The, 10, 56, 346, 354, 712
Indian Winter, An, 606
"Indians, The," 426
"Infant Speech: Effect of Systematic Reading of Stories," 12
"Information Please—Sometimes," 608
"Informational Books for Children," 608
Inhelder, Barbel, 45
Inner Chimes, 419
Innocenti, Roberto, 11, 250, 431, 539, 607
Insect Metamorphosis: From Egg to Adult, 704
Insect Zoo, 56, 581
Insects and Crawly Creatures, 580
"Inside," 431
Inside and Outside Spiders, 578
Inspirations: Stories About Women Artists, 567
Integrated Language Perspective in the Elementary School, An, 608, 661
Intellectual Freedom Manual, 658
Intent Upon Reading: A Critical Appraisal of Modern Fiction for Children, 518
Interest Factors in Reading, 40
"Interpreting Research in Children's Literature," 41
Interracial Books for Children, 358
"Interviewing Children About Their Literary Experience," 15

"Into the Eighties: BAYA's Fourth Reading Interest Survey," 40
Intrater, Roberta Grobel, 594
Investigate Nonfiction, 608
"Investigating Intelligence in Early Adolescence," 47
Invisible Hunters, The, 309
Invisible Thread, The, 570
"Invitation," 406
Invitation to the Game, 376
Invitations: Changing as Teachers and Learners K–12, 641, 645, 714
Ira Sleeps Over, 55, 233, 428, 623
Iron John, 120, 208, 281
Irvine, Joan, 602, 704
Irving, Washington, 92
Irwin, O. C., 12
Is It Larger? Is It Smaller?, 165
"Is Narrative 'Primary'?," 14
"Is Narrative "Primary"? Some Insights From Kindergartners' Pretend Readings of Stories and Information Books," 67
Is That Josie?, 5
Is This a House for a Hermit Crab?, 53, 637, 674
Is Underground, 369
Is Your Mama a Llama?, 178, 181, 428
Isaacs, Anne, 120, 199, 215, 217, 307
Isaacson, Philip M., 600
Isadora, Rachel, 52, 139, 158, 224, 247, 284, 311, 646
Ishi, Last of His Tribe, 531
Ishii, Momoko, 281
Isla, 224, 225
Island Boy, 232
Island of Ogres, 524
Island of the Blue Dolphins, 5, 43, 530, 626
Island on Bird Street, The, 540
It Could Always Be Worse, 109, 290, 636, 637
It Doesn't Always Have to Rhyme, 397, 402
It Looked Like Spilt Milk, 637
It's About Time!, 419
"It's All Right to Be Innocent Again," 120
It's Halloween, 406
It's Perfectly Normal: A Book About Changing Bodies, Growing Up, Sex, and Sexual Health, 58, 581, 583
It's Snowing! It's Snowing!, 406
It's Thanksgiving, 406
It's Too Noisy, 290, 637
Ivanhoe, 95

Jabar, Cynthia, 151
"Jack and Jill," 83, 147, 432, 685
Jack and the Bean Tree, 279, 281, 304
"Jack and the Bean Tree," 304
Jack and the Beanstalk, 65, 271, 272, 281, 302
"Jack and the Beanstalk," 237, 278, 324, 691
"Jack and the Devil," 272
"Jack and the Northwest Wind," 281
"Jack and the Robbers," 304
"Jack Be Nimble," 685
"Jack in the Giant's New Ground," 304
Jack Tales, The, 275, 281, 303, 304
"Jack the Giant Killer," 83
Jackson, Ellen, 206, 682, 696, 698
Jackson, Jesse, 112, 117
Jackson, Mary V., 126
Jackson Jones and the Puddle of Thorns, 50, 51, 648, 651
Jacob, Murv, 298, 300
Jacob Have I Loved, 59, 431, 460, 461, 625, 675
Jacobs, James S., 629
Jacobs, Joseph, 93, 270, 278, 281, 282, 289, 302
Jacobs, William Jay, 568

Jacques, Brian, 57, 351, 633, 686, 695
Jaffe, Dan, 431
Jafta, 668
Jakobsen, Kathy, 215, 424, 687, 704
Jamberry, 428
Jambo Means Hello: Swahili Alphabet Book, 158
Jamboree: Rhymes for All Times, 396, 411, 412, 418, 424, 426, 428, 430, 436, 440
James, Betsy, 682
James and the Giant Peach, 356, 606, 633
"James James Morrison Morrison Weatherby George Dupree," 394
James Marshall's Mother Goose, 147, 152
Janeczko, Paul, 59, 414, 416, 425, 442
Jansson, Tove, 357
Jaques, Faith, 147, 153
Jarrell, Randall, 283, 284, 349, 438
Jasmine's Parlour Day, 247
Jason and the Argonauts, 317
Jason and the Golden Fleece, 316
Jataka Tales, 108
Jayhawker, 535, 606
"Jazz-Man," 692
Jeanne d'Arc, 101, 102, 116
Jedera Adventure, The, 369
Jeffers, Susan, 153, 173, 282, 344, 347, 418, 424, 429, 651
Jellyfish Season, The, 712
Jenkins, Priscilla Belz, 606
Jenkins, Steve, 170, 603
Jenkinson, Edward B., 123
Jenny of the Tetons, 530
Jensen, Julie M., 643
Jeram, Anita, 167, 168
Jeremy Kooloo, 157
Jeremy Visick, 346, 367
Jericho, 45, 59, 455, 479
Jesse Bear, What Will You Wear?, 172
Jesse Jackson: A Biography, 555
Jesse's Daycare, 53, 171
Jester, R. Emile, 138
Jim Abbott: Major League Pitcher, 57
Jim and the Beanstalk, 243, 280, 281
Jimmy's Boa Bounces Back, 237, 244
Jo's Boys, 93, 99
Joan of Arc, 116
Joan's Door, 110
"Joe Magarac," 307
"John," 408
John Brown, Rose, and the Midnight Cat, 234
John Burningham's ABC, 157
"John Henry," 308
John Henry, 307, 398
John Henry: An American Legend, 62
John Newberry and His Books, 126
John Patrick Norman McHennessy—The Boy Who Was Always Late, 244
"John Steptoe: Retrospective of an Imagemaker," 297
John Treegate's Musket, 528
"Johnny and Sam: Old and New Approaches to the American Revolution," 544
Johnny Appleseed, 215, 271, 307, 308, 424, 704
Johnny Appleseed and Other Poems, 110
Johnny Crow's Garden, 103, 116
Johnny Tremain, 117, 516, 528
Johnson, Angela, 20, 52, 53, 55, 59, 139, 225, 231, 480
Johnson, Diedre, 126
Johnson, Gerald, 586
Johnson, Larry, 408
Johnson, Liz, 690
Johnson, Mauritz, 47
Johnson, Paul Brett, 233, 713

Johnson, Steve, 237
Johnson, Sylvia A., 590
Johnson, Terry D., 713
Johnston, Ginny, 650
Johnston, Julie, 59, 466
Johnston, Tony, 213, 215, 279, 311
Jolly Postman or Other People's Letters, The, 221, 237, 243, 698, 699, 701
Jonas, Ann, 53, 140, 155, 158, 161, 163, 164, 165, 166, 210, 428, 637, 650
Jones, Carol, 144, 181
Jones, Diana Wynne, 361
Jones, Hettie, 111, 417, 422
Jones, Malcolm, 272
Jones, Rebecca, 493, 674, 701
Joose, Barbara M., 429
Jordan, Alice M., 28, 99
Jorgansen, David, 109, 240, 245
Jorgensen, Gail, 181, 205
Josefina Story Quilt, The, 680
Joseph, Lynn, 219, 247
"Joshua" books, 139
Joshua by the Sea, 139
Joshua's Night Whisper, 139
Journey, 60, 462
Journey: Japanese Americans, Racism, and Renewal, The, 580, 607
Journey Back, The, 540
Journey Cake, Ho!, 269
Journey to America, 539
Journey to an 800 Number, 470
Journey to Jo'burg, 124, 489
Journey to the Center of the Earth, 96
Journey to the Planets, 602
Journey to Topaz, 117, 542, 607, 687
Journeying: Children Responding to Literature, 71
"Joy to the World," 91
Joyce, William, 6, 239, 240, 245, 701
Joyful Learning, 185
Joyful Noise: Poems for Two Voices, 440, 425, 606
Judy's Journey, 111, 117
Jukes, Mavis, 56, 231, 480
Julia and the Hand of God, 493
Julian, Dream Doctor, 483
"Julian" series, 483
Julian's Glorious Summer, 467
Julie, 57, 473, 605
Julie of the Wolves, 16, 18, 27, 69, 123, 473, 488, 631, 657
Julius, 53
Julius, the Baby of the World, 5, 53, 230, 242, 430
"July," 430
Jumanji, 30, 209, 210, 212, 215, 241, 245
Jump! The Adventures of Brer Rabbit, 270
"Jump, Jump," 411
Jump Again! More Adventures of Brer Rabbit, 274, 278, 305
"Jump or Jiggle," 685
Jump Ship to Freedom, 528, 536
Jung, Carl C., 267
Jungle, 585
Jungle Books, The, 96, 116
Junglewalk, 168
Juniper Tree and Other Tales from Grimm, The, 283
Jurmain, Suzanne, 601
Just a Dream, 241, 245, 248, 650
Just Plain Fancy, 200, 201, 220, 606
Just So Stories, 236
Just Us Women, 231
Just-So Stories, 109, 116, 236, 359
Juster, Norton, 48, 359
Justin and the Best Biscuits in the World, 483
Juvenile Miscellany, The, 99

Kahionhes, John, 324
Kaleidoscope: A Multicultural Booklist, 123, 504
Kalman, Bobbie, 686
Kalman, Maira, 221, 245
Kamen, Gloria, 173
Kane, Henry, 107
Karas, G. Brian, 54, 145, 172
Karlin, Barbara, 286
Karlin, Bernie, 161
Kate, 431, 467
Kate, Duke, 157
Kate Shelley: Bound for Legend, 560, 561
Katie and the Big Snow, 240, 245
Katz, Bobbi, 391
Katz, Welwyn Wilton, 366
Katzenberg, Jean, 340
Kaufmann, John, 584
Kaye, Marilyn, 571
Keats, Ezra Jack, 45, 53, 55, 62, 112, 117, 142,
    204, 205, 217, 221, 225, 228, 231, 307,
    308, 426, 430, 671, 708
Keats, John, 99
Keepers of Life, 325
Keepers of the Animals, 325
*Keepers of the Earth: Native American Stories and
    Environmental Activities for Children,* 324
Keepers of the Night, 325
Keeping, Charles, 424
Keeping Quilt, The, 227, 233, 680
"Keepsake," 408
Kehoe, Michael, 704
Keith, Harold, 535
Keller, Holly, 246, 247
Kellogg, Steven, 65, 109, 178, 216, 223, 236,
    237, 243, 244, 271, 272, 280, 306, 307,
    308, 311
Kelly, Eric P., 523
Kelly, Patricia P., 640
Kelsey, Alice Geer, 108
Kendall, Carol, 293, 358
Kennaway, Adrienne, 236, 243, 689
Kennedy, Dorothy M., 396, 398, 399, 403, 414,
    416, 439
Kennedy, Richard, 347, 355
Kennedy, X. J., 266, 396, 398, 399, 403, 405,
    414, 416, 429, 431, 439
Kent, Jack, 16, 181, 637, 643, 691
Kerr, Judith, 539
Kerstetter, Kristen, 632
Kesey, Ken, 243
Kesselman, Wendy, 228, 234
Kestrel, The, 369
Kettle of Hawks and Other Wildlife Groups, A, 693
Key, Alexander, 375, 690
Kherdian, David, 563
Kidd, Diana, 490, 492, 701
*Kids at Work: Lewis Hine and the Crusade Against
    Child Labor,* 600
Kids in Kennedy Middle School series, 500
"Kids of Polk Street School" series, 55, 120, 491
Kiefer, Barbara Z., 41, 212, 251, 608, 661
Killion, Bette, 651
Kimmel, Eric, 208, 276, 279, 281, 287, 288, 290,
    291, 302, 311
Kinder und Hausmärchen (Household Stories), 92
Kindl, Patricia, 347, 356
King, Laurie, 59
King, Martha L., 16
King, Stephen, 6
King and the Tortoise, The, 296
King Arthur, 84
"King Arthur," 51
King Henry's Primer, 86, 115
"King John's Christmas," 400
King Lear, 88, 304
King Midas, 314

"King Midas's Touch," 690
King of the Golden River, 93
King Phillip, 526
"King's Breakfast, The," 110, 400
King's Day: Louis XIV of France, The, 561
King's Fountain, The, 651
King's Shadow, The, 523, 536
King-Smith, Dick, 18, 54, 167, 346, 348, 349,
    375
Kingman, Lee, 33, 252
Kingsley, Charles, 96
Kinsey-Warnock, Natalie, 680
Kipling, Rudyard, 96, 99, 109, 116, 236, 243,
    270, 635, 691
Kiss the Dust, 491, 607
Kitchen, Bert, 154, 157, 160, 198
Kitchen Knight: A Tale of King Arthur, The, 320
Kjelgaard, Jim, 498
Klause, Annette Curtis, 376
Klausner, Janet, 567
Klee, Paul, 295
Klein, A. M., 414
Klein, Robin, 488
Kleven, Elisa, 224, 225, 682
Kline, Suzy, 494, 499
Kluckhohn, Clyde, 267
Knee-High Man and Other Tales, The, 305
Kneeknock Rise, 367
Knight, Amela, 570
Knight, David C., 584
Knights of the Kitchen Table, 360
Knock, Knock, Teremok!, 272
Knock at a Star, 396, 398, 399, 403, 414, 416, 439
Knots on a Counting Rope, 224
Knowlton, Jack, 591
Knoxville, Tennessee, 408
Knudson, R. R., 427
Knutson, Barbara, 279
"Koala," 428
Koala Lou, 242, 428, 686
Kobrin, Beverly, 604, 608
Kobrin Letter, The, 604
Kodama, Tatsuharu, 539
Koehn, Ilse, 541
Koertge, Ron, 24, 40, 479
Kohl, Herbert, 594
Kohl, Judith, 594
Kohlberg, Lawrence, 49
Koko's Kitten, 597, 650
Koko's Story, 597
Komaiko, Leah, 245
Konigsburg, E. L., 47, 113, 430, 470, 474, 477,
    478, 517, 523, 624
Koralek, Jenny, 323, 428
Korean Cinderella, The, 281
Korman, Gordon, 500
Koshkin, Alexander, 288, 316
Kovalski, Maryann, 145
Krahn, Fernando, 405
Kraus, Robert, 54, 140, 180, 235, 242, 428
Krauss, Ruth, 117, 172, 181, 216
Kreisler, Ken, 594
Krementz, Jill, 33
Kroeber, Theodora, 531
Krug, Judith F., 123
Krull, Kathleen, 568
Krumgold, Joseph, 30, 486
Kuklin, Susan, 578, 579
Kunhardt, Dorothy, 46, 52, 140
Kunhardt, Edith, 140
Kurelek, William, 596
Kurtz, Jane, 272
Kuskin, Karla, 32, 181, 391, 400, 407, 408, 416,
    419, 425, 426, 428, 429, 430, 691
Kutiper, Karen Sue, 404
Kwanzaa, 583

Kwon, Holly, 294

La Fontaine, 310, 312
Lacy, Lyn Ellen, 251
"Lad Who Went to the North Wind, The," 281,
    302
Ladder to the Sky, 299
Lady and the Spider, The, 650
"Lady Who Put Salt in Her Coffee, The," 97
Lady with the Alligator Purse, The, 684
Ladybug, 606
Laird, Elizabeth, 491, 607
Lake at the End of the World, The, 431, 650, 709
Lamb, Susan Condie, 234
Lampfish of Twill, The, 650
Land I Lost: Adventures of a Boy in Vietnam, The,
    430, 490
"Land of Counterpane," 407, 413
Land of Narnia, The, 370
Landsberg, Michele, 33, 623
Lang, Andrew, 93, 116, 277, 279, 290
Lang, Cecily 232
Lang, Celia, 232
Langerman, Deborah, 71
Langstaff, John, 684
Langton, Jane, 279, 360
Language Arts: An Integrated Approach, The, 15
*Language Development: Kindergarten Through
    Grade Twelve,* 48
Language in the Crib, 48
Language of Elementary School Children, The, 15
Language of Goldfish, The, 478
*Language of the Night: Essays on Fantasy and
    Science Fiction, The,* 370
Lanier, Sidney, 320
Lantern Bearers, The, 521, 536
*Larger Than Life: The Adventures of American
    Legendary Heroes,* 308
Larkin, Joanne, 668
Larrick, Nancy, 110, 395, 401, 405, 415, 416,
    419, 420, 424, 428, 432, 439, 431, 433,
    442
LaScala, Marilyn C., 441
Lasker, Joe, 560, 588, 595
Laskey, Kathryn, 112, 229, 462, 515, 532, 584
Lasky, Katherine, 229
Lass-Woodfin, Mary Jo, 504
Last Battle, The, 370
"Last Dinosaur, The," 420
Last of the Mohicans, The, 95
*Last Princess: The Story of Princess Ka'iulani of
    Hawai'i, The,* 561
Last Summer with Maizon, 485
"Last Word of a Bluebird, The," 411
Latching on to Literature: Reading Initiations
    Take Hold," 625
Latham, Jean Lee, 567
Lator, Gator, 487
Lattimore, Deborah Nourse, 217, 290, 313, 714
Lauber, Patricia, 56, 221, 578, 581, 586, 590,
    592, 593, 608, 651
Laughing Time, 405, 435
"Laughter of Children, The," 460
"Laura Ingalls Wilder's America: An
    Unflinching Assessment," 545
Lavies, Biaca, 580
Lawson, Julie, 121
Lawson, Robert, 30, 109, 116, 210, 350
Lazy Lion, 236, 243
Le Cain, Errol, 109, 286, 290, 311, 423, 424
Le Guin, Ursula K., 20, 58, 110, 341, 343, 344,
    347, 368, 370, 372, 373, 455, 680
Le Mieux, Michele, 420
Leaf, Margaret, 293, 681
Leaf, Munro, 116, 210
*Leagues Apart: The Men and Time of the Negro
    Baseball Leagues,* 568

Lear, Edward, 98, 115, 405, 416, 419, 421, 423
Learning About Biographies: A Reading-and-Writing Approach for Children, 571
Learning How to Mean: Explorations in the Functions of Language, 48
"Learning the Language of Books," 12
"Learning to Read by Reading . . . ," 12
Leatherstocking novels, 95
"Leavetaking," 430
"Leaving," 408
Leaving, The, 59, 461
Lee, Alan, 121, 365
Lee, Dennis, 414
Lee, Harper, 6
Legend Days, 530
Legend of El Dorado, The, 309
Legend of Old Befana, The, 323
Legend of Sleepy Hollow, The, 92
Legend of the Bluebonnet: An Old Tale of Texas, The, 299
Legend of William Tell, The, 424
Lehr, Susan, 60, 71
Leif the Lucky, 107
Lemming Condition, 652
Lemonade Trick, The, 360
L'Engle, Madeleine, 6, 8, 10, 11, 27, 59, 64, 110, 117, 120, 123, 342, 343, 347, 370, 374, 376, 377, 455, 468, 482, 626, 634, 653, 657, 683, 680, 700, 709
Lenski, Lois, 105, 111, 116, 117
Lent, Blair, 271, 295
Leo the Late Bloomer, 54, 235, 242, 428
Lepman, Jella, 114
Lessac, Frané, 216, 247, 408
Lester, Julius, 120, 270, 275, 303, 305, 307, 308, 606
Let the Celebrations Begin!, 539
Let the Circle Be Unbroken, 538
Let There Be Light: A Book About Windows, 601
Let's Be Enemies, 82, 83
Let's Do a Poem, 439, 442
Let's Go Outdoors, 107
"Letter from England: Great Leaping Lapins!," 352
Letter Jesters, The, 578
Letter to Amy, A, 228
Letters from a Slave Girl: The Story of Harriet Jacobs, 22, 534, 606
Letters of E. B. White, 20
Letters to Horseface: Young Mozart's Travels in Italy, 552
Letting Swift River Go, 248, 651
Levine, Ellen, 704
Levinson, Nancy Smiler, 571
Levinson, Riki, 233, 247
Levitin, Sonia, 491, 539
Levoy, Myron, 57, 542
Levstik, Linda S., 545, 608, 661
Levy, Elizabeth, 501
Levy, Constance, 58, 396, 410, 425, 431
Lewin, Betsy, 682
Lewin, Hugh, 664, 668
Lewin, Ted, 207, 246, 514, 515
Lewis, C. S., 8, 24, 33, 57, 110, 342, 347, 370, 380, 456, 624, 641
Lewis, Celeste, 233
Lewis, Claudia, 429
Lewis, J. Patrick, 288, 289, 410, 425, 495
Lewis, Richard, 110, 402, 673
"Lewis Has a Trumpet," 407
Libby On Wednesday, 57, 468, 494, 701
Librarian, The, 207
Library Bill of Rights, 656
Liestman, Vicki, 562
Life and Strange and Surprising Adventures of Robinson Crusoe, The, 89

Life and Times of the Apple, The, 598
Life and Times of the Honeybee, The, 598, 599
"Life Drawings: Some Notes on Children's Picture Book Biographies," 559
Life of a Hamster, The, 631
Light, 322, 323, 671
Light Beyond the Forest: The Quest for the Holy Grail, The, 320
Light in the Attic, A, 42, 56, 400, 406, 429, 430
Light in the Forest, The, 526
Light Princess, The, 97, 345
Lightburn, Ron, 212, 213
Like Jake and Me, 231
Lily and the Wooden Bowl, 272, 275, 276
Lily Cupboard, The, 607
Lincoln: A Photobiography, 117, 119, 553, 557, 567, 581, 606, 633, 677
Lincoln: In His Own Words, 569
Lindbergh, Reeve, 215, 271, 307, 308, 424, 704
Lindgren, Astrid, 22, 114, 355
Lindsay, Vachel, 110, 396, 439, 685
Lines or Squares, 110
Link, Lenore M., 685
Lion and the Mouse, The, 312
"Lion and the Mouse, The," 312
Lion and the Rat, The, 312
Lion and the Unicorn, The, 571, 608
Lion King, The, 119
"Lion King Roars, Goosebumps Soar," 118, 119
Lion to Guard Us, A, 524
Lion's Whiskers, The, 205, 296, 297
Lion, the Witch, and the Wardrobe, The, 24, 110, 347, 370, 641
Lioness Quartet, The, 368
Lioness Rampant, 368
Lionni, Leo, 54, 65, 66, 204, 209, 217, 236, 243, 312, 428, 606, 637, 671, 672, 676, 688, 691, 703
Lipsyte, Robert, 494
Lisa's War, 541
Lisle, Janet Taylor, 494, 650
"Listen Children," 417
"Listen to the Mustn'ts," 406
"Listening to Grownups Quarreling," 398
Listening Walk, The, 650
Literacy Through Literature, 713
"Literature and Growing Up," 6
Literature and the Reader, 40
Literature as Exploration, 60, 688
"Literature—S.O.S.!," 605
Literature: An Introduction to Fiction, Poetry and Drama, 266
Literature-Based Reading Programs at Work, 660
"Little," 407, 429
Little, Jean, 44, 57, 414, 422, 431, 459, 467, 476, 481, 482, 570, 701
Little Auto, The, 105, 116
Little Bear, 53
"Little Bear" series, 242
Little Blue and Little Yellow, 204, 428, 637, 676
"Little Burnt Face," 278
Little by Little: A Writer's Childhood, 57, 570
Little Elephant, 53
Little Engine That Could, The, 105, 240
Little Family, The Little Auto, The, 105
Little Fur Family, The, 105
"Little Goody Two Shoes," 90
Little Henry and His Bearer, 93
Little Hill, The, 110
Little House, The, 53, 105, 116, 220, 240, 245, 675
Little House Cookbook, The, 56, 602, 683
Little House in the Big Woods, 23, 31, 54, 107, 116, 531
Little House on the Prairie, 531
"Little House" series, 31, 531, 545, 624

Little Humpbacked Horse, The, 288
Little Island, The, 105, 207, 216, 430
Little Lord Fauntleroy, 95, 99, 111
Little Match Girl, The, 343
Little Men, 94
"Little Mermaid, The," 344
"Little Miss Muffet," 88
Little Old Lady Who Was Not Afraid of Anything, The, 54, 637, 676
Little Old Woman and the Hungry Cat, The, 285, 302
"Little Orphant Annie," 99
Little Plum, 209, 294, 353
Little Pretty Pocket-Book, A, 89, 115
Little Prince, The, 346, 379
Little Princess, The, 95, 111
Little Red Cap, 284, 302
"Little Red Cap," 284
Little Red Hen, The, 53, 270, 302, 310, 676, 691
"Little Red Hen, The," 16, 62, 280, 283, 623, 635
Little Red Riding Hood, 16, 211, 284, 311
"Little Red Riding Hood," 48, 269, 276
Little Rollo, 92
"Little Short Legs," 409
Little Sister and the Month Brothers, 289
Little Snowgirl, The, 279, 289, 311
Little Tim and the Brave Sea Captain, 207
Little Toot, 105, 240
Little Town on the Prairie, 531
Little Tricker the Squirrel Meets Big Double the Bear, 243
Little Women, 22, 28, 83, 93, 94, 111, 112, 115, 120, 124
Littlefield, Bill, 568
Lively, Penelope, 8, 362, 363
Lives of the Artists: Masterpieces, Messes (And What the Neighbors Thought), 568
Lives of the Writers: Comedies, Tragedies (And What the Neighbors Thought), 568
Lives of Christopher Chant, The, 361
Living Treasure: Saving the Earth's Threatened Biodiversity, 651
Livingston, Myra Cohn, 32, 219, 392, 399, 401, 412, 413, 414, 415, 419, 420, 426, 428, 429, 430, 431, 434, 442
Llama and the Great Flood: A Folktale from Peru, 309, 606
"Llama Who Had No Pajama, The," 407, 428
Llorente, Pilar Molina, 523
Lloyd, Alexander, 380
Lloyd, Megan, 412
Loban, Walter, 15, 48
Lobel, Anita, 18, 285
Lobel, Arnold, 8, 16, 21, 52, 54, 222, 243, 401, 406, 414, 425, 622, 675, 683, 698, 699
"Lobster Quadrille, The," 98
Local News, 486
Locke, John, 89
Locker, Thomas, 208, 209, 344, 420, 587
Lofting, Hugh, 109
Lofts, Pamela, 242
Lomask, William, 568
Lon Po Po: A Red Riding Hood Story from China, 48, 279, 293
London, Jack, 99, 116, 498
"Lone Dog, The," 401, 404
"Lonesome," 412
Long-Haired Girl, The, 293
Long Secret, The, 468
"Long-Ago Days," 430
Longfellow, Henry Wadsworth, 392, 423, 424
"Look Cinderella," 429
Look Through My Window, 431, 467
Loon's Necklace, The, 298
Lorax, The, 651

"Lord of the Rings, The" trilogy, 371
Lord, Bette Bao, 487
Lord, Trevor, 57
Lord of the Sky: Zeus, 316
Lost, 233
"Lost Button, A," 683
Lost Children, The, 300, 606
"Lost City of Brass, The," 290
Lost Garden, The, 570
Lost in Cyberspace, 376
Lost in the Museum, 429
Lost Lake, The, 234, 238, 430
Lost Wild America: The Story of Our Extinct and
    Vanishing Wildlife, 650
Lost Zoo, The, 110
Lostman's River, 28, 517
Lotus Seeds: Children's Pictures and Books, 251
Louie, Ai-Ling, 117, 266, 278, 279, 280, 292, 311
Louis, Daphne, 713
Love You Forever, 6
Lovelace, Maude Hart, 494
Low, Alice, 314, 315
Lowry, Lois, 5, 8, 9, 10, 39, 47, 58, 59, 341, 378,
    379, 430, 431, 455, 460, 467, 479, 481,
    494, 503, 516, 540, 605, 607, 624, 640,
    701
Lowther, Deborah, 42
Loyal Cat, The, 206, 281
Lucky Stone, The, 483
Lucy's Christmas, 204
Lucy's Summer, 204
Lueders, Edward, 416
Luka's Quilt, 673, 680
Lukens, Rebecca J., 33
"Lullaby," 428
Lumberjack, 596
Lunn, Janet, 121, 367, 517
Lurie, Alison, 126
"Lurpp Is on the Loose, The," 394, 404
"Luther and Breck," 408
Luttrell Village: Country Life in the Middle Ages,
    The, 65
Luzak, Dennis, 247
Lyddie, 22, 430, 519, 534, 632, 699
Lyle, Lyle Crocodile, 242
Lyon, George Ella, 606, 692
Lyons, Mary E., 22, 126, 534, 552, 561, 606

Macaulay, David, 56, 117, 119, 129, 202, 211,
    592, 596, 633
MacCarthy, Patricia, 159, 160
MacDonald, Amy, 54
MacDonald, Caroline, 431, 650, 709
MacDonald, George, 96, 97, 115, 344
MacDonald, Golden, (pseudonym, Margaret
    Wise Brown), 207, 430
MacDonald, Kate, 682
MacDonald, Megan, 674
MacDonald, Susie, 154, 157, 165
Macfarlane, Aidan, 44
Machine Gunners, The, 541
Machines at Work, 166
Machotka, Hana, 581, 603
Macht, Norman, 57
Mackay, Donald A., 495
Mackey, Margaret, 492
MacKinnin, Debbie, 52
MacLachan, Patricia, 23, 24, 42, 55, 56, 57, 60,
    112, 117, 120, 203, 212, 231, 232, 431,
    462, 464, 503, 532, 606, 633, 691, 709
Maclean, Morag, 146
Macmillan Book of Greek Gods and Heroes, The,
    315
Mad as a Wet Hen and Other Funny Idioms, 693

Madeline, 105, 116, 200, 202
Maestro, Guilio, 591
Magic Circle, The, 9, 342
Magic Fishbone, The, 93
Magic Listening Cap, The, 108
Magic Orange Tree and Other Haitian Folktales,
    The, 272, 274
Magic Porridge Pot, The, 281
Magic Purse, The, 279
Magic School Bus at the Waterworks, The, 117,
    651
Magic School Bus in the Time of the Dinosaurs,
    The, 56, 596
Magic School Bus Inside a Hurricane, The, 580,
    596
Magic School Bus Inside the Earth, The, 596
Magic School Bus Inside the Human Body, The,
    121
Magic School Bus on the Ocean Floor, The, 596
"Magic School Bus" series, 496, 596
Magic Spring: A Korean Folktale, 294
Magic Tapestry, The, 293
Magical Adventures of Pretty Pearl, The, 306, 342
Magician's Nephew, The, 370
Magorian, Michelle, 171
Mahurin, Tim, 157
Mahy, Margaret, 56, 58, 216, 221, 244, 279, 281,
    293, 362, 380, 569
Maid, the Mouse, and the Odd Shaped House, The,
    217
Maid of the North: Feminist Folk Tales from
    Around the World, The, 276
Ma'ii and Cousin Horned Toad, 299, 300
Maisy Goes to Bed, 140, 141
Maizon at Blue Hill, 485
Make Lemonade, 59, 470
Make Way for Ducklings, 40, 105, 116, 210
Making Babies, 583
Making Friends with Frankenstein, 406
Making of a Reader, The, 185
Making of Myth, The, 267
Making Sense: Animal Perception and
    Communication, 503
Making Your Own Movies, 678
Malam, Charles, 397
Malcolm X, 563
Malory, Sir Thomas, 85, 86, 115, 319, 320, 342
Mama Bird, Baby Birds, 139
Mama Coming and Going, 220, 231
Mama Goose: A New Mother Goose, 152
Mama One, Mama Two, 231
Mama's Going to Buy You a Mockingbird, 481
Man From the Other Side, The, 57, 536, 540
Man Who Tricked a Ghost, The, 279
Maniac Magee, 58, 70, 117, 430, 457, 472
Manitonquat, 298
Manley, Joan B., 541
Manson, Chris, 402
Manson, Christopher, 143
"Many Furs," 285
Many Lives of Benjamin Franklin, The, 562
Many Luscious Lollipops: A Book About Adjectives,
    581, 693
Many Moons, 119, 345
Maphead, 57, 375
Maps and Globes, 591
Maps: Getting from Here to There, 593
Mara, Daughter of the Nile, 521
Maraslis, Demetra, 345
Marble in the Water: Essays on Contemporary
    Writers of Fiction for Children and Young
    Adults, 504
Marc Chagall, 562
Marcellino, Fred, 218, 286, 344, 405

Marcus, Leonard S. Marcus, 126, 559, 571
Mare on the Hill, The, 208
Margaret Mead: The World Was Her Family, 563
Margaret Wise Brown: Awakened by the Moon,
    126
Mariel of Redwall, 351
Marigold Garden, 101
"Marjorie Frost Fraser," 427
Mark, Jan, 504
Mark Twain, America's Humorist, Dreamer,
    Prophet, 566
Markle, Sandra, 578, 586, 592, 603, 606
Marrin, Albert, 555, 566
Marryat, Captain Frederick, 95
Marshak, Samuel, 274, 277, 279, 281, 289
Marshall, James, 55, 140, 147, 152, 238, 244,
    270, 280, 284, 286, 312, 405, 423, 429
Martha Calling, 237, 238, 244
Martha Speaks, 237, 244
Martin, Ann, 108, 118, 491
Martin, Bill, Jr., 54, 154, 175, 176, 180, 183, 207,
    224, 436, 671
Martin, Douglas, 252
Martin, James, 592
Martin, Joseph Plumb, 570
Martin, Mary Steichen, 106
Martin, Rafe, 88, 209, 245, 272, 278, 292, 299,
    301, 311, 569
Martin, Sarah, 88
Martin, Stefan, 393
Martin Luther King, 560
Martin Luther King: The Peaceful Warrior, 558
"Martin Luther King Day," 426
Martin the Warrior, 352
Martinez, Miriam, 71, 174, 661
Maruki, Toshi, 114, 223, 250, 431, 539
Marvelous Misadventures of Sebastian, The, 369
Marvin Redpost: Why Pick on Me?, 494
Mary, Mother of Jesus, 323
"Mary, Mary, Quite Contrary," 88
Mary Cassatt, 561
Mary Had a Little Lamb, 98, 149, 150, 153, 215
"Mary Had a Little Lamb," 432
Mary Jane, 112
Mary McLeod Bethune, 563
Mary of Nazareth, 322
Mary Poppins, 97, 116, 355, 380, 691
Mary Poppins Comes Back, 355
Mary Poppins in the Park, 355
Mary Poppins Opens the Door, 355
Mary Wore Her Red Dress and Henry Wore His
    Green Sneakers, 179, 181
Marzollo, Jean, 173, 219, 685
Masefield, John, 401
Maslow, Abraham H., 50
Master Puppeteer, The, 59, 524
Matas, Carol, 541
Matchlock Gun, The, 527, 529
Math, Irwin, 599
Math Curse, 585, 586
Mather, Dr. Cotton, 126
Mathers, Petra, 235, 236, 242, 309, 682
"Matter of Taste, A," 396
Matters of Fact: Aspects of Non-fiction for
    Children, 608
Matthew's Dream, 205
Mattimeo, 352
Maudie and Me and the Dirty Book, 457
Mavor, Sally, 149, 150, 153
Max, 224
Max Found Two Sticks, 55, 204, 205, 218
Max in Hollywood, 245
Max Makes a Million, 221, 245
Maxi, the Hero, 53

Max's Dragon Shirt, 24
Max's First Word, 139
Max's Ride, 52
May, Jill P., 380
May I Bring a Friend?, 53, 244, 685
Mayer, Marianna, 118, 245, 278, 279, 286, 288, 428
Mayer, Mercer, 169, 245
Mayfield Crossing, 57
Mayne, William, 25, 55, 342, 346, 356, 365, 368, 640, 650
Mayo, Betty D., 321
Mayo, Gretchen Will, 299
Mazel and Shlimazel, or The Milk of a Lioness, 274
M. C. Higgins the Great, 113, 117, 485
McBranty, Sam, 53
McCaffrey, Anne, 58, 368, 370, 372
McCaslin, Nellie, 714
McCloskey, Robert, 22, 30, 40, 55, 63, 97, 105, 111, 116, 117, 199, 200, 207, 210, 233, 425, 430
McClung, Robert M., 583, 650
McClure, Amy A., 123, 434, 438, 442
McConaghy, June, 185
McCord, David, 8, 31, 32, 110, 394, 398, 401, 404, 411, 414, 420, 424, 428, 436, 439, 440
McCully, Emily Arnold, 169
McCurdy, Michael, 27, 204, 218, 288, 307, 417, 570, 673
McDermott, Beverly Brodsky, 109
McDermott, Dennis, 275, 299
McDermott, Gerald, 277, 278, 279, 281, 292, 295, 296, 299, 301, 303, 314, 668
McDonald, Megan, 53, 637
McDonnell, Christine, 494
McEwan, Ian, 58
McFarland, John, 312
McFarlane, Sheryl, 212, 213
McGovern, Ann, 56, 321, 563, 606
McGraw, Eloise Jarvis, 347, 514, 521, 530
McGuffey, William, 92, 98
"McGuffey Reader," 112, 626
McGuire, Richard, 52, 210
McIlwain, Mary Jane, 668
McIntosh, Jane, 585
McKay, Hilary, 57, 495
McKee, David, 240, 428
McKillip, Patricia, 372
McKinley, Robin, 58, 321, 342, 368, 372
McKissack, Frederick L., 117, 120, 565, 606
McKissack, Patricia C., 22, 55, 117, 120, 219, 555, 565, 606, 633
McLeod, Irene Rutherford, 401
McMillan, Bruce, 149, 153, 161, 693
McNaughton, Colin, 174, 176, 178, 406, 677
McNeil, Florence, 426
McNulty, Faith, 650
McPhail, David, 53, 145, 235, 242, 428, 680
McPhee, John, 602
McSwigan, Marie, 517, 540
McVitty, Walter, 272, 311
Meade, Holly, 179, 230, 673
"Mean Song," 426
Meaning Makers, The, 12, 138, 174, 186
Mears, Virginia, 668
Meddaugh, Susan, 237, 238, 244
Medearis, Angela Shelf, 606
Medieval Feast, A, 595
Meek, Margaret, 9, 174, 625, 639
Meet Addy (The American Girl Collection), 56
"Meet the Author" series, 569
Meet the Austins, 6, 120, 455, 482
Meier, Max, 623

Meigs, Cornelia, 93, 96, 126
Meltzer, Milton, 562, 569, 570, 571, 582, 599, 607
Men at Work, 107
"Mending Wall," 391, 411
Mennyms, The, 354
Mennyms in the Wilderness, The, 354
Mennyms Under Siege, The, 354
Merchant of Venice, 85
Mere Creatures: A Study of Modern Fantasy Tales for Children, 380
Merlin Dreams, 342, 365
Merlin Effect, The, 359
Mermaid Summer, The, 10, 361, 691, 709
Merriam, Eve, 32, 161, 391, 393, 396, 397, 398, 402, 403, 411, 412, 413, 414, 415, 416, 418, 419, 420, 424, 425, 426, 430, 431, 440, 698
Merrill, Jean, 346, 700
Merry Adventures of Robin Hood, 101, 116, 321
Merry Ever After: The Story of Two Medieval Weddings, 595
Merry-Go-Round Poetry Book, The, 419
Merry Pranks of Till Eulenspiegel, The, 279
Messy Baby, 139
Metamorphoses, 314
"Metaphor Man," 397
Meyers, Susan, 56, 581
Miami Giant, The, 218
Mice Are Nice, 415, 420
"Michael," 408
Mick Harte Was Here, 481
Mickelwait, Lucy, 157
Micucci, Charles, 598, 599
Middle Moffat, The, 111, 459
Middle of Somewhere: A Story of South Africa, The, 489
"Middle of the Night, The," 428
Middle Passage, The, 538
Midnight Horse, The, 360, 693
Midwife's Apprentice, The, 120, 522, 523
Mikaelsen, Ben, 496
Mike Mulligan and His Steam Shovel, 105, 116, 240, 245
Mikolaycak, Charles, 289, 322, 323, 400, 424
Mik's Mammoth, 217
Miles, Betty, 457
Miles, Miska, 112, 224
Milhous, Katherine, 289, 311, 637, 643, 689
Mill, 592
Millay, Edna St. Vincent, 110, 427
Miller, Brandon Marie, 567
Miller, Jonathan, 592
Miller, Margaret, 48, 52, 166, 589
Miller, Mary Beth, 596, 597
Miller, the Boy, and the Donkey, The, 312
Miller, William, 563
Millions of Cats, 14, 52, 104, 116, 210
Mills, Claudia, 494
Mills, Lauren, 302, 680
Milne, A. A., 5, 6, 28, 109, 116, 353, 394, 400, 407, 414, 416, 633
Milton, John, 5
Milton the Early Riser, 242
Minard, Rosemary, 276
Minarik, Else Holmelund, 53, 182, 242
Mind in Society: The Development of Higher Psychological Processes, 48
Mine for Keeps, 44, 476
Minn of the Mississippi, 598
Minor, Wendell, 579
Minpins, The, 358, 359
Miracles, 110
Mirandy and Brother Wind, 22

Miriam's Well: Stories About Women in the Bible, 322
Mirrorstone, The, 121
Mischling, Second Degree: My Childhood in Nazi Germany, 541
Misoso: Once Upon a Time Tales from Africa, 296
Miss Bianca, 350
Miss Bianca in the Salt Mines, 350
Miss Happiness and Miss Flower, 353
Miss Hickory, 353
Miss Mary Mack and Other Children's Street Rhymes, 432
Miss Nelson Has a Field Day, 238, 244
Miss Nelson Is Missing, 238, 244
Miss Rumphius, 112, 208, 228, 233, 234, 651
"Missing," 400
Missing Gator of Gumbo Limbo, 651
Missing May, 18, 19, 25, 58, 466
Missing Tarts, The, 150
Mississippi Bridge, 538
Mississippi Possum, 112
Misty of Chincoteague, 493
Mitchell, James, 652
Mitchell, Lucy Sprague, 105, 116
Mitchell, Margaree King, 227
Mitten, The, 289, 311, 637
"Mix a pancake . . . ," 99
Mixed-Up Chameleon, The, 428
Moberly, Peggy Compton, 700
Moccasin Trail, 514, 530
Mochizuki, Ken, 607
Moe, Jorgen E., 8, 53, 270, 272, 281, 285, 302, 311, 316
Moeri, Louise, 491
Moffats, The, 83, 111, 116, 459
Moffitt, John, 426, 433
Mogensen, Cauley, 236
Mohr, Nicholasa, 307, 486
Moja Means One: A Swahili Counting Book, 160, 668
Mojave, 397, 650
Mole Hill, 673
Moles and the Mireuk, The, 294
Mollel, Tololwa, 279, 296, 303
Molly's Pilgrim, 56, 488
Momaday, N. Scott, 324
Momotaro, The Peach Boy, 272, 275, 279, 294, 303
Monaghan, Lois, 63
Monarch Butterfly, 606
Monday's Troll, 406
Money, Money, Money: The Meaning of the Art and Symbols on United States Paper Currency, 601
Monjo, F. N., 107, 534, 552, 555, 556, 562
Monkey and the Crocodile, The, 312
Monkey Island, 57, 475, 633
Monkey's Haircut and Other Stories Told by the Maya, The, 307
Monroe, Jean Guard, 298, 299
Monson, Dianne, 71
Monster Garden, The, 502, 650
Montgomery, Lucy, 111, 490
Month-Brothers: A Slavic Tale, The, 274, 277, 279, 281, 289
Monthly Packet, The, 99
Montresor, Beni, 244
"Moochie," 430
Moody, Fiona, 270, 281
Moon and I, The, 569
Moon Rope/Un Lazo de la Luna, 309
"Moon's the North Wind's Cooky, The," 396
Moonlight, 169
Moorchild, The, 347

Moore, Anne Carroll, 103
Moore, Clement, 98, 115, 400
Moore, Lilian, 32, 158, 348, 391, 393, 397, 410,
    414, 416, 425, 428, 429, 430, 431, 436
Moore, Yvette, 158
Mora, Pat, 232
Moral Judgment of the Child, The, 49
Mordvinoff, Nicholas, 105
"More Leaves from a Teacher's Diary: On
    Reading," 340
"'More More More,' Said the Baby," 140
More Nonsense, 98
More Notes from a Different Drummer, 476, 504
More Stories Julian Tells, 458
More Surprises, 419
Morgan, Pierr, 289, 311, 637
Morimoto, Junko, 249, 303, 539
Morning Girl, 26, 58, 529
"Morning Has Broken," 685
Morning, Noon and Nighttime, Too, 429
Morphology of the Folktale, The, 267
Morpugo, Michael, 319, 541
Morris, Ann, 166, 590, 597
Morrison, Lillian, 398, 402, 414, 415, 416, 428
Morrison, Shirley Vittum, 608
Morrow, Honoré, 515, 532
Morrow, Lesley Mandel, 185
Morrow, Leslie, 420
Morse, Janet Crowell, 91
Morte d'Arthur, Le, 85, 115, 319, 320, 342
Morton, Miriam, 147, 441
Mosel, Arlene, 277, 281, 303
Moser, Barry, 203, 212, 243, 282, 304, 313, 316,
    317, 423
Moses, 322
Moses' Ark: Stories from the Bible, 322
Moses in the Bulrushes, 322
Moses, Grandma, 215, 400, 426
Moss, Joy F., 288, 325, 350, 714
Moss, Lloyd, 161
Moss Grown, 277, 279, 281, 304
Mossflower, 356
Most Beautiful Place in the World, The, 430, 455,
    488
Mother Goose, 90, 96, 99, 103, 153, 174, 178, 184
Mother Goose, or The Old Nursery Rhymes, 152
Mother Goose Book, The, 152
Mother Goose Rhymes, 624
Mother Goose Songbook, The, 145
Mother Goose Treasury, The, 152
Mother Goose's Melody (Newbery), 88, 115
Mother Holly, 281
"Mother to Son," 408, 425, 430, 434, 435
Motif Index of Folk-Literature, 276
Motivation and Personality, 50
Mountain Bluebird, The, 650
Mountain Light, 537
Mouse and His Child, The, 355
Mouse and the Motorcycle, The, 348, 683
Mouse Rap, The, 24, 57, 485, 699
Mousewife, The, 348
Move Over, Wheelchairs Coming Through!, 584
Moves Make the Man, The, 478, 499
Moving From One to Ten, 162
Mowat, Farley, 496, 498
Moyers, Bill, 266, 325
*Mozart: Scenes from the Childhood of the Great
    Composer,* 561
Mozart Season, The, 499
Mozart Tonight, 561
Mr. and Mrs. Pig's Evening Out, 243
Mrs. Frisby and the Rats of NIMH, 119, 343, 351,
    352, 681
Mr. Gumpy's Outing, 52, 181

*Mr. Mistoffelees with Mungojerrie and
    Rumpelteazer,* 423
Mrs. Pig's Bulk Buy, 243
Mr. Popper's Penguins, 355
Mr. Rabbit and the Lovely Present, 213, 217, 429
"Mrs. Peck Pigeon," 110, 393, 407
Mud Pony, The, 299
"Muddy Puddle, The," 414
"Mud," 396, 425
Mufaro's Beautiful Daughters: An African Tale,
    117, 281, 295, 296, 303, 633, 668
Muffin Fiend, The, 121
Müller, Jörg, 596
Mullins, Patricia, 46, 155, 159, 178, 205, 650
Mulready, William, 98
Mummies Made in Egypt, 593, 659
"Mummy Slept Late and Daddy Fixed Breakfast,"
    404, 405
Munsch, Robert, 6
Munsinger, Lynn, 400, 405, 423
Mure, Eleanor, 92
Murphy, Claire Rudolf, 597
Murphy, Jill, 180
Murphy, Jim, 17, 581, 600, 601
Murphy, Sharon, 625
Murphy, Shirley Rousseau, 215, 342
Musgrove, Margaret, 159, 217
Mushroom in the Rain, 637
Music, Music for Everyone, 228, 233
Mustard, 457, 480
My Backyard History Book, 603
"My Bed Is a Boat," 99
My Best Special Words, 112
My Black Me: A Beginning Book of Black Poetry,
    421
My Brother, My Sister, and I, 543
My Brother Sam Is Dead, 17, 117, 120, 515, 528,
    536
"My Brother," 406, 407, 429
My Buddy, the King, 57
My Daniel, 462, 606
My Doctor, 583
"My Father's Words," 429
My Feet, 167, 221
My Great-Aunt Arizona, 228, 234
My Hands, 167, 221
My Head Is Red, 428
My Hiroshima, 249, 539
"My Key," 392
My Kitchen, 179, 181
My Little Island, 216
My Mama Had a Dancing Heart, 213
My Mama Needs Me, 231
My Mom Can't See Me, 592
My Mom's A Vet, 57
*My Mother Is the Most Beautiful Woman in the
    World,* 7, 272, 289
My Mysterious World, 569
My New York, 216, 687
My Own Two Feet: A Memoir, 569
My Perfect Neighborhood, 245
My Place, 596, 651
My Prairie Christmas, 606
My Puppy Is Born, 54, 583
My Robot Buddy, 374
My Shadow, 407, 423
"My Shadow," 99
My Side of the Mountain, 10, 27, 433, 473, 526,
    623, 681, 683, 699, 701
"My Sister Is a Sissy," 406
My Son John, 203, 673
My Special Best Words, 112
"My Struggle with Facts," 608
My Visit to the Dinosaurs, 53
"My World" series, 170

Myers, Bernice, 698
Myers, Walter Dean, 20, 24, 57, 58, 59, 120, 425,
    455, 457, 467, 472, 485, 499, 500, 599,
    699
Mysteries of Harris Burdick, The, 210, 215, 714
"Mysterious Cat, The," 439
Mysterious Mr. Ross, The, 502
Mystery of Drear House, The, 502
Mystery of the Cupboard, The, 355
"Myth and Archetype in Science Fiction," 380
Mythology, 325
Mythology of Mexico and Central America, The,
    313
Mythology of North America, The, 313
Mythology of South America, The, 313

Nadelman, Ruth Lynn, 380
Naidoo, Beverley, 58, 120, 124, 489
Nail Soup, 282
Namioka, Lensey, 206, 281, 487, 488, 524
Nana Upstairs, Nana Downstairs, 226, 232
Nancy Drew, 107
"Nancy Drew" series, 18, 32, 491, 703
"Nancy Hanks," 426
Napoli, Donna Jo, 9, 342
Napping House, The, 54, 178, 181, 200, 211, 428,
    637
Narahashi, Keiko, 5, 234
Nargun and the Stars, The, 362
"Narnia" series, The, 57, 342, 370, 624
"Narrative as a Primary Act of the Mind," 9
Nash, Ogden, 400, 405, 423, 432
Natarella, Margaret A., 404
Natchev, Alexi, 201
Nate the Great, 494
Nathaniel Talking, 408
"National Book Award Acceptance Speech," 370
Nativity, The, 322
Natov, Roni, 571, 608
Natural Man, A, 307, 308
"Nature of the Reader's Satisfaction, The," 625
Navajo ABC: A Diné Alphabet Book, 159
Naylor, Phyllis Reynolds, 57, 58, 464, 494, 497,
    569, 570
Near the Window Tree, 407, 430
Neighborhood Odes, 409
Neill, John R., 109
Neitzel, Shirley, 637
Nelson, Theresa, 117, 120, 482
Nelson, Vaunda Micheaux, 57
Nesbit, Edith, 83
Nesbitt, Elizabeth, 126
Ness, Evaline, 54, 111, 278, 282
Nestful of Eggs, A, 606
Nettie's Trip South, 532, 606
"Neuteronomy," 431, 440
Neville, Emily Cheney, 490, 699, 701
New Advocate, The, 224
"New Clothes and Old," 407
New England Primer, The, 87, 92, 115
New Handbook for Storytellers, 660
New Hooked on Books, The, 622
New Illustrated Dinosaur Dictionary, The, 585,
    598
New Kid on the Block, The, 406, 429, 430
"New Look at Old Favorites: 'Charlie and the
    Chocolate Factory', A," 358
New Lottery Book of Birds and Beasts, The, 91,
    115
"New Perspective on Response to Literature, A,"
    61
New Read-Aloud Handbook, The, 33
"New Song for Old Smokey, A," 431
New Teacher, The, 233
"New Vestments, The," 405

New World, 376
New Year's Poems, 421
New York Herald Tribune, 103, 112
New York Times, 39, 402
Newbery, John, 85, 88, 89, 90, 91, 115
Newbery and Caldecott Medal Books: 1956–1965, 252
Newbery and Caldecott Medal Books 1966–1975, 252
Newbery and Caldecott Medal Books: 1976–1985, 33, 252
"Newbery Award Acceptance" speech, 378, 461, 473, 502
Newkirk, Thomas, 645
Newman, Fran, 430
News About Dinosaurs, The, 221, 590
Newsletter on Intellectual Freedom, 123, 341
Newton, Pam, 292
Newton, Robert Peck, 494
Nichols, Grace, 151, 417, 422
Nicholson, William, 104, 116
Nicodemus and the Gang, 112
"Nicodemus" series, The, 112
Nielsen, A. C., 6
Nielsen Media Center Research, 6
"Night, The," 412
Night Becomes Day, 52, 210
Night Before Christmas, The, 98
Night Crossing, 56
Night Ghosts and Hermits: Nocturnal Life on the Seashore, 651
Night Is Like an Animal, The, 10
Night Journey, The, 112, 462
Night Noises, 234
Night of the Gargoyles, 8, 210
Night on Neighborhood Street, 408
Night Swimmers, The, 465, 678
"Night Will Never Stay, The," 110, 401, 407
Nightbirds on Nantucket, 369
Nightingale, The, 341, 344
Nightjohn, 59, 533
Nightmares: Poems to Trouble Your Sleep, 123, 400, 406, 685
Nine Ducks Nine, 162
Nine-In-One Grr! Grr!, 689
Nine O'Clock Lullaby, 54
Ninio, Anat, 12, 186
Nister, Ernest, 97
Nixon, Joan Lowery, 502, 503
No Hickory, No Dickory, No Dock, 151
"No One Heard Him Call," 407
Noah's Ark, 169
"Noah's Ark," 324
Noble, Trinka H., 237, 244
Nobody Asked Me if I Wanted a Baby Sister, 231
Nodelman, Perry, 198, 252
Noisy, 141
Noisy Book, The, 105, 116
Noisy Nora, 53, 218, 230, 243, 430
Noisy Poems, 692
Nolan, Dennis, 315, 345
"Nonfiction, Language Learning, and Language Teaching," 608
Norby series, 374
Norman, Charles, 410
Norman, Howard, 299
North, Sterling, 496
North American Legends, 297, 526
North Star Shining, 110
North to Freedom, 536, 541
Northern Alphabet, A, 158, 217
Norton, Mary, 346, 357, 358, 674
Norvell, George W., 40, 418
Not A Cooper Penny In My House: Poems from the Caribbean, 408

Not So Fast, Songololo, 646
Not-So-Jolly Roger, The, 56, 360
" 'Not to Be Read on Sunday,' Centenary of *Little Women,* 1868–1968," 94
"Notable Trade Books in the Field of Social Studies," 604
Notes for Another Life, 478
Notes from a Different Drummer, 504
Nothing at All, 637
Nothing But the Truth, 49, 120, 122
Nothing Ever Happens on My Block, 218
"Novels of Katherine Paterson: Implications for the Middle School, The," 465
Now Is Your Time! The African-American Struggle for Freedom, 58, 599
Now One Foot, Now the Other, 227, 232
Now We Are Six, 110
Noyes, Alfred, 400, 424
Nuclear Energy: Troubled Past, Uncertain Future, 586
Number the Stars, 5, 10, 58, 430, 431, 455, 516, 540, 605, 607
Numbers, 160
Numbers of Things, 160
Numeroff, Laura Joffe, 677
Nürnberg Stove, The, 93
"Nursery Collection," 141
Nursery Rhyme Peek-a-Book, The, 150, 152, 181
Nursery Rhymes of London Town, 110
Nursery Story Book, The, 269, 280
Nye, Naomi Shihab, 247, 248, 417, 431

"O God Our Help in Ages Past," 91
O'Brien, Robert C., 119, 343, 352, 378, 431, 451, 650, 681, 701, 709
O'Dell, Scott, 5, 30, 43, 528, 530, 626
O'Neill, Cecily, 690
O'Neill, Mary, 425, 426, 428, 435
O'Shell, Marcia, 695
Oberg, Antoinette, 185
Ocean Parade: A Counting Book, 159, 160
"Ode to my Library," 409
"Ode to Senor Leal's Goat," 409
Odyssey, The, 11, 318
Odyssey of Homer Retold, The, 318
Of Nightingales That Weep, 524
Of Quarks, Quasars, and Quirks: Quizzical Poems for the Supersonic Age, 421
Officer Buckle and Gloria, 201
Oh, A-Hunting We Will Go, 142
"Oh, Teddy Bear," 428
Oh, That's Ridiculous!, 421
Oh, the Places You'll Go!, 6
Oh, What a Noisy Farm!, 52
Oh, What Nonsense!, 421
Ohrman, Richard, M., 267
Oink!, 203
Oink Oink, 203
Ol' Paul, the Mighty Logger, 306, 308
Old Black Fly, 158
"Old Dan Tucker," 685
Old Fashioned Girl, An, 99
Old John, 479
Old Lady Who Was Not Afraid of Anything, The, 637
Old MacDonald Had a Farm, 144, 181
"Old Man's Comforts, The," 98
"Old Mother Hubbard," 150
Old Mother Hubbard and Her Dog, 181
"Old Stormalong: The Deep Water Sailor," 308
"Old Tales for Young Tellers," 676
"Old Woman and Her Pig, The," 272, 280

Old Woman and Her Pig and Other Stories, The, 269, 272
"Old Woman in the Shoe, The," 146
Old Yeller, 457, 531
"Olive Street," 430
Oliviero, Jamie, 279, 299, 606
Olmsted, Pat, 138
Olympians, The, 314
"On a Snowy Day," 396
On Cat Mountain, 220, 281, 672
On Market Street, 154, 157
On My Honor, 49, 58, 457, 471, 477, 481, 497, 644
On the Banks of Plum Creek, 531
On the Far Side of the Mountain, 27, 426, 431, 473
On the Frontier with Mr. Audubon, 564
"On the Relation of Analytic Psychology to Poetic Art," 267
On the Road of Stars, 419
On Their Toes: A Russian Ballet School, 597
"On Three Ways of Writing for Children," 8, 380
On to Oregon!, 515, 532
"On Top of Old Smoky," 399
"On Writing for Children," 8
Once a Mouse, 55, 108, 203, 211, 292, 312
Once in a Wood: Ten Tales from Aesop, 310
Once the Hodja, 108
Once the Mullah, 108
Once Upon a Horse: A History of Horses—and How They Shaped Our History, 601
Once Upon a Recipe, 682
Once Upon a Time, 569
Once Upon America books, 514
One at a Time, 394, 398, 401, 404, 411, 424, 428, 430, 440
One Bad Thing About Father, The, 562
One Crow: A Counting Rhyme, 160
One Day in the Tropical Rain Forest, 431, 651
One Duck, Another Duck, 162
One Fall Day, 202, 203, 206
One Fine Day, 272, 290, 311, 637
One Frog Too Many, 169
One Good Horse: A Cowpuncher's Counting Book, 160
One Hundred Is a Family, 161
1 Hunter, 162
One Monday Morning, 181
One Morning in Maine, 53, 233
One Red Rooster, 160
One Sun: A Book of Terse Verse, 693
1, 2, Buckle My Shoe . . . , 88, 146, 159, 440
1, 2, 3, 156, 160
1, 2, 3 to the Zoo, 160
One Was Johnny (Nutshell Library, vol. 3), 162
One White Sail: A Caribbean Counting Book, 160
"One World," 342
Oneal, Zibby, 478
One-Eyed Cat, 471, 625
Onion Tears, 490, 492, 701
"Only Connect," 380
Only Connect: Readings on Children's Literature, 33, 380
Only My Mouth Is Smiling, 478
Only the Names Remain: The Cherokees and the Trail of Tears, 107
Onyefulu, Ifeoma, 121, 159, 162
Ooh La La, Max in Love, 245
Oom Razoom, or Go I Know Not Where, Bring Back I Know Not What, 288
Open Road, The, 351
Opening Moves: Work in Progress in the Study of Children's Language, 12
Operation Grizzly Bear, 586

Opie, Iona, 88, 147, 148, 152, 325
Opie, Peter, 88, 147, 148, 152, 325
Oppenheim, Joanne, 637, 691
Oppenheim, Shulamith Levy, 607
Optic, Oliver, 95, 107
Orbis Pictus, 86, 115
Orchard Book of Nursery Rhymes, The, 147, 153
Ordinary Jack, 493
Orgel, Doris, 316, 317
Origin of the Species, 96
Original Poems for Infant Minds, 98, 115
Orion, the Hunter, 602
Orlev, Uri, 57, 536, 540
Ormai, Stella, 598
Ormerod, Jan, 52, 139, 148, 152, 169, 284, 391,
    414
Ormondroyd, Edward, 364
Orp Goes to the Hoop, 494, 499
Orp the FBI, 494
Orphan Boy, The, 279
Orvis, 374
Osa's Pride, 55, 247, 429, 646, 668, 680
Osborne, Edgar, 92
Osborne, Jo, 682
Osborne, Mary Pope, 56, 307, 308
Other Bells for Us to Ring, 431
Other Side of Dark, The, 502
Other Way to Listen, The, 230, 234, 410, 650
"Otto," 430
Our Davie Pepper, 95
"Our Developing Knowledge of Infant
    Perception and Cognition," 44
Our Granny, 228, 229, 234
Our Home Is the Sea, 247
Our Patchwork Planet, The Story of Plate
    Tectonics, 591
Oustanding Outsides, 603
Out Loud, 397, 403
Out of the Dark, 362
Outlaws of Sherwood Forest, The, 321
Outside Child, The, 463, 467, 503
Outside Over There, 9, 64, 200, 217
"Outstanding Science Trade Books for
    Children," 604
Over in the Meadow, 684
Over in the Meadow: A Traditional Counting
    Rhyme, 142
Over Sea, Under Stone, 370
Over the Garden Wall, 110
"Over the Garden Wall," 407
"Over the River and Through the Woods," 427
Over the Water, 50, 58, 461
Ovid, 314
Owen, 242
Owens, Mary Beth, 155, 159
Owl and the Pussy Cat, The, 423
"Owl and the Pussycat, The," 98, 405
Owl and the Woodpecker, The, 244
Owl Babies, 173
Owl in Love, 347, 356
Owl in the House: A Naturalist's Diary, An, 701,
    704
Owl Moon, 30, 211, 212, 632, 650, 671
Owliver, 242
Owls in the Family, 498
Ox-Cart Man, 31, 54, 215, 218, 222, 632
Oxenbury, Helen, 52, 118, 139, 140, 143, 144,
    152, 157, 160, 175, 236, 243, 269, 280
Oxford Book of Poetry for Children, 399
Oxford Companion to Children's Literature, The,
    125
Oxford Dictionary of Nursery Rhymes, The, 147
Oxford Nursery Rhyme Book, The, 88
Ozzie On His Own, 56, 633

Pablo Picasso, 562
Pablo's Tree, 232
Pacific Crossing, 486
"Paddington Bear" series, 348
"'Paddle,' Said the Swan," 173
Paddle to the Sea, 106, 116
Pagoo, 598
Painted Desert, Green Shade: Essays on
    Contemporary Writers of Fiction for
    Children and Young Adults, 504
Painting Faces, 602
Palin, Michael, 121
Pancakes for Breakfast, 169, 683
Panchatantra stories, 292
"Pandora's Box," 690
Panzer, Nora, 427
Paper Airplane Book, The, 56, 592
Paper Crane, The, 206
Pappas, Christine C., 12, 14, 67, 608, 661
Parish, Peggy, 40, 55, 494
Park, Barbara, 40, 56, 481, 494, 699
Park, Ruth, 62, 363, 365, 488
Parke, Ross D., 48
Parker, Marilyn, 652
Parker, Nancy Winslow, 54, 142, 176, 232, 423,
    590, 601, 606
Parker, Robert Andrew, 307, 417
Parks, Van Dyke, 270, 272, 274, 278
Park's Quest, 11, 472
Parnall, Peter, 210, 230, 234, 300, 410
Parrish, Maxfield, 101
Parson, Alexandra, 704
Pascal, Francis, 500
Pass It On, 417, 422
Pass the Poetry, Please, 442
Pasternak, Boris, 417
"Pasture, The," 411
"Pat a Cake, Pat a Cake," 46
"Pat-a-Cake! Pat-a-Cake!," 142, 146
"Pat-a-cake, pat-a-cake, baker's man," 393
Pat the Bunny, 46, 52, 140
Pat the Puppy, 140
"Patch of Old Snow, A," 415
Patchen, Kenneth, 431
Patchwork Quilt, The, 227, 232, 680
Patchwork Tales, 680
Patent, Dorothy Hinshaw, 596, 631
Paterson, Katherine, 5, 8, 11, 20, 22, 24, 25, 30,
    33, 39, 56, 58, 59, 274, 294, 390, 430,
    431, 454, 459, 460, 461, 463, 464, 465,
    467, 472, 504, 519, 524, 534, 625, 632,
    633, 634, 640, 650, 657, 659, 675, 691,
    693, 699, 707
Patricia Crosses Town, 112
Patron, Susan, 282
"Patterns of Response to Literature: A One-Year
    Study of a Fifth- and Sixth-Grade
    Classroom," 15, 621, 642
Patterson, Bettina, 205
Patterson, Francine, 597, 650
Paul, Ann Whitford, 680
Paul Bunyan, 306, 308
"Paul Bunyan," 308
Paul Klee, 562
"Paul Revere Rides Ahead: Poems Teachers
    Read to Pupils in the Middle Grades,"
    422
Paul Revere's Ride, 400, 418, 423, 424
Paulsen, Gary, 20, 23, 57, 58, 456, 474, 495, 526,
    533, 534, 570, 624, 642, 684, 707
Paxton, Tom, 216, 244, 310
Paz, Octavio, 417
Peaceable Kingdom, A: The Shaker
    ABECEDARIUS, 159

"Peach," 396, 425
Peacock Pie, 109, 110
Peanut Butter and Jelly: A Play Rhyme, 181
"Peanut-Butter Sandwich," 406
Pearce, Philippa, 117, 347, 363, 364, 502
Pearson, Kit, 366, 542
Pearson, Susan, 232
Pearson, Tracey Campbell, 153
"Peas porridge hot/Peas porridge cold," 418
"Pease Porridge Hot," 146
Peck, Beth, 516
Peck, Richard, 376, 504, 570
Peck, Robert Newton, 494
Peck, Sylvia, 347
Pecos Bill, 306, 308
"Pecos Bill," 308
Pedro's Journal, 571
"Pee Wee Scouts" series, 120
Peek, Merle, 142, 179, 181
Peeling the Onion, 417
Peet, Bill, 570
Pelican Chorus, The, 405
Pelle's New Suit, 106, 595
Pelta, Kathy, 586
"Pencils," 412
Penny Whistles, 99
People, 594
People Could Fly, The, 272, 298, 306
People, Yes, The, 411
Peppe, Rodney, 153
Peppe the Lamplighter, 514
Pepper and Salt, 93, 101
Peppermint Pig, The, 496
Perez, N. A., 535, 536
Perkins, Lucy Fitch, 108
Perl, Lila, 526, 587, 603, 683
Perrault, Charles, 88, 89, 115, 210, 218, 266,
    278, 279, 280, 286, 302, 311, 429, 696
Perrault's Fairy Tales, 115
Perrine, Laurence, 390
Persephone, 316
Perseus, 316
Person, Diane Goetz, 608
Pertzoff, Alexander, 532
Pet Show!, 228
Peter, 58, 470
Peter Pan in Kensington Gardens, 103, 109, 116
Peter Parley's Method of Telling About Geography
    to Children, 92
"Peter, Peter, Pumpkin-Eater," 146
"Peter Piper," 146
Peter Rabbit and Friends Cookbook, The, 682
Peter Rabbit's Natural Foods Cookbook, 602
Peter Spier's Rain, 169, 234, 606
Peter the Great, 561
Peter's Chair, 225, 228, 231, 233, 430, 708
Peter's Pockets, 680
Peterkin Papers, The, 97, 116
Peters, David, 584
Petersham, Maud, 105, 106, 148, 152, 322
Petersham, Miska, 105, 106, 148, 152, 322
Peterson, Ralph, 661
Petry, Ann, 525
Petunia, 242, 637
Pfister, Marcus, 121
Phang, Ruth, 680
Phantom Tollbooth, The, 48, 359
Phelps, Ethel Johnston, 276
Philadelphia Adventure, The, 369
Philip, Neil, 290, 314, 415, 426
Phillips, Rita Mitchell, 55
Phoenix Rising, 378
Piaget, Jean, 45, 49
Piaget for Teachers, 45

Picard, Barbara Leonie, 318
"Pickety Fence, The," 8, 394, 404, 411
"Pickwick Portfolio," 121
"Picnic," 430
Picnic, 169
Picture Book Comes of Age, The, 252
"Picture Book History," 545
Picture Book of Benjamin Franklin, A, 562
Picture Book of Christopher Columbus, A, 562
Picture Book of Sojourner Truth, A, 560
Picture Book of Thomas Jefferson, A, 562
Picture Books for Children, 251
Piece of String Is a Wonderful Thing, A, 122
Pied Piper of Hamelin, The, 101, 400
Pied Piper Syndrome, The, 10, 504
Pienkowski, Jan, 322
Pierce, Kathryn Mitchell, 185
Pierce, Tamora, 368
Pig Pig Goes to Camp, 235, 242
Pig Pig Grows Up, 235, 242, 680
Pigeons, 650
Piggy in a Puddle, The, 176, 180
Piggybook, The, 214
Pigs Are Flying!, The, 359
Pigs from A to Z, 203
Pigs Might Fly, 349, 379
Pigs Say Oink, 141
Pilgrims of Plimoth, The, 524
Pilgrim's Progress, The, 87, 115
Pilkey, Dav, 238, 244
Pinballs, The, 459, 465, 496, 621, 632, 634, 678,
    683
Pine, Jonathon, 651
Pink and Say, 58, 249, 250, 535, 606
Pinkerton, Behave!, 237, 244
"Pinkerton" series, 244
Pinkney, Andrea Davis, 219, 483, 485, 486, 560
Pinkney, Brian, 55, 204, 205, 218, 219, 307, 408,
    568, 648, 673
Pinkney, Gloria Jean, 219
Pinkney, Jerry, 120, 219, 227, 232, 305, 307, 410,
    560, 563, 685
Pinkwater, Daniel, 121, 375, 485, 496, 692
Pioneer Twins, The, 108
Piper, Watty, 105, 240
Piping Down the Valleys Wild, 395, 401, 405, 416,
    424, 433
Pippi Goes on Board, 355
Pippi in the South Seas, 355
Pippi Longstocking, 22, 114, 355
Pippi on the Run, 355
Place for Ben, A, 231
Place My Words Are Looking For, The, 59, 414
Planet of Junior Brown, The, 485
Platt, Richard, 580
Playful Slider: The North American River Otter,
    594
Playing, 118, 139
Playing Beatie Bow, 363, 365
Playing with Plasticine, 682
Plotz, Helen, 419
Pluckett, Kirby, 56
Plume, Ilse, 109, 240, 245, 311
Pocahontas, 107, 559
"Poem," 429, 431
"Poem as a Door, The," 412
Poem for Pickle, A, 411, 432
Poem for Rodney, 408
Poem-Making: Ways to Begin Writing Poetry, 442
"Poem of Praise," 397
Poem Stew, 421, 425, 434
Poems Children Will Sit Still For, 413
Poems for Brothers, 420
Poems for Children, 390

Poems for Fathers, 419, 429
Poems for Grandmothers, 420
Poems for Jewish Holidays, 421
Poems for Mothers, 419
Poems for Sisters, 420
Poems for Youth, 110
Poems of A. Nonny Mouse, 421
Poems of Childhood, 99
Poems Selected for Young People, 110
Poems That Sing to You, 417, 425
Poetic Edda, The, 317
Poetry From A to Z: A Guide for Young Writers,
    442
Poetry Troupe, The, 691
Poetry Troupe: An Anthology of Poems to Read
    Aloud, The, 425, 432, 439, 440
Polacco, Patricia, 54, 58, 200, 201, 220, 226,
    227, 232, 233, 249, 250, 535, 606, 680,
    683
Polar Bear, Polar Bear, What Do You Hear?, 175
Polar Express, The, 117, 209, 212, 241, 245, 633
Polette, Nancy, 285, 302
Politi, Leo, 207
Polka Dot Private Eyes series, 501
Pollyanna, 111
Pomerantz, Charlotte, 162, 172, 176, 180, 216,
    247, 409, 698
Pond Year, 229, 230, 234
Pool of Fire, The, 377
Pool Party, The, 486, 487
"Poor," 412
Poor Richard in France, 107, 556
Popcorn Book, The, 683
Poppy, 348
Popular Tales from the North, 93
Porte, Barbara Ann, 55, 120, 482
Porter, A. P., 583
Porter, Connie, 56
Porter, Eleanor H., 111
Portfolio Assessment in the Reading-Writing
    Classroom, 714
Possum, 583
Possum Come A-Knockin', 243
Possum Magic, 243
"Potatoes' Dance, The," 685
Potential of Picturebooks: From Visual Literacy to
    Aesthetic Understanding, The, 212, 251
Potluck, 154, 157
Potter, Beatrix, 5, 14, 50, 53, 91, 103, 116, 222,
    348, 571, 677, 682
Powell, Ransom, 535
Power of Myth, The, 266, 325
Prairie Alphabet, A, 158
Prairie Songs, 19, 57, 519, 532, 606, 690
Prairie Visions: The Life and Times of Solomon
    Butcher, 19, 555, 606
Pratt, Charles, 230
Prayers from the Ark, 425
Predator!, 589
Predicting Growth in Reading Ability . . . , 15
Prehistoric Pinkerton, 237
Prelutsky, Jack, 33, 98, 123, 316, 394, 396, 397,
    400, 404, 406, 414, 425, 426, 430, 431,
    432, 436, 440, 492, 685
Presenting Walter Dean Myers, 504
Pretend You're a Cat, 685
"Pretending to Sleep," 430
Pretty Book of Pictures for Little Masters and
    Misses, A, 91
Pretty Poems for Children Three Feet High, 91
Price, Leontyne, 217, 220
Priceman, Marjorie, 161, 245, 421
Prichard, Mari, 125
"Prickled Pickles Don't Smile," 417

Prince Cinders, 698
Prince Henry, the Navigator, 562
Prince in Waiting, The, 377
Princess and the Curdie, The, 97
Princess and the Frog, The, 277, 279, 284, 311
Princess and the Goblin, The, 97
"Princess and the Pea, The," 92, 343
Princess Furball, 276, 281, 285
Princess Smartypants, 698
Principal's New Clothes, The, 221, 243, 698
Pringle, Laurence, 582, 584, 586, 651
"Prism in the Window," 412
Probst, Robert, 71
Promise to the Sun, A, 303
Propp, Vladimir, 267
Prose Edda, The, 317
Protecting Marie, 461
Proud Rooster and the Fox, 55
Proud Taste for Scarlet and Miniver, A, 517
Provensen, Alice, 30, 117, 152, 159, 208, 248,
    418, 423, 559, 651
Provensen, Martin, 30, 117, 152, 159, 208, 248,
    418, 423, 559, 651
"Prydain Chronicles, The," 51, 57, 341, 343, 371,
    379, 432, 624, 683
Prydain Companion, A Reference Guide to Lloyd
    Alexander's Prydain, The Chronicles, 380
Pryor, Bonnie, 54, 516, 520, 679
Psion, 376
Psychology of Childbirth, The, 44
"Ptarmigan," 411
Publisher's Weekly, 39, 40
Puritan Twins, The, 108
Purves, Alan C., 40, 60, 71
Purvey, John, 321
Purviance, Susan, 695
Pushcart War, The, 346, 357, 700
Puss in Boots, 109, 218, 270, 286, 302, 311
"Puss in Boots," 88, 324, 671
"Pussy Willow," 410
Pyk, Ann, 317
Pyle, Howard, 93, 99, 101, 116, 320, 321
Pyramid, 592
Pyramid of the Sun-Pyramid of the Moon, 682
Python's Party, 55, 244

Quackenbush, Robert, 501
"Quangle Wangle, The," 98
Quangle Wangle's Hat, The, 423
Quattlebaum, Mary, 50, 57, 648, 651
"Queen of Serpents, The," 290
Queen of the Sixth Grade, 500
"Quest," 431
Quest for a King: Searching for the Real King
    Arthur, 320
"Question, The," 408, 428, 691
Question of Trust, A, 45, 455, 497
Questioning: A Path to Critical Thinking, 640
"Questions to Ask a Butterfly," 410
Quiet, Please, 425, 698
Quilt, The, 428
Quilt Story, The, 215
"Quilts," 680

Rabbit Hill, 109, 350
Rabbit Makes a Monkey of Lion, 270, 272, 279,
    303
Rabbit's Escape, The, 295
Rabbit's Judgement, The, 273, 295
Rabble, Starkey, 467, 470, 503
Raboff, Ernest, 562
Rachel Fister's Blister, 54
Rackham, Arthur, 99, 103, 104, 109, 116, 152
Racso and the Rats of NIMH, 351

Raffi, 181
Rag Coat, The, 680
Ragged Dick, 95
Ragged Shadows, 421
"Raggedy Man, The," 99
"Rah, Rah, Peas!," 417
Railroad Book, The, 105, 106
Rain Feet, 52, 139
Rain Forest, 651
Rain Forest Secrets, 651
"Rain, Rain, Go Away," 146
Rain Rain Rivers, 207, 210, 234
Rain Talk, 229, 234
Rainbow Fish, The, 121
Rainbow People, The, 298
"Rainbow Walker," 308
Rainbows are Made: Poems by Carl Sandburg, 402, 411
Raines, Shirley C., 714
Rainy Day, A, 606
Rainy Rainy Saturday, 406
Ralph S. Mouse, 346, 348
Ramayana, The, 318
Ramona and Her Father, 22, 83, 460, 682
Ramona and Her Mother, 460
Ramona Forever, 56, 460, 626, 633, 638
Ramona Quimby, Age 8, 8, 55, 499, 500, 638, 655
"Ramona" series, 460, 492
Ramona the Brave, 54
Ramona the Pest, 460
Ramsay, Susan Hoguet, 153
Ramsey Scallop, The, 522
Rand, Ted, 207, 400, 407, 410, 411, 423, 424
Randall, Dudley, 400
Random House Book of Mother Goose, The, 52, 147, 152
Random House Book of Poetry, The, 396, 397, 414, 416, 429, 431, 432, 436
Ransome, Arthur, 277, 279, 281, 288, 302
Ransome, James, 227, 232, 233
Rappaport, Doreen, 293, 606
Rapunzel, 284
"Rapunzel," 708
Rascal: A Memoir of a Better Era, 496
Raskin, Ellen, 48, 58, 218, 502
Rasmussen, Knud, 111
Rata-Pata-Scata-Fata: A Caribbean Story, 54
Rathman, Peggy, 172, 173, 201
Rats on the Range, 55
Rattigan, Jama Kim, 226, 227, 232
Rattlebang Picnic, The, 216
Rauter, Rose, 396, 425
Raven: A Trickster Tale From the Pacific Northwest, 299, 301
"Raven the Creator," 299
Raven the Trickster, 301
Raven's Light: A Myth from the People of the Northwest Coast, 279, 299, 300, 301, 303
Rawlings, Marjorie Kinnan, 457, 496
Rawlins, Donna, 596
Rawls, Wilson, 40, 498, 634
Ray, Deborah K., 232, 423, 536
Rayevsky, Robert, 310
Raymond, Victoria, 206, 682
Raymond's Best Summer, 55
Rayner, Mary, 243
Read Aloud Handbook, The, 118
Read Aloud Rhymes for the Very Young, 416, 426, 432, 685
Read for the Fun of It: Active Programming with Books for Children, 713
"Read It Again: The Value of Repeated Readings During Storytime," 174

Reader, the Text, the Poem: The Transactional Theory of the Literary Work, The, 60, 640
Reading, 139
"Reading and Writing for Real-World Reasons," 659
Reading Comprehension, Education in 15 Countries, 12, 174
Reading for the Love of It: Best Books for Young Readers, 33, 623
"Reading Journals: Invitations to Participate in Literature," 644
Reading Miscue Inventory, 68
Reading Miscue Inventory: Alternative Procedures, 705
"Reading Preferences," 71
"Reading Preferences of American Indian and Anglo Children for Ethnicity, Gender and Story Setting," 42
"Reading Rainbow" series, 42
Reading Without Nonsense, 14
"Reading-Writing Connection: A One-Year Teacher-as-Researcher Study of Third-Fourth Grade Writers and Their Literary Experiences, The," 697
Real Books for Reading, 185
Real Mother Goose, The, 152
Real Personages of Mother Goose, The, 88
Real Plato Jones, The, 463
Real Thief, The, 350
"Real Thief: Reading Like a Writer, The," 350
Reason for the Pelican, The, 405
Rebecca of Sunnybrook Farm, 111, 116
Recipes for Art and Craft Materials, 602, 672
"Recurrent Themes in Myth and Mythmaking," 267
"Recycled," 431
"Red," 436
Red, Blue, Yellow Shoe, 44, 45, 139
Red Cap, 535
Red Dragonfly on My Shoulder, 206, 402, 425
Red Fairy Book, The, 93
Red Leaf, Yellow Leaf, 166
"Red Riding Hood," 88, 293, 649
Redbird, Duke, 414
Redwall, 351, 352, 351, 633, 686, 695
"Redwall" series, 351
Reed, Sheryl, 434, 438, 442
Reed, W. Maxwell, 106
Reeder, Carolyn, 58, 515, 518, 536, 606, 651, 700
Reef, Catherine, 566
Rees, David, 504
Reflections on a Gift of Watermelon Pickle and Other Modern Verses, 397, 398, 415, 416, 426, 427, 429, 431, 432, 433, 437, 698
Rehage, Kenneth J., 47
Reichman, Henry, 661
Reid, Barbara, 56, 205, 206, 682
Reid, Margarette S., 683
Reisburg, Veg, 682
Reiss, Johanna, 11, 539
Reiss, John J., 160, 165
Relatives Came, The, 55, 226, 232
Releasing the Imagination: Essays on Education, the Arts, and Social Change, 341
Reluctant Dragon, The, 346, 681
Remarkable Adventures of Captain Cook, The, 555
Remarkable Journey of Prince Jen, The, 371, 686
Remkiewicz, Frank, 55
Rentel, Victor, 16
Report Card on the Basal Readers, 122, 625
Rescue: The Story of How Gentiles Saved Jews in the Holocaust, 607

Rescuers, The, 350
"Research Directions: Mediating Content Through Literary Texts," 545
Response to Literature, 64
"Response to Literature," 71
Responses of Adolescents While Reading Four Short Stories, The, 68
Return, The, 491
Return of the Indian, The, 354
Return of the Wolf, 631
Rey, H. A., 105, 116, 242
Reyher, Becky, 7, 272, 289
Reynard, the Fox, 90
Rhee, Nami, 294
"Rhymes, Nursery Rhymes, and Reading in Early Childhood," 146
Rice, Eve, 52, 171, 181, 221, 232, 310, 680
Rice Without Rain, 59, 491
Rich Lizard and Other Poems, 412
Richard, Françoise, 220, 281, 672
Richards, Joan, 590
Richards, Laura, 107, 394
Richard Scarry's Best Mother Goose Ever, 152
Richter, Conrad, 526
Richter, Hans Peter, 11, 114, 686
Riddle and the Rune, The, 372
Riddle-Master of Hed, The, 372
Riddle of the Rosetta Stone: Key to Ancient Egypt, The, 578, 687
"Ride a Cock Horse," 146, 393, 418, 685
Ride a Purple Pelican, 406
Ride into Morning, A, 528
Ridicholas, Nicholas, 405
Ridlon, Marci, 397, 429
Rifles for Waite, 535
Riley, Jocelyn, 478
Riley, Linda Capus, 603
Rimonah of the Flashing Sword, 290, 291
Rinaldi, Ann, 528
"Ring a Ring o' Roses," 146
"Ring Around the Rosie," 88
Ring o' Roses, 152
Ring of Endless Light, A, 59, 482, 709
Ring Out Wild Bells, 421
Ringgold, Faith, 245, 680, 681
"Rip Van Winkle," 92
Rippere, Victoria, 57, 60
"Rise and Fall and Rise of Juvenile Nonfiction, The 1961–1988," 608
Risk 'n Roses, 57, 467, 477
Riskind, Mary, 532, 536
Ritter, Lawrence S., 568
River, The, 474
River Bank: From The Wind in the Willows, The, 351
"River Is a Piece of the Sky, The," 405
River Ran Wild, A, 248, 249, 596, 651
Riverkeeper, 597
Road from Home, The: The Story of an Armenian Girl, 563
"Road Not Taken, The," 411, 431
Road to Camlann, The, 320
Roalf, Peggy, 425
Roar and More, 181
Rob Roy, 95
Roback, Diane, 118, 119
Robart, Rose, 178, 181
Robbins, Ken, 592
Robbins, Ruth, 20, 221, 322
Robert, James, 651
Robin Hood of Sherwood Forest, 321
Robins, The, 90
Robinson, Barbara, 495
Robinson, Gail, 301

Robinson Crusoe, 28, 89, 115, 120, 475, 526
Rockaby Crocodile, 272, 278, 281
Rocking Chair Rebellion, The, 479
Rocking Horse Secret, The, 501
Rockwell, Anne, 52, 53, 157, 170, 269, 270, 272, 280, 310, 606
Rockwell, Harlow, 170, 179, 181, 583, 602
Rockwell, Thomas, 495, 684
Rodanas, Kristina, 292, 299
Rodda, Emily, 359, 488
Rodowsky, Colby F., 477
Roe, Eileen, 224
Rogasky, Barbara, 420
Rogers, Fred, 52
Rogers, Jacqueline, 322
Rogers, Jean, 55
Rogers, Theresa, 71
Rohmer, Harriet, 309, 682
Rojankovsky, Feodor, 105, 142, 152
"Role of Print as a Medium in Our Society, The," 124
Roll of Thunder Hear My Cry, 5, 57, 113, 430, 537
Roll Over! A Counting Song, 142, 181
Roller Skates, 111, 113, 116
Rolling Harvey Down the Hill, 394, 400
"Rookies" series, 498
Roomrimes, 401
Roop, Connie, 571, 600
Roop, Peter, 571, 600
Roosevelt, Theodore, 99
Roosevelt Grady, 112
Rooster Crows, The, 148, 152
"Rooster Who Went to His Uncle's Wedding, The," 272
Root, Barry, 158, 239, 245
Root Cellar, The, 121, 367, 517
Rootabaga Stories, 116
"Rope Rhyme," 394
Rosa Bonheur, 561
Rosa Parks, 563
Rosales, Melodie, 51
Roscoe, William, 98, 115
Rose Blanche, 11, 250, 431, 539, 607
Rose for Pinkerton, A, 237
Rosen, Michael, 53, 143, 144, 296, 299, 685
Rosenberg, Liz, 120, 152
Rosenberg, Susan P., 545
Rosenblatt, Louise M., 60, 71, 605, 608, 640, 688
Roser, Nancy, 71, 174, 661
Roses Sing On New Snow, 57
Rosie and the Rustlers, 217
Rosie the Riveter: Women Working on the Home Front in World War II, 567
Rosie's Walk, 168, 175, 178, 181, 182, 217, 677
Ross, Gayle, 298, 300
Ross, Tony, 270, 282, 699
Rossetti, Christina, 99, 115, 414, 431, 436
Rostkowski, Margaret I., 536, 538
Rosy Cole, She Walks in Beauty, 493
Roth, Dan, 431
Roth, Roger, 375
Roth, Susan, 205
Roth, Susan L., 269, 299, 671, 673, 680
Roth-Hano, Renée, 541
Rotner, Shelley, 594
Rough Faced Girl, The, 278, 299, 301
Round Trip, 210
Rounds, Glen, 144, 178, 181, 270, 272, 285, 302, 306, 308, 606
Rousseau, Henri, 215, 216
Routman, Regie, 641, 661, 714
Rover Boys, The, 107
Roy, Ron, 584, 677

Royal Nap, The, 54
Royston, Angela, 579, 580
R-T, Margaret, and the Rats of NIMH, 351
Rubalcaba, Jill, 279
Rubin, Cynthia, 155, 159
Ruby, 48
Ruby, Lois, 517, 606
Rudman, Marsha K., 504, 545
Ruffins, Reynold, 296
Rufus M., 111, 459
Rum Pum Pum, 181, 281
Rumble Thumble Boom, 181
Rumpelstiltskin, 217, 278, 279, 282, 283, 302, 347
"Rumpelstiltskin," 92, 269
"Runaway, The," 411
Runaway Bunny, The, 53, 105, 172
Runaway Ralph, 348
Runner, The, 463
"Running Away," 430
Rush, Barbara, 290
Ruskin, John, 93
Russ, Lavinia, 94
"Russian Cinderella, The," 288
Russo, Marisabina, 171, 180, 208, 428
Ruth Marini, Dodger Ace, 499
Ruth Marini of the Dodgers, 499
Ryan, Pam Munoz, 161
Ryder, Joanne, 234, 606, 650
Rylant, Cynthia, 18, 19, 24, 25, 54, 55, 58, 112, 182, 184, 210, 212, 226, 232, 251, 409, 430, 466, 494, 569

"S is for Snake," 410
Sable, 497
Sabuda, Robert, 119, 410
Sachar, Louis, 494
Sachs, Marilyn, 455
Sadako, 58, 250, 539
Sadako and the Thousand Paper Cranes, 250, 682
Sad-Faced Boy, 112
"Safety Pin," 397
Sage, Alison, 283
Sail Away, 166, 673
Sailor Who Captured the Sea, The, 217
Saint George and the Dragon, 200, 320, 681
Salisbury, Graham, 515, 519, 542, 543, 607
Sally Ann Thunder Ann Whirlwind Crockett, 308
Salmandastron, 352
Salt: A Russian Tale, 288, 302
Salt Hands, 650
Sam, 172
Sam, Bangs, and Moonshine, 54
Sam Johnson and the Blue Ribbon Quilt, 680
Sam Who Never Forgets, 52, 181
Sami and the Time of the Troubles, 207, 246
San Souci, Daniel, 267, 288
San Souci, Robert D., 204, 219, 267, 276, 278, 279, 281, 299, 302, 305, 306, 307, 308, 319, 606
Sancha, Sheila, 65
"Sand Dollar," 412
Sandburg, Carl, 110, 116, 391, 402, 410, 416, 423, 424, 425, 426, 564
Sanders, Eve, 159
Sanders, Marilyn, 159
Sanders, Scott R., 685
Sandra Day O'Connor: Justice for All, 563
Sanfield, Steve, 290, 306, 308
Sans Souci, Robert, 560, 561
Santayama, George, 516
Sarah, Plain and Tall, 23, 24, 42, 55, 112, 117, 431, 532, 606, 633, 691, 709
Sarah Bishop, 528
Sarah Crewe, 95, 99

"Sarah Cynthia Sylvia Stout Who Would Not Take the Garbage Out," 400
Sarah Morton's Day: A Day in the Life of a Pilgrim Girl, 585
Sarett, Lew, 440
"Satellite, Satellite," 412, 430
Sattler, Helen Roney, 582, 585, 591, 648, 650, 672
Saturday Review, The, 405
Saturdays, The, 111
Saturnalia, 59, 526, 527, 625
Sauer, Julia, 347, 363
Saunders, Susan, 563
Saving Our Wildlife, 650
Saving the Peregrine Falcon, 650
Sawyer, Ruth, 111, 116, 269
Say, Allen, 207, 211, 233, 234, 248, 430, 492, 554
Say Goodnight, 139
Say It!, 14, 197, 198
"*Say It!* Over and Over," 197
Sayers, Frances Clarke, 6
Saying Goodbye to Grandma, 480
Scary Stories to Tell in the Dark, 657
Scarry, Richard, 152
Schaeffer, Cornelia, 110
Schaffer, Amanda, 417
Scheer, George, 570
Schertle, Alice, 415, 417
Schick, Eleanor, 159
Schick, Lucy, 159
Schindler, S. D., 235
Schisse, Lillian, 570
Schlager, Norma Marian, 43
Schlein, Miriam, 431, 490, 588, 648, 650
Schmidt, Gary D., 325
Schneiper, Claudia, 623
Schnur, Steven, 58
Schoenherr, John, 30, 211, 212
Scholt, Grayce, 125
School, 169
School Bus, 166, 181
School Library Journal, 582, 655
"Schoolchild's Pocket Book," 148
Schoolcraft, Henry Rowe, 303
Schroeder, Alan, 272, 275, 276
Schroeder, Virginia C., 441
Schur, Maxine R., 219
Schwarcz, Chava, 252
Schwarcz, Joseph H., 252
Schwartz, Alvin, 48, 657
Schwartz, Amy, 229, 233
Schwartz, Howard, 290
Science Book of Weather, The, 580, 598, 606
Science Books and Films, 582
Science Experiments You Can Eat, 599
Scientific American, 608
Scieszka, Jon, 46, 56, 59, 120, 236, 237, 243, 360, 429, 585, 586, 633, 696, 698
Scioscia, Mary, 554
Scorpions, 20, 58, 425, 455, 467, 472
Scotch Twins, The, 108
Scott, Ann Herbert, 53, 172
Scott, Sally, 283, 288
Scott, Sir Walter, 95
Scott, Steve, 403
Scottish Folk-Tales and Legends, 278, 282
Scrambled Eggs Super!, 216
Scribner's Monthly Magazine, 101
Scroobious Pip, The, 423
"Sea Fever," 401
"Sea Gull," 440
Sea Is Calling Me, The, 420

Sea King: Sir Francis Drake and His Times, The, 555, 566
Sea of Gold, 108
Sea Otter Rescue: The Aftermath of an Oil Spill, 651
Sea Shapes, 165
Sea Songs, 412
Seal Child, 347
Seal Mother, The, 277, 283, 347, 639
Seal Oil Lamp, The, 299, 301, 631
Seale, Doris, 224
Search for Delicious, The, 367
"Search for Multiculturalism in Children's Books, The," 123
Searching for Dragons, 368
Searching for Shona, 542
Seascapes, 425
Seashore, 139
Seashore Book, The, 105
Season Sewn, The, 680
"Sebastian Barth" series, 120, 501
Sebesta, Sam, 71
Sebestyen, Ouida, 538
Second Mrs. Giaconda, The, 523
Second Picture Book, The, 106
"Secret Door," 413
Secret Garden, The, 28, 95, 111, 112, 116, 120
Secret of NIMH, The, 119
Secret of the Andes, 30
Secret of the Indian, The, 354
"Secret Place," 430
Secret Places, 426, 430
Secret Soldier: The Story of Deborah Sampson, The, 56, 563
"Secretary Bird," 415
Secrets of a Wildlife Watcher, 433
See How They Grow series, 579
Seed and the Vision: On the Writing and Appreciation of Children's, The, 33
Seeds: Pop Stick Glide, 593
Seeger, Elizabeth, 318
"Seeing Poem, A," 403
Seeing Stick, The, 345
Seeing Things, 403, 425
Segel, Elizabeth, 41, 545, 571
Seguin, Clare, 123
Selden, George, 350
"Selective Forgetfulness: Christopher Columbus Reconsidered," 562, 571
Selfish Giant, The, 345
Self-Portrait: Trina Schart Hyman, 569, 570
Selkie Girl, The, 277, 279, 282, 302, 347, 361
Selsam, Millicent E., 583, 584, 586, 598, 631
Selznick, Brian, 240, 245
Sendak, Maurice, 5, 9, 11, 30, 31, 33, 54, 64, 82, 83, 104, 113, 117, 118, 149, 152, 153, 177, 181, 182, 199, 200, 207, 208, 213, 216, 217, 218, 242, 283, 343, 659, 677, 683, 685, 686
Sending of Dragons, A, 372
Sense of Wonder, The, 230
Sequoyah's Gift: A Portrait of the Cherokee Leader, 567
Serfozo, Mary, 229, 234
Serious Science, 494
Serpent's Children, The, 537
Service, Robert W., 424
Seth of the Lion People, 520
Seton, Ernest Thompson, 116
"Setting Up An In-School Publishing Process," 645
Seuss, Dr. (Theodor S. Geisel), 6, 31, 105, 116, 117, 118, 126, 182, 216, 242, 651
Seven Blind Mice, 312
Seven Candles for Kwanzaa, 219

Seven Chinese Brothers, The, 279, 281, 293
Seven Days of Creation, The, 322
Seven Little Sisters Who Live on the Big Round Ball That Floats in the Air, 115
Seven Ravens, The, 211, 273, 276, 279, 284
Seventeen Against the Dealer, 463
Seven-Day Magic, 360
Sewall, Marcia, 219, 480, 524, 526
Sewell, Anna, 96
Sewing Quilts, 680
Seymour, Tres, 209
Shabanu: Daughter of the Wind, 59, 456, 491
Shades of Gray, 58, 515, 518, 536, 606, 700
Shadow, 205, 220
Shadow and Substance: Afro-American Experience in Contemporary Children's Fiction, 483, 504
Shadow Children, The, 58
Shadow Play, 598
Shadows and Reflections, 198
Shaka, King of the Zulus, 545, 561, 669
Shaker Lane, 248, 651
Shakespeare, William, 5, 85, 88, 92, 99, 416
Shannon, David, 279
Shannon, George, 209, 291, 301
Shannon, Monica, 43
Shannon, Patrick, 625
Shapes and Things, 165
Shapes, Shapes, Shapes, 165
Sharmat, Marjorie Wiseman, 494
Sharp, Margery, 350
Sharpe, Stella, 112
Sharpe, Susan, 648, 651
Shaw, Charles G., 637
Shaw, Nancy, 180
She Come Bringing Me That Little Baby Girl, 225, 231, 430
She Flew No Flags, 541
Sheep in a Jeep, 180
Shelby, Anne, 17, 53, 154, 157, 209
Sheldon, Dyan, 429, 650
Shell, 674
"Shell, The," 424
Shelley, Percy B., 99, 416
Shepard, Ernest H., 109, 116, 346, 407
Shephard, Esther, 308
Sheppard, Jeff, 52, 181
Sherlock, Philip M., 108, 279
Sherman, Josepha, 288
Sherrill, Anne, 70
Sherwood, Mrs. Martha, 93
Shetterly, Robert, 279, 303
Shetterly, Susan Hand, 299, 301
Shiloh, 58, 497
Shimin, Symeon, 172
Shining Company, The, 521
Shin's Tricycle, 539
Ship, 592, 596
Shiva: An Adventure of the Ice Age, 520
Shoes From Grandpa, 46, 178
Shoes Shoes Shoes, 590
Shooting of Dan McGrew, The, 424
Short, Kathy Gnagey, 185
"Short Talk on Poetry," 391
"Shoulder the Sky," 518, 545
Showers, Paul, 588, 650
Shrek!, 216, 243
Shreve, Susan, 499
"Shrewd Todie and Lyzer, and Mizer," 279
Shulevitz, Uri, 105, 181, 200, 207, 210, 211, 234, 288, 290, 430, 633, 650, 651, 685
Shute, Linda, 272, 275, 279, 294, 303, 311
Shy Charles, 230, 243
Sian-Tek, Lim, 108

Sibley, Brian, 370
"Sick," 400
Sick in Bed, 170
Side by Side, 416
"Sidewalk Racer, The," 398, 402, 415
Sidjakov, Nicholas, 221
Sidney, Margaret (pseudonym of Harriet Lathrop), 95
Sidney Rella and the Glass Sneaker, 696, 698
Siebert, Diane, 397, 424, 431, 650
Siegal, Aranka, 541
Sierra, 397, 424, 650
Sierra, Judy, 219, 237, 243, 673
Sign of the Beaver, The, 27, 57, 302, 431, 516, 525, 526, 527, 536, 648, 655
Sign of the Chrysanthemum, The, 524
Sills, Leslie, 567
"Silver," 110, 394
Silver Branch, The, 521
Silver Cow: A Welsh Tale, The, 283
Silver on the Tree, 371
Silver Pencil, The, 457
Silver Woven in My Hair, 342
Silverman, Erica, 49, 50, 235
Silverstein, Shel, 39, 42, 55, 62, 98, 117, 118, 400, 406, 414, 421, 425, 429, 430, 431, 492
Silvey, Anita, 126
Simmie, Lois, 414
Simmons, John S., 361, 661
Simon, Norma, 207
Simon, Seymour, 56, 501, 582, 589, 592, 598, 600, 602, 604, 606, 703
Simont, Marc, 105, 119, 218, 345, 411
Sims, Rudine (Bishop), 60, 483, 504
"Sinbad the Sailor," 89
Sinclair, Patti, 648
Sing a Song of Popcorn, 55, 393, 394, 400, 401, 404, 405, 410, 413, 416, 428, 429, 431
Sing a Song of Sixpence, 100, 115, 153
"Sing a Song of Sixpence," 146, 150
Sing Down the Moon, 530
Sing-Song, 99, 115
Sing to the Sun, 408, 409
Singer, Isaac Bashevis, 8, 271, 272, 274, 279, 289, 290
Singer, Marilyn, 8, 54, 410
Singing America, 417, 426
Singing Green: New and Selected Poems for All Seasons, The, 412
Sip of Aesop, A, 310, 312
Sir Gawain and the Green Knight, 320
"Sir Gawain and the Green Knight," 319
Sir Gawain and the Loathly Lady, 320
Sis, Peter, 161, 360, 368, 406, 558
Sister, 484
Sister Shako and Kolo the Goat, 491
Sitting at the Feet of the Past: Retelling the North American Folktale for Children, 325
Sitting in My Box, 181
Sitti's Secret, 247, 248
Skateboard Tough, 493
Sketch Book, 92
Skinnybones, 40, 56, 494, 699
Skip to My Lou, 142, 181, 684
"Skipper," 429
Skira-Venturi, Rosabianca, 562
Skurzynski, Gloria, 376, 538, 582
"Sky Bright Axe," 308
Sky Dogs, 298, 299
Sky Full of Poems, 391
Sky Is Falling, The, 5, 42
Sky Is Full of Song, The, 420, 430
Sky Songs, 412
Sky Tree, 208, 587

Skylark, 532
Slake's Limbo, 474
Slapin, Beverly, 224
Slave Dancer, The, 107, 534
Slavik, Christy Richards, 465
Sleator, William, 374, 376, 431
Sleep Out, 212, 430
Sleeping, 139
"Sleeping Beauty," 88, 286, 324, 633
Sleeping Beauty, The, 273, 283, 302
Sleeping Ugly, 696, 698
Slepian, Jan, 57, 467, 471, 476, 477
Sloane, William, 86
Slobodkin, Louis, 105, 117, 119
Slobodkina, Esphyr, 141
Slopes of War, The, 535, 536
Slote, Alfred, 374, 482, 499
Slote, Teri, 299, 303
"Slue-Foot Sue and Pecos Bill," 308
Slumps, Grunts and Snickerdoodles: What Colonial America Ate and Why, 526, 683
"Small Discovery, A," 429
Small Green Snake, 52, 179, 181, 230, 673
Small Poems, 401
"Small Poems" books, 397
Small, David, 207
Small, Terry, 424
Smedley, Constance, 108
Smith, Doris Buchanan, 63, 480
Smith, E. Boyd, 105, 116
Smith, Elizabeth, 392
Smith, Elva S., 85, 126
Smith, Frank, 14, 16, 185, 692
Smith, Hugh, 416
Smith, Janice Lee, 494
Smith, Jessie Wilcox, 94, 101
Smith, Lane, 236, 360, 586
Smith, Robert, 56
Smith, Roland, 651
Smith, Sherwood, 368
Smith, William Jay, 401, 405, 418, 435
Smoky Night, 30, 214
Snakey Riddles, 64
"Sneepies, The," 406
"Sneezles," 110
"Sneezy-Snoozer, The," 406
Sneve, Virginia Driving Hawk, 417, 422
Snopp on the Sidewalk and Other Poems, The, 406, 440
Snow, Catherine E., 12, 186
Snow on Snow on Snow, 176, 177
Snow Queen, The, 344
Snow Toward Evening, 420
"Snow Toward Evening," 415
Snow Treasure, 517, 540
Snow White, 201, 272, 278, 279, 311
"Snow White," 92, 269, 291, 689
Snow White and the Seven Dwarfs, 283, 302
"Snow White and the Seven Dwarfs," 271
Snow White in New York, 698
"Snowfall," 397, 412
Snowman, The, 54, 118, 169, 216
Snowy Day, The, 53, 112, 117, 204, 205, 221, 228, 233, 708
"Snowy Morning," 410
Snyder, Diane, 271, 272, 277, 279, 294, 303
Snyder, Zilpha Keatley, 57, 58, 368, 468, 494, 680, 699, 701
So Far From the Bamboo Grove, 543, 607
So Much, 140
Soap Bubble Magic, 598
Soap Soup and Other Verses, 408
Sobin, Dan I., 48
Sobol, Donald, 501

Social Education, 582
Sod Houses on the Prairie, 606
Sogabe, Aki, 206
Sojourner Truth: Ain't I a Woman?, 565
Soldier and Tsar in the Forest: A Russian Tale, 288
Solitary Blue, A, 463
"Solitude," 407
Solomon Grundy, 153
Soman, David, 231
Some of the Kinder Planets, 47
Somebody and the Three Blairs, 698
Someday, 694
Something BIG Has Been Here, 406
Something from Nothing, 272, 290
Something New Begins, 397, 410, 428, 429, 430, 431, 436
Something Queer series, 501
Something Sleeping in the Hall, 408
Something Special for Me, 228, 233
Something Terrible Happened, 120, 482
Song I Sang to You: A Selection of Poems, A, 412, 429
Song of el Coqui and Other Tales of Puerto Rico, The, 307
Song of Stars: An Asian Legend, A, 272
Song of the Gargoyle, 368
Song of the Swallows, 207
"Song of the Train," 404, 411, 425, 440
Song of the Trees, 538
Songs from Mother Goose, 145
Songs from the Nursery Collected by the Most Renowned, 88
Songs of Childhood, 110, 116
Songs of Innocence, 91, 115, 401
"Sonic Boom," 415
Sootface: An Ojibwa Cinderella, 267, 281
Sophie and Lou, 235, 242
Sostarich, Judith, 12, 138
Soter, Anna O., 71
Soto, Gary, 55, 58, 117, 214, 409, 486, 487, 492
Soul Looks Back in Wonder, 417, 418, 422
Sound and Sense: An Introduction to Poetry, 390
"Sound Bytes, Hamburgers and Billy Joel: Celebrating the Year of the Lifetime Reader," 652
Sound of Chariots, A, 482, 625
Sound the Jubilee, 534
Sounder, 430, 518, 538
Soup, 494
Soup Stone, The, 282, 304, 347
"Southbound on the Freeway," 431
Southey, Robert, 92, 98, 423
Southhall, Ivan, 488
Space Songs, 412
"Spaghetti," 425, 429
Sparrow Bush, The, 393
Speare, Elizabeth George, 27, 30, 57, 301, 431, 457, 516, 520, 525, 526, 527, 530, 536
Speed, Toby, 239, 245
Speidel, Sandra, 231
Sperling, Jean, 690
Sperry, Armstrong, 27, 473
"Spider and the Fly, The," 98
Spier, Peter, 141, 143, 153, 169, 234, 594, 606, 684, 704
Spin a Soft Black Song: Poems for Children, 408
Spinelli, Jerry, 58, 70, 117, 430, 457, 472
Spirals, Curves, Fanshapes, and Lines, 53, 165
Spirin, Gennady, 283, 288, 289
Spirit Child: A Story of the Nativity, 322
Spiritual Milk for Boston Babes, 86, 115
Splash, 161, 163, 164
Splash, Splash, 52, 181
Splish Splash, 403, 425, 437

Spot Bakes a Cake, 140
Spot Goes to School, 140
Spotted Eagle and the Black Crow: A Lakota Legend, 299
Spring, 579
"Spring," 427
Springer, Harriett, 621
Spying Heart: More Thoughts on Reading and Writing Books for Children, The, 504
Spyri, Johanna, 95, 111, 116
"Squeeze Is On, The," 118
Squire, James R., 10, 64, 68
"Squirrels in My Notebook," 426
St. George and the Dragon, 347
St. James, Synthia, 20, 177
St. Nicholas Magazine, 99, 101, 115
Stafford, Kim, 7, 207
Stafford, William, 207, 414, 673
Staines, Bill, 651
Stamm, Claus, 303
Stamp Collecting, 57
"Stand Back," Said the Elephant, "I'm Going to Sneeze!", 705
Stand Shining, The, 111
Stanley, Diane, 56, 289, 545, 554, 560, 669
Stanley, Fay, 561
Stanley, Henry Bear's Friend, 235, 242
Stanley, Jerry, 601, 607, 680
Stanley and Rhoda, 230, 243
Stanovich, Keith E., 15
Staples, Suzanne Fisher, 59, 456, 491
Star Boy, 217, 299, 303
"Star Boy," 299
Star Fisher, The, 537
Star Maiden, The, 299
Starbird, Kaye, 432
Stars for Sam, 106
Star-Spangled Banner, The, 684
Stars Tonight, 110
Start with a Story: Literature and Learning in Your Classroom, 714
Starting from Home: A Writer's Beginnings, 570
"Statements of Concern About Library/Media Center Resources," 658
Stateswoman to the World: A Story About Eleanor Roosevelt, 556
Staying Nine, 430, 470
Steadfast Tin Soldier, The, 343, 344, 353
Steal Away Home, 517, 606
"Steam Shovel," 397
"Steel Band Jump Up," 417
Steele, William O., 514
"Steelmaker," 308
Steichen Martin, Mary, 106
Steichen, Edward, 106, 107
Steig, William, 11, 30, 49, 54, 216, 220, 222, 243, 312, 348, 350, 633, 641, 656, 675, 691, 692, 699, 700, 709
Stein, Nancy L., 59
Stein, Sara Bonnett, 583
Steinfirst, Susan, 126
Stephens, Diane, 661
Stephens, James, 397, 414
Stepping on the Cracks, 515
Steptoe, John, 52, 55, 112, 113, 117, 139, 210, 225, 231, 233, 279, 281, 295, 296, 297, 299, 303, 311, 483, 633, 668
Sterling, Dorothy, 112
Steven Caney's Toy Book, 646
Stevens, Carla, 55, 532, 686
Stevens, Cat, 685
Stevens, Janet, 54, 153, 423, 595, 597, 704
Stevenson, James, 197, 216, 226, 232, 238, 255, 428, 570

Stevenson, Robert Lewis, 17, 28, 95, 99, 116, 393, 401, 406, 407, 413, 416, 423, 518
Stevie, 55, 117, 210, 233
Stewart, Sarah, 207
Stewig, John Warren, 282, 287, 311, 347
Sticky Beak, 476
Still as a Star: A Book of Nighttime Poems, 419
Stine, R. L., 108, 118
Stinky Cheese Man and Other Fairly Stupid Tales, The, 59, 236, 237, 633, 696, 698
Stobbs, William, 269
Stock, Catherine, 234, 246
Stockton, Frank, 99
Stolen Lake, The, 369
Stolz, Mary, 120, 226, 232, 467, 523, 651
Stone Fox, 8, 56, 460, 498
Stone Soup, 108, 277, 279, 282, 287, 302, 311, 342, 347, 689, 699
"Stone Soup," 699
Stonecutter, The, 277, 279, 292
"Stonecutter, The," 294
Stone-Faced Boy, The, 22, 430, 460
Stonewalkers, The, 502
Stonewall, 565
Stonewords, 362
"Stop, Go," 685
Stopping by Woods on a Snowy Evening, 418, 422, 424
"Stopping by Woods on a Snowy Evening," 394, 413
Stories and Readers: New Perspectives on Literature in the Elementary School, 642
Stories from the Bible, 321
Stories in the Classroom, 660
Stories Julian Tells, The, 54, 429, 493
Stories to Grow On, 643
"Stories to Solve," 291
Stories to Solve: Folktales from Around the World, 279
Storm, The, 606
Storm in the Night, 226, 232
"Stormalong," 308
Storms, 604, 606
Story, A Story, A, 109, 275, 295, 296, 303, 311, 668
Story About Ping, The, 105
Story Book of Foods from the Field, The, 106
Story Book of Things We Use, The, 106
Story Book of Things We Wear, The, 106
Story Book of Wheels, The, 106
Story of a Bad Boy, The, 95
Story of a Puppet, The, 97
Story of Babar, The, 242
Story of Birth, The, 55
Story of Dr. Dolittle, The, 109
Story of Ferdinand, The, 116, 210
Story of Johnny Appleseed, The, 562
Story of Jumping Mouse: A Native American Legend, The, 279, 299, 311
Story of King Arthur and His Knights, The, 101, 320
Story of Light, The, 269, 299
Story of Lightning and Thunder, The, 295
Story of Mankind, The, 107, 601
Story of Rosie Dock, The, 205, 651, 671
Story of the Milky Way, The, 300
Story of the Three Wise Kings, The, 323
Story of the Treasure Seekers, The, 83
Story of Wali Dad, The, 292
Story Stretchers, 714
"Story Time" series, 42
"Storyteller," 408
Storyteller's Story, A, 569

"Storyteller's Voice: Reflections on the Rewriting of Uncle Remus, The," 275
Stotan!, 499
Stoutenberg, Adrien, 307, 308
Stranded, 496
Stranger, The, 241, 245
Stranger Came Ashore, A, 10, 347, 361, 632, 639, 677
Stratemeyer, Edward, 107
Stratemeyer, Harriet, 107
Stratemeyer Pseudonyms and Series Books, 126
Strawberry Girl, 111
Street Music: City Poems, 409
Strega Nona, 54, 277, 281, 311, 429, 654
Strickland, Dorothy S., 185, 186, 420
Strickland, Michael R., 415, 420, 425
Strider, 63, 464, 626, 701
String, 578
String in the Harp, A, 365
Stringbean's Trip to the Shining Sea, 111, 117, 430, 699, 701
"Strong Black Girls: A Ten Year Old Responds to Fiction About Afro-Americans," 60
Strugnell, Ann, 297, 458
Struwwelpeter ("Shock-Headed Peter"), 98, 115
Stuart Little, 349
Stubbs, G. T., 33, 380
Students' Right to Know, The, 658
"Study of Cohesion Elements on Three Modes of Discourse," 16
"Study of the Reading Behavior of Sixth Graders, A," 12, 138
"Stupendous Pincushion, A," 405
Stupids Die, The, 238, 244
Stupids Have a Ball, The, 55, 238, 244
Stupids Step Out, The, 238, 244
Sturluson, Snorri, 317
Suddenly!, 174, 176, 178, 677
Suetake, Kinihiro, 402, 425
"Sugar Plum Tree, The," 99
Suhor, Charles, 124
Sukey and the Mermaid, 204, 219, 306
Sullivan, Charles, 425
Sullivan, George, 568
Sullivan, Howard J., 42
Sulzby, Elizabeth, 186
Summer, 54, 579
Summer Birds, The, 360
Summer of Fire: Yellowstone, 651
Summer of My German Soldier, The, 542
Summer of the Swans, The, 477, 621, 678
Summer on Wheels, 486
Summer to Die, A, 481
Summoned by Books, 6
Sun Horse, Moon Horse, 521
Sundiata: Lion King of Mali, 206
Sunflakes, 416
Sunken Treasure, 55
Sunnybank Stories: My Teacher's Gem, 82
"Sunrise," 685
Sunrises and Songs, Reading and Writing Poetry in an Elementary Classroom, 434, 438, 442
"Sunset," 411
Sunshine, 52, 169
Superfudge, 495
Surprise Party, The, 683
Surprises, 419
"Survey of the Adolescent Poetry Preferences of Seventh-, Eighth-, and Ninth-Graders, A," 404
Sussman, Susan, 651
Sutcliff, Rosemary, 319, 320, 515, 521, 524, 536

Sutherland, Zena, 33, 147, 153, 608
Swain, Gwenyth, 602
Swan Lake, 64, 199
Swamp Angel, 120, 198, 199, 215, 217, 307
Swann, Brian, 56
Swartz, Larry, 714
Swede, George, 414
Sweet, Melissa, 142, 143
Sweet Clara and the Freedom Quilt, 680
"Sweet Valley High" series, 32, 500
"Sweet Valley Twins" series, 120, 500
Sweet Whispers, Brother Rush, 363
Sweetest Fig, The, 241, 243
Swenson, May, 427, 431
Swift, Hildegarde Hoyt, 110
Swift, Jonathon, 89, 115
Swiftly Tilting Planet, A, 10, 59, 343, 376, 377
Swimmy, 672
"Swing, The," 99, 393, 401, 407, 414
"Swing Me, Swing Me," 411
"Swing Song, A," 685
Swiss Family Robinson, The, 95
Sword and the Circle, The, 319
Sword in the Stone, The, 319
Sword in the Tree, The, 521
Sword of the Spirits, The, 377
Sylvester and the Magic Pebble, 30, 54, 243, 633, 656

Table Where Rich People Sit, The, 694
Table, the Donkey, and the Stick, The, 281
Tafuri, Nancy, 52, 141, 168, 172, 173, 180, 218, 409
Tail Feathers From Mother Goose, 147, 152
Tail, Toes, Eyes, Ears, Nose, 180
Tailypo, The, 8
Take a Walk in Their Shoes, 568
Take Wing, 476
Taking Sides, 486
Talbott, Hudson, 319
Tale of a Bullfrog, The, 107
Tale of Aladdin and the Wonderful Lamp, The, 290
Tale of Custard The Dragon, The, 400, 405
Tale of Peter Rabbit, The, 5, 14, 50, 53, 103, 116, 118, 222, 655, 677
Tale of Rabbit and Coyote, The, 279, 311
"Tale of Sir Gareth of Orkney, The," 320
Tale of the Mandarin Ducks, The, 294
Tale of the Whitefoot Mouse, The, 107
Talent Is Not Enough, A, 342, 475, 504, 518, 545
Tales from Gold Mountain, 298
Tales from Grimm, 274
Tales from Moominvalley, 357
Tales from Silver Lands, 108, 309
Tales from Timbuktu, 108
Tales Mummies Tell, 578
Tales of a Chinese Grandmother, 108, 274
Tales of a Fourth Grade Nothing, 495
Tales of Peter Parley About America, 92
Tales of the Genii, 89
Tales of the Greek Heroes, The, 317
Tales of Uncle Remus: The Adventures of Brer Rabbit, The, 270, 275
"Talk to Teachers," 455
Talking About Books: Creating Literate Communities, 185
Talking Earth, The, 488, 492, 526, 648, 651, 674
Talking Eggs, The, 278, 279, 281, 305, 606
Talking Like the Rain, 414, 416
"Talking Our Way to Literacy in the Classroom Community," 642
Talking Stone, The, 526
Talking to Dragons, 367
Talking with Artists, 568

Tall Book of Mother Goose, The, 152
"Tam Lin," 283, 399
Tam Lin, 271, 272, 276, 279, 282, 302, 311, 347
Tamarindo Puppy and Other Poems, The, 409
"Tamlane," 282
Tanglewood Tales, 93
Tapahonso, Luci, 159
Tar Beach, 245, 680, 681
Taran Wanderer, 371
Tarcov, Edith H., 429
Tarot Says Beware, 493
Taste of Blackberries, A, 63, 480
Taste of Salt, 59, 124, 455, 489
Tattercoats, 278, 280, 281, 302
Tatterhood and the Hobgoblins, 302
Tattie's River Journey, 215
Taxi Taxi, 225, 226, 231
Taylor, Ann, 98, 115
Taylor, Denny, 185, 186
Taylor, Edgar, 92, 283
Taylor, Jane, 98, 115
Taylor, Mildred, 5, 11, 57, 113, 430, 492, 537, 538
Taylor, Sidney, 111, 459, 496
Taylor, Theodore, 542
Teacher's Introduction to Reader-Response Theories, A, 59
Teaching Multicultural Literature, 504
Teale, William H., 185, 186, 608
Teamates series, 499
Teasdale, Sara, 110
Teeny Tiny, 180
"Teevee," 411
Tehanu: The Last Book of Earthsea, 373
"Tell Me," 395
Tell Me Story, Mama, 225, 231
Teller of Tales, 698
Telling Line, The, 214, 252
Telling of the Tales: Five Stories, A, 307, 308
Temple, Charles, 642
Temple, Frances, 59, 124, 455, 489, 490, 522, 607
Ten Black Dots, 161
"Ten Fat Sausages . . . ," 141
Ten, Nine, Eight, 53, 160, 172
Tenniel, John, 96, 115
Tennyson, Alfred Lord, 99, 395
Tenth Good Thing About Barney, The, 233, 429
Terban, Marvin, 693
Terrapin's Pot of Sense, The, 108
Terrible Trins, The, 348
Terrific Tails, 581
Terris, Daniel, 565
Terry, Ann, 403, 405, 418, 422
Tessmer, K. M., 40
Testa, Fulvio, 310
Thank You, Jackie Robinson, 498
Thanksgiving Poems, 421
Thanksgiving Story, The, 524
That Dreadful Day, 244
That Terrible Halloween Night, 216, 238, 244
Thaxter Eton, Anne, 126
Thayer, Ernest, 423
Then Again, Maybe I Won't, 469
Theories of Myth and the Folklorist, 267
"There is no frigate like a book," 413
There Was a Place and Other Poems, 392, 412, 430, 431
"There's a Hole in the Bottom of the Sea," 142
There's a Hole in the Bucket, 684
There's a Nightmare in My Closet, 245, 428
These Happy Golden Years, 531
These Small Stones, 425
Theseus and the Minotaur, 316

They Dance in the Sky, 298, 299
They Really Like Me!, 172
Thidwick the Big-Hearted Moose, 242
Thief of Hearts, 487
Thiele, Colin, 488
Thimble Summer, 111
Thin Grin Cat, The, 405
Things to Play With, 52
Think of an Eel, 593
Thinking and Learning Together, 185
Thirteen Clocks, The, 345
Thirteen Ways to Sink a Sub, 499
This Delicious Day, 416
This House Is Made of Mud, 224
This Is the Bear, 181
This Is the Hat, 181
"This Little Pig Went to Market," 5, 103, 146
This Old Man, 181
This Same Sky: A Collection of Poems From Around the World, 417
This Star Shall Abide, 376
This Time, Tempe Wick?, 528
Thomas, Dylan, 414
Thomas, Isaiah, 88, 115
Thomas, Jane Resh, 480, 497
Thomas, Katherine Elwes, 88
Thomas, Patricia, 706
Thomas Jefferson: A Picture Book Biography, 559
Thompson, Ruth Plumly, 109
Thompson, Stith, 276, 325
Thorn Rose or the Sleeping Beauty, 286
Thorndike, Robert Ladd, 12, 174, 632
Thorne-Thomsen, Gudrun, 108
Thought and Language, 48
Thoughts Concerning Education, 89
Threadgill, Colin, 55
3NBs of Julian Drew, 478
Three Aesop Fox Fables, 312
Three Bears, The, 178, 180, 181, 280, 311
"Three Bears, The," 92, 173, 280, 304, 688
Three Bears and 15 Other Stories, The, 52, 270
Three Bears Rhyme Book, The, 428
Three Billy Goats Gruff, The, 8, 53, 178, 180, 181, 270, 272, 285, 302, 311
"Three Billy Goats Gruff, The," 173, 269, 635, 688
"Three Blind Mice, The" 146, 418, 685
Three Cool Kids, 637
Three Days on a River in a Red Canoe, 643, 701
Three Ducks Went Wandering, 677
Three Jovial Huntsmen, 153
Three Little Kittens, The, 153
"Three Little Kittens, The," 146
Three Little Pigs, The, 14, 178, 181, 270, 279, 302, 429
"Three Little Pigs, The," 60, 68, 236, 280, 283, 676
Three Little Pigs and the Big Bad Wolf, 272
Three Little Pigs and the Fox, 304
Three Little Wolves and the Big Bad Pig, The, 236, 243
Three Names, 112, 532, 606
"Three Owls, The," 103
Three Perfect Peaches, 287
Three Pigs, The, 270
"Three Pigs, The," 236
Three Princes, The, 279, 291
Three Sacks of Truth: A Story From France, 279, 287
Three Strong Women: A Tall Tale from Japan, 303
Three Voices: An Invitation to Poetry Across the Curriculum, 441
Three Wishes: An Old Story, The, 277, 279, 635, 637

Three Wonderful Beggars, The, 283, 288
Through Grandpa's Eyes, 232
Through Moon and Stars and Night Skies, 231
Through Our Eyes: Poems and Pictures About Growing Up, 392, 419
Through the Looking-Glass, 96, 98
"Throw of Threes, A," 412, 425
Throwing Things Away: From Middens to Resource Recovery, 651
"Thumbelina," 92, 344
Thunder at Gettysburg, 535
Thunder Cake, 226, 232, 683
Thunder From the Clear Sky, 526
Thurber, James, 119, 345
Thurman, Judith, 348, 430
"Tia Miseria's Pear Tree," 272
Tickle Tickle, 52, 139
"Ticky-Picky Boom-Boom," 279
Tidy Titch, 172
Tiegreen, Alan, 500
Tierney, Robert, 714
Tiger and the Rabbit, The, 108
Tiger, Tiger, Burning Bright, 24, 40, 479
Tikta Liktak: An Eskimo Legend, 301
Til All the Stars Have Fallen, 414, 416, 426, 430
Tiller, Ruth, 206
Tilley, Glenette, 568
Time, 687
Time at the Top, 364
Time For Andrew: A Ghost Story, 365
Time For Bed, 52, 172
Time Ghost, 366
Time of the Bison, 520
Time of Wonder, 200, 207, 425, 430
Time to Get Out of the Bath, Shirley, 209, 244
Time to Talk: Poems of Friendship, A, 219
Time to Wake Up!, 171, 208
"Time Trilogy, The," 377, 683
Times of My Life: A Memoir, The, 570
Tin Lizzie, 704
Tinderbox, The, 344
Tiny Tiny Boy and the Big Big Cow, The, 181
Tipi: A Center of Native American Life, The, 606
"Tippetty Witchet," 110
Titch, 53, 172, 178, 181, 430
Titherington, Jeanne, 231
Tituba of Salem Village, 525
To and Again, 109
To Baby With Love, 148, 152
To Be a Slave, 599, 606
"To Each Generation Its Own Rabbits," 608
To Kill A Mockingbird, 6
"To Look at Anything," 426, 431, 433
"To Meet Mr. Lincoln," 400, 412, 426
"To See a World in a Grain of Sand," 91
To the Moon and Back, 416, 428, 431, 432
To the Top of the World, Adventures with Arctic Wolves, 585
Toads and Diamonds, 281, 305
"Toaster," 405
Tobe, 112
Today Is Monday, 177, 180
Toddlecreek Post Office, 200, 651
Token for Children, A, 87
Token for Children of New England, A, 87
"Token of Unspoken, A," 412
Tolkien, J. R. R., 6, 57, 110, 116, 343, 347, 356, 368, 371, 379
Tollhurst, Marilyn, 698
Tolstoy, Alexi, 5
Tom, 227, 232
Tom, Chow Loy, 422
"Tom, the Piper's Son," 146
Tom & Pippo's Day, 52

Tom Sawyer, 531
Tom Swift, 107
"Tom Swift" series, 107
"Tom Tigercat," 405
Tom Tit Tot, 278, 282
Tom's Midnight Garden, 117, 347, 363, 364
Tombs of Atuan, The, 373
Tomes, Margot, 95, 284, 287, 289, 412
Tomfoolery: Trickery and Foolery with Words, 48
Tomie de Paola's Book of Poems, 391, 393, 413, 416, 429, 430
Tomie de Paola's Mother Goose, 52, 147, 152, 215
Tomlinson, Carl M., 361
Tomlinson, Theresa, 321
"Tommy Snooks and Bessie Brooks," 685
Tommy Thumb's Pretty Song Book, 88
Tompert, Ann, 303
Tongue-Cut Sparrow, The, 281
Tongues of Jade, 298
Tonight, by Sea, 490, 607
Tonight Is Carnaval, 680
Toning the Sweep, 20, 59, 480
Too Many Tamales, 55
Too Much Garbage, 651
Tool Book, 598
Tops and Bottoms, 54
"Tops and Bottoms," 306
Tops: Building and Experimenting with Spinning Toys, 646
Tortillitas Para Mama, 150
Toshi Maruki, 117
Touch Magic: Fantasy, Faerie and Folklore in the Literature of Childhood, 325, 342
Touch Wood: A Girlhood in Occupied France, 541
Tough Winter, The, 109, 350
Toughboy and Sister, 488, 526, 631
Tournament of Knights, A, 588
Toward Adolescence: The Middle School Years, 47
"Toward the 21st Century—Where Are Children's Books Going?," 120
Town Mouse, Country Mouse, 9
"Town Mouse and the Country Mouse, The," 310
Townsend, John Rowe, 33, 126, 504
Townsend's Warbler, 590
"Toy Books," 100
Toye, William, 298, 299
Traces of Life: The Origins of Humankind, 584
Tracy, Libba, 224
Trading Game, The, 499
Trains, 106
Trains, Aircraft, 106
Traitor: The Case of Benedict Arnold, 554
Transitions: From Literature to Literacy, 661
Traveling to Tondo: A Tale of the Nkundo of Zaire, 303, 311
Travers, Pamela, 116, 380, 691
Treasure Island, 28, 95, 116, 120
"Tree Coming Up," 431
"Tree House," 430
Tree in the Trail, 106
Tree in the Wood: An Old Nursery Song, The, 143
Tree Is Nice, A, 218
Tree Place and Other Poems, A, 58, 396, 410
Tree That Rains: The Flood Myth of the Huichol Indians of Mexico, The, 309, 606
Trees, 651
Trees Stand Shining: Poetry of the North American Indians, The, 417, 422
Trelease, Jim, 33, 118
Tresselt, Alvin, 119, 222, 229, 234, 289, 637
Trial Valley, 474
Tricky Tortoise, 236, 243, 689
"Trimmed-down Tales," 429
Trimmer, Mrs. Sarah, 90, 91

Tripp, Wallace, 153, 423, 705
Tristan and Iseult, 320
"Tristan and Iseult," 319
Trivas, Irene, 157
Trivias, Eugene, 236, 243
Trojan Horse, The, 316, 318
"Troll Bridge, The," 429
Trouble for Lucy, 56, 532, 680
Trouble with Tuck, The, 496
Troughton, Joanna, 299, 303
Truck, 166, 179, 181
Trucks, 53
True Adventures of Daniel Hall, The, 554
True Confessions of Charlotte Doyle, The, 18, 28, 59, 120, 401, 518
True Stories About Abraham Lincoln, 557
True Story of the 3 Little Pigs as Told by A. Wolf, The, 46, 120, 236, 243, 429, 696, 698
Trumpet of the Swan, The, 349
Trumpeter of Krakow, The, 523
"Trusting the Words," 531
Truth About Unicorns, The, 585, 601
Tseng, Jean, 293
Tseng, Mou-Sien, 293
Tub Grandfather, The, 240, 245
Tub People, 240, 245
Tuck Everlasting, 18, 21, 23, 58, 65, 341, 364, 430, 431, 634, 690
Tuck Triumphant, 497
Tucker, Nicholas, 71
Tucker Pfeffercorn, 282, 304
Tudor, Tasha, 98, 153, 159, 217, 400, 407
Tuesday, 30, 118, 170
Tunis, Edwin, 526
Tunnel, The, 214, 347
Tunnell, Michael O., 361, 380, 629
Turkle, Brinton, 169, 637, 671, 698
Turn Homeward, Hannalee, 535
Turn the Page, Please . . . ," 12
Turner, Ann, 231, 248, 520, 531, 533, 606, 651, 680
Turner, Glennette Tilley, 568
Turner, Philip, 322
Turner, Robyn Montana, 561
Turnip, The, 289, 311, 637, 643, 689
Turret, The, 350
"Turtle Dives to the Bottom of the Sea," 313
Turtle in July, 410
Twain, Mark (pseudonym of Samuel Clemens), 95, 96, 99, 115, 116
"Twelve Dancing Princesses, The," 286
Twelve Dancing Princesses, The, 278, 279, 286
Twelve Tales from Aesop, 312
12 Ways to Get to 11, 161
Twenty and Ten, 540
Twenty-One Balloons, The, 117, 357
26 Letters and 99 Cents, 159, 161
Twenty Thousand Leagues Under the Sea, 96, 115
Twilight Struggle: The Life of John Fitzgerald Kennedy, A, 565
"Twinkle Twinkle Little Star," 98
Twins, 108
"Twins" series, 108
Twisted Window, The, 503
Two Bad Ants, 241, 245
Two by Two, 206, 682
Two Cool Cows, 239
Two Eyes, a Nose, and a Mouth, 594
Two Is a Team, 112
Two of Everything, 279, 294
Two Queens of Heaven: The Story of Demeter and Aphrodite, 316
Two Short and One Long, 124
Two Years Before the Mast, 95
Tyler, Linda Wagner, 650

Uchida, Yoshiko, 108, 117, 278, 279, 303, 486, 570, 607, 687
Udry, Janice May, 82, 218
Ugly Duckling, The, 16, 343
"Ugly Duckling, The," 237
Umbrella, 229, 234
Uncegila's Seventh Spot: A Lakota Legend, 279
Uncle Bouqui of Haiti, 108
Uncle Elephant, 683
Uncle Jed's Barbershop, 227, 233
Uncle Nacho's Hat, 682
Uncle Remus, His Songs and Sayings, 93, 304
Uncle Remus Stories, 93, 116
Uncle Willie and the Soup Kitchen, 248
Uncle Wizzmo's New Used Car, 210, 637, 694
Unconditional Surrender: U.S. Grant and the Civil War, 566
Under the Blood Red Sun, 515, 519, 542, 543, 607
Under the Ground, 580
Under the Sunday Tree, 408
Under the Window, 100, 116
Underground, 592
Understanding Whole Language: From Principles to Practice, 661
Understanding Writing, 645
Understood Betsy, 111
Unsolved: Famous Real Life Mysteries, 59
"Until I Saw the Sea," 410, 425, 430
Up Goes the Skyscraper!, 54
Up in the Air, 412
Up North at the Cabin, 430
Up the Tracks to Granma's, 209
Updike, John, 415
Upon the Head of the Goat: A Childhood in Hungary, 1939–1944, 541
Upstairs Room, The, 11, 539
"Urashima Taro and the Princess of the Sea," 278
User Unfriendly, 376
Uses of Enchantment, The, 10, 268, 324
Using Nonfiction Trade Books in the Elementary Classroom, 608
Using Poetry Across the Curriculum: A Whole Language Approach, 441
"Using Predictable Materials vs. Preprimers to Teach Beginning Sight Words," 174
"Using Real Books: Research Findings on Literature-Based Reading Instruction," 629

V for Vanishing: An Alphabet of Endangered Animals, 155, 159, 205, 650
Vaës, Alain, 286
Valens, Amy, 53, 171
Valentine Poems, 421
Valerie and the Silver Pear, 683
"Valyeries, Ride, The," 685
Van Allsburg, Chris, 30, 64, 117, 155, 157, 199, 209, 210, 212, 215, 241, 245, 248, 624, 633, 650, 714
Van Clief, Sylvia Worth, 698
van der Rol, Ruud, 555, 564, 565
Van Laan, Nancy, 181, 243, 299
Van Leeuwen, Jean, 514, 515, 524, 532
Van Loon, Hendrik W., 107, 601
Van Rynbach, Iris, 282, 304, 347
Vance, Janet, 661
Vande Velde, Vivian, 376
Vander Els, Betty, 541
Vandergrift, Kay E., 33
Vanishing Manatee, The, 650
Vanishing Ozone Protecting Earth From Ultra Violet Radiation, 584
Vardell, Sylvia, 608

Vasilissa the Beautiful, 272, 274, 277, 279, 281, 288
Vassilisa the Wise: A Tale of Medieval Russia, 288
Vejigante Masquerader, 247
Velveteen Rabbit, The, 6, 41, 109, 120, 240, 245
Vennema, Peter, 560, 669
Ventura, Piero, 601
Verhoeven, Rian, 555, 564, 565
Verne, Jules, 96, 115, 376
Very Best of Friends, The, 228, 234, 429
Very Busy Spider, The, 140, 180, 183, 623, 672
"Very First Books," 139
Very Hungry Caterpillar, The, 5, 52, 140, 162, 177, 180, 183, 205, 636, 672
Very Last First Time, 247
Very Lonely Firefly, The, 141, 180
Very Quiet Cricket, The, 141, 180, 183, 672
Very Special House, A, 216
"Very Truth, The," 571
Very Worst Monster, The, 217, 241, 245
Victor and Christobel, 236
Vidal, Beatriz, 220, 309
View from the Oak, The, 594
Viguers, Ruth Hill, 126
Village by the Sea, The, 478
Village of Round and Square Houses, The, 247, 295, 296, 311, 668
Vincent, Gabrielle, 11, 242
Vinge, Joan D., 376
Viorst, Judith, 55, 233, 429, 694
Vipoint, Elfrida, 181
Visions: Stories About Women Artists, 567
"Visit, The," 430
Visit From St. Nicholas, A, 98, 115
"Visit From St. Nicholas, A," 400
Visit to William Blake's Inn, A, 30, 117, 208, 418, 423
Vison the Mink, 598
Vivas, Julie, 175, 228, 229, 234, 243, 322
Voce, Louise, 142
Voices From the Civil War: A Documentary History of the Great American Conflict, 599, 607
Voices of Readers: How We Come to Love Books, 70
Voices on the Wind: Poems for All Seasons, 420
Voigt, Cynthia, 11, 57, 83, 431, 455, 463, 478
Volarkova, Hana, 418, 430
Volcano: The Eruption and Healing of Mt. St. Helens, 581, 592
Vos, Ida, 515, 540, 542
Voyages of Dr. Dolittle, The, 109
Voyage of the Frog, The, 474
Vulpes the Red Fox, 598
Vuong, Lynette Dyer, 278, 293
Vygotsky, L. S., 48

Wabbes, Marie, 55, 533
Waber, Bernard, 55, 233, 242, 428, 623, 637
Waddell, Martin, 53, 173, 175, 180
"Waggle Taggle Gypsies," 399
Wagner, Jenny, 234
Wagner, Richard, 685
Wait for Me, Watch for Me, Eula Bee, 531
Wait Till Helen Comes, 362, 699
Waiting for Anya, 541
Waiting for Hannah, 171
Waiting for the Rain, 489
Waiting for Whales, 212
Waiting to Waltz: A Childhood, 409
Wake Up, City!, 119
Waldman, Sarah, 322, 323
Waldman, Neil, 322, 323, 400, 424
Walk Two Moons, 19, 58, 465, 503
Walker, Barbara M., 56, 291, 602, 683
Walker, Kate, 58, 470

Walking Through the Jungle, 153
"Walking to Church," 408
Wall, The, 117, 250, 431
Wallace, Ian, 247
Wallace, Karen, 593
Walsh, Jill Paton, 56, 367, 374, 431, 432
Walt Disney's Cinderella, 119
Walt Disney's Snow White, 283
Walt Whitman, 566
Walter, Mildred Pitts, 231, 483, 484
Walter, Virginia, 53
Wang, Rosalind C., 293
Wangerin, Walter, 58, 347
Wanted: Mud Blossom, 493
"War," 431
War Boy: A Country Childhood, 570
War Comes to Willy Freeman, 529
War with Grandpa, The, 56
Warburg, Sandol Stoddard, 480
Ward, Cindy, 54, 177, 180
Ward, Lynd, 14, 110
Warlow, Aidan, 9, 625
Warm Place, The, 350, 351
Warner, Gertrude Chandler, 491, 712
Warrior Goddess: Athena, The, 316
Warrior Scarlet, 521
Wasps at Home, 580
Watch Out for the Chicken Feet in Your Soup, 226, 232
Watch the Stars Come Out, 233
Watchers: A Mystery at Alton Towers, The, 58
Water Babies, The, 96
Water Sky, 27
Water: The Elements, 593
Waterman's Boy, 648, 651
Watermelons, Walnuts, and the Wisdom of Allah and Other Tales of the Hoca, 291
Waters, Kate, 585
Watership Down, 352, 380, 608
Watkins, Yoko Kawashima, 543, 607
Watson, Clyde, 148, 157, 419
Watson, Wendy, 52, 147, 148, 153, 157, 312, 400
Watson-Ellam, Linda, 714
Watts, Isaac, 91
Waugh, Sylvia, 354
Wave, The, 271
Wave in Her Pocket: Stories from Trinidad, A, 219
Wave of the Sea-Wolf, The, 206, 671
Waving: A Counting Book, 161
Way of His Own, A, 520, 536
"Way Things Are, The," 412, 431
Way Things Work, The, 56, 119, 592
Way to Sattin Shore, The, 502
Way to Start a Day, The, 210, 230, 234, 431, 650, 709
Way West: Journal of a Pioneer Woman, The, 570
Wayfarers All: From The Wind in the Willows, 351
Wayside School Gets a Little Stranger, 494
We Are All in the Dumps with Jack and Guy, 149, 153, 217, 218
We Got Here Together, 7, 207
"Weather," 415
Weaver, Lydia, 514
Weaving of a Dream: A Chinese Folktale, The, 293
WEB, The, 714
Webster, Daniel, 92
Webster, Jean, 111
Webster, Noah, 92
Wedding of the Rat Family, The, 293
Weddings, 590
Wednesday Surprise, The, 231, 430
Weaver, Constance, 661
"Wee Willie Winkie," 146, 685

Weed Is a Flower: The Life of George Washington Carver, A, 562
Week of Lullabies, A, 419
Weekend with Diego Rivera, A, 562
Weekend with Van Gogh, A, 562
Weidt, Maryann N., 556
Weil, Lisl, 561
Weir, Ruth, 48
Weisgard, Leonard, 105, 207, 643
Weiss, Harvey, 593
Weiss, Nicki, 173
Weitzman, David, 603
Well, The, 538
Weller, Frances, 650
Wells, Deborah, 639
Wells, Gordon, 12, 138, 174, 186, 632
Wells, Haru, 53
Wells, Jan, 185
Wells, Rosemary, 24, 33, 52, 139, 218, 230, 243, 430
Wendy Watson's Mother Goose, 147, 153
We're Going on a Bear Hunt, 53, 143, 144, 685
West, Delno, 555, 571
West, Jean, 555, 571
West From Home: Letters of Laura Ingalls Wilder, San Francisco, 600
Westall, Robert, 504, 541
Westcott, Nadine Bernard, 142, 144, 181, 684
"Western Wagons," 426
Western Wind, 57
Westing Game, The, 48, 502
Westmark, 369
Wet World, 207
Wexler, Jerome, 593
Whales' Song, The, 429, 650
Whaling Days, 594, 596
What About Me? 477
What Boys and Girls Like to Read, 40, 418
"What Counts as Evidence in Theories of Children's Literature?," 639
What Did I Write?, 708
"What Do We Do About Bad Biographies?," 556
What Does the Crow Know?, 578
What Game Shall We Play?, 217
What Goes Around Comes Around, 210
What Happened to the Dinosaurs?, 54, 584
"What Happens to a Dream Deferred?," 408
What Has Ten Legs and Eats Corn Flakes?, 601
What Is It?, 52, 139
"What Is Pink?," 436
What Katy Did, 94
What Katy Did at School, 94
What Katy Did Next, 94
"What Makes a Good Story?," 59
"What Makes an Appealing and Readable Science Book?," 608
What Neat Feet!, 581
"What the Gray Cat Sings," 440
"What the Stars Are Like," 299
What Whiskers Did, 116, 118
What You Know First, 203
"What's a Good Book?," 70
What's the Big Idea, Ben Franklin?, 56, 560
What's Under My Bed?, 244, 428
What's Whole in Whole Language?, 626
What's Your Name? From Ariel to Zoe, 159
Wheatley, Nadia, 596, 651
Wheelock, John Hall, 431
Wheels at Work, 598
Wheels on the Bus, The, 52, 145
When Hitler Stole Pink Rabbit, 539
"When I Am Me," 428
When I Am Old with You, 55
"When I Was Lost," 429
When I Was Nine, 570

When I Was Young in the Mountains, 54, 112, 210, 430
"When I Woke Up This Morning," 429
"When It's Thanksgiving," 410
When Jaguars Ate the Moon and Other Stories About Animals and Plants of the Americas, 298
When Shlemiel Went to Warsaw and Other Stories, 279, 289
When the Dark Comes Dancing, 419, 428
When the New Baby Comes, I'm Moving Out, 231
When the Rooster Crowed, 181
When the Tide Is Low, 234
When the Tripods Came, 377, 431, 650
When the Wind Changed, 62
When the Woods Hum, 234, 606, 650
When We Were Very Young, 110, 116
When Will I Read?, 54, 233
When Writers Read, 661
When You Were a Baby, 53
Where Are You Going, Little Mouse?, 180
Where Are You Going, Manyoni?, 246
Where Can It Be?, 140
Where Do You Get Your Ideas?," 373
Where Do You Think You're Going, Christopher Columbus?, 557, 571
Where Does It Go?, 166
Where Does the Brown Bear Go?, 173
Where Does the Trail Lead?, 219
"Where Go the Boats," 407
"Where Have All the Flowers Gone?," 685
"Where Have You Been, Dear?," 691
"Where Is It?," 426
Where Is the Green Parrot?, 52
"Where Is Thumbkin?," 141
Where Once There Was A Wood, 207, 673
Where the Buffaloes Begin, 209, 211
Where the Forest Meets the Sea, 205, 248, 651
Where the Lilies Bloom, 113, 117, 456, 474, 683
Where the Red Fern Grows, 40, 498, 634
Where the River Begins, 208
Where the River Runs: Portrait of a Refugee Family, 607
Where the Sidewalk Ends, 39, 62, 117, 400, 406, 429
"Where the Sidewalk Ends," 406
Where the Wild Things Are, 5, 9, 11, 54, 117, 118, 199, 208, 217, 677, 685
"Where Will We Run To?," 431
"Where Would You Be?," 407
Where's My Teddy?, 428
Where's Spot?, 52, 140, 174, 180
Where's the Baby?, 217, 241, 245
"Which Loved Best," 392
"Which Washington?," 426, 430
Whiff, Sniff, Nibble, and Chew: The Gingerbread Boy Retold, 698
While I Sleep, 209
"Whippety Stourie," 278, 282
Whipping Boy, The, 346, 361, 368, 626, 694
Whipple, Laura, 420
Whiskers and Rhymes, 147
"Whispers," 412
Whistle for Willie, 45, 55, 221, 227, 233, 426
"Whistling," 426
Whistling the Morning In, 428
Whitcomb Riley, James, 99
White, Dorothy, 67, 186
White, E. B., 8, 11, 20, 33, 55, 110, 117, 118, 340, 346, 349, 351, 634
White, T. H., 319
White Archer: An Eskimo Legend, The, 299, 301
White Cat, The, 302
White Deer and Other Stories From Told By the Lenape, The, 299

White Mountains, The, 377
"White Mountains Quartet," 377, 378
White on Black, 139
White Snow, Bright Snow, 117, 222, 229, 234
Whitfield, Dr. Philip, 590
Whitman, Candace, 10
Whitman, Ruth, 398
Whitman, Walt, 417
Whittier, John Greenleaf, 99, 392, 423
"Who Am I?," 428, 432
"Who Has Seen the Wind?," 99
Who Is Carrie?, 529
Who Is Frances Rain?, 366
Who Really Killed Cock Robin?, 43, 651
Who Shrank My Grandmother's House?, 395, 412, 430
Who Uses This?, 166
Who's Going to Take Care of Me?, 171
"Whodunnit," 412
Whole Language Catalog, The, 659
Who's in Rabbit's House?, 296
Whose Hat?, 166
Whose Mouse Are You?, 140, 180
Why Am I Grown So Cold? Poems of the Unknowable, 421
"Why Are Americans Afraid of Dragons?," 380
Why Can't You Unscramble an Egg? And Other Not Such Dumb Questions About Matter, 585
Why Do Grown-Ups Have All the Fun?, 171, 428
Why Do Volcanoes Erupt?, 589
Why Don't You Get a Horse, Sam Adams?, 560
Why Ducks Sleep on One Leg, 272, 311
Why Mosquitoes Buzz in People's Ears, 109, 117, 270, 275, 295, 296, 673
Why Rhino Is So Grumpy, 296
Why the Sky Is Far Away, 296, 673
Why the Sun and the Moon Live in the Sky, 272, 295
Why There Is No Arguing in Heaven, 217, 313
Wibberley, Leonard, 528
Wider Than the Sky, 399, 400, 401, 417, 428
Widow's Broom, The, 241
Wiese, Kurt, 105, 293
Wiesner, David, 30, 118, 170, 210, 234
Wiggin, Kate Douglas, 108, 111, 116
Wijngaard, Juan, 320
Wild, Margaret, 228, 234, 429, 539
Wild, Wild Cookbook, The, 683
Wild Animals I Have Known, 116
Wild Magic, 368
Wild Robin, 282, 347
Wild Swans, The, 343
"Wild Wood, The," 412
Wilde, Oscar, 344, 345
Wilder, Laura Ingalls, 23, 30, 31, 54, 68, 107, 116, 118, 531, 545, 600, 624, 683, 686, 688
"Wildlife Refuge," 405
Wildsmith, Brian, 55, 153, 178, 181, 244, 312, 322, 407, 416, 423, 693
Wilfrid Gordon McDonald Partridge, 228, 234
Will I Have a Friend?, 53, 233, 429
Will You Sign Here, John Hancock?, 552, 560
Willa and Old Miss Annie, 54
Willard, Nancy, 30, 117, 208, 418, 423, 580
Willey and the Hairy Man, 673
Williams, Garth, 242, 349, 350, 406, 682
Williams, Hazel, 505
Williams, Jay, 345, 681
Williams, Jennifer, 117
Williams, Karen Lynn, 11, 55, 246, 646, 668, 708
Williams, Linda, 54, 181, 637, 676
Williams, Margery, 6, 109 240, 245
Williams, Sue, 175, 180

Williams, Vera B., 55, 117, 121, 140, 207, 211, 218, 228, 233, 429, 430, 643, 699, 701
Williams' Doll, 224
Williamson, Ray A., 298, 299
Willie's Not the Hugging Kind, 55
Will's Mammoth, 245
Willy and Hugh, 11
Wilner, Isabel, 425, 432, 439, 440, 691
Wilson, Barbara, 278
Wilson, Budge, 59, 461
Wilson, Tona, 298
Wilson Library Bulletin, 608
Wimmer, Mike, 212
"Wind, The," 397, 401
Wind in the Door, A, 64, 116, 343, 377, 341, 342, 351, 352, 624
Wind Song, 411
"Wind Song," 393, 410
Window, 118, 248, 431, 651
"Windshield Wiper," 398, 403, 412
"Windshield Wipers' Song," 439
"Windy Nights," 99, 401, 407
Wings, 315
Winnie the Pooh, 6, 28, 109 342, 353, 380, 633
"Winnie the Pooh" series, 353
Winter, 579
Winter, Jeanette, 682
Winter, Jonah, 561, 682
Winter Across America, 592
"Winter Cardinal," 428
Winter Danger, 514
Winter Holding Spring, 120, 481
Winter Poems, 415, 420
Winter Room, The, 23
Winter Wife, The, 526
Winthrop, Elizabeth, 57, 272, 274, 277, 279, 281, 288, 322, 355
Wires and Watts: Understanding and Using Electricity, 599
Wise Brown, Margaret, 116
Wise Old Woman, The, 303
Wiseman, David, 346, 367
Wisler, G. Clifton, 535
Wisniewski, David, 206, 671
"Witch, Witch," 439
Witch of Blackbird Pond, The, 457, 525, 526
Witches' Children, 525
With Every Drop of Blood, 535, 606
Wizard of Earthsea, A, 20, 58, 341, 343, 347, 369, 372, 455, 680
Wizard of Oz, The, 109, 116, 357
"Wizard of Oz" series, 109
Wolf, Janet, 704
Wolf, Sylvia, 567
Wolfe, Art, 592
Wolferl: The First Six Years in the Life of Wolfgang Amadeus Mozart, 1756–1762, 561
Wolff, Ashley, 53, 153, 181, 203, 298, 407, 423, 673
Wolff, Virginia Euwer, 59, 470, 471, 499
Wolf-Speaker, 368
Wolkstein, Diane, 272, 274, 282, 288
Wollmann-Bonilla, J. E., 644
Wolves of Willoughby Chase, The, 369
Woman Who Fell From the Sky, The, 313
Woman Who Rides Like a Man, The, 368
"Women in America" series, 107
Women of Our Time series, 563
Womenfolk and Fairy Tales, 276
Wonder Book for Boys and Girls, The, 93
Wonder Clock, The, 93, 101
Wonderful Flight to the Mushroom Planet, The, 374
Wonderful Stories for Children, 92
"Wonderful Tar-Baby Story, The," 278, 305
Wood, Audrey, 54, 178, 181, 200, 211, 428, 637

Wood, Carl, 324
Wood, Don, 178, 200
Wood, Jakki, 142
Wood, Nancy, 299
Woodson, Jacqueline, 59, 117, 120, 457, 469, 485
Woodsong, 570
Woolard, Linda, 710
Woolf, Virginia, 6
Words About Pictures, 198, 252
Words by Heart, 538
Words With Wrinkled Knees, 413, 425
Wordsworth, William, 99
Working, 118, 139
"Working of John Henry, The," 307, 308
"Working With Mother," 414
World of Christopher Robin, The, 394, 400, 407
World of Manobozho, The, 298
World That Jack Built, The, 651
Worlds I Know, 412
Worlds of Childhood: The Art and Craft of Writing for Children, 7, 20, 33
Worlds Within: Children's Fantasy from the Middle Ages to Today, 380
Wormell, Mary, 203, 606
Worse Than Willy!, 238, 244
Worth, Valerie, 32, 348, 396, 397, 401, 425
Wounded Wolf, The, 651
"Wozzit, The," 406
"Wraggle Taggle Gypsies," 399
Wreck of the Zephyr, The, 209, 241, 245
Wrede, Patricia, C., 347, 367, 368
Wren to the Rescue, 368
Wren's Quest, 368
Wren's War, 368
Wretched Stone, The, 241, 245
Wright, Betty Ren, 9, 56, 362, 624
Wright, Blanche Fisher, 152
Wright, Joan R., 54, 606
Wright Brothers: How They Invented the Airplane, The, 553, 567
Wright-Frierson, Virginia, 234
Wrightson, Patricia, 362, 488
Wrinkle in Time, A, 11, 27, 64, 117, 123, 342, 343, 347, 370, 376, 377, 379, 626, 634, 657, 700
"Write Me a Verse," 401, 411
"Write What You Care About," 458
"Writer's Social Responsibility, A," 459
Writing and the Writer, 16, 692
Writing Books for Young People, 456
Writing Bug, The, 569
"Writing From a Minority Literature," 504
"Writing Mysteries for Children," 501
"Writing the Literature of Fact," 581
"Writing the Source: In Other Words," 458

"Writing What They Read: Reflections on Literature and Child Writers," 643
Written for Children: An Outline of English Children's Literature, 126
"Wrong Start," 425, 429
"Wumpaloons Which Never Were, The," 406
Wycliffe, John, 321
Wyeth, Andrew, 427
Wyeth, N. C., 101, 120
Wyndham, Robert, 151
Wynne-Jones, Tim, 46
Wyss, Johann David, 95

"Xerox, Candy Bar," 158
Xiong, Blia, 689

Yaccarino, Dan, 440
Yagawa, Sumiko, 274, 279, 294, 303, 311, 633, 672
Yang the Third and Her Impossible Family, 487
Yang the Youngest and His Terrible Ear, 487, 488
Yankee Doodle Boy, 570
Yankee Doodle's Literary Sampler of Prose, Poetry and Pictures, 87
Yashima, Taro (Jun Iwamatsu), 49, 55, 201, 211, 220, 229, 234, 605, 704
Yates, Elizabeth, 567
Year of Beasts, A, 55, 181, 203
Year of Birds, A, 181, 203
Year of Impossible Goodbyes, 431, 536, 543, 607
Year of the Panda, 431, 490, 648, 650
Yearling, The, 457, 496
Yee, Paul, 57, 298
Yeh-Shen: A Cinderella Story from China, 117, 266, 278, 279, 280, 292, 311
"Yell for Yellow, A," 412, 428, 436
"Yellow," 428, 436
Yellow Butter Purple Jelly Red Jam Black Bread, 393, 407, 428
Yellow Fairy Book, The, 93
Yep, Laurence, 120, 277, 279, 298, 345, 347, 487, 537, 570, 687
Yolen, Jane, 30, 121, 206, 211, 212, 248, 276, 277, 279, 282, 283, 298, 299, 302, 310, 312, 315, 319, 325, 342, 345, 347, 361, 372, 428, 517, 632, 650, 651, 671, 681, 696, 698
Yonder, 213
Yonge, Charlotte, 93, 99
Yorinks, Arthur, 218
You Be Good & I'll Be Night, 411
You Can't Catch Me!, 637, 691
You Can't Pet a Possum, 112
You Come Too, 110, 411
"You Look Ridiculous," Said the Rhinoceros to the Hippopotamus, 637
You Read to Me, I'll Read to You, 404

You Want Women to Vote, Lizzie Stanton?, 552, 565
You'll Soon Grow into Them, Titch, 55, 172, 181
"You're My Turtle," 411
Young, Ed, 48, 117, 206, 209, 250, 279, 292, 293, 294, 311, 312, 344, 345, 415, 424, 673
Young, Noela, 359
Young, Ruth, 160
Young Artist, The, 209
"Young Children's Preferences in Poetry: A National Survey of First-, Second- and Third-Graders," 404
Young Fluent Readers, 12, 15, 174
Young Folks, 95
Young Guinevere, 319
Young Merlin, 318
Young Rider, The, 56
Young Voices, 110
Your First Garden Book, 602
Your Mother Was a Neanderthal, 360
Your Own Best Secret Place, 210, 230, 234, 410, 426, 430, 694
Youth's Companion, The, 99
Yue, Charlotte, 606
Yue, David, 606

Z for Zachariah, 378, 431, 650, 701, 709
Z Was Zapped: A Play in Twenty-Six Acts, The, 155, 157
Zacharias, Thomas, 52
Zarnowski, Myra, 571
Zeely, 112, 463
Zeifert, Harriet, 52
Zeke Pippin, 49, 216, 243
Zeldis, Malcah, 407, 560
Zelinksy, Paul O., 52, 120, 145, 198, 199, 215, 217, 278, 283, 284, 464
Zemach, Harve, 276, 278, 282, 288, 302
Zemach, Margot, 109, 270, 277, 279, 282, 284, 290, 302, 311, 636, 637
Zero's Slider, 56
Zia, 531
Zimmer, Dirk, 420
Zin! Zin! Zin! A Violin, 161
Zinsser, William, 7, 20, 33
Zion, Gene, 633, 637, 706
"Zlateh the Goat," 271
Zlateh the Goat, and Other Stories, 271, 272, 289
Zolotow, Charlotte, 14, 197, 213, 217, 224, 429, 694
Zomo the Rabbit: A Trickster Tale from West Africa, 278, 295, 303
Zoom, 70, 156
Zoomrimes: Poems About Things That Go, 401
Zora Hurston and the Chinaberry Tree, 563
Zubrowski, Bernie, 598, 646
Zwerger, Lisbeth, 211, 279, 284, 310, 344

Accuracy and authenticity
  in biography, 554
  historical fiction, 518
  informational books, 581–82
Adventure
  nineteenth-century books, 95–96
Africa
  in biography, 561
  in fantasy, 350, 351, 377
  in folktales, 295–97
  in historical fiction, 533
  in picture books, 121, 159, 160, 206, 217,
    220, 246, 247
  in realistic fiction, 489
African Americans
  authorship issue, 458
  biography, 558, 560, 561, 562, 563, 564, 567,
    568, 569, 570
  fantasy, 342, 363
  folktales, 304–6
  historical fiction, 533–37, 606
  picture books, 139, 140, 148, 176–77, 204,
    205, 208, 210, 218, 219, 225, 226, 227,
    249–50
  poetry, 408–9, box 421–22
  realistic fiction, 457, 458, 463, 467, 469, 470,
    472, 479, 480, 483–85, 499, 501, 502
  stereotyping, 112
Aging
  in picture books, 228–29
  realistic fiction, 478–80
Alphabet books, 154–55
  ABC books, box 154–56
  early ABC books, 85–86
  guidelines for evaluating, box 164
American Indians (See Native Americans)
Andersen, Hans Christian, award, 31
Animals
  in fantasy, 347–53
  folktales, 270
  nineteenth-century books, 96
  personified in picture storybooks, 230,
    235–36
  realistic fiction, 496–98
Anthropomorphism
  in informational books, 584–85

Appalachia
  picture books, 210, 212
  realistic fiction, 456, 470, 474
Art
  classroom activities, 669–83
  elements of design, 210–12
  line and shape, 210
  picture storybooks, 199–21
  point of view or perspective, 211
  space, 211
  style, 212–18
  use of color, 210
  See also illustration; media
Art activities
  based on literature, 669–83
  collage pictures, 670–71
  creating endpapers, 672
  dioramas, 674–75
  displays, 674
  feltboard stories, 676
  games, 683
  graphic organizers, 677–78
  maps and timelines, 686–87
  media exploration, 671–72
  murals, 671
  museums about books, 675
  printing techniques, 672–73
  quiltmaking, 682
  roller box movie, 676
  scratchboard pictures, 672
  sewing, 680
  stencils, 673–74
  videos, 678, 680
Artifacts
  representing books, 686
Asian Americans, 211, 492, 554
  biography, 554
  historical fiction, 537, 542–44, 606
  picture books, 211, 226, 227
  realistic fiction, 487–88
Assessment (and evaluation), 704–13
  assessing literary responses, 64–69
  assessing reading abilities, 704–07
  assessment portfolios, 707
  concepts of print test, 705

determining children's literary background,
    705–6
  evaluating children's growth as readers, 709;
    box 710
  evaluating children's literary understandings,
    708–9
  evaluating the literature program, 709–10;
    box 711
  interviews, 706
  miscue analysis, 705
  ongoing observation, 706–7
  parent conferences, 707–8
  record keeping, 707
  running record, 706
  student conferences, 707
Australia
  in fantasy, 354, 362, 364, 365
  in realistic fiction, 470, 476, 488
Author illustrator visits, 652–53
Awards, children's books, 28–32, 722–31
  Appendix A, 722–31
  Edgar Allen Poe Award, 32, 730
  Hans Christian Andersen Award, 30, 729–30
  John Newbery Medal, 307, 722–25
  Laura Ingalls Wilder Award, 31, 729
  Mildred l. Batchelder Award, 30–31, 728–29
  NCTE Poetry Award, 31–32, 730
  Orbis Pictus Award, 581, 730
  Randolph Caldecott Medal, 30, 725–28
  Regina Medal, 31, 731
  Scott O'Dell Award, 32, 730

Babies' first books, 139 (See also picture books)
Batchelder, Mildred L., Award, 30–31
Beast tales, 270
Bible, 321–23
  collections, 321–22
  literary study, 321
  single story editions, 322–23
Big books, 180–84
  children create their own, 183
Biography
  accuracy and authenticity, 554–56
  authors, box 570
  autobiographies and memoirs, 569–70
  characterization, 556–57
  choice of subject, 554
  collective, 567–69
  complete, 564–67
  criteria, 554–58
  critical thinking, box 557
  fictionalized, 552
  guidelines for evaluating, box 558
  partial, 563–64
  picture book formats, 559–62
  simplified, 562–63
  style, 556
  theme, 557–58
  trends, 553
  types, 559–68
Black Americans (See African Americans)
Book clubs
  addresses, Appendix C, 743
Book discussion groups, 639–40
Book selection, 639–40
  aids, Appendix B, 732–40
  principles and guidelines, 655–65
Book talks, 637

Bookbinding
    directions, 704
Books for ages and stages,
    box 52–60
Books to begin on, 137–83 (*See* picture books)
Bookstores, in schools, 659
Britain
    in biography, 555, 561, 566
    in fantasy, 342, 346, 347, 348, 349, 351, 352,
        353, 356–57, 358–59, 361, 365, 367, 369,
        370
    folktales, 280–83
    historical fiction, 521–23
    realistic fiction, 463, 467, 479, 495, 496, 501
Buddy reading, 649

Caldecott Award, 30, 725–28
Caribbean
    historical fiction, 529, 533
    picture books, 54, 158, 160, 216, 247
    poetry, 408, 409, box 422
    realistic fiction, 489–90
Censorship
    dealing with, 657–58
    defined, 656
    increase in, 123–24
    selection vs., 656–57
Central America
    in folktales, 307–9
    realistic fiction, 488–89, 490
Chapbooks, 87–88
Characterization, 21–23
    biography, 556
    folktales, 274
    in picture storybooks, 200–201
Charts (*See* resources for teaching)
Child development, 44–51
    Elkind, David, 47
    Erikson, Erik, 50
    Gardner, Howard, 48
    Gilligan, Carol, 49
    Kohlberg, Lawrence, 49
    Maslow, Abraham, 50
    Piaget, Jean, 45–46
    Vygotsky, Lev, 47–48
Children's literature
    defined, 56
    educational values, 11–18
    guidelines for evaluating, box 27
    personal values, 8–11
China
    fantasy, 371
    folktales, 292–94
    historical fiction, 537
    picture books, 151
    realistic fiction, 490
Chinese American folktales, 298
Chinese Americans (*See* Asian Americans)
Choral reading, 439–40
Christmas
    in realistic fiction, 495
    traditional literature, 322–23
Civil War
    in fantasy, 367
    historical fiction, 535–36, 606
Classics in children's literature, 28–30
Cognitive development, 45–48
    cognitive conceit, 47
    egocentricism, 46
    zone of proximal development, 48
Concept books, 163–68, 593–94
Concept of story, 65–67
    growth of, 61–64
    See also sense of story
Controlled vocabulary books, 182–84
Cooking activities, 682–83

Counting books, 156–63
    box 160–62
    guidelines for evaluating, box 165
Craft and how-to books, 602
Crafts and construction activities, 681–82
Criteria for evaluating books (*See* guidelines for
    evaluating)
Critical thinking, 16, 20
    biography, 63
Cumulative tales, 181, 269

Death
    picture storybooks, 228
    realistic fiction, 480–82
Developmental disabilities
    in realistic fiction, 476
Didacticism
    eighteenth-century books, 90–91
    nineteenth-century poetry, 98
Dime novel, 107
Dioramas, 674
Discussion, guiding
    of books, 638–41
    of poetry, 433
Divorce
    picture storybooks, 225
    realistic fiction, 463–64
Drama and literature
    creative drama, 688
    dramatic play, 688
    dramatizing stories, 689
    improvisation, 690
    puppetry, 691
    readers' theater, 690
    story theater, 688
    values of creative drama, 688

Ecology
    theme study, web, 650
Emergent readers, 174–228
Endpapers, 220, 672
Environmental issues
    in fantasy, 377–78
    picture storybooks, 248
    realistic fiction, 473, 474, 488, 496, 498
    See also ecology
Epics, 318–21
    Iliad and Odyssey, 318
    King Arthur, 319
    Middle Ages, 318
    Ramayana, 318
    Robin Hood, 320
Eskimo
    in folktales, 299, 301
    realistic fiction, 473–74
Europe
    in historical fiction, 523–24, 538–42
Evaluating children's fiction, 18–30
    characterization, 21–23
    comparison to others, 27–28
    format, 27
    illustration, 26
    plot, 18–19
    point of view, 24–26
    setting, 19–20
    style, 23–24
    theme, 20–21
    See also guidelines for evaluating
Evaluation (*See* assessment)
Experiment books, 598–99

Fables, 310
    defined, 310
    origin, 310
Fairy tales
    modern, 343–45
    origins, 88–89

newspaper, 702
    See also folktales; wonder tales
Family stories
    nineteenth century, 93–95
    picture storybooks, 225–27
    realistic fiction, 459–66
Fantasy, 339–88
    animal, 347–53
    beginnings of modern, 343–45
    criteria, 346–47
    eccentric characters/preposterous situations,
        355–57
    extensions with children, box 352
    extraordinary worlds, 357–59
    good vs. evil, 370–71
    guidelines for evaluating, box 348
    high fantasy, 369–73
    imaginary kingdoms, 367–69
    magical powers, 360–61
    modern fairy tales, 345–46
    nineteenth-century books, 96–97
    quests and adventures, 371–73
    roots, 342–43
    science fiction, 373–79
    suspense and the supernatural, 361–63
    time shift, 362–67
    toys and dolls, 353–55
    values of, 341–43
Feltboard stories, 636
Finger rhymes, 141
Folktales, 265–338
    African, 295–97
    African American, 304–6
    Appalachian, 303–4
    Asian, 292–95
    British, 280–83
    Central and South American, 307–10
    characterization, 274
    Chinese American, 298
    Chinese and Japanese, 292–94
    collectors of, 108–9, 302–3
    crosscultural study, 281–310, box 302–3
    defined, 268
    early collections, 92–93
    Eskimo, 299, 301
    extensions with children, box 270
    French, 286, 287
    German, 283
    Jack tales, 303–4
    Jewish, 289–90
    magic objects, 277
    magical powers, 277
    Middle Eastern and Indian, 290–92
    motifs, 276–77, box 279
    Native American, 298–300
    Native American, by region, box 299
    nineteenth century, 92–93
    North American, 297–98
    origins, 266–68
    plot structure, 273
    Russian, 287–89
    Scandinavian, 285–86
    style, 274–75
    tall tales, 306–7, box 308
    themes, 275–76
    transformations, 277
    trickery, 277
    types, 269–72, box 272
    values, 268
    variants, 278, 280, box 281
    wishes, 277
Format, 26
    informational books, 593
    picture story books, 218
French folktales, 286–87

Friendship
    picture storybooks, 227
    realistic fiction, 466–68

Games
    based on books, 683
German folktales, 283–85
Grandparents
    picture storybooks, 207, 209, 226, 228, 229
    realistic fiction, 455, 462, 465, 479
Graphic organizers, 677–78
    comparison chart, 678
    semantic map, 677
    story map, 677
    Venn diagram, 678
Greek myths, 314–17
    box 315
Guidelines for evaluating (boxes)
    abc and counting books, 164
    books for the very young child, 142
    children's fiction, 29
    children's growth as readers, 710
    dealing with censorship, 658
    historical fiction, 520
    informational books, 594
    juvenile biography, 559
    literature program, 711
    modern fantasy, 348
    Mother Goose books, 149
    multicultural literature, 484
    picture storybooks, 223
    poetry anthologies, 413
    poetry for children, 399
Guidelines for reading aloud, box 635
Guides
    making and using, 645
    sample guide for *Galimoto*, 646

Harlequinades, 97
Hispanic Americans (*See* Latinos)
Hispanic folktales (*See* Central America; South
    America)
Historical fiction, 513–50
    African Americans, 537–38
    American frontier, 531–33
    American Revolution, 528–29
    ancient times, 521
    Asia, 524, 537, 543–44
    Civil War, 535–36, 606
    Colonial America, 524–28
    criteria, 517–19
    early Britain, 521
    Europe, 523–24, 539–42
    and fantasy, 517
    guidelines for evaluating, box 520
    immigrants, 536–37
    medieval times, 521–23
    Native Americans, 529, 606
    pioneers, 531–33, 606
    prehistoric times, 520–21
    slavery, in United States, 533–34
    themes in, 536
    trends in publishing, 514–15
    twentieth century, 536–44
    types, 516–17
    values, 515–16
    war, 538–44
        in Asia, 543–44
        World War I, 538–39
        World War II, 539–43
History of children's literature, 82–135
    adventure stories, 95–96
    animal stories, 96
    books of instruction, 92
    chapbooks, 87

concept of childhood, 83
didacticism, 90
eighteenth century, 90–92
fairy tales, 88–89
family stories, 93–95
fantasy and humor, 96–97
folktales, 108–9
"goodly godly" books, 86
growth of informational books, 105–7
landmarks in the development of books for
    children,
    box 115–17
magazines, 99
medieval books, 84
modern trends, 114–24
Mother Goose, 88
Newbery, John, as publisher, 89–90
nineteenth century, 92–102
picture storybooks, rise of, 103–5
poetry, 91–92, 98–99, 110–11
realistic fiction, 111–12
series books, 107–8
seventeenth century, 86–90
studying books of the past, teaching feature,
    112
twentieth century, 102–24
Homelessness
    in picture books, 248
    realistic fiction, 474, 475
Hornbooks, 85–86
Humor
    in chapbooks, 87–88
    nineteenth-century books, 96–97
    picture storybooks, 237–39
    poetry, 404–6
    realistic fiction, 492, 494–96

Identification books, 598
Illustrated book
    defined, 199
Illustration
    informational books, 590
    See also art
Illustrators
    media, 199–212
    of the nineteenth century, 100–101
    styles, 212–18
    techniques, box 673
    web, Brian Pinkney, 219
Immigrants
    in historical fiction, 536–37
    in realistic fiction, 490
India
    folktales, 291–92, 318
Indians (*See* Native Americans)
Informational books, 578–619
    accuracy and authenticity, 581
    activity books, 598
    anthropomorphism, 584
    author qualifications, 582
    awards, 581
    choosing for classroom, 604
    classroom uses, 602–6
    concept books, 593
    content and perspective, 585–88
    craft and how-to books, 602
    criteria, 581–93
    critical thinking, 603, box 604
    documents and journals, 599
    early childhood, 593
    experiment books, 598
    format, 580–81, 593
    growth of, 105, 106, 580
    guidelines for evaluating, box 594
    identification books, 598

illustration, 580, 593
language, 589
life cycle books, 598
organization, 589–90
photographic essays, 596
picture story books, 594
scientific method, 586–87
specialized topics, 601
stereotypes, 583
style, 588–89
survey books, 600
teaching feature, 604
topics, 581
trends, 578–81
types, 593–602
use with fiction, 605, box 606
writing models, 703–4
Integration
    of informational books and fiction, 605–6,
    box 606
International board on books for young people
    (IBBYP), 114

Jack tales, 303–4
Jackdaws, 687–88
    making a jackdaw, box 688
Japan
    folktales, 294
    historical fiction, 524, 543
    picture books, 223, 249, 250
Jews
    folktales, 289–90
    historical fiction, 539–41, 542
    picture storybooks, 227
    realistic fiction, 455, 462

King Arthur
    fantasy, 342, 359, 365, 370
    legends, 319, 320
Korea
    folktales, 294–95
    historical fiction, 543

Landmarks in the development of books for
    children, box 115–17
Language, sensitivty to, 692, 693
Language development, 48–49
Latinos
    biography, 561, 562, 568
    picture books, 151, 214, 217, 224, 225, 226,
    247
    realistic fiction, 486–87
Library media center, 653–59 (*See also* school
    library media center)
Life cycle books, 598
Lifetime readers, 709–12
Literacy
    influence of literature, 4, 12–13
    initial, 174–84
    key factors in development, 137
    "literacy set," 138
Literary study
    criticism, 63–64
    informal, 63–64
Literature across the curriculum, 16–18, 646–48
Literature and reading
    developing fluency, 15–16
    developing initial literacy, 137–38
    developing sense of story, 14
    research on reading aloud, 12, 13
Literature program, 620–66
    approaches to reading instruction, box 628
    author/illustrator visits, 652–53
    components, 629
    connecting literature to life, 686

curriculum possibilities, 646–48
developing appreciation, 625
developing literary awareness, 623
discovering delight in books, 622
evaluating children's literary backgrounds, 705–6
evaluating the literature program, 709–12
guiding discussions, 639–40
linking literature to life, 623
literature based reading program, 627
literature programs using real books, 626
making and using guides, 645
plans for literature program, 625–29
purposes, 622–25
study of a book, web, 526
study of a genre, webs, 311, 425
study of a single author/illustrator, web, 646
whole school program, 648

Magazines for children
    nineteenth century, 99
Magical powers
    fantasy, 360–61
    folktales, 279
Maps and timelines, 686
Media
    collage and construction 203, 204–7
        collage, 204–5
        crayon, 209
        crayon, chalk and charcoal, 209
        modeling, 205–6
        paper construction, 206
        pastel, 209
    paints, pen, and ink, 207–9
        gouache, 208
        oil paint, 209
        opaque paints, 208
        watercolor, 207
    suitability in informational books, 592
    woodcuts and similar techniques, 203–4
        etching, 203
        linoleum cuts, 203
        scratchboard, 204
        woodcut and wood engraving, 203
Medieval times
    books in, 84–85
    historical fiction, 521–23
Mental illness in realistic fiction, 477–78
Mental retardation, 476–77 (See also developmental disabilities)
Metaphor
    in poetry, 499
    visual, in picture storybooks, 200
Middle East and Southwest Asia
    in folktales, 290–92
    in picture books, 207, 247
    in realistic fiction, 456, 491
Middle eastern folktales, 290–91
Moral development, 49–50
Mother Goose
    appeal of, 146–47
    collections, 147–49
    eighteenth century, 88
    guidelines for evaluating, box 149
    Mother Goose, box 152–53
    Mother Goose books, 146–53
    nursery rhyme collections of other lands, 150–51
    origins of, 88
    single verse editions, 149–50
Motifs
    in fantasy, 342, box 347
    folktales, 276–79, box 279
Movement and literature, 685–86

Multicultural books
    cultural diversity in picture storybooks, 241, 246–48
    guidelines for evaluating, 485
    need for, 123–24
    poetry, 408–9, box 421–22
    realistic fiction, 482–91
    teaching feature, 492
    treatment of in this text, xiv
    See also African Americans; Asian Americans; Latinos; Native Americans; stereotyping
Multiliterate society, 124
Music and literature, 684–86
Mysteries
    realistic fiction, 501–3
Myths, 313–18
    creation, 313
    defined, 266, 313
    Greek and Roman, 314–17, box 315
    Hero, 314, 318–21
    Native American, 298–301
    nature, 314
    Norse, 317

NCTE Poetry Award, 32, 730
Native Americans
    biography, 559, 560, 567
    fantasy, 354–55
    folktales, myths, 298–301, box 299
    historical fiction, 529–31, 606
    picture books, 159, 206, 211, 217, 221, 224, 247
    poetry, 409, 417–18, box 422
    realistic fiction, 473, 488–89
Newbery Award, 30, 722–25
Nineteenth-century children's books, 92–102
Nonfiction
    influence on report writing, 703
    See also biography; informational books
Nursery songs, 141–45

Parents
    reading to young children, 12, 137–38
    quality of reading aloud, 138
Personality development, 50–51
Photography
    concept books, 165–66
    essays, 596–98
Physical disabilities
    in realistic fiction, 475–76
Picture books, 136–95
    ABC books, 154–55, box 157–59
    babies, for, 139–40
    bedtime stories, 172–73
    big books, 180, 183–84
    board books, 139–40
    books for beginning readers, 174–83
    common experiences of the young child in, 170–73
    concept books, 163–68
    controlled vocabulary books, 182, 184
    counting books, 156–63, box 160–62
    defined, 198–99
    finger rhymes, 141–42
    guidelines for evaluating abc and counting books, box 164
    guidelines for evaluating for the young child, box 142
    guidelines for evaluating Mother Goose books, box 149
    Mother Goose books, 146–50, box 152–53
    nursery songs, 142–45
    predictable books, 174–82
    single song editions, 142–45, 684

toy books, 140–41
    wordless books, 168–70
Picture storybooks, 196–264
    animals, personified, 135–36, 230, 235–36
    arts and artists, 202, 219
    biography, 559–62
    character, 200–202
    color, use of, 210
    content of, 222–50
    creating meaning, 199, 202
    cultural diversity, 241, 246–49
    defined, 198, 199
    design, elements of, 210–12
    endpapers, 220
    environment, stories of, 229, 248
    everyday world of the child, box 231–34
    familiar experiences, 227–28
    family stories, 225–26
    fantasy, 239–41
    folktales, modern, 236–37
    format, 218
    guidelines for evaluating, box 223
    historical fiction, 514
    homeless, stories of, 248
    humorous, 237–39
    imaginary world of the child, box 242–45
    informational, 594–96
    language of, 222
    line, use of, 210
    media of illustrations, 202–10
    metaphor in, 200
    mood, 200
    nature stories, 229–30
    older people, stories of, 228–29
    origins of, 103–5
    perspective in, 211
    study of, box 221
    style of art, 212–18
    war, stories of, 249
Pioneers
    fantasy, 374
    historical fiction, 514–15, 531–33
    realism, 462
Plot
    evaluating, 18–19
    structure in folktales, 273
Poetry, 388–452
    African American, 408–9
    anthologies, 413–15
    ballads, 399
    children's preferences for, 403–4
    choral reading, 439–40
    comprehensive collections, 413–15, box 416–17
    concrete poetry, 402–3
    creating a climate for enjoyment of, 424–26, box 427
    defined, 390–91
    discussing poetry, 433–34
    eighteenth century, 91
    elements of, 392–99
    emotional force of, 398–99
    everyday experiences, box 419
    in fantasy, 348
    figurative language, 396–98
    finding time for, 426–32
    forms of, 399–403
    free verse, 401–2
    guidelines for evaluating, box 399
    guidelines for poetry anthologies, box 413
    haiku, 402
    humorous verse, 404–6
    imagery, 395–96
    interpreters of child's world, 406–8
    limericks, 401

lyrical, 401
meaning of, 390–403
misuse of, 422
multicultural poetry, 408–9
narrative poems, 400
Native American poetry, 409, 417, 418
nature, 409–11
neglect of poetry, research, 403
nineteenth century, 98–99
personification, 397
picturebook editions of single poems, 418
picturebook editions of single poems, box 423–24
poetry/prose connections, box 428–32
poetry workshop, 438–39
poets and their books, 404–13
reading poetry aloud, 432–33
rhyme and sound, 394
rhythm, 393
selecting, 403–18
shape of a poem, 398
sharing poetry with children, 399
specialized collections, 415, box 419–22
    animal poems, box 420
    everyday experiences, box 419
    families, box 419–20
    holiday collections, box 421
    humorous poems, box 421
    multiethnic poetry, box 422–23
    nature and the seasons, box 420
    night poems, box 419
studying poetry and nature, box 433
twentieth century, development of, 110–11
using models, 435–37
versatile poets, 411–13
web, in praise of poetry, 425
writing poetry, 435–39
Poets, 404–13
Point of view, 24–26
in pictures, 211–12
Pourquoi tales, 269–70
creating with sixth graders, box 270
Predictable books, 174–80, box 180
Publishing
new markets, 114–23
number of juveniles published by decade, 114
Puppetry, 691–92
constructing puppets and stages, 691–92
selecting stories for, 691

Questioning techniques, 639–41
asking good questions, 639
children's questions, 640–641

Readers' theater, 690–91
Reading
beginning reading, 174–84
book discussion groups, 638–42, box 641
buddy reading, 649
classroom book collection, 630
creating classroom reading center, 630–31
developing fluency, 15
developing lifetime readers, 709
discussing books, 638–40
environment for, 629–32
reading aloud, 632–34
selecting books to read aloud, 633, box 635
sustained silent reading (ssr), 637
time to read, 637–38
Reading aloud, 632–34
guidelines for, box 635
poetry, 432
research on values of, 11–12
selecting books for, 633
techniques for, 634
See also endpapers; 150 books to read aloud

Reading interests, 40–50
age differences, 40–41
developmental influences, 43–51
gender differences, 40
illustrations, influence of, 41
intelligence and, 41
poetry, 418
social influences, 41–42
Realistic fiction
African Americans, 483–86
aging, 478–80
animal stories, 496–98
Asian Americans, 487–88
author's background, 458
bias and sterotyping in, 457–58
death, 480–82
defined, 456
developmental disabilities, 476–77
divorce, 463–64
early realistic fiction, 111–13
family stories, 459
finding one's self, 470–72
foster children, 465–66
friendship, 467–68
guidelines for evaluating multicultural
    literature, box 484
humorous stories, 492–96
issues, 456
Latinos, 486–87
maturity growing to, 468–75
mental illness, 477–78
mysteries, 501–3
Native Americans, 486
new freedoms of the sixties, 111
peer acceptance, 466–67
peer pressure, 466–67
physical disabilities, 466
racial and ethnic diversity, 482–91
realism in, 456–57
school stories, 499–500
series fiction, box 493–95
sexuality, 468–70
sports stories, 498–99
survival, 472–75
types of, 459
values of, 454–56
violence in, 456–57
world cultures, 488–91
Realistic folktales, 271
Record keeping, methods of, 68, 706–7
Resources for teaching (boxes)
ABC books, 156–60
American tall tale heroes, 308
approaches to reading instruction, 628
author autobiographies, 570
books about quilts and stitchery, 680
books for ages and stages, 52–60
books that introduce aspects of fantasy
    novels, 347
books that serve as writing models, 701
comprehensive poetry anthologies, 416–18
connections between poetry and prose,
    428–32
counting books, 160–63
cross-cultural study of folktale motifs, a,
    279–80
cross-cultural study of folktale types, a,
    272–73
cross-cultural study of folktale variants, a,
    281–83
developing enjoyment of poetry, 427
effective practice in reading aloud, 635
everyday world of the child, in picture books,
    231–36
fact and fiction books to use together, 606
fooling with traditional literature, 698

gods and goddesses of Greek and Roman
    mythology, 315
guide for Galimoto, a, 646
illustrators and their techniques, 673
imaginary world of the child, in picture
    books, 242–48
landmarks in the development of books for
    children, 115–17
making a jackdaw, 688
Mother Goose books, 152–54
Native American folktales by region, 302
picture book editions of single poems,
    423–24
poetry/prose connections, 428–32
popular series for children, 493–94
predictable books, 180–81
recurring themes in historical fiction, 536
specialized collections of poetry, 419–23
study of folktales by culture, a, 302–3
suggested stories for the feltboard, 637
Response to literature
books for ages and stages, box 52–60
concept of story, 65
defined, 40, 60–61
elicited by adults, 64–65
growth and change in, 43–51, 61–64
happiness binding, 68
interests and preferences, 40–43
literary miscues, 68
observing children, 64
record keeping, 68–69
research, 65–67
theories, 51–60
types, 60–61
verbal, 60–61
Robin Hood, 320–21
Robinsonades, 95
Russian folktales, 287–89

Satire, in fantasy, 357
Scandinavia
in folktales, 285–86
myths, 317–18
School library media center, 653–58
library media specialist, 654
working with parents, 658
working with public library, 659
Science fiction, 373–79
cyberspace, 375–76
introducing children to, 374
outer space, 375–76
views of the future, 376–79
visitors to earth, 375
Selection
need for, 655–57
principles of, 655–56
selection vs. censorship, 656–57
Sense of story, 12–14, 65–67
See also concept of story
Series books, 495, 496, 498, 499, 500, 501
adventure, 95
proliferation of, 95–96
realistic fiction, 491–92
realistic fiction, box 493–94
Setting, 19–20
Seventeenth- and eighteenth-century children's
    books, 86–92
Sibling rivalry
in picture storybooks, 225
realistic fiction, 225–26
Slavery, 533–35, 606
Songbooks, single editions, 141–45, 684–85
South America
in folktales, 307, 308
realistic fiction, 489–91

Stereotyping, issue of
    in early books, 112–13
    informational books, 583, 584
    picture storybooks, 223–24
    realistic fiction, 457–58
Storytelling, 634–37
    book talks, 637
    feltboard stories, box 637
    guidelines for telling stories, 635
    selecting stories to tell, 635
    storytelling aids, 676
Style, 23–24
    biography, 556
    folktales, 274–75
    informational books, 588–89
Style of art, in picture books, 212–18
    cartoon style, 216
    cultural connections, 217
    expressionism, 214
    folk art or naive style, 215–16
    Impressionism, 213–14
    personal styles, 217–18
    representational, 212–13
    Surrealism, 214–15
Survival stories
    in fantasy, 350, 374, 377–79
    historical fiction, 528, 530, 532, 534,
        539–42, 543
    realistic fiction, 472–75

Tall tales, 306–7
    tall tales, box 308
Teaching features
    asking children to tell about themselves as
        readers, 44
    "Brian Pinkney" web, 219
    creating big books with emergent readers,
        183
    creating pourquoi stories with fifth graders,
        270
    "Folktales" web, 311
    "Framework for Webbing," a, 647
    helping children evaluate informational
        books, 604
    "In Praise of Poetry" web, 425
    interviewing fictional characters, 641
    journals help children understand fantasy,
        352

learning about the art of picture storybooks,
    221
quilt making helps students review their
    study of Mexico, 682
Sign of the Beaver web, 526
"Stewards of the Earth" web, 650–51
studying books of the past, 112
studying poetry and nature, 433
teachers discuss literature about minorities,
    453
thinking critically about biography, 557
using dialogue journals, 644
whole school study one book, 562
Television
    time watched, 6
    violence, 6
Theme, 20–21
    biography, 557–58
    fantasy, 370
    folktales, 275–76
    historical fiction, box 536
Thinking skills, 9–10
    developing imagination, 9–10
    See also critical thinking
Toy books, 118–19, 140–41
Traditional literature, 266–322
    See also Bible; epics; folktales; myths; tall
        tales
Trends
    in censorship, 123
    informational books, 660–63
    publishing, 114–20
    use of books, 122–23
    writing and illustrating, 120–22
Twentieth century, 102–24
    in historical fiction, 536–43

Vietnam
    folktales, 293
    picture books, 246
    realistic fiction, 246–47

War
    American Revolution, 528–29
    Civil War, 535–36
    in fantasy, 346, 357, 367, 369, 370–71,
        377–78

in picture books, 249–50
    in realistic fiction, 490–91
    World War I and after, 538–44
Webbing techniques, 646–48
Webs
    "Brian Pinkney" web, 219
    "Folktales" web, 311
    "Framework for Webbing, A," 647
    "In Praise Of Poetry" web, 425
    Sign of the Beaver web, 526
    "Stewards of the Earth" web, 650–51
Writing
    about books, 643–45
    author's chair, 645
    books as springboards for writing, 694–95
    books that serve as writing models, box 701
    children as authors, 645
    creating alphabet books, 695
    developing sensitivity to language, 692–93
    dialogue journals, box 644
    diaries and letters, 699
    double entry draft, 644
    expository writing, 700
    fooling with folktales, fables, and myths,
        696–97
    from books, 692–704
    informational books as models, 703
    literary patterns, experimenting with,
        695–700
    log, 643
    making books, 695, 704, 705
    newspapers and newscasting, 700, 702
    report writing, 703
    research on literature and writing, 15–16
    response journals, 644
    surveys, 700–701, 703
    writing conference, 645
    writing poetry, 698
    writing program and literature, 642–45
Wilder, Laura Ingalls, Award, 31, 729
Whole language, 626
Wonder tales, 271
Woodcuts
    in early books, 85, 86, 87
    in picture books, 203
Wordless books, 168–70